INTELLECTUAL PROPERTY

PRIVATE RIGHTS, THE PUBLIC INTEREST, AND THE REGULATION OF CREATIVE ACTIVITY

Second Edition

■ ■ ■

By

Shubha Ghosh

Vilas Research Fellow, Professor of Law, & Associate Director,
Initiatives for Studies in Transformational Entrepreneurship (INSITE),
University of Wisconsin Law School, Madison, WI

Richard Gruner

Professor of Law
Director, Center for Intellectual Property Law
John Marshall Law School

Jay P. Kesan

Professor of Law
Director, Program in Intellectual Property and Technology Law
University of Illinois

Robert I. Reis

Professor of Law
State University of New York at Buffalo
School of Law

AMERICAN CASEBOOK SERIES®

WEST®

A Thomson Reuters business

Mat #41031300

© West, a Thomson business, 2007
© 2011 Thomson Reuters

    610 Opperman Drive
    St. Paul, MN 55123
    1–800–313–9378

Printed in the United States of America

ISBN: 978–0–314–26505–0

for my mother
   — S.G.

for Helen and Elizabeth
   — R.G.

for Jay, Maya and Sara
   — J.P.K.

for Ellen, JJ&J, Carl, Edna and Ruth
   — R.I.R.

PREFACE

The second edition of "Intellectual Property: Private Rights, The Public Interest, and The Regulation of Creative Activity" continues and builds on the distinctive features of the first. We move beyond the preconceptions of intellectual property having exclusively to do with science and technology to present the subject of intellectual property in a more integrated fashion, showing how similar policy and conceptual issues unite the subfields of intellectual property: trade secret, copyright, patent, trademark, and developing state and federal doctrines. This edition continues the approach of the first in examining the longstanding connection between intellectual property and creative processes. We hope by this choice of approach, we will appeal to persons interested in diverse types of creative activities and in the multiple roles that intellectual property plays in an expanding, thriving economy.

As with the first edition, our emphasis in the second is on public regulation and encouragement of creativity and the use of intellectual products. While many existing books focus squarely on the private interests protected by intellectual property, our perspective is on both the private and public interests affected by law as it regulates and promotes creative processes. Our approach makes the study of intellectual property more approachable and richer for students who can see how the doctrines of intellectual property reflect common law, statutory, and constitutional methodologies. In short, our casebook appeals to students and instructors who understand that intellectual property is not simply about technology and narrow technical industries, but about creativity, authorship, inventorship, and entrepreneurship as they arise across society.

We integrate a traditional case analysis approach with the careful consideration of statutory materials, reflecting the important roles of courts, Congress, and state legislatures in the development of intellectual property law. The cases have been carefully edited and most citations within cases have been removed for readability. We also introduce students to the constitutional and international legal materials that shape intellectual property doctrine and policy. The book is designed so that it can be used with several teaching styles whether focusing on technical legal analysis, on broader policies, or on a combination of the two. In designing the casebook, we also tried to be sensitive to the teaching of legal skills, particularly those needed by intellectual property lawyers to help creative parties as clients construct transactions and relationships that involve intellectual property.

The main innovations in the second edition are the updating of cases to present contemporary developments in the law. This edition contains the recent Supreme Court decision in *Bilski v. Kappos* as well as current materials in the ongoing Google dispute with Viacom over activities on YouTube.

New materials are included on international law, copyright, and trademark law developments, and patentable subject matter in the area of biotechnology. The second edition has an increased emphasis on contemporary issues that will make it easier to connect the materials in the book with developments in practice.

As with the first edition, this project has been a collaborative effort among the coauthors. Several additional parties have also made significant contributions to both editions.

Professor Shubha Ghosh benefitted from the resources of three supportive law schools where he had the good fortune to be a tenured full professor since the inception of this project in 2005. The University at Buffalo Law School provided a wonderful set of students from 2000 to 2006 who responded favorably to the ideas and materials collected in this casebook. Southern Methodist University Dedman School of Law provided the remarkable administrative services of Michelle Oswald and the research assistance of Gary Ross Allen, Class of 2008 and now a practitioner in the Bay Area. Finally, University of Wisconsin School of Law offered the opportunity to present the first edition to a responsive group of students from 2008 to 2010, many of whom provided comments that were useful in developing the second edition. Sue Sawatske, the consummate faculty assistant, provided professional and critical editing and word-processing services that shaped this text and the accompanying teacher's manual. Finally, comments from Mark Bartholomew, William T. McGrath, and Bill Gallagher were constructive and instrumental in identifying ways to improve the first edition. I personally hope that I have been able to integrate their suggestions in this new edition.

At the Whittier Law School, Professor Gruner would like to thank his research assistant Mark Giordano, Class of 2007, for assistance with sources and reviews of the manuscript. He also appreciates the administrative support of Henrietta Johnson, Jennifer Maniscalco, and Rosalie Robles. This project was significantly aided by a summer research stipend provided by the Whittier Law School.

At the University of Illinois, Professor Kesan would like to thank his research assistant, Jim Lovsin, for his thoughtful assistance and input on the second edition. Professor Kesan would like to thank his research assistants Mark Cassidy, Jonathan Ko, and Patty Pisut for their assistance on the earlier edition of this book. In addition, Professor Kesan would like to thank his assistant Molly Lindsey for her diligent and sustained administrative support throughout this effort.

At the State University of New York, Buffalo School of Law, Professor Reis would like to thank his secretary and conscience Dawn Fenneman for her tireless hours of typing and formatting, Professor Mark Bartholomew for his critical comments and proof reading and the numerous students over the past six years who have suffered through last minute revisions and additions to the materials. He would like to acknowledge the diligent work and commentary of Matthew Ritenburg, Class of 2009, who stayed on as a research assistant to work on these materials. Additionally, he would like to thank Dean Makau Mutua and Dean Nils Olsen for their support and encouragement.

SUMMARY OF CONTENTS

TABLE OF CONTENTS

_____

TABLE OF CASES

The principal cases are in bold type. Cases cited or discussed in the text are in roman type. References are to pages. Cases cited in principal cases and within other quoted materials are not included.

TABLE OF STATUTES

INTELLECTUAL PROPERTY

PRIVATE RIGHTS, THE PUBLIC INTEREST, AND THE REGULATION OF CREATIVE ACTIVITY

CHAPTER ONE

INTRODUCTION

■ ■ ■

Whenever humans enter into new domains of activity, law soon follows. The development of agriculture, the rise of monarchs, the expansions of empires each ushered in important changes in legal institutions. The familiar legal systems of tort, contract, and property laws reflect developments in social and economic organizations that shaped and were shaped by each body of law.

In the last century, as more human activity has moved towards the development of knowledge and the accumulation of valuable information has produced critically important resources and assets in many industries and economies, intellectual property law has become increasingly prominent. Intellectual property seems to be everywhere from newspaper headlines to the dockets of almost every court. While intellectual property law may seem to be a relatively new creation, many aspects of this body of law have a lengthy pedigree. The first pieces of legislation enacted by the first Congress in 1790 were copyright and patent statutes. These statutes were modeled upon similar legislation in England dating back to the Seventeenth and Eighteenth Centuries. Modern patent legislation can be traced back to a prototype enacted by the Republic of Venice in the Fifteenth Century. These ancient roots have generated a lush flora, which to some is a delightful garden, and to others are prickly bramble bushes. However one sees the floral arrangement, there is no doubt as to its vitality and importance.

How one sees intellectual property rests on answers to several critical questions. Where does creativity and invention come from? Are they flashes of genius without context or foundation? Do the Constitutional provisions at the heart of our current intellectual property system recognize this dependency of law on context? Who were the intended beneficiaries of these provisions? Were they those persons that were accorded rights in their intellectual creations or other persons in society who were benefited by access to the creations?

The influence of these sorts of philosophical questions on the drafters of the Constitutional provisions concerning intellectual property is debated to this date. Much of this discourse centers on the writings of John Locke, particularly the following:

> Though the earth and all inferior creatures be common to all men, yet every man has a 'property' in his own 'person.' This nobody has any right to but himself. The 'labour' of his body and the 'work' of his hands, we may say, are properly his. * * * For this 'labour' being the unquestionable property of the labourer, no man by he can have a right to what that is once joined to, at least where there is enough, and as good left in common for others.

JOHN LOCKE, TWO TREATISES ON GOVERNMENT (3rd Ed. 1698). While there may have been some debate whether Locke's views applied to the fruits of one's mind, Locke is reputed to have had a great influence on the drafting of the copyright and patent clause of the United States Constitution, Art. I, § 8, Cl. 8:

> The Congress shall have Power * * *

> To promote the Progress of Science and useful Arts, by securing for limited Times to Authors and Inventors the exclusive Right to their respective Writings and Discoveries.

When Article I, section 8, Cl. 8 speaks of securing an "exclusive right" for "limited times," it implies, upon expiration of the right having limited duration, a reversionary interest in the public commons. It also hearkens back to the last line in the quote from Locke referencing "... at least where there is enough, and as good left in common for others" For more detailed reflection and scholarship on these matters, see generally Wendy J. Gordon, *A Property Right in Self–Expression: Equality and Individualism in the Natural Law of Intellectual Property*, 102 Yale L.J. 1533, 1535 (1993); Justin Hughes, *The Philosophy of Intellectual Property*, 77 Geo. L.J. 287, 294 (1988); Adam Mossoff, *Rethinking the Development of Patents: An Intellectual History, 1550–1800*, 52 Hastings L.J. 1255 (2001); Malla Pollack, *The Owned Public Domain: The Constitutional Right Not to be Excluded—Or the Supreme Court Chose the Right Breakfast Cereal in Kellogg v. National Biscuit Co.*, 22 Hastings Comm. & Ent. L.J. 265 (2000).

In addition to these debates about the basic goals of intellectual property laws, other commentators have considered whether the evolution of intellectual property laws has reflected the timeless conflict of haves and have-nots. As Professor Jesica Litman's asks in her book *Digital Copyright*, does the history of copyright law reflect the values of benefiting society, or the protection of vested interests sometimes to the detriment or exclusion of the public interest? Likewise, Professor Lawrence Lessig raises questions in his book *Code and Other Laws of Cyberspace* concerning the economic beneficiaries in Cyberspace of limitations on access to intellectual works implemented through such diverse means as legal code and computer code. There is a subtle and significant change in Professor Lessig's position in his more recent work *The Future of Ideas: the Fate of the Commons in a Connected World*, addressing issues of the privatization of intellectual activities. These three books provide a provocative trilogy introducing both the form and substance of contemporary laws, economic structures, political and social pressures and forces behind the search for sustainable regulation and privatization of interests in intellectual works. They also present a vibrant picture of how this search for the proper scope of intellectual property rights may affect "the future of ideas."

Professor Lessig presents us with a version of the contemporary problem of private rights in plain sight. Should that which we see as part of our view of the environment or landscape in which we function be the subject of exclusion of the public from use? Should rights in a creative work that are recognized to encourage creative activities have boundaries that avoid awkward or unexpected limitations on common social activities? Or, to phrase the question slightly differently in the context of copyrights, should works that are the subject of copyrights limiting the reproduction of the works, but which are displayed in plain sight, be considered part of the commons and available for free use for some purposes? Should the boundaries of the property rights claimed by those with a copyright permit them to put limitations on that which they have not only put forth into the commons, but which can't be avoided? Building on a question raised by Professor Lessig, what if someone takes a picture in a public place which includes a building or object in which someone holds a copyright, does the holder of the copyright have the ability to exclude any or all uses of that photograph, or even the taking of the photograph itself? What if the object is a statute in Italy several hundred years old? What if it is a famous Louis Sullivan or Frank Lloyd Wright building? What if it is the Sears Tower in Chicago, or a new structure designed by a local architect? What if the building has Pepsi signs on it, or a work of original art on the exterior walls? These works are all the subject of copyright, although time may have ended the rights of the holder. But while the copyrights are in force, these are private rights concerning items in the public's common space–in plain and unavoidable view. Such rights pose a potential impediment to valuable public discourse.

Modern practices regarding the production, transmission, and copying of intellectual works have raised additional questions about the value of intellectual works that intellectual property laws should protect and where rights should be available to achieve that protection. Consider the situation of someone located in London who writes articles and reviews that are published on a web site controlled and paid for by the author with revenues derived primarily from links directing readers from this web site to other commercial web sites. Suppose someone comes and downloads these reviews and posts them on their own web site. We can call it a violation of the author's copyright, but what have they taken? Wherein lies both the value and the appropriation of that value to the detriment of the holder of the right? What are the boundaries of the right held by the copyright holder and where and under what circumstances can it be enforced? For example, can it be enforced if the right is created in London, England, and violated in Singapore? These are basic questions arising in the international application of intellectual property laws that are increasingly important given the growth in our global communication system and economy.

The impact of looking to labor in the creation of works as a sufficient basis for wide-reaching intellectual property protections has also come under increasing scrutiny in light of changing capabilities of users to access and use works via digital technologies. Consider the labor involved in completing the critical analyses and written expression incorporated in many copyrighted works. Should the ease of access and copying such works in digital forms alter the rights of the copyright holders? Should that which is "easy" to copy become a part of the commons? Is there a distinction that should be made here between works that are visible and a part of our line of sight which we do not have the power to turn off and works that are easy to access, but which are not dedicated, donated or offered to the public without the permission or control of the copyright holder?

The following excerpt from an Internet posting describes a concrete example of the types of modern disputes over intellectual works that recent trends towards easy access, copying, and redistribution have produced:

Copyright Violator: pconline.com.cn

Monday, 30 August 2004 10:35 GMT So we've tried the traditional route, we have contacted this site on numerous occasions to point out their obvious violation of our copyright (and that of other digital camera sites) but to no avail. The legal route is still open but fraught with problems. One option always available to us is to shame such websites and hope that they will see the errors of their ways. This site mixes some original content with stolen images and translated text which it then publishes as its own original work.

Phil: For the record I have personally contacted this site several times over the last year. Recently however they have taken to copying almost every original article posted here along with product photography, samples galleries, translations of our specification tables, review analysis and more. They have never responded to our emails and have continued to copy material. Images from my Sony DSC–V3 preview posted just this morning have already been copied and posted on pconline.com.cn.

Phil: For the record I have personally contacted this site several times over the last year. Recently however they have taken to copying almost every original article posted here along with product photography, samples galleries, translations of our specification tables, review analysis and more. They have never responded to our emails and have continued to copy material. Images from my Sony DSC-V3 preview posted just this morning have already been copied and posted on pconline.com.cn.

Examples of pconline.com.cn copyright violation Articles on pconline.com.cn	Taken from
http://www.pconline.com.cn/digital/dc/pingce/0408/440020.html (11 pages including samples gallery)	dpreview.com (Canon G6 preview)
http://www.pconline.com.cn/digital/dc/news/0408/439799.html (1 page comparison table)	dpreview.com (Canon G6 preview)
http://www.pconline.com.cn/digital/dc/pingce/0408/444466.html (6 pages)	dcresource.com (A95 gallery)
http://www.pconline.com.cn/digital/dc/pingce/0408/444059.html (2 pages)	dcresource.com (S70 gallery)
http://www.pconline.com.cn/digital/dc/pingce/0408/441066.html (9 pages)	steves-digicams.com (A85 review)
http://www.pconline.com.cn/digital/dc/news/0408/444792.html (3 pages, mixture of sony pr images and our own)	dpreview.com (sony news & preview)
http://www.pconline.com.cn/digital/dc/pingce/0407/422719.html (23 pages including samples, comparisons)	dpreview.com (kodak slr/c review)
http://www.pconline.com.cn/digital/dc/pingce/0407/422521.html (10 pages)	dpreview.com (fz20 & fz3 previews)
http://www.pconline.com.cn/digital/dc/news/0405/376968.html (2 pages, note the scrubbed out copyright messages)	dpreview.com (sony dsc-f88 hands-on)
http://www.pconline.com.cn/digital/dc/news/0403/334007.html (1 page)	dpreview.com (pentax *ist d review)
http://www.pconline.com.cn/digital/dc/news/0402/314289.html (1 page)	dpreview.com (pma 2004 report)
http://www.pconline.com.cn/digital/dc/news/0402/312879.html (2 pages)	dpreview.com (pma 2004 report)
http://www.pconline.com.cn/digital/dc/news/0402/310679.html (2 pages)	dpreview.com (polaroid x530 hands-on)

These copyright violations even included photographs of the author's wife as part of the improperly posted sample pictures.

Do these activities raise technological issues, copyright issues, moral issues, issues of nation state and international treaty? These are just a few of the questions that are addressed in this course. Standards governing the creation, limitation, scope, and enforcement of interests in intellectual works are being shaped by notions of fair use, moral issues of copying and respecting the labor and rights of others, issues of enablement and of treating intellectual works as free goods. These contextual forces, coupled with the temptation and anonymity of easy and remote use of intellectual works made possible by new technologies like the communication infrastructure of the Internet, are rapidly forcing us to rethink the basic principles underlying intellectual property laws. This process of rapid change in legal standards in this field make it an exciting time to study intellectual property law and to participate in the ongoing definition of intellectual property's role in increasingly complex global relations and regulations.

This book offers a rich introduction to the field of intellectual property. The cases and materials are current and span the depth and breadth of both United States and international law. When you reach the end of the tour of intellectual property topics provided by the readings here, you will, we hope, be inspired to pursue a broader knowledge of this field through readings in the many source materials that are cited throughout the book. As the cliché goes, each journey begins with a single step, and each journey is enriched by an appropriate guidebook. This guide consists of nine chapters, including the one you are reading. After this chapter, you will find one that explores the law of trade secrets, followed immediately by chapters on the three major federal bodies of intellectual property law: copyrights, patents, and trademarks. After this excursion into federal law, you move on to the state law of intellectual property with readings addressing rights of publicity, moral rights, idea protections, and interrelationships between federal and state intellectual property laws. Then the trip enters what may be less familiar terrain for you through readings addressing the worlds of digital rights in Chapter Seven and international law in Chapter Eight. Finally, Chapter Nine provides you with a glimpse of the future horizons of intellectual property laws and the forces that are likely to shape these laws in the near future. At the end of the intellectual path defined by the readings here, you will have a better sense of intellectual property law, the human activities it is designed to regulate and shape, and the future possibilities for positive interactions of creativity, innovation, and legal institutions.

One final word: the range and depth of the field of intellectual property could not be captured within the pages of this book. As a result, we have supplemented these tangible pages with an online supplement. Your instructor can provide you with the web address for the supplement and may direct you to these materials that provide added depth and substance to the discussion which follows. We hope that you make use of these materials to continue your exploration of the expanding field of intellectual property.

CHAPTER TWO

TRADE SECRETS

■ ■ ■

OVERVIEW

This chapter covers the intellectual property known as trade secrets. The first section of the chapter, Part I, defines the meaning of a trade secret under the Uniform Trade Secrets Act (UTSA), the Economic Espionage Act (EEA), and the Restatement of Torts. This section also addresses the historical context for trade secret protection.

The next section, Part II, discusses civil protection for trade secrets, specifically the protection afforded by the Uniform Trade Secrets Act (UTSA) and the Restatement of Torts. *Learning Curve Toys, Inc. v. Playwood, Inc.* describes the application of the UTSA. *DeGiorgio v. Megabyte Int'l, Inc.* and *Buffets, Inc. v. Klinke* examine the three elements necessary for information to qualify as a trade secret. *E.I. duPont deNemours & Co. v. Christopher* then provides an example of non-UTSA protection for trade secrets and explores misappropriation of trade secrets through "improper means." *Dravo v. Smith* illustrates misappropriation through "breach of confidence." Next, defenses to misappropriation and rights against others are discussed. Part II ends with an examination of civil remedies for trade secret misappropriation.

The next section, Part III, covers criminal protection for trade secrets. Part III opens with a discussion of federal protection under the Economic Espionage Act (EEA). Continuing on, the section explores the liability arising from actual theft of trade secrets, as illustrated in *United States v. Lange.* Conspiracy to steal trade secrets is then covered in *United States v. Martin.* The Chapter closes with an examination of state protection for trade secrets, illustrated by *People v. Pribich,* and a comparison between state and federal trade secret protection.

I. INTRODUCTION—WHAT IS A TRADE SECRET?

Trade secrets make up the majority of intellectual property. A trade secret may be just about anything, from the formula for a popular soft drink, to a list of customers. Unlike copyrights, trade secret protection is not limited to the expression of an idea—though something held as a trade secret may be copyrightable as well. Unlike patents, trade secrets do not require novelty to receive legal protection—though otherwise-patentable technology may be held as a trade secret.

The definition of trade secret can vary across statutory regimes. For example, the majority of states have adopted the Uniform Trade Secrets Act (UTSA), which creates civil liability for trade secret misappropriation and defines trade secret as follows:

"Trade secret" means information, including a formula, pattern, compilation, phonogram device, method, technique, or process, that: (i) derives independent economic value, actual or potential, from not being generally known to, and not being readily ascertainable by proper means by, other persons who can obtain economic value from its disclosure or use, and (ii) is the subject of efforts that are reasonable under the circumstances to maintain its secrecy.

Uniform Trade Secrets Act § 1(4).

By comparison, the federal Economic Espionage Act (EEA)—which creates criminal sanctions for theft of trade secrets—defines trade secret slightly differently:

The term "trade secret" means all forms and types of financial, business, scientific, technical, economic, or engineering information, including patterns, plans, compilations, program devices, formulas, designs, prototypes, methods, techniques, processes, procedures, programs, or codes, whether tangible or intangible, and whether or how stored, compiled, or memorialized physically, electronically, graphically, photographically, or in writing if—

(A) the owner thereof has taken reasonable measures to keep such information secret; and

(B) the information derives independent economic value, actual or potential, from not being generally known to, and not being readily ascertainable through proper means by, the public.

18 U.S.C. § 1839(3).

There are elements common to both definitions: trade secrets may be nearly any form of information, provided that (1) reasonable measures are taken to keep the information secret; and (2) the information has some economic value, through not being generally known by others.

NOTES

1. The Restatements. Before the majority of states adopted the UTSA, the common law utilized a definition of trade secrets that was drawn from the Restatement of Torts (1939) § 757:

A trade secret may consist of any formula, pattern, device or compilation of information which is used in one's business, and which gives him an opportunity to obtain an advantage over competitors who do not know or use it. It may be a formula for a chemical compound, a process of manufacturing, treating or preserving material, a pattern for a machine or other device, or a list of customers.

Several state courts still use this definition. Although discussions of trade secrets were omitted from the Restatement (Second) of Torts (1978), the American Law Institute released the Restatement (Third) of Unfair Competition in 1995, which included yet another definition:

> A trade secret is any information that can be used in the operation of a business or other enterprise and that is sufficiently valuable and secret to afford an actual or potential economic advantage over others.

Id. § 39.

2. Historical Note: The Need for Trade Protection. Roman Law recognized a cause of action called *action servi corrupti* which prohibited slaves from stealing the trade secrets of their masters and giving them to competitors. One of the earliest trade secret case in the United States is an 1837 case from Massachusetts which enforced the contractual promise of the seller of a chocolate mill not to disclose his recipe to anyone else. For more historical background, see Milton E. Babirak, Jr., *The Virginia Uniform Trade Secret Act: A Critical Summary of the Act and Case Law*, 5 VA. L.J. & TECH. 15 (2000).

3. Are Trade Secrets Property? In *E. I. Du Pont de Nemours Powder Co. v. Masland*, 244 U.S. 100, 37 S.Ct. 575, 61 L.Ed. 1016 (1917) Justice Holmes famously said, "The word property as applied to trade-marks and trade secrets is an unanalyzed expression of certain secondary consequences of the primary fact that the law makes some rudimentary requirements of good faith. Whether the plaintiffs have any valuable secret or not the defendant knows the facts, whatever they are, through a special confidence that he accepted. The property may be denied but the confidence cannot be. Therefore the starting point for the present matter is not property or due process of law, but that the defendant stood in confidential relations with the plaintiffs." *Id.* at 102. Courts have interpreted this statement over the years to stand for the proposition that trade secrets are not property but are instead rights incidental to property.

Over seventy years later, the Supreme Court revisited the issue of whether trade secrets are property in *Ruckelshaus v. Monsanto Co.*, 467 U.S. 986, 104 S.Ct. 2862, 81 L.Ed.2d 815 (1984). In *Ruckelshaus*, Monsanto claimed that governmental disclosure of a pesticide formula it held as a trade secret constituted a taking under the Fifth Amendment. The Court held that Monsanto's trade secret was property for purposes of the Taking Clause because "[t]rade secrets have many of the characteristics of more tangible forms of property," Congress spoke of trade secrets as property in the legislative history of the relevant act, and because "the Court has found other kinds of intangible interests to be property for purposes of the Fifth Amendment's Taking Clause." *Id.* at 1002–1003. After making its decision, the Court addressed Justice Holmes remarks in *E.I. du Pont*:

Contrary to EPA's contention, Brief for Appellant 29, Justice Holmes' dictum in *E. I. du Pont de Nemours Powder Co. v. Masland*, 244 U.S. 100 (1917), does not undermine our holding that a trade secret is property protected by the Fifth Amendment Taking Clause. *Masland* arose from a dispute about the disclosure of trade secrets during preparation for a trial. In his opinion for the Court, the Justice stated:

> "The case has been considered as presenting a conflict between a right of property and a right to make a full defence, and it is said that if the disclosure is forbidden to one who denies that there is a trade secret, the merits of his defence are adjudged against him before he has a chance to be heard or to prove his case. We approach the question somewhat differently. The word property as applied to trade-marks and trade secrets is an unanalyzed expression of certain secondary consequences of the primary fact that the law makes some rudimentary requirements of good faith. Whether the plaintiffs have any valuable secret or not the defendant knows the facts, whatever they are, through a special confidence that he accepted. The property may be denied but the confidence cannot be. Therefore the starting point for the present matter is not property or due process of law, but that the defendant stood in confidential relations with the plaintiffs." *Id., at 102.*

Justice Holmes did not deny the existence of a property interest; he simply deemed determination of the existence of that interest irrelevant to resolution of the case. In a case decided prior to *Masland*, the Court had spoken of trade secrets in property terms. *Board of Trade v. Christie Grain & Stock Co.*, 198 U.S. 236, 250–253 (1905) (Holmes, J., for the Court).

Id. at 1004, n. 9.

What do you think? Should the law treat trade secrets as property or are trade secrets something intangible, incidental to property?

II. CIVIL PROTECTION OF TRADE SECRETS

Trade secret protection is largely a matter of state law. States can be divided into those that have adopted the Uniform Trade Secrets Act (UTSA), and those who have not. An overwhelming majority of states have adopted some version of the UTSA. In this section, we will examine the state law of trade secrets, with a focused discussion of the UTSA, the issue of confidential disclosures, the defenses to trade secret misappropriation and rights against third parties that derive from trade secrets.

A. UNIFORM TRADE SECRETS ACT

1. Introduction

The Uniform Trade Secrets Act (UTSA) was drafted to define a standardized approach to trade secrets law as a substitute for inconsistent trade secret provisions in many common law standards prevailing in different jurisdictions. The original version of the UTSA was released by the National Conference of Commissioners on Uniform State Laws in 1979, and further amendments were added in 1985. Forty-four states and the District of Columbia have enacted the Uniform Trade Secrets Act, either in its original 1979 form or with the 1985 amendments, but several jurisdictions with active technology industries like Massachusetts, New York, and Texas have not.

2. Application of the UTSA

LEARNING CURVE TOYS, INC.
v. PLAYWOOD TOYS, INC.

United States Court of Appeals for the Seventh Circuit, 2003.
342 F.3d 714.

RIPPLE, CIRCUIT JUDGE.

PlayWood Toys, Inc. ("PlayWood") obtained a jury verdict against Learning Curve Toys, Inc. and its representatives, Roy Wilson, Harry Abraham and John Lee (collectively, "Learning Curve"), for misappropriation of a trade secret in a realistic looking and sounding toy railroad track under the Illinois Trade Secrets Act, 765 ILCS 1065/1 et seq. The jury awarded PlayWood a royalty of "8% for a license that would have been negotiated [absent the misappropriation] to last for the lifetime of the product." Although there was substantial evidence of misappropriation before the jury, the district court did not enter judgment on the jury's verdict. Instead, it granted judgment as a matter of law in favor of Learning Curve, holding that PlayWood did not have a protectable trade secret in the toy railroad track. PlayWood appealed. For the reasons set forth in the following opinion, we reverse the judgment of the district court and reinstate the jury's verdict.

Background

A. Facts

[In 1992, Robert Clausi and his brother-in-law Scott Moore began creating wooden toys under the name PlayWood Toys, Inc., a Canadian Corporation. Not having their own facilities, they contracted with Mario Borsato, who owned a woodworking facility, to manufacture toys based on PlayWood's specifications.

Clausi and Moore attended the New York Toy Fair in February, 2003, where they were approached by Roy Wilson, Learning Curve's toy designer, who explained that Learning Curve had a license to manufacture Thomas the Tank Engine ("Thomas") toys. Wilson liked PlayWood's prototypes, and raised the possibility of working together on the Thomas line. Harry Abraham, Learning Curve's vice president, and John Lee, Learning Curve's president, also stopped by and commented favorably on PlayWood's prototypes. The fair ended with the understanding that Abraham and Wilson would visit PlayWood in several days.]

On February 18, 1993, Abraham and Wilson visited PlayWood in Toronto as planned. The meeting began with a tour of Borsato's wood-working facility, where the prototypes on display at the Toy Fair had been made. After the tour, the parties went to the conference room at Borsato's facility. At this point, according to Clausi and Moore, the parties agreed to make their ensuing discussion confidential. Clausi testified:

> After we sat down in the board room, Harry [Abraham of Learning Curve] immediately said: "Look, we're going to disclose confidential information to you guys, and we're going to disclose some designs that Roy [Wilson of Learning Curve] has that are pretty confidential. If Brio were to get their hands on them, then we wouldn't like that. And we're going to do it under the basis of a confidential understanding."

And I said: "I also have some things, some ideas on how to produce the track and produce the trains now that I've had a chance to look at them for the last couple of days, and I think they're confidential as well. So if we're both okay with that, we should continue." So we did.

* * *

The parties' discussion eventually moved away from train production and focused on track design. Wilson showed Clausi and Moore drawings of Learning Curve's track and provided samples of their current product. At this point, Abraham confided to Clausi and Moore that track had posed "a bit of a problem for Learning Curve." Abraham explained that sales were terrific for Learning Curve's Thomas trains, but that sales were abysmal for its track. Abraham attributed the lack of sales to the fact that Learning Curve's track was virtually identical to that of its competitor, Brio, which had the lion's share of the track market. Because there was "no differentiation" between the two brands of track, Learning Curve's track was not even displayed in many of the toy stores that carried Learning Curve's products. Learning Curve had worked unsuccessfully for several months attempting to differentiate its track from that of Brio.

After detailing the problems with Learning Curve's existing track, Abraham inquired of Clausi whether "there was a way to differentiate" its track from Brio's track. Clausi immediately responded that he "had had a chance to look at the track and get a feel for it [over] the last few days" and that his "thoughts were that if the track were more realistic and more functional, that kids would enjoy playing with it more and it would give the retailer a reason to carry the product, especially if it looked different than the Brio track." Clausi further explained that, if the track "made noise and looked like real train tracks, that the stores wouldn't have any problem, and the Thomas the Tank line, product line would have its own different track" and could "effectively compete with Brio." Abraham and Wilson indicated that they were "intrigued" by Clausi's idea and asked him what he meant by "making noise."

Clausi decided to show Abraham and Wilson exactly what he meant. Clausi took a piece of Learning Curve's existing track from the table, drew some lines across the track (about every three-quarters of an inch), and stated: "We can go ahead and machine grooves right across the upper section ..., which would look like railway tracks, and down below machine little indentations as well so that it would look more like or sound more like real track. You would roll along and bumpity-bumpity as you go along." Clausi then called Borsato into the conference room and asked him to cut grooves into the wood * * *. Based on the sound produced by the track, Clausi told Abraham and Moore that if PlayWood procured a contract with Learning Curve to produce the track, they could call it "Clickety–Clack Track" * * *.

[When the meeting ended, Wilson took the piece of track with him. After several more meetings, PlayWood submitted a proposal, which Learning Curve rejected, saying their licensor wanted the Thomas products to be made in the United States.

In early 1994, PlayWood began to focus on the noise-producing track design. In December of 1994, Moore discovered that Learning Curve was marketing noise-producing track under the name "Clickety–Clack Track", very similar to the sample piece of track Wilson had taken from the meeting in February of 1993; Learning Curve was marketing its track as being the greatest recent innovation in wooden trains. Moore and Clausi were stunned.]

PlayWood promptly wrote a cease and desist letter to Learning Curve. The letter accused Learning Curve of stealing PlayWood's concept for the noise-producing track that it disclosed to Learning Curve "in confidence in the context of a manufacturing proposal." Learning Curve responded by seeking a declaratory judgment that it owned the concept.

Previously, on March 16, 1994, Learning Curve had applied for a patent on the noise-producing track. The patent, which was obtained on October 3, 1995, claims the addition of parallel impressions or grooves in the rails, which cause a "clacking" sound to be emitted as train wheels roll over them. The patent identifies Roy Wilson of Learning Curve as the inventor.

Clickety–Clack Track™ provided an enormous boost to Learning Curve's sales. Learning Curve had $20 million in track sales by the first quarter of 2000, and $40 million for combined track and accessory sales.

B. District Court Proceedings

[The case went to trial on PlayWood's claim against Learning Curve, Wilson, Abraham, and Lee, where the jury found for PlayWood. The judge declined to enter judgment for PlayWood.]

The district court granted Learning Curve's motion and entered judgment in its favor on the ground that PlayWood presented insufficient evidence of a trade secret. Specifically, the court determined that PlayWood did not have a trade secret in its concept for noise-producing toy railroad track under Illinois law because: (1) PlayWood did not demonstrate that its concept was unknown in the industry; (2) PlayWood's concept could have been easily acquired or duplicated through proper means; (3) PlayWood failed to guard the secrecy of its concept; (4) PlayWood's concept had no economic value; and (5) PlayWood expended no time, effort or money to develop the concept.

Discussion

A. *Trade Secret Status*

* * * The parties agree that their dispute is governed by the Illinois Trade Secrets Act ("Act"), 765 ILCS 1065/1 et seq. To prevail on a claim for misappropriation of a trade secret under the Act, the plaintiff must demonstrate that the information at issue was a trade secret, that it was misappropriated and that it was used in the defendant's business. The issue currently before us is whether there was legally sufficient evidence for the jury to find that PlayWood had a trade secret in its concept for the noise-producing toy railroad track that it revealed to Learning Curve on February 18, 1993.

The Act defines a trade secret as:

[I]nformation, including but not limited to, technical or non-technical data, a formula, pattern, compilation, program, device, method, technique, drawing, process, financial data, or list of actual or potential customers or suppliers, that:

> (1) is sufficiently secret to derive economic value, actual or potential, from not being generally known to other persons who can obtain economic value from its disclosure or use; and

> (2) is the subject of efforts that are reasonable under the circumstances to maintain its secrecy or confidentiality.

765 ILCS 1065/2(d). Both of the Act's statutory requirements focus fundamentally on the secrecy of the information sought to be protected. However, the requirements emphasize different aspects of secrecy. The first requirement, that the information be sufficiently secret to impart economic value because of its relative secrecy, "precludes trade secret protection for information generally known or understood within an industry even if not to the public at large." The second requirement, that the plaintiff take reasonable efforts to maintain the secrecy of the information, prevents a plaintiff who takes no affirmative measures to prevent others from using its proprietary information from obtaining trade secret protection.

Although the Act explicitly defines a trade secret in terms of these two requirements, Illinois courts frequently refer to six common law factors (which are derived from § 757 of the Restatement (First) of Torts) in determining whether a trade secret exists: (1) the extent to which the information is known outside of the plaintiff's business; (2) the extent to which the information is known by employees and others involved in the plaintiff's business; (3) the extent of measures taken by the plaintiff to guard the secrecy of the information; (4) the value of the information to the plaintiff's business and to its competitors; (5) the amount of time, effort and money expended by the plaintiff in developing the information; and (6) the ease or difficulty with which the information could be properly acquired or duplicated by others.

Contrary to Learning Curve's contention, we do not construe the foregoing factors as a six-part test, in which the absence of evidence on any single factor necessarily precludes a finding of trade secret protection. Instead, we interpret the common law factors as instructive guidelines for ascertaining whether a trade secret exists under the Act. The language of the Act itself makes no reference to these factors as independent requirements for trade secret status, and Illinois case law imposes no such requirement that each factor weigh in favor of the plaintiff * * *.

The existence of a trade secret ordinarily is a question of fact. As aptly observed by our colleagues on the Fifth Circuit, a trade secret "is one of the most elusive and difficult concepts in the law to define." In many cases, the existence of a trade secret is not obvious; it requires an ad hoc evaluation of all the surrounding circumstances. For this reason, the question of whether certain information constitutes a trade secret ordinarily is best "resolved by a fact finder after full presentation of evidence from each side." We do not believe that the district court was sufficiently mindful of these principles. The district court, in effect, treated the Restatement factors as requisite elements and substituted its judgment for that of the jury. PlayWood presented sufficient evidence for the jury reasonably to conclude that the Restatement factors weighed in Play-Wood's favor.

1.   Extent to which PlayWood's concept for noise-producing toy rail-road track was known outside of PlayWood's business

PlayWood presented substantial evidence from which the jury could have determined that PlayWood's concept for noise-producing toy railroad track was not generally known outside of Playwood's business. It was undisputed at trial that no similar track was on the market until Learning Curve launched Clickety–Clack Track™ in late 1994, more than a year after PlayWood first conceived of the concept. Of course, as Learning Curve correctly points out, "[m]erely being the first or only one to use particular information does not in and of itself transform otherwise general knowledge into a trade secret." "If it did, the first person to use the information, no matter how ordinary or well known, would be able to appropriate it to his own use under the guise of a trade secret." However, in this case, there was additional evidence from which the jury could have determined that PlayWood's concept was not generally known within the industry.

First, there was substantial testimony that Learning Curve had attempted to differentiate its track from that of its competitors for several months, but that it had been unable to do so successfully.

[PlayWood's expert testified that PlayWood's concept was unique, and differentiated the design from the competition. Additionally, Learning

Curve received a patent on the design, which required that it be novel. The court rejected Learning Curve's argument that PlayWood's design was not novel.]

2. Extent to which PlayWood's concept was known to employees and others involved in PlayWood's business

[The court held that this factor favored PlayWood.]

3. Measures taken by PlayWood to guard the secrecy of its concept

There also was sufficient evidence for the jury to determine that PlayWood took reasonable precautions to guard the secrecy of its concept. The Act requires the trade secret owner to take actions that are "reasonable under the circumstances to maintain [the] secrecy or confidentiality" of its trade secret; it does not require perfection. Whether the measures taken by a trade secret owner are sufficient to satisfy the Act's reasonableness standard ordinarily is a question of fact for the jury. Indeed, we previously have recognized that only in an extreme case can what is a "reasonable" precaution be determined as a matter of law, because the answer depends on a balancing of costs and benefits that will vary from case to case.

Here, the jury was instructed that it must find "by a preponderance of the evidence that PlayWood's trade secrets were given to Learning Curve as a result of a confidential relationship between the parties." By returning a verdict in favor of PlayWood, the jury necessarily found that Learning Curve was bound to PlayWood by a pledge of confidentiality. The jury's determination is amply supported by the evidence. Both Clausi and Moore testified that they entered into an oral confidentiality agreement with Abraham and Wilson before beginning their discussion on February 18, 1993 * * *. In addition to this testimony, the jury heard that Learning Curve had disclosed substantial information to PlayWood during the February 18th meeting, including projected volumes, costs and profit margins for various products, as well as drawings for toys not yet released to the public. The jury could have inferred that Learning Curve would not have disclosed such information in the absence of a confidentiality agreement. Finally, the jury also heard (from several of Learning Curve's former business associates) that Learning Curve routinely entered into oral confidentiality agreements like the one with PlayWood.

PlayWood might have done more to protect its secret. As Learning Curve points out, PlayWood gave its only prototype of the noise-producing track to Wilson without first obtaining a receipt or written confidentiality agreement from Learning Curve—a decision that proved unwise in hindsight. Nevertheless, we believe that the jury was entitled to conclude that PlayWood's reliance on the oral confidentiality agreement was reasonable under the circumstances of this case. First, it is well established that "[t]he formation of a confidential relationship imposes upon the disclosee the duty to maintain the information received in the utmost secrecy" and that "the unprivileged use or disclosure of another's trade secret becomes the basis for an action in tort." Second, both Clausi and Moore testified that they believed PlayWood had a realistic chance to "get in the door" with Learning Curve and to produce the concept as part of Learning Curve's line of Thomas products. Clausi and Moore did not anticipate that Learning Curve would violate the oral confidentiality agreement and utilize PlayWood's concept without permission; rather, they believed in good faith that they "were going to do business one day again with Learning Curve with respect to the design concept." Finally, we believe that, as part of the reasonableness inquiry, the jury could have considered the size and sophistication of the parties, as well as the relevant industry. Both PlayWood and Learning Curve were small toy companies, and PlayWood was the smaller and less experienced of the two. Viewing the evidence in the light most favorable to PlayWood, as we must, we conclude that there was sufficient evidence for the jury to determine that PlayWood took reasonable measures to protect the secrecy of its concept.

4. Value of the concept to PlayWood and to its competitors

There was substantial evidence from which the jury could have determined that PlayWood's concept had value both to PlayWood and to its competitors. It was undisputed at trial that Learning Curve's sales skyrocketed after it began to sell Clickety–Clack Track™. In addition, PlayWood's expert witness, Michael Kennedy, testified that PlayWood's concept for noise-producing track had tremendous value. Kennedy testified that the "cross-cuts and changes in the [track's] surface" imparted value to its seller by causing the track to "look different, feel different and sound different than generic track." Kennedy further testified that, in his opinion, the track would have commanded a premium royalty under a negotiated license agreement because the "invention allows its seller to differentiate itself from a host of competitors who are making a generic product with whom it is competing in a way that is proprietary and exclusive, and it gives [the seller] a significant edge over [its] competition."

[The trial court concluded that PlayWood's prototype had no economic value, as it was imperfect: the grooves were too deep to allow the train to roll smoothly. The appellate court rejected that conclusion, as PlayWood's expert testified that contracts in the toy industry were often negotiated using such imperfect prototypes, and the value in PlayWood's prototype was from the idea; the product could be perfected later, as indeed it was.]

It is irrelevant under Illinois law that PlayWood did not actually use the concept in its business. "[T]he proper criterion is not 'actual use' but whether the trade secret is 'of value' to the company."[1] Kennedy's

---

1. Both the Uniform Trade Secrets Act and the Restatement (Third) of Unfair Competition expressly reject prior use by the person asserting rights in the information as a prerequisite to trade secret protection. See Unif. Trade Secrets Act § 1 cmt. (1990) ("The broader definition in the proposed Act extends protection to a plaintiff who has not yet had an opportunity or acquired the means to put a trade secret to use."); Restatement (Third) of Unfair Competition § 39 cmt. e (1995) ("Use by the person asserting rights in the information is not a prerequisite to protection under the rule stated in this Section," in part, because such a "requirement can deny protection

testimony was more than sufficient to permit the jury to conclude that the concept was "of value" to PlayWood. It is equally irrelevant that Play-Wood did not seek to patent its concept. So long as the concept remains a secret, i.e., outside of the public domain, there is no need for patent protection. Professor Milgrim makes this point well: "Since every inventor has the right to keep his invention secret, one who has made a patentable invention has the option to maintain it in secrecy, relying upon protection accorded to a trade secret rather than upon the rights which accrue by a patent grant." 1 Roger M. Milgrim, Milgrim on Trade Secrets § 1.08[1], at 1–353 (2002). It was up to PlayWood, not the district court, to determine when and how the concept should have been disclosed to the public.

5. Amount of time, effort and money expended by PlayWood in developing its concept

PlayWood expended very little time and money developing its concept; by Clausi's own account, the cost to PlayWood was less than one dollar and the time spent was less than one-half hour. The district court determined that "[s]uch an insignificant investment is * * * insufficient as a matter of Illinois law to establish the status of a 'trade secret.' " We believe that the district court gave too much weight to the time, effort and expense of developing the track.

Although Illinois courts commonly look to the Restatement factors for guidance in determining whether a trade secret exists, as we have noted earlier, the requisite statutory inquiries under Illinois law are (1) whether the information "is sufficiently secret to derive economic value, actual or potential, from not being generally known to other persons who can obtain economic value from its disclosure or use;" and (2) whether the information "is the subject of efforts that are reasonable under the circumstances to maintain its secrecy or confidentiality." 765 ILCS 1065/2(d). A significant expenditure of time and/or money in the production of information may provide evidence of value, which is relevant to the first inquiry above. However, we do not understand Illinois law to require such an expenditure in all cases.

As pointed out by the district court, several Illinois cases have emphasized the importance of developmental costs. However, notably, none of those cases concerned the sort of innovative and creative concept that we have in this case. Indeed, several of the cases in Illinois that emphasize developmental costs concern compilations of data, such as customer lists. In that context, it makes sense to require the expenditure of significant time and money because there is nothing original or creative about the alleged trade secret. Given enough time and money, we presume that the plaintiff's competitors could compile a similar list.

Here, by contrast, we are dealing with a new toy design that has been promoted as "the first significant innovation in track design since the inception of wooden train systems." Toy designers, like many artistic

---

during periods of research and development and is particularly burdensome for innovators who do not possess the capability to exploit their innovations.").

individuals, have intuitive flashes of creativity. Often, that intuitive flash is, in reality, the product of earlier thought and practice in an artistic craft. We fail to see how the value of PlayWood's concept would differ in any respect had Clausi spent several months and several thousand dollars creating the noise-producing track. Accordingly, we conclude that Play-Wood's lack of proof on this factor does not preclude the existence of a trade secret.

6.   Ease or difficulty with which PlayWood's concept could have been properly acquired or duplicated by others

Finally, we also believe that there was sufficient evidence for the jury to determine that PlayWood's concept could not have been easily acquired or duplicated through proper means. PlayWood's expert witness, Michael Kennedy, testified: "This is a fairly simple product if you look at it. But the truth is that because it delivers feeling and sound as well as appearance, it isn't so simple as it first appears. It's a little more elegant, actually, than you might think." In addition to Kennedy's testimony, the jury heard that Learning Curve had spent months attempting to differentiate its track from Brio's before Clausi disclosed PlayWood's concept of noise-producing track. From this evidence, the jury could have inferred that, if PlayWood's concept really was obvious, Learning Curve would have thought of it earlier.

[The trial court concluded that PlayWood's design was not a trade secret, because as soon as it appeared on the market, it could have been easily reverse engineered and duplicated, destroying any trade secret protection. The appellate court agreed that it may be easy to reverse engineer, but at the time the track was disclosed confidentially to Learning Curve, it had not been disclosed to the public, and so was still secret.]

* * *

Conclusion

For the foregoing reasons, the judgment of the district court is reversed, and the jury's verdict is reinstated. The case is remanded to the district court for a jury trial on exemplary damages and for consideration of attorneys' fees by the court. PlayWood may recover its costs in this court.

MANGREN RESEARCH AND DEVELOPMENT CORP. v. NATIONAL CHEMICAL CO.

United States Court of Appeals for the Seventh Circuit, 1996.
87 F.3d 937.

ILANA DIAMOND ROVNER, CIRCUIT JUDGE.

[This case was a diversity action, brought under the Illinois Trade Secrets Act (ITSA). Mangren contended that the defendants misappropriated its trade secrets in the course of developing and marketing a competing mold release agent. At trial, the jury found for Mangren, awarding $252,684.69 in compensatory damages and $505,369.38 in exemplary damages, to which the court added Mangren's attorneys' fees and costs. Defendants contend that Mangren did not have any protectable trade secrets, or that defendants did not misappropriate any secrets.]

I.

A.

Mangren's story is one of a grass-roots operation that made good. The company was founded in 1974 by Ted Blackman and Peter Lagergren while they were chemistry students at the University of Texas. Mangren initially manufactured dog shampoo and industrial cleaners and solvents in a garage that belonged to Blackman's father-in-law. Eventually, however, the company began to produce mold release agents. Rubber and plastics manufacturers apply such agents to the molds and presses they use in the manufacturing process. Typically, the end-product is formed by filling a mold or press with a liquified rubber or plastic and then heating, which causes the liquid to solidify and to take the shape of the vessel containing it. The mold release agent is designed to prevent the solidifying substance from sticking to the mold during this process.

[In the mid–1970's, at the request of Masonite, a major consumer of mold release agents, Mangren began development of a mold release agent; after eighteen months of study, they found a chemical that suited their needs in a particular type of polytetrafluoroethylene ("PTFE"). This type of PTFE had three essential characteristics: (1) it was highly degraded; (2) it had a low molecular weight; and (3) it had low tensile strength. At the time of this discovery, PTFE was never used as the primary component of a mold release agent. Mangren's first product made use of TL–102, a PTFE; Masonite approved the product after much testing. The agent was cheap to produce, but so valuable that Mangren was able to price it high and earn a considerable profit.]

Having had considerable success selling to Masonite, Mangren decided to market its product to others as well. It first compiled a list of companies that produced molded rubber and plastic products. Yet, because not all of those manufacturers would have the equipment necessary to use Mangren's mold release agent, the company contacted each one individually, explaining its product and the equipment needed to use it. In this way, Mangren developed a list of potential customers, but only after devoting a considerable amount of time and effort to the project.

Even as its sales grew, Mangren remained a small company, never having more than six employees at any one time. Because its success depended on the uniqueness of its mold release agent, Mangren took a number of steps to ensure that its formula remained secret. First, all employees were required to sign a confidentiality agreement, and non-employees were not permitted in the company's laboratory. Once chemical ingredients were delivered to the company's premises, moreover, the labels identifying those ingredients were removed and replaced with coded labels understood only by Mangren employees. The company's financial and other records also referred to ingredients only by their code names.

B.

The seeds of the present lawsuit were planted when Mangren made two ill-fated hiring decisions in the 1980s. First, it hired Rhonda Allen in 1986 to be its office manager. Eventually, however, Allen became Mangren's sales manager, a position that provided her access to Mangren's customers and its pricing policies. In 1988, Mangren hired Larry Venable, an organic chemist, to help Blackman develop a chromium-free mold release agent. Although Venable did not have prior experience with PTFE-based mold release agents, he and Blackman succeeded in developing a chromium-free product that also used a highly degraded PTFE with low molecular weight and low tensile strength.

For reasons not relevant here, Mangren terminated the employment of Allen and Venable in 1989. After holding two intervening jobs, Venable met William Lerch early in 1990. Lerch had recently incorporated defendant National Chemical Company, Inc. ("National Chemical"), which was but one of a number of companies he then owned. Venable told Lerch about his Mangren experience and about an idea he had for developing a mold release agent to be used in the rubber industry. Lerch was excited about the prospect and inquired about the market for such a product. Venable responded that Masonite was a large user and therefore a potential customer.

The two discussed the possibility that they might be sued by Mangren if they developed a competing mold release agent. Venable was especially concerned because he realized that any product he could develop would be similar to Mangren's mold release agent. He knew, for example, that a mold release agent using TL–102—the PTFE that Mangren used—would be "potentially troublesome" and probably would prompt a lawsuit. Lerch told Venable not to worry about a misappropriation suit and explained that he had once been accused of trade secret infringement but had won the case by changing one ingredient or proportion of ingredients in creating his product. Lerch laughed and said the same thing would happen here. Shortly thereafter, Lerch and Venable incorporated defendant National Mold Release Company to manufacture the mold release agent that National Chemical would sell.

[Venable developed a mold release agent, mostly using a PTFE designated as TL–10, though he occasionally used TL–102 as well. Venable also recommended that Lerch hire Allen to market the product, and Allen was hired as a vice president and placed in charge of developing a customer base. Allen approached Mangren customers she was familiar with from her time there with news of the new product and a slightly lower price than Mangren's. Masonite in particular was interested and purchased the product after some testing.]

Venable and Allen left defendants in April 1991. Venable began to work as a consultant for Bash Corporation ("Bash"), a Chicago-based construction supply company. Venable provided Bash with a mold release agent formula that was substantially derived from defendants' formula. Allen, whom Bash had hired on Venable's recommendation, then presented Bash's product to Masonite as the same high quality product she had sold on behalf of National Chemical. Indeed, in a letter notifying Masonite of her association with Bash, Allen represented that:

> This change will not affect Masonite in any way, except for the better. You can still expect the same quality coatings and service I have provided you with in the past * * *. The only change will be in my company name and address. Even the names of the coatings will not change.

Because of its similarity to defendants' mold release agent, Bash was quickly able to qualify its product for use at Masonite and to begin selling to that company. Early in 1992, however, Bash went out of business, prompting Allen to incorporate Bash Chemical Corporation ("Bash Chemical") in Texas. That company then continued to manufacture and market the same mold release agent previously sold by the Illinois-based Bash. * * *

II.

* * *

A.

Under the ITSA, the term "trade secret" means

information, including but not limited to, technical or non-technical data, a formula, pattern, compilation, program, device, method, technique, drawing, process, financial data, or list of actual or potential customers or suppliers, that:

> (1) is sufficiently secret to derive economic value, actual or potential, from not being generally known to other persons who can obtain economic value from its disclosure; and

> (2) is the subject of efforts that are reasonable under the circumstances to maintain its secrecy or confidentiality.

This definition codifies two requirements for trade secret protection that had developed under the state's common law, both of which focus on the secrecy of the information sought to be protected. Defendants argue that Mangren failed to establish either element here.

Under the first statutory requirement, the information at issue "must be sufficiently secret to impart economic value to both its owner and its competitors because of its relative secrecy." This requirement precludes trade secret protection for information generally known within an industry even if not to the public at large. A plaintiff like Mangren must prove that the real value of the information "lies in the fact that it is not generally known to others who could benefit [from] using it." The evidence in this case presents a textbook example of information satisfying this requirement.

When Mangren first embarked on its mission to develop for Masonite a more effective mold release agent, Masonite was purchasing a product from DuPont that employed a flurotelemer as its primary ingredient. After eighteen months of intensive research and testing, Blackman and Lagergren found that a particular type of PTFE (one that was highly degraded and that had a low molecular weight and low tensile strength) would make their mold release agent more effective and less expensive than that of DuPont. When they made this discovery, the prevailing view was that such a PTFE was unsuited for the type of application that Blackman and Lagergren envisioned. Thus, Mangren was the first to successfully use this particular type of PTFE in a mold release agent. Although defendants are quick to point out that "[m]erely being the first or only one to use particular information does not in and of itself transform otherwise general knowledge into a trade secret," there was sufficient evidence for the jury to conclude that Mangren was not using general knowledge at all. A reasonable jury could find instead that Mangren had developed a distinctive formula based on information not generally known or accepted within the industry.

Mangren proved, moreover, that secrecy imparted considerable economic value to its new formula. Although its mold release agent was relatively inexpensive to produce, Mangren was able to exact a substantial price because of the product's value to the customers who used it. Masonite, in fact, attempted to find another supplier and even to develop its own mold release agent at one point, but was unable to find or to develop an equally effective product. Mangren, then, clearly satisfied the first of the statute's two requirements for a trade secret.

Defendants nonetheless contend that Mangren did not satisfy the second, as it did not make a reasonable effort to maintain the secrecy of its formula. They argue, for example, that all of Mangren's employees (of which there were never more than six at a time) knew Mangren's formula, that an observer of Mangren's premises could identify the formula's ingredients because Mangren did not replace existing labels with coded labels until ingredients had been delivered, and that Mangren could not produce signed agreements from Venable or Allen promising to maintain the confidentiality of its formula.

Arrayed against these purported deficiencies, however, is considerable evidence that the company made substantial efforts to protect the secrecy of its formula. Although Mangren was unable to produce confidentiality agreements for Venable and Allen, it presented to the jury signed agreements for other Mangren employees. Blackman testified, moreover, that each employee (including Venable and Allen) was required to sign a confidentiality agreement and that employees were further advised of the secret status of the company's mold release agent formula. Lagergren added that only Mangren employees were permitted in the company's laboratory. Mangren also demonstrated that it regularly replaced identifying labels with coded labels once ingredients were delivered to its premises. Those ingredients were then referred to in Mangren's financial and other records only by their code names. Even if Mangren could have taken further protective measures just in case, as defendants suggest, a devious potential competitor were to stake out its premises and attempt to identify the chemicals delivered there, whether or not the actions Mangren actually took were sufficient to satisfy the ITSA's reasonableness standard was a question for the jury. The evidence was certainly sufficient to enable reasonable jurors to conclude that Mangren made ample efforts to maintain the secrecy of its formula.

B.

Having determined that Mangren established a protectable trade secret in its mold release agent formula, we turn to the question of misappropriation. The ITSA defines a "misappropriation" in pertinent part as follows:

[D]isclosure or use of a trade secret of a person without express or implied consent by another person who: * * *

(B) at the time of disclosure or use, knew or had reason to know that knowledge of the trade secret was:

(I) derived from or through a person who utilized improper means to acquire it:

(II) acquired under circumstances giving rise to a duty to maintain its secrecy or limit its use; or

(III) derived from or through a person who owed a duty to the person seeking relief to maintain its secrecy or limit its use * * *.

Defendants argue that they did not "use" Mangren's trade secret under this definition because their mold release agent formula is not the same as Mangren's. Although they concede that the primary ingredient of their formula is also a highly degraded PTFE with a low molecular weight and low tensile strength, defendants emphasize that many of the other ingredients are different. Furthermore, the specific PTFE used in defendants' product is typically not the same as the one used by Mangren, although its essential characteristics are identical. Finally, defendants use a slightly smaller volume of PTFE in their mold release agent—twenty as opposed to twenty-three percent in Mangren's product. These differences, in defendants' view, should have precluded the jury from finding that they misappropriated Mangren's formula.

Defendants' argument, however, is inconsistent even with the jury instruction to which they agreed below. The jury was instructed that:

In order for you to find that defendants misappropriated one of Mangren's trade secrets, you do not have to find that defendants copied or used each and every element of the trade secret. You may find that defendants misappropriated Mangren's trade secrets even if defendants created a new product if defendants could not have done so without use of Mangren's trade secret.

That instruction, as defendants apparently conceded below, is consistent with traditional trade secret law. We observed in *In re Innovative Constr. Sys., Inc.*, 793 F.2d 875, 887 (7th Cir. 1986), for example, that "the user of another's trade secret is liable even if he uses it with modifications or improvements upon it effected by his own efforts, so long as the substance of the process used by the actor is derived from the other's secret." Although that decision involved Wisconsin law, the law of Illinois is in accord. We have observed before, in fact, that if trade secret law were not flexible enough to encompass modified or even new products that are substantially derived from the trade secret of another, the protections that law provides would be hollow indeed.

Mangren emphasizes, moreover, that the trade secret misappropriated here was not necessarily its overall formula, but the essential secret ingredient—a highly degraded PTFE having a low molecular weight and low tensile strength, which had previously been considered unsuitable for such an application.[2] Defendants do not contest that they use a similar PTFE in their mold release agent and that it was Venable, the former Mangren employee, who revealed to them that such a PTFE could be used effectively. Once Venable let defendants in on the secret and defendants then used that secret to develop their own product, there plainly was a misappropriation even if defendants' product was not identical to Mangren's. In other words, reasonable jurors could conclude from the evidence in this case that defendants' mold release agent was substantially derived from Mangren's trade secret, for defendants could not have produced their product without using that secret. Defendants were not therefore entitled to judgment as a matter of law or to a new trial on the trade secret and misappropriation issues. * * *

This hyperbolic argument misses the mark. Mangren has never suggested that because it was the first to develop a PTFE-based mold release agent, it has the exclusive right to produce and market such a product—as if it held a patent on the product, for example. Mangren would certainly have

---

2. In their reply brief and again at oral argument, defendants stridently attacked this characterization of the trade secret:

Mangren's argument seems to be that no one (at least not Venable, Allen or defendants) may ever use a PTFE similar to the one used by Mangren in its mold release formula. Mangren says this notwithstanding the fact that Blackman himself testified that Mangren used at least three different PTFEs which have the necessary characteristics for the mold release Mangren produced, and that there are dozens more of such PTFEs commercially available. If one is to take Mangren's argument literally, no one can ever use a highly degraded, low molecular weight, low tensile strength PTFE in a mold release agent without violating Mangren's alleged trade secret. Although such a conclusion makes bad law as well as bad sense, it is where Mangren's argument necessarily leads.

no claim for misappropriation if another company, after months of independent research and testing, developed a mold release agent using a similar PTFE. Under that scenario, of course, there would be no misappropriation at all because our hypothetical company would have developed its product in the same way that Mangren did—through its own ingenuity. But if, as Mangren proved to the jury's satisfaction in this case, the other company markets a PTFE-based mold release agent that it developed not through independent research and testing, but by using Mangren's trade secret, there was a misappropriation for which the law provides a remedy. That conclusion, which is actually where Mangren's argument leads, makes neither bad law nor bad sense.

IV.

Because the trial evidence amply supports the jury's verdict, the district court properly denied defendants' renewed motion for judgment as a matter of law or for a new trial. The district court's judgment is therefore

Affirmed.

NOTES

1. One Act of Misappropriation or Many? In 2002, the California Supreme court was asked to review the following question by the Ninth Circuit:

> Under the California Uniform Trade Secrets Act ("UTSA"), when does a claim for trade secret infringement arise: only once, when the initial misappropriation occurs, or with each subsequent misuse of the trade secret?

The California Supreme Court responded that continued use of misappropriated trade secrets was part of a single claim, arising at the time of initial misappropriation. *See Cadence Design Systems, Inc. v. Avant! Corp.*, 29 Cal.4th 215, 127 Cal.Rptr.2d 169, 57 P.3d 647 (2002).

2. The Continuing Relevance of the Restatement. One point to remember in approaching trade secret cases is that despite the UTSA's wide spread acceptance, the definition of a trade secret from the Restatement of Torts § 757 still is important, even in UTSA states. Courts will often give weight to the old Restatement definition and refer to it to when applying the UTSA.

3. Elements of Trade Secrets

Common to all the definitions of trade secrets are the following elements: (i) information (ii) which is valuable through not being generally known to others (iii) which the holder has tried to keep secret. Information covers a wide range of subject matter, including chemical formulae, toy designs, pricing data, investment strategies, and the ever present customer list. This section explores these three elements of a trade secret.

a. Information

DeGIORGIO v. MEGABYTE INTERNATIONAL, INC.

Supreme Court of Georgia, 1996.
266 Ga. 539, 468 S.E.2d 367.

CARLEY, JUSTICE.

[Megabyte is a distributor of computer hardware components. DeGiorgio was a salesman for Megabyte for several months before leaving to join American Megabyte Distributors, Inc. (AMDI), a newly formed competitor. At trial, Megabyte produced evidence that their customer and vendor lists, entrusted to DeGiorgio, had been faxed to AMDI's president by DeGiorgio. Megabyte was granted an interlocutory injunction by the trial court, and DeGiorgio and AMDI appealed.] * * *

2. Appellants further contend that the lists were not trade secrets which could support a grant of interlocutory injunctive relief under the Georgia Trade Secrets Act.

The lists at issue contained the identities of actual customers and vendors of Megabyte and specific information concerning them. Thus, the information on the lists was not readily ascertainable from any source other than Megabyte's business records. "Such a source would be improper if [Megabyte] had made a reasonable effort to maintain the secrecy of those customer [and vendor] lists." A review of the record reveals evidence from which the trial court could have found that Megabyte had made such a reasonable effort to maintain the secrecy of the customer and vendor lists which the trial court determined to be trade secrets. Accordingly, the trial court did not abuse its discretion in granting an interlocutory injunction under the Trade Secrets Act.

[The court then found that the injunction issued by the trial court was overly broad, and reversed that portion of the lower court's holding, before remanding the case.]

b. Value Through Secrecy

BUFFETS, INC. v. KLINKE

United States Court of Appeals for the Ninth Circuit, 1996.
73 F.3d 965.

D.W. NELSON, CIRCUIT JUDGE:

[Buffets Inc., doing business as Old Country Buffets (OCB), filed a complaint against the Klinkes for misappropriation of OCB's recipes and training manual, which OCB claimed as trade secrets. The district court, following a bench trial, entered judgment for the Klinkes.

Buffets, Inc. operates the nationwide chain of Old Country Buffet restaurants, serving all-you-can-eat food cafeteria-style for a fixed price. Dennis Scott, one of the founders of OCB, developed the menus and instituted the practice of "small batch cooking," which helps ensure freshness by only preparing small quantities at a time. Scott was an experience restaurateur, and adapted many of the recipes he was familiar with for this use. In 1989, Scott founded a new company, Evergreen Buffets, which began opening OCB restaurants. Scott's partner, Joel Brown, hired Mark Miller to work at one restaurant; Miller was later fired for alleged financial improprieties.]

In 1990, Scott met the Appellees Klinkes and gave them a tour of one of the OCB restaurants. The Klinkes were themselves successful restaurateurs, having operated a number of franchise restaurants for over 40 years. The Klinkes asked if they could buy an OCB franchise, but were told that OCB was not franchising. Paul Klinke, who was acquainted with Miller, later arranged for one of his former employees, Jack Bickle, to begin working at one of the OCB restaurants.

In March 1991, Scott, who had by now left OCB, again met with the Klinkes and told them that Miller might assist them in opening a buffet restaurant. Paul Klinke contacted Miller and Miller began working with him in April of 1991. Moreover, on March 19, 1991, Paul Klinke had dinner with Bickle and asked Bickle to provide him with OCB recipes and to get his son, Greg, a job as a cook at one of the OCB stores. Paul offered Bickle $60.00, but Bickle refused both the money and the opportunity to perform those services.

Between March 19, 1991 and April 2, 1991, Greg Klinke and Miller discussed the possibility of Greg's obtaining work at one of the OCB restaurants. On April 2, Greg applied for a job as a cook. On his application, however, he did not disclose either his true residence or his experience as a cook working for his parents. Nor did he reveal the fact that he was still on his parents' payroll.

That summer, Miller asked one of Scott's former administrative assistants to help him compile an employee's manual. Miller provided the bulk of the material for the manuals; the district court found that the new manuals were "almost exact copies of OCB position manuals." In August, Miller gave a licensed transcriber a box of recipes to retype and subsequently delivered to the Klinkes what the district court described as the "OCB recipes." The district court found that when the Klinkes first opened their buffet restaurant, Granny's, they used the copied position manuals to train their employees and the OCB recipes to prepare their dishes * * * After a bench trial, it held that neither the recipes nor the job manuals were trade secrets. * * *

Discussion

I. Trade Secret Status of the Recipes

[Washington defines a trade secret as] "information, including a formula, pattern, compilation, program, device, method, technique or process that:

(a) Derives independent economic value, actual or potential, from not being generally known to, and not being readily ascertainable by proper means by, other persons who can obtain economic value from its disclosure or use; and

(b) Is the subject of efforts that are reasonable under the circumstances to maintain its secrecy."

[T]he Washington Supreme Court makes the important distinction between copyright law and trade secrets law, noting that "[c]opyright does not protect an idea itself, only its particular expression * * *. By contrast, trade secrets law protects the author's very ideas if they possess some novelty and are undisclosed or disclosed only on the basis of confidentiality." OCB argues that novelty is not a requirement for trade secret protection; this contention, however, clearly contradicts Washington law. Moreover, contrary to OCB's assertions, the district court's finding that the recipes were more detailed than those of its competitors does not mandate a finding of novelty, for as is discussed below, the court held that even these detailed procedures were readily ascertainable.

Many of OCB's remaining arguments on appeal appear to misunderstand the logic of the district court's opinion. The district court did not hold, as OCB contends, that the recipes were not trade secrets merely because they had their origins in the public domain, but also because many of them were "basic American dishes that are served in buffets across the United States." This finding was certainly not erroneous. The recipes were for such American staples as BBQ chicken and macaroni and cheese and the procedures, while detailed, are undeniably obvious. Thus, this is not a case where material from the public domain has been refashioned or recreated in such a way so as to be an original product, but is rather an instance where the end-product is itself unoriginal.

Furthermore, OCB mischaracterizes the court's holding regarding the extent to which the recipes were readily ascertainable, suggesting that the court denied the recipes trade secret status merely because they could be reproduced. While this is not altogether incorrect, it was the reason that the recipes could be reproduced—namely, because they were little more than typical American fare—that led the court to conclude that they were readily ascertainable and thus not entitled to trade secret protection. There is thus no indication that the "defendant by an expenditure of effort might have collected the same information from sources available to the public."; rather, the alleged secrets here at issue were found to be so obvious that very little effort would be required to "discover" them.

OCB's contention that material may be protected by trade secret law even if its origins are in the public domain is thus irrelevant. Not only did the district court hold that the recipes and their procedures had their origins in well-known American cuisine, but it also maintained that in spite of their alleged innovative detail, they "[were] fairly basic" and could easily be discovered by others. A trade secrets plaintiff need not prove that every element of an information compilation is unavailable elsewhere.

Trade secrets frequently contain elements that by themselves may be in the public domain but together qualify as trade secrets. The district court here found that the recipes themselves, and not merely their different components or any earlier formulations from which they may have been derived, were readily ascertainable.

The district court further held that the recipes had no independent economic value, a finding OCB fails to address adequately on appeal. OCB's argument focuses only on that portion of the district court's opinion that held that the recipes had no independent value because OCB had not proven that its food offerings were "superior in quality to that of its rivals." This, however, was not the sole basis for the court's holding. The court held that even though OCB food tasted better than that of its rivals and few of its rivals were succeeding, "OCB [had] failed to establish by a preponderance of the evidence that its rivals [were] not succeeding because of inferior food quality." The court thus notes that there was no demonstrated relationship between the lack of success of OCB's competitors and the unavailability of the recipes, i.e., OCB failed to provide that it necessarily derived any benefit from the recipes being kept secret. The court also noted that "limiting food costs is crucial to the profitability of a buffet" and explained that OCB failed to demonstrate that its recipes play a role in limiting costs.

Further weighing against any finding of economic value was the court's finding that OCB's recipes had to be simplified because of the limited reading skills of its cooks. Given this fact, it appears unlikely that the recipes themselves conferred any economic benefit upon OCB because it was from "translated" versions of these recipes, rather than the highly detailed versions now at issue, that OCB cooks prepared its well-celebrated food. * * *

NOTES

1.   What is Generally Known? One California court attempted to answer this question as follows:

> By way of illustration, consider a hypothetical market for widgets, supplied by five widget sellers. There are 100,000 businesses engaged in industries which have been known to use widgets in their operations; however, there is no way for the widget sellers to know for sure which of those individual businesses use widgets and which do not. Seller A has a list of 500 businesses to which he has sold widgets in the recent past. That list proves a fact which is unknown to his competitors: that those 500 businesses are consumers of widgets, the product they are trying to sell. Therefore, it has independent value to those competitors, because it would allow them to distinguish those proven consumers, who are definitely part of the widget market, from the balance of the 100,000 potential consumers, who may or may not be part of the market. With that list, they would know to target their sales efforts on those 500 businesses, rather than on 500 other businesses who might never use widgets.

Now imagine the same facts, but assume that each of the other four sellers of widgets knows that the businesses on Seller A's customer list are proven widget consumers (although they do not know that those businesses buy their widgets from Seller A). Under those circumstances, Seller A's customer list has no independent economic value, because the identities of those consumers are already known to his competitors.

In both situations, the identities of the businesses which bought widgets from Seller A are unknown. The distinguishing factor is whether it is also unknown that those businesses bought widgets at all. Thus, the customer list in the first hypothetical would be a protectable trade secret, while the list in the second hypothetical would not be.

Abba Rubber Co. v. Seaquist, 235 Cal.App.3d 1, 286 Cal.Rptr. 518 (4th Dist. 1991).

2. "Not Being Generally Known To" Whom? Note that the UTSA refers to information that has value because it is not known to or readily ascertainable through proper means by *"other persons who can obtain economic value from its disclosure or use"* (emphasis added) while, the EEA refers to *"the public"* (emphasis added). The Seventh Circuit explored this slight difference between the definitions in *United States v. Lange*, 312 F.3d 263 (7th Cir. 2002), appearing *infra*:

The prosecutor's assumption is that the statutory reference in § 1839(3) to "the public" means the general public—the man in the street. Ordinary people don't have AutoCAD and 60–ton flywheels ready to hand. But is the general public the right benchmark? The statute itself does not give an answer: the word "public" could be preceded implicitly by "general" as the prosecutor supposes, but it also could be preceded implicitly by "educated" or "economically important" or any of many other qualifiers. Once we enter the business of adding words to flesh out the statute—and even the addition of "general" to "public" does this—it usually is best to ask what function the law serves. In criminal cases it also is important to inquire whether the unelaborated text is ambiguous, because if it is the language should be read to prevent surprises. * * *

A problem with using the general public as the reference group for identifying a trade secret is that many things unknown to the public at large are well known to engineers, scientists, and others whose intellectual property the Economic Espionage Act was enacted to protect. This makes the general public a poor benchmark for separating commercially valuable secrets from obscure (but generally known) information. Suppose that Lange had offered to sell Avogadro's number for $1. Avogadro's number, 6.02×10^{23}, is the number of molecules per mole of gas. It is an important constant, known to chemists since 1909 but not to the general public (or even to all recent graduates of a chemistry class). We can't believe that Avogadro's number could be called a trade secret. Other principles are known without being comprehended. Most people know that $E = mc^2$, but a pop quiz of the general public would reveal that they do not understand what this means or how it can be used productively.

One might respond that the context of the word "public" addresses this concern. The full text of § 1839(3)(B) is: "the information derives independent economic value, actual or potential, from not being generally known to, and not being readily ascertainable through proper means by, the public." Avogadro's number and other obscure knowledge is not "generally known to" the man in the street but might be deemed "readily ascertainable to" this hypothetical person. It appears in any number of scientific handbooks. Similarly one can visit a library and read Einstein's own discussion of his famous equation. Members of the general public can ascertain even abstruse information, such as Schrödinger's quantum field equation, by consulting people in the know—as high school dropouts can take advantage of obscure legal rules by hiring lawyers. But this approach uses the phrase "readily available" to treat the "general public" as if it were more technically competent, which poses the question whether it would be better to use a qualifier other than "general" in the first place.

Since only scientists or engineers could derive economic benefit from the information at issue in *Lange*, the court decided that, in this particular case, whether trade secret was valuable to the "general" public or the "economically relevant public" was immaterial to its decision.

3. Combination Trade Secret. In *Heyden Chemical Corp. v. Burrell & Neidig, Inc.*, the court addressed the question of when a combination of known information can constitute a trade secret:

> Defendants say that the Heyden processes are not secret. The claim is that they have been known to the trade for years and are, in fact, in the public domain. In support of this assertion there were offered in evidence various essays, treatises and patents dealing with the manufacture of formaldehyde and pentaerythritol. In my opinion, these exhibits served to strengthen the plaintiff's claim. According to the testimony, there are to be found in the scientific literature some 800 to 1,000 references dealing with the production of formaldehyde and 500 to 600 references dealing with the production of pentaerythritol. Of the references on the subject of formaldehyde about 30 were offered in evidence. A like number dealing with pentaerythritol were introduced. In every one of the exhibits the systems discussed differed in major particulars from those used by Heyden. In some even the ingredients used were different. But regardless of how different the process described might be, if it contained a single element to be found in the Heyden system, the exhibit was offered to show a public disclosure of the Heyden process. Time and again while being examined on a particular exhibit, the witness would be asked to explain why an engineer, unfamiliar with the Heyden process, in setting up a formaldehyde or pentaerythritol plant, would select one element of the process described in the reference and discard the rest. A satisfactory answer to the question was never given.

> The truth is, of course, that only a person who knew the Heyden process could make the selection of literature references which were offered in evidence. Dr. Elderfield of Columbia University, who appeared as an expert for the plaintiff and who was referred to as one of the leading authorities on organic chemistry, testified flatly that an engineer unfamiliar with the Heyden system could not duplicate that system by using the

information contained in the literature without long and expensive research and experimentation.

Heyden Chemical Corp. v. Burrell & Neidig, Inc., 2 N.J.Super. 467, 64 A.2d 465, 467 (Ch. Div. 1949).

c.   *Reasonable Efforts of Protection*

An owner of a trade secret must take reasonable efforts to maintain its secrecy through such methods as use of confidentiality agreements and technological and physical protections. The following case excerpt considers the characteristics of reasonable efforts to maintain the secrecy of trade secret information.

BUFFETS, INC. v. KLINKE

United States Court of Appeals for the Ninth Circuit, 1996.
73 F.3d 965.

[Author's Note: See discussion of facts from excerpt above.]

II.   Trade Secret Status of the Job Manuals

The district court held that the job manuals were not trade secrets as they were not the subject of reasonable efforts to maintain their secrecy. Commenting upon OCB's security measures, the court observed that "[g]iven the limited tenure of buffet employees, and the fact that they often move from restaurant to restaurant, a company which allows its employees to keep job position manuals cannot be heard to complain when its manuals fall into the hands of its rivals."

We see no error in the district court's ruling. In *Machen Inc. v. Aircraft Design, Inc.*, 65 Wash.App. 319, 828 P.2d 73 (1992), the Washington Court of Appeals cited the Uniform Trade Secrets Act for the proposition that "[r]easonable efforts to maintain secrecy have been held to include advising employees of the existence of a trade secret, limiting access to a trade secret on a 'need to know basis', and controlling plant access." The *Machen* court also notes that "general [protective] measures" may not be enough if they are not "designed to protect the disclosure of information." In this matter, the district court's finding that employees were allowed to take the job manuals home and keep them even though they were "supposed to be kept in the manager's office when not being used," directly addresses the reasonableness of OCB's security measures. Even if the manuals were loaned only on a "need-to-know" basis, as OCB claims, the fact that employees were advised of neither the manuals' status as secrets, nor of security measures that should be taken to prevent their being obtained by others, suggests that OCB's interest in security was minimal. * * *

Finally, OCB argues that since the Klinkes illegally obtained the manuals, the question of whether the security measures taken to protect them were reasonable is irrelevant. This argument, however, misses the mark, as the issue of whether security measures were reasonable pertains to the preliminary question of whether the material is in fact a trade secret. If it is not, then the Klinkes may be liable for stealing something, but they cannot be liable for misappropriation of trade secrets * * *. Thus, we affirm the court's finding that the manuals were not trade secrets.

The judgment of the district court is AFFIRMED.

NOTES

1. Effort Can Affect Protection. As with reasonableness standards in many other fields, courts will look to all the surrounding facts and circumstances to determine whether a trade secret owner has protected her trade secret. Of course, no amount of protection can affect information that is generally known, and hence in the public domain. But as a general rule, the more steps taken to protect a secret by the owner, the more likely it is that the secret will be protected by a court.

2. Protecting Confidential Information. The range of persons to whom a trade secret owner discloses the trade secret can affect the level of protection afforded to the trade secret. Note that in *Buffets, Inc.*, the employer allowed the employees to take the so-called secret manual home and gave it out to all the employees. Compare this with the situation in *Camp Creek Hospitality Inns, Inc. v. Sheraton Franchise Corp.*, 139 F.3d 1396 (11th Cir. 1998), where a Sheraton franchisee, provided secret marketing data to Sheraton Franchise under assurances that the data would be "kept in strict confidence." *Id.* at 1411. The court held that this was reasonable protection, allowing the owner to go forward with its trade secret misappropriation claim.

4. Non–UTSA Jurisdictions

Recall that Massachusetts, Texas, and New York have not adopted the UTSA. In these states, common law principles, as discussed in *Learning Curve* and the Restatement of Torts, apply.

The following case also illustrates the misappropriation of trade secret information through "improper means." The United States Supreme Court addressed the issue of trade secret laws in 1974, in *Kewanee Oil Co. v. Bicron Corp.*, 416 U.S. 470, 94 S.Ct. 1879, 40 L.Ed.2d 315. The Court held that federal patent laws did not preempt state trade secret laws on products that would otherwise be patentable subject matter. With respect to "improper means," the court noted that:

> The protection accorded the trade secret holder is against the disclosure or unauthorized use of the trade secret by those to whom the secret has been confided under the express or implied restriction of nondisclosure or nonuse. The law also protects the holder of a trade secret against disclosure or use when the knowledge is gained, not by the owner's volition, but by some 'improper means,' Restatement of Torts § 757(a), which may include theft, wiretapping, or even aerial reconnaissance. A trade secret law, however, does not offer protection against discovery by fair and honest means, such as by independent

invention, accidental disclosure, or by so-called reverse engineering, that is by starting with the known product and working backward to divine the process which aided in its development or manufacture.

Id. at 475–76.

E.I. duPONT deNEMOURS & COMPANY, INC. v. CHRISTOPHER

United States Court of Appeals for the Fifth Circuit, 1970.
431 F.2d 1012.

Goldberg, Circuit Judge:

This is a case of industrial espionage in which an airplane is the cloak and a camera the dagger. The defendants-appellants, Rolfe and Gary Christopher, are photographers in Beaumont, Texas. The Christophers were hired by an unknown third party to take aerial photographs of new construction at the Beaumont plant of E. I. duPont deNemours & Company, Inc. Sixteen photographs of the DuPont facility were taken from the air on March 19, 1969, and these photographs were later developed and delivered to the third party.

DuPont employees apparently noticed the airplane on March 19 and immediately began an investigation to determine why the craft was circling over the plant. By that afternoon the investigation had disclosed that the craft was involved in a photographic expedition and that the Christophers were the photographers. DuPont contacted the Christophers that same afternoon and asked them to reveal the name of the person or corporation requesting the photographs. The Christophers refused to disclose this information, giving as their reason the client's desire to remain anonymous.

Having reached a dead end in the investigation, DuPont subsequently filed suit against the Christophers, alleging that the Christophers had wrongfully obtained photographs revealing DuPont's trade secrets which they then sold to the undisclosed third party. DuPont contended that it had developed a highly secret but unpatented process for producing methanol, a process which gave DuPont a competitive advantage over other producers. This process, DuPont alleged, was a trade secret developed after much expensive and time-consuming research, and a secret which the company had taken special precautions to safeguard. The area photographed by the Christophers was the plant designed to produce methanol by this secret process, and because the plant was still under construction parts of the process were exposed to view from directly above the construction area. Photographs of that area, DuPont alleged, would enable a skilled person to deduce the secret process for making methanol. DuPont thus contended that the Christophers had wrongfully appropriated DuPont trade secrets by taking the photographs and delivering them to the undisclosed third party. In its suit DuPont asked for damages to cover the loss it had already sustained as a result of the wrongful disclosure of the trade secret and sought temporary and permanent injunctions prohibiting any further circulation of the photographs already taken and prohibiting any additional photographing of the methanol plant.

[The lower court denied motions to dismiss by the Christophers, as well as a motion for summary judgment, and granted DuPont's motion to compel the Christophers to disclose their client. The lower court allowed the Christophers' motion for interlocutory appeal.]

This is a case of first impression, for the Texas courts have not faced this precise factual issue, and sitting as a diversity court we must sensitize our *Erie* antennae to divine what the Texas courts would do if such a situation were presented to them. The only question involved in this interlocutory appeal is whether DuPont has asserted a claim upon which relief can be granted. The Christophers argued both at trial and before this court that they committed no "actionable wrong" in photographing the DuPont facility and passing these photographs on to their client because they conducted all of their activities in public airspace, violated no government aviation standard, did not breach any confidential relation, and did not engage in any fraudulent or illegal conduct. In short, the Christophers argue that for an appropriation of trade secrets to be wrongful there must be a trespass, other illegal conduct, or breach of a confidential relationship. We disagree.

It is true, as the Christophers assert, that the previous trade secret cases have contained one or more of these elements. However, we do not think that the Texas courts would limit the trade secret protection exclusively to these elements. On the contrary, in *Hyde Corporation v. Huffines*, 158 Tex. 566 (1958), the Texas Supreme Court specifically adopted the rule found in the Restatement of Torts which provides:

> "One who discloses or uses another's trade secret, without a privilege to do so, is liable to the other if (a) he discovered the secret by improper means, or (b) his disclosure or use constitutes a breach of confidence reposed in him by the other in disclosing the secret to him...."

Thus, although the previous cases have dealt with a breach of a confidential relationship, a trespass, or other illegal conduct, the rule is much broader than the cases heretofore encountered. Not limiting itself to specific wrongs, Texas adopted subsection (a) of the Restatement which recognizes a cause of action for the discovery of a trade secret by any "improper" means.

* * *

The question remaining, therefore, is whether aerial photography of plant construction is an improper means of obtaining another's trade secret. We conclude that it is and that the Texas courts would so hold. The Supreme Court of that state has declared that "the undoubted tendency of the law has been to recognize and enforce higher standards of commercial morality in the business world." That court has quoted with approval articles indicating that the proper means of gaining possession of a competitor's secret process is "through inspection and analysis" of the product in order to create a duplicate. Later another Texas court explained:

> "The means by which the discovery is made may be obvious, and the experimentation leading from known factors to presently unknown results may be simple and lying in the public domain. But these facts do not destroy the value of the discovery and will not advantage a competitor who by unfair means obtains the knowledge without paying the price expended by the discoverer."

We think, therefore, that the Texas rule is clear. One may use his competitor's secret process if he discovers the process by reverse engineering applied to the finished product; one may use a competitor's process if he discovers it by his own independent research; but one may not avoid these labors by taking the process from the discoverer without his permission at a time when he is taking reasonable precautions to maintain its secrecy. To obtain knowledge of a process without spending the time and money to discover it independently is improper unless the holder voluntarily discloses it or fails to take reasonable precautions to ensure its secrecy.

In the instant case the Christophers deliberately flew over the DuPont plant to get pictures of a process which DuPont had attempted to keep secret. The Christophers delivered their pictures to a third party who was certainly aware of the means by which they had been acquired and who may be planning to use the information contained therein to manufacture methanol by the DuPont process. The third party has a right to use this process only if he obtains this knowledge through his own research efforts, but thus far all information indicates that the third party has gained this knowledge solely by taking it from DuPont at a time when DuPont was making reasonable efforts to preserve its secrecy. In such a situation DuPont has a valid cause of action to prohibit the Christophers from improperly discovering its trade secret and to prohibit the undisclosed third party from using the improperly obtained information.

We note that this view is in perfect accord with the position taken by the authors of the Restatement. In commenting on improper means of discovery the savants of the Restatement said:

> "f. Improper means of discovery. The discovery of another's trade secret by improper means subjects the actor to liability independently of the harm to the interest in the secret. Thus, if one uses physical force to take a secret formula from another's pocket, or breaks into another's office to steal the formula, his conduct is wrongful and subjects him to liability apart from the rule stated in this Section. Such conduct is also an improper means of procuring the secret under this rule. But means may be improper under this rule even though they do not cause any other harm than that to the interest in the trade secret. Examples of such means are fraudulent misrepresentations to induce disclosure, tapping of telephone wires, eavesdropping

or other espionage. A complete catalogue of improper means is not possible. In general they are means which fall below the generally accepted standards of commercial morality and reasonable conduct.''

Restatement of Torts § 757, comment f at 10 (1939).

In taking this position we realize that industrial espionage of the sort here perpetrated has become a popular sport in some segments of our industrial community. However, our devotion to free wheeling industrial competition must not force us into accepting the law of the jungle as the standard of morality expected in our commercial relations. Our tolerance of the espionage game must cease when the protections required to prevent another's spying cost so much that the spirit of inventiveness is dampened. Commercial privacy must be protected from espionage which could not have been reasonably anticipated or prevented. We do not mean to imply, however, that everything not in plain view is within the protected vale, nor that all information obtained through every extra optical extension is forbidden. Indeed, for our industrial competition to remain healthy there must be breathing room for observing a competing industrialist. A competitor can and must shop his competition for pricing and examine his products for quality, components, and methods of manufacture. Perhaps ordinary fences and roofs must be built to shut out incursive eyes, but we need not require the discoverer of a trade secret to guard against the unanticipated, the undetectable, or the unpreventable methods of espionage now available.

In the instant case DuPont was in the midst of constructing a plant. Although after construction the finished plant would have protected much of the process from view, during the period of construction the trade secret was exposed to view from the air. To require DuPont to put a roof over the unfinished plant to guard its secret would impose an enormous expense to prevent nothing more than a school boy's trick. We introduce here no new or radical ethic since our ethos has never given moral sanction to piracy. The market place must not deviate far from our mores. We should not require a person or corporation to take unreasonable precautions to prevent another from doing that which he ought not do in the first place. Reasonable precautions against predatory eyes we may require, but an impenetrable fortress is an unreasonable requirement, and we are not disposed to burden industrial inventors with such a duty in order to protect the fruits of their efforts. 'Improper' will always be a word of many nuances, determined by time, place, and circumstances. We therefore need not proclaim a catalogue of commercial improprieties. Clearly, however, one of its commandments does say 'thou shall not appropriate a trade secret through deviousness under circumstances in which countervailing defenses are not reasonably available.'

* * * The decision of the trial court is affirmed and the case remanded to that court for proceedings on the merits.

NOTES

1. Restatement of Torts § 757. Comment b of the Restatement of Torts § 757 provides further information about the type of information that can qualify as a trade secret under the Restatement:

> b. *Definition of trade secret.* A trade secret may consist of any formula, pattern, device or compilation of information which is used in one's business, and which gives him an opportunity to obtain an advantage over competitors who do not know or use it. It may be a formula for a chemical compound, a process of manufacturing, treating or preserving materials, a pattern for a machine or other device, or a list of customers. It differs from other secret information in a business (see § 759) in that it is not simply information as to single or ephemeral events in the conduct of the business, as, for example, the amount or other terms of a secret bid for a contract or the salary of certain employees, or the security investments made or contemplated, or the date fixed for the announcement of a new policy or for bringing out a new model or the like. A trade secret is a process or device for continuous use in the operation of the business. Generally it relates to the production of goods, as, for example, a machine or formula for the production of an article. It may, however, relate to the sale of goods or to other operations in the business, such as a code for determining discounts, rebates or other concessions in a price list or catalogue, or a list of specialized customers, or a method of bookkeeping or other office management.

* * *

RESTATEMENT OF TORTS § 757, cmt. b (1939).

2. Process vs. Product. In *Phillips v. Frey*, 20 F.3d 623 (5th Cir. 1994) the trade secret owner sold collapsible single-pole deer stands that support elevated seats used by gun and bow hunters. The owner did not obtain a patent on the stands or on the process for making the stands. Instead, the process was protected as a trade secret. The defendant, a competitor of the trade secret owner, reverse engineered the product and was sued for trade secret misappropriation. The court analyzed the process-product distinction as follows:

> Although it is likely appellants used reverse engineering for the design of [their competing stand], there was no evidence that the appellants used this method to acquire the manufacturing process employed by Ambusher. A process or device may be a trade secret even where others can gain knowledge of the process from studying the manufacturer's marketed product. Although trade secret law does not offer protection against discovery by fair and honest means such as independent invention, accidental disclosure, or "reverse engineering," protection will be awarded to a trade secret holder against the disclosure or unauthorized use by those to whom the secret has been confided under either express or implied restriction of nondisclosure or by one who has gained knowledge by improper means.

Id. at 629.

3. The Limits of "Reasonable Efforts." The court makes much of the fact that the inside of the DuPont plant could only be viewed from the air. Would it have made a difference to the court if the Christophers had taken their photographs from the ground while DuPont was still constructing the plant walls? What is the outer limit of reasonable efforts to protect trade secrets? As previously noted, the more effort a trade secret owner puts into guarding his information the more likely a court will conclude the information is a trade secret. Accordingly, trade secret owners must balance the cost of protecting their information against the value of keeping it secret.

B. BREACH OF CONFIDENCE

SMITH v. DRAVO CORP.

United States Court of Appeals for the Seventh Circuit, 1953.
203 F.2d 369.

* * * In the early 1940s Leathem D. Smith, now deceased, began toying with an idea which, he believed, would greatly facilitate the ship and shore handling and transportation of cargoes. * * * He envisioned construction of ships especially designed to carry their cargo in uniformly sized steel freight containers. These devices (which, it appears, were the crux of his idea) were: equipped with high doors at one end; large enough for a man to enter easily; weather and pilfer proof; and bore collapsible legs, which (1) served to lock them (a) to the deck of the ship by fitting into recesses in the deck, or (b) to each other, when stacked, by reason of receiving sockets located in the upper four corners of each container, and (2) allowed sufficient clearance between deck and container or container and container for the facile insertion of a fork of a lift tractor, and (3) were equipped with lifting eyelets, which, together with a specially designed hoist, made possible placement of the containers upon or removal from a ship, railroad car or truck, while filled with cargo. The outer dimensions of the devices were such that they would fit compactly in standard gauge North American railroad cars, or narrow gauge South American trains, and in the holds of most water vessels.

World War II effectually prevented Smith from developing his conception much beyond the idea stage. Nevertheless blue prints were drawn in 1943, and in 1944, as a result of considerable publicity in trade journals and addresses delivered by Smith before trade associations, Agwilines, one of the principal New York ship operators, displayed great interest in the proposals. Certain refined features, particularly in dimensions and folding legs, were the result of discussions between Smith and Agwilines' officials. In 1945 production started, and in the fall of that year twelve containers were used by Agwilines in an experimental run. Relative success was experienced, with the result that, by the spring of 1946, Brodin Lines, Grace Lines, Delta Lines and Stockard, in addition to Agwilines, were leasing Safeway containers. (Leathem D. Smith Shipbuilding Company was the owner of the design and manufactured the containers. Safeway

Container Corporation purchased the finished containers from the shipbuilding company and leased them to shippers.) * * *

On June 23, 1946, Smith died in a sailing accident. The need for cash for inheritance tax purposes prompted his estate to survey his holdings for disposable assets. It was decided that the container business should be sold. Devices in process were completed but no work on new ones was started.

Defendant was interested in the Safeway container, primarily, it appears, for use by its subsidiary, the Union Barge Lines. In October 1946 it contacted Agwilines seeking information. It watched a loading operation in which Agwilines used the box. At approximately the same time, defendant approached the shipbuilding company and inquired as to the possibility of purchase of a number of the containers. It was told to communicate with Cowan, plaintiffs' eastern representative. This it did, and, on October 29, 1946, in Pittsburgh, Cowan met with defendant's officials to discuss the proposed sale of Safeways. But, as negotiations progressed, defendant demonstrated an interest in the entire container development. Thus, what started as a meeting to discuss the purchase of individual containers ended in the possible foundation for a sale of the entire business. Based upon this display of interest, Cowan sent detailed information to defendant concerning the business. This included: (1) patent applications for both the "knock-down" and "rigid" crates; (2) blue prints of both designs; (3) a miniature Safeway container; (4) letters of inquiry from possible users; (5) further correspondence with prospective users. In addition, defendant's representatives journeyed to Sturgeon Bay, Wisconsin, the home of the shipbuilding company, and viewed the physical plant, inventory and manufacturing operation.

Plaintiffs quoted a price of $150,000 plus a royalty of $10 per unit. This was rejected. Subsequent offers of $100,000 and $75,000 with royalties of $10 per container were also rejected. Negotiations continued until January 30, 1947, at which time defendant finally rejected plaintiffs' offer.

On January 31, 1947 defendant announced to Agwilines that it "intended to design and produce a shipping container of the widest possible utility" for "coastal steamship application * * * (and) use * * * on the inland rivers and * * * connecting highway and rail carriers." Development of the project moved rapidly, so that by February 5, 1947 defendant had set up a stock order for a freight container which was designed, by use of plaintiffs' patent applications, so as to avoid any claim of infringement. One differing feature was the use of skids and recesses running the length of the container, rather than legs and sockets as employed in plaintiffs' design. However, Agwilines rejected this design, insisting on an adaptation of plaintiffs' idea. In short defendant's final product incorporated many, if not all, of the features of plaintiffs' design. So conceived, it was accepted by the trade to the extent that, by March 1948, defendant had sold some 500 containers. Many of these sales were made to firms who had shown considerable prior interest in plaintiffs' design and had been included in the prospective users disclosed to defendant.

One particular feature of defendant's container differed from plaintiffs: its width was four inches less. As a result plaintiffs' product became obsolete. Their container could not be used interchangeably with defendant's; they ceased production. Consequently the prospects of disposing of the entire operation vanished.

The foregoing is the essence of plaintiffs' cause of action. Stripped of surplusage, the averment is that defendant obtained, through a confidential relationship, knowledge of plaintiffs' secret designs, plans and prospective customers, and then wrongfully breached that confidence by using the information to its own advantage and plaintiffs' detriment.

* * *

It is unquestionably lawful for a person to gain possession, through proper means, of his competitor's product and, through inspection and analysis, create a duplicate, unless, of course, the item is patented. But the mere fact that such lawful acquisition is available does not mean that he may, through a breach of confidence, gain the information in usable form and escape the efforts of inspection and analysis. "The fact that a trade secret is of such a nature that it can be discovered by experimentation or other fair and lawful means does not deprive its owner of the right to protection from those who would secure possession of it by unfair means." Nims, Unfair Competition and Trade Marks, Sec. 148.

This text citation is the distillate of many judicial decisions. Thus, in *A. O. Smith Corp. v. Petroleum Iron Works Co.*, 6 Cir., 73 F.2d 531, 538, the court said: "The mere fact that the means by which a discovery is made are obvious * * * cannot * * * advantage the competitor who by unfair means, or as the beneficiary of a broken faith, obtains the desired knowledge without himself paying the price in labor, money, or machines expended by the discoverer." And in *Shellmar Products Co. v. Allen–Qualley Co.*, 7 Cir., 36 F.2d 623, 625, this court announced: "Whether it would have been possible to have discovered and purchased the Olsen patent, without the information disclosed to appellant in confidence, it is not necessary to determine, because it is clear from the record that by a breach of confidence the information was disclosed and used as a basis for the search that was made." And in *Tabor v. Hoffman*, 118 N.Y. 30, 23 N.E. 12, 13, this is the language: "But, because this discovery may be possible by fair means, it would not justify a discovery by unfair means * * *."

It is, therefore, our conclusion, that the District Court applied an erroneous conclusion of law to the facts at hand. Here was no simple device, widely circulated, the construction of which was ascertainable at a glance. If such were the case our problem would be simple. Instead we are concerned with a relatively complex apparatus; designed to carry large and heavy amounts of cargo; proper inspection of which was, perhaps, accessible to defendant but, in no way shown to have been made. Under such circumstances the District Court's conclusion that plaintiffs no longer possessed a trade secret at the time of their negotiations with defendant was erroneous.

* * * Mr. Justice Holmes once said that the existence of the confidential relationship is the "starting point" in a cause of action such as this. *E. I. DuPont de Nemours Powder Co. v. Masland*, 244 U.S. 100, 102, 37 S.Ct. 575, 61 L.Ed. 1016. While we take a slightly different tack, there is no doubt as to the importance of this element of plaintiffs' case.

Certain it is that a non-confidential disclosure will not supply the basis for a law suit. Plaintiffs' information is afforded protection because it is secret. Promiscuous disclosures quite naturally destroy the secrecy and the corresponding protection. But this is not true where a confidence has been reposed carrying with it communication of an idea.

It is clear that no express promise of trust was exacted from defendant. There is, however, the further question of whether one was implied from the relationship of the parties. Pennsylvania has not provided us with a decision precisely in point but *Pressed Steel Car Co. v. Standard Car Co.*, 210 Pa. 464, 60 A. 4, furnishes abundant guideposts. There plaintiff delivered its blue prints to customers in order that they might acquaint themselves more thoroughly with the railroad cars they were purchasing; from these customers, defendant obtained the drawings. In holding that the customers held the plans as a result of a confidence reposed in them by plaintiff, and that the confidence was breached by delivery of the blue prints to defendant, the court said, 60 A. at page 10: "While there was no expressed restriction placed on the ownership of the prints, or any expressed limitation as to the use to which they were to be put, it it is clear * * * that the purpose for which they were delivered by the plaintiff was understood by all parties. * * * "

The quoted language is applicable and determinative. Here plaintiffs disclosed their design for one purpose, to enable defendant to appraise it with a view in mind of purchasing the business. There can be no question that defendant knew and understood this limited purpose. Trust was reposed in it by plaintiffs that the information thus transmitted would be accepted subject to that limitation. "(T)he first thing to be made sure of is that the defendant shall not fraudulently abuse the trust reposed in him. It is the usual incident of confidential relations. If there is any disadvantage in the fact that he knew the plaintiffs' secrets, he must take the burden with the good." *E. I. DuPont de Nemours Powder Co. v. Masland*, 244 U.S. 100 at page 102, 37 S.Ct. 575, at page 576, 61 L.Ed. 1016.

Nor is it an adequate answer for defendant to say that the transactions with plaintiffs were at arms length. That fact does not detract from the conclusion that but for those very transactions defendant would not have learned, from plaintiffs, of the container design. The implied limitation on the use to be made of the information had its roots in the "arms-length" transaction.

Defendant's own evidence discloses that it did not begin to design its container until after it had access to plaintiffs' plans. Defendant's engineers admittedly referred to plaintiffs' patent applications, as they said, to avoid infringement. It is not disputed that, at the urging of Agwilines, defendant revised its proposed design to incorporate the folding leg and socket principles of plaintiffs' containers. These evidentiary facts, together with the striking similarity between defendant's and plaintiffs' finished product, were more than enough to convict defendant of the improper use of the structural information obtained from plaintiffs.

NOTES

1. The Element of Knowledge. According to the court, a defendant's knowledge of the purposes for which a plaintiff disclosed its trade secrets is central to establishing a breach of confidence. Under what circumstances may a defendant legitimately claim that it lacked knowledge of the purpose for which a plaintiff disclosed its trade secrets during negotiations?

C. DEFENSES TO MISAPPROPRIATION AND RIGHTS AGAINST OTHERS

Unlike patent infringement, which is a strict liability offense, liability for trade secret misappropriation depends on how the protected information was misappropriated. It is not enough to simply use a trade secret without the permission of the owner. A party must have acquired and used the information in an improper manner.

1. The Honest Discoverer

According to § 1(2) of the Uniform Trade Secrets Act:

(2) "Misappropriation" means: (i) acquisition of a trade secret of another by a person who knows or has reason to know that the trade secret was acquired by improper means; or (ii) disclosure or use of a trade secret of another without express or implied consent by a person who (A) used improper means to acquire knowledge of the trade secret; or (B) at the time of disclosure or use knew or had reason to know that his knowledge of the trade secret was (I) derived from or through a person who has utilized improper means to acquire it; (II) acquired under circumstances giving rise to a duty to maintain its secrecy or limit its use; or (III) derived from or through a person who owed a duty to the person seeking relief to maintain its secrecy or limit its use; or (C) before a material change of his position, knew or had reason to know that it was a trade secret and that knowledge of it had been acquired by accident or mistake.

Actual independent invention is a complete defense to trade secret misappropriation. If a competitor develops a trade secret through his own efforts, or by reverse engineering, he is not liable for trade secret misappropriation. The policy is that the competitor has expended effort to independently discover the trade secret and should not held liable for his honest efforts. Note, however, it is no defense to say that the trade secret could have been developed independently. The defendant must have actually uncovered the trade secret through his efforts. *See, e.g., Boeing Co. v. Sierracin Corp.*, 108 Wash.2d 38, 738 P.2d 665 (1987) (disallowing the use of evidence showing the hypothetical ease of reverse engineering).

2. Reverse Engineering

As previously noted, one form of honest discovery is reverse engineering. The UTSA defines reverse engineering as "starting with the known product and working backward to find the method by which it was developed. The acquisition of the known product must, of course, also be by a fair and honest means, such as purchase of the item on the open market for reverse engineering to be lawful." What are the policy goals behind the lawful status of reverse engineering and what does the legality of reverse engineering imply about people's rights in the products they buy?

CHICAGO LOCK CO. v. FANBERG

United States Court of Appeals for the Ninth Circuit, 1982.
676 F.2d 400.

The Chicago Lock Company ("the Company"), a manufacturer of "tubular" locks, brought suit against Morris and Victor Fanberg, locksmiths and publishers of specialized trade books, to enjoin the unauthorized dissemination of key codes for the Company's "Ace" line of tubular locks. The District Court * * * concluded that the key codes for the Company's tubular locks were improperly acquired trade secrets and enjoined distribution of the Fanbergs' compilation of those codes. For the reasons set forth in this opinion, we reverse the District Court and order that judgment be entered in favor of the Fanbergs.

The Facts

Since 1933 the Chicago Lock Company, a manufacturer of various types of locks, has sold a tubular lock, marketed under the registered trademark "Ace," which provides greater security than other lock designs. Tubular Ace locks, millions of which have been sold, are frequently used on vending and bill changing machines and in other maximum security uses, such as burglar alarms. The distinctive feature of Ace locks (and the feature that apparently makes the locks attractive to institutional and large-scale commercial purchasers) is the secrecy and difficulty of reproduction associated with their keys.

The District Court found that the Company "has a fixed policy that it will only sell a duplicate key for the registered series 'Ace' lock to the owner of record of the lock and on request of a bona fide purchase order, letterhead or some other identifying means of the actual recorded lock owner." * * * In addition, the serial number-key code correlations are maintained by the Company indefinitely and in secrecy, the Company does not sell tubular key "blanks" to locksmiths or others, and keys to Ace locks are stamped "Do Not Duplicate." * * * If the owner of an Ace lock loses his key, he may obtain a duplicate from the Company. Alternatively, he may have a proficient locksmith "pick" the lock, decipher the tumbler configuration, and grind a duplicate tubular key. The latter procedure is quicker than the former, though more costly. The locksmith will, to avoid the need to "pick" the lock each time a key is lost, record the key code (i.e., the tumbler configuration) along with the serial number of the customer's lock * * *. Enough duplicate keys have been made by locksmiths that substantial key code data have been compiled, albeit noncommercially and on an ad hoc basis.

Appellant Victor Fanberg, the son of locksmith Morris Fanberg and a locksmith in his own right, has published a number of locksmith manuals for conventional locks. Realizing that no compilation had been made of tubular lock key codes, in 1975 Fanberg advertised in a locksmith journal, Locksmith Ledger, requesting that individual locksmiths transmit to him serial number-key code correlations in their possession in exchange for a copy of a complete compilation when finished. A number of locksmiths complied, and in late 1976 Fanberg and his father began to sell a two-volume publication of tubular lock codes, including those of Ace locks, entitled "A–Advanced Locksmith's Tubular Lock Codes." In 1976 and 1977 Fanberg advertised the manuals in the Locksmith Ledger for $49.95 and indicated that it would be supplemented as new correlations became known * * *. About 350 manuals had been sold at the time of trial. The District Court found that Fanberg "had lost or surrendered control over persons who could purchase the books," * * * meaning that nonlocksmiths could acquire the code manuals.

The books contain correlations which would allow a person equipped with a tubular key grinding machine to make duplicate keys for any listed Ace lock if the serial number of the lock was known. On some models, the serial numbers appear on the exterior of the lock face. Thus, Fanberg's manuals would make it considerably easier (and less expensive) for a person to obtain (legitimately or illegitimately) duplicate keys to Ace locks without going through the Company's screening process. This is what caused consternation to the Company and some of its customers. At no time did Fanberg seek, or the Company grant, permission to compile and sell the key codes. Nor did the individual locksmiths seek authorization from the Company or their customers before transmitting their key code data to Fanberg.

* * * The [District] [C]ourt found that the Company's high security policy for its Ace tubular locks, of which the confidential key code data were a part, was a "valuable business or trade secret-type asset" of the Company, and that the Fanbergs' publication of their compilation of these codes so undermined the Company's policy as to constitute "common law unfair competition in the form of an unfair business practice within the meaning of Section 3369 of the Civil Code of the State of California," as

broadly interpreted in *Barquis v. Merchants Collection Association*, 7 Cal.3d 94 (1972) * * *. The court enjoined the Fanbergs from publishing or distributing any lists of key code correlations for the Company's registered series Ace tubular locks * * *.

On this appeal the Fanbergs argue that the District Court erred on three grounds: (1) that the injunction against publication of their book constitutes a prior restraint prohibited by the First Amendment to the United States Constitution; (2) that the statute under which the injunction issued, former Cal.Civ.Code § 3369, is unconstitutionally vague; and (3) that the District Court applied erroneously the common law doctrine of trade secrets in concluding that the Fanbergs had committed an "unfair business practice" under Section 3369.

The Trade Secrets Claim

Appellants argue that the District Court erroneously concluded that they are liable under Section 3369 for acquiring appellee's trade secret through improper means. We agree, and on this basis we reverse the District Court.

Although the District Court's Findings of Fact and Conclusions of Law are lengthy, the thrust of its holding may be fairly summarized as follows: appellants' acquisition of appellee's serial number-key code correlations through improper means, and the subsequent publication thereof, constituted an "unfair business practice" within the meaning of Section 3369 * * *. Even though the court did not make an explicit finding that appellee's serial number-key code correlations were protectable trade secrets, both appellants and appellee premise their appeal on such an "implicit" finding * * *. We think it clear that the District Court based its decision on a theory of improper acquisition of trade secrets, and in the following discussion we assume arguendo that appellee's listing of serial number-key code correlations constituted a trade secret.

California courts have adopted the theory of trade secret protection set out in the Restatement (First) of Torts, § 757, and the comments thereto, in resolving disputes involving trade secrets * * *. Commission of this common law tort is enjoinable under the purview of "unfair competition" and "unlawful" or "unfair business practice" under Section 3369 * * *.

The pertinent portion of Section 757 of the Restatement provides:

One who discloses or uses another's trade secret, without a privilege to do so, is liable to the other if

(a) he discovered the secret by improper means, or

* * *

(c) he learned the secret from a third person with notice of the facts that it was a secret and that the third person discovered it by improper means * * *

* * *

Trade secrets are protected, therefore, in a manner akin to private property, but only when they are disclosed or used through improper means. Trade secrets do not enjoy the absolute monopoly protection afforded patented processes, for example, and trade secrets will lose their character as private property when the owner divulges them or when they are discovered through proper means. "It is well recognized that a trade secret does not offer protection against discovery by fair and honest means such as by independent invention, accidental disclosure or by so-called reverse engineering, that is, starting with the known product and working backward to divine the process." *Sinclair v. Aquarius Electronics, Inc.*, 42 Cal.App.3d 216, 226 (1974).

Thus, it is the employment of improper means to procure the trade secret, rather than mere copying or use, which is the basis of liability. Restatement (First) of Torts, § 757, comment a (1939). The Company concedes, as it must, that had the Fanbergs bought and examined a number of locks on their own, their reverse engineering (or deciphering) of the key codes and publication thereof would not have been use of "improper means." Similarly, the Fanbergs' claimed use of computer programs in generating a portion of the key code-serial number correlations here at issue must also be characterized as proper reverse engineering * * *. The trial court found that appellants obtained the serial number-key code correlations from a "comparatively small" number of locksmiths, who themselves had reverse-engineered the locks of their customers * * *. The narrow legal issue presented here, therefore, is whether the Fanbergs' procurement of these individual locksmiths' reverse engineering data is an "improper means" with respect to appellee Chicago Lock Company.

The concept of "improper means," as embodied in the Restatement, and as expressed by the Supreme Court, connotes the existence of a duty to the trade secret owner not to disclose the secret to others. See Restatement (First) of Torts, § 757, comment h (1939). "The protection accorded the trade secret holder (i.e., in this case the Company) is against the disclosure or unauthorized use of the trade secret by those to whom the secret has been confided under the express or implied restriction of disclosure or nonuse." *Kewanee Oil Co. v. Bicron Corp.*, 416 U.S. 470 (1974).

Thus, under Restatement § 757(c), appellants may be held liable if they intentionally procured the locksmiths to disclose the trade secrets in breach of the locksmiths' duty to the Company of nondisclosure. See Restatement (First) of Torts, § 757, comment h (1939). Critical to the District Court's holding, therefore, was its conclusion that the individual locksmiths, from whom the Fanbergs acquired the serial number-key code correlations, owed an implied duty to the Company not to make the disclosures. * * *

We find untenable the basis upon which the District Court concluded that the individual locksmiths owe a duty of nondisclosure to the Company. The court predicated this implied duty upon a "chain" of duties: first, that the locksmiths are in such a fiduciary relationship with their customers as to give rise to a duty not to disclose their customers' key codes without permission * * *; and second, that the lock owners are in turn under an "implied obligation (to the Company) to maintain inviolate" the serial number-key code correlations for their own locks. * * *

The court's former conclusion is sound enough: in their fiduciary relationship with lock owners, individual locksmiths are reposed with a confidence and trust by their customers, of which disclosure of the customers' key codes would certainly be a breach. This duty, however, could give rise only to an action by "injured" lock owners against the individual locksmiths, not by the company against the locksmiths or against the Fanbergs.

The court's latter conclusion, that lock owners owe a duty to the Company, is contrary to law and to the Company's own admissions. A lock purchaser's own reverse-engineering of his own lock, and subsequent publication of the serial number-key code correlation, is an example of the independent invention and reverse engineering expressly allowed by trade secret doctrine. *See Sinclair*, 42 Cal.App.3d at 226. Imposing an obligation of nondisclosure on lock owners here would frustrate the intent of California courts to disallow protection to trade secrets discovered through "fair and honest means." *See id.* Further, such an implied obligation upon the lock owners in this case would, in effect, convert the Company's trade secret into a state-conferred monopoly akin to the absolute protection that a federal patent affords. Such an extension of California trade secrets law would certainly be preempted by the federal scheme of patent regulation. * * *

Appellants, therefore, cannot be said to have procured the individual locksmiths to breach a duty of nondisclosure they owed to the Company, for the locksmiths owed no such duty. The Company's serial number-key code correlations are not subject to protection under Restatement § 757, as adopted by the California courts, because the Company has not shown a breach of any confidence reposed by it in the Fanbergs, the locksmiths, or the lock purchasers-i.e., it has failed to show the use of "improper means" by the Fanbergs required by the Restatement.

The District Court's conclusion that the Fanbergs committed an "unfair business practice" under Section 3369, therefore, must be reversed, and judgment should be entered in favor of appellants. In view of the foregoing we find it unnecessary to reach appellants' First Amendment and vagueness claims.

REVERSED AND REMANDED with instructions that judgment be entered in favor of defendants-appellants.

NOTES

1. *Social Benefits of Reverse Engineering.* In *Bonito Boats, Inc. v. Thunder Craft Boats, Inc.,* the United States Supreme Court set forth some of the benefits of reverse engineering. The Court suggested that reverse engineering "may be an essential part of innovation," "often leads to significant advances in technology," and that "the competitive reality of reverse engineering may act as a spur to . . . inventor[s], creating an incentive to develop inventions that meet the rigorous requirements of patentability." 489 U.S. 141, 160, 109 S.Ct. 971, 103 L.Ed.2d 118 (1989). It is this last benefit of reverse engineering that may be the most important. Once an innovation is patented it receives greater protection under the law and becomes available to a greater number of potential users.

3.   The Innocent Wrongful User

Under the UTSA, it is not proper to use a trade secret if "at the time of disclosure or use knew or had reason to know that his knowledge of the trade secret was (I) derived from or through a person who has utilized improper means to acquire it; (II) acquired under circumstances giving rise to a duty to maintain its secrecy or limit its use; or (III) derived from or through a person who owed a duty to the person seeking relief to maintain its secrecy or limit its use." The Court of Appeals of New York phrased it as "the discoverer of a new process or trade secret . . . has no exclusive right to it against . . . one who in good faith acquires knowledge of it without breach of contract or of a confidential relationship with the discoverer." *Speedry Chemical Products, Inc. v. Carter's Ink Co.,* 306 F.2d 328 (2d Cir. 1962). One implication is that a competitor who innocently hires an employee of a trade secret owner cannot be liable for trade secret misappropriation. But the departing employee can be liable.

Notice given by a trade secret owner to a person engaging in innocent wrongful use of a trade secret can ensure subsequent protections against further use of the trade secret. The original Restatement of Torts dealt with the notice issue as follows:

> One who learns another's trade secret from a third person without notice that it is secret and that the third person's disclosure is a breach of his duty to the other, or who learns the secret through a mistake without notice of the secrecy and the mistake,
>
>> (a) is not liable to the other for a disclosure or use of the secret prior to receipt of such notice, and
>>
>> (b) is liable to the other for a disclosure or use of the secret after the receipt of such notice, unless prior thereto he has in good faith paid value for the secret or has so changed his position that to subject him to liability would be inequitable.

RESTATEMENT OF TORTS, § 758 (1939).

Note that there are variations in the notice provisions of the statutes implementing the UTSA in different jurisdictions. For example, while the

UTSA defines misappropriation, in part, as disclosure or use by a person who "before a material change of his position, knew or had reason to know that it was a trade secret and that knowledge of it had been acquired by accident or mistake," the Virginia Act excludes the "material change" language. *See* Milton E. Babirak, Jr., *The Virginia Uniform Trade Secret Act: A Critical Summary of the Act and Case Law*, 5 VA. L.J. & TECH. 15 (2000).

D. CIVIL REMEDIES

WINSTON RESEARCH CORP. v. MINNESOTA MINING AND MANUFACTURING CO.

United States Court of Appeals for the Ninth Circuit, 1965.
350 F.2d 134.

BROWNING, CIRCUIT JUDGE.

The Mincom Division of the Minnesota Mining and Manufacturing Company developed an improved precision tape recorder and reproducer. Somewhat later, Winston Research Corporation developed a similar machine. Mincom alleged that the Winston machine was developed by former employees of Mincom, including Johnson and Tobias, by using confidential information which they had acquired while working on the Mincom machine, and sued for damages and an injunction. The district court granted Mincom an injunction, but denied damages. Both sides appealed.

I

Some background is required for an understanding of the issues.

For some uses of precision tape recorder/reproducers, the time interval between coded signals must be recorded and reproduced with great accuracy. To accomplish this, the tape must move at as constant a speed as possible during both recording and reproduction, and any changes in tape speed during recording must be duplicated as nearly as possible during reproduction. The degree to which a particular tape recorder/reproducer accomplishes, this result is measured by its "time-displacement error."

An electronic device known as a "servo" system is commonly used to reduce time-displacement error by detecting fluctuations in tape speed and immediately adjusting the speed of the motor. Machines prior to the Mincom machine employed a flywheel to inhibit fluctuation in tape speed by increasing the inertia of the system. However, the flywheel reduced the effectiveness of the servo system since the increased inertia prevented rapid adjustments in the speed of the motor.

The effectiveness of the servo system in prior machines was also reduced by resonances created by the moving parts. The range of sensitivity of the servo system was limited to exclude the frequencies of the interfering resonances. This had the disadvantage of limiting the capacity of the servo system to respond to a full range of variations in the speed of the tape.

To solve these problems Mincom eliminated the flywheel and reduced the mass of all other rotating parts. This reduced the inertia of the tape transport system, permitting rapid adjustments in tape speed. Interfering resonances were eliminated by mechanical means. This permitted use of a servo system sensitive to a wide range of frequencies, and hence capable of rapid response to a wide range of variations in tape speed. After four years of research and development based upon this approach, Mincom produced a successful machine with an unusually low time-displacement error.

In May 1962, when Mincom had substantially completed the research phase of its program and was beginning the development of a production prototype, Johnson, who was in charge of Mincom's program, left Mincom's employment. He joined Tobias * * * in forming Winston Research Corporation. In late 1962, Winston contracted with the government to develop a precision tape reproducer. Winston hired many of the technicians who had participated in the development of the Mincom machine to work on the design and development of the Winston machine.

In approximately fourteen months, Winston completed a machine having the same low time-displacement error as the Mincom machine.

* * *

IV

The district court enjoined Winston Research Corporation, Johnson, and Tobias from disclosing or using Mincom's trade secrets in any manner for a period of two years from the date of judgment—March 1, 1964. The court also required the assignment of certain patent applications to Mincom. No damages were awarded.

Winston contends that Mincom was guilty of "unclean hands" with respect to the subject matter in controversy, and should therefore have been barred from any equitable relief. The argument is based upon two circumstances.

First, the employment contracts which Mincom executed with its employees contained a provision that the contracting employee would not render services to a competitor of Mincom for a period of two years after termination of employment with Mincom. Mincom concedes that this provision is void in California. Cal. Bus. & Prof. Code, § 16600. Winston asserts that Mincom included this provision in its contracts with California employees with the deliberate purpose of misleading employees in that state as to their legal rights, and coercing them to refrain from competing with Mincom. There was no direct evidence to that effect; Winston relies entirely upon evidence that Mincom continued for many years to include the provision in contracts executed by California employees. On the other hand, the language of the contracts suggests that they contained this provision only because Mincom used the same form of employment agreement throughout its nationwide operation, and there was evidence that Mincom had never sought to enforce the provision in California. Furthermore, there was evidence that Tobias and Johnson were aware of the unenforceability of the provision in California, and no evidence that any Mincom employee was ever in fact deterred by it.

The second circumstance upon which Winston relies as establishing Mincom's "unclean hands" is that Mincom representatives allegedly offered to forego action against Winston if Winston would agree not to compete with Mincom in the precision recorder field. However, the district court found, on conflicting testimony, that the condition sought to be imposed was that Winston agree only to "refrain from *use of [Mincom's] trade secrets and confidential information* in any competition with" Mincom (italics added). We are satisfied that this district court finding was not clearly erroneous.

As we have noted, the district court enjoined disclosure or use of the specifications of Mincom's machine for a period of two years from the date of judgment. Mincom argues that the injunction should have been permanent, or at least for a substantially longer period. Winston contends that no injunctive relief was appropriate. Mincom was, of course, entitled to protection of its trade secrets for as long as they remained secret. The district court's decision to limit the duration of injunctive relief was necessarily premised upon a determination that Mincom's trade secrets would shortly be fully disclosed, through no fault of Winston, as a result of public announcements, demonstrations, and sales and deliveries of Mincom machines. Mincom has not seriously challenged this implicit finding, and we think the record fully supports it.

Mincom argues that notwithstanding public disclosure subsequent to its former employees' breach of faith, Mincom was entitled to a permanent injunction under the Shellmar rule. Winston responds that under the competing Conmar rule public disclosure of Mincom's trade secrets would end the obligation of Mincom's former employees to maintain the information in confidence, and that neither the employees nor their privies may be enjoined beyond the date of disclosure.

Thus, Winston's argument would bar any injunction at all once there was public disclosure, and Mincom's argument would require an injunction in perpetuity without regard to public disclosure. The district court rejected both extremes and granted an injunction for the period which it concluded would be sufficient both to deny Winston unjust enrichment and to protect Mincom from injury from the wrongful disclosure and use of Mincom's trade secrets by its former employees prior to public disclosure. We think the district court's approach was sound. A permanent injunction would subvert the public's interest in allowing technical employees to make full use of their knowledge and skill and in fostering research and development. On the other hand, denial of any injunction at all would leave the faithless employee unpunished where, as here, no damages were awarded; and he and his new employer would retain the benefit of a headstart over legitimate competitors who did not have access to the trade secrets until they were publicly disclosed. By enjoining use of the trade secrets for the approximate period it would require a legitimate Mincom competitor to develop a successful machine after public disclosure of the secret information, the district court denied the employees any advantage from their faithlessness, placed Mincom in the position it would have occupied if the breach of confidence had not occurred prior to the public disclosure, and imposed the minimum restraint consistent with the realization of these objectives upon the utilization of the employees' skills.

Mincom relies upon two California cases in which permanent injunctions were granted, and upon general language in another, to demonstrate that the Shellmar rule is California law. It is enough to say that the duration of injunctive relief was not an issue and was not discussed in any of these cases. In the absence of substantial reason to doubt it, we accept the district court's reasoned conclusion as to the rule the California Supreme Court would probably follow.

Mincom argues that in any event a two-year injunction from March 1, 1964, was not sufficient to overcome the wrongful advantage obtained by Winston. Mincom points out that four years were required to develop its machine, whereas Winston developed its machine in fourteen months. For this reason, and because the injunction was stayed for some time, Mincom argues that injunctive relief should be granted for at least three years from the completion of appellate review.

As we have noted, the appropriate injunctive period is that which competitors would require after public disclosure to develop a competitive machine. The time (fourteen months) which Winston in fact took with the aid of the very disclosure and use complained of by Mincom would seem to be a fair measure of the proper period. The district court granted an injunction for a somewhat longer period, presumably because the Mincom machine was built in such a way as to require some time for persons unfamiliar with it to determine the details of its construction, and to compensate for delay which Mincom encountered in the final stages of its development program because Winston had hired away Mincom's key personnel. Whether extension of the injunctive period for the latter reason was proper we need not decide, for Winston has not raised that question.

We think it was proper to make the injunctive period run from the date of judgment since public disclosure occurred at about that time. The stays subsequently granted by the district court and this court were limited in scope and do not justify an extension of the injunctive period.

Winston argues that injunctive [relief] was not appropriate because it obstructed and delayed further important research and development by Winston, and (somewhat inconsistently with its successful argument that no damages had been proved) because money damages would have afforded an adequate remedy. In deciding to grant injunctive relief, and in framing its decree, the district court evidenced a keen awareness of the impact of its decision upon the public interest. We think the court acted reasonably and within its discretion in granting a limited injunction, particularly in light of the stay granted by the district court (and subsequently extended by this court) to allow access by the interested government agencies to Winston's machine.

Winston contends that several provisions of the decree are not sufficiently "specific in terms" to satisfy Fed.R.Civ.P. Rule 65(d). As we have said, references in the decree to the general approach adopted by Mincom are to be read as limited by the particular specifications of the basic mechanical elements of the Mincom machine and their relationship to each other which are subsequently detailed in the decree. Similarly, the reference in the decree to a "shortened and widened" shaft derives the requisite specificity from a context which clearly related these generalized directions to a specific result to be achieved.

We agree with Winston that in one respect the district court's injunction was unenforceably broad. As we have noted, the district court found that "knowledge of the reasons for" the particular specifications of the Mincom machine, and "knowledge of what not to do * * * and how not to make the same mistakes" as Mincom made in arriving at these specifications were Mincom trade secrets. Disclosure or use of these "trade secrets" was enjoined. Winston argues that these provisions of the decree are too broad and indefinite, prohibit use by former Mincom employees of their personal knowledge and skill, and render these employees substantially unemployable in the work for which their specialized training and experience have equipped them. Mincom responds that the provisions are to be read narrowly as applying only to knowledge of the reasons for the particular specifications of the Mincom machine which the court held to be protectable trade secrets, and of mistakes to be avoided in developing these specifications.

Even so read, the provisions cannot stand, for their necessary effect is to prohibit conduct by Tobias, Johnson, and the other former Mincom employees in which they have a right to engage. As we have said, the general approach adopted by Mincom in the development of its machine and the basic mechanical elements incorporated in that machine were not protectible "trade secrets," since they were generally known. Mincom's former employees—and Winston—are free to utilize both in their efforts to build a machine equal or superior to the Mincom machine, so long as they do not, within the time covered by the injunction, utilize the particular specifications of the Mincom machine or their substantial equivalents. Moreover, Mincom's former employees cannot be denied the right to use their general skill, knowledge, and experience, even though acquired in part during their employment by Mincom. But the only practical way of enforcing the broad injunctive provisions here challenged would be to prohibit former Mincom employees from engaging in any development work in this area at all. They simply could not exclude their knowledge "of what not to do" and of why Mincom's machine was built as it was from any development work they might now attempt involving the general approach and basic mechanical elements of the Mincom machine.

Moreover, such broad injunctive provisions are unnecessary. The specific provisions of the decree are both sufficient and readily enforceable. If Mincom's former employees disclose or utilize the Mincom design features detailed in the district court's judgment, or their substantial equivalents, alert enforcement of the specific provisions of the decree will amply protect Mincom's rights without improperly restricting either its former employees or potential competitors.

Mincom argues that the district court should have awarded money damages as well as injunctive relief. We think the district court acted well within its discretion in declining to do so. Since Winston sold none of its machines, it had no past profits to disgorge. The evidence as to possible future profits was at best highly speculative. To enjoin future sales and at the same time make an award based on future profits from the prohibited sales would result in duplicating and inconsistent relief, and the choice which the district court made between these mutually exclusive alternatives was not an unreasonable one. There was evidence that Winston would probably sell its machine and realize profits after the injunction expired, but these sales and profits, as we have seen, would not be tainted by breach of confidence, since Winston could by that time have developed its machine from publicly disclosed information.

We have examined the other bases upon which Mincom sought damages and are satisfied that they were either too remote and speculative, or that the injunction made Mincom as nearly whole as possible. Mincom argues that Winston gained a wide variety of advantages from the improper use of Mincom's trade secrets—such as obtaining financing for its development program, securing a government contract, shortening its development program, and reducing its development costs. There is an obvious difficulty in assigning a dollar value to such matters. The two-year injunction deprived Winston of any benefit it might have gained from these advantages and shielded Mincom from any potential harm from Winston's competition which these advantages may have rendered unfair. Mincom suggests that by hiring away Mincom's skilled employees Winston hindered Mincom's development program and increased its cost, but, as we have noted, the district court expressly considered this delay and extended the period of the injunction for an equivalent period.

As noted earlier, Mincom contends that the district court erred in holding that certain items of information were not Mincom trade secrets. The first of these was knowledge of the low time-displacement error achieved in the Mincom machine and precise data as to inertia of its moving parts. Former Mincom employees were said to have used this information in the development of the Winston machine, and also to have disclosed it to others to induce them to finance Winston. Another such item was knowledge of the particular experience of Mincom's former employees, which Winston is said to have used in selecting those to be hired, and to have disclosed to aid it in obtaining financing and in securing a government development contract. A final item was the knowledge that certain government representatives were aware of the performance characteristics of Mincom's machine and were interested in acquiring equipment with such characteristics. This knowledge Winston also is said to have used in securing the government development contract.

Some of the information described clearly did not qualify as a trade secret on the record in this case; as to some the question may have been close. But, if the court erred in its refusal to classify any of these items as a trade secret, there is nothing to indicate that the error was prejudicial. The injunction itself denied Winston any benefits and protected Mincom from any adverse consequences that might have resulted from the improper disclosure and use of this information. Nothing in the record indicates that classifying the information as a trade secret would have justified either an extension of the injunctive period or an award of damages.

Winston contends that Mincom should have been denied any relief because it failed to identify the particular matters which it considered its trade secrets, either before or during trial, although Winston sought to obtain this information by both formal and informal means. The language of the memorandum of the trial court in *Futurecraft Corp. v. Clary Corp.*, upon which Winston relies, relates to the necessity for a showing by the employer that the information sought to be protected does not fall within the category of general employee knowledge and skill. We think Mincom discharged that burden with respect to the particular specifications which the district court held to be protectible. However, the fact that Mincom sought protection indiscriminately for all phases of its development program, and refused Winston's request for a more realistic statement of its claim during the initial stages of Winston's own development program, afforded an additional justification for the district court's refusal to award money damages. * * *

[Judgment Affirmed]

NOTES

1. UTSA Remedies. The UTSA offers the following remedies to injured parties:

§ 2. Injunctive Relief.

(a) Actual or threatened misappropriation may be enjoined. Upon application to the court, an injunction shall be terminated when the trade secret has ceased to exist, but the injunction may be continued for an additional reasonable period of time in order to eliminate commercial advantage that otherwise would be derived from the misappropriation.

(b) In exceptional circumstances, an injunction may condition future use upon payment of a reasonable royalty for no longer than the period of time for which use could have been prohibited. Exceptional circumstances include, but are not limited to, a material and prejudicial change of position prior to acquiring knowledge or reason to know of misappropriation that renders a prohibitive injunction inequitable.

(c) In appropriate circumstances, affirmative acts to protect a trade secret may be compelled by court order.

§ 3.   Damages.

(a) Except to the extent that a material and prejudicial change of position prior to acquiring knowledge or reason to know of misappropriation renders a monetary recovery inequitable, a complainant is entitled to recover damages for misappropriation. Damages can include both the actual loss caused by misappropriation and the unjust enrichment caused by misappropriation that is not taken into account in computing actual loss. In lieu of damages measured by any other methods, the damages caused by misappropriation may be measured by imposition of liability for a reasonable royalty for a misappropriator's unauthorized disclosure or use of a trade secret.

(b) If willful and malicious misappropriation exists, the court may award exemplary damages in an amount not exceeding twice any award made under subsection (a).

§ 4.   Attorney's Fees.

If (i) a claim of misappropriation is made in bad faith, (ii) a motion to terminate an injunction is made or resisted in bad faith, or (iii) willful and malicious misappropriation exists, the court may award reasonable attorney's fees to the prevailing party.

2.   Policy Goals. The remedies offered by the UTSA serve two different policy goals, restoration and deterrence. Injunctions and payment of "reasonable royalties" serve to make injured parties whole. While punitive measures like recovery for "unjust enrichment" and exemplary damages for "willful and malicious" misappropriation are aimed at discouraging would be wrong doers.

3.   The Adequacy of Civil Remedies. Some suggest that civil remedies no longer offer adequate protection to trade secret owners as "intellectual property thieves view civil damages as simply another cost of doing business." This lack of deterrence has led to an increase in criminal protection for trade secrets. Sylvia N. Albert, Jason A. Sanders & Jessica M. Mazzaro, *Twentieth Survey of White Collar Crime: Intellectual Property Crimes*, 42 AM. CRIM. L. REV. 631, 632–33 (2005).

III.   CRIMINAL LAWS PROTECTING TRADE SECRETS

In addition to civil laws protecting trade secrets, there are a number of criminal laws aimed at preventing trade secret misappropriation. Both federal and state criminal laws are important in protecting trade secrets.

A.   FEDERAL LAW

The 1996 Economic Espionage Act (EEA) explicitly protects trade secrets by criminalizing certain types of misappropriation, attempted misappropriation, or conspiracy to misappropriate trade secrets. Before 1996, federal mail and wire fraud statutes and the National Stolen Property Act were also the bases for federal prosecutions related to thefts of trade secrets. As one court summarizes:

> Prior to the passage of the EEA, the only federal statute directly prohibiting economic espionage was the Trade Secrets Act, 18 U.S.C. § 1905, which forbids the unauthorized disclosure of confidential government information, including trade secrets, by a government employee. However, the Trade Secrets Act was of limited value, because it did not apply to private sector employees and it provided only minor criminal sanctions of a fine and not more than one year in prison.
>
> The government often sought convictions under the National Stolen Property Act ("NSPA"), 18 U.S.C. § 2314, or the mail and wire fraud statutes, 18 U.S.C. §§ 1341 and 1343. However, the NSPA was drafted at a time when computers, biotechnology, and copy machines did not even exist, and industrial espionage often occurred without the use of mail or wire. Consequently, it soon became clear to legislators and commentators alike that a new federal strategy was needed to combat the increasing prevalence of espionage in corporate America. Congress recognized the importance of developing a systematic approach to the problem of economic espionage, and stressed that only by adopting a national scheme to protect U.S. proprietary economic information can we hope to maintain our industrial and economic edge and thus safeguard our national security. The House and Senate thus passed the Economic Espionage Act, and the President signed the bill into law on October 11, 1996.

United States v. Hsu, 155 F.3d 189, 194–195 (3d Cir. 1998).

1. Economic Espionage Act of 1996

The Economic Espionage Act (EEA), 18 U.S.C. §§ 1831–1839, contains the following provisions regarding trade secret thefts and related crimes:

18 U.S.C. § 1831 Economic Espionage

> (a) In General.—Whoever, intending or knowing that the offense will benefit any foreign government, foreign instrumentality, or foreign agent, knowingly—
>
> > (1) steals, or without authorization appropriates, takes, carries away, or conceals, or by fraud, artifice, or deception obtains a trade secret;
> >
> > (2) without authorization copies, duplicates, sketches, draws, photographs, downloads, uploads, alters, destroys, photocopies, replicates, transmits, delivers, sends, mails, communicates, or conveys a trade secret;

(3) receives, buys, or possesses a trade secret, knowing the same to have been stolen or appropriated, obtained, or converted without authorization;

(4) attempts to commit any offense described in any of paragraphs (1) through (3); or

(5) conspires with one or more other persons to commit any offense described in any of paragraphs (1) through (3), and one or more of such persons do any act to effect the object of the conspiracy, shall, except as provided in subsection (b), be fined not more than $500,000 or imprisoned not more than 15 years, or both.

(b) Organizations.—Any organization that commits any offense described in subsection (a) shall be fined not more than $10,000,000.

Section 1832 is nearly identical to Section 1831, with somewhat reduced penalties for parties not acting as foreign agents. Section 1833 creates exceptions for law enforcement officials and "whistle blowers." Section 1834 addresses the forfeiture of property derived from the theft of trade secrets. Section 1835 empowers courts to issue orders preserving the confidentiality of trade secrets during prosecution. Section 1836 allows civil actions to enjoin violations. Section 1837 extends the Act to violations committed by a citizen or permanent resident alien, and entities organized under federal or state laws. Section 1838 addresses construction with other laws. Section 1839, as was noted earlier, is the definition section, and includes the EEA's definition of "trade secret."

NOTES

1. Critical Commentary. Scholars have expressed concerns over the vagueness of the EEA, its purpose, and its potential expansion of the rights of trade secret owners. Some commentators have questioned whether the EEA has extended protection to too broad a range of information:

> Arguably, the definition of "trade secret" set forth in the EEA is broader than state law definitions, including the definition of trade secret in the Uniform Trade Secrets Act ("UTSA.") However, in another sense, the EEA definition of "trade secret" is narrower than that of the UTSA. Specifically, the EEA only applies to trade secrets that are "related to or included in a product that is produced for or placed in interstate or foreign commerce." Because of the requirement that the trade secret at issue be "included in a product," there is some question whether the EEA applies to trade secret information concerning services rather than products.

John R. Bauer et al., *Criminalization of Trade Secret Theft: On the Second Anniversary of the Economic Espionage Act*, 8 CURRENTS: INT'L TRADE L.J., Summer 1999, at 59.

Other scholars have questioned the need for the EAA since, as Professor Rochelle Dreyfuss notes, the Act allows companies to gain new tools for the acquisition of exclusive rights in old information:

One alternative available to Congress was to use its Commerce Clause authority to criminalize violations of state civil law: that is, to create criminal liability for committing the tort of misappropriation as defined by state law. Perhaps that is what the EEA was intended to do, but that conclusion is by no means clear. On the one hand, the EEA appears to track the subject matter definitions of state law, and to prohibit "unauthorized appropriation"—a term not too different from the familiar "misappropriation" of state law. At the same time, however, the statute departs from state trade secrecy law in several important respects. Its definition of unauthorized appropriation is different from that found in the states. The statute also includes state-of-mind elements, including the intent to benefit another entity and to deprive the "owner" of the secret's value, which are unknown to state causes of action—as, indeed, is the concept of owner, as opposed to rights holder. Finally, the statute creates rights against interceptions that occur outside the United States, which state laws could probably never reach, and—given its criminal nature— also departs from state legislation by substituting punishment for remedial action.

The result is something of a mongrel. The EEA's many novel provisions will provide courts with difficult questions to resolve, but since the Act is not based on federal intellectual property law, federal criminal law, or state intellectual property law, it is difficult to predict what case law and traditions courts will draw upon in resolving them.

Rochelle Cooper Dreyfuss, *Trade Secrets: How Well Should We Be Allowed to Hide Them? The Economic Espionage Act of 1996*, 9 FORDHAM INTELL. PROP. MEDIA & ENT. L.J. 1, 7–8 (1998).

2. Actual Theft of Trade Secrets

UNITED STATES v. LANGE

United States Court of Appeals for the Seventh Circuit, 2002.
312 F.3d 263.

EASTERBROOK, CIRCUIT JUDGE.

[Matthew Lange was convicted of violating 18 U.S.C. § 1832, for stealing trade secrets from his former employer, RAPCO, and attempting to sell them to a competitor. Lange denied the data met the statutory definition of a "trade secret."]

RAPCO is in the business of making aircraft parts for the aftermarket. It buys original equipment parts, then disassembles them to identify (and measure) each component. This initial step of reverse engineering, usually performed by a drafter such as Lange, produces a set of measurements and drawings. Because this case involves an effort to sell the intellectual property used to make a brake assembly, we use brakes as an illustration.

Knowing exactly what a brake assembly looks like does not enable RAPCO to make a copy. It must figure out how to make a substitute with the same (or better) technical specifications. Brakes rely on friction to slow the airplane's speed by converting kinetic energy to heat. Surfaces that do this job well are made by sintering—the forming of solid metal, usually from a powder, without melting. Aftermarket manufacturers must experiment with different alloys and compositions until they achieve a process and product that fulfils requirements set by the Federal Aviation Administration for each brake assembly. Completed assemblies must be exhaustively tested to demonstrate, to the FAA's satisfaction, that all requirements have been met; only then does the FAA certify the part for sale. For brakes this entails 100 destructive tests on prototypes, bringing a spinning 60–ton wheel to a halt at a specified deceleration measured by a dynamometer. Further testing of finished assemblies is required. It takes RAPCO a year or two to design, and obtain approval for, a complex part; the dynamometer testing alone can cost $75,000. But the process of experimenting and testing can be avoided if the manufacturer demonstrates that its parts are identical (in composition and manufacturing processes) to parts that have already been certified. What Lange, a disgruntled former employee, offered for sale was all the information required to obtain certification of several components as identical to parts for which RAPCO held certification. Lange included with the package—which he offered via the Internet to anyone willing to pay his price of $100,000—a pirated copy of AutoCAD®, the computer-assisted drawing software that RAPCO uses to maintain its drawings and specifications data. One person to whom Lange tried to peddle the data informed RAPCO, which turned to the FBI. Lange was arrested following taped negotiations that supply all the evidence necessary for conviction—if the data satisfy the statutory definition of trade secrets.

[The court considered Lange's argument that RAPCO did not take "reasonable measures to keep such information secret," and rejected it. RAPCO stored all of its drawings and data in a locked, alarmed room, and the number of copies was kept minimal. Some of the information was coded, with few people knowing the codes, and all documents carried warnings of RAPCO's intellectual property rights. RAPCO also split work among subcontractors, to ensure that no subcontractor could replicate their product.]

The second ingredient is that "the information derives independent economic value, actual or potential, from not being generally known to, and not being readily ascertainable through proper means by, the public[.]" According to Lange, all data obtained by reverse engineering some other product are "readily ascertainable . . . by the public" because everyone can do what RAPCO did: buy an original part, disassemble and measure it, and make a copy. The prosecutor responds to this contention by observing that "the public" is unable to reverse engineer an aircraft brake assembly.

[The court examined the usage of the word "public" in § 1839(3), as discussed earlier in the chapter.]

Thus it is unnecessary here to decide whether "general" belongs in front of "public"—for even if it does, the economically valuable information is not "readily ascertainable" to the general public, the educated public, the economically relevant public, or any sensible proxy for these groups.

Another line of prosecutorial argument starts with the fact that § 1832(a)(4) makes it a crime to attempt to sell trade secrets without the owner's permission. Even if Lange did not have real trade secrets in his possession, the argument goes, he thought he did and therefore may be penalized for an attempted sale. The argument finds support in [*United States v. Hsu*, 155 F.3d 189 (3rd Cir. 1998)], which held that in order to avoid graymail—the threat that to obtain a conviction the prosecutor must disclose the secret by putting it in the trial record—a case may be based on § 1832(a)(4) without disclosing all details of the trade secret. We agree with the general approach of these decisions. *Hsu* analogized the attempted sale of information believed to be a trade secret to an attempt such as shooting a corpse, believing it to be alive, or selling sugar, believing it to be cocaine. Events of this sort underlie the maxim that factual impossibility is no defense to a prosecution for attempt. This does not mean, however, that the defendant's belief alone can support a conviction. All attempt prosecutions depend on demonstrating that the defendant took a substantial step toward completion of the offense, which could have been carried out unless thwarted. Although the American Law Institute recommends a definition of attempt linked closely to intent, the Supreme Court has not embraced this view and demands in cases under federal law that the prosecutor establish a probability of success. *See, e.g., Spectrum Sports, Inc. v. McQuillan*, 506 U.S. 447, 113 S.Ct. 884 (1993) ("dangerous probability" of success is an ingredient of attempted monopolization).

An attempted murder may be thwarted by substituting a sack of flour for the intended victim; a sale of drugs may be thwarted by substituting sugar for cocaine, or rock candy for crack. These situations present a good chance of success, but for the intervention. So does "the disgruntled former employee who walks out of his former company with a computer diskette full of engineering schematics" (*Hsu*, 155 F.3d at 201)—a fair description of Lange's conduct (though diskettes are obsolete). A sale of trade secrets may be thwarted by substituting a disk with the collected works of Shakespeare for the disk that the defendant believed contained the plans for brake assemblies, or by an inadvertent failure to download the proper file. The attempted sale of the disk is a culpable substantial step. But it is far less clear that sale of information already known to the public could be deemed a substantial step toward the offense, just because the defendant is deluded and does not understand what a trade secret is. Selling a copy of Zen and the Art of Motorcycle Maintenance is not attempted economic espionage, even if the defendant thinks that the tips in the book are trade secrets; nor is sticking pins in voodoo dolls attempted murder. Booksellers and practitioners of the occult pose no social dangers, certainly none of the magnitude of those who are tricked into shooting bags of sand that have been substituted for targets of assassination. Lange was more dangerous than our bookseller but much less dangerous than our hypothetical assassin. Perhaps data purloined from an ex-employer is sufficiently likely to contain trade secrets to justify calling the preparation for sale a substantial step toward completion of the offense, and thus a culpable attempt, even if the employee stole the wrong data file and did not get his hands on the commercially valuable information. We need not pursue the subject beyond noting the plausibility of the claim and its sensitivity to the facts—what kind of data did the employee think he stole, and so on. For it is not necessary to announce a definitive rule about how dangerous the completed acts must be in trade secret cases: the judge was entitled to (and did) find that Lange had real trade secrets in his possession.

Lange wants us to proceed as if all he tried to sell were measurements that anyone could have taken with calipers after disassembling an original-equipment part. Such measurements could not be called trade secrets if, as Lange asserts, the assemblies in question were easy to take apart and measure. But no one would have paid $100,000 for metes and bounds, while Lange told his customers that the data on offer were worth more than that asking price. Which they were. What Lange had, and tried to sell, were the completed specifications and engineering diagrams that reflected all the work completed after the measurements had been taken: the metallurgical data, details of the sintering, the results of the tests, the plans needed to produce the finished goods, everything required to get FAA certification of a part supposedly identical to one that had been approved. Those details "derive[d] independent economic value, actual or potential, from not being generally known to, and not being readily ascertainable through proper means by, the public[.]" Every firm other than the original equipment manufacturer and RAPCO had to pay dearly to devise, test, and win approval of similar parts; the details unknown to the rivals, and not discoverable with tape measures, had considerable "independent economic value ... from not being generally known". A sensible trier of fact could determine that Lange tried to sell trade secrets. It was his customer's cooperation with the FBI, and not public access to the data, that prevented closing of the sale. * * *

Affirmed.

3. Conspiracy to Steal Trade Secrets

UNITED STATES v. MARTIN

United States Court of Appeals for the First Circuit, 2000.
228 F.3d 1.

TORRUELLA, CHIEF JUDGE.

[Dr. Stephen R. Martin and Caryn L. Camp were charged with ten counts of wire fraud, two counts of mail fraud, one count of conspiracy to steal trade secrets, one count of conspiracy to transport stolen goods, and one count of interstate transportation of stolen goods. Camp testified against Martin, and Martin was convicted on four counts of wire fraud, two counts of mail fraud, conspiracy to steal trade secrets, and conspiracy to transport stolen property in interstate commerce. The appeal challenged the sufficiency of the evidence.

Martin was a scientist. At the time he and Camp first came into contact, Martin was developing a company called "WDV." Sometime after they began conversing, Martin went to "Maverck." Camp was a chemist with IDEXX, which manufactured veterinary products. Martin had approached IDEXX previously with a proposal for research into HIV and feline immunodeficiency virus (FIV), which they rejected. As part of her employment, Camp had signed non-competition and non-disclosure agreements.

Camp found Martin in January, 1998, after becoming dissatisfied with her job. They began to correspond, first regarding the possibility of Camp working for WDV (and later Maverck), and then as pen-pals. During the course of this correspondence, Camp let slip minor confidential details of her work at IDEXX.]

II. Events Between May 1, 1998 and July 18, 1998

The government's first six counts of wire fraud, on which Martin was acquitted, stem from correspondence occurring prior to July 18, 1998. One count of mail fraud, on which Martin was convicted, also stems from this period.

A. Martin's Initial Requests

On May 1, in response to Camp's lengthy e-mail detailing her trip, Martin made his first explicit request for information, asking for "any info ... on the HOT topics in veterinary diagnostics." Martin renewed his request in a May 3 e-mail in which he asked a number of questions about IDEXX prices, test composition, and test use. In a subsequent message, Martin outlined his ability to avoid patent infringement with IDEXX and noted that "IDEXX is going to be in trouble very soon." On May 3, Camp responded with answers to most of Martin's questions. Attached was a letter detailing problems with a particular IDEXX product. In reference to a previous discussion about flying planes, Martin began to refer to Camp as "Ace," a moniker which would become "Agent Ace" as their "spy" business heated up.

B. Camp's Responses

On May 4, Camp wrote concerning IDEXX's legal problems. She also included "lots & lots of goodies for your next rainy day," including internal memoranda. Camp noted that the internal memoranda may have been confidential. "I feel like a spy," she commented. In a letter the next day, Camp regretted her actions, promising to "be good ... and send no more dirty secrets from Idexx...." Martin responded, claiming that he did "not want to know anything confidential about IDEXX," and asking only for "public information."

Despite Camp's repentance and Martin's denial of any desire for confidential or proprietary information, Camp continued to assemble and pass on information, an activity which she apparently viewed as ethically suspect.[3] Camp also relayed information on IDEXX's strategic plans, including a potential partnership with a company whose name, at least, was confidential. By late June, Camp appeared set on leaving IDEXX, as she commented that "I need to unload all of my stock options." Furthermore, Camp had received (and ignored) reminders of her non-compete and non-disclosure agreements; she forwarded these reminders to Martin, noting that "as a spy myself, I get a particular chuckle out of [them]," and that "my loyalty has ended." Camp and Martin began to formalize their plans for meeting at Lake Tahoe in early August, as well as for Camp's eventual move to Nevada.

* * *

E. The First Package

On July 12, Camp sent Martin a large package of information via Priority Mail, including various devices, product inserts, USDA course materials, information on her own projects, miscellaneous IDEXX product information, and "Examples of My Work," labeled "Confidential." Camp also promised to send an actual test kit, if Martin wished. The mailing and receipt of this package formed the basis of a mail fraud charge, of which Martin was ultimately convicted. After receiving the package, Martin once more praised Camp's aggressiveness, encouraged her to "keep on charging," to "keep on thinking about the competition, and how we can beat them," and promised that "lips are sealed."

III. Events Between July 19, 1998 to August 16, 1998

Correspondence during the next several weeks provided the basis for Martin's conviction on four counts of wire fraud.

A. More Questions and Answers

In several e-mails between July 19 and July 21, Camp outlined a proposal for customer-friendly additions and modifications to current IDEXX technology. Martin explained how such a test might be constructed, telling Camp that if it could be marketed successfully, she would receive "enough bonus money to buy [a] house for cash." Camp clearly understood that the proposal was for technology competitive with that of

---

3. Camp's May 7 e-mail noted that "the fun part of my week has been putting together packages of information for you ..." and celebrated "the intrigue of being Agent Ace." On June 22, she "couldn't resist playing Ace-the-Spy today ... and so I am dropping a few more things in the mail." But her fun did not come without guilt: "I know I should be shot. But I just can't resist sending you this chain of internal Idexx e-mails regarding concern of a certain competitor;" "I am probably crossing the line with this [but] I've crossed lines worse than this one." However, Camp re-assured herself that she was doing nothing wrong, that she was forwarding "nothing proprietary" but simply the "dirty secrets of an IDEXX Livestock and Poultry weekly meeting."

IDEXX, as she suggested the possibility that "[she and Martin would] own the whole market."

Camp's proposal also prompted Martin to ask about the relevance and applicability of x-Chek or similar software. Camp offered to send Martin a copy of the software IDEXX had developed for poultry and livestock testing. Martin responded the same day, writing that "he would like to play with the software you mentioned." Camp immediately replied, promising "lots of cool goodies," including the x-Chek disks. Camp also indicated that she was on the verge of "cleaning out her office" and leaving IDEXX; however, she noted that she was speaking to headhunters in addition to Martin.

Martin's response to this last message re-affirmed his intention to compete with IDEXX. Moreover, Martin acknowledged Camp's potentially illicit activity, and exhorted her to continue in her final few days at work. "Before you bag IDEXX (I am embarrassed to ask this), absorb as much information, physically and intellectually, as you can. I never had a spy before." Camp's answer bemoaned the constraints on her information gathering (because co-workers knew she was preparing to leave), detailed her continued efforts to take home both information and property, and admitted the illegality (or at least inappropriateness) of her actions. However, Camp noted that she had as of yet been unwilling to copy "confidential" documents, although she admitted that she had copied "semi-confidential" internal e-mail. The next day, Camp promised to send Martin additional kits as her last "secret agent" act.

B.   The Second Package

In Camp's last several days at IDEXX, she continued to collect products and information, which she forwarded to Martin on July 24. The package included operating manuals, IDEXX marketing materials, research and development data, a sales binder prepared by an independent contractor, as well as a binder labeled "Competition."

C.   Found Out

Unfortunately for Camp and Martin, Camp inadvertently sent her July 25 e-mail (acknowledging that July 24 was her last day and detailing the contents of her second package) to John Lawrence, the global marketing manager for Poultry/Livestock at IDEXX. Camp informed Martin of what she had done, and continued on her vacation. According to Camp, Martin later recommended that she lie to IDEXX, i.e., that she tell them that he was interested only in limited information unrelated to IDEXX core businesses. Upon her return to Maine, Camp was intercepted and interviewed by an FBI agent at the Portland airport. An August 9, 1998 search of Martin's home found the contents of Camp's second package, including the x-Chek software.

Discussion

* * *

II.   Conspiracy to Steal Trade Secrets

The jury found Martin guilty of count 13, which charged him with conspiracy to steal trade secrets in violation of the Economic Espionage Act of 1996, specifically 18 U.S.C. § 1832(a)(5). In order to find a defendant guilty of conspiracy, the prosecution must prove (1) that an agreement existed, (2) that it had an unlawful purpose, and (3) that the defendant was a voluntary participant. The government must prove that the defendant possessed both the intent to agree and the intent to commit the substantive offense. In addition, the government must prove that at least one conspirator committed an "overt act," that is, took an affirmative step toward achieving the conspiracy's purpose.

The agreement need not be express, however, as long as its existence may be inferred from the defendants' words and actions and the interdependence of activities and persons involved. A so-called "tacit" agreement will suffice. Moreover, the conspirators need not succeed in completing the underlying act, nor need that underlying act even be factually possible.

As of yet, only the Third Circuit has had the opportunity to address § 1832(a), which specifically covers private corporate espionage. *See United States v. Hsu*, 155 F.3d 189 (3d Cir.1998). The statute criminalizes the knowing theft of trade secrets, as well as attempts or conspiracies to steal trade secrets. The Act defines a "trade secret" broadly, to include both tangible property and intangible information, as long as the owner "has taken reasonable measures to keep such information secret" and the information "derives independent economic value ... from not being generally known to ... the public." 18 U.S.C. § 1839(3). This definition of trade secret "protects a wider variety" of information than most civil laws; however, "it is clear that Congress did not intend ... to prohibit lawful competition such as the use of general skills or parallel development of a similar product," *Hsu*, 155 F.3d at 196–97, although it did mean to punish "the disgruntled former employee who walks out of his former company with a computer diskette full of engineering schematics," *id.* at 201. In other words, § 1832(a) was not designed to punish competition, even when such competition relies on the know-how of former employees of a direct competitor. It was, however, designed to prevent those employees (and their future employers) from taking advantage of confidential information gained, discovered, copied, or taken while employed elsewhere.

Martin contends that the evidence is factually insufficient to establish a "meeting of the minds" or agreement to violate § 1832(a), because (1) insufficient evidence exists to establish an agreement between Martin and Camp; (2) insufficient evidence exists to prove that Martin had the necessary intent to commit an act prohibited by § 1832(a), i.e., injure the owner of the trade secret (IDEXX); and (3) the information provided by Camp to Martin did not meet the statutory definition of a trade secret under § 1839(3). As we explain below, none of these arguments are persuasive.

First, the evidence is sufficient for a reasonable jury to conclude that Martin and Camp formed an agreement regarding the theft of trade secrets. Martin's argument against the existence of an agreement relies on the facts that (a) his early e-mails specifically requested that Camp not send him confidential information, and (b) Camp did not seem to know the distinction between confidential information, proprietary information, and office gossip. However, while Martin's disclaimer and Camp's confusion indicate the lack of an explicit agreement at that time, they do not necessarily negate the existence of an agreement. A rational jury could have plausibly concluded on the basis of the evidence presented at trial that an agreement existed. By July 21, Martin had received extensive correspondence from Camp that she had either marked "confidential" or "proprietary," or had expressed some hesitation in forwarding.[4] Despite his previous protestations that he wanted nothing to do with IDEXX or its confidential information, Martin asked Camp on July 21 to "absorb as much information, physically and intellectually, as you can," and included a set of questions to direct Camp's research. Throughout June and July, Martin referred to Camp as "Agent Ace," or as his "spy." Given the type of information that Martin had already received, a reasonable jury could have concluded that, whatever Martin's original intentions, as of July 21, Camp and Martin had reached a tacit agreement by which she would send him items and information that potentially fell under the trade secret definition of 18 U.S.C. § 1839(3). In other words, sufficient evidence exists to show an agreement between Camp and Martin to violate § 1832(a).

Second, the evidence is sufficient to show that Martin intended to injure IDEXX by obtaining IDEXX trade secrets and competing against IDEXX. Although Martin consistently claimed that he had no interest in developing products that competed with IDEXX, and hence had no intention of injuring IDEXX economically, his correspondence with Camp detailed a plan of competition. Martin had, among other things, considered the possibility of starting a competing veterinary lab, and had asked Camp to think, in particular, about ways to compete with tests that IDEXX manufactured. A reasonable jury could have found that Martin intended to use the information gained from Camp, particularly information on IDEXX's costs and customer dissatisfaction with IDEXX, to create a more successful competitor with greater capability to injure IDEXX.

Third, Martin's final argument—that he actually received no trade secrets—even if true, is irrelevant. Martin has only been found guilty of a conspiracy to steal trade secrets, rather than the underlying offense. The relevant question to determine whether a conspiracy existed was whether Martin intended to violate the statute. *See Hsu*, 155 F.3d at 198 ("[T]he crimes charged—attempt and conspiracy—do not require proof of the existence of an actual trade secret, but, rather, proof only of one's attempt

---

4. Some of the information Martin received in their early correspondence clearly had the potential to fall within the § 1839 definition of trade secret: for example, cost information unavailable to the public included in Camp's message of May 2, a confidential IDEXX business plan included in Camp's June 8 message, and a customer list included in Camp's July 1 message.

or conspiracy with intent to steal a trade secret."). The key question is whether Martin intended to steal trade secrets. A rational jury, considering the information Camp had already sent Martin, could have concluded that his further queries indicated such an intention.

A reasonable jury could therefore have concluded that Martin and Camp formed an agreement by which Camp conveyed information and property to Martin that potentially fell under the definition of a trade secret in 18 U.S.C. § 1839. As a result, sufficient evidence existed to convict Martin of conspiracy to steal trade secrets.

Conclusion

A careful reading of the seven-month e-mail communication between Dr. Stephen Martin and Caryn Camp could lead to the conclusion Martin and his counsel urge—that this is simply a pen-pal relationship between a lonely Maine lab technician and a reclusive California scientist. However, the evidence could also lead a reader to the conclusion that something far more sinister was afoot: that an originally harmless communication mushroomed into a conspiracy to steal trade secrets and transport stolen property interstate, and that the electronic mail and U.S. mails were used to further a scheme to defraud IDEXX. Because we find there was sufficient evidence for a reasonable jury to conclude the latter beyond any reasonable doubt, we AFFIRM the defendant's conviction on all counts.

Notes

1. Criminal Liability for Business Organizations. Companies can be convicted of the same crimes as individuals under the EEA. In *United States v. Yang*, 281 F.3d 534 (6th Cir. 2002), the defendant and his corporation were charged with a conspiracy to commit theft of a trade secret under § 1832 and attempted theft of a trade secret. Both were convicted, and the company was given the statutory maximum fine of $5,000,000. An appellate court later vacated the fine on the ground that the trial judge in the case did not give an adequate reason for imposing the maximum corporate fine.

2. The Defense of Legal Impossibility. *United States v. Hsu*, 155 F.3d 189 (3d Cir. 1998) was the first appellate case to examine the Economic Espionage Act. The case involved a sting operation in which no trade secrets were actually misappropriated. In evaluating whether an attempted criminal misappropriation of trade secrets was present, the court analyzed the defense of legal impossibility as follows:

> We hold that legal impossibility is not a defense to a charge of attempted misappropriation of trade secrets in violation of 18 U.S.C. § 1832(a)(4). We agree with the district court's conclusion that a charge of "attempt" under the EEA requires proof of the same elements used in other modern attempt statutes, including the Model Penal Code. A defendant is guilty of attempting to misappropriate trade secrets if, "acting with the kind of culpability otherwise required for commission of the crime, he ... purposely does or omits to do anything that, under the circumstances as he believes them to be, is an act or omission constituting a substantial step

in a course of conduct planned to culminate in his commission of the crime." Thus, the defendant must (1) have the intent needed to commit a crime defined by the EEA, and must (2) perform an act amounting to a "substantial step" toward the commission of that crime.

Id. at 202.

B. STATE PROTECTION

Prior to the enactment of the EEA, several states enacted statutes criminalizing thefts of trade secrets. The following California criminal statute is an one example of these early attempts to curb trade secret thefts through the imposition of criminal sanctions.

California Penal Code § 499c(b):

(b) Every person is guilty of theft who, with intent to deprive or withhold the control of a trade secret from its owner, or with an intent to appropriate a trade secret to his or her own use or to the use of another, does any of the following:

(1) Steals, takes, carries away, or uses without authorization, a trade secret.

(2) Fraudulently appropriates any article representing a trade secret entrusted to him or her.

(3) Having unlawfully obtained access to the article, without authority makes or causes to be made a copy of any article representing a trade secret.

(4) Having obtained access to the article through a relationship of trust and confidence, without authority and in breach of the obligations created by that relationship, makes or causes to be made, directly from and in the presence of the article, a copy of any article representing a trade secret.

(c) Every person who promises, offers or gives, or conspires to promise or offer to give, to any present or former agent, employee or servant of another, a benefit as an inducement, bribe or reward for conveying, delivering or otherwise making available an article representing a trade secret owned by his or her present or former principal, employer or master, to any person not authorized by the owner to receive or acquire the trade secret and every present or former agent, employee, or servant, who solicits, accepts, receives or takes a benefit as an inducement, bribe or reward for conveying, delivering or otherwise making available an article representing a trade secret owned by his or her present or former principal, employer or master, to any person not authorized by the owner to receive or acquire the trade secret, shall be punished by imprisonment in the state prison, or in a county jail not exceeding one year, or by a fine not exceeding five thousand dollars ($5,000), or by both that fine and imprisonment.

PEOPLE v. PRIBICH

California Court of Appeal, Second District, 1994.
21 Cal.App.4th 1844, 27 Cal.Rptr.2d 113.

Boris Pribich appeals after a jury convicted him of one count of the theft of trade secrets (Pen. Code § 499c, subd. (b)(2)) and found the offense to be a misdemeanor petty theft. The court suspended imposition of sentence, placed appellant on summary probation for three years, ordered him to pay restitution of $400, and stayed payment of a $1,000 fine. Appellant contends that the evidence was insufficient to support his conviction and that there were various jury instruction errors. We find the evidence insufficient as to a requisite element of the offense and reverse.

Facts

[In April of 1990, Hancock, an officer of Aquatec, a water cooler company, hired Boris Pribich to work on a freonless cooler, using a thermal chip. Aquatec held patents on methods of using such a chip in water coolers. Pribich fell behind his anticipated schedule, which concerned Aquatec, as they wanted to display the cooler at an October trade show. Aquatec wanted to give Pribich the chance to succeed, and provided staff, workspace, and permission to work at home on his own computer.]

Hancock was familiar with some of the information in appellant's computer at work, such as graphs and equations on the performance of thermal electric chips. This information was necessary to Aquatec's objective of improving the performance of the thermal electric chip. Hancock thus considered the information in appellant's computer at work to constitute trade secrets belonging to Aquatec, since the information dealt with Aquatec's product and was not available to the general public.

To protect such trade secrets, Aquatec did not allow nonemployees to go into the building without being escorted and required employees to sign a confidentiality agreement. Even the sales people employed at Aquatec who had confidentiality agreements with the company were not permitted to view appellant's work product because, as Hancock stated, "We didn't want our competitors tipped off, we did not want the people to know what we were working on. And Aquatec is a start up company and could easily be outdone by someone with a large amount of cash and no one was going in our engineering department without a confidential[ity] agreement." According to Hancock, the information in appellant's work computer "would be of great interest . . . to our competitors."

Appellant was repeatedly absent from work, fell behind schedule, and Hancock became increasingly concerned that appellant could not finish his project to enable Aquatec to have an operating unit of its new product to demonstrate at the trade show in October of 1990. On September 17 and 19, 1990, Hancock asked appellant to have all the documents he had on his project available at the plant and to bring all the Aquatec documents and computer files or programs that he had at home to the plant. On

September 20, Hancock asked appellant whether he brought all the information that had been requested and reminded appellant of the confidentiality agreement that he had signed. Appellant advised Hancock that the computer program was his property and stated, "You are a prick, I can be a prick, too." Hancock requested appellant to go to his work area and show another employee, Yongky Muljadi, what he was doing on the computer so that Muljadi could be brought up to date on appellant's project.

Hancock then called the company's patent counsel to alert him of the events. Appellant was very upset at that time. He showed Muljadi the files on the computer screen and claimed they belonged to him. However, based on the code letters of the files, Muljadi concluded that some of them were not appellant's files. Appellant proceeded to delete the files he claimed were his. After deleting the files, appellant left the building and never came back to work.

Hancock thereafter hired a computer consultant, Robert Torchon, to retrieve the data in appellant's work computer. Torchon and Muljadi were unable to retrieve the data. Hancock then contacted appellant and demanded that all the computer files and programs and other materials be returned to Aquatec. Appellant refused to do so, unless Aquatec paid a fair or reasonable price for them. Aquatec did not produce for the October trade show any prototype of a water cooler using a thermal electric chip.

On October 12, 1990, a Los Angeles police officer served a search warrant at appellant's residence. The police found two computers, computer discs, programs and numerous papers. The police officer who served the warrant used a Turbo Basic program to obtain computer printouts generated from diskettes found in appellant's house. Most of the computer files found in appellant's house had "BAS" or "DWG" extension code letters, such as the code letters observed by Muljadi on the screen of appellant's work computer before appellant deleted the files.

According to Hancock, some of the documents obtained from appellant's home pertained to the work appellant was doing for Aquatec, constituted drawings of certain components that go into the coolers and certain information on the thermal electric cooler, and were deemed by Hancock to be proprietary documents or trade secrets of Aquatec. The documents included information about a heat exchanger, a heat problem in the thermal electric chip, and a bottle cap designed by Aquatec. A computer printout and computer programs, calculations, tests and graphs regarding the performance of Aquatec's new cooler were also discovered pursuant to the search warrant. Appellant was not supposed to have retained those items seized and should have returned them to Aquatec as Hancock had requested.

In appellant's defense at trial, Dr. Martin Balaban, a mechanical engineer employed by Union Carbide to design heat exchangers and a consultant for the Rand Corp., testified that none of the prosecution's documentary evidence obtained from appellant's computer at home included any original concepts which could have given Aquatec an advantage over competitors who did not know of those documents. Moreover, the prosecution evidence included a document which showed appellant's coefficient of performance for a week when he was sick, another document constituting a milestone chart in which appellant outlined his project schedule, and other documents reflecting concepts which were in the public domain, though the exact numbers and dimensions set forth in the documents were not generally available to the public. According to Balaban, based upon his professional engineering expertise, it is not possible to make a thermal electric water cooler for the home or office which would be energy efficient and marketable.

Appellant claimed that he did not erase the files at work which belonged to Aquatec. As a part of his employment with Aquatec, he was required to use two computer programs, Auto Cad and Turbo Basic. Before he left Aquatec, appellant removed his Turbo Basic program, of which he was the registered owner, and a game-type program which he had in his work computer. He removed the programs in Muljadi's presence. When Hancock contacted appellant at home and demanded the program which he had taken, appellant claimed that he owned the programs and he never offered to sell them to Hancock. Appellant merely offered to convert his files into stand alone files, which could be used without the Turbo Basic program. Appellant admitted that most of the documents seized by the police at his home dealt with Aquatec's New Century water cooler project.

The jury found appellant not guilty of one of the two charged offenses, the unauthorized deletion of computer data. (Pen.Code, § 502, subd. (c)(4).) However, appellant was found guilty of the theft of trade secrets as a misdemeanor. (Pen.Code, § 499c, subd. (b)(2).)

Discussion

To satisfy the elements of the crime with which appellant was charged, the fraudulent appropriation of an article representing a trade secret entrusted to him, the prosecution must, of course, establish that the article appropriated represented a trade secret. Penal Code section 499c, subdivision (a)(9) defines a trade secret, in pertinent part, as "any scientific or technical information, design, process, procedure, formula, computer program or information stored in a computer . . . which is secret and is not generally available to the public, and which gives one who uses it an advantage over competitors who do not know of or use the trade secret; and a trade secret shall be presumed to be secret when the owner thereof takes measures to prevent it from becoming available to persons other than those selected by the owner to have access thereto for limited purposes." One of the requisite elements of a trade secret is lacking in the present case. Specifically, there is no evidence that any of the items allegedly fraudulently appropriated by appellant and retrieved from his computer at home would give "one who uses [any of the items] an advantage over competitors who do not know of or use the trade secret."

In the present case, Hancock testified that he was familiar with some of the information in appellant's computer at work, which included graphs and mathematical models relating to the performance of thermal electric chips, that he considered the items observed on appellant's computer at work as trade secrets and that the items in appellant's computer at work would be of "great interest" to a competitor. However, Hancock described the information in appellant's computer at work and not in his computer at home. It was the information in appellant's computer at home which had been appropriated and which was alleged to constitute trade secrets. Although Hancock indicated that a computer printout reflecting information retrieved from appellant's computer at home contained a proprietary or trade secret of Aquatec, he stated only that "a lot of it is very familiar" and "looks like material that I saw on the screen that [appellant] was working on and certain other graphs I have certainly seen." However, Hancock could not indicate "the exact coding" for the printout. Such testimony by Hancock insufficiently addresses the items purportedly fraudulently appropriated by appellant, i.e., the numerous items generated from appellant's computer at home.

Most significantly, Hancock did not establish that the items seized from appellant's computer at home could give "one who uses it an advantage over competitors." Hancock did indicate that one of the items retrieved from appellant's computer was a milestone chart or work schedule which was not a technical document but which he considered proprietary to Aquatec. Hancock would not have wanted anyone to know appellant's work schedule because it would have revealed where Aquatec was at any point in time regarding its product development. However, Hancock did not specifically allege any advantage a competitor could obtain by theoretical access to such information. For example, there was no indication that any unspecified company could or would have worked any faster or differently if it had access to appellant's work schedule. * * *

Apart from whether a "substantial" competitive advantage is required for a violation of Penal Code section 499c, we find that the element of the offense that the prosecution establish the item appropriated give "one who uses it an advantage over competitors who do not know of or use the trade secret" requires more than merely conclusory and generalized allegations. Hancock asserted that the information in appellant's computer at work would be of "great interest" to a competitor and stated his desire not to have any competitors know appellant's work schedule, which was in appellant's computer at home. However, such statements do not reveal, except by an insufficient and generalized assumption, that any competitive advantage would specifically flow from the revelation of the information.

Indeed, it appears most unlikely that any competitive advantage could have been obtained by knowledge of appellant's work schedule or other information because, as indicated by the uncontradicted testimony of appellant's expert witness, it was impossible in light of known scientific principles to make a thermal electric water cooler for the home or office which would be energy efficient and marketable. Hancock himself acknowledged that one of the items retrieved from appellant's computer revealed appellant's opinion that the model under study was not suited for low-cost thermal electric modes and "was not working very well." Moreover, appellant's expert witness repeatedly stated during direct and cross-examination that none of the documents obtained from appellant's computer at home would give anyone who had them any advantage over competitors.

We note that in the prosecutor's argument to the jury, he belittled the defense expert's testimony regarding the lack of any advantage over competitors and urged that it was unrealistic to believe that no competitive advantage could ensue from the information, but the prosecutor pointed to no evidence at trial supporting this conclusion. Nor can we find in the record any substantial evidence as to this element of the offense.

Disposition

The judgment is reversed, and the trial court is directed to dismiss the information and to order any restitution and fine paid by appellant be remitted to him.

Notes

1. Differences in Federal and State Law. Compare *Pribich* with *United v. Martin* and *United v. Hsu*, discussed *supra*. In the first case, the prosecutor failed to show that the information which was taken was a trade secret and this failure led to a reversal of the defendant's conviction. In the second set of cases brought under federal law, the existence of a trade secret did not need to be shown in order to obtain a conviction for a conspiracy to commit misappropriation of a trade secret. Are these decisions inconsistent or at least troubling?

2. Preemption of State Trade Secret Laws by Federal Intellectual Property Laws. In *Kewanee Oil Co. v. Bicron Corp.*, 416 U.S. 470, 483, 94 S.Ct. 1879, 40 L.Ed.2d 315 (1974), the United States Supreme Court addressed the question of "whether those items which are proper subjects for consideration for a patent may also have available the alternative protection accorded by trade secret law." The Court found no preemption:

> Certainly the patent policy of encouraging invention is not disturbed by the existence of another form of incentive to invention. In this respect the two systems are not and never would be in conflict. Similarly, the policy that matter once in the public domain must remain in the public domain is not incompatible with the existence of trade secret protection. By definition a trade secret has not been placed in the public domain.

Kewanee, 416 U.S. at 484. Consequently, subject matter qualifying for protection under the federal patent regime could also enjoy trade secret protection under state law.

As is discussed greater detail in Chapter Six, the Supreme Court continued this analysis in *Bonito Boats, Inc. v. Thunder Craft Boats, Inc.*, 489 U.S.

141, 109 S.Ct. 971, 103 L.Ed.2d 118 (1989). In that case, the Court examined the "limits the operation of the federal patent system places on the States' ability to offer substantial protection to utilitarian and design ideas which the patent laws leave otherwise unprotected." The Court described the scope of preemption of states laws (including state trade secret laws) by federal patent laws as follows:

> States may not offer patent-like protection to intellectual creations which would otherwise remain unprotected as a matter of federal law. Both the novelty and the nonobviousness requirements of federal patent law are grounded in the notion that concepts within the public grasp, or those so obvious that they readily could be, are the tools of creation available to all. They provide the baseline of free competition upon which the patent system's incentive to creative effort depends. A state law that substantially interferes with the enjoyment of an unpatented utilitarian or design conception which has been freely disclosed by its author to the public at large impermissibly contravenes the ultimate goal of public disclosure and use which is the centerpiece of federal patent policy. Moreover, through the creation of patent-like rights, the States could essentially redirect inventive efforts away from the careful criteria of patentability developed by Congress over the last 200 years.

Bonito Boats, 489 U.S. at 156–57. Trade secret protection and patent protection are complementary intellectual property regimes. Yet, trade secret protection is weaker than patent protection because, unlike patent law, trade secret law includes the doctrines of independent invention and reverse engineering. Therefore, trade secret protection is not patent-like protection. Moreover, while trade secret protection may last indefinitely, as explained in Chapter 4, patent protection usually may only extend twenty years from the date of filing. Do the Court's analyses in *Kewanee Oil* and *Bonito Boats* apply consistent tests for determining the scope of preemption of state trade secret laws (criminal or civil) by federal patent laws?

3.   Historical Note: States created specific trade secret theft statutes like the California criminal legislation described above in response to failed attempts to prosecute defendants for trade secret thefts under larceny statutes. For example, in *Commonwealth v. Engleman*, 336 Mass. 66, 142 N.E.2d 406 (1957), the Massachusetts Supreme Court held that the larceny statute then in effect in that state did not include trade secrets as a type of property that could be the subject of a larceny offense. In response to this case, the Massachusetts legislature revised its criminal laws to make a theft of a trade secret a form of larceny. *See* M.G.L.A. § 30.

CHAPTER THREE

COPYRIGHT: PUBLIC AND PRIVATE RIGHTS

■ ■ ■

OVERVIEW

The justification for creating private rights in authors and inventors lies as recognition for enriching the public and the eventuality of return to the public domain. Copyright in the United States is a matter of Federal statutory creation pursuant to Article I, Section 8, clause 8 of the Constitution:

> "[T]he Congress shall have power * * * to promote the progress of science and useful arts, by securing for limited times to authors and inventors the exclusive right to their respective writings and discoveries."

Coverage of Copyright is divided in two chapters. *Chapter Three* focuses on the creation, elements and issues of copyright common to analog and digital regimes. *Chapter Seven* continues the exposition of copyright issues in the context of Digital Rights Management problems facing content holder rights and the public interest in the creation, publication and distribution of copyright materials.

Section I of this chapter summarizes the history of copyright under English law, Colonial actions and early state legislative and judicial approaches prior to the Copyright Act of 1790. The Copyright Act of 1790 chose not to confirm prior common law or State legislative activities. Instead, the act created a new federal copyright as a singular interest pursuant to the authority granted Congress under the Constitution. Section II explores the Constitutional and statutory basis for copyright by examining the scope of copyright subject matter. Section III presents three legal prerequisites for copyright: originality, fixation, and legal formalities (the last being less important under current Copyright law). Section IV presents issues pertaining to the subject matter of copyright by laying out the basics of copyright infringement and remedies. This section also explores copyrights in pictorial, graphic, and sculptural works, software, and architecture. Section V turns to the challenging problem of derivative works. Sections VI and VII explore two important aspect of authorship: copyright ownership and moral rights. Section VIII examines fair use, a critical limitation on copyright. Section IX concludes the chapter by discussing the duration of copyright.

I. THE PREQUEL AND FOUNDATIONS OF COPYRIGHT

A. THE PUBLIC DOMAIN: IDENTIFYING AND DEFINING

The Public Domain intellectual content use is conceptual, rather than tangible. It represents the relative rights, duties, privileges, powers and immunities that exist between and among members of the public entitled to access, use and share in the richness of the public domain. (*See generally*, Hohfeld, *Fundamental Legal Conceptions as Applied in Judicial Reasoning*, 26 Yale L.J. 710, 746–47 (1917)). The Public Domain is an inclusive concept and is often in critical analysis or common parlance referred to as the intellectual commons, or simply commons. (*See generally*, Jessica Litman, *The Public Domain*, 39 Emory L.J. 965, 975 (1990); Boyle, *The Public Domain: Foreword: The Opposite of Property?* 66 Law & Contemp. Prob. 1 (Winter/Spring, 2003)). The Public Domain may also be thought of as the status quo ante in the natural order of things. It is the common right before society privatized selected intellectual activities, functions and content by property based limitations and controls over the rights of the public to free and unfettered use of the public domain. (*See generally*, Samuel Oddi, *The Tragicomedy of the Public Domain in Intellectual Property Law*, 25 Hastings Comm. & Ent. L.J. 1 (2003)). It is not a static set of constructs, but rather vibrant and responsive to social, political, economic, technological, normative and legal forces in securing sustainable balance between private interests and the public beneficial use of intellectual content. The public domain reflects the ebb and flow of attribution and incentive to foster creativity and the need for vigilance and empirical proof that privatization does not stifle competition and innovation. Global concern with proposed digitalization of written works, art and artifacts highlight the extraordinary character of this repository of creative necessity. The University Southern California has an ongoing decade long program for digitalization of the artifacts of early settlement. The French government has a digitalization project for preserving the exterior art incorporated in buildings and structures. The initial Google Book Project (now litigation and settlement agreement) and the recently announced HP agreement to digitalize books in the University of Michigan library attest to the forces set in motion for securing the public domain for public use.

Consider this definition posited by the American Association of Law Libraries and others in an amicus brief filed in *Eldred v. Ashcroft*, 537 U.S. 186, 123 S.Ct. 769, 154 L.Ed.2d 683 (2003):

> "The public domain is the priceless repository of works that are ineligible for copyright, were created before copyright law existed,

have had their copyrights expire, or have been freely given to the public by their authors.'' (No. 01–618, at 4)

In this context copyright is a bundle of rights carved out of what would otherwise be in the public domain. (*See generally*, Pamela Samuelson, *Mapping the Digital Public Domain: Threats and Opportunities*, 66 Law & Contemp. Probs. 147 (Winter/Spring 2003)). In the case of *Graham v. John Deere Co.*, 383 U.S. 1, 86 S.Ct. 684, 15 L.Ed.2d 545 (1966), Mr. Justice Clark reminds us of this fundamental perspective applicable to copyrights as well as patents, when he notes that:

> At the outset it must be remembered that the federal patent power stems from a specific constitutional provision which authorizes the Congress 'To promote the Progress of * * * useful Arts, by securing for limited Times to * * * Inventors the exclusive Right to their * * * Discoveries.' Art. I, § 8, cl. 8. The clause is both a grant of power and a limitation. * * * The Congress in the exercise of the patent power may not overreach the restraints imposed by the stated constitutional purpose. Nor may it enlarge the patent monopoly without regard to the innovation, advancement or social benefit gained thereby. Moreover, Congress may not authorize the issuance of patents whose effects are to remove existent knowledge from the public domain, or to restrict free access to materials already available. Innovation, advancement, and things which add to the sum of useful knowledge are inherent requisites in a patent system which by constitutional command must 'promote the Progress of * * * useful Arts.' This is the standard expressed in the Constitution and it may not be ignored. * * * (Id., at 5)

Deliberations of federal courts considering the force of legislative requirements necessary to perfect rights under the copyright statutes had repeatedly held that failure to comply with these mandatory elements left these interests in the public domain. These early decisions reinforced the proposition that at the end of the term of the private right the protected material fell back into the public domain.

Why during these past centuries has the Public Domain been a relatively passive doctrine in protecting public rights of use? Why has it not been the subject of judicial action seeking to ensure the public right against excessive diminution or dilution? Why has there been limited empirical validation whether privatization encourages or discourages ''progress,'' the sin qua non of copyright and patent monopolies? Some of these answers will become self evident in the cases and materials that follow. For a starting point, however, consider the following.

First, private rights were initially few, limited in time, content and scope. The public good was served by encouragement of publication and the sharing of ideas, remembering that from the beginning ideas were not copyrightable. Until recently, there doesn't appear to have been a widespread perception of ''scarcity'' nor concern regarding intellectual content available for use in the public domain.

Second, during the early to later parts of the 20th Century, intellectual property became a significant part of the wealth of nations, particularly the United States. (See Steven Wilf, *The Making of the Post–War Paradigm in American Intellectual Property Law*, 31 COLUM. J.L. & ARTS 139 (2008).) See also Reis, *The Sony Legacy: Secondary Liability Perspectives*, 3 Akron Intell. Prop. L.J. 205 (March 2010).

Third, judicial actions have generally been brought to enforce recognized rights the value of which justifies the transaction. This partially may explain why almost every case concerned some aspect of enforcing a copyright in the context of an adversarial proceeding, not seeking to enforce or secure recognition for the broader public right. Justices in decisions through and including *Sony Betamax*, however, accounted for the public domain interest in their decision making. This perspective may have altered after *Eldred* and as part and parcel of the Digital Rights Management quandary addressed in Chapter Seven *Metro-Goldwyn–Mayer Studios Inc. v. Grokster, Ltd.*, 545 U.S. 913, 125 S.Ct. 2764, 162 L.Ed.2d 781 (2005) [hereinafter *Grokster*].

Concern for public domain rights has been exacerbated by the pace of technological change in analog and digital structures. These changes affect the creation, use and distribution of content. Global populations have been enabled through digital devices, applications and transmission to "use" content, both privately and in the public domain. Most contemporary digital uses were never conceived or anticipated in paradigms which balance the public interest in the creation and enforcement of intellectual property rights.

The question remains why are we highlighting the public domain in the context of understanding copyright? Is it because of growing public sentiment and political pressure regarding the public beneficial interest in intellectual content and the integrity of the public domain? It behooves those who seek to understand copyright to appreciate the implications of public domain issues as rules change to accommodate existing private rights and ensure the necessary balance for a sustainable future. (See e.g., the victory celebration of the Swedish "Pirate Party" in electing candidates for copyright and intellectual property right reform to the EU Congress.) (http://www.piratpartiet.se/international/english) The contagion of political action is spreading through Europe like wildfire. (http://www.gulf-imes.com/site/topics/article.asp?cu_no=2 & item_no=296947 & version=1 & template_id=39 & parent_id=21)

Reis, *The Public Trust Doctrine in the Intellectual Commons–Who Has Standing to Represent the Public Interest?* (Paper presented, IPSC Berkeley (Summer 2006).) See also, *Google Books Library Project—An enhanced card catalog of the world's books.* "The Library Project's aim is simple: make it easier for people to find relevant books—specifically, books they wouldn't find any other way such as those that are out of print—while carefully respecting authors' and publishers' copyrights. Our ultimate goal is to work with publishers and libraries to create a comprehensive, searchable, virtual card catalog of all books in all languages that helps users discover new books and publishers discover new readers. (http: //books.google.com/googlebooks/library.html) See also, (http://www.tech flash.com/seattle/2009/10/hp_amazon _team_on_rare_book_reprints.html) a project of HP, the University of Michigan with Amazon to distribute digitalized books. The Google Book Project and proposed settlement agreements have demonstrated both limitations with interests represented in the adversarial process, as well internal and international response as reminders that the end is the public beneficial interest and progress in the arts and sciences.

B. AN ABBREVIATED COPYRIGHT TIMELINE

1787 – James Madison submitted a provision "to secure to literary authors their copyrights for a limited time." ***May 31, 1790*** *–First copyright law enacted with a term of 14 years, renewal 14 years covering Books, maps, and charts.* ***1831*** *– First general revision. Music added. Term 28 years, renewal 14 years.* ***1856*** *– Added Dramatic compositions.* ***1865*** *– Photographs added.* ***1870*** *– Second general revision. Works of art added. Authors given right to create derivative works including translations and dramatizations.* ***1897*** *– Public performance of music added.* ***1909*** *– Effective date third general revision of copyright law. Classes of unpublished works added. Term measured from date of publication, renewal increased to 28 years.* ***1912*** *– Motion pictures.* ***1972*** *– Limited copyright protection to sound recordings.* ***1974*** *–1971 Universal Copyright Convention revised at Paris, France.* ***1978*** *– Effective date of 1976 copyright law. Term life of the author and 50 years.* ***1980*** *· Computer programs added.* ***1984*** *– Semiconductor Chip Protection Act.* ***1989*** *- Berne Convention.* ***1990*** *– Section 511 Federal and State employees not immune from copyright infringement.* ***1990*** *– Computer Software Rental Amendments Act.* ***1990*** *– Architectural works. Visual Artists Rights Act gave visual artists moral rights of attribution and integrity.* ***1992*** *– Renewal registration optional.* ***1992*** *– Digital Audio Home Recording Act authorizes serial copy management systems in digital audio recorders and imposed royalties on sale of digital audio recording devices and media.* ***1998*** *– Sonny Bono Copyright Term Extension life of the author plus 70 years after the author's death.* ***1998*** *– The Digital Millennium Copyright Act.* ***2002*** *– The Technology, Education, and Copyright Harmonization (TEACH) Act of 2002.*

II. CONSTITUTIONAL AND STATUTORY BASES FOR COPYRIGHT

BAKER v. SELDEN

Supreme Court of the United States, 1879.
101 U.S. 99, ___ S.Ct. ___, 25 L.Ed. 841.

Mr. Justice Bradley delivered the opinion of the court.

Charles Selden, the testator of the complainant in this case, in the year 1859 took the requisite steps for obtaining the copyright of a book, entitled "Selden's Condensed Ledger, or Book-keeping Simplified," the object of which was to exhibit and explain a peculiar system of book-keeping. In 1860 and 1861, he took the copyright of several other books, containing additions to and improvements upon the said system. The bill of complaint was filed against the defendant, Baker, for an alleged infringement of these copyrights. The latter, in his answer, denied that Selden was the author or designer of the books, and denied the infringement charged, and contends on the argument that the matter alleged to be infringed is not a lawful subject of copyright. * * *

The book or series of books of which the complainant claims the copyright consists of an introductory essay explaining the system of book-keeping referred to, to which are annexed certain forms or banks, consisting of ruled lines, and headings, illustrating the system and showing how it is to be used and carried out in practice. This system effects the same results as book-keeping by double entry; but, by a peculiar arrangement of columns and headings, presents the entire operation, of a day, a week, or a month, on a single page, or on two pages facing each other, in an account-book. The defendant uses a similar plan so far as results are concerned; but makes a different arrangement of the columns, and uses different headings. If the complainant's testator had the exclusive right to the use of the system explained in his book, it would be difficult to contend that the defendant does not infringe it, notwithstanding the difference in his form of arrangement; but if it be assumed that the system is open to public use, it seems to be equally difficult to contend that the books made and sold by the defendant are a violation of the copyright of the complainant's book considered merely as a book explanatory of the system. Where the truths of a science or the methods of an art are the common property of the whole world, any author has the right to express the one, or explain and use the other, in his own way. As an author, Selden explained the system in a particular way. It may be conceded that Baker makes and uses account-books arranged on substantially the same system; but the proof fails to show that he has violated the copyright of Selden's book, regarding the latter merely as an explanatory work; or that he has infringed Selden's right in any way, unless the latter became entitled to an exclusive right in the system. * * *

It cannot be pretended, and indeed it is not seriously urged, that the ruled lines of the complainant's account-book can be claimed under any special class of objects, other than books, named in the law of copyright existing in 1859. The law then in force was that of 1831, and specified only books, maps, charts, musical compositions, prints, and engravings. An account-book, consisting of ruled lines and blank columns, cannot be called by any of these names unless by that of a book.

There is no doubt that a work on the subject of book-keeping, though only explanatory of well-known systems, may be the subject of a copyright; but, then, it is claimed only as a book. Such a book may be explanatory either of old systems, or of an entirely new system; and, considered as a book, as the work of an author, conveying information on the subject of book-keeping, and containing detailed explanations of the art, it may be a very valuable acquisition to the practical knowledge of the community. But there is a clear distinction between the book, as such, and the art which it is intended to illustrate. The mere statement of the proposition is so evident, that it requires hardly any argument to support it. The same distinction may be predicated of every other art as well as that of book-keeping. A treatise on the composition and use of medicines, be they old or new; on the construction and use of ploughs, or watches, or churns; or on the mixture and application of colors for painting or dyeing; or on the mode of drawing lines to produce the effect of perspective,-would be the subject of copyright; but no one would contend that the copyright of the treatise would give the exclusive right to the art or manufacture described therein. The copyright of the book, if not pirated from other works, would be valid without regard to the novelty, or want of novelty, of its subject-matter. The novelty of the art or thing described or explained has nothing to do with the validity of the copyright. To give to the author of the book an exclusive property in the art described therein, when no examination of its novelty has ever been officially made, would be a surprise and a fraud upon the public. That is the province of letters-patent, not of copyright. The claim to an invention or discovery of an art or manufacture must be subjected to the examination of the Patent Office before an exclusive right therein can be obtained; and it can only be secured by a patent from the government.

The difference between the two things, letters-patent and copyright, may be illustrated by reference to the subjects just enumerated. Take the case of medicines. Certain mixtures are found to be of great value in the healing art. If the discoverer writes and publishes a book on the subject (as regular physicians generally do), he gains no exclusive right to the manufacture and sale of the medicine; he gives that to the public. If he desires to acquire such exclusive right, he must obtain a patent for the mixture as a new art, manufacture, or composition of matter. He may copyright his book, if he pleases; but that only secures to him the exclusive right of printing and publishing his book. So of all other inventions or discoveries.

The copyright of a book on perspective, no matter how many drawings and illustrations it may contain, gives no exclusive right to the modes of drawing described, though they may never have been known or used before. By publishing the book, without getting a patent for the art, the latter is given to the public. The fact that the art described in the book by illustrations of lines and figures which are reproduced in practice in the application of the art, makes no difference. Those illustrations are the mere language employed by the author to convey his ideas more clearly. Had he used words of description instead of diagrams (which merely stand in the place of words), there could not be the slightest doubt that others, applying the art to practical use, might lawfully draw the lines and diagrams which were in the author's mind, and which he thus described by words in his book.

The copyright of a work on mathematical science cannot give to the author an exclusive right to the methods of operation which he propounds, or to the diagrams which he employs to explain them, so as to prevent an engineer from using them whenever occasion requires. The very object of publishing a book on science or the useful arts is to communicate to the world the useful knowledge which it contains. But this object would be frustrated if the knowledge could not be used without incurring the guilt of piracy of the book. And where the art it teaches cannot be used without employing the methods and diagrams used to illustrate the book, or such as are similar to them, such methods and diagrams are to be considered as necessary incidents to the art, and given therewith to the public; not given for the purpose of publication in other works explanatory of the art, but for the purpose of practical application.

Of course, these observations are not intended to apply to ornamental designs, or pictorial illustrations addressed to the taste. Of these it may be said, that their form is their essence, and their object, the production of pleasure in their contemplation. This is their final end. They are as much the product of genius and the result of composition, as are the lines of the poet or the historian's period. On the other hand, the teachings of science and the rules and methods of useful art have their final end in application and use; and this application and use are what the public derive from the publication of a book which teaches them. But as embodied and taught in a literary composition or book, their essence consists only in their statement. This alone is what is secured by the copyright. The use by another of the same methods of statement, whether in words or illustrations, in a book published for teaching the art, would undoubtedly be an infringement of the copyright.

Recurring to the case before us, we observe that Charles Selden, by his books, explained and described a peculiar system of book-keeping, and illustrated his method by means of ruled lines and blank columns, with proper headings on a page, or on successive pages. Now, whilst no one has a right to print or publish his book, or any material part thereof, as a book intended to convey instruction in the art, any person may practice and use the art itself which he has described and illustrated therein. The use of the art is a totally different thing from a publication of the book explaining it. The copyright of a book on book-keeping cannot secure the exclusive right to make, sell, and use account-books prepared upon the plan set forth in such book. Whether the art might or might not have been patented, is a question which is not before us. It was not patented, and is open and free to the use of the public. And, of course, in using the art, the ruled lines and headings of accounts must necessarily be used as incident to it.

The plausibility of the claim put forward by the complainant in this case arises from a confusion of ideas produced by the peculiar nature of the art described in the books which have been made the subject of copyright. In describing the art, the illustrations and diagrams employed happen to correspond more closely than usual with the actual work performed by the operator who uses the art. Those illustrations and diagrams consist of ruled lines and headings of accounts; and it is similar ruled lines and headings of accounts which, in the application of the art, the book-keeper makes with his pen, or the stationer with his press; whilst in most other cases the diagrams and illustrations can only be represented in concrete forms of wood, metal, stone, or some other physical embodiment. But the principle is the same in all. The description of the art in a book, though entitled to the benefit of copyright, lays no foundation for an exclusive claim to the art itself. The object of the one is explanation; the object of the other is use. The former may be secured by copyright. The latter can only be secured, if it can be secured at all, by letters-patent. * * *

The conclusion to which we have come is, that blank account-books are not the subject of copyright; and that the mere copyright of Selden's book did not confer upon him the exclusive right to make and use account-books, ruled and arranged as designated by him and described and illustrated in said book.

SATAVA v. LOWRY

United States Court of Appeals for the Ninth Circuit, 2003.
323 F.3d 805.

GOULD, CIRCUIT JUDGE.

In the Copyright Act, Congress sought to benefit the public by encouraging artists' creative expression. Congress carefully drew the contours of copyright protection to achieve this goal. It granted artists the exclusive right to the original expression in their works, thereby giving them a financial incentive to create works to enrich our culture. But it denied artists the exclusive right to ideas and standard elements in their works, thereby preventing them from monopolizing what rightfully belongs to the public. In this case, we must locate the faint line between unprotected idea and original expression in the context of realistic animal sculpture. We must decide whether an artist's lifelike glass-in-glass sculptures of jellyfish are protectable by copyright. Because we conclude that the sculptures are composed of unprotectable ideas and standard elements, and also that the combination of those unprotectable elements is unprotectable, we reverse the judgment of the district court. * * *

Plaintiff Richard Satava is a glass artist from California. In the late 1980s, Satava was inspired by the jellyfish display at an aquarium. He began experimenting with jellyfish sculptures in the glass-in-glass medium and, in 1990, began selling glass-in-glass jellyfish sculptures. The sculptures sold well, and Satava made more of them. By 2002, Satava was designing and creating about three hundred jellyfish sculptures each month. Satava's sculptures are sold in galleries and gift shops in forty states, and they sell for hundreds or thousands of dollars, depending on size. Satava has registered several of his works with the Register of Copyrights.

Satava describes his sculptures as "vertically oriented, colorful, fanciful jellyfish with tendril-like tentacles and a rounded bell encased in an outer layer of rounded clear glass that is bulbous at the top and tapering toward the bottom to form roughly a bullet shape, with the jellyfish portion of the sculpture filling almost the entire volume of the outer, clearglass shroud." Satava's jellyfish appear lifelike. They resemble the pelagia colorata that live in the Pacific Ocean. * * *

During the 1990s, defendant Christopher Lowry, a glass artist from Hawaii, also began making glass-in-glass jellyfish sculptures. Lowry's sculptures look like Satava's, and many people confuse them: * * *

Glass-in-glass sculpture is a centuries-old art form that consists of a glass sculpture inside a second glass layer, commonly called the shroud. The artist creates an inner glass sculpture and then dips it into molten glass, encasing it in a solid outer glass shroud. The shroud is malleable before it cools, and the artist can manipulate it into any shape he or she desires.

Satava filed suit against Lowry accusing him of copyright infringement. Satava requested, and the district court granted, a preliminary injunction, enjoining Lowry from making sculptures that resemble Satava's. Lowry appealed to us. * * *

Copyright protection is available for "original works of authorship fixed in any tangible medium of expression, now known or later developed, from which they can be perceived, reproduced, or otherwise communicated, either directly or with the aid of a machine or device." 17 U.S.C. § 102(a). Copyright protection does not, however, "extend to any idea, procedure, process, system, method of operation, concept, principle, or discovery...." 17 U.S.C. § 102(b).

It follows from these principles that no copyright protection may be afforded to the idea of producing a glass-in-glass jellyfish sculpture or to elements of expression that naturally follow from the idea of such a sculpture. See *Aliotti v. R. Dakin & Co.*, 831 F.2d 898, 901 (9th Cir.1987) ("No copyright protection may be afforded to the idea of producing stuffed dinosaur toys or to elements of expression that necessarily follow from the idea of such dolls."). Satava may not prevent others from copying aspects of his sculptures resulting from either jellyfish physiology or from their depiction in the glass-in-glass medium. See id. ("Appellants therefore may place no reliance upon any similarity in expression resulting from either the physiognomy of dinosaurs or from the nature of stuffed animals.").

Satava may not prevent others from depicting jellyfish with tendril-like tentacles or rounded bells, because many jellyfish possess those body parts. He may not prevent others from depicting jellyfish in bright colors, because many jellyfish are brightly colored. He may not prevent others from depicting jellyfish swimming vertically, because jellyfish swim vertically in nature and often are depicted swimming vertically. See id. at 901 n. 1 (noting that a Tyrannosaurus stuffed animal's open mouth was not an element protected by copyright because Tyrannosaurus "was a carnivore and is commonly pictured with its mouth open").

Satava may not prevent others from depicting jellyfish within a clear outer layer of glass, because clear glass is the most appropriate setting for an aquatic animal. See id. (noting that a Pterodactyl stuffed animal's depiction as a mobile hanging from the ceiling was not protectable because Pterodactyl "was a winged creature and thus is appropriate for such treatment"). He may not prevent others from depicting jellyfish "almost filling the entire volume" of the outer glass shroud, because such proportion is standard in glass-in-glass sculpture. And he may not prevent others from tapering the shape of their shrouds, because that shape is standard in glass-in-glass sculpture.

Satava's glass-in-glass jellyfish sculptures, though beautiful, combine several unprotectable ideas and standard elements. These elements are part of the public domain. They are the common property of all, and Satava may not use copyright law to seize them for his exclusive use.

It is true, of course, that a combination of unprotectable elements may qualify for copyright protection. *Apple Computer, Inc. v. Microsoft Corp.*, 35 F.3d 1435, 1446 (9th Cir.1994); *United States v. Hamilton*, 583 F.2d 448, 451 (9th Cir.1978) (Kennedy, J.) ("[O]riginality may be found in taking the commonplace and making it into a new combination or arrangement."). * * * But it is not true that any combination of unprotectable elements automatically qualifies for copyright protection. Our case law suggests, and we hold today, that a combination of unprotectable elements is eligible for copyright protection only if those elements are numerous enough and their selection and arrangement original enough that their combination constitutes an original work of authorship. * * *

The combination of unprotectable elements in Satava's sculpture falls short of this standard. The selection of the clear glass, oblong shroud, bright colors, proportion, vertical orientation, and stereotyped jellyfish form, considered together, lacks the quantum of originality needed to merit copyright protection. See *Hamilton*, 583 F.2d at 451 ("Trivial elements of compilation and arrangement, of course, are not copyrightable because they fall below the threshold of originality."). These elements are so commonplace in glass-in-glass sculpture and so typical of jellyfish physiology that to recognize copyright protection in their combination effectively would give Satava a monopoly on lifelike glass-in-glass sculptures of single jellyfish with vertical tentacles. * * * Because the quantum of originality Satava added in combining these standard and stereotyped elements must be considered "trivial" under our case law, Satava cannot prevent other artists from combining them.

Our analysis above suggests that the "merger doctrine" might apply in this case. Under the merger doctrine, courts will not protect a copyrighted work from infringement if the idea underlying the copyrighted work can be expressed in only one way, lest there be a monopoly on the underlying idea. *CDN Inc. v. Kapes*, 197 F.3d 1256, 1261 (9th Cir.1999). In light of our holding that Satava cannot prevent other artists from using the standard and stereotyped elements in his sculptures, or the combination of those elements, we find it unnecessary to consider the application of the merger doctrine.

We do not mean to suggest that Satava has added nothing copyrightable to his jellyfish sculptures. He has made some copyrightable contributions: the distinctive curls of particular tendrils; the arrangement of certain hues; the unique shape of jellyfishes' bells. To the extent that these and other artistic choices were not governed by jellyfish physiology or the glass-in-glass medium, they are original elements that Satava theoretically may protect through copyright law. Satava's copyright on these original elements (or their combination) is "thin," however, comprising no more than his original contribution to ideas already in the public domain. Stated another way, Satava may prevent others from copying the original features he contributed, but he may not prevent others from copying elements of expression that nature displays for all observers, or that the glass-in-glass medium suggests to all sculptors. Satava possesses a thin copyright that protects against only virtually identical copying. See *Ets–Hokin v. Skyy Spirits, Inc.*, 323 F.3d at 766 (9th Cir.2003) ("When we apply the limiting doctrines, subtracting the unoriginal elements, Ets Hokin is left with ... a 'thin' copyright, which protects against only virtually identical copying."); Apple, 35 F.3d at 1439 ("When the range of protectable expression is narrow, the appropriate standard for illicit copying is virtual identity.").

We do not hold that realistic depictions of live animals cannot be protected by copyright. In fact, we have held to the contrary. See *Kamar Int'l, Inc. v. Russ Berrie and Co.*, 657 F.2d 1059, 1061 (9th Cir.1981). We recognize, however, that the scope of copyright protection in such works is narrow. See *Herbert Rosenthal Jewelry Corp. v. Kalpakian*, 446 F.2d 738, 741 (9th Cir.1971) ("Any inference of copying based upon similar appearance lost much of its strength because both [works] were lifelike representations of a natural creature."). Nature gives us ideas of animals in their natural surroundings: an eagle with talons extended to snatch a mouse; a grizzly bear clutching a salmon between its teeth; a butterfly emerging from its cocoon; a wolf howling at the full moon; a jellyfish swimming through tropical waters. These ideas, first expressed by nature, are the common heritage of humankind, and no artist may use copyright law to prevent others from depicting them.

An artist may, however, protect the original expression he or she contributes to these ideas. An artist may vary the pose, attitude, gesture, muscle structure, facial expression, coat, or texture of animal. An artist may vary the background, lighting, or perspective. Such variations, if original, may earn copyright protection. Because Satava's jellyfish sculptures contain few variations of this type, the scope of his copyright is narrow.

We do not mean to short-change the legitimate need of creative artists to protect their original works. After all, copyright law achieves its high purpose of enriching our culture by giving artists a financial incentive to create. But we must be careful in copyright cases not to cheat the public domain. Only by vigorously policing the line between idea and expression can we ensure both that artists receive due reward for their original creations and that proper latitude is granted other artists to make use of ideas that properly belong to us all.

NOTES

1. The Supreme Court's decision in *Baker v. Selden* creates an important exception from the subject matter of copyright. The decision also draws boundaries between the subject matter of patent and that of copyright. What exactly does the Court exclude from copyright protection? Would what the Court excludes from copyright protection be covered by some other field of intellectual property? Or does the decision in *Baker* create subject matter that is not protected by law and therefore left open for the public to use?

2. The Supreme Court's decision in *Baker v. Selden* provides the basis for the list of statutory exceptions from copyright under Section 102(b) of the Copyright Act. More about this provision in the discussion of copyright and computer programs below.

3. The Ninth Circuit's decision in *Satava* is included to provoke discussion and to illustrate the broader issue of the boundaries of copyright protection. Would it be accurate to say that the court is excluding the realistic depiction of nature from the scope of copyright protection? Can you think of reasons why such a reading of the case would be too broad? The artist worked hard and showed an incredible amount of craftsmanship in creating the glass statues. Why should that not be protected by copyright law? Think of this question again after you have read and discussed the *Feist* decision below.

III. THE PREREQUISITES OF COPYRIGHT

A. ORIGINALITY

Once subject matter is determined to be within the purview of copyright, the question is whether the act of authorship meets the criteria for protection. As the *Feist* case below notes, originality is a requirement of copyright. What does this mean? Is there a minimum threshold of originality required by the Constitution for copyright protection? Can there be one or more persons who claim authorship of identical or similar "original" expressions? Does the proposition that copyright is not intended as a reward for hard work, but rather for the contribution of the author to the public benefit set any standard to determine the degree of originality required for protection? (See generally, Denicola, *Copyright in Collections of Facts: A Theory for the Protection of Nonfiction Literary Works*, 81 Colum. L. Rev. 516 (1981)). How are these questions addressed in the cases that follow?

§ 102. Subject matter of copyright: In general

(a) Copyright protection subsists, in accordance with this title, in original works of authorship fixed in any tangible medium of expression, now known or later developed, from which they can be perceived, reproduced, or otherwise communicated, either directly or with the aid of a machine or device.

The following case highlights a number of fundamental distinctions between facts and expression and addresses that minimal level of originality warranting protection under the Copyright Act.

FEIST PUBLICATIONS, INC. v. RURAL TELEPHONE SERVICE COMPANY, INC.

Supreme Court of the United States, 1991.
499 U.S. 340, 111 S.Ct. 1282, 113 L.Ed.2d 358.

JUSTICE O'CONNOR delivered the opinion of the Court.

This case requires us to clarify the extent of copyright protection available to telephone directory white pages.

Rural Telephone Service Company, Inc., is a certified public utility that provides telephone service to several communities in northwest Kansas. It is subject to a state regulation that requires all telephone companies operating in Kansas to issue annually an updated telephone directory. Accordingly, as a condition of its monopoly franchise, Rural publishes a typical telephone directory, consisting of white pages and yellow pages. The white pages list in alphabetical order the names of Rural's subscribers, together with their towns and telephone numbers. The yellow pages list Rural's business subscribers alphabetically by category and feature classified advertisements of various sizes. Rural distributes its directory free of charge to its subscribers, but earns revenue by selling yellow pages advertisements.

Feist Publications, Inc. is a publishing company that specializes in area-wide telephone directories.

Unlike a typical directory, which covers only a particular calling area, Feist's area-wide directories cover a much larger geographical range, reducing the need to call directory assistance or consult multiple directories. The Feist directory that is the subject of this litigation covers 11 different telephone service areas in 15 counties and contains 46,878 white pages listings—compared to Rural's approximately 7,700 listings. Like Rural's directory, Feist's is distributed free of charge and includes both white pages and yellow pages. Feist and Rural compete vigorously for yellow pages advertising.

As the sole provider of telephone service in its service area, Rural obtains subscriber information quite easily. Persons desiring telephone service must apply to Rural and provide their names and addresses; Rural then assigns them a telephone number. Feist is not a telephone company, let alone one with monopoly status, and therefore lacks independent access to any subscriber information. To obtain white pages listings for its area-wide directory, Feist approached each of the 11 telephone companies operating in northwest Kansas and offered to pay for the right to use its white pages listings.

Of the 11 telephone companies, only Rural refused to license its listings to Feist. Rural's refusal created a problem for Feist, as omitting these listings would have left a gaping hole in its area-wide directory, rendering it less attractive to potential yellow pages advertisers. In a decision subsequent to that which we review here, the District Court determined that this was precisely the reason Rural refused to license its listings. The refusal was motivated by an unlawful purpose "to extend its monopoly in telephone service to a monopoly in yellow pages advertising." *Rural Telephone Service Co. v. Feist Publications, Inc.,* 737 F.Supp. 610, 622 (Kan.1990).

Unable to license Rural's white pages listings, Feist used them without Rural's consent. Feist began by removing several thousand listings that fell outside the geographic range of its area-wide directory, then hired personnel to investigate the 4,935 that remained. These employees verified the data reported by Rural and sought to obtain additional information. As a result, a typical Feist listing includes the individual's street address; most of Rural's listings do not. Notwithstanding these additions, however, 1,309 of the 46,878 listings in Feist's 1983 directory were identical to listings in Rural's 1982–1983 white pages. * * * Four of these were fictitious listings that Rural had inserted into its directory to detect copying.

Rural sued for copyright infringement in the District Court for the District of Kansas taking the position that Feist, in compiling its own directory, could not use the information contained in Rural's white pages. Rural asserted that Feist's employees were obliged to travel door-to-door or conduct a telephone survey to discover the same information for themselves. Feist responded that such efforts were economically impractical and, in any event, unnecessary because the information copied was beyond the scope of copyright protection. The District Court granted summary judgment to Rural, explaining that "[c]ourts have consistently held that telephone directories are copyrightable" and citing a string of lower court decisions. * * * In an unpublished opinion, the Court of Appeals for the Tenth Circuit affirmed "for substantially the reasons given by the district court." * * * We granted certiorari, 498 U.S. 808, 111 S.Ct. 40, 112 L.Ed.2d 17 (1990), to determine whether the copyright in Rural's directory protects the names, towns, and telephone numbers copied by Feist.

II

A

This case concerns the interaction of two well-established propositions. The first is that facts are not copyrightable; the other, that compilations of facts generally are. Each of these propositions possesses an impeccable pedigree. That there can be no valid copyright in facts is universally understood. The most fundamental axiom of copyright law is that "[n]o author may copyright his ideas or the facts he narrates." *Harper & Row, Publishers, Inc. v. Nation Enterprises,* 471 U.S. 539, 556,

105 S.Ct. 2218, 2228, 85 L.Ed.2d 588 (1985). Rural wisely concedes this point, noting in its brief that "[f]acts and discoveries, of course, are not themselves subject to copyright protection." * * * At the same time, however, it is beyond dispute that compilations of facts are within the subject matter of copyright. Compilations were expressly mentioned in the Copyright Act of 1909, and again in the Copyright Act of 1976.

There is an undeniable tension between these two propositions. Many compilations consist of nothing but raw data—*i.e.,* wholly factual information not accompanied by any original written expression. On what basis may one claim a copyright in such a work? Common sense tells us that 100 uncopyrightable facts do not magically change their status when gathered together in one place. Yet copyright law seems to contemplate that compilations that consist exclusively of facts are potentially within its scope.

The key to resolving the tension lies in understanding why facts are not copyrightable. The *sine qua non* of copyright is originality. To qualify for copyright protection, a work must be original to the author. See *Harper & Row, supra,* at 547–549, 105 S.Ct., at 2223–2224. Original, as the term is used in copyright, means only that the work was independently created by the author (as opposed to copied from other works), and that it possesses at least some minimal degree of creativity. 1 M. Nimmer & D. Nimmer, Copyright §§ 2.01[A], [B] (1990) (hereinafter Nimmer). To be sure, the requisite level of creativity is extremely low; even a slight amount will suffice. The vast majority of works make the grade quite easily, as they possess some creative spark, "no matter how crude, humble or obvious" it might be. *Id.,* § 1.08 [C] [1]. Originality does not signify novelty; a work may be original even though it closely resembles other works so long as the similarity is fortuitous, not the result of copying. To illustrate, assume that two poets, each ignorant of the other, compose identical poems. Neither work is novel, yet both are original and, hence, copyrightable. See *Sheldon v. Metro–Goldwyn Pictures Corp.,* 81 F.2d 49, 54 (2d Cir. 1936).

Originality is a constitutional requirement. The source of Congress' power to enact copyright laws is Article I, § 8, cl. 8, of the Constitution, which authorizes Congress to "secur[e] for limited Times to Authors ... the exclusive Right to their respective Writings." In two decisions from the late 19th century—*The Trade–Mark Cases,* 100 U.S. 82, 25 L.Ed. 550 (1879); and *Burrow–Giles Lithographic Co. v. Sarony,* 111 U.S. 53, 4 S.Ct. 279, 28 L.Ed. 349 (1884)—this Court defined the crucial terms "authors" and "writings." In so doing, the Court made it unmistakably clear that these terms presuppose a degree of originality.

In *The Trade–Mark Cases,* the Court addressed the constitutional scope of "writings." For a particular work to be classified "under the head of writings of authors," the Court determined, "originality is required." 100 U.S., at 94. The Court explained that originality requires independent creation plus a modicum of creativity: "[W]hile the word *writings* may be liberally construed, as it has been, to include original designs for engraving, prints, & c., it is only such as are *original,* and are founded in the creative powers of the mind. The writings which are to be protected are *the fruits of intellectual labor,* embodied in the form of books, prints, engravings, and the like." *Ibid.* (emphasis in original).

In *Burrow–Giles,* the Court distilled the same requirement from the Constitution's use of the word "authors." The Court defined "author," in a constitutional sense, to mean "he to whom anything owes its origin; originator; maker." 111 U.S., at 58, 4 S.Ct., at 281 (internal quotation marks omitted). As in *The Trade–Mark Cases,* the Court emphasized the creative component of originality. It described copyright as being limited to "original intellectual conceptions of the author," 111 U.S., at 58, 4 S.Ct., at 281, and stressed the importance of requiring an author who accuses another of infringement to prove "the existence of those facts of originality, of intellectual production, of thought, and conception." *Id.,* at 59–60, 4 S.Ct., at 281–282.

The originality requirement articulated in *The Trade–Mark Cases* and *Burrow–Giles* remains the touchstone of copyright protection today. See *Goldstein v. California,* 412 U.S. 546, 561–562, 93 S.Ct. 2303, 2312, 37 L.Ed.2d 163 (1973). It is the very "premise of copyright law." *Miller v. Universal City Studios, Inc.,* 650 F.2d 1365, 1368 (5th Cir. 1981). Leading scholars agree on this point. As one pair of commentators succinctly puts it: "The originality requirement is *constitutionally mandated* for all works." Patterson & Joyce, Monopolizing the Law: The Scope of Copyright Protection for Law Reports and Statutory Compilations, 36 UCLA L.Rev. 719, 763, n. 155 (1989) (emphasis in original) (hereinafter Patterson & Joyce). Accord, *id.,* at 759–760, and n. 140; Nimmer § 1.06[A] ("[O]riginality is a statutory as well as a constitutional requirement"); *id.,* § 1.08[C][1] ("[A] modicum of intellectual labor . . . clearly constitutes an essential constitutional element").

It is this bedrock principle of copyright that mandates the law's seemingly disparate treatment of facts and factual compilations. "No one may claim originality as to facts." *Id.,* § 2.11[A], p. 2–157. This is because facts do not owe their origin to an act of authorship. The distinction is one between creation and discovery: The first person to find and report a particular fact has not created the fact; he or she has merely discovered its existence. To borrow from *Burrow–Giles,* one who discovers a fact is not its "maker" or "originator." 111 U.S., at 58, 4 S.Ct., at 281. "The discoverer merely finds and records." Nimmer § 2.03[E]. Census takers, for example, do not "create" the population figures that emerge from their efforts, in a sense, they copy these figures from the world around them. Denicola, Copyright in Collections of Facts: A Theory for the Protection of Nonfiction Literary Works, 81 Colum.L.Rev. 516, 525 (1981) (hereinafter Denicola). Census data therefore do not trigger copyright because these data are not "original" in the constitutional sense. Nimmer § 2.03[E]. The same is true of all facts—scientific, historical, biographical, and news of the day. "[T]hey may not be copyrighted and are part of the public domain available to every person." *Miller, supra,* at 1369.

Factual compilations, on the other hand, may possess the requisite originality. The compilation author typically chooses which facts to include, in what order to place them, and how to arrange the collected data so that they may be used effectively by readers. These choices as to selection and arrangement, so long as they are made independently by the compiler and entail a minimal degree of creativity, are sufficiently original that Congress may protect such compilations through the copyright laws. Nimmer §§ 2.11[D], 3.03; Denicola 523, n. 38. Thus, even a directory that contains absolutely no protectible written expression, only facts, meets the constitutional minimum for copyright protection if it features an original selection or arrangement. See *Harper & Row,* 471 U.S., at 547, 105 S.Ct., at 2223. Accord, Nimmer § 3.03.

This protection is subject to an important limitation. The mere fact that a work is copyrighted does not mean that every element of the work may be protected. Originality remains the *sine qua non* of copyright; accordingly, copyright protection may extend only to those components of a work that are original to the author. Patterson & Joyce 800–802; Jane Ginsburg, Creation and Commercial Value: Copyright Protection of Works of Information, 90 Colum.L.Rev. 1865, 1868, and n. 12 (1990) (hereinafter Ginsburg). Thus, if the compilation author clothes facts with an original collocation of words, he or she may be able to claim a copyright in this written expression. Others may copy the underlying facts from the publication, but not the precise words used to present them. In *Harper & Row,* for example, we explained that President Ford could not prevent others from copying bare historical facts from his autobiography, see 471 U.S., at 556–557, 105 S.Ct., at 2228–2229, but that he could prevent others from copying his "subjective descriptions and portraits of public figures." *Id.,* at 563, 105 S.Ct., at 2232. Where the compilation author adds no written expression but rather lets the facts speak for themselves, the expressive element is more elusive. The only conceivable expression is the manner in which the compiler has selected and arranged the facts. Thus, if the selection and arrangement are original, these elements of the work are eligible for copyright protection. See Patry, *Copyright in Compilations of Facts (or Why the "White Pages" Are Not Copyrightable),* 12 Com. & Law 37, 64 (Dec. 1990) (hereinafter Patry). No matter how original the format, however, the facts themselves do not become original through association. See Patterson & Joyce 776.

This inevitably means that the copyright in a factual compilation is thin. Notwithstanding a valid copyright, a subsequent compiler remains free to use the facts contained in another's publication to aid in preparing a competing work, so long as the competing work does not feature the same selection and arrangement. As one commentator explains it: "[N]o matter how much original authorship the work displays, the facts and ideas it exposes are free for the taking. . . . [T]he very same facts and ideas may be divorced from the context imposed by the author, and restated or reshuffled by second comers, even if the author was the first to discover the facts or to propose the ideas." Ginsburg 1868.

It may seem unfair that much of the fruit of the compiler's labor may be used by others without compensation. As Justice Brennan has correctly observed, however, this is not "some unforeseen byproduct of a statutory scheme." *Harper & Row,* 471 U.S., at 589, 105 S.Ct., at 2245 (dissenting opinion). It is, rather, "the essence of copyright," *ibid.,* and a constitutional requirement. The primary objective of copyright is not to reward the labor of authors, but "[t]o promote the Progress of Science and useful Arts." Art. I, § 8, cl. 8. Accord, *Twentieth Century Music Corp. v. Aiken,* 422 U.S. 151, 156, 95 S.Ct. 2040, 2044, 45 L.Ed.2d 84 (1975). To this end, copyright assures authors the right to their original expression, but encourages others to build freely upon the ideas and information conveyed by a work. *Harper & Row, supra,* 471 U.S., at 556–557, 105 S.Ct., at 2228–2229. This principle, known as the idea/expression or fact/expression dichotomy, applies to all works of authorship. As applied to a factual compilation, assuming the absence of original written expression, only the compiler's selection and arrangement may be protected; the raw facts may be copied at will. This result is neither unfair nor unfortunate. It is the means by which copyright advances the progress of science and art.

This Court has long recognized that the fact/expression dichotomy limits severely the scope of protection in fact-based works. More than a century ago, the Court observed: "The very object of publishing a book on science or the useful arts is to communicate to the world the useful knowledge which it contains. But this object would be frustrated if the knowledge could not be used without incurring the guilt of piracy of the book." *Baker v. Selden,* 101 U.S. 99, 103, 25 L.Ed. 841 (1880).

We reiterated this point in *Harper & Row:*

"[N]o author may copyright facts or ideas. The copyright is limited to those aspects of the work—termed 'expression'—that display the stamp of the author's originality.

[C]opyright does not prevent subsequent users from copying from a prior author's work those constituent elements that are not original— for example ... facts, or materials in the public domain—as long as such use does not unfairly appropriate the author's original contributions." 471 U.S., at 547–548, 105 S.Ct., at 2223–2224 (citation omitted).

This, then, resolves the doctrinal tension: Copyright treats facts and factual compilations in a wholly consistent manner. Facts, whether alone or as part of a compilation, are not original and therefore may not be copyrighted. A factual compilation is eligible for copyright if it features an original selection or arrangement of facts, but the copyright is limited to the particular selection or arrangement. In no event may copyright extend to the facts themselves.

B

As we have explained, originality is a constitutionally mandated prerequisite for copyright protection. The Court's decisions announcing this rule predate the Copyright Act of 1909, but ambiguous language in the 1909 Act caused some lower courts temporarily to lose sight of this requirement.

The 1909 Act embodied the originality requirement, but not as clearly as it might have. See Nimmer § 2.01. The subject matter of copyright was set out in §§ 3 and 4 of the Act. Section 4 stated that copyright was available to "all the writings of an author." 35 Stat. 1076. By using the words "writings" and "author"—the same words used in Article I, § 8, of the Constitution and defined by the Court in *The Trade–Mark Cases* and *Burrow–Giles*—the statute necessarily incorporated the originality requirement articulated in the Court's decisions. It did so implicitly, however, thereby leaving room for error.

Section 3 was similarly ambiguous. It stated that the copyright in a work protected only "the copyrightable component parts of the work." It thus stated an important copyright principle, but failed to identify the specific characteristic—originality—that determined which component parts of a work were copyrightable and which were not.

Most courts construed the 1909 Act correctly, notwithstanding the less-than-perfect statutory language. They understood from this Court's decisions that there could be no copyright without originality. See Patterson & Joyce 760–761. As explained in the Nimmer treatise: "The 1909 Act neither defined originality, nor even expressly required that a work be 'original' in order to command protection. However, the courts uniformly inferred the requirement from the fact that copyright protection may only be claimed by 'authors'.... It was reasoned that since an author is 'the ... creator, originator' it follows that a work is not the product of an author unless the work is original." Nimmer § 2.01 (footnotes omitted) (citing cases).

But some courts misunderstood the statute. See, *e.g., Leon v. Pacific Telephone & Telegraph Co.,* 91 F.2d 484 (CA9 1937); *Jeweler's Circular Publishing Co. v. Keystone Publishing Co.,* 281 F. 83 (CA2 1922). These courts ignored §§ 3 and 4, focusing their attention instead on § 5 of the Act. Section 5, however, was purely technical in nature: It provided that a person seeking to register a work should indicate on the application the type of work, and it listed 14 categories under which the work might fall. One of these categories was "[b]ooks, including composite and cyclopaedic works, directories, gazetteers, and other compilations." § 5(a). Section 5 did not purport to say that all compilations were automatically copyrightable. Indeed, it expressly disclaimed any such function, pointing out that "the subject-matter of copyright [i]s defined in section four." Nevertheless, the fact that factual compilations were mentioned specifically in § 5 led some courts to infer erroneously that directories and the like were copyrightable *per se,* "without any further or precise showing of original—personal—authorship." Ginsburg 1895.

Making matters worse, these courts developed a new theory to justify the protection of factual compilations. Known alternatively as "sweat of the brow" or "industrious collection," the underlying notion was that copyright was a reward for the hard work that went into compiling facts. The classic formulation of the doctrine appeared in *Jeweler's Circular Publishing Co.,* 281 F., at 88:

> "The right to copyright a book upon which one has expended labor in its preparation does not depend upon whether the materials which he has collected consist or not of matters which are public juris, or whether such materials show literary skill *or originality,* either in thought or in language, or anything more than industrious collection. The man who goes through the streets of a town and puts down the names of each of the inhabitants, with their occupations and their street number, acquires material of which he is the author" (emphasis added).

The "sweat of the brow" doctrine had numerous flaws, the most glaring being that it extended copyright protection in a compilation beyond selection and arrangement—the compiler's original contributions—to the facts themselves. Under the doctrine, the only defense to infringement was independent creation. A subsequent compiler was "not entitled to take one word of information previously published," but rather had to "independently wor[k] out the matter for himself, so as to arrive at the same result from the same common sources of information." *Id.,* at 88–89 (internal quotation marks omitted). "Sweat of the brow" courts thereby eschewed the most fundamental axiom of copyright law—that no one may copyright facts or ideas. See *Miller v. Universal City Studios, Inc.,* 650 F.2d, at 1372 (criticizing "sweat of the brow" courts because "ensur[ing] that later writers obtain the facts independently . . . is precisely the scope of protection given . . . copyrighted matter, and the law is clear that facts are not entitled to such protection").

Decisions of this Court applying the 1909 Act make clear that the statute did not permit the "sweat of the brow" approach. The best example is *International News Service v. Associated Press,* 248 U.S. 215, 39 S.Ct. 68, 63 L.Ed. 211 (1918). In that decision, the Court stated unambiguously that the 1909 Act conferred copyright protection only on those elements of a work that were original to the author. International News Service had conceded taking news reported by Associated Press and publishing it in its own newspapers. Recognizing that § 5 of the Act specifically mentioned " 'periodicals, including newspapers,' " § 5(b), the Court acknowledged that news articles were copyrightable. *Id.,* at 234, 39 S.Ct., at 70. It flatly rejected, however, the notion that the copyright in an article extended to the factual information it contained: "[T]he news element—the information respecting current events contained in the literary production—is not the creation of the writer, but is a report of matters that ordinarily are *publici juris;* it is the history of the day." *Ibid.*

Without a doubt, the "sweat of the brow" doctrine flouted basic copyright principles. Throughout history, copyright law has "recognize[d] a greater need to disseminate factual works than works of fiction or fantasy." *Harper & Row,* 471 U.S., at 563, 105 S.Ct., at 2232. Accord, Gorman, Fact or Fancy: The Implications for Copyright, 29 J. Copyright Soc. 560, 563 (1982). But "sweat of the brow" courts took a contrary view; they handed out proprietary interests in facts and declared that authors are absolutely precluded from saving time and effort by relying upon the facts contained in prior works. In truth, "[i]t is just such wasted effort that the proscription against the copyright of ideas and facts ... [is] designed to prevent." *Rosemont Enterprises, Inc. v. Random House, Inc.,* 366 F.2d 303, 310 (CA2 1966), cert. denied 385 U.S. 1009, 87 S.Ct. 714, 17 L.Ed.2d 546 (1967). "Protection for the fruits of such research ... may in certain circumstances be available under a theory of unfair competition. But to accord copyright protection on this basis alone distorts basic copyright principles in that it creates a monopoly in public domain materials without the necessary justification of protecting and encouraging the creation of 'writings' by 'authors.'" Nimmer § 3.04, p. 3–23 (footnote omitted).

C

"Sweat of the brow" decisions did not escape the attention of the Copyright Office. When Congress decided to overhaul the copyright statute and asked the Copyright Office to study existing problems, see *Mills Music, Inc. v. Snyder,* 469 U.S. 153, 159, 105 S.Ct. 638, 642, 83 L.Ed.2d 556 (1985), the Copyright Office promptly recommended that Congress clear up the confusion in the lower courts as to the basic standards of copyrightability. The Register of Copyrights explained in his first report to Congress that "originality" was a "basic requisit[e]" of copyright under the 1909 Act, but that "the absence of any reference to [originality] in the statute seems to have led to misconceptions as to what is copyrightable matter." Report of the Register of Copyrights on the General Revision of the U.S. Copyright Law, 87th Cong., 1st Sess., p. 9 (H. Judiciary Comm. Print 1961). The Register suggested making the originality requirement explicit. *Ibid.*

Congress took the Register's advice. In enacting the Copyright Act of 1976, Congress dropped the reference to "all the writings of an author" and replaced it with the phrase "original works of authorship." 17 U.S.C. § 102(a). In making explicit the originality requirement, Congress announced that it was merely clarifying existing law: "The two fundamental criteria of copyright protection [are] originality and fixation in tangible form. ... The phrase 'original works of authorship,' which is purposely left undefined, is intended to incorporate without change *the standard of originality established by the courts under the present [1909] copyright statute.*" H.R.Rep. No. 94–1476, p. 51 (1976) (emphasis added) (hereinafter

H.R.Rep.); S.Rep. No. 94–473, p. 50 (1975), U.S.Code Cong. & Admin.News 1976, pp. 5659, 5664 (emphasis added) (hereinafter S.Rep.). This sentiment was echoed by the Copyright Office: "Our intention here is to maintain the *established standards* of originality...." Supplementary Report of the Register of Copyrights on the General Revision of U.S. Copyright Law, 89th Cong., 1st Sess., pt. 6, p. 3 (H. Judiciary Comm. Print 1965) (emphasis added).

To ensure that the mistakes of the "sweat of the brow" courts would not be repeated, Congress took additional measures. For example, § 3 of the 1909 Act had stated that copyright protected only the "copyrightable component parts" of a work, but had not identified originality as the basis for distinguishing those component parts that were copyrightable from those that were not. The 1976 Act deleted this section and replaced it with § 102(b), which identifies specifically those elements of a work for which copyright is not available: "In no case does copyright protection for an original work of authorship extend to any idea, procedure, process, system, method of operation, concept, principle, or discovery, regardless of the form in which it is described, explained, illustrated, or embodied in such work." Section 102(b) is universally understood to prohibit any copyright in facts. *Harper & Row, supra,* at 547, 556, 105 S.Ct., at 2223, 2228. Accord, Nimmer § 2.03[E] (equating facts with "discoveries"). As with § 102(a), Congress emphasized that § 102(b) did not change the law, but merely clarified it: "Section 102(b) in no way enlarges or contracts the scope of copyright protection under the present law. Its purpose is to restate ... that the basic dichotomy between expression and idea remains unchanged." H.R.Rep., at 57; S.Rep., at 54, U.S.Code Cong. & Admin.News 1976, p. 5670.

Congress took another step to minimize confusion by deleting the specific mention of "directories ... and other compilations" in § 5 of the 1909 Act. As mentioned, this section had led some courts to conclude that directories were copyrightable *per se* and that every element of a directory was protected. In its place, Congress enacted two new provisions. First, to make clear that compilations were not copyrightable *per se*, Congress provided a definition of the term "compilation." Second, to make clear that the copyright in a compilation did not extend to the facts themselves, Congress enacted § 103.

The definition of "compilation" is found in § 101 of the 1976 Act. It defines a "compilation" in the copyright sense as "a work formed by the collection and assembling of preexisting materials or of data *that* are selected, coordinated, or arranged *in such a way that* the resulting work as a whole constitutes an original work of authorship" (emphasis added).

The purpose of the statutory definition is to emphasize that collections of facts are not copyrightable *per se*. It conveys this message through its tripartite structure, as emphasized above by the italics. The statute identifies three distinct elements and requires each to be met for a work to qualify as a copyrightable compilation: (1) the collection and assembly of pre-existing material, facts, or data; (2) the selection, coordination, or arrangement of those materials; and (3) the creation, by virtue of the particular selection, coordination, or arrangement, of an "original" work of authorship. "[T]his tripartite conjunctive structure is self-evident, and should be assumed to 'accurately express the legislative purpose.'" Patry 51, quoting *Mills Music,* 469 U.S., at 164, 105 S.Ct., at 645.

At first glance, the first requirement does not seem to tell us much. It merely describes what one normally thinks of as a compilation—a collection of pre-existing material, facts, or data. What makes it significant is that it is not the *sole* requirement. It is not enough for copyright purposes that an author collects and assembles facts. To satisfy the statutory definition, the work must get over two additional hurdles. In this way, the plain language indicates that not every collection of facts receives copyright protection. Otherwise, there would be a period after "data."

The third requirement is also illuminating. It emphasizes that a compilation, like any other work, is copyrightable only if it satisfies the originality requirement ("an *original* work of authorship"). Although § 102 states plainly that the originality requirement applies to all works, the point was emphasized with regard to compilations to ensure that courts would not repeat the mistake of the "sweat of the brow" courts by concluding that fact-based works are treated differently and measured by some other standard. As Congress explained it, the goal was to "make plain that the criteria of copyrightable subject matter stated in section 102 apply with full force to works ... containing preexisting material." H.R.Rep., at 57; S.Rep., at 55, U.S.Code Cong. & Admin.News 1976, p. 5670.

The key to the statutory definition is the second requirement. It instructs courts that, in determining whether a fact-based work is an original work of authorship, they should focus on the manner in which the collected facts have been selected, coordinated, and arranged. This is a straightforward application of the originality requirement. Facts are never original, so the compilation author can claim originality, if at all, only in the way the facts are presented. To that end, the statute dictates that the principal focus should be on whether the selection, coordination, and arrangement are sufficiently original to merit protection.

Not every selection, coordination, or arrangement will pass muster. This is plain from the statute. It states that, to merit protection, the facts must be selected, coordinated, or arranged "in such a way" as to render the work as a whole original. This implies that some "ways" will trigger copyright, but that others will not. See Patry 57, and n. 76. Otherwise, the phrase "in such a way" is meaningless and Congress should have defined "compilation" simply as "a work formed by the collection and assembly of preexisting materials or data that are selected, coordinated, or arranged." That Congress did not do so is dispositive. In accordance with "the established principle that a court should give effect, if possible, to every clause and word of a statute," *Moskal v. United States,* 498 U.S. 103, 109–

110, 111 S.Ct. 461, 466, 112 L.Ed.2d 449 (1990) (internal quotation marks omitted), we conclude that the statute envisions that there will be some fact-based works in which the selection, coordination, and arrangement are not sufficiently original to trigger copyright protection.

As discussed earlier, however, the originality requirement is not particularly stringent. A compiler may settle upon a selection or arrangement that others have used; novelty is not required. Originality requires only that the author make the selection or arrangement independently (*i.e.,* without copying that selection or arrangement from another work), and that it display some minimal level of creativity. Presumably, the vast majority of compilations will pass this test, but not all will. There remains a narrow category of works in which the creative spark is utterly lacking or so trivial as to be virtually nonexistent. See generally *Bleistein v. Donaldson Lithographing Co.,* 188 U.S. 239, 251, 23 S.Ct. 298, 300, 47 L.Ed. 460 (1903) (referring to "the narrowest and most obvious limits"). Such works are incapable of sustaining a valid copyright. Nimmer § 2.01[B].

Even if a work qualifies as a copyrightable compilation, it receives only limited protection. This is the point of § 103 of the Act. Section 103 explains that "[t]he subject matter of copyright ... includes compilations," § 103(a), but that copyright protects only the author's original contributions—not the facts or information conveyed:

> "The copyright in a compilation ... extends only to the material contributed by the author of such work, as distinguished from the preexisting material employed in the work, and does not imply any exclusive right in the preexisting material." § 103(b).

As § 103 makes clear, copyright is not a tool by which a compilation author may keep others from using the facts or data he or she has collected. "The most important point here is one that is commonly misunderstood today: copyright ... has no effect one way or the other on the copyright or public domain status of the preexisting material." H.R.Rep., at 57; S.Rep., at 55, U.S.Code Cong. & Admin. News 1976, p. 5670. The 1909 Act did not require, as "sweat of the brow" courts mistakenly assumed, that each subsequent compiler must start from scratch and is precluded from relying on research undertaken by another. See, *e.g., Jeweler's Circular Publishing Co.,* 281 F., at 88–89. Rather, the facts contained in existing works may be freely copied because copyright protects only the elements that owe their origin to the compiler—the selection, coordination, and arrangement of facts.

In summary, the 1976 revisions to the Copyright Act leave no doubt that originality, not "sweat of the brow," is the touchstone of copyright protection in directories and other fact-based works. Nor is there any doubt that the same was true under the 1909 Act. The 1976 revisions were a direct response to the Copyright Office's concern that many lower courts had misconstrued this basic principle, and Congress emphasized repeatedly that the purpose of the revisions was to clarify, not change, existing law. The revisions explain with painstaking clarity that copyright requires originality, § 102(a); that facts are never original, § 102(b); that the copyright in a compilation does not extend to the facts it contains, § 103(b); and that a compilation is copyrightable only to the extent that it features an original selection, coordination, or arrangement, § 101.

The 1976 revisions have proven largely successful in steering courts in the right direction. A good example is *Miller v. Universal City Studios, Inc.*, 650 F.2d, at 1369–1370: "A copyright in a directory ... is properly viewed as resting on the originality of the selection and arrangement of the factual material, rather than on the industriousness of the efforts to develop the information. Copyright protection does not extend to the facts themselves, and the mere use of information contained in a directory without a substantial copying of the format does not constitute infringement" (citation omitted). Additionally, the Second Circuit, which almost 70 years ago issued the classic formulation of the "sweat of the brow" doctrine in *Jeweler's Circular Publishing Co.*, has now fully repudiated the reasoning of that decision. See, *e.g., Financial Information, Inc. v. Moody's Investors Service, Inc.*, 808 F.2d 204, 207 (CA2 1986), cert. denied, 484 U.S. 820, 108 S.Ct. 79, 98 L.Ed.2d 42 (1987); *Financial Information, Inc. v. Moody's Investors Service, Inc.*, 751 F.2d 501, 510 (CA2 1984) (Newman, J., concurring); *Hoehling v. Universal City Studios, Inc.*, 618 F.2d 972, 979 (CA2 1980). Even those scholars who believe that "industrious collection" should be rewarded seem to recognize that this is beyond the scope of existing copyright law. See Denicola 516 ("[T]he very vocabulary of copyright is ill suited to analyzing property rights in works of nonfiction"); *id.*, at 520–521, 525; Ginsburg 1867, 1870.

III

There is no doubt that Feist took from the white pages of Rural's directory a substantial amount of factual information. At a minimum, Feist copied the names, towns, and telephone numbers of 1,309 of Rural's subscribers. Not all copying, however, is copyright infringement. To establish infringement, two elements must be proven: (1) ownership of a valid copyright, and (2) copying of constituent elements of the work that are original. See *Harper & Row*, 471 U.S., at 548, 105 S.Ct., at 2224. The first element is not at issue here; Feist appears to concede that Rural's directory, considered as a whole, is subject to a valid copyright because it contains some foreword text, as well as original material in its yellow pages advertisements. See Brief for Petitioner 18; Pet. for Cert. 9.

The question is whether Rural has proved the second element. In other words, did Feist, by taking 1,309 names, towns, and telephone numbers from Rural's white pages, copy anything that was "original" to Rural? Certainly, the raw data does not satisfy the originality requirement. Rural may have been the first to discover and report the names, towns, and telephone numbers of its subscribers, but this data does not " 'ow[e] its origin' " to Rural. *Burrow–Giles*, 111 U.S., at 58, 4 S.Ct., at 281. Rather, these bits of information are uncopyrightable facts; they existed before Rural reported them and would have continued to exist if Rural had never published a telephone directory. The originality requirement "rule[s] out protecting ... names, addresses, and telephone numbers of which the plaintiff by no stretch of the imagination could be called the author." Patterson & Joyce 776.

Rural essentially concedes the point by referring to the names, towns, and telephone numbers as "preexisting material." * * * Brief for Respondent 17. Section 103(b) states explicitly that he copyright in a compilation does not extend to "the preexisting material employed in the work."

The question that remains is whether Rural selected, coordinated, or arranged these uncopyrightable facts in an original way. As mentioned, originality is not a stringent standard; it does not require that facts be presented in an innovative or surprising way. It is equally true, however, that the selection and arrangement of facts cannot be so mechanical or routine as to require no creativity whatsoever. The standard of originality is low, but it does exist. See Patterson & Joyce 760, n. 144 ("While this requirement is sometimes characterized as modest, or a low threshold, it is not without effect") (internal quotation marks omitted; citations omitted). As this Court has explained, the Constitution mandates some minimal degree of creativity, see *The Trade–Mark Cases,* 100 U.S., at 94; and an author who claims infringement must prove "the existence of ... intellectual production, of thought, and conception." *Burrow–Giles, supra,* 111 U.S., at 59–60, 4 S.Ct., at 281–282.

The selection, coordination, and arrangement of Rural's white pages do not satisfy the minimum constitutional standards for copyright protection. As mentioned at the outset, Rural's white pages are entirely typical. Persons desiring telephone service in Rural's service area fill out an application and Rural issues them a telephone number. In preparing its white pages, Rural simply takes the data provided by its subscribers and lists it alphabetically by surname. The end product is a garden-variety white pages directory, devoid of even the slightest trace of creativity.

Rural's selection of listings could not be more obvious: It publishes the most basic information—name, town, and telephone number—about each person who applies to it for telephone service. This is "selection" of a sort, but it lacks the modicum of creativity necessary to transform mere selection into copyrightable expression. Rural expended sufficient effort to make the white pages directory useful, but insufficient creativity to make it original.

We note in passing that the selection featured in Rural's white pages may also fail the originality requirement for another reason. Feist points out that Rural did not truly "select" to publish the names and telephone numbers of its subscribers; rather, it was required to do so by the Kansas Corporation Commission as part of its monopoly franchise. See 737 F.Supp., at 612. Accordingly, one could plausibly conclude that this selection was dictated by state law, not by Rural.

Nor can Rural claim originality in its coordination and arrangement of facts. The white pages do nothing more than list Rural's subscribers in alphabetical order. This arrangement may, technically speaking, owe its origin to Rural; no one disputes that Rural undertook the task of alphabetizing the names itself. But there is nothing remotely creative about arranging names alphabetically in a white pages directory. It is an age-old practice, firmly rooted in tradition and so commonplace that it has come to be expected as a matter of course. * * * It is not only unoriginal, it is practically inevitable. This time-honored tradition does not possess the minimal creative spark required by the Copyright Act and the Constitution.

We conclude that the names, towns, and telephone numbers copied by Feist were not original to Rural and therefore were not protected by the copyright in Rural's combined white and yellow pages directory. As a constitutional matter, copyright protects only those constituent elements of a work that possess more than a *de minimis* quantum of creativity. Rural's white pages, limited to basic subscriber information and arranged alphabetically, fall short of the mark. As a statutory matter, 17 U.S.C. § 101 does not afford protection from copying to a collection of facts that are selected, coordinated, and arranged in a way that utterly lacks originality. Given that some works must fail, we cannot imagine a more likely candidate. Indeed, were we to hold that Rural's white pages pass muster, it is hard to believe that any collection of facts could fail.

Because Rural's white pages lack the requisite originality, Feist's use of the listings cannot constitute infringement. This decision should not be construed as demeaning Rural's efforts in compiling its directory, but rather as making clear that copyright rewards originality, not effort. As this Court noted more than a century ago, " 'great praise may be due to the plaintiffs for their industry and enterprise in publishing this paper, yet the law does not contemplate their being rewarded in this way.' " *Baker v. Selden,* 101 U.S., at 105.

The judgment of the Court of Appeals is Reversed.

NOTES

1. What standards are noted in *Feist* with regard to minimal levels of creativity? Could single words in ordinary usage qualify? Or, would a collection of two or more words in short phrases, such as "you're fired" meet the standard for originality? Is the standard quantitative, qualitative or both?

Originality must be understood as applying to the author's expression as distinguished from underlying ideas or facts which are not protected under the Copyright Act as noted in 17 U.S.C § 102(b):

"In no case does copyright protection for an original work of authorship extend to any idea, procedure, process, system, method of operation, concept, principle, or discovery, regardless of the form in which it is described, explained, illustrated, or embodied in such work."

Thus, only the author's original expression fixed in a tangible medium is protected.

2.   During the course of a presentation at a conference, a paper was presented which contained a notice at the bottom of the first page stipulating that the paper was a draft of an article for future publication. The stipulation continued that the paper could not be quoted, cited or otherwise referenced and that any such act would be unauthorized and in violation of the author's copyright. The paper had a number of ideas that stimulated members of the audience for use in other contexts than that of the presentation. What was protected by the notice, what use if any could be made of these ideas and did use of them without indicating the source or in any manner giving attribution violate the author's copyrights? Why?

3.   The requirement of originality may be one of the few remaining substantive limitations on copyrightability. The issue arises frequently, particularly as applied to data bases and compilations.

Dealers and collectors of coins, stamps, baseball cards and other collectables, as well as sellers and purchasers of preowned items in commodity markets, such as automobiles, cameras or guitars need to be informed of market value based on scarcity, condition, initial cost and demand. This service is often provided by compendiums and data bases that include both fact and judgment. The facts, as noted in Feist, are not copyrightable. That leaves the judgment of the compiler/author to meet the threshold of original expression for copyright protection.

In *CDN Inc. v. Kenneth A. Kapes*, 197 F.3d 1256 (9th Cir. 1999) the court determined that a wholesale price guide for coins met the standards for originality and was protected under the copyright laws. The creation of a price list for used coins involves setting a series of discrete rankings, explaining what qualifies for each classification and establishing the objective and subjective measures applied to the pricing. This represents not only the objective facts that inhere in the commodity, but judgment of condition and other factors affecting value. The data base is expression and the application of experience and knowledge the element of originality. While a person may copy coin descriptions relative to facts, such as dates during which coins of a particular description were minted, judgments of condition and scarcity are protected.

4.   The legal profession has long known that words and expression are the stock in trade of lawyers. Some expression is original and as such would warrant protection under the copyright laws. This creates interesting issues for a profession that doesn't relish reinventing the wheel and freely copies instruments that have been demonstrated to work and give the appearance to the recipient of a verified status. The language of conveyance in deeds, the language of trust creation, and the language of wills demonstrate the pragmatic assurance of repetition. On occasion, lawyers have been known to adopt expression in letters they receive in the next letters they send because they are comfortable with known consequences. Legal "forms" perform this function. They represent accepted versions of necessary facts and essential elements to accomplish a given legal task. To the extent that standardization

saves time and labor and eliminates uncertainty, the use of forms is a valuable element in the routine practice of law.

How much creativity and original expression is in a legal form? How often do forms follow closely the language and content of statutes or decisions? What if the forms are computer based and provide that required information can simply be typed into the form and saved as a discrete document? Is the program copyrightable? What if the form cannot only be filled in, but when there are other forms that require the same data, the data is automatically entered in these forms as well? Does this interactivity make the process or forms used copyrightable? Is there a quantitative measure that determines whether the use of a grouping of forms constitutes a copying of someone else's selection of judgment in form selection and is this copyrightable? Does the grouping constitute a compilation protectable under that provision of the statute? See, *Ross, Brovins & Oehmke, P.C., doing business as LawMode v. Lexis Nexis Group*, 463 F.3d 478 (6th Cir. 2006) where Lexis was found not to have violated the copyright of LawMode. LawMode both compiled and organized a set of Michigan legal forms. The compilation and organization of forms can constitute a collection and assembling of preexisting facts and materials, which qualifies as an original work of authorship under 17 U.S.C. § 101. In this case, Lexis forms and those of LawMode showed sufficient differences to warrant the work by Lexis being original to them and not a copy from LawMode. Likewise, the organization around a table of contents which itself followed the table of contents of a Michigan public domain classification on the internet did not constitute a protected work of authorship for copyright in LawMode.

5.   See also *Southco, Inc. v. Kanebridge Corporation*, 390 F.3d 276 (3rd Cir. 2004) where the plaintiff, a manufacturer of fasteners using screws and other materials as components; developed a system using number codes to identify specific screws and materials and their characteristics. These codes were included in a published book for use by their employees and customers. The digits in the numbering system individually represented a specific characteristic of the product, in this case screws. The handbook was copyrighted. The court held that the numbers were not original expression, but rather simply a variation on standard reference methodologies for identification. The court noted that Southco product numbers were not original. Each number was fixed by the underlying rules governing the digits' use to designate descriptors and elements of the product or component to which it referred. The use of numbers for this purpose constitutes an idea which cannot be copyrighted and the part numbers and elements do not exhibit creativity or originality as required for copyright protection.

Problem:

Despite the minimization of requirements for the creation of a copyright, there may be some issues of ambiguity that remain in actual application. Consider the following fact pattern and identify the problems and issues relative to whether there is a copyright and who might have it?

Sandy and Joan were roommates at the Universe University, Mid–State Somewhere. They roomed together since their freshman year at school and were finally seniors. Sandy had some strange habits, such as singing full throttle while in the shower. At first it annoyed Joan, but after awhile she came to enjoy the fresh lyrics Sandy made up each day as a tale of her ongoing experiences. Sandy was a talented musician and could play the piano, violin and a few other instruments. She had perfect pitch and a great ear for matching notes to lyric.

In every song she sang, there was one bar toward the end of the lyrics and accompanying notes that was repeated. The lyrics were pure nonsense utterings with discordant music. She considered it her signature.

Sarah never sang her songs in public. It wasn't that she was shy; it was that these songs were very personal to her and she wasn't ready to share them with others. Obviously, she felt different about her close friend and roommate hearing her singing in the shower, but even here, she wouldn't sing for her as a "performance."

Sometime in their third year, Joan started writing down Sandy's lyrics. She did this without informing Sandy what she was doing. She tried to close her eyes, hear the tune and write the notes to match the lyrics and actually came very close to that which Sandy had composed.

After awhile, Joan thought of a better method for accomplishing her ends. She purchased a small digital recorder and set it in the sink on her side of the bathroom when Sandy was about to enter the shower. She then copied the recording to her computer and with software applications she purchased was able to transcribe the notes and match them to the lyrics. These notes were then scored using a template in the program along with the words of the song.

After graduation, Joan took the lyrics and score to a local producer of records. She represented herself as the author. She also tendered a recording of her singing the words with her boyfriend playing the piano to accompany her.

The record producer was excited enough after listening to the demonstration recording to offer Joan a recording contract. A few months later her first compact disk was released. It hit the charts running and was an unqualified commercial success. The press presented her as a talented composer and performer. They reveled in the purity of the words and music.

Sandy left for Europe after graduation. She was living, studying and working in Paris, France. She still sang her heart out in the shower. One day while out with some new friends she heard a broadcast of a song she instantly knew was something she'd composed in the shower. If there was any doubt, it was removed by the infamous nonsense signature she always inserted in her music. Stunned, confused and somewhat angry, she called her father in New York and told him about the recordings. She had always thought that someday she would write her songs down and perform them for the public. In fact, in the months before she left for Paris she had taken the time to write out all of her songs and score in a notebook given to her by Joan at graduation. Sandy felt betrayed by her long time friend.

Her father referred the matter to the intellectual property group in his law firm. He requested a review of the situation as told to him by his daughter and confirmed by a short investigation that turned up the facts and scenario noted above. Based on the facts, which if any rights were perfected and valid? Based on the facts, was the right infringed; if so how? What facts have to be shown to demonstrate infringement? If Sandy wishes to pursue her rights, does she need to do anything further before filing her law suit?

Would it have made any difference if Sandy discovered that Joan was recording her singing, thought it "a little funny" and didn't tell Joan to stop?

B. FIXATION

In order for a work of authorship to be protected by copyright law, not only must that work be original, it must also be fixed in a tangible medium of expression. This requirement is derived from the Constitutional language that copyright protection attaches to "writings". The Copyright Act defines the fixation requirement as follows:

> A work is "fixed" in a tangible medium of expression when its embodiment in a copy or phonorecord, by or under the authority of the author, is sufficiently permanent or stable to permit it to be perceived, reproduced, or otherwise communicated for a period of more than transitory duration. A work consisting of sounds, images, or both, that are being transmitted, is "fixed" for purposes of this title if a fixation of the work is being made simultaneously with its transmission.

Another way to state the fixation requirement is as extending copyright protection only to works that are recorded by some medium. Live performances are not protected by copyright law. If a live performance is recorded, copyright law protects against unauthorized copying, distribution, adaptation, and public performances of the recording. In other words, an unauthorized recording of the life performance is not prohibited by traditional copyright law although as we will see in Chapter Seven, more recent provisions of the Copyright Act do protect against such unauthorized recordings of live performances. Notice that a recording must be made or authorized by the author to count as a fixation under the statute. There have been some interesting cases in the past as to whether a fixation occurs when a new technology arises. For example, should the broadcast of live programs on television constitute a fixation? How about the storage of digital information in the random access memory (RAM) of a computer? In general, courts have dealt with new technologies by expanding the definition of fixation to fit new technologies within the scope of copyright. Those interested are encouraged to read *United States v. Martignon*, 492 F.3d 140 (2d Cir. 2007) (analyzing constitutionality of provision criminalizing unauthorized fixation of live performances).

C. COPYRIGHT FORMALITIES

The statutory prerequisites of publication, deposit, registration and notice were originally mandatory. The failure to include the proper notice or inscription, deposit copies of the work with the designated office and register the work were considered conditions precedent, the failure of which left the work in the public domain. Why were the early legislators and courts concerned with compliance with these conditions to the creation of a copyright? What interest(s) were they attempting to protect and did those interests include the rights of the public in the public domain?

Over the years, each of these conditions has either been eliminated or diminished in importance to the point that under present legislative requirements a work does not have to be published, no notice of copyright is required to be inscribed on copies of the work and deposit of the work and registration is treated as a condition subsequent not to perfection, but as provided in 17 U.S.C. § 411(b) " * * * no action for infringement of the copyright in any United States work shall be instituted until registration of the copyright claim has been made in accordance with this title."

1. The statutory requirement of an inscription on each copy in which a right is claimed was addressed by the court in *American Tobacco Company v. Emil Werckmeister*, 207 U.S. 284, 28 S.Ct. 72, 52 L.Ed. 208 (1907). The issue arose in the context of an original painting displayed in the Royal Academy in London. There were notices that the work was copyrighted, but that notice was not inscribed on the painting itself. The painting and the copyright were later sold to a private collector. A photograph of the painting, the title and description of the painting were deposited with the Librarian of Congress as required for copyright under the Copyright Act. The court held that original works of art were not copies intended for publication and didn't require an inscription. Copies of the work, including photographs, however, would have to be inscribed to protect the "copyright" which is an exclusive right to the "multiplication" of copies distinct from the work itself.

Why was notice or inscription required during the early periods of copyright in the United States? Who was the intended beneficiary, the author, the public or both? What distinct interests do each have that notice would have protected?

2. The case of *Washingtonian Pub. Co., Inc. v. Pearson*, 306 U.S. 30, 59 S.Ct. 397, 83 L.Ed. 470 (1939) addressed the changes affecting the requirement to deposit with the register of copyrights under the 1909 revisions of the Copyright Act. The act put the onus on the register to give notice if he found an undue delay in making the required deposit and if there was a failure to comply with the requirement three months from the date of notice, the proprietor would be subject to a fine and the copyright would become null and void. The failure to file doesn't void the copyright; it is the failure to file after notice is provided under section thirteen of the act that works the forfeiture.

The majority held that Congress had the power and authority to change the statutory requirements from a condition precedent to a condition subsequent. A lengthy dissent by Justice Black, however, informs us of the purpose of conditions precedent and the protection of the public interest in each and every one of the early requirements to the vesting of copyright interests. It was Justice Black's position that this requirement was a condition precedent to the vesting of a private interest from the first copyright act in 1790 to the revision in 1909. Justice Black believed that the language of the 1909 revision was neither clear nor compelling as to a legislative intent to do away with deposit as a condition precedent. The deposit performed two essential purposes: (1) it provided a complete record and information about the work which was the subject matter of the copyright, available to the public for inspection and (2) it served to preserve the work for the "diffusion of public knowledge."

One must therefore ask in light of the decision of the court in this case, why the requirement of deposit was altered and of what effect on the underlying purpose of the granting of copyrights. Why would Congress and the court diminish an act considered essential to the perfection of an "inchoate" interest for over a century by minimizing and treating it as "prefatory," rather than "mandatory" in the vesting of a private interest?

Who benefited by these requirements and who benefited by their removal? Can you describe the public interest in removal or retention of these prerequisites? And finally, list the elements necessary to perfect a copyright interest in 2006.

3. The 1976 Copyright Act removed the formal requirements of registration, publication, and notice to obtain copyright protection. Under contemporary law, copyright is created as soon as a work is fixed in a tangible medium of expression. However, as discussed below under infringement and remedies, timely registration is still required in order to bring a suit for copyright infringement and to obtain statutory remedies and attorney's fees. As this edition was being prepared for publication, the United States Supreme Court clarified an important point about the requirement for copyright registration under the Copyright Act of 1976. In *Reed Elsevier, Inc. v. Muchnick*, ___ U.S. ___, 130 S.Ct. 1237, 176 L.Ed.2d 17, (2010), the Court ruled that the Copyright Act's registration requirement is a precondition to filing a copyright infringement claim which does not restrict a federal court's subject matter jurisdiction with respect to infringement suits involving unregistered works. The case involved a class action lawsuit brought by freelance writers whose settlement was challenged on the grounds that the district court lacked subject matter jurisdiction because some of the works in the class were unregistered. Copyright formalities are important to know because of works created before the 1976 Copyright Act and because of their role in copyright infringement suits under the 1976 Copyright Act.

IV.   THE SUBJECT MATTER OF COPYRIGHT, BOUNDARIES AND ENFORCEMENT

The Copyright Act (17 U.S.C. § 102) enumerates specific categories of creative expression to which copyright is applicable. In reviewing the provisions of this section of the Act, how do the provisions of subpart (a), the enumerated categories (1) through (8) and the qualifications of (b) refine what can be copyrighted and the extent to which each of these delineations remain dynamic and compliant through changing times?

(1) literary works;

(2) musical works, including any accompanying words;

(3) dramatic works, including any accompanying music;

(4) pantomimes and choreographic works;

(5) pictorial, graphic, and sculptural works;

(6) motion pictures and other audiovisual works;

(7) sound recordings; and

(8) architectural works.

The cases and materials in this survey section provide a rich context illustrating the breadth of copyright subject matter, boundaries, rights, infringement and enforcement. The burden of proof to demonstrate copyright infringement rests on the plaintiff. The nature of the subject matter and infringing activity, proof of access and copying and defenses are context sensitive. It is context which determines the subject matter qualification for copyright protection, the requisites of proof of copying, the exclusions permitting "copying" or other use under doctrines of fair use, parody, or other considerations. These cases exemplify the process of copyright claims and enforcement. They highlight the lack of protection accorded copyright holders against work original to the second author. "Access" and proof of "copying" are essential elements to infringement. While the burden of proof to show a copyright infringement rests on the plaintiff, the nature of proof of access and copying are likely to adapt in the digital environment.

§ 106. Exclusive rights in copyrighted works

Subject to sections 107 [Fair Use] through 122 [Satellite Transmissions], the owner of copyright under this title has the exclusive rights to do and to authorize any of the following:

(1) to reproduce the copyrighted work in copies or phonorecords;

(2) to prepare derivative works based upon the copyrighted work;

(3) to distribute copies or phonorecords of the copyrighted work to the public by sale or other transfer of ownership, or by rental, lease, or lending;

(4) in the case of literary, musical, dramatic, and choreographic works, pantomimes, and motion pictures and other audiovisual works, to perform the copyrighted work publicly;

(5) in the case of literary, musical, dramatic, and choreographic works, pantomimes, and pictorial, graphic, or sculptural works, including the individual images of a motion picture or other audiovisual work, to display the copyrighted work publicly; and

(6) in the case of sound recordings, to perform the copyrighted work publicly by means of a digital audio transmission.

In each of the cases that follow, identify the subject matter, the alleged violation, and facts necessary to prove infringement and the nature and validity of the defenses set forth by the defendant.

A. COPYRIGHT INFRINGEMENT AND REMEDIES

BOISSON v. BANIAN, LTD.

United States Court of Appeals for the Second Circuit, 2001.
273 F.3d 262.

CARDAMONE, CIRCUIT JUDGE.

Plaintiffs Judi Boisson and her wholly-owned company, American Country Quilts and Linens, Inc., d/b/a Judi Boisson American Country, brought suit in the United States District Court for the Eastern District of New York (Platt, J.), alleging that defendants Vijay Rao and his wholly-owned company Banian Ltd., illegally copied two quilt designs for which plaintiffs had obtained copyright registrations. Following a bench trial, the trial court, in denying the claims of copyright infringement, ruled that defendants' quilts were not substantially similar to what it deemed were the protectible elements of plaintiffs' works. Plaintiffs have appealed this ruling. Copying the creative works of others is an old story, one often accomplished by the copyist changing or disfiguring the copied work to pass it off as his own. Stealing the particular expression of another's ideas is rightly condemned in the law because pirating the expression of the author's creative ideas risks diminishing the author's exclusive rights to her work, or as a poet said, taking all that she may be or all that she has been.

In reviewing this decision, we find plaintiffs' copyrights cover more elements than were recognized by the trial court, and that though the trial court articulated the proper test when comparing the contested works, its application of that test was too narrow. It failed not only to account for the protectible elements we identify, but also to consider the overall look and feel brought about by the creator's arrangement of unprotectible elements. Hence, we disagree with part of the district court's ruling and find some instances of copyright infringement. The trial court's disposition of those claims must therefore be reversed and remanded for a determination as to what remedies should be awarded. * * *

Copyright infringement is established by proving "ownership of a valid copyright" and "copying of constituent elements of the work that are original." *Feist Publ'ns, Inc. v. Rural Tel. Serv. Co.*, 499 U.S. 340, 361, 111 S.Ct. 1282, 113 L.Ed.2d 358 (1991). Throughout the following analysis the key consideration is the extent to which plaintiffs' work is original. See id. at 361–64, 111 S.Ct. 1282. * * *

The Copyright Act provides that a "certificate of [copyright] registration made before or within five years after first publication of the work shall constitute prima facie evidence of the validity of the copyright." 17 U.S.C. § 410(c) (1994). Boisson secured certificates of registration for both "School Days" quilts in 1991, the same year in which she designed them, so that we must presume she holds valid copyrights. Although such a presumption may be rebutted, *Folio Impressions, Inc. v. Byer Cal.*, 937 F.2d 759, 763 (2d Cir.1991), the district court found there was insufficient proof to support defendants' argument that plaintiffs deliberately misled the Copyright Office when submitting their applications. * * *

The element of copying breaks down into two parts. Plaintiffs must first show that defendants "actually copied" their quilts. *Streetwise Maps, Inc. v. Vandam, Inc.*, 159 F.3d 739, 747 (2d Cir.1998). Actual copying may be established by direct or indirect evidence. *Laureyssens v. Idea Group, Inc.*, 964 F.2d 131, 140 (2d Cir.1992). Indirect evidence may include proof of "access to the copyrighted work, similarities that are probative of copying between the works, and expert testimony." Id. The district court made a finding that actual copying had occurred, and because defendants do not dispute that finding, actual copying is also established. But not all copying results in copyright infringement, even if the plaintiff has a valid copyright. *Feist Publ'ns*, 499 U.S. at 361, 111 S.Ct. 1282. Plaintiffs must also demonstrate "substantial similarity" between defendants' quilts and the protectible elements of their own quilts. *Streetwise Maps*, 159 F.3d at 747; accord *Laureyssens*, 964 F.2d at 140.

Plaintiffs' certificates of registration constitute prima facie evidence of the validity not only of their copyrights, but also of the originality of their works. *Gaste v. Kaiserman*, 863 F.2d 1061, 1066 (2d Cir.1988) ("We also note that on the issue of originality, as compared to the issue of compliance with statutory formalities, it is even clearer that copyright registration created a presumption of validity."). Yet copyright protection extends only to a particular expression of an idea, and not to the idea itself. *Folio Impressions*, 937 F.2d at 765; accord *Beaudin v. Ben & Jerry's Homemade, Inc.*, 95 F.3d 1, 2 (2d Cir.1996); *Reyher v. Children's Television Workshop*, 533 F.2d 87, 91 (2d Cir.1976). Simply because a work is copyrighted does not mean every element of that work is protected.

Copyright law does not define the term "originality." Rather, courts have derived its meaning from art. I, § 8, cl. 8 of the United States Constitution, which authorizes Congress "To promote the Progress of Science and useful Arts, by securing for limited Times to Authors and Inventors the exclusive Right to their respective Writings and Discoveries." See *Feist Publ'ns*, 499 U.S. at 346, 111 S.Ct. 1282. Originality does not mean that the work for which copyright protection is sought must be either novel or unique, *In re Trade–Mark Cases*, 100 U.S. 82, 94, 25 L.Ed. 550 (1879), it simply means a work independently created by its author, one not copied from pre-existing works, and a work that comes from the exercise of the creative powers of the author's mind, in other words, "the fruits of [the author's] intellectual labor." Id. The Supreme Court gave an example when it said, in upholding the validity of a copyright to a photo of Oscar Wilde, the photographer made a " 'useful, new, harmonious, characteristic, and graceful picture ... entirely from his own mental conception, to which he gave visible form by posing the [subject] and arranging the costume, draperies, and other various accessories ... so as to present graceful outlines.' " *Burrow–Giles Lithographic Co. v. Sarony*, 111 U.S. 53, 60, 4 S.Ct. 279, 28 L.Ed. 349 (1884).

If a work is not original, then it is unprotectible. Likewise an element within a work may be unprotectible even if other elements, or the work as a whole, warrant protection. Some material is unprotectible because it is in the public domain, which means that it "is free for the taking and cannot be appropriated by a single author even though it is included in a copyrighted work." *Computer Assocs. Int'l, Inc. v. Altai, Inc.*, 982 F.2d 693, 710 (2d Cir.1992). * * *

Following the bench trial, the district court found some elements of plaintiffs' quilts were unprotectible (i.e., not original) because they were in the public domain: (1) the alphabet, (2) formation of the alphabet using six rows of five blocks across and four icons in the last row, and (3) color. Although that court expressed doubt as to whether copyright protection would extend to the shapes of the letters used in the quilts, it did not rule on that issue. These determinations as to originality may be overturned only if clearly erroneous. See *Matthew Bender & Co. v. West Publ'g Co.*, 158 F.3d 674, 681 (2d Cir.1998). A finding is clearly erroneous if, upon reviewing the entire record, we are left with "the definite and firm conviction" that a mistake was made. *Anderson v. City of Bessemer*, 470 U.S. 564, 573, 105 S.Ct. 1504, 84 L.Ed.2d 518 (1985).

1. Use of Alphabet

Passing now to the court's ruling, it correctly determined that the alphabet is in the public domain, a finding plaintiffs do not dispute. Nor could they object, considering the applicable regulations provide no copyright protection for "familiar symbols or designs" or "mere variations of ... lettering." 37 C.F.R. § 202.1(a) (2000).

2. Layouts of Alphabet

To support its finding that the layouts of plaintiffs' quilts were not protected by copyright, the district court relied upon evidence submitted by defendants showing that alphabet quilts have been in existence for over a century, suggesting that such layouts were also in the public domain. One circa 1900 quilt displayed letters and icons in blocks arranged in the same format used in "School Days I." From this evidence the court reasoned that such formation belonged to the public domain. Although it made specific findings only as to the block formation in "School Days I," we presume for purposes of our discussion that, in the absence of a specific finding as to the "School Days II" format, the trial court intended its findings on unprotectibility to extend to the layouts of both of plaintiffs' quilts.

These findings are clearly erroneous. Not only did plaintiffs obtain valid certificates of copyright registration, but also the alphabetical arrangement of the letters in the five-by-six block format required some minimum degree of creativity, which is all that is required for copyrightability. Moreover, unlike the use of letters, no federal regulation establishes that the use of this layout is unprotectible. These factors create a presumption that the layout is original and therefore a protectible element. Therefore, if defendants want to contest this presumption, they bear the burden of proving that this particular layout is not original. Cf. *Gaste*, 863 F.2d at 1064 (explaining that burden of proof is on defendant in infringement action who claims the plaintiff's copyright registration is invalid). At trial, defendants asserted that the particular layout of plaintiffs' quilts was copied from the public domain, but they presented insufficient proof to establish that proposition.

As noted earlier, a plaintiff attempting to prove actual copying on the part of a defendant is entitled to use direct or indirect evidence. Indirect evidence of access and substantial similarity to the plaintiff's work can "support an inference" that copying took place. *Streetwise Maps*, 159 F.3d at 747. Scholars disagree as to whether a defendant may also rely upon circumstantial evidence to show that a plaintiff copied from the public domain. Compare Jessica Litman, The Public Domain, 39 Emory L.J. 965, 1002–03 (1990) (explaining that a defendant is not entitled to any inference that a plaintiff copied from the public domain simply by showing access and substantial similarity to the public domain work), with Russ VerSteeg, Rethinking Originality, 34 Wm. & Mary L.Rev. 801, 874–75 & n. 328 (1993) (permitting a defendant to show copying on the part of the plaintiff through circumstantial evidence that the plaintiff had access and created a work substantially similar to a public domain work). Assuming arguendo that an inference is allowable, defendants in the case at hand nevertheless fall short of proving Boisson copied from the public domain.

Access may be established directly or inferred from the fact that a work was widely disseminated or that a party had a reasonable possibility of viewing the prior work. See generally 4 Melville B. Nimmer & David Nimmer, Nimmer on Copyright, § 13.02[A] (2001) (describing the ways in which access can be shown). Defendants proffered no evidence that Boisson owned an alphabet quilt prior to designing "School Days I" or "School Days II." Instead they point to Boisson's affirmative answer when asked at her deposition whether she had "seen an alphabet design in any other quilts." Boisson was not asked what these quilts looked like or when she saw them relative to designing her own quilts, or whether they bore any resemblance to her own designs.

Moreover, having seen an alphabet design would not conclusively establish that Boisson saw one from which she copied the arrangement of letters for her "School Days" quilts. As defendants' own proof reveals, alphabet quilts are not limited to the formations found in either the 1900 quilt or plaintiffs' quilts. Some quilts display letters out of order; some display three letters in the first and last rows with five letters in each of the middle rows; one has six letters in rows with icons placed in the border; another has varying numbers of letters in each row with icons or quilting designs in the remaining blocks; while still others have five rows of five letters with the "Z" by itself in a corner or followed by numbers representing the year the quilt was made. Nor are all letters of the alphabet always displayed or even displayed with each letter in its own block.

3. Shapes of Letters

The trial judge made no explicit finding with respect to the shapes of the letters of the alphabet. Instead, the court stated it was "questionable" whether plaintiffs could copyright the shapes of the letters used, and it cited the regulation that provides "mere variations of typographic ornamentation" are not copyrightable. 37 C.F.R. § 202.1(a). At this juncture, we hesitate to say that letter shapes are unprotectible in this context, but in the absence of a trial court finding, it is not necessary for us to reach this issue.

4. Color

Color by itself is not subject to copyright protection. See 37 C.F.R. § 202.1(a). Nevertheless, "[a]n original combination or arrangement of colors should be regarded as an artistic creation capable of copyright protection." 1 Nimmer & Nimmer, supra, § 2.14, at 2–178.4. We have previously declined to single out color as an individual element when conducting a copyright infringement analysis. In Streetwise Maps, 159 F.3d at 748, we determined that "instead of examining the [plaintiff's and defendants'] maps feature-by-feature, viewing the individual colors chosen by [plaintiff] as the protected elements upon which defendants encroached, we focus on the overall manner in which [plaintiff] selected, coordinated, and arranged the expressive elements in its map, including color, to depict the map's factual content" (emphasis added).

IV Substantial Similarity: Ordinary Observer v. More Discerning Observer

Having found that plaintiffs' quilts are entitled to copyright protection and that defendants actually copied at least some elements of plaintiffs' quilts, we turn our analysis to defendants' contention that its quilts were not substantially similar to plaintiffs'. We review de novo the district court's determination with respect to substantial similarity because credibility is not at stake and all that is required is a visual comparison of the products-a task we may perform as well as the district court. Folio Impressions, 937 F.2d at 766; accord Nihon Keizai Shimbun, Inc. v. Comline Bus. Data, Inc., 166 F.3d 65, 70 (2d Cir.1999).

Generally, an allegedly infringing work is considered substantially similar to a copyrighted work if "the ordinary observer, unless he set out to detect the disparities, would be disposed to overlook them, and regard their aesthetic appeal as the same." Folio Impressions, 937 F.2d at 765. Yet in Folio Impressions, the evidence at trial showed the plaintiff designer had copied the background for its fabric from a public domain document and "contributed nothing, not even a trivial variation." 937 F.2d at 764. Thus, part of the plaintiff's fabric was not original and therefore not protectible. We articulated the need for an ordinary observer to be "more discerning" in such circumstances.

> [T]he ordinary observer would compare the finished product that the fabric designs were intended to grace (women's dresses), and would be inclined to view the entire dress-consisting of protectible and unprotectible elements-as one whole. Here, since only some of the design enjoys copyright protection, the observer's inspection must be more discerning.

Id. at 765–66. Shortly after Folio Impressions was decided, we reiterated that a "more refined analysis" is required where a plaintiff's work is not "wholly original," but rather incorporates elements from the public domain. *Key Publ'ns, Inc. v. Chinatown Today Publ'g Enters., Inc.*, 945 F.2d 509, 514 (2d Cir.1991). In these instances, "[w]hat must be shown is substantial similarity between those elements, and only those elements, that provide copyrightability to the allegedly infringed compilation." Id. In contrast, where the plaintiff's work contains no material imported from the public domain, the "more discerning" test is unnecessary. *Hamil Am., Inc. v. GFI*, 193 F.3d 92, 101–02 (2d Cir.1999), cert. denied, 528 U.S. 1160, 120 S.Ct. 1171, 145 L.Ed.2d 1080 (2000). In the case at hand, because the alphabet was taken from the public domain, we must apply the "more discerning" ordinary observer test.

In applying this test, a court is not to dissect the works at issue into separate components and compare only the copyrightable elements. *Knitwaves*, 71 F.3d at 1003. To do so would be to take the "more discerning" test to an extreme, which would result in almost nothing being copyrightable because original works broken down into their composite parts would usually be little more than basic unprotectible elements like letters, colors and symbols. Id. This outcome-affording no copyright protection to an original compilation of unprotectible elements-would be contrary to the Supreme Court's holding in *Feist Publications*.

Although the "more discerning" test has not always been identified by name in our case law, we have nevertheless always recognized that the test is guided by comparing the "total concept and feel" of the contested works. *Knitwaves*, 71 F.3d at 1003. For example, in *Streetwise Maps*, 159 F.3d at 748, we found no infringement-not because the plaintiff's map consisted of public domain facts such as street locations, landmasses, bodies of water and landmarks, as well as color-but rather "because the total concept and overall feel created by the two works may not be said to be substantially similar." In *Nihon Keizai Shimbun*, 166 F.3d at 70–71, we conducted a side-by-side comparison of the articles and abstracts at issue to determine whether a copyright infringement had occurred. Looking beyond the unprotected facts, we analyzed how alike or different the abstracts were in their structure and organization of the facts. Id. at 71.

Likewise, when evaluating claims of infringement involving literary works, we have noted that while liability would result only if the protectible elements were substantially similar, our examination would encompass "the similarities in such aspects as the total concept and feel, theme, characters, plot, sequence, pace, and setting of the [plaintiff's] books and the [defendants'] works." *Williams*, 84 F.3d at 588; see also id. at 590 ("[A] scattershot approach cannot support a finding of substantial similarity because it fails to address the underlying issue: whether a lay observer would consider the works as a whole substantially similar to one another."). But see *Fisher–Price, Inc. v. Well–Made Toy Mfg. Corp.*, 25 F.3d 119, 123–24 (2d Cir.1994) (pre-dating *Knitwaves* and comparing feature-by-feature only the protectible elements of copyrighted dolls).

In the present case, while use of the alphabet may not provide a basis for infringement, we must compare defendants' quilts and plaintiffs' quilts on the basis of the arrangement and shapes of the letters, the colors chosen to represent the letters and other parts of the quilts, the quilting patterns, the particular icons chosen and their placement. Our analysis of the "total concept and feel" of these works should be instructed by common sense. Cf. *Hamil Am.*, 193 F.3d at 102 (noting that the ordinary observer test involves an examination of "total concept and feel," which in turn can be guided by "good eyes and common sense"). It is at this juncture that we part from the district court, which never considered the arrangement of the whole when comparing plaintiffs' works with defendants'. With this concept in mind, we pass to a comparison of the quilts at issue.

V Comparison

A. "School Days I" v. "ABC Green" Versions

"School Days I" consists of six horizontal rows, each row containing five blocks, with a capital letter or an icon in each block. The groupings of blocks in each row are as follows: A–E; F–J; K–O; P–T; U–Y; and Z with four icons following in the last row. The four icons are a cat, a house, a single-starred American flag and a basket. "ABC Green Version I" displays the capital letters of the alphabet in the same formation. The four icons in the last row are a cow jumping over the moon, a sailboat, a bear and a star. "ABC Green Version II" is identical to "ABC Green Version I," except that the picture of the cow jumping over the moon is somewhat altered, the bear is replaced by a teddy bear sitting up and wearing a vest that looks like a single-starred American flag, and the star in the last block is represented in a different color.

All three quilts use a combination of contrasting solid color fabrics or a combination of solid and polka-dotted fabrics to represent the blocks and letters. The following similarities are observed in plaintiffs' and defendants' designs: "A" is dark blue on a light blue background; "B" is red on a white background; "D" is made of polka-dot fabric on a light blue background; "F" on plaintiffs' "School Days I" is white on a pink background, while the "F" on defendants' "ABC Green" versions is pink on a white background; "G" has a green background; "H" and "L" are each a shade of blue on a white background; "M" in each quilt is a shade of yellow on a white background. "N" is green on a white background; "O" is blue on a polka-dot background; "P" is polka-dot fabric on a yellow background; "Q" is brown on a light background; "R" is pink on a gray/purple background. "S" is white on a red background; "T" is blue on a white background; "U" is gray on a white background; "V" is white on a gray background; "W" is pink on a white background; "X" is purple in all quilts, albeit in different shades, on a light background; "Y" is a shade of yellow on the same light background; and "Z" is navy blue or black, in all the quilts.

Boisson also testified that defendants utilized the same unique shapes as she had given to the letters "J," "M," "N," "P," "R" and "W." With respect to the quilting patterns, "School Days I" and the "ABC Green" versions feature diamond-shaped quilting within the blocks and a "wavy" pattern in the plain white border that surrounds the blocks. The quilts are also edged with a 3/8″ green binding.

From this enormous amount of sameness, we think defendants' quilts sufficiently similar to plaintiffs' design as to demonstrate illegal copying. In particular, the overwhelming similarities in color choices lean toward a finding of infringement. See 1 Nimmer & Nimmer, supra, § 2.14, at 2–178.4 ("[S]imilarity of color arrangements may create an inference of copying of other protectible subject matter."), quoted in *Primcot Fabrics, Dep't of Prismatic Fabrics, Inc. v. Kleinfab Corp.*, 368 F.Supp. 482, 485 (S.D.N.Y.1974). Although the icons chosen for each quilt are different and defendants added a green rectangular border around their rows of blocks, these differences are not sufficient to cause even the "more discerning" observer to think the quilts are other than substantially similar insofar as the protectible elements of plaintiffs' quilt are concerned. See *Williams*, 84 F.3d at 588 ("[D]issimilarity between some aspects of the works will not automatically relieve the infringer of liability." (emphasis removed)); *Sheldon v. Metro–Goldwyn Pictures Corp.*, 81 F.3d 49, 56 (2d Cir.1936) ("[I]t is enough that substantial parts were lifted; no plagiarist can excuse the wrong by showing how much of his work he did not pirate."). Moreover, the substitution in "ABC Green Version II" of the teddy bear wearing a flag vest as the third icon causes this version of defendants' quilt to look even more like plaintiffs' quilt that uses a single-starred American flag as its third icon. Consequently, both of defendants' "ABC Green" quilts infringed plaintiffs' copyright on its "School Days I" quilt.

B.   "School Days I" v. "ABC Navy"

We agree with the district court, however, that Rao did not infringe on plaintiffs' design in "School Days I" when he created "ABC Navy." While both quilts utilize an arrangement of six horizontal rows of five blocks each, "ABC Navy" does not have its four icons in the last row. Rather, the teddy bear with the flag vest is placed after the "A" in the first row, the cow jumping over the moon is placed after the "L" in the third row, the star is placed after the "S" in the fifth row, and the sailboat is placed after the "Z" in the last row. Further, the colors chosen to represent the letters and the blocks in "ABC Navy" are, for the most part, entirely different from "School Days I." Defendants dropped the use of polka-dot fabric, and plaintiffs did not even offer a color comparison in their proposed findings of fact to the district court, as they had with each of the "ABC Green" versions. The quilting pattern in the plain white border is changed to a "zig-zag" in "ABC Navy," as opposed to plaintiffs' "wavy" design. Finally, although defendants use a binding around the edge of their quilt, in this instance it is blue instead of green.

Looking at these quilts side-by-side, we conclude they are not substantially similar to one another. Just as we rejected defendants' earlier argument and held that what few differences existed between "School Days I" and the "ABC Green" quilts could not preclude a finding of infringement, plaintiffs' emphasis on the similarity in style between some of the letters between "School Days I" and "ABC Navy" cannot support a finding of infringement. See *Williams*, 84 F.3d at 588 ("[W]hen the similarities between the protected elements of plaintiff's work and the allegedly infringing work are of 'small import quantitatively or qualitatively[,]' the defendant will be found innocent of infringement."). Because no observer, let alone a "more discerning" observer, would likely find the two works to be substantially similar, no copyright violation could properly be found.

[AUTHOR'S NOTE: The rest of the court's analysis is omitted, but follows in this vein.]

CONCLUSION

For the reasons stated above, we affirm the judgment of the district court insofar as it found no infringement on the part of defendants with respect to their "ABC Navy" quilt as compared to plaintiffs' "School Days I" and "School Days II" quilts and their "ABC Green Version I" and "ABC Green Version II" quilts as compared to plaintiffs' "School Days II" quilt. We reverse the judgment of the district court with respect to plaintiffs' remaining claims, and find defendants' versions I and II of their "ABC Green" quilts infringed on plaintiffs' "School Days I" quilt. Accordingly, we remand the case to the district court for it to determine the appropriate remedies.

BOISSON v. BANIAN

United States District Court, Eastern District of New York, 2003.
280 F. Supp.2d 10.

[AUTHOR'S NOTE: The following is the discussion of the copyright remedies portion of the opinion on remand.]

A. Statutory Damages

17 U.S.C. § 504 ("Section 504") provides that a copyright infringer shall be liable for either actual damages and profits or statutory damages.

17 U.S.C. § 504(a)(emphasis added). *Stevens v. Aeonian Press, Inc.*, 2002 WL 31387224 *1 (S.D.N.Y. October 23, 2002). A plaintiff who seeks statutory damages is currently entitled to collect in the range of $750 to $30,000 for each work that is infringed upon. In cases filed before the statutory amendments setting damages in this range, the prior range of $500 to $20,000 is the applicable statutory range.

In addition to the statutory range of damages, Section 504 provides that if a plaintiff proves willful infringement, the court has discretion to increase the statutory award up to $100,000 ($150,000 pursuant to the 1999 Amendments). See 17 U.S.C. § 504(c)(2). In *Yurman Design, Inc. v. PAJ, Inc.*, 262 F.3d 101 (2d Cir.2001), the court noted that a defendant's conduct can be considered willful if "the defendant had knowledge that [his] conduct represented infringement or perhaps recklessly disregarded the possibility." Id. at 112.

On the other hand, if it is shown that the infringer was not aware, and had no reason to be aware of the infringement, he can be declared an innocent infringer. An innocent infringer is not absolved of all liability. Instead, the finding of innocence allows the court to exercise its discretion to fashion the proper equitable remedy. *Fitzgerald Pub. Co., Inc. v. Baylor Pub. Co., Inc.*, 807 F.2d 1110, 1117 (2d Cir.1986). In such instances, the court has discretion to reduce the statutory award to $200. 17 U.S.C. 504(c).

A finding that an infringement is not willful does not necessarily mean that the infringement is innocent and that the infringer is entitled to a reduction in damages. See *Fitzgerald*, 807 F.2d at 1115. Instead, the court considers a variety of factors when exercising its discretion to determine the proper award, within the statutory range. Such factors include the plaintiff's lost revenues, defendant's profits, the value of the copyright and the deterrent effect of the award. *Stevens*, 2002 WL 31387224 *1.

B.   Injunctive Relief

The Copyright Act gives the court discretion to grant temporary and permanent injunctions deemed reasonably necessary to prevent future infringements. 17 U.S.C. § 502(a). Permanent injunctions are appropriate only where infringement has been found and there is a substantial likelihood of future infringements. See *Central Point Software, Inc. v. Global Software & Accessories, Inc.*, 880 F.Supp. 957, 966 (E.D.N.Y.1995). On the other hand, permanent injunctive relief will not be awarded in cases where there is no history of infringement, the defendant is cooperative in ceasing to sell infringing products and there does not exist any probability of future infringement. See *Dolori Fabrics, Inc. v. Limited, Inc.*, 662 F.Supp. 1347, 1358 (S.D.N.Y.1987).

C.   Attorney's Fees

In addition to the remedies above, the court in a copyright action has the discretion to award full costs to the prevailing party. As part of these costs, the court may award a reasonable attorney's fee. 17 U.S.C. § 505; see *Matthew Bender & Co. v. West Publishing Co.*, 240 F.3d 116, 120 (2d Cir.2001).

The standard to apply when deciding whether a party has "prevailed" is the same for plaintiffs and defendants. *Fogerty v. Fantasy, Inc.*, 510 U.S. 517, 534, 114 S.Ct. 1023, 127 L.Ed.2d 455 (1994); *Earth Flag, Ltd. v. Alamo Flag Co.*, 154 F.Supp.2d 663, 665 (S.D.N.Y.2001). A party need not be successful on all claims to be deemed the "prevailing party" under the Copyright Act. Instead, a party may be deemed prevailing if it succeeds on a significant issue in litigation that achieves some benefits that the party sought in bringing suit. *Screenlife Establishment v. Tower Video, Inc.*, 868 F.Supp. 47, 50 (S.D.N.Y.1994).

Prevailing party status does not require an award of fees. See *Fogerty*, 510 U.S. at 534, 114 S.Ct. 1023 (noting that attorney's fees are not be awarded automatically, but rather the decision is within the court's discretion). Instead, the court considers the conduct of the non-prevailing party. The factors considered when determining whether an award of fees is appropriate include frivolousness, motivation, objective unreasonableness, and the need to advance considerations of compensation and deterrence. Id. The factor of objective reasonableness is entitled to "substantial weight" when determining whether an award of fees is warranted. *Matthew Bender*, 240 F.3d at 122; *Video–Cinema Films, Inc. v. Cable News Network, Inc.*, 2003 WL 1701904 *1 (S.D.N.Y. March 31, 2003).

With the above-referenced principals in mind, the court turns to the merits of Plaintiff's claims for relief.

II.   Disposition of Plaintiff's Claims

A.   Statutory Damages

Plaintiff here has elected to seek statutory damages. Because this suit was filed in 1997, the range of $500 to $20,000 is the applicable statutory range.

As noted above, the determination of the proper amount of the award requires the court to consider whether the infringement was willful, innocent, or neither. In addition, the court considers the plaintiff's lost revenues, defendant's profits, the value of the copyright and the deterrent effect of the award. Stevens, 2002 WL 31387224 *1.

1.   Wilfulness or Innocence

It is Plaintiff's contention that the striking similarity between the copyrighted quilt and the infringing quilts warrants a finding of willfulness. Acceptance of this argument, however, would turn all infringements into willful infringements, which is clearly beyond the scope of the law. The court turns, therefore, to consider other facts in this case.

The evidence developed shows that Defendant had access to Plaintiff's catalogs. However, there is no evidence that Defendant used the catalogs and copyrighted designs to engage in infringing activities. Mere access to the catalogs is, in this case, insufficient to establish willfulness. The next evidence offered by Plaintiff in support of a finding of willfulness is a conversation in which Defendant engaged at a 1995 quilt trade show. Another trader approached Rao at the trade show, and, after observing one of the alphabet quilts, the trader made the comment "I carry Judi Boisson quilts as well," seemingly hinting that the trader thought Rao's quilts to be Plaintiff's designs. It is Plaintiff's contention that this comment should have alerted Defendant to the point that he should have investigated the matter, and his failure to take action warrants a finding of reckless disregard, and thus willfulness. Defendant counters by explaining that he thought the trader simply meant that he carried Judi Boisson quilts in addition to other quilts. While it is difficult to ascertain the true meaning of the comment, both proposals are plausible. Regardless of the actual intention of the trader who made the comment, the court would be hard-pressed to conclude that one vague, out-of-context comment warrants a finding of reckless disregard. In sum, after review of the extensive evidence developed at trial of this matter, the court concludes that there is no evidence to support a finding of willful infringement.

As noted above, statutory damages can be reduced to $200 in cases where the infringer was unaware, and had no reason to be aware, of the infringement. Defendant contends that the infringement here was completely innocent and a reduction in damages is therefore appropriate.

A finding that an infringement was not willful does not necessarily lead to the conclusion that the infringement was innocent. Fitzgerald, 807 F.2d at 1115. In light of this standard and the facts developed at trial, the court concludes that the infringement can be deemed neither willful nor innocent. The catalogs in Defendant's possession make it clear that Defendant had access to Plaintiff's copyrighted designs. While the possession of these catalogs does not necessarily lead to the conclusion that Defendant knew of, or recklessly disregarded, the possibility of infringement, the court concludes that Defendant had reason to be aware of the infringement. Thus, a finding of innocent infringement is improper here. The court therefore rejects the invitation to increase or decrease the statutory damage award and turns to consider the appropriate award within the statutory range.

2. Other Factors

In determining the appropriate level of statutory damages, the court looks at a number of factors in addition to willfulness, including the value of the copyright, expenses saved and profits gained by the defendant, lost revenues by the plaintiff, defendant's cooperation in providing records, and the need to deter the defendant and others from future infringing activity. *Fitzgerald*, 807 F.2d at 1117. While this court is required to consider such factors, there is broad discretion in determining the amount of an award. Id. at 1116.

a. Value of Plaintiff's Copyright

On the whole, little evidence is provided as to the value of the Plaintiff's copyright on the School Days I quilt. It is noted that Plaintiff designed that quilt herself and sold the quilt for a number of years for a significant profit. However, no evidence has been presented to demonstrate a reduction in the value of Plaintiff's copyright. Furthermore, it seems clear that Defendant did not mass market his quilts. He sold only 153 of the infringing quilts for a profit of $3,306. Moreover, he promptly withdrew the infringing quilts from the market upon initiation of the lawsuit. In light of all of these facts, and in the absence of any concrete evidence of a devaluation of Plaintiff's copyright, the court would be hard pressed to conclude that there has been a significant devaluation to warrant the high end of statutory damages.

b. Saved Expenses

The next factor that may be considered is any expenses saved as a result of the infringement. Plaintiff argues that the School Days I quilt took her at least one month to design despite her extensive arts background and her many years of experience. Thus, Plaintiff contends that it would have taken Defendant even more time to design such a quilt, an expense which has been saved via Defendant's infringement. The evidence is clear, however, that the quilts draw heavily on designs in the public domain, known as Amish quilts. Even assuming that Plaintiff's contention regarding design time is true, there is no evidence whatsoever as to the monetary value of the saved expense. The only materials Plaintiff used to create the School Days I design were a pencil and some tracing paper, and while the court could include the cost of such materials in the final damages figure, the number would obviously be quite small. As to saved labor expenses, there is no evidence offered as to what that expense would be, nor is there any reason to believe that Defendant would have worked on a similar schedule as the Plaintiff. Perhaps it would have taken Defendant a mere few hours to design a similar quilt on his own, or perhaps it would have taken six months.

Although there is no way to definitively assess the design expenses saved by Defendant, there is no doubt that some expenses were saved. The court therefore will exercise its discretion to award $1,000 to Plaintiff to represent expenses saved by Defendant.

c. Defendant's Profits

As to profits reaped by Defendant as a result of the infringing activity, Defendant has provided evidence of 153 ABC Green quilts sold for a gross revenue of $7,150 and a profit of $3,306. Plaintiff has continually argued that Defendant has been uncooperative in providing documentation of sales and profits. While a defendant's lack of cooperation in providing records is a factor which the court can consider in assessing statutory damages, Plaintiff's contention here is simply wrong. Defendant has been cooperative in providing records, and the records indicate clearly a net profit of $3,306 on the infringing quilts. Plaintiff correctly points to a number of cases which courts have awarded statutory damages which far exceed defendant's actual profits. See *Odegard, Inc. v. Costikyan Classic Carpets*, 963 F.Supp. 1328, 1342 (S.D.N.Y.1997) (awarding statutory damages of $25,000 for one infringement where there is no showing of lost profits by plaintiff or revenue gained by defendant); See also *Lauratex Textile Corp. v. Allton Knitting Mills, Inc.*, 519 F.Supp. 730, 733 (S.D.N.Y. 1981) (awarding statutory damages of $40,000 where defendant's profits were $5,177).

When relying to the foregoing authorities, however, Plaintiff fails to note that both cases dealt with a defendant who was a willful infringer within the definition of 17 U.S.C. § 504(c). In *Odegard*, the defendant repeatedly acted dishonestly in relation to both the plaintiff and the court. Similarly, in *Lauratex*, the defendant was a willful infringer who had been served with six copyright infringement claims in the previous three years. In other words, while the court clearly has discretion to award statutory damages in excess of actual profits reaped, courts have exercised that discretion in light of additional circumstances which are lacking in this case. Still, however, in light of this documentation provided by the Defendant, the court will award the $3,306 reaped by Defendant to the Plaintiff as part of the statutory damages.

d. Plaintiff's Lost Revenue

In addition to profits reaped by the defendant, the court can look at plaintiff's lost revenue as a result of the infringement. Plaintiff, however, has provided no evidence as to lost revenue. Plaintiff claims that she lost revenue and valuable customers as a result of Defendant's action, but such claims are nothing more than blanket statements with no supporting evidence. While Plaintiff need not prove lost revenue for statutory damages, the court still has complete discretion in considering any lost revenue to make a final determination of statutory damages. See *Odegard*, 963 F.Supp. at 1340 (S.D.N.Y.1997) (noting that only in the case of actual damages, but not statutory damages, plaintiff bears the burden to demonstrate that but for the infringement, there would have been greater sales).

e. Deterrence

The final factor which the court considers is the need to deter the defendant and others from future infringing activity. With regards to the Defendant, an increase in statutory damages would do little to deter future infringing activity. Upon being advised of the initial lawsuit, Defendant promptly ceased selling all quilts involved with the lawsuit, and he continued to do so until receiving a final court order of non-infringement. It is clear that Defendant was entirely cooperative in this lawsuit, and an increase in damages is not necessary to deter Defendant. Although no damages award appears absolutely necessary to deter Defendant from future infringement, the court will not ignore this factor. Instead, to make it clear that damages will not be limited to profits alone and to deter others from infringement, the court will award Plaintiff $500 in statutory damages to deter future infringing conduct by Defendant and others in the industry.

In light of the foregoing, the court awards to Plaintiff a total of $4,806 in statutory damages.

B. Injunctive Relief

The issue as to the propriety of injunctive relief is whether or not Defendant poses a threat of future infringement. Plaintiff argues that there is a threat of continuing infringement because Defendant has continually created new designs by making modifications to previous designs, specifically pointing to Defendant's creation of the ABC Navy quilt as a modification of the ABC Green quilts. Defendant correctly points out, however, that such design by modification is commonplace in the quilting industry. Furthermore, even though the ABC Navy quilt was based on a modification of an infringing quilt, the Navy quilt was found to be non-infringing by both the District Court and the Court of Appeals. Thus, it would be improper for the court to base a finding of a substantial likelihood of future infringement on an action which was never declared to be an infringement.

Defendant points out a number of additional factors which the court considers. Specifically, Defendant has no history of copyright infringement, and he immediately ceased selling the designs when advised of the initial lawsuit. Furthermore, Defendant did not resume selling any of the designs even after the District Court entered a finding of non-infringement, and continued to withhold the designs from the market until a final decision from the Court of Appeals. Finally, Defendant has thus far fully complied with the settlement agreement reached with Plaintiff pertaining to the star-design quilts.

All of these factors weigh strongly against finding a substantial likelihood of future infringement, and thus the court is reluctant to award a permanent injunction against defendant. See *Dolori Fabrics.*, 662 F.Supp. at 1358 (declining to award a permanent injunction where there was no history of infringement, defendant was fully cooperative in ceasing to sell infringing products, and there was no evidence of a probability of future infringement) Furthermore, Defendant argues that a permanent injunction would harm his reputation as a quilt dealer, and that harm outweighs any potential benefit gained by the injunction. The court is reluctant to recognize that injunctive relief would have any drastic effects on Defendant's business as a quilt retailer, especially since Defendant repeatedly stipulated to a permanent injunction in his many settlement offers throughout the course of litigation. In any event, the requisite threat of future infringing activity is lacking completely in this case, and the court therefore declines to award a permanent injunction.

C. Attorney's Fees

Both parties contend that they have prevailed and should therefore be awarded full attorney's fees. After identifying the prevailing party, the court will turn to consider the factors necessary to determine whether an fee award is warranted.

1. Prevailing Party

The first issue of contention here is whether Plaintiff or Defendant is the prevailing party. Plaintiff initially brought suit claiming a number of infringements. Boisson claimed that defendant's ABC Green Version I, ABC Green Version II, and ABC Navy quilts each infringed on plaintiff's School Days I and School Days II quilts. Although Plaintiff also initially claimed infringement on her Pastel Twinkle Star quilts, this matter was settled before litigation on the alphabet quilts.

The ultimate result of this litigation was that only the ABC Green quilts infringed on plaintiff's School Days I quilt. All other claims were decided in Defendant's favor. Due to the mixed outcome of the initial claims brought by plaintiff, each party claims that they are the prevailing party within the meaning of 17 U.S.C. § 505. It is clear, however, that Boisson succeeded on a significant aspect of her initial lawsuit, and thus it is appropriate to declare Plaintiff as the prevailing party within the meaning of the Copyright Act.

2. Frivolousness

Neither the actions of Plaintiff nor Defendant can be deemed frivolous. Because there was nothing frivolous about either party's actions, this factor has no bearing on the decision of whether or not to award attorney's fees.

3. Motivation

Defendant's motivation throughout the course of litigation was simply to defend his right to produce and sell quilts which he felt he was entitled to sell. In view of the fact that the District Court and Court of Appeals came to different decisions as to the infringement, it is evident that this was not a clear-cut case to decide. Both parties had a good-faith belief in the merits of their cases, and the litigation was simply an effort to assert those beliefs. Furthermore, Plaintiff made settlement demands throughout the litigation for monetary damages in the amount of $175,000, which far exceeds the statutory maximum. Defendant's refusal to accept this settlement offer was in no way motivated by a bad-faith effort. Thus, this factor alone would not support an award of attorney's fees to the plaintiff. See *Warner Bros., Inc. v. Dae Rim Trading, Inc.*, 877 F.2d 1120, 1127 (2d Cir.1989) (holding that a prevailing plaintiff is not entitled to attorney's fees where defendant litigated in good faith against unreasonable settlement demands from plaintiff).

4. Objective Unreasonableness

The third discretionary factor which courts consider, and the factor that is entitled to substantial weight, is whether the legal or factual arguments put forth by the losing party were objectively unreasonable.

See *Matthew Bender*, 240 F.3d at 122. In this case, there is no basis to conclude that Defendant's actions were objectively unreasonable. It is first worth noting that not only did Defendant's claim survive attempts at summary judgment at the trial level, but the District Court ultimately decided the case in Defendant's favor. See *Williamson v. Pearson Educ., Inc.*, 2001 WL 1262964 (S.D.N.Y.2001); *CK Co. v. Burger King Corp.*, 1995 WL 29488 (S.D.N.Y.1995), aff'd., 122 F.3d 1055, 1995 WL 595526 (2d Cir.1995) (declining to conclude objective unreasonableness and award attorney's fees to the prevailing defendant despite the fact plaintiff's case did not survive summary judgment). Though the Court of Appeals ultimately reversed the trial court's decision in part, Defendant was nonetheless successful on a number of claims. Furthermore, Defendant's primary argument on appeal was that Plaintiff's copyrights were invalid because her designs were copied from the public domain. Although the Court of Appeals ultimately concluded that there was not enough evidence to support this claim, there is still no basis to conclude that Defendant's actions were objectively unreasonable. See *EMI Catalogue Partnership v. CBS/Fox Co.*, 1996 WL 280813 (S.D.N.Y.1996) (holding that losing plaintiff's claim was not objectively unreasonable, even though it was unsuccessful, because plaintiff survived summary judgment and some claims were settled in plaintiff's favor prior to a jury verdict).

5. Deterrence and Compensation

The final factor to consider is the need to advance notions of compensation and deterrence. Given the nature of this case, the court does not conclude that an award of attorney's fees is necessary to advance considerations of deterrence. As noted earlier, Defendant was entirely cooperative in ceasing any potentially infringing activity upon being served with this lawsuit. Defendant continued to cease selling all quilts involved until the final disposition by the Court of Appeals. Furthermore, Defendant made multiple attempts to settle this matter for a monetary value which was significantly greater than the current award. Given all of these circumstances, the court does not find any need to further notions of deterrence or compensation, and thus declines to award attorney's fees to the prevailing plaintiff. See *Infinity Broad. Corp. v. Kirkwood*, 63 F.Supp.2d 420, 427–28 (S.D.N.Y.1999) (declining to award attorney's fees where defendant was not a rip-off artist and was entirely responsible and cooperative throughout the course of litigation); See also *Abeshouse v. Ultragraphics, Inc.*, 754 F.2d 467 (2d Cir.1985) (declining to award attorney's fees where infringing party gained little profit from the infringing action and made many unsuccessful attempts to reasonably settle the matter).

B. § 102(A)(5)—PICTORIAL, GRAPHIC AND SCULPTURAL WORKS

17 U.S.C.A. § 101—Definitions:

"Pictorial, graphic, and sculptural works include two-dimensional and three-dimensional works of fine, graphic, and applied art, photographs, prints and art reproductions, maps, globes, charts, diagrams, models, and technical drawings, including architectural plans. Such works shall include works of artistic craftsmanship insofar as their form but not their mechanical or utilitarian aspects are concerned; the design of a useful article, as defined in this section, shall be considered a pictorial, graphic, or sculptural work only if, and only to the extent that, such design incorporates pictorial, graphic, or sculptural features that can be identified separately from, and are capable of existing independently of, the utilitarian aspects of the article."

PIVOT POINT INTERN., INC. v. CHARLENE PRODUCTS, INC.

United State Court of Appeals for the Seventh Circuit, 2004.
372 F.3d 913.

RIPPLE, CIRCUIT JUDGE.

* * *

Pivot Point develops and markets educational techniques and tools for the hair design industry. It was founded in 1965 by Leo Passage, an internationally renowned hair designer. One aspect of Pivot Point's business is the design and development of mannequin heads, "slip-ons" (facial forms that slip over a mannequin head) and component hair pieces.

In the mid–1980s, Passage desired to develop a mannequin that would imitate the "hungry look" of high-fashion, runway models. Passage believed that such a mannequin could be marketed as a premium item to cutting-edge hair-stylists and to stylists involved in hair design competitions. Passage then worked with a German artist named Horst Heerlein to create an original sculpture of a female human head. Although Passage discussed his vision with Heerlein, Passage did not give Heerlein any specific dimensional requirements. From Passage's description, Heerlein created a sculpture in plaster entitled "Mara."

Wax molds of Mara were made and sent to Pivot Point's manufacturer in Hong Kong. The manufacturer created exact reproductions of Mara in polyvinyl chloride ("PVC"). The manufacturer filled the PVC form with a liquid that expands and hardens into foam. The process of creating the Mara sculpture and of developing the mannequin based on the sculpture took approximately eighteen months. * * *

At a trade show in 1989, Charlene, a wholesaler of beauty products founded by Mr. Yau, displayed its own "Liza" mannequin, which was very close in appearance to Pivot Point's Mara. In addition to the strikingly similar facial features, Liza also exhibited a double hairline that the early Mara mannequins possessed.

On September 24, 1989, Pivot Point noticed Charlene for copyright infringement. When Charlene refused to stop importing and selling the Liza mannequin, Pivot Point filed this action. * * *

The central issue in this case is whether the Mara mannequin is subject to copyright protection. This issue presents, at bottom, a question of statutory interpretation. We therefore begin our analysis with the language of the statute. Two provisions contained in 17 U.S.C. § 101 are at the center of our inquiry. The first of these is the description of pictorial, graphic and sculptural works. * * * The definition section further provides that "[a] 'useful article' is an article having an intrinsic utilitarian function that is not merely to portray the appearance of the article or to convey information. An article that is normally a part of a useful article is considered a 'useful article.'" 17 U.S.C. § 101. As is clear from the definition of pictorial, graphic and sculptural work, only "useful article[s]," as the term is further defined, are subject to the limitation contained in the emphasized language above. If an article is not "useful" as the term is defined in § 101, then it is a pictorial, graphic and sculptural work entitled to copyright protection (assuming the other requirements of the statute are met).

1. Usefulness

Pivot Point submits that the Mara mannequin is not a "useful article" for purposes of § 101 because its "inherent nature is to portray the appearance of runway models. Its value," continues Pivot Point, "resides in how well it portrays the appearance of runway models, just as the value of a bust-depicting Cleopatra, for example, . . .-would be in how well it approximates what one imagines the subject looked like." * * *

Charlene presents us with a different view. It suggests that * * * the Mara mannequin does have a useful function other than portraying an image of a high-fashion runway model. According to Charlene, Mara also is marketed and used for practicing the art of makeup application. Charlene points to various places in the record that establish that Mara is used for this purpose and is, therefore, a useful article subject to the limiting language of § 101.

Pivot Point strongly disputes that the record establishes such a use and argues that the district court's reliance on Charlene's alleged proof improperly resolves an issue of fact against the non-moving party in contravention of Federal Rule of Civil Procedure 56. Indeed, our own review of the record leads us to believe that many of the documents cited by Charlene are susceptible to more than one interpretation.

Nevertheless, we shall assume that the district court correctly ruled that Mara is a useful article and proceed to examine whether, despite that usefulness, it is amenable to copyright protection.

2. Separability

We return to the statutory language. A useful article falls within the definition of pictorial, graphic or sculptural works "only if, and only to the extent that, such design incorporates pictorial, graphic, or sculptural features that can be identified separately from, and are capable of existing independently of, the utilitarian aspects of the article." 17 U.S.C. § 101. It is common ground between the parties and, indeed, among the courts that have examined the issue, that this language, added by the 1976 Act, was intended to distinguish creative works that enjoy protection from elements of industrial design that do not. See H.R.Rep. No. 94–1476, at 55 (1976), reprinted in 1976 U.S.C.C.A.N. 5659, 5668 (stating that the purpose behind this language was "to draw as clear a line as possible between copyrightable works of applied art and uncopyrighted works of industrial design"). Although the Congressional goal was evident, application of this language has presented the courts with significant difficulty. Indeed, one scholar has noted: "Of the many fine lines that run through the Copyright Act, none is more troublesome than the line between protectible pictorial, graphic and sculptural works and unprotectible utilitarian elements of industrial design." Paul Goldstein, 1 Copyright § 2.5.3, at 2:56 (2d ed.2004).

The difficulty in the application of this language would not have come, in all likelihood, as a surprise to the Congressional drafters. The language employed by Congress is not the language of a bright-line rule of universal application. Indeed, the circuits that have addressed the interpretative problem now before us uniformly have recognized that the wording of the statute does not supply categorical direction, but rather requires the Copyright Office and the courts "to continue their efforts to distinguish applied art and industrial design." Robert C. Denicola, Applied Art & Industrial Design: A Suggested Approach to Copyright in Useful Articles, 67 Minn. L.Rev. 707, 730 (1983). In short, no doubt well-aware of the myriad of factual scenarios to which its policy guidance would have to be applied, Congress wisely chose to provide only general policy guidance to be implemented on a case-by-case basis through the Copyright Office and the courts.

Even though the words of the statute do not yield a definitive answer, we believe that the statutory language nevertheless provides significant guidance in our task. We therefore shall examine in more detail what that language has to tell us, and we return to the necessary starting point of our task, § 101.

The statutory language provides that "the design of a useful article ... shall be considered a pictorial, graphic, or sculptural work only if, and only to the extent that, such design incorporates pictorial, graphic, or sculptural features that can be identified separately from and are capable of existing independently of, the utilitarian aspects of the article." Although the italicized clause contains two operative phrases-"can be identified separately from" and "are capable of existing independently of"-we believe, as have the other courts that have grappled with this issue, that Congress, in amending the statute, intended these two phrases to state a single, integrated standard to determine when there is sufficient separateness between the utilitarian and artistic aspects of a work to justify copyright protection.

Certainly, one approach to determine whether material can be "identified separately," and the most obvious, is to rely on the capacity of the artistic material to be severed physically from the industrial design. See *Mazer v. Stein*, 347 U.S. 201, 74 S.Ct. 460, 98 L.Ed. 630 (1954) (holding that a statuette incorporated into the base of a lamp is copyrightable). When a three-dimensional article is the focus of the inquiry, reliance on physical separability can no doubt be a helpful tool in ascertaining whether the artistic material in question can be separated from the industrial design. As Professor Denicola points out, however, such an approach really is not of much use when the item in question is two-dimensional. See Denicola, supra, at 744. Indeed, because this provision, by its very words, was intended to apply to two-dimensional material, it is clear that a physical separability test cannot be the exclusive test for determining copyrightability.

It seems to be common ground between the parties and, indeed, among the courts and commentators, that the protection of the copyright statute also can be secured when a conceptual separability exists between the material sought to be copyrighted and the utilitarian design in which that material is incorporated. The difficulty lies not in the acceptance of that proposition, which the statutory language clearly contemplates, but in its application. As noted by Pivot Point, the following tests have been suggested for determining when the artistic and utilitarian aspects of useful articles are conceptually separable: 1) the artistic features are "primary" and the utilitarian features "subsidiary," *Kieselstein–Cord*, 632 F.2d at 993; 2) the useful article "would still be marketable to some significant segment of the community simply because of its aesthetic qualities," Melville B. Nimmer & David Nimmer, 1 Nimmer on Copyright § 2.08[B][3], at 2–101 (2004); 3) the article "stimulate[s] in the mind of the beholder a concept that is separate from the concept evoked by its utilitarian function," Carol Barnhart, 773 F.2d at 422 (Newman, J., dissenting); 4) the artistic design was not significantly influenced by functional considerations, see Brandir Int'l, 834 F.2d at 1145 (adopting the test forwarded in Denicola, supra, at 741); 5) the artistic features "can stand alone as a work of art traditionally conceived, and ... the useful article in which it is embodied would be equally useful without it," Goldstein, 1 Copyright § 2.5.3, at 2:67; and 6) the artistic features are not utilitarian, see William F. Patry, 1 Copyright Law & Practice 285 (1994).
* * *

In articulating a meaningful approach to conceptual separability, we note that we are not the first court of appeals to deal with this problem. The work of our colleagues in the other circuits provides significant insights into our understanding of Congressional intent. Indeed, even when those judges have disagreed on the appropriate application of the Congressional mandate to the case before them, their insight yield a bountiful harvest for those of us who now walk the same interpretative path.

Among the circuits, the Court of Appeals for the Second Circuit has had occasion to wrestle most comprehensively with the notion of "conceptual separability." Its case law represents, we believe, an intellectual journey that has explored the key aspects of the problem. We therefore turn to a study of the key stages of doctrinal development in its case law. * * *

The Second Circuit first grappled with the issue of conceptual separability in *Kieselstein–Cord v. Accessories by Pearl, Inc.*, 632 F.2d 989 (2d Cir.1980). In that case, Kieselstein–Cord, a jewelry designer, had created a line of decorative and jeweled belt buckles inspired by works of art; he obtained copyright registrations for his designs. When the line was successful, Accessories by Pearl, Inc., ("Pearl") copied the designs and marketed its own, less-expensive versions of the belt buckles. Kieselstein–Cord then sued Pearl for copyright infringement; however, Pearl claimed that the belt buckles were not copyrightable because they were " 'useful articles' with no 'pictorial, graphic, or sculptural features that can be identified separately from, and are capable of existing independently of, the utilitarian aspects' of the buckles." Id. at 991–92. The Second Circuit disagreed. Although it did not articulate a specific test for evaluating conceptual separability, it focused on the "primary" and "subsidiary" elements of the article and concluded:

> We see in appellant's belt buckles conceptually separable sculptural elements, as apparently have the buckles' wearers who have used them as ornamentation for parts of the body other than the waist. The primary ornamental aspect of the Vaquero and Winchester buckles is conceptually separable from their subsidiary utilitarian function. This conclusion is not at variance with the expressed congressional intent to distinguish copyrightable applied art and uncopyrightable industrial design. Pieces of applied art, these buckles may be considered jewelry, the form of which is subject to copyright protection.

Id. at 993 (internal citations omitted). * * *

The Second Circuit revisited the issue of conceptual separability in *Carol Barnhart Inc. v. Economy Cover Corp.*, 773 F.2d 411 (2d Cir.1985). In that case, Carol Barnhart, a provider of retail display items, developed four mannequins consisting of human torsos for the display of shirts and jackets. It obtained copyright registrations for each of the forms. When a competitor, Economy Cover, copied the designs, Carol Barnhart claimed infringement of that copyright. The Second Circuit held that the designs were not copyrightable. It explained:

> [W]hile copyright protection has increasingly been extended to cover articles having a utilitarian dimension, Congress has explicitly refused copyright protection for works of applied art or industrial design which have aesthetic or artistic features that cannot be identified separately from the useful article. Such works are not copyrightable regardless of the fact that they may be "aesthetically satisfying and valuable."

Applying these principles, we are persuaded that since the aesthetic and artistic features of the Barnhart forms are inseparable from the forms' use as utilitarian articles the forms are not copyrightable.... [Barnhart] stresses that the forms have been responded to as sculptural forms, and have been used for purposes other than modeling clothes, e.g., as decorating props and signs without any clothing or accessories. While this may indicate that the forms are "aesthetically satisfying and valuable," it is insufficient to show that the forms possess aesthetic or artistic features that are physically or conceptually separable from the forms' use as utilitarian objects to display clothes. On the contrary, to the extent the forms possess aesthetically pleasing features, even when these features are considered in the aggregate, they cannot be conceptualized as existing independently of their utilitarian function.

Id. at 418 (internal citations omitted). The court also rejected the argument that Kieselstein–Cord was controlling. The majority explained that what distinguished the Kieselstein–Cord buckles from the Barnhart forms was "that the ornamented surfaces of the buckles were not in any respect required by their functions; the artistic and aesthetic features would thus be conceived as having been added to, or superimposed upon, an otherwise utilitarian article." Id. at 419.

Perhaps the most theoretical and comprehensive discussion of "conceptual separability," as opposed to physical separability, can be found in the dissenting opinion of Judge Newman in *Carol Barnhart*, 773 F.2d at 419. After reviewing the possible ways to determine conceptual separability, Judge Newman set forth his choice and rationale:

How, then, is "conceptual separateness" to be determined? In my view, the answer derives from the word "conceptual." For the design features to be "conceptually separate" from the utilitarian aspects of the useful article that embodies the design, the article must stimulate in the mind of the beholder a concept that is separate from the concept evoked by its utilitarian function. The test turns on what may reasonably be understood to be occurring in the mind of the beholder or, as some might say, in the "mind's eye" of the beholder....

. . .

The "separateness" of the utilitarian and non-utilitarian concepts engendered by an article's design is itself a perplexing concept. I think the requisite "separateness" exists whenever the design creates in the mind of the ordinary observer two different concepts that are not inevitably entertained simultaneously. Again, the example of the artistically designed chair displayed in a museum may be helpful. The ordinary observer can be expected to apprehend the design of a chair whenever the object is viewed. He may, in addition, entertain the concept of a work of art, but, if this second concept is engendered in the observer's mind simultaneously with the concept of the article's utilitarian function, the requisite "separateness" does not exist. The test is not whether the observer fails to recognize the object as a chair but only whether the concept of the utilitarian function can be displaced in the mind by some other concept. That does not occur, at least for the ordinary observer, when viewing even the most artistically designed chair. It may occur, however, when viewing some other object if the utilitarian function of the object is not perceived at all; it may also occur, even when the utilitarian function is perceived by observation, perhaps aided by explanation, if the concept of the utilitarian function can be displaced in the observer's mind while he entertains the separate concept of some non-utilitarian function. The separate concept will normally be that of a work of art.

Id. at 422–23.* * *

The Second Circuit soon addressed conceptual separability again in *Brandir International, Inc. v. Cascade Pacific Lumber Co.*, 834 F.2d 1142 (2d Cir.1987). That case involved the work of an artist, David Levine; specifically, Levine had created a sculpture of thick, interwoven wire. A cyclist friend of Levine's realized that the sculpture could, with modification, function as a bicycle rack and thereafter put Levine in touch with Brandir International, Inc. ("Brandir"). The artist and the Brandir engineers then worked to modify the sculpture to produce a workable and marketable bicycle rack. Their work culminated in the "Ribbon Rack," which Brandir began marketing in 1979. Shortly thereafter, Cascade Pacific Lumber Co. ("Cascade") began selling a similar product, and, in response, Brandir applied for copyright protection and began placing copyright notices on its racks. The Copyright Office, however, rejected the registration on the ground that the rack did not contain any element that was "capable of independent existence as a copyrightable pictorial, graphic or sculptural work apart from the shape of the useful article." Id. at 1146.

The court first considered the possible tests for conceptual separability in light of its past decisions and, notably, attempted to reconcile its earlier attempts:

Perhaps the differences between the majority and the dissent in *Carol Barnhart* might have been resolved had they had before them the Denicola article on Applied Art and Industrial Design: A Suggested Approach to Copyright in Useful Articles, [67 Minn. L.Rev. 707 (1983)].... Denicola argues that "the statutory directive requires a distinction between works of industrial design and works whose origins lie outside the design process, despite the utilitarian environment in which they appear." He views the statutory limitation of copyrightability as "an attempt to identify elements whose form and appearance reflect the unconstrained perspective of the artist," such features not being the product of industrial design. Id. at 742. "Copyrightability, therefore, should turn on the relationship between the proffered work and the process of industrial design." Id. at 741. He suggests that "the dominant characteristic of industrial design is the influence of nonaesthetic, utilitarian concerns" and hence concludes that copyrightability "ultimately should depend on the extent to which the work reflects artistic expression uninhibited by functional considerations." Id. To state the Denicola test in the language of conceptual separability, if design elements reflect a merger of aesthetic and functional considerations, the artistic aspects of a work cannot be said to be conceptually separable from the utilitarian elements. Conversely, where design elements can be identified as reflecting the designer's artistic judgment exercised independently of functional influences, conceptual separability exists.

We believe that Professor Denicola's approach provides the best test for conceptual separability and, accordingly, adopt it here for several reasons. First, the approach is consistent with the holdings of our previous cases. In *Kieselstein–Cord*, for example, the artistic aspects of the belt buckles reflected purely aesthetic choices, independent of the buckles' function, while in *Carol Barnhart* the distinctive features of the torsos—the accurate anatomical design and the sculpted shirts and collars—showed clearly the influence of functional concerns.... Second, the test's emphasis on the influence of utilitarian concerns in the design process may help ... "alleviate the de facto discrimination against nonrepresentational art that has regrettably accompanied much of the current analysis." Id. at 745.

Id. at 1145 (footnotes omitted).

Applying Professor Denicola's test to the Ribbon Rack, the court found that the rack was not copyrightable. The court stated that, "[h]ad Brandir merely adopted one of the existing sculptures as a bicycle rack, neither the application to a utilitarian end nor commercialization of that use would have caused the object to forfeit its copyrighted status." Id. at 1147. However, when the Ribbon Rack was compared to earlier sculptures, continued the court, it was "in its final form essentially a product of industrial design." Id. * * *

* * * There is one final Second Circuit case that bears comment. In *Mattel, Inc. v. Goldberger Doll Manufacturing Co.*, 365 F.3d 133 (2d Cir.2004), the Second Circuit rejected the idea that a particular expression of features on a doll's face was not subject to copyright protection. The case arose out of the alleged copying of the facial features of Mattel's Barbie dolls by Goldberger Doll Manufacturing when creating its "Rockettes 2000" doll. On Goldberger's motion for summary judgment, the district court held that "copyright protection did not extend to Barbie's eyes, nose, and mouth...." Id. at 134. The Second Circuit reversed. Although it did not speak specifically in terms of conceptual separability, the court's reasoning is nevertheless instructive; it stated:

the proposition that standard or common features are not protected is inconsistent with copyright law. To merit protection from copying, a work need not be particularly novel or unusual. It need only have been "independently created" by the author and possess "some minimal degree of creativity." *Feist Publ'ns, Inc. v. Rural Tel. Serv.*

Co., 499 U.S. 340, 345, 111 S.Ct. 1282, 113 L.Ed.2d 358 (1991)....
There are innumerable ways of making upturned noses, bow lips, and
widely spaced eyes. Even if the record had shown that many dolls
possess upturned noses, bow lips, and wide-spread eyes, it would not
follow that each such doll-assuming it was independently created and
not copied from others-would not enjoy protection from copying.

Id. at 135 (footnotes and parallel citations omitted). Additionally, the court
noted the scope of the copyright protection that the Barbie dolls enjoyed:

The copyright does not protect ideas; it protects only the author's
particularized expression of the idea. Thus, Mattel's copyright in a
doll visage with an upturned nose, bow lips, and widely spaced eyes
will not prevent a competitor from making dolls with upturned noses,
bow lips, and widely spaced eyes, even if the competitor has taken the
idea from Mattel's example, so long as the competitor has not copied
Mattel's particularized expression. An upturned nose, bow lips, and
wide eyes are the "idea" of a certain type of doll face. That idea
belongs not to Mattel but to the public domain. But Mattel's copyright
will protect its own particularized expression of that idea and bar a
competitor from copying Mattel's realization of the Barbie features.

Id. at 136 (citations omitted).

* * *

Each of these cases differs in the object at issue and the method by
which the court evaluated whether the object was entitled to copyright
protection. Yet, each court attempted to give effect to "the expressed
congressional intent to distinguish copyrightable applied art and uncopyrightable industrial design." *Kieselstein–Cord*, 632 F.2d at 993; see also
Carol Barnhart, 773 F.2d at 417–18 (reviewing legislative history in detail
and concluding that, although "copyright protection has increasingly been
extended to cover articles having a utilitarian dimension," Congress did
not intend all useful articles that are "aesthetically satisfying or valuable"
to be copyrightable); *Brandir Int'l*, 834 F.2d at 1145 (adopting Professor
Denicola's test that makes copyrightability dependent upon "the extent to
which the work reflects artistic expression uninhibited by functional
considerations"). * * *

The Second Circuit cases exhibit a progressive attempt to forge a
workable judicial approach capable of giving meaning to the basic Congressional policy decision to distinguish applied art from uncopyrightable
industrial art or design. In *Kieselstein–Cord*, the Second Circuit attempted
to distinguish artistic expression from industrial design by focusing on the
present use of the item, i.e., the "primary ornamental aspect" versus the
"subsidiary utilitarian function" of the object at issue. 632 F.2d at 993. In
Carol Barnhart, the Second Circuit moved closer to a process-oriented
approach:

What distinguishes those [Kieselstein–Cord] buckles from the Barnhart forms is that the ornamented surfaces of the buckles were not in

any respect required by their utilitarian functions; the artistic and aesthetic features could thus be conceived of as having been added to, or superimposed upon, an otherwise utilitarian article. The unique artistic design was wholly unnecessary to performance of the utilitarian function. In the case of the Barnhart forms, on the other hand, the features claimed to be aesthetic or artistic, e.g., the life-size configuration of the breasts and the width of the shoulders, are inextricably intertwined with the utilitarian feature, the display of clothes. Whereas a model of a human torso, in order to serve its utilitarian function, must have some configuration of the chest and some width of shoulders, a belt buckle can serve its function satisfactorily without any ornamentation of the type that renders the Kieselstein–Cord buckles distinctive.

773 F.2d at 419. Thus, it was the fact that the creator of the torsos was driven by utilitarian concerns, such as how display clothes would fit on the end product, that deprived the human torsos of copyright protection.

This process-oriented approach for conceptual separability-focusing on the process of creating the object to determine whether it is entitled to copyright protection-is more fully articulated in *Brandir* and indeed reconciles the earlier case law pertaining to conceptual separability.

[T]he approach is consistent with the holdings of our previous cases. In *Kieselstein–Cord*, for example, the artistic aspects of the belt buckles reflected purely aesthetic choices, independent of the buckles' function, while in *Carol Barnhart* the distinctive features of the torsos-the accurate anatomical design and the sculpted shirts and collars-showed clearly the influence of functional concerns. Though the torsos bore artistic features, it was evident the designer incorporated those features to further the usefulness of the torsos as mannequins. * * *

Furthermore, *Brandir* is not inconsistent with the more theoretical rendition of Judge Newman in his *Carol Barnhart* dissent-that "the requisite 'separateness' exists whenever the design creates in the mind of an ordinary observer two different concepts that are not inevitably entertained simultaneously." 773 F.2d at 422. When a product has reached its final form as a result of predominantly functional or utilitarian considerations, it necessarily will be more difficult for the observer to entertain simultaneously two different concepts-the artistic object and the utilitarian object. In such circumstances, *Brandir* has the added benefit of providing a more workable judicial methodology by articulating the driving principle behind conceptual separability-the influence of industrial design. When the ultimate form of the object in question is "as much the result of utilitarian pressures as aesthetic choices," "[f]orm and function are inextricably intertwined," and the artistic aspects of the object cannot be separated from its utilitarian aspects for purposes of copyright protection. *Brandir*, 834 F.2d at 1147.

Conceptual separability exists, therefore, when the artistic aspects of an article can be "conceptualized as existing independently of their utilitarian function." *Carol Barnhart*, 773 F.2d at 418. This independence is necessarily informed by "whether the design elements can be identified as reflecting the designer's artistic judgment exercised independently of functional influences." *Brandir*, 834 F.2d at 1145. If the elements do reflect the independent, artistic judgment of the designer, conceptual separability exists. Conversely, when the design of a useful article is "as much the result of utilitarian pressures as aesthetic choices," id. at 1147, the useful and aesthetic elements are not conceptually separable.

Applying this test to the Mara mannequin, we must conclude that the Mara face is subject to copyright protection. It certainly is not difficult to conceptualize a human face, independent of all of Mara's specific facial features, i.e., the shape of the eye, the upturned nose, the angular cheek and jaw structure, that would serve the utilitarian functions of a hair stand and, if proven, of a makeup model. Indeed, one is not only able to conceive of a different face than that portrayed on the Mara mannequin, but one easily can conceive of another visage that portrays the "hungry look" on a high-fashion runway model. Just as Mattel is entitled to protection for "its own particularized expression" of an "upturned nose[ ], bow lips, and widely spaced eyes," *Mattel*, 365 F.3d at 136, so too is Heerlein (and, therefore, Pivot Point as assignee of the copyright registration) entitled to have his expression of the "hungry look" protected from copying.

Mara can be conceptualized as existing independent from its use in hair display or make-up training because it is the product of Heerlein's artistic judgment. When Passage approached Heerlein about creating the Mara sculpture, Passage did not provide Heerlein with specific dimensions or measurements; indeed, there is no evidence that Heerlein's artistic judgment was constrained by functional considerations. Passage did not require, for instance, that the sculpture's eyes be a certain width to accommodate standard-sized eyelashes, that the brow be arched at a certain angle to facilitate easy make-up application or that the sculpture as a whole not exceed certain dimensional limits so as to fit within Pivot Point's existing packaging system. Such considerations, had they been present, would weigh against a determination that Mara was purely the product of an artistic effort. By contrast, after Passage met with Heerlein to discuss Passage's idea for a "hungry-look" model, Heerlein had carte blanche to implement that vision as he saw fit. Consequently, this is not a situation, such as was presented to the Second Circuit in *Carol Barnhart*, in which certain features ("accurate anatomical design and the sculpted shirts and collars") were included in the design for purely functional reasons. *Brandir*, 834 F.2d at 1145. Furthermore, unlike "the headless, armless, backless styrene torsos" which "were little more than glorified coat-racks used to display clothing in stores," *Hart*, 86 F.3d at 323, the creative aspects of the Mara sculpture were meant to be seen and admired. Thus, because Mara was the product of a creative process unfettered by functional concerns, its sculptural features "can be identified separately from, and are capable of existing independently of," its utilitarian aspects.

It therefore meets the requirements for conceptual separability and is subject to copyright protection.

Conclusion

The Mara mannequin is subject to copyright protection. We therefore must reverse the summary judgment in favor of Charlene Products and Mr. Yau; the case is remanded for a trial on Pivot Point's infringement claim.

KANNE, CIRCUIT JUDGE, dissenting.

Writing for the majority, Judge Ripple has applied his usual thorough and scholarly approach to this difficult intellectual property problem; however, I cannot join the majority opinion because I am not persuaded that the "Mara" mannequin is copyrightable. All functional items have aesthetic qualities. If copyright provided protection for functional items simply because of their aesthetic qualities, Congress's policy choice that gives less protection in patent than copyright would be undermined. See *American Dental Ass'n v. Delta Dental Plans Ass'n*, 126 F.3d 977, 980 (7th Cir.1997). * * *

Mara, on the other hand, has only functional attributes. Thus, any physical separation of a portion of her would not be independent of her utilitarian aspects. She is sold to beauty schools as a teaching device; students style her hair and apply makeup as realistic training for such pursuits on live subjects. A mannequin head without a neck, or with different eyes and musculature, would not serve the utilitarian purpose of applying makeup or teaching the art of matching hair styles to facial features. As the district court explained: "Beauty students style hair to flatter the face, not to be worn on featureless ovoids. The use of a mannequin head in training students of beauty schools lies in its aesthetic qualities." There is nothing in Mara that we could physically remove that would not be part of Mara's utility as a teaching aid. Like mannequins of human torsos, *Carol Barnhart Inc. v. Economy Cover Corp.*, 773 F.2d 411, 418–19 (2d Cir.1985), mannequins of human faces are not physically separable from their functional purpose and are therefore not copyrightable. * * *

Problematically, the majority's test for conceptual separability seems to bear little resemblance to the statute. The statute asks two questions: Does the useful article incorporate "sculptural features that can be identified separately from the utilitarian aspects" of the article? And are these features "capable of existing independently" from the utilitarian aspects? The copyright statute is concerned with protecting only non-utilitarian features of the useful article. To be copyrightable, the statute requires that the useful article's functionality remain intact once the copyrightable material is separated. In other words, Pivot Point needs to show that Mara's face is not a utilitarian "aspect" of the product "Mara," but rather a separate non-utilitarian "feature." The majority, by looking only to whether the features could also "be conceptualized as existing

independently of their utilitarian function" and ignoring the more important question of whether the features themselves are utilitarian aspects of
the useful article, mistakenly presupposes that utilitarian aspects of a
useful article can be copyrighted. If we took away Mara's facial features,
her functionality would be greatly diminished or eliminated, thus proving
that her features cannot be copyrighted.

NOTES

1.   Can you conceptualize the distinction between works of literature or
art and a work of multiple copies? Does one copyright a singular art object
and then produce copies of the same under the protection of copyright? Does
that art lose copyright protection because it has become a functional commercial object? Does the *Pivot Point* decision clarify or add complexity to differentiate function from art? The mannequin was used for functional purposes, yet
the court treated the aesthetic features as art and expression. Do these
questions evolve around whether the object was intended as art, or as an
ingredient in a functional setting? Was there independence to the art of a
female head with no makeup or hair that would have given it a "life of its'
own?" Does it make any difference that it was a competitor who copied the
likeness of the female head? Both the district court and the dissent believed
the head was utilitarian. Does Professor Goldstein's "conceptual separation"
test noted in the decision create a bright line for review purposes? Do these
cases represent a continuing saga of attempting to secure a competitive
advantage ancillary to trademark under copyright statutes? What if this were
not an exact copy, but rather an assimilation of the concept (idea), coupled
with the fact (a head with two eyes, lips, ears and a hair line) that was similar
to lifelike proportion, but with different hairline and differently shaped eyes
and lips? Does this constitute original expression per *Mazer*?

2.   The line between aesthetic and functional, a distinction that can be
traced back to the *Baker v. Selden* decision, continues to be explored in
copyright cases involving software and those involving architectural works.

C. SOFTWARE

COMPUTER ASSOCIATES INTERN, INC. v. ALTAI

United States Court of Appeals for the Second Circuit, 1992.
982 F.2d 693.

WALKER, CIRCUIT JUDGE:

In recent years, the growth of computer science has spawned a
number of challenging legal questions, particularly in the field of copyright law. As scientific knowledge advances, courts endeavor to keep pace,
and sometimes-as in the area of computer technology-they are required to
venture into less than familiar waters. This is not a new development,
though. "From its beginning, the law of copyright has developed in
response to significant changes in technology." *Sony Corp. v. Universal
City Studios, Inc.*, 464 U.S. 417, 430, 104 S.Ct. 774, 782, 78 L.Ed.2d 574
(1984).

Article I, section 8 of the Constitution authorizes Congress "[t]o promote the Progress of Science and useful Arts, by securing for limited Times to Authors and Inventors the exclusive Right to their respective Writings and Discoveries." The Supreme Court has stated that "[t]he economic philosophy behind the clause ... is the conviction that encouragement of individual effort by personal gain is the best way to advance public welfare...." *Mazer v. Stein*, 347 U.S. 201, 219, 74 S.Ct. 460, 471, 98 L.Ed. 630 (1954). The author's benefit, however, is clearly a "secondary" consideration. See *United States v. Paramount Pictures, Inc.*, 334 U.S. 131, 158, 68 S.Ct. 915, 929, 92 L.Ed. 1260 (1948). "[T]he ultimate aim is, by this incentive, to stimulate artistic creativity for the general public good." *Twentieth Century Music Corp. v. Aiken*, 422 U.S. 151, 156, 95 S.Ct. 2040, 2044, 45 L.Ed.2d 84 (1975).

Thus, the copyright law seeks to establish a delicate equilibrium. On the one hand, it affords protection to authors as an incentive to create, and, on the other, it must appropriately limit the extent of that protection so as to avoid the effects of monopolistic stagnation. In applying the federal act to new types of cases, courts must always keep this symmetry in mind. Id.

Among other things, this case deals with the challenging question of whether and to what extent the "non-literal" aspects of a computer program, that is, those aspects that are not reduced to written code, are protected by copyright. While a few other courts have already grappled with this issue, this case is one of first impression in this circuit. As we shall discuss, we find the results reached by other courts to be less than satisfactory. Drawing upon long-standing doctrines of copyright law, we take an approach that we think better addresses the practical difficulties embedded in these types of cases. In so doing, we have kept in mind the necessary balance between creative incentive and industrial competition.

Certain elementary facts concerning the nature of computer programs are vital to the following discussion. The Copyright Act defines a computer program as "a set of statements or instructions to be used directly or indirectly in a computer in order to bring about a certain result." 17 U.S.C. § 101. In writing these directions, the programmer works "from the general to the specific." *Whelan Assocs., Inc. v. Jaslow Dental Lab., Inc.*, 797 F.2d 1222, 1229 (3d Cir.1986), cert. denied, 479 U.S. 1031, 107 S.Ct. 877, 93 L.Ed.2d 831 (1987).

The first step in this procedure is to identify a program's ultimate function or purpose. An example of such an ultimate purpose might be the creation and maintenance of a business ledger. Once this goal has been achieved, a programmer breaks down or "decomposes" the program's ultimate function into "simpler constituent problems or 'subtasks,'" * * * which are also known as subroutines or modules. * * * In the context of a business ledger program, a module or subroutine might be responsible for the task of updating a list of outstanding accounts receivable. Sometimes, depending upon the complexity of its task, a subroutine may be broken down further into sub-subroutines.

Having sufficiently decomposed the program's ultimate function into its component elements, a programmer will then arrange the subroutines or modules into what are known as organizational or flow charts. Flow charts map the interactions between modules that achieve the program's end goal.

In order to accomplish these intra-program interactions, a programmer must carefully design each module's parameter list. A parameter list, according to the expert appointed and fully credited by the district court, Dr. Randall Davis, is "the information sent to and received from a subroutine." See Report of Dr. Randall Davis, at 12. The term "parameter list" refers to the form in which information is passed between modules (e.g. for accounts receivable, the designated time frame and particular customer identifying number) and the information's actual content (e.g. 8/91–7/92; customer No. 3). Id. With respect to form, interacting modules must share similar parameter lists so that they are capable of exchanging information.

In fashioning the structure, a programmer will normally attempt to maximize the program's speed, efficiency, as well as simplicity for user operation, while taking into consideration certain externalities such as the memory constraints of the computer upon which the program will be run.

Once each necessary module has been identified, designed, and its relationship to the other modules has been laid out conceptually, the resulting program structure must be embodied in a written language that the computer can read. This process is called "coding," and requires two steps. *Whelan*, 797 F.2d at 1230. First, the programmer must transpose the program's structural blue-print into a source code. This step has been described as "comparable to the novelist fleshing out the broad outline of his plot by crafting from words and sentences the paragraphs that convey the ideas." * * * The source code may be written in any one of several computer languages, such as COBAL, FORTRAN, BASIC, EDL, etc., depending upon the type of computer for which the program is intended. *Whelan*, 797 F.2d at 1230. Once the source code has been completed, the second step is to translate or "compile" it into object code. Object code is the binary language comprised of zeros and ones through which the computer directly receives its instructions.

After the coding is finished, the programmer will run the program on the computer in order to find and correct any logical and syntactical errors. This is known as "debugging" and, once done, the program is complete.

The subject of this litigation originates with one of CA's marketed programs entitled CA–SCHEDULER. CA–SCHEDULER is a job scheduling program designed for IBM mainframe computers. Its primary functions are straightforward: to create a schedule specifying when the computer should run various tasks, and then to control the computer as it executes the schedule. CA–SCHEDULER contains a sub-program entitled ADAPTER, also developed by CA. ADAPTER is not an independently marketed product of CA; it is a wholly integrated component of CA–SCHEDULER and has no capacity for independent use.

Nevertheless, ADAPTER plays an extremely important role. It is an "operating system compatibility component," which means, roughly speaking, it serves as a translator. An "operating system" is itself a program that manages the resources of the computer, allocating those resources to other programs as needed. The IBM System 370 family of computers, for which CA–SCHEDULER was created, is, depending upon the computer's size, designed to contain one of three operating systems: DOS/VSE, MVS, or CMS. As the district court noted, the general rule is that "a program written for one operating system, e.g., DOS/VSE, will not, without modification, run under another operating system such as MVS." * * * ADAPTER's function is to translate the language of a given program into the particular language that the computer's own operating system can understand. * * *

A program like ADAPTER, which allows a computer user to change or use multiple operating systems while maintaining the same software, is highly desirable. It saves the user the costs, both in time and money, that otherwise would be expended in purchasing new programs, modifying existing systems to run them, and gaining familiarity with their operation. The benefits run both ways. The increased compatibility afforded by an ADAPTER-like component, and its resulting popularity among consumers, makes whatever software in which it is incorporated significantly more marketable.

Starting in 1982, Altai began marketing its own job scheduling program entitled ZEKE. The original version of ZEKE was designed for use in conjunction with a VSE operating system. By late 1983, in response to customer demand, Altai decided to rewrite ZEKE so that it could be run in conjunction with an MVS operating system.

At that time, James P. Williams ("Williams"), then an employee of Altai and now its President, approached Claude F. Arney, III ("Arney"), a computer programmer who worked for CA. Williams and Arney were longstanding friends, and had in fact been co-workers at CA for some time before Williams left CA to work for Altai's predecessor. Williams wanted to recruit Arney to assist Altai in designing an MVS version of ZEKE.

At the time he first spoke with Arney, Williams was aware of both the CA–SCHEDULER and ADAPTER programs. However, Williams was not involved in their development and had never seen the codes of either program. When he asked Arney to come work for Altai, Williams did not know that ADAPTER was a component of CA–SCHEDULER. * * *

Arney went to work creating OSCAR at Altai's offices using the ADAPTER source code. The district court accepted Williams' testimony that no one at Altai, with the exception of Arney, affirmatively knew that Arney had the ADAPTER code, or that he was using it to create OS-

CAR/VSE. However, during this time period, Williams' office was adjacent to Arney's. Williams testified that he and Arney "conversed quite frequently" while Arney was "investigating the source code of ZEKE" and that Arney was in his office "a number of times daily, asking questions." In three months, Arney successfully completed the OSCAR/VSE project. In an additional month he developed an OSCAR/MVS version. When the dust finally settled, Arney had copied approximately 30% of OSCAR's code from CA's ADAPTER program. The first generation of OSCAR programs was known as OSCAR 3.4. From 1985 to August 1988, Altai used OSCAR 3.4 in its ZEKE product, as well as in programs entitled ZACK and ZEBB. In late July 1988, CA first learned that Altai may have appropriated parts of ADAPTER. After confirming its suspicions, CA secured copyrights on its 2.1 and 7.0 versions of CA–SCHEDULER. CA then brought this copyright and trade secret misappropriation action against Altai.

Apparently, it was upon receipt of the summons and complaint that Altai first learned that Arney had copied much of the OSCAR code from ADAPTER. After Arney confirmed to Williams that CA's accusations of copying were true, Williams immediately set out to survey the damage. Without ever looking at the ADAPTER code himself, Williams learned from Arney exactly which sections of code Arney had taken from ADAPTER.

Upon advice of counsel, Williams initiated OSCAR's rewrite. The project's goal was to save as much of OSCAR 3.4 as legitimately could be used, and to excise those portions which had been copied from ADAPTER. Arney was entirely excluded from the process, and his copy of the ADAPTER code was locked away. Williams put eight other programmers on the project, none of whom had been involved in any way in the development of OSCAR 3.4. Williams provided the programmers with a description of the ZEKE operating system services so that they could rewrite the appropriate code. The rewrite project took about six months to complete and was finished in mid-November 1989. The resulting program was entitled OSCAR 3.5.

From that point on, Altai shipped only OSCAR 3.5 to its new customers. Altai also shipped OSCAR 3.5 as a "free upgrade" to all customers that had previously purchased OSCAR 3.4. While Altai and Williams acted responsibly to correct Arney's literal copying of the ADAPTER program, copyright infringement had occurred. * * *

We address * * * CA's appeal from the district court's rulings that: (1) Altai was not liable for copyright infringement in developing OSCAR 3.5; and (2) in developing both OSCAR 3.4 and 3.5, Altai was not liable for misappropriating CA's trade secrets.

CA makes two arguments. First, CA contends that the district court applied an erroneous method for determining whether there exists substantial similarity between computer programs, and thus, erred in determining that OSCAR 3.5 did not infringe the copyrights held on the different versions of its CA–SCHEDULER program. CA asserts that the test applied by the district court failed to account sufficiently for a computer program's non-literal elements. Second, CA maintains that the district court erroneously concluded that its state law trade secret claims had been preempted by the federal Copyright Act. See 17 U.S.C. § 301(a). We shall address each argument in turn.

In any suit for copyright infringement, the plaintiff must establish its ownership of a valid copyright, and that the defendant copied the copyrighted work. * * * The plaintiff may prove defendant's copying either by direct evidence or, as is most often the case, by showing that (1) the defendant had access to the plaintiff's copyrighted work and (2) that defendant's work is substantially similar to the plaintiff's copyrightable material.

As a general matter, and to varying degrees, copyright protection extends beyond a literary work's strictly textual form to its non-literal components. As we have said, "[i]t is of course essential to any protection of literary property ... that the right cannot be limited literally to the text, else a plagiarist would escape by immaterial variations." *Nichols v. Universal Pictures Co.*, 45 F.2d 119, 121 (2d Cir.1930) (L. Hand, J.), cert. denied, 282 U.S. 902, 51 S.Ct. 216, 75 L.Ed. 795 (1931). Thus, where "the fundamental essence or structure of one work is duplicated in another," 3 Nimmer, § 13.03[A][1], at 13–24, courts have found copyright infringement. * * *

It is now well settled that the literal elements of computer programs, i.e., their source and object codes, are the subject of copyright protection. * * * Here, as noted earlier, Altai admits having copied approximately 30% of the OSCAR 3.4 program from CA's ADAPTER source code, and does not challenge the district court's related finding of infringement.

In this case, the hotly contested issues surround OSCAR 3.5. As recounted above, OSCAR 3.5 is the product of Altai's carefully orchestrated rewrite of OSCAR 3.4. After the purge, none of the ADAPTER source code remained in the 3.5 version; thus, Altai made sure that the literal elements of its revamped OSCAR program were no longer substantially similar to the literal elements of CA's ADAPTER.

CA argues that, despite Altai's rewrite of the OSCAR code, the resulting program remained substantially similar to the structure of its ADAPTER program. As discussed above, a program's structure includes its non-literal components such as general flow charts as well as the more specific organization of inter-modular relationships, parameter lists, and macros. In addition to these aspects, CA contends that OSCAR 3.5 is also substantially similar to ADAPTER with respect to the list of services that both ADAPTER and OSCAR obtain from their respective operating systems. We must decide whether and to what extent these elements of computer programs are protected by copyright law. * * *

As a caveat, we note that our decision here does not control infringement actions regarding categorically distinct works, such as certain types of screen displays. These items represent products of computer programs, rather than the programs themselves, and fall under the copyright rubric of audiovisual works. If a computer audiovisual display is copyrighted separately as an audiovisual work, apart from the literary work that generates it (i.e., the program), the display may be protectable regardless of the underlying program's copyright status. See *Stern Elecs., Inc. v. Kaufman*, 669 F.2d 852, 855 (2d Cir.1982) (explaining that an audiovisual works copyright, rather than a copyright on the underlying program, extended greater protection to the sights and sounds generated by a computer video game because the same audiovisual display could be generated by different programs). Of course, the copyright protection that these displays enjoy extends only so far as their expression is protectable. See *Data East USA, Inc. v. Epyx, Inc.*, 862 F.2d 204, 209 (9th Cir.1988). In this case, however, we are concerned not with a program's display, but the program itself, and then with only its non-literal components. In considering the copyrightability of these components, we must refer to venerable doctrines of copyright law.

1) Idea vs. Expression Dichotomy

It is a fundamental principle of copyright law that a copyright does not protect an idea, but only the expression of the idea. See *Baker v. Selden*, 101 U.S. 99, 25 L.Ed. 841 (1879); *Mazer v. Stein*, 347 U.S. 201, 217, 74 S.Ct. 460, 470, 98 L.Ed. 630 (1954). This axiom of common law has been incorporated into the governing statute. Section 102(b) of the Act provides:

> In no case does copyright protection for an original work of authorship extend to any idea, procedure, process, system, method of operation, concept, principle, or discovery, regardless of the form in which it is described, explained, illustrated, or embodied in such work.

17 U.S.C. § 102(b). See also House Report, at 5670 ("Copyright does not preclude others from using ideas or information revealed by the author's work.").

Congress made no special exception for computer programs. To the contrary, the legislative history explicitly states that copyright protects computer programs only "to the extent that they incorporate authorship in programmer's expression of original ideas, as distinguished from the ideas themselves." Id. at 5667; see also id. at 5670 ("Section 102(b) is intended ... to make clear that the expression adopted by the programmer is the copyrightable element in a computer program, and that the actual processes or methods embodied in the program are not within the scope of copyright law.").

Similarly, the National Commission on New Technological Uses of Copyrighted Works ("CONTU") established by Congress to survey the issues generated by the interrelationship of advancing technology and copyright law, see Pub.L. No. 93–573, § 201, 88 Stat. 1873 (1974), recommended, inter alia, that the 1976 Copyright Act "be amended ... to make it explicit that computer programs, to the extent that they embody the author's original creation, are proper subject matter for copyright." See National Commission on New Technological Uses of Copyrighted Works, Final Report 1 (1979) (hereinafter "CONTU Report"). To that end, Congress adopted CONTU's suggestions and amended the Copyright Act by adding, among other things, a provision to 17 U.S.C. § 101 which defined the term "computer program." See Pub.L. No. 96–517, § 10(a), 94 Stat. 3028 (1980). CONTU also "concluded that the idea-expression distinction should be used to determine which aspects of computer programs are copyrightable." CONTU Report, at 44.

Drawing the line between idea and expression is a tricky business. Judge Learned Hand noted that "[n]obody has ever been able to fix that boundary, and nobody ever can." *Nichols*, 45 F.2d at 121. Thirty years later his convictions remained firm. "Obviously, no principle can be stated as to when an imitator has gone beyond copying the 'idea,' and has borrowed its 'expression,'" Judge Hand concluded. "Decisions must therefore inevitably be ad hoc." *Peter Pan Fabrics, Inc. v. Martin Weiner Corp.*, 274 F.2d 487, 489 (2d Cir.1960).

The essentially utilitarian nature of a computer program further complicates the task of distilling its idea from its expression. * * * In order to describe both computational processes and abstract ideas, its content "combines creative and technical expression." * * * The variations of expression found in purely creative compositions, as opposed to those contained in utilitarian works, are not directed towards practical application. For example, a narration of Humpty Dumpty's demise, which would clearly be a creative composition, does not serve the same ends as, say, a recipe for scrambled eggs-which is a more process oriented text. Thus, compared to aesthetic works, computer programs hover even more closely to the elusive boundary line described in § 102(b).

The doctrinal starting point in analyses of utilitarian works, is the seminal case of *Baker v. Selden*, 101 U.S. 99, 25 L.Ed. 841 (1879). * * * The Court held that:

> The fact that the art described in the book by illustrations of lines and figures which are reproduced in practice in the application of the art, makes no difference. Those illustrations are the mere language employed by the author to convey his ideas more clearly. Had he used words of description instead of diagrams (which merely stand in the place of words), there could not be the slightest doubt that others, applying the art to practical use, might lawfully draw the lines and diagrams which were in the author's mind, and which he thus described by words in his book.

The copyright of a work on mathematical science cannot give to the author an exclusive right to the methods of operation which he propounds, or to the diagrams which he employs to explain them, so as to prevent an engineer from using them whenever occasion requires.

Id. at 103.* * *

While *Baker v. Selden* provides a sound analytical foundation, it offers scant guidance on how to separate idea or process from expression, and moreover, on how to further distinguish protectable expression from that expression which "must necessarily be used as incident to" the work's underlying concept. * * *

2) Substantial Similarity Test for Computer Program Structure: Abstraction–Filtration–Comparison

* * * As discussed herein, we think that district courts would be well-advised to undertake a three-step procedure, based on the abstractions test utilized by the district court, in order to determine whether the non-literal elements of two or more computer programs are substantially similar. This approach breaks no new ground; rather, it draws on such familiar copyright doctrines as merger, scenes a faire, and public domain. In taking this approach, however, we are cognizant that computer technology is a dynamic field which can quickly outpace judicial decisionmaking. Thus, in cases where the technology in question does not allow for a literal application of the procedure we outline below, our opinion should not be read to foreclose the district courts of our circuit from utilizing a modified version.

In ascertaining substantial similarity under this approach, a court would first break down the allegedly infringed program into its constituent structural parts. Then, by examining each of these parts for such things as incorporated ideas, expression that is necessarily incidental to those ideas, and elements that are taken from the public domain, a court would then be able to sift out all non-protectable material. Left with a kernel, or possible kernels, of creative expression after following this process of elimination, the court's last step would be to compare this material with the structure of an allegedly infringing program. The result of this comparison will determine whether the protectable elements of the programs at issue are substantially similar so as to warrant a finding of infringement. It will be helpful to elaborate a bit further.

Step One: Abstraction

As the district court appreciated, * * * the theoretic framework for analyzing substantial similarity expounded by Learned Hand in the *Nichols* case is helpful in the present context. In *Nichols*, we enunciated what has now become known as the "abstractions" test for separating idea from expression:

> Upon any work . . . a great number of patterns of increasing generality will fit equally well, as more and more of the incident is left out. The last may perhaps be no more than the most general statement of what the [work] is about, and at times might consist only of its title; but there is a point in this series of abstractions where they are no longer protected, since otherwise the [author] could prevent the use of his "ideas," to which, apart from their expression, his property is never extended.

Nichols, 45 F.2d at 121.

While the abstractions test was originally applied in relation to literary works such as novels and plays, it is adaptable to computer programs. In contrast to the Whelan approach, the abstractions test "implicitly recognizes that any given work may consist of a mixture of numerous ideas and expressions." 3 Nimmer § 13.03[F], at 13–62.34–63.

As applied to computer programs, the abstractions test will comprise the first step in the examination for substantial similarity. Initially, in a manner that resembles reverse engineering on a theoretical plane, a court should dissect the allegedly copied program's structure and isolate each level of abstraction contained within it. This process begins with the code and ends with an articulation of the program's ultimate function. Along the way, it is necessary essentially to retrace and map each of the designer's steps-in the opposite order in which they were taken during the program's creation.

As an anatomical guide to this procedure, the following description is helpful:

> At the lowest level of abstraction, a computer program may be thought of in its entirety as a set of individual instructions organized into a hierarchy of modules. At a higher level of abstraction, the instructions in the lowest-level modules may be replaced conceptually by the functions of those modules. At progressively higher levels of abstraction, the functions of higher-level modules conceptually replace the implementations of those modules in terms of lower-level modules and instructions, until finally, one is left with nothing but the ultimate function of the program.... A program has structure at every level of abstraction at which it is viewed. At low levels of abstraction, a program's structure may be quite complex; at the highest level it is trivial. * * *

Step Two: Filtration

Once the program's abstraction levels have been discovered, the substantial similarity inquiry moves from the conceptual to the concrete. Professor Nimmer suggests, and we endorse, a "successive filtering method" for separating protectable expression from non-protectable material. See generally 3 Nimmer § 13.03[F]. This process entails examining the structural components at each level of abstraction to determine whether their particular inclusion at that level was "idea" or was dictated by considerations of efficiency, so as to be necessarily incidental to that idea; required by factors external to the program itself; or taken from the public domain and hence is nonprotectable expression. * * * The structure of any given program may reflect some, all, or none of these considerations. Each case requires its own fact specific investigation.

Strictly speaking, this filtration serves "the purpose of defining the scope of plaintiff's copyright." *Brown Bag Software v. Symantec Corp.*, 960 F.2d 1465, 1475 (9th Cir.) (endorsing "analytic dissection" of computer programs in order to isolate protectable expression), cert. denied, 506 U.S. 869, 113 S.Ct. 198, 121 L.Ed.2d 141 (1992). By applying well developed doctrines of copyright law, it may ultimately leave behind a "core of protectable material." 3 Nimmer § 13.03[F][5], at 13–72. Further explication of this second step may be helpful.

(a) Elements Dictated by Efficiency

The portion of *Baker v. Selden*, discussed earlier, which denies copyright protection to expression necessarily incidental to the idea being expressed, appears to be the cornerstone for what has developed into the doctrine of merger. The doctrine's underlying principle is that "[w]hen there is essentially only one way to express an idea, the idea and its expression are inseparable and copyright is no bar to copying that expression." *Concrete Machinery Co. v. Classic Lawn Ornaments, Inc.*, 843 F.2d 600, 606 (1st Cir.1988). Under these circumstances, the expression is said to have "merged" with the idea itself. In order not to confer a monopoly of the idea upon the copyright owner, such expression should not be protected. See *Herbert Rosenthal Jewelry Corp. v. Kalpakian*, 446 F.2d 738, 742 (9th Cir.1971).

CONTU recognized the applicability of the merger doctrine to computer programs. In its report to Congress it stated that:

> [C]opyrighted language may be copied without infringing when there is but a limited number of ways to express a given idea.... In the computer context, this means that when specific instructions, even though previously copyrighted, are the only and essential means of accomplishing a given task, their later use by another will not amount to infringement.

CONTU Report, at 20. While this statement directly concerns only the application of merger to program code, that is, the textual aspect of the program, it reasonably suggests that the doctrine fits comfortably within the general context of computer programs.

Furthermore, when one considers the fact that programmers generally strive to create programs "that meet the user's needs in the most efficient manner," * * * the applicability of the merger doctrine to computer programs becomes compelling. In the context of computer program design, the concept of efficiency is akin to deriving the most concise logical proof or formulating the most succinct mathematical computation. Thus, the more efficient a set of modules are, the more closely they approximate the idea or process embodied in that particular aspect of the program's structure.

While, hypothetically, there might be a myriad of ways in which a programmer may effectuate certain functions within a program,-i.e., express the idea embodied in a given subroutine-efficiency concerns may so narrow the practical range of choice as to make only one or two forms of expression workable options. See 3 Nimmer § 13.03[F][2], at 13–63; see also *Whelan*, 797 F.2d at 1243 n. 43 ("It is true that for certain tasks there are only a very limited number of file structures available, and in such cases the structures might not be copyrightable. . . ."). Of course, not all program structure is informed by efficiency concerns. * * * It follows that in order to determine whether the merger doctrine precludes copyright protection to an aspect of a program's structure that is so oriented, a court must inquire "whether the use of this particular set of modules is necessary efficiently to implement that part of the program's process" being implemented. * * * If the answer is yes, then the expression represented by the programmer's choice of a specific module or group of modules has merged with their underlying idea and is unprotected. * * *

Another justification for linking structural economy with the application of the merger doctrine stems from a program's essentially utilitarian nature and the competitive forces that exist in the software marketplace. * * * Working in tandem, these factors give rise to a problem of proof which merger helps to eliminate.

Efficiency is an industry-wide goal. Since, as we have already noted, there may be only a limited number of efficient implementations for any given program task, it is quite possible that multiple programmers, working independently, will design the identical method employed in the allegedly infringed work. Of course, if this is the case, there is no copyright infringement. See *Roth Greeting Cards v. United Card Co.*, 429 F.2d 1106, 1110 (9th Cir.1970); Sheldon, 81 F.2d at 54.

Under these circumstances, the fact that two programs contain the same efficient structure may as likely lead to an inference of independent creation as it does to one of copying. See 3 Nimmer § 13.03[F][2], at 13–65; cf. *Herbert Rosenthal Jewelry Corp.*, 446 F.2d at 741 (evidence of independent creation may stem from defendant's standing as a designer of previous similar works). Thus, since evidence of similarly efficient structure is not particularly probative of copying, it should be disregarded in the overall substantial similarity analysis. See 3 Nimmer § 13.03[F][2], at 13–65.

(b) Elements Dictated By External Factors

We have stated that where "it is virtually impossible to write about a particular historical era or fictional theme without employing certain 'stock' or standard literary devices," such expression is not copyrightable. *Hoehling v. Universal City Studios, Inc.*, 618 F.2d 972, 979 (2d Cir.), cert. denied, 449 U.S. 841, 101 S.Ct. 121, 66 L.Ed.2d 49 (1980). For example, the Hoehling case was an infringement suit stemming from several works on the Hindenberg disaster. There we concluded that similarities in representations of German beer halls, scenes depicting German greetings such as "Heil Hitler," or the singing of certain German songs would not lead to a finding of infringement because they were " 'indispensable, or at least standard, in the treatment of' " life in Nazi Germany. Id. (quoting Alexander v. Haley, 460 F.Supp. 40, 45 (S.D.N.Y.1978)). This is known as the scenes a faire doctrine, and like "merger," it has its analogous application to computer programs. * * *

Professor Nimmer points out that "in many instances it is virtually impossible to write a program to perform particular functions in a specific computing environment without employing standard techniques." 3 Nimmer § 13.03[F][3], at 13–65. This is a result of the fact that a programmer's freedom of design choice is often circumscribed by extrinsic considerations such as (1) the mechanical specifications of the computer on which a particular program is intended to run; (2) compatibility requirements of other programs with which a program is designed to operate in conjunction; (3) computer manufacturers' design standards; (4) demands of the industry being serviced; and (5) widely accepted programming practices within the computer industry. Id. at 13–66–71.

(c) Elements taken From the Public Domain

Closely related to the non-protectability of scenes a faire, is material found in the public domain. Such material is free for the taking and cannot be appropriated by a single author even though it is included in a copyrighted work. See *E.F. Johnson Co. v. Uniden Corp. of America*, 623 F.Supp. 1485, 1499 (D.Minn.1985). We see no reason to make an exception to this rule for elements of a computer program that have entered the public domain by virtue of freely accessible program exchanges and the like. See 3 Nimmer § 13.03[F][4]. Thus, a court must also filter out this material from the allegedly infringed program before it makes the final inquiry in its substantial similarity analysis.

Step Three: Comparison

The third and final step of the test for substantial similarity that we believe appropriate for non-literal program components entails a comparison. Once a court has sifted out all elements of the allegedly infringed program which are "ideas" or are dictated by efficiency or external factors, or taken from the public domain, there may remain a core of protectable expression. In terms of a work's copyright value, this is the golden nugget. * * * At this point, the court's substantial similarity inquiry focuses on whether the defendant copied any aspect of this protected expression, as well as an assessment of the copied portion's relative importance with respect to the plaintiff's overall program. * * *

3) Policy Considerations

We are satisfied that the three step approach we have just outlined not only comports with, but advances the constitutional policies underlying the Copyright Act. * * * CA and some amici argue against the type of approach that we have set forth on the grounds that it will be a disincentive for future computer program research and development. At bottom, they claim that if programmers are not guaranteed broad copyright protection for their work, they will not invest the extensive time, energy and funds required to design and improve program structures. While they have a point, their argument cannot carry the day. The interest of the copyright law is not in simply conferring a monopoly on industrious persons, but in advancing the public welfare through rewarding artistic creativity, in a manner that permits the free use and development of non-protectable ideas and processes. * * *

Recently, the Supreme Court has emphatically reiterated that "[t]he primary objective of copyright is not to reward the labor of authors...." *Feist Publications, Inc. v. Rural Tel. Serv. Co.,* 499 U.S. 340, 349, 111 S.Ct. 1282, 1290, 113 L.Ed.2d 358 (1991) (emphasis added). While the *Feist* decision deals primarily with the copyrightability of purely factual compilations, its underlying tenets apply to much of the work involved in computer programming. *Feist* put to rest the "sweat of the brow" doctrine in copyright law. Id. at 361, 111 S.Ct. at 1295. The rationale of that doctrine "was that copyright was a reward for the hard work that went into compiling facts." Id. at 353, 111 S.Ct. at 1291. The Court flatly rejected this justification for extending copyright protection, noting that it "eschewed the most fundamental axiom of copyright law-that no one may copyright facts or ideas." Id.* * *

Generally, we think that copyright registration-with its indiscriminating availability-is not ideally suited to deal with the highly dynamic technology of computer science. Thus far, many of the decisions in this area reflect the courts' attempt to fit the proverbial square peg in a round hole. * * * [A]t least one commentator have suggested that patent registration, with its exacting up-front novelty and non-obviousness requirements, might be the more appropriate rubric of protection for intellectual property of this kind. See Randell M. Whitmeyer, Comment, A Plea for Due Processes: Defining the Proper Scope of Patent Protection for Computer Software, 85 Nw.U.L.REV. 1103, 1123–25 (1991); see also *Lotus Dev. Corp. v. Borland Int'l, Inc.,* 788 F.Supp. 78, 91 (D.Mass.1992) (discussing the potentially supplemental relationship between patent and copyright protection in the context of computer programs). In any event, now that more than 12 years have passed since CONTU issued its final report, the resolution of this specific issue could benefit from further legislative investigation-perhaps a CONTU II. In the meantime, Congress has made clear that computer programs are literary works entitled to copyright protection. Of course, we shall abide by these instructions, but in so doing we must not impair the overall integrity of copyright law. While incentive based arguments in favor of broad copyright protection are perhaps attractive from a pure policy perspective, see *Lotus Dev. Corp.,* 740 F.Supp. at 58, ultimately, they have a corrosive effect on certain fundamental tenets of copyright doctrine. If the test we have outlined results in narrowing the scope of protection, as we expect it will, that result flows from applying, in accordance with Congressional intent, long-standing principles of copyright law to computer programs. Of course, our decision is also informed by our concern that these fundamental principles remain undistorted. * * * [Author's note: The court goes on to apply the three step test to the facts of this case and to analyze the possible preemption of the trade secret claim by the copyright claim.]

CONCLUSION

In adopting the above three step analysis for substantial similarity between the non-literal elements of computer programs, we seek to insure two things: (1) that programmers may receive appropriate copyright protection for innovative utilitarian works containing expression; and (2) that non-protectable technical expression remains in the public domain for others to use freely as building blocks in their own work. At first blush, it may seem counter-intuitive that someone who has benefitted to some degree from illicitly obtained material can emerge from an infringement suit relatively unscathed. However, so long as the appropriated material consists of non-protectable expression, "[t]his result is neither unfair nor unfortunate. It is the means by which copyright advances the progress of science and art." * * *

Furthermore, we underscore that so long as trade secret law is employed in a manner that does not encroach upon the exclusive domain of the Copyright Act, it is an appropriate means by which to secure compensation for software espionage.

D. ARCHITECTURAL WORKS

T–PEG, INC. v. VERMONT TIMBER WORKS, INC.

United States Court of Appeals, First Circuit, 2006.
459 F.3d 97.

LYNCH, CIRCUIT JUDGE.

This case is the first occasion for us to address a copyright infringement suit under the Architectural Works Copyright Protection Act ("AWCPA"), Pub.L. No. 101–650, §§ 701–706, 104 Stat. 5089, 5133–34 (1990) (codified in scattered sections of 17 U.S.C.), which created a new category of copyrightable subject matter for "architectural works." 17 U.S.C. § 102(a)(8).

The plaintiffs, T–Peg, Inc. and Timberpeg East, Inc. (collectively, "Timberpeg"), sell both architectural designs and the associated packages of material for the construction of timberframed homes. Timberpeg created architectural plans for a home for Stanley Isbitski in Salisbury, New Hampshire. The central feature of those plans was the timberframed main house, although the plans did not show a completed final architectural design for the actual timberframe. The plaintiffs registered their second set of preliminary plans as an architectural work with the Copyright Office, and maintained ownership over the copyright in the work embodied in the plans.

Isbitski, however, never purchased a construction materials package and final plans from Timberpeg. He did file the registered plans with the Town of Salisbury in order to get a building permit. Isbitski hired defendant, Vermont Timber Works, Inc. ("VTW"), to erect a timberframe for his home. VTW erected its timberframe, but Isbitski never completed his home. A later owner bought the property and completed the home.

Timberpeg filed suit against both Isbitski and VTW, claiming, inter alia, that the timberframe designed through shop drawings and constructed by VTW for Isbitski infringed Timberpeg's copyright in the architectural work. This appeal concerns only the copyright infringement claim against VTW. * * *

III.

Before turning to the specific arguments on appeal, we discuss the governing framework of copyright law and the AWCPA. The AWCPA extended copyright protection to a class of works called "architectural works," 17 U.S.C. § 102(a)(8), which are defined as

> "the design of a building as embodied in any tangible medium of expression, including a building, architectural plans, or drawings. The work includes the overall form as well as the arrangement and composition of spaces and elements in the design, but does not include individual standard features." 17 U.S.C. § 101.

Timberpeg argues that this definition is broad, and that VTW's timberframe (as reflected in the shop drawings and as constructed) infringes Timberpeg's copyright in the architectural work as embodied in its second, registered preliminary plans and including a particular configuration of elements which together form the work.

We first briefly lay out the requirements of a claim of copyright infringement.

A. *Copyright Infringement*

Under the Copyright Act, "[c]opyright protection subsists ... in original works of authorship fixed in any tangible medium of expression, now known or later developed, from which they can be perceived, reproduced, or otherwise communicated, either directly or with the aid of a machine or device." 17 U.S.C. § 102(a). An "architectural work" is a work of authorship. *Id.* § 102(a)(8). A copyright holder has certain exclusive rights to the work, including the right to reproduce all or any part of the copyrighted work. *Id.* § 106; see also *Johnson v. Gordon*, 409 F.3d 12, 17 (1st Cir.2005). One infringes a copyright when he or she violates one of the exclusive rights to a work held by a copyright owner, and the owner has the right to sue for infringement. *See* 17 U.S.C. § 501.

"To establish copyright infringement under the Copyright Act, 'two elements must be proven: (1) ownership of a valid copyright, and (2) copying of constituent elements of the work that are original.' " *Johnson,* 409 F.3d at 17 (quoting *Feist Publ'ns, Inc. v. Rural Tel. Serv. Co.,* 499 U.S. 340, 361, 111 S.Ct. 1282, 113 L.Ed.2d 358 (1991)); see also *Yankee Candle Co. v. Bridgewater Candle Co.,* 259 F.3d 25, 33 (1st Cir.2001); *Segrets, Inc. v. Gillman Knitwear Co.,* 207 F.3d 56, 60 (1st Cir.2000). Proving "copying of constituent elements of the work that are original" (the second element of the *Feist* test) itself involves two steps: the plaintiff must show (a) that the defendant actually copied the work as a factual matter, either through direct evidence or through indirect means, *see Yankee Candle Co.,* 259 F.3d at 33; *Segrets,* 207 F.3d at 60, and (b) that the defendant's "copying of the copyrighted material was so extensive that it rendered the infringing and copyrighted works 'substantially similar,' " * * *

In an infringement action, the burden is on the plaintiff to prove these elements. *Id.* VTW does not challenge Timberpeg's ownership of a valid copyright in this case. This leaves the question of whether VTW "cop[ied] constituent elements of the work that are original." * * *

B. *The Architectural Works Copyright Protection Act*

Historically, copyright law provided limited protection to works of architecture. Architectural plans, while not explicitly mentioned in the Copyright Act of 1976, were covered under a provision affording protection to "pictorial, graphic, and sculptural works." 17 U.S.C. § 102(a)(5)[.] * * *

This began to change with the accession of the United States to the Berne Convention for the Protection of Literary and Artistic Works, Sept. 9, 1886, *as last revised* July 24, 1971 *and amended* Sept. 28, 1979, S. Treaty Doc. No. 99–27, 1161 U.N.T.S. 30. The Berne Convention requires protection for "works of . . . architecture" as distinct from "illustrations, maps, plans, sketches and three-dimensional works relative to . . . architecture." * * * The United States joined the Berne Convention with the passage of the Berne Convention Implementation Act of 1988 ("BCIA")[.] * * * While the BCIA amended the definition of "pictorial, graphic, and sculptural works" to explicitly include "architectural plans," * * * (codified at 17 U.S.C. § 101), it did not explicitly extend protection to "architectural works," as distinct from architectural plans.

To ensure United States' compliance with the requirements of the Berne Convention, the AWCPA was signed into law on December 1, 1990. * * * The AWCPA added "architectural works" as a new category of copyrightable works. 17 U.S.C. § 102(a)(8). The legislative history makes it clear that "[p]rotection for architectural plans, drawings, and models as pictorial, graphic, or sculptural works under section 102(a)(5) . . . is unaffected by" the AWCPA. * * *

The definition of an "architectural work," 17 U.S.C. § 101, quoted in full above, has three main components. First, an "architectural work" is the "design of a building as embodied in any tangible medium of expression." * * * The definition provides three exemplars of such a tangible medium of expression—"a building, architectural plans, or drawings"— although these are not the only possible media of expression. * * * According to the legislative history for the AWCPA, "there was concern that a defendant with access to the plans or drawings could construct an identical building but escape liability so long as the plans or drawings were not copied." * * * To close this potential gap, the bill was reworded to expand the definition of an architectural work to encompass a building design "as embodied in any tangible medium of expression." * * *

This more expansive definition means that the holder of a copyright in an architectural plan (such as Timberpeg) has two forms of protection, one under the provision for an "architectural work" under 17 U.S.C. § 102(a)(8), and another under the provision for a "pictorial, graphical, or sculptural work" under 17 U.S.C. § 102(a)(5). The legislative history confirms this point. * * * The two avenues of protection are slightly different in scope, as discussed below. As Timberpeg made clear in its motion for reconsideration before the district court, its "central theory" is based on the protection afforded architectural works under § 102(a)(8) rather than the protection afforded architectural plans under § 102(a)(5).

The second component of the definition is that an architectural work "includes the overall form as well as the arrangement and composition of spaces and elements in the design." 17 U.S.C. § 101. According to the legislative history,

> [t]he phrase 'arrangement and composition of spaces and elements' recognizes that: (1) creativity in architecture frequently takes the form of a selection, coordination, or arrangement of unprotectible elements into an original, protectible whole; (2) an architect may incorporate new, protectible design elements into otherwise standard, unprotectible building features; and (3) interior architecture may be protected.

H.R.Rep. No. 101–735, *reprinted in* 1990 U.S.C.C.A.N. at 6949.

Finally, the definition excludes from the protectable "architectural work" "individual standard features." 17 U.S.C. § 101. The legislative history provides examples of such individual standard features: "common windows, doors, and other staple building components." * * * Non-standard individual features reflecting some amount of originality are not necessarily excluded from copyright protection. * * * Furthermore, while individual standard features may not be individually copyrightable, as the quoted legislative history above confirms, the combination of such standard features may be copyrightable.* * *

Under the Copyright Act, architectural works are, in at least one sense, "subject to a standard of copyrightability more generous than that accorded pictorial, graphic or sculptural works." * * * Under 17 U.S.C. § 101, pictorial, graphic, and sculptural works ... include works of artistic craftsmanship insofar as their form *but not their mechanical or utilitarian aspects* are concerned; the design of a useful article, as defined in this section, shall be considered a pictorial, graphic, or sculptural work only if, and only to the extent that, such design incorporates pictorial, graphic, or sculptural features that can be identified separately from, and are capable of existing independently of, the utilitarian aspects of the article.

* * * The requirement that the protectable elements of a pictorial, graphic, or sculptural work be separated from the "utilitarian aspects" of the work under 17 U.S.C. § 102(a)(5) is known as the "separability test." By contrast, there is no separability test for an architectural work. In the AWCPA, Congress purposefully did not impose such a separability test for determining the copyrightability of architectural works. * * * ("[T]he copyrightability of architectural works shall not be evaluated under the separability test applicable to pictorial, graphic, or sculptural works.").

IV.

* * * On appeal, the arguments center around whether there is a genuine issue of material fact as to substantial similarity. The district court, at least in its first order, also concluded that no reasonable jury could conclude that VTW had actually copied Timberpeg's plans. Since copying is a necessary element of a copyright infringement claim, see *Johnson,* 409 F.3d at 17–18, we would uphold summary judgment if the district court were correct on this ground, and we may affirm on any ground supported by the record, see *Senior,* 449 F.3d at 216. We briefly discuss the evidence of copying and conclude that the district court was not correct.

A. *Actual Copying*

Copying may be proven through direct or circumstantial evidence. * * * Timberpeg points both to direct and to circumstantial evidence of copying, sufficient to create a material issue of fact for a jury.

For direct evidence, Timberpeg points to the letter from VTW's attorneys stating that Isbitski "represented to [VTW] that he paid for and owned a set of plans, which he provided to [VTW] that were drawn by Timberpeg." Timberpeg argues that this letter is an admission by VTW that it relied on the registered preliminary plans. VTW, like the district court, rejects Timberpeg's reliance on the letters, arguing that the letters were not admissions, but to the contrary, state that VTW did not copy Timberpeg's plans. The letter from VTW's attorney does not say whether the plans referenced are the second, registered preliminary plans (about which there is a dispute as to whether VTW saw the plans) or the first, unregistered preliminary plans (which VTW acknowledges it received, but states it did not rely on). This is a factual dispute about the meaning of the admission by counsel, and that issue cannot be resolved on summary judgment.

In the absence of direct evidence of copying—such direct evidence is rare, * * * one of the ways to indirectly establish that the defendant copied the plaintiff's work is to provide evidence that (1) the defendant "enjoyed access to the copyrighted work," and so had the opportunity to copy the work, and (2) "a sufficient degree of similarity exists between the copyrighted work and the allegedly infringing work to give rise to an inference of actual copying." * * * The similarity inquiry used to indirectly establish copying is referred to as "*probative* similarity" and is "somewhat akin to, but different than, the requirement of substantial similarity" that must be shown to prove copyright infringement. * * *

As to access, Timberpeg argues that VTW had access to its registered preliminary plans both because Isbitski had made those plans public by filing them with the Town of Salisbury, and because VTW could have received the plans directly from Isbitski. A trier of fact may impute access when there is "evidence that a third party with whom both the plaintiff and defendant were dealing had possession of plaintiff's work," and the "plaintiff's and defendant's dealings took place concurrently." 4 Nimmer & Nimmer, *supra*, § 13.02[A]. That is the case here.

As to whether there is a genuine issue of material fact as to "probative similarity"—whether "a sufficient degree of similarity exists between the copyrighted work and the allegedly infringing work to give rise to an inference of actual copying"—this analysis merges somewhat with the question of "substantial similarity" (although they are separate questions). We discuss below the similarities and dissimilarities between Timberpeg's registered plans and VTW's frame in the context of the substantial similarity inquiry. We conclude that a reasonable jury could find a sufficient degree of probative similarity exists between Timberpeg's architectural work and VTW's frame "to give rise to an inference of actual copying" for the same reasons a jury could find there is substantial similarity.

B. *Substantial Similarity*

The substantial similarity inquiry "entails proof that the copying was so extensive that it rendered the works so similar that the later work represented a wrongful appropriation of expression." *Johnson,* 409 F.3d at 18. The inquiry focuses not on every aspect of the copyrighted work, but on those " 'aspects of the plaintiff's work [that] are protectible under copyright laws and whether whatever copying took place appropriated those [protected] elements.' " *Id.* at 19 (second alteration in original) (quoting *Matthews v. Freedman,* 157 F.3d 25, 27 (1st Cir.1998)); *see also Feist,* 499 U.S. at 361 (noting that wrongful copying requires showing of "copying of constituent elements of the work *that are original*" (emphasis added)). Summary judgment on substantial similarity is "unusual" but can be warranted on the right set of facts. See *Segrets,* 207 F.3d at 62. "Summary judgment on [substantial similarity] is appropriate only when a rational factfinder, correctly applying the pertinent legal standards, would be compelled to conclude that no substantial similarity exists between the copyrighted work and the allegedly infringing work." *Johnson,* 409 F.3d at 18.

The copyrighted work at issue is Timberpeg's architectural work as embodied in the second preliminary plans. As for the allegedly infringing works, there are both VTW's shop drawings and the frame as actually erected by VTW. The parties have assumed that the frame as erected matches VTW's shop drawings. VTW's shop drawings also reflect certain other features that VTW did not actually build—the exterior walls and the actual staircase (although VTW did build the posts that define the stair bay). We include these features as part of the allegedly infringing work when conducting the similarity analysis.

Substantial similarity can be measured by the "ordinary observer" test. *Id.* Under that test, two works will be said to be substantially similar if a reasonable, ordinary observer, upon examination of the two works, would "conclude that the defendant unlawfully appropriated the plaintiff's protectable expression." *Id.* The two works need not be exact copies to be substantially similar. Differences between the works have some effect on the inquiry, but the mere existence of differences is insufficient to end the matter in the defendant's favor. Id.; see also *Concrete Mach. Co. v. Classic Lawn Ornaments, Inc.,* 843 F.2d 600, 608 (1st Cir.1988) ("Slight or trivial variations between works will not preclude a finding of infringement under the ordinary observer test."). "If the points of dissimilarity not only exceed the points of similarity, but indicate that the remaining points of similarity are, within the context of plaintiff's work, of minimal importance, either quantitatively or qualitatively, then no infringement results." 4 Nimmer & Nimmer, *supra,* § 13.03[B][1][a].

The record shows * * * [a number of similarities] of the following similarities between VTW's shop drawings and Timberpeg's registered plans * * *.

* * * Keeping in mind the definition of an "architectural work" as "includ[ing] the overall form as well as the arrangement and composition of spaces and elements in the design," 17 U.S.C. § 101, we conclude that there are genuine issues of material fact as to substantial similarity.

The district court erred in failing to consider those similarities that went to the "overall form" of the building as well as the "arrangement and composition of spaces and elements." The district court found that the only similarities were in "the idea of a twenty-eight by forty-four foot part of a house, with a stair bay located in a particular position" and so found that no reasonable jury could conclude that VTW's shop drawings were substantially similar to Timberpeg's registered plans.

In fact, the relevant similarities here go beyond those recognized by the district court. At issue here is a particular combination of elements in Timberpeg's architectural work: a portion of a home featuring a timber-frame with a backwards-L-shaped footprint, with a particular arrangement of posts, with certain dimensions and a bump-out along the western wall, featuring a central switchback staircase, with a lofted second floor of a certain floor area and in a certain location, with a certain roof pitch with certain dimensions, and certain wall heights. A reasonable jury, properly considering this combination of elements, could conclude that VTW's frame was substantially similar to Timberpeg's registered plans.

* * * The district court and VTW emphasized that VTW designed only a frame, while Timberpeg's plans did not contain a complete frame design. * * * The question here is whether a reasonable jury could conclude that VTW's frame as drawn and built is substantially similar to

Timberpeg's *architectural work* (which includes "the overall form as well as the arrangement and composition of spaces and elements in the design") as embodied in the second preliminary plans for the Isbitski house. This does not necessarily turn on whether Timberpeg created a complete frame design or not.

* * * Copyright protection exists not only in the architectural work taken as a whole (which includes a particular floor plan and arrangement of external features), but also in protectable portions of the work. Timberpeg bases its claims here on a combination of elements, which, taken together, are protectable under the definition of an architectural work in 17 U.S.C. § 101. As the legislative history for the AWCPA states, "[t]he phrase 'arrangement and composition of spaces and elements' recognizes that ... creativity in architecture frequently takes the form of a selection, coordination, or arrangement of unprotectible elements into an original, protectible whole." H.R.Rep. No. 101–735, *reprinted in* 1990 U.S.C.C.A.N. at 6949. A jury could reasonably conclude that VTW's frame is substantially similar to these protectable elements of Timberpeg's architectural work. The fact that VTW's frame might not necessarily result in *other* elements being taken from Timberpeg's architectural work is not dispositive.

VTW also considers the differences in the posts between Timberpeg's plan and VTW's frame to be dispositive. * * * Timberpeg argues that differences in almost all of the posts are measured on the scale of inches rather than feet. VTW has not argued that Timberpeg is wrong on this point, and has not demonstrated that no reasonable jury would find the differences insignificant. VTW makes general statements that certain posts have a different size, orientation, or notching, but the actual measure of the differences is important to evaluating substantial similarity; a difference of a few feet obviously weighs more strongly against substantial similarity than a difference of a few inches. * * *

VTW also relies on the difference in the size of the kitchen bump-out and the fact that Timberpeg's second preliminary plan contemplated a common rafter style, whereas the VTW frame featured a bent style * * * is evidence for the jury to weigh.

This analysis alone requires reversal. We also comment on one other point to give guidance to the district court and to clarify an earlier decision of ours.

Timberpeg and VTW both introduced reports prepared by expert witnesses. The district court rejected any reference to expert affidavits in the context of substantial similarity * * *. We have not, however, uniformly rejected the use of expert testimony on substantial similarity. *See Johnson,* 409 F.3d at 20 (noting that the plaintiff's "burden of establishing both probative similarity ... and substantial similarity ... [are] dependent on three purported similarities (points one, two, and seven in Mr. John's [expert] report)"). Moreover, the need for expert testimony may be greater in cases involving complex subject matters where an ordinary observer may find it difficult to properly evaluate the similarity of two works without the aid of expert testimony. As Nimmer notes, "[a] special challenge is posed in adjusting the traditional categories of substantial similarity to the burgeoning areas of technology protected by copyright." 4 Nimmer & Nimmer, *supra*, § 13.03[E][4]. * * *

The issue of whether VTW's shop drawings and constructed frame were substantially similar to Timberpeg's architectural work as embodied in the second preliminary plans for the Isbitski home is one for a jury to decide after trial. At present there are genuine issues of material fact both as to copying and as to substantial similarity, making the question one that cannot be resolved on summary judgment.

We reverse.

V. DERIVATIVE WORKS

The statutory definition of a derivative work is set forth in 17 U.S.C. § 101.

A "derivative work" is a work based upon one or more preexisting works, such as a translation, musical arrangement, dramatization, fictionalization, motion picture version, sound recording, art reproduction, abridgment, condensation, or any other form in which a work may be recast, transformed, or adapted. A work consisting of editorial revisions, annotations, elaborations, or other modifications which, as a whole, represent an original work of authorship, is a "derivative work".

The statute also specifically notes the terms of compilations and derivative works:

§ 103. Subject matter of copyright: Compilations and derivative works

(a) The subject matter of copyright as specified by section 102 includes compilations and derivative works, but protection for a work employing preexisting material in which copyright subsists does not extend to any part of the work in which such material has been used unlawfully.

(b) The copyright in a compilation or derivative work extends only to the material contributed by the author of such work, as distinguished from the preexisting material employed in the work, and does not imply any exclusive right in the preexisting material. The copyright in such work is independent of, and does not affect or enlarge the scope, duration, ownership, or subsistence of, any copyright protection in the preexisting material.

The report of the House (H.R. REP. 94–1476, 1976 U.S.C.C.A.N. 5659) provides this analysis of compilations and derivative rights:

SECTION 103. COMPILATIONS AND DERIVATIVE WORKS

Section 103 complements section 102: A compilation or derivative work is copyrightable if it represents an "original work of authorship" and falls within one or more of the categories listed in section 102. Read together, the two sections make plain that the criteria of copyrightable subject matter stated in section 102 apply with full force to works that are entirely original and to those containing preexisting material. Section 103(b) is also intended to define, more sharply and clearly than does section 7 of the present law, the important interrelationship and correlation between protection of preexisting and of "new" material in a particular work. The most important point here is one that is commonly misunderstood today: copyright in a "new version" covers only the material added by the later author, and has no effect one way or the other on the copyright or public domain status of the preexisting material.

Between them the terms "compilations" and "derivative works" which are defined in section 101, comprehend every copyrightable work that employs preexisting material or data of any kind. There is necessarily some overlapping between the two, but they basically represent different concepts. A "compilation" results from a process of selecting, bringing together, organizing, and arranging previously existing material of all kinds, regardless of whether the individual items in the material have been or ever could have been subject to copyright. A "derivative work," on the other hand, requires a process of recasting, transforming, or adapting "one or more preexisting works"; the "preexisting work" must come within the general subject matter of copyright set forth in section 102, regardless of whether it is or was ever copyrighted.

See generally, Goldstein, *Derivative Rights and Derivative Works in Copyright* 30 J. Copyright Soc'y 209 (1983); see also Cohen, *When Does a Work Infringe the Derivative Works Right of A Copyright Owner?*, 17 Cardozo Arts & Ent. L.J. 623 (1999).

SCHROCK v. LEARNING CURVE INTERN., INC.

United States Court of Appeals for the Seventh Circuit, 2009.
586 F.3d 513.

SYKES, CIRCUIT JUDGE.

HIT Entertainment ("HIT") owns the copyright to the popular "Thomas & Friends" train characters, and it licensed Learning Curve International ("Learning Curve") to make toy figures of its characters. Learning Curve in turn hired Daniel Schrock, a professional photographer, to take pictures of the toys for promotional materials. Learning Curve used Schrock's services on a regular basis for about four years and thereafter continued to use some of his photographs in its advertising and on product packaging. After Learning Curve stopped giving him work, Schrock registered his photos for copyright protection and sued Learning Curve and HIT for infringement.

The district court granted summary judgment for the defendants, holding that Schrock has no copyright in the photos. The court classified the photos as "derivative works" under the Copyright Act-derivative, that is, of the "Thomas & Friends" characters, for which HIT owns the copyright-and held that Schrock needed permission from Learning Curve (HIT's licensee) not only to make the photographs but also to copyright them. Because Schrock had permission to make but not permission to copyright the photos, the court dismissed his claim for copyright infringement.

We reverse. We assume for purposes of this decision that the district court correctly classified Schrock's photographs as derivative works. It does not follow, however, that Schrock needed authorization from Learning Curve to copyright the photos. As long as he was authorized to make the photos (he was), he owned the copyright in the photos to the extent of their incremental original expression. In requiring permission to make and permission to copyright the photos, the district court relied on language in *Gracen v. Bradford Exchange*, 698 F.2d 300 (7th Cir.1983), suggesting that both are required for copyright in a derivative work. We have more recently explained, however, that copyright in a derivative work arises by operation of law-not through authority from the owner of the copyright in the underlying work-although the parties may alter this default rule by agreement. See *Liu v. Price Waterhouse LLP*, 302 F.3d 749, 755 (7th Cir.2002). Schrock created the photos with permission and therefore owned the copyright to the photos provided they satisfied the other requirements for copyright and the parties did not contract around the default rule.

We also take this opportunity to clarify another aspect of *Gracen* that is prone to misapplication. *Gracen* said that "a derivative work must be substantially different from the underlying work to be copyrightable." 698 F.2d at 305. This statement should not be understood to require a heightened standard of originality for copyright in a derivative work. We have more recently explained that "the only 'originality' required for [a] new work to be copyrightable ... is enough expressive variation from public-domain or other existing works to enable the new work to be readily distinguished from its predecessors." *Bucklew v. Hawkins, Ash, Baptie & Co., LLP*, 329 F.3d 923, 929 (7th Cir.2003). Here, Schrock's photos of Learning Curve's "Thomas & Friends" toys possessed sufficient incremental original expression to qualify for copyright.

I. Background

HIT is the owner of the copyright in the "Thomas & Friends" properties, and Learning Curve is a producer and distributor of children's toys. HIT and Learning Curve entered into a licensing agreement granting Learning Curve a license to create and market toys based on HIT's characters. HIT and Learning Curve maintain (through an affidavit of HIT's vice-president of licensing) that HIT retained all intellectual-property rights in the works produced under the license. The licensing agreement, however, is not in the record.

In 1999 Learning Curve retained Daniel Schrock to take product photographs of its toys, including those based on HIT's characters, for use in promotional materials. On numerous occasions during the next four years, Schrock photographed several lines of Learning Curve's toys, including many of the "Thomas & Friends" toy trains, related figures, and train-set accessories. * * * Schrock invoiced Learning Curve for this work, and some of the invoices included "usage restrictions" purporting to limit Learning Curve's use of his photographs to two years. Learning Curve paid the invoices in full-in total more than $400,000.

Learning Curve stopped using Schrock's photography services in mid–2003 but continued to use some of his photos in its printed advertising, on packaging, and on the internet. In 2004 Schrock registered his photos for copyright protection and sued HIT and Learning Curve for infringement; he also alleged several state-law claims. HIT and Learning Curve moved for summary judgment, arguing primarily that Schrock's photos were derivative works and not sufficiently original to claim copyright protection, and that neither HIT nor Learning Curve ever authorized Schrock to copyright the photos. They argued in the alternative that Schrock granted them an unlimited oral license to use the photos. * * *

As a general matter, a plaintiff asserting copyright infringement must prove: "(1) ownership of a valid copyright, and (2) copying of constituent elements of the work that are original." *Feist Publ'ns, Inc. v. Rural Tel. Serv. Co.*, 499 U.S. 340, 361, 111 S.Ct. 1282, 113 L.Ed.2d 358 (1991). There is no dispute here about copying; Learning Curve used Schrock's photos in its promotional materials. The focus instead is on the validity of Schrock's asserted copyright in the photos. The Copyright Act provides that "[c]opyright protection subsists ... in original works of authorship fixed in any tangible medium of expression ... from which they can be perceived, reproduced, or otherwise communicated, either directly or with the aid of a machine or device." 17 U.S.C. § 102(a). In this circuit, copyrightability is an issue of law for the court. *Gaiman v. McFarlane*, 360 F.3d 644, 648–49 (7th Cir.2004). * * *

The Copyright Act specifically grants the author of a derivative work copyright protection in the incremental original expression he contributes as long as the derivative work does not infringe the underlying work. * * * The copyright in a derivative work, however, "extends only to the material contributed by the author of such work, as distinguished from the preexisting material employed in the work." 17 U.S.C. § 103(b).

A. Photographs as Derivative Works

Whether photographs of a copyrighted work are derivative works is the subject of deep disagreement among courts and commentators alike. See 1 Melville B. Nimmer & David Nimmer, Nimmer on Copyright § 3.03[C][1], at 3–20.3 (Aug.2009). The district court held that Schrock's photos came within the definition of derivative works because they "recast, transformed, or adapted" the three-dimensional toys into a different, two-dimensional medium. * * *

The classification of Schrock's photos as derivative works does not affect the applicable legal standard for determining copyrightability, although as we have noted, it does determine the scope of copyright protection. Accordingly, we will assume without deciding that each of Schrock's photos qualifies as a derivative work within the meaning of the Copyright Act.

B. Originality and Derivative Works

As a constitutional and statutory matter, "[t]he sine qua non of copyright is originality." *Feist Publ'ns, Inc.*, 499 U.S. at 345, 111 S.Ct. 1282; see 17 U.S.C. § 102. Originality in this context "means only that the work was independently created by the author ... and that it possesses at least some minimal degree of creativity." *Feist Publ'ns, Inc.*, 499 U.S. at 345, 111 S.Ct. 1282. The Supreme Court emphasized in *Feist* that "the requisite level of creativity is extremely low; even a slight amount will suffice." Id. The Court also explained that "[o]riginality does not signify novelty; a work may be original even though it closely resembles other works." Id. What is required is "independent creation plus a modicum of creativity." Id. at 346, 111 S.Ct. 1282.

Federal courts have historically applied a generous standard of originality in evaluating photographic works for copyright protection. * * * In some cases, the original expression may be found in the staging and creation of the scene depicted in the photograph. See, e.g., *Mannion v. Coors Brewing Co.*, 377 F.Supp.2d 444, 452 (S.D.N.Y.2005). But in many cases, the photographer does not invent the scene or create the subject matter depicted in it. Rather, the original expression he contributes lies in the rendition of the subject matter-that is, the effect created by the combination of his choices of perspective, angle, lighting, shading, focus, lens, and so on. See id.; *Rogers v. Koons*, 960 F.2d 301, 307 (2d Cir.1992) ("Elements of originality in a photograph may include posing the subjects, lighting, angle, selection of film and camera, evoking the desired expression, and almost any other variant involved."). Most photographs contain at least some originality in their rendition, see *Mannion*, 377 F.Supp.2d at 452 ("Unless a photograph replicates another work with total or near-total fidelity, it will be at least somewhat original in the rendition."), except perhaps for a very limited class of photographs that can be characterized as "slavish copies" of an underlying work, *Bridgeman Art Library, Ltd. v. Corel Corp.*, 25 F.Supp.2d 421, 427 (S.D.N.Y.1998) (finding no originality in transparencies of paintings where the goal was to reproduce those works exactly and thus to minimize or eliminate any individual expression).

Our review of Schrock's photographs convinces us that they do not fall into the narrow category of photographs that can be classified as "slavish copies," lacking any independently created expression. To be sure, the photographs are accurate depictions of the three-dimensional "Thomas & Friends" toys, but Schrock's artistic and technical choices combine to create a two-dimensional image that is subtly but nonetheless sufficiently his own. This is confirmed by Schrock's deposition testimony describing his creative process in depicting the toys. Schrock explained how he used various camera and lighting techniques to make the toys look more "life like," "personable," and "friendly." He explained how he tried to give the toys "a little bit of dimension" and that it was his goal to make the toys "a little bit better than what they look like when you actually see them on the shelf." The original expression in the representative sample is not particularly great (it was not meant to be), but it is enough under the applicable standard to warrant the limited copyright protection accorded derivative works under § 103(b).

The defendants' [second] argument is that it is not enough that Schrock's photographs might pass the ordinary test for originality; they claim that as derivative works, the photos are subject to a higher standard of originality. A leading copyright commentator disagrees. The Nimmer treatise maintains that the quantum of originality required for copyright in a derivative work is the same as that required for copyright in any other work. See 1 Nimmer on Copyright § 3.01, at 3–2, § 3.03[A], at 3–7. More particularly, Nimmer says the relevant standard is whether a derivative work contains a "nontrivial" variation from the preexisting work "sufficient to render the derivative work distinguishable from [the] prior work in any meaningful manner." Id. § 3.03[A], at 3–10. The caselaw generally follows this formulation. See, e.g., *Eden Toys, Inc. v. Florelee Undergarment Co.*, 697 F.2d 27, 34–35 (2d Cir.1982) (holding that numerous minor changes in an illustration of Paddington Bear were sufficiently nontrivial because they combined to give Paddington a "different, cleaner 'look' ''); *Millworth Converting Corp. v. Slifka*, 276 F.2d 443, 445 (2d Cir.1960) (holding that embroidered reproduction of a public-domain embroidery of Peter Pan was sufficiently distinguishable because the latter gave a "three-dimensional look" to the former embroidery).

Learning Curve and HIT argue that our decision in *Gracen* established a more demanding standard of originality for derivative works. *Gracen* involved an artistic competition in which artists were invited to submit paintings of the character Dorothy from the Metro–Goldwyn–Mayer ("MGM") movie The Wizard of Oz. Participating artists were given a still photograph of Dorothy from the film as an exemplar, and the paintings were solicited and submitted with the understanding that the best painting would be chosen for a series of collector's plates. *Gracen*, 698 F.2d at 301. * * *

The concern expressed in *Gracen* was that a derivative work could be so similar in appearance to the underlying work that in a subsequent infringement suit brought by a derivative author, it would be difficult to separate the original elements of expression in the derivative and underlying works in order to determine whether one derivative work infringed another. The opinion offered the example of artists A and B who both painted their versions of the Mona Lisa, a painting in the public domain. See *Gracen*, 698 F.2d at 304. "[I]f the difference between the original and A's reproduction is slight, the difference between A's and B's reproductions will also be slight, so that if B had access to A's reproductions the trier of fact will be hard-pressed to decide whether B was copying A or copying the Mona Lisa itself." Id.

No doubt this concern is valid. But nothing in the Copyright Act suggests that derivative works are subject to a more exacting originality requirement than other works of authorship. Indeed, we have explained since *Gracen* that "the only 'originality' required for [a] new work to by copyrightable ... is enough expressive variation from public-domain or other existing works to enable the new work to be readily distinguished from its predecessors." * * * *

We think *Gracen* must be read in light of [cases] on which it relied, and [cases] which followed it. And doing so reveals the following general principles: (1) the originality requirement for derivative works is not more demanding than the originality requirement for other works; and (2) the key inquiry is whether there is sufficient nontrivial expressive variation in the derivative work to make it distinguishable from the underlying work in some meaningful way. This focus on the presence of nontrivial "distinguishable variation" adequately captures the concerns articulated in *Gracen* without unduly narrowing the copyrightability of derivative works. It is worth repeating that the copyright in a derivative work is thin, extending only to the incremental original expression contributed by the author of the derivative work. See 17 U.S.C. § 103(b).

As applied to photographs, we have already explained that the original expression in a photograph generally subsists in its rendition of the subject matter. If the photographer's rendition of a copyrighted work varies enough from the underlying work to enable the photograph to be distinguished from the underlying work (aside from the obvious shift from three dimensions to two, see supra n.3), then the photograph contains sufficient incremental originality to qualify for copyright. Schrock's photos of the "Thomas & Friends" toys are highly accurate product photos but contain minimally sufficient variation in angle, perspective, lighting, and dimension to be distinguishable from the underlying works; they are not "slavish copies." Accordingly, the photos qualify for the limited derivative-work copyright provided by § 103(b). * * * However narrow that copyright might be, it at least protects against the kind of outright copying that occurred here. * * *

C. Authorization and Derivative Works

To be copyrightable, a derivative work must not be infringing. See 17 U.S.C. § 103(a). * * * The owner of the copyright in the underlying work has the exclusive right to "prepare derivative works based upon the copyrighted work," 17 U.S.C. § 106(2), and "it is a copyright infringement to make or sell a derivative work without a license from the owner of the copyright on the work from which the derivative work is derived," * * *

This means the author of a derivative work must have permission to make the work from the owner of the copyright in the underlying work; *Gracen* suggested, however, that the author of a derivative work must also have permission to copyright it. 698 F.2d at 303–04 ("[T]he question is not whether Miss Gracen was licensed to make a derivative work but whether she was also licensed to exhibit [her] painting and to copyright it.... Even if [*Gracen*] was authorized to exhibit her derivative works, she may not have been authorized to copyright them."). The district court relied on this language from *Gracen* to conclude that Schrock has no copyright in his photos because he was not authorized by Learning Curve to copyright them. This was error.

First, *Gracen's* language presupposing a permission-to-copyright requirement was dicta; the case was actually decided on nonoriginality grounds. Id. at 305. More importantly, the dicta was mistaken; there is nothing in the Copyright Act requiring the author of a derivative work to obtain permission to copyright his work from the owner of the copyright in the underlying work. To the contrary, the Act provides that copyright in a derivative work, like copyright in any other work, arises by operation of law once the author's original expression is fixed in a tangible medium. "Copyright protection subsists ... in original works of authorship fixed in any tangible medium of expression," 17 U.S.C. § 102(a), and "[t]he subject matter of copyright ... includes ... derivative works," id. § 103(a). "Copyright in a work protected under this title vests initially in the author or authors of the work." Id. § 201(a); see also *Schiller & Schmidt, Inc. v. Nordisco Corp.*, 969 F.2d 410, 413 (7th Cir.1992) ("The creator of the [intellectual] property is the owner...."). While the author of an original work "may obtain a certificate of copyright, which is 'prima facie evidence' of its validity," *JCW Invs., Inc. v. Novelty, Inc.*, 482 F.3d 910, 915 (7th Cir.2007), "copyright protection begins at the moment of creation of 'original works of authorship,'" id. at 914. This principle applies with equal force to derivative works.

The leading treatise on copyright law confirms this basic understanding. "[T]he right to claim copyright in a noninfringing derivative work arises by operation of law, not through authority from the copyright owner of the underlying work." 1 Nimmer on Copyright § 3.06, at 3–34.34. * * *

In this case, the evidence submitted with the summary-judgment motion does not establish as a matter of law that the parties adjusted Schrock's rights by contract. * * * We cannot tell, however, whether the parties altered this default rule in their agreements. We note that HIT apparently attempted to do so, at least vis-à-vis Learning Curve; it claims that its licensing agreement with Learning Curve expressly retained the intellectual-property rights in all works that were based upon its copyrights. HIT also claims that the licensing agreement prohibited Learning Curve from granting any third parties copyright protection in derivative works based on HIT's copyright. As we have noted, however, the licensing agreement is not in the record.

[REVERSED AND REMANDED]

NOTES

1.   The language of the Copyright Act provides for multiple copyrights in the original work as well as derivatives. Thus, there can be a copyright in the first author, and one in the author of the new derivative material. Both copyrights exist independently of one another and both copyrights have their respective terms and rights of renewal. See generally *Nom Music, Inc. v. William Kaslin*, 343 F.2d 198 (2d Cir. 1965) involving a copyright in the lyrics and melody line of "A Thousand Miles Away" published in 1956 with a statutory copyright secured by Keel Music Publishing Co. Keel assigned its copyright to the plaintiff, but claims it was forfeited for failure to record the assignment in a timely manner. Meanwhile, plaintiff altered the piano arrangement and registered the second version. The court held there were two copyrights, each with lives of their own.

2.   In an attempt to make a movie with R rated content morally acceptable, Clean Flicks of Colorado purchased DVDs of movies, used DeCSS technologies to bypass encryption controls, edited out the "offensive" audio and video portions, and burned the resulting content to a DVD without encryption limitations and controls. Plaintiff Motion Picture Studios sued under Title 17 U.S.C. § 106(1) claiming infringement of their right to reproduce, under § 106(2) infringement of their derivative rights under § 106(2), and infringement of their exclusive right to distribute the materials under § 106(3). Among other defenses, Clean Flicks raised fair use and transformative rights. See *Clean Flicks of Colorado, LLC v. Soderbergh*, 433 F.Supp.2d 1236 (D.Ct. Colo. 2006).

VI.   SELECTED PROBLEMS OF AUTHORSHIP AND CO–AUTHORSHIP

17 U.S.C.A., § 201. Ownership of copyright

(a) **Initial Ownership.**—Copyright in a work protected under this title vests initially in the author or authors of the work. The authors of a joint work are co-owners of copyright in the work.

(b) **Works Made for Hire.**—In the case of a work made for hire, the employer or other person for whom the work was prepared is considered the author for purposes of this title, and, unless the parties have expressly agreed otherwise in a written instrument signed by them, owns all of the rights comprised in the copyright.

The basic proposition is that the person or entity for whom the work was created is the author and owns the copyright as such under copyright law if (1) the work was that of an employee within the scope of employment as understood in agency law; or (2) the parties have expressly agreed that the preparer shall have, or be assigned ownership of the copyright; or (3) it can be clearly demonstrated that the work was not within the scope of employment, or that the work was one of a party acting in the capacity of "independent contractor." Conversely, works that would ordinarily be considered those of an independent contractor or outside the scope of employment can by contractual agreement be treated as "works for hire."

Whether a party is an employee or independent contractor or whether the work was prepared within the ordinary scope of employment of a party otherwise an employee is a mixed question of fact and law. The following case illustrates the distinction between employee and independent contractor and the relevance for copyright ownership.

CCNV v. REID

Supreme Court of the United States, 1989.
490 U.S. 730, 109 S.Ct. 2166, 104 L.Ed.2d 811.

JUSTICE MARSHALL delivered the opinion of the Court.

In this case, an artist and the organization that hired him to produce a sculpture contest the ownership of the copyright in that work. To resolve this dispute, we must construe the "work made for hire" provisions of the Copyright Act of 1976 (Act or 1976 Act), 17 U.S.C. §§ 101 and 201(b), and in particular, the provision in § 101, which defines as a "work made for hire" a "work prepared by an employee within the scope of his or her employment" (hereinafter § 101(1)). * * *

Petitioners are the Community for Creative Non–Violence (CCNV), a nonprofit unincorporated association dedicated to eliminating homelessness in America, and Mitch Snyder, a member and trustee of CCNV. In the fall of 1985, CCNV decided to participate in the annual Christmastime Pageant of Peace in Washington, D.C., by sponsoring a display [of a sculpture] to dramatize the plight of the homeless. * * * Snyder made inquiries to locate an artist to produce the sculpture. He was referred to respondent James Earl Reid, a Baltimore, Maryland, sculptor. In the course of two telephone calls, Reid agreed to sculpt the three human figures. CCNV agreed to make the steam grate and pedestal for the statue. Reid proposed that the work be cast in bronze, at a total cost of approximately $100,000 and taking six to eight months to complete. Snyder rejected that proposal because CCNV did not have sufficient funds, and because the statue had to be completed by December 12 to be included in the pageant. Reid then suggested, and Snyder agreed, that the sculpture would be made of a material known as "Design Cast 62," a synthetic substance that could meet CCNV's monetary and time constraints, could be tinted to resemble bronze, and could withstand the elements. The parties agreed that the project would cost no more than $15,000, not including Reid's services, which he offered to donate. The parties did not sign a written agreement. Neither party mentioned copyright.

After Reid received an advance of $3,000, he made several sketches of figures in various poses. At Snyder's request, Reid sent CCNV a sketch of a proposed sculpture showing the family in a crèche like setting: the mother seated, cradling a baby in her lap; the father standing behind her, bending over her shoulder to touch the baby's foot. Reid testified that

Snyder asked for the sketch to use in raising funds for the sculpture. Snyder testified that it was also for his approval. Reid sought a black family to serve as a model for the sculpture. Upon Snyder's suggestion, Reid visited a family living at CCNV's Washington shelter but decided that only their newly born child was a suitable model. While Reid was in Washington, Snyder took him to see homeless people living on the streets. Snyder pointed out that they tended to recline on steam grates, rather than sit or stand, in order to warm their bodies. From that time on, Reid's sketches contained only reclining figures.

Throughout November and the first two weeks of December 1985, Reid worked exclusively on the statue, assisted at various times by a dozen different people who were paid with funds provided in installments by CCNV. On a number of occasions, CCNV members visited Reid to check on his progress and to coordinate CCNV's construction of the base. CCNV rejected Reid's proposal to use suitcases or shopping bags to hold the family's personal belongings, insisting instead on a shopping cart. Reid and CCNV members did not discuss copyright ownership on any of these visits.

On December 24, 1985, 12 days after the agreed-upon date, Reid delivered the completed statue to Washington. There it was joined to the steam grate and pedestal prepared by CCNV and placed on display near the site of the pageant. Snyder paid Reid the final installment of the $15,000. The statue remained on display for a month. In late January 1986, CCNV members returned it to Reid's studio in Baltimore for minor repairs. Several weeks later, Snyder began making plans to take the statue on a tour of several cities to raise money for the homeless. Reid objected, contending that the Design Cast 62 material was not strong enough to withstand the ambitious itinerary. He urged CCNV to cast the statue in bronze at a cost of $35,000, or to create a master mold at a cost of $5,000. Snyder declined to spend more of CCNV's money on the project.

In March 1986, Snyder asked Reid to return the sculpture. Reid refused. He then filed a certificate of copyright registration for "Third World America" in his name and announced plans to take the sculpture on a more modest tour than the one CCNV had proposed. Snyder, acting in his capacity as CCNV's trustee, immediately filed a competing certificate of copyright registration.

Snyder and CCNV then commenced this action against Reid and his photographer, Ronald Purtee, seeking return of the sculpture and a determination of copyright ownership. [The District Court found the sculpture to be a work made for hire. The Court of Appeals reversed and found that Reid was the copyright owner.] * * * We granted certiorari to resolve a conflict among the Courts of Appeals over the proper construction of the "work made for hire" provisions of the Act. * * * We now affirm. * * *

The Copyright Act of 1976 provides that copyright ownership "vests initially in the author or authors of the work." 17 U.S.C. § 201(a). As a general rule, the author is the party who actually creates the work, that is, the person who translates an idea into a fixed, tangible expression entitled to copyright protection. § 102. The Act carves out an important exception, however, for "works made for hire." If the work is for hire, "the employer or other person for whom the work was prepared is considered the author" and owns the copyright, unless there is a written agreement to the contrary. § 201(b). Classifying a work as "made for hire" determines not only the initial ownership of its copyright, but also the copyright's duration, § 302(c), and the owners' renewal rights, § 304(a), termination rights, § 203(a), and right to import certain goods bearing the copyright, § 601(b)(1). See 1 M. Nimmer & D. Nimmer, Nimmer on Copyright § 5.03[A], pp. 5–10 (1988). The contours of the work for hire doctrine therefore carry profound significance for freelance creators-including artists, writers, photographers, designers, composers, and computer programmers-and for the publishing, advertising, music, and other industries which commission their works.

Section 101 of the 1976 Act provides that a work is "for hire" under two sets of circumstances:

"(1) a work prepared by an employee within the scope of his or her employment; or

(2) a work specially ordered or commissioned for use as a contribution to a collective work, as a part of a motion picture or other audiovisual work, as a translation, as a supplementary work, as a compilation, as an instructional text, as a test, as answer material for a test, or as an atlas, if the parties expressly agree in a written instrument signed by them that the work shall be considered a work made for hire."

Petitioners do not claim that the statue satisfies the terms of § 101(2). Quite clearly, it does not. Sculpture does not fit within any of the nine categories of "specially ordered or commissioned" works enumerated in that subsection, and no written agreement between the parties establishes "Third World America" as a work for hire.

The dispositive inquiry in this case therefore is whether "Third World America" is "a work prepared by an employee within the scope of his or her employment" under § 101(1). The Act does not define these terms. In the absence of such guidance, four interpretations have emerged. The first holds that a work is prepared by an employee whenever the hiring party retains the right to control the product. * * * Petitioners take this view. * * * A second, and closely related, view is that a work is prepared by an employee under § 101(1) when the hiring party has actually wielded control with respect to the creation of a particular work. * * * A third view is that the term "employee" within § 101(1) carries its common-law agency law meaning. * * * Finally, respondent and numerous amici curiae contend that the term "employee" only refers to "formal, salaried" employees. * * *

The Act nowhere defines the terms "employee" or "scope of employment." It is, however, well established that "[w]here Congress uses terms that have accumulated settled meaning under . . . the common law, a court must infer, unless the statute otherwise dictates, that Congress means to incorporate the established meaning of these terms." * * * In the past, when Congress has used the term "employee" without defining it, we have concluded that Congress intended to describe the conventional master-servant relationship as understood by common-law agency doctrine. * * * Nothing in the text of the work for hire provisions indicates that Congress used the words "employee" and "employment" to describe anything other than " 'the conventional relation of employer and employé.' " * * * On the contrary, Congress' intent to incorporate the agency law definition is suggested by § 101(1)'s use of the term, "scope of employment," a widely used term of art in agency law. See Restatement (Second) of Agency § 228 (1958) (hereinafter Restatement).

In past cases of statutory interpretation, when we have concluded that Congress intended terms such as "employee," "employer," and "scope of employment" to be understood in light of agency law, we have relied on the general common law of agency, rather than on the law of any particular State, to give meaning to these terms. * * * Establishment of a federal rule of agency, rather than reliance on state agency law, is particularly appropriate here given the Act's express objective of creating national, uniform copyright law by broadly pre-empting state statutory and common-law copyright regulation. See 17 U.S.C. § 301(a). We thus agree with the Court of Appeals that the term "employee" should be understood in light of the general common law of agency.

In contrast, neither test proposed by petitioners is consistent with the text of the Act. The exclusive focus of the right to control the product test on the relationship between the hiring party and the product clashes with the language of § 101(1), which focuses on the relationship between the hired and hiring parties. The right to control the product test also would distort the meaning of the ensuing subsection, § 101(2). Section 101 plainly creates two distinct ways in which a work can be deemed for hire: one for works prepared by employees, the other for those specially ordered or commissioned works which fall within one of the nine enumerated categories and are the subject of a written agreement. The right to control the product test ignores this dichotomy by transforming into a work for hire under § 101(1) any "specially ordered or commissioned" work that is subject to the supervision and control of the hiring party

The actual control test * * * fares only marginally better when measured against the language and structure of § 101. Under this test, independent contractors who are so controlled and supervised in the creation of a particular work are deemed "employees" under § 101(1). Thus work for hire status under § 101(1) depends on a hiring party's actual control of, rather than right to control, the product. * * * Section 101 clearly delineates between works prepared by an employee and commissioned works. Sound though other distinctions might be as a matter of copyright policy, there is no statutory support for an additional dichotomy between commissioned works that are actually controlled and supervised by the hiring party and those that are not.

We therefore conclude that the language and structure of § 101 of the Act do not support either the right to control the product or the actual control approaches. The structure of § 101 indicates that a work for hire can arise through one of two mutually exclusive means, one for employees and one for independent contractors, and ordinary canons of statutory interpretation indicate that the classification of a particular hired party should be made with reference to agency law. * * *

We turn, finally, to an application of § 101 to Reid's production of "Third World America." In determining whether a hired party is an employee under the general common law of agency, we consider the hiring party's right to control the manner and means by which the product is accomplished. Among the other factors relevant to this inquiry are the skill required; the source of the instrumentalities and tools; the location of the work; the duration of the relationship between the parties; whether the hiring party has the right to assign additional projects to the hired party; the extent of the hired party's discretion over when and how long to work; the method of payment; the hired party's role in hiring and paying assistants; whether the work is part of the regular business of the hiring party; whether the hiring party is in business; the provision of employee benefits; and the tax treatment of the hired party. See Restatement § 220(2) (setting forth a nonexhaustive list of factors relevant to determining whether a hired party is an employee). No one of these factors is determinative.

Examining the circumstances of this case in light of these factors, we agree with the Court of Appeals that Reid was not an employee of CCNV but an independent contractor. True, CCNV members directed enough of Reid's work to ensure that he produced a sculpture that met their specifications. But the extent of control the hiring party exercises over the details of the product is not dispositive. Indeed, all the other circumstances weigh heavily against finding an employment relationship. Reid is a sculptor, a skilled occupation. Reid supplied his own tools. He worked in his own studio in Baltimore, making daily supervision of his activities from Washington practicably impossible. Reid was retained for less than two months, a relatively short period of time. During and after this time, CCNV had no right to assign additional projects to Reid. Apart from the deadline for completing the sculpture, Reid had absolute freedom to decide when and how long to work. CCNV paid Reid $15,000, a sum dependent on "completion of a specific job, a method by which independent contractors are often compensated." * * * Reid had total discretion in hiring and paying assistants. "Creating sculptures was hardly 'regular business' for CCNV." * * *. Indeed, CCNV is not a business at all. Finally, CCNV did not pay payroll or Social Security taxes, provide any employee benefits, or contribute to unemployment insurance or workers' compensation funds.

Because Reid was an independent contractor, whether "Third World America" is a work for hire depends on whether it satisfies the terms of § 101(2). This petitioners concede it cannot do. Thus, CCNV is not the author of "Third World America" by virtue of the work for hire provisions of the Act. However, as the Court of Appeals made clear, CCNV nevertheless may be a joint author of the sculpture if, on remand, the District Court determines that CCNV and Reid prepared the work "with the intention that their contributions be merged into inseparable or interdependent parts of a unitary whole." 17 U.S.C. § 101. In that case, CCNV and Reid would be co-owners of the copyright in the work. See § 201(a).

NOTES

1.   There is often a pecking order regarding decision-making powers in a joint authorship work. How joint authors make decisions regarding their relative rights in their respective contributions and interests raises another set of questions. What if they cannot agree on issues during authorship regarding content or expression? What if one decides there is no further need for the other and terminates the relationship or usurps the collective opportunity? Are their copyright interests joint, joint and several or several? Can either or both take their separate portion and go their own way, or assign their interests? If they have a joint authorship copyright, what of their renewal rights? If they each assign their interests to separate persons, can each of their assignees make use of the whole?

2.   Creative work contexts are often lonely and collaboration not only distributes the burden, but permits mutual synergies to expand creative horizons. Like any relationship, however, there are issues as to the parties' intentions, respective contributions and rights. The case that follows details the interplay joint authors experience during the creative process.

MAURIZIO v. GOLDSMITH

United States District Court, S.D. New York, 2000.
84 F.Supp.2d 455.

* * *

A.   Goldsmith and Maurizio Agree to Work Together

Goldsmith and Maurizio first met during the summer of 1989 at a social event hosted by RKO Pavilion ("Pavilion"), a movie production company. At the time, both were aspiring novelists. By the end of that year, they had become friendly.

In or around June 1989, Goldsmith started writing FWC (First Wives' Club). Initially, Goldsmith intended FWC as a movie script, but by November 1989, however, Goldsmith decided to write the story as a novel. By January 1990, Goldsmith had completed the first hundred pages of the manuscript. By March 1990, Al Zuckerman ("Zuckerman"), an agent with Writers' House, Inc., had agreed to represent Goldsmith based on his evaluation of a 20–30 page synopsis of FWC constructed by Goldsmith.

Zuckerman advised Goldsmith that, before he could sell the novel, he would need either a complete manuscript of FWC or a revised partial manuscript and a promotional outline of the entire book. The latter option was more feasible for Goldsmith, and she decided to pursue Maurizio's assistance.

In March 1990, Maurizio declined two requests from Goldsmith to "write the outline." * * * On April 7, 1990, Goldsmith "got down on her hands and knees and begged" Maurizio to work with her, telling her it would be "a big opportunity for both of [them]." On that date, Maurizio agreed to "give it a shot." * * * According to Brendan Gunning, Maurizio's friend, Goldsmith was excited to work with Maurizio because Maurizio would be able to help Goldsmith structure the plot and had the mechanics that Goldsmith lacked for putting together a novel. * * * Goldsmith told Gunning at that time that Maurizio was "going to plot the book and do the outline."

According to Maurizio, Goldsmith proposed to pay her $10,000 to work on the outline, regardless of whether it was successfully sold. * * * At various times Goldsmith told Maurizio that if the book were sold, they would both "make a lot of money off of [the] book" and "be rich." * * * Also, Goldsmith promised to introduce Maurizio "as a co-writer of the novel and the outline of the novel" to Zuckerman. * * *

B. Goldsmith and Maurizio Begin to Work Together

At the time that Goldsmith and Maurizio agreed to work together, Goldsmith had completed drafts of a dozen early chapters of FWC, and Maurizio used these chapters to start the outline. * * * On April 10, 1990, Goldsmith and Maurizio met for several hours at Maurizio's home. On that day Goldsmith prepared a document called the "Outline for the Outline," which she shared with Maurizio. * * * The two discussed characters to be created, the characters' personalities, how to proceed on the chapters yet to be written, and "how to fill in the blanks and . . . get to [certain] points." * * * They also discussed the placement of certain characters in certain chapters and performed an exercise of simultaneously writing a few paragraphs to compare each other's writing.

From April 10–20, they began writing outlines for the next few chapters, and attempted to construct one-sentence descriptions for subsequent chapters. They then considered what other chapters needed to be created or rearranged. Maurizio took notes of their conversations and wrote new sections of the outline expressing the ideas they generated. Maurizio would show portions of the outline to Goldsmith who provided written comments. * * *

C. Goldsmith Proposes Co–Authorship

On April 20, 1990, Goldsmith presented the completed chapter outlines to Zuckerman. Afterwards, Goldsmith told Maurizio that the meeting with Zuckerman went very well, and that they were both going to "make a lot of money." * * * According to Maurizio, Goldsmith presented her with an orchid and proposed that they co-write the entire novel. Maurizio understood this to mean that when she co-wrote the novel, she would be credited as a co-author.

D.   Maurizio's Contributions

Maurizio claims that, from the time she and Goldsmith began to work together until May 14, she worked on the outline nearly daily and that she and Goldsmith met or talked about the outline every day. * * * On May 10, 1990, a 62–page outline was completed. However, before a hard copy was printed, Maurizio mistakenly deleted the entire outline from the computer. Maurizio reconstructed the outline by May 14, 1990. * * * Goldsmith thanked her for her "heroic retrieval."

On May 15, 1990, Goldsmith delivered the reconstructed outline and about 250 pages of FWC text which she had written to Zuckerman. * * * A few days later, Zuckerman told Goldsmith that he wanted to make changes to the outline and "be more actively involved in the project." * * *

After delivering the outline to Zuckerman but before receiving feedback from him, Goldsmith gave Maurizio a check for $1,000 for her work. On the memo portion of the check, Goldsmith wrote "for typing services." Maurizio objected to this because she was not a typist. Goldsmith thus wrote her a second check that substituted the word "loan" in the memo portion. They agreed on this term because they planned to settle accounts at a later time. * * *

Maurizio contends that she made numerous contributions to the outline. Her efforts allegedly included creating new characters, assisting Goldsmith with the articulation of a premise, constructing ideas or premises of her own which Goldsmith would agree or disagree with, and substantially contributing to the creation and personae of the second wives and the husbands, who were principal characters of FWC. However, Maurizio does not dispute that every draft of the outline contains the following notation: "The First Wives Club, by Justine Rendal." * * *

Beyond her contributions to the outline, Maurizio contends that she wrote two draft chapters of FWC. Maurizio called the first of these "Bad Day at Black Rock." She admits that she "began to write it as an outline and it started to become a chapter." * * * She first told Goldsmith that she was writing this chapter on April 20, 1990. At that time she gave Goldsmith the first page of the chapter and Goldsmith encouraged her to finish it. Maurizio gave the completed chapter to Goldsmith around April 23, 1990. * * * Goldsmith read it and made some handwritten comments. * * * Around that same time, Maurizio also offered to write, and then wrote, a second chapter, which she called "He–Man and Wonder Woman." Maurizio asserts that she agreed to write the chapter after Goldsmith asked her how she felt about writing sex scenes. Maurizio wrote the chapter and presented it to Goldsmith, who read it and told Maurizio it was terrific. * * * Around this time, the two agreed that after the outline was completed they would divide up the chapters and go to East Hampton during the summer to complete the novel. * * *

E. Goldsmith Refuses Maurizio Co–Authorship Credit

According to Maurizio, she and Goldsmith always planned to work out a formal co-authorship agreement. On May 15, 1990, Maurizio attempted to formalize their agreement, asking for co-authorship credit and twenty-five percent of the profits from the book. * * * Goldsmith reacted to this request "very badly. She acted shocked, appalled." (*Id.* at 353:10–15). Maurizio characterized Goldsmith's reaction as "freaking out," and stated that Goldsmith "absolutely refused to give [her] credit in any way." On May 18, 1990, Maurizio again approached Goldsmith about co-authorship credit, but Goldsmith again refused to give her credit. On May 21, 1990, Goldsmith told her that Zuckerman wanted a number of changes to the outline, and that Goldsmith was going to "shelve it" for a while. * * * Goldsmith never introduced Maurizio as a co-writer to Zuckerman, as she had promised. * * *

It is not disputed that the parties never agreed to write the rest of FWC together, and that Maurizio did nothing with respect to FWC after the reconstruction of the outline on May 14, 1990.

F. Goldsmith's Completion of FWC

On May 21, 1990, Goldsmith told Maurizio that she was going on vacation and indefinitely postponing the writing of the remainder of FWC. * * * Instead, Goldsmith went to East Hampton with Gunning, and, according to Gunning, he completed writing FWC after discussions with Goldsmith that were based in part on the outline. * * *

Maurizio learned about Goldsmith's completion of FWC on January 23, 1991 through an article in the New York Post about Goldsmith's sale of FWC to Paramount. * * * She demanded a twenty-five percent credit as co-author, but Goldsmith told her that under no circumstances would she give Maurizio co-authorship credit. * * *

In March 1992, when FWC was published, Maurizio obtained a copy of the book and placed marks on it indicating the precise language and ideas that she claims were hers. * * * Maurizio claims that her language appears on 27 of FWC's 480 pages, seven of which comprise the chapter "Masters of the Universe," which Maurizio claims is her chapter "He–Man and Wonder Woman." Regarding the other chapter Maurizio allegedly wrote, "Bad Day at Black Rock," Maurizio admits that her chapter appears in FWC in "reworked" form. * * *

G. Copyright Act Claims

This Court has held that the statute of limitations provides grounds for dismissal of Maurizio's joint authorship claim and grounds for limitation of her copyright infringement claim. Beyond the statute of limitations argument, however, Goldsmith argues that summary judgment is proper as to both of these claims because there are no genuine issues of material fact and Goldsmith is entitled to judgment as a matter of law. This Court disagrees. Maurizio's claim for joint authorship will be addressed first.

1. Joint Authorship

Maurizio's second claim is for joint authorship under the Copyright Act and an accounting in connection therewith. The Copyright Act defines a "joint work" as follows:

> [A] work prepared by two or more authors with the intention that their contributions be merged into inseparable or interdependent parts of a unitary whole. 17 U.S.C. § 101.

The Second Circuit has established a two-part test for joint authorship, whereby each putative co-author must have (1) intended, at the time of creation, to be a co-author and (2) made independently copyrightable contributions to the work. *Thomson v. Larson*, 147 F.3d 195, 200 (2d Cir.1998); *Childress v. Taylor*, 945 F.2d 500, 507–08 (2d Cir.1991) 945 F.2d 500, 507–08 (2d Cir.1991). * * * Goldsmith argues that there is no genuine issue of material fact as to either element of the test, and that she is entitled to judgment as a matter of law. For the reasons that follow, this Court holds that judgment as a matter of law is improper as to both elements.

a. Intent

"Focusing on whether the putative joint authors regarded themselves as joint authors is especially important in circumstances ... where one person is indisputably the dominant author of the work and the only issue is whether that person is the sole author or she and another are joint authors." *Childress*, 945 F.2d at 508. In this case, Goldsmith is indisputably the dominant author. She contends that Maurizio has failed to present sufficient evidence that Goldsmith intended FWC to be co-authored by Maurizio. For the following reasons, this Court finds that a genuine issue of material fact exists regarding Goldsmith's intent.

Maurizio has proffered sufficient evidence that, during the time that she made her contributions, Goldsmith intended Maurizio to be a co-author of FWC. On April 20, 1990, Maurizio contends that Goldsmith, orchid in hand, asked her to co-write the novel, at the same time renewing an earlier promise that they would both "make a lot of money" from the book. * * * From that date until May 10, 1990, Maurizio allegedly worked on the outline and wrote two draft chapters. There is no evidence that Goldsmith changed her mind about co-authorship until May 15, 1990, when she rejected Maurizio's request for co-authorship credit and twenty-five percent of the profits from the book. Goldsmith's April 20 request and her subsequent silence about co-authorship until May 15 constitute evidence upon which a trier of fact could reasonably find intent of joint authorship by Goldsmith during the time that Maurizio made her contributions.

Goldsmith argues that the Second Circuit holdings in *Childress* and *Thomson* mandate summary judgment. However, these cases are distinguishable from the present case. In *Childress,* the Second Circuit upheld the district court's grant of summary judgment to plaintiff Childress as to defendant Taylor's joint authorship counterclaim. The Second Circuit agreed with the district court that "there is no evidence from which a trier of fact could infer that Childress had the state of mind required for joint authorship.... There is no evidence that Childress ever contemplated, much less would have accepted, crediting the play as 'written by Alice Childress and Clarice Taylor.' " Childress, 945 F.2d at 509. In the present case, however, Goldsmith's April 20 proposal constitutes the type of evidence lacking in *Childress.*

In *Thomson,* the Second Circuit upheld the district court's conclusion, made after a bench trial, that Thomson, a dramaturg, was not a joint author of the Broadway musical *Rent.* 147 F.3d at 199. Among the evidence that Thomson offered to show that the author, Larson, intended the play to be a joint work was a statement Larson had made to Thomson that he would " 'always acknowledge [Thomson's] contribution' " and " 'would never say that [he] wrote what [Thomson] did.' " The Second Circuit upheld the district judge's determination that Larson's statement was consistent with the view that Larson was the sole author of *Rent. Id. Thomson* fails to mandate summary judgment in the present case for two reasons. First, the district judge had made his determination after a bench trial, not on a motion for summary judgment. Second, Goldsmith's request that Maurizio co-author FWC with her, made before much of Maurizio's work on the outline and draft chapters of FWC, constitutes stronger evidence of intent than the statement attributed to Larson in *Thomson.* Indeed, a trier of fact could reasonably find intent based on Goldsmith's April 20 request that Maurizio co-author FWC, followed by Maurizio's work on the outline and draft chapters until May 10, 1990.

b. *Copyrightable Contribution*

Even if Maurizio establishes the requisite intent on Goldsmith's part, Maurizio's asserted contributions to FWC must be copyrightable. Copyright protection extends to "original works of authorship fixed in any tangible medium of expression." 17 U.S.C. § 102(a). For the following reasons, this Court finds that genuine issues of fact exist as to the copyrightability of Maurizio's contributions that render summary judgment improper.

As noted above, only tangible forms of expression are protected by the Copyright Act. "Ideas, refinements, and suggestions, standing alone, are not the subjects of copyrights." * * * Maurizio contends not only that her ideas and suggestions were incorporated into FWC, but also that some of her language, that is, her expression, appears in the novel. While her ideas and suggestions are not copyrightable, language which she produced as a tangible form of expression (in the outline or draft chapters) and which was intended to and did indeed merge with Goldsmith's work in FWC may be copyrightable. Maurizio claims that her language appears on 27 of FWC's 480 pages, and much of this language appears in the outline and draft chapters. Most notable is the language in the FWC chapter "Masters of the Universe," * * * which Maurizio alleges she originally wrote in her draft chapter "He–Man and Wonder Woman." * * * Thus, this Court holds that at least some of the language allegedly contributed by Maurizio is copyrightable. Whether and to what extent the language is indeed Maurizio's expression is an issue of fact not properly considered at this time.

For a contribution to be copyrightable, originality is also required. To be original, an author's work must (1) be independently created by the author and (2) possess at least a minimal degree of creativity. *Feist Publications, Inc. v. Rural Tel. Serv. Co.,* 499 U.S. 340, 345, 111 S.Ct. 1282, 113 L.Ed.2d 358 (1991); *Matthew Bender & Co. v. West Publ'g Co.,* 158 F.3d 674, 681 (2d Cir.1998). "To be sure, the requisite level of creativity is extremely low; even a slight amount will suffice. The vast majority of works make the grade quite easily, as they possess some creative spark, 'no matter how crude humble or obvious' it might be." *Feist,* 499 U.S. at 345, 111 S.Ct. 1282 * * * Applying these standards to the facts of this case, the question of whether the language was independently created by Maurizio is disputed, and thus one for the trier of fact. Further, this Court holds that at least a portion of the language Maurizio claims as hers contains a sufficient degree of creativity. In sum, questions remain as to the originality of Maurizio's contributions which make summary judgment improper at this time.

c. Goldsmith's Derivative Work Argument

Goldsmith argues that even if Maurizio was a joint author of the outline and draft chapters, she was not a joint author of FWC itself because the novel is Goldsmith's derivative work of these earlier joint works. * * * In *Weissmann v. Freeman,* the Second Circuit held that "[e]ven though one co-author has the right to revise a joint work in order to create an individual derivative work, the other co-author acquires no property rights in the newly created work prepared without his involvement." 868 F.2d 1313, 1318 (1989) * * * Goldsmith also points to *Ashton–Tate v. Ross,* where the Ninth Circuit held that "[j]oint authorship in a prior work is insufficient to make one a joint author of a derivative work." 916 F.2d 516, 522 (9th Cir.1990).

This argument fails because, considering the evidence, a trier of fact could reasonably find that, at the time Maurizio made her contributions to the outline and draft chapters, both parties intended that these contributions were being made as part of the development of FWC itself, and that some of Maurizio's contributions might be "merged" with Goldsmith's work in FWC. In other words, the parties did not necessarily intend that the outline and draft chapters were simply ends in themselves. Rather, they may have been intended to be a part of the process of completing the final product—FWC. This was not the situation in either *Weissmann* or *Ashton–Tate.*

Further, even if no reasonable trier of fact could find Maurizio to be a joint author of FWC (considering it as distinct from the underlying works, as Goldsmith's derivative work argument does), summary judgment would be improper because a joint author must account to his co-author for use of their joint work in a derivative work. *See Weissmann v. Freeman,* 868 F.2d 1313, 1318; *see also Ashton–Tate,* 916 F.2d at 522. Thus, Goldsmith would have to account to Maurizio for Goldsmith's use of the outline and draft chapters in constructing FWC.

2. *Copyright Infringement*

Maurizio's first claim, argued in the alternative to her joint authorship claim, is for copyright infringement of the outline and draft chapters which she purportedly created. "To prevail in an action for copyright infringement, 'a plaintiff must show [1] ownership of a valid copyright and [2] the defendant's infringement by unauthorized copying.' " *Debitetto v. Alpha Books,* 7 F.Supp.2d 330, 333 (S.D.N.Y.1998) (quoting *Laureyssens v. Idea Group, Inc., Laureyssens v. Idea Group, Inc.,* 964 F.2d 131, 139 (2d Cir.1992)). If unauthorized copying occurred, the " 'plaintiff must then show that the copying amounts to an improper appropriation by demonstrating that substantial similarity [of] protected material exists between the two works.' " *Id.* (quoting *Laureyssens,* 964 F.2d at 140).

Goldsmith argues that "the minimal bits of expression claimed by Maurizio, much of which consists of only sentence fragments, are not independently copyrightable and, accordingly, not subject to infringement." * * * However, the "minimal bits of expression" that Goldsmith points to are not the *source* of infringement here, but rather the alleged *product* of infringement. The *sources* of the infringement are the 62–page outline and draft chapters allegedly written by Maurizio.

This Court does hold that, under Maurizio's version of the facts in this case, the outline was jointly authored by Maurizio and Goldsmith. "[A]n action for infringement between joint owners will not lie because an individual cannot infringe his own copyright." *Weissmann,* 868 F.2d at 1318. Therefore, the outline in this case cannot be a source of infringement. A successful infringement claim must be based on the draft chapters which Maurizio allegedly wrote.

As discussed *supra,* copyright protection extends to original, tangible forms of expression. The draft chapters pass this test. Further, there appears to be little question that at least some copying occurred. This Court cannot say that the works are not substantially similar. Further, even though the language at issue constitutes a very small portion of the complete novel of FWC, "no plagiarist can excuse the wrong by showing how much of his work he did not pirate." *Sheldon v. Metro–Goldwyn Pictures Corp.,* 81 F.2d 49, 56 (2d Cir.1936) (Hand, J.); *accord Nihon*

Keizai Shimbun, Inc. v. Comline Bus. Data, Inc., 166 F.3d 65, 72 (2d Cir.1999).

* * * [Summary Judgment Denied]

ARTHUR RUTENBERG HOMES, INC. v. DREW HOMES, INC.

United States Court of Appeals, Eleventh Circuit, 1994.
29 F.3d 1529.

HILL, SENIOR CIRCUIT JUDGE:

This case presents an issue of copyright law. Appellant Arthur Rutenberg Homes, Inc. ("Rutenberg"), filed a complaint against Drew Homes, Inc. ("Drew Homes"), and its president and sole shareholder, Andrew J. Vecchio, Jr. Rutenberg claimed copyright infringement and common law unfair competition arising out of Drew Homes' use of certain architectural drawings and plans on which Rutenberg claimed to hold the copyright. Drew Homes counterclaimed alleging trade defamation and seeking a declaratory judgment that Rutenberg's copyright was invalid. The case ultimately proceeded to trial on Rutenberg's copyright infringement claim and Drew Homes' counterclaim for declaratory relief.

The case was tried, by agreement, before a United States Magistrate Judge who found that Rutenberg did not own a valid copyright at the time of the alleged infringement. 829 F.Supp. 1314. For the following reasons, we reverse.

The Creation of the Copyright

The undisputed facts are that in 1987, Chrysalis Homes Associates ("Chrysalis") engaged an architectural firm, the Heise Group, Inc. ("Heise"), to prepare for Chrysalis original architectural drawings of single family homes. At that time, Chrysalis and Heise verbally agreed that any resulting architectural drawings would be owned by Chrysalis.

Pursuant to this agreement, Heise created an architectural drawing entitled the "Verandah II" on which, as agreed, Heise placed a copyright notice identifying Chrysalis as the copyright owner. On March 21, 1988, Chrysalis secured a Certificate of Copyright Registration on the "Verandah II" drawings. The copyright registration identified Chrysalis as both the author of the drawings, by "work-for-hire," and the copyright claimant. Chrysalis' claim of authorship by "work-for-hire" apparently reflected the common practice at the time where drawings were created for an employer by an "independent contractor."

Two years later, the Eleventh Circuit decided in *M.G.B. Homes Inc. v. Ameron Homes, Inc.,* 903 F.2d 1486 (11th Cir.1990), that the "work-for-hire" doctrine does not confer authorship upon the home builder employer of the independent contractor who creates home floor plans. Chrysalis realized then that Heise was the author, and, therefore, original copyright owner of the "Verandah II" plans.

Shortly thereafter, Chrysalis secured a written "Certificate of Release" from Heise reciting and confirming that Heise had, from the beginning, assigned all of its rights, interest and ownership in the copyright for the "Verandah II" plans to Chrysalis.

Subsequently, Chrysalis wound up its business and sold its "Verandah II" plans to the Arthur Rutenberg Corporation ("ARC"). On February 19, 1990, Chrysalis assigned its copyright in the "Verandah II" plans to ARC. The written copyright assignments for the "Verandah II" plans from Heise to Chrysalis and from Chrysalis to ARC were duly recorded in the United States Copyright Office. As part of a corporate reorganization, ARC assigned all of its copyrights, including "Verandah II", to Rutenberg on January 1, 1991. This assignment was also recorded in the copyright office.

Rutenberg's claim for copyright infringement arises out of Drew Homes' alleged use of the "Verandah II" plans in preparing its own architectural drawings for a house constructed by it in 1991.

While this action was pending, Rutenberg applied for and received from the copyright office a Certificate of Supplementary Copyright Registration correcting the original "Verandah II" copyright registration to reflect Heise as the author, and Chrysalis as owner by assignment, and not the author by "work-for-hire".

The Ownership of the Copyright

The original owner of the copyright in the "Verandah II" drawings was Heise, the author. Heise was the owner because the Copyright Act of 1976 provides that ownership vests in the author (Heise) as the party who actually creates the work. 17 U.S.C. § 201(a). *M.G.B. Homes* made clear that Chrysalis did not obtain ownership under the "work-for-hire" doctrine.

It is uncontroverted, however, that Heise and Chrysalis entered into an oral agreement that Heise would prepare these plans for Chrysalis, and that the copyright in the "Verandah II" plan would be owned by Chrysalis. Heise, in fact, placed a copyright notice on the drawings identifying Chrysalis as the copyright owner. At this point, Chrysalis held, at least, a contractual right by oral assignment to the copyright in the "Verandah II" drawings.

Copyright ownership, however, can be conveyed only by a writing signed by the owner of the copyright. 17 U.S.C. § 204(a) provides:

> A transfer of copyright ownership, other than by operation of law, is not valid unless an instrument of conveyance, or a note or memorandum of transfer, is in writing and signed by the owner of the rights conveyed or such owner's duly authorized agent.

Chrysalis, therefore, could have become the owner of the copyright only if there were such a writing.

There is no dispute that a "Certificate of Release" was signed by Heise in early 1990, or that there were subsequent written assignments of the "Verandah II" copyright from Chrysalis to ARC, dated February 19, 1990 and from ARC to Rutenberg, effective January 1, 1991. All these writings satisfy Section 204(a)'s requirement for writing and were recorded in the copyright office prior to the allegedly infringing acts.

Despite these written assignments of ownership, however, the trial court concluded that Rutenberg "loses on its copyright claim solely because it did not own a valid copyright at the time of the suggested infringement." The trial court based its conclusion on the following analysis: only the copyright owner can register a copyright. Since Chrysalis was not the author of the "Verandah II" drawings (M.G.B. Homes, Inc.), it was not entitled to register the copyright at all, since at the time of registration it was not the owner of the copyright, there being no written assignment prior to registration. Therefore, the registration was void from the beginning.

The trial court appears, however, to have extended *M.G.B. Homes, Inc.,* beyond its holding that the "work-for-hire" doctrine does not confer authorship upon the employer of an independent contractor. It does not hold that actual ownership, mistakenly registered as authorship resulting from "work-for-hire," may not be shown by assignment from the independent contractor author.

Indeed, in *M.G.B. Homes, Inc.,* no basis for ownership was asserted except "work-for-hire." In that case, if the party claiming ownership did not acquire that ownership as the result of "work-for-hire," that party had no other basis on which to assert ownership. In this case, however, Chrysalis was the owner of a contractual right in the copyright by assignment from the beginning. Its subsequent registration of that copyright merely contained a statement, erroneous after *M.G.B. Homes, Inc.,* of how it came to acquire that ownership.

But certainly, if registration does not confer copyright, neither can erroneous registration take it away. Copyright ownership and the effect of mistaken copyright registration are separate and distinct issues.

Copyright inheres in authorship and exists whether or not it is ever registered. The Copyright Act makes clear that registration is a separate issue from the existence of the copyright itself:

Section 408. Copyright Registration in General.

(a) REGISTRATION PERMISSIVE.—At any time during the subsistence of copyright in any published or unpublished work, the owner of a copyright or of any exclusive right in the work may obtain registration of the copyright.... *Such a registration is not a condition of copyright protection.*

(emphasis supplied); see also M. Nimmer & D. Nimmer, 3 *Nimmer on Copyright* § 7.16[A], (1992).

Unlike the claimant in *M.G.B. Homes,* Rutenberg's claim to owner-ship of the copyright is not that the plans were created as a "work-for-hire," but rather that they were assigned by the original author to Chrysalis and subsequently to ARC and then to it. As there is no dispute that these assignments did occur, and in writing, all prior to the alleged infringement by Drew Homes, we conclude that Rutenberg did *own* a valid copyright at the time of the alleged infringement.

The Effect of the Inaccurate Registration

Copyright registration is a pre-requisite to the institution of a copy-right infringement lawsuit. 17 U.S.C. § 411(a) provides that "no action for infringement of the copyright in any work shall be instituted until registration of the copyright claim has been made...." Furthermore, as noted above, only the copyright owner may apply for registration. *See* 17 U.S.C. § 408(a). Therefore, the dispositive issue in this case is whether Chrysalis was the owner of the "Verandah II" copyright *at the time of the original registration in 1988* so that the registration had legal effect. If so, then Rutenberg as a valid subsequent assignee could bring this action to enforce its copyright on the original registration. If not, then despite being the owner of the copyright, Rutenberg would not hold a valid registration and could not bring this action.

Resolution of this issue requires that we inquire when Chrysalis obtained ownership of the copyright in the "Verandah II" plans. Was ownership transferred in 1988 upon the execution of the "Verandah II" plans pursuant to the agreement between Chrysalis and Heise to create the plans with the express understanding and agreement that Chrysalis would own the copyright? Or did Chrysalis obtain ownership only in early 1990, well after the initial registration of the copyright, when Heise executed a written memorandum of this agreement, as required by 17 U.S.C. § 204(a)?

Many courts have held that the requirements of 17 U.S.C. § 204(a) can be satisfied by an oral assignment later ratified or confirmed by a written memorandum of the transfer. In *Eden Toys, Inc. v. Florelee Undergarment Co., Inc.,* 697 F.2d 27 (2d Cir.1982) the Second Circuit reasoned that:

> [S]ince the purpose of the provision is to protect copyright holders from persons mistakenly or fraudulently claiming oral licenses, the "note or memorandum of the transfer" need not be made at the time when the license is initiated; the requirement is satisfied by the copyright owner's late execution of a writing which confirms the agreement.... *In this case, in which the copyright holder appears to have no dispute with its licensee on this matter, it would be anomalous to permit a third-party infringer to invoke this provision against the licensee.*

Id. at 36 (citations omitted) (emphasis added).

Every court which has considered the issue has arrived at the same result. See e.g., *Valente–Kritzer Video v. Pinckney,* 881 F.2d 772 (9th Cir.1989) *cert. denied* 493 U.S. 1062, 110 S.Ct. 879, 107 L.Ed.2d 962 (1990); *Great Southern Homes, Inc. v. Johnson & Thompson Realtors,* 797 F.Supp. 609 (M.D.Tenn.1992); *Kenbrooke Fabrics Inc. v. SoHo Fashions, Inc.,* 690 F.Supp. 298 (S.D.N.Y.1988). *Accord* M. Nimmer & D. Nimmer, 3 *Nimmer on Copyright* § 10.03[A], at 10–36 (1992).

In a case closely on point with this case, *Dan–Dee Imports, Inc. v. Well–Made Toy Mfg. Corp.,* 524 F.Supp. 615 (E.D.N.Y.1981), the defense was raised that plaintiff's copyright registration was ineffective since it was secured prior to the execution of a written memorandum of transfer from the author. The district court in a well-reasoned opinion rejected this argument:

> Furthermore, the regulations respecting registration do not clearly preclude issuance of a copyright to an applicant who has only received oral assignment prior to the registration since a "claimant" includes "a person or organization that has obtained ... *the contractual right* to claim legal title to the copyright in an application for copyright registration." 37 C.F.R. § 202.3(a)(3)(ii) n. 1 (emphasis added).

> * * *

> Accordingly, this Court holds that Dan–Dee was not required to have written evidence of the transfer from [the author] as a prerequisite to the issuance of copyright registration for the [copyrighted work], although such proof would, of course, be necessary on its copyright infringement claim.

Id. at 618–19.

The regulation relied upon by the court in *Dan–Dee Imports* remains in full force and effect. See 37 C.F.R. § 202.3(a)(3)(ii) n. 1 (1993). Since we have previously concluded that Chrysalis had at least a contractual right to legal title to the copyright at the time of its original copyright registration, it was a proper claimant under the regulation, and its registration, therefore, was valid.

This result is consistent with Section 204(a)'s allowance for a "note or memorandum of the transfer" in lieu of a formal "instrument of conveyance" which one court has noted "apparently codifies the judge made rule under the 1909 Act that if a prior oral grant is subsequently confirmed in writing, this will validate the grant *ab initio* as of the time of the oral grant." *Great Southern Homes, Inc. v. Johnson & Thompson Realtors,* 797 F.Supp. at 612.

This Court today adopts the reasoning of the cases cited above and holds that Chrysalis was not required to have written evidence of the assignment from Heise as a prerequisite to application for and the issuance of a valid copyright registration. Therefore, in this case, Chrysalis effectively registered its copyright on the "Verandah II" drawings in March of 1988, and its subsequent assignee Rutenberg both owned the copyright in and held a validly registered copyright on the "Verandah II" plans at the time of the alleged infringement.

While the trial court appears to have felt that Drew Homes did copy the "Verandah II" plans, he did not address that issue squarely because, having concluded that Rutenberg did not own a valid copyright at the time of the infringement, he did not think it necessary. The trial court has heard the evidence and can, we anticipate, make findings on the infringement issue without further proceedings. The judge may wish to hear from counsel on the issue.

The judgment is VACATED and the case is REMANDED for further proceedings.

NOTES

See also, *Morris v. Business Concepts, Inc.*, 259 F.3d 65 (2d Cir. 2001) where the parties had an ongoing relationship as follows:

> For eight years, Morris wrote a series of articles for *Allure* magazine, published by The Condé Nast Publications, Inc. ("Condé Nast"). The column was entitled "Mood News." Every year the parties entered into a written agreement requiring monthly articles in which Morris would retain ownership, subject to a ninety day exclusive publication right in Condé Nast. The publisher by this account was not the author, but did copyright the issues in which the articles appeared. See *Feist.* Morris, retained the copyright but did not register her copyright interest. The court held the registration by Condé Nast did not satisfy the registration requirements of the author and that Morris had no right to bring an action in federal court against others who violated her copyright. See also, John Marascalco v. Fantasy, Inc., 953 F.2d 469 (9th Cir. 1991) regarding rights of renewal and rights of assignee of author.

Is this consistent with the language of 17 U.S.C. § 201 below:

> **(c) Contributions to Collective Works.**—Copyright in each separate contribution to a collective work is distinct from copyright in the collective work as a whole, and vests initially in the author of the contribution. In the absence of an express transfer of the copyright or of any rights under it, the owner of copyright in the collective work is presumed to have acquired only the privilege of reproducing and distributing the contribution as part of that particular collective work, any revision of that collective work, and any later collective work in the same series.

In *New York Times, Co., Inc. v. Tasini*, 533 U.S. 483, 121 S.Ct. 2381, 150 L.Ed.2d 500 (2001), the Supreme Court addressed claims by freelance journalists that publication of newspaper articles in electronic databases by newspapers was copyright infringement. The newspapers sought a defense in the words "any revision of that collective work" under the paragraph above. The Court ruled that an electronic publication was not a revision since the individual articles would be distributed separately from the collective work when reproduced in electronic form.

VII. MORAL RIGHTS

Attribution arises as a multifaceted issue in a number of copyright cases. It often appears with related claims under section 43(a) of the Lanham Act. See 15 U.S.C. § 1125(a) (1988). Steven King has a notable reputation which he rightfully seeks to protect. In *King v. Innovation Books,* 976 F.2d 824 (2d Cir. 1992) one finds the scenario of a movie based on his short story "The Lawnmower Man." King was not involved in writing the movie and had no voice in approving or disapproving in the screenplay or production. Any attribution of his involvement with having written the original script was the issue with the movie. "[T]he film and advertising seen by King contained both possessory information (Stephen King's) and 'based upon'" information. (Id. at 827–828). The court considered both copyright and Lanham Act claims and determined that "based upon" was an accurate representation which protected King from further implication with the actual writing or production.

While the concept of moral rights has been uniquely of European application, it is increasingly a concern among American holders of copyrights as a necessary, non property element of their creative bundle of rights. *Gilliam v. American Broadcasting Companies, Inc.,* 538 F.2d 14 (2d Cir. 1976) addresses a cause of action for defamation of an artist's work. This course of action finds its roots in the continental concept of droit moral, or moral right, which may generally be summarized as the right of an artist to have his work attributed to him in the form in which the artist created it.

Moral rights have also been recognized in the context of site specific art, integrated art and VARA. If the work requires a "site specific" setting does that constitute a part of the author's copyright similar to the right of publication, copying or performing? Is there a distinction between "site specific" and integrated art? Certainly, the object of art (sculpture, painting or other work) can be copyrighted, but can the setting constitute a part of the overall expression for these purposes? What is the nature of the interest that is protected by this form of "right?" Is this a moral right? Is it a right of attribution? Is this a right that affects the "use" of that which is copyrighted and attribution which has an impact on the artist similar to the concerns expressed by Steven King in *King v. Innovation Books*, 976 F.2d 824 (2d Cir. 1992)?

DAVID PHILLIPS v. PEMBROKE REAL ESTATE, INC.

United States Court of Appeals, First Circuit, 2006.
459 F.3d 128.

LIPEZ, CIRCUIT JUDGE.

This case raises important questions about the application of the Visual Artists Rights Act of 1990 ("VARA"), 17 U.S.C. § 106A, to "site-specific art", which is a subset of "integrated art". A work of "integrated art" is comprised of two or more physical objects that must be presented together as the artist intended for the work to retain its meaning and integrity. In a work of "site-specific art", one of the component physical objects is the location of the art. To remove a work of site-specific art from its original site is to destroy it.

I.

David Phillips brought suit against Pembroke Real Estate, Inc. in federal district court, asserting that the removal of any or all of his work, consisting of multiple pieces of sculpture and stonework, from Eastport Park in South Boston would violate his statutory rights under VARA * * * The district court ruled that VARA recognized integrated art, and that most of Phillips' sculptures and stonework in the Park constituted "one integrated 'work of visual art'"—with the remaining pieces being "individual free-standing pieces of sculpture, which are not integrated into the other pieces." It also held that Phillips' integrated work of art was an example of site-specific art. But the court held that Pembroke could remove Phillips' works from the Park pursuant to VARA's so-called "public presentation" exception. *See* 17 U.S.C. § 106A(c)(2).

Phillips challenges that reading of the public presentation exception on appeal. Although we disagree with the district court's reasoning (we hold that VARA does not apply to site-specific art at all), we affirm the decision of the district court permitting Pembroke to remove Phillips' works from the Park.

II.

A.   The artist

Phillips is a nationally recognized sculptor who works primarily with stone and bronze forms that he integrates into local environs. In many of his sculptures, the design of the stones is incorporated into the landscape. * * *

C.   Phillips' work in the Park

In 1999, Pembroke commissioned Phillips to work on the Park in conjunction with the development of the World Trade Center East office building that forms the Park's western border. Phillips worked closely with Halvorson on the design of the Park. * * *

To establish the terms of the commission, Phillips and Pembroke executed two contracts in August 1999. Under the "Eastport Park Artwork Agreement", Phillips created approximately twenty-seven sculptures for the Park, comprised of fifteen abstract bronze and granite pieces and twelve realistic bronze sculptures of various aquatic creatures, including frogs, crabs, and shrimp. Under the "Eastport Park Stonework Agreement", Phillips was responsible for the design and installation of stone walls, granite stones inlaid into the Park's walkways, and other landscape design elements. Most of Phillips' work in the Park is organized along the diagonal axis running from the northeast to the southwest corner, at the center of which is his large spherical sculpture entitled "Chords", the centerpiece of the Park, which Phillips personally carved from granite. * * *

D. Pembroke's redesign of the Park and the preliminary injunction

In 2001, Pembroke decided to alter the Park. * * * Banks' redesign plan called for the removal and relocation of Phillips' sculptures. Phillips protested. In January 2003, Pembroke agreed to retain Phillips' rough stone walls and all but one of his sculptures. The new redesign plan would also relocate some of the granite paving and change several walkways and finished granite objects. Objecting to this revised plan, Phillips filed suit in federal district court, seeking injunctive relief under VARA and MAPA.

On August 21, 2003, following a nonevidentiary hearing, the district court issued a temporary restraining order enjoining Pembroke from altering the Park. * * *

A. Statutory Background

VARA states in relevant part that the "author of a work of visual art":

> (3) subject to the limitations set forth in section 113(d), shall have the right—
>
>> (A) to prevent any intentional distortion, mutilation, or other modification of that work which would be prejudicial to his or her honor or reputation, and any intentional distortion, mutilation, or modification of that work is a violation of that right, and
>>
>> (B) to prevent any destruction of a work of recognized stature, and any intentional or grossly negligent destruction of that work is a violation of that right.

17 U.S.C. § 106(A)(a)(3)(A) and (B). As an exception, § 106A(c)(2) states that:

> The modification of a work of visual art which is the result of conservation, or of the public presentation, including lighting and placement, of the work is not a destruction, distortion, mutilation, or other modification described in subsection (a)(3) unless the modification is caused by gross negligence.

This is the public presentation exception. A "work of visual art" is defined as including "a painting, drawing, print or sculpture, existing in a single copy" or in a limited edition. 17 U.S.C. § 101.

In *Carter v. Helmsley–Spear, Inc.,* 71 F.3d 77 (2d Cir.1995), the Second Circuit, citing VARA's legislative history, explained that VARA:

> protects both the reputations of certain visual artists and the works of art they create. It provides these artists with the rights of "attribution" and "integrity".... These rights are analogous to those protected by Article 6 *bis* of the Berne Convention, which are commonly known as "moral rights." The theory of moral rights is that they

result in a climate of artistic worth and honor that encourages the author in the arduous act of creation.

Id. at 83 (citing H.R.Rep. No. 101–514, at 5, *reprinted in* 1990 U.S.C.C.A.N. 6915, 6917). "VARA grants three rights: the right of attribution, the right of integrity and, in the case of works of visual art of 'recognized stature,' the right to prevent destruction." *Id.*

The right of attribution generally consists of the right of an artist to be recognized by name as the author of his work or to publish anonymously or pseudonymously, the right to prevent the author's work from being attributed to someone else, and to prevent the use of the author's name on works created by others, including distorted editions of the author's original work. The right of integrity allows the author to prevent any deforming or mutilating changes to his work, even after title in the work has been transferred. *Id.* at 81 * * *.

In other words, these moral rights protect what an artist retains after relinquishing ownership (and/or copyright) of the tangible object that the artist has created. * * *

B.   Site-specific art

During the preliminary injunction hearing, one of Phillips' experts, Daniel Ranalli, a professor of art history at Boston University, stated:

Beginning at least with the last third of the 20th century, and continuing through the present, the notion of *sculpture* has undergone a radical redefinition. In essence, sculpture has come off [of] its pedestal, functioning in the space in and around its site, and playing an integral role in *defining* that space.

Phillips I, 288 F.Supp.2d at 95. According to the district court's summary, another of Phillips' experts, Richard Barreto, Executive Director of the Urban Arts Institute of the Massachusetts College of Art, who is involved in the selection of artists to create art in public spaces, testified that:

[T]oday the concept of "site specificity" is the "rallying cry" of public artists who seek to create a piece that derives enhanced meaning from its environment. Much of modern sculpture does not exist separate from its context, but rather integrates its context with the work to form, ideally, a seamless whole. *Id.*

Essentially, for site-specific art, the location of the work is an integral element of the work. Because the location of the work contributes to its meaning, site-specific art is destroyed if it is moved from its original site. * * *

As Halvorson stated in an affidavit, "[t]his view contrasts with so-called 'plop-art' where a separately conceived art object is simply placed in a space." *Phillips I,* 288 F.Supp.2d at 95. A piece of plop-art does not incorporate its surroundings. Site-specific art is the opposite of plop-art. In summary, as the district court found below, "[t]he undisputed expert testimony is that in site-specific sculpture, the artist incorporates the environment as one of the media with which he works." * * *

A. The district court's understanding of site-specific art and VARA

To help explain our holding that VARA does not apply to site-specific art, we must begin with a restatement of the district court's view of the interaction between VARA and site-specific art. On the one hand, the district court accepted the concept of site-specific art. It credited the unopposed testimony of Ranalli, Phillips' expert, "that for site specific art, the location of the work is a constituent element of the work." * * * The district court understood that "[u]nder this approach, because the location defines the art, site-specific sculpture is destroyed if it is moved from the site." * * * The district court also found that "[t]o move Phillips' integrated work of visual art (i.e., the sculptures, boulders, and granite paths along the axis ... described in the VARA discussion) to another location ... would be to alter it physically," * * *.

On the other hand, in the section of its opinion addressing Phillips' site-specificity argument—entitled " 'Public–Presentation' Exclusion"— the district court noted that "Section 106A(c)(2) has been interpreted to exclude from VARA's protection 'site-specific' works, works that would be modified if they were moved." * * * It then referenced *Soho I* ("[T]he point of VARA 'is not ... to preserve a work of visual art *where* it is, but rather to preserve as work *as* it is,' " * * * (" '[N]owhere in VARA does the statute make any legal distinction between site-specific or free-standing works,' " * * *. The district court concluded "that an artist has no right to the placement or public presentation of his sculpture under the exception in § 106A(c)(2)." * * * In short, the district court found that while VARA applies to site-specific art, the public presentation exception permits the removal of site-specific art, e.g., Phillips' work in the Park.

Without in any way diminishing our respect for the district court's careful handling of this difficult case, we find its analysis of VARA's relationship to site-specific art unpersuasive. By definition, site-specific art integrates its location as one of its elements. Therefore, the removal of a site-specific work from its location necessarily destroys that work of art. Here, the district court concluded that VARA recognized site-specific art as a type of integrated art, and then concluded that VARA treats site-specific art the same way that it treats other integrated art. However, a work of integrated art, unless it is a site-specific work, is not destroyed by removal from its location.

By concluding that VARA applies to site-specific art, and then allowing the removal of site-specific art pursuant to the public presentation exception, the district court purports to protect site-specific art under VARA's general provisions, and then permit its destruction by the application of one of VARA's exceptions. To us, this is not a sensible reading of VARA's plain meaning. Either VARA recognizes site-specific art and protects it, or it does not recognize site-specific art at all.

* * * We agree with Phillips that the premise of the public presentation exception is artwork that can be moved in some fashion, such as paintings or sculptures—that is, art that is not permanently affixed or "integrated" in such a way that the mere act of moving it would destroy it. The possibility of change without destruction is implicit in the public presentation exception. The public presentation exception defines the types of changes, such as those in lighting and placement that do not constitute "destruction, distortion, or mutilation". But Phillips draws a startling conclusion from the public presentation exception's focus on permissible change in the presentation of a work of visual art: because the public presentation exception addresses itself only to "plop-art", that is, those works of art subject to temporary changes in such matters as lighting and placement, and declares further that such modifications of a work of visual art are not "destroying, distorting, or mutilating" them, the public presentation exception does not apply to site-specific art, which, as everyone acknowledges, cannot be removed from its location without destroying it. This approach leaves Phillips with the district court's holding that VARA applies to site-specific art, minus the court's related holding that the public presentation exception permits the removal of such art. In this way, the tension that we identified in the district court's decision disappears.

* * * Phillips argues that VARA essentially creates a dual regime—words that mean one thing as applied to non-site-specific art have a different meaning when applied to site-specific art. Beyond his reading of the public presentation exception itself, Phillips cites only one other provision of VARA in support of his dual regime argument— § 113(d)(1)(A) of VARA, the so-called "building exception", which excludes from VARA's protection "a work of visual art [that] has been incorporated or made a part of a building in such a way that removing the work from the building will cause the destruction, distortion, mutilation, or other modification of the work as described in section 106A(a)(3)." Phillips asserts that because VARA provides an exception to VARA for artwork attached to buildings, but does not contain a similar provision for site-specific art (understood as art attached to real property), VARA must protect site-specific art.

With both the public presentation and building exceptions, Phillips is arguing that VARA's silence on a subject is actually evidence that the statute addresses that subject. To say the least, this is an odd way to read a statute. If VARA actually established such a complicated, dual regime, we would expect that the phrase "site-specific", or some equivalent, would appear in the language of the statute. There is no such phrase anywhere. Indeed, we would expect much more than just a reference to site-specific art. We would expect an elaboration of how to differentiate between site-specific and non-site-specific art (plop-art). That elaboration is nowhere to be found.

Moreover, the creation of a dual regime—which would require us, essentially, to rewrite VARA—has potentially far-reaching effects beyond the protection of Phillips' work in the Park. Once a piece of art is considered site-specific, and protected by VARA, such objects could not be altered by the property owner absent consent of the artist. Such a conclusion could dramatically affect real property interests and laws.

For example, as Pembroke argues in its brief, Phillips' work in the Park "lies within a rapidly changing urban area and extends beyond Eastport Park to Boston Harbor." If a dual regime were created, there is the potential that:

> not only would Pembroke's ability to move [Phillips'] work or alter Eastport Park be subject to Phillips' approval, but also the owners of nearby property who had nothing to do with the purchase or installation of Phillips' works would be subject to claims that what they do with *their* property has somehow affected the site and has, as a result, altered or destroyed Phillips' works.

* * * Ultimately, we agree with Pembroke's position that "[t]here is no basis for Phillips' claim that VARA establishes two different regulatory regimes: one for free-standing works of art . . . and one for site-specific art that can never be moved and must always be displayed." VARA's plain language also requires us to reject the district court's approach to site-specific art. VARA does not protect site-specific art and then permit its destruction by removal from its site pursuant to the statute's public presentation exception. VARA does not apply to site-specific art at all.

* * * We do not denigrate the value or importance of site-specific art, which unmistakably enriches our culture and the beauty of our public spaces. We have simply concluded, for all of the reasons stated, that the plain language of VARA does not protect site-specific art. If such protection is necessary, Congress should do the job. We cannot do it by rewriting the statute in the guise of statutory interpretation.

Affirmed.

NOTES

Do you think that despite adequate compensation and intent, the statute doesn't protect the artist's "moral right?" How could you ensure the art stayed where it was intended under state law?

For a wonderful and easily understood case on moral rights under the VARA, see generally *Kahle v. Gonzales*, 474 F.3d 665 (9th Cir. 2007).

VIII. THE INHERENT LIMITATIONS OF COPYRIGHT: FAIR USE

A. FAIR USE AS OF RIGHT

The early case law abounds with attempts to delineate the interest copyright protected. The scope of protected interest may well have been dependant on the theory upon which it was based and the purpose intended to be served. Those that adopted the premise of natural rights that expression was an integral part of the human persona, or that everyone was entitled to the fruits of their labor and sweat of the brow, might consider the right was inclusive of original expression and any fruit it might subsequently bear. Those that interpret the constitution based on prior history of copyright and use might limit the protected elements to that of the Stationary act and later the Statute of Anne, citation. That would include the common law right of first publication and the right to make copies of the specific expression disclosed in distribution to the public. Constructions of this nature are reminiscent of the common law notion of possessory interest and the need to devise legal mechanisms to protect the interest if physical possession were shared. It is also consistent as a justification for "securing" the private right in furtherance of the stated objective of "progress" set forth in the Constitution.

Fair use was perceived as a right at common law, not a defense. It served to maximize public user of shared publications. *Stowe* reminds that use by the public did not necessarily diminish value to the original author relative to subsequent works she might produce, unless the product of another was clearly to the better. The right was based on competition which ideally serves to assure progress. Do you think that competition is a catalyst for progress?

STOWE v. THOMAS

Circuit Court, E.D. Pennsylvania.
23 Fed. Cas. 201.

The act of congress (Act Feb. 3, 1831 [4 Stat. 436]) respecting copyrights gives to the "author of any book" the "sole right and liberty of printing, reprinting, publishing and vending such book:" and if any other person shall print, publish or import, &c., "any copy of such book" without the consent, &c., affixes certain penalties for the infringement of copy-right. With this act in force, Mrs. Harriet Beecher Stowe published in 1850–52, a romance called "Uncle Tom's Cabin: or Life among the Lowly." The copy-right had been duly secured. The book became very popular, and soon after its publication Mrs. Stowe "employed at much expense Hugo Rudolph Hutton, a competent German scholar of ability and critical knowledge of the German language, as also of the English, to translate and copy it into the German language." Dr. Hutton was assisted in his labours by Mrs. Stowe's husband: and by these individuals, at her expense, her said book, as she alleged, had "been fully, completely, accurately and recognized translated and copied, printed and published in the German language;" and in that form duly secured by copy-right. With this original and translation before the public, the defendant made a second translation into German. It appeared in chapters, in the columns of a daily newspaper, Die Freie Presse; the type before distribution being used to print a re-publication in pamphlet form. The ordinary formalities to secure copy-right had been taken in regard to this translation. The Die

Freie Presse was printed at Philadelphia and circulated extensively among the German population with which that place and adjoining parts of Pennsylvania are known to abound. There being no considerable dispute about facts, the question on this bill for injunction was, whether the translation was an infringement of Mrs. Stowe's copy-right in the original.

GRIER, CIRCUIT JUSTICE.

In the balance of opinions among learned jurists, we must endeavour to find some ascertained principles of the common law as established by judicial decision on which to found our conclusion. In order to decide what is an infringement of an author's rights, we must inquire what constitutes literary property, and what is recognized as such by the act of congress. And secured and protected thereby.

An author may be said to be the creator or inventor, both of the ideas contained in his book, and the combination of words to represent them. Before publication he has the exclusive possession of his invention. His dominion is perfect. But when he has published his book, and given his thoughts, sentiments, knowledge or discoveries to the world, he can have no longer an exclusive possession of them. Such an appropriation becomes impossible, and is inconsistent with the object of publication. The author's conceptions have become the common property of his readers, who cannot be deprived of the use of them, nor of their right to communicate them to another clothed in their own language, by lecture or by treatise.

The claim of literary property, therefore, after publication, cannot be in the ideas, sentiments, or the creations of the imagination of the poet or novelist as dissevered from the language, idiom, style, or the outward semblance and exhibition of them. His exclusive property in the creation of his mind, cannot be vested in the author as abstractions, but only in the concrete form which he has given them, and the language in which he has clothed them. When he has sold his book, the only property which be reserves to himself, or which the law gives to him, is the exclusive right to multiply the copies of that particular combination of characters which exhibits to the eyes of another the ideas intended to be conveyed. This is what the law terms copy, or copyright. Curt. Copyr. 9–11, et seq.

The statute of 8 Anne, c. 19 (which so far as it describes the rights and property of an author, is but declaratory of the common law), is entitled, "An act for the encouragement of learning, by vesting the copies of printed books in the authors, &c." It gives the author "the sole right of printing and reprinting such book or books," and describes those who infringe the author's rights, as persons "printing, reprinting, or importing such book or books" without the license of the author. Our acts of congress give substantially the same description both of the author's rights and what is an infringement of them.

Now, although the legal definition of a "book" may be much more extensive than that given by lexicographers, and may include a sheet of music as well as a bound volume; yet, it necessarily conveys the idea, of thought or conceptions clothed in language or in musical characters, written, printed or published. Its identity does not consist merely in the ideas, knowledge or information communicated, but in the same conceptions clothed in the same words, which make it the same composition. 2 Bl. Comm. 406. A 'copy' of a book must, therefore, be a transcript of the language in which the conceptions of the author are clothed; of something printed and embodied in a tangible shape. The same conceptions clothed in another language cannot constitute the same composition, nor can it be called a transcript or "copy" of the same "book." have seen a literal translation of Burns' poems into French prose; but to call it a copy of the original, would be as ridiculous as the translation itself.

The notion that a translation is a piracy of the original composition, is founded on the analogy assumed between copy-right and patents for inventions, and where the infringing machine is only a change of the form or proportions of the original, while it embodies the principle or essence of the invention. But as the author's exclusive property in a literary composition or his copy-right, consists only in a right to multiply copies of his book, and enjoy the profits therefrom, and not in an exclusive right to his conceptions and inventions, which may be termed the essence of his composition, the argument from the supposed analogy is fallacious. Hence, in questions of infringement of copyright, the inquiry is not, whether the defendant has used the thoughts, conceptions, information or discoveries promulgated by the original, but whether his composition may be considered a new work, requiring invention, learning and judgment, or only a mere transcript of the whole or parts of the original, with merely colourable variations. Hence, also, the many cases to be found in the reports, which decide that a bonâ fide abridgment of a book is not an infringement of copyright.

To make a good translation of a work, often requires more learning, talent and judgment, than was required to write the original. Many can transfer from one language to another, but few can translate. To call the translations of an author's ideas and conceptions into another language, a copy of his book, would be an abuse of terms, and arbitrary judicial legislation.

Although the question now under consideration, was not directly in issue in the great case of Millar v. Taylor (4 Burrows, 2303), yet the inference that a translation is not an infringement of copyright, is a logical result, and stated by the judges themselves as a necessary corollary, from the principles of law then decided by the court. That case exhausted the argument, and has finally settled the question as to the nature of the property which an author has in his works; and it is, that after publication, his property consists in the "right of copy," which signifies "the sole right of printing, publishing and selling his literary composition or book," not that he has such a property in his original conceptions, that he alone can use them in the composition of a new work, or clothe them in a different dress by translation. He may be incompetent to such a task, or to make a new work out of his old materials, and neither the common law nor the statute give him such a monopoly, even of his own creations.

An author, says Lord Mansfield, has the same property in his book, which the king has to the English translation of the Bible. "Yet if any man should turn the Psalms, or the writings of Solomon, or Job, into verse, the king could not stop the printing or sale of such a work. It is the author's work; the king has no power or control over the subject-matter. His power rests in property. His whole right rests upon the foundation of property in the copy." Mr. Justice Willes, in answer to the question, "Wherein consists the identity of a book?" says, "Certainly, bonâ fide imitations, translations and abridgments are different, and in respect of property, may be considered new works." And Mr. Justice Aston observes: "The publication of a composition does not give away the property in the work. But the right of copy still remains in the author. No more passes to the public from the free will and consent of the author, than unlimited use of every advantage that the purchaser can reap from the doctrine and sentiments which the work contains. He may improve it, imitate it, translate it, oppose its sentiments; but he buys no right to publish the identical work."

The distinction taken by some writers on the subject of literary property, between the works which are publici juris, and of those which are subject to copyright, has no foundation, in fact, if the established doctrine of the cases be true, and the author's property in a published book consists only in a right of copy. By the publication of Mrs. Stowe's book, the creations of the genius and imagination of the author have become as much public property as those of Homer or Cervantes. [Uncle Tom and Topsy are as much publici juris as Don Quixote and Sancho Panza.](fn omitted) All her conceptions and inventions may be used and abused by imitators, play-rights and poetasters. [They are no longer her own-those who have purchased her book, may clothe them in English doggerel, in German or Chinese prose. Her absolute dominion and property in the creations of her genius and imagination have been voluntarily relinquished.] All that now remains is the copyright of her book; the exclusive right to print, reprint and vend it, and those only can be called infringers of her rights, or pirates of her property, who are guilty of printing, publishing, importing or vending without her license, "copies of her book." A translation may, in loose phraseology, be called a transcript or copy of her thoughts or conceptions, but in no correct sense can it be called a copy of her book.

Bill dismissed, with costs.

NOTE

1. A number of contrasts are worth noting after reading the *Stowe* case. Notice that the decision in *Folsom v. Marsh,* 6 Hunt, Mer. Mag. 175, 9 Fed. Cas. 342 (C.C. Mass. 1841), was not acknowledged by the court in *Stowe,* even though decided almost a decade earlier. *Folsom* was a bill in equity claiming that the letters and other writings of George Washington were complied in a duly copyrighted work: "The Writings of George Washington" in 12 Volumes.

The case involved the alleged infringement of a second book, abridged in form, of 866 pages, about half of which was verbatim that of the copyrighted work.

Justice Story noted in the opinion:

> "So, in cases of copyright, it is often exceedingly obvious, that the whole substance of one work has been copied from another, with slight omissions and formal differences only, which can be treated in no other way than as studied evasions; whereas, in other cases, the identity of the two works in substance, and the question of piracy, often depend upon a nice balance of the comparative use made in one of the materials of the other; the nature, extent, and value of the materials thus used; the objects of each work; and the degree to which each writer may be fairly presumed to have resorted to the same common sources of information, or to have exercised the same common diligence in the selection and arrangement of the materials. Thus, for example, no one can doubt that a reviewer may fairly cite largely from the original work, if his design be really and truly to use the passages for the purposes of fair and reasonable criticism. On the other hand, it is as clear, that if he thus cites the most important parts of the work, with a view, not to criticize, but to supersede the use of the original work, and substitute the review for it, such a use will be deemed in law a piracy. A wide interval might, of course, exist between these two extremes, calling for great caution and involving great difficulty, where the court is approaching the dividing middle line which separates the one from the other. So, it has been decided that a fair and bona fide abridgment of an original work, is not a piracy of the copyright of the author. . . . But, then, what constitutes a fair and bona fide abridgment, in the sense of the law, is one of the most difficult points, under particular circumstances, which can well arise for judicial discussion. It is clear, that a mere selection, or different arrangement of parts of the original work, so as to bring the work into a smaller compass, will not be held to be such an abridgment. There must be real, substantial condensation of the materials, and intellectual labor and judgment bestowed thereon; and not merely the facile use of the scissors; or extracts of the essential parts, constituting the chief value of the original work. . . ." *Folsom*, at 9 Fed. Cas. 342, 345.

The fair use standard incorporated in the statutory revision in 1976 is premised on the decision articulated in *Folsom,* not the literal copying of all, but of less than all the copyrighted work. This lies in sharp contrast to the decision in the *Stowe* case. Beyond adoption of the more protective standard for right exclusion of use by others, it also forces a finding of infringement, the pleading of fair use as an affirmative defense and shifts the burden of proof to the public user. This changes not only ultimate liability, but the chilling effects of risk calculation on use and "progress." This has not gone unnoticed among scholars and the courts. In essence it has changed the use and function of paradigms of "transformative" analysis. See e.g., *Arriba* and *Perfect 10 v. Amazon* and Google, See section VIII (D).

2.   An excellent analysis and history of fair use, including the impact of Justice Story's decision in Folsom will be found in John Tehranian, *Et Tu,*

Fair Use? The Triumph of Natural Law Copyright, 38 U.C. Davis L. Rev. 465 (2005).

B.   THE FUNCTION OF FAIR USE-
THE HOUSE REPORT

With the 1976 revision of the Copyright Act, fair use was considered an equitable common law doctrine applied by the court as a defense and limitation on copyrights. This construction, although noted in revisionist comments, House Report and cases which follow, is also thought to change the original nature and function of Fair Use. First, it treats Fair Use as a defense, rather than an affirmative right of use. Second, by setting forth four elements that are to be taken into consideration, it does not weight the factors, nor indicate the relationship of any or all to the determination of fair use as a defense. Fair use has been viewed by many as a "safety valve" for the rights of the public use in the grey area between private rights and the public domain. In light of increased term limits and the expanding coverage of content, fair use is a critical concept in maintaining balance between public use and private rights.

§ 107.   Limitations on exclusive rights: Fair use

Notwithstanding the provisions of sections 106 and 106A, the fair use of a copyrighted work, including such use by reproduction in copies or phonorecords or by any other means specified by that section, for purposes such as criticism, comment, news reporting, teaching (including multiple copies for classroom use), scholarship, or research, is not an infringement of copyright. In determining whether the use made of a work in any particular case is a fair use the factors to be considered shall include—

(1) the purpose and character of the use, including whether such use is of a commercial nature or is for nonprofit educational purposes;

(2) the nature of the copyrighted work;

(3) the amount and substantiality of the portion used in relation to the copyrighted work as a whole; and

(4) the effect of the use upon the potential market for or value of the copyrighted work.

The fact that a work is unpublished shall not itself bar a finding of fair use if such finding is made upon consideration of all the above factors.

HOUSE REPORT FAIR USE

H.R. REP. 94–1476, 1976 U.S.C.C.A.N. 5659.
5678–5680

Section 107. Fair Use

General background of the problem

"The judicial doctrine of fair use, one of the most important and well established limitations on the exclusive right of copyright owners, would be given express statutory recognition for the first time in section 107. The claim that a defendant's acts constituted a fair use rather than an infringement has been raised as a defense in innumerable copyright actions over the years, and there is ample case law recognizing the existence of the doctrine and applying it. The examples enumerated at page 24 of the Register's 1961 Report, while by no means exhaustive, give some idea of the sort of activities the courts might regard as fair use under the circumstances: 'Quotation of excerpts in a review or criticism for purposes of illustration or comment; quotation of short passages in a scholarly or technical work, for illustration or clarification of the author's observations; use in a parody of some of the content of the work parodied; summary of an address or article, with brief quotations, in a news report; reproduction by a library of a portion of a work to replace part of a damaged copy; reproduction by a teacher or student of a small part of a work to illustrate a lesson; reproduction of a work in legislative or judicial proceedings or reports; incidental and fortuitous reproduction, in a news-reel or broadcast, of a work located in the scene of an event being reported.'

Although the courts have considered and ruled upon the fair use doctrine over and over again, no real definition of the concept has ever emerged. Indeed, since the doctrine is an equitable rule of reason, no generally applicable definition is possible, and each case raising the question must be decided on its own facts. On the other hand, the courts have evolved a set of criteria which, though in no case definitive or determinative, provide some gauge for balancing the equities. These criteria have been stated in various ways, but essentially they can all be reduced to the four standards which have been adopted in section 107: '(1) the purpose and character of the use, including whether such use is of a commercial nature or is for non-profit educational purposes; (2) the nature of the copyrighted work; (3) the amount and substantiality of the portion used in relation to the copyrighted work as a whole; and (4) the effect of the use upon the potential market for or value of the copyrighted work.'

These criteria are relevant in determining whether the basic doctrine of fair use, as stated in the first sentence of section 107, applies in a particular case: 'Notwithstanding the provisions of section 106, the fair use of a copyrighted work, including such use by reproduction in copies or phonorecords or by any other means specified by that section, for purposes such as criticism, comment, news reporting, teaching (including multiple copies for classroom use), scholarship, or research, is not an infringement of copyright.'

The specific wording of section 107 as it now stands is the result of a process of accretion, resulting from the long controversy over the related problems of fair use and the reproduction (mostly by photocopying) of copyrighted material for educational and scholarly purposes. For example, the reference to fair use 'by reproduction in copies of phonorecords, or by any other means' is mainly intended to make clear that the doctrine has as much application to photocopying and taping as to older forms of use; it is not intended to give these kinds of reproduction any special status under the fair use provision or to sanction any reproduction beyond the normal and reasonable limits of fair use. Similarly, the newly-added reference to 'multiple copies for classroom use' is a recognition that, under the proper circumstances of fairness, the doctrine can be applied to reproductions of multiple copies for the members of a class.

The Committee has amended the first of the criteria to be considered—'the purpose and character of the use'—to state explicitly that this factor includes a consideration of 'whether such use is of a commercial nature or is for non-profit educational purposes.' This amendment is not intended to be interpreted as any sort of not-for-profit limitation on educational uses of copyrighted works. It is an express recognition that, as under the present law, the commercial or non-profit character of an activity, while not conclusive with respect to fair use, can and should be weighed along with other factors in fair use decisions.

General intention behind the provision

The statement of the fair use doctrine in section 107 offers some guidance to users in determining when the principles of the doctrine apply. However, the endless variety of situations and combinations of circumstances that can arise in particular cases precludes the formulation of exact rules in the statute. The bill endorses the purpose and general scope of the judicial doctrine of fair use, but there is no disposition to freeze the doctrine in the statute, especially during a period of rapid technological change. Beyond a very broad statutory explanation of what fair use is and some of the criteria applicable to it, the courts must be free to adapt the doctrine to particular situations on a case-by-case basis. Section 107 is intended to restate the present judicial doctrine of fair use, not to change, narrow, or enlarge it in any way.''

C. FAIR USE IN PARODY

CAMPBELL v. ACUFF–ROSE MUSIC, INC.

Supreme Court of the United States, 1994.
510 U.S. 569, 114 S.Ct. 1164, 127 L.Ed.2d 500.

JUSTICE SOUTER delivered the opinion of the Court.

We are called upon to decide whether 2 Live Crew's commercial parody of Roy Orbison's song, "Oh, Pretty Woman," may be a fair use within the meaning of the Copyright Act of 1976, 17 U.S.C. § 107 (1988 ed. and Supp. IV). Although the District Court granted summary judgment for 2 Live Crew, the Court of Appeals reversed, holding the defense of fair use barred by the song's commercial character and excessive borrowing. Because we hold that a parody's commercial character is only one element to be weighed in a fair use enquiry, and that insufficient consideration was given to the nature of parody in weighing the degree of copying, we reverse and remand.

In 1964, Roy Orbison and William Dees wrote a rock ballad called "Oh, Pretty Woman" and assigned their rights in it to respondent Acuff–Rose Music, Inc. * * * Acuff–Rose registered the song for copyright protection.

Petitioners Luther R. Campbell, Christopher Wongwon, Mark Ross, and David Hobbs are collectively known as 2 Live Crew, a popular rap music group. In 1989, Campbell wrote a song entitled "Pretty Woman," which he later described in an affidavit as intended, "through comical lyrics, to satirize the original work. . . ." On July 5, 1989, 2 Live Crew's manager informed Acuff–Rose that 2 Live Crew had written a parody of "Oh, Pretty Woman," that they would afford all credit for ownership and authorship of the original song to Acuff–Rose, Dees, and Orbison, and that they were willing to pay a fee for the use they wished to make of it.

Almost a year later, after nearly a quarter of a million copies of the recording had been sold, Acuff–Rose sued 2 Live Crew and its record company, Luke Skyywalker Records, for copyright infringement. * * *

It is uncontested here that 2 Live Crew's song would be an infringement of Acuff–Rose's rights in "Oh, Pretty Woman," under the Copyright Act of 1976, 17 U.S.C. § 106 (1988 ed. and Supp. IV), but for a finding of fair use through parody. From the infancy of copyright protection, some opportunity for fair use of copyrighted materials has been thought necessary to fulfill copyright's very purpose, "[t]o promote the Progress of Science and useful Arts. . . ." U.S. Const., Art. I, § 8, cl. 8. For as Justice Story explained, "[i]n truth, in literature, in science and in art, there are, and can be, few, if any, things, which in an abstract sense, are strictly new and original throughout. Every book in literature, science and art, borrows, and must necessarily borrow, and use much which was well known and used before." *Emerson v. Davies*, 8 F.Cas. 615, 619 (No. 4,436) (CCD

Mass.1845). Similarly, Lord Ellenborough expressed the inherent tension in the need simultaneously to protect copyrighted material and to allow others to build upon it when he wrote, "while I shall think myself bound to secure every man in the enjoyment of his copy-right, one must not put manacles upon science." *Cary v. Kearsley*, 4 Esp. 168, 170, 170 Eng.Rep. 679, 681 (K.B.1803). In copyright cases brought under the Statute of Anne of 1710, English courts held that in some instances "fair abridgements" would not infringe an author's rights, see W. Patry, The Fair Use Privilege in Copyright Law 6–17 (1985) (hereinafter Patry); Leval, Toward a Fair Use Standard, 103 Harv.L.Rev. 1105 (1990) (hereinafter Leval), and although the First Congress enacted our initial copyright statute, Act of May 31, 1790, 1 Stat. 124, without any explicit reference to "fair use," as it later came to be known, the doctrine was recognized by the American courts nonetheless. * * *

In *Folsom v. Marsh*, 9 F.Cas. 342 (No. 4,901) (CCD Mass. 1841), Justice Story distilled the essence of law and methodology from the earlier cases: "look to the nature and objects of the selections made, the quantity and value of the materials used, and the degree in which the use may prejudice the sale, or diminish the profits, or supersede the objects, of the original work." Id., at 348. * * *

The first factor in a fair use enquiry is "the purpose and character of the use, including whether such use is of a commercial nature or is for nonprofit educational purposes." § 107(1). This factor draws on Justice Story's formulation, "the nature and objects of the selections made." *Folsom v. Marsh*, supra, at 348. The enquiry here may be guided by the examples given in the preamble to § 107, looking to whether the use is for criticism, or comment, or news reporting, and the like, see § 107. The central purpose of this investigation is to see, in Justice Story's words, whether the new work merely "supersede[s] the objects" of the original creation, *Folsom v. Marsh*, supra, at 348.

This Court has only once before even considered whether parody may be fair use, and that time issued no opinion because of the Court's equal division. *Benny v. Loew's Inc.*, 239 F.2d 532 (CA9 1956), aff'd sub nom. *Columbia Broadcasting System, Inc. v. Loew's Inc.*, 356 U.S. 43, 78 S.Ct. 667, 2 L.Ed.2d 583 (1958). Suffice it to say now that parody has an obvious claim to transformative value, as Acuff–Rose itself does not deny. Like less ostensibly humorous forms of criticism, it can provide social benefit, by shedding light on an earlier work, and, in the process, creating a new one. We thus line up with the courts that have held that parody, like other comment or criticism, may claim fair use under § 107. See, e.g., *Fisher v. Dees*, 794 F.2d 432 (CA9 1986) ("When Sonny Sniffs Glue," a parody of "When Sunny Gets Blue," is fair use); *Elsmere Music, Inc. v. National Broadcasting Co.*, 482 F.Supp. 741 SDNY), aff'd, 623 F.2d 252 (CA2 1980) ("I Love Sodom," a "Saturday Night Live" television parody of "I Love New York," is fair use); see also House Report, p. 65; Senate Report, p. 61, U.S.Code Cong. & Admin.News 1976, pp. 5659, 5678 ("[U]se in a parody of some of the content of the work parodied" may be fair use).

The germ of parody lies in the definition of the Greek parodeia, quoted in Judge Nelson's Court of Appeals dissent, as "a song sung alongside another." * * * Modern dictionaries accordingly describe a parody as a "literary or artistic work that imitates the characteristic style of an author or a work for comic effect or ridicule," or as a "composition in prose or verse in which the characteristic turns of thought and phrase in an author or class of authors are imitated in such a way as to make them appear ridiculous." For the purposes of copyright law, the nub of the definitions, and the heart of any parodist's claim to quote from existing material, is the use of some elements of a prior author's composition to create a new one that, at least in part, comments on that author's works. See, e.g., *Fisher v. Dees*, supra, at 437; *MCA, Inc. v. Wilson*, 677 F.2d 180, 185 (CA2 1981). If, on the contrary, the commentary has no critical bearing on the substance or style of the original composition, which the alleged infringer merely uses to get attention or to avoid the drudgery in working up something fresh, the claim to fairness in borrowing from another's work diminishes accordingly (if it does not vanish), and other factors, like the extent of its commerciality, loom larger. Parody needs to mimic an original to make its point, and so has some claim to use the creation of its victim's (or collective victims') imagination, whereas satire can stand on its own two feet and so requires justification for the very act of borrowing. * * *

While we might not assign a high rank to the parodic element here, we think it fair to say that 2 Live Crew's song reasonably could be perceived as commenting on the original or criticizing it, to some degree. 2 Live Crew juxtaposes the romantic musings of a man whose fantasy comes true, with degrading taunts, a bawdy demand for sex, and a sigh of relief from paternal responsibility. The later words can be taken as a comment on the naiveté of the original of an earlier day, as a rejection of its sentiment that ignores the ugliness of street life and the debasement that it signifies. It is this joinder of reference and ridicule that marks off the author's choice of parody from the other types of comment and criticism that traditionally have had a claim to fair use protection as transformative works.

The language of the statute makes clear that the commercial or nonprofit educational purpose of a work is only one element of the first factor enquiry into its purpose and character. Section 107(1) uses the term "including" to begin the dependent clause referring to commercial use, and the main clause speaks of a broader investigation into "purpose and character." As we explained in *Harper & Row*, Congress resisted attempts to narrow the ambit of this traditional enquiry by adopting categories of presumptively fair use, and it urged courts to preserve the breadth of their traditionally ample view of the universe of relevant evidence. 471 U.S., at 561, 105 S.Ct. at 2230; House Report, p. 66, U.S.Code Cong. & Admin.News 1976, pp. 5659, 5679. Accordingly, the mere fact that a use is educational and not for profit does not insulate it from a finding of infringement, any more than the commercial character of a use bars a finding of fairness. If, indeed, commerciality carried presumptive force against a finding of fairness, the presumption would swallow nearly all of the illustrative uses listed in the preamble paragraph of § 107, including news reporting, comment, criticism, teaching, scholarship, and research, since these activities "are generally conducted for profit in this country." *Harper & Row*, supra, at 592, 105 S.Ct., at 2246 (Brennan, J., dissenting). Congress could not have intended such a rule, which certainly is not inferable from the common-law cases, arising as they did from the world of letters in which Samuel Johnson could pronounce that "[n]o man but a blockhead ever wrote, except for money." 3 Boswell's Life of Johnson 19 (G. Hill ed. 1934). * * *

The second statutory factor, "the nature of the copyrighted work," § 107(2), draws on Justice Story's expression, the "value of the materials used." *Folsom v. Marsh*, 9 F.Cas., at 348. This factor calls for recognition that some works are closer to the core of intended copyright protection than others, with the consequence that fair use is more difficult to establish when the former works are copied. * * * This fact, however, is not much help in this case, or ever likely to help much in separating the fair use sheep from the infringing goats in a parody case, since parodies almost invariably copy publicly known, expressive works. * * *

The third factor asks whether "the amount and substantiality of the portion used in relation to the copyrighted work as a whole," § 107(3) (or, in Justice Story's words, "the quantity and value of the materials used," Folsom v. Marsh, supra, at 348) are reasonable in relation to the purpose of the copying. Here, attention turns to the persuasiveness of a parodist's justification for the particular copying done, and the enquiry will harken back to the first of the statutory factors, for, as in prior cases, we recognize that the extent of permissible copying varies with the purpose and character of the use. * * * The facts bearing on this factor will also tend to address the fourth, by revealing the degree to which the parody may serve as a market substitute for the original or potentially licensed derivatives. * * *

The fourth fair use factor is "the effect of the use upon the potential market for or value of the copyrighted work." § 107(4). It requires courts to consider not only the extent of market harm caused by the particular actions of the alleged infringer, but also "whether unrestricted and widespread conduct of the sort engaged in by the defendant ... would result in a substantially adverse impact on the potential market" for the original.

Since fair use is an affirmative defense, its proponent would have difficulty carrying the burden of demonstrating fair use without favorable evidence about relevant markets. In moving for summary judgment, 2 Live Crew left themselves at just such a disadvantage when they failed to address the effect on the market for rap derivatives, and confined themselves to uncontroverted submissions that there was no likely effect on the market for the original. They did not, however, thereby subject themselves to the evidentiary presumption applied by the Court of Appeals. In assessing the likelihood of significant market harm, the Court of Appeals quoted from language in Sony that " '[i]f the intended use is for commercial gain, that likelihood may be presumed. But if it is for a noncommercial purpose, the likelihood must be demonstrated.' " * * *The court reasoned that because "the use of the copyrighted work is wholly commercial, . . . we presume that a likelihood of future harm to Acuff–Rose exists. * * * In so doing, the court resolved the fourth factor against 2 Live Crew, just as it had the first, by applying a presumption about the effect of commercial use, a presumption which as applied here we hold to be error.

We do not, of course, suggest that a parody may not harm the market at all, but when a lethal parody, like a scathing theater review, kills demand for the original, it does not produce a harm cognizable under the Copyright Act. * * *

This distinction between potentially remediable displacement and unremediable disparagement is reflected in the rule that there is no protectible derivative market for criticism. The market for potential derivative uses includes only those that creators of original works would in general develop or license others to develop. Yet the unlikelihood that creators of imaginative works will license critical reviews or lampoons of their own productions removes such uses from the very notion of a potential licensing market.

In explaining why the law recognizes no derivative market for critical works, including parody, we have, of course, been speaking of the later work as if it had nothing but a critical aspect. But the later work may have a more complex character, with effects not only in the arena of criticism but also in protectible markets for derivative works, too. In that sort of case, the law looks beyond the criticism to the other elements of the work, as it does here. 2 Live Crew's song comprises not only parody but also rap music, and the derivative market for rap music is a proper focus of enquiry. * * *

Although 2 Live Crew submitted uncontroverted affidavits on the question of market harm to the original, neither they, nor Acuff–Rose, introduced evidence or affidavits addressing the likely effect of 2 Live Crew's parodic rap song on the market for a nonparody, rap version of "Oh, Pretty Woman." And while Acuff–Rose would have us find evidence of a rap market in the very facts that 2 Live Crew recorded a rap parody of "Oh, Pretty Woman" and another rap group sought a license to record a rap derivative, there was no evidence that a potential rap market was harmed in any way by 2 Live Crew's parody, rap version. The fact that 2 Live Crew's parody sold as part of a collection of rap songs says very little about the parody's effect on a market for a rap version of the original, either of the music alone or of the music with its lyrics. * * *

It was error for the Court of Appeals to conclude that the commercial nature of 2 Live Crew's parody of "Oh, Pretty Woman" rendered it presumptively unfair. No such evidentiary presumption is available to address either the first factor, the character and purpose of the use, or the fourth, market harm, in determining whether a transformative use, such as parody, is a fair one. The court also erred in holding that 2 Live Crew had necessarily copied excessively from the Orbison original, considering the parodic purpose of the use. We therefore reverse the judgment of the Court of Appeals and remand the case for further proceedings consistent with this opinion.

D. FAIR USE, REVERSE ENGINEERING, AND INTEROPERABILITY

In the context of complex computer programs, applications and operating systems, whether in memory, or as a ROM module as part of the hardware, 17 U.S.C. § 102(b) informs that any " * * * procedure, process, system, method of operation, concept, principle, or discovery, regardless of the form in which it is described, explained, illustrated, or embodied in such work" is excluded as the subject matter of copyright. Computer machine language, usually in the form of non-volatile memory, controls basic functions and input-output routines of the computer. These system calls can vary from one computer system to another. What if, as here, a computer software application has been designed to operate on a specific proprietary platform that has different system calls than a PC Compatible computer? What if a software developer has to reverse engineer the operating system of the hardware device they wish to emulate by reading its machine language and copying it to a PC in order to write routines to accomplish the same ends on a PC as the original hardware device for which it was designed? Are the routines, processes and input/output code protected elements under copyright? If not, may both protected and unprotected material be copied to get at the unprotected elements? What "bright line" of permissive copying and use can you discern from the case that follows?

SONY COMPUTER ENTERTAINMENT, INC. v. CONNECTIX CORPORATION

United States Court of Appeals, Ninth Circuit, 2000.
203 F.3d 596.

CANBY, CIRCUIT JUDGE:

In this case we are called upon once again to apply the principles of copyright law to computers and their software, to determine what must be protected as expression and what must be made accessible to the public as function. Sony Computer Entertainment, Inc., which brought this copyright infringement action, produces and markets the Sony PlayStation console, a small computer with hand controls that connects to a television console and plays games that are inserted into the PlayStation on compact discs (CDs). Sony owns the copyright on the basic input-output system or BIOS, which is the software program that operates its PlayStation. Sony has asserted no patent rights in this proceeding.

The defendant is the Connectix Corporation, which makes and sells a software program called "Virtual Game Station." The purpose of the Virtual Game Station is to emulate on a regular computer the functioning of the Sony PlayStation console, so that computer owners who buy the Virtual Game Station software can play Sony PlayStation games on their computers. The Virtual Game Station does not contain any of Sony's copyrighted material. In the process of producing the Virtual Game Station, however, Connectix repeatedly copied Sony's copyrighted BIOS during a process of "reverse engineering" that Connectix conducted in order to find out how the Sony PlayStation worked. Sony claimed infringement and sought a preliminary injunction. The district court concluded that Sony was likely to succeed on its infringement claim because Connectix's "intermediate copying" was not a protected "fair use" under 17 U.S.C. § 107. The district court enjoined Connectix from selling the Virtual Game Station or from copying or using the Sony BIOS code in the development of other Virtual Game Station products.

Connectix now appeals. We reverse and remand with instructions to dissolve the injunction. The intermediate copies made and used by Connectix during the course of its reverse engineering of the Sony BIOS were protected fair use, necessary to permit Connectix to make its non-infringing Virtual Game Station function with PlayStation games. Any other intermediate copies made by Connectix do not support injunctive relief, even if those copies were infringing.

The district court also found that Sony is likely to prevail on its claim that Connectix's sale of the Virtual Game Station program tarnishes the Sony PlayStation mark under 15 U.S.C. § 1125. We reverse that ruling as well.

I. Background

A. *The products*

Sony is the developer, manufacturer and distributor of both the Sony PlayStation and Sony PlayStation games. * * * The PlayStation system consists of a console (essentially a mini-computer), controllers, and software that produce a three-dimensional game for play on a television set. The PlayStation games are CDs that load into the top of the console. The PlayStation console contains both (1) hardware components and (2) software known as firmware that is written onto a read-only memory (ROM) chip. The firmware is the Sony BIOS. Sony has a copyright on the BIOS. It has claimed no patent relevant to this proceeding on any component of the PlayStation. PlayStation is a registered trademark of Sony.

Connectix's Virtual Game Station is software that "emulates" the functioning of the PlayStation console. That is, a consumer can load the Virtual Game Station software onto a computer, load a PlayStation game into the computer's CD–ROM drive, and play the PlayStation game. The Virtual Game Station software thus emulates both the hardware and firmware components of the Sony console. The Virtual Game Station does not play PlayStation games as well as Sony's PlayStation does. * * *

B. Reverse engineering

Copyrighted software ordinarily contains both copyrighted and unprotected or functional elements. *Sega Enters. Ltd. v. Accolade, Inc.,* 977 F.2d 1510, 1520 (9th Cir.1992) (amended opinion); see 17 U.S.C. § 102(b) (Copyright protection does not extend to any "idea, procedure, process, system, method of operation, concept, principle, or discovery" embodied in the copyrighted work.). Software engineers designing a product that must be compatible with a copyrighted product frequently must "reverse engineer" the copyrighted product to gain access to the functional elements of the copyrighted product. * * *

Reverse engineering encompasses several methods of gaining access to the functional elements of a software program. They include: (1) reading about the program; (2) observing "the program in operation by using it on a computer;" (3) performing a "static examination of the individual computer instructions contained within the program;" and (4) performing a "dynamic examination of the individual computer instructions as the program is being run on a computer." *Id.* at 846. Method (1) is the least effective, because individual software manuals often misdescribe the real product. See id. It would be particularly ineffective in this case because Sony does not make such information available about its PlayStation. Methods (2), (3), and (4) require that the person seeking access load the target program on to a computer, an operation that necessarily involves copying the copyrighted program into the computer's random access memory or RAM.

Method (2), observation of a program, can take several forms. The functional elements of some software programs, for example word processing programs, spreadsheets, and video game displays may be discernible by observation of the computer screen. See *Sega,* 977 F.2d at 1520. * * * Here, the software program is copied each time the engineer boots up the computer, and the computer copies the program into RAM.

* * * Operations systems, system interface procedures, and other programs like the Sony BIOS are not visible to the user when they are operating. See *id.* One method of "observing" the operation of these programs is to run the program in an emulated environment. In the case of the Sony BIOS, this meant operating the BIOS on a computer with software that simulated the operation of the PlayStation hardware; operation of the program, in conjunction with another program known as a "debugger," permitted the engineers to observe the signals sent between the BIOS and other programs on the computer. This latter method required copying the Sony BIOS from a chip in the PlayStation onto the computer. The Sony BIOS was copied again each time the engineers booted up their computer and the computer copied the program into RAM. All of this copying was intermediate; that is, none of the Sony copyrighted

material was copied into, or appeared in, Connectix's final product, the Virtual Game Station.

Methods (3) and (4) constitute "disassembly" of object code into source code. In each case, engineers use a program known as a "disassembler" to translate the ones and zeros of binary machine-readable object code into the words and mathematical symbols of source code. This translated source code is similar to the source code used originally to create the object code but lacks the annotations drafted by the authors of the program that help explain the functioning of the source code. In a static examination of the computer instructions, method (3), the engineer disassembles the object code of all or part of the program. The program must generally be copied one or more times to perform disassembly. In a dynamic examination of the computer instructions, method (4), the engineer uses the disassembler program to disassemble parts of the program, one instruction at a time, while the program is running. This method also requires copying the program and * * * may require additional copying of the program into RAM every time the computer is booted up.

C. *Connectix's reverse engineering of the Sony BIOS*

Connectix began developing the Virtual Game Station for Macintosh on about July 1, 1998. In order to develop a PlayStation emulator, Connectix needed to emulate both the PlayStation hardware and the firmware (the Sony BIOS).

Connectix first decided to emulate the PlayStation's hardware. In order to do so, Connectix engineers purchased a Sony PlayStation console and extracted the Sony BIOS from a chip inside the console. Connectix engineers then copied the Sony BIOS into the RAM of their computers and observed the functioning of the Sony BIOS in conjunction with the Virtual Game Station hardware emulation software as that hardware emulation software was being developed by Connectix. The engineers observed the operation of the Sony BIOS through use of a debugging program that permitted the engineers to observe the signals sent between the BIOS and the hardware emulation software. During this process, Connectix engineers made additional copies of the Sony BIOS every time they booted up their computer and the Sony BIOS was loaded into RAM.

Once they had developed the hardware emulation software, Connectix engineers also used the Sony BIOS to "debug" the emulation software. In doing so, they repeatedly copied and disassembled discrete portions of the Sony BIOS.

Connectix also used the Sony BIOS to begin development of the Virtual Game Station for Windows. Specifically, they made daily copies to RAM of the Sony BIOS and used the Sony BIOS to develop certain Windows-specific systems for the Virtual Game Station for Windows. Although Connectix had its own BIOS at the time, Connectix engineers used the Sony BIOS because it contained CD–ROM code that the Connectix BIOS did not contain.

* * * During development of the Virtual Game Station, Connectix contacted Sony and requested "technical assistance" from Sony to complete the development of the Virtual Game Station. Connectix and Sony representatives met during September 1998. Sony declined Connectix's request for assistance.

* * * At MacWorld, Connectix marketed the Virtual Game Station as a "PlayStation emulator." The materials stated that the Virtual Game Station permits users to play "their favorite Playstation games" on a computer "even if you don't yet have a Sony PlayStation console."

* * * Connectix admits that it copied Sony's copyrighted BIOS software in developing the Virtual Game Station but contends that doing so was protected as a fair use under 17 U.S.C. § 107. * * *

A. *Fair use*

The fair use issue arises in the present context because of certain characteristics of computer software. The object code of a program may be copyrighted as expression, 17 U.S.C. § 102(a), but it also contains ideas and performs functions that are not entitled to copyright protection. See 17 U.S.C. § 102(b). Object code cannot, however, be read by humans. The unprotected ideas and functions of the code therefore are frequently undiscoverable in the absence of investigation and translation that may require copying the copyrighted material. We conclude that, under the facts of this case and our precedent, Connectix's intermediate copying and use of Sony's copyrighted BIOS was a fair use for the purpose of gaining access to the unprotected elements of Sony's software.

The general framework for analysis of fair use is established by statute, 17 U.S.C. § 107. We have applied this statute and the fair use doctrine to the disassembly of computer software in the case of *Sega Enterprises Ltd. v. Accolade, Inc.,* 977 F.2d 1510 (9th Cir.1992) (amended opinion). Central to our decision today is the rule set forth in *Sega:*

> [W]here disassembly is the *only way to gain access to the ideas and functional elements embodied in a copyrighted computer program* and where there is a legitimate reason for seeking such access, disassembly is a fair use of the copyrighted work, as a matter of law.

Id. at 1527–28 (emphasis added). In *Sega*, we recognized that intermediate copying could constitute copyright infringement even when the end product did not itself contain copyrighted material. *Id.* at 1518–19. But this copying nonetheless could be protected as a fair use if it was "necessary" to gain access to the functional elements of the software itself. *Id.* at 1524–26. We drew this distinction because the Copyright Act protects expression only, not ideas or the functional aspects of a software program. See *id.* at 1524 (citing 17 U.S.C. § 102(b)). We also recognized that, in the case of computer programs, this idea/expression distinction poses "unique problems" because computer programs are "in essence, utilitarian articles—articles that accomplish tasks. As such, they contain many logical, structural, and visual display elements that are dictated by the function to be performed, by considerations of efficiency, or by external factors such as compatibility requirements and industry demands." *Id.* Thus, the fair use doctrine preserves public access to the ideas and functional elements embedded in copyrighted computer software programs. This approach is consistent with the " 'ultimate aim [of the Copyright Act], to stimulate artistic creativity for the general public good.' " *Sony Corp. of Am. v. Universal City Studios, Inc.,* 464 U.S. 417, 432, 104 S.Ct. 774, 78 L.Ed.2d 574 (1984) (quoting *Twentieth Century Music Corp. v. Aiken,* 422 U.S. 151, 156, 95 S.Ct. 2040, 45 L.Ed.2d 84 (1975)).

We turn then to the statutory fair use factors, as informed by our precedent in *Sega.*

1. *Nature of the copyrighted work*

Under our analysis of the second statutory factor, nature of the copyrighted work, we recognize that "some works are closer to the core of intended copyright protection than others." *Campbell v. Acuff–Rose Music, Inc.,* 510 U.S. 569, 586, 114 S.Ct. 1164, 127 L.Ed.2d 500 (1994). Sony's BIOS lies at a distance from the core because it contains unprotected aspects that cannot be examined without copying. See *Sega,* 977 F.2d at 1526. We consequently accord it a "lower degree of protection than more traditional literary works." *Id.* As we have applied this standard, Connectix's copying of the Sony BIOS must have been "necessary" to have been fair use. See *id.* at 1524–26. We conclude that it was.

There is no question that the Sony BIOS contains unprotected functional elements. Nor is it disputed that Connectix could not gain access to these unprotected functional elements without copying the Sony BIOS. * * * Consequently, if Connectix was to gain access to the functional elements of the Sony BIOS it had to be through a form of reverse engineering that required copying the Sony BIOS onto a computer. Sony does not dispute this proposition.

The question then becomes whether the methods by which Connectix reverse-engineered the Sony BIOS were necessary to gain access to the unprotected functional elements within the program. We conclude that they were. Connectix employed several methods of reverse engineering (observation and observation with partial disassembly) each of which required Connectix to make intermediate copies of copyrighted material. Neither of these methods renders fair use protection inapplicable. *Sega* expressly sanctioned disassembly. See *id.* at 1527–28. We see no reason to distinguish observation of copyrighted software in an emulated computer environment. Both methods require the reverse engineer to copy protected as well as unprotected elements of the computer program. Because this intermediate copying is the gravamen of the intermediate infringement claim, see 17 U.S.C. § 106(1); *Sega,* 977 F.2d at 1518–19, and both methods of reverse engineering require it, we find no reason inherent in these methods to prefer one to another as a matter of copyright law. Connectix presented evidence that it observed the Sony BIOS in an emulated environment to observe the functional aspects of the Sony BIOS.

When this method of reverse engineering was unsuccessful, Connectix engineers disassembled discrete portions of the Sony BIOS to view directly the ideas contained therein. We conclude that intermediate copying in this manner was "necessary" within the meaning of *Sega*.

* * * The district court did not focus on whether Connectix's copying of the Sony BIOS was necessary for access to functional elements. Instead, it found that Connectix's copying and *use* of the Sony BIOS to develop its own software exceeded the scope of *Sega*. See Order at 17 ("[T]hey disassembled Sony's code not just to study the concepts. They actually used that code in the development of [their] product."). This rationale is unpersuasive. * * * [T]he distinction between "studying" and "use" is unsupported in *Sega*. Moreover, reverse engineering is a technically complex, frequently iterative process. * * * Within the limited context of a claim of intermediate infringement, we find the semantic distinction between "studying" and "use" to be artificial, and decline to adopt it for purposes of determining fair use.

* * * Sony contends that Connectix's reverse engineering of the Sony BIOS should be considered unnecessary on the rationale that Connectix's decision to observe the Sony BIOS in an emulated environment required Connectix to make more intermediate copies of the Sony BIOS than if Connectix had performed a complete disassembly of the program. Under this logic, at least some of the intermediate copies were not necessary within the meaning of *Sega*. This construction stretches *Sega* too far. The "necessity" we addressed in *Sega* was the necessity of the method, i.e., disassembly, not the necessity of the number of times that method was applied. * * * In any event, the interpretation advanced by Sony would be a poor criterion for fair use. Most of the intermediate copies of the Sony BIOS were made by Connectix engineers when they booted up their computers and the Sony BIOS was copied into RAM. But if Connectix engineers had left their computers turned on throughout the period during which they were observing the Sony BIOS in an emulated environment, they would have made far fewer intermediate copies of the Sony BIOS (perhaps as few as one per computer). Even if we were inclined to supervise the engineering solutions of software companies in minute detail, and we are not, our application of the copyright law would not turn on such a distinction. Such a rule could be easily manipulated. More important, the rule urged by Sony would require that a software engineer, faced with two engineering solutions that each require intermediate copying of protected and unprotected material, often follow the *least efficient solution*. * * * This is precisely the kind of "wasted effort that the proscription against the copyright of ideas and facts . . . [is] designed to prevent." *Feist Publications, Inc. v. Rural Tel. Serv. Co.*, 499 U.S. 340, 354, 111 S.Ct. 1282, 113 L.Ed.2d 358 (1991) (internal quotation marks omitted). Such an approach would erect an artificial hurdle in the way of the public's access to the ideas contained within copyrighted software programs. These are "aspects that were expressly denied copyright protection by Congress." *Sega*, 977 F.2d at 1526 (citing 17 U.S.C. § 102(b)). We

decline to erect such a barrier in this case. If Sony wishes to obtain a lawful monopoly on the functional concepts in its software, it must satisfy the more stringent standards of the patent laws. * * * The second statutory factor strongly favors Connectix.

2. Amount and substantiality of the portion used

With respect to the third statutory factor, amount and substantiality of the portion used in relation to the copyrighted work as a whole, Connectix disassembled parts of the Sony BIOS and copied the entire Sony BIOS multiple times. This factor therefore weighs against Connectix. But as we concluded in *Sega*, in a case of intermediate infringement when the final product does not itself contain infringing material, this factor is of "very little weight." * * *

3. Purpose and character of the use

Under the first factor, purpose and character of the use, we inquire into whether Connectix's Virtual Game Station:

> "merely supersedes the objects of the original creation, or instead adds something new, with a further purpose or different character, altering the first with new expression, meaning, or message; it asks, in other words, whether and to what extent the new work is "transformative.""

Campbell v. Acuff–Rose Music, Inc., 510 U.S. 569, 579, 114 S.Ct. 1164, 127 L.Ed.2d 500 (1994) * * * As an initial matter, we conclude that the district court applied an erroneous legal standard; the district court held that Connectix's commercial purpose in copying the Sony BIOS gave rise to a "presumption of unfairness that ... can be rebutted by the characteristics of a particular commercial use." * * * Since *Sega,* however, the Supreme Court has rejected this presumption as applied to the first and fourth factor of the fair use analysis. *Acuff–Rose,* 510 U.S. at 584, 594, 114 S.Ct. 1164 (clarifying *Sony,* 464 U.S. at 451, 104 S.Ct. 774). Instead, the fact that Connectix's copying of the Sony BIOS was for a commercial purpose is only a "separate factor that tends to weigh against a finding of fair use." *Id.* at 585, 114 S.Ct. 1164 * * *

We find that Connectix's Virtual Game Station is modestly transformative. The product creates a new platform, the personal computer, on which consumers can play games designed for the Sony PlayStation. This innovation affords opportunities for game play in new environments, specifically anywhere a Sony PlayStation console and television are not available, but a computer with a CD–ROM drive is. More important, the Virtual Game Station itself is a wholly new product, notwithstanding the similarity of uses and functions between the Sony PlayStation and the Virtual Game Station. The expressive element of software lies as much in the organization and structure of the object code that runs the computer as it does in the visual expression of that code that appears on a computer screen. See 17 U.S.C. § 102(a) (extending copyright protection to original works of authorship that "can be perceived, reproduced, or otherwise communicated, either directly or with the aid of a machine or device"). Sony does not claim that the Virtual Game Station itself contains object code that infringes Sony's copyright. We are therefore at a loss to see how Connectix's drafting of entirely new object code for its VGS program could not be transformative, despite the similarities in function and screen output.

Finally, we must weigh the extent of any transformation in Connectix's Virtual Game Station against the significance of other factors, including commercialism, that militate against fair use. * * * Connectix's commercial use of the copyrighted material was an intermediate one, and thus was only "indirect or derivative." * * * Moreover, Connectix reverse-engineered the Sony BIOS to produce a product that would be compatible with games designed for the Sony PlayStation. We have recognized this purpose as a legitimate one under the first factor of the fair use analysis. * * * Upon weighing these factors, we find that the first factor favors Connectix.

The district court ruled, however, that the Virtual Game Station was not transformative on the rationale that a computer screen and a television screen are interchangeable, and the Connectix product therefore merely "supplants" the Sony PlayStation console. * * * The district court clearly erred. For the reasons stated above, the Virtual Game Station is transformative and does not merely supplant the PlayStation console. In reaching its decision, the district court apparently failed to consider the expressive nature of the Virtual Game Station software itself. Sony's reliance on *Infinity Broadcast Corp. v. Kirkwood,* 150 F.3d 104 (2d Cir.1998), suffers from the same defect. The *Infinity* court reasoned that a "change of format, though useful, is not technically a transformation." *Id.* at 108 n. 2. But the infringing party in that case was merely taking copyrighted radio transmissions and retransmitting them over telephone lines; there was no new expression. *Id.* at 108. *Infinity* does not change our conclusion; the purpose and character of Connectix's copying points toward fair use.

4. *Effect of the use upon the potential market*

We also find that the fourth factor, effect of the use upon the potential market, favors Connectix. Under this factor, we consider

> not only the extent of market harm caused by the particular actions of the alleged infringer, but also "whether unrestricted and widespread conduct of the sort engaged in by the defendant ... would result in a substantially adverse impact on the potential market" for the original.

Acuff–Rose, 510 U.S. at 590, 114 S.Ct. 1164 (quoting 3 M. Nimmer & D. Nimmer, *Nimmer on Copyright,* § 13.05[A][4], at 13–102.61 (1993)). Whereas a work that merely supplants or supersedes another is likely to cause a substantially adverse impact on the potential market of the original, a transformative work is less likely to do so. * * *

The district court found that "[t]o the extent that such a substitution [of Connectix's Virtual Game Station for Sony PlayStation console] occurs, Sony will lose console sales and profits." * * * We recognize that this may be so. But because the Virtual Game Station is transformative, and does not merely supplant the PlayStation console, the Virtual Game Station is a legitimate competitor in the market for platforms on which Sony and Sony-licensed games can be played. * * * For this reason, some economic loss by Sony as a result of this competition does not compel a finding of no fair use. Sony understandably seeks control over the market for devices that play games Sony produces or licenses. The copyright law, however, does not confer such a monopoly. * * * ("[A]n attempt to monopolize the market by making it impossible for others to compete runs counter to the statutory purpose of promoting creative expression and cannot constitute a strong equitable basis for resisting the invocation of the fair use doctrine."). This factor favors Connectix.

The four statutory fair use factors must be "weighed together, in light of the purposes of copyright." *Acuff–Rose,* 510 U.S. at 578, 114 S.Ct. 1164. Here, three of the factors favor Connectix; one favors Sony, and it is of little weight. Of course, the statutory factors are not exclusive, *Harper & Row,* 471 U.S. at 560, 105 S.Ct. 2218, but we are unaware of other factors not already considered that would affect our analysis. Accordingly, we conclude that Connectix's intermediate copying of the Sony BIOS during the course of its reverse engineering of that product was a fair use under 17 U.S.C. § 107, as a matter of law. With respect to its claim of copyright infringement, Sony has not established either a likelihood of success on the merits or that the balance of hardships tips in its favor. See *Cadence Design Sys., Inc. v. Avant! Corp.,* 125 F.3d 824, 826 (9th Cir.1997), *cert. denied,* 523 U.S. 1118, 118 S.Ct. 1795, 140 L.Ed.2d 936 (1998). Accordingly, we need not address defenses asserted by Connectix under 17 U.S.C. § 117(a)(1) and our doctrine of copyright misuse. We reverse the district court's grant of a preliminary injunction on the ground of copyright infringement. * * *

Conclusion

Connectix's reverse engineering of the Sony BIOS extracted from a Sony PlayStation console purchased by Connectix engineers is protected as a fair use. Other intermediate copies of the Sony BIOS made by Connectix, if they infringed Sony's copyright, do not justify injunctive relief. For these reasons, the district court's injunction is dissolved and the case is remanded to the district court. We also reverse the district court's finding that Connectix's Virtual Game Station has tarnished the Sony PlayStation mark.

Reversed And Remanded.

NOTES

Does *Connectix* inform your understanding of the protected elements of copyright and areas in which copy rights are relative, ambulatory and changing with context and technology? See generally, Paul Goldstein, *Fair Use in a Changing World*, 50 J. COPYRIGHT SOC'Y U.S.A. 133 (2003); Wendy J. Gordon, *Fair Use: Threat or Threatened?*, 55 CASE W. RES. L. REV. 903, 906 (2005); David Nimmer, "Fairest of Them All" and Other Fairy Tales of Fair Use Factors, 66 Law & Contemp. Prob. 263 (Winter/Spring 2003); Samuel Oddi, The Tragicomedy of the Public Domain in Intellectual Property Law, 25 Hastings Comm. & Ent. L.J. 1 (2002).

What constitutes expression in the "transformative" code created by Connectix? What constituted expression in the original Bios of the Sony consol?

After reading the entire case, could one simply conclude that fair use permits copying to reach unprotected elements of computer programs or machine level instructions so long as protected expression is not copied or integrated in the "fair user" work?

Is this case an example of the distinction between copying and use of content? What is the protected interest of copyright? What is the purpose of copyright for the public good?

If facts, ideas and processes are not the subject of copyright, then does fair use play a significant role as a pathway in protecting access to matter in the Public Domain? Does this beg the question of whether uses that constitute the body of fair use are representative of the public's right of use in the public domain. In what way does fair use in this context function as a "limitation on copyright?" Does that mean because of fair use, the bundle of rights included in copyright are limited, or does it mean that rights are absolute, but subject to limited use by the public under the equitable (now statutory) designation of "fair use?"

E. FAIR USE IN TIME SHIFTING: SONY BETAMAX

New technologies have accorded users the ability to record over the air broadcasts of radio and television, as well as content accessible through the internet. Sony was one of the first manufacturers to bring a "machine" to consumer use for the purpose of video tape recording of home movies, as well as over the air broadcasts. Sony was sued by several content owners because these copies by the end user's were alleged to violate their copyrights and because Sony through the *Betamax* VTR enabled them to engage in these acts of infringement.

Why did the content rights holder no bring actions against the individuals who were actively engaged in copying? Why did they sue the manufacturer of equipment that permitted the end users to copy? The multitude of practical and policy issues behind this decision find further exposition in the context of Digital Rights Management, Chapter Seven, albeit the seeds were present in the case that follows. On what basis could a suit be brought against the manufacturer of equipment that had the potential to permit copyright infringement? What would be the theory of liability? Is there a basis for contributory liability under the Copyright Act? What acts would constitute the basis for manufacturer liability? What facts and circumstances protect the manufacturer? This has often been called the *Betamax* "bright line." After reading the case, can you formulate that bright line?

There are a number of values fundamental to society and democratic institutions noted in the *Betamax* decision. Can you identify the range of and specific values affected by Copyright?

SONY CORPORATION OF AMERICA v. UNIVERSAL CITY STUDIOS, INC.

Supreme Court of the United States, 1984.
464 U.S. 417, 104 S.Ct. 774, 78 L.Ed.2d 574.

JUSTICE STEVENS delivered the opinion of the Court.

Petitioners manufacture and sell home video tape recorders. Respondents own the copyrights on some of the television programs that are broadcast on the public airwaves. Some members of the general public use video tape recorders sold by petitioners to record some of these broadcasts, as well as a large number of other broadcasts. The question presented is whether the sale of petitioners' copying equipment to the general public violates any of the rights conferred upon respondents by the Copyright Act.

* * * Respondents alleged that some individuals had used Betamax video tape recorders (VTR's) to record some of respondents' copyrighted works which had been exhibited on commercially sponsored television and contended that these individuals had thereby infringed respondents' copyrights. Respondents further maintained that petitioners were liable for the copyright infringement allegedly committed by Betamax consumers because of petitioners' marketing of the Betamax VTR's. Respondents sought no relief against any Betamax consumer. Instead, they sought money damages and an equitable accounting of profits from petitioners, as well as an injunction against the manufacture and marketing of Betamax VTR's.

* * * [T]he District Court denied respondents all the relief they sought and entered judgment for petitioners. 480 F.Supp. 429 (1979). The United States Court of Appeals for the Ninth Circuit reversed the District Court's judgment on respondent's copyright claim, holding petitioners liable for contributory infringement * * * 659 F.2d 963 (1981). We granted certiorari, 457 U.S. 1116, 102 S.Ct. 2926, 73 L.Ed.2d 1328 (1982) * * * We now reverse.

* * * In summary, [the findings of the District court] * * * reveal that the average member of the public uses a VTR principally to record a

program he cannot view as it is being televised and then to watch it once at a later time. This practice, known as "time-shifting," enlarges the television viewing audience. For that reason, a significant amount of television programming may be used in this manner without objection from the owners of the copyrights on the programs. For the same reason, even the two respondents in this case, who do assert objections to time-shifting in this litigation, were unable to prove that the practice has impaired the commercial value of their copyrights or has created any likelihood of future harm. Given these findings, there is no basis in the Copyright Act upon which respondents can hold petitioners liable for distributing VTR's to the general public. The Court of Appeals' holding * * * would enlarge the scope of respondents' statutory monopolies to encompass control over an article of commerce that is not the subject of copyright protection. Such an expansion of the copyright privilege is beyond the limits of the grants authorized by Congress.

I

The two respondents in this action, Universal Studios, Inc. and Walt Disney Productions, produce and hold the copyrights on a substantial number of motion pictures and other audiovisual works. * * * Petitioner Sony manufactures millions of Betamax video tape recorders and markets these devices through numerous retail establishments. * * * Sony's Betamax VTR is a mechanism consisting of three basic components: (1) a tuner, which receives electromagnetic signals transmitted over the television band of the public airwaves and separates them into audio and visual signals; (2) a recorder, which records such signals on a magnetic tape; and (3) an adapter, which converts the audio and visual signals on the tape into a composite signal that can be received by a television set. * * *

The respondents and Sony both conducted surveys of the way the Betamax machine was used by several hundred owners during a sample period in 1978. Although there were some differences in the surveys, they both showed that the primary use of the machine for most owners was "time-shifting,"—the practice of recording a program to view it once at a later time, and thereafter erasing it. Time-shifting enables viewers to see programs they otherwise would miss because they are not at home, are occupied with other tasks, or are viewing a program on another station at the time of a broadcast that they desire to watch. * * * Sony's survey indicated that over 80% of the interviewees watched at least as much regular television as they had before owning a Betamax. Respondents offered no evidence of decreased television viewing by Betamax owners. Sony introduced considerable evidence describing television programs that could be copied without objection from any copyright holder, with special emphasis on sports, religious, and educational programming. For example, their survey indicated that 7.3% of all Betamax use is to record sports events, and representatives of professional baseball, football, basketball, and hockey testified that they had no objection to the recording of their televised events for home use. * * *

The District Court concluded that noncommercial home use recording of material broadcast over the public airwaves was a fair use of copyrighted works and did not constitute copyright infringement. It emphasized the fact that the material was broadcast free to the public at large, the noncommercial character of the use, and the private character of the activity conducted entirely within the home. Moreover, the court found that the purpose of this use served the public interest in increasing access to television programming, an interest that "is consistent with the First Amendment policy of providing the fullest possible access to information through the public airwaves. *Columbia Broadcasting System, Inc. v. Democratic National Committee,* 412 U.S. 94, 102 [93 S.Ct. 2080, 2086, 36 L.Ed.2d 772]." 480 F.Supp., at 454. * * * Even when an entire copyrighted work was recorded, the District Court regarded the copying as fair use "because there is no accompanying reduction in the market for 'plaintiff's original work.' " Ibid.

As an independent ground of decision, the District Court also concluded that Sony could not be held liable as a contributory infringer even if the home use of a VTR was considered an infringing use. The District Court noted that Sony had no direct involvement with any Betamax purchasers who recorded copyrighted works off the air. Sony's advertising was silent on the subject of possible copyright infringement, but its instruction booklet contained the following statement:

"Television programs, films, videotapes and other materials may be copyrighted. Unauthorized recording of such material may be contrary to the provisions of the United States copyright laws." *Id.,* at 436.

The District Court assumed that Sony had constructive knowledge of the probability that the Betamax machine would be used to record copyrighted programs, but found that Sony merely sold a "product capable of a variety of uses, some of them allegedly infringing." Id., at 461. It reasoned:

"Selling a staple article of commerce e.g., a typewriter, a recorder, a camera, a photocopying machine technically contributes to any infringing use subsequently made thereof, but this kind of 'contribution,' if deemed sufficient as a basis for liability, would expand the theory beyond precedent and arguably beyond judicial management.

"Commerce would indeed be hampered if manufacturers of staple items were held liable as contributory infringers whenever they 'constructively' knew that some purchasers on some occasions would use their product for a purpose which a court later deemed, as a matter of first impression, to be an infringement." *Ibid.*

Finally, the District Court discussed the respondents' prayer for injunctive relief, noting that they had asked for an injunction either preventing the future sale of Betamax machines, or requiring that the machines be rendered incapable of recording copyrighted works off the air. The court stated that it had "found no case in which the manufacturers, distributors, retailers, and advertisors of the instrument enabling the infringement were sued by the copyright holders," and that the request for relief in this case "is unique." 480 F.Supp., at 465.

It concluded that an injunction was wholly inappropriate because any possible harm to respondents was outweighed by the fact that "the Betamax could still legally be used to record noncopyrighted material or material whose owners consented to the copying. An injunction would deprive the public of the ability to use the Betamax for this noninfringing off-the-air recording." 480 F.Supp., at 468.

The Court of Appeals' Decision

The Court of Appeals reversed the District Court's judgment on respondents' copyright claim. It did not set aside any of the District Court's findings of fact. Rather, it concluded as a matter of law that the home use of a VTR was not a fair use because it was not a "productive use." * * * It therefore held that it was unnecessary for plaintiffs to prove any harm to the potential market for the copyrighted works, but then observed that it seemed clear that the cumulative effect of mass reproduction made possible by VTR's would tend to diminish the potential market for respondents' works. 659 F.2d, at 974.

On the issue of contributory infringement, the Court of Appeals first rejected the analogy to staple articles of commerce such as tape recorders or photocopying machines. It noted that such machines "may have substantial benefit for some purposes" and do not "even remotely raise copyright problems." *Id.,* at 975. VTR's, however, are sold "for the primary purpose of reproducing television programming" and "virtually all" such programming is copyrighted material. *Ibid.* The Court of Appeals concluded, therefore, that VTR's were not suitable for any substantial noninfringing use even if some copyright owners elect not to enforce their rights.

The Court of Appeals also rejected the District Court's reliance on Sony's lack of knowledge that home use constituted infringement. Assuming that the statutory provisions defining the remedies for infringement applied also to the non-statutory tort of contributory infringement, the court stated that a defendant's good faith would merely reduce his damages liability but would not excuse the infringing conduct. It held that Sony was chargeable with knowledge of the homeowner's infringing activity because the reproduction of copyrighted materials was either "the most conspicuous use" or "the major use" of the Betamax product. *Ibid.* * * *

II

* * * The monopoly privileges that Congress may authorize are neither unlimited nor primarily designed to provide a special private benefit. Rather, the limited grant is a means by which an important public purpose may be achieved. It is intended to motivate the creative activity of authors and inventors by the provision of a special reward, and to allow

the public access to the products of their genius after the limited period of exclusive control has expired.

* * * "The sole interest of the United States and the primary object in conferring the monopoly lie in the general benefits derived by the public from the labors of authors. It is said that reward to the author or artist serves to induce release to the public of the products of his creative genius." *United States v. Paramount Pictures,* 334 U.S. 131, 158, 68 S.Ct. 915, 929, 92 L.Ed. 1260.

As the text of the Constitution makes plain, it is Congress that has been assigned the task of defining the scope of the limited monopoly that should be granted to authors or to inventors in order to give the public appropriate access to their work product. Because this task involves a difficult balance between the interests of authors and inventors in the control and exploitation of their writings and discoveries on the one hand, and society's competing interest in the free flow of ideas, information, and commerce on the other hand, our patent and copyright statutes have been amended repeatedly. * * *

"The enactment of copyright legislation by Congress under the terms of the Constitution is not based upon any natural right that the author has in his writings, . . . but upon the ground that the welfare of the public will be served and progress of science and useful arts will be promoted by securing to authors for limited periods the exclusive rights to their writings.

* * *

"In enacting a copyright law Congress must consider . . . two questions: First, how much will the legislation stimulate the producer and so benefit the public, and, second, how much will the monopoly granted be detrimental to the public? The granting of such exclusive rights, under the proper terms and conditions, confers a benefit upon the public that outweighs the evils of the temporary monopoly." H.R.Rep. No. 2222, 60th Cong., 2d Sess. 7 (1909).

From its beginning, the law of copyright has developed in response to significant changes in technology. * * * Indeed, it was the invention of a new form of copying equipment—the printing press—that gave rise to the original need for copyright protection. * * * [R]epeatedly, as new developments have occurred in this country, it has been the Congress that has fashioned the new rules that new technology made necessary. Thus, long before the enactment of the Copyright Act of 1909, 35 Stat. 1075, it was settled that the protection given to copyrights is wholly statutory. *Wheaton v. Peters,* 33 U.S. (8 Peters) 591, 661–662, 8 L.Ed. 1055 (1834). The remedies for infringement "are only those prescribed by Congress." *Thompson v. Hubbard,* 131 U.S. 123, 151, 9 S.Ct. 710, 720, 33 L.Ed. 76 (1889).

By enacting the Sound Recording Amendment of 1971, 85 Stat. 391, Congress also provided the solution to the "record piracy" problems that had been created by the development of the audio tape recorder. Sony argues that the legislative history of that Act, see especially H.Rep. No. 487, 92nd Cong., 1st Sess., p. 7, indicates that Congress did not intend to prohibit the private home use of either audio or video tape recording equipment. In view of our disposition of the contributory infringement issue, we express no opinion on that question.

The judiciary's reluctance to expand the protections afforded by the copyright without explicit legislative guidance is a recurring theme. * * * Sound policy, as well as history, supports our consistent deference to Congress when major technological innovations alter the market for copyrighted materials. Congress has the constitutional authority and the institutional ability to accommodate fully the varied permutations of competing interests that are inevitably implicated by such new technology.

In a case like this, in which Congress has not plainly marked our course, we must be circumspect in construing the scope of rights created by a legislative enactment which never contemplated such a calculus of interests. In doing so, we are guided by Justice Stewart's exposition of the correct approach to ambiguities in the law of copyright: "The limited scope of the copyright holder's statutory monopoly, like the limited copyright duration required by the Constitution, reflects a balance of competing claims upon the public interest: Creative work is to be encouraged and rewarded, but private motivation must ultimately serve the cause of promoting broad public availability of literature, music, and the other arts. The immediate effect of our copyright law is to secure a fair return for an 'author's' creative labor. But the ultimate aim is, by this incentive, to stimulate artistic creativity for the general public good. 'The sole interest of the United States and the primary object in conferring the monopoly,' this Court has said, 'lie in the general benefits derived by the public from the labors of authors.' * * * When technological change has rendered its literal terms ambiguous, the Copyright Act must be construed in light of this basic purpose." * * *

Copyright protection "subsists ... in original works of authorship fixed in any tangible medium of expression." 17 U.S.C. § 102(a). This protection has never accorded the copyright owner complete control over all possible uses of his work. * * * Rather, the Copyright Act grants the copyright holder "exclusive" rights to use and to authorize the use of his work in five qualified ways, including reproduction of the copyrighted work in copies. *Id.,* § 106 * * * All reproductions of the work, however, are not within the exclusive domain of the copyright owner; some are in the public domain. Any individual may reproduce a copyrighted work for a "fair use;" the copyright owner does not possess the exclusive right to such a use. Compare *id.,* § 106, with *id.,* § 107.

While the law has never recognized an author's right to absolute control of his work, the natural tendency of legal rights to express themselves in absolute terms to the exclusion of all else is particularly pronounced in the history of the constitutionally sanctioned monopolies of the copyright and the patent.

"Anyone who violates any of the exclusive rights of the copyright owner," that is, anyone who trespasses into his exclusive domain by using or authorizing the use of the copyrighted work in one of the five ways set forth in the statute, "is an infringer of the copyright."* * * Conversely, anyone who is authorized by the copyright owner to use the copyrighted work in a way specified in the statute or who makes a fair use of the work is not an infringer of the copyright with respect to such use. * * *

The two respondents in this case do not seek relief against the Betamax users who have allegedly infringed their copyrights. * * * As was made clear by their own evidence, the copying of the respondents' programs represents a small portion of the total use of VTR's. It is, however, the taping of respondents own copyrighted programs that provides them with standing to charge Sony with contributory infringement. To prevail, they have the burden of proving that users of the Betamax have infringed their copyrights and that Sony should be held responsible for that infringement.

III

The Copyright Act does not expressly render anyone liable for infringement committed by another. In contrast, the Patent Act expressly brands anyone who "actively induces infringement of a patent" as an infringer, 35 U.S.C. § 271(b), and further imposes liability on certain individuals labeled "contributory" infringers, *id.*, § 271(c). The absence of such express language in the copyright statute does not preclude the imposition of liability for copyright infringements on certain parties who have not themselves engaged in the infringing activity. * * * For vicarious liability is imposed in virtually all areas of the law, and the concept of contributory infringement is merely a species of the broader problem of identifying the circumstances in which it is just to hold one individual accountable for the actions of another. * * *

Respondents argue that *Kalem* stands for the proposition that supplying the "means" to accomplish an infringing activity and encouraging that activity through advertisement are sufficient to establish liability for copyright infringement. This argument rests on a gross generalization that cannot withstand scrutiny. The producer in *Kalem* did not merely provide the "means" to accomplish an infringing activity; the producer supplied the work itself, albeit in a new medium of expression. Petitioners in the instant case do not supply Betamax consumers with respondents' works; respondents do. Petitioners supply a piece of equipment that is generally capable of copying the entire range of programs that may be televised: those that are uncopyrighted, those that are copyrighted but may be copied without objection from the copyright holder, and those that the copyright holder would prefer not to have copied. The Betamax can be used to make authorized or unauthorized uses of copyrighted works, but the range of its potential use is much broader than the particular infringing use of the film *Ben Hur* involved in *Kalem*. *Kalem* does not support respondents' novel theory of liability.

Justice Holmes stated that the producer had "contributed" to the infringement of the copyright, and the label "contributory infringement" has been applied in a number of lower court copyright cases involving an ongoing relationship between the direct infringer and the contributory infringer at the time the infringing conduct occurred. In such cases, as in other situations in which the imposition of vicarious liability is manifestly just, the "contributory" infringer was in a position to control the use of copyrighted works by others and had authorized the use without permission from the copyright owner. * * * This case, however, plainly does not fall in that category. The only contact between Sony and the users of the Betamax that is disclosed by this record occurred at the moment of sale. The District Court expressly found that "no employee of Sony, Sonam or DDBI had either direct involvement with the allegedly infringing activity or direct contact with purchasers of Betamax who recorded copyrighted works off-the-air." 480 F.Supp., at 460. And it further found that "there was no evidence that any of the copies made by Griffiths or the other individual witnesses in this suit were influenced or encouraged by [Sony's] advertisements." *Ibid.*

If vicarious liability is to be imposed on petitioners in this case, it must rest on the fact that they have sold equipment with constructive knowledge of the fact that their customers may use that equipment to make unauthorized copies of copyrighted material. There is no precedent in the law of copyright for the imposition of vicarious liability on such a theory. The closest analogy is provided by the patent law cases to which it is appropriate to refer because of the historic kinship between patent law and copyright law. The two areas of the law, naturally, are not identical twins, and we exercise the caution which we have expressed in the past in applying doctrine formulated in one area to the other. * * *

We have consistently rejected the proposition that a similar kinship exists between copyright law and trademark law, and in the process of doing so have recognized the basic similarities between copyrights and patents. * * * Given the fundamental differences between copyright law and trademark law, in this copyright case we do not look to the standard for contributory infringement * * * which was crafted for application in trademark cases. * * * Sony certainly does not "intentionally induce[ ]" its customers to make infringing uses of respondents' copyrights, nor does it supply its products to identified individuals known by it to be engaging in continuing infringement of respondents' copyrights, see *id.*, at 855, 102 S.Ct., at 2188.

In the Patent Code both the concept of infringement and the concept of contributory infringement are expressly defined by statute. * * * The prohibition against contributory infringement is confined to the knowing sale of a component especially made for use in connection with a particular patent. There is no suggestion in the statute that one patentee may object to the sale of a product that might be used in connection with other patents. Moreover, the Act expressly provides that the sale of a "staple article or commodity of commerce suitable for substantial noninfringing use" is not contributory infringement.

When a charge of contributory infringement is predicated entirely on the sale of an article of commerce that is used by the purchaser to infringe a patent, the public interest in access to that article of commerce is necessarily implicated. A finding of contributory infringement does not, of course, remove the article from the market altogether; it does, however, give the patentee effective control over the sale of that item. Indeed, a finding of contributory infringement is normally the functional equivalent of holding that the disputed article is within the monopoly granted to the patentee. * * *

For that reason, in contributory infringement cases arising under the patent laws the Court has always recognized the critical importance of not allowing the patentee to extend his monopoly beyond the limits of his specific grant. These cases deny the patentee any right to control the distribution of unpatented articles unless they are "unsuited for any commercial noninfringing use." * * *

A. *Authorized Time Shifting*

Each of the respondents owns a large inventory of valuable copyrights, but in the total spectrum of television programming their combined market share is small. The exact percentage is not specified, but it is well below 10%. * * * If they were to prevail, the outcome of this litigation would have a significant impact on both the producers and the viewers of the remaining 90% of the programming in the Nation. * * * Nevertheless the findings of the District Court make it clear that time-shifting may enlarge the total viewing audience and that many producers are willing to allow private time-shifting to continue, at least for an experimental time period. * * *

The District Court found:

"Even if it were deemed that home-use recording of copyrighted material constituted infringement, the Betamax could still legally be used to record noncopyrighted material or material whose owners consented to the copying. An injunction would deprive the public of the ability to use the Betamax for this noninfringing off-the-air recording.

"Defendants introduced considerable testimony at trial about the potential for such copying of sports, religious, educational and other programming. This included testimony from representatives of the Offices of the Commissioners of the National Football, Basketball, Baseball and Hockey Leagues and Associations, the Executive Director of National Religious Broadcasters and various educational communications agencies. Plaintiffs attack the weight of the testimony offered and also contend that an injunction is warranted because infringing uses outweigh noninfringing uses."

> "Whatever the future percentage of legal versus illegal home-use recording might be, an injunction which seeks to deprive the public of the very tool or article of commerce capable of some noninfringing use would be an extremely harsh remedy, as well as one unprecedented in copyright law." 480 F.Supp., at 468.

Although the District Court made these statements in the context of considering the propriety of injunctive relief, the statements constitute a finding that the evidence concerning "sports, religious, educational, and other programming" was sufficient to establish a significant quantity of broadcasting whose copying is now authorized, and a significant potential for future authorized copying. That finding is amply supported by the record. * * *

If there are millions of owners of VTR's who make copies of televised sports events, religious broadcasts, and educational programs such as *Mister Rogers' Neighborhood,* and if the proprietors of those programs welcome the practice, the business of supplying the equipment that makes such copying feasible should not be stifled simply because the equipment is used by some individuals to make unauthorized reproductions of respondents' works. The respondents do not represent a class composed of all copyright holders. Yet a finding of contributory infringement would inevitably frustrate the interests of broadcasters in reaching the portion of their audience that is available only through time-shifting.

Of course, the fact that other copyright holders may welcome the practice of time-shifting does not mean that respondents should be deemed to have granted a license to copy their programs. Third party conduct would be wholly irrelevant in an action for direct infringement of respondents' copyrights. But in an action for *contributory* infringement against the seller of copying equipment, the copyright holder may not prevail unless the relief that he seeks affects only his programs, or unless he speaks for virtually all copyright holders with an interest in the outcome. In this case, the record makes it perfectly clear that there are many important producers of national and local television programs who find nothing objectionable about the enlargement in the size of the television audience that results from the practice of time-shifting for private home use. * * *

In the context of television programming, some producers evidently believe that permitting home viewers to make copies of their works off the air actually enhances the value of their copyrights. Irrespective of their reasons for authorizing the practice, they do so, and in significant enough numbers to create a substantial market for a non-infringing use of the Sony VTR's. * * * No one could dispute the legitimacy of that market if the producers had authorized home taping of their programs in exchange for a license fee paid directly by the home user. The legitimacy of that market is not compromised simply because these producers have authorized home taping of their programs without demanding a fee from the home user. The copyright law does not require a copyright owner to charge a fee for the use of his works, and as this record clearly demonstrates, the owner of a copyright may well have economic or noneconomic reasons for permitting certain kinds of copying to occur without receiving direct compensation from the copier. It is not the role of the courts to tell copyright holders the best way for them to exploit their copyrights: even if respondents' competitors were ill-advised in authorizing home videotaping, that would not change the fact that they have created a substantial market for a paradigmatic non-infringing use of petitioners' product.

B. *Unauthorized Time–Shifting*

Even unauthorized uses of a copyrighted work are not necessarily infringing. An unlicensed use of the copyright is not an infringement unless it conflicts with one of the specific exclusive rights conferred by the copyright statute. *Twentieth Century Music Corp. v. Aiken,* 422 U.S. 151, 154–155, 95 S.Ct. 2040, 2043, 45 L.Ed.2d 84. Moreover, the definition of exclusive rights in § 106 of the present Act is prefaced by the words "subject to sections 107 through 118." Those sections describe a variety of uses of copyrighted material that "are not infringements of copyright notwithstanding the provisions of § 106." The most pertinent in this case is § 107, the legislative endorsement of the doctrine of "fair use." * * *

That section identifies various factors * * * that enable a Court to apply an "equitable rule of reason" analysis to particular claims of infringement. * * * Although not conclusive, the first factor requires that "the commercial or nonprofit character of an activity" be weighed in any fair use decision. * * * If the Betamax were used to make copies for a commercial or profit-making purpose, such use would presumptively be unfair. The contrary presumption is appropriate here, however, because the District Court's findings plainly establish that time-shifting for private home use must be characterized as a noncommercial, nonprofit activity. Moreover, when one considers the nature of a televised copyrighted audiovisual work, see 17 U.S.C. § 107(2), and that timeshifting merely enables a viewer to see such a work which he had been invited to witness in its entirety free of charge, the fact that the entire work is reproduced, see *id.,* at § 107(3), does not have its ordinary effect of militating against a finding of fair use. * * *

This is not, however, the end of the inquiry because Congress has also directed us to consider "the effect of the use upon the potential market for or value of the copyrighted work." *Id.,* at § 107(4). The purpose of copyright is to create incentives for creative effort. Even copying for noncommercial purposes may impair the copyright holder's ability to obtain the rewards that Congress intended him to have. But a use that has no demonstrable effect upon the potential market for, or the value of, the copyrighted work need not be prohibited in order to protect the author's incentive to create. The prohibition of such noncommercial uses

would merely inhibit access to ideas without any countervailing benefit.
* * *

Thus, although every commercial use of copyrighted material is presumptively an unfair exploitation of the monopoly privilege that belongs to the owner of the copyright, noncommercial uses are a different matter. A challenge to a noncommercial use of a copyrighted work requires proof either that the particular use is harmful, or that if it should become widespread, it would adversely affect the potential market for the copyrighted work. Actual present harm need not be shown; such a requirement would leave the copyright holder with no defense against predictable damage. Nor is it necessary to show with certainty that future harm will result. What is necessary is a showing by a preponderance of the evidence that *some* meaningful likelihood of future harm exists. If the intended use is for commercial gain, that likelihood may be presumed. But if it is for a noncommercial purpose, the likelihood must be demonstrated.

In this case, respondents failed to carry their burden with regard to home time-shifting. The District Court described respondents' evidence as follows:

> "Plaintiffs' experts admitted at several points in the trial that the time-shifting without librarying would result in 'not a great deal of harm.' Plaintiffs' greatest concern about time-shifting is with 'a point of important philosophy that transcends even commercial judgment.' They fear that with any Betamax usage, 'invisible boundaries' are passed: 'the copyright owner has lost control over his program.' " 480 F.Supp., at 467.

* * *

There was no need for the District Court to say much about past harm. "Plaintiffs have admitted that no actual harm to their copyrights has occurred to date." *Id.,* at 451.

On the question of potential future harm from time-shifting, the District Court offered a more detailed analysis of the evidence. It rejected respondents' "fear that persons 'watching' the original telecast of a program will not be measured in the live audience and the ratings and revenues will decrease," by observing that current measurement technology allows the Betamax audience to be reflected. *Id.,* at 466. * * * It rejected respondents' prediction "that live television or movie audiences will decrease as more people watch Betamax tapes as an alternative," with the observation that "[t]here is no factual basis for [the underlying] assumption." *Ibid.* * * * It rejected respondents' "fear that time-shifting will reduce audiences for telecast reruns," and concluded instead that "given current market practices, this should aid plaintiffs rather than harm them." *Ibid.* * * * And it declared that respondents' suggestion "that theater or film rental exhibition of a program will suffer because of time-shift recording of that program" "lacks merit." 480 F.Supp., at 467.

* * * After completing that review, the District Court restated its overall conclusion several times, in several different ways. "Harm from time-shifting is speculative and, at best, minimal." *Ibid.* "The audience benefits from the time-shifting capability have already been discussed. It is not implausible that benefits could also accrue to plaintiffs, broadcasters, and advertisers, as the Betamax makes it possible for more persons to view their broadcasts." *Ibid.* "No likelihood of harm was shown at trial, and plaintiffs admitted that there had been no actual harm to date." *Id.,* at 468–469. "Testimony at trial suggested that Betamax may require adjustments in marketing strategy, but it did not establish even a likelihood of harm." *Id.,* at 469. "Television production by plaintiffs today is more profitable than it has ever been, and, in five weeks of trial, there was no concrete evidence to suggest that the Betamax will change the studios' financial picture." *Ibid.*

The District Court's conclusions are buttressed by the fact that to the extent time-shifting expands public access to freely broadcast television programs, it yields societal benefits. Earlier this year, in *Community Television of Southern California v. Gottfried,* 459 U.S. 498, __–__, n. 12, 103 S.Ct. 885, 891–892, 74 L.Ed.2d 705 (1983), we acknowledged the public interest in making television broadcasting more available. Concededly, that interest is not unlimited. But it supports an interpretation of the concept of "fair use" that requires the copyright holder to demonstrate some likelihood of harm before he may condemn a private act of time-shifting as a violation of federal law.

When these factors are all weighed in the "equitable rule of reason" balance, we must conclude that this record amply supports the District Court's conclusion that home time-shifting is fair use. In light of the findings of the District Court regarding the state of the empirical data, it is clear that the Court of Appeals erred in holding that the statute as presently written bars such conduct. * * *

Congress has plainly instructed us that fair use analysis calls for a sensitive balancing of interests. The distinction between "productive" and "unproductive" uses may be helpful in calibrating the balance, but it cannot be wholly determinative. Although copying to promote a scholarly endeavor certainly has a stronger claim to fair use than copying to avoid interrupting a poker game, the question is not simply two-dimensional. For one thing, it is not true that all copyrights are fungible. Some copyrights govern material with broad potential secondary markets. Such material may well have a broader claim to protection because of the greater potential for commercial harm. Copying a news broadcast may have a stronger claim to fair use than copying a motion picture. And, of course, not all uses are fungible. Copying for commercial gain has a much weaker claim to fair use than copying for personal enrichment. But the notion of social "productivity" cannot be a complete answer to this analysis. A teacher who copies to prepare lecture notes is clearly productive. But so is a teacher who copies for the sake of broadening his personal understanding of his specialty. Or a legislator who copies for the sake of broadening her understanding of what her constituents are watching; or a constituent who copies a news program to help make a decision on how to vote.

Making a copy of a copyrighted work for the convenience of a blind person is expressly identified by the House Committee Report as an example of fair use, with no suggestion that anything more than a purpose to entertain or to inform need motivate the copying. In a hospital setting, using a VTR to enable a patient to see programs he would otherwise miss has no productive purpose other than contributing to the psychological well-being of the patient. Virtually any time-shifting that increases viewer access to television programming may result in a comparable benefit. The statutory language does not identify any dichotomy between productive and nonproductive time-shifting, but does require consideration of the economic consequences of copying.

In summary, the record and findings of the District Court lead us to two conclusions. First, Sony demonstrated a significant likelihood that substantial numbers of copyright holders who license their works for broadcast on free television would not object to having their broadcasts time-shifted by private viewers. And second, respondents failed to demonstrate that time-shifting would cause any likelihood of nonminimal harm to the potential market for, or the value of, their copyrighted works. The Betamax is, therefore, capable of substantial noninfringing uses. Sony's sale of such equipment to the general public does not constitute contributory infringement of respondent's copyrights.

V

"The direction of Art. I is that *Congress* shall have the power to promote the progress of science and the useful arts. When, as here, the Constitution is permissive, the sign of how far Congress has chosen to go can come only from Congress." *Deepsouth Packing Co. v. Laitram Corp.,* 406 U.S. 518, 530, 92 S.Ct. 1700, 1707, 32 L.Ed.2d 273 (1972).

One may search the Copyright Act in vain for any sign that the elected representatives of the millions of people who watch television every day have made it unlawful to copy a program for later viewing at home, or have enacted a flat prohibition against the sale of machines that make such copying possible.

It may well be that Congress will take a fresh look at this new technology, just as it so often has examined other innovations in the past. But it is not our job to apply laws that have not yet been written. Applying the copyright statute, as it now reads, to the facts as they have been developed in this case, the judgment of the Court of Appeals must be reversed.

It is so ordered.

NOTES

1. As noted at the beginning of the case, this action was not against actual copyright infringers, the end users in the home, but rather against Sony as the manufacturer of the mechanisms for "copying." If you were a manufacturer of product capable of recording infringing materials, how would you protect yourself after *Sony Betamax*? This case may be thought the precursor of digital copy issues in *A & M Records, Inc. v. Napster, Inc.*, 114 F.Supp.2d 896 (N.D. Cal. 2000); 239 F.3d 1004 (9th Cir. 2001); *Metro-Goldwyn–Mayer Studios Inc. v. Grokster, Ltd.*, 545 U.S. 913, 125 S.Ct. 2764, 162 L.Ed.2d 781 (2005). How do these cases inform what you might have recommended in light of issues involving XM Radio devices enabling end users to record broadcasts without appropriate manufacturer licenses?

2. Can you identify the issues articulated and weighted in the decision making process balancing the rights of the public as fair use with private content right holder interests?

3. Does the *Betamax* bright line only apply to manufacturers? Was there a bright line for end user non-infringement? What if the actions of the end user were clearly thought to be infringing, would that possibly have made a difference in the outcome of the case? Some of the questions will assume a different character in chapter seven.

IX. THE COPYRIGHT TERM EXTENSION ACT OF 1998 (CTEA)

The past two centuries have witnessed a continuing succession of extended term interest in copyright. CTEA set new term limits for works created after the effective date of the amendments and at the same time extended the term for existing works about to expire. New works are now protected for the "life of the author and 70 years after the author's death." (17 U.S.C § 302) Likewise, there have been increases in the substantive reach of the copyright. How do these expansions of private right serve the underlying purposes of the Constitution? Was anyone a party to deliberations, or with standing in judicial actions, that demanded these legal changes account for the public interest? What makes CTEA unique is the juxtaposition of public anticipation of the enrichment of the public domain by expiring private content rights being restored to unfettered public use and the shock of loss created by the term extension and the failure of those expiring rights to enter the public domain.

The level of public concern may be an indication of implications of CTEA. This has been analogized to the environmental awakening of the 1960s. Who has standing to represent the public's interest in the public domain? Does the public have a right to expect that content which was subject to copyright would return to the public domain during their lifetimes? What role will the courts play in ensuring proper interpretation of the limitations of powers given to Congress in the furtherance of the Constitutional purpose? These questions lie at the very foundation and essence of democratic institutions and governance.

The question of who has standing to represent the public interest requires that the majority opinion and both dissents in *Eldred* be included for your review (the dissent are found on the companion web site to this work). The dissents speak to an interpretation of the public beneficial interest in intellectual content distinct from the majority opinion. History reminds us that it was the dissent of Justice Douglas in *Sierra Club v. Morton*, 405 U.S. 727, 741, 92 S.Ct. 1361, 31 L.Ed.2d 636 (1972) that forever memorialized standing for public interest groups in environmental litigation. See Christopher D. Stone, Should Trees Have Standing? Toward Legal Rights for Natural Objects, 45 S. CALIF. L. REV. 450 (1972); Joseph Sax, The Public Trust Doctrine in Natural Resource Law: Effective Judicial Intervention, 68 MICH. L. REV 471 (1970).

The dissents also pose numerous questions concerning the role of the court and raise fundamental issues of democratic governance. Separation of powers requires restraint, tempered by obligation ensuring that no branch exceeds the proper delegation of authority under the Constitution. Questions implicating rights in the public domain are fundamental to the delegation of copyright powers to congress. Do questions of this nature require political redress?

17 U.S.C. 302 (as amended through 1998)

§ 302. Duration of copyright: Works created on or after January 1, 1978

(a) In General.—Copyright in a work created on or after January 1, 1978, subsists from its creation and, except as provided by the following subsections, endures for a term consisting of the life of the author and 70 years after the author's death.

(b) Joint Works.—In the case of a joint work prepared by two or more authors who did not work for hire, the copyright endures for a term consisting of the life of the last surviving author and 70 years after such last surviving author's death.

(c) Anonymous Works, Pseudonymous Works, and Works Made for Hire.—In the case of an anonymous work, a pseudonymous work, or a work made for hire, the copyright endures for a term of 95 years from the year of its first publication, or a term of 120 years from the year of its creation, whichever expires first. * * *

(d) Records Relating to Death of Authors.—Any person having an interest in a copyright may at any time record in the Copyright Office a statement of the date of death of the author of the copyrighted work, or a statement that the author is still living on a particular date. * * *

(e) Presumption as to Author's Death.—After a period of 95 years from the year of first publication of a work, or a period of 120 years from the year of its creation, whichever expires first, any person who obtains from the Copyright Office a certified report that the records provided by subsection (d) disclose nothing to indicate that the author of the work is living, or died less than 70 years before, is entitled to the benefit of a presumption that the author has been dead for at least 70 years. Reliance in good faith upon this presumption shall be a complete defense to any action for infringement under this title.

(Pub.L. 94–553, Title I, § 101, Oct. 19, 1976, 90 Stat. 2572; Pub.L. 105–298, Title I, § 102(b), Oct. 27, 1998, 112 Stat. 2827.)

ERIC ELDRED v. JOHN D. ASHCROFT

Supreme Court of the United States, 2003.
537 U.S. 186, 123 S.Ct. 769, 154 L.Ed.2d 683.

JUSTICE GINSBURG delivered the opinion of the Court.

This case concerns the authority the Constitution assigns to Congress to prescribe the duration of copyrights. The Copyright and Patent Clause of the Constitution, Art. I, § 8, cl. 8, provides as to copyrights: "Congress shall have Power ... [t]o promote the Progress of Science ... by securing [to Authors] for limited Times ... the exclusive Right to their ... Writings." In 1998, in the measure here under inspection, Congress enlarged the duration of copyrights by 20 years. Copyright Term Extension Act (CTEA), Pub.L. 105–298, §§ 102(b) and (d), 112 Stat. 2827–2828 (amending 17 U.S.C. §§ 302, 304). As in the case of prior extensions, principally in 1831, 1909, and 1976, Congress provided for application of the enlarged terms to existing and future copyrights alike.

Petitioners are individuals and businesses whose products or services build on copyrighted works that have gone into the public domain. They seek a determination that the CTEA fails constitutional review under both the Copyright Clause's "limited Times" prescription and the First Amendment's free speech guarantee. Under the 1976 Copyright Act, copyright protection generally lasted from the work's creation until 50 years after the author's death. Pub.L. 94–553, § 302(a), 90 Stat. 2572 (1976 Act). Under the CTEA, most copyrights now run from creation until 70 years after the author's death. 17 U.S.C. § 302(a). Petitioners do not challenge the "life-plus-70-years" time span itself. "Whether 50 years is enough, or 70 years too much," they acknowledge, "is not a judgment meet for this Court." Brief for Petitioners 14. Congress went awry, petitioners maintain, not with respect to newly created works, but in enlarging the term for published works with existing copyrights. The "limited Tim[e]" in effect when a copyright is secured, petitioners urge, becomes the constitutional boundary, a clear line beyond the power of Congress to extend. See *ibid.* As to the First Amendment, petitioners contend that the CTEA is a content-neutral regulation of speech that fails inspection under the heightened judicial scrutiny appropriate for such regulations.

In accord with the District Court and the Court of Appeals, we reject petitioners' challenges to the CTEA. In that 1998 legislation, as in all previous copyright term extensions, Congress placed existing and future copyrights in parity. In prescribing that alignment, we hold, Congress acted within its authority and did not transgress constitutional limitations.

I

A

We evaluate petitioners' challenge to the constitutionality of the CTEA against the backdrop of Congress' previous exercises of its authority under the Copyright Clause. The Nation's first copyright statute, enacted in 1790, provided a federal copyright term of 14 years from the date of publication, renewable for an additional 14 years if the author survived the first term. Act of May 31, 1790, ch. 15, § 1, 1 Stat. 124 (1790 Act). The 1790 Act's renewable 14–year term applied to existing works (*i.e.,* works already published and works created but not yet published) and future works alike. *Ibid.* Congress expanded the federal copyright term to 42 years in 1831 (28 years from publication, renewable for an additional 14 years), and to 56 years in 1909 (28 years from publication, renewable for an additional 28 years). Act of Feb. 3, 1831, ch. 16, §§ 1, 16, 4 Stat. 436, 439 (1831 Act); Act of Mar. 4, 1909, ch. 320, §§ 23–24, 35 Stat. 1080–1081 (1909 Act). Both times, Congress applied the new copyright term to existing and future works, 1831 Act §§ 1, 16; 1909 Act §§ 23–24; to qualify for the 1831 extension, an existing work had to be in its initial copyright term at the time the Act became effective, 1831 Act §§ 1, 16.

In 1976, Congress altered the method for computing federal copyright terms. 1976 Act §§ 302–304. For works created by identified natural persons, the 1976 Act provided that federal copyright protection would run from the work's creation, not—as in the 1790, 1831, and 1909 Acts— its publication; protection would last until 50 years after the author's death. § 302(a). In these respects, the 1976 Act aligned United States copyright terms with the then-dominant international standard adopted under the Berne Convention for the Protection of Literary and Artistic Works. See H.R.Rep. No. 94–1476, p. 135 (1976), U.S.Code Cong. & Admin.News 1976, p.5659. For anonymous works, pseudonymous works, and works made for hire, the 1976 Act provided a term of 75 years from publication or 100 years from creation, whichever expired first. § 302(c).

These new copyright terms, the 1976 Act instructed, governed all works not published by its effective date of January 1, 1978, regardless of when the works were created. §§ 302–303. For published works with existing copyrights as of that date, the 1976 Act granted a copyright term of 75 years from the date of publication, §§ 304(a) and (b), a 19–year increase over the 56–year term applicable under the 1909 Act.

The measure at issue here, the CTEA, installed the fourth major duration extension of federal copyrights. Retaining the general structure of the 1976 Act, the CTEA enlarges the terms of all existing and future copyrights by 20 years. For works created by identified natural persons, the term now lasts from creation until 70 years after the author's death.

17 U.S.C. § 302(a). This standard harmonizes the baseline United States copyright term with the term adopted by the European Union in 1993. See Council Directive 93/98/EEC of 29 October 1993 Harmonizing the Term of Protection of Copyright and Certain Related Rights, 1993 Official J. Eur. Coms. (L290), p. 9 (EU Council Directive 93/98). For anonymous works, pseudonymous works, and works made for hire, the term is 95 years from publication or 120 years from creation, whichever expires first. 17 U.S.C. § 302(c).

Paralleling the 1976 Act, the CTEA applies these new terms to all works not published by January 1, 1978. §§ 302(a), 303(a). For works published before 1978 with existing copyrights as of the CTEA's effective date, the CTEA extends the term to 95 years from publication. §§ 304(a) and (b). Thus, in common with the 1831, 1909, and 1976 Acts, the CTEA's new terms apply to both future and existing copyrights.

B

Petitioners' suit challenges the CTEA's constitutionality under both the Copyright Clause and the First Amendment. On cross-motions for judgment on the pleadings, the District Court entered judgment for the Attorney General (respondent here). 74 F.Supp.2d 1 (D.D.C.1999). The court held that the CTEA does not violate the "limited Times" restriction of the Copyright Clause because the CTEA's terms, though longer than the 1976 Act's terms, are still limited, not perpetual, and therefore fit within Congress' discretion. *Id.,* at 3. The court also held that "there are no First Amendment rights to use the copyrighted works of others." *Ibid.*

The Court of Appeals for the District of Columbia Circuit affirmed. 239 F.3d 372 (2001). In that court's unanimous view, *Harper & Row, Publishers, Inc. v. Nation Enterprises,* 471 U.S. 539, 105 S.Ct. 2218, 85 L.Ed.2d 588 (1985), foreclosed petitioners' First Amendment challenge to the CTEA. 239 F.3d, at 375. Copyright, the court reasoned, does not impermissibly restrict free speech, for it grants the author an exclusive right only to the specific form of expression; it does not shield any idea or fact contained in the copyrighted work, and it allows for "fair use" even of the expression itself. *Id.,* at 375–376.

A majority of the Court of Appeals also upheld the CTEA against petitioners' contention that the measure exceeds Congress' power under the Copyright Clause. Specifically, the court rejected petitioners' plea for interpretation of the "limited Times" prescription not discretely but with a view to the "preambular statement of purpose" contained in the Copyright Clause: "To promote the Progress of Science." *Id.,* at 377–378. Circuit precedent, *Schnapper v. Foley,* 667 F.2d 102 (C.A.D.C.1981), the court determined, precluded that plea. In this regard, the court took into account petitioners' acknowledgment that the preamble itself places no substantive limit on Congress' legislative power. 239 F.3d, at 378.

The appeals court found nothing in the constitutional text or its history to suggest that "a term of years for a copyright is not a 'limited

Time' if it may later be extended for another 'limited Time.' " *Id.,* at 379. The court recounted that "the First Congress made the Copyright Act of 1790 applicable to subsisting copyrights arising under the copyright laws of the several states." *Ibid.* That construction of Congress' authority under the Copyright Clause "by [those] contemporary with [the Constitution's] formation," the court said, merited "very great" and in this case "almost conclusive" weight. *Ibid.* (quoting *Burrow–Giles Lithographic Co. v. Sarony,* 111 U.S. 53, 57, 4 S.Ct. 279, 28 L.Ed. 349 (1884)). As early as *McClurg v. Kingsland,* 1 How. 202, 11 L.Ed. 102 (1843), the Court of Appeals added, this Court had made it "plain" that the same Clause permits Congress to "amplify the terms of an existing patent." 239 F.3d, at 380. The appeals court recognized that this Court has been similarly deferential to the judgment of Congress in the realm of copyright. *Ibid.* (citing *Sony Corp. of America v. Universal City Studios, Inc.,* 464 U.S. 417, 104 S.Ct. 774, 78 L.Ed.2d 574 (1984); *Stewart v. Abend,* 495 U.S. 207, 110 S.Ct. 1750, 109 L.Ed.2d 184 (1990)).

Concerning petitioners' assertion that Congress might evade the limitation on its authority by stringing together "an unlimited number of 'limited Times,' " the Court of Appeals stated that such legislative misbehavior "clearly is not the situation before us." 239 F.3d, at 379. Rather, the court noted, the CTEA "matches" the baseline term for "United States copyrights [with] the terms of copyrights granted by the European Union." *Ibid.* "[I]n an era of multinational publishers and instantaneous electronic transmission," the court said, "harmonization in this regard has obvious practical benefits" and is "a 'necessary and proper' measure to meet contemporary circumstances rather than a step on the way to making copyrights perpetual." *Ibid.*

Judge Sentelle dissented in part. He concluded that Congress lacks power under the Copyright Clause to expand the copyright terms of existing works. *Id.,* at 380–384. The Court of Appeals subsequently denied rehearing and rehearing en banc. 255 F.3d 849 (2001).

We granted certiorari to address two questions: whether the CTEA's extension of existing copyrights exceeds Congress' power under the Copyright Clause; and whether the CTEA's extension of existing and future copyrights violates the First Amendment. 534 U.S. 1126 and 1160, 122 S.Ct. 1062 and 1170, 151 L.Ed.2d 966 and 152 L.Ed.2d 115 (2002). We now answer those two questions in the negative and affirm.

II

A

We address first the determination of the courts below that Congress has authority under the Copyright Clause to extend the terms of existing copyrights. Text, history, and precedent, we conclude, confirm that the Copyright Clause empowers Congress to prescribe "limited Times" for copyright protection and to secure the same level and duration of protection for all copyright holders, present and future.

The CTEA's baseline term of life plus 70 years, petitioners concede, qualifies as a "limited Tim[e]" as applied to future copyrights. Petitioners contend, however, that existing copyrights extended to endure for that same term are not "limited." Petitioners' argument essentially reads into the text of the Copyright Clause the command that a time prescription, once set, becomes forever "fixed" or "inalterable." The word "limited," however, does not convey a meaning so constricted. At the time of the Framing, that word meant what it means today: "confine[d] within certain bounds," "restrain[ed]," or "circumscribe[d]." S. Johnson, A Dictionary of the English Language (7th ed. 1785); see T. Sheridan, A Complete Dictionary of the English Language (6th ed. 1796) ("confine[d] within certain bounds"); Webster's Third New International Dictionary 1312 (1976) ("confined within limits"; "restricted in extent, number, or duration"). Thus understood, a time span appropriately "limited" as applied to future copyrights does not automatically cease to be "limited" when applied to existing copyrights. And as we observe, *infra*, at 783, there is no cause to suspect that a purpose to evade the "limited Times" prescription prompted Congress to adopt the CTEA.

To comprehend the scope of Congress' power under the Copyright Clause, "a page of history is worth a volume of logic." *New York Trust Co. v. Eisner,* 256 U.S. 345, 349, 41 S.Ct. 506, 65 L.Ed. 963 (1921) (Holmes, J.). History reveals an unbroken congressional practice of granting to authors of works with existing copyrights the benefit of term extensions so that all under copyright protection will be governed evenhandedly under the same regime. As earlier recounted, see *supra,* at 775, the First Congress accorded the protections of the Nation's first federal copyright statute to existing and future works alike. 1790 Act § 1. Since then, Congress has regularly applied duration extensions to both existing and future copyrights. 1831 Act §§ 1, 16; 1909 Act §§ 23–24; 1976 Act §§ 302–303; 17 U.S.C. §§ 302–304.

Because the Clause empowering Congress to confer copyrights also authorizes patents, congressional practice with respect to patents informs our inquiry. We count it significant that early Congresses extended the duration of numerous individual patents as well as copyrights. See, *e.g.,* Act of Jan. 7, 1808, ch. 6, 6 Stat. 70 (patent); Act of Mar. 3, 1809, ch. 35, 6 Stat. 80 (patent); Act of Feb. 7, 1815, ch. 36, 6 Stat. 147 (patent); Act of May 24, 1828, ch. 145, 6 Stat. 389 (copyright); Act of Feb. 11, 1830, ch. 13, 6 Stat. 403 (copyright); see generally Ochoa, Patent and Copyright Term Extension and the Constitution: A Historical Perspective, 49 J. Copyright Soc. 19 (2001). The courts saw no "limited Times" impediment to such extensions; renewed or extended terms were upheld in the early days, for example, by Chief Justice Marshall and Justice Story sitting as circuit justices. See *Evans v. Jordan,* 8 F. Cas. 872, 874 (No. 4,564) (CC Va. 1813) (Marshall, J.) ("Th[e] construction of the constitution which admits the renewal of a patent, is not controverted. A renewed patent . . . confers the same rights, with an original."), aff'd, 9 Cranch 199, 3 L.Ed. 704 (1815); *Blanchard v. Sprague,* 3 F. Cas. 648, 650 (No. 1,518) (CC Mass. 1839)

(Story, J.) ("I never have entertained any doubt of the constitutional authority of congress" to enact a 14–year patent extension that "operates retrospectively"); see also *Evans v. Robinson,* 8 F. Cas. 886, 888 (No. 4,571) (CC Md. 1813) (Congresses "have the exclusive right ... to limit the times for which a patent right shall be granted, and are not restrained from renewing a patent or prolonging" it.).

Further, although prior to the instant case this Court did not have occasion to decide whether extending the duration of existing copyrights complies with the "limited Times" prescription, the Court has found no constitutional barrier to the legislative expansion of existing patents. *McClurg v. Kingsland,* 1 How. 202, 11 L.Ed. 102 (1843), is the path setting precedent. The patentee in that case was unprotected under the law in force when the patent issued because he had allowed his employer briefly to practice the invention before he obtained the patent. Only upon enactment, two years later, of an exemption for such allowances did the patent become valid, retroactive to the time it issued. *McClurg* upheld retroactive application of the new law. The Court explained that the legal regime governing a particular patent "depend[s] on the law as it stood at the emanation of the patent, together with such changes as have been since made; for though they may be retrospective in their operation, that is not a sound objection to their validity." *Id.,* at 206. Neither is it a sound objection to the validity of a copyright term extension, enacted pursuant to the same constitutional grant of authority, that the enlarged term covers existing copyrights.

Congress' consistent historical practice of applying newly enacted copyright terms to future and existing copyrights reflects a judgment stated concisely by Representative Huntington at the time of the 1831 Act: "[J]ustice, policy, and equity alike forb[id]" that an "author who had sold his [work] a week ago, be placed in a worse situation than the author who should sell his work the day after the passing of [the] act." 7 Cong. Deb. 424 (1831); accord, Symposium, The Constitutionality of Copyright Term Extension, 18 Cardozo Arts & Ent. L.J. 651, 694 (2000) (Prof. Miller) ("[S]ince 1790, it has indeed been Congress's policy that the author of yesterday's work should not get a lesser reward than the author of tomorrow's work just because Congress passed a statute lengthening the term today."). The CTEA follows this historical practice by keeping the duration provisions of the 1976 Act largely in place and simply adding 20 years to each of them. Guided by text, history, and precedent, we cannot agree with petitioners' submission that extending the duration of existing copyrights is categorically beyond Congress' authority under the Copyright Clause.

Satisfied that the CTEA complies with the "limited Times" prescription, we turn now to whether it is a rational exercise of the legislative authority conferred by the Copyright Clause. On that point, we defer substantially to Congress. *Sony,* 464 U.S., at 429, 104 S.Ct. 774 ("[I]t is Congress that has been assigned the task of defining the scope of the limited monopoly that should be granted to authors ... in order to give the public appropriate access to their work product.'').

The CTEA reflects judgments of a kind Congress typically makes, judgments we cannot dismiss as outside the Legislature's domain. As respondent describes, see Brief for Respondent 37–38, a key factor in the CTEA's passage was a 1993 European Union (EU) directive instructing EU members to establish a copyright term of life plus 70 years. EU Council Directive 93/98, Art. 1(1), p. 11; see 144 Cong. Rec. S12377–S12378 (daily ed. Oct. 12, 1998) (statement of Sen. Hatch). Consistent with the Berne Convention, the EU directed its members to deny this longer term to the works of any non-EU country whose laws did not secure the same extended term. See Berne Conv. Art. 7(8); P. Goldstein, International Copyright § 5.3, p. 239 (2001). By extending the baseline United States copyright term to life plus 70 years, Congress sought to ensure that American authors would receive the same copyright protection in Europe as their European counterparts. The CTEA may also provide greater incentive for American and other authors to create and disseminate their work in the United States. See Perlmutter, Participation in the International Copyright System as a Means to Promote the Progress of Science and Useful Arts, 36 Loyola (LA) L.Rev. 323, 330 (2002) (''[M]atching th[e] level of [copyright] protection in the United States [to that in the EU] can ensure stronger protection for U.S. works abroad and avoid competitive disadvantages vis-à-vis foreign right holders.''); see also id., at 332 (the United States could not ''play a leadership role'' in the give-and-take evolution of the international copyright system, indeed it would ''lose all flexibility,'' ''if the only way to promote the progress of science were to provide incentives to create new works'').

In addition to international concerns, Congress passed the CTEA in light of demographic, economic, and technological changes, Brief for Respondent 25–26, 33, and nn. 23 and 24, and rationally credited projections that longer terms would encourage copyright holders to invest in the restoration and public distribution of their works, id., at 34–37; see H.R.Rep. No. 105–452, p. 4 (1998) (term extension ''provide[s] copyright owners generally with the incentive to restore older works and further disseminate them to the public'').

Congress also heard testimony from Register of Copyrights Marybeth Peters and others regarding the economic incentives created by the CTEA. According to the Register, extending the copyright for existing works ''could ... provide additional income that would finance the production and publication of new works.'' House Hearings 158. ''Authors would not be able to continue to create,'' the Register explained, ''unless they earned income on their finished works. The public benefits not only from an author's original work but also from his or her further creations. Although this truism may be illustrated in many ways, one of the best examples is Noah Webster [,] who supported his entire family from the earnings on his speller and grammar during the twenty years he took to complete his dictionary.'' Id., at 165.

In sum, we find that the CTEA is a rational enactment; we are not at liberty to second-guess congressional determinations and policy judgments of this order, however debatable or arguably unwise they may be. Accordingly, we cannot conclude that the CTEA—which continues the unbroken congressional practice of treating future and existing copyrights in parity for term extension purposes—is an impermissible exercise of Congress' power under the Copyright Clause.

B

Petitioners' Copyright Clause arguments rely on several novel readings of the Clause. We next address these arguments and explain why we find them unpersuasive.

1

Petitioners contend that even if the CTEA's 20–year term extension is literally a "limited Tim[e]," permitting Congress to extend existing copyrights allows it to evade the "limited Times" constraint by creating effectively perpetual copyrights through repeated extensions. We disagree.

As the Court of Appeals observed, a regime of perpetual copyrights "clearly is not the situation before us." 239 F.3d, at 379. Nothing before this Court warrants construction of the CTEA's 20–year term extension as a congressional attempt to evade or override the "limited Times" constraint. Critically, we again emphasize, petitioners fail to show how the CTEA crosses a constitutionally significant threshold with respect to "limited Times" that the 1831, 1909, and 1976 Acts did not. See *supra,* at 775–776; Austin, *supra* n. 13, at 56 ("If extending copyright protection to works already in existence is constitutionally suspect," so is "extending the protections of U. S copyright law to works by foreign authors that had already been created and even first published when the federal rights attached."). Those earlier Acts did not create perpetual copyrights, and neither does the CTEA.

2

Petitioners dominantly advance a series of arguments all premised on the proposition that Congress may not extend an existing copyright absent new consideration from the author. They pursue this main theme under three headings. Petitioners contend that the CTEA's extension of existing copyrights (1) overlooks the requirement of "originality," (2) fails to "promote the Progress of Science," and (3) ignores copyright's *quid pro quo.*

Petitioners' "originality" argument draws on *Feist Publications, Inc. v. Rural Telephone Service Co.,* 499 U.S. 340, 111 S.Ct. 1282, 113 L.Ed.2d 358 (1991). In *Feist,* we observed that "[t]he *sine qua non* of copyright is originality," *id.,* at 345, 111 S.Ct. 1282, and held that copyright protection is unavailable to "a narrow category of works in which the creative spark is utterly lacking or so trivial as to be virtually nonexistent," *id.,* at 359, 111 S.Ct. 1282. Relying on *Feist,* petitioners urge that even if a work is sufficiently "original" to qualify for copyright protection in the first instance, any extension of the copyright's duration is impermissible because, once published, a work is no longer original.

Feist, however, did not touch on the duration of copyright protection. Rather, the decision addressed the core question of copyrightability, *i.e.,* the "creative spark" a work must have to be eligible for copyright protection at all. Explaining the originality requirement, *Feist* trained on the Copyright Clause words "Authors" and "Writings." *Id.,* at 346–347, 111 S.Ct. 1282. The decision did not construe the "limited Times" for which a work may be protected, and the originality requirement has no bearing on that prescription.

More forcibly, petitioners contend that the CTEA's extension of existing copyrights does not "promote the Progress of Science" as contemplated by the preambular language of the Copyright Clause. Art. I, § 8, cl. 8. To sustain this objection, petitioners do not argue that the Clause's preamble is an independently enforceable limit on Congress' power. See 239 F.3d, at 378 (Petitioners acknowledge that "the preamble of the Copyright Clause is not a substantive limit on Congress' legislative power." (internal quotation marks omitted)). Rather, they maintain that the preambular language identifies the sole end to which Congress may legislate; accordingly, they conclude, the meaning of "limited Times" must be "determined in light of that specified end." Brief for Petitioners 19. The CTEA's extension of existing copyrights categorically fails to "promote the Progress of Science," petitioners argue, because it does not stimulate the creation of new works but merely adds value to works already created.

As petitioners point out, we have described the Copyright Clause as "both a grant of power and a limitation," *Graham v. John Deere Co. of Kansas City,* 383 U.S. 1, 5, 86 S.Ct. 684, 15 L.Ed.2d 545 (1966), and have said that "[t]he primary objective of copyright" is "[t]o promote the Progress of Science," *Feist,* 499 U.S., at 349, 111 S.Ct. 1282. The "constitutional command," we have recognized, is that Congress, to the extent it enacts copyright laws at all, create a "system" that "promote[s] the Progress of Science." *Graham,* 383 U.S., at 6, 86 S.Ct. 684.

We have also stressed, however, that it is generally for Congress, not the courts, to decide how best to pursue the Copyright Clause's objectives. See *Stewart v. Abend,* 495 U.S., at 230, 110 S.Ct. 1750 ("Th[e] evolution of the duration of copyright protection tellingly illustrates the difficulties Congress faces.... [I]t is not our role to alter the delicate balance Congress has labored to achieve."); *Sony,* 464 U.S., at 429, 104 S.Ct. 774 ("[I]t is Congress that has been assigned the task of defining the scope of [rights] that should be granted to authors or to inventors in order to give the public appropriate access to their work product."); *Graham,* 383 U.S., at 6, 86 S.Ct. 684 ("Within the limits of the constitutional grant, the Congress may, of course, implement the stated purpose of the Framers by selecting the policy which in its judgment best effectuates the constitutional aim."). The justifications we earlier set out for Congress' enactment of the CTEA, *supra,* at 781–782, provide a rational basis for the conclusion that the CTEA "promote[s] the Progress of Science."

On the issue of copyright duration, Congress, from the start, has routinely applied new definitions or adjustments of the copyright term to both future works and existing works not yet in the public domain. Such consistent congressional practice is entitled to "very great weight, and when it is remembered that the rights thus established have not been disputed during a period of [over two] centur[ies], it is almost conclusive." *Burrow–Giles Lithographic Co. v. Sarony,* 111 U.S., at 57, 4 S.Ct. 279. Indeed, "[t]his Court has repeatedly laid down the principle that a contemporaneous legislative exposition of the Constitution when the founders of our Government and framers of our Constitution were actively participating in public affairs, acquiesced in for a long term of years, fixes the construction to be given [the Constitution's] provisions." *Myers v. United States,* 272 U.S. 52, 175, 47 S.Ct. 21, 71 L.Ed. 160 (1926). Congress' unbroken practice since the founding generation thus overwhelms petitioners' argument that the CTEA's extension of existing copyrights fails *per se* to "promote the Progress of Science."

Closely related to petitioners' preambular argument, or a variant of it, is their assertion that the Copyright Clause "imbeds a quid pro quo." Brief for Petitioners 23. They contend, in this regard, that Congress may grant to an "Autho[r]" an "exclusive Right" for a "limited Tim[e]," but only in exchange for a "Writin[g]." Congress' power to confer copyright protection, petitioners argue, is thus contingent upon an exchange: The author of an original work receives an "exclusive Right" for a "limited Tim[e]" in exchange for a dedication to the public thereafter. Extending an existing copyright without demanding additional consideration, petitioners maintain, bestows an unpaid-for benefit on copyright holders and their heirs, in violation of the *quid pro quo* requirement.

We can demur to petitioners' description of the Copyright Clause as a grant of legislative authority empowering Congress "to secure a bargain—this for that." *Id.,* at 16; see *Mazer v. Stein,* 347 U.S. 201, 219, 74 S.Ct. 460, 98 L.Ed. 630 (1954) ("The economic philosophy behind the clause empowering Congress to grant patents and copyrights is the conviction that encouragement of individual effort by personal gain is the best way to advance public welfare through the talents of authors and inventors in 'Science and useful Arts.'"). But the legislative evolution earlier recalled demonstrates what the bargain entails. Given the consistent placement of existing copyright holders in parity with future holders, the author of a work created in the last 170 years would reasonably comprehend, as the "this" offered her, a copyright not only for the time in place when protection is gained, but also for any renewal or extension legislated during that time. Congress could rationally seek to "promote ... Progress" by including in every copyright statute an express guarantee that authors would receive the benefit of any later legislative extension of the copyright term. Nothing in the Copyright Clause bars Congress from creating the same incentive by adopting the same position as a matter of unbroken practice. See Brief for Respondent 31–32.

Neither *Sears, Roebuck & Co. v. Stiffel Co.,* 376 U.S. 225, 84 S.Ct. 784, 11 L.Ed.2d 661 (1964), nor *Bonito Boats, Inc. v. Thunder Craft Boats, Inc.,* 489 U.S. 141, 109 S.Ct. 971, 103 L.Ed.2d 118 (1989), is to the contrary. In both cases, we invalidated the application of certain state laws as inconsistent with the federal patent regime. *Sears,* 376 U.S., at 231–233, 84 S.Ct. 784; *Bonito,* 489 U.S., at 152, 109 S.Ct. 971. Describing Congress' constitutional authority to confer patents, *Bonito Boats* noted: "The Patent Clause itself reflects a balance between the need to encourage innovation and the avoidance of monopolies which stifle competition without any concomitant advance in the 'Progress of Science and useful Arts.'" *Id.,* at 146, 109 S.Ct. 971. *Sears* similarly stated that "[p]atents are not given as favors ... but are meant to encourage invention by rewarding the inventor with the right, limited to a term of years fixed by the patent, to exclude others from the use of his invention." 376 U.S., at 229, 84 S.Ct. 784. Neither case concerned the extension of a patent's duration. Nor did either suggest that such an extension might be constitutionally infirm. Rather, *Bonito Boats* reiterated the Court's unclouded understanding: "It is for Congress to determine if the present system" effectuates the goals of the Copyright and Patent Clause. 489 U.S., at 168, 109 S.Ct. 971. And as we have documented, see *supra,* at 779–781, Congress has many times sought to effectuate those goals by extending existing patents.

We note, furthermore, that patents and copyrights do not entail the same exchange, and that our references to a *quid pro quo* typically appear in the patent context. See, *e.g., J.E.M. Ag Supply, Inc. v. Pioneer Hi–Bred International, Inc.,* 534 U.S. 124, 142, 122 S.Ct. 593, 151 L.Ed.2d 508 (2001) ("The disclosure required by the Patent Act is 'the *quid pro quo* of the right to exclude.'" (quoting *Kewanee Oil Co. v. Bicron Corp.,* 416 U.S. 470, 484, 94 S.Ct. 1879, 40 L.Ed.2d 315 (1974))); *Bonito Boats,* 489 U.S., at 161, 109 S.Ct. 971 ("the *quid pro quo* of substantial creative effort required by the federal [patent] statute"); *Brenner v. Manson,* 383 U.S. 519, 534, 86 S.Ct. 1033, 16 L.Ed.2d 69 (1966) ("The basic *quid pro quo* ... for granting a patent monopoly is the benefit derived by the public from an invention with substantial utility."); *Pennock v. Dialogue,* 2 Pet. 1, 23, 7 L.Ed. 327 (1829) (If an invention is already commonly known and used when the patent is sought, "there might be sound reason for presuming, that the legislature did not intend to grant an exclusive right," given the absence of a *"quid pro quo."*). This is understandable, given that immediate disclosure is not the objective of, but is *exacted from,* the patentee. It is the price paid for the exclusivity secured. See *J.E.M. Ag Supply,* 534 U.S., at 142, 122 S.Ct. 593. For the author seeking copyright protection, in contrast, disclosure is the desired objective, not something exacted from the author in exchange for the copyright. Indeed, since the 1976 Act, copyright has run from creation, not publication. See 1976 Act § 302(a); 17 U.S.C. § 302(a).

Further distinguishing the two kinds of intellectual property, copyright gives the holder no monopoly on any knowledge. A reader of an author's writing may make full use of any fact or idea she acquires from her reading. See § 102(b). The grant of a patent, on the other hand, does prevent full use by others of the inventor's knowledge. See Brief for Respondent 22; *Alfred Bell & Co. v. Catalda Fine Arts,* 191 F.2d 99, 103, n. 16 (C.A.2 1951) (The monopoly granted by a copyright "is not a monopoly of knowledge. The grant of a patent does prevent full use being made of knowledge, but the reader of a book is not by the copyright laws prevented from making full use of any information he may acquire from his reading." (quoting W. Copinger, Law of Copyright 2 (7th ed.1936))). In light of these distinctions, one cannot extract from language in our patent decisions—language not trained on a grant's duration—genuine support for petitioners' bold view. Accordingly, we reject the proposition that a *quid pro quo* requirement stops Congress from expanding copyright's term in a manner that puts existing and future copyrights in parity.

3

As an alternative to their various arguments that extending existing copyrights violates the Copyright Clause *per se,* petitioners urge heightened judicial review of such extensions to ensure that they appropriately pursue the purposes of the Clause. See Brief for Petitioners 31–32. Specifically, petitioners ask us to apply the "congruence and proportionality" standard described in cases evaluating exercises of Congress' power under § 5 of the Fourteenth Amendment. See, *e.g., City of Boerne v. Flores,* 521 U.S. 507, 117 S.Ct. 2157, 138 L.Ed.2d 624 (1997). But we have never applied that standard outside the § 5 context; it does not hold sway for judicial review of legislation enacted, as copyright laws are, pursuant to Article I authorization.

Section 5 authorizes Congress to *enforce* commands contained in and incorporated into the Fourteenth Amendment. Amdt. 14, § 5 ("The Congress shall have power to *enforce,* by appropriate legislation, the provisions of this article." (emphasis added)). The Copyright Clause, in contrast, empowers Congress to *define* the scope of the substantive right. See *Sony,* 464 U.S., at 429, 104 S.Ct. 774. Judicial deference to such congressional definition is "but a corollary to the grant to Congress of any Article I power." *Graham,* 383 U.S., at 6, 86 S.Ct. 684. It would be no more appropriate for us to subject the CTEA to "congruence and proportionality" review under the Copyright Clause than it would be for us to hold the Act unconstitutional *per se.*

For the several reasons stated, we find no Copyright Clause impediment to the CTEA's extension of existing copyrights.

III

Petitioners separately argue that the CTEA is a content-neutral regulation of speech that fails heightened judicial review under the First Amendment. We reject petitioners' plea for imposition of uncommonly strict scrutiny on a copyright scheme that incorporates its own speech-protective purposes and safeguards. The Copyright Clause and First Amendment were adopted close in time. This proximity indicates that, in the Framers' view, copyright's limited monopolies are compatible with free speech principles. Indeed, copyright's purpose is to *promote* the creation and publication of free expression. As *Harper & Row* observed: "[T]he Framers intended copyright itself to be the engine of free expression. By establishing a marketable right to the use of one's expression, copyright supplies the economic incentive to create and disseminate ideas." 471 U.S., at 558, 105 S.Ct. 2218.

In addition to spurring the creation and publication of new expression, copyright law contains built-in First Amendment accommodations. See *id.,* at 560, 105 S.Ct. 2218. First, it distinguishes between ideas and expression and makes only the latter eligible for copyright protection. Specifically, 17 U.S.C. § 102(b) provides: "In no case does copyright protection for an original work of authorship extend to any idea, procedure, process, system, method of operation, concept, principle, or discovery, regardless of the form in which it is described, explained, illustrated, or embodied in such work." As we said in *Harper & Row,* this "idea/expression dichotomy strike[s] a definitional balance between the First Amendment and the Copyright Act by permitting free communication of facts while still protecting an author's expression." 471 U.S., at 556, 105 S.Ct. 2218 (internal quotation marks omitted). Due to this distinction, every idea, theory, and fact in a copyrighted work becomes instantly available for public exploitation at the moment of publication. See *Feist,* 499 U.S., at 349–350, 111 S.Ct. 1282.

Second, the "fair use" defense allows the public to use not only facts and ideas contained in a copyrighted work, but also expression itself in certain circumstances. Codified at 17 U.S.C. § 107, the defense provides: "[T]he fair use of a copyrighted work, including such use by reproduction in copies ..., for purposes such as criticism, comment, news reporting, teaching (including multiple copies for classroom use), scholarship, or research, is not an infringement of copyright." The fair use defense affords considerable "latitude for scholarship and comment," *Harper & Row,* 471 U.S., at 560, 105 S.Ct. 2218, and even for parody, see *Campbell v. Acuff–Rose Music, Inc.,* 510 U.S. 569, 114 S.Ct. 1164, 127 L.Ed.2d 500 (1994) (rap group's musical parody of Roy Orbison's "Oh, Pretty Woman" may be fair use).

The CTEA itself supplements these traditional First Amendment safeguards. First, it allows libraries, archives, and similar institutions to "reproduce" and "distribute, display, or perform in facsimile or digital form" copies of certain published works "during the last 20 years of any term of copyright ... for purposes of preservation, scholarship, or research" if the work is not already being exploited commercially and further copies are unavailable at a reasonable price. 17 U.S.C. § 108(h); see Brief for Respondent 36. Second, Title II of the CTEA, known as the Fairness in Music Licensing Act of 1998, exempts small businesses, restaurants, and like entities from having to pay performance royalties on music played from licensed radio, television, and similar facilities. 17 U.S.C. § 110(5)(B); see Brief for Representative F. James Sensenbrenner, Jr., et al. as *Amici Curiae* 5–6, n. 3.

Finally, the case petitioners principally rely upon for their First Amendment argument, *Turner Broadcasting System, Inc. v. FCC,* 512 U.S. 622, 114 S.Ct. 2445, 129 L.Ed.2d 497 (1994), bears little on copyright. The statute at issue in *Turner* required cable operators to carry and transmit broadcast stations through their proprietary cable systems. Those "must-carry" provisions, we explained, implicated "the heart of the First Amendment," namely, "the principle that each person should decide for himself or herself the ideas and beliefs deserving of expression, consideration, and adherence." *Id.,* at 641, 114 S.Ct. 2445.

The CTEA, in contrast, does not oblige anyone to reproduce another's speech against the carrier's will. Instead, it protects authors' original expression from unrestricted exploitation. Protection of that order does not raise the free speech concerns present when the government compels or burdens the communication of particular facts or ideas. The First Amendment securely protects the freedom to make—or decline to make—one's own speech; it bears less heavily when speakers assert the right to make other people's speeches. To the extent such assertions raise First Amendment concerns, copyright's built-in free speech safeguards are generally adequate to address them. We recognize that the D.C. Circuit spoke too broadly when it declared copyrights "categorically immune from challenges under the First Amendment." 239 F.3d, at 375. But when, as in this case, Congress has not altered the traditional contours of copyright protection, further First Amendment scrutiny is unnecessary. See *Harper & Row,* 471 U.S., at 560, 105 S.Ct. 2218; cf. *San Francisco Arts & Athletics, Inc. v. United States Olympic Comm.,* 483 U.S. 522, 107 S.Ct. 2971, 97 L.Ed.2d 427 (1987).

IV

If petitioners' vision of the Copyright Clause held sway, it would do more than render the CTEA's duration extensions unconstitutional as to existing works. Indeed, petitioners' assertion that the provisions of the CTEA are not severable would make the CTEA's enlarged terms invalid even as to tomorrow's work. The 1976 Act's time extensions, which set the pattern that the CTEA followed, would be vulnerable as well.

As we read the Framers' instruction, the Copyright Clause empowers Congress to determine the intellectual property regimes that, overall, in that body's judgment, will serve the ends of the Clause. See *Graham,* 383 U.S., at 6, 86 S.Ct. 684 (Congress may "implement the stated purpose of the Framers by selecting the policy which *in its judgment* best effectuates the constitutional aim." (emphasis added)). Beneath the facade of their inventive constitutional interpretation, petitioners forcefully urge that Congress pursued very bad policy in prescribing the CTEA's long terms. The wisdom of Congress' action, however, is not within our province to second-guess. Satisfied that the legislation before us remains inside the domain the Constitution assigns to the First Branch, we affirm the judgment of the Court of Appeals.

It is so ordered.

NOTES

Although Eldred was a party to the action for interests claimed in the public domain, the majority opinion minimizes his private interest and do not appear to accord him standing to represent the public interest. The question remains, was there anyone in this case representing the public interest?

How does one handle the proliferation of scholarship that posits the court had it wrong on the meaning of "progress" in the Constitution? See generally Malla Pollack, "What Is Congress Supposed to Promote? Defining 'Progress' in Article I, Section 8, Clause 8 of the U.S. Constitution, or Introducing the Progress Clause" 80 *Nebraska L. Rev. 754* (2002): See also, Vivian J. Fong, Progress: Are We Making Progress?: The Constitution As A Touchstone For Creating Consistent Patent Law And Policy, Fong11U.Pa.J.Const.L.1163 (2009); Dotan Oliar The (Constitutional) Convention On IP: A New Reading, 57 UCLA L. Rev. 421 (December, 2009).

Is the door closed to further review by the Court as currently constituted? Is this reflected in the 9th Circuit treatment of *Kahle v. Gonzales*, 474 F.3d 665, 666–667 (9th Cir. 2007) *Certiorari Denied* Kahle v. Mukasey, 552 U.S. 1096, 128 S.Ct. 958, 169 L.Ed.2d 724 (U.S. Jan. 07, 2008) (NO. 07–189). Where does this leave issues relative to the impact and validation of the coincidence of interest between the private copyright and the benefit to the public intended by the Constitution? Is the matter now binding against any challenge that term extension inhibits rather than fosters progress, or more simply, causes harm to the public?

Note that the Court concludes that a rational basis for extending the term of copyright for works already protected by copyright was to create incentives for publishing and distributing these works in new forms and through new media. This conclusion is consistent with an important background to the dispute: the growth of digital media and new forms of distribution. But the Court ignores one important fact in reaching this conclusion: Eldred was poised to enter the digital market for works as soon as they entered the public domain. What was Eldred's incentive to enter these markets? Note that he would not have a copyright in the public domain works. (Make sure you understand why not.) Does the Court overstate the case for copyright extension? Would there not be other incentives beside copyright protection to create, publish, and distribute new works? Before you become too comfortable with an affirmative answer to this last question, also ask yourself whether recognizing these other incentives would not obviate the need for copyright law. If people do not need the copyright incentive, then what purpose does copyright serve? Does the Court reach the right result and apply a correct analysis in the *Eldred* decision?

Digital media creates special problems for copyright. We examine these special issues in Chapter Seven. One compelling problem that builds on the issues in this chapter and are highlighted in Chapter Seven is posed by the Google Book Project. As of the writing of this edition, Google is locked in a dispute with copyright owners over its scanning of all of the books in the libraries of major United States universities. Google contends that the scanning of these books into digital form for search purposes is fair use. Is there a basis for that contention? The copyright owners and Google are engaged in a settlement whereby copyright owners will be compensated and Google will be able to continue with its scanning and distribution of scanned books for search purposes. Notice that one difficult and important issue is what rights does Google and the public have in the scanned copies of all existing books. In other words, who owns the Google's digital library. Can copyright law handle this issue? Can other areas of intellectual property? Do we need new laws?

X.   THE "ORPHAN ACT"

1.   The Library of Congress Orphan Act Hearings

[Federal Register: January 26, 2005 (Volume 70, Number 16)] [Page 3739–3743]

"The Copyright Office seeks to examine the issues raised by 'orphan works,'" i.e., copyrighted works whose owners are difficult or even impossible to locate. Concerns have been raised that the uncertainty surrounding ownership of such works might needlessly discourage subsequent creators and users from incorporating such works in new creative efforts or making such works available to the public. This notice requests written comments from all interested parties. Specifically, the Office is seeking comments on whether there are compelling concerns raised by orphan works that merit a legislative, regulatory or other solution, and what type of solution could effectively address these concerns without conflicting with the legitimate interests of authors and right holders.

* * * The Copyright Act of 1976 made it substantially easier for an author to obtain and maintain copyright in his or her creative works. Today, copyright subsists the moment an original work of authorship is fixed in a tangible form—it need not be registered with the Copyright Office or published with notice to obtain protection. While registration of claims to copyright with the Copyright Office is encouraged and provides important benefits to copyright holders, it is not required as a condition to copyright protection. Under the 1909 Act, renewal registration was required to maintain protection beyond an initial 28-year term. Failure to register the renewal during the last year of the first term resulted in complete loss of protection. The 1976 Act removed the renewal requirement going forward, but kept it for works copyrighted before 1978. It was not until 1992 that the renewal requirement was abolished altogether. These changes, as well as other changes in the 1976 Act and in the Berne

Convention Implementation Act of 1988, were important steps toward harmonizing U.S. copyright law with international treaties.

* * * Concerns have been raised, however, as to whether current copyright law imposes inappropriate burdens on users, including subsequent creators, of works for which the copyright owner cannot be located (hereinafter referred to as "orphan" works). The issue is whether orphan works are being needlessly removed from public access and their dissemination inhibited. If no one claims the copyright in a work, it appears likely that the public benefit of having access to the work would outweigh whatever copyright interest there might be. Such concerns were raised in connection with the adoption of the life plus 50 copyright term with the 1976 Act and the 20–year term extension enacted with the Sonny Bono Copyright Term Extension Act of 1998.

* * * Prior to the 1976 Act, the term of protection was limited to 28 years if the copyright was not renewed. Under this system, if the copyright owner was no longer interested in exploiting the work, or a corporate owner no longer existed, or, in the case of individual copyright owners, there were no interested heirs to claim the copyright, then the work entered the public domain. Of course, it also meant that some copyrights were unintentionally allowed to enter the public domain, for instance, where the claimant was unaware that renewal had to occur within the one year window at the end of the first term or that the copyright was up for renewal. The legislative history to the 1976 Act reflects Congress' recognition of the concern raised by some that eliminating renewal requirements would take a large number of works out of the public domain and that for a number of those older works it might be difficult or impossible to identify the copyright owner in order to obtain permissions. Congress nevertheless determined that the renewal system should be discarded, in part, because of the "inadvertent and unjust loss of copyright" it in some cases caused. More recently, in the mid–1990s, Congress heard concerns that the Copyright Term Extension Act would exacerbate problems in film preservation by maintaining copyright protection for older motion pictures for which the copyright owner is difficult to identify. Also, in our study on Digital Distance Education published in 1999, the Copyright Office identified several "problems with licensing" that educators asserted in attempting to use copyrighted materials in digital formats, including that "it can be time-consuming, difficult or even impossible to locate the copyright owner or owners."

A situation often described is one where a creator seeks to incorporate an older work into a new work (e.g., old photos, footage or recordings) and is willing to seek permission, but is not able to identify or locate the copyright owner(s) in order to seek permission. While in such circumstances the user might be reasonably confident that the risk of an infringement claim against this use is unlikely, under the current system the copyright in the work is still valid and enforceable, and the risk cannot be completely eliminated. Moreover, even where the user only copies portions of the work in a manner that would not likely be deemed infringing under the doctrine of fair use, it is asserted by some that the fair use defense is often too unpredictable as a general matter to remove the uncertainty in the user's mind. Some have claimed that many potential users of orphan works, namely individuals and small entities, may not have access to legal advice on these issues and cannot fully assess risk themselves. Moreover, even if they are able to determine with some certainty that there is little or no risk of losing a lawsuit, they may not be able to afford any risk of having to bear the cost of defending themselves in litigation.

* * * Given the high costs of litigation and the inability of most creators, scholars and small publishers to bear those costs, the result is that orphan works often are not used—even where there is no one who would object to the use.

This uncertainty created by copyright in orphan works has the potential to harm an important public policy behind copyright: To promote the dissemination of works by creating incentives for their creation and dissemination to the public. First, the economic incentive to create may be undermined by the imposition of additional costs on subsequent creators wishing to use material from existing works. Subsequent creators may be dissuaded from creating new works incorporating existing works for which the owner cannot be found because they cannot afford the risk of potential liability or even of litigation. Second, the public interest may be harmed when works cannot be made available to the public due to uncertainty over its copyright ownership and status, even when there is no longer any living person or legal entity claiming ownership of the copyright or the owner no longer has any objection to such use.

Empirical analysis of data on trends in copyright registrations and renewals over the last century suggests that a large number of works may fall into the category of orphan works.

Based on data of registrations of claims to copyright and their subsequent renewal under the 1909 Act, it appears that, overall, well less than half of all registered copyrighted works were renewed under the old copyright system. Because renewal was required to maintain protection of a work, this data suggests that, at least in many cases, there was insufficient interest a mere 28 years later to maintain copyright protection. The empirical data does not indicate why any particular works were not renewed, and no doubt, a certain portion of those works were not renewed due to inadvertence, mistake or ignorance on the part of the owner. With respect to many of these works, however, particularly those owned by legal entities or other sophisticated copyright owners, it can be assumed that the work no longer had sufficient economic value to the copyright claimant to merit renewal. Libraries and scholars have argued that those works that have so little economic value that they fail to merit the small expense and effort of renewal may nevertheless have scholarly or educational value and should not be needlessly barred from such use. (Footnotes omitted)

NOTES

1. The final report was released by the Library of Congress and dated January 2006. The report itself is copyrighted and posted in a protected PDF format. This raises some interesting questions about the government copyright. (See 17 U.S.C. § 105 and Judiciary Committee, house report 94–1476 at 5672. copyright.gov/orphan/.) The report of the Copyright Office and text of proposed legislation highlight problems of Orphan Works and the functionality of permitting use of works for which the copyright owner cannot be found in a search of the record.

2. Circa 1961 Frederick Durrenmatt's short novel "Traps" was printed and released in English. It appears to have only had one printing and was by 1964 listed as out of print. Recalling that the Orphan Act appears to be addressed to "copyrighted works whose owners are difficult or even impossible to locate" where would one begin to look for the author under these circumstances? Does this fully take into consideration the underlying purpose of the copyright to begin with? Should the Orphan Act also consider only one printing a negation of copyright obligation by depriving the public of a realistic right to read and benefit from the work? Should there be a condition subsequent that the author use best efforts to maintain the "inprint" status of the work?

3. Suppose after extended search a copy is found in a "rare" and "out of print" bookstore. Suppose the purchaser fears loss of access to the work again, having read it once in 1962. Can the purchaser photocopy the book? Can the purchaser "scan" the book and create a PDF file of the scan? Would either of these two actions violate the copyright of the author? If so, what right(s) would be violated? What if the PDF file were shared on the internet? Would that constitute a violation and would it alter the situation in the questions above?

CHAPTER FOUR

PATENT

■ ■ ■

OVERVIEW

Article I, Section 8, Clause 8, of the United States Constitution provides the basis for patent law. It states: "[The Congress shall have Power ...] [t]o promote the Progress of Science and useful Arts, by securing for limited Times to Authors and Inventors the exclusive Right to their respective Writings and Discoveries." U.S. Const. art. I, § 8, cl. 8. The First Congress passed the Patent Act of 1790. In effect since 1953, Congress passed the Patent Act of 1952, 35 U.S.C. §§ 1–376. The Patent Act of 1952 grants patent protection for 17 years from the date of issuance. As of January 1, 1995, patent protection extends for 20 years from the date of filing, to conform with international trade agreements.

Under federal law, a patent grants the patent holder the exclusive right to prevent others from making, using, or selling any patented invention within the United States and importing a patented invention. Liability is also established for inducing infringement and contributory infringement. Under section 271 of the Patent Act, supplying "components" of patented products, processes, or methods may constitute infringement. In Justice Black's words, "a patent is the grant of a statutory monopoly ... meant to encourage invention by rewarding the inventor with the right, limited to a term of years fixed by the patent, to exclude others from the use of his invention." *Sears, Roebuck & Co. v. Stiffel Co.,* 376 U.S. 225, 231, 84 S.Ct. 784, 11 L.Ed.2d 661 (1964).

There is an underlying assumption in patent law that a period of exclusivity is necessary to balance the costs of innovation and commercial exploitation. Without incentives to insure long-term gain, such as an exclusive right to prevent others from using a patented invention, the necessary initial expenditure is unlikely. At the same time, a period of exclusivity for the inventor comes with a cost to the public. There is a "quid pro quo" presumption that an inventor is only entitled to a patent when the public receives something of value in exchange. There are those who feel the "quid pro quo" metaphor is outdated, misleading, incomplete, and overused. The metaphor mischievously encroached on copyright law in the *Eldred* case, and more recent theories take into consideration the importance of reciprocity and trust in the innovation process. Shubha Ghosh, *Patents and the Regulatory State: Rethinking the Patent Bargain Metaphor after* Eldred, 19 BERKELEY TECH. L.J. 1315 (2004). To balance the public's interests with those of inventors, inventors are prohibited from patenting things readily available to the public.

The Patent Act of 1952 requires inventions covered by utility patents to be useful, novel, and nonobvious. These requirements ensure the public benefits from a patented product or process. The Patent Act goes further to encourage disclosure. An inventor could hypothetically keep an invention secret, but if the secret is uncovered, there is no remedy under patent law (there may be protection granted under the law of trade secrets). The Patent Act also establishes patent protection for designs and plants. In order to obtain a design patent, a design must be new, original, ornamental, and nonobvious. Plants must be a distinct, new variety to receive patent-like protection. This chapter focuses on the most common type of patent, the utility patent.

I. INTRODUCTION TO PATENT LAW

A. BRIEF HISTORY

Modern patent law traces its origins to 15th century Venice, which had a coherent patent system similar to our own. The Venetian patent system created incentives for inventors to divulge their creations. An inventor could register any device that met the requirements of being "new and ingenious," "not previously made in this commonwealth," and "reduced to perfection." In exchange for registration of their inventions, inventors received an exclusive right to bar all others, in the territory, from making similar devices for a fixed term of 10 years. Novelty, nonobviousness, enablement, and disclosure continue to be conditions of patent protection today.

In England, the development of patent law went through a number of changes reflecting different policy considerations. In the mid–16th century, the patent system sought to induce the introduction of new technology into England by foreign craftsman. The English hoped that the granting of exclusive rights granted through patent protection would be enticing to skilled immigrants. The policy of attracting immigrants through patent protection ultimately failed as emigrants from England left to settle in foreign countries and the Crown's colonies.

In the 17th century, the granting of patent protection to favored courtiers of the royal court led to outcry against the Crown and its patent letters. Parliament responded by passing The Statute of Monopolies, a predecessor of modern antitrust laws, which attempted to limit patent protection to the true and first inventor, a policy later adopted by the United States. Despite its disdain for monopolies, the Statute of Monopolies recognized the economic value of legitimate patents.

England began to put more emphasis on the value of disclosure in the 18th century. Judge Mansfield underscored that the contribution of technical knowledge to society was as important, if not more important, than the introduction of an invention or technology. The Judge's words led to a greater emphasis being placed on the requirement of describing an invention clearly and completely. While debatable, the shift of emphasis to the dissemination of technical expertise, as opposed to the introduction new products, seemed to have been a greater success at drawing new industry to England.

The English patent system passed on to the American colonies, and after the revolution, individual states granted patent protection. The first Constitutional Convention nationalized the patent system in the Patent Act of 1790. Thomas Jefferson was instrumental in the implementation of the national patent system. He contributed to the original statute, and served as the first patent administrator.

The original patent system required registration instead of a formal examination process. The 1836 revision of the Patent Act changed the registration system to formal examination, which made it harder to earn patent protection. As the number of patent examinations increased, the application requirements became more stringent. One such requirement, the "inventive leap," eventually became the modern "nonobviousness" requirement.

In the early half of the 20th century, patent protection alternated between strong protection and disfavor. During World War II, despite a rapid increase in innovation, excluding domestic competitors by means of a patent was considered unpatriotic. After the war, a desire for greater patent protection led Congress to pass the Patent Act of 1952. The 1952 revision codified the ideas of "novelty" and "infringement."

Even though the 1952 revision defined infringement, and further delineated the conditions for patent protection, circuit courts continued to hold diverse opinions about patents. During the 1960s, the patent office granted patents more freely then it had before, but the courts rarely upheld them. Motivated in part by a desire to unify patent doctrine, The Federal Courts Improvement Act of 1982 created the Court of Appeals for the Federal Circuit, sometimes referred as CAFC. Among its other duties, the Court of Appeals for the Federal Circuit hears all patent appeals. There are some doubts as to whether the Court of Appeals for the Federal Circuit has succeeded in unifying patent law or whether the court is in broad transition. R. Polk Wagner & Lee Petherbridge, *Is the Federal Circuit Succeeding? An Empirical Assessment of Judicial Performance*, 152 U. PA. L. REV. 1105 (2004) ("We also find that the significantly different approaches to claim construction followed by individual Federal Circuit judges has led to panel dependency; claim construction analysis is clearly affected by the composition of the three-judge panel that hears and decides the case.").

Recent studies show that the Court of Appeals for the Federal Circuit may have a "pro-patent" bias, as patents are more likely to be held valid than they were before 1982. *See* John R. Allison & Mark A. Lemley, *Empirical Evidence on the Validity of Litigated Patents*, 26 AM. INTELL. PROP. ASSN. Q.J. 185 (1998); injunctions are granted more often then in the past; and monetary damages are higher then they were prior to the formation of the court. *See* Robert P. Merges, *Commercial Success and Patent Standards: Economic Perspectives on Innovations*, 76 CAL. L. REV. 803, 820–21 (1988). The Court of Appeals for the Federal Circuit may also be responsible for an expansion in the scope of patent protection. In addition to the creation of Court of Appeals for the Federal Circuit, the expansion of the global economy has also put pressure on the government to broaden patent protection.

Protection of United States patents overseas has become a greater priority for the government, then it was in the past. The United States has made a number of reciprocal agreements to expand patent protection internationally. The negotiations over these agreements have not always gone smoothly, due to cultural and historical differences with other nations. For instance, the United States is unique in its "first to invent" priority rule, where the right of patent protection goes to the inventor who can demonstrate that he was the first to conceive of an idea and reduce it to practice with reasonable diligence. Most other countries use a "first to file" system that minimizes administrative burdens by simply giving the priority right to the first to file a valid application. If the project of international patent system integration is to be successful, both the United States and other nations will need to make compromises.

B. INTERNATIONAL PATENT CONCERNS

For the most part, patent protection only extends within the country that issues the patent, but inventors may also obtain patent protection in countries that have signed reciprocal protective agreements with their home nation. The United States is party to four agreements that allow inventors from foreign counties to receive equal patent protection in this country. The International Convention for the Protection of Industrial Property (Paris Convention), the Agreement on Trade–Related Aspects of Intellectual Property Rights (TRIPS), part of the General Agreement on Tariffs and Trade (GATT), and the Patent Cooperation Treaty (PCT). These four agreements help minimize the costs of obtaining global patent protection for citizens of the signatory nations.

1. The Paris Convention

The Paris Convention was instituted in 1883, adopted by the United States in 1887, and last revised in 1967. Over 100 countries recognize the Convention, which establishes reciprocal rights and sets rules to establish priority.

The Convention ensures that patents acquired in signatory countries will provide the same patent protection for patentees regardless of their nationality. Article 2 of the Convention states:

> Nationals of any country of the Union shall, as regards the protection of industrial property, enjoy in all the other countries of the Union the advantages that their respective laws now grant, or may hereafter grant, to nationals; all without prejudice to the rights specially provided for by this Convention. Consequently, they shall have the same protection as the latter, and the same legal remedy against any infringement of their rights, provided that the conditions and formalities imposed upon nationals are complied with. Paris Convention for the Protection of Industrial Property, Art. 2.

This provision assures inventors that patents acquired in a foreign country will provide the same protections granted to the country's nationals, but it does not guarantee that patent protection will be the same from country to country. It simply provides assurance that signatory countries will treat all patent holders equally.

Establishing a right of priority, Article 4 states: "[a]ny filing that is equivalent to a regular national filing under the domestic legislation of any country of the Union or under bilateral or multilateral treaties concluded between countries of the Union shall be recognized as giving rise to the right of priority." Paris Convention for the Protection of Industrial Property, Art. 4. The right to priority establishes a filing date that holds for subsequent filings in other signatory countries during a given period. For utility patents, the period of priority is 12 months. In other words, if someone files an application in a signatory country, and then files a second application in another signatory country, the filing date of the first filed application is assigned to the second application, so long as 12 months have not passed since the first application was filed.

The 12 month grace period gives inventors time to decide whether they want to pursue filing in another country. Pursuing an application in another country requires obtaining translations, adhering to foreign patent law requirements, and quite likely the aid of international counsel. One consideration is whether the costs of the application are worth the protection gained in the foreign country.

2. The Patent Cooperation Treaty

The Patent Cooperation Treaty (PCT), promulgated in 1970, was implemented with the goal of ameliorating the process of applying in multiple countries by providing a more unified filing procedure. A patent holder may file a single international application and designate in which countries he is seeking patent protection. This process creates efficiency, for both applicants and national patent offices, by eliminating duplicative examinations and other administrative burdens. The PCT establishes procedures for international applications, searches, and preliminary examinations. Countries that are party to the PCT designate a Receiving Office to receive applications, ensure that applications comply with regulations, and forward applications to the International Bureau, and a designated International Searching Authority. The World Intellectual Property Organization (WIPO) currently serves as the International Bureau who acts as a central repository for international applications. The International Searching Authorities, generally the patent offices of signatory countries, conduct international searches for prior art, relevant in finding whether an invention is new and nonobvious.

International Search Authorities compile a Search Report and transmit it to the International Bureau and the applicant. After receiving the Search Report, the applicant may amend their application if they wish. After deciding whether to amend, the applicant may proceed in one of two ways. It can ask the International Bureau to send the Search Report and the application to countries of its choosing who will determine the patentability of the application based on its own standards. Alternatively, the applicant could have the International Bureau send the report to an International Preliminary Examining Authority who will conduct an International Preliminary Examination to determine whether the patent claims are novel, involve an inventive step, and are industrially applicable. The International Preliminary Examining Authority sends a written opinion to the International Bureau, the applicant, and the designated countries' patent offices. Frustratingly, the Preliminary Examination is not binding. The domestic patent offices of each country maintain the right to determine patentability.

Although the process seems complicated, and the result depends on the domestic patent laws of each country, the PCT offers advantages for both applicants and member countries. Usually, the agency that examines domestic applications in a member country acts as a Receiving Office. As a result, most applicants can file a single application in their own country and in their own language. The applicant can opt to receive a Preliminary Examination Report before deciding whether to continue with the international application process, and then, provide supplemental materials and translations if necessary. Ultimately, the applicant will know the opinion of at least one patent office before it decides whether to continue with the international application process. Furthermore, the Preliminary Examination Report aids the local patent offices in their examinations, saving both time and money. Since the number of patent applications worldwide have increased, providing a timely examination is increasingly difficult. The PCT also has provisions that extend the period for holding priority rights once an international application has been filed.

Although the PCT does not establish a single patentability standard, it is a step towards global harmonization. As the world's economies integrate, the need for global harmonization becomes increasingly apparent. Harmonization will necessitate compromise on a number of fundamental issues. The United States is not an exception; it remains one of the few countries with a "first to invent" priority rule as opposed to the "first to file" priority rule which most countries follow.

3. The General Agreement on Tariffs and Trade and the TRIPS Agreement

Unlike the Paris Convention and the Patent Cooperation Treaty, the General Agreement on Tariffs and Trade (GATT) was not originally intended to include intellectual property issues. First signed in 1947, the World Trade Organization (WTO) administered GATT with a focus on commodities and manufactured goods. Expectations were that international intellectual property concerns would be addressed by the World Intellectual Property Organization (WIPO), as the United Nations mandated WIPO to administer intellectual property matters in 1974. However, at the Uruguay round of negotiations to revise GATT in 1993, the agenda grew to cover "Trade-related Aspects of Intellectual Property," known as TRIPS, which brought substantive harmonization to world patent law, including changes to the patent law of the United States.

In order to comply with TRIPS, the United States changed its patent term from 17 years from issuance to 20 years from filing. Additional changes allow for an extension of the patent term due to unexpected delays during prosecution. The United States also made its "first to invent" system open to foreign countries, so that foreign inventors may present evidence to establish priority in the United States. The definition of infringement was amended to include an unauthorized offer to sell or import. The United States further added a procedure to file a "provisional application" requiring a specification and drawing, but not a single claim. For inventors in the United States, the TRIPS agreement effects confidentiality when filing in foreign counties, in order to make the patent laws of the United States more similar to the rest of the countries in the WTO.

Other member nations have had to accommodate the patentability standards of the United States. Nations that wish to join the WTO are required to include an inventive step requirement to patentability, similar to the nonobvious requirement in the United States and an "industrial application" prerequisite to patent protection that acts like the utility requirement. To help establish global harmonization, WTO member nations have the right to control the importation of patented goods.

Like the Paris Convention, signatories of the TRIPS agreement must give foreign patent applicants the same rights as domestic applicants. A "most-favored-nation" standard is enforced to ensure equal treatment under TRIPS. This standard extends any advantage or favor granted by one member country to another to all other members. The TRIPS agreement also establishes minimum standards for the protection of intellectual property including a 20 year period of protection running from the date of filing. Patentees also have the right to prevent third parties from making, using, offering for sale, selling, or importing any patented invention. Even though the TRIPS agreement takes substantial steps towards achieving global harmonization, it remains to be seen if an international patent system will ever be established.

4. International Jurisprudence

In addition to international treaties, there is some hope that harmonization can come through similar jurisprudence. United States jurisprudence is increasingly having a greater influence in foreign countries, for instance Japan, as more foreign legal professionals study at U.S. Law Schools. The influence of United States jurisprudence is clear in Japanese patent claim interpretation, the courts' power to review patent validity, parallel importation, and infringement damages. Toshiko Takenaka, *Harmonizing the Japanese System with Its U.S. Counterpart Through Judge-made Law: Interaction Between Japanese and U.S. Case Law Developments*, 7 PAC. RIM L. & POL'Y J. 249 (1998).

C. OVERVIEW OF THE PATENT DOCUMENT

A patent must include a drawing, a specification, and at least one claim. Section 113 is the drawing requirement, and a specification is required by Section 112. Section 112 establishes that a specification should include: (1) a written description of the invention, (2) that is clear and concise, (3) which should enable any person skilled in the art to make and use the invention described, and (4) discloses the best mode for carrying out the invention. Section 112 also introduces the concept of claims.

Claims demarcate the boundaries of patent protection. Claims, like the "metes and bounds" of real property, are used to determine the scope of the intellectual property patented. Claims define the boundaries of protection using limitations that confine intellectual property either by qualia or by steps in a process. Claims may be written as either independent of, or dependent on, the limitations of other claims. When there is a question of infringement, claims determine the extent of an inventor's protection.

To get an idea of what a patent looks like, look at U.S. Patent No. 6,186,636: APPARATUS FOR ILLUMINATING A PORTABLE ELECTRONIC OR COMPUTING DEVICE. Generally, the final three digits of the Patent Number are used as shorthand for referring to the patent. In this case, U.S. Patent No. 6,186,636 would be referred to as the '636 patent. The date of issue is located directly below the patent number. Additionally, on the front page of a patent, one can find the title of the invention, the inventor, the filing date of the invention, references cited, and a helpful abstract of the invention.

US006186636B1

(12) **United States Patent**   (10) **Patent No.:**   **US 6,186,636 B1**

Naghi et al.   (45) **Date of Patent:**   **Feb. 13, 2001**

(54) **APPARATUS FOR ILLUMINATING A PORTABLE ELECTRONIC OR COMPUTING DEVICE**

(75) Inventors: **David Naghi**, Los Angeles; **Gilbert Fregoso**, Santa Ana, both of CA (US)

(73) Assignee: **Design Rite, LLC.**, Fontana, CA (US)

(*) Notice: Under 35 U.S.C. 154(b), the term of this patent shall be extended for 0 days.

(21) Appl. No.: **09/330,322**

(22) Filed: **Jun. 11, 1999**

(51) Int. Cl.[7] **F21V 33/00**

(52) U.S. Cl. **362/85**; 362/84; 362/253; 362/285; 362/109; 362/198; 362/311

(58) Field of Search 362/311, 335, 362/326, 194, 197, 198, 199, 418, 419, 190, 800, 109, 85; 439/502, 504

(56) **References Cited**

U.S. PATENT DOCUMENTS

D. 238,959	2/1976	Kurokawa	D26/107 X
D. 251,687	4/1979	Kurokawa	D26/107
D. 377,840	2/1997	Chang	D26/62
D. 418,240	12/1999	Sherman	D26/63
1,651,307	11/1927	Wilkinson	362/226 X
3,065,339	11/1962	Fahey, Jr.	362/308 X
4,312,507	1/1982	Smith et al. .	
5,091,832	2/1992	Tortola et al. .	
5,122,937	* 6/1992	Stoudemire	362/109
5,122,941	* 6/1992	Gross et al.	362/276
5,136,477	* 8/1992	Lemmy	362/198
5,172,974	12/1992	Riban .	
5,183,325	* 2/1993	Hurdle	362/109
5,203,622	4/1993	Sottile .	
5,379,201	* 1/1995	Friedman	362/191
5,486,986	1/1996	Brada .	
5,590,950	1/1997	Hildebrand .	
5,615,945	* 4/1997	Tseng	362/226
5,707,137	1/1998	Hon .	
5,803,572	9/1998	Brada .	
5,868,487	2/1999	Polley et al. .	
5,899,553	5/1999	Howell .	

FOREIGN PATENT DOCUMENTS

2 113 818 A	12/1981	(GB) .
WO 92/06327	4/1992	(WO) .

OTHER PUBLICATIONS

"Ultimate Palmtop Computer Lights®" internet web page printout; http://www.std.com/sfl/3.pct.html; printed Mar. 2, 2000.

Book light product internet web page printout; http://store1.yimg.com/I/parksherman_1550_902141; printed Mar. 2, 2000.

"The Ittybitty Book Light" internet web page printout; http://www.zelco.com/10013.jpg; printed Mar. 2, 2000.

Sierra Gold Marketing "SGM28367" Clip On Light product web page printout; http://www.sgm.simplenet.com/boutique/special/sgm28367.htm.printed Mar. 2, 2000.

Amazon.com product web page printout for "Adventure Book Light and Flashlight" by Lumatec; http://www.amazon.com/exec/obidos/ASIN/b00000IJZM/104–9549104–0986847; printed Mar. 2, 2000.

Igo.com product web page printout for "NBL–100 Notebook Light" by Interex; http://www.igo.com/cgi–bin/ncommerce3/ProductDisplay?prmenbr=1&prrfnbr=522530; printed Jul. 21, 2000.

Taiwan Lighting, lamps on p. 69.

* cited by examiner

Primary Examiner—Sandra O'Shea
Assistant Examiner—Ali Alavi
(74) *Attorney, Agent, or Firm*—Lyon & Lyon LLP

(57) **ABSTRACT**

An illumination device that can use a white light diode in a flexible arm plugs into, and is powered through, a utility power jack of a portable computing device or a utility port of a portable computing device.

27 Claims, 1 Drawing Sheet

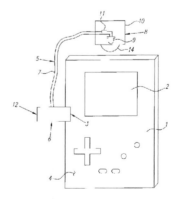

Patents generally include drawings. Arrows and numbers label important features. In the '636 patent, there is one drawing on page 2 of the patent.

U.S. Patent   Feb. 13, 2001   US 6,186,636 B1

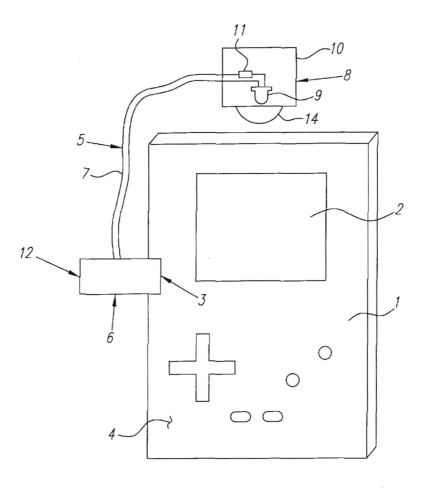

FIG. 1

The numbers on the drawing correspond to a written description of the invention in the specification. The specification of the '636 patent begins on page 3. It includes the Background of the Invention, a Summary of the Invention, a Brief Description of the Drawings, and the Detailed Description of the Preferred Embodiment.

US 6,186,636 B1

1

APPARATUS FOR ILLUMINATING A PORTABLE ELECTRONIC OR COMPUTING DEVICE

Field of the Invention

The present invention is in the field of lighting devices for portable electronic or computing devices.

BACKGROUND OF THE INVENTION

Compact electronic devices with a viewing screen or keypads have become very common and quite popular. Such devices have been popular for a number of years in connection with hand-held, portable, battery-powered gaming devices. A well-known example of such a device, that has sold millions of units, is the GAME BOY® device sold by Nintendo. More recently, other electronic devices have also included viewing screens, such as portable video cameras and cellular phones. And, of course, portable computers have long had viewing screens. Although the complexity and cost of such devices can vary greatly, it is common for such devices to use a generally flat, liquid crystal display screen.

Flat, liquid crystal display screens work very well in a well-lit area. However, when such devices are used in dimly lit areas, or at night, it can be difficult, if not impossible, for a user to see anything in the viewing screen. This problem is magnified when such a screen is used in a device that is meant to be portable, and especially when it is a small device.

If a portable device is sufficiently complex, and generally more expensive, such as a portable laptop computer, the device can include lighting within the actual device. An example of such lighting is a portable laptop computer with a backlit screen. However, this solution is not always economically practical, nor does it necessarily solve the problem in smaller devices. Also, if an electronic device does not have a viewing screen, then this option is not even available.

To solve this problem, especially in connection with hand-held, portable, battery-powered gaming devices, a number of different solutions have been proposed. Such solutions have typically included add-on devices with their own source of electrical power. These devices can be designed to fit onto the electronic device or be designed for use in connection with the electronic device. However, because such devices use their own source of electrical power, they tend to be rather bulky and heavy. In addition, the second source of electrical power increases cost and creates the possibility of another source of power failure.

Accordingly, there is a long felt need for a simple, economical, device that can illuminate portable electronic or computing devices without the drawbacks associated with prior illumination devices.

SUMMARY OF THE INVENTION

The present invention is generally directed to an apparatus for illuminating a portable electronic device that plugs into the electronic device and is powered by the power source of the electrical device through an electronic connection to a utility power jack of the electronic device. The present invention is also generally directed to an apparatus for illuminating a portable computing device with a display screen that plugs into the computing device and is powered by the power source of the computing device through an electronic connection to a port in connection with a power source.

2

In a first, separate aspect of the present invention, the illumination device is a light emitting diode. A white light diode is especially preferred.

In another, separate aspect of the present invention, the illumination apparatus includes a plug that has a second utility power jack or port adapted to receive a second plug that is in electrical communication with the utility power jack or port.

In still another, separate aspect of the present invention, the illumination apparatus can include a flexible arm. This flexible arm can be adjusted as to adjust the height or angle of the illumination device relative to the portable electronic or computing device. In addition, other devices, such as a diffuser, a magnifier, or a regulator for varying the intensity of light, can also be added to the illumination apparatus.

Accordingly, it is a primary object of the present invention to provide a low-cost, practical and improved illumination apparatus for a portable electronic device that is powered by a utility jack of the electronic device.

It is also a primary object of the present invention to provide a low-cost, practical and improved illumination apparatus for a portable computing device that is powered by a utility port of the computing device.

This and further objects and advantages will be apparent to those skilled in the art in connection with the drawing and the detailed description of the preferred embodiment set forth below.

BRIEF DESCRIPTION OF THE DRAWINGS

FIG. 1 is a schematic representation of a preferred embodiment of the present invention.

DETAILED DESCRIPTION OF THE PREFERRED EMBODIMENT

FIG. 1 illustrates how a preferred embodiment of the present invention can be used with a portable electronic game device, such as a GAME BOY® device. Although this drawing depicts a portable electronic game device, the invention is adaptable to any portable electronic device that has a utility power jack in electrical connection with a power source, such as a cellular phone or a video camera.

In the preferred embodiment shown in FIG. 1, the electronic device 1 has a viewing screen 2, a power source and a utility power jack. The power source and utility power jacks are not visible and are shown generally as 3 and 4, because their location and configuration will vary depending upon the design of a given portable electronic device. The power source 3 may be self-contained, such as batteries in a battery compartment. The power source 3 may or may not be augmented by a plug-in capability to a non-portable power source, such as a wall outlet.

The illumination apparatus, shown generally as 5, includes a plug, shown generally as 6, for plugging the illumination apparatus 5 into the utility power jack 4 of the electronic device 1. The exact configuration of the plug 6 should be designed so as to mate with the utility power jack 4 and create a mechanical and electrical connection between the utility power jack 4 and the plug 6 when the apparatus 5 is plugged into the electronic device 1.

The illumination apparatus 5 also includes a body 7 and an illumination device 8. The body 7 connects the illumination device 8 to the plug 6, and the body is preferably comprised of a flexible arm. The illumination device 8 is electrically connected to the utility power jack 4 through the plug 6 and the body 7 so that the illumination device 8 is

Starting with the phrase "What is claimed is," the claims follow the written description on page 4 at the bottom of column 3. The claims continue on page 5 of the '636 patent.

US 6,186,636 B1

3

powered by the power source **2** when the illumination apparatus **5** is plugged into the electronic device **1**. The electrical connection between the illumination device **8** and the plug **6** can be by any suitable means, such as by a wire (not shown). It is especially preferred that the body **7** can be adjusted, when the apparatus **5** is plugged into the utility power jack **4**, to adjust the height and/or the angle of the illumination device **8** relative to the electronic device **1**.

In the preferred embodiment of the present invention, the illumination device **8** is comprised of a light emitting diode ("LED") **9** housed in a case housing **10**. The housing **10** can also include suitable electronics, such as a resistor **11**, or a regulator (not shown) for varying the intensity of light given off by the LED. In an especially preferred embodiment, the LED **9** is a white light diode. The housing can also include additional features, such as a diffuser lens **14**, The diffuser **14** can alternatively be replaced by a magnifier **14**. The diffuser **14** can alternatively be replaced by a magnifier **14**.

When the plug **6** of the illumination apparatus **5** is plugged into the utility power jack **4** of the electronic device **1**, it necessarily occupies the connection that the utility power jack **4** would otherwise provide to a user of the electronic device **1**. Because a user of the electronic device **1** might need to connect some other device to the utility power jack **4**, it is especially preferred that the plug **6** be constructed so as to include a second utility power jack **12**. The second utility power jack **12** is adapted to receive a second plug and provide a mechanical and electrical connection for the second plug equivalent to that which is provided by the utility power jack **4**. Thus, the second utility power jack **12** will provide electrical communication for the second plug with the utility power jack **4** when the second plug is plugged into the plug **6** and the plug **6** is plugged into the utility power jack **4**.

The present invention is also adaptable to a portable computing device with a display screen that is not illuminated by the portable computing device. In such an embodiment, the illumination apparatus is plugged into a utility port of the computing device in electrical connection with a power source instead of the utility power jack **4** of the electronic device **1**. In such a device, the utility port can be any port that allows connection of additional products or communication devices, or cables, or any additional accessory or product. The illumination apparatus can have a second utility port adapted to receive a second plug that is in electrical communication with the utility port when the second plug is plugged into the plug and the plug is plugged into the utility port. In all other respects, the structure and function of the illumination apparatus would be the same as for the illumination apparatus **5** described above in connection with electronic device **1**.

It will be readily apparent to those skilled in the art that still further changes and modifications in the actual concepts described herein can readily be made without departing from the spirit and scope of the invention as defined by the following claims.

What is claimed is:

1. An apparatus for illuminating a portable electronic or computing device having a utility power jack in electrical connection with a power source, comprising:

a plug for plugging the apparatus into the utility power jack;

a body connected to the plug; and

an illumination device attached to the body and to be electrically connected to the utility power jack through the plug and the body. the illumination device including

4

a light emitting diode to illuminate the portable electronic device;

wherein the illumination device is powered by the power source when the apparatus is plugged into the utility power jack.

2. A method of illuminating a non-backlit display screen of a handheld portable video game device having a utility power jack in electrical connection with a power source, comprising:

providing an apparatus including a plug for plugging the apparatus into the utility power jack, a body connected to the plug, and a light emitting diode attached to the body and to be electrically connected to the utility power jack through the plug and the body;

coupling the plug of the apparatus with the utility jack of the handheld portable video game device so as to power the light emitting diode; and

illuminating the non-backlit display screen of the handheld portable video game device with the light emitting diode.

3. An apparatus as recited in claim **1**, wherein the apparatus is adapted for use with a handheld portable video game device.

4. An apparatus as recited in claim **1**, wherein the handheld portable video same device has a non-backlit display screen.

5. An apparatus for illuminating a portable electronic or computing device having a first utility power jack in electrical connection with a power source, comprising: with the first

a first plug for plugging the apparatus into the first utility power jack the first plug having a second utility power jack to receive a second plug that is in electrical communication utility power jack when the second plugged into the second utility jack and the first plug is plugged into the first utility power jack;

a body connected to the first plug; and

an illumination device attached to the body and to be electrically connected to the first utility power jack through the first plug and the body

wherein the illumination device is powered by the power source when the apparatus is plugged into the first utility power jack.

6. An apparatus for illuminating a portable electronic or computing device having a first utility power jack in electrical connection with a power source, comprising:

a first plug for plugging the apparatus into the first utility power jack, the first plug having a second utility power jack to receive a second plug that is in electrical communication with the first utility power jack when the second plug is plugged into the second utility power jack and the first plug is plugged into the first utility power jack,

a body connected to the first plug; and

an illumination device attached to the body and to be electrically connected to the first utility power jack through the first plug and the body, the illumination device including a light emitting diode;

wherein the illumination device is powered by the power source when the apparatus is plugged into the first utility power jack.

7. An apparatus as recited in claim **1**, wherein the body is comprised of a flexible arm.

8. An apparatus as recited in claim **1**, wherein the body can be adjusted, when the apparatus is plugged into the

US 6,186,636 B1

5	6

utility power jack, to adjust the height of the illumination device relative to the portable electronic device.

9. An apparatus as recited in claim 1, wherein the body can be adjusted, when the apparatus is plugged into the utility power jack, to adjust the angle of the illumination device relative to the portable electronic device.

10. An apparatus as recited in claim 1, wherein the body further comprises a diffuser for diffusing light given off by the illumination device.

11. An apparatus as recited in claim 1, wherein the body further comprises a magnifier.

12. An apparatus as recited in claim 1, wherein the body further comprises a regulator for varying the intensity of light given off by the illumination device.

13. An apparatus as recited in claim 1, wherein the light emitting diode is a white light emitting diode.

14. An apparatus for illuminating a non-backlit display screen of a handheld portable video game device having a utility port in electrical connection with a power source, comprising:

a plug for plugging the apparatus into the utility port;

a body connected to the plug; and

a light emitting diode ("LED") attached to the body and to be electrically connected to the utility port through the plug and the body, the light emitting diode to illuminate the non-backlit display screen of the handheld portable video game device;

wherein the LED is powered by the power source when the apparatus is plugged into the utility port.

15. An apparatus as recited in claim 14, wherein the LED is a white light emitting diode.

16. An apparatus for illuminating a non-backlit display screen of a handheld portable video game device having a first utility port in electrical connection with a power source, comprising:

a first plug for plugging the apparatus into the first utility port, the first plug having a second utility port to receive a second plug that is in electrical communication with the first utility port when the second plug is plugged into the second utility port and the first plug is plugged into the first utility port;

a body connected to the first plug; and

a light emitting diode ("LED") attached to the body and to be electrically connected to the first utility port through the first plug and the body;

wherein the LED is powered by the power source when the apparatus is plugged into the first utility port.

17. An apparatus as recited in claim 14, wherein the body is comprised of a flexible arm.

18. An apparatus as recited in claim 14, wherein the body can be adjusted, when the apparatus is plugged into the utility port, to adjust the height of the LED relative to the portable computing device.

19. An apparatus as recited in claim 14, wherein the body can be adjusted, when the apparatus is plugged into the utility port, to adjust the angle of the LED relative to the portable computing device.

20. An apparatus as recited in claim 14, wherein the body further comprises a diffuser for diffusing light given off by the LED.

21. An apparatus as recited in claim 20, wherein the body further comprises a magnifier.

22. A method as recited in claim 2, wherein the light emitting diode is a white light emitting diode.

23. A method as recited in claim 2, wherein the body is comprised of a flexible arm.

24. A method as recited in claim 2, wherein the body further comprises a magnifier.

25. A method as recited in claim 2, wherein the body further comprises a diffuser for diffusing light given off by the illumination device.

26. A method as recited in claim 2, wherein the body further comprises a regulator for varying the intensity of light given off by the illumination device, and the method further comprises adjusting the regulator to regulate an intensity of light given off by the illumination device.

27. A method as recited in claim 2, wherein the plug has a second utility power jack adapted to receive a second plug that is in electrical communication with the utility power jack when the second plug is plugged into the second utility powerjack and the plug is plugged into the utility power jack, and the method further comprises coupling a second plug to the second utility jack.

* * * * *

An applicant must file a patent application with the Patent and Trademark Office (PTO) in order to obtain a patent. The application process is known as "patent prosecution," and the record of a patent's application proceedings is called the "prosecution history." If the PTO rejects the application, the applicant may appeal to the Board of Patent Appeals and Interferences. If the Board denies the appeal, the applicant may file an additional appeal in the Court of Appeals for the Federal Circuit (CAFC).

Inventors are also required to attest to their "inventorship," the belief that they are the first inventor. Since the United States uses a "first to invent" system, only the first, true inventor is entitled to patent protection and priority. The inventor may assign his rights or share patent protection through joint inventorship, but "first to invent" determines priority. If there is a dispute about inventorship, the first inventor is determined using a proceeding known as "interference."

Infringement of a patent involves making, using, offering for sale, or selling any patented invention within the United States or its territories. Importing patented inventions, or their components, may also qualify as infringement. Patent holders, who believe infringement has occurred, may seek relief in the federal court system. District courts first hear patent claims; on appeal, all patent claims go to the Court of Appeals for the Federal Circuit. If the U.S. government infringes a patent, the patent holder may sue in the United States Court of Federal Claims.

Courts offer two types of remedies for infringement. They may award damages or grant injunctive relief. Damages may include lost profits and, if the injured party can show willful infringement, attorney's fees. Defenses to infringement include: invalidation, inequitable conduct, and patent misuse. General defenses such as laches, equitable estoppel, and expiration of the statutory period of protection may also be used.

We begin by examining which inventions are patentable. Then we consider the conditions for patentability and nonobviousness. Finally, we study infringement, defenses, and remedies.

II.   PATENTABILITY—WHAT IS PATENTABLE?

A.   SECTION 101: INVENTIONS PATENTABLE

Section 101 of the Patent Act describes the inventions and discoveries eligible for patent protection, also known as "patentable subject matter." Section 101 defines the scope of patentability as:

> Whoever invents or discovers any new and useful process, machine, manufacture, or composition of matter, or any new and useful improvement thereof, may obtain a patent therefor, subject to the conditions and requirements of this title.

35 U.S.C. § 101.

The scope of patentability under Section 101 is quite broad. It includes both concrete things like "machine[s]" and intangibles like "process[es]" and "useful improvement[s]." The breadth of Section 101 may prompt one to ask, "What is excluded?" Are natural or mental processes patentable? How about a DNA sequence or an "improvement" to a living organism?

1.   Patentable Subject Matter

DIAMOND v. CHAKRABARTY

Supreme Court of the United States, 1980.
447 U.S. 303, 100 S.Ct. 2204, 65 L.Ed.2d 144.

MR. CHIEF JUSTICE BURGER delivered the opinion of the Court.

We granted certiorari to determine whether a live, human-made micro-organism is patentable subject matter under 35 U.S.C. § 101.

I

In 1972, respondent Chakrabarty, a microbiologist, filed a patent application, assigned to the General Electric Co. The application asserted

36 claims related to Chakrabarty's invention of "a bacterium from the genus *Pseudomonas* containing therein at least two stable energy-generating plasmids, each of said plasmids providing a separate hydrocarbon degradative pathway."[1] This human-made, genetically engineered bacterium is capable of breaking down multiple components of crude oil. Because of this property, which is possessed by no naturally occurring bacteria, Chakrabarty's invention is believed to have significant value for the treatment of oil spills.

Chakrabarty's patent claims were of three types: first, process claims for the method of producing the bacteria; second, claims for an inoculum comprised of a carrier material floating on water, such as straw, and the new bacteria; and third, claims to the bacteria themselves. The patent examiner allowed the claims falling into the first two categories, but rejected claims for the bacteria. His decision rested on two grounds: (1) that micro-organisms are "products of nature," and (2) that as living things they are not patentable subject matter under 35 U.S.C. § 101.

Chakrabarty appealed the rejection of these claims to the Patent Office Board of Appeals, and the Board affirmed the Examiner on the second ground.[3] Relying on the legislative history of the 1930 Plant Patent Act, in which Congress extended patent protection to certain asexually reproduced plants, the Board concluded that § 101 was not intended to cover living things such as these laboratory created micro-organisms.

The Court of Customs and Patent Appeals, by a divided vote, reversed
* * *.

II

The Constitution grants Congress broad power to legislate to "promote the Progress of Science and useful Arts, by securing for limited Times to Authors and Inventors the exclusive Right to their respective Writings and Discoveries." Art. I, § 8, cl. 8. The patent laws promote this progress by offering inventors exclusive rights for a limited period as an incentive for their inventiveness and research efforts. The authority of Congress is exercised in the hope that "[t]he productive effort thereby fostered will have a positive effect on society through the introduction of new products and processes of manufacture into the economy, and the emanations by way of increased employment and better lives for our citizens." *Kewanee Oil Co. v. Bicron Corp.*, 416 U.S. 470, at 480 (1974).

---

1. Plasmids are hereditary units physically separate from the chromosomes of the cell. In prior research, Chakrabarty and an associate discovered that plasmids control the oil degradation abilities of certain bacteria. In particular, the two researchers discovered plasmids capable of degrading camphor and octane, two components of crude oil. In the work represented by the patent application at issue here, Chakrabarty discovered a process by which four different plasmids, capable of degrading four different oil components, could be transferred to and maintained stably in a single *Pseudomonas* bacterium, which itself has no capacity for degrading oil.

3. The Board concluded that the new bacteria were not "products of nature," because *Pseudomonas* bacteria containing two or more different energy-generating plasmids are not naturally occurring.

The question before us in this case is a narrow one of statutory interpretation requiring us to construe 35 U.S.C. § 101, which provides:

"Whoever invents or discovers any new and useful process, machine, manufacture, or composition of matter, or any new and useful improvement thereof, may obtain a patent therefor, subject to the conditions and requirements of this title."

Specifically, we must determine whether respondent's micro-organism constitutes a "manufacture" or "composition of matter" within the meaning of the statute.

III

In cases of statutory construction we begin, of course, with the language of the statute. And "unless otherwise defined, words will be interpreted as taking their ordinary, contemporary common meaning." We have also cautioned that courts "should not read into the patent laws limitations and conditions which the legislature has not expressed."

Guided by these canons of construction, this Court has read the term "manufacture" in § 101 in accordance with its dictionary definition to mean "the production of articles for use from raw or prepared materials by giving to these materials new forms, qualities, properties, or combinations, whether by hand-labor or by machinery." *American Fruit Growers, Inc. v. Brogdex Co.*, 283 U.S. 1, 11, 51 S.Ct. 328, 330, 75 L.Ed. 801 (1931). Similarly, "composition of matter" has been construed consistent with its common usage to include "all compositions of two or more substances and . . . all composite articles, whether they be the results of chemical union, or of mechanical mixture, or whether they be gases, fluids, powders or solids." *Shell Development Co. v. Watson*, 149 F.Supp. 279, 280 (D.C. 1957). In choosing such expansive terms as "manufacture" and "composition of matter," modified by the comprehensive "any," Congress plainly contemplated that the patent laws would be given wide scope.

The relevant legislative history also supports a broad construction. The Patent Act of 1793, authored by Thomas Jefferson, defined statutory subject matter as "any new and useful art, machine, manufacture, or composition of matter, or any new or useful improvement [thereof]." Act of Feb. 21, 1793, § 1, 1 Stat. 319. The Act embodied Jefferson's philosophy that "ingenuity should receive a liberal encouragement." 5 Writings of Thomas Jefferson 75–76 (Washington ed. 1871). Subsequent patent statutes in 1836, 1870, and 1874 employed this same broad language. In 1952, when the patent laws were recodified, Congress replaced the word "art" with "process," but otherwise left Jefferson's language intact. The Committee Reports accompanying the 1952 Act inform us that Congress intended statutory subject matter to "include anything under the sun that is made by man." S.Rep.No.1979, 82d Cong., 2d Sess., 5 (1952); H.R.Rep. No.1923, 82d Cong., 2d Sess., 6 (1952).

This is not to suggest that § 101 has no limits or that it embraces every discovery. The laws of nature, physical phenomena, and abstract ideas have been held not patentable. Thus, a new mineral discovered in the earth or a new plant found in the wild is not patentable subject matter. Likewise, Einstein could not patent his celebrated law that $E=mc^2$; nor could Newton have patented the law of gravity. Such discoveries are "manifestations of . . . nature, free to all men and reserved exclusively to none." *Funk Brothers Seed Co. v. Kalo Inoculant Co.*, 333 U.S. 127, at 130 (1948).

Judged in this light, respondent's micro-organism plainly qualifies as patentable subject matter. His claim is not to a hitherto unknown natural phenomenon, but to a nonnaturally occurring manufacture or composition of matter—a product of human ingenuity "having a distinctive name, character [and] use." The point is underscored dramatically by comparison of the invention here with that in *Funk*. There, the patentee had discovered that there existed in nature certain species of root-nodule bacteria which did not exert a mutually inhibitive effect on each other. He used that discovery to produce a mixed culture capable of inoculating the seeds of leguminous plants. Concluding that the patentee had discovered "only some of the handiwork of nature," the Court ruled the product nonpatentable:

> "Each of the species of root-nodule bacteria contained in the package infects the same group of leguminous plants which it always infected. No species acquires a different use. The combination of species produces no new bacteria, no change in the six species of bacteria, and no enlargement of the range of their utility. Each species has the same effect it always had. The bacteria perform in their natural way. Their use in combination does not improve in any way their natural functioning. They serve the ends nature originally provided and act quite independently of any effort of the patentee."

Here, by contrast, the patentee has produced a new bacterium with markedly different characteristics from any found in nature and one having the potential for significant utility. His discovery is not nature's handiwork, but his own; accordingly it is patentable subject matter under § 101.

IV

Two contrary arguments are advanced, neither of which we find persuasive.

(A)

The petitioner's first argument rests on the enactment of the 1930 Plant Patent Act, which afforded patent protection to certain asexually reproduced plants, and the 1970 Plant Variety Protection Act, which authorized protection for certain sexually reproduced plants but excluded bacteria from its protection.[7] In the petitioner's view, the passage of these

---

7. The Plant Patent Act of 1930, 35 U.S.C. § 161, provides in relevant part:

Acts evidences congressional understanding that the terms "manufacture" or "composition of matter" do not include living things; if they did, the petitioner argues, neither Act would have been necessary.

We reject this argument. Prior to 1930, two factors were thought to remove plants from patent protection. The first was the belief that plants, even those artificially bred, were products of nature for purposes of the patent law. This position appears to have derived from the decision of the patent office in *Ex parte Latimer*, 1889 Dec.Com.Pat. 123, in which a patent claim for fiber found in the needle of the *Pinus australis* was rejected. The Commissioner reasoned that a contrary result would permit "patents [to] be obtained upon the trees of the forest and the plants of the earth, which of course would be unreasonable and impossible." *Id.*, at 126. The Latimer case, it seems, came to "se[t] forth the general stand taken in these matters" that plants were natural products not subject to patent protection. Thorne, Relation of Patent Law to Natural Products, 6 J. Pat.Off.Soc. 23, 24 (1923). The second obstacle to patent protection for plants was the fact that plants were thought not amenable to the "written description" requirement of the patent law. See 35 U.S.C. § 112. Because new plants may differ from old only in color or perfume, differentiation by written description was often impossible.

In enacting the Plant Patent Act, Congress addressed both of these concerns. It explained at length its belief that the work of the plant breeder "in aid of nature" was patentable invention. And it relaxed the written description requirement in favor of "a description . . . as complete as is reasonably possible." 35 U.S.C. § 162. No Committee or Member of Congress, however, expressed the broader view, now urged by the petitioner, that the terms "manufacture" or "composition of matter" exclude living things. The sole support for that position in the legislative history of the 1930 Act is found in the conclusory statement of Secretary of Agriculture Hyde, in a letter to the Chairmen of the House and Senate Committees considering the 1930 Act, that "the patent laws . . . at the present time are understood to cover only inventions or discoveries in the field of inanimate nature." Secretary Hyde's opinion, however, is not entitled to controlling weight. His views were solicited on the administration of the new law and not on the scope of patentable subject matter—an area beyond his competence. Moreover, there is language in the House and Senate Committee Reports suggesting that to the extent Congress considered the matter it found the Secretary's dichotomy unpersuasive. The Reports observe:

"Whoever invents or discovers and asexually reproduces any distinct and new variety of plant, including cultivated sports, mutants, hybrids, and newly found seedlings, other than a tuber propagated plant or a plant found in an uncultivated state, may obtain a patent therefor...."

The Plant Variety Protection Act of 1970, provides in relevant part:

"The breeder of any novel variety of sexually reproduced plant (other than fungi, bacteria, or first generation hybrids) who has so reproduced the variety, or his successor in interest, shall be entitled to plant variety protection therefor...." 84 Stat. 1547, 7 U.S.C. § 2402(a).

"There is a clear and logical distinction *between the discovery of a new variety of plant and of certain inanimate things*, such, for example, as a new and useful natural mineral. The mineral is created wholly by nature unassisted by man.... On the other hand, a plant discovery resulting from cultivation is unique, isolated, and is not repeated by nature, nor can it be reproduced by nature unaided by man...."

Congress thus recognized that the relevant distinction was not between living and inanimate things, but between products of nature, whether living or not, and human-made inventions. Here, respondent's micro-organism is the result of human ingenuity and research. Hence, the passage of the Plant Patent Act affords the Government no support.

Nor does the passage of the 1970 Plant Variety Protection Act support the Government's position. As the Government acknowledges, sexually reproduced plants were not included under the 1930 Act because new varieties could not be reproduced true-to-type through seedlings. Brief for Petitioner 27, n. 31. By 1970, however, it was generally recognized that true-to-type reproduction was possible and that plant patent protection was therefore appropriate. The 1970 Act extended that protection. There is nothing in its language or history to suggest that it was enacted because § 101 did not include living things.

In particular, we find nothing in the exclusion of bacteria from plant variety protection to support the petitioner's position. The legislative history gives no reason for this exclusion. As the Court of Customs and Patent Appeals suggested, it may simply reflect congressional agreement with the result reached by that court in deciding *In re Arzberger*, 27 C.C.P.A. (Pat.) 1315, 112 F.2d 834 (1940), which held that bacteria were not plants for the purposes of the 1930 Act. Or it may reflect the fact that prior to 1970 the Patent Office had issued patents for bacteria under § 101. In any event, absent some clear indication that Congress "focused on [the] issues * * * directly related to the one presently before the Court," there is no basis for reading into its actions an intent to modify the plain meaning of the words found in § 101.

(B)

The petitioner's second argument is that micro-organisms cannot qualify as patentable subject matter until Congress expressly authorizes such protection. His position rests on the fact that genetic technology was unforeseen when Congress enacted § 101. From this it is argued that resolution of the patentability of inventions such as respondent's should be left to Congress. The legislative process, the petitioner argues, is best equipped to weigh the competing economic, social, and scientific considerations involved, and to determine whether living organisms produced by genetic engineering should receive patent protection. In support of this position, the petitioner relies on our recent holding in *Parker v. Flook*, 437 U.S. 584, 98 S.Ct. 2522, 57 L.Ed.2d 451 (1978), and the statement that the judiciary "must proceed cautiously when ... asked to extend patent rights into areas wholly unforeseen by Congress." *Id.*, at 596.

It is, of course, correct that Congress, not the courts, must define the limits of patentability; but it is equally true that once Congress has spoken it is "the province and duty of the judicial department to say what the law is." *Marbury v. Madison*, 1 Cranch 137, 177 (1803). Congress has performed its constitutional role in defining patentable subject matter in § 101; we perform ours in construing the language Congress has employed. In so doing, our obligation is to take statutes as we find them, guided, if ambiguity appears, by the legislative history and statutory purpose. Here, we perceive no ambiguity. The subject-matter provisions of the patent law have been cast in broad terms to fulfill the constitutional and statutory goal of promoting "the Progress of Science and the useful Arts" with all that means for the social and economic benefits envisioned by Jefferson. Broad general language is not necessarily ambiguous when congressional objectives require broad terms.

Nothing in *Flook* is to the contrary. That case applied our prior precedents to determine that a "claim for an improved method of calculation, even when tied to a specific end use, is unpatentable subject matter under § 101." The Court carefully scrutinized the claim at issue to determine whether it was precluded from patent protection under "the principles underlying the prohibition against patents for 'ideas' or phenomena of nature." We have done that here. *Flook* did not announce a new principle that inventions in areas not contemplated by Congress when the patent laws were enacted are unpatentable *per se*.

To read that concept into *Flook* would frustrate the purposes of the patent law. This Court frequently has observed that a statute is not to be confined to the "particular application[s] ... contemplated by the legislators." This is especially true in the field of patent law. A rule that unanticipated inventions are without protection would conflict with the core concept of the patent law that anticipation undermines patentability. Mr. Justice Douglas reminded that the inventions most benefiting mankind are those that "push back the frontiers of chemistry, physics, and the like." *Great A. & P. Tea Co. v. Supermarket Corp.*, 340 U.S. 147, 154, 71 S.Ct. 127, 131, 95 L.Ed. 162 (1950) (concurring opinion). Congress employed broad general language in drafting § 101 precisely because such inventions are often unforeseeable.

To buttress his argument, the petitioner, with the support of *amicus*, points to grave risks that may be generated by research endeavors such as respondent's. The briefs present a gruesome parade of horribles. Scientists, among them Nobel laureates, are quoted suggesting that genetic research may pose a serious threat to the human race, or, at the very least, that the dangers are far too substantial to permit such research to proceed apace at this time. We are told that genetic research and related technological developments may spread pollution and disease, that it may result in a loss of genetic diversity, and that its practice may tend to depreciate the value of human life. These arguments are forcefully, even passionately, presented; they remind us that, at times, human ingenuity seems unable to control fully the forces it creates—that with Hamlet, it is sometimes better "to bear those ills we have than fly to others that we know not of."

It is argued that this Court should weigh these potential hazards in considering whether respondent's invention is patentable subject matter under § 101. We disagree. The grant or denial of patents on micro-organisms is not likely to put an end to genetic research or to its attendant risks. The large amount of research that has already occurred when no researcher had sure knowledge that patent protection would be available suggests that legislative or judicial fiat as to patentability will not deter the scientific mind from probing into the unknown any more than Canute could command the tides. Whether respondent's claims are patentable may determine whether research efforts are accelerated by the hope of reward or slowed by want of incentives, but that is all.

What is more important is that we are without competence to entertain these arguments—either to brush them aside as fantasies generated by fear of the unknown, or to act on them. The choice we are urged to make is a matter of high policy for resolution within the legislative process after the kind of investigation, examination, and study that legislative bodies can provide and courts cannot. That process involves the balancing of competing values and interests, which in our democratic system is the business of elected representatives. Whatever their validity, the contentions now pressed on us should be addressed to the political branches of the Government, the Congress and the Executive, and not to the courts.

We have emphasized in the recent past that "[o]ur individual appraisal of the wisdom or unwisdom of a particular [legislative] course . . . is to be put aside in the process of interpreting a statute." Our task, rather, is the narrow one of determining what Congress meant by the words it used in the statute; once that is done our powers are exhausted. Congress is free to amend § 101 so as to exclude from patent protection organisms produced by genetic engineering. Cf. 42 U.S.C. § 2181(a), exempting from patent protection inventions "useful solely in the utilization of special nuclear material or atomic energy in an atomic weapon." Or it may chose to craft a statute specifically designed for such living things. But, until Congress takes such action, this Court must construe the language of § 101 as it is. The language of that section fairly embraces respondent's invention.

Accordingly, the judgment of the Court of Customs and Patent Appeals is

Affirmed.

MR. JUSTICE BRENNAN, with whom MR. JUSTICE WHITE, MR. JUSTICE MARSHALL, and MR. JUSTICE POWELL join, dissenting.

I agree with the Court that the question before us is a narrow one. Neither the future of scientific research, nor even, the ability of respondent Chakrabarty to reap some monopoly profits from his pioneering work, is at stake. Patents on the processes by which he has produced and employed the new living organism are not contested. The only question we need decide is whether Congress, exercising its authority under Art. I, § 8, of the Constitution, intended that he be able to secure a monopoly on the living organism itself, no matter how produced or how used. Because I believe the Court has misread the applicable legislation, I dissent.

The patent laws attempt to reconcile this Nation's deep seated antipathy to monopolies with the need to encourage progress. Given the complexity and legislative nature of this delicate task, we must be careful to extend patent protection no further than Congress has provided. In particular, were there an absence of legislative direction, the courts should leave to Congress the decisions whether and how far to extend the patent privilege into areas where the common understanding has been that patents are not available.

In this case, however, we do not confront a complete legislative vacuum. The sweeping language of the Patent Act of 1793, as re-enacted in 1952, is not the last pronouncement Congress has made in this area. In 1930 Congress enacted the Plant Patent Act affording patent protection to developers of certain asexually reproduced plants. In 1970 Congress enacted the Plant Variety Protection Act to extend protection to certain new plant varieties capable of sexual reproduction. Thus, we are not dealing— as the Court would have it—with the routine problem of "unanticipated inventions." *Ante*, at 2211. In these two Acts, Congress has addressed the general problem of patenting animate inventions and has chosen carefully limited language granting protection to some kinds of discoveries, but specifically excluding others. These Acts strongly evidence a congressional limitation that excludes bacteria from patentability.[2]

First, the Acts evidence Congress' understanding, at least since 1930, that § 101 does not include living organisms. If newly developed living organisms not naturally occurring had been patentable under § 101, the plants included in the scope of the 1930 and 1970 Acts could have been patented without new legislation. Those plants, like the bacteria involved in this case, were new varieties not naturally occurring. Although the Court, rejects this line of argument, it does not explain why the Acts were necessary unless to correct a pre-existing situation. I cannot share the Court's implicit assumption that Congress was engaged in either idle exercises or mere correction of the public record when it enacted the 1930 and 1970 Acts. And Congress certainly thought it was doing something significant. The Committee Reports contain expansive prose about the previously unavailable benefits to be derived from extending patent pro-

---

2. But even if I agreed with the Court that the 1930 and 1970 Acts were not dispositive, I would dissent. This case presents even more cogent reasons than *Deepsouth Packing Co.* not to extend the patent monopoly in the face of uncertainty. At the very least, these Acts are signs of legislative attention to the problems of patenting living organisms, but they give no affirmative indication of congressional intent that bacteria be patentable. The caveat of *Parker v. Flook*, 437 U.S. 584, 596 (1978), an admonition to "proceed cautiously when we are asked to extend patent rights into areas wholly unforeseen by Congress," therefore becomes pertinent. I should think the necessity for caution is that much greater when we are asked to extend patent rights into areas Congress has foreseen and considered but has not resolved.

tection to plants. Because Congress thought it had to legislate in order to make agricultural "human-made inventions" patentable and because the legislation Congress enacted is limited, it follows that Congress never meant to make items outside the scope of the legislation patentable.

Second, the 1970 Act clearly indicates that Congress has included bacteria within the focus of its legislative concern, but not within the scope of patent protection. Congress specifically excluded bacteria from the coverage of the 1970 Act. 7 U.S.C. § 2402(a). The Court's attempts to supply explanations for this explicit exclusion ring hollow. It is true that there is no mention in the legislative history of the exclusion, but that does not give us license to invent reasons. The fact is that Congress, assuming that animate objects as to which it had not specifically legislated could not be patented, excluded bacteria from the set of patentable organisms.

The Court protests that its holding today is dictated by the broad language of § 101, which cannot "be confined to the 'particular application[s] ... contemplated by the legislators.'" But as I have shown, the Court's decision does not follow the unavoidable implications of the statute. Rather, it extends the patent system to cover living material even though Congress plainly has legislated in the belief that § 101 does not encompass living organisms. It is the role of Congress, not this Court, to broaden or narrow the reach of the patent laws. This is especially true where, as here, the composition sought to be patented uniquely implicates matters of public concern.

NOTES

1. *Chakrabarty* Includes Agricultural Biotechnology. The U.S. Supreme Court in *J.E.M. Ag Supply, Inc. v. Pioneer Hi-Bred International, Inc.,* 534 U.S. 124, 122 S.Ct. 593, 151 L.Ed.2d 508 (2001) (see the on-line supplement to this book) held that *Chakrabarty's* broad interpretation of § 101 includes plant life and the products of plant innovation such as genetically modified seeds and plants.

2. Naturally Occurring Organisms. In *Funk Bros. Seed Co. v. Kalo Inoculant Co.,* 333 U.S. 127, 68 S.Ct. 440, 92 L.Ed. 588 (1948), the Supreme Court invalidated a patent that claimed a combination of nitrogen fixing bacteria that could be used to inoculate a variety of leguminous plants. The process is enabled by infecting the plants' roots with bacteria. Due to a well-known inhibitory effect different species had on each other, it was generally thought that combining different species of bacteria to inoculate different varieties of leguminous plants would not be successful. Contrary to these teachings, the patentee discovered a combination of bacteria that could co-exist and inoculate all leguminous plants. The Supreme Court found that the combination "may have been the product of skill, [but] it certainly was not the product of invention." The Court held that the combination of bacteria was not patentable subject matter.

3. Natural Products. May natural products be patented under Section 101? Consider *Parke-Davis & Co. v. H. K. Mulford & Co.,* 189 F. 95

(C.C.S.D.N.Y. 1911). Jokichi Takamine discovered how to isolate a purified product; that he called adrenalin, from the suprarenal glands of animals. He claimed "the active principle," or the substance possessing the physiological characteristics and reactions of the suprarenal glands free from gland tissue, not just the process of purification. Judge Learned Hand reasoned, "Takamine was the first to make it available for any use by removing it from the other gland tissue in which it was found, and, while it is of course possible logically to call this a purification of the principle, it became for every practical purpose a new thing commercially and therapeutically. That was a good ground for a patent." Is human intervention sufficient to validate a patent? What kind of involvement is necessary?

The PTO has had a practice of issuing patent claims directed to isolated DNA (i.e., DNA that exists outside of the body). In *Association for Molecular Pathology v. United States Patent and Trademark Office*, 2010 WL 1233416 (S.D.N.Y. Mar. 29, 2010), plaintiffs sought summary judgment on a declaration of invalidity against patent claims directed to isolated DNA and methods of use for diagnosis of breast and ovarian cancer. Judge Sweet, who noted that some commentators have called the PTO's practice "a lawyer's trick" granted plaintiff's motion for summary judgment holding that the claims in-suit were invalid because they do not qualify as eligible subject matter. Defendants appealed, and as this edition went to press, the appeal was pending.

4. Natural Phenomena. In *Metabolite Laboratories, Inc. v. Laboratory Corp. of America Holdings*, 370 F.3d 1354 (Fed. Cir. 2004), *cert. dismissed*, 548 U.S. 124, 126 S.Ct. 2921, 165 L.Ed.2d 399 (2006), the Federal Circuit held that a patented method for detecting vitamin deficiencies was valid without addressing the issue of patenting natural phenomena. The Court granted certiorari to review the patent on grounds it improperly sought "to claim a monopoly over a basic scientific relationship." The patentee discovered a correlation between elevated levels of homocysteine in warm-blooded animals and folate (folic acid) and cobalamin (vitamin B_{12}) deficiencies. The Court dismissed the case, holding that the writ of certiorari was improvidently granted, but the dissent felt that the patent was likely invalid because it was "an unpatentable 'natural phenomenon.' "

5. Research in the Field of Biotechnology. As research in biotechnology generates greater commercial opportunities, scientists and their research sponsors increasingly seek to protect commercial interests through intellectual property law. The incentives of traditional scientific research, and those created by commercial exploitation are incongruent. Although disclosure is encouraged by both patent law and the norms of scientific research, it has been urged that more effective means of influencing researchers' behavior are possible if one takes into account the norms and incentives that guide behavior in the scientific community. There are concerns about the potential impact of commercial incentives on the traditions of open communication and free flow of information within the scientific community if efforts are not taken to keep some research in the public domain. Rebecca S. Eisenberg, *Proprietary Rights and the Norms of Science in Biotechnology Research*, 97 YALE L.J. 177 (1987).

Some argue that the law must go more to stimulate the creation, disclosure, and development of inventive or creative works. Rather than granting stronger intellectual property rights, building contexts in which "communality" is more beneficial to inventors than property rights could change the norms that guide scientific research. Reliance on norms to preserve a public domain in biotechnology would likely require considerable governmental efforts. Agencies such as the National Institutes of Health (NIH), could implement these changes. Measures should be taken to guard against "the corrosive effect of norm violators and industry actors who seek property rights simply in order to maximize revenue." Arti Kaur Rai, *Regulating Scientific Research: Intellectual Property Rights and the Norms of Science,* 94 Nw. U. L. Rev. 77 (1999).

Scott Kieff responds to Rai and Eisenberg's concerns, arguing that the use of patents in the basic biological research community should be encouraged. Kieff believes Rai mischaracterized the norms in the biological research communities of the 1980's, and that patents are essential for bringing needed resources to the community. Scott Kieff, *Facilitating Scientific Research Intellectual Property Rights and the Norms of Science—A Response to Rai and Eisenberg,* 95 Nw. U. L. Rev. 691 (2001).

6. Patenting Federally Supported Inventions. Inventors may patent federally funded inventions under the Bayh–Dole Act. The NIH has pursued patent rights for thousands of gene fragments of unknown function. It is not clear that this policy of promoting the patenting of federally funded inventions furthers the transfer of new technologies for commercial development. Rebecca S. Eisenberg, *A Technology Policy Perspective on the NIH Gene Patenting Controversy,* 55 U. Pitt. L. Rev. 633 (1994). Some parties advocate reforming the Bayh–Dole Act to give funding agencies greater discretion to determine when discoveries are to be dedicated to the public domain. Arti K. Rai & Rebecca S. Eisenberg, *Bayh–Dole Reform and the Progress of Biomedicine,* 66 Law & Contemp. Probs., Winter/Spring 2003, at 289.

2. What Is a Process?

According to *Chakrabarty,* Section 101 may include "anything under the sun that is made by man," yet Section 101 specifically mentions, "any new and useful *process, machine, manufacture, or composition of matter* ..." (emphasis added). The abstract nature of processes begs the question, "what is a process for purposes of the statute?" Section 100 unhelpfully states: "[t]he term 'process' means process, art or method, and includes a new use of a known process, machine, manufacture, composition of matter, or material." Despite the Act's vagueness, laws of nature, natural phenomena, and abstract ideas appear not to be patentable subject matter. As the information technology space dramatically grew in the late 20th century, courts struggled with applying § 101 "process" to information technology innovation. In *State Street Bank & Trust Co. v. Signature Financial Group, Inc.,* 149 F.3d 1368 (Fed. Cir. 1998), the Federal Circuit took a broad view of statutory subject matter. Judge Rich, writing for the court, held a patent claim directed to a data processing system for implementing a mutual fund strategy was statutory subject matter because it produced "a useful, concrete and tangible result." The court's broad view was based on *In re Alappat*, 33 F.3d 1526 (Fed. Cir. 1994) (en banc). The Federal Circuit made clear that the *State Street* "useful, concrete and tangible result" test applied to § 101 "process" in *AT & T Corp. v. Excel Communications, Inc.*, 172 F.3d 1352 (Fed. Cir. 1999). To be sure, the *State Street* test facilitated an increased number of patent applications claiming information technology processes.

Following the *AT & T Corp.* decision, Congress enacted the First Inventor Defense Act of 1999, which is codified at Section 273. The statute provides a defense to patent infringement of "method" claims "if such person, acting in good faith, actually reduced the subject matter to practice at least 1 year before the effective filing date of such patent, and commercially used the subject matter before the effective filing date of such patent." Section 273(b)(1). Moreover, the statute defines method as "a method of doing or conducting business." Section 273(a)(3).

One decade after *State Street* was decided, in *In re Bilski*, 545 F.3d 943 (Fed. Cir. 2008) (en banc), a fractured Federal Circuit changed course and took a restrictive view of "process." The court discarded the *State Street* test, and articulated the machine-or-transformation test based on the Supreme Court's Section 101 jurisprudence. The Supreme Court granted certiorari, and decided *Bilski v. Kappos*. While reading the case, compare Justice Kennedy's and Justice Stevens' interpretations of Section 101 and Section 273.

BILSKI v. KAPPOS

Supreme Court of the United States, 2010.
561 U.S. ___, 130 S.Ct. 3218, ___ L.Ed.2d ___, 2010 WL 2555192.

KENNEDY, J., delivered the opinion of the Court, except for Parts II–B–2 and II–C–2. ROBERTS, C.J., and THOMAS and ALITO, JJ., joined the opinion in full, and SCALIA, J., joined except for Parts II–B–2 and II–C–2. STEVENS, J., filed an opinion concurring in the judgment, in which GINSBURG, BREYER, and SOTOMAYOR, JJ., joined. BREYER, J., filed an opinion concurring in the judgment, in which SCALIA, J., joined as to Part II.

JUSTICE KENNEDY delivered the opinion of the Court, except as to Parts II–B–2 and II–C–2.

The question in this case turns on whether a patent can be issued for a claimed invention designed for the business world. The patent application claims a procedure for instructing buyers and sellers how to protect against the risk of price fluctuations in a discrete section of the economy. Three arguments are advanced for the proposition that the claimed invention is outside the scope of patent law: (1) it is not tied to a machine and does not transform an article; (2) it involves a method of conducting business; and (3) it is merely an abstract idea. The Court of Appeals ruled that the first mentioned of these, the so-called machine-or-transformation test, was the sole test to be used for determining the patentability of a "process" under the Patent Act, 35 U.S.C. § 101.

I

Petitioners' application seeks patent protection for a claimed invention that explains how buyers and sellers of commodities in the energy market can protect, or hedge, against the risk of price changes. The key claims are claims 1 and 4. Claim 1 describes a series of steps instructing how to hedge risk. Claim 4 puts the concept articulated in claim 1 into a simple mathematical formula. Claim 1 consists of the following steps:

> "(a) initiating a series of transactions between said commodity provider and consumers of said commodity wherein said consumers purchase said commodity at a fixed rate based upon historical averages, said fixed rate corresponding to a risk position of said consumers;

> "(b) identifying market participants for said commodity having a counter-risk position to said consumers; and

> "(c) initiating a series of transactions between said commodity provider and said market participants at a second fixed rate such that said series of market participant transactions balances the risk position of said series of consumer transactions."

The remaining claims explain how claims 1 and 4 can be applied to allow energy suppliers and consumers to minimize the risks resulting from fluctuations in market demand for energy. * * *

The patent examiner rejected petitioners' application, explaining that it " 'is not implemented on a specific apparatus and merely manipulates [an] abstract idea and solves a purely mathematical problem without any limitation to a practical application, therefore, the invention is not directed to the technological arts.' " The Board of Patent Appeals and Interferences affirmed, concluding that the application involved only mental steps that do not transform physical matter and was directed to an abstract idea.

The United States Court of Appeals for the Federal Circuit heard the case en banc and affirmed. The case produced five different opinions. Students of patent law would be well advised to study these scholarly opinions.

Chief Judge Michel wrote the opinion of the court. The court rejected its prior test for determining whether a claimed invention was a patentable "process" under § 101–whether it produces a " 'useful, concrete, and tangible result' "-as articulated in *State Street Bank & Trust Co. v. Signature Financial Group, Inc.*, 149 F.3d 1368, 1373 (1998), and *AT & T Corp. v. Excel Communications, Inc.*, 172 F.3d 1352, 1357 (1999). The court held that "[a] claimed process is surely patent-eligible under § 101 if: (1) it is tied to a particular machine or apparatus, or (2) it transforms a particular article into a different state or thing." [*In re Bilski*, 545 F.3d 943,] 954. The court concluded this "machine-or-transformation test" is "the sole test governing § 101 analyses," *id.*, at 955, and thus the "test for determining patent eligibility of a process under § 101," *id.*, at 956.

Applying the machine-or-transformation test, the court held that petitioners' application was not patent eligible. Judge Dyk wrote a separate concurring opinion, providing historical support for the court's approach.

Three judges wrote dissenting opinions. Judge Mayer argued that petitioners' application was "not eligible for patent protection because it is directed to a method of conducting business." *Id.*, at 998. He urged the adoption of a "technological standard for patentability." *Id.*, at 1010. Judge Rader would have found petitioners' claims were an unpatentable abstract idea. Only Judge Newman disagreed with the court's conclusion that petitioners' application was outside of the reach of § 101. She did not say that the application should have been granted but only that the issue should be remanded for further proceedings to determine whether the application qualified as patentable under other provisions.

This Court granted certiorari.

II

A

Section 101 defines the subject matter that may be patented under the Patent Act:

> "Whoever invents or discovers any new and useful process, machine, manufacture, or composition of matter, or any new and useful improvement thereof, may obtain a patent therefor, subject to the conditions and requirements of this title."

Section 101 thus specifies four independent categories of inventions or discoveries that are eligible for protection: processes, machines, manufactures, and compositions of matter. "In choosing such expansive terms ... modified by the comprehensive 'any,' Congress plainly contemplated that the patent laws would be given wide scope." *Diamond v. Chakrabarty*, 447 U.S. 303, 308, 100 S.Ct. 2204, 65 L.Ed.2d 144 (1980). Congress took this permissive approach to patent eligibility to ensure that " 'ingenuity should receive a liberal encouragement.' " *Id.*, at 308–309, 100 S.Ct. 2204 (quoting 5 Writings of Thomas Jefferson 75–76 (H. Washington ed. 1871)).

The Court's precedents provide three specific exceptions to § 101's broad patent-eligibility principles: "laws of nature, physical phenomena, and abstract ideas." *Chakrabarty, supra*, at 309, 100 S.Ct. 2204. While these exceptions are not required by the statutory text, they are consistent with the notion that a patentable process must be "new and useful." And, in any case, these exceptions have defined the reach of the statute as a matter of statutory stare decisis going back 150 years. See *Le Roy v. Tatham*, 14 How. 156, 174–175, 14 L.Ed. 367 (1853). The concepts covered by these exceptions are "part of the storehouse of knowledge of all men ... free to all men and reserved exclusively to none." *Funk Brothers Seed Co. v. Kalo Inoculant Co.*, 333 U.S. 127, 130, 68 S.Ct. 440, 92 L.Ed. 588 (1948).

The § 101 patent-eligibility inquiry is only a threshold test. Even if an invention qualifies as a process, machine, manufacture, or composition of matter, in order to receive the Patent Act's protection the claimed invention must also satisfy "the conditions and requirements of this title." § 101. Those requirements include that the invention be novel, *see* § 102, nonobvious, *see* § 103, and fully and particularly described, *see* § 112.

The present case involves an invention that is claimed to be a "process" under § 101. Section 100(b) defines "process" as:

> "process, art or method, and includes a new use of a known process, machine, manufacture, composition of matter, or material."

The Court first considers two proposed categorical limitations on "process" patents under § 101 that would, if adopted, bar petitioners' application in the present case: the machine-or-transformation test and the categorical exclusion of business method patents.

B

1

Under the Court of Appeals' formulation, an invention is a "process" only if: "(1) it is tied to a particular machine or apparatus, or (2) it transforms a particular article into a different state or thing." 545 F.3d, at 954. This Court has "more than once cautioned that courts 'should not read into the patent laws limitations and conditions which the legislature has not expressed.' " *Diamond v. Diehr*, 450 U.S. 175, 182, 101 S.Ct. 1048, 67 L.Ed.2d 155 (1981) (quoting *Chakrabarty, supra*, at 308, 100 S.Ct. 2204; some internal quotation marks omitted). In patent law, as in all statutory construction, "[u]nless otherwise defined, 'words will be interpreted as taking their ordinary, contemporary, common meaning.' " *Diehr, supra*, at 182, 101 S.Ct. 1048 (quoting *Perrin v. United States*, 444 U.S. 37, 42, 100 S.Ct. 311, 62 L.Ed.2d 199 (1979)). The Court has read the § 101 term "manufacture" in accordance with dictionary definitions, * * * and approved a construction of the term "composition of matter" consistent with common usage[.]

Any suggestion in this Court's case law that the Patent Act's terms deviate from their ordinary meaning has only been an explanation for the exceptions for laws of nature, physical phenomena, and abstract ideas. *See Parker v. Flook*, 437 U.S. 584, 588–589, 98 S.Ct. 2522, 57 L.Ed.2d 451 (1978). This Court has not indicated that the existence of these well-established exceptions gives the Judiciary carte blanche to impose other limitations that are inconsistent with the text and the statute's purpose and design. Concerns about attempts to call any form of human activity a "process" can be met by making sure the claim meets the requirements of § 101.

Adopting the machine-or-transformation test as the sole test for what constitutes a "process" (as opposed to just an important and useful clue) violates these statutory interpretation principles. Section 100(b) provides that "[t]he term 'process' means process, art or method, and includes a new use of a known process, machine, manufacture, composition of matter, or material." The Court is unaware of any " 'ordinary, contemporary, common meaning,' " *Diehr*, supra, at 182, 101 S.Ct. 1048, of the definitional terms "process, art or method" that would require these terms to be tied to a machine or to transform an article. Respondent urges the Court to look to the other patentable categories in § 101–machines, manufactures, and compositions of matter-to confine the meaning of "process" to a machine or transformation, under the doctrine of noscitur a sociis. Under this canon, "an ambiguous term may be given more precise content by the neighboring words with which it is associated." *United States v. Stevens*, 559 U.S. ___, ___, 130 S.Ct. 1577, 1587, 176 L.Ed.2d 435 (2010) (internal quotation marks omitted). This canon is inapplicable here, for § 100(b) already explicitly defines the term "process."

The Court of Appeals incorrectly concluded that this Court has endorsed the machine-or-transformation test as the exclusive test. It is true that *Cochrane v. Deener*, 94 U.S. 780, 788, 24 L.Ed. 139 (1877), explained that a "process" is "an act, or a series of acts, performed upon the subject-matter to be transformed and reduced to a different state or thing." More recent cases, however, have rejected the broad implications of this dictum; and, in all events, later authority shows that it was not intended to be an exhaustive or exclusive test. *Gottschalk v. Benson*, 409 U.S. 63, 70, 93 S.Ct. 253, 34 L.Ed.2d 273 (1972), noted that "[t]ransformation and reduction of an article 'to a different state or thing' is the clue to the patentability of a process claim that does not include particular machines." At the same time, it explicitly declined to "hold that no process patent could ever qualify if it did not meet [machine or transformation] requirements." *Id.*, at 71, 93 S.Ct. 253. *Flook* took a similar approach, "assum[ing] that a valid process patent may issue even if it does not meet [the machine-or-transformation test]." 437 U.S., at 588, n. 9, 98 S.Ct. 2522.

This Court's precedents establish that the machine-or-transformation test is a useful and important clue, an investigative tool, for determining whether some claimed inventions are processes under § 101. The machine-or-transformation test is not the sole test for deciding whether an invention is a patent-eligible "process."

2

It is true that patents for inventions that did not satisfy the machine-or-transformation test were rarely granted in earlier eras, especially in the Industrial Age, as explained by Judge Dyk's thoughtful historical review. But times change. Technology and other innovations progress in unexpected ways. For example, it was once forcefully argued that until recent times, "well-established principles of patent law probably would have prevented the issuance of a valid patent on almost any conceivable computer program." *Diehr*, 450 U.S., at 195, 101 S.Ct. 1048 (STEVENS, J., dissenting). But this fact does not mean that unforeseen innovations such as computer programs are always unpatentable. Section 101 is a "dynamic provision designed to encompass new and unforeseen inventions." *J.E.M. Ag Supply, Inc. v. Pioneer Hi–Bred Int'l, Inc.*, 534 U.S. 124, 135, 122 S.Ct. 593, 151 L.Ed.2d 508 (2001). A categorical rule denying patent protection for "inventions in areas not contemplated by Congress ... would frustrate the purposes of the patent law." *Chakrabarty*, 447 U.S., at 315, 100 S.Ct. 2204.

The machine-or-transformation test may well provide a sufficient basis for evaluating processes similar to those in the Industrial Age-for example, inventions grounded in a physical or other tangible form. But there are reasons to doubt whether the test should be the sole criterion for determining the patentability of inventions in the Information Age. As numerous amicus briefs argue, the machine-or-transformation test would create uncertainty as to the patentability of software, advanced diagnostic medicine techniques, and inventions based on linear programming, data compression, and the manipulation of digital signals.

In the course of applying the machine-or-transformation test to emerging technologies, courts may pose questions of such intricacy and refinement that they risk obscuring the larger object of securing patents for valuable inventions without transgressing the public domain. The dissent by Judge Rader refers to some of these difficulties. 545 F.3d, at 1015. As a result, in deciding whether previously unforeseen inventions qualify as patentable "process[es]," it may not make sense to require courts to confine themselves to asking the questions posed by the machine-or-transformation test. Section 101's terms suggest that new technologies may call for new inquiries.

It is important to emphasize that the Court today is not commenting on the patentability of any particular invention, let alone holding that any of the above-mentioned technologies from the Information Age should or should not receive patent protection. This Age puts the possibility of innovation in the hands of more people and raises new difficulties for the patent law. With ever more people trying to innovate and thus seeking patent protections for their inventions, the patent law faces a great challenge in striking the balance between protecting inventors and not granting monopolies over procedures that others would discover by independent, creative application of general principles. Nothing in this opinion should be read to take a position on where that balance ought to be struck.

C

1

Section 101 similarly precludes the broad contention that the term "process" categorically excludes business methods. The term "method," which is within § 100(b)'s definition of "process," at least as a textual matter and before consulting other limitations in the Patent Act and this Court's precedents, may include at least some methods of doing business.

The Court is unaware of any argument that the " 'ordinary, contemporary, common meaning,' " *Diehr, supra,* at 182, 101 S.Ct. 1048, of "method" excludes business methods. Nor is it clear how far a prohibition on business method patents would reach, and whether it would exclude technologies for conducting a business more efficiently.

The argument that business methods are categorically outside of § 101's scope is further undermined by the fact that federal law explicitly contemplates the existence of at least some business method patents. Under 35 U.S.C. § 273(b)(1), if a patent-holder claims infringement based on "a method in [a] patent," the alleged infringer can assert a defense of prior use. For purposes of this defense alone, "method" is defined as "a method of doing or conducting business." § 273(a)(3). In other words, by allowing this defense the statute itself acknowledges that there may be business method patents. Section 273's definition of "method," to be sure, cannot change the meaning of a prior-enacted statute. But what § 273 does is clarify the understanding that a business method is simply one kind of "method" that is, at least in some circumstances, eligible for patenting under § 101.

A conclusion that business methods are not patentable in any circumstances would render § 273 meaningless. This would violate the canon against interpreting any statutory provision in a manner that would render another provision superfluous. This principle, of course, applies to interpreting any two provisions in the U.S.Code, even when Congress enacted the provisions at different times. This established rule of statutory interpretation cannot be overcome by judicial speculation as to the subjective intent of various legislators in enacting the subsequent provision. Finally, while § 273 appears to leave open the possibility of some business method patents, it does not suggest broad patentability of such claimed inventions.

2

Interpreting § 101 to exclude all business methods simply because business method patents were rarely issued until modern times revives many of the previously discussed difficulties. * * *

In searching for a limiting principle, this Court's precedents on the unpatentability of abstract ideas provide useful tools. Indeed, if the Court of Appeals were to succeed in defining a narrower category or class of patent applications that claim to instruct how business should be conducted, and then rule that the category is unpatentable because, for instance, it represents an attempt to patent abstract ideas, this conclusion might well be in accord with controlling precedent. * * *

III

Even though petitioners' application is not categorically outside of § 101 under the two broad and atextual approaches the Court rejects today, that does not mean it is a "process" under § 101. Petitioners seek to patent both the concept of hedging risk and the application of that concept to energy markets. Rather than adopting categorical rules that might have wide-ranging and unforeseen impacts, the Court resolves this case narrowly on the basis of this Court's decisions in *Benson*, *Flook*, and *Diehr*, which show that petitioners' claims are not patentable processes because they are attempts to patent abstract ideas. Indeed, all members of the Court agree that the patent application at issue here falls outside of § 101 because it claims an abstract idea.

In *Benson*, the Court considered whether a patent application for an algorithm to convert binary-coded decimal numerals into pure binary code was a "process" under § 101. 409 U.S., at 64–67, 93 S.Ct. 253. * * * The Court * * * held the application at issue was not a "process," but an unpatentable abstract idea. * * *

In *Flook*, the Court considered the next logical step after *Benson*. The applicant there attempted to patent a procedure for monitoring the conditions during the catalytic conversion process in the petrochemical and oil-refining industries. The application's only innovation was reliance on a mathematical algorithm. 437 U.S., at 585–586, 98 S.Ct. 2522. *Flook* held the invention was not a patentable "process." * * * The Court concluded that the process at issue there was "unpatentable under § 101, not because it contain[ed] a mathematical algorithm as one component, but because once that algorithm [wa]s assumed to be within the prior art, the application, considered as a whole, contain[ed] no patentable invention." *Id.*, at 594, 98 S.Ct. 2522. As the Court later explained, *Flook* stands for the proposition that the prohibition against patenting abstract ideas "cannot be circumvented by attempting to limit the use of the formula to a particular technological environment" or adding "insignificant postsolution activity." *Diehr*, 450 U.S., at 191–192, 101 S.Ct. 1048.

Finally, in *Diehr*, the Court established a limitation on the principles articulated in *Benson* and *Flook*. The application in *Diehr* claimed a previously unknown method for "molding raw, uncured synthetic rubber into cured precision products," using a mathematical formula to complete some of its several steps by way of a computer. 450 U.S., at 177, 101 S.Ct. 1048. * * * [T]he Court concluded that because the claim was not "an attempt to patent a mathematical formula, but rather [was] an industrial process for the molding of rubber products," it fell within § 101's patentable subject matter. *Id.*, at 192–193, 101 S.Ct. 1048.

In light of these precedents, it is clear that petitioners' application is not a patentable "process." Claims 1 and 4 in petitioners' application explain the basic concept of hedging, or protecting against risk: "Hedging is a fundamental economic practice long prevalent in our system of commerce and taught in any introductory finance class." 545 F.3d, at 1013 (Rader, J., dissenting). The concept of hedging, described in claim 1 and reduced to a mathematical formula in claim 4, is an unpatentable abstract idea, just like the algorithms at issue in *Benson* and *Flook*. Allowing petitioners to patent risk hedging would pre-empt use of this approach in all fields, and would effectively grant a monopoly over an abstract idea.

* * *

Today, the Court once again declines to impose limitations on the Patent Act that are inconsistent with the Act's text. The patent application here can be rejected under our precedents on the unpatentability of abstract ideas. The Court, therefore, need not define further what constitutes a patentable "process," beyond pointing to the definition of that term provided in § 100(b) and looking to the guideposts in *Benson*, *Flook*, and *Diehr*.

And nothing in today's opinion should be read as endorsing interpretations of § 101 that the Court of Appeals for the Federal Circuit has used in the past. *See, e.g.*, *State Street*, 149 F.3d, at 1373; *AT & T Corp.*, 172 F.3d, at 1357. It may be that the Court of Appeals thought it needed to make the machine-or-transformation test exclusive precisely because its case law had not adequately identified less extreme means of restricting business method patents, including (but not limited to) application of our opinions in *Benson*, *Flook*, and *Diehr*. In disapproving an exclusive machine-or-transformation test, we by no means foreclose the Federal Circuit's development of other limiting criteria that further the purposes of the Patent Act and are not inconsistent with its text.

The judgment of the Court of Appeals is affirmed.

It is so ordered.

JUSTICE STEVENS, with whom JUSTICE GINSBURG, JUSTICE BREYER, and JUSTICE SOTOMAYOR join, concurring in the judgment.

In the area of patents, it is especially important that the law remain stable and clear. The only question presented in this case is whether the so-called machine-or-transformation test is the exclusive test for what constitutes a patentable "process" under 35 U.S.C. § 101. It would be possible to answer that question simply by holding, as the entire Court agrees, that although the machine-or-transformation test is reliable in most cases, it is not the exclusive test.

I agree with the Court that, in light of the uncertainty that currently pervades this field, it is prudent to provide further guidance. But I would take a different approach. Rather than making any broad statements about how to define the term "process" in § 101 or tinkering with the bounds of the category of unpatentable, abstract ideas, I would restore patent law to its historical and constitutional moorings.

For centuries, it was considered well established that a series of steps for conducting business was not, in itself, patentable. In the late 1990's, the Federal Circuit and others called this proposition into question. Congress quickly responded to a Federal Circuit decision with a stopgap measure designed to limit a potentially significant new problem for the business community. It passed the First Inventors Defense Act of 1999

(1999 Act), 113 Stat. 1501A–555 (codified at 35 U.S.C. § 273), which provides a limited defense to claims of patent infringement, see § 273(b), for "method[s] of doing or conducting business," § 273(a)(3). Following several more years of confusion, the Federal Circuit changed course, overruling recent decisions and holding that a series of steps may constitute a patentable process only if it is tied to a machine or transforms an article into a different state or thing. This "machine-or-transformation test" excluded general methods of doing business as well as, potentially, a variety of other subjects that could be called processes.

The Court correctly holds that the machine-or-transformation test is not the sole test for what constitutes a patentable process; rather, it is a critical clue.[1] But the Court is quite wrong, in my view, to suggest that any series of steps that is not itself an abstract idea or law of nature may constitute a "process" within the meaning of § 101. The language in the Court's opinion to this effect can only cause mischief. The wiser course would have been to hold that petitioners' method is not a "process" because it describes only a general method of engaging in business transactions-and business methods are not patentable. More precisely, although a process is not patent-ineligible simply because it is useful for conducting business, a claim that merely describes a method of doing business does not qualify as a "process" under § 101.

* * *

II

Before explaining in more detail how I would decide this case, I will comment briefly on the Court's opinion. The opinion is less than pellucid in more than one respect, and, if misunderstood, could result in confusion or upset settled areas of the law. * * *

* * *

The Court, in sum, never provides a satisfying account of what constitutes an unpatentable abstract idea. Indeed, the Court does not even explain if it is using the machine-or-transformation criteria. The Court essentially asserts its conclusion that petitioners' application claims an abstract idea. This mode of analysis (or lack thereof) may have led to the correct outcome in this case, but it also means that the Court's musings on this issue stand for very little.

* * *

IV

Because the text of § 101 does not on its face convey the scope of patentable processes, it is necessary, in my view, to review the history of

---

1. Even if the machine-or-transformation test may not define the scope of a patentable process, it would be a grave mistake to assume that anything with a " 'useful, concrete and tangible result,' " *State Street Bank & Trust v. Signature Financial Group, Inc.*, 149 F.3d 1368, 1373 (C.A.Fed.1998), may be patented.

our patent law in some detail. This approach yields a much more straight-forward answer to this case than the Court's. As I read the history, it strongly supports the conclusion that a method of doing business is not a "process" under § 101.

* * *

V

Despite the strong historical evidence that a method of doing business does not constitute a "process" under § 101, petitioners nonetheless argue-and the Court suggests in dicta, *ante* that a subsequent law, the First Inventor Defense Act of 1999, "must be read together" with § 101 to make business methods patentable. This argument utilizes a flawed method of statutory interpretation and ignores the motivation for the 1999 Act.

In 1999, following a Federal Circuit decision that intimated business methods could be patented, see *State Street*, 149 F.3d 1368, Congress moved quickly to limit the potential fallout. Congress passed the 1999 Act, codified at 35 U.S.C. § 273, which provides a limited defense to claims of patent infringement, see § 273(b), regarding certain "method[s] of doing or conducting business," § 273(a)(3).

It is apparent, both from the content and history of the Act, that Congress did not in any way ratify *State Street* (or, as petitioners contend, the broadest possible reading of *State Street*). The Act merely limited one potential effect of that decision: that businesses might suddenly find themselves liable for innocently using methods they assumed could not be patented. The Act did not purport to amend the limitations in § 101 on eligible subject matter. Indeed, Congress placed the statute in Part III of Title 35, which addresses "Patents and Protection of Patent Rights," rather than in Part II, which contains § 101 and addresses "Patentability of Inventions and Grant of Patents." Particularly because petitioners' reading of the 1999 Act would expand § 101 to cover a category of processes that have not "historically been eligible" for patents, *Diehr*, 450 U.S., at 184, 101 S.Ct. 1048, we should be loathe to conclude that Congress effectively amended § 101 without saying so clearly. We generally presume that Congress "does not, one might say, hide elephants in mouseholes." *Whitman v. American Trucking Assns., Inc.*, 531 U.S. 457, 468, 121 S.Ct. 903, 149 L.Ed.2d 1 (2001).

The Act therefore is, at best, merely evidence of 1999 legislative views on the meaning of the earlier, 1952 Act. "[T]he views of a subsequent Congress," however, "form a hazardous basis for inferring the intent of an earlier one." *United States v. Price*, 361 U.S. 304, 313, 80 S.Ct. 326, 4 L.Ed.2d 334 (1960). When a later statute is offered as "an expression of how the ... Congress interpreted a statute passed by another Congress ... a half century before," "such interpretation has very little, if any, significance." *Rainwater v. United States*, 356 U.S. 590, 593, 78 S.Ct. 946, 2 L.Ed.2d 996 (1958).

Furthermore, even assuming that Congress' views at the turn of the 21st century could potentially serve as a valid basis for interpreting a statute passed in the mid–20th century, the First Inventor Defense Act does not aid petitioners because it does not show that the later Congress itself understood § 101 to cover business methods. If anything, it shows that a few judges on the Federal Circuit understood § 101 in that manner and that Congress understood what those judges had done. The Act appears to reflect surprise and perhaps even dismay that business methods might be patented. Thus, in the months following *State Street*, congressional authorities lamented that "business methods and processes . . . until recently were thought not to be patentable," H.R.Rep. No. 106–464, p. 121 (1999). The fact that Congress decided it was appropriate to create a new *defense* to claims that business method patents were being infringed merely demonstrates recognition that such claims could create a significant new problem for the business community.

* * *

In light of its history and purpose, I think it obvious that the 1999 Congress would never have enacted § 273 if it had foreseen that this Court would rely on the provision as a basis for concluding that business methods are patentable. Section 273 is a red herring; we should be focusing our attention on § 101 itself.

VI

The constitutionally mandated purpose and function of the patent laws bolster the conclusion that methods of doing business are not "processes" under § 101.

The Constitution allows Congress to issue patents "[t]o promote the Progress of . . . useful Arts," Art. I, § 8, cl. 8. This clause "is both a grant of power and a limitation." *Graham*, 383 U.S., at 5, 86 S.Ct. 684. It "reflects a balance between the need to encourage innovation and the avoidance of monopolies which stifle competition without any concomitant advance in the 'Progress of Science and useful Arts.'" *Bonito Boats*, 489 U.S., at 146, 109 S.Ct. 971. * * *

* * *

The Court has kept this "constitutional standard" in mind when deciding what is patentable subject matter under § 101. For example, we have held that no one can patent "laws of nature, natural phenomena, and abstract ideas." *Diehr*, 450 U.S., at 185, 101 S.Ct. 1048. These "are the basic tools of scientific and technological work," *Benson*, 409 U.S., at 67, 93 S.Ct. 253, and therefore, if patented, would stifle the very progress that Congress is authorized to promote[.]

Without any legislative guidance to the contrary, there is a real concern that patents on business methods would press on the limits of the "standard expressed in the Constitution," *Graham*, 383 U.S., at 6, 86 S.Ct. 684, more likely stifling progress than "promot[ing]" it. U.S. Const.,

Art. I, § 8, cl. 8. I recognize that not all methods of doing business are the same, and that therefore the constitutional "balance," *Bonito Boats*, 489 U.S., at 146, 109 S.Ct. 971, may vary within this category. Nevertheless, I think that this balance generally supports the historic understanding of the term "process" as excluding business methods. And a categorical analysis fits with the purpose, as Thomas Jefferson explained, of ensuring that " 'every one might know when his actions were safe and lawful,' " *Graham*, 383 U.S., at 10, 86 S.Ct. 684. * * *

* * *

The constitutional standard for patentability is difficult to apply with any precision, and Congress has significant discretion to "implement the stated purpose of the Framers by selecting the policy which in its judgment best effectuates the constitutional aim," *Graham*, 383 U.S., at 6, 86 S.Ct. 684. But Congress has not, either explicitly or implicitly, determined that patents on methods of doing business would effectuate this aim. And as I understand their practical consequences, it is hard to see how they would.

VII

The Constitution grants to Congress an important power to promote innovation. In its exercise of that power, Congress has established an intricate system of intellectual property. The scope of patentable subject matter under that system is broad. But it is not endless. In the absence of any clear guidance from Congress, we have only limited textual, historical, and functional clues on which to rely. Those clues all point toward the same conclusion: that petitioners' claim is not a "process" within the meaning of § 101 because methods of doing business are not, in themselves, covered by the statute. In my view, acknowledging as much would be a far more sensible and restrained way to resolve this case. Accordingly, while I concur in the judgment, I strongly disagree with the Court's disposition of this case.

JUSTICE BREYER, with whom JUSTICE SCALIA joins as to Part II, concurring in the judgment.

I

I agree with JUSTICE STEVENS that a "general method of engaging in business transactions" is not a patentable "process" within the meaning of 35 U.S.C. § 101. * * * I would therefore decide this case on that ground, and I join JUSTICE STEVENS's opinion in full.

I write separately, however, in order to highlight the substantial agreement among many Members of the Court on many of the fundamental issues of patent law raised by this case. In light of the need for clarity and settled law in this highly technical area, I think it appropriate to do so.

II

In addition to the Court's unanimous agreement that the claims at issue here are unpatentable abstract ideas, it is my view that the following four points are consistent with both the opinion of the Court and Justice STEVENS' opinion concurring in the judgment:

First, although the text of § 101 is broad, it is not without limit. "[T]he underlying policy of the patent system [is] that 'the things which are worth to the public the embarrassment of an exclusive patent,' ... must outweigh the restrictive effect of the limited patent monopoly." *Graham v. John Deere Co. of Kansas City*, 383 U.S. 1, 10–11, 86 S.Ct. 684, 15 L.Ed.2d 545 (1966) (quoting Letter from Thomas Jefferson to Isaac McPherson (Aug. 13, 1813), in 6 Writings of Thomas Jefferson 181 (H. Washington ed.)). The Court has thus been careful in interpreting the Patent Act to "determine not only what is protected, but also what is free for all to use." *Bonito Boats, Inc. v. Thunder Craft Boats, Inc.*, 489 U.S. 141, 151, 109 S.Ct. 971, 103 L.Ed.2d 118 (1989). In particular, the Court has long held that "[p]henomena of nature, though just discovered, mental processes, and abstract intellectual concepts are not patentable" under § 101, since allowing individuals to patent these fundamental principles would "wholly pre-empt" the public's access to the "basic tools of scientific and technological work." *Gottschalk v. Benson*, 409 U.S. 63, 67, 72, 93 S.Ct. 253, 34 L.Ed.2d 273 (1972).

Second, in a series of cases that extend back over a century, the Court has stated that "[t]ransformation and reduction of an article to a different state or thing is the clue to the patentability of a process claim that does not include particular machines." *Diehr, supra,* at 184, 101 S.Ct. 1048. Application of this test, the so-called "machine-or-transformation test," has thus repeatedly helped the Court to determine what is "a patentable 'process.' " *Flook, supra,* at 589, 98 S.Ct. 2522.

Third, while the machine-or-transformation test has always been a "useful and important clue," it has never been the "sole test" for determining patentability. *Ante.* Rather, the Court has emphasized that a process claim meets the requirements of § 101 when, "considered as a whole," it "is performing a function which the patent laws were designed to protect (e.g., transforming or reducing an article to a different state or thing)." *Diehr, supra,* at 192, 101 S.Ct. 1048. The machine-or-transformation test is thus an important example of how a court can determine patentability under § 101, but the Federal Circuit erred in this case by treating it as the exclusive test.

Fourth, although the machine-or-transformation test is not the only test for patentability, this by no means indicates that anything which produces a " 'useful, concrete, and tangible result,' " *State Street Bank & Trust Co. v. Signature Financial Group, Inc.*, 149 F.3d 1368, 1373 (C.A.Fed.1998), is patentable. "[T]his Court has never made such a statement and, if taken literally, the statement would cover instances where this Court has held the contrary." *Laboratory Corp. of America*

Holdings v. Metabolite Laboratories, Inc., 548 U.S. 124, 136, 126 S.Ct. 2921, 165 L.Ed.2d 399 (2006) (BREYER, J., dissenting from dismissal of certiorari as improvidently granted). Indeed, the introduction of the "useful, concrete, and tangible result" approach to patentability, associated with the Federal Circuit's *State Street* decision, preceded the granting of patents that "ranged from the somewhat ridiculous to the truly absurd." *In re Bilski*, 545 F.3d 943, 1004 (C.A.Fed.2008) (Mayer, J., dissenting) To the extent that the Federal Circuit's decision in this case rejected that approach, nothing in today's decision should be taken as disapproving of that determination.

In sum, it is my view that, in reemphasizing that the "machine-or-transformation" test is not necessarily the sole test of patentability, the Court intends neither to de-emphasize the test's usefulness nor to suggest that many patentable processes lie beyond its reach.

III

With these observations, I concur in the Court's judgment.

NOTES

1.   Applying the Majority Opinion to the Next Case. Remember that only Parts I, II–A, II–B–1, II–C–1, and III of Justice Kennedy's opinion are the majority opinion. Keeping this in mind, there are two important principles to take away from the majority opinion. First, the Federal Circuit's machine-or-transformation test, while "an important and useful clue," is not the exclusive test for the eligibility of processes under Section 101. Second, business methods are not categorically excluded from Section 101. Thus, *Bilski* appears to stand for the proposition that processes associated with some technology are eligible under Section 101. Put another way, while *Diehr*-type processes continue to be eligible subject matter under Section 101, both *Benson*-type and *Flook*-type processes continue not to be eligible under Section 101.

2.   Grant–Vacate–Remand. The day after *Bilski* was handed down, the Supreme Court granted certiorari petitions in two cases raising a Section 101 issue, vacated the judgments, and remanded the cases to the Federal Circuit "for further consideration in light of *Bilski v. Kappos.*" The first case, *Classen Immunotherapies, Inc. v. Biogen Idec*, involves a challenge to the validity of a patent claim directed to determining an immunization schedule. The second case, *Mayo Collaborative Services v. Prometheus Laboratories*, involves a challenge to the validity of patent claims directed to iterative drug dosing. Are these two methods eligible processes?

B.   UTILITY

An invention must be "new and useful" to be patentable under Section 101. The novelty requirement of Section 102 addresses the condition that an invention be "new." The "useful" condition of Section 101 has become a requirement of "utility," insuring a "quid pro quo" between the inventor and the public, and has not historically limited the scope of patentable subject matter to a large degree. In *Lowell v. Lewis*, 15 F. Cas. 1018, 1019 (C.C.D. Mass. 1817), Justice Story commented that, "All that the law requires, that the invention should not be frivolous or injurious to the well-being, good policy, or sound morals of society. The word 'useful,' therefore, is incorporated into the act in contradiction to mischievous or immoral." Does this standard continue to insure a public benefit? Consider the case that follows.

BRENNER v. MANSON

Supreme Court of the United States, 1966.
383 U.S. 519, 86 S.Ct. 1033, 16 L.Ed.2d 69.

MR. JUSTICE FORTAS delivered the opinion of the Court.

[The Patent Office rejected a patent application for a process of making certain known steroids on grounds that the application did not fulfill the utility requirement of 35 U.S.C. § 101. According to the Patent Office, the applicant, Manson, failed "to disclose any utility for" the chemical compound produced in the process. In response, a reference showing that "steroids of a class which included the compound in question were undergoing screening for possible tumor-inhibiting effects in mice" was not enough to save the application. The Board of Appeals stated, "It is our view that the statutory requirement of usefulness of a product cannot be presumed merely because it happens to be closely related to another compound which is known to be useful." On Appeal, the Court of Customs and Patent Appeals reversed. The court found "where a claimed process produces a known product it is not necessary to show utility for the product," so long as the product "is not alleged to be detrimental to the public interest."] * * *

Certiorari was granted, to resolve this running dispute over what constitutes 'utility' in chemical process claims. * * *

It is not remarkable that differences arise as to how the test of usefulness is to be applied to chemical processes. Even if we knew precisely what Congress meant in 1790 when it devised the 'new and useful' phraseology and in subsequent re-enactments of the test, we should have difficulty in applying it in the context of contemporary chemistry where research is as comprehensive as man's grasp and where little or nothing is wholly beyond the pale of 'utility'—if that word is given its broadest reach.

Respondent does not—at least in the first instance—rest upon the extreme proposition, advanced by the court below, that a novel chemical process is patentable so long as it yields the intended product and so long as the product is not itself 'detrimental.' Nor does he commit the outcome of his claim to the slightly more conventional proposition that any process is 'useful' within the meaning of § 101 if it produces a compound whose potential usefulness is under investigation by serious scientific researchers, although he urges this position, too, as an alternative basis for affirming the decision of the CCPA. Rather, he begins with the much more orthodox argument that his process has a specific utility which would entitle him to a declaration of interference even under the Patent Office's reading of § 101. The claim is that the supporting affidavits filed pursuant to Rule 204(b), by reference to Ringold's 1956 article, reveal that an adjacent homologue of the steroid yielded by his process has been demonstrated to have tumor-inhibiting effects in mice, and that this discloses the requisite utility. We do not accept any of these theories as an adequate basis for overriding the determination of the Patent Office that the 'utility' requirement has not been met.

Even on the assumption that the process would be patentable were respondent to show that the steroid produced had a tumor-inhibiting effect in mice, we would not overrule the Patent Office finding that respondent has not made such a showing. The Patent Office held that, despite the reference to the adjacent homologue, respondent's papers did not disclose a sufficient likelihood that the steroid yielded by his process would have similar tumor-inhibiting characteristics. Indeed, respondent himself recognized that the presumption that adjacent homologues have the same utility has been challenged in the steroid field because of 'a greater known unpredictability of compounds in that field.' In these circumstances and in this technical area, we would not overturn the finding of the Primary Examiner, affirmed by the Board of Appeals and not challenged by the CCPA.

The second and third points of respondent's argument present issues of much importance. Is a chemical process 'useful' within the meaning of § 101 either (1) because it works—i.e., produces the intended product? or (2) because the compound yielded belongs to a class of compounds now the subject of serious scientific investigation? These contentions present the basic problem for our adjudication. Since we find no specific assistance in the legislative materials underlying § 101, we are remitted to an analysis of the problem in light of the general intent of Congress, the purposes of the patent system, and the implications of a decision one way or the other.

In support of his plea that we attenuate the requirement of 'utility,' respondent relies upon Justice Story's well-known statement that a 'useful' invention is one 'which may be applied to a beneficial use in society, in contradistinction to an invention injurious to the morals, health, or good order of society, or frivolous and insignificant'—and upon the assertion that to do so would encourage inventors of new processes to publicize the event for the benefit of the entire scientific community, thus widening the search for uses and increasing the fund of scientific knowledge. Justice Story's language sheds little light on our subject. Narrowly read, it does no more than compel us to decide whether the invention in question is 'frivolous and insignificant'—a query no easier of application than the one built into the statute. Read more broadly, so as to allow the patenting of any invention not positively harmful to society, it places such a special meaning on the word 'useful' that we cannot accept it in the absence of evidence that Congress so intended. There are, after all, many things in this world which may not be considered 'useful' but which, nevertheless are totally without a capacity for harm.

It is true, of course, that one of the purposes of the patent system is to encourage dissemination of information concerning discoveries and inventions. And it may be that inability to patent a process to some extent discourages disclosure and leads to greater secrecy than would otherwise be the case. The inventor of the process, or the corporate organization by which he is employed, has some incentive to keep the invention secret while uses for the product are searched out. However, in light of the highly developed art of drafting patent claims so that they disclose as little useful information as possible—while broadening the scope of the claim as widely as possible—the argument based upon the virtue of disclosure must be warily evaluated. Moreover, the pressure for secrecy is easily exaggerated, for if the inventor of a process cannot himself ascertain a 'use' for that which his process yields, he has every incentive to make his invention known to those able to do so. Finally, how likely is disclosure of a patented process to spur research by others into the uses to which the product may be put? To the extent that the patentee has power to enforce his patent, there is little incentive for others to undertake a search for uses.

Whatever weight is attached to the value of encouraging disclosure and of inhibiting secrecy, we believe a more compelling consideration is that a process patent in the chemical field, which has not been developed and pointed to the degree of specific utility, creates a monopoly of knowledge which should be granted only if clearly commanded by the statute. Until the process claim has been reduced to production of a product shown to be useful, the metes and bounds of that monopoly are not capable of precise delineation. It may engross a vast, unknown, and perhaps unknowable area. Such a patent may confer power to block off whole areas of scientific development, without compensating benefit to the public. The basic quid pro quo contemplated by the Constitution and the Congress for granting a patent monopoly is the benefit derived by the public from an invention with substantial utility. Unless and until a process is refined and developed to this point—where specific benefit exists in currently available form—there is insufficient justification for permitting an applicant to engross what may prove to be a broad field.

These arguments for and against the patentability of a process which either has no known use or is useful only in the sense that it may be an object of scientific research would apply equally to the patenting of the product produced by the process. Respondent appears to concede that with respect to a product, as opposed to a process, Congress has struck the balance on the side of nonpatentability unless 'utility' is shown. Indeed, the decisions of the CCPA are in accord with the view that a product may not be patented absent a showing of utility greater than any adduced in the present case. We find absolutely no warrant for the proposition that although Congress intended that no patent be granted on a chemical compound whose sole 'utility' consists of its potential role as an object of use-testing, a different set of rules was meant to apply to the process which yielded the unpatentable product. That proposition seems to us little more than an attempt to evade the impact of the rules which concededly govern patentability of the product itself.

This is not to say that we mean to disparage the importance of contributions to the fund of scientific information short of the invention of something 'useful,' or that we are blind to the prospect that what now seems without 'use' may tomorrow command the grateful attention of the public. But a patent is not a hunting license. It is not a reward for the search, but compensation for its successful conclusion. '(A) patent system must be related to the world of commerce rather than to the realm of philosophy. * * *'

The judgment of the CCPA is reversed.

Reversed.

[Dissent by MR. JUSTICE HARLAN, joined by MR. JUSTICE DOUGLAS on the issue of patentability omitted]

NOTES

1.   Animal Models. In *In re Brana*, 51 F.3d 1560 (Fed. Cir. 1995), the Federal Circuit held that a chemical compound, effective at treating lympho-cystic leukemia tumors in mice, had sufficient utility to satisfy the statutory requirement. Distinguishing patent law and Food and Drug Administration (FDA) approval, the court stated, "Usefulness in patent law, and in particular in the context of pharmaceutical inventions, necessarily includes the expecta-tion of further research and development. The stage at which an invention in this field becomes useful is well before it is ready to be administered to humans." The court found that animal models could demonstrate the utility of drugs intended for humans. How is *Brana* different from *Brenner*?

2.   Specific Utility. In *In re Fisher*, 421 F.3d 1365 (Fed. Cir. 2005), the PTO rejected a patent application seeking to claim expressed sequence tags (ESTs), nucleotide sequences used in molecular genetics. The ESTs in ques-tion could be used for mapping the maize genome, checking levels of a gene being expressed, as primers for PCR, for identifying polymorphisms, isolating promoters, controlling protein expression, and locating genetic molecules on other plants and organisms. The Federal Circuit held that none of the petitioner's disclosed "uses" constituted "specific" or "substantial" utility, and that "an application must show that an invention is useful to the public as disclosed in its current form, not that it may prove useful at some future date after further research."

3.   Moral Utility. In *Juicy Whip, Inc. v. Orange Bang, Inc.*, 185 F.3d 1364 (Fed. Cir. 1999), Orange Bang challenged Juicy Whip's patent on a "Post–Mix Beverage Dispenser with an Associated Simulated Display of Beverage." The patent claimed a beverage dispenser that appears to have a reservoir that mixes the beverage when, in fact, there is "no fluid connection" between the display reservoir and the actual beverage that is dispensed. The district court found the patent "deceptive" and held it invalid under Section 101. On appeal, the Federal Court found that there is "no basis in section 101 to hold

that inventions can be ruled unpatentable for lack of utility simply because they have the capacity to fool some members of public." The Federal Circuit found that Congress has the power to limit patentable subject matter if it wishes, and that other agencies such as the Federal Trade Commission (FTC) and the FDA are perfectly capable of regulating deceptive trade practices—a job not delegated to the PTO.

C. SECTION 102: CONDITIONS FOR PATENTABILITY; NOVELTY AND LOSS OF RIGHT TO PATENT

1. Novelty

a. What Is "Known or Used?"

Section 102 includes a novelty requirement and statutory bars that preclude inventors from patenting subject matter that is not truly "new" or "anticipated." "Novelty" requires an invention or discovery to be new compared to prior art. Generally, "statutory bars" discourage delay when seeking patent protection. Section 102 works to prevent removal of inventions from the public domain, and to prevent inventors from commercially exploiting a period of exclusivity beyond the statutory term. At the same time, it gives inventors time to determine whether obtaining a patent is worthwhile, and supports prompt disclosure of new inventions to the public.

The first subsection of Section 102 has two parts. Section 102(a) states:

A person shall be entitled to a patent unless—

> (a) the invention was known or used by others in this country,
>
> > or patented or described in a printed publication in this or a foreign country, before the invention thereof by the applicant for patent, or . . .

35 U.S.C. § 102(a).

Section 102(a) addresses "known or used" particularly "in this country." The second part of Section 102(b), applies "in this or a foreign country" to inventions "patented or described in a printed publication." We first look at what it means to be "known or used."

ROSAIRE v. BAROID SALES DIVISION, NATIONAL LEAD COMPANY

United States Court of Appeals for the Fifth Circuit, 1955.
218 F.2d 72.

Before HOLMES and TUTTLE, CIRCUIT JUDGES, and ALLRED, DISTRICT JUDGE.

TUTTLE, CIRCUIT JUDGE.

In this suit for patent infringement there is presented to us for determination the correctness of the judgment of the trial court, based on findings of fact and conclusions of law, holding that the two patents involved in the litigation were invalid and void and that furthermore there had been no infringement by defendant.

The Rosaire and Horvitz patents relate to methods of prospecting for oil or other hydrocarbons. The inventions are based upon the assumption that gases have emanated from deposits of hydrocarbons which have been trapped in the earth and that these emanations have modified the surrounding rock. The methods claimed involve the steps of taking a number of samples of soil from formations which are not themselves productive of hydrocarbons, either over a horizontal area or vertically down a well bore, treating each sample, as by grinding and heating in a closed vessel, to cause entrained or absorbed hydrocarbons therein to evolve as a gas, quantitatively measuring the amount of hydrocarbon gas so evolved from each sample, and correlating the measurements with the locations from which the samples were taken.

Plaintiff claims that in 1936 he and Horvitz invented this new method of prospecting for oil. In due course the two patents in suit, Nos. 2,192,525 and 2,324,085, were issued thereon. Horvitz assigned his interest to Rosaire.

Appellant alleged that appellee Baroid began infringing in 1947; that he learned of this in 1949 and asked Baroid to take a license, but no license agreement was worked out, and this suit followed, seeking an injunction and an accounting.

In view of the fact that the trial court's judgment that the patents were invalid, would of course dispose of the matter if correct, we turn our attention to this issue. Appellee's contention is that the judgment of the trial court in this respect should be supported on two principal grounds. The first is that the prior art, some of which was not before the patent office, anticipated the two patents; the second is that work carried on by one Teplitz for the Gulf Oil Corporation invalidated both patents by reason of the relevant provisions of the patent laws which state that an invention is not patentable if it 'was known or used by others in this country' before the patentee's invention thereof, 35 U.S.C.A. § 102(a). Appellee contends that Teplitz and his coworkers knew and extensively used in the field the same alleged inventions before any date asserted by Rosaire and Horvitz.

On this point appellant himself in his brief admits that 'Teplitz conceived of the idea of extracting and quantitatively measuring entrained or absorbed gas from the samples of rock, rather than relying upon the free gas in the samples. We do not deny that Teplitz conceived of the methods of the patents in suit.' And further appellant makes the following admission: 'We admit that the Teplitz–Gulf work was done before Rosaire and Horvitz conceived of the inventions. We will show, however, that Gulf did not apply for patent until 1939, did not publish Teplitz's ideas, and did not otherwise give the public the benefit of the experimental work.'

* * *

In support of their respective positions, both appellant and appellee stress the language in our opinion in the case of *Pennington v. National Supply Co.*, 5 Cir., 95 F.2d 291, 294, where, speaking through Judge Holmes, we said:

> Appellant insists that the court erred in considering the prior use of the Texas machine, because that machine was abandoned by the Texas Company and was not successful until modified and rebuilt. As to this, it does not appear that the Texas machine was a failure, since it drilled three wells for the Texas Company, which was more than was usually accomplished by the rotary drilling machines then in use.

"An unsuccessful experiment which is later abandoned does not negative novelty in a new and successful device." *T. H. Symington Co. v. National Malleable Castings Co.*, 250 U.S. 383, 386; *Clark Thread Co. v. Willimantic Linen Co.*, 140 U.S. 481, 489. Nevertheless, the existence and operation of a machine, abandoned after its completion and sufficient use to demonstrate its practicability, is evidence that the same ideas incorporated in a later development along the same line do not amount to invention. *Corona Cord Tire Co. v. Dovan Chemical Corporation*, 276 U.S. 358. If the prior machine does not anticipate, it would not have done so if it had been neither unsuccessful nor abandoned. Novelty is ascribed to new things, without regard to the successful and continued use of old things. Correlatively, it is denied to old things, without regard to the circumstances which caused their earlier applications to be unsatisfactory or their use to be abandoned.

The question as to whether the work of Teplitz was 'an unsuccessful experiment,' as claimed by appellant, or was a successful trial of the method in question and a reduction of that method to actual practice, as contended by appellee, is, of course, a question of fact. On this point the trial court made the following finding of fact:

> I find as a fact, by clear and substantial proof beyond a reasonable doubt, that Abraham J. Teplitz and his coworkers with Gulf Oil Corporation and its Research Department during 1935 and early 1936, before any date claimed by Rosaire, spent more than a year in the oil fields and adjacent territory around Palestine, Texas, taking and analyzing samples both over an area and down drill holes, exactly as called for in the claims of the patents which Rosaire and Horvitz subsequently applied for and which are here in suit.

> This Teplitz work was a successful and adequate field trial of the prospecting method involved and a reduction to practice of that method. The work was performed in the field under ordinary conditions without any deliberate attempt at concealment or effort to

exclude the public and without any instructions of secrecy to the employees performing the work.

As we view it, if the court's findings of fact are correct then under the statute as construed by the courts, we must affirm the finding of the trial court that appellee's patents were invalid. As to the finding of fact we are to affirm unless we conclude that it is "clearly erroneous." Rule 52, Fed.Rules Civ.Proc., 28 U.S.C.A.

A close analysis of the evidence on which the parties rely to resolve this question clearly demonstrates that there was sufficient evidence to sustain the finding of the trial court that there was more here than an unsuccessful or incomplete experiment. It is clear that the work was not carried forward, but that appears to be a result of two things: (1) that the geographical area did not lend itself properly to the test, and (2) that the "entire gas prospecting program was therefore suspended in September of 1936, in order that the accumulated information might be thoroughly reviewed." It will be noted that the program was not suspended to test the worth of the method but to examine the data that was produced by use of the method involved. The above quotation came from one of the recommendations at the end of Teplitz's report, and was introduced on behalf of the appellant himself.

Expert testimony presented by witnesses Rogers, Eckhardt and Weaver supported appellee's contention.

With respect to the argument advanced by appellant that the lack of publication of Teplitz's work deprived an alleged infringer of the defense of prior use, we find no case which constrains us to hold that where such work was done openly and in the ordinary course of the activities of the employer, a large producing company in the oil industry, the statute is to be so modified by construction as to require some affirmative act to bring the work to the attention of the public at large.

While there is authority for the proposition that one of the basic principles underlying the patent laws is the enrichment of the art, and that a patent is given to encourage disclosure of inventions, no case we have found requires a holding that, under the circumstances that attended the work of Teplitz, the fact of public knowledge must be shown before it can be urged to invalidate a subsequent patent. The case of *Corona Cord Tire Co. v. Dovan Chemical Corporation, supra,* is authority for the opposing view, that taken by the court below. In that case the Supreme Court said:

> In 1916, while with the Norwalk Company, Kratz prepared D.P.G. and demonstrated its utility as a rubber accelerator by making test slabs of vulcanized or cured rubber with its use. Every time that he produced such a slab he recorded his test in cards which he left with the Norwalk Company and kept a duplicate of his own. * * * This work was known to, and was participated in, by his associate in the Norwalk Company, his immediate superior and the chief chemist of

the company, Dr. Russell, who fully confirms Kratz's records and statement.

Corona Cord Tire Co. v. Dovan Chemical Corporation, 276 U.S. 358, 378, 379, 48 S.Ct. 380, 386, 72 L.Ed. 610.

The court further states in the *Corona* case at page 382 of 276 U.S., at page 387 of 48 S.Ct.:

> But, even if we ignore this evidence of Kratz's actual use of D.P.G. in these rubber inner tubes which were sold, what he did at Norwalk, supported by the evidence of Dr. Russell, his chief, and by the indubitable records that are not challenged, leaves no doubt in our minds that he did discover in 1916 the strength of D.P.G. as an accelerator as compared with the then known accelerators, and that he then demonstrated it by a reduction of it to practice in production of cured or vulcanized rubber.

> This constitutes priority in this case.

* * *

Concluding, as we do, that the trial court correctly held that patents invalid, it is not necessary to consider the question of infringement. The judgment of the trial court is affirmed.

NOTES

1. "Constructive" Reduction to Practice? In *Application of Borst*, 345 F.2d 851 (C.C.P.A. 1965), the appellant sought to patent a means for controlling a relatively large neutron output safely and effectively by varying a small and easily controlled neutron input source. An unpublished classified memorandum, later declassified before the appellant's filing, discussed the method. The Court of Customs and Patent Appeals found that prior "knowledge" does not require a reduction to practice, either actual or constructive. The court held, "Rather, the criterion should be whether the disclosure is sufficient to enable one skilled in the art to reduce the disclosed invention to practice."

2. Inherent Anticipation. What about the "accidental" anticipation of an invention? In a number of cases, products have been produced unintentionally or inherently. Chemical processes often produce unknown, unintended, or accidental products that demonstrate a useful application later.

In *Tilghman v. Proctor*, 102 U.S. (12 Otto) 707, 26 L.Ed. 279 (1880), the Supreme Court held that a patent on a process of separating fatty acids was not anticipated by a process for lubricating a steam engine with tallow that incidentally caused the separation of fatty acids:

> They revealed no process for the manufacture of fat acids. If the acids were accidentally unwittingly produced, whilst the operators were in pursuit of other and different results, without exciting attention and without it even being known what was done or how it had been done, it would be absurd to say that this was an anticipation of Tilghman's discovery.

The result in *Tilghman* suggests that a production process anticipates a later "invention" only when the first producer was aware of the product produced or the first producer was attempting to produce the specific product.

Does the amount of the product made inherently matter? In *Application of Seaborg*, 328 F.2d 996 (C.C.P.A. 1964), the Court of Customs and Patent Appeals reversed a finding of anticipation by the Board of Patent Appeals and Interferences related to claims on a new transuranic element, known as Americium, with an atomic number of 95. The court did not find anything warranting extrapolation of the "doctrine of inherency" to a case where the claimed product "was produced in such minuscule amounts and under such conditions that its presence was undetectable." The fact that a reactor described in Fermi's U.S. Patent No. 2,708,656 would create element 95 inherently in miniscule amounts was not enough to anticipate Seaborg's claims.

A line of cases has distinguished *Tilghman* and *Application of Seaborg*. When a patented process inherently produces an unknown form of a specific chemical product and the product is appreciated or sold, that patent can anticipate and preclude future claims. In *Smithkline Beecham Corp. v. Apotex Corp.*, 403 F.3d 1331 (Fed. Cir. 2005), a patent covered a process that inherently produced trace amounts of an unknown, hemihydrate form of a compound used as an anti-depressant. The court held that this patented process anticipated a different, later patent on the previously unknown hemihydrate form of the anti-depressant. In *Abbott Labs. v. Geneva Pharmaceuticals, Inc.*, 182 F.3d 1315 (Fed. Cir. 1999), sales of a product created an "on sale" bar precluding a patent of an unknown crystalline form of terazosin hydrochloride, a pharmaceutical compound used for the treatment of hypertension and benign prostatic hyperplasia. The process used to make terazosin hydrochloride inherently produced the unknown crystalline form.

In patent law, inherency addresses characteristics or qualities of a technology that exist, but not explicitly described. Generally, inventions and discoveries of value are missed through ignorance or inadvertence and later come into dispute. Anticipation, the on-sale bar, priority disputes, double-patenting, and enablement are all areas in which the inherency doctrine causes confusion. The Federal Circuit has recently made the doctrine more clear, and coherent. For a summary, see Dan L. Burk & Mark A. Lemley, *Inherency*, 47 WM. & MARY L. REV. 371 (2005).

b.   What Does It Mean to Be "Patented or Described in a Printed Publication?"

Section 102(a) and Section 102(b) share the language "patented or described in a printed publication." Section 102(b) is a statutory bar. It sets a critical date, the date one year before filing, as a bar for patent protection. The conditions of Section 102 (b) are:

> b) the invention was patented or described in a printed publication
> . . .
>
> in this or a foreign country . . .
>
> or in public use or on sale in this country,

more than one year prior to the date of the application for patent in the United States * * *

35 U.S.C. § 102(b).

The next case discusses how prior art references are treated for purposes of Section 102(b).

IN RE HALL

United States Court of Appeals for the Federal Circuit, 1986.
781 F.2d 897.

BALDWIN, CIRCUIT JUDGE.

This is an appeal from the decision of the U.S. Patent and Trademark Office's (PTO) former Board of Appeals, adhered to on reconsideration by the Board of Patent Appeals and Interferences (board), sustaining the final rejection of claims 1–25 of reissue Application No. 343,922, filed January 29, 1982, based principally on a "printed publication" bar under 35 U.S.C. §§ 102(b). The reference is a doctoral thesis. Because appellant concedes that his claims are unpatentable if the thesis is available as a "printed publication" more than one year prior to the application's effective filing date of February 27, 1979, the only issue is whether the thesis is available as such a printed publication. On the record before us, we affirm the board's decision.

Background

A protest was filed during prosecution of appellant's reissue application which included in an appendix a copy of the dissertation "1,4–*a*-Glucanglukohydrolase ein amylotylisches Enzym ..." by Peter Foldi (Foldi thesis or dissertation). The record indicates that in September 1977, Foldi submitted his dissertation to the Department of Chemistry and Pharmacy at Freiburg University in the Federal Republic of Germany, and that Foldi was awarded a doctorate degree on November 2, 1977 * * *.

The examiner made a final rejection of the application claims. He said: "On the basis of the instant record it is reasonable to assume that the Foldi thesis was available (accessible) prior to February 27, 1979." He also pointed out that there was no evidence to the contrary and asked the appellant to state his "knowledge of any inquiry which may have been made regarding 'availability' beyond that presently referred to in the record." Appellant did not respond.

By letter, the PTO's Scientific Library asked Dr. Will whether the Foldi dissertation was made available to the public by being cataloged and placed in the main collection. Dr. Will replied in an October 20, 1983 letter, as translated:

> Our dissertations, thus also the Foldi dissertation, are indexed in a special dissertations catalogue, which is part of the general users' catalogue. In the stacks they are likewise set apart in a special dissertation section, which is part of the general stacks.

In response to a further inquiry by the PTO's Scientific Library requesting (1) the exact date of indexing and cataloging of the Foldi dissertation or (2) "the time such procedures normally take," Dr. Will replied in a June 18, 1984 letter:

> The Library copies of the Foldi dissertation were sent to us by the faculty on November 4, 1977. Accordingly, the dissertation most probably was available for general use toward the beginning of the month of December, 1977.

The board held that the unrebutted evidence of record was sufficient to conclude that the Foldi dissertation had an effective date as prior art more than one year prior to the filing date of the appellant's initial application. In rejecting appellant's argument that the evidence was not sufficient to establish a specific date when the dissertation became publicly available, the board said:

> We rely on the librarian's affidavit of express facts regarding the *specific* dissertation of interest and his description of the routine treatment of dissertations in general, in the ordinary course of business in his library.

On appeal, appellant raises two arguments: (1) the § 102(b) "printed publication" bar requires that the publication be accessible to the interested public, but there is no evidence that the dissertation was properly indexed in the library catalog prior to the critical date; and (2) even if the Foldi thesis were cataloged prior to the critical date, the presence of a single cataloged thesis in one university library does not constitute sufficient accessibility of the publication's teachings to those interested in the art exercising reasonable diligence.

Opinion

The statutory phrase "printed publication" has been interpreted to give effect to ongoing advances in the technologies of data storage, retrieval, and dissemination. *In re Wyer*, 655 F.2d 221, 226 (CCPA 1981). Because there are many ways in which a reference may be disseminated to the interested public, "public accessibility" has been called the touchstone in determining whether a reference constitutes a "printed publication" bar under 35 U.S.C. § 102(b). The § 102 publication bar is a legal determination based on underlying fact issues, and therefore must be approached on a case-by-case basis. The proponent of the publication bar must show that prior to the critical date the reference was sufficiently accessible, at least to the public interested in the art, so that such a one by examining the reference could make the claimed invention without further research or experimentation.

Relying on *In re Bayer*, 568 F.2d 1357, 1361 (CCPA 1978), appellant argues that the Foldi thesis was not shown to be accessible because Dr. Will's affidavits do not say when the thesis was indexed in the library catalog and do not chronicle the procedures for receiving and processing a thesis in the library.

As the board pointed out in its decision, the facts in *Bayer* differ from those here. Bayer, who was himself the author of the dissertation relied upon by the PTO, submitted a declaration from the university librarian which detailed the library's procedures for receiving, cataloging, and shelving of theses and attested to the relevant dates that Bayer's thesis was processed. The evidence showed that cataloging and shelving thesis copies routinely took many months from the time they were first received from the faculty and that during the interim the theses were accumulated in a private library office accessible only to library employees. In particular, processing of Bayer's thesis was shown to have been completed after the critical date.

On those facts the CCPA held that Bayer's thesis was not sufficiently accessible and could not give rise to the § 102(b) publication bar. But the court did not hold, as appellant would have it, that accessibility can only be shown by evidence establishing a *specific* date of cataloging and shelving before the critical date. While such evidence would be desirable, in lending greater certainty to the accessibility determination, the realities of routine business practice counsel against requiring such evidence. The probative value of routine business practice to show the performance of a specific act has long been recognized. Therefore, we conclude that competent evidence of the general library practice may be relied upon to establish an approximate time when a thesis became accessible.

In the present case, Dr. Will's affidavits give a rather general library procedure as to indexing, cataloging, and shelving of theses. Although no specific dates are cited (except that the thesis was received on November 4, 1977), Dr. Will's affidavits consistently maintain that inasmuch as the Foldi dissertation was received by the library in early November 1977, the dissertation "most probably was available for general use toward the beginning of the month of December, 1977." The only reasonable interpretation of the affidavits is that Dr. Will was relying on his library's general practice for indexing, cataloging, and shelving theses in estimating the time it would have taken to make the dissertation available to the interested public. Dr. Will's affidavits are competent evidence, and in these circumstances, persuasive evidence that the Foldi dissertation was accessible prior to the critical date. Reliance on an approximation found in the affidavits such as "toward the beginning of the month of December, 1977" works no injustice here because the critical date, February 27, 1978, is some two and one half months later. Moreover, it is undisputed that appellant proffered no rebuttal evidence.

Based on what we have already said concerning "public accessibility," and noting that the determination rests on the facts of each case, we reject appellant's legal argument that a single cataloged thesis in one university library does not constitute sufficient accessibility to those interested in the art exercising reasonable diligence.

We agree with the board that the evidence of record consisting of Dr. Will's affidavits establishes a prima facie case for unpatentability of the claims under the § 102(b) publication bar. It is a case which stands unrebutted.

Accordingly, the board's decision sustaining the rejection of appellant's claims is *affirmed*.

NOTES

1.   Section 102(a) or Section 102(b)? Both Sections 102(a) and 102(b) use the language "patented or described in a printed publication." What is the difference between Section 102(a) and Section 102(b)'s bar on inventions patented or described in a printed publication in this or a foreign country? What does Section 102(a) protect against that 102(b) does not? To whom is each section directed? Does the one year statutory period make sense?

2.   "Printed Publication?" In *In re Klopfenstein*, 380 F.3d 1345 (Fed. Cir. 2004), the appellants applied for a patent for preparing foods comprising extruded soy cotyledon fiber. Although it was known that extrusion of these fibers created foodstuffs that reduce serum cholesterol levels, while raising HDL cholesterol levels, it was not known that double extrusion increased the effect. The Patent and Trademark Office and the Board of Patent Appeals and Interferences denied the patent application on grounds that the invention described had previously been described in a printed publication more than one year before the date of the patent application. The "printed publication" referenced by the court was a poster with printed slides that the applicants presented with an associate at two different conferences. The court held that the poster was a "printed publication" despite it never having been indexed, distributed, or copied. The court found that "public accessibility has been the criterion by which a prior art reference will be judged for the purposes of § 102(b)," and that the slide presentations were sufficiently publicly accessible to count as a "printed publication." Is it strange that inventors can invalidate their own claims? Do safeguards exist against invalidating one's own invention?

3.   Distinguishing Earlier Patents. In *United States v. Adams*, 383 U.S. 39, 86 S.Ct. 708, 15 L.Ed.2d 572 (1966), Adams invented a practical, water-activated, constant potential battery which could be fabricated and stored indefinitely without any fluid in its cells. Even though earlier patents disclosed the composition of the electrodes Adams used in his invention, the Court found, "it is fundamental that claims are to be construed in the light of the specifications and both are to be read with a view to ascertaining the invention." Adams was not claiming a simple battery, his invention was a battery activated by adding water, having additional utility, particularly in military use.

4.   Foreign Patents. In *Carter Products v. Colgate–Palmolive*, 130 F.Supp. 557, 566 (D.Md. 1955), *aff'd*, 230 F.2d 855 (4th Cir. 1956), *cert denied*, 352 U.S. 843, 77 S.Ct. 43, 1 L.Ed.2d 59 (1956), the patent in question was related to a composition used in producing a soap or a detergent lather without resorting to any manual or mechanical whipping or an agitating operation. When analyzing foreign patents, the court held that "nothing is to be treated as patented by a foreign patent except what is actually claimed."

The court also found that a prior, "typewritten" Argentine patent was not a "printed publication" by statutory standards due to limitations on the availability of the patent in its entirety.

2. Priority

a. Section 102(g)

While most of the world uses a "first to file" rule, wherein the first applicant to file a valid patent is awarded patent protection, the United States has a "first to invent" regime. The inventor that first conceives an invention, and reduces the invention to practice with reasonable due diligence, is entitled to patent protection if he completes the application process. Usually, the court considers the inventor the first to reduce the invention to practice. If however, the inventor is not the first to reduce his invention to practice, he may still be considered the first inventor, if he is the first to conceive of the invention and exercises due diligence. Disputes over who was the first to invent are resolved by an administrative "interference" proceeding.

Section 102(g) provides guidance for interferences. It states:

A person shall be entitled to a patent unless—

(g)(1) during the course of an interference conducted under section 135 or section 291, another inventor involved therein establishes, to the extent permitted in section 104,

that before such person's invention thereof the invention was made by such other inventor and not abandoned, suppressed, or concealed, or

(2) before such person's invention thereof, the invention was made in this country by another inventor who had not abandoned, suppressed, or concealed it.

In determining priority of invention under this subsection, there shall be considered not only

the respective dates of conception and reduction to practice of the invention,

but also the reasonable diligence of one who was first to conceive and last to reduce to practice, from a time prior to conception by the other.

35 U.S.C. § 102(g).

The following case addresses how an inventor may show priority.

FUJIKAWA v. WATTANASIN

United States Court of Appeals for the Federal Circuit, 1996.
93 F.3d 1559.

CLEVENGER, CIRCUIT JUDGE.

Yoshihiro Fujikawa et al. (Fujikawa) appeal from two decisions of the Board of Patent Appeals and Interferences of the United States Patent &

Trademark Office (Board) granting priority of invention in two related interferences to Sompong Wattanasin, and denying Fujikawa's motion to add an additional sub-genus count to the interferences. We affirm.

I

These interferences pertain to a compound and method for inhibiting cholesterol biosynthesis in humans and other animals. The compound count recites a genus of novel mevalonolactones. The method count recites a method of inhibiting the biosynthesis of cholesterol by administering to a "patient in need of said treatment" an appropriate dosage of a compound falling within the scope of the compound count.

The real parties in interest are Sandoz Pharmaceuticals Corporation (Sandoz), assignee of Wattanasin, and Nissan Chemical Industries, Ltd. (Nissan), assignee of Fujikawa.

The inventive activity of Fujikawa, the senior party, occurred overseas. Fujikawa can thus rely only on his effective filing date, August 20, 1987, to establish priority. 35 U.S.C. § 102(g). Whether Wattanasin is entitled to priority as against Fujikawa therefore turns on two discrete questions. First, whether Wattanasin has shown conception coupled with diligence from just prior to Fujikawa's effective filing date until reduction to practice. Second, whether Wattanasin suppressed or concealed the invention between reduction to practice and filing. With respect to the first question, Fujikawa does not directly challenge the Board's holdings on Wattanasin's conception or diligence, but rather contends that the Board incorrectly fixed the date of Wattanasin's reduction to practice. As for the second question, Fujikawa contends that the Board erred in concluding that Wattanasin had not suppressed or concealed the invention. Fujikawa seeks reversal, and thus to establish priority in its favor, on either ground.

II

The Board divided Wattanasin's inventive activity into two phases. The first phase commenced in 1979 when Sandoz began searching for drugs which would inhibit the biosynthesis of cholesterol. Inventor Wattanasin was assigned to this project in 1982, and during 1984–1985 he synthesized three compounds falling within the scope of the compound count. When tested *in vitro,* each of these compounds exhibited some cholesterol-inhibiting activity, although not all the chemicals were equally effective. Still, according to one Sandoz researcher, Dr. Damon, these test results indicated that, to a high probability, the three compounds "would be active when administered *in vivo* to a patient to inhibit cholesterol biosynthesis, i.e. for the treatment of hypercholesteremia or atherosclerosis." Notwithstanding these seemingly positive results, Sandoz shelved Wattanasin's project for almost two years, apparently because the level of *in vitro* activity in two of the three compounds was disappointingly low.

By January 1987, however, interest in Wattanasin's invention had revived, and the second phase of activity began. Over the next several months, four more compounds falling within the scope of the compound count were synthesized. In October, these compounds were tested for *in vitro* activity, and each of the four compounds yielded positive results. Again, however, there were significant differences in the level of *in vitro* activity of the four compounds. Two of the compounds in particular, numbered 64–935 and 64–936, exhibited *in vitro* activity significantly higher than that of the other two compounds, numbered 64–933 and 64–934.

Soon after, in December 1987, the three most active compounds *in vitro* were subjected to additional *in vivo* testing. For Sandoz, one primary purpose of these tests was to determine the *in vivo* potency of the three compounds relative to that of Compactin, a prior art compound of known cholesterol-inhibiting potency. From the results of the *in vivo* tests, reproduced in the margin, Sandoz calculated an ED_{50}[2] for each of the compounds and compared it to the ED_{50} of Compactin. Only one of the compounds, compound 64–935, manifested a better ED_{50} than Compactin: an ED_{50} of 0.49 as compared to Compactin's ED_{50} of 3.5. All of the tests performed by Sandoz were conducted in accordance with established protocols.

During this period, Sandoz also began to consider whether, and when, a patent application should be filed for Wattanasin's invention. Several times during the second phase of activity, the Sandoz patent committee considered the question of Wattanasin's invention but decided that it was too early in the invention's development to file a patent application. Each time, however, the patent committee merely deferred decision on the matter and specified that it would be taken up again at subsequent meetings. Finally, in January 1988, with the *in vivo* testing completed, the Committee assigned Wattanasin's invention an "A" rating which meant that the invention was ripe for filing and that a patent application should be prepared. The case was assigned to a Ms. Geisser, a young patent attorney in the Sandoz patent department with little experience in the pharmaceutical field.

Over the next several months the Sandoz patent department collected additional data from the inventor which was needed to prepare the patent application. This data gathering took until approximately the end of May 1988. At that point, work on the case seems to have ceased for several months until Ms. Geisser began preparing a draft sometime in the latter half of 1988. The parties dispute when this preparation began. Fujikawa contends that it occurred as late as October, and that Ms. Geisser was spurred to begin preparing the draft application by the discovery that a patent to the same subject matter had been issued to a third party, Picard. Fujikawa, however, has no evidence to support that contention. In con-

---

2. The ED_{50} of a compound represents the effective concentration, measured in milligrams of compound per kilogram of laboratory specimen, which inhibits cholesterol biosynthesis by 50%.

trast, Sandoz contends that Ms. Geisser began the draft as early as August, and that she was already working on the draft when she first heard of Picard's patent. The evidence of record, and in particular the testimony of Ms. Geisser, supports that version of events. In any event, the draft was completed in November and, after several turn-arounds with the inventor, ultimately filed in March of 1989.

Both Wattanasin and Fujikawa requested an interference with Picard. The requests were granted and a three-party interference between Picard, Fujikawa, and Wattanasin was set up. Early in the proceedings, however, Picard filed a request for an adverse judgment presumably because he could not antedate Fujikawa's priority date. What remained was a two-party interference between Fujikawa and Wattanasin. Ultimately, for reasons not significant to this appeal, the interference was divided into two interferences: one relating to the method count and one relating to the compound count. The Board decided each of these interferences adverse to Fujikawa.

With respect to the compound count, the Board made two alternative findings regarding reduction to practice. First, it found that the *in vitro* results in October 1987 showed sufficient practical utility for the compound so as to constitute a reduction to practice as of the date of those tests. In the alternative, the Board held, the *in vivo* tests which showed significant activity in the 64–935 compound at doses of 1.0 and 0.1 mg were sufficient to show practical utility. Consequently, Wattanasin had reduced the compound to practice, at the latest, as of December 1987. Since Fujikawa did not challenge Wattanasin's diligence for the period between Fujikawa's effective filing date of August 20, 1987 and Wattanasin's reduction to practice in either October or December 1987, the Board held that Wattanasin was *de facto* the first inventor of the compound count. Finally, the Board found that the seventeen month period (counting from the *in vitro* testing) or fifteen month period (counting from the *in vivo* testing) between Wattanasin's reduction to practice and filing was not sufficient to raise an inference of suppression or concealment given the complexity of the invention, and therefore awarded priority of the compound count to Wattanasin. In reaching this conclusion, the Board rejected Fujikawa's argument that Wattanasin was spurred to file by Picard because it held that spurring by Picard, a third party, had no legal effect in a priority dispute between Fujikawa and Wattanasin.

With respect to the method count, the Board determined that Wattanasin reduced to practice in December 1987 on the date that *in vivo* testing of the 64–935 compound was concluded. In reaching that conclusion, the Board first noted that a reduction to practice must include every limitation of the count. Consequently, Wattanasin's early *in vitro* testing could not constitute a reduction to practice of the *method* count, since that count recites administering the compound to a "patient." The *in vivo* testing, however, met the limitations of the count since the word "patient" was sufficiently broad to include the laboratory rats to whom the compounds were administered. The *in vivo* testing also proved that 64–935 had practical utility because the compound displayed significant cholesterol inhibiting activity at doses of 1.0 and 0.1 mg. Given this date of reduction to practice, the Board again held that Wattanasin was the *de facto* first inventor of the count and that the delay in filing of fifteen months was not sufficient to trigger an inference of suppression or concealment. The Board therefore awarded priority of the method count to Wattanasin. * * *

III

* * *

B

Turning to the method count, the Board found that Wattanasin reduced the method to practice in December 1987 when successful *in vivo* testing of the compound was completed. This finding, too, was based on testimony that the *in vivo* data for one of the compounds tested, 64–935, showed significant cholesterol inhibiting activity in the laboratory rats tested.

Fujikawa challenges the Board's holding by referring to an anomaly in the test data of the 64–935 compound which it contends undercuts the reliability of the *in vivo* tests. In particular, Fujikawa points to the fact that the compound's potency was less at a dosage of 0.3 mg than it was at a dosage of 0.1 mg. On the basis of this aberration, Fujikawa's expert, Dr. Holmlund, testified that this test data was unreliable and could not support a finding that the compound was pharmacologically active.

It is clear from the Board's opinion, however, that to the extent Dr. Holmlund was testifying that this aberration would lead one of ordinary skill to completely reject these test results, the Board did not accept his testimony. This decision of the Board was not clear error. Admittedly, the decreased potency at 0.3 mg is curious. The question remains, however, as to how much this glitch in the data would undercut the persuasiveness of the test results as a whole in the mind of one of ordinary skill. Each party presented evidence on this point and the Board resolved this disputed question of fact by finding that the test results as a whole were sufficient to establish pharmacological activity in the minds of those skilled in the art. In doing so, the Board properly exercised its duty as fact finder, and we therefore affirm its finding on this point.[7]

---

7. Before the Board, Fujikawa additionally argued that *in vivo* testing cannot establish reduction to practice of the method count because it does not fulfill every limitation of the count. In particular, Fujikawa argued that only human beings can be considered "patients in need of" cholesterol biosynthesis inhibition, as required by the count. As noted above, the Board rejected this argument and held that the term "patient" in the count is broad enough to encompass mammals, such as the laboratory rats tested *in vivo*.

In its brief to this court, Fujikawa renews this argument. In the process, however, Fujikawa seems to add an additional ground which it did not argue before the Board below. We are not absolutely certain, but it appears that Fujikawa is now contending that *in vivo* testing cannot constitute a reduction to practice because the rats tested were, from all that would appear, healthy animals, rather than animals in need of cholesterol biosynthesis inhibition. To the extent that Fujikawa's argument before this court is directed to this novel ground not raised below, we

As noted above, Fujikawa does not challenge the Board's conclusions that Wattanasin conceived prior to Fujikawa's effective date or that Wattanasin pursued the invention with diligence from just prior to Fujikawa's date until his reductions to practice in October and December 1987. Consequently, we affirm the Board's finding that Wattanasin has shown conception coupled with diligence from just prior to Fujikawa's effective date of August 20, 1987 up to the date he reduced the invention to practice in October 1987, for the compound, or December 1987, for the method.

IV

Having determined that Wattanasin was the *de facto* first inventor, the remaining question before the Board was whether Wattanasin had suppressed or concealed the invention between the time he reduced to practice and the time he filed his patent application. Suppression or concealment of the invention by Wattanasin would entitle Fujikawa to priority. 35 U.S.C. § 102(g).

Suppression or concealment is a question of law which we review de novo. *Brokaw v. Vogel*, 429 F.2d 476, 480 (1970). Our case law distinguishes between two types of suppression and concealment: cases in which the inventor deliberately suppresses or conceals his invention, and cases in which a legal inference of suppression or concealment is drawn based on "too long" a delay in filing a patent application. *Paulik v. Rizkalla*, 760 F.2d 1270, 1273 (Fed. Cir. 1985) (in banc).

Fujikawa first argues that there is evidence of intentional suppression or concealment in this case. Intentional suppression refers to situations in which an inventor "designedly, and with the view of applying it indefinitely and exclusively for his own profit, withholds his invention from the public." *Id.* (quoting *Kendall v. Winsor*, 62 U.S. (21 How.) 322, 328 (1858)). Admittedly, Sandoz was not overly efficient in preparing a patent application, given the time which elapsed between its reduction to practice in late 1987 and its ultimate filing in March 1989. Intentional suppression, however, requires more than the passage of time. It requires evidence that the inventor intentionally delayed filing in order to prolong the period during which the invention is maintained in secret. Fujikawa presented no evidence that Wattanasin delayed filing for this purpose. On the contrary, all indications are that throughout the period between reduction to practice and filing, Sandoz moved slowly (one might even say fitfully), but inexorably, toward disclosure. We therefore hold that Wattanasin did not intentionally suppress or conceal the invention in this case.

Absent intentional suppression, the only question is whether the 17 month period between the reduction to practice of the compound, or the 15 month period between reduction to practice of the method, and Wattanasin's filing justify an *inference* of suppression or concealment. The

---

consider the argument waived and decline to address it. To the extent that Fujikawa is still arguing that the count requires administration of the compound to a human, we disagree, and affirm the Board's decision on this point.

Board held that these facts do not support such an inference. As the Board explained: "In our view, this hiatus in time is not sufficiently long to raise the inference that Wattanasin suppressed or concealed the invention considering the nature and complexity of the invention here."

Fujikawa attacks this finding of the Board on two grounds. First, it contends that the Board should not have held that a 15 or 17 month delay is *per se* insufficient to raise an inference of suppression or concealment without examining the circumstances surrounding the delay and whether, in view of those circumstances, Wattanasin's delay was reasonable. Second, Fujikawa argues that the Board failed to consider evidence that Wattanasin was spurred to file by the issuance of a patent to a third party, Picard, directed to the same genus of compounds invented by Wattanasin. Evidence that a first inventor was spurred to disclose by the activities of a second inventor has always been an important factor in priority determinations because it creates an inference that, but for the efforts of the second inventor, "the public would never have gained knowledge of [the invention]." *Brokaw*, 429 F.2d at 480. Here, however, the Board expressly declined to consider the evidence of spurring because it held that spurring by a third party who is not a party to the interference is irrelevant to a determination of priority as between Wattanasin and Fujikawa. We first address Fujikawa's arguments concerning spurring.

A

We are not certain that the Board is correct that third party spurring is irrelevant in determining priority. After all, "[w]hat is involved here is a policy question as to which of the two rival inventors has the greater right to a patent." *Brokaw*, 429 F.2d at 480. Resolution of this question could well be affected by the fact that one of the inventors chose to maintain his invention in secrecy until disclosure by another spurred him to file, even when the spurrer was a third party not involved in the interference. We need not resolve that question here, however, because we hold that no reasonable fact finder could have found spurring on the facts of this case. The only evidence in the record on the question of spurring is the testimony of Ms. Geisser who expressly testified that she had already begun work on the Wattanasin draft application before she learned of Picard's patent, in other words, that she had not been spurred by Picard. Consequently, we leave the question of the relevance of third party spurring for another case.

B

Fujikawa's other argument also requires us to examine the evidence of record in this case. As Fujikawa correctly notes, this court has not set strict time limits regarding the minimum and maximum periods necessary to establish an inference of suppression or concealment. Rather, we have recognized that "it is not the time elapsed that is the controlling factor but the total conduct of the first inventor." *Young v. Dworkin*, 489 F.2d 1277, 1285 (CCPA 1974) (Rich, J., concurring). Thus, the circumstances surrounding the first inventor's delay and the reasonableness of that delay are important factors which must be considered in deciding questions of suppression or concealment. Fujikawa again correctly notes that the Board's opinion gives short shrift to the question of whether *this* delay on the facts of *this* case was reasonable. In seeking reversal of the Board's decision, Fujikawa asks us to assess the factual record for ourselves to determine whether Wattanasin engaged in sufficient disclosure-related activity to justify his 17–month delay in filing. The facts of record, however, do not support Fujikawa's position.

In our view, the circumstances in this case place it squarely within the class of cases in which an inference of suppression or concealment is not warranted. We acknowledge, of course, that each case of suppression or concealment must be decided on its own facts. Still, the rich and varied case law which this court has developed over many years provides some guidance as to the type of behavior which warrants an inference of suppression or concealment. In this case Wattanasin delayed approximately 17 months between reduction to practice and filing. During much of that period, however, Wattanasin and Sandoz engaged in significant steps towards perfecting the invention and preparing an application. For example, we do not believe any lack of diligence can be ascribed to Wattanasin for the period between October and December 1987 when *in vivo* testing of the invention was taking place. Similarly, at its first opportunity following the *in vivo* testing, the Sandoz patent committee approved Wattanasin's invention for filing. This takes us up to the end of January 1988.

Over the next several months, until May 1988, the Sandoz patent department engaged in the necessary collection of data from the inventor and others in order to prepare Wattanasin's patent application. We are satisfied from the record that this disclosure-related activity was sufficient to avoid any inference of suppression or concealment during this period. Also, as noted above, the record indicates that by August 1988, Ms. Geisser was already at work preparing the application, and that work continued on various drafts until Wattanasin's filing date in March 1989. Thus, the only real period of unexplained delay in this case is the approximately three month period between May and August of 1988.

Given a total delay of 17 months, an unexplained delay of three months, the complexity of the subject matter at issue, and our sense from the record as a whole that throughout the delay Sandoz was moving, albeit slowly, towards filing an application, we conclude that this case does not warrant an inference of suppression or concealment. Consequently, we affirm the Board on this point.

C

Finally, Fujikawa contends that assuming *in vitro* tests are sufficient to establish reduction to practice, Wattanasin reduced the compound count to practice in 1984 when he completed *in vitro* testing of his first three compounds falling within the scope of the count. If so, Fujikawa argues, the delay between reduction to practice and filing was greater than four years, and an inference of suppression or concealment is justified.

We reject this argument in view of *Paulik v. Rizkalla*, 760 F.2d 1270 (Fed.Cir.1985) (in banc). In *Paulik,* we held that a suppression or concealment could be negated by renewed activity prior to an opposing party's effective date. There, inventor Paulik reduced his invention to practice and submitted an invention disclosure to his employer's patent department. For four years the patent department did nothing with the disclosure. Then, just two months before Rizkalla's effective date, the patent department allegedly picked up Paulik's disclosure and worked diligently to prepare a patent application which it ultimately filed. We held that although Paulik could not rely on his original date of reduction to practice to establish priority, he could rely on the date of renewed activity in his priority contest with Rizkalla. In large measure, this decision was driven by the court's concern that denying an inventor the benefit of his renewed activity, might "discourage inventors and their supporters from working on projects that had been 'too long' set aside, because of the impossibility of relying, in a priority contest, on either their original work or their renewed work." *Id.* at 1275–76.

Paulik's reasoning, if not its holding, applies squarely to this case. A simple hypothetical illustrates why this is so. Imagine a situation similar to the one facing Sandoz in early 1987. A decisionmaker with limited funds must decide whether additional research funds should be committed to a project which has been neglected for over two years. In making this decision, the decisionmaker would certainly take into account the likelihood that the additional research might yield valuable patent rights. Furthermore, in evaluating the probability of securing those patent rights, an important consideration would be the earliest priority date to which the research would be entitled, especially in situations where the decisionmaker knows that he and his competitors are "racing" toward a common goal. Thus, the right to rely on renewed activity for purposes of priority would encourage the decisionmaker to fund the additional research. Conversely, denying an inventor the benefit of renewed activity would discourage the decisionmaker from funding the additional research.

Here, Wattanasin returned to his abandoned project well before Fujikawa's effective date and worked diligently towards reducing the invention to practice a second time. For the reasons explained above, we hold that, on these facts, Wattanasin's earlier reduction to practice in 1984 does not bar him from relying on his earliest date of renewed activity for purposes of priority.

* * *

VI

For the reasons we set forth above, the decision of the Board is, in all respects,

AFFIRMED.

NOTES

1.   What are the advantages and disadvantages of a "first to invent" system? A "first to invent" system rewards the first, true inventor, whereas a "first to file" system may unfairly burden small, independent inventors and favor larger entities that hire inventors and lawyers to patent inventions. Are there American values at stake? Would a "first to file" system create greater or lesser incentives for inventors to disclose their inventions? Would statutory bars continue to be necessary?

Conversely, a "first to file" system creates less administrative burden for the patent examining agency. In a "first to invent" system, one may be asked to prove the date of invention. Costs of a "first to invent" vs. "first to file" system would seem to favor a "first to file" system. Since most of the world uses a first file system, switching to a first to file system would encourage comity between United States and foreign nations. Why shouldn't the United States switch to a "first to file" system? What are the adverse incentives created by a "first to file" system?

There have been different proposals to move the U.S. patent system in line with first to file systems. Although adoption of a first to file system would simplify the rule and eliminate USPTO administration costs, such a drastic change may not be realistic. A proposal to supplement priority proceedings by granting a one-year grace period to domestic applicants who do not want to apply for patents outside of the United States is more likely to be passed. Until there is reform, the first to invent rule and the cost of administering expensive interference proceedings most likely will remain in place. Toshiko Takenaka, *Rethinking the United States First-to-Invent Principle from a Comparative Law Perspective: A Proposal to Restructure § 102 Novelty and Priority Provisions,* 39 HOUS. L. REV. 621 (2002).

2.   When is an invention first conceived? Can an invention be reduced to a practice before being conceived? In *Invitrogen Corp. v. Clontech Labs., Inc.,* 429 F.3d 1052 (Fed. Cir. 2005), the court held that the conception necessary to show priority was not adequately demonstrated if the inventors did not appreciate important qualities of the claimed invention even though the invention had been already reduced to practice. In *Invitrogen,* the patents related to a genetically modified enzyme, reverse transcriptase called "Rnase H minus" that facilitated DNA replication. Scientists at Columbia University made the same mutations for reverse transcriptase years before Invitrogen, but did not discover the properties of "Rnase H minus" until after Invitrogen had done so.

3.   Joint Inventors: § 116 Inventors. What happens when inventors collaborate on an invention? What level of participation must one have to be a joint inventor? In *Hess v. Advanced Cardiovascular Systems, Inc.,* 106 F.3d 976 (Fed. Cir. 1997), two doctors patented a balloon angioplasty catheter. An engineer, Mr. Hess, who had made suggestions about the balloon's construction, claimed to be a joint inventor. The court held that the inventors named in an issued patent are presumptively correct, and that one must show, by

clear and convincing evidence that the suggestions and contributions of third persons amount to co-inventorship. The court found that "Mr. Hess did no more than a skilled salesman would do in explaining how his employer's product could be used to meet a customer's requirements. The extensive research and development work that produced the catheter was done by Drs. Simpson and Robert."

In *Nartron Corp. v. Schukra U.S.A., Inc.*, 558 F.3d 1352 (Fed. Cir. 2009), the Federal Circuit, applying *Hess* to reverse a district court's grant of summary judgment on inventorship, stated that "[t]his is not a case in which a person claims to be an inventor because he has suggested a non-obvious combination of prior art elements to the named inventors. Such an individual may be a co-inventor." *Id.* at 1358. Does *Nartron* suggest that co-inventors must make patentable contributions to the claimed invention?

Section 116 states:

When an invention is made by two or more persons jointly, they shall apply for patent jointly and each make the required oath, except as otherwise provided in this title. Inventors may apply for a patent jointly even though (1) they did not physically work together or at the same time, (2) each did not make the same type or amount of contribution, or (3) each did not make a contribution to the subject matter of every claim of the patent.

If a joint inventor refuses to join in an application for patent or cannot be found or reached after diligent effort, the application may be made by the other inventor on behalf of himself and the omitted inventor. The Director, on proof of the pertinent facts and after such notice to the omitted inventor as he prescribes, may grant a patent to the inventor making the application, subject to the same rights which the omitted inventor would have had if he had been joined. The omitted inventor may subsequently join in the application.

Whenever through error a person is named in an application for patent as the inventor, or through error an inventor is not named in an application, and such error arose without any deceptive intention on his part, the Director may permit the application to be amended accordingly, under such terms as he prescribes.

35 U.S.C. § 116.

4. *Abandonment, Suppression, and Concealment.* Under Section 102(g), an inventor may lose his right of priority if he abandons, suppresses, or conceals his invention even if he was the first to reduce the invention to practice. Abandonment, suppression, and concealment may be explicit or inferred. An unreasonable delay prior to filing may lead to a finding of inferred abandonment, suppression, or concealment. Section 102(c) specifically states that "[a person shall be entitled to a patent unless] he has abandoned the invention." Even so, there is no set time limit for when an invention is abandoned.

In *Griffith v. Kanamaru*, 816 F.2d 624 (Fed. Cir. 1987), the Federal Circuit held that a three month cessation in work towards reduction to practice was not a reasonable delay for purposes of Section 102(g). A university professor stopped work on an amino-carnitine compound to await the matriculation of a graduate student and to solicit more funding for the research. The court held that the three month period of inactivity did not fulfill the "reasonable diligence" requirement of 102(g), allowing the Japanese inventor to sustain a challenge to his right of priority.

In *Paulik v. Rizkalla*, 760 F.2d 1270, 1273 (Fed. Cir. 1985) (en banc), the Federal Circuit held that a four and a half year period of inactivity by a party was permissible, as long that party can show that it renewed its activity, and exhibited diligence, prior to the earliest date that the other party was entitled. Paulik reduced to practice a process for producing alkylidiene diesters in November 1970, and submitted a preliminary disclosure to the patent department of his assignee, the Monsanto Company. After initially choosing not to pursue patent protection, Paulik's assignee filed an application on June 30, 1975. Rizkalla chose to depend on a filing date of March 10, 1975, for the interference proceeding. Despite almost five years of delay by Paulik, the Federal Circuit held that he was not barred from trying to prove "reasonable diligence" in the form of resumed activity prior to the earliest date that Rizkalla was entitled.

5. International Agreements. Section 102(g)(1) refers to Section 104, which grants inventors from NAFTA and WTO countries the same priority rights as U.S. inventors. In essence, Section 102(g) gives foreign inventors the rights of native inventors under the United States' "first to invent" system. Since the WTO has more than 100 members, including Mexico and Canada, most of the industrialized world can raise questions of priority in the United States.

6. Disclosure in Patent Applications: Section 102(e). What happens when an inventor discloses an invention in a patent but does not claim it? In *Alexander Milburn Co. v. Davis–Bournonville Co.*, 270 U.S. 390, 46 S.Ct. 324, 70 L.Ed. 651 (1926), the defendant claimed that the plaintiff's patent was invalid because the invention had been described in a patent application filed prior to the plaintiff's. The prior application disclosed the subject matter of the plaintiff's invention, an improved welding apparatus, but did not claim it. The district court and the Court of Appeals both held that the first patent applicant was not a prior inventor because of his failure to claim the subject matter. The Supreme Court granted a writ of certiorari and held: "It is said that without a claim the thing described is not reduced to practice. But this seems to us to rest on a false theory helped out by the fiction that by a claim it is reduced to practice ... A description that would bar a patent if printed in a periodical or in an issued patent is equally effective in an application so far as reduction to practice goes."

The Patent Act of 1952 codified the idea that disclosure in a previous application precludes later claimants.

Section 102(e) states:

A person shall be entitled to a patent unless—

(e) the invention was described in (1) an application for patent, published under section 122(b), by another filed in the United States before the invention by the applicant for patent or (2) a patent granted on an application for patent by another filed in the United States before the invention by the applicant for patent, except that an international application filed under the treaty defined in section 351(a) shall have the effects for the purposes of this subsection of an application filed in the United States only if the international application designated the United States and was published under Article 21(2) of such treaty in the English language . . .

35 U.S.C. § 102(e).

7. The Disclosure–Dedication Rule. The basis of the disclosure-dedication rule is the idea that things are dedicated to the public when they are disclosed. In *Pfizer, Inc. v. Teva Pharmaceuticals, USA, Inc.*, 429 F.3d 1364 (Fed. Cir. 2005), the Federal Circuit clarified the disclosure-dedication rule by stating that "the public notice function of patents suggests that before unclaimed subject matter is deemed to have been dedicated to the public, that unclaimed subject matter must have been identified by the patentee as an alternative to a claim limitation."

8. Conception and Reduction to Practice. Generally, in order to be the first, true inventor, one must conceive the invention and reduce the conception of the idea to practice. Joint inventorship and assignment of rights are exceptions to this general rule. What happens when someone conceives an idea but another party reduces it to practice?

In *Applegate v. Scherer*, 332 F.2d 571 (C.C.P.A. 1964), an appeal from an interference proceeding was heard to decide who invented a method for controlling sea lampreys using 3–trifluoromethyl–4–nitrophenol. Because sea lampreys had created havoc for commercial and game fish in the Great Lakes, the Fish and Wildlife Service of the Department of the Interior looked for chemical compounds to control the lampreys without causing undue harm to desirable fish species. In earlier tests, a different compound, 3–bromo–4–nitrophenol, was found to be efficacious. Unfortunately, the production of 3–bromo–4–nitrophenol proved to be difficult. Applegate, working for the Department of the Interior, solicited Scherer's help. Scherer sent a letter suggesting that the Department try using 3–trifluoromethyl–4–nitrophenol, a compound that was effective.

On appeal, Applegate argued that to complete an invention there had to have been an actual reduction to practice. The court held:

> Appellants seem to propose that there cannot be a conception of an invention of the type here involved in the absence of knowledge that the invention will work. Such knowledge, necessarily, can rest only on an actual reduction to practice. To adopt this proposition would mean, as a practical matter, that one could never communicate an invention thought up by him to another who is to try it out, for, when the tester succeeds, the one who does no more than exercise ordinary skill would be rewarded and the innovator would not be. Such cannot be the law. A contrary intent is implicit in the statutes and in a multitude of precedents.

Id. at 573–74. In the Patent Act of 1952, Section 102(f) states: "[A person shall be entitled to a patent unless] . . . he did not himself invent the subject matter sought to be patented."

9. Foreign Patent Applications: Section 102(d). In *In re Kathawala*, 9 F.3d 942 (Fed. Cir. 1993), Kathawala filed a patent application for a group of new compounds that had the ability to inhibit a key enzyme during the biosynthesis of cholesterol. Kathawala filed his application in the United States on April 11, 1985, more than a year after November 21, 1983, when he had filed counterpart applications in Greece and Spain. Kathawala initially filed his application in the United States on November 22, 1982, however when he filed abroad, in 1983, he expanded his claims to include certain ester derivatives of the originally claimed compounds. Subsequently, Kathawala filed a continuation-in-part application for those ester derivatives. Both foreign patents issued prior to the instant application in the United States, the Greek patent on October 2, 1984, and the Spanish patent on January 21, 1985. Because Kathawala filed his U.S. application claiming the esters more than one year after he filed his corresponding foreign applications, and those foreign applications issued as patents prior to the U.S. filing date, the examiner rejected the claims under 35 U.S.C. § 102(d). Section 102(d) states:

> [A person shall be entitled to a patent unless] ... the invention was first patented or caused to be patented, or was the subject of an inventor's certificate, by the applicant or his legal representatives or assigns in a foreign country prior to the date of the application for patent in this country on an application for patent or inventor's certificate filed more than twelve months before the filing of the application in the United States.

35 U.S.C. § 102(d).

The court held that when an applicant files a foreign application fully disclosing his invention, the reference in Section 102(d) to "invention ... patented" necessarily includes all disclosed aspects of the invention. Thus, the Section 102(d) bar applies even when the foreign patent does not claim all aspects of the invention. The court held that Kathawala was barred under 35 U.S.C. § 102(d) from obtaining a U.S. patent.

If Kathawala's original application had issued, what result would you expect? What international effects are there if the USPTO takes an extraordinary amount of time issuing a U.S. Patent?

3. Statutory Bars

Statutory bars do not discriminate between inventors and third parties. If anyone sells, offers for sale, publicly uses, patents, or describes an invention in a printed publication more than a year before the filing date of the patent application, the invention cannot receive patent protection. Defining the conditions for patentability, such as what constitutes a "printed publication," are difficult. Under Section 102(b), inventions that are in "public use" or "on sale" a year before filing cannot receive patent protection.

a. *What Is "Public Use?"*

Prior to the enactment of the Patent Act of 1952, the law barred "prior use." One of the first cases dealing with the effect on patentability of prior use by the patentee was *Pennock v. Dialogue*, 27 U.S. (2 Pet.) 1, 7 L.Ed. 327 (1829). In *Pennock*, a patent was granted in 1818 for a process of making hose in which the sections were joined in such a way that the joints resisted pressure as well as the other parts. The invention had been completed in 1811, and the patentee had sold 13,000 feet of hose between the completion of the invention and the grant of the patent. Since knowledge of the invention could not be acquired through the product, the inventor argued that he did not intend to dedicate the invention to the public.

In response, the trial court found "[i]f the public, with the knowledge and tacit consent of the inventor, be permitted to use the invention, without opposition, it is a fraud on the public afterwards to take out a patent." On appeal, the Supreme Court affirmed, stating: "If an inventor should be permitted to hold back from the knowledge of the public the secrets of his invention; if he should . . . make[ ] and sell his invention publicly, and thus gather the whole profits . . . it would materially retard the progress of science and the useful arts."

The strict interpretation of statutory bars as favoring prompt disclosure encourages patent owners to patent early or forgo patent protection altogether. The Supreme Court's interpretation of "public use" in the following case may surprise you.

EGBERT v. LIPPMANN

Supreme Court of the United States, 1881.
104 U.S. (14 Otto) 333, 26 L.Ed. 755.

MR. JUSTICE WOODS delivered the opinion of the court.

This suit was brought for an alleged infringement of the complainant's reissued letters-patent, No. 5216, dated Jan. 7, 1873, for an improvement in corset-springs.

The original letters bear date July 17, 1866, and were issued to Samuel H. Barnes. The reissue was made to the complainant, under her then name, Frances Lee Barnes, executrix of the original patentee. * * *

The evidence on which the defendants rely to establish a prior public use of the invention consists mainly of the testimony of the complainant.

She testifies that Barnes invented the improvement covered by his patent between January and May, 1855; that between the dates named the witness and her friend Miss Cugier were complaining of the breaking of their corset-steels. Barnes, who was present, and was an intimate friend of the witness, said he thought he could make her a pair that would not break. At their next interview he presented her with a pair of corset-steels which he himself had made. The witness wore these steels a long time. In 1858 Barnes made and presented to her another pair, which she also wore a long time. When the corsets in which these steels were used wore out, the witness ripped them open and took out the steels and put them in new corsets. This was done several times.

It is admitted, and, in fact, is asserted, by complainant, that these steels embodied the invention afterwards patented by Barnes and covered by the reissued letters-patent on which this suit is brought.

Joseph H. Sturgis, another witness for complainant, testifies that in 1863 Barnes spoke to him about two inventions made by himself, one of which was a corset-steel, and that he went to the house of Barnes to see them. Before this time, and after the transactions testified to by the complainant, Barnes and she had intermarried. Barnes said his wife had a pair of steels made according to his invention in the corsets which she was then wearing, and if she would take them off he would show them to witness. Mrs. Barnes went out, and returned with a pair of corsets and a pair of scissors, and ripped the corsets open and took out the steels. Barnes then explained to witness how they were made and used.

This is the evidence presented by the record, on which the defendants rely to establish the public use of the invention by the patentee's consent and allowance.

The question for our decision is, whether this testimony shows a public use within the meaning of the statute.

We observe, in the first place, that to constitute the public use of an invention it is not necessary that more than one of the patented articles should be publicly used. The use of a great number may tend to strengthen the proof, but one well-defined case of such use is just as effectual to annul the patent as many. For instance, if the inventor of a mower, a printing-press, or a railway-car makes and sells only one of the articles invented by him, and allows the vendee to use it for two years, without restriction or limitation, the use is just as public as if he had sold and allowed the use of a great number.

We remark, secondly, that, whether the use of an invention is public or private does not necessarily depend upon the number of persons to whom its use is known. If an inventor, having made his device, gives or sells it to another, to be used by the donee or vendee, without limitation or restriction, or injunction of secrecy, and it is so used, such use is public, even though the use and knowledge of the use may be confined to one person.

We say, thirdly, that some inventions are by their very character only capable of being used where they cannot be seen or observed by the public eye. An invention may consist of a lever or spring, hidden in the running gear of a watch, or of a rachet, shaft, or cog-wheel covered from view in the recesses of a machine for spinning or weaving. Nevertheless, if its inventor sells a machine of which his invention forms a part, and allows it to be used without restriction of any kind, the use is a public one. So, on the other hand, a use necessarily open to public view, if made in good faith solely to test the qualities of the invention, and for the purpose of experiment, is not a public use within the meaning of the statute. *Elizabeth v. Pavement Company*, 97 U.S. 126.

Tested by these principles, we think the evidence of the complainant herself shows that for more than two years before the application for the original letters there was, by the consent and allowance of Barnes, a public use of the invention, covered by them. He made and gave to her two pairs of corset-steels, constructed according to his device, one in 1855 and one in 1858. They were presented to her for use. He imposed no obligation of secrecy, nor any condition or restriction whatever. They were not presented for the purpose of experiment, nor to test their qualities. No such claim is set up in her testimony. The invention was at the time complete, and there is no evidence that it was afterwards changed or improved. The donee of the steels used them for years for the purpose and in the manner designed by the inventor. They were not capable of any other use. She might have exhibited them to any person, or made other steels of the same kind, and used or sold them without violating any condition or restriction imposed on her by the inventor.

According to the testimony of the complainant, the invention was completed and put into use in 1855. The inventor slept on his rights for eleven years. Letters-patent were not applied for till March, 1866. In the mean time, the invention had found its way into general, and almost universal, use. A great part of the record is taken up with the testimony of the manufacturers and venders of corset-steels, showing that before he applied for letters the principle of his device was almost universally used in the manufacture of corset-steels. It is fair to presume that having learned from this general use that there was some value in his invention, he attempted to resume, by his application, what by his acts he had clearly dedicated to the public.

"An abandonment of an invention to the public may be evinced by the conduct of the inventor at any time, even within the two years named in the law. The effect of the law is that no such consequence will necessarily follow from the invention being in public use or on sale, with the inventor's consent and allowance, at any time within the two years before his application; but that, if the invention is in public use or on sale prior to that time, it will be conclusive evidence of abandonment, and the patent will be void." *Elizabeth v. Pavement Company, supra.*

We are of opinion that the defense of two years' public use, by the consent and allowance of the inventor, before he made application for letters-patent, is satisfactorily established by the evidence.

Mr. Justice Miller dissenting.

The sixth section of the act of July 4, 1836, c. 357, makes it a condition of the grant of a patent that the invention for which it was asked should not, at the time of the application for a patent, "have been in public use or on sale with the consent or allowance" of the inventor or discoverer. Section fifteen of the same act declares that it shall be a good defense to an action for infringement of the patent, that it had been in public use or on sale with the consent or allowance of the patentee before his application. This was afterwards modified by the seventh section of the act of March 3, 1839, c. 88, which declares that no patent shall be void on that ground unless the prior use has been for more than two years before the application.

This is the law under which the patent of the complainant is held void by the opinion just delivered. The previous part of the same section requires that the invention must be one "not known or used by others" before the discovery or invention made by the applicant. In this limitation, though in the same sentence as the other, the word "public" is not used, so that the use by others which would defeat the applicant, if without his consent, need not be public; but where the use of his invention is by his consent or allowance, it must be public or it will not have that affect.

The reason of this is undoubtedly that, if without his consent others have used the machine, composition, or manufacture, it is strong proof that he was not the discoverer or first inventor. In that case he was not entitled to a patent. If the use was with his consent or allowance, the fact that such consent or allowance was first obtained is evidence that he was the inventor, and claimed to be such. In such case, he was not to lose his right to a patent, unless the use which he permitted was such as showed an intention of abandoning his invention to the public. It must, in the language of the act, be in public use or on sale. If on sale, of course the public who buy can use it, and if used in public with his consent, it may be copied by others. In either event there is an end of his exclusive right of use or sale.

The word *public* is, therefore, an important member of the sentence. A private use with consent, which could lead to no copy or reproduction of the machine, which taught the nature of the invention to no one but the party to whom such consent was given, which left the public at large as ignorant of this as it was before the author's discovery, was no abandonment to the public, and did not defeat his claim for a patent. If the little steep spring inserted in a single pair of corsets, and used by only one woman, covered by her outer-clothing, and in a position always withheld from public observation, is a *public* use of that piece of steel, I am at a loss to know the line between a private and a public use.

The opinion argues that the use was public, because, with the consent of the inventor to its use, no limitation was imposed in regard to its use in public. It may be well imagined that a prohibition to the party so permitted against exposing her use of the steel spring to public observation would have been supposed to be a piece of irony. An objection quite the opposite of this suggested by the opinion is, that the invention was incapable of a public use. That is to say, that while the statute says the right to the patent can only be defeated by a use which is public, it is equally fatal to the claim, when it is permitted to be used at all, that the article can never be used in public.

I cannot on such reasoning as this eliminate from the statute the word *public*, and disregard its obvious importance in connection with the remainder of the act, for the purpose of defeating a patent otherwise meritorious.

b. The Experimental Use Exception

The experimental use exception is a limited exception to the "public use" bar. The experimental use exception increases both efficiency and the quality of innovation by giving inventors time to perfect their inventions. If further experimentation is necessary to reduce an invention to practice or to disclose its best mode, the PTO may deny a patent application. At the same time, there is the concern that inventors may exploit their inventions commercially, and delay filing for a patent in an attempt to extend the statutory period of exclusivity beyond the limit. Consider how the two policies work in the following case.

CITY OF ELIZABETH v. AMERICAN NICHOLSON PAVEMENT CO.

Supreme Court of the United States, 1877.
97 U.S. (7 Otto) 126, 24 L.Ed. 1000.

MR. JUSTICE BRADLEY delivered the opinion of the court.

This suit was brought by the American Nicholson Pavement Company against the city of Elizabeth, N. J., George W. Tubbs, and the New Jersey Wood–Paving Company, a corporation of New Jersey, upon a patent issued to Samuel Nicholson, dated Aug. 20, 1867, for a new and improved wooden pavement, being a second reissue of a patent issued to said Nicholson Aug. 8, 1854. The reissued patent was extended in 1868 for a further term of seven years. A copy of it is appended to the bill; and, in the specification, it is declared that the nature and object of the invention consists in providing a process or mode of constructing wooden block pavements upon a foundation along a street or roadway with facility, cheapness, and accuracy, and also in the creation and construction of such a wooden pavement as shall be comparatively permanent and durable, by so uniting and combining all its parts, both superstructure and foundation, as to provide against the slipping of the horses' feet, against noise, against unequal wear, and against rot and consequent sinking away from below.

* * *

The bill charges that the defendants infringed this patent by laying down wooden pavements in the city of Elizabeth, N. J., constructed in substantial conformity with the process patented, and prays an account of profits, and an injunction.

* * *

[The defendants] averred that the alleged invention of Nicholson was in public use, with his consent and allowance, for six years before he applied for a patent, on a certain avenue in Boston called the Mill-dam;

and contended that said public use worked an abandonment of the pretended invention.

* * *

The next question to be considered is, whether Nicholson's invention was in public use or on sale, with his consent and allowance, for more than two years prior to his application for a patent * * * It is contended by the appellants that the pavement which Nicholson put down by way of experiment, on Mill-dam Avenue in Boston, in 1848, was publicly used for the space of six years before his application for a patent, and that this was a public use within the meaning of the law.

To determine this question, it is necessary to examine the circumstances under which this pavement was put down, and the object and purpose that Nicholson had in view. It is perfectly clear from the evidence that he did not intend to abandon his right to a patent. He had filed a *caveat* in August, 1847, and he constructed the pavement in question by way of experiment, for the purpose of testing its qualities. The road in which it was put down, though a public road, belonged to the Boston and Roxbury Mill Corporation, which received toll for its use; and Nicholson was a stockholder and treasurer of the corporation. The pavement in question was about seventy-five feet in length, and was laid adjoining to the toll-gate and in front of the toll-house. It was constructed by Nicholson at his own expense, and was placed by him where it was, in order to see the effect upon it of heavily loaded wagons, and of varied and constant use; and also to ascertain its durability, and liability to decay. Joseph L. Lang, who was toll-collector for many years, commencing in 1849, familiar with the road before that time, and with this pavement from the time of its origin, testified as follows:

> Mr. Nicholson was there almost daily, and when he came he would examine the pavement, would often walk over it, cane in hand, striking it with his cane, and making particular examination of its condition. He asked me very often how people liked it, and asked me a great many questions about it. I have heard him say a number of times that this was his first experiment with this pavement, and he thought that it was wearing very well. The circumstances that made this locality desirable for the purpose of obtaining a satisfactory test of the durability and value of the pavement were: that there would be a better chance to lay it there; he would have more room and a better chance than in the city; and, besides, it was a place where most everybody went over it, rich and poor. It was a great thoroughfare out of Boston. It was frequently travelled by teams having a load of five or six tons, and some larger. As these teams usually stopped at the toll-house, and started again, the stopping and starting would make as severe a trial to the pavement as it could be put to.

This evidence is corroborated by that of several other witnesses in the cause; the result of the whole being that Nicholson merely intended this piece of pavement as an experiment, to test its usefulness and durability. Was this a public use, within the meaning of the law?

An abandonment of an invention to the public may be evinced by the conduct of the inventor at any time, even within the two years named in the law. The effect of the law is, that no such consequence will necessarily follow from the invention being in public use or on sale, with the inventor's consent and allowance, at any time within two years before his application; but that, if the invention is in public use or on sale prior to that time, it will be conclusive evidence of abandonment, and the patent will be void.

But, in this case, it becomes important to inquire what is such a public use as will have the effect referred to. That the use of the pavement in question was public in one sense cannot be disputed. But can it be said that the invention was in public use? The use of an invention by the inventor himself, or of any other person under his direction, by way of experiment, and in order to bring the invention to perfection, has never been regarded as such a use.

Now, the nature of a street pavement is such that it cannot be experimented upon satisfactorily except on a highway, which is always public.

When the subject of invention is a machine, it may be tested and tried in a building, either with or without closed doors. In either case, such use is not a public use, within the meaning of the statute, so long as the inventor is engaged, in good faith, in testing its operation. He may see cause to alter it and improve it, or not. His experiments will reveal the fact whether any and what alterations may be necessary. If durability is one of the qualities to be attained, a long period, perhaps years, may be necessary to enable the inventor to discover whether his purpose is accomplished. And though, during all that period, he may not find that any changes are necessary, yet he may be justly said to be using his machine only by way of experiment; and no one would say that such a use, pursued with a *bona fide* intent of testing the qualities of the machine, would be a public use, within the meaning of the statute. So long as he does not voluntarily allow others to make it and use it, and so long as it is not on sale for general use, he keeps the invention under his own control, and does not lose his title to a patent.

It would not be necessary, in such a case, that the machine should be put up and used only in the inventor's own shop or premises. He may have it put up and used in the premises of another, and the use may inure to the benefit of the owner of the establishment. Still, if used under the surveillance of the inventor, and for the purpose of enabling him to test the machine, and ascertain whether it will answer the purpose intended, and make such alterations and improvements as experience demonstrates to be necessary, it will still be a mere experimental use, and not a public use, within the meaning of the statute.

Whilst the supposed machine is in such experimental use, the public may be incidentally deriving a benefit from it. If it be a grist-mill, or a carding-machine, customers from the surrounding country may enjoy the use of it by having their grain made into flour, or their wool into rolls, and still it will not be in public use, within the meaning of the law.

But if the inventor allows his machine to be used by other persons generally, either with or without compensation, or if it is, with his consent, put on sale for such use, then it will be in public use and on public sale, within the meaning of the law.

If, now, we apply the same principles to this case, the analogy will be seen at once. Nicholson wished to experiment on his pavement. He believed it to be a good thing, but he was not sure; and the only mode in which he could test it was to place a specimen of it in a public roadway. He did this at his own expense, and with the consent of the owners of the road. Durability was one of the qualities to be attained. He wanted to know whether his pavement would stand, and whether it would resist decay. Its character for durability could not be ascertained without its being subjected to use for a considerable time. He subjected it to such use, in good faith, for the simple purpose of ascertaining whether it was what he claimed it to be. Did he do any thing more than the inventor of the supposed machine might do, in testing his invention? The public had the incidental use of the pavement, it is true; but was the invention in public use, within the meaning of the statute? We think not. The proprietors of the road alone used the invention, and used it at Nicholson's request, by way of experiment. The only way in which they could use it was by allowing the public to pass over the pavement.

Had the city of Boston, or other parties, used the invention, by laying down the pavement in other streets and places, with Nicholson's consent and allowance, then, indeed, the invention itself would have been in public use, within the meaning of the law; but this was not the case. Nicholson did not sell it, nor allow others to use it or sell it. He did not let it go beyond his control. He did nothing that indicated any intent to do so. He kept it under his own eyes, and never for a moment abandoned the intent to obtain a patent for it.

* * *

It is sometimes said that an inventor acquires an undue advantage over the public by delaying to take out a patent, inasmuch as he thereby preserves the monopoly to himself for a longer period than is allowed by the policy of the law; but this cannot be said with justice when the delay is occasioned by a *bona fide* effort to bring his invention to perfection, or to ascertain whether it will answer the purpose intended. His monopoly only continues for the allotted period, in any event; and it is the interest of the public, as well as himself, that the invention should be perfect and properly tested, before a patent is granted for it. Any attempt to use it for a profit, and not by way of experiment, for a longer period than two years before the application, would deprive the inventor of his right to a patent.

* * *

NOTES

1.   What qualifies as "experimentation?" In order to qualify for the experimental use exception, an inventor must maintain control and obtain feedback from any prototypes in use. In *Lough v. Brunswick Corp.*, 86 F.3d 1113 (Fed. Cir. 1996), an inventor made six prototypes of a seal system for marine motors that he installed in his own boat and those of his friends but did not gather feedback about the performance of the prototypes or maintain supervision over them. The court held that experimentation could not exist without control over the invention.

In *Baxter Int'l, Inc. v. COBE Laboratories, Inc.*, 88 F.3d 1054 (Fed. Cir. 1996), a patent concerning a seal centrifuge for separating blood into its components was declared invalid under the "public use" bar despite clear control over the invention. A third party researcher used the centrifuge, that was reduced to practice, for furthering his own research. Even though the centrifuge was used in a private laboratory, the court held that use of the centrifuge by a researcher unassociated with the inventor constituted "public use." The centrifuge did not qualify for the experimental use exception.

The court in *In re Theis*, 610 F.2d 786 (C.C.P.A. 1979), held that the burden of establishing experimental use should be on the party claiming the exception. Generally, there has been concern that inventors will claim experimental use to extend their period of exclusivity for commercial gain. In *Thesis*, the court held that the purpose of experimental use must be to complete the invention. Market testing does not qualify as experimental use as it is a means of commercial exploitation.

Not every use that has a competitive benefit is disqualified as non-experimental commercial exploitation. In *Invitrogen Corp. v. Biocrest Mfg., L.P.*, 424 F.3d 1374 (Fed. Cir. 2005), the case dealt with a patent for a process to improve the ability of E. coli cells to take up exogenous DNA molecules and replicate this DNA. The patent holder had used its claimed process in its private laboratories to "further other projects," for more than a year before filing a patent application. Even though the process increases efficiency of producing "competent" E. coli cells, the Federal Circuit held that Invitrogen's use did not constitute commercial exploitation, therefore asserting the experimental use exception was unnecessary.

2.   Research Exception 35 U.S.C. § 271(e)(1). Congress enacted Section 271(e)(1) as a research exception "solely for uses reasonably related to the development and submission of information under a Federal law which regulates the manufacture, use, or sale of drugs or veterinary biological products." The provision allows for basic research, clinical trials, and provisionally protects studies that support the creation of generic drugs.

3.   The Incentives for the Experimental Use Exception. Patent protection counterintuitively promotes scientific and technological progress through

the grant of exclusive rights. As most research uses previous discoveries as its foundation, exclusive rights may interfere with scientific progress. Rebecca Eisenberg suggests that a carefully formulated experimental use exemption from patent infringement liability is needed to accommodate the sometime irreconcilable conflicts between scientific progress and the granting of exclusive rights. Rebecca Eisenberg, *Patents in the Progress of Science: Exclusive Rights and Experimental Use,* 56 U. CHI. L. REV. 1017 (1989).

Rochelle Dreyfuss advocates a broader experimental use exception for medical academia and university research. She believes that a broader experimental use defense would be most beneficial in areas where the benefits of research were already in the public domain. Rochelle Dreyfuss, *Protecting the Public Domain of Science: Has the Time for an Experimental Use Defendant Arrived?,* 46 ARIZ. L. REV. 457 (2004).

c. What Does "on Sale" Mean?

What constitutes a sale or an offer for sale? In *Metallizing Engineering Co. v. Kenyon Bearing & Auto Parts Co.,* 153 F.2d 516 (2d Cir.), *cert. denied,* 328 U.S. 840, 66 S.Ct. 1016, 90 L.Ed. 1615 (1946), Judge Hand writing for the court addressed whether a secret process of conditioning metal for bonding could be patented after products created using the process had been sold for more than a year. The court reasoned that "the sale of the product was irrelevant, since no knowledge could possibly be acquired of the machine in that way." Judge Hand had previously analyzed the issue in *Peerless Roll Leaf Co. v. H. Griffin & Sons Co.,* 29 F.2d 646 (2d Cir. 1928). In that case, he found that no distinction existed between selling a product created by private use of a secret process, and selling a product where the patentable invention is necessarily contained in the product. The "public sale" bar applies to both types of sales if the inventor has commercially exploited the invention. Judge Hand wrote: "[an inventor] shall not exploit his discovery competitively after it is ready for patenting; he must content himself with either secrecy, or legal monopoly."

What happens if an inventor sells or offers to sell an invention that has not been reduced to practice?

PFAFF v. WELLS ELECTRONICS, INC.

Supreme Court of the United States, 1998.
525 U.S. 55, 119 S.Ct. 304, 142 L.Ed.2d 261.

JUSTICE STEVENS delivered the opinion of the Court.

Section 102(b) of the Patent Act of 1952 provides that no person is entitled to patent an "invention" that has been "on sale" more than one year before filing a patent application. We granted certiorari to determine whether the commercial marketing of a newly invented product may mark the beginning of the 1–year period even though the invention has not yet been reduced to practice.

I

On April 19, 1982, petitioner, Wayne Pfaff, filed an application for a patent on a computer chip socket. Therefore, April 19, 1981, constitutes the critical date for purposes of the on-sale bar of 35 U.S.C. § 102(b); if the 1–year period began to run before that date, Pfaff lost his right to patent his invention.

Pfaff commenced work on the socket in November 1980, when representatives of Texas Instruments asked him to develop a new device for mounting and removing semiconductor chip carriers. In response to this request, he prepared detailed engineering drawings that described the design, the dimensions, and the materials to be used in making the socket. Pfaff sent those drawings to a manufacturer in February or March 1981.

Prior to March 17, 1981, Pfaff showed a sketch of his concept to representatives of Texas Instruments. On April 8, 1981, they provided Pfaff with a written confirmation of a previously placed oral purchase order for 30,100 of his new sockets for a total price of $91,155. In accord with his normal practice, Pfaff did not make and test a prototype of the new device before offering to sell it in commercial quantities.

The manufacturer took several months to develop the customized tooling necessary to produce the device, and Pfaff did not fill the order until July 1981. The evidence therefore indicates that Pfaff first reduced his invention to practice in the summer of 1981. The socket achieved substantial commercial success before Patent No. 4,491,377 ('377 patent) issued to Pfaff on January 1, 1985.

After the patent issued, petitioner brought an infringement action against respondent, Wells Electronics, Inc., the manufacturer of a competing socket. Wells prevailed on the basis of a finding of no infringement. When respondent began to market a modified device, petitioner brought this suit, alleging that the modifications infringed six of the claims in the '377 patent.

After a full evidentiary hearing before a Special Master, the District Court held that two of those claims (1 and 6) were invalid because they had been anticipated in the prior art. Nevertheless, the court concluded that four other claims (7, 10, 11, and 19) were valid and three (7, 10, and 11) were infringed by various models of respondent's sockets. Adopting the Special Master's findings, the District Court rejected respondent's § 102(b) defense because Pfaff had filed the application for the '377 patent less than a year after reducing the invention to practice.

The Court of Appeals reversed, finding all six claims invalid. Four of the claims (1, 6, 7, and 10) described the socket that Pfaff had sold to Texas Instruments prior to April 8, 1981. Because that device had been offered for sale on a commercial basis more than one year before the patent application was filed on April 19, 1982, the court concluded that those claims were invalid under § 102(b). That conclusion rested on the court's view that as long as the invention was "substantially complete at the time of sale," the 1–year period began to run, even though the invention had not yet been reduced to practice. The other two claims (11 and 19) described a feature that had not been included in Pfaff's initial design, but the Court of Appeals concluded as a matter of law that the additional feature was not itself patentable because it was an obvious addition to the prior art. Given the court's § 102(b) holding, the prior art included Pfaff's first four claims.

Because other courts have held or assumed that an invention cannot be "on sale" within the meaning of § 102(b) unless and until it has been reduced to practice, and because the text of § 102(b) makes no reference to "substantial completion" of an invention, we granted certiorari.

II

The primary meaning of the word "invention" in the Patent Act unquestionably refers to the inventor's conception rather than to a physical embodiment of that idea. The statute does not contain any express requirement that an invention must be reduced to practice before it can be patented. Neither the statutory definition of the term in § 100 nor the basic conditions for obtaining a patent set forth in § 101 make any mention of "reduction to practice." The statute's only specific reference to that term is found in § 102(g), which sets forth the standard for resolving priority contests between two competing claimants to a patent. That subsection provides:

> In determining priority of invention there shall be considered not only the respective dates of conception and reduction to practice of the invention, but also the reasonable diligence of one who was first to conceive and last to reduce to practice, from a time prior to conception by the other.

Thus, assuming diligence on the part of the applicant, it is normally the first inventor to conceive, rather than the first to reduce to practice, who establishes the right to the patent.

It is well settled that an invention may be patented before it is reduced to practice. In 1888, this Court upheld a patent issued to Alexander Graham Bell even though he had filed his application before constructing a working telephone. Chief Justice Waite's reasoning in that case merits quoting at length:

> It is quite true that when Bell applied for his patent he had never actually transmitted telegraphically spoken words so that they could be distinctly heard and understood at the receiving end of his line, but in his specification he did describe accurately and with admirable clearness his process, that is to say, the exact electrical condition that must be created to accomplish his purpose, and he also described, with sufficient precision to enable one of ordinary skill in such matters to make it, a form of apparatus which, if used in the way pointed out, would produce the required effect, receive the words, and carry them to and deliver them at the appointed place. The particular

instrument which he had, and which he used in his experiments, did not, under the circumstances in which it was tried, reproduce the words spoken, so that they could be clearly understood, but the proof is abundant and of the most convincing character, that other instruments, carefully constructed and made exactly in accordance with the specification, without any additions whatever, have operated and will operate successfully. A good mechanic of proper skill in matters of the kind can take the patent and, by following the specification strictly, can, without more, construct an apparatus which, when used in the way pointed out, will do all that it is claimed the method or process will do. . . .

"The law does not require that a discoverer or inventor, in order to get a patent for a process, must have succeeded in bringing his art to the highest degree of perfection. It is enough if he describes his method with sufficient clearness and precision to enable those skilled in the matter to understand what the process is, and if he points out some practicable way of putting it into operation." The Telephone Cases, 126 U.S. 1, 535–536 (1888).

When we apply the reasoning of *The Telephone Cases* to the facts of the case before us today, it is evident that Pfaff could have obtained a patent on his novel socket when he accepted the purchase order from Texas Instruments for 30,100 units. At that time he provided the manufacturer with a description and drawings that had "sufficient clearness and precision to enable those skilled in the matter" to produce the device. The parties agree that the sockets manufactured to fill that order embody Pfaff's conception as set forth in claims 1, 6, 7, and 10 of the '377 patent. We can find no basis in the text of § 102(b) or in the facts of this case for concluding that Pfaff's invention was not "on sale" within the meaning of the statute until after it had been reduced to practice.

III

Pfaff nevertheless argues that longstanding precedent, buttressed by the strong interest in providing inventors with a clear standard identifying the onset of the 1–year period, justifies a special interpretation of the word "invention" as used in § 102(b). We are persuaded that this nontextual argument should be rejected.

As we have often explained, most recently in *Bonito Boats, Inc. v. Thunder Craft Boats, Inc.*, 489 U.S. 141, 151 (1989), the patent system represents a carefully crafted bargain that encourages both the creation and the public disclosure of new and useful advances in technology, in return for an exclusive monopoly for a limited period of time. The balance between the interest in motivating innovation and enlightenment by rewarding invention with patent protection on the one hand, and the interest in avoiding monopolies that unnecessarily stifle competition on the other, has been a feature of the federal patent laws since their inception. As this Court explained in 1871:

Letters patent are not to be regarded as monopolies . . . but as public franchises granted to the inventors of new and useful improvements for the purpose of securing to them, as such inventors, for the limited term therein mentioned, the exclusive right and liberty to make and use and vend to others to be used their own inventions, as tending to promote the progress of science and the useful arts, and as matter of compensation to the inventors for their labor, toil, and expense in making the inventions, and reducing the same to practice for the public benefit, as contemplated by the Constitution and sanctioned by the laws of Congress. *Seymour v. Osborne*, 11 Wall. 516, 533–534.

Consistent with these ends, § 102 of the Patent Act serves as a limiting provision, both excluding ideas that are in the public domain from patent protection and confining the duration of the monopoly to the statutory term.

We originally held that an inventor loses his right to a patent if he puts his invention into public use before filing a patent application. "His voluntary act or acquiescence in the public sale and use is an abandonment of his right." *Pennock v. Dialogue*, 2 Pet. 1, 24, 7 L.Ed. 327 (1829) (Story, J.). A similar reluctance to allow an inventor to remove existing knowledge from public use undergirds the on-sale bar.

Nevertheless, an inventor who seeks to perfect his discovery may conduct extensive testing without losing his right to obtain a patent for his invention—even if such testing occurs in the public eye. The law has long recognized the distinction between inventions put to experimental use and products sold commercially. In 1878, we explained why patentability may turn on an inventor's use of his product.

It is sometimes said that an inventor acquires an undue advantage over the public by delaying to take out a patent, inasmuch as he thereby preserves the monopoly to himself for a longer period than is allowed by the policy of the law; but this cannot be said with justice when the delay is occasioned by a *bona fide* effort to bring his invention to perfection, or to ascertain whether it will answer the purpose intended. His monopoly only continues for the allotted period, in any event; and it is the interest of the public, as well as himself, that the invention should be perfect and properly tested, before a patent is granted for it. *Any attempt to use it for a profit, and not by way of experiment, for a longer period than two years before the application, would deprive the inventor of his right to a patent.* *Elizabeth v. American Nicholson Pavement Co.*, 97 U.S. 126, 137, 24 L.Ed. 1000 (1877) (emphasis added).

The patent laws therefore seek both to protect the public's right to retain knowledge already in the public domain and the inventor's right to control whether and when he may patent his invention. The Patent Act of 1836, 5 Stat. 117, was the first statute that expressly included an on-sale bar to the issuance of a patent. Like the earlier holding in *Pennock*, that provision precluded patentability if the invention had been placed on sale at any time before the patent application was filed. In 1839, Congress ameliorated that requirement by enacting a 2–year grace period in which the inventor could file an application.

In *Andrews v. Hovey*, 123 U.S. 267, 274 (1887), we noted that the purpose of that amendment was "to fix a period of limitation which should be certain;" it required the inventor to make sure that a patent application was filed "within two years from the completion of his invention." In 1939, Congress reduced the grace period from two years to one year.

Petitioner correctly argues that these provisions identify an interest in providing inventors with a definite standard for determining when a patent application must be filed. A rule that makes the timeliness of an application depend on the date when an invention is "substantially complete" seriously undermines the interest in certainty. Moreover, such a rule finds no support in the text of the statute. Thus, petitioner's argument calls into question the standard applied by the Court of Appeals, but it does not persuade us that it is necessary to engraft a reduction to practice element into the meaning of the term "invention" as used in § 102(b).

The word "invention" must refer to a concept that is complete, rather than merely one that is "substantially complete." It is true that reduction to practice ordinarily provides the best evidence that an invention is complete. But just because reduction to practice is sufficient evidence of completion, it does not follow that proof of reduction to practice is necessary in every case. Indeed, both the facts of *The Telephone Cases* and the facts of this case demonstrate that one can prove that an invention is complete and ready for patenting before it has actually been reduced to practice.

We conclude, therefore, that the on-sale bar applies when two conditions are satisfied before the critical date. First, the product must be the subject of a commercial offer for sale. An inventor can both understand and control the timing of the first commercial marketing of his invention. The experimental use doctrine, for example, has not generated concerns about indefiniteness, and we perceive no reason why unmanageable uncertainty should attend a rule that measures the application of the on-sale bar of § 102(b) against the date when an invention that is ready for patenting is first marketed commercially. In this case the acceptance of the purchase order prior to April 8, 1981, makes it clear that such an offer had been made, and there is no question that the sale was commercial rather than experimental in character.

Second, the invention must be ready for patenting. That condition may be satisfied in at least two ways: by proof of reduction to practice before the critical date; or by proof that prior to the critical date the inventor had prepared drawings or other descriptions of the invention that were sufficiently specific to enable a person skilled in the art to practice the invention. In this case the second condition of the on-sale bar is satisfied because the drawings Pfaff sent to the manufacturer before the critical date fully disclosed the invention.

The evidence in this case thus fulfills the two essential conditions of the on-sale bar. * * *

The judgment of the Court of Appeals finds support not only in the text of the statute but also in the basic policies underlying the statutory scheme, including § 102(b). When Pfaff accepted the purchase order for his new sockets prior to April 8, 1981, his invention was ready for patenting. The fact that the manufacturer was able to produce the socket using his detailed drawings and specifications demonstrates this fact. Furthermore, those sockets contained all the elements of the invention claimed in the '377 patent. Therefore, Pfaff's '377 patent is invalid because the invention had been on sale for more than one year in this country before he filed his patent application. Accordingly, the judgment of the Court of Appeals is affirmed.

NOTES

1. **Conception and Sale.** In *Sparton Corp. v. United States*, 399 F.3d 1321 (Fed. Cir. 2005), the court held that the "on sale" bar did not apply to a contracted sale of an anti-submarine warfare sonobuoy. Sparton had entered into a contract with the Navy to provide sonobuoys, but the contract described a different sonobuoy device. Sparton substituted one sonobuoy device for another as permitted by the U.C.C. (the sonobuoys would be considered conforming goods under the contract. *See* U.C.C. §§ 2–106, 2–311). The contract did not disclose the patented device at the time of the offer of sale, and at the time the contract was accepted the invention had not been conceived of.

2. **Misappropriation of an Invention.** There is no misappropriation exception to Section 102(b). In *Evans Cooling Systems, Inc. v. General Motors*, 125 F.3d 1448 (Fed. Cir. 1997), the inventor alleged that the defendant "stole" his patented invention, a reverse cooling system for internal combustion engines, during a demonstration it had requested. Facing patent infringement charges instead of misappropriation, the defendant asserted that the invention had been on sale for more than a year before the plaintiff filed his patent application. Generally, fraudulent use by a misappropriator will not invalidate a patent. In *Evans*, however, the Federal Circuit found that there is no misappropriation exception to the "on sale" bar, and although the patent was invalid, the inventor could file a state court action for misappropriation of a trade secret.

3. **A Publication and Foreign Plant Sale.** A plant patent was at issue in *In re Elsner*, 381 F.3d 1125 (Fed. Cir. 2004). The Federal Circuit found that a combination of foreign sales that put one of ordinary skill in the art in possession of the plant itself, and a publication, that identifies the plant, might serve as a statutory bar to patent protection under Section 102(b). The court reasoned:

[B]ecause the public may have had access to the claimed inventions through the foreign sales of the plants, from which the claimed plants may be reproduced, it may fairly be said that the PBR applications are adequately enabled. Because the published applications, combined with the foreign sales of the plants, placed the claimed inventions in the possession of the public, we therefore hold that they are proper § 102(b) anticipatory references that may bar patentability.

Id. at 1129.

4. A Higher Standard? Both Sections 102(b) and 271 use the language "offer for sale." Timothy R. Holbrook believes that courts should construe the phrase "offer for sale" broadly when ruling on invalidity and infringement. He "strongly suggest[s] that the two provisions should be interpreted identically and should require something less than a formal commercial offer." This would put the United States more in line with other nations' patent laws, strengthen patent protection, and give inventors greater certainty of what constitutes a violation of the "on sale bar." Timothy R. Holbrook, *Liability for the "Threat of a Sale": Assessing Patent Infringement For Offering to Sell an Invention And Implications for the on Sale Patentability Bar And Other Forms of Infringement*, 43 Santa Clara L. Rev. 751 (2003).

D.   SECTION 103: CONDITIONS FOR PATENTABILITY; NONOBVIOUS SUBJECT MATTER

For an invention to be patentable, nonobviousness is required in addition to novelty. The nonobviousness requirement traces its origin to the common law. In *Cuno Engr. Corp. v. Automatic Devices Corp.*, 314 U.S. 84, 62 S.Ct. 37, 86 L.Ed. 58 (1941), the Supreme Court held that, "the new device ... must reveal the flash of creative genius and not merely the skill of the calling." In *Hotchkiss v. Greenwood*, 52 U.S. (11 How.) 248, 13 L.Ed. 683 (1850), the Court found a method of making doorknobs had "an absence of that degree of skill and ingenuity, which constitute essential elements of every invention." In *Great Atlantic & Pacific Tea Co. v. Supermarket Equipment Corp.*, 340 U.S. 147, 71 S.Ct. 127, 95 L.Ed. 162 (1950), the Court refused to find "invention" in a countertop extension for customers waiting to pay the cashier. The Court held, "a standard of invention appears to have been used that is less exacting than that required where a combination is made up entirely of old components." In an effort to create a single objective test, Congress codified a nonobviousness requirement in Section 103 of the Patent Act of 1952.

Nevertheless, by 1965 a single test, to determine the standard of invention necessary to show nonobviousness, still had not emerged. To resolve the confusion of the lower courts, the Supreme Court consolidated a number of cases in the case below.

GRAHAM v. JOHN DEERE CO. OF KANSAS CITY

Supreme Court of the United States, 1966.
383 U.S. 1, 86 S.Ct. 684, 15 L.Ed.2d 545.

MR. JUSTICE CLARK delivered the opinion of the Court.

After a lapse of 15 years, the Court again focuses its attention on the patentability of inventions under the standard of Art. I, s 8, cl. 8, of the Constitution and under the conditions prescribed by the laws of the United States. Since our last expression on patent validity, *A. & P. Tea Co. v. Supermarket Equipment Corp.*, 340 U.S. 147, 71 S.Ct. 127, 95 L.Ed. 162 (1950), the Congress has for the first time expressly added a third statutory dimension to the two requirements of novelty and utility that had been the sole statutory test since the Patent Act of 1793. This is the test of obviousness, i.e., whether "the subject matter sought to be patented and the prior art are such that the subject matter as a whole would have been obvious at the time the invention was made to a person having ordinary skill in the art to which said subject matter pertains. Patentability shall not be negatived by the manner in which the invention was made." § 103 of the Patent Act of 1952.

The questions, involved in each of the companion cases before us, are what effect the 1952 Act had upon traditional statutory and judicial tests of patentability and what definitive tests are now required. We have concluded that the 1952 Act was intended to codify judicial precedents embracing the principle long ago announced by this Court in *Hotchkiss v. Greenwood*, 11 How. 248, 13 L.Ed. 683 (1851), and that, while the clear language of § 103 places emphasis on an inquiry into obviousness, the general level of innovation necessary to sustain patentability remains the same.

I.

The Cases.

(a). No. 11, Graham v. John Deere Co., an infringement suit by petitioners, presents a conflict between two Circuits over the validity of a single patent on a 'Clamp for vibrating Shank Plows.' The invention, a combination of old mechanical elements, involves a device designed to absorb shock from plow shanks as they plow through rocky soil and thus to prevent damage to the plow. In 1955, the Fifth Circuit had held the patent valid under its rule that when a combination produces an "old result in a cheaper and otherwise more advantageous way," it is patentable. The Eighth Circuit held, in the case at bar, that there was no new result in the patented combination and that the patent was, therefore, not valid. We granted certiorari. Although we have determined that neither Circuit applied the correct test, we conclude that the patent is invalid under § 103 and, therefore, we affirm the judgment of the Eighth Circuit.

* * *

III.

The difficulty of formulating conditions for patentability was heightened by the generality of the constitutional grant and the statutes implementing it, together with the underlying policy of the patent system that 'the things which are worth to the public the embarrassment of an exclusive patent,' as Jefferson put it, must outweigh the restrictive effect of the limited patent monopoly. The inherent problem was to develop some means of weeding out those inventions which would not be disclosed or devised but for the inducement of a patent.

This Court formulated a general condition of patentability in 1851 in *Hotchkiss v. Greenwood*, 11 How. 248, 13 L.Ed. 683. The patent involved a mere substitution of materials—porcelain or clay for wood or metal in doorknobs—and the Court condemned it, holding:

> (U)nless more ingenuity and skill ... were required ... than were possessed by an ordinary mechanic acquainted with the business, there was an absence of that degree of skill and ingenuity which constitute essential elements of every invention. In other words, the improvement is the work of the skilful mechanic, not that of the inventor.

Hotchkiss, by positing the condition that a patentable invention evidence more ingenuity and skill than that possessed by an ordinary mechanic acquainted with the business, merely distinguished between new and useful innovations that were capable of sustaining a patent and those that were not. The *Hotchkiss* test laid the cornerstone of the judicial evolution suggested by Jefferson and left to the courts by Congress. The language in the case, and in those which followed, gave birth to "invention" as a word of legal art signifying patentable inventions. Yet, as this Court has observed, "(t)he truth is, the word ("invention") cannot be defined in such manner as to afford any substantial aid in determining whether a particular device involves an exercise of the inventive faculty or not." *McClain v. Ortmayer*, 141 U.S. 419, 427 (1891). Its use as a label brought about a large variety of opinions as to its meaning both in the Patent Office, in the courts, and at the bar. The *Hotchkiss* formulation, however, lies not in any label, but in its functional approach to questions of patentability. In practice, *Hotchkiss* has required a comparison between the subject matter of the patent, or patent application, and the background skill of the calling. It has been from this comparison that patentability was in each case determined.

IV.

The 1952 Patent Act.

The Act sets out the conditions of patentability in three sections. An analysis of the structure of these three sections indicates that patentability is dependent upon three explicit conditions: novelty and utility as articulated and defined in § 101 and § 102, and nonobviousness, the new statutory formulation, as set out in § 103. The first two sections, which trace closely the 1874 codification, express the 'new and useful' tests which have always existed in the statutory scheme and, for our purposes here, need no clarification. The pivotal section around which the present controversy centers is § 103. It provides:

§ 103.   Conditions for patentability; non-obvious subject matter

A patent may not be obtained though the invention is not identically disclosed or described as set forth in section 102 of this title, if the differences between the subject matter sought to be patented and the prior art are such that the subject matter as a whole would have been obvious at the time the invention was made to a person having ordinary skill in the art to which said subject matter pertains. Patentability shall not be negatived by the manner in which the invention was made.

The section is cast in relatively unambiguous terms. Patentability is to depend, in addition to novelty and utility, upon the 'non-obvious' nature of the 'subject matter sought to be patented' to a person having ordinary skill in the pertinent art.

The first sentence of this section is strongly reminiscent of the language in *Hotchkiss*. Both formulations place emphasis on the pertinent art existing at the time the invention was made and both are implicitly tied to advances in that art. The major distinction is that Congress has emphasized "nonobviousness" as the operative test of the section, rather than the less definite "invention" language of *Hotchkiss* that Congress thought had led to "a large variety" of expressions in decisions and writings. In the title itself the Congress used the phrase "Conditions for patentability; non-obvious subject matter," thus focusing upon "nonobviousness" rather than "invention."

* * *

It is undisputed that this section was, for the first time, a statutory expression of an additional requirement for patentability, originally expressed in *Hotchkiss*. It also seems apparent that Congress intended by the last sentence of § 103 to abolish the test it believed this Court announced in the controversial phrase "flash of creative genius," used in *Cuno Engineering Corp. v. Automatic Devices Corp.*, 314 U.S. 84 (1941).

It is contended, however, by some of the parties and by several of the amici that the first sentence of § 103 was intended to sweep away judicial precedents and to lower the level of patentability. Others contend that the Congress intended to codify the essential purpose reflected in existing judicial precedents—the rejection of insignificant variations and innovations of a commonplace sort—and also to focus inquiries under § 103 upon nonobviousness, rather than upon "invention," as a means of achieving more stability and predictability in determining patentability and validity.

* * *

V.

While the ultimate question of patent validity is one of law, *A. & P. Tea Co. v. Supermarket Equipment Corp.*, *supra*, 340 U.S. at 155, 71 S.Ct. at 131, the § 103 condition, which is but one of three conditions, each of which must be satisfied, lends itself to several basic factual inquiries. Under § 103, the scope and content of the prior art are to be determined; differences between the prior art and the claims at issue are to be ascertained; and the level of ordinary skill in the pertinent art resolved. Against this background, the obviousness or nonobviousness of the subject matter is determined. Such secondary considerations as commercial success, long felt but unsolved needs, failure of others, etc., might be utilized to give light to the circumstances surrounding the origin of the subject matter sought to be patented. As indicia of obviousness or nonobviousness, these inquiries may have relevancy.

This is not to say, however, that there will not be difficulties in applying the nonobviousness test. What is obvious is not a question upon which there is likely to be uniformity of thought in every given factual context. The difficulties, however, are comparable to those encountered daily by the courts in such frames of reference as negligence and scienter, and should be amenable to a case-by-case development. We believe that strict observance of the requirements laid down here will result in that uniformity and definiteness which Congress called for in the 1952 Act.

Although we conclude here that the inquiry which the Patent Office and the courts must make as to patentability must be beamed with greater intensity on the requirements of § 103, it bears repeating that we find no change in the general strictness with which the overall test is to be applied. We have been urged to find in § 103 a relaxed standard, supposedly a congressional reaction to the 'increased standard' applied by this Court in its decisions over the last 20 or 30 years. The standard has remained invariable in this Court. Technology, however, has advanced— and with remarkable rapidity in the last 50 years. Moreover, the ambit of applicable art in given fields of science has widened by disciplines unheard of a half century ago. It is but an evenhanded application to require that those persons granted the benefit of a patent monopoly be charged with an awareness of these changed conditions. The same is true of the less technical, but still useful arts. He who seeks to build a better mousetrap today has a long path to tread before reaching the Patent Office.

VI.

We now turn to the application of the conditions found necessary for patentability to the cases involved here:

A. The Patent in Issue in No. 11, Graham v. John Deere Co.

This patent, No. 2,627,798 (hereinafter called the '798 patent) relates to a spring clamp which permits plow shanks to be pushed upward when they hit obstructions in the soil, and then springs the shanks back into normal position when the obstruction is passed over. The device, which we show diagrammatically in the accompanying sketches (See Fig. 1), is fixed to the plow frame as a unit. The mechanism around which the controversy center is basically a hinge. The top half of it, known as the upper plate (marked 1 in the sketches), is a heavy metal piece clamped to the plow frame (2) and is stationary relative to the plow frame. The lower half of the hinge, known as the hinge plate (3), is connected to the rear of the upper plate by a hinge pin (4) and rotates downward with respect to it. The shank (5), which is bolted to the forward end of the hinge plate (at 6), runs beneath the plate and parallel to it for about nine inches, passes through a stirrup (7), and then continues backward for several feet curving down toward the ground. The chisel (8), which does the actual plowing, is attached to the rear end of the shank. As the plow frame is pulled forward, the chisel rips through the soil, thereby plowing it. In the normal position, the hinge plate and the shank are kept tight against the upper plate by a spring (9), which is atop the upper plate. A rod (10) runs through the center of the spring, extending down through holes in both plates and the shank. Its upper end is bolted to the top of the spring while its lower end is hooked against the underside of the shank.

When the chisel hits a rock or other obstruction in the soil, the obstruction forces the chisel and the rear portion of the shank to move upward. The shank is pivoted (at 11) against the rear of the hinge plate and pries open the hinge against the closing tendency of the spring. (See sketch labeled 'Open Position' Fig. 1.) This closing tendency is caused by the fact that, as the hinge is opened, the connecting rod is pulled downward and the spring is compressed. When the obstruction is passed over, the upward force on the chisel disappears and the spring pulls the shank and hinge plate back into their original position. The lower, rear portion of the hinge plate is constructed in the form of a stirrup (7) which brackets the shank, passing around and beneath it. The shank fits loosely into the stirrup (permitting a slight up and down play). The stirrup is designed to prevent the shank from recoiling away from the hinge plate, and thus prevents excessive strain on the shank near its bolted connection. The stirrup also girds the shank, preventing it from fishtailing from side to side.

In practical use, a number of spring-hinge-shank combinations are clamped to a plow frame, forming a set of ground-working chisels capable of withstanding the shock of rocks and other obstructions in the soil without breaking the shanks.

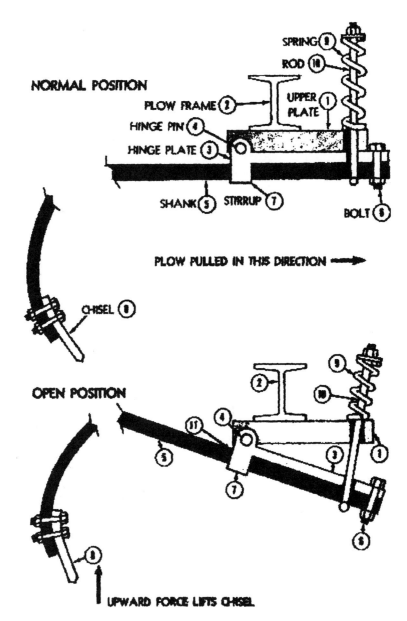

NORMAL POSITION

SPRING 9
ROD 10
PLOW FRAME 2
UPPER PLATE 1
HINGE PIN 4
HINGE PLATE 3
SHANK 5 STIRRUP 7
BOLT 6

PLOW PULLED IN THIS DIRECTION ⟶

CHISEL 8

OPEN POSITION

UPWARD FORCE LIFTS CHISEL

Fig. 1

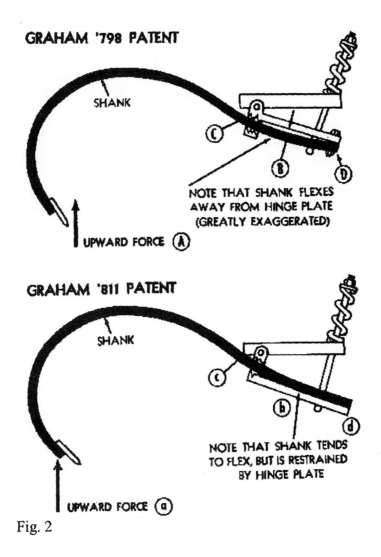

Fig. 2

Background of the Patent.

Chisel plows, as they are called, were developed for plowing in areas where the ground is relatively free from rocks or stones. Originally, the shanks were rigidly attached to the plow frames. When such plows were used in the rocky, glacial soils of some of the Northern States, they were found to have serious defects. As the chisels hit buried rocks, a vibratory motion was set up and tremendous forces were transmitted to the shank near its connection to the frame. The shanks would break. Graham, one of the petitioners, sought to meet that problem, and in 1950 obtained a patent, U.S. No. 2,493,811 (hereinafter '811), on a spring clamp where solved some of the difficulties. Graham and his companies manufactured and sold the '811 clamps. In 1950, Graham modified the '811 structure and filed for a patent. That patent, the one in issue, was granted in 1953.

This suit against competing plow manufacturers resulted from charges by petitioners that several of respondents' devices infringed the '798 patent. * * *

We confine our discussion to the prior patent of Graham, '811, and to the Glencoe clamp device, both among the references asserted by respondents. The Graham '811 and '798 patent devices are similar in all elements, save two: (1) the stirrup and the bolted connection of the shank to the hinge plate do not appear in '811; and (2) the position of the shank is reversed, being placed in patent '811 above the hinge plate, sandwiched between it and the upper plate. The shank is held in place by the spring rod which is hooked against the bottom of the hinge plate passing through a slot in the shank. Other differences are of no consequence to our examination. In practice the '811 patent arrangement permitted the shank to wobble or fishtail because it was not rigidly fixed to the hinge plate; moreover, as the hinge plate was below the shank, the latter caused wear on the upper plate, a member difficult to repair or replace.

* * *

Graham did not urge before the Patent Office the greater "flexing" qualities of the '798 patent arrangement which he so heavily relied on in the courts. The sole element in patent '798 which petitioners argue before us is the interchanging of the shank and hinge plate and the consequences flowing from this arrangement. The contention is that this arrangement— which petitioners claim is not disclosed in the prior art—permits the shank to flex under stress for its entire length. As we have sketched (see sketch, 'Graham '798 Patent' Fig. 2), when the chisel hits an obstruction the resultant force (A) pushes the rear of the shank upward and the shank pivots against the rear of the hinge plate at (C). The natural tendency is for that portion of the shank between the pivot point and the bolted connection (i.e., between C and D) to bow downward and away from the hinge plate. The maximum distance (B) that the shank moves away from the plate is slight—for emphasis, greatly exaggerated in the sketches. This is so because of the strength of the shank and the short—nine inches or so—length of that portion of the shank between (C) and (D). On the contrary, in patent '811 (see sketch, 'Graham '811 Patent' Fig. 2), the pivot point is the upper plate at point (c); and while the tendency for the shank to bow between points (c) and (d) is the same as in '798, the shank is restricted because of the underlying hinge plate and cannot flex as freely. In practical effect, the shank flexes only between points (a) and (c), and not along the entire length of the shank, as in '798. Petitioners say that this difference in flex, though small, effectively absorbs the tremendous forces of the shock of obstructions whereas prior art arrangements failed.

The Obviousness of the Differences.

We cannot agree with petitioners. We assume that the prior art does not disclose such an arrangement as petitioners claim in patent '798. Still we do not believe that the argument on which petitioners' contention is bottomed supports the validity of the patent. The tendency of the shank to flex is the same in all cases. If free-flexing, as petitioners now argue, is the crucial difference above the prior art, then it appears evident that the desired result would be obtainable by not boxing the shank within the confines of the hinge. The only other effective place available in the arrangement was to attach it below the hinge plate and run it through a stirrup or bracket that would not disturb its flexing qualities. Certainly a person having ordinary skill in the prior art, given the fact that the flex in the shank could be utilized more effectively if allowed to run the entire length of the shank, would immediately see that the thing to do was what Graham did, i.e., invert the shank and the hinge plate.

* * *

We find no nonobvious facets in the '798 arrangement. The wear and repair claims were sufficient to overcome the patent examiner's original conclusions as to the validity of the patent. However, some of the prior art, notably Glencoe, was not before him. There the hinge plate is below the shank but, as the courts below found, all of the elements in the '798 patent are present in the Glencoe structure. Furthermore, even though the position of the shank and hinge plate appears reversed in Glencoe, the mechanical operation is identical. The shank there pivots about the underside of the stirrup, which in Glencoe is above the shank. In other words, the stirrup in Glencoe serves exactly the same function as the heel of the hinge plate in '798. The mere shifting of the wear point to the heel of the '798 hinge plate from the stirrup of Glencoe—itself a part of the hinge plate—presents no operative mechanical distinctions, much less nonobvious differences.

* * *

NOTES

1. "Person Having Ordinary Skill in the Art." Who qualifies as a person having ordinary skill in the art? Sometimes abbreviated as PHOSITA, the person having ordinary skill in the art of patent law is comparable to the hypothetical reasonable person used to decide many legal issues. In the PHOSITA standard, the emphasis is on "ordinary." To determine "ordinary skill" one must take into account several factors. In *Environmental Designs, Ltd. v. Union Oil Co.*, 713 F.2d 693, 697 (Fed.Cir.1983), *cert. denied*, 464 U.S. 1043, 104 S.Ct. 709, 79 L.Ed.2d 173 (1984), the court listed six factors relevant to a determination of ordinary skill: the education of the inventor, the types of problems encountered in the art, prior art solutions, the rapidity of innovation, the sophistication of technology, and the educational level of workers active in the field. In *International Cellucotton Prods. Co. v. Sterilek Co.*, 94 F.2d 10 (2d Cir. 1938), when attempting to discern a PHOSITA's skill, Judge Hand said "we are to impute to him knowledge of all that is not only in his immediate field, but in all fields nearly akin to that field." Thus, a PHOSITA presumptively has comprehensive knowledge of all pertinent art, despite possessing only "ordinary skill."

2. Secondary Considerations. The Court in *Graham* put forth secondary considerations for a finding of obviousness: "Such secondary considerations as commercial success, long felt but unsolved needs, failure of others, etc., might be utilized to give light to the circumstances surrounding the origin of the subject matter sought to be patented. As indicia of obviousness or nonobviousness, these inquiries may have relevancy."

In *Hybritech, Inc. v. Monoclonal Antibodies, Inc.*, 802 F.2d 1367 (Fed. Cir. 1986), *cert. denied*, 480 U.S. 947, 107 S.Ct. 1606, 94 L.Ed.2d 792 (1987), the Federal Circuit reversed a finding of obviousness based in part on secondary considerations. The invention in question, monoclonal antibodies used in immunometric assays, was capable of detecting such biological conditions as pregnancy, cancer growth hormone deficiency, and hepatitis faster, and more accurately, than polyclonal antibody assays. Although references predicted the use of monoclonal antibodies in assays, the court held that the invention was not obvious. The court stated: "[o]bjective evidence such as commercial success, failure of others, long-felt need, and unexpected results must be considered before a conclusion on obviousness is reached and is not merely 'icing on the cake,' as the district court stated at trial." The court supported its finding of nonobviousness by pointing out Hybritech's commercial success that resulted in a sales increase of over seven million dollars in one year.

In *Merck & Co. v. Teva Pharm. USA, Inc.*, 395 F.3d 1364 (Fed. Cir. 2005), on the other hand, the Federal Circuit rejected evidence of Merck's commercial success as unpersuasive. Under another patent, Merck had the right to exclude others from using a weekly dosing schedule that helped to minimize commercial competition. The Federal Circuit held, "in this context that fact has minimal probative value on the issue of obviousness." The court reasoned, "Commercial success is relevant because the law presumes an idea would successfully have been brought to market sooner, in response to market forces, had the idea been obvious to persons skilled in the art. Thus, the law deems evidence of (1) commercial success, and (2) some causal relation or "nexus" between an invention and commercial success of a product embodying that invention, probative of whether an invention was non-obvious." The court found Merck's patent for Fosamax invalid on grounds of obviousness.

3. More on Secondary Considerations—Teaching Away and Suggestions in the Prior Art. Some other factors to be considered when evaluating obviousness are whether prior references teach that a practice is unadvisable, or whether a modification produces new and unexpected results when compared to the prior references.

In *Arkie Lures, Inc. v. Gene Larew Tackle, Inc.*, 119 F.3d 953 (Fed. Cir. 1997), Larew, a retired engineer, invented a salty plastisol fishing lure. Manufacturers were skeptical of Larew's idea because salt might reduce the plastic's tensile strength and because mixing salt with plastic might cause an explosion. Despite the skepticism, Larew prevailed and found a manufacturer willing to produce his lures that were an instant commercial success. The Federal Circuit reversed the lower court's finding of obviousness. Conversely, in *In re Huang*, 100 F.3d 135 (Fed. Cir. 1996), results expected of a person having ordinary skill in the art led to a showing of obviousness. The claimed invention was a shock-absorbing tennis grip where the polyurethane/textile ratio was 0.180. Because prior art disclosed that polyurethane/textile ratios between 0.1111 and 0.142 increased shock absorption, the court held that Huang's increase of the ratio to 0.180 was obvious.

4. *Analogous Prior Art.* For purpose of Section 103 analysis there are limitations on which prior art an invention may be compared to. In *In re Clay*, 966 F.2d 656 (Fed. Cir. 1992), the Federal Circuit reversed a finding of obviousness by the Board of Patent Appeals and Interferences. The process in question was one for storing refined liquid hydrocarbon product in a storage tank that had a dead volume between the tank bottom and the outlet port. The process involved adding gel to the tank to displace the remaining liquid hydrocarbon, and then dissolving the gel with a degrading agent. The Board of Patent Appeals and Interferences compared the invention to two other patents: Hetherington's '294 patent on displacing dead space liquid with inflatable bladders and Sydansk's '949 patent on improving oil production by producing the permeability of hydrocarbon bearing formation using a gel.

The Federal Circuit found that "[a]lthough § 103 does not, by its terms, define the 'art to which [the] subject matter [sought to be patented] pertains,' this determination is frequently couched in terms of whether the art is analogous or not, i.e., whether the art is 'too remote to be treated as prior art.'" The court also set two criteria for determining whether prior art is analogous: (1) whether the art is from the same field of endeavor, regardless of the problem addressed, and (2) if the reference is not within the field of the inventor's endeavor, whether the reference is still reasonably pertinent to the particular problem with which the inventor is involved. The court held that Sydansk's '949 patent was in the field of endeavor of extraction, whereas Clay's invention was in the field of endeavor of storage.

5. *Standards of Obviousness.* There have been a number of standards for obviousness over the years: "more than combining references" (*Great Atlantic & Pacific Tea Co.*), "flash of creative genius" (*Cuno*), and "synergism" *Sakraida v. Ag Pro, Inc.*, 425 U.S. 273, 96 S.Ct. 1532, 47 L.Ed.2d 784 (1976). All of which have been discredited by either Section 103, or by *Stratoflex, Inc. v. Aeroquip Corp.*, 713 F.2d 1530 (Fed. Cir. 1983). In *Stratoflex*, polytetrafluoroethylene (PTFE) tubing was the invention in dispute. The Federal Circuit held:

> A requirement for "synergism" or a "synergistic effect" is nowhere found in the statute, 35 U.S.C. When present, for example in a chemical case, synergism may point toward nonobviousness, but its absence has no place in evaluating the evidence on obviousness. The more objective findings suggested in Graham, supra, are drawn from the language of the statute and are fully adequate guides for evaluating the evidence relating to compliance with 35 U.S.C. § 103 . . .

> The reference to a "combination patent" is equally without support in the statute. There is no warrant for judicial classification of patents, whether into "combination" patents and some other unnamed and undefined class or otherwise. Nor is there warrant for differing treatment or consideration of patents based on a judicially devised label. Reference to "combination" patents is, moreover, meaningless. Virtually all patents are "combination patents," if by that label one intends to describe

patents having claims to inventions formed of a combination of elements. It is difficult to visualize, at least in the mechanical-structural arts, a "non-combination" invention, i.e., an invention consisting of a single element. Such inventions, if they exist, are rare indeed.

Id. at 1540.

E. COMBINING REFERENCES

After the Federal Circuit was created in 1982, the court provided uniformity to the law of obviousness by emphasizing both Section 103 and *Graham*. To guard against hindsight-based analysis when combining prior art references, the court also developed the teaching-suggestion-motivation test.

As the test was applied for over 15 years, some commentators, including the authors, were concerned that the Federal Circuit's application of the teaching-suggestion-motivation test lowered the most important requirement for patentability. A Motion for Leave to File Amicus Curiae Brief and Brief of Twenty–Four Intellectual Property Law Professors As Amici Curiae in Support of Petitioner, *KSR Intern. Co. v. Teleflex, Inc.*, 550 U.S. 398, 127 S.Ct. 1727, 167 L.Ed.2d 705 (2007), 2005 WL 1334163. In the following case, the Supreme Court considered the appropriate test for determining nonobviousness.

KSR INTERNATIONAL CO. v. TELEFLEX INC.

Supreme Court of the United States, 2007.
550 U.S. 398, 127 S.Ct. 1727, 167 L.Ed.2d 705.

JUSTICE KENNEDY delivered the opinion of the Court.

Teleflex Incorporated and its subsidiary Technology Holding Company-both referred to here as Teleflex-sued KSR International Company for patent infringement. The patent at issue, United States Patent No. 6,237,565 B1, is entitled "Adjustable Pedal Assembly With Electronic Throttle Control." The patentee is Steven J. Engelgau, and the patent is referred to as "the Engelgau patent." Teleflex holds the exclusive license to the patent.

Claim 4 of the Engelgau patent describes a mechanism for combining an electronic sensor with an adjustable automobile pedal so the pedal's position can be transmitted to a computer that controls the throttle in the vehicle's engine. When Teleflex accused KSR of infringing the Engelgau patent by adding an electronic sensor to one of KSR's previously designed pedals, KSR countered that claim 4 was invalid under the Patent Act, 35 U.S.C. § 103, because its subject matter was obvious.

Section 103 forbids issuance of a patent when "the differences between the subject matter sought to be patented and the prior art are such that the subject matter as a whole would have been obvious at the time the invention was made to a person having ordinary skill in the art to which said subject matter pertains."

In *Graham v. John Deere Co. of Kansas City*, 383 U.S. 1, 86 S.Ct. 684, 15 L.Ed.2d 545 (1966), the Court set out a framework for applying the statutory language of § 103, language itself based on the logic of the earlier decision in *Hotchkiss v. Greenwood*, 11 How. 248, 13 L.Ed. 683 (1851), and its progeny. The analysis is objective:

> "Under § 103, the scope and content of the prior art are to be determined; differences between the prior art and the claims at issue are to be ascertained; and the level of ordinary skill in the pertinent art resolved. Against this background the obviousness or nonobviousness of the subject matter is determined. Such secondary considerations as commercial success, long felt but unsolved needs, failure of others, etc., might be utilized to give light to the circumstances surrounding the origin of the subject matter sought to be patented."

While the sequence of these questions might be reordered in any particular case, the factors continue to define the inquiry that controls. If a court, or patent examiner, conducts this analysis and concludes the claimed subject matter was obvious, the claim is invalid under § 103.

Seeking to resolve the question of obviousness with more uniformity and consistency, the Court of Appeals for the Federal Circuit has employed an approach referred to by the parties as the "teaching, suggestion, or motivation" test (TSM test), under which a patent claim is only proved obvious if "some motivation or suggestion to combine the prior art teachings" can be found in the prior art, the nature of the problem, or the knowledge of a person having ordinary skill in the art. KSR challenges that test, or at least its application in this case. Because the Court of Appeals addressed the question of obviousness in a manner contrary to § 103 and our precedents, we granted certiorari. We now reverse.

I

* * *

B

KSR, a Canadian company, manufactures and supplies auto parts, including pedal systems. Ford Motor Company hired KSR in 1998 to supply an adjustable pedal system for various lines of automobiles with cable-actuated throttle controls. KSR developed an adjustable mechanical pedal for Ford and obtained U.S. Patent No. 6,151,986 (filed July 16, 1999) ('986) for the design. In 2000, KSR was chosen by General Motors Corporation (GMC or GM) to supply adjustable pedal systems for Chevrolet and GMC light trucks that used engines with computer-controlled throttles. To make the '986 pedal compatible with the trucks, KSR merely took that design and added a modular sensor.

Teleflex is a rival to KSR in the design and manufacture of adjustable pedals. As noted, it is the exclusive licensee of the Engelgau patent. Engelgau filed the patent application on August 22, 2000 as a continuation of a previous application for U.S. Patent No. 6,109,241, which was filed on

January 26, 1999. He has sworn he invented the patent's subject matter
on February 14, 1998. The Engelgau patent discloses an adjustable electronic pedal described in the specification as a "simplified vehicle control
pedal assembly that is less expensive, and which uses fewer parts and is
easier to package within the vehicle." Engelgau, col. 2, lines 2–5. Claim 4
of the patent, at issue here, describes:

> "A vehicle control pedal apparatus comprising:
>
> a support adapted to be mounted to a vehicle structure;
>
> an adjustable pedal assembly having a pedal arm moveable in for[e]
> and aft directions with respect to said support;
>
> a pivot for pivotally supporting said adjustable pedal assembly with
> respect to said support and defining a pivot axis; and
>
> an electronic control attached to said support for controlling a vehicle
> system;
>
> said apparatus characterized by said electronic control being respon-
> sive to said pivot for providing a signal that corresponds to pedal arm
> position as said pedal arm pivots about said pivot axis between rest
> and applied positions wherein the position of said pivot remains
> constant while said pedal arm moves in fore and aft directions with
> respect to said pivot."

We agree with the District Court that the claim discloses "a position-
adjustable pedal assembly with an electronic pedal position sensor attached to the support member of the pedal assembly. Attaching the sensor
to the support member allows the sensor to remain in a fixed position
while the driver adjusts the pedal." 298 F.Supp.2d, at 586–587.

Before issuing the Engelgau patent the U.S. Patent and Trademark
Office (PTO) rejected one of the patent claims that was similar to, but
broader than, the present claim 4. The claim did not include the requirement that the sensor be placed on a fixed pivot point. The PTO concluded
the claim was an obvious combination of the prior art disclosed in Redding
and Smith, explaining:

> " 'Since the prior ar[t] references are from the field of endeavor, the
> purpose disclosed . . . would have been recognized in the pertinent art
> of Redding. Therefore it would have been obvious . . . to provide the
> device of Redding with the . . . means attached to a support member
> as taught by Smith.' "

In other words Redding provided an example of an adjustable pedal and
Smith explained how to mount a sensor on a pedal's support structure,
and the rejected patent claim merely put these two teachings together.

Although the broader claim was rejected, claim 4 was later allowed
because it included the limitation of a fixed pivot point, which distinguished the design from Redding's. Engelgau had not included Asano
among the prior art references, and Asano was not mentioned in the
patent's prosecution. Thus, the PTO did not have before it an adjustable

pedal with a fixed pivot point. The patent issued on May 29, 2001 and was assigned to Teleflex.

Upon learning of KSR's design for GM, Teleflex sent a warning letter informing KSR that its proposal would violate the Engelgau patent. " 'Teleflex believes that any supplier of a product that combines an adjustable pedal with an electronic throttle control necessarily employs technology covered by one or more' " of Teleflex's patents. *Id.*, at 585. KSR refused to enter a royalty arrangement with Teleflex; so Teleflex sued for infringement, asserting * * * that KSR's pedal system for GM infringed claim 4 of the Engelgau patent. * * *

C

The District Court granted summary judgment in KSR's favor. After reviewing the pertinent history of pedal design, the scope of the Engelgau patent, and the relevant prior art, the court considered the validity of the contested claim. By direction of 35 U.S.C. § 282, an issued patent is presumed valid. The District Court applied *Graham*'s framework to determine whether under summary-judgment standards KSR had overcome the presumption and demonstrated that claim 4 was obvious in light of the prior art in existence when the claimed subject matter was invented.

The District Court determined, in light of the expert testimony and the parties' stipulations, that the level of ordinary skill in pedal design was " 'an undergraduate degree in mechanical engineering (or an equivalent amount of industry experience) [and] familiarity with pedal control systems for vehicles.' " 298 F.Supp.2d, at 590. The court then set forth the relevant prior art, including the patents and pedal designs described above.

Following *Graham*'s direction, the court compared the teachings of the prior art to the claims of Engelgau. It found "little difference." 298 F.Supp.2d, at 590. Asano taught everything contained in claim 4 except the use of a sensor to detect the pedal's position and transmit it to the computer controlling the throttle. That additional aspect was revealed in sources such as the '068 patent and the sensors used by Chevrolet.

Under the controlling cases from the Court of Appeals for the Federal Circuit, however, the District Court was not permitted to stop there. The court was required also to apply the TSM test. The District Court held KSR had satisfied the test. It reasoned (1) the state of the industry would lead inevitably to combinations of electronic sensors and adjustable pedals, (2) Rixon provided the basis for these developments, and (3) Smith taught a solution to the wire chafing problems in Rixon, namely locating the sensor on the fixed structure of the pedal. This could lead to the combination of Asano, or a pedal like it, with a pedal position sensor.

The conclusion that the Engelgau design was obvious was supported, in the District Court's view, by the PTO's rejection of the broader version of claim 4. Had Engelgau included Asano in his patent application, it reasoned, the PTO would have found claim 4 to be an obvious combination of Asano and Smith, as it had found the broader version an obvious combination of Redding and Smith. As a final matter, the District Court held that the secondary factor of Teleflex's commercial success with pedals based on Engelgau's design did not alter its conclusion. The District Court granted summary judgment for KSR.

With principal reliance on the TSM test, the Court of Appeals reversed. It ruled the District Court had not been strict enough in applying the test, having failed to make " 'finding[s] as to the specific understanding or principle within the knowledge of a skilled artisan that would have motivated one with no knowledge of [the] invention' ... to attach an electronic control to the support bracket of the Asano assembly." 119 Fed.Appx., at 288. The Court of Appeals held that the District Court was incorrect that the nature of the problem to be solved satisfied this requirement because unless the "prior art references address[ed] the precise problem that the patentee was trying to solve," the problem would not motivate an inventor to look at those references.

Here, the Court of Appeals found, the Asano pedal was designed to solve the " 'constant ratio problem' " that is, to ensure that the force required to depress the pedal is the same no matter how the pedal is adjusted-whereas Engelgau sought to provide a simpler, smaller, cheaper adjustable electronic pedal. As for Rixon, the court explained, that pedal suffered from the problem of wire chafing but was not designed to solve it. In the court's view Rixon did not teach anything helpful to Engelgau's purpose. Smith, in turn, did not relate to adjustable pedals and did not "necessarily go to the issue of motivation to attach the electronic control on the support bracket of the pedal assembly." When the patents were interpreted in this way, the Court of Appeals held, they would not have led a person of ordinary skill to put a sensor on the sort of pedal described in Asano.

That it might have been obvious to try the combination of Asano and a sensor was likewise irrelevant, in the court's view, because " ' "[o]bvious to try" has long been held not to constitute obviousness.' "

The Court of Appeals also faulted the District Court's consideration of the PTO's rejection of the broader version of claim 4. * * * [T]he court held, the District Court was obliged first to presume that the issued patent was valid and then to render its own independent judgment of obviousness based on a review of the prior art. The fact that the PTO had rejected the broader version of claim 4 * * * had no place in that analysis.

The Court of Appeals further held that genuine issues of material fact precluded summary judgment. * * *

II

A

We begin by rejecting the rigid approach of the Court of Appeals. Throughout this Court's engagement with the question of obviousness, our cases have set forth an expansive and flexible approach inconsistent with the way the Court of Appeals applied its TSM test here. To be sure, *Graham* recognized the need for "uniformity and definiteness." Yet the principles laid down in Graham reaffirmed the "functional approach" of *Hotchkiss*, 11 How. 248, 13 L.Ed. 683. To this end, *Graham* set forth a broad inquiry and invited courts, where appropriate, to look at any secondary considerations that would prove instructive.

Neither the enactment of § 103 nor the analysis in Graham disturbed this Court's earlier instructions concerning the need for caution in granting a patent based on the combination of elements found in the prior art . For over a half century, the Court has held that a "patent for a combination which only unites old elements with no change in their respective functions ... obviously withdraws what is already known into the field of its monopoly and diminishes the resources available to skillful men." *Great Atlantic & Pacific Tea Co. v. Supermarket Equipment Corp.*, 340 U.S. 147, 152, 71 S.Ct. 127, 95 L.Ed. 162 (1950). This is a principal reason for declining to allow patents for what is obvious. The combination of familiar elements according to known methods is likely to be obvious when it does no more than yield predictable results. * * *

* * *

* * * When a work is available in one field of endeavor, design incentives and other market forces can prompt variations of it, either in the same field or a different one. If a person of ordinary skill can implement a predictable variation, § 103 likely bars its patentability. For the same reason, if a technique has been used to improve one device, and a person of ordinary skill in the art would recognize that it would improve similar devices in the same way, using the technique is obvious unless its actual application is beyond his or her skill. * * * [A] court must ask whether the improvement is more than the predictable use of prior art elements according to their established functions.

Following these principles may be more difficult in other cases than it is here because the claimed subject matter may involve more than the simple substitution of one known element for another or the mere application of a known technique to a piece of prior art ready for the improvement. Often, it will be necessary for a court to look to interrelated teachings of multiple patents; the effects of demands known to the design community or present in the marketplace; and the background knowledge possessed by a person having ordinary skill in the art, all in order to determine whether there was an apparent reason to combine the known elements in the fashion claimed by the patent at issue. To facilitate review, this analysis should be made explicit. As our precedents make clear, however, the analysis need not seek out precise teachings directed to the specific subject matter of the challenged claim, for a court can take account of the inferences and creative steps that a person of ordinary skill in the art would employ.

B

When it first established the requirement of demonstrating a teaching, suggestion, or motivation to combine known elements in order to show that the combination is obvious, the Court of Customs and Patent Appeals captured a helpful insight. As is clear from cases such as [*United States v.*] *Adams* [383 U.S. 39 (1966)], a patent composed of several elements is not proved obvious merely by demonstrating that each of its elements was, independently, known in the prior art. Although common sense directs one to look with care at a patent application that claims as innovation the combination of two known devices according to their established functions, it can be important to identify a reason that would have prompted a person of ordinary skill in the relevant field to combine the elements in the way the claimed new invention does. This is so because inventions in most, if not all, instances rely upon building blocks long since uncovered, and claimed discoveries almost of necessity will be combinations of what, in some sense, is already known.

Helpful insights, however, need not become rigid and mandatory formulas; and when it is so applied, the TSM test is incompatible with our precedents. The obviousness analysis cannot be confined by a formalistic conception of the words teaching, suggestion, and motivation, or by overemphasis on the importance of published articles and the explicit content of issued patents. The diversity of inventive pursuits and of modern technology counsels against limiting the analysis in this way. In many fields it may be that there is little discussion of obvious techniques or combinations, and it often may be the case that market demand, rather than scientific literature, will drive design trends. Granting patent protection to advances that would occur in the ordinary course without real innovation retards progress and may, in the case of patents combining previously known elements, deprive prior inventions of their value or utility.

In the years since the Court of Customs and Patent Appeals set forth the essence of the TSM test, the Court of Appeals no doubt has applied the test in accord with these principles in many cases. There is no necessary inconsistency between the idea underlying the TSM test and the *Graham* analysis. But when a court transforms the general principle into a rigid rule that limits the obviousness inquiry, as the Court of Appeals did here, it errs.

C

The flaws in the analysis of the Court of Appeals relate for the most part to the court's narrow conception of the obviousness inquiry reflected in its application of the TSM test. In determining whether the subject matter of a patent claim is obvious, neither the particular motivation nor the avowed purpose of the patentee controls. What matters is the objective reach of the claim. If the claim extends to what is obvious, it is invalid under § 103. One of the ways in which a patent's subject matter can be proved obvious is by noting that there existed at the time of invention a known problem for which there was an obvious solution encompassed by the patent's claims.

The first error of the Court of Appeals in this case was to foreclose this reasoning by holding that courts and patent examiners should look only to the problem the patentee was trying to solve. The Court of Appeals failed to recognize that the problem motivating the patentee may be only one of many addressed by the patent's subject matter. The question is not whether the combination was obvious to the patentee but whether the combination was obvious to a person with ordinary skill in the art. Under the correct analysis, any need or problem known in the field of endeavor at the time of invention and addressed by the patent can provide a reason for combining the elements in the manner claimed.

The second error of the Court of Appeals lay in its assumption that a person of ordinary skill attempting to solve a problem will be led only to those elements of prior art designed to solve the same problem. The primary purpose of Asano was solving the constant ratio problem; so, the court concluded, an inventor considering how to put a sensor on an adjustable pedal would have no reason to consider putting it on the Asano pedal. Common sense teaches, however, that familiar items may have obvious uses beyond their primary purposes, and in many cases a person of ordinary skill will be able to fit the teachings of multiple patents together like pieces of a puzzle. Regardless of Asano's primary purpose, the design provided an obvious example of an adjustable pedal with a fixed pivot point; and the prior art was replete with patents indicating that a fixed pivot point was an ideal mount for a sensor. The idea that a designer hoping to make an adjustable electronic pedal would ignore Asano because Asano was designed to solve the constant ratio problem makes little sense. A person of ordinary skill is also a person of ordinary creativity, not an automaton.

The same constricted analysis led the Court of Appeals to conclude, in error, that a patent claim cannot be proved obvious merely by showing that the combination of elements was "obvious to try." When there is a design need or market pressure to solve a problem and there are a finite number of identified, predictable solutions, a person of ordinary skill has good reason to pursue the known options within his or her technical grasp. If this leads to the anticipated success, it is likely the product not of innovation but of ordinary skill and common sense. In that instance the fact that a combination was obvious to try might show that it was obvious under § 103.

The Court of Appeals, finally, drew the wrong conclusion from the risk of courts and patent examiners falling prey to hindsight bias. A factfinder should be aware, of course, of the distortion caused by hindsight bias and must be cautious of arguments reliant upon *ex post* reasoning. Rigid preventative rules that deny factfinders recourse to common sense, however, are neither necessary under our case law nor consistent with it.

We note the Court of Appeals has since elaborated a broader conception of the TSM test than was applied in the instant matter. *See, e.g., DyStar Textilfarben GmbH & Co. Deutschland KG v. C.H. Patrick Co.*, 464 F.3d 1356, 1367 (2006). Those decisions, of course, are not now before us and do not correct the errors of law made by the Court of Appeals in this case. The extent to which they may describe an analysis more consistent with our earlier precedents and our decision here is a matter for the Court of Appeals to consider in its future cases. What we hold is that the fundamental misunderstandings identified above led the Court of Appeals in this case to apply a test inconsistent with our patent law decisions.

III

When we apply the standards we have explained to the instant facts, claim 4 must be found obvious. We agree with and adopt the District Court's recitation of the relevant prior art and its determination of the level of ordinary skill in the field. As did the District Court, we see little difference between the teachings of Asano and Smith and the adjustable electronic pedal disclosed in claim 4 of the Engelgau patent. A person having ordinary skill in the art could have combined Asano with a pedal position sensor in a fashion encompassed by claim 4, and would have seen the benefits of doing so.

* * *

B

The District Court was correct to conclude that, as of the time Engelgau designed the subject matter in claim 4, it was obvious to a person of ordinary skill to combine Asano with a pivot-mounted pedal position sensor. There then existed a marketplace that created a strong incentive to convert mechanical pedals to electronic pedals, and the prior art taught a number of methods for achieving this advance. The Court of Appeals considered the issue too narrowly by, in effect, asking whether a pedal designer writing on a blank slate would have chosen both Asano and a modular sensor similar to the ones used in the Chevrolet truckline and disclosed in the '068 patent. The District Court employed this narrow inquiry as well, though it reached the correct result nevertheless. The proper question to have asked was whether a pedal designer of ordinary skill, facing the wide range of needs created by developments in the field of endeavor, would have seen a benefit to upgrading Asano with a sensor.

In automotive design, as in many other fields, the interaction of multiple components means that changing one component often requires the others to be modified as well. Technological developments made it clear that engines using computer-controlled throttles would become standard. As a result, designers might have decided to design new pedals from scratch; but they also would have had reason to make pre-existing pedals work with the new engines. Indeed, upgrading its own pre-existing model led KSR to design the pedal now accused of infringing the Engelgau patent.

For a designer starting with Asano, the question was where to attach the sensor. The consequent legal question, then, is whether a pedal designer of ordinary skill starting with Asano would have found it obvious to put the sensor on a fixed pivot point. The prior art discussed above leads us to the conclusion that attaching the sensor where both KSR and Engelgau put it would have been obvious to a person of ordinary skill.

The '936 patent taught the utility of putting the sensor on the pedal device, not in the engine. Smith, in turn, explained to put the sensor not on the pedal's footpad but instead on its support structure. And from the known wire-chafing problems of Rixon, and Smith's teaching that "the pedal assemblies must not precipitate any motion in the connecting wires," Smith, col. 1, lines 35–37, the designer would know to place the sensor on a nonmoving part of the pedal structure. The most obvious nonmoving point on the structure from which a sensor can easily detect the pedal's position is a pivot point. The designer, accordingly, would follow Smith in mounting the sensor on a pivot, thereby designing an adjustable electronic pedal covered by claim 4.

Just as it was possible to begin with the objective to upgrade Asano to work with a computer-controlled throttle, so too was it possible to take an adjustable electronic pedal like Rixon and seek an improvement that would avoid the wire-chafing problem. Following similar steps to those just explained, a designer would learn from Smith to avoid sensor movement and would come, thereby, to Asano because Asano disclosed an adjustable pedal with a fixed pivot.

Teleflex indirectly argues that the prior art taught away from attaching a sensor to Asano because Asano in its view is bulky, complex, and expensive. The only evidence Teleflex marshals in support of this argument, however, is the Radcliffe declaration, which merely indicates that Asano would not have solved Engelgau's goal of making a small, simple, and inexpensive pedal. * * * Teleflex may have made a plausible argument that Asano is inefficient as compared to Engelgau's preferred embodiment, but to judge Asano against Engelgau would be to engage in the very hindsight bias Teleflex rightly urges must be avoided. Accordingly, Teleflex has not shown anything in the prior art that taught away from the use of Asano.

Like the District Court, finally, we conclude Teleflex has shown no secondary factors to dislodge the determination that claim 4 is obvious. Proper application of *Graham* and our other precedents to these facts therefore leads to the conclusion that claim 4 encompassed obvious subject matter. As a result, the claim fails to meet the requirement of § 103.

We need not reach the question whether the failure to disclose Asano during the prosecution of Engelgau voids the presumption of validity given to issued patents, for claim 4 is obvious despite the presumption. We nevertheless think it appropriate to note that the rationale underlying the presumption-that the PTO, in its expertise, has approved the claim-seems much diminished here.

IV

A separate ground the Court of Appeals gave for reversing the order for summary judgment was the existence of a dispute over an issue of material fact. * * * Nothing in the declarations proffered by Teleflex prevented the District Court from reaching the careful conclusions underlying its order for summary judgment in this case.

* * *

We build and create by bringing to the tangible and palpable reality around us new works based on instinct, simple logic, ordinary inferences, extraordinary ideas, and sometimes even genius. These advances, once part of our shared knowledge, define a new threshold from which innovation starts once more. And as progress beginning from higher levels of achievement is expected in the normal course, the results of ordinary innovation are not the subject of exclusive rights under the patent laws. Were it otherwise patents might stifle, rather than promote, the progress of useful arts. See U.S. Const., Art. I, § 8, cl. 8. These premises led to the bar on patents claiming obvious subject matter established in *Hotchkiss* and codified in § 103. Application of the bar must not be confined within a test or formulation too constrained to serve its purpose.

KSR provided convincing evidence that mounting a modular sensor on a fixed pivot point of the Asano pedal was a design step well within the grasp of a person of ordinary skill in the relevant art. Its arguments, and the record, demonstrate that claim 4 of the Engelgau patent is obvious. In rejecting the District Court's rulings, the Court of Appeals analyzed the issue in a narrow, rigid manner inconsistent with § 103 and our precedents. The judgment of the Court of Appeals is reversed, and the case remanded for further proceedings consistent with this opinion.

NOTES

1. The *KSR* Court's reason to combine formulation is undoubtedly broader than the teaching-suggestion-motivation test, but what is the outer limit of the Court's holding? Did the *KSR* Court articulate what is not a reason to combine? Post–*KSR*, courts have been hesitant to hold patents invalid under Section 103, but the PTO has found religion in *KSR* and rejects many applications as obvious under Section 103. What is your opinion? Was the "teaching-suggestion-motivation test" too narrow? What are the pros and cons of having a narrow test?

2. Notice that the facts of *KSR* do not present good arguments for *Graham* secondary considerations of obviousness. How do the *Graham* secondary considerations of obviousness work in the *KSR* framework? Moreover, in *KSR*, the PHOSITA was not disputed. Does the *KSR* framework change the PHOSITA standard?

3. Obviousness in Biotechnology. In *In re Kubin*, 561 F.3d 1351 (Fed. Cir. 2009), the Federal Circuit refused "to cabin *KSR* to the 'predictable arts' (as opposed to the 'unpredictable art' of biotechnology)." *Id.* at 1360. Specifically, the court affirmed the Board of Patent Appeals and Interferences finding that the applicant's claim "to a classic biotechnology invention—the isolation and sequencing of a human gene that encodes a particular domain of a protein" was obvious. *Id.* at 1352.

4. Network Science and the Increase of Patents. Professor Strandburg analyzed the recent surge of patenting using "network science" which takes into account the role of relationship patterns in collective behavior. By studying citation references, the study demonstrated that a lower patentability standard is the most likely explanation of the increase in patenting rather than increased technological progress or the enlarged breadth of patented technologies. Katherine J. Strandburg et al., *Law and the Science of Networks: An Overview and an Application to the "Patent Explosion,"* 21 BERKELEY TECH. L.J. 1293 (2006).

F. DISCLOSURE AND CLAIMING: SECTION 112: SPECIFICATION AND OTHER APPLICATION REQUIREMENTS

Patent prosecution is the name given to the process of applying for patent protection. During the prosecution process, inventors interact with examiners from the United States Patent and Trademark Office. This interaction, which involves office actions and rejections, eventually determines what the inventor must disclose and what exclusionary rights are granted to him. This process establishes the quid pro quo of patent protection. Arguably, Section 112's requirements are the most important in the process of disclosing and claiming an invention.

Paragraphs one and two of Section 112 list four requirements: a written description, enablement, best mode, and particularly pointing out and distinctly claiming the subject matter regarded as the invention. Paragraphs three, four, and five list the two types of claims available, independent and dependent. Independent claims are not limited by any other claims whereas Dependent claims reference another claim and are bound by its limitations. Finally, paragraph six describes the claiming of an element using the means plus function language.

[1] The specification shall contain a written description of the invention, and of the manner and process of making and using it, in such full, clear, concise, and exact terms as to enable any person skilled in the art to which it pertains, or with which it is most nearly connected, to make and use the same, and shall set forth the best mode contemplated by the inventor of carrying out his invention.

[2] The specification shall conclude with one or more claims particularly pointing out and distinctly claiming the subject matter which the applicant regards as his invention.

[3]   A claim may be written in independent or, if the nature of the case admits, in dependent or multiple dependent form.

[4]   Subject to the following paragraph, a claim in dependent form shall contain a reference to a claim previously set forth and then specify a further limitation of the subject matter claimed. A claim in dependent form shall be construed to incorporate by reference all the limitations of the claim to which it refers.

[5]   A claim in multiple dependent form shall contain a reference, in the alternative only, to more than one claim previously set forth and then specify a further limitation of the subject matter claimed. A multiple dependent claim shall not serve as a basis for any other multiple dependent claim. A multiple dependent claim shall be construed to incorporate by reference all the limitations of the particular claim in relation to which it is being considered.

[6]   An element in a claim for a combination may be expressed as a means or step for performing a specified function without the recital of structure, material, or acts in support thereof, and such claim shall be construed to cover the corresponding structure, material, or acts described in the specification and equivalents thereof.

35 U.S.C. § 112.

1.   The Enablement Requirement

CONSOLIDATED ELECTRIC LIGHT CO. v. McKEESPORT LIGHT CO.

Supreme Court of the United States, 1895.
159 U.S. 465, 16 S.Ct. 75, 40 L.Ed. 221.

This was a bill in equity, filed by the Consolidated Electric Light Company against the McKeesport Light Company, to recover damages for the infringement of letters patent No. 317,076, issued May 12, 1885, to the Electro–Dynamic Light Company, assignee of Sawyer and Man, for an electric light. The defendants justified under certain patents to Thomas A. Edison, particularly No. 223,898, issued January 27, 1880; denied the novelty and utility of the complainant's patent; and averred that the same had been fraudulently and illegally procured. The real defendant was the Edison Electric Light Company, and the case involved a contest between what are known as the Sawyer and Man and the Edison systems of electric lighting.

In their application, Sawyer and Man stated that their invention related to "that class of electric lamps employing an incandescent conductor enclosed in a transparent, hermetically sealed vessel or chamber, from which oxygen is excluded, and ... more especially to the incandescing conductor, its substance, its form, and its combination with the other elements composing the lamp. Its object is to secure a cheap and effective apparatus; and our improvement consists, first, of the combination, in a lamp chamber, composed wholly of glass, as described in patent No. 205,144," upon which this patent was declared to be an improvement, "of an incandescing conductor of carbon made from a vegetable fibrous material, in contradistinction to a similar conductor made from mineral or gas carbon, and also in the form of such conductor so made from such vegetable carbon, and combined in the lighting circuit with the exhausted chamber of the lamp."

The following drawings exhibit the substance of the invention:

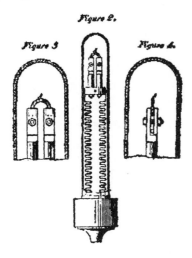

The specification further stated that:

In the practice of our invention, we have made use of carbonized paper, and also wood carbon. We have also used such conductors or burners of various shapes, such as pieces with their lower ends secured to their respective supports, and having their upper ends united so as to form an inverted V-shaped burner. We have also used conductors of varying contours,—that is, with rectangular bends instead of curvilinear ones; but we prefer the arch shape.

No especial description of making the illuminating carbon conductors, described in this specification, and making the subject-matter of this improvement, is thought necessary, as any of the ordinary methods of forming the material to be carbonized to the desired shape and size, and carbonizing it while confined in retorts in powdered carbon, substantially according to the methods in practice before the date of this improvement, may be adopted in the practice thereof by any one skilled in the arts appertaining to the making of carbons for electric lighting or for other use in the arts.

* * *

The advantages resulting from the manufacture of the carbon from vegetable fibrous or textile material instead of mineral or gas carbon are many. Among them may be mentioned the convenience afforded for cutting and making the conductor in the desired form and size, the purity and equality of the carbon obtained, its susceptibility to tempering, both as to hardness and resistance, and its toughness and durability. We have used such burners in closed or hermetically sealed transparent chambers, in a vacuum, in nitrogen gas, and in hydrogen gas; but we have obtained the best results in a vacuum, or an attenuated atmosphere of nitrogen gas, the great desideratum being to exclude oxygen or other gases capable of combining with carbon at high temperatures from the incandescing chamber, as is well understood.

The claims were as follows:

(1) An incandescing conductor for an electric lamp, of carbonized fibrous or textile material, and of an arch or horseshoe shape, substantially as hereinbefore set forth.

(2) The combination, substantially as hereinbefore set forth, of an electric circuit and an incandescing conductor of carbonized fibrous material, included in and forming part of said circuit, and a transparent, hermetically sealed chamber, in which the conductor is enclosed.

(3) The incandescing conductor for an electric lamp, formed of carbonized paper, substantially as described.

(4) An incandescing electric lamp consists of the following elements in combination: First, an illuminating chamber made wholly of glass hermetically sealed, and out of which all carbon-consuming gas has been exhausted or driven; second, an electric-circuit conductor passing through the glass wall of said chamber, and hermetically sealed therein, as described; third, an illuminating conductor in said circuit, and forming part thereof within said chamber, consisting of carbon made from a fibrous or textile material, having the form of an arch or loop, substantially as described, for the purpose specified.

The commercial Edison lamp used by the appellee, and which is illustrated below, is composed of a burner, A, made of carbonized bamboo of a peculiar quality, discovered by Mr. Edison to be highly useful for the purpose, and having a length of about 6 inches, a diameter of about 5/1000 of an inch, and an electrical resistance of upward of 100 ohms. This filament of carbon is bent into the form of a loop, and its ends are secured by good electrical and mechanical connections to two fine platinum wires, B, B. These wires pass through a glass stem, C, the glass being melted and fused upon the platinum wires. A glass globe, D, is fused to the glass stem, C. This glass globe has originally attached to it, at the point d, a glass tube, by means of which a connection is made with highly organized and refined exhausting apparatus, which produces in the globe a high vacuum, whereupon the glass tube is melted off by a flame, and the globe is closed by the fusion of the glass at the point d.

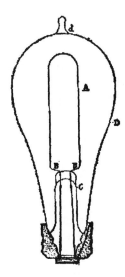

Upon a hearing in the circuit court before Mr. Justice Bradley, upon pleadings and proofs, the court held the patent to be invalid, and dismissed the bill. Thereupon complainant appealed to this court.

MR. JUSTICE BROWN, after stating the facts in the foregoing language, delivered the opinion of the court.

In order to obtain a complete understanding of the scope of the Sawyer and Man patent, it is desirable to consider briefly the state of the art at the time the application was originally made, which was in January, 1880.

Two general forms of electric illumination had for many years been the subject of experiments more or less successful, one of which was known as the ''arc light,'' produced by the passage of a current of electricity between the points of two carbon pencils placed end to end, and slightly separated from each other. In its passage from one point to the other through the air, the electric current took the form of an arc, and gave the name to the light. This form of light had been produced by Sir Humphry Davy as early as 1810, and, by successive improvements in the carbon pencils and in their relative adjustment to each other, had come into general use as a means of lighting streets, halls, and other large spaces; but by reason of its intensity, the uncertain and flickering character of the light, and the rapid consumption of the carbon pencils, it was wholly unfitted for domestic use. The second form of illumination is what is known as the 'incandescent system,' and consists generally in the passage of a current of electricity through a continuous strip or piece of refractory material, which is a conductor of electricity, but a poor conductor; in other words, a conductor offering a considerable resistance to the flow of the current through it. It was discovered early in this century that various substances might be heated to a white heat by passing a sufficiently strong current of electricity through them. The production of a light in this way does not in any manner depend upon the consumption or wearing away of the conductor, as it does in the arc light. The third system was a combination of the two others, but it never seems to have come into general use, and is unimportant in giving a history of the art.

For many years prior to 1880, experiments had been made by a large number of persons, in various countries, with a view to the production of an incandescent light which could be made available for domestic purposes, and could compete with gas in the matter of expense. Owing partly to a failure to find a proper material, which should burn but not consume, partly to the difficulty of obtaining a perfect vacuum in the globe in which the light was suspended, and partly to a misapprehension of the true principle of incandescent lighting, these experiments had not been attended with success; although it had been demonstrated as early as 1845 that, whatever material was used, the conductor must be enclosed in an art-tight bulb, to prevent it from being consumed by the oxygen in the atmosphere. The chief difficulty was that the carbon burners were subject to a rapid disintegration or evaporation, which electricians assumed was due to the disrupting action of the electric current, and hence the conclusion was reached that carbon contained in itself the elements of its own destruction, and was not a suitable material for the burner of an incandescent lamp.

It is admitted that the lamp described in the Sawyer and Man patent is no longer in use, and was never a commercial success; that it does not embody the principle of high resistance with a small illuminating surface; that it does not have the filament burner of the modern incandescent lamp; that the lamp chamber is defective; and that the lamp manufactured by the complainant, and put upon the market, is substantially the Edison lamp; but it is said that, in the conductor used by Edison (a particular part of the stem of the bamboo, lying directly beneath the siliceous cuticle, the peculiar fitness for which purpose was undoubtedly discovered by him), he made use of a fibrous or textile material covered by the patent to Sawyer and Man, and is therefore an infringer. It was admitted, however, that the third claim—for a conductor of carbonized paper—was not infringed.

The two main defenses to this patent are (1) that it is defective upon its face, in attempting to monopolize the use of all fibrous and textile materials for the purpose of electric illuminations; and (2) that Sawyer and Man were not in fact the first to discover that these were better adapted than mineral carbons to such purposes.

Is the complainant entitled to a monopoly of all fibrous and textile materials for incandescent conductors? If the patentees had discovered in fibrous and textile substances a quality common to them all, or to them generally, as distinguishing them from other materials, such as minerals, etc., and such quality or characteristic adapted them peculiarly to incandescent conductors, such claim might not be too broad. If, for instance, minerals or porcelains had always been used for a particular purpose, and a person should take out a patent for a similar article of wood, and woods generally were adapted to that purpose, the claim might not be too broad, though defendant used wood of a different kind from that of the patentee. But if woods generally were not adapted to the purpose, and yet the patentee had discovered a wood possessing certain qualities, which gave it a peculiar fitness for such purpose, it would not constitute an infringement for another to discover and use a different kind of wood, which was found to contain similar or superior qualities. The present case is an apt illustration of this principle. Sawyer and Man supposed they had discovered in carbonized paper the best material for an incandescent conductor. Instead of confining themselves to carbonized paper, as they might properly have done, and in fact did in their third claim, they made a broad claim for every fibrous or textile material, when in fact an examination of over 6,000 vegetable growths showed that none of them possessed the peculiar qualities that fitted them for that purpose. Was everybody, then, precluded by this broad claim from making further investigation? We think not.

The injustice of so holding is manifest in view of the experiments made, and continued for several months, by Mr. Edison and his assistants, among the different species of vegetable growth, for the purpose of ascertaining the one best adapted to an incandescent conductor. Of these he found suitable for his purpose only about three species of bamboo, one species of cane from the valley of the Amazon (impossible to be procured in quantities on account of the climate), and one or two species of fibers from the agave family. Of the special bamboo, the walls of which have a thickness of about 3/8 of an inch, he used only about 20/1000 of an inch in thickness. In this portion of the bamboo the fibers are more nearly parallel, the cell walls are apparently smallest, and the pithy matter between the fibers is at its minimum. It seems that carbon filaments cannot be made of wood,—that is, exogenous vegetable growth,—because the fibers are not parallel, and the longitudinal fibers are intercepted by radial fibers. The cells composing the fibers are all so large that the resulting carbon is very porous and friable. Lamps made of this material proved of no commercial value. After trying as many as 30 or 40 different woods of exogenous growth, he gave them up as hopeless. But finally, while experimenting with a bamboo strip which formed the edge of a palm-leaf fan, cut into filaments, he obtained surprising results. After microscopic examination of the material, he dispatched a man to Japan to make arrangements for securing the bamboo in quantities. It seems that the characteristic of the bamboo which makes it particularly suitable is that the fibers run more nearly parallel than in other species of wood. Owing to this, it can be cut up into filaments having parallel fibers, running throughout their length, and producing a homogeneous carbon. There is no generic quality, however, in vegetable fibers, because they are fibrous, which adapts them to the purpose. Indeed, the fibers are rather a disadvantage. If the bamboo grew solid, without fibers, but had its peculiar cellular formation, it would be a perfect material, and incandescent lamps would last at least six times as long as at present. All vegetable fibrous growths do not have a suitable cellular structure. In some the cells are so large that they are valueless for that purpose. No exogenous, and very few endogenous, growths are suitable. The messenger whom he dispatched to different parts of Japan and China sent him about 40 different kinds of bamboo, in such quantities as to enable him to make a number of lamps, and from a test of these different species he ascertained which was best for the purpose. From this it appears very clearly that there is no such quality common to fibrous and textile substances generally as makes them suitable for an incandescent conductor, and that the bamboo which was finally pitched upon, and is now generally used, was not selected because it was of vegetable growth, but because it contained certain peculiarities in its fibrous structure which distinguished it from every other fibrous substance. The question really is whether the imperfectly successful experiments of Sawyer and Man, with carbonized paper and wood carbon, conceding all that is claimed for them, authorize them to put under tribute the results of the brilliant discoveries made by others.

It is required by Rev. St. § 4888, that the application shall contain "a written description of the device, and of the manner and process of making constructing, compounding, and using it in such full, clear, concise, and exact terms as to enable any person, skilled in the art or science to which it appertains or with which it is most nearly connected, to make, construct, compound, and use the same." The object of this is to apprise the public of what the patentee claims as his own, the courts of what they are called upon to construe, and competing manufacturers and dealers of exactly what they are bound to avoid. *Grant v. Raymond*, 6 Pet. 218, 247. If the description be so vague and uncertain that no one can tell, except by independent experiments, how to construct the patented device, the patent is void.

* * *

Applying this principle to the patent under consideration, how would it be possible for a person to know what fibrous or textile material was adapted to the purpose of an incandescent conductor, except by the most careful and painstaking experimentation? If, as before observed, there were some general quality, running through the whole fibrous and textile kingdom, which distinguished it from every other, and gave it a peculiar fitness for the particular purpose, the man who discovered such quality might justly be entitled to a patent; but that is not the case here. An examination of materials of this class carried on for months revealed nothing that seemed to be adapted to the purpose; and even the carbonized paper and wood carbons specified in the patent, experiments with which first suggested their incorporation therein, were found to be so inferior to the bamboo, afterwards discovered by Edison, that the complainant was forced to abandon its patent in that particular, and take up with the material discovered by its rival. Under these circumstances, to hold that one who had discovered that a certain fibrous or textile material answered the required purpose should obtain the right to exclude everybody from the whole domain of fibrous and textile materials, and thereby shut out any further efforts to discover a better specimen of that class than the patentee had employed, would be an unwarranted extension of his monopoly, and operate rather to discourage than to promote invention. If Sawyer and Man had discovered that a certain carbonized paper would answer the purpose, their claim to all carbonized paper would, perhaps, not be extravagant; but the fact that paper happens to belong to the fibrous kingdom did not invest them with sovereignty over this entire kingdom, and thereby practically limit other experimenters to the domain of minerals.

In fact, such a construction of this patent as would exclude competitors from making use of any fibrous or textile material would probably defeat itself, since, if the patent were infringed by the use of any such material, it would be anticipated by proof of the prior use of any such material. In this connection it would appear, not only that wood charcoal had been constantly used since the days of Sir Humphry Davy for arc lighting, but that in the English patent to Greener and Staite, of 1846, for an incandescent light, "charcoal, reduced to a state of powder," was one of the materials employed. So also, in the English patent of 1841 to De Moleyns, "a finely pulverized boxwood charcoal or plumbago" was used for an incandescent electric lamp. Indeed, in the experiments of Sir Humphry Davy, early in the century, pieces of well-burned charcoal were heated to a vivid whiteness by the electric current, and other experiments were made which evidently contemplated the use of charcoal heated to the point of incandescence. Mr. Broadnax, the attorney who prepared the application, it seems, was also of opinion that a broad claim for vegetable carbons could not be sustained, because charcoal had been used before in incandescent lighting. There is undoubtedly a good deal of testimony tending to show that, for the past 50 or 60 years, the word "charcoal" has been used in the art, not only to designate carbonized wood, but mineral or hard carbons, such as were commonly employed for the carbon pencils of arc lamps. But we think it quite evident that, in the patents and experiments above referred to, it was used in its ordinary sense of charcoal obtained from wood. The very fact of the use of such word to designate mineral carbons indicates that such carbons were believed to possess peculiar properties required for illumination, that before that had been supposed to belong to wood charcoal.

We have not found it necessary in this connection to consider the amendments that were made to the original specification, upon which so much stress was laid in the opinion of the court below, since we are all agreed that the claims of this patent, with the exception of the third, are too indefinite to be the subject of a valid monopoly.

As these suggestions are of themselves sufficient to dispose of the case adversely to the complainant, a consideration of the question of priority of invention, or rather of the extent and results of the Sawyer and Man experiments, which was so fully argued upon both sides, and passed upon by the court below, becomes unnecessary.

For the reasons above stated, the decree of the circuit court is affirmed.

NOTES

1. "Undue Experimentation." Paragraphs one and two of Section 112 are the modern equivalent to Rev. Stat. § 4888. *Consolidated Electric* illustrates the principle that inventors must disclose "to enable any person skilled in the art" to use or make their invention. To determine whether an inventor has satisfied the enablement requirement, the Federal Circuit asks whether "undue experimentation" is required to make or use an invention. To determine whether disclosure requires "undue experimentation," the Federal Circuit considers "(1) the quantity of experimentation necessary, (2) the amount of direction or guidance presented, (3) the presence or absence of working examples, (4) the nature of the invention, (5) the state of the prior art, (6) the relative skill of those in the art, (7) the predictability or unpredictability of the art, and (8) the breadth of the claims." *In re Wands*, 858 F.2d 731 (Fed. Cir. 1988).

2. Timing. Enablement is measured at the time of filing of the patent application. In other words, inventors must show that they understood the invention on the filing date. The Federal Circuit has found that the sufficiency of a patent's disclosure must be judged as of its filing date. Any information or technological advancement proffered after the filing date is not considered. The date of invention establishes priority, and the filing date may be used to prove or disprove possession of an invention.

2. The Written Description Requirement

The written description requirement of Section 112 aims to prevent applicants from claiming more than they disclosed after they file their application, or claiming new subject matter that the applicant had not previously thought of. Section 132 prohibits the introduction of new matter.

§ 132. Notice of rejection; reexamination

(a) Whenever, on examination, any claim for a patent is rejected, or any objection or requirement made, the Director shall notify the applicant thereof, stating the reasons for such rejection, or objection or requirement, together with such information and references as may be useful in judging of the propriety of continuing the prosecution of his application; and if after receiving such notice, the applicant persists in his claim for a patent, with or without amendment, the application shall be reexamined. No amendment shall introduce new matter into the disclosure of the invention.

* * *

35 U.S.C. § 132.

The written description requirement is also used to resolve questions of "priority." Section 120 outlines how an early disclosure can save a filing date.

§ 120.   Benefit of earlier filing date in the United States

An application for patent for an invention disclosed in the manner provided by the first paragraph of section 112 of this title in an application previously filed in the United States, or as provided by section 363 of this title, which is filed by an inventor or inventors named in the previously filed application shall have the same effect, as to such invention, as though filed on the date of the prior application, if filed before the patenting or abandonment of or termination of proceedings on the first application or on an application similarly entitled to the benefit of the filing date of the first application and if it contains or is amended to contain a specific reference to the earlier filed application. No application shall be entitled to the benefit of an earlier filed application under this section unless an amendment containing the specific reference to the earlier filed application is submitted at such time during the pendency of the application as required by the Director. The Director may consider the failure to submit such an amendment within that time period as a waiver of any benefit under this section. The Director may establish procedures, including the payment of a surcharge, to accept an unintentionally delayed submission of an amendment under this section.

35 U.S.C. § 120.

ARIAD PHARMACEUTICALS, INC. v. ELI LILLY & CO.

United States Court of Appeals for the Federal Circuit, 2010.
598 F.3d 1336.

LOURIE, CIRCUIT JUDGE.

Ariad Pharmaceuticals, Inc., Massachusetts Institute of Technology, the Whitehead Institute for Biomedical Research, and the President and Fellows of Harvard College (collectively, "Ariad") brought suit against Eli Lilly & Company ("Lilly") in the United States District Court for the District of Massachusetts, alleging infringement of U.S. Patent 6,410,516 ("the '516 patent"). After trial, at which a jury found infringement, but found none of the asserted claims invalid, a panel of this court reversed the district court's denial of Lilly's motion for judgment as a matter of law ("JMOL") and held the asserted claims invalid for lack of written description. *Ariad Pharms., Inc. v. Eli Lilly & Co.*, 560 F.3d 1366 (Fed.Cir.2009).

Ariad petitioned for rehearing *en banc,* challenging this court's interpretation of 35 U.S.C. § 112, first paragraph, as containing a separate written description requirement. Because of the importance of the issue, we granted Ariad's petition and directed the parties to address whether § 112, first paragraph, contains a written description requirement separate from the enablement requirement and, if so, the scope and purpose of that requirement. We now reaffirm that § 112, first paragraph, contains a written description requirement separate from enablement, and we again reverse the district court's denial of JMOL and hold the asserted claims of the '516 patent invalid for failure to meet the statutory written description requirement.

BACKGROUND

The '516 patent relates to the regulation of gene expression by the transcription factor NF-êB. The inventors of the '516 patent were the first to identify NF-êB and to uncover the mechanism by which NF-êB activates gene expression underlying the body's immune responses to infection. The inventors discovered that NF-êB normally exists in cells as an inactive complex with a protein inhibitor, named "IêB" ("Inhibitor of kappa B"), and is activated by extracellular stimuli, such as bacterial-produced lipopolysaccha rides, through a series of biochemical reactions that release it from IêB. Once free of its inhibitor, NF-êB travels into the cell nucleus where it binds to and activates the transcription of genes containing a NF-êB recognition site. The activated genes (e.g., certain cytokines), in turn help the body to counteract the extracellular assault. The production of cytokines can, however, be harmful in excess. Thus the inventors recognized that artificially interfering with NF-êB activity could reduce the harmful symptoms of certain diseases, and they filed a patent application on April 21, 1989, disclosing their discoveries and claiming methods for regulating cellular responses to external stimuli by reducing NF-êB activity in a cell.

Ariad brought suit against Lilly * * * the day the '516 patent issued. Ariad alleged infringement of claims 80, 95, 144, and 145 by Lilly's Evista® and Xigris® pharmaceutical products. The asserted claims, re-written to include the claims from which they depend, are as follows:

80. [A method for modifying effects of external influences on a eukaryotic cell, which external influences induce NF-êB-mediated intracellular signaling, the method comprising altering NF-êB activity in the cells such that NF-êB-mediated effects of external influences are modified, wherein NF-êB activity in the cell is reduced] wherein reducing NF-êB activity comprises reducing binding of NF-êB to NF-êB recognition sites on genes which are transcriptionally regulated by NF-êB.

95. [A method for reducing, in eukaryotic cells, the level of expression of genes which are activated by extracellular influences which induce NF-êBmediated intracellular signaling, the method comprising reducing NF-êB activity in the cells such that expression of said genes is reduced], carried out on human cells.

144. [A method for reducing bacterial lipopolysaccharide-induced expression of cytokines in mammalian cells, which method comprises reducing NF-êB activity in the cells so as to reduce bacterial lipopoly-

saccharide-induced expression of said cytokines in the cells] wherein reducing NF-êB activity comprises reducing binding of NF-êB to NF-êB recognition sites on genes which are transcriptionally regulated by NF-êB.

145. [A method for reducing bacterial lipopolysaccharide-induced expression of cytokines in mammalian cells, which method comprises reducing NF-êB activity in the cells so as to reduce bacterial lipopoly-saccharide-induced expression of said cytokines in the cells], carried out on human cells.

The claims are thus genus claims, encompassing the use of all substances that achieve the desired result of reducing the binding of NF-êB to NF-êB recognition sites. Furthermore, the claims, although amended during prosecution, use language that corresponds to language present in the priority application. Specifically, the asserted claims recite methods of reducing NF-êB activity, and more specifically reducing binding of NF-êB to NF-êB recognition sites, in cells in response to external influences like bacterial lipopolysaccha rides. The specification filed on April 21, 1989, similarly recites the desired goal of reducing NF-êB activity and binding to NF-êB recognition sites in cells in response to such external influences. The specification also hypothesizes three types of molecules with the potential to reduce NF-êB activity in cells: decoy, dominantly interfering, and specific inhibitor molecules.

* * * [T]he district court held a fourteen-day jury trial on the issues of infringement and validity. The jury rendered a special verdict finding infringement of claims 80 and 95 with respect to Evista® and claims 144 and 145 with respect to Xigris®. The jury also found that the asserted claims were not invalid for anticipation, lack of enablement, or lack of written description. The court denied without opinion Lilly's motions for JMOL and, in the alternative, a new trial. * * * [T]he court [then] conducted a four-day bench trial on Lilly's additional defenses of unpatentable subject matter, inequitable conduct, and prosecution laches, ruling in favor of Ariad on all three issues. *Ariad Pharms., Inc. v. Eli Lilly & Co.*, 529 F.Supp.2d 106 (D.Mass.2007).

Lilly timely appealed to this court, and on April 3, 2009, a panel affirmed in part and reversed in part. The panel upheld the district court's finding of no inequitable conduct, but reversed the jury's verdict on written description, holding the asserted claims invalid for lack of an adequate written description as required by 35 U.S.C. § 112, first paragraph. Ariad petitioned for rehearing *en banc,* challenging the existence of a written description requirement in § 112, first paragraph, separate from the enablement requirement. * * * In light of the controversy concerning the distinctness and proper role of the written description requirement, we granted Ariad's petition, vacating the prior panel opinion and directing the parties to brief two questions:

(1) Whether 35 U.S.C. § 112, paragraph 1, contains a written description requirement separate from an enablement requirement?

(2) If a separate written description requirement is set forth in the statute, what is the scope and purpose of that requirement?

In addition to the parties' briefs, the court received twenty-five amicus briefs. Of those, seventeen were filed in support of Lilly, one was filed in support of Ariad, and seven were filed in support of neither party. The majority, including a brief filed by the United States, were filed in support of this court's current written description doctrine. * * *

DISCUSSION

I.

Although the parties differ in their answers to the court's questions, their positions converge more than they first appear. Ariad, in answering the court's first question, argues that § 112, first paragraph, does *not* contain a written description requirement separate from enablement. Yet, in response to this court's second question on the scope and purpose of a written description requirement, Ariad argues that the statute contains two description requirements: "Properly interpreted, the statute requires the specification to describe (i) what the invention is, and (ii) how to make and use it." Appellee Br. 1. Ariad reconciles this apparent contradiction by arguing that the legal sufficiency of its two-prong description requirement is judged by whether it enables one of skill in the art to make and use the claimed invention. Thus, according to Ariad, in order to enable the invention, the specification must first identify *"what* the invention is, for otherwise it fails to inform a person of skill in the art what to make and use." *Id.* at 30. Yet Ariad argues that this first step of "identifying" the invention applies only in the context of priority (*i.e.*, claims amended during prosecution; priority under 35 U.S.C. §§ 119, 120; and interferences) because original claims "constitute their own description." *Id.* at 44.

Lilly, in contrast, answers the court's first question in the affirmative, arguing that two hundred years of precedent support the existence of a statutory written description requirement separate from enablement. Thus, Lilly argues that the statute requires, first, a written description of the invention and, second, a written description of how to make and use the invention so as to enable one of skill in the art to make and use it. Finally, Lilly asserts that this separate written description requirement applies to all claims-both original and amended-to ensure that inventors have actually invented the subject matter claimed.

Thus, although the parties take diametrically opposed positions on the existence of a written description requirement separate from enablement, both agree that the specification must contain a written description of the invention to establish what the invention is. The dispute, therefore, centers on the standard to be applied and whether it applies to original claim language.

A.

As in any case involving statutory interpretation, we begin with the language of the statute itself. Section 112, first paragraph, reads as follows:

> The specification shall contain a written description of the invention, and of the manner and process of making and using it, in such full, clear, concise, and exact terms as to enable any person skilled in the art to which it pertains, or with which it is most nearly connected, to make and use the same, and shall set forth the best mode contemplated by the inventor of carrying out his invention.

According to Ariad, a plain reading of the statute reveals two components: a written description (i) of the invention, and (ii) of the manner and process of making and using it. Yet those two components, goes Ariad's argument, must be judged by the final prepositional phrase; both written descriptions must be "in such full, clear, concise, and exact terms as to enable any person skilled in the art ... to make and use the same." Specifically, Ariad parses the statute as follows:

> The specification shall contain
>
> [A]   a written description
>
> [i]   of the invention, and
>
> [ii]   of the manner and process of making and using it,
>
> [B]   in such full, clear, concise, and exact terms as to enable any person skilled in the art to which it pertains, or with which it is most nearly connected, to make and use the same ...

Ariad argues that its interpretation best follows the rule of English grammar that prepositional phrases (here, "of the invention," "of the manner and process of making and using it," and "in such full, clear, concise, and exact terms") modify another word in the sentence (here, "written description"), and that it does not inexplicably ignore the comma after "making and using it" or sever the "description of the invention" from the requirement that it be in "full, clear, concise, and exact terms," leaving the description without a legal standard.

Ariad also argues that earlier versions of the Patent Act support its interpretation. Specifically, Ariad contends that the first Patent Act, adopted in 1790, and its immediate successor, adopted in 1793, required a written description of the invention that accomplished two purposes: (i) to distinguish the invention from the prior art, and (ii) to enable a person skilled in the art to make and use the invention. Ariad then asserts that when Congress assigned the function of defining the invention to the claims in 1836, Congress amended the written description requirement so that it served a single purpose: enablement.

Lilly disagrees, arguing that § 112, first paragraph, contains three separate requirements. Specifically, Lilly parses the statute as follows:

(1) "The specification shall contain a written description of the invention, *and*"

(2) "The specification shall contain a written description . . . of the manner and process of making and using it, in such full, clear, concise, and exact terms as to enable any person skilled in the art to which it pertains, or with which it is most nearly connected, to make and use the same, *and*"

(3) "The specification . . . shall set forth the best mode contemplated by the inventor of carrying out the invention."

Lilly argues that Ariad's construction ignores a long line of judicial precedent interpreting the statute's predecessors to contain a separate written description requirement, an interpretation Congress adopted by reenacting the current language of § 112, first paragraph, without significant amendment.

We agree with Lilly and read the statute to give effect to its language that the specification "shall contain a written description of the invention" and hold that § 112, first paragraph, contains two separate description requirements: a "written description [i] of the invention, *and* [ii] of the manner and process of making and using [the invention].["] 35 U.S.C. § 112, ¶ 1 (emphasis added). On this point, we do not read Ariad's position to be in disagreement as Ariad concedes the existence of a written description requirement. Instead Ariad contends that the written description requirement exists, not for its own sake as an independent statutory requirement, but only to identify the invention that must comply with the enablement requirement.

But, unlike Ariad, we see nothing in the statute's language or grammar that unambiguously dictates that the adequacy of the "written description of the invention" must be determined solely by whether that description identifies the invention so as to enable one of skill in the art to make and use it. The prepositional phrase "in such full, clear, concise, and exact terms as to enable any person skilled in the art . . . to make and use the same" modifies only "the written description . . . of the manner and process of making and using [the invention]," as Lilly argues, without violating the rules of grammar. That the adequacy of the description of the manner and process of *making* and *using* the invention is judged by whether that description enables one skilled in the art to *make* and *use* the same follows from the parallelism of the language.

While Ariad agrees there is a requirement to describe the invention, a few amici appear to suggest that the only description requirement is a requirement to describe enablement. If Congress had intended enablement to be the sole description requirement of § 112, first paragraph, the statute would have been written differently. Specifically, Congress could have written the statute to read, "The specification shall contain a written description of the invention, in such full, clear, concise, and exact terms as to enable any person skilled in the art . . . to make and use the same," or "The specification shall contain a written description of the manner and process of making and using the invention, in such full, clear, concise, and exact terms as to enable any person skilled in the art . . . to make and use the same." Under the amicis' construction a portion of the statute-either "and of the manner and process of making and using it" or "[a written description] of the invention"-becomes surplusage, violating the rule of statutory construction that Congress does not use unnecessary words.

Furthermore, since 1793, the Patent Act has expressly stated that an applicant must provide a written description of the invention, and after the 1836 Act added the requirement for claims, the Supreme Court applied this description requirement separate from enablement. Congress recodified this language in the 1952 Act, and nothing in the legislative history indicates that Congress intended to rid the Act of this requirement. On the contrary, "Congress is presumed to be aware of a[ ] . . . judicial interpretation of a statute and to adopt that interpretation when it reenacts a statute without change." *Forest Grove Sch. Dist. v. T.A.*, ___ U.S. ___, ___, 129 S.Ct. 2484, 2492, 174 L.Ed.2d 168 (2009) (quoting *Lorillard v. Pons*, 434 U.S. 575, 580, 98 S.Ct. 866, 55 L.Ed.2d 40 (1978)).

Finally, a separate requirement to describe one's invention is basic to patent law. Every patent must describe an invention. It is part of the *quid pro quo* of a patent; one describes an invention, and, if the law's other requirements are met, one obtains a patent. The specification must then, of course, describe how to make and use the invention (*i.e.,* enable it), but that is a different task. A description of the claimed invention allows the United States Patent and Trademark Office ("PTO") to examine applications effectively; courts to understand the invention, determine compliance with the statute, and to construe the claims; and the public to understand and improve upon the invention and to avoid the claimed boundaries of the patentee's exclusive rights.

B.

Ariad argues that Supreme Court precedent comports with its reading of the statute and provides no support for a written description requirement separate from enablement. Specifically, Ariad asserts that in *Evans v. Eaton*, 20 U.S. (7 Wheat.) 356, 433–34, 5 L.Ed. 472 (1822), the Supreme Court recognized just two requirements under § 3 of the 1793 Act, the requirements "to enable" the invention and "to distinguish" it from all things previously known. And, goes Ariad's argument, since the 1836 Act, which removed the latter language and added the requirement for claims, the Court has consistently held that a patent applicant need fulfill but a single "written description" requirement, the measure of which is enablement.

Lilly disagrees and reads *Evans* as acknowledging a written description requirement separate from enablement. Lilly further contends that the Court has continually confirmed the existence of a separate written description requirement, including in *O'Reilly v. Morse*, 56 U.S. (15 How.) 62, 14 L.Ed. 601 (1853) under the 1836 Act; *Schriber–Schroth Co. v. Cleveland Trust Co.*, 305 U.S. 47, 59 S.Ct. 8, 83 L.Ed. 34 (1938), under the

1870 Act; and more recently in *Festo Corp. v. Shoketsu Kinzoku Kogyo Kabushiki Co.*, 535 U.S. 722, 736, 122 S.Ct. 1831, 152 L.Ed.2d 944 (2002).

Like Lilly, we also read Supreme Court precedent as recognizing a written description requirement separate from an enablement requirement even after the introduction of claims. Specifically, in *Schriber–Schroth*, the Court held that a patent directed to pistons for a gas engine with "extremely rigid" webs did not adequately describe amended claims that recited flexible webs under the then-in-force version of § 112, first paragraph. The Court ascribed two purposes to this portion of the statute, only the first of which involved enablement:

> [1] to require the patentee to describe his invention so that others may construct and use it after the expiration of the patent and [2] to inform the public during the life of the patent of the limits of the monopoly asserted, so that it may be known which features may be safely used or manufactured without a license and which may not.

[305 U.S.] at 57. The Court then concluded that even if the original specification enabled the use of a flexible web, the claim could derive no benefit from it because "that was not the invention which [the patentee] *described* by his references to an extremely rigid web." *Id.* at 58–59 (emphasis added). Although the Court did not expressly state that it was applying a description of the invention requirement separate from enablement, that is exactly what the Court did.

Further, both before and after *Schriber–Schroth*, the Court has stated that the statute serves a purpose other than enablement. In *Gill v. Wells*, 89 U.S. (22 Wall.) 1, 22 L.Ed. 699 (1874), the Court held invalid a reissue patent for claiming a combination not described in the original application, but the Court also emphasized the need for all patents to meet the "three great ends" of § 26, only one of which was enablement. Specifically, the Court stated:

> (1.) That the government may know what they have granted and what will become public property when the term of the monopoly expires. (2.) That licensed persons desiring to practice the invention may know, during the term, how to make, construct, and use the invention. (3.) That other inventors may know what part of the field of invention is unoccupied.

Id. at 25–26. Finally, most recently in *Festo*, the Court recited three requirements for § 112, first paragraph, and noted a written description requirement separate from the others:

> [T]he patent application must *describe, enable, and set forth the best mode* of carrying out the invention. These latter requirements must be satisfied before issuance of the patent, for exclusive patent rights are given in exchange for disclosing the invention to the public. What is claimed by the patent application must be the same as what is disclosed in the specification; otherwise the patent should not issue.

The patent also should not issue if the other requirements of § 112 are not satisfied. . . .

535 U.S. at 736 (emphasis added) (internal citations omitted). As a subordinate federal court, we may not so easily dismiss such statements as dicta but are bound to follow them. While Ariad points to statements in other cases that support its view not one disavows the existence of a separate written description requirement.

A separate written description requirement also does not conflict with the function of the claims. 35 U.S.C. § 112, ¶ 2. Claims define the subject matter that, after examination, has been found to meet the statutory requirements for a patent. Their principal function, therefore, is to provide notice of the boundaries of the right to exclude and to define limits; it is not to describe the invention, although their original language contributes to the description and in certain cases satisfies it. Claims define and circumscribe, the written description discloses and teaches.

C.

In addition to the statutory language and Supreme Court precedent supporting the existence of a written description requirement separate from enablement, *stare decisis* impels us to uphold it now. * * * If the law of written description is to be changed, contrary to sound policy and the uniform holdings of this court, the settled expectations of the inventing and investing communities, and PTO practice, such a decision would require good reason and would rest with Congress.

* * *

E.

In contrast to amended claims, the parties have more divergent views on the application of a written description requirement to original claims. Ariad argues that *Regents of the University of California v. Eli Lilly & Co.*, 119 F.3d 1559 (Fed.Cir.1997), extended the requirement beyond its proper role of policing priority as part of enablement and transformed it into a heightened and unpredictable general disclosure requirement in place of enablement. Rather, Ariad argues, the requirement to describe what the invention is does not apply to original claims because original claims, as part of the original disclosure, constitute their own written description of the invention. Thus, according to Ariad, as long as the claim language appears *in ipsis verbis* in the specification as filed, the applicant has satisfied the requirement to provide a written description of the invention.

Lilly responds that the written description requirement applies to all claims and requires that the specification objectively demonstrate that the applicant actually invented-was in possession of-the claimed subject matter. Lilly argues that § 112 contains no basis for applying a different standard to amended versus original claims and that applying a separate written description requirement to original claims keeps inventors from claiming beyond their inventions and thus encourages innovation in new technological areas by preserving patent protection for actual inventions.

Again we agree with Lilly. If it is correct to read § 112, first paragraph, as containing a requirement to provide a separate written description of the invention, as we hold here, Ariad provides no principled basis for restricting that requirement to establishing priority. Certainly nothing in the language of § 112 supports such a restriction; the statute does not say "The specification shall contain a written description of the invention *for purposes of determining priority.*" And although the issue arises primarily in cases involving priority, Congress has not so limited the statute, and neither will we.

Furthermore, while it is true that original claims are part of the original specification, *In re Gardner*, 480 F.2d 879, 879 (CCPA 1973), that truism fails to address the question whether original claim language necessarily discloses the subject matter that it claims. Ariad believes so, arguing that original claims identify whatever they state, *e.g.,* a perpetual motion machine, leaving only the question whether the applicant has enabled anyone to make and use such an invention. We disagree that this is always the case. Although many original claims will satisfy the written description requirement, certain claims may not. For example, a generic claim may define the boundaries of a vast genus of chemical compounds, and yet the question may still remain whether the specification, including original claim language, demonstrates that the applicant has invented species sufficient to support a claim to a genus. The problem is especially acute with genus claims that use functional language to define the boundaries of a claimed genus. In such a case, the functional claim may simply claim a desired result, and may do so without describing species that achieve that result. But the specification must demonstrate that the applicant has made a generic invention that achieves the claimed result and do so by showing that the applicant has invented species sufficient to support a claim to the functionally-defined genus.

* * *

Ariad argues that *Eli Lilly* constituted a change in the law, imposing new requirements on biotechnology inventions. We disagree. Applying the written description requirement outside of the priority context in our 1997 *Eli Lilly* decision merely faithfully applied the statute, consistent with Supreme Court precedent and our case law dating back at least to our predecessor court's *Ruschig* decision. Neither the statute nor legal precedent limits the written description requirement to cases of priority or distinguishes between original and amended claims. The application of the written description requirement to original language was raised in *Fiers*, *Eli Lilly*, and *Enzo*, and is raised again by the parties here. Once again we reject Ariad's argument and hold that generic language in the application as filed does not automatically satisfy the written description requirement.

F.

Since its inception, this court has consistently held that § 112, first paragraph, contains a written description requirement separate from enablement, and we have articulated a "fairly uniform standard," which we now affirm. *Vas–Cath Inc. v. Mahurkar*, 935 F.2d 1555, 1562–63 (Fed.Cir.1991). Specifically, the description must "clearly allow persons of ordinary skill in the art to recognize that [the inventor] invented what is claimed." *Id.* at 1563. In other words, the test for sufficiency is whether the disclosure of the application relied upon reasonably conveys to those skilled in the art that the inventor had possession of the claimed subject matter as of the filing date.

The term "possession," however, has never been very enlightening. It implies that as long as one can produce records documenting a written description of a claimed invention, one can show possession. But the hallmark of written description is disclosure. Thus, "possession as shown in the disclosure" is a more complete formulation. Yet whatever the specific articulation, the test requires an objective inquiry into the four corners of the specification from the perspective of a person of ordinary skill in the art. Based on that inquiry, the specification must describe an invention understandable to that skilled artisan and show that the inventor actually invented the invention claimed.

This inquiry, as we have long held, is a question of fact. Thus, we have recognized that determining whether a patent complies with the written description requirement will necessarily vary depending on the context. *Capon v. Eshhar*, 418 F.3d 1349, 1357–58 (Fed.Cir.2005). Specifically, the level of detail required to satisfy the written description requirement varies depending on the nature and scope of the claims and on the complexity and predictability of the relevant technology. For generic claims, we have set forth a number of factors for evaluating the adequacy of the disclosure, including "the existing knowledge in the particular field, the extent and content of the prior art, the maturity of the science or technology, [and] the predictability of the aspect at issue." *Id.* at 1359.

* * *

II.

Because we reaffirm our written description doctrine, we see no reason to deviate from the panel's application of that requirement to the facts of this case. As such, we adopt that analysis, as follows, as the decision of the *en banc* court.

A.

We review the denial of Lilly's motion for JMOL without deference. Under First Circuit law, JMOL is warranted pursuant to Fed.R.Civ.P. 50(a)(1) where "there is no legally sufficient evidentiary basis for a reasonable jury to find" for the non-moving party. *Guilloty Perez v. Pierluisi*, 339 F.3d 43, 50 (1st Cir.2003) (quotations omitted). "A patent is presumed to be valid, and this presumption only can be overcome by clear and convincing evidence to the contrary." *Enzo*, 424 F.3d at 1281.

Ariad explains that developing the subject matter of the '516 patent "required years of hard work, great skill, and extraordinary creativity-so much so that the inventors first needed to discover, give names to, and describe previously unknown cellular components as a necessary predicate for their inventions." Lilly offered the undisputed expert testimony of David Latchman that the field of the invention was particularly unpredictable. Thus, this invention was made in a new and unpredictable field where the existing knowledge and prior art was scant.

B.

Ariad claims methods comprising the single step of reducing NF-êB activity. Lilly argues that the asserted claims are not supported by a written description because the specification of the '516 patent fails to adequately disclose how the claimed reduction of NF-êB activity is achieved. The parties agree that the specification of the '516 patent hypothesizes three classes of molecules potentially capable of reducing NF-êB activity: specific inhibitors, dominantly interfering molecules, and decoy molecules. Lilly contends that this disclosure amounts to little more than a research plan, and does not satisfy the patentee's *quid pro quo* as described in Rochester. Ariad responds that Lilly's arguments fail as a matter of law because Ariad did not actually claim the molecules. According to Ariad, because there is no term in the asserted claims that corresponds to the molecules, it is entitled to claim the methods without describing the molecules. Ariad's legal assertion, however, is flawed.

In *Rochester*, as discussed above, we held very similar method claims invalid for lack of written description. Ariad attempts to categorically distinguish Rochester, Fiers, and Eli Lilly, because in those cases, the claims explicitly included the non-described compositions. For example, in *Rochester*, the method claims recited a broad type of compound that we held was inadequately described in the specification of the patent:

> 1. A method for selectively inhibiting PGHS–2 activity in a human host, comprising administering a non-steroidal compound that selectively inhibits activity of the PGHS–2 gene product to a human host in need of such treatment.

Ariad's attempt to distinguish these cases is unavailing. Regardless whether the asserted claims recite a compound, Ariad still must describe some way of performing the claimed methods, and Ariad admits that the specification suggests only the use of the three classes of molecules to achieve NF-êB reduction. Thus, to satisfy the written description requirement for the asserted claims, the specification must demonstrate that Ariad possessed the claimed methods by sufficiently disclosing molecules capable of reducing NF-êB activity so as to "satisfy the inventor's obligation to disclose the technologic knowledge upon which the patent is based, and to demonstrate that the patentee was in possession of the invention that is claimed." *Capon*, 418 F.3d at 1357.

C.

Alternatively, Ariad argues that the specification of the '516 patent and the expert testimony of Tom Kadesch provided the jury with substantial evidence of adequate written description of the claimed methods. "A determination that a patent is invalid for failure to meet the written description requirement of 35 U.S.C. § 112, ¶ 1 is a question of fact, and we review a jury's determinations of facts relating to compliance with the written description requirement for substantial evidence." *PIN/NIP, Inc. v. Platte Chem. Co.*, 304 F.3d, 1235, 1243 (Fed.Cir.2002).

Much of Ariad's written description evidence, however, is legally irrelevant to the question of whether the disclosure of the '516 patent conveys to those skilled in the art that the inventors were in possession of the claimed generic invention on April 21, 1989–the effective filing date of the '516 patent. The parties disputed the effective filing date of the '516 patent, and in a detailed and well-crafted special verdict form, the jury was asked to choose between the two possible dates: April 21, 1989, and November 13, 1991. The jury chose 1989 and neither party appealed that determination. Presumably because of uncertainty over the priority date, much of Ariad's evidence was actually directed to the later date. Because written description is determined as of the filing date-April 21, 1989, in this case-evidence of what one of ordinary skill in the art knew in 1990 or 1991 cannot provide substantial evidence to the jury that the asserted claims were supported by adequate written description.

In accordance with *Rochester*, the '516 patent must adequately describe the claimed methods for reducing NF-êB activity, including adequate description of the molecules that Ariad admits are necessary to perform the methods. The specification of the '516 patent hypothesizes three classes of molecules potentially capable of reducing NF-êB activity: specific inhibitors, dominantly interfering molecules, and decoy molecules. We review the specification's disclosure of each in turn to determine whether there is substantial evidence to support the jury's verdict that the written description evidenced that the inventor possessed the claimed invention.

* * *

* * * The '516 patent discloses no working or even prophetic examples of methods that reduce NF-êB activity, and no completed syntheses of any of the molecules prophesized to be capable of reducing NF-êB activity. The state of the art at the time of filing was primitive and uncertain, leaving Ariad with an insufficient supply of prior art knowledge with which to fill the gaping holes in its disclosure.

Whatever thin thread of support a jury might find in the decoy-molecule hypothetical simply cannot bear the weight of the vast scope of these generic claims. Here, the specification at best describes decoy molecule structures and hypothesizes with no accompanying description that they could be used to reduce NF-êB activity. Yet the asserted claims are far broader. We therefore conclude that the jury lacked substantial evidence for its verdict that the asserted claims were supported by adequate written description, and thus hold the asserted claims invalid.

CONCLUSION

For the foregoing reasons, we hold that the asserted claims of the '516 patent are invalid for lack of written description, and we do not address the other validity issues that were before the panel. We also reinstate Part II of the panel decision reported at 560 F.3d 1366 (Fed.Cir.2009), affirming the district court's finding of no inequitable conduct. The judgment below is

REVERSED IN PART AND AFFIRMED IN PART

[NEWMAN, CIRCUIT JUDGE, additional views omitted]

[GAJARSA, CIRCUIT JUDGE, concurring omitted]

RADER, CIRCUIT JUDGE, with whom LINN, CIRCUIT JUDGE, joins, dissenting-in-part and concurring-in-part.

The Constitution of the United States gives Congress, not the courts, the power to promote the progress of the useful arts by securing exclusive rights to inventors for limited times. Art. I, § 8, cl. 8. Yet this court proclaims itself the body responsible for achieving the "right balance" between upstream and downstream innovation. Ante at 28. The Patent Act, however, has already established the balance by requiring that a patent application contain "a written description of the invention, and of the manner and process of making and using it, *in such full, clear, concise, and exact terms as to enable any person skilled in the art to which it pertains ... to make and use the same.*" 35 U.S.C. § 112, ¶ 1 (emphasis added). In rejecting that statutory balance in favor of an undefined "written description" doctrine, this court ignores the problems of standardless decision making and serious conflicts with other areas of patent law. Because the Patent Act already supplies a better test, I respectfully dissent.

I.

The frailties of this court's "written description" doctrine have been exhaustively documented in previous opinions. These earlier writings document the embarrassingly thin (perhaps even mistaken) justifications for the minting of this new description doctrine in 1997 and the extensive academic criticism of this product of judicial imagination. For present purposes I will only recount those frailties of this court's relatively recent justifications for a doctrine of its own making.

First and foremost, the separate written description requirement that the court petrifies today has no statutory support. As noted, § 112, first paragraph, reads as follows:

> The specification shall contain a written description of the invention, and of the manner and process of making and using it, in such full, clear, concise, and exact terms as to enable any person skilled in the art to which it pertains, or with which it is most nearly connected, to make and use the same, and shall set forth the best mode contemplated by the inventor of carrying out his invention.

This language, while cumbersome, is unambiguous. It says that the written descriptions of the invention and of the manner and process of making and using the invention are both judged by whether they are in such full, clear, concise, and exact terms as to enable a person skilled in the art to make and use the invention. The reason for a description doctrine is clear: to ensure that the inventor fully discloses the invention in exchange for an exclusive right. The test for the adequacy of the specification that describes the invention is also clear: Is the description sufficient to enable a person of ordinary skill in the art to make and use the claimed invention? Nowhere does the paragraph require that the inventor satisfy some quixotic possession requirement.

This court, however, calves the "written description of the invention" language out of its context in the rest of the paragraph. In this court's strained reading, the prepositional phrases that follow apply only to a "written description . . . of the manner and process of making and using" the invention, not to a "written description of the invention." The practical effect of the court's interpretation is that the written description of the invention contained in the specification need not be full. It need not be clear. It need not be concise. It need not be exact. And, of course, it need not enable. Instead, it must satisfy a vague possession notion.

To support its reading of the statute, the court relies on a new doctrine of statutory interpretation that it calls "parallelism." Before today, parallelism would have been simply disfavored under the maxim that the law does not use redundant language, a maxim that has actually been used by courts before. (Indeed, even the court uses this maxim when it fits its purpose.) If Congress had intended enablement to test only the sufficiency of the written description of the manner and process of making and using the invention, then it would have simply required "a written description . . . of the manner and process of making and using it in such full, clear, concise, and exact terms as to enable any person skilled in the art . . . to *do so.*" Note also that the comma after "it" in the statute as written is meaningless under the court's interpretation.

Moreover, if "parallelism" is indeed the right test, then it conflicts with the court's separate argument that the written description of the invention test has been separate from the enablement test since the 1793 Act. A close look at Section 3 of the 1793 Act reveals that the "parallelism" there connects the enablement clause to both written description requirements:

> [E]very inventor, before he can receive a patent shall . . . deliver a written description *of his invention,* and of the manner of *using,* or

process of *compounding* the same, in such full, clear and exact terms
. . . to enable any person skilled . . . to *make, compound,* and use, the
same.

Act of Feb. 27, 1793, 1 Stat. 318, 321–22, ch. 11, § 3 (emphasis added).

In reality, the court simply sidesteps the conflict between its position
and the language of the statute by suggesting that Supreme Court
precedent has settled this issue. Of course, that is a question for the
Supreme Court to answer, but reading the statute as it is written is in fact
fully consistent with cases like *Schriber–Schroth Co. v. Cleveland Trust
Co.*, 305 U.S. 47, 59 S.Ct. 8, 83 L.Ed. 34 (1938).

Specifically, the description doctrine under a correct reading of the
statute shows that a specification satisfies the "written description of the
invention" requirement when it tells a person of skill in the art what the
invention is. In other words, a proper reading of the statutory description
requirement recognizes that the enablement requirement identifies the
invention and tells a person of ordinary skill *what* to make and use. Of
course, the original claims must always, by statute, "particularly point[ ]
out and distinctly claim[ ] the subject matter which the applicant regards
as his invention." § 112, ¶ 2. *Schriber–Schroth*, as the court acknowledges,
dealt with amended claims, as did *Mackay Radio & Tel. Co. v. Radio Corp.
of Am.*, 306 U.S. 86, 59 S.Ct. 427, 83 L.Ed. 506 (1939), and *Gill v. Wells*,
89 U.S. (22 Wall.) 1, 22 L.Ed. 699 (1874). These cases stand only for the
unremarkable proposition that an applicant cannot add new matter to an
original disclosure. Thus Supreme Court precedent is fully consistent with
the logical reading of the statute and impeaches this court's *ultra vires*
imposition of a new written description requirement for original claims,
an imposition that first arose in *Regents of the University of California v.
Eli Lilly & Co.*, 119 F.3d 1559, 1566–69 (Fed.Cir.1997).

* * *

II.

Eli Lilly was not only new law, it also is in tension with other areas of
long-established law: claim construction and blocking patents, to name
just two.

The doctrine of claim construction, a doctrine that is framed by the
first two paragraphs of § 112 presents an undeniable conflict of monu-
mental proportions. As *Phillips* confirmed, and this court has confirmed
and reconfirmed, claims must be read " 'in view of the specification' " to
determine their meaning. 415 F.3d at 1315 (quoting *Markman v. Westview
Instruments*, 52 F.3d 967, 979 (Fed.Cir.1995).

If this court followed its own rule and ensured that claims do not
enlarge what the inventor has described, then the claims would never
have a scope that exceeds the disclosure in the rest of the specification.
Thus, this court would never find a claim that "lacks support" (again,
whatever that means) in the rest of the patent document. In other words,

this court's new written description doctrine only has meaning if this court ignores its own claim construction rules. This court essentially claims unfettered power to err twice-both in construing the claims so broad as to exceed the scope of the rest of the specification and then to invalidate those claims because it reads the specification as failing to "support" this court's own broad conception of the claimed subject matter.

"A 'blocking patent' is an earlier patent that must be licensed in order to practice a later patent. This often occurs, for instance, between a pioneer patent and an improvement patent." *Prima Tek II, L.L.C. v. A–Roo Co.*, 222 F.3d 1372, 1379 n. 2 (Fed.Cir.2000). The Supreme Court has long acknowledged the "well established" rule that "an improver cannot appropriate the basic patent of another and that the improver without a license is an infringer and may be sued as such." *Temco Elec. Motor Co. v. Apco Mfg. Co.*, 275 U.S. 319, 328, 48 S.Ct. 170, 72 L.Ed. 298 (1928). This blocking condition can exist even where the original patentee "failed to contemplate" an additional element found in the improvement patent. *A.B. Dick Co. v. Burroughs Corp.*, 713 F.2d 700, 703 (Fed.Cir.1983).

Blocking conditions conceivably occur often where a pioneering patent claims a genus and an improvement patent later claims a species of that genus. These blocking patents often serve the market well by pressuring both inventors to license their innovations to each other and beyond.

After *Eli Lilly*, however, the value of these blocking situations will disappear unless the pioneering patentee "possessed," yet for some reason chose not to claim, the improvement. That situation, of course, would rarely, if ever, happen. Unfortunately the new *Eli Lilly* doctrine effectively prevents this long-standing precept of patent law. For example, although "[i]mprovement and selection inventions are ubiquitous in patent law; such developments do not cast doubt on enablement of the original invention," *CFMT, Inc. v. Yieldup Int'l Corp.*, 349 F.3d 1333, 1340 (Fed.Cir.2003), they apparently do cast doubt on the written description of the original invention. Without this new rule, downstream and upstream innovators in this case would have benefited from the ability to cross license. Under the new regime, mere improvements will likely invalidate genus patents. The principle of unintended consequences once again counsels against judicial adventurism.

III.

Under this new doctrine, patent applicants will face a difficult burden in discerning proper claiming procedure under this court's unpredictable written description of the invention requirement. * * * As it stands, the court's inadequate description of its written description requirement acts as a wildcard on which the court may rely when it faces a patent that it feels is unworthy of protection.

A reading of the statute, on the other hand, supplies a strong enablement test with a neutral, empirical, and predictable test:

Enablement already requires inventors to disclose how to *make* (re-produce, replicate, manufacture) and how to *use* the invention (by definition rendering it a "useful art"). Therefore, because the competitor can make the invention, it can then acquire the DNA sequence or any other characteristic whenever it desires. Meantime the competitor can use, exploit, commercialize (outside the patent term) or improve upon and design around (within the patent term) as much of the invention as it cares to make. In other words, the statutory standard for sufficiency of disclosure serves masterfully the values of the patent system.

Enzo, 323 F.3d at 980–81 (RADER, J., dissenting).

In sum, the statute supplies a test for description that has operated marvelously for decades, if not centuries. If this court perceives a need for renewed attention to description requirements, it should strengthen its enablement jurisprudence instead of making new rules. Invention of new technologies strengthens and advances the "useful arts," but invention of new doctrines frustrates and confuses the law.

[LINN, CIRCUIT JUDGE, dissenting-in-part and concurring-in-part omitted]

NOTES

1. Applying Written Description in Priority Disputes. In *Vas–Cath Inc. v. Mahurkar*, 935 F.2d 1555 (Fed. Cir. 1991), Vas–Cath sued Mahurkar seeking a declaratory judgment that Vas–Cath's cathers did not infringe Mahurkar's patents directed to a double lumen catheter. Vas–Cath alleged that Mahurkar's patents were invalid as anticipated: the patents were not entitled to the filing date of an abandoned design application because its drawings did not provide an adequate "written description" of the claimed invention. On appeal, the Federal Circuit held that "drawings alone *may* be sufficient to provide the 'written description of the invention' required by § 112, first paragraph."

3. Definite Claiming: "Clear and Concise"

ORTHOKINETICS, INC. v. SAFETY TRAVEL CHAIRS, INC.

United States Court of Appeals for the Federal Circuit, 1986.
806 F.2d 1565.

MARKEY, CHIEF JUDGE.

Orthokinetics, Inc. (Orthokinetics) appeals * * * a judgment notwithstanding the verdict (JNOV) holding that * * * claims 1–5 of its U.S. Patent Re. 30,867 ('867 patent) are invalid under § 112 * * *

Background

I. The Claimed Inventions

Orthokinetics manufactures products for invalids and handicapped individuals, including pediatric wheelchairs. It is the assignee * * * of the '867 patent reissued to Edward J. Gaffney (Gaffney) on February 16, 1982, entitled "Travel Chair."

* * *

The '867 reissue patent discloses a collapsible pediatric wheelchair which facilitates the placing of wheelchair-bound persons, particularly children, in and out of an automobile. Orthokinetics asserted infringement of claims 1 through 5 by Safety. Claim 1 reads [underscoring indicates language added by reissue]:

1.   In a wheel chair having a seat portion, a front leg portion, and a rear wheel assembly, the improvement wherein said front leg portion is so dimensioned as to be insertable through the space between the doorframe of an automobile and one of the seats thereof whereby said front leg is placed in support relation to the automobile and will support the seat portion from the automobile in the course of subsequent movement of the wheel chair into the automobile, and the *retractor* means for *assisting the attendant in* retracting said rear wheel assembly upwardly independently of any change in the position of the front leg portion with respect to the seat portion *while the front leg portion is supported on the automobile* and to a position which clears the space beneath the rear end of the chair and permits the chair seat portion and retracted rear wheel assembly to be swung over and set upon said automobile seat.

* * *

II. Procedural History

Orthokinetics introduced the Travel Chair to the market in November of 1973. In 1978, Safety Travel Chairs, Inc. (STC) began to sell similar chairs manufactured by Entron, Inc. (Entron). William J. Pivacek, Clark Chipman, and William J. Cole established STC and were the stockholders and officers of STC and Entron. When Orthokinetics sued STC, Entron, Pivacek, Chipman, and Cole, it alleged * * * infringement of claims 1–5 of [the '867 patent,] and demanded a jury trial. Safety answered that the patents were invalid and not infringed * * *

III. Summary of the District Court's Opinion

On June 14, 1985, the district court filed a 69–page unpublished opinion, vacated its January 30 and July 17, 1984 judgments, and dismissed the complaint and counterclaim. It granted Safety's JNOV motion on validity * * * The district court held claims 1–5 of the '867 patent invalid as: (1) indefinite under § 112 * * *

D. The '867 Patent

(i) Indefiniteness

The jury found that Safety failed to prove by clear and convincing evidence that the '867 patent was invalid because of claim language that does not particularly point out and distinctly claim the invention. 35 U.S.C. § 112, 2d ¶. The district court determined otherwise and granted Safety's motion for JNOV.

Claim 1, from which the rest of the claims depend, contains the limitation: "wherein said front leg portion is so dimensioned as to be insertable through the space between the doorframe of an automobile and one of the seats thereof."

Noting the testimony of Orthokinetics' expert, Mr. Hobbs, who said the dimensions of the front legs depend upon the automobile the chair is designed to suit, the district court stated:

> In response to this testimony, which clearly and convincingly establishes that claim 1 of the ['867] patent does not describe the invention in "full, clear, concise and exact terms," Orthokinetics points only to the conclusory statements of Hobbs, Gaffney and expert witness William McCoy, Jr., that the patent is, in fact definite. These conclusory statements are not an adequate basis for the jury to reject Safety's defense. The undisputed, specific testimony of Gaffney and Hobbs demonstrates that an individual desiring to build a non-infringing travel chair cannot tell whether that chair violates the ['867] patent until he constructs a model and tests the model on vehicles ranging from a Honda Civic to a Lincoln Continental to a Checker cab. Without those cars, "so dimensioned" is without meaning.

The foregoing statement employs two measures impermissible in law: (1) it requires that claim 1 "describe" the invention, which is the role of the disclosure portion of the specification, not the role of the claims; and (2) it applied the "full, clear, concise, and exact" requirement of the first paragraph of § 112 to the claim, when that paragraph applies only to the disclosure portion of the specification, not to the claims. The district court spoke, inappropriately, of indefiniteness of the "patent," and did not review the claim for indefiniteness under the second paragraph of § 112.

A decision on whether a claim is invalid under § 112, 2d ¶, requires a determination of whether those skilled in the art would understand what is claimed when the claim is read in light of the specification.

It is undisputed that the claims require that one desiring to build and use a travel chair must measure the space between the selected automobile's doorframe and its seat and then dimension the front legs of the travel chair so they will fit in that particular space in that particular automobile. Orthokinetics' witnesses, who were skilled in the art, testified that such a task is evident from the specification and that one of ordinary skill in the art would easily have been able to determine the appropriate dimensions. The jury had the right to credit that testimony and no reason exists for the district court to have simply discounted that testimony as "conclusory".

The claims were intended to cover the use of the invention with various types of automobiles. That a particular chair on which the claims read may fit within some automobiles and not others is of no moment. The phrase "so dimensioned" is as accurate as the subject matter permits, automobiles being of various sizes. As long as those of ordinary skill in the art realized that the dimensions could be easily obtained, § 112, 2d ¶ requires nothing more. The patent law does not require that all possible lengths corresponding to the spaces in hundreds of different automobiles be listed in the patent, let alone that they be listed in the claims.

Compliance with the second paragraph of § 112 is generally a question of law. On the record before us, we observe no failure of compliance with the statute, and thus no basis on § 112 grounds for disturbing the jury's verdict. The district court's grant of Safety's motion for JNOV for claim indefiniteness was in error and must be reversed.

* * *

NOTES

1. Claiming a Method or an Apparatus. In *IPXL Holdings, L.L.C. v. Amazon.com, Inc.*, 430 F.3d 1377 (Fed. Cir. 2005), the patent holder claimed that Amazon's "one-click" system infringed his patent for an "Electronic Fund Transfer or Transaction System." The court held that a claim reciting both the system and a method for using the system is indefinite:

> [I]t is unclear whether infringement of claim 25 occurs when one creates a system that allows the user to change the predicted transaction information or accept the displayed transaction, or whether infringement occurs when the user actually uses the input means to change transaction information or uses the input means to accept a displayed transaction. Because claim 25 recites both a system and the method for using that system, it does not apprise a person of ordinary skill in the art of its scope, and it is invalid under section 112, paragraph 2.

Id. at 1384. Thus, the court held that Amazon's "one-click" system did not infringe.

4. Best Mode

SPECTRA–PHYSICS, INC. v. COHERENT, INC.

United States Court of Appeals for the Federal Circuit, 1987.
827 F.2d 1524.

RICH, CIRCUIT JUDGE.

These are cross-appeals from the December 16, 1985, judgment of the United States District Court for the Northern District of California holding both of Coherent's patents in suit, No. 4,378,600 entitled "Gas Laser" issued on March 29, 1983, to James L. Hobart (the Hobart patent) and No. 4,376,328 entitled "Method of Constructing Gaseous Laser" issued on March 15, 1983, to Wayne S. Mefferd (the Mefferd patent), invalid for lack of enabling disclosure under 35 U.S.C. § 112, first paragraph * * *

Background

A. Ion Lasers—In General

The Hobart patent is directed to an ion laser structure and the Mefferd patent to a method of fabricating an ion laser. The discharge through the laser is extremely hot—up to 6000°C. The exterior of the laser, however, must operate at room temperature, requiring dissipation of large amounts of heat by external cooling. It is also important that gas pressure be uniformly controlled along the discharge tube. [For cooling purposes, the Hobart laser has copper cups attached to the inside of a ceramic tube.]

* * *

D. The Importance of Brazing

Both the Hobart and Mefferd patents stress the importance of the bond between the copper cups and the ceramic tube. Poor thermal contact between them results in higher disc temperatures which in turn impedes the gas flow through the tube. For the laser to be reliable, the copper-ceramic bond must also be able to withstand repeated heat cycling. Due to the differing rates of thermal expansion of copper and alumina, the bond is subject to compressive forces as the laser heats up and tensile stress during cooling.

Dr. Hobart initially approached the problem of how to make the critical copper to ceramic bond by experimenting with soldering. These attempts were unsuccessful and no attempt was made to even try to solder together any laser shaped parts. Wayne Mefferd was then brought in to solve the attachment problem. His solution was brazing.

While the patent specifications disclose pulse soldering as one method of attachment, brazing is clearly the preferred method. In this process, a brazing shim is placed between the copper cup and the inner wall of the ceramic tube and the whole assembly is heated to the melting point of the braze material.

* * *

The patents further disclose "TiCuSil" as the preferred brazing material. This material is a copper silver eutectic (an alloy whose ingredients are proportioned to have the lowest possible melting point) with a small percentage of titanium added for making a ceramic to metal seal under what is known as the active metal process. In this process, the titanium invades and wets the ceramic so that the copper-silver braze material can hold the copper to the ceramic. In the absence of an active metal alloy component such as titanium, the ceramic must be premetalized with, for example, moly-manganese (MoMn), to provide a metallic surface to which the copper-silver braze material will adhere.

The TiCuSil active metal process is preferred because it requires only one step and avoids the need for premetalization. In addition, the copper cups cannot be electrically connected because this destroys the evenly graduated electrical potential down the bore of the tube which is required for the laser to operate. Thus, any premetalization must be in circular stripes along the inner surface of the tube so that each copper cup can be brazed or soldered to a different stripe.

E.   Patentee Coherent's Six–Stage Braze Cycle

Mefferd's six-stage cycle produced a reliable braze joint between the copper cups and the ceramic tube. Because this approach worked, Coherent continued to use TiCuSil and never investigated the moly-manganese process or further experimented with soldering. Neither the Hobart patent nor the Mefferd patent, however, discloses the braze cycle or any additional information on brazing copper to ceramic using TiCuSil.

F.   Spectra's "Cold Disc" Lasers

Dave Wright, head of research at Spectra, and his technician Martin Riley, worked on so-called "cold disc" lasers of the type in suit in the late 1970's. They referred to these lasers as "cold disc" lasers because the process of brazing the copper cups to the ceramic tube provided good thermal conduction as contrasted with the earlier radiatively cooled lasers which ran hot. Wright and Riley, however, had only limited success with cold disc lasers, in part because they could not make a satisfactory bond between the copper cups and the alumina ceramic tube. Upon repeated heat cycling, the ceramic would crack and cause the copper to break away, overheat, and melt, which destroyed the operation of the tube. After two and a half years, Wright was unable to make a TiCuSil braze joint which was reliable enough for a commercially acceptable product and Spectra temporarily abandoned the project.

Spectra resumed work on the cold disc project in 1981 after Coherent introduced its INNOVA laser embodying the inventions of the patents in suit. Because of their uncertainty about brazing, Spectra hired a brazing expert, Dr. Leonard Reed, to develop a moly-manganese process for attaching the cups to the ceramic tube. After nearly a year of experimentation, Dr. Reed developed Spectra's proprietary moly-manganese process. This involved using precision ceramic tubing and a special computerized striping tool which ground circular rings away from a coat of moly-manganese metallization painted on the entire inside of the tube.

* * *

The Decision Below

Spectra brought a declaratory judgment action against Coherent asking a holding of invalidity and non-infringement of both patents. Coherent counterclaimed for infringement and an adjudication of validity.

* * *

After entering judgment on the jury verdict, the district court withdrew the judgment and asked the parties to prepare proposed findings of fact and conclusions of law on several additional issues including disclosure of best mode and enablement under § 112, co-inventorship of the shield claims by Dr. Rempel, another Coherent employee, and inequitable conduct. The court ruled in favor of Coherent on all of these issues except enablement. On that issue, the court held both patents invalid for failure to disclose the six-stage braze cycle used by Coherent to manufacture the laser. The court found that the best mode requirement was satisfied, however, because neither Hobart nor Mefferd deliberately or accidentally concealed brazing as the best mode of attaching the copper cups to the ceramic tube.

Coherent appeals from the judgment with respect to lack of enablement and seeks reinstatement of the jury verdict that the shield claims are valid and infringed by Spectra. Coherent also appeals the portion of the judgment finding the remaining (non-shield) claims invalid for obviousness because of an erroneous jury instruction and requests a remand for a new trial on these claims.

Spectra cross-appeals from the judgment as it relates to best mode, inventorship of the shield claims, and derivation of the claimed subject matter from Wright and Riley. Spectra also appeals the denial of its request for attorney fees.

Opinion

1. Introduction—Adequate Disclosure Under § 112, 1st Paragraph

To constitute adequate disclosure under the first paragraph of 35 U.S.C. § 112, a patent specification must set forth both the manner and process of making and using the invention (the enablement requirement) and the best mode contemplated by the inventor of carrying out the invention (the best mode requirement). The difference between these two is explained in *In re Gay*, 309 F.2d 769, 135 USPQ 311 (CCPA 1962):

> The essence of [the enablement requirement] is that a specification shall disclose an invention in such a manner as will enable one skilled in the art to make and utilize it. *Separate and distinct* from [enablement] is [the best mode requirement], the essence of which requires the inventor to disclose the best mode *contemplated by him,* as of the time he executes the application, of carrying out his invention. Manifestly, the sole purpose of this latter requirement is to restrain inventors from applying for patents while at the same time concealing from the public preferred embodiments of their inventions which they have in fact conceived.

> . . . The question of whether an inventor has or has not disclosed what he feels is his best mode is, however, a question separate and distinct from the question of the *sufficiency* of his disclosure to satisfy the requirements of [enablement].

Id. at 772, 135 USPQ at 315 (emphasis in original).

Thus, compliance with the best mode requirement focuses on a different matter than does compliance with the enablement requirement. Enablement looks to placing the subject matter of the claims generally in the possession of the public. If, however, the applicant develops specific instrumentalities or techniques which are recognized at the time of filing as the best way of carrying out the invention, then the best mode requirement imposes an obligation to disclose that information to the public as well.

The situation before us is one in which the patent specifications disclose more than one means for making the claimed invention, but do not adequately disclose the best means actually known to the inventors. The district court recognized that the specifications were inadequate under § 112, but incorrectly based its decision on a lack of enablement. As we explain, the problem is really one of best mode, and thus, while we disagree with the district court's views on these issues, the judgment that the patents are both invalid was correct and must be sustained.

2. *Enablement*

* * *

To be enabling under § 112, a patent specification must disclose sufficient information to enable those skilled in the art to make and use the claimed invention. The district court held both of the patents in suit invalid for lack of enablement based on their failure to disclose Coherent's six-stage braze cycle for brazing TiCuSil. The court found that the braze cycle was "necessary to the enjoyment of the invention [sic]."

Coherent's braze cycle, however, is applicable only to TiCuSil brazing, which is just one of the ways to make and use the claimed inventions. The Hobart patent calls for "means for attaching" the copper cups to the inside of the ceramic tube and Mefferd has essentially the same step of "permanently securing" the cups to the tube. The specifications identify as suitable attachment techniques the alternatives of TiCuSil brazing, moly-manganese brazing, and low-temperature pulse-soldering.

If an invention pertains to an art where the results are predictable, e.g., mechanical as opposed to chemical arts, a broad claim can be enabled by disclosure of a single embodiment, and is not invalid for lack of enablement simply because it reads on another embodiment of the invention which is inadequately disclosed. Thus, it is sufficient here with respect to enablement that the patents disclose at least one attachment means which would enable a person of ordinary skill in the art to make and use the claimed inventions. Because the patents disclose the alternatives of moly-manganese brazing and pulse-soldering, their failure to also disclose Coherent's TiCuSil braze cycle is not fatal to enablement under § 112.

Spectra argues that the patents' references to the "moly-manganese process" is only in regard to low-temperature pulse-soldering, not brazing. We disagree. A fair reading of that paragraph as part of the general discussion of brazing, given that moly-manganese brazing was the most common method of bonding metal to ceramic, is that one skilled in the art would recognize that moly-manganese brazing was an alternative means of attachment. Spectra's Dave Wright, among others, testified that moly-manganese brazing was common in the industry and was well-known for brazing copper to ceramic.

The district court ignored the moly-manganese process, however, for the erroneous reason that it was "neither described nor advocated in the patents in suit." A patent need not teach, and preferably omits, what is well known in the art. While there is no elaboration of moly-manganese brazing in the patent specifications, the district court found that brazing was an old and well-known technique when the applications were filed. * * *

As for the court's statement that moly-manganese was not "advocated" in the patents, this is another matter entirely. We can only surmise that the court somehow confused the enablement requirement with the best mode. Nonenablement is the failure to disclose *any* mode, and does not depend on the applicant advocating a particular embodiment or method for making the invention. In practical terms, where only an alternative embodiment is enabled, the disclosure of the best mode may be inadequate. But that is a question separate and distinct from the question whether the specification enabled one to make the invention at all. * * *

3. *Best Mode*

* * *

Because the best mode provision of § 112 speaks in terms of the best mode "contemplated by the inventor," there is no objective standard by which to judge the adequacy of a best mode disclosure. Instead, only evidence of "concealment," whether accidental or intentional, is considered. The specificity of disclosure required to comply with the best mode requirement must be determined by the knowledge of facts within the possession of the inventor at the time of filing the application.

Compliance with the best mode requirement, because it depends on the applicant's state of mind, is a question of fact subject to the clearly erroneous standard of review. This assumes, however, a proper legal understanding of the best mode requirement, which we find missing from the district court's analysis. In general, we do not disagree with the facts as found by the district court. It is only the court's ultimate conclusion that the best mode requirement was satisfied that we reject.

In analyzing compliance with the best mode requirement, the district court focused only on the generic rather than the specific information known to the inventors and found that neither Mefferd nor Hobart intentionally, deliberately, or accidentally "concealed the braze technique as the best mode of attaching the heat web to the alumina tube." (Findings of Fact 4 and 8.) The patent specifications make clear, however, that the best mode contemplated by the inventors, as least as far as the critical "means for attaching" the copper cups to the ceramic tube is concerned, was more than just brazing in general—it was TiCuSil active metal brazing. Coherent acknowledges as much by its references to TiCuSil as the "preferred" brazing material and by the fact that Coherent never used anything else.

The appropriate question then is not whether the inventors disclosed TiCuSil brazing *at all*—they did—but whether TiCuSil brazing was *adequately* disclosed. Even though there may be a general reference to the best mode, the quality of the disclosure may be so poor as to effectively result in concealment.

The facts found by the district court, when placed in the proper framework, plainly demonstrate that the TiCuSil brazing technique used by Coherent was not adequately disclosed. The court stated in findings of fact under the heading "ENABLEMENT":

> 2. The use to which Coherent put the TiCuSil braze material was, and was known to be by Coherent at the time, contrary to criteria for the use of TiCuSil as contained in the literature.

and again,

> 9. The references to brazing as used in the patents and the extraneous texts (Kohl, Wesgo Brochure) relied upon by Coherent, do not describe for the benefit of one skilled in the art of laser construction the manner in which the Mefferd method is usable for the construction of the Hobart apparatus by means of [TiCuSil] brazing.

The district court also found that the inventors were aware of the problems associated with TiCuSil:

> 4. The known difficulty recognized by Hobart and Mefferd in working with TiCuSil as a braze material for the purpose to which they put it is reflected in Hobart's disclosure dated March 1, 1979 ... that the titanium-copper-silver process is "not in high favor in the ceramic industry" and "not preferred as compared with what is called the moly-manganese technique which produces stronger and also less leak-prone seals" and essentially the same language in the May, 1979 patent disclosure signed by all of Hobart, Mefferd and Johnston.

Coherent admits that its braze cycle is not disclosed in either patent nor is it contained in the prior art. Instead, it maintains that its braze cycle is unique to its ovens, and because the performance of industrial ovens varies considerably, the actual parameters would be meaningless to someone who used a different oven. In support of its position, Coherent cites *In re Gay*, 309 F.2d at 769, 135 USPQ at 316, which states that "[n]ot every last detail is to be described, else patent specifications would turn into production specifications, which they were never meant to be." In doing so, however, Coherent was not discussing whether it had complied with the best mode requirement because the court had held in its favor on that issue; it was discussing whether it had complied with the enablement requirement on which the court had held against it.

First, it is not up to the courts to decide *how* an inventor should disclose the best mode, but *whether* he has done so adequately under the statute. Second, far from being a "production specification," Coherent did not disclose *any* details about its brazing process. It is this complete lack of detail which effectively resulted in its concealment.

Where the district court went wrong on the law while reaching the right result is starkly revealed in its conclusions of law. Under the heading of "BEST MODE" is this conclusion:

> 4. There was no concealment deliberate or otherwise by Hobart or Mefferd of the brazing process as the best mode of bonding the heating web to the alumina tube.

As we have pointed out, however, this refers to brazing in general, not the actual brazing cycle with TiCuSil and all of the parameters which Coherent found to be its best mode, admittedly not disclosed. In contrast, but under the heading "ENABLEMENT," is the key conclusion of law which supports our conclusion and the judgment, reading as follows:

> 3. The six stage braze cycle employed by Coherent, and developed by it, are [sic, is] necessary to the enjoyment of the invention taught by the patents in suit by a person skilled in the art of laser construction, and are [sic] not *sufficiently disclosed* by the patents in suit. [Original emphasis.]

For reasons above explained, Coherent's failure to disclose its "six stage braze cycle" fully supports the defense of non-compliance with the best mode requirement of the first paragraph of § 112 although the inventions as broadly claimed could be practiced without knowledge of it, which means that the patent specifications are enabling. The trial court evidently had a grasp on the essential facts but somehow got them into the wrong legal pigeonholes. With the aid of lawyers, this is not difficult to do.

Spectra's claim in this declaratory judgment complaint that the two patents in suit are invalid must therefore be sustained on the ground that they fail to disclose the best mode contemplated by the inventors for practicing their respective inventions.

* * *

Conclusion

The judgment of the district court that the Hobart and Mefferd patents are both invalid is affirmed but on a different ground than that relied on by the court below. We hold that both patents are invalid under § 112, first paragraph, for failure to disclose the best mode, not for lack of enablement as the district court held.

AFFIRMED

NOTES

1. Is Best Mode Necessary? The United States is the only nation that requires a best mode disclosure. Often foreign applicants need to amend their foreign filings in order to meet the best mode requirement. Even so, 35 U.S.C. § 132 forbids the addition of new matter to patent applications, which often results in foreign applicants losing their priority date. If other nations do not believe that best mode disclosure is important, why does the United States? Does best mode disclosure simply raise the level of the enablement requirement?

In *Chemcast Corp. v. Arco Industries*, 913 F.2d 923 (Fed. Cir. 1990), the Federal Circuit set forth a two part test for best mode disclosure:

> [A] proper best mode analysis has two components. The first is whether, at the time the inventor filed his patent application, he knew of a mode of practicing his claimed invention that he considered to be better than any other. This part of the inquiry is wholly subjective, and resolves whether the inventor must disclose any facts in addition to those sufficient for enablement. If the inventor in fact contemplated such a preferred mode, the second part of the analysis compares what he knew with what he disclosed—is the disclosure adequate to enable one skilled in the art to practice the best mode or, in other words, has the inventor "concealed" his preferred mode from the "public"? Assessing the *adequacy* of the disclosure, as opposed to its *necessity*, is largely an objective inquiry that depends upon the scope of the claimed invention and the level of skill in the art.

Id. at 927–28. Are the two parts of the test compatible or do they counter each other?

5. Section 112 Paragraph 6: "Means Plus Function"

IN RE DONALDSON CO.

United States Court of Appeals for the Federal Circuit, 1994.
16 F.3d 1189.

RICH, CIRCUIT JUDGE.

The Donaldson Company (Donaldson) appeals from the January 30, 1991 decision of the Board of Patent Appeals and Interferences (Board) of the United States Patent and Trademark Office (PTO), reaffirmed on reconsideration on April 17, 1991, sustaining the Examiner's rejection of claim 1 of reexamination application Serial No. 90/001,776 (Schuler application) under 35 U.S.C. § 103. We reverse.

I. Background

A. The Invention

The present invention relates to industrial air-filtering devices often referred to as "dust collectors."

* * *

One problem with conventional collectors is that the dust accumulated in the hopper tends to harden or cake, thus interfering with the free movement of the accumulated dust downward to the auger screw. To overcome this problem, the Schuler collector takes advantage of the fact that every pulse of air from the nozzles causes the pressure within the dirty-air chamber to increase momentarily. At least one wall of the hopper of the Schuler collector is made from a flexible material which in essence transforms the hopper into a diaphragm-like structure which expands outward in response to the temporary pressure increases. This movement breaks up any dust that may have hardened or caked onto the hopper. This flexible-wall, diaphragm-like structure also provides the additional advantages of deadening the sounds of the cleaning pulses and expanding the volume of the dirty-air chamber, thus allowing the air pulses to act more vigorously on the filters.

Claim 1, the only claim on appeal, reads, as follows:

An air filter assembly for filtering air laden with particulate matter, said assembly comprising:

a housing having a clean air chamber and a filtering chamber, said housing having an upper wall, a closed bottom, and a plurality of side walls depending from said upper wall;

a clean air outlet from said clean air chamber in one of said side walls;

a dirty air inlet to said filtering chamber positioned in a wall of said housing in a location generally above said clean air outlet;

means separating said clean air chamber from said filtering chamber including means mounting a plurality of spaced-apart filter elements within said filtering chamber, with each of said elements being in fluid communication with said air outlet;

pulse-jet cleaning means, intermediate said outlet and said filter elements, for cleaning each of said filter elements; and

a lowermost portion in said filtering chamber arranged and constructed for the collection of particulate matter, said portion having *means, responsive to pressure increases in said chamber caused by said cleaning means, for moving particulate matter in a downward direction* to a bottommost point in said portion for subsequent transfer to a location exterior to said assembly.

B. The Board Decision

In its initial January 30, 1991 decision, the Board relied solely upon the dust collector disclosed in U.S. Patent No. 3,421,295 (Swift patent) to affirm the Examiner's rejection of claim 1.

[T]he Board did not interpret the "means, responsive to pressure increases in said chamber caused by said cleaning means, for moving particulate matter in a downward direction" language recited in the last paragraph of claim 1 as limited to the flexible wall, diaphragm-like structure disclosed in Schuler's specification, and equivalents thereof.

Indeed, the Board specifically stated at page 2 of its decision on reconsideration mailed April 17, 1991:

> It is axiomatic that particular features or limitations appearing in the specification are *not* to be read into the claims of an application. [citations omitted] Thus, contrary to [Donaldson's] argument, a flexible sloping surface is *not* a feature of the air filtering apparatus of claim 1 which distinguishes it over the air filtering apparatus of Swift.

C. Donaldson's Assertions

For purposes of this appeal, Donaldson effectively concedes that Swift teaches or suggests each and every element of the apparatus recited in Schuler's claim 1 except for the "means, responsive to pressure increases in said chamber caused by said cleaning means, for moving particulate matter in a downward direction" recited in the last segment of claim 1. As to this limitation, Donaldson argues that the Board erred in holding that Swift teaches or suggests such a means as it is described in Schuler's specification. Donaldson further argues that the Board's error in this regard is the result of a fundamental legal error by the Board, namely the Board's failure to obey the statutory mandate of 35 U.S.C. § 112, paragraph six, in construing this claim.

II.   Discussion

* * *

In this case, the PTO erred in its construction of the "means-plus-function" language recited in the last segment of Schuler's claim 1, and this error consequently led the PTO to impose an improper obviousness rejection.

B.   35 U.S.C. § 112, Paragraph Six

When statutory interpretation is at issue, the plain and unambiguous meaning of a statute prevails in the absence of clearly expressed legislative intent to the contrary. The statutory language at issue in this case reads:

> An element in a claim for a combination may be expressed as a means or step for performing a specified function without the recital of structure, material, or acts in support thereof, and such claim *shall be construed* to cover the corresponding structure, material, or acts described in the specification and equivalents thereof.

35 U.S.C. § 112, paragraph 6 (1988).

The plain and unambiguous meaning of paragraph six is that one construing means-plus-function language in a claim must look to the specification and interpret that language in light of the corresponding structure, material, or acts described therein, and equivalents thereof, to the extent that the specification provides such disclosure. Paragraph six does not state or even suggest that the PTO is exempt from this mandate, and there is no legislative history indicating that Congress intended that the PTO should be. Thus, this court must accept the plain and precise language of paragraph six. Accordingly, because no distinction is made in paragraph six between prosecution in the PTO and enforcement in the courts, or between validity and infringement, we hold that paragraph six applies regardless of the context in which the interpretation of means-plus-function language arises, i.e., whether as part of a patentability determination in the PTO or as part of a validity or infringement determination in a court.

The Commissioner argues that his interpretation is entitled to deference in view of what the Commissioner alleges is the PTO's sweeping and long-standing practice of not applying paragraph six during examination. We disagree. The fact that the PTO may have failed to adhere to a statutory mandate over an extended period of time does not justify its continuing to do so. In addition, paragraph six facially covers every situation involving the interpretation of means-plus-function language, and the Commissioner's attempts to create an ambiguity in paragraph six where none exists are to no avail. The fact that paragraph six does not specifically state that it applies during prosecution in the PTO does not mean that paragraph six is ambiguous in this respect. Quite the contrary, we interpret the fact that paragraph six fails to distinguish between prosecution in the PTO and enforcement in the courts as indicating that Congress did not intend to create any such distinction.

In addition, Section 112 as a whole relates to requirements for the specification and claims without regard to whether a patent or patent application is involved. Moreover, Section 112 is found in Chapter 11 of Title 35, titled "Application for Patent," which supports our holding that section 112, paragraph six, governs the interpretation of "means" clauses in a claim for a combination when being examined in pending applications.

The Commissioner argues that Congress enacted paragraph six to codify the "reverse doctrine of equivalents" for means-plus-function claim language, a claim interpretation tool which finds application only in the litigation context, wherefore Congress must have intended paragraph six to apply only in the context of post-issuance infringement and validity actions. We see no merit in this imaginative reasoning, and no support for it has been cited. The record is clear on why paragraph six was enacted. In *Halliburton Oil Well Cementing Co. v. Walker*, 329 U.S. 1, 67 S.Ct. 6, 91 L.Ed. 3 (1946), the Supreme Court held that means-plus-function language could not be employed at the exact point of novelty in a combination claim. Congress enacted paragraph six, originally paragraph three, to statutorily overrule that holding. The fact that the question of how to treat means-plus-function language came to Congress's attention through the context of infringement litigation does not suggest that Congress did not intend paragraph six to apply to all interpretations of means-plus-function claim language. Furthermore, there is no legislative history suggesting that Congress's purpose in enacting paragraph six was to codify the reverse doctrine of equivalents, and thus there is no reason to believe that Congress intended to limit the application of paragraph six to post-issuance claim interpretation.

Contrary to suggestions by the Commissioner, our holding does not conflict with the principle that claims are to be given their "broadest reasonable interpretation" during prosecution. Generally speaking, this claim interpretation principle remains intact. Rather, our holding in this case merely sets a limit on how broadly the PTO may construe means-plus-function language under the rubric of "reasonable interpretation." Per our holding, the "broadest reasonable interpretation" that an examiner may give means-plus-function language is that statutorily mandated in paragraph six. Accordingly, the PTO may not disregard the structure disclosed in the specification corresponding to such language when rendering a patentability determination.

Our holding similarly does not conflict with the second paragraph of section 112. Indeed, we agree with the general principle espoused in *In re Lundberg*, 244 F.2d at 547–48 (CCPA 1957), that the sixth paragraph of section 112 does not exempt an applicant from the requirements of the first two paragraphs of that section. Although paragraph six statutorily provides that one may use means-plus-function language in a claim, one is still subject to the requirement that a claim "particularly point out and distinctly claim" the invention. Therefore, if one employs means-plus-function language in a claim, one must set forth in the specification an adequate disclosure showing what is meant by that language. If an applicant fails to set forth an adequate disclosure, the applicant has in effect failed to particularly point out and distinctly claim the invention as required by the second paragraph of section 112.

Also contrary to suggestions by the Commissioner, our holding does not conflict with the general claim construction principle that limitations found only in the specification of a patent or patent application should not be imported or read into a claim. The Commissioner confuses impermissibly imputing limitations from the specification into a claim with properly referring to the specification to determine the meaning of a particular word or phrase recited in a claim. What we are dealing with in this case is the construction of a limitation already in the claim in the form of a means-plus-function clause and a statutory mandate on how that clause must be construed.

C. *Application of Paragraph Six to Claims*

For the foregoing reasons, the PTO was required by statute to look to Schuler's specification and construe the "means" language recited in the last segment of claim 1 as limited to the corresponding structure disclosed in the specification and equivalents thereof. The particular means language of claim 1 at issue reads:

> means, responsive to pressure increases in said chamber caused by said cleaning means, for moving particulate matter in a downward

direction to a bottommost point in said [lowermost] portion for subsequent transfer to a location exterior to said assembly.

In the "Summary of the Invention" section of his specification, Schuler states:

> A lowermost portion of the assembly is arranged and constructed to collect the removed particulate matter. The collection *portion* includes a sloping surface constructed of a material *which flexes in response to the pressure differentials created within the chamber* during the operation of the pulse-jet cleaning means.
>
> . . . .
>
> [t]he sloping *surface* of the collection portion of the assembly *moves outward, or flexes, as the pressure increases within the chamber* with each operation of the pulse-jet means. The flexing movement allows the air entraining the dust from the filter element to travel towards the collection area, thereby helping to prevent the removed dust from being re-deposited on a neighboring filter element. Also, the flexing surface dampens the noise and vibrations of the pulse jet cleaning means, and moves the dust collected on its surface towards the collection area for subsequent removal from the assembly itself.

Schuler Patent, Col. 2, lines 6–12, 28–39. In discussing a preferred embodiment of his dust collector, Schuler further describes the "means, responsive to pressure" recited in claim 1 as follows:

> The larger surface area is designed and arranged to act as a diaphragm which is movably responsive to the pressure differentials created within the dirty air chamber by the operation of the pulse jet cleaning means. The diaphragm is preferably made from a flexible, reinforced rubber sheet material. However, any material sufficiently strong and flexible could be used, i.e., a relatively thin metal panel which will flex. The diaphragm movement caused by the operation of the pulse jet cleaning means will be explained in detail below.

Schuler Patent, Col. 6, lines 21–31. The further explanation referred to reads:

> During the operation of the pulse-jet cleaning means the larger, sloping surface or diaphragm moves outward or away from the filter elements in response to the increase in pressure within the dirty air chamber. As the pressure diminishes, the surface flexes back to its normal position.
>
> The pressure-responsive, flexing movement of the larger sloping surface accomplishes four important functions: (1) the movement allows air entraining the removed dust to move downwardly towards the hopper; (2) it helps prevent the removed dust and particulate matter from being re-deposited onto adjacent elements; (3) it helps to dampen the noise and the vibrations of the pulse-jet cleaning means; and (4) it helps to move the particulate matter which has settled on the diaphragm surface towards the auger screw.

Schuler Patent, Col. 7, lines 42–61.

A review of the foregoing excerpts leads to the inescapable conclusion that Schuler's specification defines the "means, responsive to pressure increases in said chamber ..., for moving particulate matter in a downward direction" language recited in claim 1 as a flexible-wall, diaphragm-like structure, such that the hopper is made up of at least one flexible wall which expands outward upon pressure increases, thus causing caked-on dust to break loose from the wall of the hopper and fall towards the auger screw due to gravity.

D. Swift

The Swift collector does not teach or suggest the flexible-wall, diaphragm-like structure claimed by Schuler. Indeed, there is no teaching or suggestion in Swift that the hopper walls therein be anything but rigid and non-responsive to any pressure increases within the collector. Consequently, it would not have been obvious to one of ordinary skill in the art to modify Swift to obtain Schuler's flexible-wall, diaphragm-like structure. In this regard, we note that the Board itself specifically held at page 6 of its initial decision that the examiner had failed to establish a *prima facie* case of obviousness as to claims 2, 3, and 5, because Swift and the other references relied upon by the examiner

> fail to disclose or render obvious the feature of the lowermost portion of the claimed apparatus comprising the flexible sloping surface which flexes in response to increases in pressure in the apparatus caused by the pulse-jet cleaning means whereby filtered particulate matter is moved in a downward direction.

* * *

In summary, Schuler's claimed collector would not have been obvious in view of Swift's collector having hopper walls which are rigid and non-responsive to pressure increases within the collector. In addition, even if the issue of anticipation under section 102 were before us, which it is not, the Commissioner could not have argued anticipation because he has failed to establish that the rigid hopper wall structure in Swift's collector is an "equivalent" of the flexible wall, diaphragm-like hopper structure in Schuler's claim 1 collector.

Conclusion

For the foregoing reasons, we hold, as a matter of law, that Swift does not render the structure defined by claim 1 obvious under 35 U.S.C. § 103, and therefore we reverse the decision of the Board. On the record before us, we see no reason to remand this case for further findings as to "equivalents" as suggested by the Commissioner.

REVERSED.

Notes

1. Single Element Claims and "means plus function." A single element claim written in "means plus function" language is invalid. The rejected claim in *In re Hyatt*, 708 F.2d 712, 712–13 (Fed. Cir. 1983) stated:

> A Fourier transform processor for generating Fourier transformed incremental output signals in response to incremental input signals, said Fourier transform processor comprising incremental means for incrementally generating the Fourier transformed incremental output signals in response to the incremental input signals.

Because it was a single element claim, Judge Rich rejected it, stating "[t]he long-recognized problem with a single means claim is that it covers every conceivable means for achieving the stated result, while the specification discloses at most only those means known to the inventor." *Id.* at 714.

G. THE APPLICANT'S OATH AND DUTY OF CANDOR: SECTION 115 AND 37 C.F.R. 1.56

In addition to the disclosure and claim requirements, Section 115 requires a patent applicant to take an oath. The goal of Section 115 is to prevent applicants from being dishonest with the PTO about whether they invented the subject matter under consideration for a patent.

§ 115. Oath of applicant

The applicant shall make oath that he believes himself to be the original and first inventor of the process, machine, manufacture, or composition of matter, or improvement thereof, for which he solicits a patent; and shall state of what country he is a citizen. Such oath may be made before any person within the United States authorized by law to administer oaths, or, when, made in a foreign country, before any diplomatic or consular officer of the United States authorized to administer oaths, or before any officer having an official seal and authorized to administer oaths in the foreign country in which the applicant may be, whose authority is proved by certificate of a diplomatic or consular officer of the United States, or apostille of an official designated by a foreign country which, by treaty or convention, accords like effect to apostilles of designated officials in the United States, and such oath shall be valid if it complies with the laws of the state or country where made. When the application is made as provided in this title by a person other than the inventor, the oath may be so varied in form that it can be made by him. For purposes of this section, a consular officer shall include any United States citizen serving overseas, authorized to perform notarial functions pursuant to section 1750 of the Revised Statutes, as amended (22 U.S.C. 4221).

35 U.S.C. § 115.

Patent applicants also have a duty of candor under 37 C.F.R. § 1.56. In essence, this duty requires all "[i]ndividuals associated with the filing or prosecution of a patent application" to disclose information material to patentability of pending claims to the PTO. 37 C.F.R. § 1.56 (2009). Section 1.56 defines materiality, and also provides that a non-attorney involved in patent prosecution (e.g., an inventor) may discharge their duty of candor by disclosing the material information to their attorney. Because patent prosecution is an ex parte administrative process, the PTO does not have the resources to ensure compliance with Section 1.56. Accordingly, the duty of candor is policed in litigation.

During litigation, the alleged infringer may allege that the patentee engaged in inequitable conduct (i.e., a breach of the duty of candor) during prosecution of one or more claims of the asserted patent. If the court finds the patentee engaged in inequitable conduct, then, as a matter of equity, the entire patent is unenforceable. Inequitable conduct requires (1) intent to deceive and (2) materiality.

Relying on litigation, however, has created its own problems. In *Burlington Industries, Inc. v. Dayco Corp.*, 849 F.2d 1418, 1422 (1988), the Federal Circuit remarked "the habit of charging inequitable conduct in almost every major patent case has become an absolute plague." The Federal Circuit can combat the plague by raising either the intent to deceive or materiality necessary for a finding of inequitable conduct. Yet, when the court makes it harder to establish inequitable conduct, the duty of candor is not effectively policed. There is little ex ante incentive to disclose all material information to the PTO when the duty of candor is not effectively policed.

KINGSDOWN MEDICAL CONSULTANTS, LTD. v. HOLLISTER INCORPORATED

United States Court of Appeals for the Federal Circuit, 1988.
863 F.2d 867.

MARKEY, CHIEF JUDGE.

Kingsdown Medical Consultants, Ltd. and E.R. Squibb & Sons, Inc., (Kingsdown) appeal from a judgment of the United States District Court for the Northern District of Illinois holding U.S. Patent No. 4,460,363 ('363) unenforceable because of inequitable conduct before the United States Patent and Trademark Office (PTO). We reverse and remand.

BACKGROUND

Kingsdown sued Hollister Incorporated (Hollister) for infringement of claims 2, 4, 5, 9, 10, 12, 13, 14, 16, 17, 18, 27, 28, and 29 of Kingsdown's '363 patent. The district court held the patent unenforceable because of Kingsdown's conduct in respect of claim 9 and reached no other issue.

The invention claimed in the '363 patent is a two-piece ostomy appliance for use by patients with openings in their abdominal walls for release of waste.

The two pieces of the appliance are a pad and a detachable pouch. The pad is secured to the patient's body encircling the abdominal wall opening. Matching coupling rings are attached to the pad and to the pouch. When engaged, the rings provide a water tight seal. Disengaging the rings allows for removal of the pouch.

A. The Prosecution History

Kingsdown filed its original patent application in February 1978. The '363 patent issued July 17, 1984. The intervening period of more than six-and-a-half years saw a complex prosecution, involving the submission, rejection, amendment, re-numbering, etc., of 118 claims, a continuation application, an appeal, a petition to make special, and citation and discussion of 44 references.

After a series of office actions and amendments, Kingsdown submitted claim 50. With our emphasis on the language of interest here, claim 50 read:

> A coupling for an ostomy appliance comprising a pad or dressing having a generally circular aperture for passage of the stoma, said *pad or dressing aperture encircled by a coupling member* and an ostomy bag also having a generally circular aperture for passage of the stoma, said *bag aperture encircled by a second coupling member,* one of said coupling members being two opposed walls of closed looped annular channel form and the other coupling member of closed loop form having a rib or projection dimensioned to be gripped between the mutaully (sic) opposed channel walls when said coupling members are connected, said rib or projection having a thin resilient deflectible seal strip extending therefrom, which, when said rib or projection is disposed between said walls, springs away therefrom to sealingly engage one of said walls, and in which each coupling member is formed of resilient synthetic plastics material.

The examiner found that claim 50 contained allowable subject matter, but rejected the claim for indefiniteness under 35 U.S.C. § 112, second paragraph, objecting to "encircled", because the coupling ring could not, in the examiner's view, "encircle" the aperture in the pad, the ring and aperture not being "coplanar." The examiner had not in earlier actions objected to "encircled" to describe similar relationships in other claims. Nor had the examiner found the identical "encircled" language indefinite in original claims 1 and 6 which were combined to form claim 50.

To render claim 50 definite, and thereby overcome the § 112 rejection, Kingsdown amended the claim. With our emphasis on the changed language, amended claim 50 read:

> A coupling for an ostomy appliance comprising a pad or dressing having *a body contacting surface and an outer surface with* a generally circular aperture for passage of the stoma *extending through* said pad or dressing, a coupling member *extending outwardly from said outer pad or dressing surface and encircling the intersection of said aperture*

and said outer pad or dressing surface, and an ostomy bag also having a generally circular aperture *in one bag wall* for passage of the stoma *with* a second coupling member *affixed to said bag wall around the periphery of said bag wall aperture and extending outwardly from said bag wall,* one of said coupling members being two opposed walls of closed looped *annular* channel form and the other coupling member of closed loop form having a rib or projection dimensioned to be gripped between the mutually opposed channel walls when said coupling members are connected, said rib or projection having a thin resilient deflectible seal strip extending therefrom, which, when said rib or projection is disposed between said walls, springs away therefrom to sealingly engage one of said walls, and in which each coupling member is formed of resilient synthetic plastic material.

To avoid the § 112 rejection, Kingsdown had thus added the pad's two surfaces, replaced "aperture encircled", first occurrence, with "encircling the intersection of said aperture and said outer pad or dressing surface", and deleted "encircled", second occurrence. In an advisory action, the examiner said the changes in claim language overcame the § 112 rejection and that amended claim 50 would be allowable.

While Kingsdown's appeal of other rejected claims was pending, Kingsdown's patent attorney saw a two-piece ostomy appliance manufactured by Hollister. Kingsdown engaged an outside counsel to file a continuation application and withdrew the appeal.

Thirty-four claims were filed with the continuation application, including new and never-before-examined claims and 22 claims indicated as corresponding to claims allowed in the parent application. In prosecuting the continuation, a total of 44 references, including 14 new references, were cited and 29 claims were substituted for the 34 earlier filed, making a total of 63 claims presented. Kingsdown submitted a two-column list, one column containing the claim numbers of 22 previously allowed claims, the other column containing the claim numbers of the 21 claims in the continuation application that corresponded to those previously allowed claims. That list indicated, incorrectly, that claim 43 in the continuation application corresponded to allowed claim 50 in the parent application. Claim 43 actually corresponded to the unamended claim 50 that had been rejected for indefiniteness under § 112. Claim 43 was renumbered as the present claim 9 in the '363 patent.

There was another claim 43. It was in the parent application and was combined with claim 55 of the parent application to form claim 61 in the continuation. Claim 55 contained the language of amended claim 50 relating to "encircled." It was allowed as submitted and was not involved in any discussion of indefiniteness. Claim 61 became claim 27 of the patent. Claim 27 reads as follows:

An ostomy appliance comprising a pad or dressing having a body contacting surface and an outer surface with an aperture for passage of the stoma extending through said pad or dressing, *a coupling member extending outwardly from said pad or dressing and encircling the intersection of said aperture and the outer surface of said pad or dressing* and an ostomy bag also having an aperture in one bag wall for passage of the stoma with a second coupling member affixed to said bag wall around the periphery of said bag wall aperture and extending outwardly from said bag wall, said bag coupling member being two opposed walls of closed loop channel form and said pad or dressing coupling member being a closed loop form having a rib or projection dimensioned to be gripped between the opposed channel walls when said coupling members are connected, and a thin resilient seal strip extending at an angle radially inward from an inner surface of said rib or projection which engages the outer surface of said inner channel wall and wherein said rib or projection has a peripheral bead extending therefrom in a direction opposite said deflectible seal strip and said outer channel wall has a complementary bead on its inner surface, each of said two beads having an annular surface inclined to the common axis of said coupling members when connected, the arrangement being such that said two annular surfaces are in face-to-face contact when said two members are in their mutually coupled positions. (emphasis provided)

B.   The District Court

* * *

Having examined the prosecution history, the district court found that the examiner could have relied on the representation that claim 43 corresponded to allowable claim 50 and rejected Kingsdown's suggestion that the examiner must have made an independent examination of claim 43 * * *.

The district court found the materiality element of inequitable conduct, because allowability of claim 50 turned on the amendment overcoming the § 112 rejection in the parent application. Kingsdown's knowledge of materiality was inferred from claim 50's having been deemed allowable in the parent application only after the change in claim language.

The court found the deceitful intent element of inequitable conduct, because Kingsdown was grossly negligent in not noticing the error, or, in the alternative, because Kingsdown's acts indicated an intent to deceive the PTO.

The court found that Kingsdown's patent attorney was grossly negligent in not catching the misrepresentation because a mere ministerial review of the language of amended claim 50 in the parent application and of claim 43 in the continuing application would have uncovered the error, and because Kingsdown's patent attorney had * * * several opportunities to make that review.

The district court stated that the narrower language of amended claim 50 gave Hollister a possible defense, i.e., that Hollister's coupling member does not encircle the intersection of the aperture and the pad surface because it has an intervening "floating flange" member. The court inferred motive to deceive the PTO because Kingsdown's patent attorney viewed the Hollister appliance after he had amended claim 50 and before the continuation application was filed. The court expressly declined to make any finding on whether the accused device would or would not infringe any claims, but stated that Kingsdown's patent attorney must have perceived that Hollister would have a defense against infringement of the amended version of claim 50 that it would not have against the unamended version.

* * *

ISSUE

Whether the district court's finding of intent to deceive was clearly erroneous, rendering its determination that inequitable conduct occurred an abuse of discretion.

OPINION

We confront a case of first impression, in which inequitable conduct has been held to reside in an incorrect inclusion in a continuation application of a claim that contained allowable subject matter, but had been rejected as indefinite in the parent application.

Inequitable conduct resides in failure to disclose material information, or submission of false material information, with an intent to deceive, and those two elements, materiality and intent, must be proven by clear and convincing evidence. The findings on materiality and intent are subject to the clearly erroneous standard of Rule 52(a) Fed.R.Civ.P. and are not to be disturbed unless this court has a definite and firm conviction that a mistake has been committed.

"To be guilty of inequitable conduct, one must have intended to act inequitably." *FMC Corp. v. Manitowoc Co., Inc.*, 835 F.2d 1411, 1415, 5 USPQ2d 1112, 1115 (Fed.Cir.1987). Kingsdown's attorney testified that he was not aware of the error until Hollister mentioned it in March 1987, and the experts for both parties testified that they saw no evidence of deceptive intent. As above indicated, the district court's finding of Kingsdown's intent to mislead is based on the alternative grounds of: (a) gross negligence; and (b) acts indicating an intent to deceive. Neither ground, however, supports a finding of intent in this case.

a. Negligence

The district court inferred intent based on what it perceived to be Kingsdown's gross negligence. Whether the intent element of inequitable conduct is present cannot always be inferred from a pattern of conduct that may be described as gross negligence. That conduct must be sufficient to require a finding of deceitful intent in the light of all the circumstances. We are not convinced that deceitful intent was present in Kingsdown's negligent filing of its continuation application or, in fact, that its conduct even rises to a level that would warrant the description "gross negligence."

It is well to be reminded of what actually occurred in this case-a ministerial act involving two claims, which, because both claims contained allowable subject matter, did not result in the patenting of anything anticipated or rendered obvious by anything in the prior art and thus took nothing from the public domain. In preparing and filing the continuation application, a newly-hired counsel for Kingsdown had two versions of "claim 50" in the parent application, an unamended rejected version and an amended allowed version. As is common, counsel renumbered and transferred into the continuation all (here, 22) claims "previously allowed". In filing its claim 43, it copied the "wrong", i.e., the rejected, version of claim 50. That error led to the incorrect listing of claim 43 as corresponding to allowed claim 50 and to incorporation of claim 43 as claim 9 in the patent. In approving the continuation for filing, Kingsdown's regular attorney did not, as the district court said, "catch" the mistake.

In view of the relative ease with which others also overlooked the differences in the claims, Kingsdown's failure to notice that claim 43 did not correspond to the amended and allowed version of claim 50 is insufficient to warrant a finding of an intent to deceive the PTO. Undisputed facts indicating that relative ease are: (1) the similarity in language of the two claims; (2) the use of the same claim number, 50, for the amended and unamended claims; (3) the multiplicity of claims involved in the prosecution of both applications; (4) the examiner's failure to reject claims using "encircled" in the parent application's first and second office actions, making its presence in claim 43 something less than a glaring error; (5) the two-year interval between the rejection/amendment of claim 50 and the filing of the continuation; (6) failure of the examiner to reject claim 43 under § 112 or to notice the differences between claim 43 and amended claim 50 during what must be presumed, absent contrary evidence, to have been an examination of the continuation; and (7) the failure of Hollister to notice the lack of correspondence between claim 43 and the amended version of claim 50 during three years of discovery and until after it had carefully and critically reviewed the file history 10 to 15 times with an eye toward litigation. That Kingsdown did not notice its mistake during more than one opportunity of doing so, does not in this case, and in view of Hollister's frequent and focused opportunities, establish that Kingsdown intended to deceive the PTO.

We do not, of course, condone inattention to the duty of care owed by one preparing and filing a continuation application. Kingsdown's counsel may have been careless, but it was clearly erroneous to base a finding of intent to deceive on that fact alone.

* * *

Thus the first basis for the district court's finding of deceitful intent (what it viewed as "gross negligence") cannot stand.

b. Acts

The district court also based its finding of deceitful intent on the separate and alternative inferences it drew from Kingsdown's acts in viewing the Hollister device, in desiring to obtain a patent that would "cover" that device, and in failing to disclaim or reissue after Hollister charged it with inequitable conduct. The district court limited its analysis here to claim 9 and amended claim 50.

It should be made clear at the outset of the present discussion that there is nothing improper, illegal or inequitable in filing a patent application for the purpose of obtaining a right to exclude a known competitor's product from the market; nor is it in any manner improper to amend or insert claims intended to cover a competitor's product the applicant's attorney has learned about during the prosecution of a patent application. Any such amendment or insertion must comply with all statutes and regulations, of course, but, if it does, its genesis in the marketplace is simply irrelevant and cannot of itself evidence deceitful intent.

* * *

Faced with Hollister's assertion that an experienced patent attorney would knowingly and intentionally transfer into a continuing application a claim earlier rejected for indefiniteness, without rearguing that the claim was not indefinite, the district court stated that "how an experienced patent attorney could allow such conduct to take place" gave it "the greatest difficulty." A knowing failure to disclose and knowingly false statements are always difficult to understand. However, a transfer of numerous claims *en masse* from a parent to a continuing application, as the district court stated, is a ministerial act. As such, it is more vulnerable to errors which by definition result from inattention, and is less likely to result from the scienter involved in the more egregious acts of omission and commission that have been seen as reflecting the deceitful intent element of inequitable conduct in our cases.

* * *

We are forced to the definite and firm conviction that a mistake has been committed, amounting to an abuse of discretion. The district court's finding of deceitful intent was clearly erroneous.

* * *

CONCLUSION

Having determined that the district court's finding of intent is clearly erroneous, the panel reverses the judgment based on a conclusion of inequitable conduct before the PTO and remands the case for such further proceedings as the district court may deem appropriate.

REVERSED AND REMANDED.

H. PATENT REFORM

Patent litigation is a rare occurrence, 99% of patent owners never file suit to enforce their rights. Yet, $4.33 billion dollars are spent per year to obtain patents. One explanation for this inconsistency is the differing values of patents. Litigated patents are distinguishable from non-litigated patents in that they tend to be more complex, take longer to prosecute, and the large companies that obtain most patents are not the ones that tend to enforce them. John R. Allison, Mark A. Lemley, Kimberly A. Moore, and R. Derek Trunkey, *Valuable Patents*, 92 GEO. L.J. 435 (2004).

A recent study on the outcomes of patent infringement cases found that patent holders win about 25% of the cases, accused infringers win the other 75%, and approximately 45% of litigated patents are invalidated. Paul M. Janicke & LiLan Ren, *Who Wins Patent Infringement Cases?*, 34 AIPLA Q.J. 1 (2006). These findings may be helpful in finding efficient ways to promote innovation, and may help in eliminating inefficiency at the PTO.

There is also debate about whether the PTO may be "rationally ignorant." One argument holds that the PTO may be rationally ignorant of the objective validity of the patents it examines as gathering all of the information necessary to make failsafe validity decisions would require an enormous investment of time and resources. Mark A. Lemley, *Rational Ignorance at the Patent Office*, 95 NW. U. L. REV. 1495 (2001). It is argued that, due to the small number of patents litigated, validity may be more efficiently established through the litigation process. Under this rationale, allowing invalid patents to pass through the PTO is not bad policy.

The countervailing argument holds that rational ignorance should be constrained, and that the PTO should strive for an optimal level of ignorance. Shubha Ghosh & Jay P. Kesan, *What Do Patents Purchase? In Search of Optimal Ignorance in the Patent Office*, 40 HOUS. L. REV. 1219 (2004). While the constraints on the PTO's ability to process the vast quantities of information necessary to assess patents need to be recognized, the needs of society must be the guide when assessing constraints on information.

In order to have an optimal patent system, the role of the PTO in granting patents, and the role of the courts in policing their use, must be defined. The social costs and benefits of the patent system should be considered for all affected actors including patentees, competitors, improvers, and the like.

A look at the interaction between PTO and the Court of Appeals for the Federal Circuit reveals that the level of deference the Federal Circuit grants the PTO's findings is less than the level of deference it gives to other governmental agencies. Some believe that the Federal Circuit should give the PTO's decisions *Chevron* deference and dispense with *de novo* review of patent validity questions, particularly when making determinations of nonobviousness. Craig Allen Nard, *Deference, Defiance, and the Useful Arts*, 56 OHIO ST. L.J. 1415 (1995).

Reversals of the PTO's patent denials, in the Federal Circuit, may be responsible for the recent upsurge in patent filings and patents granted. Some suggest that greater deference to the PTO's denials represents an important mechanism for curtailing the "gold rush" to patent, especially in the fields of biotechnology and computer software. Arti Rai, *Addressing the Patent Gold Rush: The Role of Deference to the PTO Patent Denials*, 2 WASH. U. J.L. & POL'Y 199 (2000). In addition to making changes in the administration of the patent system, some commentators seek broader patent reform.

It is widely recognized that the PTO often grants overly broad patents. One proposal to address this issue is to increase the quantity and quality of the information that patentees are required to give the Patent Office to discourage patentees from engaging in opportunistic behavior with the PTO. Jay P. Kesan, *Carrots and Sticks to Create a Better Patent System*, 17 BERKELEY TECH. L.J. 763 (2002). One suggested incentive is to grant presumptions of validity only in cases where the patentee has presented an expanded information disclosure statement to the PTO. A suggested disincentive is the of use fee-shifting strategies like transferring litigation costs to patent holding plaintiffs, whose claims have been invalidated or revoked based on categories of prior art that are likely to have been discovered by a diligent patentee.

There have been a number of proposals to streamline or reform the patent system including the creation of bounties, switching back to a registration system, and implementation of a dual patent invalidation system with oppositions. For a summary, see Jay P. Kesan, *Why "Bad" Patents Survive in the Market and How Should We Change?—The Private and Social Costs of Patents*, 55 EMORY L.J. 61 (2006). Although patents may be revoked through the reexamination process, it is mechanically awkward, and while the process is designed to be a curative it may actually derogate legitimate policy objectives. Mark D. Janis, *Rethinking Reexamination: Toward a Viable Administrative Revocation System for U.S. Patent Law*, 11 HARV. J.L. & TECH. 1 (1997). Critics of reexamination call for the "amputation" of the reexamination process under the American Inventors Protection Act of 1999, and want reexamination replaced with a prosthetic invalidation procedure. Kristen Jakobsen Osenga, *Rethinking Reexamination Reform: Is It Time for Corrective Surgery, or Is It Time to Amputate?* 14 FORDHAM INTELL. PROP. MEDIA & ENT. L.J. 217 (2003). It remains to be seen if Congress will adopt any of these proposals. In 2007, the U.S. House of Representatives passed Patent Reform legislation that, among other things, included a PTO post-grant opposition proceeding similar to European opposition proceedings. H.R. 1980 § 6(f), 110th Cong. (as passed by House, Sep. 7, 2007). This type of legislation, however, was not passed by the Senate.

III. INFRINGEMENT

The Patent Act says the following about infringement:

(a) Except as otherwise provided in this title, whoever without authority makes, uses, offers to sell, or sells any patented invention, within the United States or imports into the United States any patented invention during the term of the patent therefor, infringes the patent.

(b) Whoever actively induces infringement of a patent shall be liable as an infringer.

(c) Whoever offers to sell or sells within the United States or imports into the United States a component of a patented machine, manufacture, combination or composition, or a material or apparatus for use in practicing a patented process, constituting a material part of the invention, knowing the same to be especially made or especially adapted for use in an infringement of such patent, and not a staple article or commodity of commerce suitable for substantial noninfringing use, shall be liable as a contributory infringer.

35 U.S.C. § 271. Under Section 271(a), infringement occurs when one or more of the listed activities takes place. Thus, one may infringe by making without using or selling, using without making or selling, or by selling without using or making.

A. DIRECT INFRINGEMENT

PHILLIPS v. AWH CORP.

United States Court of Appeals for the Federal Circuit, 2005.
415 F.3d 1303.

BRYSON, CIRCUIT JUDGE.

Edward H. Phillips invented modular, steel-shell panels that can be welded together to form vandalism-resistant walls. The panels are especially useful in building prisons because they are load-bearing and impact-resistant, while also insulating against fire and noise. Mr. Phillips obtained a patent on the invention, U.S. Patent No. 4,677,798 ("the '798 patent"), and he subsequently entered into an arrangement with AWH Corporation, Hopeman Brothers, Inc., and Lofton Corporation (collectively "AWH") to market and sell the panels. That arrangement ended in 1990. In 1991, however, Mr. Phillips received a sales brochure from AWH that suggested to him that AWH was continuing to use his trade secrets and patented technology without his consent. In a series of letters in 1991 and 1992, Mr. Phillips accused AWH of patent infringement and trade secret misappropriation. Correspondence between the parties regarding the matter ceased after that time.

In February 1997, Mr. Phillips brought suit in the United States District Court for the District of Colorado charging AWH with misappropriation of trade secrets and infringement of claims 1, 21, 22, 24, 25, and 26 of the '798 patent. The district court dismissed the trade secret misappropriation claim as barred by Colorado's three-year statute of limitations.

With regard to the patent infringement issue, the district court focused on the language of claim 1, which recites "further means disposed inside the shell for increasing its load bearing capacity comprising internal steel baffles extending inwardly from the steel shell walls." The court interpreted that language as "a means . . . for performing a specified function," subject to 35 U.S.C. § 112, paragraph 6, which provides that such a claim "shall be construed to cover the corresponding structure, material, or acts described in the specification and equivalents thereof." Looking to the specification of the '798 patent, the court noted that "every textual reference in the Specification and its diagrams show baffle deployment at an angle other than 90 to the wall faces" and that "placement of the baffles at such angles creates an intermediate interlocking, but not solid, internal barrier." The district court therefore ruled that, for purposes of the '798 patent, a baffle must "extend inward from the steel shell walls at an oblique or acute angle to the wall face" and must form part of an interlocking barrier in the interior of the wall module. Because Mr. Phillips could not prove infringement under that claim construction, the district court granted summary judgment of noninfringement.

Mr. Phillips appealed with respect to both the trade secret and patent infringement claims. A panel of this court affirmed on both issues. *Phillips v. AWH Corp.*, 363 F.3d 1207 (Fed.Cir.2004). As to the trade secret claim, the panel unanimously upheld the district court's ruling that the claim was barred by the applicable statute of limitations. As to the patent infringement claims, the panel was divided. The majority sustained the district court's summary judgment of noninfringement, although on different grounds. The dissenting judge would have reversed the summary judgment of noninfringement.

The panel first determined that because the asserted claims of the '798 patent contain a sufficient recitation of structure, the district court erred by construing the term "baffles" to invoke the "means-plus-function" claim format authorized by section 112, paragraph 6. Nonetheless, the panel concluded that the patent uses the term "baffles" in a restrictive manner. Based on the patent's written description, the panel held that the claim term "baffles" excludes structures that extend at a 90 degree angle from the walls. The panel noted that the specification repeatedly refers to the ability of the claimed baffles to deflect projectiles and that it describes the baffles as being "disposed at such angles that bullets which might penetrate the outer steel panels are deflected." '798 patent, col. 2, ll. 13–15. In addition, the panel observed that nowhere in the patent is there any disclosure of a baffle projecting from the wall at a right angle and that baffles oriented at 90 degrees to the wall were found in the prior art. Based on "the specification's explicit descriptions," the panel concluded "that the patentee regarded his invention as panels providing impact or projectile resistance and that the baffles must be oriented at angles other than 90." The panel added that the patent specification "is intended to support and inform the claims, and here it makes it unmistakably clear that the invention involves baffles angled at other than 90." The panel therefore upheld the district court's summary judgment of noninfringement.

The dissenting judge argued that the panel had improperly limited the claims to the particular embodiment of the invention disclosed in the specification, rather than adopting the "plain meaning" of the term "baffles." The dissenting judge noted that the parties had stipulated that "baffles" are a "means for obstructing, impeding, or checking the flow of something," and that the panel majority had agreed that the ordinary meaning of baffles is "something for deflecting, checking, or otherwise regulating flow." In the dissent's view, nothing in the specification redefined the term "baffles" or constituted a disclaimer specifically limiting the term to less than the full scope of its ordinary meaning. Instead, the dissenting judge contended, the specification "merely identifies impact resistance as one of several objectives of the invention." In sum, the dissent concluded that "there is no reason to supplement the plain meaning of the claim language with a limitation from the preferred embodiment." Consequently, the dissenting judge argued that the court should have adopted the general purpose dictionary definition of the term baffle, i.e., "something for deflecting, checking, or otherwise regulating flow," and therefore should have reversed the summary judgment of noninfringement.

This court agreed to rehear the appeal en banc and vacated the judgment of the panel. We now affirm the portion of the district court's judgment addressed to the trade secret misappropriation claims. However, we reverse the portion of the court's judgment addressed to the issue of infringement.

I

Claim 1 of the '798 patent is representative of the asserted claims with respect to the use of the term "baffles." It recites:

> Building modules adapted to fit together for construction of fire, sound and impact resistant security barriers and rooms for use in securing records and persons, comprising in combination, an outer shell ..., sealant means ... and further means disposed inside the shell for increasing its load bearing capacity comprising internal steel baffles extending inwardly from the steel shell walls.

As a preliminary matter, we agree with the panel that the term "baffles" is not means-plus-function language that invokes 35 U.S.C. § 112, paragraph 6. To be sure, the claim refers to "means disposed inside the shell for increasing its load bearing capacity," a formulation that would ordinarily be regarded as invoking the means-plus-function claim format. However, the claim specifically identifies "internal steel baffles" as structure that performs the recited function of increasing the shell's load-bearing capacity. In contrast to the "load bearing means" limitation, the reference to "baffles" does not use the word "means," and we have held that the absence of that term creates a rebuttable presumption that section 112, paragraph 6, does not apply.

* * * Accordingly, we must determine the correct construction of the structural term "baffles," as used in the '798 patent.

II

The first paragraph of section 112 of the Patent Act, 35 U.S.C. § 112, states that the specification

> shall contain a written description of the invention, and of the manner and process of making and using it, in such full, clear, concise, and exact terms as to enable any person skilled in the art to which it pertains ... to make and use the same....

The second paragraph of section 112 provides that the specification

> shall conclude with one or more claims particularly pointing out and distinctly claiming the subject matter which the applicant regards as his invention.

Those two paragraphs of section 112 frame the issue of claim interpretation for us. The second paragraph requires us to look to the language of the claims to determine what "the applicant regards as his invention." On the other hand, the first paragraph requires that the specification describe the invention set forth in the claims. The principal question that this case presents to us is the extent to which we should resort to and rely on a patent's specification in seeking to ascertain the proper scope of its claims.

This is hardly a new question. The role of the specification in claim construction has been an issue in patent law decisions in this country for nearly two centuries. We addressed the relationship between the specification and the claims at some length in our en banc opinion in *Markman v. Westview Instruments, Inc.*, 52 F.3d 967, 979–81 (Fed.Cir.1995) (en banc), *aff'd*, 517 U.S. 370, 116 S.Ct. 1384, 134 L.Ed.2d 577 (1996). We again summarized the applicable principles in *Vitronics Corp. v. Conceptronic, Inc.*, 90 F.3d 1576 (Fed.Cir.1996), and more recently in *Innova/Pure Water, Inc. v. Safari Water Filtration Systems, Inc.*, 381 F.3d 1111 (Fed. Cir.2004). What we said in those cases bears restating, for the basic principles of claim construction outlined there are still applicable, and we reaffirm them today. We have also previously considered the use of dictionaries in claim construction. What we have said in that regard requires clarification.

A

It is a "bedrock principle" of patent law that "the claims of a patent define the invention to which the patentee is entitled the right to exclude." *Innova*, 381 F.3d at 1115. That principle has been recognized since at least 1836, when Congress first required that the specification include a portion in which the inventor "shall particularly specify and point out the part, improvement, or combination, which he claims as his own invention or discovery." Act of July 4, 1836, ch. 357, § 6, 5 Stat. 117, 119. In the following years, the Supreme Court made clear that the claims are "of primary importance, in the effort to ascertain precisely what it is that is patented." *Merrill v. Yeomans*, 94 U.S. 568, 570, 24 L.Ed. 235 (1876). Because the patentee is required to "define precisely what his invention is," the Court explained, it is "unjust to the public, as well as an evasion of the law, to construe it in a manner different from the plain import of its terms." *White v. Dunbar*, 119 U.S. 47, 52, 7 S.Ct. 72, 30 L.Ed. 303 (1886).

We have frequently stated that the words of a claim "are generally given their ordinary and customary meaning." *Vitronics*, 90 F.3d at 1582. We have made clear, moreover, that the ordinary and customary meaning of a claim term is the meaning that the term would have to a person of ordinary skill in the art in question at the time of the invention, i.e., as of the effective filing date of the patent application.

The inquiry into how a person of ordinary skill in the art understands a claim term provides an objective baseline from which to begin claim interpretation. That starting point is based on the well-settled understanding that inventors are typically persons skilled in the field of the invention and that patents are addressed to and intended to be read by others of skill in the pertinent art.

Importantly, the person of ordinary skill in the art is deemed to read the claim term not only in the context of the particular claim in which the disputed term appears, but in the context of the entire patent, including the specification. This court explained that point well in *Multiform Desiccants, Inc. v. Medzam, Ltd.*, 133 F.3d 1473, 1477 (Fed.Cir.1998):

> It is the person of ordinary skill in the field of the invention through whose eyes the claims are construed. Such person is deemed to read the words used in the patent documents with an understanding of their meaning in the field, and to have knowledge of any special meaning and usage in the field. The inventor's words that are used to describe the invention-the inventor's lexicography-must be understood and interpreted by the court as they would be understood and interpreted by a person in that field of technology. Thus the court starts the decisionmaking process by reviewing the same resources as would that person, *viz.*, the patent specification and the prosecution history.

B

In some cases, the ordinary meaning of claim language as understood by a person of skill in the art may be readily apparent even to lay judges, and claim construction in such cases involves little more than the application of the widely accepted meaning of commonly understood words. In such circumstances, general purpose dictionaries may be helpful. In many cases that give rise to litigation, however, determining the ordinary and customary meaning of the claim requires examination of terms that have a particular meaning in a field of art. Because the meaning of a claim term as understood by persons of skill in the art is often not immediately apparent, and because patentees frequently use terms idiosyncratically, the court looks to "those sources available to the public that show what a person of skill in the art would have understood disputed claim language to mean." *Innova*, 381 F.3d at 1116. Those sources include "the words of the claims themselves, the remainder of the specification, the prosecution history, and extrinsic evidence concerning relevant scientific principles, the meaning of technical terms, and the state of the art."

1

Quite apart from the written description and the prosecution history, the claims themselves provide substantial guidance as to the meaning of particular claim terms.

To begin with, the context in which a term is used in the asserted claim can be highly instructive. To take a simple example, the claim in this case refers to "steel baffles," which strongly implies that the term "baffles" does not inherently mean objects made of steel. This court's cases provide numerous similar examples in which the use of a term within the claim provides a firm basis for construing the term.

Other claims of the patent in question, both asserted and unasserted, can also be valuable sources of enlightenment as to the meaning of a claim term. Because claim terms are normally used consistently throughout the patent, the usage of a term in one claim can often illuminate the meaning of the same term in other claims. Differences among claims can also be a useful guide in understanding the meaning of particular claim terms. For example, the presence of a dependent claim that adds a particular limitation gives rise to a presumption that the limitation in question is not present in the independent claim.

2

The claims, of course, do not stand alone. Rather, they are part of "a fully integrated written instrument," *Markman*, 52 F.3d at 978, consisting principally of a specification that concludes with the claims. For that reason, claims "must be read in view of the specification, of which they are a part." As we stated in *Vitronics*, the specification "is always highly relevant to the claim construction analysis. Usually, it is dispositive; it is the single best guide to the meaning of a disputed term." 90 F.3d at 1582.

* * *

The importance of the specification in claim construction derives from its statutory role. The close kinship between the written description and the claims is enforced by the statutory requirement that the specification describe the claimed invention in "full, clear, concise, and exact terms."

35 U.S.C. § 112, para. 1. In *Renishaw*, this court summarized that point succinctly:

> Ultimately, the interpretation to be given a term can only be determined and confirmed with a full understanding of what the inventors actually invented and intended to envelop with the claim. The construction that stays true to the claim language and most naturally aligns with the patent's description of the invention will be, in the end, the correct construction.

Consistent with that general principle, our cases recognize that the specification may reveal a special definition given to a claim term by the patentee that differs from the meaning it would otherwise possess. In such cases, the inventor's lexicography governs. In other cases, the specification may reveal an intentional disclaimer, or disavowal, of claim scope by the inventor. In that instance as well, the inventor has dictated the correct claim scope, and the inventor's intention, as expressed in the specification, is regarded as dispositive.

The pertinence of the specification to claim construction is reinforced by the manner in which a patent is issued. The Patent and Trademark Office ("PTO") determines the scope of claims in patent applications not solely on the basis of the claim language, but upon giving claims their broadest reasonable construction "in light of the specification as it would be interpreted by one of ordinary skill in the art." *In re Am. Acad. of Sci. Tech. Ctr.*, 367 F.3d 1359, 1364 (Fed.Cir.2004). Indeed, the rules of the PTO require that application claims must "conform to the invention as set forth in the remainder of the specification and the terms and phrases used in the claims must find clear support or antecedent basis in the description so that the meaning of the terms in the claims may be ascertainable by reference to the description." 37 C.F.R. § 1.75(d)(1). It is therefore entirely appropriate for a court, when conducting claim construction, to rely heavily on the written description for guidance as to the meaning of the claims.

3

In addition to consulting the specification, we have held that a court "should also consider the patent's prosecution history, if it is in evidence." *Markman*, 52 F.3d at 980. The prosecution history, which we have designated as part of the "intrinsic evidence," consists of the complete record of the proceedings before the PTO and includes the prior art cited during the examination of the patent. *Autogiro*, 384 F.2d at 399. Like the specification, the prosecution history provides evidence of how the PTO and the inventor understood the patent. Furthermore, like the specification, the prosecution history was created by the patentee in attempting to explain and obtain the patent. Yet because the prosecution history represents an ongoing negotiation between the PTO and the applicant, rather than the final product of that negotiation, it often lacks the clarity of the specification and thus is less useful for claim construction purposes.

C

Although we have emphasized the importance of intrinsic evidence in claim construction, we have also authorized district courts to rely on extrinsic evidence, which "consists of all evidence external to the patent and prosecution history, including expert and inventor testimony, dictionaries, and learned treatises." *Markman*, 52 F.3d at 980. However, while extrinsic evidence "can shed useful light on the relevant art," we have explained that it is "less significant than the intrinsic record in determining 'the legally operative meaning of claim language.'" *C.R. Bard, Inc. v. U.S. Surgical Corp.*, 388 F.3d 858, 862 (Fed.Cir.2004), quoting *Vanderlande Indus. Nederland BV v. Int'l Trade Comm'n*, 366 F.3d 1311, 1318 (Fed.Cir.2004).

Within the class of extrinsic evidence, the court has observed that dictionaries and treatises can be useful in claim construction. We have especially noted the help that technical dictionaries may provide to a court "to better understand the underlying technology" and the way in which one of skill in the art might use the claim terms. *Vitronics*, 90 F.3d at 1584 n. 6. Because dictionaries, and especially technical dictionaries, endeavor to collect the accepted meanings of terms used in various fields of science and technology, those resources have been properly recognized as among the many tools that can assist the court in determining the meaning of particular terminology to those of skill in the art of the invention. Such evidence, we have held, may be considered if the court deems it helpful in determining "the true meaning of language used in the patent claims." *Markman*, 52 F.3d at 980.

We have also held that extrinsic evidence in the form of expert testimony can be useful to a court for a variety of purposes, such as to provide background on the technology at issue, to explain how an invention works, to ensure that the court's understanding of the technical aspects of the patent is consistent with that of a person of skill in the art, or to establish that a particular term in the patent or the prior art has a particular meaning in the pertinent field. However, conclusory, unsupported assertions by experts as to the definition of a claim term are not useful to a court. Similarly, a court should discount any expert testimony "that is clearly at odds with the claim construction mandated by the claims themselves, the written description, and the prosecution history, in other words, with the written record of the patent." *Key Pharms.*, 161 F.3d at 716.

* * *

In sum, extrinsic evidence may be useful to the court, but it is unlikely to result in a reliable interpretation of patent claim scope unless considered in the context of the intrinsic evidence. Nonetheless, because extrinsic evidence can help educate the court regarding the field of the invention and can help the court determine what a person of ordinary skill in the art would understand claim terms to mean, it is permissible for the district court in its sound discretion to admit and use such evidence. In exercising that discretion, and in weighing all the evidence bearing on claim construction, the court should keep in mind the flaws inherent in each type of evidence and assess that evidence accordingly.

III

Although the principles outlined above have been articulated on numerous occasions, some of this court's cases have suggested a somewhat different approach to claim construction, in which the court has given greater emphasis to dictionary definitions of claim terms and has assigned a less prominent role to the specification and the prosecution history. The leading case in this line is *Texas Digital Systems, Inc. v. Telegenix, Inc.*, 308 F.3d 1193 (Fed.Cir.2002).

A

In *Texas Digital*, the court noted that "dictionaries, encyclopedias and treatises are particularly useful resources to assist the court in determining the ordinary and customary meanings of claim terms." 308 F.3d at 1202. Those texts, the court explained, are "objective resources that serve as reliable sources of information on the established meanings that would have been attributed to the terms of the claims by those of skill in the art," and they "deserve no less fealty in the context of claim construction" than in any other area of law. The court added that because words often have multiple dictionary meanings, the intrinsic record must be consulted to determine which of the different possible dictionary meanings is most consistent with the use of the term in question by the inventor. If more than one dictionary definition is consistent with the use of the words in the intrinsic record, the court stated, "the claim terms may be construed to encompass all such consistent meanings."

* * *

The *Texas Digital* court explained that it advanced the methodology set forth in that opinion in an effort to combat what this court has termed "one of the cardinal sins of patent law-reading a limitation from the written description into the claims," *SciMed Life Sys.*, 242 F.3d at 1340. The court concluded that it is improper to consult "the written description and prosecution history as a threshold step in the claim construction process, before any effort is made to discern the ordinary and customary meanings attributed to the words themselves." *Texas Digital*, 308 F.3d at 1204. To do so, the court reasoned, "invites a violation of our precedent counseling against importing limitations into the claims."

* * *

B

Although the concern expressed by the court in *Texas Digital* was valid, the methodology it adopted placed too much reliance on extrinsic sources such as dictionaries, treatises, and encyclopedias and too little on intrinsic sources, in particular the specification and prosecution history.

While the court noted that the specification must be consulted in every case, it suggested a methodology for claim interpretation in which the specification should be consulted only after a determination is made, whether based on a dictionary, treatise, or other source, as to the ordinary meaning or meanings of the claim term in dispute. Even then, recourse to the specification is limited to determining whether the specification excludes one of the meanings derived from the dictionary, whether the presumption in favor of the dictionary definition of the claim term has been overcome by "an explicit definition of the term different from its ordinary meaning," or whether the inventor "has disavowed or disclaimed scope of coverage, by using words or expressions of manifest exclusion or restriction, representing a clear disavowal of claim scope." 308 F.3d at 1204. In effect, the *Texas Digital* approach limits the role of the specification in claim construction to serving as a check on the dictionary meaning of a claim term if the specification requires the court to conclude that fewer than all the dictionary definitions apply, or if the specification contains a sufficiently specific alternative definition or disavowal. That approach, in our view, improperly restricts the role of the specification in claim construction.

* * *

To avoid importing limitations from the specification into the claims, it is important to keep in mind that the purposes of the specification are to teach and enable those of skill in the art to make and use the invention and to provide a best mode for doing so. One of the best ways to teach a person of ordinary skill in the art how to make and use the invention is to provide an example of how to practice the invention in a particular case. Much of the time, upon reading the specification in that context, it will become clear whether the patentee is setting out specific examples of the invention to accomplish those goals, or whether the patentee instead intends for the claims and the embodiments in the specification to be strictly coextensive. The manner in which the patentee uses a term within the specification and claims usually will make the distinction apparent.

In the end, there will still remain some cases in which it will be hard to determine whether a person of skill in the art would understand the embodiments to define the outer limits of the claim term or merely to be exemplary in nature. While that task may present difficulties in some cases, we nonetheless believe that attempting to resolve that problem in the context of the particular patent is likely to capture the scope of the actual invention more accurately than either strictly limiting the scope of the claims to the embodiments disclosed in the specification or divorcing the claim language from the specification.

In *Vitronics*, this court grappled with the same problem and set forth guidelines for reaching the correct claim construction and not imposing improper limitations on claims. The underlying goal of our decision in *Vitronics* was to increase the likelihood that a court will comprehend how a person of ordinary skill in the art would understand the claim terms. In that process, we recognized that there is no magic formula or catechism for conducting claim construction. Nor is the court barred from considering any particular sources or required to analyze sources in any specific sequence, as long as those sources are not used to contradict claim meaning that is unambiguous in light of the intrinsic evidence. For example, a judge who encounters a claim term while reading a patent might consult a general purpose or specialized dictionary to begin to understand the meaning of the term, before reviewing the remainder of the patent to determine how the patentee has used the term. The sequence of steps used by the judge in consulting various sources is not important; what matters is for the court to attach the appropriate weight to be assigned to those sources in light of the statutes and policies that inform patent law. In *Vitronics*, we did not attempt to provide a rigid algorithm for claim construction, but simply attempted to explain why, in general, certain types of evidence are more valuable than others. Today, we adhere to that approach and reaffirm the approach to claim construction outlined in that case, in *Markman*, and in *Innova*. We now turn to the application of those principles to the case at bar.

IV

A

The critical language of claim 1 of the '798 patent—"further means disposed inside the shell for increasing its load bearing capacity comprising internal steel baffles extending inwardly from the steel shell walls"— imposes three clear requirements with respect to the baffles. First, the baffles must be made of steel. Second, they must be part of the load-bearing means for the wall section. Third, they must be pointed inward from the walls. Both parties, stipulating to a dictionary definition, also conceded that the term "baffles" refers to objects that check, impede, or obstruct the flow of something. The intrinsic evidence confirms that a person of skill in the art would understand that the term "baffles," as used in the '798 patent, would have that generic meaning.

The other claims of the '798 patent specify particular functions to be served by the baffles. For example, dependent claim 2 states that the baffles may be "oriented with the panel sections disposed at angles for deflecting projectiles such as bullets able to penetrate the steel plates." The inclusion of such a specific limitation on the term "baffles" in claim 2 makes it likely that the patentee did not contemplate that the term "baffles" already contained that limitation. Independent claim 17 further supports that proposition. It states that baffles are placed "projecting inwardly from the outer shell at angles tending to deflect projectiles that penetrate the outer shell." That limitation would be unnecessary if persons of skill in the art understood that the baffles inherently served such a function. Dependent claim 6 provides an additional requirement for the baffles, stating that "the internal baffles of both outer panel sections overlap and interlock at angles providing deflector panels extending from one end of the module to the other." If the baffles recited in claim 1 were inherently placed at specific angles, or interlocked to form an intermediate barrier, claim 6 would be redundant.

The specification further supports the conclusion that persons of ordinary skill in the art would understand the baffles recited in the '798 patent to be load-bearing objects that serve to check, impede, or obstruct flow. At several points, the specification discusses positioning the baffles so as to deflect projectiles. The patent states that one advantage of the invention over the prior art is that "[t]here have not been effective ways of dealing with these powerful impact weapons with inexpensive housing." While that statement makes clear the invention envisions baffles that serve that function, it does not imply that in order to qualify as baffles within the meaning of the claims, the internal support structures must serve the projectile-deflecting function in all the embodiments of all the claims. The specification must teach and enable all the claims, and the section of the written description discussing the use of baffles to deflect projectiles serves that purpose for claims 2, 6, 17, and 23, which specifically claim baffles that deflect projectiles.

The specification discusses several other purposes served by the baffles. For example, the baffles are described as providing structural support. The patent states that one way to increase load-bearing capacity is to use "at least in part inwardly directed steel baffles 15, 16." '798 patent, col. 4, II. 14–15. The baffle 16 is described as a "strengthening triangular baffle." Importantly, Figures 4 and 6 do not show the baffles as part of an "intermediate interlocking, but not solid, internal barrier." In those figures, the baffle 16 simply provides structural support for one of the walls, as depicted below:

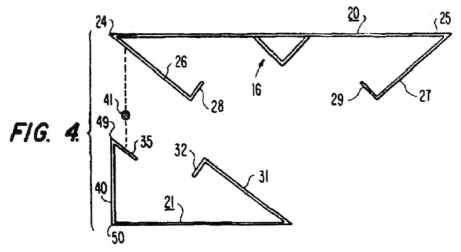

FIG. 6.

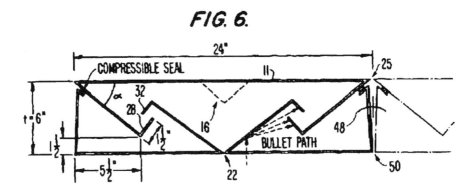

Other uses for the baffles are listed in the specification as well. In Figure 7, the overlapping flanges "provide for overlapping and interlocking the baffles to produce substantially an intermediate barrier wall between the opposite [wall] faces":

FIG. 7.

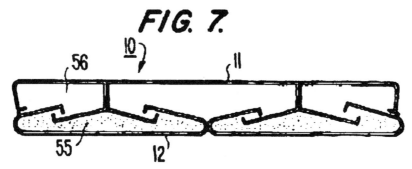

Those baffles thus create small compartments that can be filled with either sound and thermal insulation or rock and gravel to stop projectiles. By separating the interwall area into compartments (see, e.g., compartment 55 in Figure 7), the user of the modules can choose different types of material for each compartment, so that the module can be "easily custom tailored for the specific needs of each installation." When material is placed into the wall during installation, the baffles obstruct the flow of material from one compartment to another so that this "custom tailoring" is possible.

The fact that the written description of the '798 patent sets forth multiple objectives to be served by the baffles recited in the claims confirms that the term "baffles" should not be read restrictively to require that the baffles in each case serve all of the recited functions. We have held that "[t]he fact that a patent asserts that an invention achieves several objectives does not require that each of the claims be construed as limited to structures that are capable of achieving all of the objectives." *Liebel–Flarsheim*, 358 F.3d at 908. Although deflecting projectiles is one of the advantages of the baffles of the '798 patent, the patent does not require that the inward extending structures always be capable of performing that function. Accordingly, we conclude that a person of skill in the art would not interpret the disclosure and claims of the '798 patent to mean that a structure extending inward from one of the wall faces is a "baffle" if it is at an acute or obtuse angle, but is not a "baffle" if it is disposed at a right angle.

B

Invoking the principle that "claims should be so construed, if possible, as to sustain their validity," *Rhine v. Casio, Inc.*, 183 F.3d 1342, 1345 (Fed.Cir.1999), AWH argues that the term "baffles" should be given a restrictive meaning because if the term is not construed restrictively, the asserted claims would be invalid.

While we have acknowledged the maxim that claims should be construed to preserve their validity, we have not applied that principle broadly, and we have certainly not endorsed a regime in which validity analysis is a regular component of claim construction. Instead, we have limited the maxim to cases in which "the court concludes, after applying all the available tools of claim construction, that the claim is still ambiguous." *Liebel–Flarsheim*, 358 F.3d at 911. In such cases, we have looked to whether it is reasonable to infer that the PTO would not have issued an invalid patent, and that the ambiguity in the claim language should therefore be resolved in a manner that would preserve the patent's validity.

* * *

In this case, unlike in *Klein* and other cases in which the doctrine of construing claims to preserve their validity has been invoked, the claim term at issue is not ambiguous. Thus, it can be construed without the need to consider whether one possible construction would render the claim invalid while the other would not. The doctrine of construing claims to preserve their validity, a doctrine of limited utility in any event, therefore has no applicability here.

In sum, we reject AWH's arguments in favor of a restrictive definition of the term "baffles." Because we disagree with the district court's claim construction, we reverse the summary judgment of noninfringement. In light of our decision on claim construction, it is necessary to remand the infringement claims to the district court for further proceedings.

* * *

VI

In our order granting rehearing en banc, we asked the parties to brief various questions, including the following: "Consistent with the Supreme Court's decision in *Markman v. Westview Instruments*, 517 U.S. 370, 116 S.Ct. 1384, 134 L.Ed.2d 577 (1996), and our en banc decision in *Cybor Corp. v. FAS Technologies, Inc.*, 138 F.3d 1448 (Fed.Cir.1998), is it appropriate for this court to accord any deference to any aspect of trial court claim construction rulings? If so, on what aspects, in what circumstances, and to what extent?" After consideration of the matter, we have decided not to address that issue at this time. We therefore leave undisturbed our prior en banc decision in *Cybor*.

Each party shall bear its own costs for this appeal.

AFFIRMED IN PART, REVERSED IN PART, DISMISSED IN PART, and REMANDED.

[LOURIE, CIRCUIT JUDGE, concurring in part and dissenting in part omitted].

MAYER, CIRCUIT JUDGE, with whom PAULINE NEWMAN, CIRCUIT JUDGE, joins, dissenting.

Now more than ever I am convinced of the futility, indeed the absurdity, of this court's persistence in adhering to the falsehood that claim construction is a matter of law devoid of any factual component. Because any attempt to fashion a coherent standard under this regime is pointless, as illustrated by our many failed attempts to do so, I dissent.

This court was created for the purpose of bringing consistency to the patent field. Instead, we have taken this noble mandate, to reinvigorate the patent and introduce predictability to the field, and focused inappropriate power in this court. In our quest to elevate our importance, we have, however, disregarded our role as an appellate court; the resulting mayhem has seriously undermined the legitimacy of the process, if not the integrity of the institution.

In the name of uniformity, *Cybor Corp. v. FAS Technologies, Inc.*, 138 F.3d 1448 (Fed.Cir.1998) (en banc), held that claim construction does not involve subsidiary or underlying questions of fact and that we are, therefore, unbridled by either the expertise or efforts of the district court. What we have wrought, instead, is the substitution of a black box, as it so pejoratively has been said of the jury, with the black hole of this court. Out of this void we emit "legal" pronouncements by way of "interpretive necromancy"; these rulings resemble reality, if at all, only by chance. Regardless, and with a blind eye to the consequences, we continue to struggle under this irrational and reckless regime, trying every alternative-dictionaries first, dictionaries second, never dictionaries, etc., etc., etc.

Again today we vainly attempt to establish standards by which this court will interpret claims. But after proposing no fewer than seven questions, receiving more than thirty *amici curiae* briefs, and whipping the bar into a frenzy of expectation, we say nothing new, but merely restate what has become the practice over the last ten years-that we will decide cases according to whatever mode or method results in the outcome we desire, or at least allows us a seemingly plausible way out of the case. I am not surprised by this. Indeed, there can be no workable standards by which this court will interpret claims so long as we are blind to the factual component of the task.

* * *

While this court may persist in the delusion that claim construction is a purely legal determination, unaffected by underlying facts, it is plainly not the case. Claim construction is, or should be, made in context: a claim should be interpreted both from the perspective of one of ordinary skill in the art and in view of the state of the art at the time of invention. These questions, which are critical to the correct interpretation of a claim, are inherently factual. They are hotly contested by the parties, not by resort to case law as one would expect for legal issues, but based on testimony and documentary evidence. During so called *Markman* "hearings," which are often longer than jury trials, parties battle over experts offering conflicting evidence regarding who qualifies as one of ordinary skill in the art; the meaning of patent terms to that person; the state of the art at the time of the invention; contradictory dictionary definitions and which would be consulted by the skilled artisan; the scope of specialized terms; the problem a patent was solving; what is related or pertinent art; whether a construction was disallowed during prosecution; how one of skill in the art would understand statements during prosecution; and on and on. In order to reconcile the parties' inconsistent submissions and arrive at a sound interpretation, the district court is required to sift through and weigh volumes of evidence. While this court treats the district court as an intake clerk, whose only role is to collect, shuffle and collate evidence, the reality, as revealed by conventional practice, is far different.

Even if the procedures employed by the district court did not show that it is engaging in factfinding, the nature of the questions underlying claim construction illustrate that they are factual and should be reviewed in accordance with Rule 52(a). For each patent, for example, who qualifies as one of ordinary skill in the art will differ, just as the state of the art at the time of invention will differ. These subsidiary determinations are specific, multifarious and not susceptible to generalization; as such their resolution in one case will bear very little, if at all, on the resolution of subsequent cases. That the determination of the meaning of a particular term in one patent will not necessarily bear on the interpretation of the same term in a subsequent patent illustrates this point; while the term is the same, the underlying factual context is different. It further proves that these questions (e.g., who qualifies as one of ordinary skill in the art and what was the state of the art at the time of invention, among others) are implicitly being determined in each case; because we refuse to acknowledge either their existence or importance, however, the manner of their resolution is never elucidated. Finally, that claim construction is dependent on underlying factual determinations has been verified by our experience, which shows that reviewing these questions *de novo* has not clarified the law, but has instead "distort[ed] the appellate process," causing confusion among the district courts and bar. *See Cooter*, 496 U.S. at 404, 110 S.Ct. 2447 (quoting *Pierce*, 487 U.S. at 561, 108 S.Ct. 2541).

Our purely *de novo* review of claim interpretation also cannot be reconciled with the Supreme Court's instructions regarding obviousness.

While ultimately a question of law, obviousness depends on several underlying factual inquiries. *Graham v. John Deere Co.*, 383 U.S. 1, 17, 86 S.Ct. 684, 15 L.Ed.2d 545 (1966). "Under [section] 103, the scope and content of the prior art are to be determined; differences between the prior art and the claims at issue are to be ascertained; and the level of ordinary skill in the pertinent art resolved."

To a significant degree, each of these factual inquiries is also necessary to claim construction. Before beginning claim construction, "the scope and content of the prior art [should] be determined," to establish context. The "differences between the prior art and the claims at issue [should] be ascertained," to better define what the inventor holds out as the invention. And, the foundation for both the obviousness and claim construction determinations is "the level of ordinary skill in the pertinent art." These underlying factual considerations receive the level of deference due under Rule 52(a) when considering obviousness, but they are scrutinized *de novo* in the claim construction context. As directed by the Supreme Court, however, it is especially important in the patent field, "where so much depends upon familiarity with specific scientific problems and principles not usually contained in the general storehouse of knowledge and experience," to give deference to the district court's findings of fact. *Graver Tank & Mfg. Co. v. Linde Air Prods. Co.*, 339 U.S. 605, 609–10, 70 S.Ct. 854, 94 L.Ed. 1097 (1950).

While the court flails about in an attempt to solve the claim construction "conundrum," the solution to our plight is straightforward. We simply must follow the example of every other appellate court, which, regarding the vast majority of factual questions, reviews the trial court for clear error. This equilibrium did not come about as the result of chance or permissive appellate personalities, but because two centuries of experience has shown that the trial court's factfinding ability is "unchallenged." *Salve Regina Coll. v. Russell*, 499 U.S. 225, 233, 111 S.Ct. 1217, 113 L.Ed.2d 190 (1991). Time has similarly revealed that it is more economical for the district court to find facts.

Therefore, not only is it more efficient for the trial court to construct the record, the trial court is *better,* that is, more accurate, by way of both position and practice, at finding facts than appellate judges. Our rejection of this fundamental premise has resulted, not surprisingly, in several serious problems, including increased litigation costs, needless consumption of judicial resources, and uncertainty, as well as diminished respect for the court and less "decisional accuracy." We should abandon this unsound course.

If we persist in deciding the subsidiary factual components of claim construction without deference, there is no reason why litigants should be required to parade their evidence before the district courts or for district courts to waste time and resources evaluating such evidence. It is excessive to require parties, who "have already been forced to concentrate their energies and resources on persuading the trial judge that their account of the facts is the correct one," to "persuade three more judges at the appellate level." *Anderson*, 470 U.S. at 575, 105 S.Ct. 1504. If the proceedings before the district court are merely a "tryout on the road," *id.* (quoting *Wainwright v. Sykes*, 433 U.S. 72, 90, 97 S.Ct. 2497, 53 L.Ed.2d 594 (1977)), as they are under our current regimen, it is wasteful to require such proceedings at all. Instead, all patent cases could be filed in this court; we would determine whether claim construction is necessary, and, if so, the meaning of the claims. Those few cases in which claim construction is not dispositive can be remanded to the district court for trial. In this way, we would at least eliminate the time and expense of the charade currently played out before the district court.

Eloquent words can mask much mischief. The court's opinion today is akin to rearranging the deck chairs on the Titanic-the orchestra is playing as if nothing is amiss, but the ship is still heading for Davey Jones' locker.

NOTES

1. Federal Circuit Claim Construction Cases. The *Phillips* opinion discusses several of the Federal Circuit's important pre-*Phillips* claim construction decisions.

First, *Markman v. Westview Instruments, Inc.*, 52 F.3d 967 (Fed. Cir. 1995) (en banc) is arguably the most important patent case in 25 years because it changed patent litigation. *Markman* held that claim construction is a question of law. The holding had two consequences. First, a trial judge determines the meaning of the claims before trial, and then the jury determines infringement. Pre-trial claim construction is called a *Markman* hearing. Second, because claim construction is a question of law, the Federal Circuit's standard of review for claim construction is de novo. Two judges did not agree with the de novo standard of review. Judge Mayer (concurring) and Judge Newman (dissenting) argued that claim construction is a mixed question of law and fact because claim construction is a legal conclusion based technical facts. Notice that 10 years later, Judge Mayer expressed similar concerns in his dissent in *Phillips*, which was joined by Judge Newman.

Second, *Vitronics Corp. v. Conceptronic, Inc.*, 90 F.3d 1576 (Fed. Cir. 1996) carefully applied *Markman* to reverse judgment as a matter of law of noninfringement based on a district court's claim construction. The Federal Circuit held that the meaning of the claim term "solder reflow temperature" could be determined entirely from the intrinsic evidence and it was error for the district court to rely on extrinsic evidence. Third, the Federal Circuit again used detailed *Markman* analysis to vacate summary judgment of noninfringement based on a district court's claim construction of the claim term "operatively connected" in *Innova/Pure Water, Inc. v. Safari Water Filtration Systems, Inc.* 381 F.3d 1111 (Fed. Cir. 2004).

2. Supreme Court and Claim Construction. In *Markman v. Westview Instruments, Inc.*, 517 U.S. 370, 116 S.Ct. 1384, 134 L.Ed.2d 577 (1996), the Supreme Court affirmed the Federal Circuit. Writing for a unanimous Court, Justice Souter framed the issue as "whether the interpretation of a so-called patent claim, the portion of the patent document that defines the scope of the

patentee's rights, is a matter of law reserved entirely for the court, or subject to a Seventh Amendment guarantee that a jury will determine the meaning of any disputed term of art about which expert testimony is offered." *Id.* at 372. The Court engaged in Seventh Amendment analysis to reach its conclusion. Recall that Judge Mayer in his dissent in *Phillips* pointed out that the Supreme Court's *Markman* opinion cannot be read to endorse the Federal Circuit's view that claim construction is subject to de novo review. Judge Mayer showed that the Supreme Court was silent on that issue.

3. Costs of Claim Interpretation. The interpretation of claims is necessary to define inventions' scope. However, interpretation is not without cost. When deciding upon an interpretation methodology one should consider the information costs it imposes on both the patentee and patent observers. Christopher A. Cotropia analyzes the cost of interpreting claims using external definitional sources such as dictionaries, and the patent specification, in *Patent Claim Interpretation and Information Costs,* 9 Lewis & Clark L. Rev. 57 (2005). He finds that full use of the specification early in the process of claim interpretation minimizes information costs.

B. DOCTRINE OF EQUIVALENTS

GRAVER TANK & MFG. CO., INC. ET AL. v. LINDE AIR PRODUCTS CO.

Supreme Court of the United States, 1950.
339 U.S. 605, 70 S.Ct. 854, 94 L.Ed. 1097.

Mr. Justice Jackson delivered the opinion of the Court.

Linde Air Products Co., owner of the Jones patent for an electric welding process and for fluxes to be used therewith, brought an action for infringement against Lincoln and the two Graver companies. The trial court held four flux claims valid and infringed and certain other flux claims and all process claims invalid. The Court of Appeals affirmed findings of validity and infringement as to the four flux claims but reversed the trial court and held valid the process claims and the remaining contested flux claims. We granted certiorari and reversed the judgment of the Court of Appeals insofar as it reversed that of the trial court, and reinstated the District Court decree. Rehearing was granted, limited to the question of infringement of the four valid flux claims and to the applicability of the doctrine of equivalents to findings of fact in this case.

At the outset it should be noted that the single issue before us is whether the trial court's holding that the four flux claims have been infringed will be sustained. Any issue as to the validity of these claims was unanimously determined by the previous decision in this Court and attack on their validity cannot be renewed now by reason of limitation on grant of rehearing. The disclosure, the claims, and the prior art have been adequately described in our former opinion and in the opinions of the courts below.

In determining whether an accused device or composition infringes a valid patent, resort must be had in the first instance to the words of the claim. If accused matter falls clearly within the claim, infringement is made out and that is the end of it.

But courts have also recognized that to permit imitation of a patented invention which does not copy every literal detail would be to convert the protection of the patent grant into a hollow and useless thing. Such a limitation would leave room for—indeed encourage—the unscrupulous copyist to make unimportant and insubstantial changes and substitutions in the patent which, though adding nothing, would be enough to take the copied matter outside the claim, and hence outside the reach of law. One who seeks to pirate an invention, like one who seeks to pirate a copyrighted book or play, may be expected to introduce minor variations to conceal and shelter the piracy. Outright and forthright duplication is a dull and very rare type of infringement. To prohibit no other would place the inventor at the mercy of verbalism and would be subordinating substance to form. It would deprive him of the benefit of his invention and would foster concealment rather than disclosure of inventions, which is one of the primary purposes of the patent system.

The doctrine of equivalents evolved in response to this experience. The essence of the doctrine is that one may not practice a fraud on a patent. Originating almost a century ago in the case of *Winans v. Denmead*, 15 How. 330, it has been consistently applied by this Court and the lower federal courts, and continues today ready and available for utilization when the proper circumstances for its application arise. "To temper unsparing logic and prevent an infringer from stealing the benefit of an invention" a patentee may invoke this doctrine to proceed against the producer of a device "if it performs substantially the same function in substantially the same way to obtain the same result." *Sanitary Refrigerator Co. v. Winters*, 280 U.S. 30, 42. The theory on which it is founded is that "if two devices do the same work in substantially the same way, and accomplish substantially the same result, they are the same, even though they differ in name, form, or shape." *Machine Co. v. Murphy*, 97 U.S. 120, 125. The doctrine operates not only in favor of the patentee of a pioneer or primary invention, but also for the patentee of a secondary invention consisting of a combination of old ingredients which produce new and useful results, although the area of equivalence may vary under the circumstances. The wholesome realism of this doctrine is not always applied in favor of a patentee but is sometimes used against him. Thus, where a device is so far changed in principle from a patented article that it performs the same or a similar function in a substantially different way, but nevertheless falls within the literal words of the claim, the doctrine of equivalents may be used to restrict the claim and defeat the patentee's action for infringement. In its early development, the doctrine was usually applied in cases involving devices where there was equivalence in mechanical components. Subsequently, however, the same principles were also applied to compositions, where there was equivalence between chemical ingredients. Today the doctrine is applied to mechanical or chemical equivalents in compositions or devices.

What constitutes equivalency must be determined against the context of the patent, the prior art, and the particular circumstances of the case. Equivalence, in the patent law, is not the prisoner of a formula and is not an absolute to be considered in a vacuum. It does not require complete identity for every purpose and in every respect. In determining equivalents, things equal to the same thing may not be equal to each other and, by the same token, things for most purposes different may sometimes be equivalents. Consideration must be given to the purpose for which an ingredient is used in a patent, the qualities it has when combined with the other ingredients, and the function which it is intended to perform. An important factor is whether persons reasonably skilled in the art would have known of the interchangeability of an ingredient not contained in the patent with one that was.

A finding of equivalence is a determination of fact. Proof can be made in any form: through testimony of experts or others versed in the technology; by documents, including texts and treatises; and, of course, by the disclosures of the prior art. Like any other issue of fact, final determination requires a balancing of credibility, persuasiveness and weight of evidence. It is to be decided by the trial court and that court's decision, under general principles of appellate review, should not be disturbed unless clearly erroneous. Particularly is this so in a field where so much depends upon familiarity with specific scientific problems and principles not usually contained in the general storehouse of knowledge and experience.

In the case before us, we have two electric welding compositions or fluxes: the patented composition, Unionmelt Grade 20, and the accused composition, Lincolnweld 660. The patent under which Unionmelt is made claims essentially a combination of alkaline earth metal silicate and calcium fluoride; Unionmelt actually contains, however, silicates of calcium and magnesium, two alkaline earth metal silicates. Lincolnweld's composition is similar to Unionmelt's, except that it substitutes silicates of calcium and manganese—the latter not an alkaline earth metal—for silicates of calcium and magnesium. In all other respects, the two compositions are alike. The mechanical methods in which these compositions are employed are similar. They are identical in operation and produce the same kind and quality of weld.

The question which thus emerges is whether the substitution of the manganese which is not an alkaline earth metal for the magnesium which is, under the circumstances of this case, and in view of the technology and the prior art, is a change of such substance as to make the doctrine of equivalents inapplicable; or conversely, whether under the circumstances the change was so insubstantial that the trial court's invocation of the doctrine of equivalents was justified.

Without attempting to be all-inclusive, we note the following evidence in the record: Chemists familiar with the two fluxes testified that manganese and magnesium were similar in many of their reactions. There is testimony by a metallurgist that alkaline earth metals are often found in manganese ores in their natural state and that they serve the same purpose in the fluxes; and a chemist testified that "in the sense of the patent" manganese could be included as an alkaline earth metal. Much of this testimony was corroborated by reference to recognized texts on inorganic chemistry. Particularly important, in addition, were the disclosures of the prior art, also contained in the record. The Miller patent, No. 1,754,566, which preceded the patent in suit, taught the use of manganese silicate in welding fluxes. Manganese was similarly disclosed in the Armor patent, No. 1,467,825, which also described a welding composition. And the record contains no evidence of any kind to show that Lincolnweld was developed as the result of independent research or experiments.

It is not for this Court to even essay an independent evaluation of this evidence. This is the function of the trial court. And, as we have heretofore observed, "To no type of case is this ... more appropriately applicable than to the one before us, where the evidence is largely the testimony of experts as to which a trial court may be enlightened by scientific demonstrations. This trial occupied some three weeks, during which, as the record shows, the trial judge visited laboratories with counsel and experts to observe actual demonstrations of welding as taught by the patent and of the welding accused of infringing it, and of various stages of the prior art. He viewed motion pictures of various welding operations and tests and heard many experts and other witnesses." 336 U.S. 271, 274–275.

The trial judge found on the evidence before him that the Lincolnweld flux and the composition of the patent in suit are substantially identical in operation and in result. He found also that Lincolnweld is in all respects equivalent to Unionmelt for welding purposes. And he concluded that "for all practical purposes, manganese silicate can be efficiently and effectually substituted for calcium and magnesium silicates as the major constituent of the welding composition." These conclusions are adequately supported by the record; certainly they are not clearly erroneous.

It is difficult to conceive of a case more appropriate for application of the doctrine of equivalents. The disclosures of the prior art made clear that manganese silicate was a useful ingredient in welding compositions. Specialists familiar with the problems of welding compositions understood that manganese was equivalent to and could be substituted for magnesium in the composition of the patented flux and their observations were confirmed by the literature of chemistry. Without some explanation or indication that Lincolnweld was developed by independent research, the trial court could properly infer that the accused flux is the result of imitation rather than experimentation or invention. Though infringement was not literal, the changes which avoid literal infringement are colorable only. We conclude that the trial court's judgment of infringement respecting the four flux claims was proper, and we adhere to our prior decision on this aspect of the case.

Affirmed.

NOTES

1. The Doctrine of Equivalents: Approaches and Justifications. Is the doctrine of equivalents truly necessary? In *Pennwalt Corp. v. Durand–Wayland, Inc.*, 708 F.2d 492 (9th Cir. 1983), the court held that the doctrine of equivalents must be applied on an element-by-element basis. Nevertheless, the doctrine still creates ambiguity about what patents protect. The doctrine has been used to cover an accused device when the patentee has not claimed what their patent enabled. More legitimately, when claims that would cover the technology literally are unavailable, the doctrine extends patent protection to cover technology developed after the patent has issued. In *The Doctrine of Equivalents in Patent Law: Questions that* Pennwalt *did not Answer*, 137 U. PA. L. REV. 673 (1989), Martin J. Adelman and Gary L. Francione argue that substantial justice could be achieved without the confusing doctrine of equivalents.

What justifies the doctrine of equivalents? A number of the theories fall short in their justifications. The equitable justification of the doctrine does not fit with the notice function of patent claims, and is inconsistent with patent law's utilitarian grounding. The "friction theory" justifies the doctrine of equivalents on shortcomings of the patent prosecution system, such as the limitations of language, and prosecutorial mistakes. Michael J. Meurer & Craig Allen Nard propose a refinement theory based on the idea that "inventors fail to obtain the full claim breadth they are entitled to when they have not sufficiently refined their claims during patent prosecution to capture equivalent technology." Thus, the doctrine of equivalents allows patent applicants to avoid refinement costs. The theory reveals that there is a need to balance refinement cost savings and the innovation incentives created by the doctrine of equivalents against the possible harm to competition and rent-seeking costs it creates. Michael J. Meurer & Craig Allen Nard, *Invention, Refinement, and Patent Claim Scope: A New Perspective on the Doctrine of Equivalents*, 93 GEO. L.J. 1947 (2005).

WARNER–JENKINSON COMPANY, INC. v. HILTON DAVIS CHEMICAL CO.

Supreme Court of the United States, 1997.
520 U.S. 17, 117 S.Ct. 1040, 137 L.Ed.2d 146.

JUSTICE THOMAS delivered the opinion of the Court.

Nearly 50 years ago, this Court in *Graver Tank & Mfg. Co. v. Linde Air Products Co.*, 339 U.S. 605 (1950), set out the modern contours of what is known in patent law as the "doctrine of equivalents." Under this doctrine, a product or process that does not literally infringe upon the express terms of a patent claim may nonetheless be found to infringe if there is "equivalence" between the elements of the accused product or process and the claimed elements of the patented invention. Petitioner, which was found to have infringed upon respondent's patent under the doctrine of equivalents, invites us to speak the death of that doctrine. We decline that invitation. The significant disagreement within the Court of Appeals for the Federal Circuit concerning the application of *Graver Tank* suggests, however, that the doctrine is not free from confusion. We therefore will endeavor to clarify the proper scope of the doctrine.

I

The essential facts of this case are few. Petitioner Warner–Jenkinson Co. and respondent Hilton Davis Chemical Co. manufacture dyes. Impurities in those dyes must be removed. Hilton Davis holds United States Patent No. 4,560,746 ('746 patent), which discloses an improved purification process involving "ultrafiltration." The '746 process filters impure dye through a porous membrane at certain pressures and pH levels, resulting in a high purity dye product.

The '746 patent issued in 1985. As relevant to this case, the patent claims as its invention an improvement in the ultrafiltration process as follows:

"In a process for the purification of a dye ... the improvement which comprises: subjecting an aqueous solution ... to ultrafiltration through a membrane having a nominal pore diameter of 5–15 Angstroms under a hydrostatic pressure of approximately 200 to 400 p.s.i.g., *at a pH from approximately 6.0 to 9.0*, to thereby cause separation of said impurities from said dye...." (emphasis added).

The inventors added the phrase "at a pH from approximately 6.0 to 9.0" during patent prosecution. At a minimum, this phrase was added to distinguish a previous patent (the "Booth" patent) that disclosed an ultrafiltration process operating at a pH above 9.0. The parties disagree as to why the low-end pH limit of 6.0 was included as part of the claim.

In 1986, Warner–Jenkinson developed an ultrafiltration process that operated with membrane pore diameters assumed to be 5–15 Angstroms, at pressures of 200 to nearly 500 p.s.i.g., and at a pH of 5.0. Warner–Jenkinson did not learn of the '746 patent until after it had begun commercial use of its ultrafiltration process. Hilton Davis eventually learned of Warner–Jenkinson's use of ultrafiltration and, in 1991, sued Warner–Jenkinson for patent infringement.

As trial approached, Hilton Davis conceded that there was no literal infringement, and relied solely on the doctrine of equivalents. Over Warner–Jenkinson's objection that the doctrine of equivalents was an equitable doctrine to be applied by the court, the issue of equivalence was included among those sent to the jury. The jury found that the '746 patent was not invalid and that Warner–Jenkinson infringed upon the patent under the doctrine of equivalents. The jury also found, however, that Warner–Jenkinson had not intentionally infringed, and therefore awarded only 20% of the damages sought by Hilton Davis. The District Court denied Warner–Jenkinson's post-trial motions, and entered a permanent injunction prohibiting Warner–Jenkinson from practicing ultrafiltration below 500 p.s.i.g. and below 9.01 pH. A fractured en banc Court of Appeals for the Federal Circuit affirmed.

The majority below held that the doctrine of equivalents continues to exist and that its touchstone is whether substantial differences exist between the accused process and the patented process. The court also held that the question of equivalence is for the jury to decide and that the jury in this case had substantial evidence from which it could conclude that the Warner–Jenkinson process was not substantially different from the ultrafiltration process disclosed in the '746 patent.

There were three separate dissents, commanding a total of 5 of 12 judges. Four of the five dissenting judges viewed the doctrine of equivalents as allowing an improper expansion of claim scope, contrary to this Court's numerous holdings that it is the claim that defines the invention and gives notice to the public of the limits of the patent monopoly. The fifth dissenter, the late Judge Nies, was able to reconcile the prohibition against enlarging the scope of claims and the doctrine of equivalents by applying the doctrine to each element of a claim, rather than to the accused product or process "overall." As she explained it, "the 'scope' is not enlarged if courts do not go beyond the substitution of equivalent elements." All of the dissenters, however, would have found that a much narrowed doctrine of equivalents may be applied in whole or in part by the court.

We granted certiorari * * * and now reverse and remand.

II

In *Graver Tank* we considered the application of the doctrine of equivalents to an accused chemical composition for use in welding that differed from the patented welding material by the substitution of one chemical element. The substituted element did not fall within the literal terms of the patent claim, but the Court nonetheless found that the "question which thus emerges is whether the substitution [of one element for the other] ... is a change of such substance as to make the doctrine of equivalents inapplicable; or conversely, whether under the circumstances the change was so insubstantial that the trial court's invocation of the doctrine of equivalents was justified." The Court also described some of the considerations that go into applying the doctrine of equivalents:

> "What constitutes equivalency must be determined against the context of the patent, the prior art, and the particular circumstances of the case. Equivalence, in the patent law, is not the prisoner of a formula and is not an absolute to be considered in a vacuum. It does not require complete identity for every purpose and in every respect. In determining equivalents, things equal to the same thing may not be equal to each other and, by the same token, things for most purposes different may sometimes be equivalents. Consideration must be given to the purpose for which an ingredient is used in a patent, the qualities it has when combined with the other ingredients, and

the function which it is intended to perform. An important factor is whether persons reasonably skilled in the art would have known of the interchangeability of an ingredient not contained in the patent with one that was."

Considering those factors, the Court viewed the difference between the chemical element claimed in the patent and the substitute element to be "colorable only," and concluded that the trial court's judgment of infringement under the doctrine of equivalents was proper.

A

Petitioner's primary argument in this Court is that the doctrine of equivalents, as set out in *Graver Tank* in 1950, did not survive the 1952 revision of the Patent Act, 35 U.S.C. § 100 et seq., because it is inconsistent with several aspects of that Act. In particular, petitioner argues: (1) the doctrine of equivalents is inconsistent with the statutory requirement that a patentee specifically "claim" the invention covered by a patent, 35 U.S.C. § 112; (2) the doctrine circumvents the patent reissue process— designed to correct mistakes in drafting or the like—and avoids the express limitations on that process, 35 U.S.C. §§ 251–252; (3) the doctrine is inconsistent with the primacy of the Patent and Trademark Office (PTO) in setting the scope of a patent through the patent prosecution process; and (4) the doctrine was implicitly rejected as a general matter by Congress' specific and limited inclusion of the doctrine in one section regarding "means" claiming, 35 U.S.C. § 112, P6. All but one of these arguments were made in *Graver Tank* in the context of the 1870 Patent Act, and failed to command a majority.

The 1952 Patent Act is not materially different from the 1870 Act with regard to claiming, reissue, and the role of the PTO. Compare, *e.g.*, 35 U.S.C. § 112 ("The specification shall conclude with one or more claims particularly pointing out and distinctly claiming the subject matter which the applicant regards as his invention") with The Consolidated Patent Act of 1870, ch. 230, § 26, 16 Stat. 198, 201 (the applicant "shall particularly point out and distinctly claim the part, improvement, or combination which he claims as his invention or discovery"). Such minor differences as exist between those provisions in the 1870 and the 1952 Acts have no bearing on the result reached in *Graver Tank*, and thus provide no basis for our overruling it. In the context of infringement, we have already held that pre–1952 precedent survived the passage of the 1952 Act. *See Aro Mfg. Co. v. Convertible Top Replacement Co.*, 365 U.S. 336, 342 (1961) (new section defining infringement "left intact the entire body of case law on direct infringement"). We see no reason to reach a different result here.

Petitioner's fourth argument for an implied congressional negation of the doctrine of equivalents turns on the reference to "equivalents" in the "means" claiming provision of the 1952 Act. Section 112, P6, a provision not contained in the 1870 Act, states:

"An element in a claim for a combination may be expressed as a means or step for performing a specified function without the recital of structure, material, or acts in support thereof, and such claim shall be construed to cover the corresponding structure, material, or acts described in the specification *and equivalents thereof.*" (Emphasis added.)

Thus, under this new provision, an applicant can describe an element of his invention by the result accomplished or the function served, rather than describing the item or element to be used (*e.g.,* "a means of connecting Part A to Part B," rather than "a two-penny nail"). Congress enacted § 112, P6 in response to *Halliburton Oil Well Cementing Co. v. Walker*, 329 U.S. 1, which rejected claims that "do not describe the invention but use 'conveniently functional language at the exact point of novelty,'" 329 U.S. 1, 8 (1946) (citation omitted) * * *. Section 112, P6 now expressly allows so-called "means" claims, with the proviso that application of the broad literal language of such claims must be limited to only those means that are "equivalent" to the actual means shown in the patent specification. This is an application of the doctrine of equivalents in a restrictive role, narrowing the application of broad literal claim elements. We recognized this type of role for the doctrine of equivalents in *Graver Tank* itself. The added provision, however, is silent on the doctrine of equivalents as applied where there is no literal infringement.

Because § 112, P6 was enacted as a targeted cure to a specific problem, and because the reference in that provision to "equivalents" appears to be no more than a prophylactic against potential side effects of that cure, such limited congressional action should not be overread for negative implications. Congress in 1952 could easily have responded to *Graver Tank* as it did to the *Halliburton* decision. But it did not. Absent something more compelling than the dubious negative inference offered by petitioner, the lengthy history of the doctrine of equivalents strongly supports adherence to our refusal in *Graver Tank* to find that the Patent Act conflicts with that doctrine. Congress can legislate the doctrine of equivalents out of existence any time it chooses. The various policy arguments now made by both sides are thus best addressed to Congress, not this Court.

B

We do, however, share the concern of the dissenters below that the doctrine of equivalents, as it has come to be applied since *Graver Tank*, has taken on a life of its own, unbounded by the patent claims. There can be no denying that the doctrine of equivalents, when applied broadly, conflicts with the definitional and public-notice functions of the statutory claiming requirement. Judge Nies identified one means of avoiding this conflict:

> "[A] distinction can be drawn that is not too esoteric between substitution of an equivalent for a component *in* an invention and enlarging the metes and bounds of the invention *beyond* what is claimed.

* * *

"Where a claim to an invention is expressed as a combination of elements, as here, 'equivalents' in the sobriquet 'Doctrine of Equivalents' refers to the equivalency of an *element* or *part* of the invention with one that is substituted in the accused product or process.

* * *

"This view that the accused device or process must be more than 'equivalent' *overall* reconciles the Supreme Court's position on infringement by equivalents with its concurrent statements that 'the courts have no right to enlarge a patent beyond the scope of its claims as allowed by the Patent Office.' The 'scope' is not enlarged if courts do not go beyond the substitution of equivalent elements." (emphasis in original).

We concur with this apt reconciliation of our two lines of precedent. Each element contained in a patent claim is deemed material to defining the scope of the patented invention, and thus the doctrine of equivalents must be applied to individual elements of the claim, not to the invention as a whole. It is important to ensure that the application of the doctrine, even as to an individual element, is not allowed such broad play as to effectively eliminate that element in its entirety. So long as the doctrine of equivalents does not encroach beyond the limits just described, or beyond related limits to be discussed, we are confident that the doctrine will not vitiate the central functions of the patent claims themselves.

III

Understandably reluctant to assume this Court would overrule Graver Tank, petitioner has offered alternative arguments in favor of a more restricted doctrine of equivalents than it feels was applied in this case. We address each in turn.

A

Petitioner first argues that *Graver Tank* never purported to supersede a well-established limit on non-literal infringement, known variously as "prosecution history estoppel" and "file wrapper estoppel." According to petitioner, any surrender of subject matter during patent prosecution, regardless of the reason for such surrender, precludes recapturing any part of that subject matter, even if it is equivalent to the matter expressly claimed. Because, during patent prosecution, respondent limited the pH element of its claim to pH levels between 6.0 and 9.0, petitioner would have those limits form bright lines beyond which no equivalents may be claimed. Any inquiry into the reasons for a surrender, petitioner claims, would undermine the public's right to clear notice of the scope of the patent as embodied in the patent file.

We can readily agree with petitioner that *Graver Tank* did not dispose of prosecution history estoppel as a legal limitation on the doctrine of equivalents. But petitioner reaches too far in arguing that the reason for an amendment during patent prosecution is irrelevant to any subsequent estoppel. In each of our cases cited by petitioner and by the dissent below, prosecution history estoppel was tied to amendments made to avoid the prior art, or otherwise to address a specific concern—such as obviousness—that arguably would have rendered the claimed subject matter unpatentable. Thus, in *Exhibit Supply Co. v. Ace Patents Corp.*, 315 U.S. 126, Chief Justice Stone distinguished inclusion of a limiting phrase in an original patent claim from the "very different" situation in which "the applicant, in order to meet objections in the Patent Office, *based on references to the prior art*, adopted the phrase as a substitute for the broader one" previously used. 315 U.S. 126, 136 (1942) (emphasis added). Similarly, in *Keystone Driller Co. v. Northwest Engineering Corp.*, 294 U.S. 42 (1935), estoppel was applied where the initial claims were "rejected on the prior art," and where the allegedly infringing equivalent element was outside of the revised claims and within the prior art that formed the basis for the rejection of the earlier claims.

It is telling that in each case this Court probed the reasoning behind the Patent Office's insistence upon a change in the claims. In each instance, a change was demanded because the claim as otherwise written was viewed as not describing a patentable invention at all—typically because what it described was encompassed within the prior art. But, as the United States informs us, there are a variety of other reasons why the PTO may request a change in claim language. And if the PTO has been requesting changes in claim language without the intent to limit equivalents or, indeed, with the expectation that language it required would in many cases allow for a range of equivalents, we should be extremely reluctant to upset the basic assumptions of the PTO without substantial reason for doing so. Our prior cases have consistently applied prosecution history estoppel only where claims have been amended for a limited set of reasons, and we see no substantial cause for requiring a more rigid rule invoking an estoppel regardless of the reasons for a change.

In this case, the patent examiner objected to the patent claim due to a perceived overlap with the Booth patent, which revealed an ultrafiltration process operating at a pH above 9.0. In response to this objection, the phrase "at a pH from approximately 6.0 to 9.0" was added to the claim. While it is undisputed that the upper limit of 9.0 was added in order to distinguish the Booth patent, the reason for adding the lower limit of 6.0 is unclear. The lower limit certainly did not serve to distinguish the Booth patent, which said nothing about pH levels below 6.0. Thus, while a lower limit of 6.0, by its mere inclusion, became a material *element* of the claim, that did not necessarily preclude the application of the doctrine of equivalents as to that element. Where the reason for the change was not related to avoiding the prior art, the change may introduce a new element, but it does not necessarily preclude infringement by equivalents of that element.

We are left with the problem, however, of what to do in a case like the one at bar, where the record seems not to reveal the reason for including the lower pH limit of 6.0. In our view, holding that certain reasons for a claim amendment may avoid the application of prosecution history estoppel is not tantamount to holding that the *absence* of a reason for an amendment may similarly avoid such an estoppel. Mindful that claims do indeed serve both a definitional and a notice function, we think the better rule is to place the burden on the patent-holder to establish the reason for an amendment required during patent prosecution. The court then would decide whether that reason is sufficient to overcome prosecution history estoppel as a bar to application of the doctrine of equivalents to the element added by that amendment. Where no explanation is established, however, the court should presume that the PTO had a substantial reason related to patentability for including the limiting element added by amendment. In those circumstances, prosecution history estoppel would bar the application of the doctrine equivalents as to that element. The presumption we have described, one subject to rebuttal if an appropriate reason for a required amendment is established, gives proper deference to the role of claims in defining an invention and providing public notice, and to the primacy of the PTO in ensuring that the claims allowed cover only subject matter that is properly patentable in a proffered patent application. Applied in this fashion, prosecution history estoppel places reasonable limits on the doctrine of equivalents, and further insulates the doctrine from any feared conflict with the Patent Act.

Because respondent has not proffered in this Court a reason for the addition of a lower pH limit, it is impossible to tell whether the reason for that addition could properly avoid an estoppel. Whether a reason in fact exists, but simply was not adequately developed, we cannot say. On remand, the Federal Circuit can consider whether reasons for that portion of the amendment were offered or not and whether further opportunity to establish such reasons would be proper.

B

Petitioner next argues that even if *Graver Tank* remains good law, the case held only that the absence of substantial differences was a *necessary* element for infringement under the doctrine of equivalents, not that it was *sufficient* for such a result. Relying on *Graver Tank*'s references to the problem of an "unscrupulous copyist" and "piracy," petitioner would require judicial exploration of the equities of a case before allowing application of the doctrine of equivalents. To be sure, Graver Tank refers to the prevention of copying and piracy when describing the benefits of the doctrine of equivalents. That the doctrine produces such benefits, however, does not mean that its application is limited only to cases where those particular benefits are obtained.

Elsewhere in *Graver Tank* the doctrine is described in more neutral terms. And the history of the doctrine as relied upon by *Graver Tank* reflects a basis for the doctrine not so limited as petitioner would have it. In *Winans v. Denmead*, 56 U.S. 330 (1854), we described the doctrine of equivalents as growing out of a legally implied term in each patent claim that "the claim extends to the thing patented, however its form or proportions may be varied." Under that view, application of the doctrine of equivalents involves determining whether a particular accused product or process infringes upon the patent claim, where the claim takes the form—half express, half implied—of "X and its equivalents."

Machine Co. v. Murphy, 97 U.S. 120, 125 (1878), on which *Graver Tank* also relied, offers a similarly intent-neutral view of the doctrine of equivalents:

> "The substantial equivalent of a thing, in the sense of the patent law, is the same as the thing itself; so that if two devices do the same work in substantially the same way, and accomplish substantially the same result, they are the same, even though they differ in name, form, or shape."

If the essential predicate of the doctrine of equivalents is the notion of identity between a patented invention and its equivalent, there is no basis for treating an infringing equivalent any differently than a device that infringes the express terms of the patent. Application of the doctrine of equivalents, therefore, is akin to determining literal infringement, and neither requires proof of intent.

Petitioner also points to *Graver Tank*'s seeming reliance on the absence of independent experimentation by the alleged infringer as supporting an equitable defense to the doctrine of equivalents. The Federal Circuit explained this factor by suggesting that an alleged infringer's behavior, be it copying, designing around a patent, or independent experimentation, indirectly reflects the substantiality of the differences between the patented invention and the accused device or process. According to the Federal Circuit, a person aiming to copy or aiming to avoid a patent is imagined to be at least marginally skilled at copying or avoidance, and thus intentional copying raises an inference—rebuttable by proof of independent development—of having only insubstantial differences, and intentionally designing around a patent claim raises an inference of substantial differences. This explanation leaves much to be desired. At a minimum, one wonders how ever to distinguish between the intentional copyist making minor changes to lower the risk of legal action, and the incremental innovator designing around the claims, yet seeking to capture as much as is permissible of the patented advance.

But another explanation is available that does not require a divergence from generally objective principles of patent infringement. In both instances in *Graver Tank* where we referred to independent research or experiments, we were discussing the known interchangeability between the chemical compound claimed in the patent and the compound substituted by the alleged infringer. The need for independent experimentation thus could reflect knowledge—or lack thereof—of interchangeability possessed by one presumably skilled in the art. The known interchangeability of substitutes for an element of a patent is one of the express objective factors noted by *Graver Tank* as bearing upon whether the accused device is substantially the same as the patented invention. Independent experimentation by the alleged infringer would not always reflect upon the objective question whether a person skilled in the art would have known of the interchangeability between two elements, but in many cases it would likely be probative of such knowledge.

Although *Graver Tank* certainly leaves room for petitioner's suggested inclusion of intent-based elements in the doctrine of equivalents, we do not read it as requiring them. The better view, and the one consistent with *Graver Tank*'s predecessors and the objective approach to infringement, is that intent plays no role in the application of the doctrine of equivalents.

C

Finally, petitioner proposes that in order to minimize conflict with the notice function of patent claims, the doctrine of equivalents should be limited to equivalents that are disclosed within the patent itself. A milder version of this argument, which found favor with the dissenters below, is that the doctrine should be limited to equivalents that were known at the time the patent was issued, and should not extend to after-arising equivalents.

As we have noted, with regard to the objective nature of the doctrine, a skilled practitioner's knowledge of the interchangeability between claimed and accused elements is not relevant for its own sake, but rather for what it tells the fact-finder about the similarities or differences between those elements. Much as the perspective of the hypothetical "reasonable person" gives content to concepts such as "negligent" behavior, the perspective of a skilled practitioner provides content to, and limits on, the concept of "equivalence." Insofar as the question under the doctrine of equivalents is whether an accused element is equivalent to a claimed element, the proper time for evaluating equivalency—and thus knowledge of interchangeability between elements—is at the time of infringement, not at the time the patent was issued. And rejecting the milder version of petitioner's argument necessarily rejects the more severe proposition that equivalents must not only be known, but must also be actually disclosed in the patent in order for such equivalents to infringe upon the patent.

IV

The various opinions below, respondents, and *amici* devote considerable attention to whether application of the doctrine of equivalents is a task for the judge or for the jury. However, despite petitioner's argument below that the doctrine should be applied by the judge, in this Court petitioner makes only passing reference to this issue.

* * *

Because resolution of whether, or how much of, the application of the doctrine of equivalents can be resolved by the court is not necessary for us to answer the question presented, we decline to take it up. The Federal Circuit held that it was for the jury to decide whether the accused process was equivalent to the claimed process. There was ample support in our prior cases for that holding * * *. Whether, if the issue were squarely presented to us, we would reach a different conclusion than did the Federal Circuit is not a question we need decide today.

V

All that remains is to address the debate regarding the linguistic framework under which "equivalence" is determined. Both the parties and the Federal Circuit spend considerable time arguing whether the so-called "triple identity" test—focusing on the *function* served by a particular claim element, the *way* that element serves that function, and the *result* thus obtained by that element—is a suitable method for determining equivalence, or whether an "insubstantial differences" approach is better. There seems to be substantial agreement that, while the triple identity test may be suitable for analyzing mechanical devices, it often provides a poor framework for analyzing other products or processes. On the other hand, the insubstantial differences test offers little additional guidance as to what might render any given difference "insubstantial."

In our view, the particular linguistic framework used is less important than whether the test is probative of the essential inquiry: Does the accused product or process contain elements identical or equivalent to each claimed element of the patented invention? Different linguistic frameworks may be more suitable to different cases, depending on their particular facts. A focus on individual elements and a special vigilance against allowing the concept of equivalence to eliminate completely any such elements should reduce considerably the imprecision of whatever language is used. An analysis of the role played by each element in the context of the specific patent claim will thus inform the inquiry as to whether a substitute element matches the function, way, and result of the claimed element, or whether the substitute element plays a role substantially different from the claimed element. With these limiting principles as a backdrop, we see no purpose in going further and micro-managing the Federal Circuit's particular word-choice for analyzing equivalence. We expect that the Federal Circuit will refine the formulation of the test for equivalence in the orderly course of case-by-case determinations, and we leave such refinement to that court's sound judgment in this area of its special expertise.

VI

Today we adhere to the doctrine of equivalents. The determination of equivalence should be applied as an objective inquiry on an element-by-element basis. Prosecution history estoppel continues to be available as a defense to infringement, but if the patent-holder demonstrates that an amendment required during prosecution had a purpose unrelated to patentability, a court must consider that purpose in order to decide whether an estoppel is precluded. Where the patent-holder is unable to establish such a purpose, a court should presume that the purpose behind the required amendment is such that prosecution history estoppel would apply. Because the Court of Appeals for the Federal Circuit did not consider all of the requirements as described by us today, particularly as related to prosecution history estoppel and the preservation of some meaning for each element in a claim, we reverse and remand for further proceedings consistent with this opinion.

FESTO CORP. v. SHOKETSU KINZOKU KOGYO KABUSHIKI CO., LTD.

Supreme Court of the United States, 2002.
535 U.S. 722, 122 S.Ct. 1831, 152 L.Ed.2d 944.

JUSTICE KENNEDY delivered the opinion of the Court.

This case requires us to address once again the relation between two patent law concepts, the doctrine of equivalents and the rule of prosecution history estoppel. The Court considered the same concepts in *Warner–Jenkinson Co. v. Hilton Davis Chemical Co.*, 520 U.S. 17 (1997), and reaffirmed that a patent protects its holder against efforts of copyists to evade liability for infringement by making only insubstantial changes to a patented invention. At the same time, we appreciated that by extending protection beyond the literal terms in a patent the doctrine of equivalents can create substantial uncertainty about where the patent monopoly ends. If the range of equivalents is unclear, competitors may be unable to determine what is a permitted alternative to a patented invention and what is an infringing equivalent.

To reduce the uncertainty, *Warner–Jenkinson* acknowledged that competitors may rely on the prosecution history, the public record of the patent proceedings. In some cases the Patent and Trademark Office (PTO) may have rejected an earlier version of the patent application on the ground that a claim does not meet a statutory requirement for patentability. When the patentee responds to the rejection by narrowing his claims, this prosecution history estops him from later arguing that the subject matter covered by the original, broader claim was nothing more than an equivalent. Competitors may rely on the estoppel to ensure that their own devices will not be found to infringe by equivalence.

In the decision now under review the Court of Appeals for the Federal Circuit held that by narrowing a claim to obtain a patent, the patentee surrenders all equivalents to the amended claim element. Petitioner asserts this holding departs from past precedent in two respects. First, it applies estoppel to every amendment made to satisfy the requirements of the Patent Act and not just to amendments made to avoid pre-emption by an earlier invention, *i.e.*, the prior art. Second, it holds that when estoppel arises, it bars suit against every equivalent to the amended claim element. The Court of Appeals acknowledged that this holding departed from its own cases, which applied a flexible bar when considering what claims of equivalence were estopped by the prosecution history. Petitioner argues that by replacing the flexible bar with a complete bar the Court of Appeals cast doubt on many existing patents that were amended during the application process when the law, as it then stood, did not apply so rigorous a standard.

We granted certiorari to consider these questions.

I

Petitioner Festo Corporation owns two patents for an improved magnetic rodless cylinder, a piston-driven device that relies on magnets to move objects in a conveying system. The device has many industrial uses and has been employed in machinery as diverse as sewing equipment and the Thunder Mountain ride at Disney World. Although the precise details of the cylinder's operation are not essential here, the prosecution history must be considered.

Petitioner's patent applications, as often occurs, were amended during the prosecution proceedings. The application for the first patent, the Stoll Patent (U.S. Patent No. 4,354,125), was amended after the patent examiner rejected the initial application because the exact method of operation was unclear and some claims were made in an impermissible way. (They were multiply dependent.) The inventor, Dr. Stoll, submitted a new application designed to meet the examiner's objections and also added certain references to prior art. The second patent, the Carroll Patent (U.S. Patent No. 3,779,401), was also amended during a reexamination proceeding. The prior art references were added to this amended application as well. Both amended patents added a new limitation—that the inventions contain a pair of sealing rings, each having a lip on one side, which would prevent impurities from getting on the piston assembly. The amended Stoll Patent added the further limitation that the outer shell of the device, the sleeve, be made of a magnetizable material.

After Festo began selling its rodless cylinder, respondents (whom we refer to as SMC) entered the market with a device similar, but not identical, to the ones disclosed by Festo's patents. SMC's cylinder, rather than using two one-way sealing rings, employs a single sealing ring with a two-way lip. Furthermore, SMC's sleeve is made of a nonmagnetizable alloy. SMC's device does not fall within the literal claims of either patent, but petitioner contends that it is so similar that it infringes under the doctrine of equivalents.

SMC contends that Festo is estopped from making this argument because of the prosecution history of its patents. The sealing rings and the magnetized alloy in the Festo product were both disclosed for the first time in the amended applications. In SMC's view, these amendments narrowed the earlier applications, surrendering alternatives that are the very points of difference in the competing devices—the sealing rings and the type of alloy used to make the sleeve. As Festo narrowed its claims in these ways in order to obtain the patents, says SMC, Festo is now estopped from saying that these features are immaterial and that SMC's device is an equivalent of its own.

The United States District Court for the District of Massachusetts disagreed. It held that Festo's amendments were not made to avoid prior art, and therefore the amendments were not the kind that give rise to estoppel. A panel of the Court of Appeals for the Federal Circuit affirmed. We granted certiorari, vacated, and remanded in light of our intervening decision in *Warner–Jenkinson v. Hilton Davis Chemical Co.*, 520 U.S. 17 (1997). After a decision by the original panel on remand, the Court of Appeals ordered rehearing en banc to address questions that had divided its judges since our decision in *Warner–Jenkinson*.

The en banc court reversed, holding that prosecution history estoppel barred Festo from asserting that the accused device infringed its patents under the doctrine of equivalents. The court held, with only one judge dissenting, that estoppel arises from any amendment that narrows a claim to comply with the Patent Act, not only from amendments made to avoid prior art. More controversial in the Court of Appeals was its further holding: When estoppel applies, it stands as a complete bar against any claim of equivalence for the element that was amended. The court acknowledged that its own prior case law did not go so far. Previous decisions had held that prosecution history estoppel constituted a flexible bar, foreclosing some, but not all, claims of equivalence, depending on the purpose of the amendment and the alterations in the text. The court concluded, however, that its precedents applying the flexible-bar rule should be overruled because this case-by-case approach has proved unworkable. In the court's view a complete-bar rule, under which estoppel bars all claims of equivalence to the narrowed element, would promote certainty in the determination of infringement cases.

Four judges dissented from the decision to adopt a complete bar. In four separate opinions, the dissenters argued that the majority's decision to overrule precedent was contrary to *Warner–Jenkinson* and would unsettle the expectations of many existing patentees. Judge Michel, in his dissent, described in detail how the complete bar required the Court of Appeals to disregard 8 older decisions of this Court, as well as more than 50 of its own cases.

We granted certiorari.

II

The patent laws "promote the Progress of Science and useful Arts" by rewarding innovation with a temporary monopoly. U.S. Const., Art. I, § 8, cl. 8. The monopoly is a property right; and like any property right, its boundaries should be clear. This clarity is essential to promote progress, because it enables efficient investment in innovation. A patent holder should know what he owns, and the public should know what he does not. For this reason, the patent laws require inventors to describe their work in "full, clear, concise, and exact terms," 35 U.S.C. § 112, as part of the delicate balance the law attempts to maintain between inventors, who rely on the promise of the law to bring the invention forth, and the public, which should be encouraged to pursue innovations, creations, and new ideas beyond the inventor's exclusive rights.

Unfortunately, the nature of language makes it impossible to capture the essence of a thing in a patent application. The inventor who chooses to patent an invention and disclose it to the public, rather than exploit it in secret, bears the risk that others will devote their efforts toward exploiting the limits of the patent's language:

> "An invention exists most importantly as a tangible structure or a series of drawings. A verbal portrayal is usually an afterthought written to satisfy the requirements of patent law. This conversion of machine to words allows for unintended idea gaps which cannot be satisfactorily filled. Often the invention is novel and words do not exist to describe it. The dictionary does not always keep abreast of the inventor. It cannot. Things are not made for the sake of words, but words for things." *Autogiro Co. of America v. United States*, 384 F.2d 391, 397 (Ct. Cl. 1967).

The language in the patent claims may not capture every nuance of the invention or describe with complete precision the range of its novelty. If patents were always interpreted by their literal terms, their value would be greatly diminished. Unimportant and insubstantial substitutes for certain elements could defeat the patent, and its value to inventors could be destroyed by simple acts of copying. For this reason, the clearest rule of patent interpretation, literalism, may conserve judicial resources but is not necessarily the most efficient rule. The scope of a patent is not limited to its literal terms but instead embraces all equivalents to the claims described.

It is true that the doctrine of equivalents renders the scope of patents less certain. It may be difficult to determine what is, or is not, an equivalent to a particular element of an invention. If competitors cannot be certain about a patent's extent, they may be deterred from engaging in legitimate manufactures outside its limits, or they may invest by mistake in competing products that the patent secures. In addition the uncertainty may lead to wasteful litigation between competitors, suits that a rule of literalism might avoid. These concerns with the doctrine of equivalents, however, are not new. Each time the Court has considered the doctrine, it has acknowledged this uncertainty as the price of ensuring the appropriate incentives for innovation, and it has affirmed the doctrine over dissents that urged a more certain rule. When the Court in *Winans v. Denmead* first adopted what has become the doctrine of equivalents, it stated that "the exclusive right to the thing patented is not secured, if the public are at liberty to make substantial copies of it, varying its form or proportions." *Id.*, at 343. The dissent argued that the Court had sacrificed the objective of "fullness, clearness, exactness, preciseness, and particularity, in the description of the invention." *Id.*, at 347 (opinion of Campbell, J.).

The debate continued in *Graver Tank & Mfg. Co. v. Linde Air Products Co.*, 339 U.S. 605 (1950), where the Court reaffirmed the doctrine. Graver Tank held that patent claims must protect the inventor not only from those who produce devices falling within the literal claims of the patent but also from copyists who "make unimportant and insubstantial changes and substitutions in the patent which, though adding nothing, would be enough to take the copied matter outside the claim, and hence outside the reach of law." *Id.*, at 607. Justice Black, in dissent, objected that under the doctrine of equivalents a competitor "cannot rely on what the language of a patent claims. He must be able, at the peril of heavy infringement damages, to forecast how far a court relatively unversed in a particular technological field will expand the claim's language...."

Most recently, in *Warner–Jenkinson*, the Court reaffirmed that equivalents remain a firmly entrenched part of the settled rights protected by the patent. A unanimous opinion concluded that if the doctrine is to be discarded, it is Congress and not the Court that should do so:

> "The lengthy history of the doctrine of equivalents strongly supports adherence to our refusal in *Graver Tank* to find that the Patent Act conflicts with that doctrine. Congress can legislate the doctrine of equivalents out of existence any time it chooses. The various policy arguments now made by both sides are thus best addressed to Congress, not this Court." 520 U.S., at 28.

III

Prosecution history estoppel requires that the claims of a patent be interpreted in light of the proceedings in the PTO during the application process. Estoppel is a "rule of patent construction" that ensures that claims are interpreted by reference to those "that have been cancelled or rejected." *Schriber–Schroth Co. v. Cleveland Trust Co.*, 311 U.S. 211, 220 (1940). The doctrine of equivalents allows the patentee to claim those insubstantial alterations that were not captured in drafting the original patent claim but which could be created through trivial changes. When, however, the patentee originally claimed the subject matter alleged to infringe but then narrowed the claim in response to a rejection, he may not argue that the surrendered territory comprised unforeseen subject matter that should be deemed equivalent to the literal claims of the issued patent. On the contrary, "by the amendment [the patentee] recognized and emphasized the difference between the two phrases[,] ... and the difference which [the patentee] thus disclaimed must be regarded as material." *Exhibit Supply Co. v. Ace Patents Corp.*, 315 U.S. 126, 136–137 (1942).

A rejection indicates that the patent examiner does not believe the original claim could be patented. While the patentee has the right to appeal, his decision to forgo an appeal and submit an amended claim is taken as a concession that the invention as patented does not reach as far as the original claim. Were it otherwise, the inventor might avoid the

PTO's gatekeeping role and seek to recapture in an infringement action the very subject matter surrendered as a condition of receiving the patent.

Prosecution history estoppel ensures that the doctrine of equivalents remains tied to its underlying purpose. Where the original application once embraced the purported equivalent but the patentee narrowed his claims to obtain the patent or to protect its validity, the patentee cannot assert that he lacked the words to describe the subject matter in question. The doctrine of equivalents is premised on language's inability to capture the essence of innovation, but a prior application describing the precise element at issue undercuts that premise. In that instance the prosecution history has established that the inventor turned his attention to the subject matter in question, knew the words for both the broader and narrower claim, and affirmatively chose the latter.

A

The first question in this case concerns the kinds of amendments that may give rise to estoppel. Petitioner argues that estoppel should arise when amendments are intended to narrow the subject matter of the patented invention, for instance, amendments to avoid prior art, but not when the amendments are made to comply with requirements concerning the form of the patent application. In *Warner–Jenkinson* we recognized that prosecution history estoppel does not arise in every instance when a patent application is amended. Our "prior cases have consistently applied prosecution history estoppel only where claims have been amended for a limited set of reasons," such as "to avoid the prior art, or otherwise to address a specific concern—such as obviousness—that arguably would have rendered the claimed subject matter unpatentable." 520 U.S., at 30–32. While we made clear that estoppel applies to amendments made for a "substantial reason related to patentability," *id.*, at 33, we did not purport to define that term or to catalog every reason that might raise an estoppel. Indeed, we stated that even if the amendment's purpose were unrelated to patentability, the court might consider whether it was the kind of reason that nonetheless might require resort to the estoppel doctrine.

Petitioner is correct that estoppel has been discussed most often in the context of amendments made to avoid the prior art * * * It does not follow, however, that amendments for other purposes will not give rise to estoppel. Prosecution history may rebut the inference that a thing not described was indescribable. That rationale does not cease simply because the narrowing amendment, submitted to secure a patent, was for some purpose other than avoiding prior art.

We agree with the Court of Appeals that a narrowing amendment made to satisfy any requirement of the Patent Act may give rise to an estoppel. As that court explained, a number of statutory requirements must be satisfied before a patent can issue. The claimed subject matter must be useful, novel, and not obvious. 35 U.S.C. §§ 101–103. In addition, the patent application must describe, enable, and set forth the best mode of carrying out the invention. § 112. These latter requirements must be satisfied before issuance of the patent, for exclusive patent rights are given in exchange for disclosing the invention to the public. What is claimed by the patent application must be the same as what is disclosed in the specification; otherwise the patent should not issue. The patent also should not issue if the other requirements of § 112 are not satisfied, and an applicant's failure to meet these requirements could lead to the issued patent being held invalid in later litigation.

Petitioner contends that amendments made to comply with § 112 concern the form of the application and not the subject matter of the invention. The PTO might require the applicant to clarify an ambiguous term, to improve the translation of a foreign word, or to rewrite a dependent claim as an independent one. In these cases, petitioner argues, the applicant has no intention of surrendering subject matter and should not be estopped from challenging equivalent devices. While this may be true in some cases, petitioner's argument conflates the patentee's reason for making the amendment with the impact the amendment has on the subject matter.

Estoppel arises when an amendment is made to secure the patent and the amendment narrows the patent's scope. If a § 112 amendment is truly cosmetic, then it would not narrow the patent's scope or raise an estoppel. On the other hand, if a § 112 amendment is necessary and narrows the patent's scope—even if only for the purpose of better description—estoppel may apply. A patentee who narrows a claim as a condition for obtaining a patent disavows his claim to the broader subject matter, whether the amendment was made to avoid the prior art or to comply with § 112. We must regard the patentee as having conceded an inability to claim the broader subject matter or at least as having abandoned his right to appeal a rejection. In either case estoppel may apply.

B

Petitioner concedes that the limitations at issue—the sealing rings and the composition of the sleeve—were made for reasons related to § 112, if not also to avoid the prior art. Our conclusion that prosecution history estoppel arises when a claim is narrowed to comply with § 112 gives rise to the second question presented: Does the estoppel bar the inventor from asserting infringement against any equivalent to the narrowed element or might some equivalents still infringe? The Court of Appeals held that prosecution history estoppel is a complete bar, and so the narrowed element must be limited to its strict literal terms. Based upon its experience the Court of Appeals decided that the flexible-bar rule is unworkable because it leads to excessive uncertainty and burdens legitimate innovation. For the reasons that follow, we disagree with the decision to adopt the complete bar.

Though prosecution history estoppel can bar challenges to a wide range of equivalents, its reach requires an examination of the subject matter surrendered by the narrowing amendment. The complete bar avoids this inquiry by establishing a *per se* rule; but that approach is inconsistent with the purpose of applying the estoppel in the first place—to hold the inventor to the representations made during the application process and to the inferences that may reasonably be drawn from the amendment. By amending the application, the inventor is deemed to concede that the patent does not extend as far as the original claim. It does not follow, however, that the amended claim becomes so perfect in its description that no one could devise an equivalent. After amendment, as before, language remains an imperfect fit for invention. The narrowing amendment may demonstrate what the claim is not; but it may still fail to capture precisely what the claim is. There is no reason why a narrowing amendment should be deemed to relinquish equivalents unforeseeable at the time of the amendment and beyond a fair interpretation of what was surrendered. Nor is there any call to foreclose claims of equivalence for aspects of the invention that have only a peripheral relation to the reason the amendment was submitted. The amendment does not show that the inventor suddenly had more foresight in the drafting of claims than an inventor whose application was granted without amendments having been submitted. It shows only that he was familiar with the broader text and with the difference between the two. As a result, there is no more reason for holding the patentee to the literal terms of an amended claim than there is for abolishing the doctrine of equivalents altogether and holding every patentee to the literal terms of the patent.

This view of prosecution history estoppel is consistent with our precedents and respectful of the real practice before the PTO. While this Court has not weighed the merits of the complete bar against the flexible bar in its prior cases, we have consistently applied the doctrine in a flexible way, not a rigid one. We have considered what equivalents were surrendered during the prosecution of the patent, rather than imposing a complete bar that resorts to the very literalism the equivalents rule is designed to overcome.

The Court of Appeals ignored the guidance of *Warner–Jenkinson*, which instructed that courts must be cautious before adopting changes that disrupt the settled expectations of the inventing community. In that case we made it clear that the doctrine of equivalents and the rule of prosecution history estoppel are settled law. The responsibility for changing them rests with Congress. Fundamental alterations in these rules risk destroying the legitimate expectations of inventors in their property. The petitioner in *Warner–Jenkinson* requested another bright-line rule that would have provided more certainty in determining when estoppel applies but at the cost of disrupting the expectations of countless existing patent holders. We rejected that approach: "To change so substantially the rules of the game now could very well subvert the various balances the PTO sought to strike when issuing the numerous patents which have not yet expired and which would be affected by our decision." * * * As *Warner–Jenkinson* recognized, patent prosecution occurs in the light of our case law. Inventors who amended their claims under the previous regime had no reason to believe they were conceding all equivalents. If they had known, they might have appealed the rejection instead. There is no justification for applying a new and more robust estoppel to those who relied on prior doctrine.

In *Warner–Jenkinson* we struck the appropriate balance by placing the burden on the patentee to show that an amendment was not for purposes of patentability:

> "Where no explanation is established, however, the court should presume that the patent application had a substantial reason related to patentability for including the limiting element added by amendment. In those circumstances, prosecution history estoppel would bar the application of the doctrine of equivalents as to that element."

When the patentee is unable to explain the reason for amendment, estoppel not only applies but also "bars the application of the doctrine of equivalents as to that element." These words do not mandate a complete bar; they are limited to the circumstance where "no explanation is established." They do provide, however, that when the court is unable to determine the purpose underlying a narrowing amendment—and hence a rationale for limiting the estoppel to the surrender of particular equivalents—the court should presume that the patentee surrendered all subject matter between the broader and the narrower language.

Just as *Warner–Jenkinson* held that the patentee bears the burden of proving that an amendment was not made for a reason that would give rise to estoppel, we hold here that the patentee should bear the burden of showing that the amendment does not surrender the particular equivalent in question. This is the approach advocated by the United States, and we regard it to be sound. The patentee, as the author of the claim language, may be expected to draft claims encompassing readily known equivalents. A patentee's decision to narrow his claims through amendment may be presumed to be a general disclaimer of the territory between the original claim and the amended claim * * *. There are some cases, however, where the amendment cannot reasonably be viewed as surrendering a particular equivalent. The equivalent may have been unforeseeable at the time of the application; the rationale underlying the amendment may bear no more than a tangential relation to the equivalent in question; or there may be some other reason suggesting that the patentee could not reasonably be expected to have described the insubstantial substitute in question. In those cases the patentee can overcome the presumption that prosecution history estoppel bars a finding of equivalence.

This presumption is not, then, just the complete bar by another name. Rather, it reflects the fact that the interpretation of the patent must begin with its literal claims, and the prosecution history is relevant to construing those claims. When the patentee has chosen to narrow a claim, courts may presume the amended text was composed with awareness of this rule and that the territory surrendered is not an equivalent of the territory claimed. In those instances, however, the patentee still might rebut the presumption that estoppel bars a claim of equivalence. The patentee must show that at the time of the amendment one skilled in the art could not reasonably be expected to have drafted a claim that would have literally encompassed the alleged equivalent.

IV

On the record before us, we cannot say petitioner has rebutted the presumptions that estoppel applies and that the equivalents at issue have been surrendered. Petitioner concedes that the limitations at issue—the sealing rings and the composition of the sleeve—were made in response to a rejection for reasons under § 112, if not also because of the prior art references. As the amendments were made for a reason relating to patentability, the question is not whether estoppel applies but what territory the amendments surrendered. While estoppel does not effect a complete bar, the question remains whether petitioner can demonstrate that the narrowing amendments did not surrender the particular equivalents at issue. On these questions, respondents may well prevail, for the sealing rings and the composition of the sleeve both were noted expressly in the prosecution history. These matters, however, should be determined in the first instance by further proceedings in the Court of Appeals or the District Court.

The judgment of the Federal Circuit is vacated, and the case is remanded for further proceedings consistent with this opinion.

It is so ordered.

NOTES

1. **Prosecution History Estoppel.** There are differing views on the effectiveness of prosecution history estoppel. One view holds that prosecution history estoppel creates an ex ante effect encouraging the disclosure of information during patent prosecution. Increased disclosure helps to narrow the scope of claims and facilitate claim interpretation for later inventors and litigators. Those holding this view support a strong form of prosecution history estoppel. R. Polk Wagner, *Reconsidering Estoppel: Patent Administration and the Failure of* Festo, 151 U. PA. L. REV. 159 (2002). The contrary view is that prosecution history is not intended to guide claim interpretation. By treating prosecution histories as such, there exists a danger of overinterpretation. In *On Preparatory Texts And Proprietary Technologies: The Place of Prosecution Histories and Patent Claim Interpretation*, 47 UCLA L. REV. 183 (1999), John R. Thomas writes, "The pages of prosecution histories are turned not so much by those seeking the meaning of patent claims but by those who would destroy them."

2. **Prosecution History Estoppel Framework.** Consider the following framework for combining *Warner–Jenkinson* and *Festo*. While prosecution history estoppel (PHE) is a flexible bar that is a case-by-case analysis, PHE is operationlized by two rebuttable presumptions.

The first presumption, which deals with whether PHE applies to a particular claim element, provides that all changes to claims were for reasons related to patentability. The first presumption may be rebutted with evidence showing that an amendment during prosecution had a purpose unrelated to patentability. For example, clarifying amendments like spelling errors or correcting antecedent basis have a purpose unrelated to patentability. The second presumption, which deals with whether PHE bars a particular equivalent, provides that a narrowing amendment surrenders all equivalents between the original claim and the amended claim. The second presumption may be rebutted by showing (1) the equivalent was unforeseeable at time of the application, (2) the amendment has a tangential relation to the equivalent, and (3) any other reason suggesting the patentee could not have been reasonably been expected to have drafted a claim that would have literally encompassed the equivalent. The third category, which is a catch-all, is called "indescribable".

3. Prosecution History Estoppel and Foreseeability. In *Festo Corp. v. Shoketsu Kinzoku Kogyo Kabushiki*, 493 F.3d 1368 (Fed. Cir. 2007), the Federal Circuit provided guidance on showing that the equivalent was unforeseeable at the time of application to rebut the presumption that a narrowing amendment surrenders all equivalents between the original claim and the amended claim. The court stated "An equivalent is foreseeable if one skilled in the art would have known that an alternative existed in the field of art as defined by the original claim scope, even if the suitability of the alternative for the particular purposes defined by the amended claim scope were unknown." *Id.* at 1382. In dissent, Judge Newman recited the majority's foreseeability formulation and stated "even if unforeseeable as a matter of fact, even if technologically unexpected or unlikely, the equivalent must be ruled to be foreseeable if the structure is later found to be a usable equivalent." *Festo*, 493 F.3d at 1384 (Newman, J., dissenting).

Is the *Festo* court's foreseeability formulation broad or narrow? What policy goals are served by broad and narrow foreseeability formulations?

C. CONTRIBUTORY INFRINGEMENT

DSU MEDICAL CORP. v. JMS CO., LTD.

United States Court of Appeals for the Federal Circuit, 2006.
471 F.3d 1293.

RADER, CIRCUIT JUDGE.

DSU Medical Corporation (DSU) and Medisystems Corporation (MDS) (collectively DSU) sued JMS Company, Limited (JMS) and JMS North America (collectively JMS) and ITL Corporation Pty, Limited (ITL) for patent infringement, inducement to infringe, and contributory infringement of United States Patent Nos. 5,112,311 ('311) and 5,266,072 ('072). After a six-week jury trial produced a unanimous verdict, the United States District Court for the Northern District of California entered a final judgment finding claims 46–47, and 50–52 of the '311 patent invalid as obvious. The trial court also entered a final judgment, pursuant to the unanimous verdict, of infringement against JMS and JMS North American on claims 49, 53, and 54 of the '311 patent, and of non-infringement for ITL. The jury awarded total damages of \$5,055,211 for infringement against JMS and JMS North America, and the trial court entered a final judgment holding both jointly and severally liable for the award. Finding no reversible error, this court affirms.

I.

The '311 and '072 patents claim a guarded, winged-needle assembly. The invention reduces the risk of accidental needle-stick injuries. Needle puncture wounds can transmit blood-borne diseases such as Hepatitis B and AIDS. The '311 and '072 patented inventions effectively guard standard winged-needle-sets to prevent needle-stick injuries.

The '311 patent claims a "slotted, locking guard for shielding a needle, and a winged needle assembly including a needle, a winged needle hub, and a slotted, locking guard." '311, col.1, l. 8–11. This invention includes both "[a] slotted guard for locking a needle in a shielded position as the needle is removed from the patient", and "a guarded winged needle assembly ... slidably mounted within the guard." *Id.*, abstract. Figures 5–6 illustrate one embodiment of the patented invention:

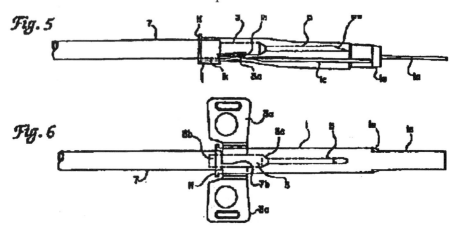

Figure 5 is a side view of a needle, winged needle hub (3), and slotted needle guard (1). '311 patent, col. 3, ll. 4–6. In this depiction, the needle (5) remains retracted within the needle guard (1). Figure 6 shows the same needle from above. '311 patent, col. 3, ll. 7–10.

Mr. David Utterberg, a co-inventor of the '311 patent, owns DSU and MDS. DSU owns the '311 patent; MDS has an exclusive license to make and sell the '311 invention for large-bore needles, including Arterial–Venous Fistula (AVF) sets used for dialysis and aphaeresis. MDS markets AVF needles under the brand names "MasterGuard" and "PointGuard."

The alleged infringing device, made by ITL (an Australian company) sells under the name Platypus ™ Needle Guard (Platypus). ITL manufactures the Platypus in Malaysia and Singapore. The Platypus needle guard is a "stand-alone" product: a small configured piece of plastic. This plastic guard structure is not attached to any other device. In other words, the Platypus does not include a needle, but only a sheathing structure. Some claims of the '311 patent recite both a slotted guard and a guarded winged needle assembly. Before use, the Platypus resembles an open clamshell (open-shell configuration). During use, the halves of the clam shell close to form the needle guard (closed-shell configuration). The following illustration shows the Platypus in open-and closed-shell configuration:

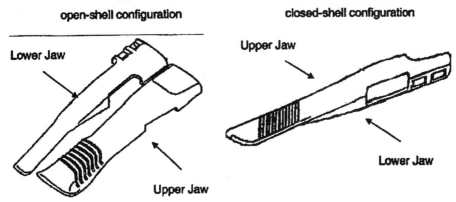

The Platypus has an upper and a lower "jaw." When closed, the upper jaw extends around and overlaps the inner, lower jaw. During use, a medical technician closes the Platypus and locks it around tubing connected to the winged needle assembly. When the technician removes the needle from a patient, the worker slides the guard down the tube until the needle assembly's wings meet and pry the jaws apart. The wings and their attached needle assembly slide into and through the guard, forcing the jaws ever wider as the wings make their way into a notched opening at the guard's back. Ultimately the wings slide into the rear opening. At that point, the jaws close around the used needle.

JMS is a large Japanese medical supply business that competes with MDS in the United States market. Beginning in June 1999, JMS purchased Platypus needle guards from ITL, entering into an agreement to distribute the Platypus worldwide (the Supply Agreement). Under the Supply Agreement, JMS bought open-shell configuration Platypus guard units from ITL in Singapore and Malaysia. JMS generally closed the Platypus guards around needle sets before distributing them to customers.

DSU alleges that the Platypus infringes the '311 patent. DSU also alleges that JMS and ITL contributed to and induced each other's infringement. JMS sought to sell ITL's infringing Platypus until it could produce its substitute non-infringing product, the WingEater. ITL offered to supply its infringing Platypus. DSU additionally seeks damages from JMS because it "stole" MDS's ability to renew a MasterGuard exclusive license with a former customer, Fresenius USA Manufacturing, Inc. (Fresenius).

* * *

III.

The jury found that JMS North America and JMS directly and contributorily infringed, and that JMS additionally induced JMS North America to infringe. However, the jury returned a verdict of non-infringement in favor of ITL. The jury entered a verdict finding that ITL did not engage in contributory infringement or inducement to infringe. The trial court denied DSU's motion for new trial on the jury's verdict that ITL did not contributorily infringe or induce infringement. This court reviews a denial of a motion for a new trial after a jury trial for an abuse of discretion.

A.

On appeal, DSU argues that ITL committed contributory infringement. According to DSU, the Platypus, which ITL sold to JMS, had no substantial noninfringing use. Therefore, DSU argues, ITL committed contributory infringement as a matter of law. ITL responds that it made and sold "most Platypus guards" outside of the United States. ITL also contends that the record contains no evidence that the Platypus was used in an infringing manner in the United States.

The Platypus sets that came into the United States fall within three categories:

(1) JMS imported into the United States approximately 30 million Platypus guards that, prior to importation into the United States, it had already assembled into the closed-shell configuration, combined with needle sets. These units accounted for the vast majority of Platypus sales in the United States.

(2) Fresenius purchased approximately 3.5 million Platypus guards, in the open-shell configuration without needle sets. ITL billed JMS for the shipments and shipped them to Fresenius in the United States at JMS's request. Fresenius ultimately decided that guards without needle sets did not meet FDA regulations, and it returned about 3 million.

(3) ITL sent approximately 15,000 Platypus in the open-shell configuration to JMS in San Francisco. DSU introduced no evidence that those units were ever put into the closed-shell configuration in the United States.

Additionally, the record contained evidence that when instructed to do so by JMS, ITL would ship Platypus guard units F.O.B. into the United States. The record also shows, however, that ITL only sold the Platypus in its open-shell configuration.

Therefore, this court must determine whether the jury's verdict is against the clear weight of the evidence. Under § 271(c):

> [w]hoever offers to sell or sells *within the United States* ... a component of a patented machine, manufacture, combination or composition ... constituting a material part of the invention, *knowing* the same to be especially made or especially adapted for use in an infringement of such patent, and not a staple article or commodity of commerce *suitable for substantial noninfringing use,* shall be liable as a contributory infringer.

In discussing 35 U.S.C. § 271(c), the Supreme Court stated:

> One who makes and sells articles which are only adapted to be used in a patented combination will be presumed to intend the natural consequences of his acts; he will be presumed to intend that they shall be used in the combination of the patent.

Metro–Goldwyn–Mayer Studios, Inc. v. Grokster, Ltd., 545 U.S. 913, 125 S.Ct. 2764, 2777, 162 L.Ed.2d 781 (2005). In addition, the patentee always has the burden to show direct infringement for each instance of indirect infringement. Thus, to prevail on contributory infringement, DSU must have shown that ITL made and sold the Platypus, that the Platypus has no substantial non-infringing uses in its closed-shell configuration, that ITL engaged in conduct (made sales) within the United States that contributed to another's direct infringement, and that JMS engaged in an act of direct infringement on those sales that ITL made in the United States.

The trial court properly applied these legal principles. The trial court determined that the record showed that ITL supplied the Platypus, that the Platypus had no substantial non-infringing uses in its closed-shell configuration, and that ITL intended to make the Platypus that resulted in the potential for contributory infringement as a product designed for use in the patented combination. In fact, even beyond the minimal intent requirement for contributory infringement, ITL acted with the knowledge of the '311 patent and knowledge that the component was especially made or adapted for use in an infringing manner. However, the district court denied the motion for a new trial because the record does not show that "the alleged contributory act ha[d] a direct nexus to a specific act of direct infringement." In denying the new trial, the court stated:

> And while it is true that Plaintiffs introduced evidence that "ITL sold and shipped millions of 'stand alone' guards directly to United States customers, including JMS [North America] and end-users like Fresenius," *there was no direct evidence* at trial establishing that these guards were actually closed and used as an act of direct infringement in the United States.

Upon review of the record, this court perceives, as well, an absence of evidence of direct infringement to which ITL contributed *in* the United States. Under the terms of the '311 patent, the Platypus only infringes in the closed-shell configuration. When open, the Platypus, for instance, lacks a "slot" as well as other claimed features. ITL only contributed to placing the Platypus into the closed-shell configuration in Malaysia (category 1, above); not in the United States. Section 271(c) has a territorial limitation requiring contributory acts to occur in the United States. Furthermore, this court cannot reverse a jury verdict of non-infringement on mere inferences that the Platypus guard units sold in the United States (i.e., the open-shell configuration in categories 2 and 3, above) were put into the infringing closed-shell configuration. The record does not show that the Platypus guards ITL shipped into the United States in the open-shell configuration were ever put into an infringing configuration, i.e., closed-shell. On categories 2 and 3, above, the record contains no evidence of direct infringement, i.e., that the open-shell Platypus guards imported by ITL were sold or used in their closed-shell configuration. As a result, the trial court did not abuse its discretion in denying DSU's motion for new trial on ITL's contributory infringement.

On the issue of induced infringement, DSU argues that ITL induced infringement by inducing JMS to sell the closed-shell configuration in the United States. The district court denied DSU's motion for a new trial on the ground that, although JMS directly infringed, ITL did not intend JMS to infringe.

B.

RESOLUTION OF CONFLICTING PRECEDENT

Section III. B., only, is considered en banc.

Opinion for the court filed by CIRCUIT JUDGE RADER, with NEWMAN, LOURIE, SCHALL, BRYSON, GAJARSA, LINN, DYK, PROST, and MOORE, CIRCUIT JUDGES, join. Concurring opinion filed by MICHEL, CHIEF JUDGE, and MAYER, CIRCUIT JUDGE.

This court addresses Part III. B., of this opinion en banc. This section addresses, in the context of induced infringement, "the required intent . . . to induce the specific acts of [infringement] or additionally to cause an infringement." *MEMC Elec. Materials, Inc. v. Mitsubishi Materials Silicon Corp.*, 420 F.3d 1369, 1378 n. 4 (Fed.Cir.2005) (citing *MercExchange, L.L.C. v. eBay, Inc.*, 401 F.3d 1323, 1332 (Fed.Cir.2005)). This section clarifies that intent requirement by holding en banc that, as was stated in *Manville Sales Corp. v. Paramount Systems, Inc.*, 917 F.2d 544, 554 (Fed.Cir.1990), "[t]he plaintiff has the burden of showing that the alleged infringer's actions induced infringing acts and that he knew or should have known his actions would induce actual infringements." The requirement that the alleged infringer knew or should have known his actions would induce actual infringement necessarily includes the requirement that he or she knew of the patent.

DSU claims the district court improperly instructed the jury on the state of mind necessary to prove inducement to infringe under 35 U.S.C. § 271(b). This court reviews the legal sufficiency of jury instructions on an issue of patent law without deference to the district court. "This Court reviews jury instructions in their entirety and 'only orders a new trial when errors in the instructions as a whole clearly mislead the jury.'" *Chiron*, 363 F.3d at 1258 (quoting *Delta–X Corp. v. Baker Hughes Prod. Tools, Inc.*, 984 F.2d 410, 415 (Fed.Cir.1993)).

Under section 271(b), "[w]hoever actively induces infringement of a patent shall be liable as an infringer." 35 U.S.C. § 271(b). To establish liability under section 271(b), a patent holder must prove that once the defendants knew of the patent, they "actively and *knowingly* aid[ed] and abett[ed] another's direct infringement." *Water Technologies Corp. v. Calco, Ltd.*, 850 F.2d 660, 668 (Fed.Cir.1988) (emphasis in original). However, "knowledge of the acts alleged to constitute infringement" is not enough. *Warner–Lambert Co. v. Apotex Corp.*, 316 F.3d 1348, 1363 (Fed.Cir.2003) (citation omitted). The "mere knowledge of possible infringement by others does not amount to inducement; specific intent and action to induce infringement must be proven."

DSU asked the court to instruct the jury, purportedly in accordance with *Hewlett–Packard Co. v. Bausch & Lomb, Inc.*, 909 F.2d 1464 (Fed. Cir.1990), that to induce infringement, the inducer need only intend to cause the *acts* of the third party that constitute direct infringement. The trial court gave the following instruction to the jury:

> In order to induce infringement, there must first be an act of direct infringement and proof that the defendant knowingly induced infringement with the intent to encourage the infringement. The defendant must have intended to cause the acts that constitute the direct infringement and must have known or should have known than[sic] its action would cause the direct infringement. Unlike direct infringement, which must take place within the United States, induced infringement does not require any activity by the indirect infringer in this country, as long as the direct infringement occurs here.

Thus, the court charged the jury in accordance with *Manville*. The statute does not define whether the purported infringer must intend to induce the infringement or whether the purported infringer must merely intend to engage in the acts that induce the infringement regardless of whether it knows it is causing another to infringe. DSU complains that the instruction is incorrect because it requires that the inducer possess specific intent to encourage another's infringement, and not merely that the inducer had knowledge of the acts alleged to constitute infringement.

In *Grokster*, which was a copyright case, the Supreme Court cited with approval this court's decision in Water Technologies when it discussed inducement of infringement, stating:

> The rule on inducement of infringement as developed in the early cases is no different today. Evidence of "active steps ... taken to encourage direct infringement," such as advertising an infringing use or instructing how to engage in an infringing use, show an affirmative intent that the product be used to infringe, and a showing that

infringement was encouraged overcomes the law's reluctance to find liability when a defendant merely sells a commercial product suitable for some lawful use.

Grokster, 125 S.Ct. at 2779 (citation and footnote omitted). As a result, if an entity offers a product with the object of promoting its use to infringe, as shown by clear expression or other affirmative steps taken to foster infringement, it is then liable for the resulting acts of infringement by third parties. "The inducement rule ... premises liability on purposeful, culpable expression and conduct...."

Grokster, thus, validates this court's articulation of the state of mind requirement for inducement. In *Manville*, this court held that the "alleged infringer must be shown ... to have *knowingly* induced infringement," 917 F.2d at 553, not merely knowingly induced the *acts* that constitute direct infringement. This court explained its "knowing" requirement:

> It must be established that the defendant possessed specific intent to encourage another's infringement and not merely that the defendant had knowledge of the acts alleged to constitute inducement. The plaintiff has the burden of showing that the alleged infringer's actions induced infringing acts *and* that he knew or should have known his actions would induce actual infringements.

In *Water Technologies*, also cited with approval by the Supreme Court, this court clarified: "While proof of intent is necessary, direct evidence is not required; rather, circumstantial evidence may suffice." 850 F.2d at 668. Although this court stated "that proof of actual intent to cause the acts which constitute the infringement is a necessary prerequisite to finding active inducement," *Hewlett–Packard*, 909 F.2d at 1469, *Grokster* has clarified that the intent requirement for inducement requires more than just intent to cause the acts that produce direct infringement. Beyond that threshold knowledge, the inducer must have an affirmative intent to cause direct infringement. In the words of a recent decision, inducement requires " 'that the alleged infringer knowingly induced infringement and possessed specific intent to encourage another's infringement.' " *MEMC Elec.*, 420 F.3d at 1378 (Fed.Cir.2005) (quoting *Minn. Mining & Mfg. Co. v. Chemque, Inc.*, 303 F.3d 1294, 1304–05 (Fed.Cir. 2002)). Accordingly, inducement requires evidence of culpable conduct, directed to encouraging another's infringement, not merely that the inducer had knowledge of the direct infringer's activities. Accordingly, the district court correctly instructed the jury in this case.

C.

The district court denied DSU's motion for a new trial on the issue of inducement to infringe. This court reviews a denial of a motion for a new trial after a jury trial for abuse of discretion, affirming on any basis that supports the verdict. In denying the motion for new trial, the trial court stated:

Fundamental principles of law hold that it is up to the jury to make determinations of witness credibility, to decide the existence of any factual inferences, and to determine the weight to be attributed to any direct or indirect evidence. Although Plaintiffs introduced circumstantial evidence which permitted inferences of ITL's intentions, it is up to the Jury to decide whether or not to draw any inference and to consider the weight of any such evidence. Assessing competing evidence is what the law asks juries to do, and the Court declines to take over this fundamental role of the Jury.

The jury heard evidence about the commercial transactions between ITL and JMS, including JMS's intention to sell ITL's Platypus to Fresenius until JMS could get its own WingEater approved by the Food and Drug Administration (FDA) and ready for market. The jury also heard evidence that Mr. Utterberg's lawyer informed ITL in January 1997 that the Platypus infringed the '311 patent. Additionally, the jury learned that ITL contacted an Australian attorney, who concluded that its Platypus would not infringe. JMS and ITL then also obtained letters from U.S. patent counsel advising that the Platypus did not infringe. Mr. William Mobbs, one of the owners of ITL who had participated in the design of the Platypus, testified that ITL had no intent to infringe the '311 patent.

Thus, on this record, the jury was well within the law to conclude that ITL did not induce JMS to infringe by purposefully and culpably encouraging JMS's infringement. To the contrary, the record contains evidence that ITL did not believe its Platypus infringed. Therefore, it had no intent to infringe. Accordingly, the record supports the jury's verdict based on the evidence showing a lack of the necessary specific intent. The trial court certainly did not abuse its discretion.

* * *

VII.

In conclusion, this court affirms the trial court's grant of summary judgment of non-infringement on the combination claims (combination of guard and needle assembly) and on the open-shell configuration of the stand-alone claims. This court affirms the trial court's evidentiary rulings. This court also affirms the trial court's denial of all of the post-trial motions, affirming entry of the final judgment in its entirety.

* * *

AFFIRMED

MICHEL, CHIEF JUDGE, and MAYER, CIRCUIT JUDGE, concurring.

Although we agree with the court's analysis in Section III.B, we do not consider it necessary to address this issue en banc. DSU misreads *Hewlett–Packard* as if we had said "proof of actual intent to cause the acts which constitute the infringement is a necessary *and sufficient* prerequisite to finding active inducement," but we did not. There is no actual conflict between *Hewlett–Packard* and *Manville* and, thus, no need for intervention by the full court. Such rare intervention should be reserved for real conflicts as well as cases of exceptional importance. *See* Fed. R.App. P. 35(a). In our opinion, the panel was free to conclude that the district court correctly rejected DSU's proffered jury instruction because, misunderstanding *Hewlett–Packard*, DSU did not correctly state the law.

Moreover, we write to make clear that we do not set forth a new standard here as to what satisfies the "knowledge of the patent" requirement in cases brought under 35 U.S.C. § 271(b). There is no dispute that ITL Corporation Pty, Ltd., had actual knowledge of United States Patent No. 5,112,311. Accordingly, the "knowledge of the patent" issue is not before us.

JAZZ PHOTO CORP. v. UNITED STATES

United States Court of Appeals for the Federal Circuit, 2006.
439 F.3d 1344.

LOURIE, CIRCUIT JUDGE.

The United States and Fuji Photo Film Co., Ltd. ("Fuji") appeal from the final decision of the Court of International Trade ordering the United States Bureau of Customs and Border Protection ("Customs") to release for entry certain Jazz Photo Corporation ("Jazz") lens-fitted film packages ("LFFPs") from two shipments that were denied entry by Customs on August 25 and 26, 2004, and ordering Customs to allow Jazz to complete the process of segregating the two shipments of LFFPs under the supervision of Customs. Customs excluded the two shipments of Jazz's LFFPs based on a General Exclusion Order and Order to Cease and Desist ("Exclusion Order") of the United States International Trade Commission (the "Commission") issued June 2, 1999, under Section 337 of the Tariff Act of 1930, as amended, 19 U.S.C. § 1337 ("Section 337"). Because the Court of International Trade did not err in holding that Jazz proved the affirmative defense of first sale and permissible repair for the LFFPs released for importation, did not err in ordering Customs to allow Jazz to complete the process of segregating the two shipments of Jazz's LFFPs under Customs' supervision, * * *, we affirm.

Background

This is the fourth case to come before this court involving Jazz's importation of LFFPs, also known as "disposable cameras," "single use cameras," or "one-time use cameras." The initial proceeding began in 1998, when Fuji filed a complaint at the Commission, alleging that 27 respondents, including Jazz, were violating Section 337 by importing into the United States articles that infringed fifteen patents owned by Fuji or by importing articles that were produced by means of a process covered by the claims of Fuji's patents. *Jazz Photo Corp. v. Int'l Trade Comm'n*, 264 F.3d 1094, 1098 (Fed. Cir. 2001) ("Jazz I"). The Commission held that 26 respondents, including Jazz, infringed all or most of the claims in suit of fourteen of Fuji's patents and it issued an Exclusion Order on June 2, 1999, prohibiting the importation into the United States of certain LFFPs. We stayed the Commission's order pending appeal. On August 21, 2001, we reversed the Commission's judgment of patent infringement "with respect to LFFPs for which the patent right was exhausted by first sale in the United States, and that were permissibly repaired," and affirmed the Commission's order for all other cameras.

Fuji also filed a second action at the Commission in June 2001 seeking institution of a formal enforcement proceeding to enforce the Exclusion Order and to impose civil penalties. *Fuji Photo Film Co., Ltd. v. Int'l Trade Comm'n*, 386 F.3d 1095, 1097–98 (Fed. Cir. 2004) ("Jazz II"). In May 2002, the administrative law judge found that Jazz had violated the Exclusion Order with respect to some LFFPs imported by Jazz from August 21, 2001, through December 12, 2003; that determination became the final determination of the Commission on July 27, 2004. Subsequently, on January 14, 2005, the Commission imposed a $13,675,000 civil penalty against Jazz.

In addition to the two actions before the Commission, Fuji filed suit against Jazz for patent infringement in the United States District Court for the District of New Jersey on June 23, 1999, seeking damages and injunctive relief for direct and indirect infringement of its LFFP patents between 1995 and August 21, 2001. *Fuji Photo Film Co. Ltd. v. Jazz Photo Corp.*, 394 F.3d 1368, 1371 (Fed. Cir. 2005) ("Jazz III"). After a jury trial, the court entered judgment on March 18, 2003, that Jazz was liable for willful infringement of Fuji's patents and awarded damages of $29,765,280.60. We affirmed that court's judgment on January 14, 2005.

The present appeal arises from Customs' decision to exclude from entry two shipments of LFFPs that Jazz imported at the Port of Los Angeles/Long Beach on August 25 and 26, 2004. All the subject LFFPs were "reloaded" cameras, also known as "refurbished" cameras, that were initially manufactured by Fuji or one of its licensees (Kodak, Concord, or Konica) and, after being used by consumers and collected following photo processing, were processed by Polytech Enterprise Limited ("Polytech") in China. That processing included fitting the camera with new film, and in some instances with new flash batteries, repairing the camera case to exclude light following the film reloading operation, repackaging, and relabeling under Jazz's trademark. Some of the subject LFFPs were processed using spent disposable cameras or "shells" that Polytech obtained from a collector of shells, Photo Recycling Enterprise, Inc. ("Photo Recycling"). The remaining subject LFFPs were processed using shells that Jazz acquired from a company known as Seven Buck's, Inc. ("Seven Buck's") and provided to Polytech. Jazz's inventory control system identified the reloaded cameras processed using Photo Recycling's shells separately from the reloaded cameras processed using Seven Buck's shells.

Customs concluded that Jazz had failed to prove that the subject LFFPs were outside the scope of the Exclusion Order and excluded the two shipments from entry on September 24 and 26, 2004. Jazz then filed a protest to Customs' decision under 19 U.S.C. § 1514(a), and Customs denied Jazz's protest on September 29, 2004. On October 4, 2004, Jazz challenged Customs' denial of its administrative protest in the Court of International Trade under 28 U.S.C. § 1581(a), seeking an order that the subject LFFPs were admissible into the United States and an order directing Customs to release the subject LFFPs.

After a bench trial, the Court of International Trade held on November 17, 2004, that Jazz established by a preponderance of the evidence that the subject LFFPs processed using Photo Recycling's shells were first sold in the United States and permissibly repaired, and thus that those LFFPs should be released by Customs for entry. The court also held that Jazz did not establish by a preponderance of the evidence that the subject LFFPs processed using Seven Buck's shells were first sold in the United States, and thus that those LFFPs were properly excluded from entry by Customs.

The court made factual findings supporting its conclusions on three issues: permissible repair, first sale, and segregation. First, the court relied on the testimony of Michal Zawodny, the Quality Assurance Manager for Jazz, in concluding that Polytech refurbished all of the subject LFFPs in a process that constituted permissible repair. Second, the court credited the testimony of Leon Silvera, the President of Photo Recycling, in holding that the subject LFFPs processed using Photo Recycling's shells were first sold in the United States. The court relied in part on a "presumption of regularity," reasoning that any "new single use cameras identified by the Exclusion Order that are commercially imported by anyone other than Fuji or one of its licensees would be unlawful imports and presumed to be excluded from the U.S. market." The court also observed that while this presumption does not extend to the LFFPs called "tourist" cameras because the Exclusion Order contains an exception allowing noncommercial importations, there was "no record evidence from which the court may conclude that the subject merchandise actually includes cameras refurbished from tourist shells." At the same time, the court found that the subject LFFPs processed using Seven Buck's shells were not first sold in the United States. Finally, the court found that the subject LFFPs processed using Seven Buck's shells were located in Master Lot Number 463, and thus could be segregated from the subject LFFPs made using Photo Recycling's shells that were not included in Master Lot Number 463.

On November 17, 2004, the court entered final judgment in favor of Jazz as to the subject LFFPs processed using Photo Recycling's shells, and in favor of the government as to the subject LFFPs processed using Seven Buck's shells. The government and Fuji timely appealed that portion of the court's order permitting entry of the subject LFFPs processed using

Photo Recycling's shells, and Jazz filed a cross-appeal contesting the exclusion of the subject LFFPs made using Seven Buck's shells.

Jazz's cross-appeal has now been rendered moot by the May 16, 2005 order of the United States Bankruptcy Court for the District of New Jersey that, pursuant to the parties' settlement agreement, ordered the sale of substantially all of Jazz's assets to Ribi Tech Products LLC ("Ribi"). Ribi subsequently took ownership of the subject LFFPs processed using Seven Buck's shells and exported them for sale overseas. Thus, the only portion of the Final Judgment on appeal is the entry and segregation of the subject LFFPs processed using Photo Re cycling's shells. We have jurisdiction pursuant to 28 U.S.C. § 1295(a)(5).

Discussion

* * *

As a threshold matter, it is important to state that this case has not been mooted by the release of the subject LFFPs processed using Photo Recycling's shells into the stream of commerce following the Final Judgment. "Mootness of an action relates to the basic dispute between the parties, not merely the relief requested. Thus, although subsequent acts may moot a request for particular relief or a count, the constitutional requirement of a case or controversy may be supplied by the availability of other relief." *Intrepid v. Pollock*, 907 F.2d 1125, 1131 (Fed. Cir. 1990) * * *

Here, although the release of the subject LFFPs processed using Photo Recycling's shells into the stream of commerce removed the possibility of the relief originally requested, viz., exclusion of the goods from entry, the government may still seek other relief by demanding redelivery of the goods and imposing liquidated damages on Jazz for failure to redeliver. Therefore, there remains a "definite and concrete" controversy between Jazz and the government concerning the exclusion of the subject LFFPs processed using Photo Recycling's shells.

I.   Entry of the Subject LFFPs

A.   Affirmative Defense

1.   First Sale

On appeal, the government argues that the Court of International Trade erred as a matter of law in holding that Jazz had demonstrated a patent-exhausting first sale for the subject LFFPs processed using Photo Recycling's shells. The government asserts that under the first sale defense articulated in *Jazz I*, Jazz did not satisfy its burden. According to the government, the court's reliance, even in part, upon the presumption of regularity is incorrect for three reasons: first, the Exclusion Order does not prohibit the importation of used foreign LFFPs that were not first sold in the United States; second, the Exclusion Order allows the importation of foreign LFFPs by tourists that were not first sold in the United States; and third, ample evidence in the record rebuts any presumption that commercial quantities of unauthorized LFFPs were not in the United States market. The government points out that Jazz was able to import substantial quantities of infringing LFFPs notwithstanding the Exclusion Order; the Commission found that 90% of the LFFPs imported by Jazz from 1995 to December 2003 were found to have infringed Fuji's patents. Fuji essentially repeats the arguments made by the government on this issue and also contends that the testimony credited by the court was inadmissible as lay opinion and hearsay. Fuji also argues that absent a presumption of regularity, there is no credible evidence as to the place of first sale for at least 15% of the subject LFFPs processed using Photo Recycling's shells.

Jazz responds that the court correctly applied the presumption of regularity, albeit in a limited way, to hold that the subject LFFPs processed using Photo Recycling's shells satisfied the first sale requirement. Jazz points out that the court only applied the presumption of regularity to new LFFPs or single use cameras that had not been repaired, and did not apply the presumption to cameras repaired abroad whose importation had previously been held to infringe Fuji's patents or violate the Exclusion Order. According to Jazz, the court properly applied the presumption of regularity because the government did not offer clear evidence to the contrary rebutting the presumption. Jazz also argues that the court properly held that Jazz overcame the presumption of correctness attached to Customs' decision to exclude the subject LFFPs because the government did not present a case-in-chief and the only evidence admitted at trial as to whether the subject LFFPs satisfied the first sale and permissible repair defense was provided by Jazz.

We agree with Jazz that the court did not err in holding that Jazz satisfied the first sale defense for the subject LFFPs processed using Photo Recycling's shells. We articulated the affirmative defense of first sale and permissible repair in *Jazz I*, holding that the "unrestricted sale of a patented article, by or with the authority of the patentee, 'exhausts' the patentee's right to control further sale and use of that article by enforcing the patent under which it was first sold." 264 F.3d at 1105. We reasoned that "when a patented device has been lawfully sold in the United States, subsequent purchasers inherit the same immunity under the doctrine of patent exhaustion" so long as the device has been permissibly repaired. The party raising the affirmative defense has the burden of establishing it by a preponderance of the evidence. Moreover, we have defined preponderance of the evidence in civil actions to mean "the greater weight of evidence, evidence which is more convincing than the evidence which is offered in opposition to it." *Hale v. Dep't of Transp., Fed. Aviation Admin.*, 772 F.2d 882, 885 (Fed. Cir. 1985).

Here, Jazz bears the burden of proving by a preponderance of the evidence its affirmative defense, and the trial court has the responsibility to weigh the evidence and evaluate the credibility of witnesses to determine whether Jazz satisfied its burden. At trial, Jazz relied on evidence from Silvera to establish its affirmative defense of first sale. Silvera testified that Photo Recycling obtained approximately 80% of its shells from national retailers in the United States operating internal photo processing labs, 10% to 15% of its shells from independent photo processors or small, wholesale photo finishing labs in the United States, and the remaining 10% to 12% of its shells from shell collectors in the United States. He also testified that, as an industry standard, at least 85% of disposable cameras developed at photo processing locations, such as national retailers or independent photo processors, were usually purchased from that same location. Further, Silvera testified that Photo Recycling required that the shells it purchased from shell collectors be accompanied by letter certifications indicating the shells in the cartons had been collected from photo processors in the United States. In addition, Silvera testified that Photo Recycling sold over 90% of the shells it had collected to Polytech.

Based on Silvera's demeanor, demonstrated knowledge of Photo Recycling's business activities, and general knowledge of the business of collecting spent shells, the trial court credited his testimony and made factual findings corresponding to his assertions. The trial court then concluded that Jazz had presented "sufficient, unrebutted evidence to establish that the shells collected by Photo Recycling and subsequently used by Polytech in producing LFFPs at issue in this case were collected from photo processors in the United States." We conclude that the trial court's factual determinations were not clearly erroneous and its legal conclusion was not erroneous as a matter of law.

To be sure, Jazz did not present direct evidence that each of the subject LFFPs processed using Photo Recycling's shells were first sold in the United States; Jazz's case is circumstantial. However, Jazz may carry its burden by presenting its case based upon circumstantial evidence * * *. Here, the circumstantial evidence offered by Silvera tended to show that the subject LFFPs processed using Photo Recycling's shells were first sold in the United States. Because the court was entitled to give weight to that evidence, we see no error in the court's conclusion that Jazz met its burden.

* * *

To meet its burden of proof, Jazz was not required to prove to a certainty that there were no used foreign shells, infringing shells, and tourist shells in the subject LFFPs processed using Photo Recycling's shells. Here, the theoretical possibility that used foreign shells, infringing shells, and tourist shells may exist in Photo Recycling's shells did not necessarily mean that the specific LFFPs at issue in this case were processed from those shells. Indeed, the government did not present any evidence at trial that any of the Photo Recycling shells used to make the subject LFFPs actually used foreign shells, infringing shells, or tourist shells. The court thus credited testimony offered by Silvera that there was a "very tiny" number or de minimis amount of tourist shells that were first sold outside the United States that "could possibly have been among the shells Photo Recycling collected from photo processors in the United States.''

Moreover, the Commission's ruling that Jazz imported infringing cameras into the United States from August 21, 2001, through December 12, 2003, does not establish that the Photo Recycling shells used to make the subject LFFPs included infringing shells. Similarly, that used foreign shells could have been imported into the United States does not establish that the Photo Recycling shells used to make the subject LFFPs were processed using any of those shells. We recognize that the government was not required to present evidence that the LFFPs at issue were actually processed from used foreign shells, infringing shells, and tourist shells. However, in the absence of such conflicting evidence, the court was entitled to give weight to Jazz's evidence. Accordingly, there is no error in the court's conclusion that Jazz established first sale by a preponderance of the evidence.

2.   Permissible Repair

On appeal, the government argues that the Court of International Trade erred in holding that Jazz established permissible repair for the subject LFFPs processed using Photo Recycling's shells because Jazz did not carry its burden of demonstrating that the repair process consisted of no more than the eight permissible steps identified in *Jazz I*. According to the government, the court's failure to identify "various minor operations" in Polytech's processing of the cameras is important because there is evidence in the record that Polytech engaged in full-back replacements in the past, which amounted to impermissible reconstruction. The government also contends that the court improperly relied on two 2003 videotapes as depicting the repair process performed by Polytech, pointing out that the videotapes did not accurately reflect the process used to make the subject LFFPs. Fuji essentially repeats the arguments made by the government on this issue and also contends that issue preclusion prevents the court from relying on the two 2003 videotapes to establish permissible repair because, in a separate enforcement proceeding decided by the Commission in 2004, *Jazz II*, the Commission found that those same videotapes were not sufficient to show permissible repair.

Jazz responds that the court's failure to identify "various minor operations" did not mean that the subject LFFPs were impermissibly repaired because Polytech had stopped engaging in full-back replacements at the time the subject LFFPs were produced. According to Jazz, the government's argument that the various minor operations included full-back replacements is mere speculation that is unsupported by evidence. Jazz also argues that the court's reliance on the two 2003 videotapes as showing permissible repair was proper because the Commission's finding as to the admissibility of a piece of evidence has no preclusive or binding effect on a court's determination regarding that same evidence in a separate proceeding. Jazz points out that the two videotapes were offered for a narrower purpose in this case than in the enforcement proceeding before the Commission, and that Zawodny testified as to all the steps of permissible repair depicted in the videotapes.

We agree with Jazz that the trial court did not err in holding that the subject LFFPs were permissibly repaired in accordance with the standard set forth in *Jazz I*. We held in *Jazz I* that the following eight steps were permissible repair, not prohibited reconstruction: "(1) removing the cardboard cover, (2) cutting open the plastic casing, (3) inserting new film and a container to receive the film, (4) replacing the winding wheel for certain cameras, (5) replacing the battery for flash cameras, (6) resetting the counter, (7) resealing the outer case, and (8) adding a new cardboard cover." 264 F.3d at 1099. We reasoned:

> "The decisions of [the Supreme] Court require the conclusion that reconstruction of a patented entity, comprised of unpatented elements, is limited to such a true reconstruction of the entity as to 'in fact make a new' article, after the entity, viewed as a whole, has become spent. In order to call the monopoly, conferred by the patent grant, into play for a second time, it must, indeed, be a second creation of the patented entity.... Mere replacement of individual unpatented parts, one at a time, whether of the same part repeatedly or different parts successively, is no more than the lawful right of the owner to repair his property." This right of repair, provided that the activity does not "in fact make a new article," accompanies the article to succeeding owners.

Id. at 1103. Here, the subject LFFPs were permissibly repaired under the standard set forth in *Jazz I* because the steps did not in fact make a new single use camera.

The trial court found, based on Zawodny's testimony, that the processing undertaken by Polytech for the subject LFFPs was:

> [1] opening of the body of the shell, [2] replacement of the advance wheel, [3] replacement of the film and of the battery (if a flash camera), [4] resetting the counter, [5] closing and repairing the case using original parts except for the additional molded part referred to above, [6] repackaging the refurbished camera, and [7] various minor operations incidental to these processes.

The government does not challenge the trial court's holding that the first six steps constituted permissible repair under *Jazz I*. However, the government argues that the court did not properly determine whether "various minor operations" constituted permissible repair. We disagree. While there is no bright-line test for determining whether a device has been permissibly repaired, it does not turn on minor details. Here, the court characterized the seventh step as "various minor operations incidental to the first six steps." Because the first six steps did not make a new single use camera, it follows that minor operations which were incidental to those steps also did not make a new single use camera. Moreover, even if the trial court did not identify the specifics of each minor operation, the fact that they were incidental to the first six steps indicates that the court considered them to be known processes that were permissible repair. We thus discern no error in the court's conclusion that those "various minor operations" did not make a new single use camera and thus constituted permissible repair.

* * *

B. Segregation of Jazz's LFFPs

On appeal, the government argues that the Court of International Trade erred in ordering Customs to supervise Jazz's segregation of the LFFPs that the court deemed to be admissible and to release those LFFPs. The government contends that the court exceeded its authority by directing Customs to assist in the segregation and in ordering the release of the goods. According to the government, compliance with the court's order imposed significant administrative demands upon Customs; Jazz, not Customs, should have been responsible for segregating the admissible LFFPs from the inadmissible LFFPs.

Jazz responds that supervision by Customs was necessary to segregate the goods because the subject LFFPs were stored in a bonded warehouse owned by Customs. Jazz also contends that Customs' regulations and laws require that importers segregate commingled goods under the supervision of Customs. According to Jazz, even if the court erred in ordering Customs to supervise Jazz's segregation of goods, the government has not shown how it was prejudiced by that error and does not justify reversal of the court's order.

We agree with Jazz that the trial court did not err in ordering Customs to supervise the segregation of the subject LFFPs. 19 CFR § 19.4(b)(1) provides that in Customs warehouses Customs "shall supervise all transportation, receipts, deliveries, sampling, recordkeeping, repacking, manipulation, destruction, physical and procedural security, conditions of storage, and safety in the warehouse as required by law and regulations." Under the regulation, Customs is obligated to supervise certain activities in its warehouse and that supervision is mandatory, not discretionary. Here, the subject LFFPs were stored in a Customs warehouse, and the segregation of those goods necessarily involved manipulation of the merchandise. Because Customs was required to supervise the segregation of the subject LFFPs in its warehouse, we see no error in the trial court's order.

* * *

Conclusion

The Court of International Trade did not err in holding that Jazz established, by a preponderance of the evidence, the affirmative defense of first sale and permissible repair for the subject LFFPs processed using Photo Recycling's shells [and] did not err in ordering Customs to allow Jazz to complete the process of segregating the subject LFFPs under Customs' supervision, * * *. The decision of that court is therefore

AFFIRMED.

NOTES

1. Knowledge Requirement for Inducement. Recall that Judge Michel in his concurrence in *DSU Medical* emphasized that the majority did not articulate a new standard for knowledge of the patent under Section 271(b) because the defendant had actual knowledge of one of the patents-in-suit. In *SEB v. Montgomery Ward & Co.*, 594 F.3d 1360 (Fed Cir. 2010), the Federal Circuit addressed the knowledge requirement. While not purporting to define the boundaries of knowledge of the patent required for inducement, the court affirmed a jury finding of induced infringement by reasoning that knowledge of the patent includes deliberate indifference.

2. Indirect Infringement of Method Claims. In *NTP, Inc. v. Research In Motion, LTD.*, 418 F.3d 1282 (Fed. Cir. 2005), the patentee asserted method claims directed to receiving email over a wireless network against the defendant's popular product, the BlackBerry. The defendant, a Canadian Corporation with its principal place of business in Ontario, had a relay component of its wireless network located in Canada.

The patentee alleged the defendant's BlackBerry indirectly infringed the asserted method claims. Specifically, the patentee alleged both inducement and contributory infringement. Indirect infringement requires an act of direct infringement. Here, the patentee argued that the defendant's customer's directly infringed the asserted method claims. The Federal Circuit held "a process cannot be used 'within' the United States as required by section 271(a) unless each of the steps is performed within this country." *Id.* at 1318. Because the defendant's relay was located in Canada, there was no direct infringement by the defendant's customers. Accordingly, the court held there was no indirect infringement by the defendant.

3. Joint Infringement of Method Claims. In *BMC Resources, Inc. v. Paymentech L.P.*, 498 F.3d 1373 (Fed. Cir. 2007), the Federal Circuit first recognized joint infringement of a method claim, which is a subset of direct infringement.

The patentee asserted method claims directed to a method for processing debit transactions without a pin number. Neither the defendant nor any other third-party, including debit networks and financial institutions, individually practiced every step of anyone of the asserted claims. Accordingly, the defendant could not be liable for either direct infringement or indirect infringement because direct infringement of a method claim requires every step be met by an accused product or service, and indirect infringement requires an underlying act of direct infringement. The Federal Circuit held that one who has "control or direction" over multiple parties, and the group practices every step of claim, is liable for joint infringement. The court reasoned that "[i]t would be unfair indeed for the mastermind ... to escape infringement liability." *Id.* at 1381. Nevertheless, the defendant escaped liability because there was no evidence that the defendant had control or direction over third-party debit networks or financial institutions.

Muniauction, Inc. v. Thompson Corp., 532 F.3d 1318 (Fed. Cir. 2008) elaborated on the *BMC Resources* control-or-direction test. In *Muniauction*, the patentee asserted method claims directed to a method for performing original issuer municipal bond auctions over an electronic network. The Federal Circuit first set the direction-or-control test along a spectrum. While a mastermind clearly satisfies the control-or-direction test, mere arms-length cooperation between multiple parties does not. Then the Federal Circuit stated that the control-or-direction test "is satisfied in situations where the law would traditionally hold the accused direct infringer vicariously liable for the acts committed by another party that are required to complete performance of the claimed method." *Id.* at 1330. Nonetheless, the defendant escaped liability because it did not have control or direction over the bidders.

Is there any statutory basis for joint infringement? What are the policy reasons for joint infringement?

4. **Right to Repair.** Two Supreme Court cases, on the same patent litigation, form the Court's most important expression of the right to repair: *Aro Manufacturing Co. v. Convertible Top Replacement Co.* 365 U.S. 336, 81 S.Ct. 599, 5 L.Ed.2d 592 (1961) ("Aro I") and *Aro Manufacturing Co. v. Convertible Top Replacement Co.*, 377 U.S. 476, 84 S.Ct. 1526, 12 L.Ed.2d 457 (1964) ("Aro II"). The patent at issue was for the mechanics and cloth skin that together form a top for convertible cars. A number of car manufactures used the patent. Some, like General Motors, acquired a license under the patent, while others, like Ford did not. When the patent holder sued a manufacturer of replacement cloth tops, The Supreme Court held that when General Motors' customers purchased a car with a properly licensed car top, they received an implied right to repair the top, but that Ford's customers did not. As no direct infringement had occurred on the part of General Motors, or its customers, the defendant was not liable for selling replacement tops for General Motors' vehicles, but was liable of contributory infringement for selling replacement tops for Ford cars.

IV. DEFENSES

A. INVALIDITY

The Patent Act states that a patent has a presumption of validity:

> A patent shall be presumed valid. Each claim of a patent ... shall be presumed valid independently of the validity of other claims; dependent or multiple dependent claims shall be presumed valid even though dependent upon an invalid claim.... The burden of establishing invalidity of a patent or any claim thereof shall rest on the party asserting such invalidity.

The following shall be defenses in any action involving the validity or infringement of a patent and shall be pleaded:

> (1) Noninfringement, absence of liability for infringement or unenforceability,

> (2) Invalidity of the patent or any claim in suit on any ground specified in ... this title as a condition for patentability,

(3) Invalidity of the patent or any claim in suit for failure to comply with any requirement of . . . this title.

(4) Any other fact or act made a defense by this title.

35 U.S.C. § 282.

B. PATENT MISUSE

The patent misuse defense is analogous to an antitrust claim by the defendant against the plaintiff. In a typical patent misuse situation, the licensee is required to purchase a product not covered by the patent in order to receive the license, a behavior known as "tying."

The Supreme Court explained the reasoning behind patent misuse in *Motion Picture Patents Co. v. Universal Film Manufacturing Co.*, 243 U.S. 502, 37 S.Ct. 416, 61 L.Ed. 871 (1917), a case where the defendant required the licensees of its motion picture projector to use it only with films covered under another patent it held:

> [The] rules of law make it very clear that the scope of the grant which may be made to an inventor in a patent, pursuant to the statute, must be limited to the invention described in the claims of his patent * * *

> Plainly, [the] language of the statute and the established rules * * * restrict the patent granted on a machine, such as we have in this case, to the mechanism described in the patent as necessary to produce the described results. It is not concerned with and has nothing to do with the materials with which or on which the machine operates. The grant is of the exclusive right to use the mechanism to produce the result with any appropriate material, and the materials with which the machine is operated are no part of the patented machine or of the combination which produces the patented result. The difference is clear and vital between the exclusive right to use the machine which the law gives to the inventor and the right to use it exclusively with prescribed materials to which such a license notice as we have here seeks to restrict it.

Id. at 511–12. The Patent Act expressly excludes certain conduct from the patent misuse defense:

> (d) No patent owner otherwise entitled to relief for infringement or contributory infringement of a patent shall be denied relief or deemed guilty of misuse or illegal extension of the patent right by reason of his having done one or more of the following: (1) derived revenue from acts which if performed by another without his consent would constitute contributory infringement of the patent; (2) licensed or authorized another to perform acts which if performed without his consent would constitute contributory infringement of the patent; (3) sought to enforce his patent rights against infringement or contributory infringement; (4) refused to license or use any rights to the patent; or (5) conditioned the license of any rights to the patent or the

sale of the patented product on the acquisition of a license to rights in another patent or purchase of a separate product, unless, in view of the circumstances, the patent owner has market power in the relevant market for the patent or patented product on which the license or sale is conditioned.

35 USC § 271(d).

More recently, in *Illinois Tool Works Inc. v. Independent Ink, Inc.*, 547 U.S. 28, 126 S.Ct. 1281, 164 L.Ed.2d 26 (2006), the Supreme Court addressed whether there is presumption of market power in a patented product based on the mere fact that the product is patented. The Court held that just because a tying product is patented does not mean that this is a presumption of market power in a patented product, abrogating precedent in patent law and antitrust law.

C. LACHES

The defense of laches is a claim by the defendant that the patentee unreasonably delayed filing suit after becoming aware of the alleged infringement resulting in material prejudice to the defendant.

In *A.C. Aukerman Co. v. R.L. Chaides Construction Co.*, 1993 WL 379548 (N.D. Cal. 1993) the plaintiff, A.C. Aukerman (Aukerman), held patents on a method and mold apparatus for slip-forming concrete highway barrier walls. Defendant R.L. Chaides (Chaides) purchased the patented mold from a manufacturer of construction equipment licensed by Aukerman. After Aukerman informed Chaides that it intended to enforce its patent rights, Chaides represented that its infringement was de minimis and amounted to only $200–300 a year. Based on this representation, Aukerman decided not to pursue Chaides and instead focused on others who were engaged in significant infringement. After its representation to Aukerman, Chaides went on to perform concrete wall construction work worth more than $5.7 million and to build two additional molds without Aukerman's knowledge or authorization.

At trial Chaides asserted a number of defenses, among them the defense of laches. The *Aukerman* court, on remand from the Federal Circuit, set forth the requirements of laches:

> In order to invoke the defense of laches, a defendant has the burden to prove: (1) the plaintiff's delay in filing suit was unreasonable and inexcusable and (2) the defendant was materially prejudiced by the delay. Prejudice to the defendant may be economic or evidentiary. Economic prejudice may arise where a defendant incurs damages which would have been prevented had the suit been brought earlier. Evidentiary prejudice may arise where the delay prevents defendant from presenting a full and fair defense on the merits, due to the death of critical witnesses, the dimming of memories, or the unavailability of records, thereby undermining the court's ability to determine the facts.

Id. at *4 (citing *A.C. Aukerman Co. v. R.L. Chaides Constr. Co.*, 960 F.2d 1020, 1032 (Fed. Cir. 1992) (en banc)). The court went on to say: "A court must also consider and weigh any reason the plaintiff offers to justify its delay (e.g. other litigation, negotiations with the accused, the extent of infringement, etc.). A patentee may also preclude the application of a laches defense by demonstrating that the infringer has engaged in 'egregious conduct' which causes the balance of equities to shift significantly in plaintiff's favor. A presumption of laches arises where the patentee delays in bringing suit for more than six years after the time the plaintiff knew or reasonably should have known of the alleged infringer's activities." *Id.* at *4–5.

Because more than six years passed between when Aukerman first became aware of Chaides' infringement and when it filed suit, the court found the presumption of laches existed. Nevertheless, it held that Chaides was precluded from raising the defense of laches because its' construction of additional molds constituted egregious behavior and because Aukerman's delay was reasonable as it was based on Chaides' representation of de minimis infringement.

D. EQUITABLE ESTOPPEL

R.L. Chaides also unsuccessfully asserted the defense of equitable estoppel, which is a claim that the defendant reasonably relied on the plaintiff's assertion that it would not bring an infringement claim. The *Aukerman* court, on remand from the Federal Circuit, set forth the requirements of equitable estoppel:

> To establish the defense of estoppel, a defendant must prove the following three elements: (1) the patentee, through misleading conduct, led the defendant to reasonably infer that it did not intend to enforce its patent against the defendant, (2) the defendant relied on that conduct and (3) due to its reliance, the defendant will be materially prejudiced if the patentee's suit is allowed to proceed. Conduct may include specific statements, action, inaction or silence where the patentee had a duty to speak. No presumption is applicable to the defense of equitable estoppel.

Id. at *5 (citing *A.C. Aukerman Co. v. R.L. Chaides Constr. Co.*, 960 F.2d at 1028*)*. The court held that Aukerman's failure to sue could have only led Chaides to believe that Aukerman was waiving its rights regarding Chaides de minimis infringement. However, such a waiver did not give Chaides the right to increase the scope of its infringement.

E. TERM LIMIT

The term limit defense is a claim that the allegedly infringing activity took place after the patent term had run out and therefore did not constitute infringement.

In *Paper Converting Machine Co. v. Magna–Graphics Corp.*, 745 F.2d 11 (Fed. Cir. 1984) the plaintiff, Paper Converting Machine Co. (Paper Converting), held a patent for machines "incorporating the sequential rewinding approach" to paper towel and toilet paper manufacture. The lower court found defendant Magna–Graphics guilty of manufacturing and selling a machine that infringed upon Paper Converting's patent and enjoined Magna–Graphics from any future infringing activity. Before the court handed down its ruling, Magna–Graphics had contracted to sell a second machine. Knowing that Paper Converting's patent would soon be expiring, Magna–Graphics sought a legal way to fulfill its contract. Magna–Graphics solution was to deliver the completed machine after Paper Converting's patent had expired. During the period in which the patent was still valid, Magna–Graphics purposefully did not completely assemble the machine and instead tested it in a substantially complete form. Magna–Graphics' claim was that Paper–Converting's patent only covered the completed machine and that by only substantially building the machine during the patent's term no violation had occurred.

The court found Magna–Graphics' assertions without merit stating:

If without fear of liability a competitor can assemble a patented item past the point of testing, the last year of the patent becomes worthless whenever it deals with a long lead-time article. Nothing would prohibit the unscrupulous competitor from aggressively marketing its own product and constructing it to all but the final screws and bolts, as Magna–Graphics did here. . . . That the machine was not operated in its optimum mode is inconsequential: imperfect practice of an invention does not avoid infringement.

Id. at 19–20. Thus, one may not wait out a patent's expiration all the while manufacturing a product for sale on the day of the patent's expiration. To assert a term limits defense successfully, one must not have engaged in substantially infringing activities during the patent's term.

V. REMEDIES

Sections 283 and 284 of the Patent Act describe the two types of remedies courts may grant for patent infringement: injunctions and damages.

A. INJUNCTIVE RELIEF

The several courts having jurisdiction of cases under this title may grant injunctions in accordance with the principles of equity to prevent the violation of any right secured by patent, on such terms as the court deems reasonable.

35 U.S.C. § 283.

Courts may grant two types of injunctions: the preliminary injunction and the permanent injunction. A preliminary injunction is an injunction that stops the allegedly infringing action so that the plaintiff does not suffer additional damages during the pendency of trial. If the plaintiff's claim of infringement is successful, the court will then issue a permanent injunction barring the defendant's infringing action going forward.

eBAY INC. v. MERCEXCHANGE, L.L.C.

Supreme Court of the United States, 2006.
547 U.S. 388, 126 S.Ct. 1837, 164 L.Ed.2d 641.

JUSTICE THOMAS delivered the opinion of the Court.

Ordinarily, a federal court considering whether to award permanent injunctive relief to a prevailing plaintiff applies the four-factor test historically employed by courts of equity. Petitioners eBay Inc. and Half.com, Inc., argue that this traditional test applies to disputes arising under the Patent Act. We agree and, accordingly, vacate the judgment of the Court of Appeals.

I

Petitioner eBay operates a popular Internet Web site that allows private sellers to list goods they wish to sell, either through an auction or at a fixed price. Petitioner Half.com, now a wholly owned subsidiary of eBay, operates a similar Web site. Respondent MercExchange, L.L.C., holds a number of patents, including a business method patent for an electronic market designed to facilitate the sale of goods between private individuals by establishing a central authority to promote trust among participants. *See* U.S. Patent No. 5,845,265. MercExchange sought to license its patent to eBay and Half.com, as it had previously done with other companies, but the parties failed to reach an agreement. MercExchange subsequently filed a patent infringement suit against eBay and Half.com in the United States District Court for the Eastern District of Virginia. A jury found that MercExchange's patent was valid, that eBay and Half.com had infringed that patent, and that an award of damages was appropriate.

Following the jury verdict, the District Court denied MercExchange's motion for permanent injunctive relief. 275 F.Supp.2d 695 (2003). The Court of Appeals for the Federal Circuit reversed, applying its "general rule that courts will issue permanent injunctions against patent infringement absent exceptional circumstances." 401 F.3d 1323, 1339 (2005). We granted certiorari to determine the appropriateness of this general rule.

II

According to well-established principles of equity, a plaintiff seeking a permanent injunction must satisfy a four-factor test before a court may grant such relief. A plaintiff must demonstrate: (1) that it has suffered an irreparable injury; (2) that remedies available at law, such as monetary damages, are inadequate to compensate for that injury; (3) that, considering the balance of hardships between the plaintiff and defendant, a remedy in equity is warranted; and (4) that the public interest would not be disserved by a permanent injunction. *See, e.g., Weinberger v. Romero–Barcelo*, 456 U.S. 305, 311–313, 102 S.Ct. 1798, 72 L.Ed.2d 91 (1982). The decision to grant or deny permanent injunctive relief is an act of equitable discretion by the district court, reviewable on appeal for abuse of discretion.

These familiar principles apply with equal force to disputes arising under the Patent Act. As this Court has long recognized, "a major departure from the long tradition of equity practice should not be lightly implied." Nothing in the Patent Act indicates that Congress intended such a departure. To the contrary, the Patent Act expressly provides that injunctions "may" issue "in accordance with the principles of equity." 35 U.S.C. § 283.

To be sure, the Patent Act also declares that "patents shall have the attributes of personal property," § 261, including "the right to exclude others from making, using, offering for sale, or selling the invention," § 154(a)(1). According to the Court of Appeals, this statutory right to exclude alone justifies its general rule in favor of permanent injunctive relief. But the creation of a right is distinct from the provision of remedies for violations of that right. Indeed, the Patent Act itself indicates that patents shall have the attributes of personal property "[s]ubject to the provisions of this title," 35 U.S.C. § 261, including, presumably, the provision that injunctive relief "may" issue only "in accordance with the principles of equity," § 283.

This approach is consistent with our treatment of injunctions under the Copyright Act. Like a patent owner, a copyright holder possesses "the right to exclude others from using his property." *Fox Film Corp. v. Doyal*, 286 U.S. 123, 127, 52 S.Ct. 546, 76 L.Ed. 1010 (1932). Like the Patent Act, the Copyright Act provides that courts "may" grant injunctive relief "on such terms as it may deem reasonable to prevent or restrain infringement of a copyright." 17 U.S.C. § 502(a). And as in our decision today, this Court has consistently rejected invitations to replace traditional equitable considerations with a rule that an injunction automatically follows a determination that a copyright has been infringed.

Neither the District Court nor the Court of Appeals below fairly applied these traditional equitable principles in deciding respondent's motion for a permanent injunction. Although the District Court recited the traditional four-factor test, it appeared to adopt certain expansive principles suggesting that injunctive relief could not issue in a broad swath of cases. Most notably, it concluded that a "plaintiff's willingness to license its patents" and "its lack of commercial activity in practicing the patents" would be sufficient to establish that the patent holder would not suffer irreparable harm if an injunction did not issue. But traditional equitable principles do not permit such broad classifications. For example, some patent holders, such as university researchers or self-made inventors, might reasonably prefer to license their patents, rather than undertake efforts to secure the financing necessary to bring their works to market themselves. Such patent holders may be able to satisfy the traditional four-factor test, and we see no basis for categorically denying them the opportunity to do so. To the extent that the District Court adopted such a categorical rule, then, its analysis cannot be squared with the principles of equity adopted by Congress. The court's categorical rule is also in tension with *Continental Paper Bag Co. v. Eastern Paper Bag Co.*, 210 U.S. 405, 422–430, 28 S.Ct. 748, 52 L.Ed. 1122 (1908), which rejected the contention that a court of equity has no jurisdiction to grant injunctive relief to a patent holder who has unreasonably declined to use the patent.

In reversing the District Court, the Court of Appeals departed in the opposite direction from the four-factor test. The court articulated a "general rule," unique to patent disputes, "that a permanent injunction will issue once infringement and validity have been adjudged." 401 F.3d, at 1338. The court further indicated that injunctions should be denied only in the "unusual" case, under "exceptional circumstances" and " 'in rare instances ... to protect the public interest.' " Just as the District Court erred in its categorical denial of injunctive relief, the Court of Appeals erred in its categorical grant of such relief.

Because we conclude that neither court below correctly applied the traditional four-factor framework that governs the award of injunctive relief, we vacate the judgment of the Court of Appeals, so that the District Court may apply that framework in the first instance. In doing so, we take no position on whether permanent injunctive relief should or should not issue in this particular case, or indeed in any number of other disputes arising under the Patent Act. We hold only that the decision whether to grant or deny injunctive relief rests within the equitable discretion of the district courts, and that such discretion must be exercised consistent with traditional principles of equity, in patent disputes no less than in other cases governed by such standards.

Accordingly, we vacate the judgment of the Court of Appeals and remand the case for further proceedings consistent with this opinion.

It is so ordered.

Chief Justice Roberts, with whom Justice Scalia and Justice Ginsburg join, concurring.

I agree with the Court's holding that "the decision whether to grant or deny injunctive relief rests within the equitable discretion of the district courts, and that such discretion must be exercised consistent with traditional principles of equity, in patent disputes no less than in other cases governed by such standards," and I join the opinion of the Court. That opinion rightly rests on the proposition that "a major departure from the long tradition of equity practice should not be lightly implied." *Weinberger v. Romero–Barcelo*, 456 U.S. 305, 320, 102 S.Ct. 1798, 72 L.Ed.2d 91 (1982).

From at least the early 19th century, courts have granted injunctive relief upon a finding of infringement in the vast majority of patent cases. This "long tradition of equity practice" is not surprising, given the difficulty of protecting a right to *exclude* through monetary remedies that allow an infringer to *use* an invention against the patentee's wishes-a difficulty that often implicates the first two factors of the traditional four-factor test. This historical practice, as the Court holds, does not *entitle* a patentee to a permanent injunction or justify a *general rule* that such injunctions should issue. The Federal Circuit itself so recognized in *Roche Products, Inc. v. Bolar Pharmaceutical Co.*, 733 F.2d 858, 865–867 (1984). At the same time, there is a difference between exercising equitable discretion pursuant to the established four-factor test and writing on an entirely clean slate. "Discretion is not whim, and limiting discretion according to legal standards helps promote the basic principle of justice that like cases should be decided alike." Martin v. Franklin Capital Corp., 546 U.S. 132, 139, 126 S.Ct. 704, 710, 163 L.Ed.2d 547 (2005). When it comes to discerning and applying those standards, in this area as others, "a page of history is worth a volume of logic." *New York Trust Co. v. Eisner*, 256 U.S. 345, 349, 41 S.Ct. 506, 65 L.Ed. 963 (1921) (opinion for the Court by Holmes, J.).

JUSTICE KENNEDY, with whom JUSTICE STEVENS, JUSTICE SOUTER, and JUSTICE BREYER join, concurring.

The Court is correct, in my view, to hold that courts should apply the well-established, four-factor test-without resort to categorical rules-in deciding whether to grant injunctive relief in patent cases. THE CHIEF JUSTICE is also correct that history may be instructive in applying this test. The traditional practice of issuing injunctions against patent infringers, however, does not seem to rest on "the difficulty of protecting a right to *exclude* through monetary remedies that allow an infringer to *use* an invention against the patentee's wishes." Both the terms of the Patent Act and the traditional view of injunctive relief accept that the existence of a right to exclude does not dictate the remedy for a violation of that right. To the extent earlier cases establish a pattern of granting an injunction against patent infringers almost as a matter of course, this pattern simply illustrates the result of the four-factor test in the contexts then prevalent. The lesson of the historical practice, therefore, is most helpful and instructive when the circumstances of a case bear substantial parallels to litigation the courts have confronted before.

In cases now arising trial courts should bear in mind that in many instances the nature of the patent being enforced and the economic function of the patent holder present considerations quite unlike earlier cases. An industry has developed in which firms use patents not as a basis for producing and selling goods but, instead, primarily for obtaining licensing fees. *See* FTC, To Promote Innovation: The Proper Balance of Competition and Patent Law and Policy, ch. 3, pp. 38–39 (Oct.2003), available at http:// www. ftc. gov/ os/ 2003/ 10/innovationrpt.pdf (as visited May 11, 2006, and available in Clerk of Court's case file). For these firms, an injunction, and the potentially serious sanctions arising from its violation, can be employed as a bargaining tool to charge exorbitant fees to companies that seek to buy licenses to practice the patent. When the patented invention is but a small component of the product the companies seek to produce and the threat of an injunction is employed simply for undue leverage in negotiations, legal damages may well be sufficient to compensate for the infringement and an injunction may not serve the public interest. In addition injunctive relief may have different consequences for the burgeoning number of patents over business methods, which were not of much economic and legal significance in earlier times. The potential vagueness and suspect validity of some of these patents may affect the calculus under the four-factor test.

The equitable discretion over injunctions, granted by the Patent Act, is well suited to allow courts to adapt to the rapid technological and legal developments in the patent system. For these reasons it should be recognized that district courts must determine whether past practice fits the circumstances of the cases before them. With these observations, I join the opinion of the Court.

NOTES

1. Preliminary Injunctions. Courts apply a four-factor test for preliminary injunctions: (1) likelihood of success of the merits, (2) irreparable injury, (3) balance of hardships, and (4) public interest. In *H.H. Robertson Comp. v. United Steel Deck, Inc.* 820 F.2d 384 (Fed. Cir. 1987), the Federal Circuit noted that prior litigation history and strong positions on infringement and validity are important considerations in the preliminary injunction analysis. Nevertheless, the Federal Circuit has "cautioned ... that a preliminary injunction is a drastic and extraordinary remedy that is not to be routinely granted." *Intel Corp. v. ULSI Sys. Tech., Inc.*, 995 F.2d 1566, 1568 (Fed. Cir. 1993).

2. Supreme Court and Equitable Relief in Patent Law. Declaratory judgments, particularly (in)validity and (non)infringement frequently occur in patent litigation. *See* 28 U.S.C. § 2201 (2006). In *MedImmune, Inc. v. Genentech, Inc.*, 549 U.S. 118, 127 S.Ct. 764, 166 L.Ed.2d 604 (2007), the Supreme Court reversed the Federal Circuit and held that a patent licensee had declaratory judgment standing to seek a declaration of invalidity and enforcement on the underlying patent even though the licensee had not terminated the license. The Federal Circuit has understood *MedImmune* as setting aside nearly all of its declaratory judgment jurisdiction jurisprudence. *SanDisk Corp. v. STMicroelectronics, NV*, 480 F.3d 1372, 1380 (Fed. Cir. 2007).

eBay arguably raised the standard for patentees obtaining permanent injunctions. On the other hand, the Federal Circuit recognizes post-*MedImmune* that "the now more lenient legal standard facilitates or enhances the availability of declaratory judgment jurisdiction in patent cases." *Micron Tech., Inc. v. Mosaid Techs., Inc.* 518 F.3d 897, 902 (Fed. Cir. 2008). Are the two cases decided strictly doctrinally, or are there policy reasons that motivated the Supreme Court to raise the standard for obtaining one form of equitable relief for patentees and lower the standard for obtaining another form of equitable relief for accused infringers? Does Justice Kennedy's concurrence in *eBay* provide any answers?

B. DAMAGES

Upon finding for the claimant the court shall award the claimant damages adequate to compensate for the infringement, but in no event less than a reasonable royalty for the use made of the invention by the infringer, together with interest and costs as fixed by the court.

When the damages are not found by a jury, the court shall assess them. In either event the court may increase the damages up to three times the amount found or assessed. Increased damages under this paragraph shall not apply to provisional rights under section 154(d) of this title.

The court may receive expert testimony as an aid to the determination of damages or of what royalty would be reasonable under the circumstances.

35 U.S.C. § 284.

RITE–HITE CORP. v. KELLEY CO., INC.

United States Court of Appeals for the Federal Circuit, 1995.
56 F.3d 1538.

LOURIE, CIRCUIT JUDGE

Kelley Company appeals from a decision of the United States District Court for the Eastern District of Wisconsin, awarding damages for the infringement of U.S. Patent 4,373,847, owned by Rite–Hite Corporation. *Rite–Hite Corp. v. Kelley Co.*, 774 F. Supp. 1514 (E.D. Wis. 1991). The district court determined, inter alia, that Rite–Hite was entitled to lost profits for lost sales of its devices that were in direct competition with the infringing devices, but which themselves were not covered by the patent in suit. The appeal has been taken in banc to determine whether such damages are legally compensable under 35 U.S.C. § 284. We affirm in part, vacate in part, and remand.

Background

On March 22, 1983, Rite–Hite sued Kelley, alleging that Kelley's "Truk Stop" vehicle restraint infringed Rite–Hite's U.S. Patent 4,373,847 ("the '847 patent"). The '847 patent, issued February 15, 1983, is directed to a device for securing a vehicle to a loading dock to prevent the vehicle from separating from the dock during loading or unloading. Any such separation would create a gap between the vehicle and dock and create a danger for a forklift operator.

Rite–Hite distributed all its products through its wholly-owned and operated sales organizations and through independent sales organizations

(ISOs). During the period of infringement, the Rite–Hite sales organizations accounted for approximately 30 percent of the retail dollar sales of Rite–Hite products, and the ISOs accounted for the remaining 70 percent. Rite–Hite sued for its lost profits at the wholesale level and for the lost retail profits of its own sales organizations. Shortly after this action was filed, several ISOs moved to intervene, contending that they were "exclusive licensees" of the '847 patent by virtue of "Sales Representative Agreements" and "Dok–Lok Supplement" agreements between themselves and Rite–Hite. The court determined that the ISOs were exclusive licensees and accordingly, on August 31, 1984, permitted them to intervene. The ISOs sued for their lost retail profits.

The district court bifurcated the liability and damage phases of the trial and, on March 5, 1986, held the '847 patent to be not invalid and to be infringed by the manufacture, use, and sale of Kelley's Truk Stop device. The court enjoined further infringement. The judgment of liability was affirmed by this court.

On remand, the damage issues were tried to the court. Rite–Hite sought damages calculated as lost profits for two types of vehicle restraints that it made and sold: the "Manual Dok–Lok" model 55 (MDL–55), which incorporated the invention covered by the '847 patent, and the "Automatic Dok–Lok" model 100 (ADL–100), which was not covered by the patent in suit. The ADL–100 was the first vehicle restraint Rite–Hite put on the market and it was covered by one or more patents other than the patent in suit. The Kelley Truk Stop restraint was designed to compete primarily with Rite–Hite's ADL–100. Both employed an electric motor and functioned automatically, and each sold for $1,000–$1,500 at the wholesale level, in contrast to the MDL–55, which sold for one-third to one-half the price of the motorized devices. Rite–Hite does not assert that Kelley's Truk Stop restraint infringed the patents covering the ADL–100.

* * *

The court awarded Rite–Hite as a manufacturer the wholesale profits that it lost on lost sales of the ADL–100 restraints, MDL–55 restraints, and restraint-leveler packages. It also awarded to Rite–Hite as a retailer and to the ISOs reasonable royalty damages on lost ADL–100, MDL–55, and restraint-leveler sales caused by Kelley's infringing sales. Finally, prejudgment interest, calculated without compounding, was awarded. Kelley's infringement was found to be not willful.

On appeal, Kelley contends that the district court erred as a matter of law in its determination of damages. Kelley does not contest the award of damages for lost sales of the MDL–55 restraints; however, Kelley argues that (1) the patent statute does not provide for damages based on Rite–Hite's lost profits on ADL–100 restraints because the ADL–100s are not covered by the patent in suit; (2) lost profits on unpatented dock levelers are not attributable to demand for the '847 invention and, therefore, are not recoverable losses; (3) the ISOs have no standing to sue for patent infringement damages; and (4) the court erred in calculating a reasonable royalty based as a percentage of ADL–100 and dock leveler profits. Rite–Hite and the ISOs challenge the district court's refusal to award lost retail profits and its award of prejudgment interest at a simple, rather than a compound, rate.

We affirm the damage award with respect to Rite–Hite's lost profits as a manufacturer on its ADL–100 restraint sales, affirm the court's computation of a reasonable royalty rate, vacate the damage award based on the dock levelers, and vacate the damage award with respect to the ISOs because they lack standing. We remand for dismissal of the ISOs' claims and for a redetermination of damages consistent with this opinion. The issues raised by Rite–Hite are unpersuasive.

Discussion

* * *

A.   Kelley's Appeal

I.   *Lost Profits on the ADL–100 Restraints*

The district court's decision to award lost profits damages pursuant to 35 U.S.C. § 284 turned primarily upon the quality of Rite–Hite's proof of actual lost profits. The court found that, "but for" Kelley's infringing Truk Stop competition, Rite–Hite would have sold * * * additional ADL–100 * * * and MDL–55 restraints. The court reasoned that awarding lost profits fulfilled the patent statute's goal of affording complete compensation for infringement and compensated Rite–Hite for the ADL–100 sales that Kelley "anticipated taking from Rite–Hite when it marketed the Truk Stop against the ADL–100." Rite–Hite, 774 F. Supp. at 1540. The court stated, "the rule applied here therefore does not extend Rite–Hite's patent rights excessively, because Kelley could reasonably have foreseen that its infringement of the '847 patent would make it liable for lost ADL–100 sales in addition to lost MDL–55 sales." The court further reasoned that its decision would avoid what it referred to as the "whip-saw" problem, whereby an infringer could avoid paying lost profits damages altogether by developing a device using a first patented technology to compete with a device that uses a second patented technology and developing a device using the second patented technology to compete with a device that uses the first patented technology.

Kelley maintains that Rite–Hite's lost sales of the ADL–100 restraints do not constitute an injury that is legally compensable by means of lost profits. It has uniformly been the law, Kelley argues, that to recover damages in the form of lost profits a patentee must prove that, "but for" the infringement, it would have sold a product covered by the patent in suit to the customers who bought from the infringer. Under the circumstances of this case, in Kelley's view, the patent statute provides only for damages calculated as a reasonable royalty. Rite–Hite, on the other hand, argues that the only restriction on an award of actual lost profits damages for patent infringement is proof of causation-in-fact. A patentee, in its view, is entitled to all the profits it would have made on any of its products "but for" the infringement. Each party argues that a judgment in favor of the other would frustrate the purposes of the patent statute. Whether the lost profits at issue are legally compensable is a question of law, which we review de novo.

Our analysis of this question necessarily begins with the patent statute. Implementing the constitutional power under Article I, section 8, to secure to inventors the exclusive right to their discoveries, Congress has provided in 35 U.S.C. § 284 as follows:

> Upon finding for the claimant the court shall award the claimant damages adequate to compensate for the infringement, but in no event less than a reasonable royalty for the use made of the invention by the infringer, together with interest and costs as fixed by the court.

The statute thus mandates that a claimant receive damages "adequate" to compensate for infringement. Section 284 further instructs that a damage award shall be "in no event less than a reasonable royalty"; the purpose of this alternative is not to direct the form of compensation, but to set a floor below which damage awards may not fall. Thus, the language of the statute is expansive rather than limiting. It affirmatively states that damages must be adequate, while providing only a lower limit and no other limitation.

The Supreme Court spoke to the question of patent damages in *General Motors*, stating that, in enacting § 284, Congress sought to "ensure that the patent owner would in fact receive full compensation for 'any damages' [the patentee] suffered as a result of the infringement." *General Motors*, 461 U.S. at 654. Thus, while the statutory text states tersely that the patentee receive "adequate" damages, the Supreme Court has interpreted this to mean that "adequate" damages should approximate those damages that will fully compensate the patentee for infringement. Further, the Court has cautioned against imposing limitations on patent infringement damages, stating: "When Congress wished to limit an element of recovery in a patent infringement action, it said so explicitly." *General Motors*, 461 U.S. at 653

In *Aro Mfg. Co. v. Convertible Top Replacement Co.*, 377 U.S. 476 (1964), the Court discussed the statutory standard for measuring patent infringement damages, explaining:

> The question to be asked in determining damages is "how much had the Patent Holder and Licensee suffered by the infringement. And that question [is] primarily: had the Infringer not infringed, what would the Patentee Holder–Licensee have made?"

This surely states a "but for" test. In accordance with the Court's guidance, we have held that the general rule for determining actual damages to a patentee that is itself producing the patented item is to determine the sales and profits lost to the patentee because of the infringement. To recover lost profits damages, the patentee must show a reasonable probability that, "but for" the infringement, it would have made the sales that were made by the infringer.

Panduit Corp. v. Stahlin Bros. Fibre Works, Inc., 575 F.2d 1152 (6th Cir. 1978), articulated a four-factor test that has since been accepted as a useful, but non-exclusive, way for a patentee to prove entitlement to lost profits damages. The *Panduit* test requires that a patentee establish: (1) demand for the patented product; (2) absence of acceptable non-infringing substitutes; (3) manufacturing and marketing capability to exploit the demand; and (4) the amount of the profit it would have made. A showing under *Panduit* permits a court to reasonably infer that the lost profits claimed were in fact caused by the infringing sales, thus establishing a patentee's prima facie case with respect to "but for" causation. A patentee need not negate every possibility that the purchaser might not have purchased a product other than its own, absent the infringement. The patentee need only show that there was a reasonable probability that the sales would have been made "but for" the infringement. When the patentee establishes the reasonableness of this inference, e.g., by satisfying the *Panduit* test, it has sustained the burden of proving entitlement to lost profits due to the infringing sales. The burden then shifts to the infringer to show that the inference is unreasonable for some or all of the lost sales.

Applying *Panduit*, the district court found that Rite–Hite had established "but for" causation. In the court's view, this was sufficient to prove entitlement to lost profits damages on the ADL–100. Kelley does not challenge that Rite–Hite meets the *Panduit* test and therefore has proven "but for" causation; rather, Kelley argues that damages for the ADL–100, even if in fact caused by the infringement, are not legally compensable because the ADL–100 is not covered by the patent in suit.

Preliminarily, we wish to affirm that the "test" for compensability of damages under § 284 is not solely a "but for" test in the sense that an infringer must compensate a patentee for any and all damages that proceed from the act of patent infringement. Notwithstanding the broad language of § 284, judicial relief cannot redress every conceivable harm that can be traced to an alleged wrongdoing. For example, remote consequences, such as a heart attack of the inventor or loss in value of shares of common stock of a patentee corporation caused indirectly by infringement are not compensable. Thus, along with establishing that a particular injury suffered by a patentee is a "but for" consequence of infringement, there may also be a background question whether the asserted injury is of the type for which the patentee may be compensated.

Judicial limitations on damages, either for certain classes of plaintiffs or for certain types of injuries have been imposed in terms of "proximate cause" or "foreseeability." Such labels have been judicial tools used to limit legal responsibility for the consequences of one's conduct that are too remote to justify compensation. The general principles expressed in the common law tell us that the question of legal compensability is one "to be determined on the facts of each case upon mixed considerations of logic, common sense, justice, policy and precedent." *See* 1 Street, Foundations of Legal Liability 110 (1906) (quoted in W. Page Keeton et al., Prosser & Keeton on the Law of Torts § 42, at 279 (5th ed. 1984)).

We believe that under § 284 of the patent statute, the balance between full compensation, which is the meaning that the Supreme Court has attributed to the statute, and the reasonable limits of liability encompassed by general principles of law can best be viewed in terms of reasonable, objective foreseeability. If a particular injury was or should have been reasonably foreseeable by an infringing competitor in the relevant market, broadly defined, that injury is generally compensable absent a persuasive reason to the contrary. Here, the court determined that Rite–Hite's lost sales of the ADL–100, a product that directly competed with the infringing product, were reasonably foreseeable. We agree with that conclusion. Being responsible for lost sales of a competitive product is surely foreseeable; such losses constitute the full compensation set forth by Congress, as interpreted by the Supreme Court, while staying well within the traditional meaning of proximate cause. Such lost sales should therefore clearly be compensable.

Recovery for lost sales of a device not covered by the patent in suit is not of course expressly provided for by the patent statute. Express language is not required, however. Statutes speak in general terms rather than specifically expressing every detail. Under the patent statute, damages should be awarded "where necessary to afford the plaintiff full compensation for the infringement." *General Motors*, 461 U.S. at 654. Thus, to refuse to award reasonably foreseeable damages necessary to make Rite–Hite whole would be inconsistent with the meaning of § 284.

Kelley asserts that to allow recovery for the ADL–100 would contravene the policy reason for which patents are granted: "To promote the progress of ... the useful arts." U.S. Const., art. I, § 8, cl. 8. Because an inventor is only entitled to exclusivity to the extent he or she has invented and disclosed a novel, nonobvious, and useful device, Kelley argues, a patent may never be used to restrict competition in the sale of products not covered by the patent in suit. In support, Kelley cites antitrust case law condemning the use of a patent as a means to obtain a "monopoly" on unpatented material.

These cases are inapposite to the issue raised here. The present case does not involve expanding the limits of the patent grant in violation of the antitrust laws; it simply asks, once infringement of a valid patent is found, what compensable injuries result from that infringement, i.e., how may the patentee be made whole. Rite–Hite is not attempting to exclude its competitors from making, using, or selling a product not within the scope of its patent. The Truk Stop restraint was found to infringe the '847 patent, and Rite–Hite is simply seeking adequate compensation for that infringement; this is not an antitrust issue. Allowing compensation for such damage will "promote the Progress of ... the useful Arts" by providing a stimulus to the development of new products and industries.

Kelley further asserts that, as a policy matter, inventors should be encouraged by the law to practice their inventions. This is not a meaningful or persuasive argument, at least in this context. A patent is granted in exchange for a patentee's disclosure of an invention, not for the patentee's use of the invention. There is no requirement in this country that a patentee make, use, or sell its patented invention. If a patentee's failure to practice a patented invention frustrates an important public need for the invention, a court need not enjoin infringement of the patent. Accordingly, courts have in rare instances exercised their discretion to deny injunctive relief in order to protect the public interest. Whether a patentee sells its patented invention is not crucial in determining lost profits damages. Normally, if the patentee is not selling a product, by definition there can be no lost profits. However, in this case, Rite–Hite did sell its own patented products, the MDL–55 and the ADL–100 restraints.

Kelley next argues that to award lost profits damages on Rite–Hite's ADL–100s would be contrary to precedent. Citing *Panduit*, Kelley argues that case law regarding lost profits uniformly requires that "the intrinsic value of the patent in suit is the only proper basis for a lost profits award." Kelley argues that each prong of the *Panduit* test focuses on the patented invention; thus, Kelley asserts, Rite–Hite cannot obtain damages consisting of lost profits on a product that is not the patented invention.

Generally, the *Panduit* test has been applied when a patentee is seeking lost profits for a device covered by the patent in suit. However, *Panduit* is not the sine qua non for proving "but for" causation. If there are other ways to show that the infringement in fact caused the patentee's lost profits, there is no reason why another test should not be acceptable. Moreover, other fact situations may require different means of evaluation, and failure to meet the *Panduit* test does not ipso facto disqualify a loss from being compensable.

In any event, the only *Panduit* factor that arguably was not met in the present fact situation is the second one, absence of acceptable non-infringing substitutes. Establishment of this factor tends to prove that the patentee would not have lost the sales to a non-infringing third party rather than to the infringer. That, however, goes only to the question of proof. Here, the only substitute for the patented device was the ADL–100, another of the patentee's devices. Such a substitute was not an "acceptable, non-infringing substitute" within the meaning of *Panduit* because, being patented by Rite–Hite, it was not available to customers except from Rite–Hite. Rite–Hite therefore would not have lost the sales to a third party. The second *Panduit* factor thus has been met. If, on the other hand, the ADL–100 had not been patented and was found to be an acceptable substitute, that would have been a different story, and Rite–Hite would have had to prove that its customers would not have obtained the ADL–100 from a third party in order to prove the second factor of *Panduit*.

Kelley's conclusion that the lost sales must be of the patented invention thus is not supported. Kelley's concern that lost profits must relate to the "intrinsic value of the patent" is subsumed in the "but for" analysis; if the patent infringement had nothing to do with the lost sales, "but for" causation would not have been proven. However, "but for" causation is conceded here. The motive, or motivation, for the infringement is irrelevant if it is proved that the infringement in fact caused the loss. We see no basis for Kelley's conclusion that the lost sales must be of products covered by the infringed patent.

Kelley has thus not provided, nor do we find, any justification in the statute, precedent, policy, or logic to limit the compensability of lost sales of a patentee's device that directly competes with the infringing device if it is proven that those lost sales were caused in fact by the infringement. Such lost sales are reasonably foreseeable and the award of damages is necessary to provide adequate compensation for infringement under 35 U.S.C. § 284. Thus, Rite–Hite's ADL–100 lost sales are legally compensable and we affirm the award of lost profits on the 3,283 sales lost to Rite–Hite's wholesale business in ADL–100 restraints.

II.   *Damages on the Dock Levelers*

Based on the "entire market value rule," the district court awarded lost profits on 1,692 dock levelers that it found Rite–Hite would have sold with the ADL–100 and MDL–55 restraints. Kelley argues that this award must be set aside because Rite–Hite failed to establish that the dock levelers were eligible to be included in the damage computation under the entire market value rule. We agree.

When a patentee seeks damages on unpatented components sold with a patented apparatus, courts have applied a formulation known as the "entire market value rule" to determine whether such components should be included in the damage computation, whether for reasonable royalty purposes * * * Early cases invoking the entire market value rule required that for a patentee owning an "improvement patent" to recover damages calculated on sales of a larger machine incorporating that improvement, the patentee was required to show that the entire value of the whole machine, as a marketable article, was "properly and legally attributable" to the patented feature. Subsequently, our predecessor court held that damages for component parts used with a patented apparatus were recoverable under the entire market value rule if the patented apparatus "was of such paramount importance that it substantially created the value of the component parts." *Marconi Wireless Telegraph Co. v. United States*, 99 Ct. Cl. 1 (Ct. Cl. 1942), aff'd in part and vacated in part, 320 U.S. 1 (1943). We have held that the entire market value rule permits recovery of damages based on the value of a patentee's entire apparatus containing several features when the patent-related feature is the "basis for customer demand." *State Indus.*, 883 F.2d at 1580.

The entire market value rule has typically been applied to include in the compensation base unpatented components of a device when the unpatented and patented components are physically part of the same machine. The rule has been extended to allow inclusion of physically separate unpatented components normally sold with the patented components. However, in such cases, the unpatented and patented components together were considered to be components of a single assembly or parts of a complete machine, or they together constituted a functional unit.

In *Paper Converting*, this court articulated the entire market value rule in terms of the objectively reasonable probability that a patentee would have made the relevant sales. Furthermore, we may have appeared to expand the rule when we emphasized the financial and marketing dependence of the unpatented component on the patented component. *See id.* In *Paper Converting*, however, the rule was applied to allow recovery of profits on the unpatented components only because all the components together were considered to be parts of a single assembly. The references to "financial and marketing dependence" and "reasonable probability" were made in the context of the facts of the case and did not separate the rule from its traditional moorings.

Specifically, recovery was sought for the lost profits on sales of an entire machine for the high speed manufacture of paper rolls comprising several physically separate components, only one of which incorporated the invention. The machine was comprised of the patented "rewinder" component and several auxiliary components, including an "unwind stand" that supported a large roll of supply paper to the rewinder, a "core loader" that supplied paperboard cores to the rewinder, an "embosser" that embossed the paper and provided a special textured surface, and a "tail sealer" that sealed the paper's trailing end to the finished roll. Although we noted that the auxiliary components had "separate usage" in that they each separately performed a part of an entire rewinding operation, the components together constituted one functional unit, including the patented component, to produce rolls of paper. The auxiliary components derived their market value from the patented rewinder because they had no useful purpose independent of the patented rewinder.

Similarly, our subsequent cases have applied the entire market value rule only in situations in which the patented and unpatented components were analogous to a single functioning unit. *See, e.g., Kalman v. Berlyn Corp.*, 914 F.2d 1473 (Fed. Cir. 1990) (affirming award of damages for filter screens used with a patented filtering device); *TWM*, 789 F.2d at 901 (affirming award of damages for unpatented wheels and axles sold with patented vehicle suspension system); *Kori Corp. v. Wilco Marsh Buggies & Draglines, Inc.*, 761 F.2d 649 (Fed. Cir.) (affirming an award of damages for unpatented uppers of an improved amphibious vehicle having a patented pontoon structure), cert. denied, 474 U.S. 902 (1985).

Thus, the facts of past cases clearly imply a limitation on damages, when recovery is sought on sales of unpatented components sold with patented components, to the effect that the unpatented components must function together with the patented component in some manner so as to produce a desired end product or result. All the components together must be analogous to components of a single assembly or be parts of a complete machine, or they must constitute a functional unit. Our precedent has not extended liability to include items that have essentially no functional relationship to the patented invention and that may have been sold with an infringing device only as a matter of convenience or business advantage. We are not persuaded that we should extend that liability. Damages on such items would constitute more than what is "adequate to compensate for the infringement."

The facts of this case do not meet this requirement. The dock levelers operated to bridge the gap between a loading dock and a truck. The patented vehicle restraint operated to secure the rear of the truck to the loading dock. Although the two devices may have been used together, they did not function together to achieve one result and each could effectively have been used independently of each other. The parties had established positions in marketing dock levelers long prior to developing the vehicle restraints. Rite–Hite and Kelley were pioneers in that industry and for many years were primary competitors. Although following Rite–Hite's introduction of its restraints onto the market, customers frequently solicited package bids for the simultaneous installation of restraints and dock levelers, they did so because such bids facilitated contracting and construction scheduling, and because both Rite–Hite and Kelley encouraged this linkage by offering combination discounts. The dock levelers were thus sold by Kelley with the restraints only for marketing reasons, not because they essentially functioned together. We distinguish our conclusion to permit damages based on lost sales of the unpatented (not covered by the patent in suit) ADL–100 devices, but not on lost sales of the unpatented dock levelers, by emphasizing that the Kelley Truk Stops were devices competitive with the ADL–100s, whereas the dock levelers were merely items sold together with the restraints for convenience and business advantage. It is a clear purpose of the patent law to redress competitive damages resulting from infringement of the patent, but there is no basis for extending that recovery to include damages for items that are neither competitive with nor function with the patented invention. Promotion of the useful arts requires one, but not the other. These facts do not establish the functional relationship necessary to justify recovery under the entire market value rule. Therefore, the district court erred as a matter of law in including them within the compensation base. Accordingly, we vacate the court's award of damages based on the dock leveler sales.

* * *

IV. Computation of Reasonable Royalty

The district court found that Rite–Hite as a manufacturer was entitled to an award of a reasonable royalty on 502 infringing restraint or restraint-leveler sales for which it had not proved that it contacted the Kelley customer prior to the infringing Kelley sale. The court awarded a royalty equal to approximately fifty percent of Rite–Hite's estimated lost profits per unit sold to retailers. Further, the court found that Rite–Hite as a retailer was entitled to a reasonable royalty amounting to approximately one-third its estimated lost distribution income per infringing sale.

Kelley challenges the amount of the royalty as grossly excessive and legally in error.

A patentee is entitled to no less than a reasonable royalty on an infringer's sales for which the patentee has not established entitlement to lost profits. The royalty may be based upon an established royalty, if there is one, or if not, upon the supposed result of hypothetical negotiations between the plaintiff and defendant. The hypothetical negotiation requires the court to envision the terms of a licensing agreement reached as the result of a supposed meeting between the patentee and the infringer at the time infringement began. "One challenging only the court's finding as to amount of damages awarded under the 'reasonable royalty' provision of § 284, therefore, must show that the award is, in view of all the evidence, either so outrageously high or so outrageously low as to be unsupportable as an estimation of a reasonably royalty." *Lindemann Maschinenfabrik GmbH v. American Hoist & Derrick Co.*, 895 F.2d 1403 (Fed. Cir. 1990).

The district court here conducted the hypothetical negotiation analysis. It determined that Rite–Hite would have been willing to grant a competitor a license to use the '847 invention only if it received a royalty of no less than one-half of the per unit profits that it was foregoing. In so determining, the court considered that the '847 patent was a "pioneer" patent with manifest commercial success; that Rite–Hite had consistently followed a policy of exploiting its own patents, rather than licensing to competitors; and that Rite–Hite would have had to forego a large profit by granting a license to Kelley because Kelley was a strong competitor and Rite–Hite anticipated being able to sell a large number of restraints and related products. *See Deere & Co. v. International Harvester Co.*, 710 F.2d 1551, 1559 (Fed. Cir. 1983) (court may consider impact of anticipated collateral sales); *Georgia–Pacific Corp. v. United States Plywood Corp.*, 318 F. Supp. 1116, (S.D.N.Y. 1970) (wide range of factors relevant to hypothetical negotiation), modified and aff'd, 446 F.2d 295 (2d Cir.), cert. denied, 404 U.S. 870 (1971). It was thus not unreasonable for the district court to find that an unwilling patentee would only license for one-half its expected lost profits and that such an amount was a reasonable royalty. The fact that the award was not based on the infringer's profits did not make it an unreasonable award. Furthermore, the fact that the award was based on and was a significant portion of the patentee's profits also does not make the award unreasonable. The language of the statute requires "damages adequate to compensate," which does not include a royalty that a patentee who does not wish to license its patent would find unreasonable.

We conclude that the district court made no legal error and was not clearly erroneous in determining the reasonable royalty rate. Accordingly, we affirm the trial court's calculation of a reasonable royalty rate. However, because we vacate the court's decision to include dock levelers in the royalty base, we remand for a redetermination of damages based only on the sale of the infringing restraints and not on the restraint-leveler packages.

B. Rite–Hite's Cross Appeal

Rite–Hite and the ISOs sought damages based on lost profits at the retail level for ADL–100 and MDL–55 restraints and dock levelers. The district court denied the award on the basis that both Rite–Hite and the ISOs failed to meet their evidentiary burden of proving lost profits. Rite–Hite has not persuaded us that the court's decision was erroneous. As for the ISOs, this issue is mooted by the above rulings.

Rite–Hite also argues that the district court erred in awarding interest at a simple rather than a compound rate because, as a matter of law, prejudgment interest must be compounded. We disagree. It has been recognized that "an award of compound rather than simple interest assures that the patent owner is fully compensated." *Fromson v. Western Litho Plate & Supply Co.*, 13 uspq2D 1856, 1862, 1989 wl 149268 (E.D. Mo. 1989), aff'd mem., 909 F.2d 1495 (Fed. Cir. 1990). However, the determination whether to award simple or compound interest is a matter largely within the discretion of the district court. Rite–Hite has not persuaded us that the court abused its discretion in awarding interest at a simple rate.

Conclusion

On Kelley's appeal, we affirm the district court's decision that Rite–Hite is entitled to an award of lost profit damages based on its lost business in ADL–100 restraints. We affirm the court's determination of the reasonable royalty rate. We vacate the awards to the ISOs and vacate the damage award based on the dock levelers. We remand for the court to dismiss the ISOs as plaintiffs and recalculate damages to Rite–Hite. On Rite–Hite's cross-appeal, we affirm.

[NIES, CIRCUIT JUDGE dissenting and concurring in result omitted]

[NEWMAN, CIRCUIT JUDGE concurring in-part and dissenting in-part omitted]

C. ATTORNEY'S FEES

The court in exceptional cases may award reasonable attorney fees to the prevailing party.

35 U.S.C. § 285.

For information about design and plant patents please see the on-line supplement to this book.

CHAPTER FIVE

TRADEMARKS: CREATING SIGNPOSTS FOR CONSUMERS IN THE MARKETPLACE

■ ■ ■

OVERVIEW

A trademark is "any word, symbol, or device, or any combination thereof [that is] (1) used by a person or (2) which a person has a bona fide intention to use in commerce and applies to register on the principal register, * * * to identify or distinguish his or her goods, including a unique product, from those manufactured or sold by others and to indicate the source of the goods, even if that source is unknown." 15 U.S.C. § 1127.

Notice the key words in the definition. Trademark is a word, symbol, or device, or any combination thereof, or simply put a mark. This mark is used to distinguish the goods (and services) of one manufacturer or seller from those of another. The definition envisions the following three part relationship:

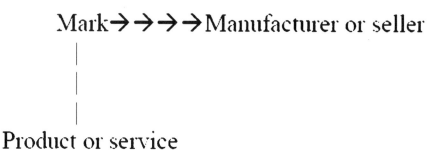

In other words, a mark is attached to a product or service to refer to the manufacturing or selling source of the product of the service. Notice if any one of these prongs is missing, we no longer have a trademark. For example, if the mark is not attached to a product or service, but is referring to a manufacturer or seller, the mark is serving as a trade name.

If the mark is attached to a product or service, but is not referring to a manufacturer or seller, the mark is serving as a generic name. A trademark exists when this three part relationship exists.

Trademarks serve a unique function in the scheme of intellectual property in that they are tied almost exclusively to the function of buying and selling goods and services. A predominant objective of trademark law is to prevent consumer confusion in the marketplace. If anyone has traveled to a bazaar in a developing country or even a farmer's market in the United States, one may have been struck by the absence of brands or labels on products that are often displayed in bulk in bins or crates placed in stalls. Sometimes there may be a name attached to the stall to help identify the source of the wares. More often, word of mouth or some characteristic of the product (its size or shape) may give some sense of where it came from. In large marketplaces that are national in scope, trademarks serve to allow consumers to distinguish between products that may have been produced on opposite sides of the country, or the globe. Trademarks are also unusual in the intellectual property scheme because rights are created by use in commerce. Federal trademark registration in fact requires use in interstate commerce. Furthermore, use must be continued to maintain one's rights. Therefore, it is possible to have trademark rights without registration even though registration offers significant advantages to the trademark owner.

The previous discussion raises many points about trademarks. First, trademark law, like all intellectual property, is international in scope. The issues of international trademark law will be discussed in the chapter on international law.

Second, trademarks cover any word, symbol, or device, or any combination of these three. There is a separate category of marks called service marks which are used "to identify and distinguish the services of others and to indicate the source of services, even if that source is unknown." The law of trademarks and service marks overlap, and therefore in this chapter, as is typical practice, we will use the word trademark to include both trademarks and service marks. The definition of service marks states that "[t]itles, character names, and other distinctive features of radio or television programs may be registered as service marks notwithstanding that they, or the programs, may advertise the goods of the sponsor." See 15 USC § 1127. This means that distinctive features of your favorite television shows may be used as service marks to brand the program themselves or other products that might spin off from the programs. In fact, many musicians register their stage names or band names as trademarks.

Trademark law also applies to certification marks and collective marks. Certification marks are trademarks used by certification organizations (such as the Good Housekeeping Seal of Approval or California Organic Farmers Association or the American Bar Association) to certify that a product or service meets a specified quality standard. Collective marks are used by collective bodies, such as unions or trade associations, to represent the affiliation with the body. See 15 USC § 1054.

Third, trademarks should be distinguished from trade names or commercial names. The last two are defined as "any name used by a person to identify his or her business or vocation." See 15 USC § 1127. Federal trademark law protects trade names or commercial name only to the extent that the same name is used as a trademark. Trade names and commercial names are protected through state law, and each state has its own registration process for registering these names when a business is formed. The only exception to this rule is that federal law protects some trade names, such as the Red Cross, that are federally created corporate entities. Notice that a non-profit entity can own trademarks, trade names, or commercial names. Here are some examples of these concepts. The word Hilton when used to refer to the corporation is a trade name. When the same word Hilton is used to refer to a brand of a hotel, it is being used as a trademark (specifically a service mark). When the word Planned Parenthood is used to refer to the non-profit organization, it is being used as a trade name. When the same word is being used to brand the services provided by that organization, the word is being used as a trademark. As with any word, you need to be careful of the context to understand how the word is being used and what meaning it has.

Federal trademark law is codified in the Lanham Act, also referred to as the Trademark Act of 1946. There were several Trademark Acts before this one, but because of a restrictive reading of the commerce clause that existed before the 1930's, these federal acts were narrow in their scope. See *The Trade–Mark Cases*, 100 U.S. (10 Otto) 82, 25 L.Ed. 550 (1879). Trademark law also includes some state law, particularly the state law of unfair competition. Our discussion in this chapter will focus almost exclusively on the Lanham Act with a brief mention of state law. Discussion of international law is left for another chapter.

The organization of this chapter falls into three broad issues: (1) what can be trademarked, (2) how trademarks are protected, and (3) the scope of trademark rights. The first issue will focus on trademark prosecution, or the process of securing trademark rights at the federal level. Since trademark prosecution entails interacting with the United States Patent and Trademark Office (USPTO), these materials will provide some insight into the administrative side of trademark law. The second issue will focus on trademark infringement and therefore will largely have a focus on litigation. However, keep in mind that the validity of the trademark is an issue for both prosecution and litigation. Therefore, most of the issues under issue (1) will also apply under issue (2). Finally, we will consider defenses and remedies in trademark infringement actions, a topic that will allow us to explore the limits on trademark rights.

I. WHAT CAN BE TRADEMARKED?

A. TRADEMARK AND OTHER IP

1. Trademarks and Trade Names: Overlapping Approaches

ALDERMAN v. IDITAROD PROPERTIES, INC.

Supreme Court of Alaska, 2001.
32 P.3d 373.

CARPENETI, JUSTICE.

During the 1998 Anchorage tourist season, both Robert Gottstein's Iditarod Properties and Caleb and Barbara Alderman's Alaska Guestours operated separate trolley tours named "Fourth Avenue Theater Trolley Tours" from the front of the historic Fourth Avenue Theatre owned by Iditarod. Iditarod sued the Aldermans for trade name infringement. A jury found that the Aldermans had infringed Iditarod's trade name "Fourth Avenue Theatre" and had breached a lease agreement for the use of the theater's ticket booth. The Aldermans appeal numerous issues including the application of trade name law, the jury verdict, the interpretation of the business name registration statute, the amendment of the pleadings, and the award of attorney's fees. We affirm on all issues. * * *

A. Trademark and Trade Name Law in General

1. *Terminology: trade name v. trademark*

In the modern legal vernacular, "trade name" means a symbol used to distinguish companies, partnerships, and businesses. By contrast, "trademark" refers to symbols used to distinguish goods and services. This distinction blurs somewhat when talking about a service company- does "Fourth Avenue Theatre" distinguish the business or the services provided? Because "Fourth Avenue Theatre" is more typical of a business name and the dispute here is over its use as a business name, we treat this as a case involving a trade name rather than a trademark.

The distinction between trade name and trademark, however, is generally not a critical distinction, and we conclude that it is not in this case. The United States Supreme Court noted the identity of protection for trademarks and trade names:

Whether the name of a corporation is to be regarded as a trade-mark, a trade-name, or both, is not entirely clear under the decisions. To some extent the two terms overlap, but there is a difference, more or less definitely recognized, which is that, generally speaking, the former is applicable to the vendible commodity to which it is affixed, the latter to a business and its good will. A corporate name seems to fall more appropriately into the latter class. But the precise difference is not often material, since the law affords protection against its appropriation in either view, upon the same fundamental principles. *American Steel Foundries v. Robertson*, 269 U.S. 372, 380, 46 S.Ct. 160, 70 L.Ed. 317 (1926) (citation omitted).

Protection of trade names and trademarks is the same because trade names and trademarks serve the same basic purposes. "Although trade names [and] trademarks ... are used differently, they [both] serve the same basic purposes, that is, to identify a business and its products or services, to create a consumer demand therefore, and to protect any goodwill which one may create as to his goods or services." *Younker v. Nationwide Mut. Ins. Co.*, 175 Ohio St. 1, 191 N.E.2d 145, 149 (1963).

The same basic rules apply equally to trade names and trademarks. Trademarks and trade names are classified in the same four categories. Analysis of infringement for both trademarks and trade names is done under a likelihood-of-confusion test. Trade names, like trademarks and other types of trade symbols, are protected against use that is likely to cause confusion even if the related infringing use is non-competitive. The term "trademark infringement" covers the use of one party's trade name as a trademark on another's goods or services as well as the use of one party's trademark as part of another's corporate name. Because the same basic rules and rationales apply equally to trade names and trademarks, we rely on trademark infringement case law in a trade name case such as this.

2. *General concepts of trade name and trademark law*

"Two elements must be proved to establish a prima facie case of unfair or deceptive acts or practices under the Alaska Act: (1) that the defendant is engaged in trade or commerce; and (2) that in the conduct of trade or commerce, an unfair act or practice has occurred." * * * Neither party contests that the Aldermans are engaged in trade or commerce. Thus, the focus is on establishing an unfair act or practice.

According to AS 45.50.471(a)(3), it is an unfair act or practice to "caus[e] a likelihood of confusion or misunderstanding as to the source, sponsorship, or approval, or another person's affiliation, connection, or association with or certification of goods or services"—in other words, trademark or trade name infringement. In general, to establish an unfair act or practice like trade name infringement, "the law has traditionally required proof of two basic elements: (1) Validity-that the public recognizes plaintiff's symbol as identifying his [business] and distinguishing [it] from those of others, and (2) Infringement—that defendant's actions cause a likelihood of confusion among the relevant buyer class." Validity could be shown in either of two ways: (a) that the symbol was inherently distinctive, or (b) that even if not inherently distinctive, the symbol has become distinctive through the acquisition of "secondary meaning," the mental association in buyers' minds between the trade name and a single business. Infringement is shown by analysis under a multi-factor likelihood-of-confusion test.

B. "Fourth Avenue Theatre" Is a Valid Trade Name.

1. General types of trade names

There are four types of trade names: (1) arbitrary or fanciful, (2) suggestive, (3) descriptive (including geographic or personal name), and (4) generic. They differ in level of distinctiveness. Arbitrary, fanciful, and suggestive trade names are the most distinctive and qualify for protection under the Lanham Act or common law. Generic names are entirely non-distinctive and cannot receive such protection. In the middle are descriptive trade names, which may or may not receive protection depending on whether they have achieved a secondary meaning.

Arbitrary, fanciful, and suggestive trade names are inherently distinctive. An arbitrary trade name is a common word or symbol that is applied in a manner not suggestive or descriptive of the business. Examples of arbitrary trade names and trademarks are Sun Microsystems, Stork Club (as a night club), and Nova (as a television series). A fanciful trade name is a word coined expressly for use as a trade name or an obscure or archaic term not inherently familiar to buyers. Examples of fanciful trade names and trademarks include Exxon, Polaroid, and Clorox. Arbitrary and fanciful trade names are broadly protected as strong trade names because their novelty identifies them uniquely to consumers; the recognition of an arbitrary or fanciful name is almost entirely a reflection of the reputation developed by the single user.

Suggestive terms "connote, rather than describe," some particular product or service; they require "use of the consumer's ingenuity to envisage the nature of the product or service." Some examples of trade names and trademarks held to be suggestive rather than descriptive are Citibank, Orange Crush, and Tie Rak. The concept of suggestive trademarks developed to avoid the draconian result of the 1905 Trademark Act's lack of protection for descriptive marks. Courts could uphold the registration of trademarks that were only subtly "descriptive" by placing them in the inherently distinctive category of suggestive trademarks.

Generic names lie at the other end of the distinctiveness spectrum and are not protected. Generic names are the actual names of the goods or services and, thus, cannot be distinctive of a unique source. Some examples of terms held to be generic are Discount Mufflers, Convenient Store, and Lite Beer. Generic names are not protectable as trade names because doing so would effectively remove words of common usage from the commercial vernacular. To permit exclusive trade name rights in a generic name would grant the owner of the generic name a monopoly because a competitor could not describe his business by its common generic term.

Descriptive terms fall between generic names and suggestive trade names in distinctiveness. A term is descriptive if it describes the intended purpose, function, or use of the goods, the size of the goods, the class of the users of the goods, a desirable characteristic of the goods, the nature of goods, or the end effect upon the user. Some examples of trade names and trademarks found to be descriptive are Beer Nuts, Fashion–knit, and Raisin–Bran.

Descriptive terms are categorized as inherently non-distinctive and, as such, entitled to protection only upon a showing of "secondary meaning" or a mental connection between the trade name and a single business. The United States Supreme Court has stated two reasons for this extra requirement for protection. First, because descriptive terms can be truthfully applied to a whole range of goods and services, a descriptive term cannot, per se, function to identify and distinguish the goods or services of only one seller in the marketplace. A descriptive term merely informs the buyer of an alleged quality of the product but does not help the consumer to distinguish between products of different sellers. Second, descriptive terms are regarded as words in the "public domain" in the sense that all sellers should be free to truthfully use these terms to describe their merchandise. "[O]ne competitor will not be permitted to impoverish the language of commerce by preventing his fellows from fairly describing their own goods."

A subcategory of descriptive terms is the geographically descriptive term. Examples include ALASKA, Bank of America, and Boston. Proof of secondary meaning is required for protection of geographically descriptive names for the same reasons that secondary meaning is required for descriptive names. Personal names are another subcategory of descriptive names. Examples include Gucci and Waterman. They too are considered inherently non-distinctive for reasons similar to those for descriptive terms and gain protection only by secondary meaning.

2. *Composite trade names*

Terms that are a combination of two or more types are called composite names. The proper analysis of a composite is to look at the name as a whole, not to dissect it into its component parts. Thus, a composite generic-descriptive name may result in a protectable trade name. The United States Supreme Court has stated the reason for this anti-dissection rule: "The commercial impression of a trade mark is derived from it as a whole, not from its elements separated and considered in detail. For this reason it should be considered in its entirety...." The anti-dissection rule is not violated, however, by separately analyzing the component parts as a step in making the ultimate determination of probable customer reaction to the composite as a whole * * *.

3. *"Fourth Avenue Theatre" is a composite descriptive name*

The Aldermans argue that "Fourth Avenue Theatre" is not a distinctive name entitled to protection. They suggest that "Fourth Avenue Theatre" is a geographically descriptive name, and, without more, is not distinctive enough to warrant trade name protection. Iditarod does not dispute that "Fourth Avenue Theatre" is a descriptive name, arguing instead that the name has gained secondary meaning and is thus protectable.

"Fourth Avenue Theatre" is a composite name. "Fourth Avenue" is geographically descriptive. "Theater" is generic of a type of business. Looking at the whole, "Fourth Avenue Theatre" is still a descriptive name. As a composite descriptive trade name, "Fourth Avenue Theatre" must have acquired a secondary meaning in the minds of consuming public to be entitled to protection against infringement.

4. Secondary meaning generally

Marks which are merely descriptive of a product are not inherently distinctive. When used to describe a product, they do not inherently identify a particular source, and hence cannot be protected. However, descriptive marks may acquire the distinctiveness which will allow them to be protected under the Act. Section 2 of the Lanham Act provides that a descriptive mark that otherwise could not be registered under the Act may be registered if it "has become distinctive of the applicant's goods in commerce." This acquired distinctiveness is generally called "secondary meaning."

Secondary meaning refers to the meaning developed second in time. The primary or original meaning of a name is the general understanding of the words before the trade name gained distinction. In this case, the original meaning of the words "Fourth Avenue Theatre" is a movie house located on Fourth Avenue in some city. Over time, the name "Fourth Avenue Theatre" may attain secondary meaning when consumers identify the name with the one specific, historic landmark theater on Fourth Avenue in Anchorage.

The more descriptive the term, the closer it is to a generic name, and the greater the evidentiary burden on the party attempting to prove secondary meaning. Like all trade names, descriptive trade names fall on a spectrum of distinctiveness. Some terms are only slightly descriptive and need only a minimum quantum of evidence to prove secondary meaning. Other terms are highly descriptive and may need a substantial quantity of significant secondary-meaning evidence to be protectable as a trade name.

In this case, "Fourth Avenue Theatre" is highly descriptive because the words alone describe a business and its location in common terms. The words could refer to any theater on Fourth Avenue. Accordingly, a substantial amount of evidence would be needed to prove secondary meaning.

Factors that support finding secondary meaning include both direct and circumstantial evidence. Direct evidence factors are consumer testimony and consumer surveys. Circumstantial evidence factors include (1) exclusivity, length, and manner of use; (2) amount and manner of advertising; (3) amount of sales and number of customers; (4) established place in the market; and (5) proof of intentional copying. Some courts add a sixth factor: unsolicited media coverage. "[N]o single factor is determinative, and every element need not be proved." * * *

The party seeking to establish the trade name is not required to prove that the term is recognized as a trade name by all prospective purchasers in the relevant market nor even by a majority of them. Instead, secondary meaning exists if a "significant number of prospective purchasers" connect the term with a particular entity. Many courts require only that a "substantial part" of the buying class makes such an association.

> 5. *The jury finding that "Fourth Avenue Theatre" had acquired a secondary meaning was supported by the evidence.*

The Aldermans contend that the superior court erred as a matter of law in determining that "Fourth Avenue Theatre" was a trade name. Whether or not a symbol has acquired secondary meaning is a question of fact. In this case, Iditarod has provided sufficient evidence-both direct and circumstantial-to support the jury finding of secondary meaning.

Iditarod presented direct evidence of its trade name "Fourth Avenue Theatre" by the letters from its customers using that name. Evidence that buyers sent letters to a company with the trade name, rather than the corporate name, as the addressee tends to prove consumer association between the trade name and the corporate source. In the instant case, Iditarod has presented three letters addressed to the "Fourth Avenue Theatre." This partially supports the jury's determination that "Fourth Avenue Theatre" has secondary meaning.

Three of the circumstantial evidence factors (exclusivity, length, and manner of use; established place in the market; and amount and manner of advertising) also support the finding of secondary meaning. The factor of exclusivity, length, and manner of use strongly favors Iditarod. The Fourth Avenue Theatre first opened around 1947. Even the Aldermans considered it to be a historic landmark in Anchorage. When Iditarod purchased the Fourth Avenue Theatre in 1991, it restored the theater to its original appearance and continued to use its original name.

The Fourth Avenue Theatre's established place in the market is shown by its appearance in newspapers and trade journals. Dictionaries, trade journals, magazines, and newspapers using a trade name to identify a business show that the business is commonly associated with that trade name. If the business is recognized by its trade name in professional circles, the buyer class is also likely to recognize the business by the trade name. Here, Iditarod has presented substantial evidence showing the use of the trade name "Fourth Avenue Theatre" in newspapers and trade journals.

Advertising also helps support a finding of secondary meaning. Iditarod has provided substantial evidence of its advertising for the Fourth Avenue Theatre.

In sum, Iditarod presented ample direct and circumstantial evidence of secondary meaning. We conclude that the jury verdict finding that the name "Fourth Avenue Theatre" had acquired secondary meaning was supported by the evidence.

*6.   Iditarod's trade name gained its secondary
meaning prior to use by the Aldermans.*

The general rule of priority for inherently distinctive trade names is that the first or senior user is entitled to legal protection. Priority for inherently non-distinctive trade names like "Fourth Avenue Theatre" is more complex. Because rights by secondary meanings are gained solely by public recognition and association, the issue of priority and ownership is not which party first used the name, but which party first achieved secondary meaning in the trade name. This would logically require a rule awarding priority to the party who was the first in a race to acquire secondary meaning. Instead, the rule has evolved to "an easier-to-apply, but stricter, surrogate test: the senior user must prove the existence of secondary meaning in its mark at the time and place that the junior user first began use of that mark."

Almost all of Iditarod's evidence of secondary meaning existed prior to the Aldermans' alleged first use. The Aldermans claim that they used the name "Fourth Avenue Theater Trolley Tours" in the fall of 1997. Only Iditarod's marginally relevant supplier invoices post-date the fall of 1997; the remainder of Iditarod's evidence of secondary meaning pre-dates the Aldermans' first use. Thus, the same evidence that strongly supports the finding of secondary meaning also supports a finding that the secondary meaning had developed before the Aldermans' first alleged use. We conclude that the jury verdict finding that the trade name "Fourth Avenue Theatre" belonged to Iditarod was supported by the evidence.

C.   The Aldermans' Use of the Name "Fourth Avenue Theater
Trolley Tours" Infringed Iditarod's Trade Name

1.   Trade name infringement does not require direct competition

The Aldermans argue that there can be no likelihood of confusion unless there is competition. They correctly state that the trade name "Fourth Avenue Theatre" does not automatically protect all conceivable goods or services emanating from that business. The Aldermans then suggest that the scope of protection for the trade name is limited to goods or services already in existence.

This is wrong. Despite the terminology "unfair competition," the vast majority of modern decisions have adopted the rule that competition is not necessary between the parties for there to be a likelihood of confusion. "Confusion, or the likelihood of confusion, not competition, is the real test of trademark infringement."

There are four reasons for this broad protection of a trade name. First, protection from trade name use by non-competing businesses prevents placing the trade name holder's reputation in another's hands. Second, it protects consumers from confusion. Third, it allows a zone of natural expansion. Fourth, it prevents unjust enrichment of the junior user-"reaping where one has not sown" and "riding the coat-tails" of the senior user.

The related goods doctrine is the modern rule. This doctrine extends trade name protection beyond businesses in direct competition to businesses that are related. "The [junior's] use need not be the same as, nor one in competition with, the original use in order to infringe." Instead, the junior's use will infringe if it is likely to cause consumer confusion.

2. Likelihood of confusion generally

"Likelihood of confusion" is the basic test of both common-law trademark infringement and federal statutory trademark infringement. State statutes modeled after the Lanham Act also use the same likelihood-of-confusion test.

The test has been stated in these terms: An appreciable number of reasonable buyers must be likely to be confused by the names for trade name infringement or unfair trade practice liability. "Appreciable number" escapes a numerical value, but most courts find that a majority of confused customers is not needed. Some courts have found survey evidence of even low percentages of actual confusion to be strong evidence of a likelihood of confusion. "Likely" has been interpreted as synonymous with probable, but not merely possible, confusion.

"Confusion" is a broad concept. Many courts have recognized not only point-of-sale confusion, but also post-sale confusion, pre-sale confusion, and even reverse confusion (where the junior user's advertising swamps the market and consumers are likely to think that the senior user's goods or services are those of the junior). Also, "confusion" is not limited to confusion as to the source of goods or services; "confusion" includes confusion as to "affiliation, connection, or association."

The relevant class of people is purchasers and potential customers. Both the senior and junior users' customers should be considered. "Brand indifferent" customers are not relevant to the likelihood-of-confusion determination.

In determining infringement of a trade name, the court must take into account the goods and services of the contesting companies. Goods-related factors are important to consider in determining infringement of a trade name by another's use of a trade name. "The trade name interests that [the senior user] seeks to protect relate to the quality and reputation of the goods it produces [or the services it provides]."

There are at least three ways to prove a likelihood of confusion: (1) survey evidence; (2) evidence of actual confusion; or (3) argument based on a clear inference arising from a comparison of the conflicting marks and the context of their use. While not required, actual confusion is a powerful indicator of a likelihood of confusion. "There can be no more positive or substantial proof of the likelihood of confusion than proof of actual confusion."

The factors used to determine the likelihood of confusion vary from court to court, but most courts appear to have derived their tests from the factors listed in the Restatement of Torts. In the instant case, the trial court used a six-factor test in its instructions to the jury:

Likelihood of confusion is also determined by evaluating the following factors:

(1) the degree of similarity of the names;

(2) the manner and method in which the plaintiff and defendant used the names;

(3) the strength of the name, "4th Avenue Theatre";

(4) the length of time the parties used the names without evidence of actual confusion;

(5) the intent of a party in adopting the name, "Fourth Avenue Theater," that is, whether there was an intent to confuse;

(6) other factors about the name, "Fourth Avenue Theater" that would tend to reduce any tendency to confuse the purchaser about the source or origin of the trolley service

This formulation is not erroneous.

3. The jury finding of a likelihood of confusion was supported by the evidence

"The jury's finding on the likelihood of confusion issue is factual and must be affirmed if it was based on substantial evidence. . . ." The jury found that "Fourth Avenue Theatre" would likely be confused with "Fourth Avenue Theater Trolley Tours." Substantial evidence supports this finding.

Regarding the strength of the trade name, Iditarod presented substantial evidence of secondary meaning. The stronger the evidence of secondary meaning, the stronger the mark, and the greater the scope of protection because confusion is more likely. This evidence of secondary meaning supports the jury's finding.

Other evidence shows that both Iditarod and the Aldermans provided tourist attractions that operated side-by-side. The similarities between their businesses indicate the danger that consumers will mistakenly assume an association between related businesses.

The evidence also shows that the disputed trade names are similar in sight, sound, and meaning. Here, "Fourth Avenue Theatre" is exactly the same as the first part of the name "Fourth Avenue Theater Trolley Tours." The addition of the descriptive "Trolley Tours" does not avoid a likelihood of confusion.

Evidence of actual confusion also strongly supports a finding of likely confusion. Both sides acknowledge that once Iditarod started its trolley service, there was actual consumer confusion.

Iditarod also presented evidence that the Aldermans intentionally infringed the trade name. The evidence shows that the Aldermans registered the name "Fourth Avenue Theater Trolley Tours" soon after the falling out with Iditarod and selected a trolley parking spot partially in front of the theater. Because this evidence raises the inference that the Aldermans intentionally infringed Iditarod's trade name, it also supports the jury finding.

Finally, Iditarod proved a likelihood of expansion when it presented evidence that it launched its own trolley tour business in the spring of 1998. We conclude that the jury's finding of likely confusion was amply supported by the evidence. * * *

[The Supreme Court of Alaska affirmed the jury's finding that the Aldermans infringed Iditarod's trade name.]

NOTES

1. Business attorneys, whether they work in intellectual property or not, should know something about trade names and business names. The *Alderman* case provides an excellent overview of the issues and gives some insight into state practice. Many general lessons can be learned. First, note the court's discussion of trade names and trademarks. The court concludes that there is little difference between the two. That conclusion is generally correct for the purposes of unfair competition, the issue in this case. Remember however that trade names and trademarks are two different things, the first referring to the name of a business and the second to the brand on a product or service that allows consumers to distinguish the source of the product or service. The Overview section gave an example of how the same word might function as either a trade name or a trademark depending upon the context (the example was "Hilton"). Can you think of other examples? How about the names of musicians, such as Bruce Springsteen, often referred to as The Boss, or Cher or Madonna? How about law firm names? Are they trade names or trademarks, or either depending on the context? What is the relevant context for each? For a theoretical discussion of the role of trademarks as language, see Barton Beebe, *The Semiotic Analysis of Trademark Law*, 51 UCLA L. REV. 621 (2004); Mark A. Lemley, *The Modern Lanham Act and the Death of Common Sense*, 108 YALE L. J. 1687 (1999); Graeme B. Dinwoodie, *The Death of Ontology: A Teleological Approach to Trademark Law*, 84 IOWA L. REV. 611 (1999).

2. The Alderman case also provides some useful discussion about the registration process at the state level. Review the discussion which occurs towards the end of the case. Keep it in mind and compare it with the discussion of federal registration that follows.

3. The case also discusses the standard for likelihood of confusion. Review it. We will encounter this standard again in the materials on trademark infringement.

4. In order to start organizing these various concepts, think of the relationship between federal and state law as follows. Trademarks are protected under both federal and state law. State law protection for trademarks occurs through state unfair competition law. Most states also have a state

registration system for trademarks. Federal protection occurs through the Lanham Act, which creates a system of federal registration for trademarks. The Lanham Act also provides protection for trademarks against infringement for both federally registered and unregistered trademarks. Trade names are protected only under state law which creates a system for registration for trade names and provides protection against infringement through state unfair competition law.

5.   A trade name is protected by federal trademark law only to the extent that the trade name is used as a trademark, i.e. to distinguish a business' goods and services from that of its competitors. Federal law, however, does not create a registration scheme for trade names. Do you think it should? Or is there some compelling reason to make trade name registration wholly a matter of state law? Is it potentially confusing that the same word can be used either as a trade name, protected under state law, or a trademark, protected under both federal and state law? Do cases like Alderman reduce any potential confusion by simplifying the differences?

2.   Trademarks, Copyrights, and Patents

DASTAR CORPORATION v. TWENTIETH CENTURY FOX FILM CORPORATION

Supreme Court of the United States, 2003.
539 U.S. 23, 123 S.Ct. 2041, 156 L.Ed.2d 18.

JUSTICE SCALIA delivered the opinion of the Court.

In this case, we are asked to decide whether § 43(a) of the Lanham Act, 15 U.S.C. § 1125(a), prevents the unaccredited copying of a work, and if so, whether a court may double a profit award under § 1117(a), in order to deter future infringing conduct.

I

In 1948, three and a half years after the German surrender at Reims, General Dwight D. Eisenhower completed Crusade in Europe, his written account of the allied campaign in Europe during World War II. Doubleday published the book, registered it with the Copyright Office in 1948, and granted exclusive television rights to an affiliate of respondent Twentieth Century Fox Film Corporation (Fox). Fox, in turn, arranged for Time, Inc., to produce a television series, also called Crusade in Europe, based on the book, and Time assigned its copyright in the series to Fox. The television series, consisting of 26 episodes, was first broadcast in 1949. It combined a soundtrack based on a narration of the book with film footage from the United States Army, Navy, and Coast Guard, the British Ministry of Information and War Office, the National Film Board of Canada, and unidentified "Newsreel Pool Cameramen." In 1975, Doubleday renewed the copyright on the book as the " 'proprietor of copyright in a work made for hire.' " * * * Fox, however, did not renew the copyright on the Crusade television series, which expired in 1977, leaving the television series in the public domain.

In 1988, Fox reacquired the television rights in General Eisenhower's book, including the exclusive right to distribute the Crusade television series on video and to sublicense others to do so. Respondents SFM Entertainment and New Line Home Video, Inc., in turn, acquired from Fox the exclusive rights to distribute Crusade on video. SFM obtained the negatives of the original television series, restored them, and repackaged the series on videotape; New Line distributed the videotapes.

Enter petitioner Dastar. In 1995, Dastar decided to expand its product line from music compact discs to videos. Anticipating renewed interest in World War II on the 50th anniversary of the war's end, Dastar released a video set entitled World War II Campaigns in Europe. To make Campaigns, Dastar purchased eight beta cam tapes of the *original* version of the Crusade television series, which is in the public domain, copied them, and then edited the series. Dastar's Campaigns series is slightly more than half as long as the original Crusade television series. Dastar substituted a new opening sequence, credit page, and final closing for those of the Crusade television series; inserted new chapter-title sequences and narrated chapter introductions; moved the "recap" in the Crusade television series to the beginning and retitled it as a "preview"; and removed references to and images of the book. Dastar created new packaging for its Campaigns series and (as already noted) a new title.

Dastar manufactured and sold the Campaigns video set as its own product. The advertising states: "Produced and Distributed by: *Entertainment Distributing*" (which is owned by Dastar), and makes no reference to the Crusade television series. Similarly, the screen credits state "DASTAR CORP presents" and "an ENTERTAINMENT DISTRIBUTING Production," and list as executive producer, producer, and associate producer employees of Dastar. * * * The Campaigns videos themselves also make no reference to the Crusade television series, New Line's Crusade videotapes, or the book. Dastar sells its Campaigns videos to Sam's Club, Costco, Best Buy, and other retailers and mail-order companies for $25 per set, substantially less than New Line's video set.

In 1998, respondents Fox, SFM, and New Line brought this action alleging that Dastar's sale of its Campaigns video set infringes Doubleday's copyright in General Eisenhower's book and, thus, their exclusive television rights in the book. Respondents later amended their complaint to add claims that Dastar's sale of Campaigns "without proper credit" to the Crusade television series constitutes "reverse passing off" in violation of § 43(a) of the Lanham Act, 60 Stat. 441, 15 U.S.C. § 1125(a), and in violation of state unfair-competition law. * * * On cross-motions for summary judgment, the District Court found for respondents on all three counts, *id.,* at 54a–55a, treating its resolution of the Lanham Act claim as controlling on the state-law unfair-competition claim because "the ultimate test under both is whether the public is likely to be deceived or confused," *id.,* at 54a. The court awarded Dastar's profits to respondents and doubled them pursuant to § 35 of the Lanham Act, 15 U.S.C. § 1117(a), to deter future infringing conduct by petitioner.

The Court of Appeals for the Ninth Circuit affirmed the judgment for respondents on the Lanham Act claim, but reversed as to the copyright claim and remanded. 34 Fed.Appx. 312, 316 (2002). (It said nothing with regard to the state-law claim.) With respect to the Lanham Act claim, the Court of Appeals reasoned that "Dastar copied substantially the entire *Crusade in Europe* series created by Twentieth Century Fox, labeled the resulting product with a different name and marketed it without attribution to Fox[, and] therefore committed a 'bodily appropriation' of Fox's series." *Id.,* at 314. It concluded that "Dastar's 'bodily appropriation' of Fox's original [television] series is sufficient to establish the reverse passing off." *Ibid.* The court also affirmed the District Court's award under the Lanham Act of twice Dastar's profits. We granted certiorari. 537 U.S. 1099, 123 S.Ct. 816, 154 L.Ed.2d 767 (2003).

II

The Lanham Act was intended to make "actionable the deceptive and misleading use of marks," and "to protect persons engaged in ... commerce against unfair competition." 15 U.S.C. § 1127. While much of the Lanham Act addresses the registration, use, and infringement of trademarks and related marks, § 43(a), 15 U.S.C. § 1125(a) is one of the few provisions that goes beyond trademark protection. As originally enacted, § 43(a) created a federal remedy against a person who used in commerce either "a false designation of origin, or any false description or representation" in connection with "any goods or services." 60 Stat. 441. As the Second Circuit accurately observed with regard to the original enactment, however—and as remains true after the 1988 revision—§ 43(a) "does not have boundless application as a remedy for unfair trade practices," *Alfred Dunhill, Ltd. v. Interstate Cigar Co.,* 499 F.2d 232, 237 (C.A.2 1974). "[B]ecause of its inherently limited wording, § 43(a) can never be a federal 'codification' of the overall law of 'unfair competition,'" 4 J. McCarthy, Trademarks and Unfair Competition § 27:7, p. 27–14 (4th ed. 2002) (McCarthy), but can apply only to certain unfair trade practices prohibited by its text.

Although a case can be made that a proper reading of § 43(a), as originally enacted, would treat the word "origin" as referring only "to the geographic location in which the goods originated," *Two Pesos, Inc. v. Taco Cabana, Inc.,* 505 U.S. 763, 777, 112 S.Ct. 2753, 120 L.Ed.2d 615 (1992) (STEVENS, J., concurring in judgment), the Courts of Appeals considering the issue, beginning with the Sixth Circuit, unanimously concluded that it "does not merely refer to geographical origin, but also to origin of source or manufacture," *Federal–Mogul–Bower Bearings, Inc. v. Azoff,* 313 F.2d 405, 408 (C.A.6 1963), thereby creating a federal cause of action for traditional trademark infringement of unregistered marks. See 4 McCarthy § 27:14; *Two Pesos, supra,* at 768, 112 S.Ct. 2753. Moreover, every Circuit to consider the issue found § 43(a) broad enough to encompass reverse passing off. See, *e.g., Williams v. Curtiss–Wright Corp.,* 691 F.2d 168, 172 (C.A.3 1982); *Arrow United Indus., Inc. v. Hugh Richards,*

Inc., 678 F.2d 410, 415 (C.A.2 1982); *F.E.L. Publications, Ltd. v. Catholic Bishop of Chicago,* 214 USPQ 409, 416, 1982 WL 19198 (C.A.7 1982); *Smith v. Montoro,* 648 F.2d 602, 603 (C.A.9 1981); *Bangor Punta Operations, Inc. v. Universal Marine Co.,* 543 F.2d 1107, 1109 (C.A.5 1976). The Trademark Law Revision Act of 1988 made clear that § 43(a) covers origin of production as well as geographic origin. Its language is amply inclusive, moreover, of reverse passing off—if indeed it does not implicitly adopt the unanimous court-of-appeals jurisprudence on that subject. See, *e.g., ALPO Petfoods, Inc. v. Ralston Purina Co.,* 913 F.2d 958, 963–964, n. 6 (C.A.D.C.1990) (Thomas, J.).

Thus, as it comes to us, the gravamen of respondents' claim is that, in marketing and selling Campaigns as its own product without acknowledging its nearly wholesale reliance on the Crusade television series, Dastar has made a "false designation of origin, false or misleading description of fact, or false or misleading representation of fact, which . . . is likely to cause confusion . . . as to the origin . . . of his or her goods." § 43(a). See, *e.g.,* Brief for Respondents 8, 11. That claim would undoubtedly be sustained if Dastar had bought some of New Line's Crusade videotapes and merely repackaged them as its own. Dastar's alleged wrongdoing, however, is vastly different: It took a creative work in the public domain—the Crusade television series—copied it, made modifications (arguably minor), and produced its very own series of videotapes. If "origin" refers only to the manufacturer or producer of the physical "goods" that are made available to the public (in this case the videotapes), Dastar was the origin. If, however, "origin" includes the creator of the underlying work that Dastar copied, then someone else (perhaps Fox) was the origin of Dastar's product. At bottom, we must decide what § 43(a)(1)(A) of the Lanham Act means by the "origin" of "goods."

III

The dictionary definition of "origin" is "[t]he fact or process of coming into being from a source," and "[t]hat from which anything primarily proceeds; source." Webster's New International Dictionary 1720–1721 (2d ed.1949). And the dictionary definition of "goods" (as relevant here) is "[w]ares; merchandise." *Id.,* at 1079. We think the most natural understanding of the "origin" of "goods"—the source of wares—is the producer of the tangible product sold in the marketplace, in this case the physical Campaigns videotape sold by Dastar. The concept might be stretched (as it was under the original version of § 43(a)) to include not only the actual producer, but also the trademark owner who commissioned or assumed responsibility for ("stood behind") production of the physical product. But as used in the Lanham Act, the phrase "origin of goods" is in our view incapable of connoting the person or entity that originated the ideas or communications that "goods" embody or contain. Such an extension would not only stretch the text, but it would be out of accord with the history and purpose of the Lanham Act and inconsistent with precedent.

Section 43(a) of the Lanham Act prohibits actions like trademark infringement that deceive consumers and impair a producer's goodwill. It forbids, for example, the Coca–Cola Company's passing off its product as Pepsi–Cola or reverse passing off Pepsi–Cola as its product. But the brand-loyal consumer who prefers the drink that the Coca–Cola Company or PepsiCo sells, while he believes that that company produced (or at least stands behind the production of) that product, surely does not necessarily believe that that company was the "origin" of the drink in the sense that it was the very first to devise the formula. The consumer who buys a branded product does not automatically assume that the brand-name company is the same entity that came up with the idea for the product, or designed the product—and typically does not care whether it is. The words of the Lanham Act should not be stretched to cover matters that are typically of no consequence to purchasers.

It could be argued, perhaps, that the reality of purchaser concern is different for what might be called a communicative product—one that is valued not primarily for its physical qualities, such as a hammer, but for the intellectual content that it conveys, such as a book or, as here, a video. The purchaser of a novel is interested not merely, if at all, in the identity of the producer of the physical tome (the publisher), but also, and indeed primarily, in the identity of the creator of the story it conveys (the author). And the author, of course, has at least as much interest in avoiding passing off (or reverse passing off) of his creation as does the publisher. For such a communicative product (the argument goes) "origin of goods" in § 43(a) must be deemed to include not merely the producer of the physical item (the publishing house Farrar, Straus and Giroux, or the video producer Dastar) but also the creator of the content that the physical item conveys (the author Tom Wolfe, or—assertedly—respondents).

The problem with this argument according special treatment to communicative products is that it causes the Lanham Act to conflict with the law of copyright, which addresses that subject specifically. The right to copy, and to copy without attribution, once a copyright has expired, like "the right to make [an article whose patent has expired]—including the right to make it in precisely the shape it carried when patented—passes to the public." *Sears, Roebuck & Co. v. Stiffel Co.,* 376 U.S. 225, 230, 84 S.Ct. 784, 11 L.Ed.2d 661 (1964); see also *Kellogg Co. v. National Biscuit Co.,* 305 U.S. 111, 121–122, 59 S.Ct. 109, 83 L.Ed. 73 (1938). "In general, unless an intellectual property right such as a patent or copyright protects an item, it will be subject to copying." *TrafFix Devices, Inc. v. Marketing Displays, Inc.,* 532 U.S. 23, 29, 121 S.Ct. 1255, 149 L.Ed.2d 164 (2001). The rights of a patentee or copyright holder are part of a "carefully crafted bargain," *Bonito Boats, Inc. v. Thunder Craft Boats, Inc.,* 489 U.S. 141, 150–151, 109 S.Ct. 971, 103 L.Ed.2d 118 (1989), under which, once the patent or copyright monopoly has expired, the public may use the invention or work at will and without attribution. Thus, in construing the Lanham Act, we have been "careful to caution against misuse or overextension" of trademark and related protections into areas traditionally occupied by patent or copyright. *TrafFix*, 532 U.S., at 29, 121 S.Ct. 1255. "The Lanham Act," we have said, "does not exist to reward manufacturers for their innovation in creating a particular device; that is the purpose of the patent law and its period of exclusivity." *Id.*, at 34, 121 S.Ct. 1255. Federal trademark law "has no necessary relation to invention or discovery," *In re Trade–Mark Cases*, 100 U.S. 82, 94, 25 L.Ed. 550 (1879), but rather, by preventing competitors from copying "a source-identifying mark," "reduce[s] the customer's costs of shopping and making purchasing decisions," and "helps assure a producer that it (and not an imitating competitor) will reap the financial, reputation-related rewards associated with a desirable product," *Qualitex Co. v. Jacobson Products Co.*, 514 U.S. 159, 163–164, 115 S.Ct. 1300, 131 L.Ed.2d 248 (1995) (internal quotation marks and citation omitted). Assuming for the sake of argument that Dastar's representation of itself as the "Producer" of its videos amounted to a representation that it originated the creative work conveyed by the videos, allowing a cause of action under § 43(a) for that representation would create a species of mutant copyright law that limits the public's "federal right to 'copy and to use'" expired copyrights, *Bonito Boats, supra*, at 165, 109 S.Ct. 971.

When Congress has wished to create such an addition to the law of copyright, it has done so with much more specificity than the Lanham Act's ambiguous use of "origin." The Visual Artists Rights Act of 1990, § 603(a), 104 Stat. 5128, provides that the author of an artistic work "shall have the right ... to claim authorship of that work." 17 U.S.C. § 106A(a)(1)(A). That express right of attribution is carefully limited and focused: It attaches only to specified "work[s] of visual art," § 101, is personal to the artist, §§ 106A(b) and (e), and endures only for "the life of the author," § 106A(d)(1). Recognizing in § 43(a) a cause of action for misrepresentation of authorship of noncopyrighted works (visual or otherwise) would render these limitations superfluous. A statutory interpretation that renders another statute superfluous is of course to be avoided. *E.g., Mackey v. Lanier Collection Agency & Service, Inc.*, 486 U.S. 825, 837, and n. 11, 108 S.Ct. 2182, 100 L.Ed.2d 836 (1988).

Reading "origin" in § 43(a) to require attribution of uncopyrighted materials would pose serious practical problems. Without a copyrighted work as the basepoint, the word "origin" has no discernable limits. A video of the MGM film Carmen Jones, after its copyright has expired, would presumably require attribution not just to MGM, but to Oscar Hammerstein II (who wrote the musical on which the film was based), to Georges Bizet (who wrote the opera on which the musical was based), and to Prosper Merimee (who wrote the novel on which the opera was based). In many cases, figuring out who is in the line of "origin" would be no simple task. Indeed, in the present case it is far from clear that respondents have that status. Neither SFM nor New Line had anything to do with the production of the Crusade television series—they merely were licensed to distribute the video version. While Fox might have a claim to being in the line of origin, its involvement with the creation of the television series was limited at best. Time, Inc., was the principal, if not the exclusive, creator, albeit under arrangement with Fox. And of course it was neither Fox nor Time, Inc., that shot the film used in the Crusade television series. Rather, that footage came from the United States Army, Navy, and Coast Guard, the British Ministry of Information and War Office, the National Film Board of Canada, and unidentified "Newsreel Pool Cameramen." If anyone has a claim to being the *original* creator of the material used in both the Crusade television series and the Campaigns videotapes, it would be those groups, rather than Fox. We do not think the Lanham Act requires this search for the source of the Nile and all its tributaries.

Another practical difficulty of adopting a special definition of "origin" for communicative products is that it places the manufacturers of those products in a difficult position. On the one hand, they would face Lanham Act liability for *failing* to credit the creator of a work on which their lawful copies are based; and on the other hand they could face Lanham Act liability for *crediting* the creator if that should be regarded as implying the creator's "sponsorship or approval" of the copy, 15 U.S.C. § 1125(a)(1)(A). In this case, for example, if Dastar had simply "copied [the television series] as Crusade in Europe and sold it as Crusade in Europe," without changing the title or packaging (including the original credits to Fox), it is hard to have confidence in respondents' assurance that they "would not be here on a Lanham Act cause of action," Tr. of Oral Arg. 35.

Finally, reading § 43(a) of the Lanham Act as creating a cause of action for, in effect, plagiarism—the use of otherwise unprotected works and inventions without attribution—would be hard to reconcile with our previous decisions. For example, in *Wal–Mart Stores, Inc. v. Samara Brothers, Inc.*, 529 U.S. 205, 120 S.Ct. 1339, 146 L.Ed.2d 182 (2000), we considered whether product-design trade dress can ever be inherently distinctive. Wal–Mart produced "knockoffs" of children's clothes designed and manufactured by Samara Brothers, containing only "minor modifications" of the original designs. *Id.,* at 208, 120 S.Ct. 1339. We concluded that the designs could not be protected under § 43(a) without a showing that they had acquired "secondary meaning," *id.,* at 214, 120 S.Ct. 1339, so that they " 'identify the source of the product rather than the product itself,' " *id.,* at 211, 120 S.Ct. 1339 (quoting *Inwood Laboratories, Inc. v. Ives Laboratories, Inc.,* 456 U.S. 844, 851, n. 11, 102 S.Ct. 2182, 72 L.Ed.2d 606 (1982)). This carefully considered limitation would be entirely pointless if the "original" producer could turn around and pursue a reverse-passing-off claim under exactly the same provision of the Lanham Act. Samara would merely have had to argue that it was the "origin" of the designs that Wal–Mart was selling as its own line. It was not, because "origin of goods" in the Lanham Act referred to the producer of the clothes, and not the producer of the (potentially) copyrightable or patentable designs that the clothes embodied.

Similarly under respondents' theory, the "origin of goods" provision of § 43(a) would have supported the suit that we rejected in *Bonito Boats,* 489 U.S. 141, 109 S.Ct. 971, where the defendants had used molds to duplicate the plaintiff's unpatented boat hulls (apparently without crediting the plaintiff). And it would have supported the suit we rejected in *TrafFix,* 532 U.S. 23, 121 S.Ct. 1255: The plaintiff, whose patents on flexible road signs had expired, and who could not prevail on a trade-dress claim under § 43(a) because the features of the signs were functional, would have had a reverse-passing-off claim for unattributed copying of his design.

In sum, reading the phrase "origin of goods" in the Lanham Act in accordance with the Act's common-law foundations (which were *not* designed to protect originality or creativity), and in light of the copyright and patent laws (which *were*), we conclude that the phrase refers to the producer of the tangible goods that are offered for sale, and not to the author of any idea, concept, or communication embodied in those goods. Cf. 17 U.S.C. § 202 (distinguishing between a copyrighted work and "any material object in which the work is embodied"). To hold otherwise would be akin to finding that § 43(a) created a species of perpetual patent and copyright, which Congress may not do. See *Eldred v. Ashcroft,* 537 U.S. 186, 208, 123 S.Ct. 769, 154 L.Ed.2d 683 (2003).

The creative talent of the sort that lay behind the Campaigns videos is not left without protection. The original film footage used in the Crusade television series could have been copyrighted, see 17 U.S.C. § 102(a)(6), as was copyrighted (as a compilation) the Crusade television series, even though it included material from the public domain, see § 103(a). Had Fox renewed the copyright in the Crusade television series, it would have had an easy claim of copyright infringement. And respondents' contention that Campaigns infringes Doubleday's copyright in General Eisenhower's book is still a live question on remand. If, moreover, the producer of a video that substantially copied the Crusade series were, in advertising or promotion, to give purchasers the impression that the video was quite different from that series, then one or more of the respondents might have a cause of action—not for reverse passing off under the "confusion . . . as to the origin" provision of § 43(a)(1)(A), but for misrepresentation under the "misrepresents the nature, characteristics [or] qualities" provision of § 43(a)(1)(B). For merely saying it is the producer of the video, however, no Lanham Act liability attaches to Dastar.

* * * Because we conclude that Dastar was the "origin" of the products it sold as its own, respondents cannot prevail on their Lanham Act claim. We thus have no occasion to consider whether the Lanham Act permitted an award of double petitioner's profits. The judgment of the Court of Appeals for the Ninth Circuit is reversed, and the case is remanded for further proceedings consistent with this opinion.

It is so ordered.

TRAFFIX DEVICES, INC. v. MARKETING DISPLAYS, INC.

Supreme Court of the United States, 2001.
532 U.S. 23, 121 S.Ct. 1255, 149 L.Ed.2d 164.

JUSTICE KENNEDY delivered the opinion of the Court.

Temporary road signs with warnings like "Road Work Ahead" or "Left Shoulder Closed" must withstand strong gusts of wind. An inventor named Robert Sarkisian obtained two utility patents for a mechanism built upon two springs (the dual-spring design) to keep these and other outdoor signs upright despite adverse wind conditions. The holder of the now-expired Sarkisian patents, respondent Marketing Displays, Inc. (MDI), established a successful business in the manufacture and sale of sign stands incorporating the patented feature. MDI's stands for road signs were recognizable to buyers and users (it says) because the dual-spring design was visible near the base of the sign.

This litigation followed after the patents expired and a competitor, TrafFix Devices, Inc., sold sign stands with a visible spring mechanism that looked like MDI's. MDI and TrafFix products looked alike because they were. When TrafFix started in business, it sent an MDI product abroad to have it reverse engineered, that is to say copied. Complicating matters, TrafFix marketed its sign stands under a name similar to MDI's. MDI used the name "WindMaster," while TrafFix, its new competitor, used "WindBuster."

MDI brought suit under the Trademark Act of 1946 (Lanham Act), 60 Stat. 427, as amended, 15 U.S.C. § 1051 et seq., against TrafFix for trademark infringement (based on the similar names), trade dress infringement (based on the copied dual-spring design), and unfair competition. TrafFix counterclaimed on antitrust theories. After the United States District Court for the Eastern District of Michigan considered cross-motions for summary judgment, MDI prevailed on its trademark claim for the confusing similarity of names and was held not liable on the antitrust counterclaim; and those two rulings, affirmed by the Court of Appeals, are not before us.

I

We are concerned with the trade dress question. The District Court ruled against MDI on its trade dress claim. * * * After determining that the one element of MDI's trade dress at issue was the dual-spring design, * * * it held that "no reasonable trier of fact could determine that MDI has established secondary meaning" in its alleged trade dress * * *. In other words, consumers did not associate the look of the dual-spring design with MDI. As a second, independent reason to grant summary judgment in favor of TrafFix, the District Court determined the dual-spring design was functional. On this rationale secondary meaning is irrelevant because there can be no trade dress protection in any event. In ruling on the functional aspect of the design, the District Court noted that Sixth Circuit precedent indicated that the burden was on MDI to prove that its trade dress was nonfunctional, and not on TrafFix to show that it was functional (a rule since adopted by Congress, see 15 U.S.C. § 1125(a)(3) (1994 ed., Supp. V)), and then went on to consider MDI's arguments that the dual-spring design was subject to trade dress protection. Finding none of MDI's contentions persuasive, the District Court concluded MDI had not "proffered sufficient evidence which would enable a reasonable trier of fact to find that MDI's vertical dual-spring design is non-functional." * * * Summary judgment was entered against MDI on its trade dress claims.

The Court of Appeals for the Sixth Circuit reversed the trade dress ruling. * * * The Court of Appeals held the District Court had erred in ruling MDI failed to show a genuine issue of material fact regarding whether it had secondary meaning in its alleged trade dress * * * and had erred further in determining that MDI could not prevail in any event because the alleged trade dress was in fact a functional product configuration. * * * The Court of Appeals suggested the District Court committed legal error by looking only to the dual-spring design when evaluating MDI's trade dress. Basic to its reasoning was the Court of Appeals' observation that it took "little imagination to conceive of a hidden dual-spring mechanism or a tri or quad-spring mechanism that might avoid infringing [MDI's] trade dress." * * * The Court of Appeals explained that "[i]f TrafFix or another competitor chooses to use [MDI's] dual-spring design, then it will have to find some other way to set its sign apart to avoid infringing [MDI's] trade dress." * * * It was not sufficient, according to the Court of Appeals, that allowing exclusive use of a particular feature such as the dual-spring design in the guise of trade dress would "hinde[r] competition somewhat." Rather, "[e]xclusive use of a feature must 'put competitors at a significant non-reputation-related disadvantage' before trade dress protection is denied on functionality grounds." * * * (quoting *Qualitex Co. v. Jacobson Products Co.*, 514 U.S. 159, 165, 115 S.Ct. 1300, 131 L.Ed.2d 248 (1995)). In its criticism of the District Court's ruling on the trade dress question, the Court of Appeals took note of a split among Courts of Appeals in various other Circuits on the issue whether the existence of an expired utility patent forecloses the possibility of the patentee's claiming trade dress protection in the product's design. * * * Compare *Sunbeam Products, Inc. v. West Bend Co.*, 123 F.3d 246 (C.A.5 1997) (holding that trade dress protection is not foreclosed), *Thomas & Betts Corp. v. Panduit Corp.*, 138 F.3d 277 (C.A.7 1998) (same), and *Midwest Industries, Inc. v. Karavan Trailers, Inc.*, 175 F.3d 1356 (C.A.Fed.1999) (same), with *Vornado Air Circulation Systems, Inc. v. Duracraft Corp.*, 58 F.3d 1498, 1500 (C.A.10 1995) ("Where a product configuration is a significant inventive component of an invention covered by a utility patent ... it cannot receive trade dress protection"). To resolve the conflict, we granted certiorari. * * *

II

It is well established that trade dress can be protected under federal law. The design or packaging of a product may acquire a distinctiveness which serves to identify the product with its manufacturer or source; and a design or package which acquires this secondary meaning, assuming other requisites are met, is a trade dress which may not be used in a manner likely to cause confusion as to the origin, sponsorship, or approval of the goods. In these respects protection for trade dress exists to promote competition. As we explained just last Term, see *Wal–Mart Stores, Inc. v. Samara Brothers, Inc.*, 529 U.S. 205, 120 S.Ct. 1339, 146 L.Ed.2d 182 (2000), various Courts of Appeals have allowed claims of trade dress infringement relying on the general provision of the Lanham Act which provides a cause of action to one who is injured when a person uses "any word, term name, symbol, or device, or any combination thereof . . . which is likely to cause confusion . . . as to the origin, sponsorship, or approval of his or her goods." 15 U.S.C. § 1125(a)(1)(A). Congress confirmed this statutory protection for trade dress by amending the Lanham Act to recognize the concept. Title 15 U.S.C. § 1125(a)(3) (1994 ed., Supp. V) provides: "In a civil action for trade dress infringement under this chapter for trade dress not registered on the principal register, the person who asserts trade dress protection has the burden of proving that the matter sought to be protected is not functional." This burden of proof gives force to the well-established rule that trade dress protection may not be claimed for product features that are functional. *Qualitex,* supra, at 164–165, 115 S.Ct. 1300; *Two Pesos, Inc. v. Taco Cabana, Inc.*, 505 U.S. 763, 775, 112 S.Ct. 2753, 120 L.Ed.2d 615 (1992). And in *Wal–Mart*, supra, we were careful to caution against misuse or overextension of trade dress. We noted that "product design almost invariably serves purposes other than source identification." Id., at 213, 120 S.Ct. 1339.

Trade dress protection must subsist with the recognition that in many instances there is no prohibition against copying goods and products. In general, unless an intellectual property right such as a patent or copyright protects an item, it will be subject to copying. As the Court has explained, copying is not always discouraged or disfavored by the laws which preserve our competitive economy. *Bonito Boats, Inc. v. Thunder Craft Boats, Inc.*, 489 U.S. 141, 160, 109 S.Ct. 971, 103 L.Ed.2d 118 (1989). Allowing competitors to copy will have salutary effects in many instances. "Reverse engineering of chemical and mechanical articles in the public domain often leads to significant advances in technology." Ibid.

The principal question in this case is the effect of an expired patent on a claim of trade dress infringement. A prior patent, we conclude, has vital significance in resolving the trade dress claim. A utility patent is strong evidence that the features therein claimed are functional. If trade dress protection is sought for those features the strong evidence of functionality based on the previous patent adds great weight to the statutory presumption that features are deemed functional until proved otherwise by the party seeking trade dress protection. Where the expired patent claimed the features in question, one who seeks to establish trade dress protection must carry the heavy burden of showing that the feature is not functional, for instance by showing that it is merely an ornamental, incidental, or arbitrary aspect of the device.

In the case before us, the central advance claimed in the expired utility patents (the Sarkisian patents) is the dual-spring design; and the dual-spring design is the essential feature of the trade dress MDI now seeks to establish and to protect. The rule we have explained bars the trade dress claim, for MDI did not, and cannot, carry the burden of overcoming the strong evidentiary inference of functionality based on the disclosure of the dual-spring design in the claims of the expired patents.

The dual springs shown in the Sarkisian patents were well apart (at either end of a frame for holding a rectangular sign when one full side is the base) while the dual springs at issue here are close together (in a frame designed to hold a sign by one of its corners). As the District Court recognized, this makes little difference. The point is that the springs are necessary to the operation of the device. The fact that the springs in this very different-looking device fall within the claims of the patents is illustrated by MDI's own position in earlier litigation. In the late 1970's, MDI engaged in a long-running intellectual property battle with a company known as Winn–Proof. Although the precise claims of the Sarkisian patents cover sign stands with springs "spaced apart," U.S. Patent No. 3,646,696, col. 4; U.S. Patent No. 3,662,482, col. 4, the Winn–Proof sign stands (with springs much like the sign stands at issue here) were found to infringe the patents by the United States District Court for the District of Oregon, and the Court of Appeals for the Ninth Circuit affirmed the judgment. *Sarkisian v. Winn–Proof Corp.*, 697 F.2d 1313 (1983). Although the Winn–Proof traffic sign stand (with dual springs close together) did not appear, then, to infringe the literal terms of the patent claims (which called for "spaced apart" springs), the Winn–Proof sign stand was found to infringe the patents under the doctrine of equivalents, which allows a finding of patent infringement even when the accused product does not fall within the literal terms of the claims. Id., at 1321–1322; see generally Warner–Jenkinson Co. v. Hilton Davis Chemical Co., 520 U.S. 17, 117 S.Ct. 1040, 137 L.Ed.2d 146 (1997). In light of this past ruling-a ruling procured at MDI's own insistence-it must be concluded the products here at issue would have been covered by the claims of the expired patents.

The rationale for the rule that the disclosure of a feature in the claims of a utility patent constitutes strong evidence of functionality is well illustrated in this case. The dual-spring design serves the important purpose of keeping the sign upright even in heavy wind conditions; and, as confirmed by the statements in the expired patents, it does so in a unique and useful manner. As the specification of one of the patents recites, prior art "devices, in practice, will topple under the force of a strong wind." U.S. Patent No. 3,662,482, col. 1. The dual-spring design allows sign stands to resist toppling in strong winds. Using a dual-spring design rather than a single spring achieves important operational advantages.

For example, the specifications of the patents note that the "use of a pair of springs . . . as opposed to the use of a single spring to support the frame structure prevents canting or twisting of the sign around a vertical axis," and that, if not prevented, twisting "may cause damage to the spring structure and may result in tipping of the device." U.S. Patent No. 3,646,696, col. 3. In the course of patent prosecution, it was said that "[t]he use of a pair of spring connections as opposed to a single spring connection . . . forms an important part of this combination" because it "forc[es] the sign frame to tip along the longitudinal axis of the elongated ground-engaging members." App. 218. The dual-spring design affects the cost of the device as well; it was acknowledged that the device "could use three springs but this would unnecessarily increase the cost of the device." Id., at 217. These statements made in the patent applications and in the course of procuring the patents demonstrate the functionality of the design. MDI does not assert that any of these representations are mistaken or inaccurate, and this is further strong evidence of the functionality of the dual-spring design.

III

In finding for MDI on the trade dress issue the Court of Appeals gave insufficient recognition to the importance of the expired utility patents, and their evidentiary significance, in establishing the functionality of the device. The error likely was caused by its misinterpretation of trade dress principles in other respects. As we have noted, even if there has been no previous utility patent the party asserting trade dress has the burden to establish the nonfunctionality of alleged trade dress features. MDI could not meet this burden. Discussing trademarks, we have said " '[i]n general terms, a product feature is functional,' and cannot serve as a trademark, 'if it is essential to the use or purpose of the article or if it affects the cost or quality of the article.' " *Qualitex*, 514 U.S., at 165, 115 S.Ct. 1300 (quoting *Inwood Laboratories, Inc. v. Ives Laboratories, Inc.*, 456 U.S. 844, 850, n. 10, 102 S.Ct. 2182, 72 L.Ed.2d 606 (1982)). Expanding upon the meaning of this phrase, we have observed that a functional feature is one the "exclusive use of [which] would put competitors at a significant non-reputation-related disadvantage." 514 U.S., at 165, 115 S.Ct. 1300. The Court of Appeals in the instant case seemed to interpret this language to mean that a necessary test for functionality is "whether the particular product configuration is a competitive necessity." 200 F.3d, at 940. See also *Vornado*, 58 F.3d, at 1507 ("Functionality, by contrast, has been defined both by our circuit, and more recently by the Supreme Court, in terms of competitive need"). This was incorrect as a comprehensive definition. As explained in *Qualitex*, supra, and *Inwood*, supra, a feature is also functional when it is essential to the use or purpose of the device or when it affects the cost or quality of the device. The *Qualitex* decision did not purport to displace this traditional rule. Instead, it quoted the rule as *Inwood* had set it forth. It is proper to inquire into a "significant non-reputation-related disadvantage" in cases of esthetic functionality, the question involved in *Qualitex*. Where the design is functional under the

Inwood formulation there is no need to proceed further to consider if there is a competitive necessity for the feature. In *Qualitex*, by contrast, esthetic functionality was the central question, there having been no indication that the green-gold color of the laundry press pad had any bearing on the use or purpose of the product or its cost or quality.

The Court has allowed trade dress protection to certain product features that are inherently distinctive. *Two Pesos*, 505 U.S., at 774, 112 S.Ct. 2753. In *Two Pesos*, however, the Court at the outset made the explicit analytic assumption that the trade dress features in question (decorations and other features to evoke a Mexican theme in a restaurant) were not functional. Id., at 767, n. 6, 112 S.Ct. 2753. The trade dress in those cases did not bar competitors from copying functional product design features. In the instant case, beyond serving the purpose of informing consumers that the sign stands are made by MDI (assuming it does so), the dual-spring design provides a unique and useful mechanism to resist the force of the wind. Functionality having been established, whether MDI's dual-spring design has acquired secondary meaning need not be considered.

There is no need, furthermore, to engage, as did the Court of Appeals, in speculation about other design possibilities, such as using three or four springs which might serve the same purpose. * * * Here, the functionality of the spring design means that competitors need not explore whether other spring juxtapositions might be used. The dual-spring design is not an arbitrary flourish in the configuration of MDI's product; it is the reason the device works. Other designs need not be attempted.

Because the dual-spring design is functional, it is unnecessary for competitors to explore designs to hide the springs, say, by using a box or framework to cover them, as suggested by the Court of Appeals. Ibid. The dual-spring design assures the user the device will work. If buyers are assured the product serves its purpose by seeing the operative mechanism that in itself serves an important market need. It would be at cross-purposes to those objectives, and something of a paradox, were we to require the manufacturer to conceal the very item the user seeks.

In a case where a manufacturer seeks to protect arbitrary, incidental, or ornamental aspects of features of a product found in the patent claims, such as arbitrary curves in the legs or an ornamental pattern painted on the springs, a different result might obtain. There the manufacturer could perhaps prove that those aspects do not serve a purpose within the terms of the utility patent. The inquiry into whether such features, asserted to be trade dress, are functional by reason of their inclusion in the claims of an expired utility patent could be aided by going beyond the claims and examining the patent and its prosecution history to see if the feature in question is shown as a useful part of the invention. No such claim is made here, however. MDI in essence seeks protection for the dual-spring design alone. The asserted trade dress consists simply of the dual-spring design, four legs, a base, an upright, and a sign. MDI has pointed to nothing arbitrary about the components of its device or the way they are assembled. The Lanham Act does not exist to reward manufacturers for their innovation in creating a particular device; that is the purpose of the patent law and its period of exclusivity. The Lanham Act, furthermore, does not protect trade dress in a functional design simply because an investment has been made to encourage the public to associate a particular functional feature with a single manufacturer or seller. The Court of Appeals erred in viewing MDI as possessing the right to exclude competitors from using a design identical to MDI's and to require those competitors to adopt a different design simply to avoid copying it. MDI cannot gain the exclusive right to produce sign stands using the dual-spring design by asserting that consumers associate it with the look of the invention itself. Whether a utility patent has expired or there has been no utility patent at all, a product design which has a particular appearance may be functional because it is "essential to the use or purpose of the article" or "affects the cost or quality of the article." *Inwood*, 456 U.S., at 850, n. 10, 102 S.Ct. 2182.

TrafFix and some of its amici argue that the Patent Clause of the Constitution, Art. I, § 8, cl. 8, of its own force, prohibits the holder of an expired utility patent from claiming trade dress protection. * * * We need not resolve this question. If, despite the rule that functional features may not be the subject of trade dress protection, a case arises in which trade dress becomes the practical equivalent of an expired utility patent, that will be time enough to consider the matter. The judgment of the Court of Appeals is reversed, and the case is remanded for further proceedings consistent with this opinion.

NOTES

1. The two principal cases are important in identifying the relationship between trademark law and the two other principal areas of federal intellectual property protection, copyright and patent. In *Dastar*, the Court limits the use of trademark law to protect an interest protected by copyright law. Notice that the issue raised by the case may be a limited one because of the unusual facts of the case. If the copyright owner had registered the copyright interest properly, then it may not have needed to rely on trademark law to push its legal claims. On the other hand, if the Court had ruled the other way in the case, a registered copyright owner would have claims under both copyright and trademark law. Is there a problem with multiple intellectual property claims over the same subject matter? Who is hurt if such multiple claims are allowed? Is the Court's reasoning persuasive in limiting trademark claims in cases like *Dastar*? Some argue that the Court does not adequately protect the attribution right of authors. In this regard, recall the discussion of moral rights in Chapter Three. Is trademark law a good way to recognize attribution rights? Does copyright law need to be reformed?

2. The *Traffix Devices* case forced the Court to draw the line between trade dress, a type of trademark for product packaging and design, and patent protection. Think about this decision in greater detail after reading *Wal–Mart*,

below. Does the Court do a good job in distinguishing patent from trademark protection? Does the doctrine of functionality work? How does it compare with the Court's decision in *Baker v Selden*, discussed in Chapter Three?

B. FEDERAL TRADEMARK REGISTRATION

There are three requirements for federal trademark registration on the Principal Register: (1) the mark must be used in interstate commerce; (2) the mark must be distinctive; and (3) the mark must not be barred from registration under 15 USC § 1052, which creates several bases for refusing registration of a mark. Note that these requirements will also apply for protection of a unregistered trademark against infringement under the Lanham Act. To understand this point, note that in a federal action for infringement, the trademark owner must show that the trademark is valid. She can do this by showing either that the mark is registered at the federal level or that the mark has been used in interstate commerce and is distinctive. Federal registration initially provides prima facie evidence of validity. After five years of continuous registration and use, federal registration provides conclusive evidence of validity. See 15 USC § 1115 (a)–(b).

The process of procuring federal trademark registration is called trademark prosecution. Trademark prosecution occurs through the filing of an application with the United States Patent and Trademark Office (USPTO). There are two types of applications: use applications and intent-to-use applications, or ITU's. See 15 USC § 1151 (a)–(b). After the filing of the use application and the submission of the requisite fees and affidavits, the trademark is published in the Official Gazette for opposition purposes. See 15 USC § 1162. Any person who believes that he would be damaged by registration of the mark can file for an opposition within thirty days of the mark's publication in the Gazette, the period can be extended for another thirty days upon written request during the first thirty day period, and further extensions can be obtained for good cause prior to the expiration of the first extension. See 15 USC § 1163. If the mark is not successfully opposed, then the mark is registered on the Principal Register. The procedure for ITU's is a bit more complicated. If the mark is not successfully opposed, then the applicant receives a notice of allowance. Within six months of the notice of allowance, the applicant must establish use of the mark in interstate commerce. Upon written request before the expiration of the first six month period, the time to respond can be extended for another six months. Upon another written request and for cause, the period can then be additionally extended for another 24 months. In effect, the applicant using an ITU has up to 36 months to establish use in interstate commerce after the notice of allowance. See 15 USC § 1151(d).

After registration on the Principal Register, the trademark owner must maintain the mark and continue to use the mark to maintain his rights. Under 15 USC § 1058 (a)–(b), the owner must pay fees and submit affidavits continued use starting at the end of the six years following the date of registration and at the end of each successive ten year period following the date of registration. In addition, anyone who believes that he is or will be damaged by the registration of the mark can bring an administrative action for cancellation under 15 USC § 1064 within five years from the registration of the mark or anytime if the grounds for cancellation is that the mark is generic or the mark is a certification mark that is not being properly used. (The grounds for cancelling certification marks are provided in 15 USC § 1064 (5).) If the mark has been registered and used continuously for five consecutive years, then the mark is incontestable and can be challenged only if the mark is generic or the mark is a collective mark that is not being property used. Incontestability also means that the mark is conclusively valid in an infringement suit.

Trademarks can also be federally registered on the Supplemental Register. The applicant must specifically state in her application that registration is sought on the Supplemental Register. Otherwise, the presumption is that registration is on the Principal Register. See 15 USC §§ 1091–1096. Registration on the Supplemental Register allows the trademark owner to sue in federal court for trademark infringement but provides none of the evidentiary advantages of registration on the Principal Register, such as presumptions of validity or constructive notice, and does not allow the owner to stop unauthorized importation of the mark. Registration on the Supplemental Register is usually sought for descriptive marks or surnames that might not meet the distinctiveness standard required for the Principal Register. As a strategy, a trademark owner may seek registration of the mark on the Supplemental Register to obtain federal rights, develop the required distinctiveness through use of the mark and marketing of the product or service, and then choose to file an application for registration of the Principal Register. Note that five years continuous use of the mark does provide prima facie evidence of distinctiveness. See 15 USC § 1052 (f).

1. Use or Intent to Use in Interstate Commerce

MOUNTAIN TOP BEVERAGE GROUP, INC. v. WILDLIFE BREWING N.B., INC.

United States District Court, S.D. Ohio, 2003.
338 F.Supp. 2d 827.

DLOTT, DISTRICT JUDGE

This case involves the manufacture and sale of competing malt liquor products bearing the name "Wildcat." On July 19, 1993, Third–Party Defendant BLSS filed an Intent to Use trademark application ("ITU application") with the United States Patent and Trademark Office ("USPTO") to register "X 40 Wildcat" as a trademark on the USPTO's Principal Register in connection with beer and malt liquor. An ITU application allows a trademark applicant to begin the federal registration process without actually using the mark at the time of application. The USPTO then issues a Notice of Allowance stating that a mark is in compliance with formalities and is registrable. Within six months an ITU applicant must file a Statement of Use ("SOU") and specimen or facsimile of the mark in order to successfully register its trademark. The applicant may request and receive a number of extensions of time in which to file the SOU, so long as the SOU issues no later than thirty-six months after the Notice of Allowance. The SOU is a verified statement that the mark is in use in commerce, specifying the date on which the mark was used in commerce, the goods in connection with which the mark was used, and the manner in which the mark is used in connection with the goods. Subject to examination of the SOU, the mark is then registered on the Principal Register. On August 28, 2000, the last possible day in which BLSS could file its SOU without abandoning its trademark application, BLSS filed its SOU to register the Wildcat mark, and on November 13, 2001, "40 Wildcat" ("The Wildcat mark") was registered on the Principal Register of the USPTO.

BLSS's SOU consisted of a photograph of a bottle with the mark affixed to it and the signed statement of Brady Skinner, president of BLSS, that "[a]pplicant is using the mark in commerce on or in connection with the following goods: malt liquor in class 32. The mark was first used at least as early as August 22, 2000, and first used in commerce at least as early as August 22, 2000. Applicant is using the mark in interstate commerce. The SOU provides no details as to how the mark was used, no information indicating whether there were any sales or interstate transportation of the goods, no details as to what quantity of the goods was produced, nor what revenue the goods had earned.

Defendants have established through depositions of Mountain Top personnel and through answers to interrogatories that from the 1993 filing date of the ITU application until the commencement of this action, neither Plaintiff nor its predecessor BLSS had made any sales of any products bearing the Wildcat mark, nor conducted any advertising or marketing of any products bearing the Wildcat mark. Defendants have established that there are no items bearing the Wildcat mark being marketed, sold, distributed or otherwise provided by Plaintiff. Although Plaintiff, as required by statute, enclosed an image of a Wildcat product in its SOU, a true sample of packaging that could be used on a product eligible for sale was not available until at least August 30, 2000 because the labels required by ATF were not approved until then. Further, Defendants have shown that Plaintiff had not yet contracted with a brewer to produce a Wildcat product at the time the SOU was filed, and the brewer with whom Skinner companies were in contact ("Frederick Brewing") could not even quote a price until September of 2000, let alone have produced a shipment of the actual brew.

There was no sale of goods bearing the Wildcat mark by any Skinner company until January 10, 2001, when Frederick Brewing Company sold a shipment to KABCo. The shipment was later destroyed by one of the

Skinner companies because Mountain Top did not want to sell its Wildcat product while Wildlife's Wildcat products were sold in the market. The interaction between BLSS, Mountain Top, KABCo and Heartland Distributing company is somewhat complicated, but suffice to say, all are solely owned or majority controlled by Brady L. Skinner.

The evidence shows that the Wildcat product shown in the SOU was a "dummy sample." Bert Smith, an operations employee of KABCo, testified in his deposition that a "dummy sample" of a Wildcat product was created and shown by local salespeople to retailers in the summer of 2000 although he couldn't be sure if the display actually occurred or by whom and to whom the sample might have been shown. Smith clarified that he did not in fact know if a salesperson had ever shown the dummy sample. Smith also testified that there was no chance that the dummy sample contained the actual brew to be sold. He stated that there were no items bearing Wildcat marks marketed, sold, distributed, or otherwise provided by Mountain Top or BLSS. Brady Skinner, president of BLSS and majority shareholder of Mountain Top, testified that he personally never placed an order for any Wildcat product with David Snyder (the head of Frederick Brewing's parent company), and that Bert Smith would be the only other person authorized to do so.

In early 1999, while BLSS' ITU application to register its Wildcat mark was pending, BLSS learned that Defendants Wildlife and Sorenson were using the name "Wildcat" in connection with the manufacture and sale of either beer or malt liquor or both. Shortly thereafter, BLSS notified Defendants Wildlife and Sorenson of BLSS' ITU application and informed Wildlife and Sorenson that their use of the name Wildcat constituted infringement of BLSS' pending Wildcat trademark. After a second letter from BLSS to Wildlife and Sorenson in February of 2001, Wildlife and Sorenson responded in March of 2001 with a letter to BLSS asserting that Sorenson was the owner of the common law trademark "Wildcat" and any use of the mark Wildcat by BLSS would constitute infringement.

On December 3, 2001, BLSS assigned its Wildcat mark to Mountain Top. On December 5, 2001, Mountain Top commenced the instant action against Defendants Wildlife and Sorenson and against Defendant PBC, the company that manufactures Wildlife's Wildcat products, alleging federal claims of trademark infringement and false designation of origin, and related state law claims of deceptive trade practices, tortious interference with economic relations and unfair competition, and asking the Court to cancel Wildlife's Ohio state registration of the marks "Wild Cat Ice" and "Wild Cat Malt Liquor." Defendants Wildlife and Sorenson counterclaimed, alleging a federal claim of false designation of origin and related state and common law claims of trademark infringement, unfair competition, dilution of mark, tarnishment, and injury to business reputation, unfair business practices, deceptive trade practices, and tortious interference with a contract and business relationship. All Defendants seek cancellation of Mountain Top's trademark on the grounds that it was never "used in commerce." * * *

The term "commerce," as used in § 1127 means interstate and foreign commerce. Because the power of Congress to register a mark stems from the Commerce Clause of the Constitution, a trademark must be used in interstate or foreign commerce as that is the commerce Congress may lawfully regulate. Defining "use" is significantly more problematic. After the 1988 Trademark Law Revision Act ("TLRA") the quantum of use necessary to support a registration changed. Prior to the 1989 effective date of the TLRA, an applicant had to be using the mark in commerce before applying for registration. Requiring use as a foundation to registration meant greater economic risk, so under that system, the quantum of use necessary to support a registration was a "token use." A sale or transportation of a mark in commerce made primarily to serve as a foundation for federal registration was a sufficient "use" so long as the transaction was bona fide and the applicant intended to continue using the mark.

However, some uses fell below even the "token use" standard. See, e.g. *La Societe Anonyme des Parfums le Galion v. Jean Patou, Inc.*, 495 F.2d 1265 (2d Cir. 1974) (only eighty-nine bottles of perfume sold over twenty years is a "meager trickle" which cannot create common law trademark rights sufficient to preclude foreign importer waiting to enter U.S. market); *D.M. & Antique Import Corp. v. Royal Saxe Corp.*, 311 F.Supp. 1261 (S.D.N.Y. 1969) (initial sale to personal friend followed six years later by a $400 shipment held insufficient to support registration); *Richardson–Vicks, Inc. v. Franklin Mint Corp.*, 216 U.S.P.Q. 989 (T.T.A.B. 1982) (one sale of $1.27 followed by no sales for four years is an impermissible "attempt to reserve a trademark"); *Clairol, Inc. v. Holland Hall Prods.*, 165 U.S.P.Q. 214 (T.T.A.B. 1970) (initial sale followed by two years of token shipments of less than $1.00 per month to wholesalers, not customers, held insufficient).

Sales presentations, under certain circumstances, could meet the "token use" bar. However, when an applicant relied on a sales presentation to qualify as "transportation" for "use in commerce" purposes, the trademarked product shown had to be "an actual product of the nature for which registration is sought. The shipment of sample packaging alone before the product is in existence is insufficient and was held to not even constitute a token use by shipment of the product."

Even in a sale situation, if goods were contracted for and sold although they did not yet exist, "until they are in actual physical existence the mark has not been 'used.' " Even under the "token use" standard, displaying samples in bottles without the necessary labeling did not qualify as use. In one oft-cited Seventh Circuit case, a company gave out a few samples in bottles that did not have the labeling required for sale to the public. The Court held that "[s]uch transactions are the sort of pre-marketing maneuvers that * * * cases hold insufficient to establish rights in a trademark." *Zazu Designs v. L'Oreal, S.A.*, 979 F.2d 499, 505 (7th Cir. 1992). A bona fide use in trade also requires that the mark "be affixed to the merchandise actually intended to bear the mark in commercial transactions." *Blue Bell, Inc. v. Farah Manufacturing Co., Inc.* 508 F.2d 1260, 1267 (5th Cir. 1975).

The TLRA has eliminated such "token" uses to support trademark registration. The TLRA created ITU applications, which allow an applicant to apply to register a mark without first having used the mark in commerce, thereby eliminating the economic risks associated with pre-TLRA use-based applications. Consequently, in the post-TLRA era, mere "token" use is no longer sufficient to support federal trademark registration. The revised § 45 of the Lanham Act, 15 U.S.C. § 1127 states that "[t]he term 'use in commerce' means the bona fide use of a mark in the ordinary course of trade, and not made merely to reserve a right in a mark." The raised standard of use necessary to support federal registration of a trademark in the post-TLRA era is "entirely consistent with the traditional rules governing common law ownership of trademarks." [As one court] explains, "In the absence of registration, rights to a mark traditionally have depended on the very same elements that are now included in the statutory definition: the bona fide use of a mark in commerce that was not made merely to reserve a mark for later exploitation." * * * "The talismanic test for use in commerce remains whether or not the use was sufficiently public to identify or distinguish the marked goods in an appropriate segment of the public mind as those of the adopter of the mark." * * * The pre-TLRA cases are still instructive, however, because if a use does not meet the "token use" standard, then that use certainly will not rise to the level necessary to support today's federal trademark registration obtained through an ITU application.

Mountain Top argues that Defendants have not met their burden of overcoming the presumption of validity of Mountain Top's mark because they have merely alleged the same set of facts that the USPTO had before it when it deemed the mark registrable. This argument is unpersuasive. The USPTO received a bare allegation of use and a picture of a bottle with the mark affixed to it. Defendants have satisfactorily rebutted the presumption of validity of Mountain Top's mark by bringing forth significant evidence through depositions and interrogatories that establishes that neither Plaintiff nor Third–Party Defendant BLSS has ever sold or marketed any products bearing the Wildcat mark, and, in fact, BLSS had never even contracted with a brewer to produce a Wildcat product at the time the SOU was filed.

Defendants' evidence is unrebutted: the only evidence of the "use in commerce" to which BLSS swore in the 2000 SOU is a dummy sample of a Wildcat bottle containing liquid that was not the actual Wildcat brew. Neither Plaintiff Mountain Top nor Third–Party Defendant BLSS has provided evidence-whether by documents or testimony based on personal knowledge-that the dummy sample was ever shown to retailers. The only two individuals authorized to order production of goods bearing the Wildcat mark (1) had no personal knowledge of the "use" and (2) did not place any orders for goods bearing the Wildcat mark. Further, Bert Smith testified that there was no chance that the dummy sample contained the actual brew to be sold. The evidence Mountain Top has produced that it used the Wildcat mark in commerce therefore consists solely of the affidavit of Brady Skinner, asserting a legal rather than factual conclusion, attached to the SOU.

Moreover, even if the display of the dummy sample actually did occur, showing samples in bottles lacking the necessary labeling where the sample did not contain the merchandise actually intended to bear the mark does not constitute "use" as a matter of law. Both *Zazu* and *Blue Bell* indicate that such a display does not qualify as even "token use." Mountain Top has produced no evidence by which a trier of fact could reasonably find it used the Wildcat mark. This Court finds that Mountain Top does not satisfy the "use in commerce" requirement of federal trademark registration as a matter of law. This Court therefore orders the cancellation of Plaintiff's federally registered Wildcat trademark. Because Plaintiff's federal trademark claims depend on its ownership of a valid trademark, those claims must fail.

Plaintiff also asserts a tortious interference with prospective economic relations claim. "The torts of interference with business relationships and contract rights generally occur when a person, without a privilege to do so, induces or otherwise purposely causes a third person not to enter into or continue a business relation with another, or not to perform a contract with another." Taking the evidence in the light most favorable to Plaintiff, there is no evidence that Defendants purposefully induced a third party not to enter a contract or continue a business relationship with Mountain Top, nor that Mountain Top suffered any harm directly resulting from Defendants' actions. Plaintiff's claims for tortious interference with prospective economic relations must therefore fail. Because the rest of Plaintiff's claims depend on its ownership of a valid trademark, its remaining claims against Defendants Wildlife, Sorenson, and PBC must also fail. Defendant PBC's motion for summary judgment and the portion of Defendants Wildlife and Sorenson's motion for summary judgment on Plaintiff's federal claims of trademark infringement and false designation of origin, and state law claims of deceptive trade practices, tortious interference with economic relations and unfair competition are therefore GRANTED.

2. Distinctive to Consumers

KELLOGG COMPANY v. TOUCAN GOLF, INC.

United States Court of Appeals, Sixth Circuit, 2003.
337 F.3d 616.

SUHRHEINRICH, CIRCUIT JUDGE.

Kellogg, a Delaware corporation based in Battle Creek, Michigan, is the largest producer of breakfast cereal in the world. On July 24, 1963, Kellogg first introduced Toucan Sam on boxes of "Froot Loops" cereal. Kellogg has used Toucan Sam on Froot Loops boxes, and in every print and television advertisement for the cereal, since. Toucan Sam is an anthropomorphic cartoon toucan. He is short and stout and walks upright. He is nearly always smiling with a pleasant and cheery demeanor, but looking nothing similar to a real toucan. He has a royal and powder blue body and an elongated and oversized striped beak, colored shades of orange, red, pink, and black. He has human features, such as fingers and toes, and only exhibits his wings while flying. Moreover, in television advertisements over the past forty years, Toucan Sam has been given a voice. He speaks with a British accent, allowing him to fervently sing the praises of the cereal he represents, and to entice several generations of children to "follow his nose" because "it always knows" where to find the Froot Loops.

Kellogg is the holder of five federally-registered Toucan Sam marks at issue in this case. The first was registered on August 18, 1964, under United States Patent and Trademark Office (USPTO) Reg. No. 775,496, and consists of a simplistic toucan design, drawn with an exaggerated, striped beak, standing in profile with hands on hips and smiling. The second mark was registered March 20, 1984, under USPTO Reg. No. 1,270,940, and consists of an updated version of the same toucan, standing and smiling with his mouth open widely; and pointing his left index finger upward. The third mark is for the word mark, "Toucan Sam." This mark was registered on June 18, 1985, under USPTO Reg. No. 1,343,023. The fourth mark, registered on June 21, 1994, under USPTO Reg. No. 1,840,-746, is a shaded drawing of Toucan Sam flying, with wings spread, and smiling. The fifth mark, registered January 31, 1995, under USPTO Reg. No. 1,876,803, is essentially the same drawing as in the fourth mark, except unshaded. Together the five registrations indicate that Kellogg's marks are for use in the breakfast cereal industry, and on clothing.

Figure 5–1: TGI's Toucan

[Author's Note: Unfortunately, Kellogg did not grant permission for us to reproduce the Toucan Sam logo. However, you can readily find a copy on the Internet by doing a search of "Toucan Sam."]

In 1994, Peter Boyko created TGI, an Ohio corporation with its principal place of business in Mansfield, Ohio, with his wife, Janice Boyko, and daughter. TGI is a manufacturer of golf equipment, mainly putter heads. TGI creates putter heads from polycarbonate plastics, purchases shafts and grips from outside sources, and then assembles and sells the putters. Principally, TGI's clientele consists of companies who use TGI's goods as promotional gifts at charity events. For this purpose, TGI prints the name or logo of its client on the putter head or other piece of equipment being sold. TGI rarely, if ever, sells directly to retailers or the public.

TGI likewise uses a toucan drawing, known as "GolfBird" or "Lady GolfBird," to represent its products. TGI has placed this logo on letterhead, business cards, its web site, and even on the outside of its building in Mansfield. GolfBird has a multi-colored body, and TGI displays GolfBird in a myriad of color schemes for different purposes. Invariably, however, she has a long, narrow, yellow beak with a black tip, not disproportionate to or unlike that of a real toucan. GolfBird is always seen perched upon a golf iron as if it were a tree branch. She has no human features whatsoever, and resembles a real toucan in all aspects except, perhaps, her variable body coloring.

TGI has not registered its GolfBird logo with the USPTO. On December 15, 1994, however, TGI did file an "intent to use" application with the USPTO for the word mark "Toucan Gold." The application, as later amended, sought to use the mark in relation to "golf clubs and golf putters." Specifically, TGI planned to use the mark for its newest line of putters which consist of a putter head on a Boron Graphite shaft. On August 29, 1995, the USPTO published TGI's application for opposition. Kellogg filed an opposition with the TTAB, asserting that TGI's proposed use of the mark "Toucan Gold" for golf-related merchandise infringed upon Kellogg's Toucan Sam marks under the Lanham Act by creating a likelihood of consumer confusion. On May 19, 1999, the TTAB dismissed the opposition without testimony.

On July 16, 1999, Kellogg appealed the TTAB decision to the district court below. In its complaint, Kellogg again claimed that TGI's use of the word mark "Toucan Gold" created a likelihood of confusion among consumers with respect to Kellogg's Toucan Sam word mark. Kellogg added a likelihood of confusion claim with respect to the GolfBird logo as well. Furthermore, Kellogg added a dilution claim under the Federal Trademark Dilution Act of 1995 (FTDA). On September 6, 2001, after a four day bench trial, the district court dismissed Kellogg's complaint. The judgment was then entered on September 10. The court found that confusion was highly unlikely, principally because Kellogg is in the business of selling cereal, whereas TGI is in the business of selling putters. Moreover, the court found no dilution because the parties' marks are "visually and verbally distinct."

III. Analysis

Essentially, Kellogg seeks to block the registration of the "Toucan Gold" word mark, and to prevent further commercial use of both the word mark and the GolfBird logo. To this end, Kellogg asserts that there is a Lanham Act violation because there exists a likelihood that consumers will be confused as to the source of TGI's products. Moreover, Kellogg asserts that, regardless of our confusion analysis, TGI's use of its marks dilutes the fame of Kellogg's marks, and therefore TGI is in violation of the FTDA.

A. Likelihood of Confusion

In order to show trademark infringement under the Lanham Act, and that TGI is not entitled to registration, Kellogg must show that TGI's use of its marks constitutes use "in commerce" of a "reproduction, counterfeit, copy, or colorable imitation of a registered mark in connection with the sale, offering for sale, distribution, or advertising of any goods or services on or in connection with which such use is likely to cause confusion, or to cause mistake, or to deceive...."

This Court has established an eight-part test for determining when a likelihood of confusion exists between the origins of two products. The factors are: (1) the strength of the plaintiff's mark; (2) the relatedness of the goods or services offered by the parties; (3) similarity of the marks; (4) any evidence of actual confusion; (5) the marketing channels used by the parties; (6) the probable degree of purchaser care and sophistication; (7) the defendant's intent; and (8) the likelihood of either party expanding its product line using the marks. Thus, the question here, as in all trademark cases, is whether we believe consumers of TGI's golf equipment are likely to think it was manufactured by Kellogg. None of the factors is dispositive, but the factors guide us in our ultimate determination.

1. Strength of Kellogg's Marks

The first factor of the test focuses on the distinctiveness of a mark and the public's ability to recognize it. * * * [W]e recognized a spectrum of distinctiveness for trademarks, ranging from "generic" to "fanciful." For example, the word "cereal" is generic, whereas the names "Xerox" and "Kodak" are fanciful, having been completely fabricated by the trademark holders.

We find the "Toucan Sam" word mark and logo each to be fanciful. Kellogg completely created the name "Toucan Sam." Kellogg also completely fabricated Toucan Sam's logo design. He does not resemble a real toucan. His unique shape, coloring, size, and demeanor are entirely the creation of Kellogg, and not reminiscent of anything seen in the wild. Therefore, as a logo, he is also a fanciful mark and distinctive.

In further support of the strength of its Toucan Sam marks, Kellogg has submitted survey information indicating that 94% of Americans recognize Toucan Sam, and 81% of children who recognize him correspond him with Froot Loops. Moreover, Kellogg has submitted extensive records detailing the massive amount of time, money, and effort expended in regard to the marketing of Toucan Sam and Froot Loops. We need not delve into Kellogg's records; we find the fact that Kellogg is the largest cereal maker in the world, that Froot Loops is one of its best selling cereals, and that Toucan Sam has appeared in every print and television advertisement for Froot Loops since 1963 enough to establish that Toucan Sam is visually recognizable by an overwhelming cross-section of American consumers. Coupling that with his distinctiveness, Toucan Sam is a very strong mark.

2. Relatedness of the Products

In consideration of the second factor, we must examine the relatedness of the goods and services offered by each party. We have established three benchmarks regarding the relatedness of parties' goods and services. First, if the parties compete directly, confusion is likely if the marks are sufficiently similar; second, if the goods and services are somewhat related, but not competitive, then the likelihood of confusion will turn on other factors; finally, if the products are unrelated, confusion is highly unlikely.

TGI makes golf equipment, mainly putter heads. TGI also sells bag tags, divot tools, and full sets of clubs, but has never sold any merchandise unrelated to golf.

Kellogg is primarily a producer of breakfast cereal, but has branched off from cereal and sold products in other industries on a limited basis. It has also at times licensed its name and characters to outside companies. Kellogg asserts before this Court that it has sufficiently entered the golf equipment industry. In support of this claim, Kellogg presents a catalog, wherein it offers for sale golf balls and golf shirts on which is imprinted the picture of Toucan Sam. Moreover, Kellogg has presented a mass-marketed 1982 animated television advertisement wherein Toucan Sam is portrayed soliciting his Froot Loops on a golf course, and interacting with a golf-playing bear. Kellogg claims these materials indicate that the Toucan Sam marks are related not only to the manufacture of breakfast cereal, but to the golf equipment industry as well.

However, Kellogg, although it is the largest producer of breakfast cereal nationally, has not presented evidence that its golf "equipment" has been marketed nationally. The golf balls and shirts are available on a limited basis, either through the aforementioned catalog—which is not widely distributed—or through select local theme stores, such as Kellogg's own "Cereal City" in Battle Creek, Michigan. Moreover, the commercial in which Toucan Sam plays golf is nonetheless an advertisement for Froot Loops, not golf equipment. The district court found that Kellogg's presence in the golf industry was insignificant, and nothing more than a marketing tool to further boost sales of its cereal. We agree. We find that one thirty second advertisement does not render Toucan Sam a golfer, nor does a novelty catalog make Kellogg a player in the golfing industry. In any event, trademark law is grounded on a likelihood of confusion standard. We find that no consumer would associate Kellogg with top-line golf equipment based on Kellogg's extremely limited licensing of its characters on novelty items. We also believe that if any consumers ever did associate

Kellogg and Toucan Sam with golf based on the 1982 commercial, it is highly unlikely that they would still do so twenty years after the advertisement last aired. We find the parties' products completely unrelated. And under the benchmarks established in this Circuit, the second factor therefore supports a conclusion that confusion is not likely to occur.

3. Similarity of the Marks

Kellogg argues that it can prove a likelihood of confusion notwithstanding the unrelatedness of the goods. It has presented several cases to demonstrate that courts have held for trademark owners relying heavily on the similarity of the marks, even where the parties' goods were in different product markets.

But here, the parties' goods are completely unrelated, and the "Toucan Sam" and "Toucan Gold" word marks are similar only in that they each contain the common word "toucan." Although the name "Toucan Sam" is itself fanciful and distinctive, use of the word "toucan" for cereal is merely arbitrary. Kellogg has taken an everyday word and applied it to a setting where it is not naturally placed. As opposed to a fanciful mark, an arbitrary mark is distinctive only within its product market and entitled to little or no protection outside of that area. Thus, * * * here TGI has not used any distinctive portion of Kellogg's word mark at all. Admittedly, we would have a far different case had TGI attempted to use a mark such as "Toucan Sam Gold" for its line of products, because the "Toucan Sam" word mark, in its entirety, is fanciful and likely transcends its market in the same way "Frito Lay" and the "Mc" prefix do. Kellogg has not cornered the market on all potential uses of the common bird name "toucan" in commerce, only on uses of "Toucan Sam." In regard to the word marks, TGI's apparently similar use is therefore not enough to overcome the unrelatedness of the goods.

As for the logos, the actual Toucan Sam design is fanciful. Hence, if TGI's GolfBird is similar to Toucan Sam's design, there may be a Lanham Act violation in spite of the unrelated goods. But we find GolfBird dissimilar to Toucan Sam. GolfBird resembles a real toucan. She has the look and proportions of a toucan that one would encounter in the wild. Toucan Sam is anthropomorphic, with a discolored, misshaped beak. His body type is not the same as that of a real toucan; and he smiles and has several other human features. We therefore find no similarity between Toucan Sam and GolfBird.

4. The Other Confusion Factors

The other five factors can be disposed of quickly. Kellogg has presented no evidence of actual customer confusion. Thus, we need not consider that factor.

The parties do not use similar avenues of commerce. Kellogg distributes Froot Loops through regular wholesale and retail channels. Kellogg advertises its product nationally on television and in print. Conversely,

TGI distributes its product primarily at trade shows and over the internet. TGI does not sell its golf equipment via retail outlets or advertise on television or radio

TGI's clientele is primarily, and almost exclusively, comprised of corporations and wealthy golfers. We find each of these groups to be sufficiently sophisticated, so as not to believe that Kellogg, a cereal company, has manufactured a golf club named "Toucan Gold." Moreover, we find the two industries sufficiently separate, so that there will rarely, if ever, exist a consumer who is looking for Kellogg's product in the golf equipment market.

Next, there is no evidence to suggest that Boyko chose his toucan marks in order to dishonestly trade on Kellogg's marks. Again, the goods are so unrelated as to dispose of this factor with little discussion. Boyko testified that he chose the name "toucan" because of any bird's obvious connection to the game of golf, as evidenced through golfing terms such as "eagle," "birdie," and "albatross." The district court found his testimony on this issue credible, and Kellogg has presented no evidence to cause us to doubt that Boyko's intent was not dishonorable.

Lastly, there is no evidence to suggest that TGI has any desire to enter the cereal game, or that Kellogg has any plan to begin manufacturing golf equipment on a full-scale basis. As stated above, we do not believe Kellogg's limited licensing of golf balls and golf shirts with a Toucan Sam logo, nor the single 1982 advertisement wherein Toucan Sam parades around a golf course, announces Kellogg's entry into the golf market, or its intention to do so.

Accordingly, we find no likelihood of confusion between TGI's use of its marks-the word mark "Toucan Gold" and its GolfBird logo; and Kellogg's marks-the word mark "Toucan Sam" and the Toucan Sam design. In fact, the only of the eight factors we find in favor of Kellogg is the strength of its marks. The products sold by each party are wholly unrelated; the similarity between the word marks or the bird designs is not enough to overcome this unrelatedness; and TGI's clientele is not the sort to believe that Kellogg now manufactures golf clubs. We affirm the decision of the district court and find no likelihood of confusion.

B. *Dilution*

Kellogg also raises claims of trademark dilution under the FTDA of 1995. The FTDA amended § 43 of the Lanham Act to include a remedy for "dilution of famous marks." 15 U.S.C. § 1125. "Dilution" is defined as "the lessening of the capacity of a famous mark to identify and distinguish goods and services." Kellogg believes that TGI's marks dilute the fame of the Toucan Sam marks, and that Kellogg may oppose TGI's marks on that ground and obtain relief under the FTDA. The district court rejected Kellogg's argument.

Dilution law, unlike traditional trademark infringement law, does not exist to protect the public. It is not based on a likelihood of confusion standard, but only exists to protect the quasi-property rights a holder has in maintaining the integrity and distinctiveness of his mark. We have developed a five part test to determine whether dilution has occurred under the FTDA: the senior mark must be (1) famous; and (2) distinctive. Use of the junior mark must (3) be in commerce; (4) have begun subsequent to the senior mark becoming famous; and (5) cause dilution of the distinctive quality of the senior mark.

The first four factors are not in dispute and require no discussion. The only factor before this Court is whether TGI has diluted Kellogg's Toucan Sam marks. The Supreme Court has held that, under the plain language of the FTDA, for a plaintiff to show dilution, he must demonstrate actual dilution, and not merely the likelihood of dilution.

The plaintiff need not show actual loss of sales or profit, but the mere fact that customers might see the junior mark and associate it with a famous mark does not establish dilution. In *V Secret v. Moseley*, 537 U.S. 418 (2003), the defendant created a lingerie shop called "Victor's Little Secret." The owners of the more famous lingerie-related mark "Victoria's Secret" sued under the FTDA. The Supreme Court held that the plaintiff's claim failed, even though it presented evidence that consumers had associated the two marks. The plaintiff did not present any empirical evidence that consumers no longer clearly understood to which products the "Victoria's Secret" mark was related, and thus failed to demonstrate the "lessening of the capacity of the Victoria's Secret mark to identify and distinguish goods or services sold in Victoria's Secret stores or advertised in its catalogs." Likewise, here, Kellogg has presented no evidence that TGI's use of its toucan marks has caused consumers no longer to recognize that Toucan Sam represents only Froot Loops. In fact, Kellogg's own 1991 study indicated that 94% of children recognize Toucan Sam and 81% of children relate him to Froot Loops. Kellogg performed another study in 1997–after TGI started business-wherein it determined that 94% of adults likewise recognized Toucan Sam. Kellogg has failed to present evidence that any segment of the population recognizes Toucan Sam as the spokesbird only for Froot Loops in lesser numbers than it did before TGI started using its toucan marks. Accordingly, we affirm the decision of the district court and deny Kellogg's FTDA claims.

Kellogg asks this Court for a remand on this issue in light of the fact that the Supreme Court decided Moseley and clarified the dilution standard after the briefing stage in this case. Kellogg believes it is entitled to the opportunity to present empirical evidence of actual dilution before the district court. We find a remand inappropriate. In Moseley, the Supreme Court provided a stricter standard for proving dilution than the likelihood of dilution standard that was previously employed by this Court. We find Kellogg's proffered empirical evidence insufficient even to meet the lesser standard.

MENASHE v. V SECRET CATALOGUE, INC.

United States District Court, S.D.N.Y, 2006.
409 F.Supp. 2d 412.

BAER, DISTRICT JUDGE.

A.   Plaintiff's Adoption of the Mark

On or about June 1, 2004, Menashe, a publicist, and Quock, a fashion model and actress, embarked on a joint business venture to produce and launch a line of women's underwear. Sometime in July 2004, they decided to name their line "SEXY LITTLE THINGS." Also in July 2004, Quock purchased 400 sample pieces of plain stock underwear from a manufacturer in China and in late July or early August 2004, heat pressed her designs consisting of words and logos onto the stock underwear. She also heat pressed the Mark onto the back of the underwear where a label would normally be attached.

In late July or early August 2004, Menashe and Quock came up with the phrase "SEXY LITTLE THING, SEXY LITTLE THINGS," a variation of their chosen name that they believed yielded many creative possibilities for design and advertising. On August 31, 2004, Quock registered the domain name www.sexylittle things.com in preparation for building a website to sell the underwear line over the Internet. Subsequently, on September 13, 2004, after searching the website of the United States Patent and Trademark Office ("USPTO") and finding that the Mark was available, Menashe and Quock filed an intent-to-use ("ITU") application with the USPTO for "SEXY LITTLE THING, SEXY LITTLE THINGS" for lingerie. About ten days later, Quock hired a website designer to create the www.sexylittle things.com site.

By early September 2004, Quock initiated negotiations with her manufacturer in China to silkscreen print her designs on bulk shipments of underwear. In October 2004, she sent the manufacturer eight designs to make prototype prints, and started negotiations for an order of 6,000 pieces of underwear. The manufacturer sent Quock the eight prototypes on November 13, 2004. By then, she had also sent the manufacturer diagrams for the production of labels carrying the mark "SEXY LITTLE THINGS."

Meanwhile, Plaintiffs had also set about publicizing their line. Sometime in September or October 2004, Quock did an interview with www. ediets.com, and an article that mentioned the name of Plaintiffs' line and the www.sexylittle things.com website appeared online at the ediets.com website in the week of November 19, 2004. On August 19, 2004, Quock did a photo shoot for Stuff Magazine in which she modeled a pair of "SEXY LITTLE THINGS" underwear. The photographs were published in Stuff Magazine in March of 2005 with an accompanying article that featured Quock's venture into women's lingerie, but did not mention the name of the line. In late September or early October 2004, Quock did an interview with Beyond Fitness magazine in which she promoted her underwear line, but was unaware whether the article was ever published. In mid-November, she flew to Milan for a photo shoot featuring "SEXY LITTLE THINGS" underwear. The photographs were never published.

On October 14, 2004, Quock e-mailed Menashe an outline of a business plan for the underwear line and indicated that they were ready to seek buyers. Sometime in November 2004, Quock contacted a friend who was a buyer for Fred Segal stores about selling the underwear line in boutiques in Los Angeles, California. As noted below, this effort too was never consummated.

On November 16, 2004, Menashe received a letter from Victoria's Secret's outside counsel informing her that Victoria's Secret had been using "SEXY LITTLE THINGS" as a trademark for lingerie since prior to the filing date of Plaintiffs' ITU application. The letter warned that "SEXY LITTLE THING, SEXY LITTLE THINGS," the subject of Plaintiffs' ITU application, was confusingly similar to Victoria's Secret's mark and, if used, would constitute trademark infringement. Further, the letter demanded that Plaintiffs cease and desist all plans to use "SEXY LITTLE THING, SEXY LITTLE THINGS," abandon their ITU application, and transfer the domain name www.sexylittle things.com to Victoria's Secret. Finally, the letter requested a response by November 19, 2004.

Victoria's Secret's letter caused Plaintiffs to halt production of their underwear project, instruct Stuff Magazine not to mention the name of their underwear line, discontinue other publicity efforts, stop development of their website, and cease their attempts to find retail outlets for their product. Plaintiffs also ordered two trademark investigations into Victoria's Secret's claims to the Mark. They were informed that no one had used the Mark prior to the filing of their ITU application. One investigation reported that Victoria's Secret's Resort 2005 catalogue, which had been sent with the cease and desist letter as proof of Victoria's Secret's use of the Mark, was not mailed out until December 28, 2004. At trial—while it stretches credulity—Menashe testified that since the time she received the cease and desist letter, she has not been in a Victoria's Secret store or looked at a Victoria's Secret catalogue to see whether Victoria's Secret was selling merchandise under the name "SEXY LITTLE THINGS." Quock testified that she did not visit a Victoria's Secret store nor look at a Victoria's Secret catalogue until some time after receipt of the cease and desist letter, when she walked into a Victoria's Secret store and saw a display for "SEXY LITTLE THINGS."

B. Victoria's Secret's Adoption and Use of the Mark

As early as Fall 2002, Victoria's Secret began to develop the concept and marketing for a panty collection. Victoria's Secret's decision to expand its panty business stemmed from a desire to capitalize on a major fashion trend that appeared to herald "decorated bottoms"—seen in the popularity of low rise pants and the vogue among young women for wearing lingerie style items as outerwear. Sometime between March 30 and June

1, 2004, Victoria's Secret's marketing department settled on the name "SEXY LITTLE THINGS" for its panty collection. The collection, characterized as "fun, flirty, and playfully sexy," was designed to appeal to women in their twenties and early thirties, and was comprised of over eighty items that included panties, camisoles, and other underwear. Some of these items were already being sold in Victoria Secret stores as general merchandise prior to the introduction of the "SEXY LITTLE THINGS" collection (the "Collection"), but the majority of the items were placed in stores for the first time when the Collection was rolled out in July 2004.

On or around July 28, 2004, the Collection was scheduled to make its first appearance in five Victoria's Secret stores in Ohio, Michigan, and California. On that date, the mark "SEXY LITTLE THINGS" was displayed with the Collection in four of the five stores in the form of hangtags, store signage, permanent fixtures, or in window exposures. For example, in one of the Ohio stores, denominated Easton #1300, the Mark appeared as a large illuminated sign on a "focal wall," a specially constructed vertical unit of nine compartments, each compartment containing a plastic "buttock" on which a pair of panties was displayed. In that store, the Mark also appeared prominently on hangtags attached to hangers that displayed panties, on labels adhered to pull-out compartments of something called a "panty bar"-a horizontal case that displayed merchandise in each compartment-and with window displays of the same merchandise. Further, on July 28, 2004, the testimony recites that the "selling environments" for "SEXY LITTLE THINGS" merchandise, comprising the various described displays, opened to consumers in the Ohio roll-out stores.

The roll-out at the Briarwood, Michigan store was delayed owing to technical difficulties related to signage. Maria Thurston, a co-manager of the Briarwood store from October 2001 until November 27, 2004, testified that while construction for a "panty boutique" was completed on July 28, 2004, no "SEXY LITTLE THINGS" signs appeared in the store until the second week of September 2004. Ms. Thurston also testified that through September 2004, she never received brand guides from corporate headquarters with instructions for displaying "SEXY LITTLE THINGS" merchandise in the store.

The "SEXY LITTLE THINGS" collection was rolled out to more Victoria's Secret stores in September and October 2004, and by October 19, 2004, the Collection was available to consumers in all nine hundred and twenty-three Victoria's Secret retail lingerie stores nationwide. In each of the stores, there was some form of focal wall or table signage that displayed the "SEXY LITTLE THINGS" mark together with garments from the Collection. No labels displaying the Mark were sewn on the merchandise, however, until June 2005. Moreover, when the Collection was rolled out, store receipts did not indicate that the consumer had bought a "SEXY LITTLE THINGS" item.

The Collection was also available to consumers through catalogues and online. The Collection, according to the uncontradicted testimony and exhibits, first appeared in the Major Fall 2 edition of the Victoria's Secret catalogue that was mailed out to approximately 2.9 million consumers nationwide between September 4, 2004 and September 9, 2004. Because Victoria's Secret Direct simultaneously makes most of its catalogues available online through its website, the Major Fall 2 catalogue became available online on or about September 9, 2004. Beginning with the Major Fall 2 edition, the Collection has appeared in approximately twenty-two editions of the Victoria's Secret catalogue.

Typically, the catalogues contained several pages dedicated to the display of "SEXY LITTLE THINGS" merchandise. The Mark was prominently displayed on these pages together with "SEXY LITTLE THINGS" items. Occasionally, together with "SEXY LITTLE THINGS" merchandise, these pages also displayed a few items from Victoria's Secret's other trademarked collections, sub-brands such as Angels by Victoria, Body by Victoria, and Very Sexy, so as to suggest to the consumer various looks that could be created using pieces from different collections. When this happened, the catalogue copy stated the name of the collection to which the item belonged. In addition, a few items advertised as part of the "SEXY LITTLE THINGS" collection were advertised in other editions of the catalogue as part of another trademarked collection or simply as general merchandise not belonging to any particular collection.

In the period July 31, 2004 through November 19, 2005, Victoria's Secret sold over thirteen million units of "SEXY LITTLE THINGS" merchandise for total sales of $119,052,756. The "SEXY LITTLE THINGS" brand accounted for approximately 4% of Victoria Secret Stores' total company sales for fiscal year 2005.

On November 11, 2004, Victoria's Secret applied to register "SEXY LITTLE THINGS" for lingerie on the USPTO's Principal Register based on first use in commerce dating from July 28, 2004. At about this time, Victoria's Secret learned of Plaintiffs' ITU application for "SEXY LITTLE THING, SEXY LITTLE THINGS" and of their registration of the domain name www.sexylittle things.com. On November 15, 2004, Victoria's Secret's outside counsel sent Plaintiffs a cease and desist letter.

On March 28, 2005, the USPTO suspended further action on Victoria's Secret's trademark application pending the disposition of Plaintiffs' ITU application. On September 13, 2005, the USPTO published Plaintiffs' ITU application for opposition in the Official Gazette. Victoria's Secret filed its notice of opposition to Plaintiffs' application on September 30, 2005, on the grounds that Victoria's Secret has priority of use as to the Mark, and that registration of Plaintiffs' "SEXY LITTLE THING, SEXY LITTLE THINGS" mark for identical goods would be likely to cause consumer confusion. That action is still pending before the Trademark Trial and Appeal Board ("TTAB"). On January 11, 2005, Plaintiffs filed the instant action for declaratory judgment of trademark non-infringement * * *.

1. Protectability of the Mark

To merit trademark protection, a mark "must be capable of distinguishing the products it marks from those of others." As set forth by Judge Friendly in the landmark case of *Abercrombie & Fitch Co. v. Hunting World, Inc.* [537 F.2d 4 (2d Cir. 1976)], the four categories of terms to be considered in determining the protectability of a mark, listed in order of the degree of protection accorded, are (i) generic, (ii) descriptive, (iii) suggestive, and (iv) arbitrary or fanciful. A descriptive term "forthwith conveys an immediate idea of the ingredients, qualities or characteristics of the goods." In contrast, a suggestive term "requires imagination, thought and perception to reach a conclusion as to the nature of the goods." Suggestive marks are automatically protected because they are inherently distinctive * * *. Descriptive marks are not inherently distinctive and may only be protected on a showing of secondary meaning, i.e. that the purchasing public associates the mark with a particular source.

Classification of a mark is a question of fact. The fact-finder must decide, based on the evidence, whether prospective purchasers would perceive the mark to be suggestive or merely descriptive. A composite mark-one comprising more than one term-must be assessed as a whole and not by its parts. A leading trademark authority has proposed the following three-part test to distinguish suggestive from descriptive marks: (i) whether the purchaser must use some imagination to connect the mark to some characteristic of the product; (ii) whether competitors have used the term descriptively or rather as a trademark; and (iii) whether the proposed use would deprive competitors of a way to describe their goods.

Applying this three-part test, I find "SEXY LITTLE THINGS" to be suggestive. First, while the term describes the erotically stimulating quality of the trademarked lingerie, it also calls to mind the phrase "sexy little thing" popularly used to refer to attractive lithe young women. Hence, the Mark prompts the purchaser to mentally associate the lingerie with its targeted twenty to thirty year-old consumers. Courts have classified marks that both describe the product and evoke other associations as inherently distinctive. See, e.g., *Blisscraft of Hollywood v. United Plastics, Co.*, 294 F.2d 694, 700 (2d Cir.1961) ("POLY PITCHER" for polyethylene pitchers is a fanciful mark because it is reminiscent of Molly Pitcher of Revolutionary time) * * *. The second factor is not at issue here as neither party has submitted evidence of competitors' usage of the term. Considering the third factor, however, it is hard to believe that Victoria's Secret's use of the Mark will deprive competitors of ways to describe their lingerie products. Indeed, Victoria's Secret's own descriptions of its lingerie in its catalogues and website illustrate that there are numerous ways to describe provocative underwear.

2. Priority

Plaintiffs' alternative contention is that even though the Mark may be suggestive, Victoria's Secret has used it in a descriptive manner, i.e.

that Victoria's Secret used the words "sexy little things" to describe its lingerie rather than to identify itself as the source of the goods. Although not crystal clear, the thrust of Plaintiffs' argument appears to be that Victoria's Secret never sold a distinct collection of lingerie under the "SEXY LITTLE THINGS" mark, and hence the term could not have been used as a trademark, but only as a description of various items of underwear drawn from Victoria's Secret's several sub-brands or from the retailer's general merchandise. Consequently, Victoria's Secret is not entitled to priority in the Mark.

The Second Circuit has held that "the right to exclusive use of a trademark derives from its appropriation and subsequent use in the marketplace." *La Societe Anonyme des Parfums Le Galion v. Jean Patou, Inc.*, 495 F.2d 1265, 1271 (2d Cir. 1974). A single use suffices to prove priority if the proponent demonstrates that his subsequent use was "deliberate and continuous." Id. at 1272. The later filing of an ITU application by another party does not defeat these use-based rights. The use must, however, be bona fide "use in commerce" as defined in 15 U.S.C. Section 1127. Under this statute, the mark must be "placed in any manner on the goods or their containers or the displays associated therewith or on tags or labels affixed thereto." 15 U.S.C. § 1127(1)(A). Prominent use of a mark in a catalog with a picture and description of the product constitutes a display associated with goods and not mere advertising because of the "point of sale" nature of the display. * * * The same principle can reasonably be extended to "point of sale" website displays. Whether or not a term has been used as a trademark must be determined from the perspective of the prospective purchaser.

At trial, Plaintiffs highlighted the delay in the roll-out of the Collection to the Briarwood, Michigan store. They painstakingly pointed to evidence that a few items sold as "SEXY LITTLE THINGS" had previously been sold under one of Victoria's Secret's other trademarks, or as part of a store's general merchandise. Plaintiffs also made much of the fact that in Victoria's Secret's catalogues and on its website, a few items from other trademarked collections were included in pages displaying "SEXY LITTLE THINGS" lingerie. Finally, Plaintiffs argued that the late introduction of sewn-in garment labels bearing the Mark and the delay in indicating on receipts that an item was from the "SEXY LITTLE THINGS" collection proved that there was no "SEXY LITTLE THINGS" collection prior to the filing of their ITU application.

Plaintiffs' determination to ignore the model for the underwear fails to overcome the overwhelming evidence that Victoria's Secret used "SEXY LITTLE THINGS" as a trademark in commerce beginning on July 28, 2004. Commencing on that date, the prominent use of the Mark in four stores on focal wall and table signage, on hangtags, and in window and floor displays in close association with the lingerie satisfies the "use in commerce" requirement of 15 U.S.C. Section 1127. Similarly, Victoria's

Secret's prominent use of the Mark in its catalogues beginning on September 4, 2004, and on its website beginning on or about September 9, 2004, together with pictures and descriptions of the goods meets the Lands' End test, as both mediums were "point of sale" displays. Moreover, Victoria's Secret produced abundant testimony that, dating from July 28, 2004, it continuously used the Mark in association with lingerie sold through its retail stores, catalogues, and online. That Victoria's Secret sold a few garments as part of more than one collection, or that it occasionally included garments from other collections in the catalogue spreads showing "SEXY LITTLE THINGS" lingerie do not detract from such trademark use. Prospective purchasers of underwear, whose perception is determinative on the question of trademark use here, are unlikely to undertake the type of microscopic scrutiny Plaintiffs engaged in to unearth these details for purposes of this litigation. I find that because Victoria's Secret made bona fide trademark use of "SEXY LITTLE THINGS" in commerce before Plaintiffs filed their ITU application, and has continued to use that Mark in commerce, Victoria Secret has acquired priority in the Mark. Consequently, Plaintiffs are not entitled to a declaratory judgment of non-infringement under the Lanham Act or at common law.

C. Cybersquatting

Plaintiffs contend that a declaration of no-cybersquatting is proper because they registered the domain name www.sexylittle things.com in good faith and did not know, nor should have known, of Victoria's Secret's use of the Mark. Victoria's Secret responds that this Court has no jurisdiction over this claim because Plaintiffs did not obtain Lanham Act rights through mere registration of their domain name, and there is no actual case or controversy because Victoria's Secret never threatened Plaintiffs with suit for cybersquatting.

I agree with Victoria's Secret that Plaintiffs have failed to establish the existence of an actual case or controversy related to cybersquatting. Victoria's Secret's cease and desist letter may not reasonably be read to threaten Plaintiffs with suit for cybersquatting. The letter made no reference to cybersquatting. Victoria's Secret did demand that Plaintiffs transfer their domain name to it, but this demand was in a separate paragraph and logically unconnected to the sections of the letter that discuss infringement, the only sections that may be read to threaten litigation. Moreover, 15 U.S.C. Section 1125(d)(1)(A), which regulates cybersquatting, requires a showing that the defendant "has a bad faith intent to profit" from a mark. As Plaintiffs claim that they registered the domain name in good faith, they had no reason to fear liability for cybersquatting. Consequently, Plaintiffs fail to persuade me that they had a real and reasonable apprehension of liability for cybersquatting as required for jurisdiction under the Declaratory Judgment Act, and this Court lacks subject matter jurisdiction over this claim.

3. Not Otherwise Barred by Statute

IN RE CALIFORNIA INNOVATIONS, INC.

United States Court of Appeals, Federal Circuit, 2003.
329 F.3d 1334.

RADER, CIRCUIT JUDGE

California Innovations, Inc. (CA Innovations), a Canadian-based corporation, appeals the Trademark Trial and Appeal Board's refusal to register its mark-CALIFORNIA INNOVATIONS. Citing section 2(e)(3) of the Lanham Act, 15 U.S.C. § 1052(e)(3) (2000), the Board concluded that the mark was primarily geographically deceptively misdescriptive. Because the Board applied an outdated standard in its analysis under § 1052(e)(3), this court vacates the Board's decision and remands.

I.

CA Innovations filed an intent-to-use trademark application, Serial No. 74/650,703, on March 23, 1995, for the composite mark CALIFORNIA INNOVATIONS and Design. The application sought registration for the following goods:

automobile visor organizers, namely, holders for personal effects, and automobile trunk organizers for automotive accessories in International Class 12; backpacks in International Class 18; thermal insulated bags for food and beverages, thermal insulated tote bags for food or beverages, and thermal insulated wraps for cans to keep the containers cold or hot in International Class 21; and nylon, vinyl, polyester and/or leather bags for storage and storage pouches in International Class 22.

The United States Patent and Trademark Office (PTO) initially refused registration based on an alleged likelihood of confusion with some prior registrations. At the PTO's request, applicant disclaimed the CALIFORNIA component of the mark. Applicant also amended its identification and classification of goods to conform to the examiner's suggestions. Thereafter, the PTO issued a notice of publication. The mark was published for opposition on September 29, 1998. No opposition was ever filed.

In July 1999, the PTO reasserted jurisdiction over the application under 37 C.F.R. § 2.84(a) and refused registration under § 1052(e)(3), concluding that the mark was primarily geographically deceptively misdescriptive. Applicant filed a timely notice for reconsideration with the PTO and a notice of appeal to the Board in November 2000. After the PTO refused to reconsider its decision, CA Innovations renewed its appeal to the Board. On February 20, 2002, the Board upheld the PTO's refusal to register applicant's mark and concluded that the mark was primarily geographically deceptively misdescriptive.

This court reviews the Board's "legal conclusions, such as its interpretations of the Lanham Act," without deference. Under a proper legal standard, the Board's determination of geographic misdescription is a factual finding. This court upholds the Board's factual findings "unless they are unsupported by substantial evidence."

II.

The Lanham Act addresses geographical marks in three categories. The first category, § 1052(a), identifies geographically deceptive marks:

No trademark by which the goods of the applicant may be distinguished from the goods of others shall be refused registration on the principal register on account of its nature unless it-(a) Consists of or comprises immoral, deceptive, or scandalous matter; or matter which may disparage or falsely suggest a connection with persons, living or dead, institutions, beliefs, or national symbols, or bring them into contempt, or disrepute.

15 U.S.C. § 1052(a) (2000). Although not expressly addressing geographical marks, § 1052(a) has traditionally been used to reject geographic marks that materially deceive the public. A mark found to be deceptive under § 1052(a) cannot receive protection under the Lanham Act. To deny a geographic mark protection under § 1052(a), the PTO must establish that (1) the mark misrepresents or misdescribes the goods, (2) the public would likely believe the misrepresentation, and (3) the misrepresentation would materially affect the public's decision to purchase the goods. This test's central point of analysis is materiality because that finding shows that the misdescription deceived the consumer.

The other two categories of geographic marks are (1) "primarily geographically descriptive" marks and (2) "primarily geographically deceptively misdescriptive" marks under § 1052(e). The North American Free Trade Agreement, [hereinafter NAFTA] has recently changed these two categories. Before the NAFTA changes, § 1052(e) and (f) stated:

No trademark by which the goods of the applicant may be distinguished from the goods of others shall be refused registration on the principal register on account of its nature unless it-

(e) Consists of a mark which ...

(2) when used on or in connection with the goods of the applicant is primarily geographically descriptive or deceptively misdescriptive of them.

* * *

(f) Except as expressly excluded in paragraphs (a) (d) of this section, nothing in this chapter shall prevent the registration of a mark used by the applicant which has become distinctive of the applicant's goods in commerce.

15 U.S.C. § 1052(e)(2) and (f) (1988). The law treated these two categories of geographic marks identically. Specifically, the PTO generally placed a "primarily geographically descriptive" or "deceptively misdescriptive"

mark on the supplemental register. Upon a showing of acquired distinctiveness, these marks could qualify for the principal register.

Thus, in contrast to the permanent loss of registration rights imposed on deceptive marks under § 1052(a), pre-NAFTA § 1052(e)(2) only required a temporary denial of registration on the principal register. Upon a showing of distinctiveness, these marks could acquire a place on the principal register. As permitted by pre-NAFTA § 1052(f), a mark could acquire distinctiveness or "secondary meaning" by showing that "in the minds of the public, the primary significance of a product feature or term is to identify the source of the product rather than the product itself."

In the pre-NAFTA era, the focus on distinctiveness overshadowed the deceptiveness aspect of § 1052(e)(2) and made it quite easy for the PTO to deny registration on the principal register to geographically deceptively misdescriptive marks under § 1052(e)(2). On the other hand, the deception requirement of § 1052(a) protected against fraud and could not be overlooked. Therefore, the PTO had significantly more difficulty denying registration based on that higher standard.

Before NAFTA, in *In re Nantucket*, 209 USPQ 868, 870, 1981 WL 48122 (TTAB 1981), the Board used a three-prong test to detect either primarily geographically descriptive or deceptively misdescriptive marks. Under the Board's test, the only substantive inquiry was whether the mark conveyed primarily a geographical connotation. On appeal in *In re Nantucket*, this court's predecessor rejected that test:

> The board's test rests mechanistically on the one question of whether the mark is recognizable, at least to some large segment of the public, as the name of a geographical area. NANTUCKET is such. That ends the board's test. Once it is found that the mark is the name of a known place, i.e., that it has "a readily recognizable geographic meaning," the next question, whether applicant's goods do or do not come from that place, becomes irrelevant under the board's test, for if they do, the mark is "primarily geographically descriptive"; if they don't, the mark is "primarily geographically deceptively misdescriptive." Either way, the result is the same, for the mark must be denied registration on the principal register unless resort can be had to § 2(f).

In re Nantucket, Inc., 677 F.2d 95, 97–98 (CCPA 1982). Thus *In re Nantucket*, for the first time, set forth a goods-place association requirement. Id. at 99–100. In other words, this court required a geographically deceptively misdescriptive mark to have more than merely a primary geographic connotation. Specifically, the public must also associate the goods in question with the place identified by the mark-the goods-place association requirement. However, this court did not require a showing that the goods-place association was material to the consumer's decision before rejection under § 1052(e).

In *In re Loew's Theatres, Inc.*, 769 F.2d 764, 767–69 (Fed.Cir. 1985), this court expressly permitted a goods-place association without any showing that the place is "well-known" or "noted" for the goods in question. The *Loew's* court explained: "[I]f the place is noted for the particular goods, a mark for such goods which do not originate there is likely to be deceptive under § 2(a) and not registrable under any circumstances." Id. at 768, n. 6. Clarifying that pre-NAFTA § 1052(e)(2) does not require a "well-known" place, this court noted:

> The PTO's burden is simply to establish that there is a reasonable predicate for its conclusion that the public would be likely to make the particular goods/place association on which it relies.... The issue is not the fame or exclusivity of the place name, but the likelihood that a particular place will be associated with particular goods.

Id.

As noted, the Lanham Act itself does not expressly require different tests for geographically misleading marks. In order to implement the Lanham Act prior to the NAFTA amendments, the PTO used a low standard to reject marks for geographically deceptive misdescriptiveness under pre-NAFTA § 1052(e), which was relatively simple to meet. In contrast, the PTO required a much more demanding finding to reject for geographical deception under § 1052(a). This distinction was justified because rejection under subsection (a) was final, while rejection under pre-NAFTA subsection (e)(2) was only temporary, until the applicant could show that the mark had become distinctive. The more drastic consequence establishes the propriety of the elevated materiality test in the context of a permanent ban on registration under § 1052(a).

NAFTA and its implementing legislation obliterated the distinction between geographically deceptive marks and primarily geographically deceptively misdescriptive marks. Article 1712 of NAFTA provides:

> 1. Each party [United States, Mexico, Canada] shall provide, in respect of geographical indications, the legal means for interested persons to prevent:
>
>> (a) the use of any means in the designation or presentation of a good that indicates or suggests that the good in question originates in a territory, region or locality other than the true place of origin, in a manner that misleads the public as to the geographical origin of the good....

See NAFTA, Dec. 17, 1992, art. 1712, 32 I.L.M. 605, 698. This treaty shifts the emphasis for geographically descriptive marks to prevention of any public deception. Accordingly, the NAFTA Act amended § 1052(e) to read:

> No trademark by which the goods of the applicant may be distinguished from the goods of others shall be refused registration on the principal register on account of its nature unless it-
>
>> (e) Consists of a mark which (1) when used on or in connection with the goods of the applicant is merely descriptive or deceptively misdescriptive of them, (2) when used on or in connection with the goods of the applicant is primarily geographically descriptive of them, except as

indications of regional origin may be registrable under section 4 [15 USCS § 1054], (3) when used on or in connection with the goods of the applicant is primarily geographically deceptively misdescriptive of them, (4) is primarily merely a surname, or (5) comprises any matter that, as a whole, is functional.

(f) Except as expressly excluded in subsections (a), (b), (c), (d), (e)(3), and (e)(5) of this section, nothing herein shall prevent the registration of a mark used by the applicant which has become distinctive of the applicant's goods in commerce. 15 U.S.C. § 1052(e)–(f) (2000).

Recognizing the new emphasis on prevention of public deception, the NAFTA amendments split the categories of geographically descriptive and geographically deceptively misdescriptive into two subsections (subsections (e)(2) and (e)(3) respectively). Under the amended Lanham Act, subsection (e)(3)-geographically deceptive misdescription-could no longer acquire distinctiveness under subsection (f). Accordingly, marks determined to be primarily geographically deceptively misdescriptive are permanently denied registration, as are deceptive marks under § 1052(a).

Thus, § 1052 no longer treats geographically deceptively misdescriptive marks differently from geographically deceptive marks. Like geographically deceptive marks, the analysis for primarily geographically deceptively misdescriptive marks under § 1052(e)(3) focuses on deception of, or fraud on, the consumer. The classifications under the new § 1052 clarify that these two deceptive categories both receive permanent rejection. Accordingly, the test for rejecting a deceptively misdescriptive mark is no longer simple lack of distinctiveness, but the higher showing of deceptiveness.

The legislative history of the NAFTA Act confirms the change in standard for geographically deceptively misdescriptive marks. In a congressional record statement, which appears to be the equivalent of a committee report, the Senate Judiciary Committee acknowledges the new standard for these marks:

> [T]he bill creates a distinction in subsection 2(e) of the Trademark Act between geographically "descriptive" and "misdescriptive" marks and amends subsections 2(f) and 23(a) of the Act to preclude registration of "primarily geographically deceptively misdescriptive" marks on the principal and supplemental registers, respectively. The law as it relates to "primarily geographically descriptive" marks would remain unchanged.

139 Cong. Rec. S 16,092 (1993).

The amended Lanham Act gives geographically deceptively misdescriptive marks the same treatment as geographically deceptive marks under § 1052(a). Because both of these categories are subject to permanent denial of registration, the PTO may not simply rely on lack of distinctiveness to deny registration, but must make the more difficult showing of public deception. In other words, by placing geographically deceptively misdescriptive marks under subsection (e)(3) in the same fatal circumstances as deceptive marks under subsection (a), the NAFTA Act also elevated the standards for identifying those deceptive marks.

Before NAFTA, the PTO identified and denied registration to a primarily geographically deceptively misdescriptive mark with a showing that (1) the primary significance of the mark was a generally known geographic location, and (2) "the public was likely to believe the mark identified the place from which the goods originate and that the goods did not come from there." *In re Loew's,* 769 F.2d at 768. The second prong of the test represents the "goods-place association" between the mark and the goods at issue. This test raised an inference of deception based on the likelihood of a goods-place association that did not reflect the actual origin of the goods. A mere inference, however, is not enough to establish the deceptiveness that brings the harsh consequence of non-registrability under the amended Lanham Act. As noted, NAFTA and the amended Lanham Act place an emphasis on actual misleading of the public.

Therefore, the relatively easy burden of showing a naked goods-place association without proof that the association is material to the consumer's decision is no longer justified, because marks rejected under § 1052(e)(3) can no longer obtain registration through acquired distinctiveness under § 1052(f). To ensure a showing of deceptiveness and misleading before imposing the penalty of non-registrability, the PTO may not deny registration without a showing that the goods-place association made by the consumer is material to the consumer's decision to purchase those goods. This addition of a materiality inquiry equates this test with the elevated standard applied under § 1052(a). See *House of Windsor,* [221 USPQ 53, 56–579 (TTAB 1983)] (establishing "a 'materiality' test to distinguish marks that fall within the proscription of Section 2(e)(2) from those that fall also within the proscription of Section 2(a)"). This also properly reflects the presence of the deceptiveness criterion often overlooked in the "primarily geographically deceptively misdescriptive" provision of the statute.

The shift in emphasis in the standard to identify primarily geographically deceptively misdescriptive marks under § 1052(e)(3) will bring that section into harmony with § 1052(a). Both sections involve proof of deception with the consequence of non-registrability. The adherence to the pre-NAFTA standard designed to focus on distinctiveness would almost read the term "deceptively" out of § 1052(e)(3), which is the term that the NAFTA amendments to the Lanham Act has reemphasized. Accordingly, under the amended Lanham Act, both subsection (a) and subsection (e)(3) share a similar legal standard * * *.

Thus, due to the NAFTA changes in the Lanham Act, the PTO must deny registration under § 1052(e)(3) if (1) the primary significance of the mark is a generally known geographic location, (2) the consuming public is likely to believe the place identified by the mark indicates the origin of the goods bearing the mark, when in fact the goods do not come from that place, and (3) the misrepresentation was a material factor in the consumer's decision.

As a result of the NAFTA changes to the Lanham Act, geographic deception is specifically dealt with in subsection (e)(3), while deception in general continues to be addressed under subsection (a). Consequently, this court anticipates that the PTO will usually address geographically deceptive marks under subsection (e)(3) of the amended Lanham Act rather than subsection (a). While there are identical legal standards for deception in each section, subsection (e)(3) specifically involves deception involving geographic marks.

III.

* * * The parties agree that CA Innovations' goods do not originate in California.

Under the first prong of the test-whether the mark's primary significance is a generally known geographic location-a composite mark such as the applicant's proposed mark must be evaluated as a whole * * *.

The Board found that "the word CALIFORNIA is a prominent part of applicant's mark and is not overshadowed by either the word INNOVATIONS or the design element." Although the mark may also convey the idea of a creative, laid-back lifestyle or mindset, the Board properly recognized that such an association does not contradict the primary geographic significance of the mark. Even if the public may associate California with a particular life-style, the record supports the Board's finding that the primary meaning remains focused on the state of California. Nonetheless, this court declines to review at this stage the Board's finding that CA Innovations' composite mark CALIFORNIA INNOVATIONS and Design is primarily geographic in nature. Rather the PTO may apply the entire new test on remand.

The second prong of the test requires proof that the public is likely to believe the applicant's goods originate in California. The Board stated that the examining attorney submitted excerpts from the Internet and the NEXIS database showing "some manufacturers and distributors of backpacks, tote bags, luggage, computer cases, and sport bags ... headquartered in California." The Board also acknowledged articles "which make reference to companies headquartered in California which manufacture automobile accessories such as auto organizers," as well as the "very serious apparel and sewn products industry" in California.

A great deal of the evidence cited in this case relates to the fashion industry, which is highly prevalent in California due to Hollywood's influence on this industry. However, clothing and fashion have nothing to do with the products in question. At best, the record in this case shows some general connection between the state of California and backpacks and automobile organizers. However, because CA Innovations has limited its appeal to insulated bags and wraps, the above referenced evidence is immaterial. Therefore, this opinion has no bearing on whether the evidence of record supports a rejection of the application with regard to any goods other than those identified in CA Innovations' application under International Class 21, namely insulated bags and wraps.

CA Innovations argues that the examining attorney provided no evidence at all concerning insulated bags for food and wraps for cans in California. The Government contends that the evidence shows some examples of a lunch bag, presumed to be insulated, and insulated backpacks. According to the government, the evidence supports a finding of a goods-place association between California and insulated bags and wraps. This court has reviewed the publications and listings supplied by the examining attorney. At best, the evidence of a connection between California and insulated bags and wraps is tenuous. Even if the evidence supported a finding of a goods-place association, the PTO has yet to apply the materiality test in this case. This court declines to address that issue and apply the new standard in the first instance. Accordingly, this court vacates the finding of the Board that CA Innovations' mark is primarily geographically deceptively misdescriptive, and remands the case for further proceedings. On remand, the Board shall apply the new three-prong standard.

NOTES

1. As the *Mountain Top* case states, the ITU application was introduced in 1989 in order to correct disadvantages the US trademarks had with respect to rest of the world. Prior to 1989, the applicant had to establish use in the United States in order to proceed with trademark prosecution. This requirement reflected the fact that trademark law in the United States follows from Congress' powers under the Commerce Clause, rather than under the Intellectual Property Clause. Other countries, however, did not have the use in commerce requirement, and therefore prosecution could proceed without actual use. This put US trademark owners at a disadvantage with respect to the rest of the world in establishing priority of rights. The ITU was implemented to cure this inequity and to put US trademark prosecution on parity with the rest of the world.

2. Notice the requirements for proof of use. These issues can arise both in prosecution and in an infringement action, as the cases show. What types of evidence are required to establish use in commerce? How does the requirement affect the development of marks and the marketing of products and services at the national level? Consider the requirement of bona fide use? How easy is this standard to meet?

3. Distinctiveness is the heart of trademark law much like originality is for copyright and novelty and nonobviousness are for patent. From reading the *Kellogg* and the *Menasche* cases, do you get the sense that the standard is easy to meet or hard? Notice that there are two types of distinctiveness: inherent distinctiveness and acquired distinctiveness through secondary meaning. For completely fabricated marks, inherent distinctiveness is easy to show. The difficulty arises with marks that are on the border between suggestive and descriptive. One way to draw that distinction is between marks

that describe literally some quality of the product or service and marks that are more metaphorical. The latter marks are suggestive. Does this way to distinguish between suggestive and descriptive marks seem consistent with the test used in *Menasche*? Is the distinction ultimately an arbitrary one?

4. The *Menasche* case illustrates the development of trademarks both in real space and in cyberspace. We will discuss cybersquatting in more detail later on in the chapter. Recognize from this case that domain names are another type of naming and registration system having to do with establishing addresses on the Internet. As we will explore in this chapter, domain name registration and trademark registration are related in ways that show how the Internet has become more commercialized over time. Do you agree with the court that there was no issue of cybersquatting in the case?

5. The *Menasche* case also offers a nice glimpse into cease and desist letter practice and into the standards for declaratory judgments. Review the case for what is required to have standing to bring a declaratory judgment suit.

6. Under 15 USC § 1052(a)–(f), some marks cannot be registered per se. These marks are of the following type:

- immoral, deceptive, or scandalous matter
- matter which may disparage or falsely suggest a connection with persons, living or dead, institutions, beliefs, or national symbols, or bring them into contempt or disrepute
- After January 1, 1995: geographic indication with respect to wines and spirits that identifies a place other than the origin of the wines or spirits
- flags, coat of arms, or insignia of the United States, of any state or municipality, or foreign nation
- name, portrait or signature of particular living person, except with consent
- name, portrait or signature of a deceased President of the United States during the life of his widow, unless the widow consents
- mark that resembles a registered mark and is likely to cause confusion, deception or mistake, unless the USPTO determines such confusion, deception, or mistake is unlikely
- mark that is primarily geographically deceptively misdescriptive of the product or service
- matter that is functional

The USPTO has recently addressed the protection of insignia of Native American tribes by creating a register of Native American tribal insignia. This register does not create any federally protected rights under trademark or other federal law. Instead, the register is used to establish notice and to prevent the registration of Native American tribal insignia that would offend the exclusions from registration under § 1052. For more information on the register, see the discussion on the USPTO website at http://www.uspto.gov/web/offices/tac/tribalfaq.htm

7. Under 15 USC § 1052(f), the following can be registered only if the applicant can show that the mark has acquired distinctiveness:

- descriptive or deceptively misdescriptive marks

- primarily geographically descriptive marks

- surname

8. A deceptively misdescriptive mark is a strange beast indeed. But think of a mark like Everready for a battery. It is misdescriptive for the battery since batteries do stop working. The mark may be deceptive for the unknowing if the fact that the battery was marketed as always ready was material to the purchasing decision. But if the mark has secondary meaning, that it has acquired distinctiveness, then it can be registered.

9. Geographic indicators are a type of mark that indicates the geographic origin of a product or service. As we will see, the United States has historically been reluctant to adopt protections for geographic indicators because of the potential anti-competitive effects. The argument against them is easy to see. If a company gets a trademark on New England Clam Chowder, then no other company that sells clam chowder from New England can use that mark without being an infringer. The second company must find some other mark that does not use New England even if that company in fact is from New England. Consumer might lose from this outcome in two ways. First, there is the possibility of reduced competition. Second, consumers may not know what the second company is selling when it starts marketing its clam chowder with a name that does not include the protected mark. Advocates for geographic indicators, however, argue that such protection is necessary to protect the authenticity of the product or service and to protect regional or local industry.

As the Federal Circuit's discussion in the *California Innovations* case indicates, courts in the United States have been hesitant to extend trademark protection to geographic marks absent a showing of secondary meaning, starting in the late Nineteenth Century with Justice Holmes opinion, from the Massachusetts Supreme Court, in *American Waltham Watch Co. v. United States Watch Co.*, 173 Mass. 85, 53 N.E. 141 (1899) (holding that manufacturer of watches with Waltham brand, indicating origin from Waltham, Mass., could enjoin competitor from use of the word Waltham if secondary meaning had been established). The requirement of secondary meaning, however, may not be consistent with requirements under international law, which mandates somewhat stronger protection. We will discuss the mandates under international law in more detail in the chapter on international law.

In order to comply with international obligations, United States trademark law protects geographic indicators in six ways. The first is through the special protection for wines and spirits after January 1, 1995. Second, geographically descriptive marks can be protected if there is secondary meaning. Third, geographically misdescriptive marks can never be protected. The last two rules should be understood together. The first of the two allows registration of the mark for the company that used New England Clam Chowder as its mark if there is secondary meaning in the mark; in other words, if an association has been established in the consumer's mind between the mark and the source. The second of the two states that if a company in Florida uses the mark New England Clam Chowder, then it cannot register the mark unless the clam chowder is made in New England. Acquired geographic associations can be the basis for the registration, but deceptive geographic associations cannot.

A fourth way in which geographic indicators obtain protection under the Lanham Act is through a § 43(a) claim for "false designation of origin." This type of claim is discussed in more detail in the sections below on trade dress and infringement.

A fifth way in which geographic indicators are protected under the Lanham Act is the protection for collective and certification marks. An element of each of these types of marks can be geographic. For example, if a trade organization calls itself the Florida Orange Growers Association, the geographic identification of the product can be protected as part of the certification or collective designation.

A sixth, and final, way for geographic indicators to be protected is through common law trademark protection. In *Institut National des Appellations d'Origine v. Brown–Forman Corp.*, 47 U.S.P.Q. 2d 1875 (TTAB 1998), the board held that the word Cognac was protected through usage as a geographic indicator for brandy that originated in France. In that case, the board was considering protection of the mark as a collective mark, but looked to common law usage to determine the meaning of the mark.

For a comparative perspective on protection of geographic indicators, see Molly Torsen, *Apples and Oranges: French and American Models of Geographic Indications Policies Demonstrate an International Lack of Consensus*, 95 Trademark Rep. 1415 (2005).

10. The *California Innovations* case offers a discussion of the history of the geographically misdescriptive category and its current application. Notice that one new, and essential, element for a rejection is material. If, in the New England Clam Chowder example, it is not material to the consumer whether the clam chowder was actually from New England, then there cannot be a rejection under 1052(e)(3). Does the materiality standard make the Lanham Act more protective or less protective of geographic indicators? Is the materiality requirement consistent with the traditional United States reluctance to protect geographic indicators or with the advocates of protection? Or is the requirement a compromise between the two positions? For an incisive analysis of the Federal Circuit's decision, see Mary LaFrance, *Innovations Palpitations: The Confusing Status of Geographic Misdescriptive Trademarks*, 12 J. INTELL. PROP. LAW. 125 (2003) (arguing that the reading of a materiality requirement into the standard for geographic misdescriptive trademarks is inconsistent with the statutory language and legislative intent of the statute). As we will see in the chapter on international law, the TRIPS requirement requires fairly strong protection for geographic indicators and the inclusion of a materiality requirement is arguably inconsistent with obligations under TRIPS.

C. WHAT COUNTS AS A TRADEMARK?

A trademark can be "any word, symbol, device or combination thereof." But does "any" encompass every? Trademark registration has been obtained for smells (for perfumes) and sounds (the famous NBC chimes), but tastes (for drinks) have been more difficult to register. These exceptions have to do, in part, with administrative issues. The trademark prosecution process requires that the mark be submitted and published. How do you publish a taste? Some of these administrative hurdles can be overcome through clever legal drafting of a description of the mark, as occurs with sound. Policy against trademark protection provides a more difficult hurdle. Since federal trademark registration, especially when the mark becomes incontestable, allows the owner to keep anyone from using the identical or similar mark in way that is likely to cause confusion among consumers, the potential market power given by trademarks is of concern, especially for trademarks of dubious distinctiveness. These issues are explored in this section by consideration of two categories of trademarks: trade dress and famous marks.

Remember in reading these cases that much of the debate over protection has to do with the requirement that the owner show secondary meaning in order to obtain protection. A requirement of secondary meaning means that protection should not be granted unless the mark has acquired distinctiveness among consumers. Essentially, the requirement of secondary meaning serves to protect consumer reliance on a mark that has been established in the marketplace.

1. Trade Dress

TWO PESOS, INC. v. TACO CABANA, INC.

Supreme Court of the United States, 1992.
505 U.S. 763, 112 S.Ct. 2753, 120 L.Ed.2d 615.

JUSTICE WHITE delivered the opinion of the Court.

The issue in this case is whether the trade dress of a restaurant may be protected under § 43(a) of the Trademark Act of 1946 (Lanham Act), based on a finding of inherent distinctiveness, without proof that the trade dress has secondary meaning.

[Author's note: The Court noted the following definition of trade dress from the jury instructions in a footnote: " '[T]rade dress' is the total image of the business. Taco Cabana's trade dress may include the shape and general appearance of the exterior of the restaurant, the identifying sign, the interior kitchen floor plan, the decor, the menu, the equipment used to serve food, the servers' uniforms and other features reflecting on the total image of the restaurant."]

Respondent Taco Cabana, Inc., operates a chain of fast-food restaurants in Texas. The restaurants serve Mexican food. The first Taco

Cabana restaurant was opened in San Antonio in September 1978, and five more restaurants had been opened in San Antonio by 1985. Taco Cabana describes its Mexican trade dress as "a festive eating atmosphere having interior dining and patio areas decorated with artifacts, bright colors, paintings and murals. The patio includes interior and exterior areas with the interior patio capable of being sealed off from the outside patio by overhead garage doors. The stepped exterior of the building is a festive and vivid color scheme using top border paint and neon stripes. Bright awnings and umbrellas continue the theme."

In December 1985, a Two Pesos, Inc., restaurant was opened in Houston. Two Pesos adopted a motif very similar to the foregoing description of Taco Cabana's trade dress. Two Pesos restaurants expanded rapidly in Houston and other markets, but did not enter San Antonio. In 1986, Taco Cabana entered the Houston and Austin markets and expanded into other Texas cities, including Dallas and El Paso where Two Pesos was also doing business.

In 1987, Taco Cabana sued Two Pesos in the United States District Court for the Southern District of Texas for trade dress infringement and for theft of trade secrets under Texas common law. The case was tried to a jury, which was instructed to return its verdict in the form of answers to five questions propounded by the trial judge. The jury's answers were: Taco Cabana has a trade dress; taken as a whole, the trade dress is nonfunctional; the trade dress is inherently distinctive; the trade dress has not acquired a secondary meaning in the Texas market; and the alleged infringement creates a likelihood of confusion on the part of ordinary customers as to the source or association of the restaurant's goods or services. Because, as the jury was told, Taco Cabana's trade dress was protected if it either was inherently distinctive or had acquired a secondary meaning, judgment was entered awarding damages to Taco Cabana. In the course of calculating damages, the trial court held that Two Pesos had intentionally and deliberately infringed Taco Cabana's trade dress.

The Court of Appeals ruled that the instructions adequately stated the applicable law and that the evidence supported the jury's findings. In particular, the Court of Appeals rejected petitioner's argument that a finding of no secondary meaning contradicted a finding of inherent distinctiveness.

In so holding, the court below followed precedent in the Fifth Circuit * * *. The Court of Appeals noted that this approach conflicts with decisions of other courts, particularly the holding of the Court of Appeals for the Second Circuit * * * that § 43(a) protects unregistered trademarks or designs only where secondary meaning is shown. We granted certiorari to resolve the conflict among the Courts of Appeals on the question whether trade dress that is inherently distinctive is protectible under § 43(a) without a showing that it has acquired secondary meaning. We find that it is, and we therefore affirm.

The Lanham Act was intended to make "actionable the deceptive and misleading use of marks" and "to protect persons engaged in ... commerce against unfair competition. Section 43(a) "prohibits a broader range of practices than does § 32," which applies to registered marks, ... but it is common ground that § 43(a) protects qualifying unregistered trademarks and that the general principles qualifying a mark for registration under § 2 of the Lanham Act are for the most part applicable in determining whether an unregistered mark is entitled to protection under § 43(a).

A trademark is defined in 15 U.S.C. § 1127 as including "any word, name, symbol, or device or any combination thereof" used by any person "to identify and distinguish his or her goods, including a unique product, from those manufactured or sold by others and to indicate the source of the goods, even if that source is unknown." In order to be registered, a mark must be capable of distinguishing the applicant's goods from those of others. § 1052. Marks are often classified in categories of generally increasing distinctiveness; following the classic formulation set out by Judge Friendly, they may be (1) generic; (2) descriptive; (3) suggestive; (4) arbitrary; or (5) fanciful. The Court of Appeals followed this classification and petitioner accepts it. The latter three categories of marks, because their intrinsic nature serves to identify a particular source of a product, are deemed inherently distinctive and are entitled to protection. In contrast, generic marks—those that "refe[r] to the genus of which the particular product is a species," * * * are not registrable as trademarks.

Marks which are merely descriptive of a product are not inherently distinctive. When used to describe a product, they do not inherently identify a particular source, and hence cannot be protected. However, descriptive marks may acquire the distinctiveness which will allow them to be protected under the Act. Section 2 of the Lanham Act provides that a descriptive mark that otherwise could not be registered under the Act may be registered if it "has become distinctive of the applicant's goods in commerce." This acquired distinctiveness is generally called "secondary meaning." The concept of secondary meaning has been applied to actions under § 43(a).

The general rule regarding distinctiveness is clear: An identifying mark is distinctive and capable of being protected if it either (1) is inherently distinctive or (2) has acquired distinctiveness through secondary meaning.

The Court of Appeals determined that the District Court's instructions were consistent with the foregoing principles and that the evidence supported the jury's verdict. Both courts thus ruled that Taco Cabana's trade dress was not descriptive but rather inherently distinctive, and that it was not functional. None of these rulings is before us in this case, and for present purposes we assume, without deciding, that each of them is correct. In going on to affirm the judgment for respondent, the Court of Appeals * * * held that Taco Cabana's inherently distinctive trade dress was entitled to protection despite the lack of proof of secondary meaning.

It is this issue that is before us for decision, and we agree with its resolution by the Court of Appeals. There is no persuasive reason to apply to trade dress a general requirement of secondary meaning which is at odds with the principles generally applicable to infringement suits under § 43(a). Petitioner devotes much of its briefing to arguing issues that are not before us, and we address only its arguments relevant to whether proof of secondary meaning is essential to qualify an inherently distinctive trade dress for protection under § 43(a).

Petitioner argues that the jury's finding that the trade dress has not acquired a secondary meaning shows conclusively that the trade dress is not inherently distinctive. The Court of Appeals' disposition of this issue was sound:

> Two Pesos' argument—that the jury finding of inherent distinctive-ness contradicts its finding of no secondary meaning in the Texas market—ignores the law in this circuit. While the necessarily imper-fect (and often prohibitively difficult) methods for assessing secondary meaning address the empirical question of current consumer associa-tion, the legal recognition of an inherently distinctive trademark or trade dress acknowledges the owner's legitimate proprietary interest in its unique and valuable informational device, regardless of whether substantial consumer association yet bestows the additional empirical protection of secondary meaning.

* * * Recognizing that a general requirement of secondary meaning imposes "an unfair prospect of theft [or] financial loss" on the developer of fanciful or arbitrary trade dress at the outset of its use, petitioner suggests that such trade dress should receive limited protection without proof of secondary meaning. Petitioner argues that such protection should be only temporary and subject to defeasance when over time the dress has failed to acquire a secondary meaning. This approach is also vulnerable for the reasons given by the Court of Appeals. If temporary protection is available from the earliest use of the trade dress, it must be because it is neither functional nor descriptive, but an inherently distinctive dress that is capable of identifying a particular source of the product. Such a trade dress, or mark, is not subject to copying by concerns that have an equal opportunity to choose their own inherently distinctive trade dress. To terminate protection for failure to gain secondary meaning over some unspecified time could not be based on the failure of the dress to retain its fanciful, arbitrary, or suggestive nature, but on the failure of the user of the dress to be successful enough in the marketplace. This is not a valid basis to find a dress or mark ineligible for protection. The user of such a trade dress should be able to maintain what competitive position it has and continue to seek wider identification among potential customers.

This brings us to the line of decisions by the Court of Appeals for the Second Circuit that would find protection for trade dress unavailable absent proof of secondary meaning, a position that petitioner concedes would have to be modified if the temporary protection that it suggests is to be recognized * * *. The Court of Appeals held that unregistered marks did not enjoy the "presumptive source association" enjoyed by registered marks and hence could not qualify for protection under § 43(a) without proof of secondary meaning. The court's rationale seemingly denied protection for unregistered, but inherently distinctive, marks of all kinds, whether the claimed mark used distinctive words or symbols or distinctive product design. The court thus did not accept the arguments that an unregistered mark was capable of identifying a source and that copying such a mark could be making any kind of a false statement or representation under § 43(a).

This holding is in considerable tension with the provisions of the Lanham Act. If a verbal or symbolic mark or the features of a product design may be registered under § 2, it necessarily is a mark "by which the goods of the applicant may be distinguished from the goods of others," 60 Stat. 428, and must be registered unless otherwise disqualified. Since § 2 requires secondary meaning only as a condition to registering descriptive marks, there are plainly marks that are registrable without showing secondary meaning. These same marks, even if not registered, remain inherently capable of distinguishing the goods of the users of these marks. Furthermore, the copier of such a mark may be seen as falsely claiming that his products may for some reason be thought of as originating from the plaintiff.

The Fifth Circuit was quite right, * * * in this case, to follow the *Abercrombie* classifications consistently and to inquire whether trade dress for which protection is claimed under § 43(a) is inherently distinctive. If it is, it is capable of identifying products or services as coming from a specific source and secondary meaning is not required. This is the rule generally applicable to trademarks, and the protection of trademarks and trade dress under § 43(a) serves the same statutory purpose of preventing deception and unfair competition. There is no persuasive reason to apply different analysis to the two.

It would be a different matter if there were textual basis in § 43(a) for treating inherently distinctive verbal or symbolic trademarks differently from inherently distinctive trade dress. But there is none. The section does not mention trademarks or trade dress, whether they be called generic, descriptive, suggestive, arbitrary, fanciful, or functional. Nor does the concept of secondary meaning appear in the text of § 43(a). Where secondary meaning does appear in the statute, 15 U.S.C. § 1052 (1982 ed.), it is a requirement that applies only to merely descriptive marks and not to inherently distinctive ones. We see no basis for requiring secondary meaning for inherently distinctive trade dress protection under § 43(a) but not for other distinctive words, symbols, or devices capable of identifying a producer's product.

Engrafting onto § 43(a) a requirement of secondary meaning for inherently distinctive trade dress also would undermine the purposes of the Lanham Act. Protection of trade dress, no less than of trademarks, serves the Act's purpose to "secure to the owner of the mark the goodwill of his business and to protect the ability of consumers to distinguish among competing producers. National protection of trademarks is desirable, Congress concluded, because trademarks foster competition and the maintenance of quality by securing to the producer the benefits of good reputation." By making more difficult the identification of a producer with its product, a secondary meaning requirement for a nondescriptive trade dress would hinder improving or maintaining the producer's competitive position.

Suggestions that under the Fifth Circuit's law, the initial user of any shape or design would cut off competition from products of like design and shape are not persuasive. Only nonfunctional, distinctive trade dress is protected under § 43(a). The Fifth Circuit holds that a design is legally functional, and thus unprotectible, if it is one of a limited number of equally efficient options available to competitors and free competition would be unduly hindered by according the design trademark protection. This serves to assure that competition will not be stifled by the exhaustion of a limited number of trade dresses.

On the other hand, adding a secondary meaning requirement could have anticompetitive effects, creating particular burdens on the startup of small companies. It would present special difficulties for a business, such as respondent, that seeks to start a new product in a limited area and then expand into new markets. Denying protection for inherently distinctive nonfunctional trade dress until after secondary meaning has been established would allow a competitor, which has not adopted a distinctive trade dress of its own, to appropriate the originator's dress in other markets and to deter the originator from expanding into and competing in these areas.

As noted above, petitioner concedes that protecting an inherently distinctive trade dress from its inception may be critical to new entrants to the market and that withholding protection until secondary meaning has been established would be contrary to the goals of the Lanham Act. Petitioner specifically suggests, however, that the solution is to dispense with the requirement of secondary meaning for a reasonable, but brief, period at the outset of the use of a trade dress. If § 43(a) does not require secondary meaning at the outset of a business' adoption of trade dress, there is no basis in the statute to support the suggestion that such a requirement comes into being after some unspecified time.

JUSTICE THOMAS, concurring in the judgment.

Section 43(a) made actionable (before being amended) "any false description or representation, including words or other symbols tending falsely to describe or represent," when "use[d] in connection with any goods or services." This language codified, among other things, the related common-law torts of technical trademark infringement and passing off.

At common law, words or symbols that were arbitrary, fanciful, or suggestive (called "inherently distinctive" words or symbols, or "trademarks") were presumed to represent the source of a product, and the first user of a trademark could sue to protect it without having to show that the word or symbol represented the product's source in fact. That presumption did not attach to personal or geographic names or to words or symbols that only described a product (called "trade names"), and the user of a personal or geographic name or of a descriptive word or symbol could obtain relief only if he first showed that his trade name did in fact represent not just the product, but a producer (that the good or service had developed "secondary meaning"). Trade dress, which consists not of words or symbols, but of a product's packaging (or "image," more broadly), seems at common law to have been thought incapable ever of being inherently distinctive, perhaps on the theory that the number of ways to package a product is finite. Thus, a user of trade dress would always have had to show secondary meaning in order to obtain protection.

Over time, judges have come to conclude that packages or images may be as arbitrary, fanciful, or suggestive as words or symbols, their numbers limited only by the human imagination. A particular trade dress, then, is now considered as fully capable as a particular trademark of serving as a "representation or designation" of source under § 43(a). As a result, the first user of an arbitrary package, like the first user of an arbitrary word, should be entitled to the presumption that his package represents him without having to show that it does so in fact. This rule follows, in my view, from the language of § 43(a), and this rule applies under that section without regard to the rules that apply under the sections of the Lanham Act that deal with registration.

WAL–MART STORES, INC. v. SAMARA BROTHERS, INC.

Supreme Court of the United States, 2000.
529 U.S. 205, 120 S.Ct. 1339, 146 L.Ed.2d 182.

JUSTICE SCALIA delivered the opinion of the Court.

In this case, we decide under what circumstances a product's design is distinctive, and therefore protectible, in an action for infringement of unregistered trade dress under § 43(a).

Respondent Samara Brothers, Inc., designs and manufactures children's clothing. Its primary product is a line of spring/summer one-piece seersucker outfits decorated with appliques of hearts, flowers, fruits, and the like. A number of chain stores, including JCPenney, sell this line of clothing under contract with Samara.

Petitioner Wal–Mart Stores, Inc., is one of the Nation's best known retailers, selling among other things children's clothing. In 1995, Wal–Mart contracted with one of its suppliers, Judy–Philippine, Inc., to manufacture a line of children's outfits for sale in the 1996 spring/summer season. Wal–Mart sent Judy–Philippine photographs of a number of garments from Samara's line, on which Judy–Philippine's garments were to be based; Judy–Philippine duly copied, with only minor modifications, 16 of Samara's garments, many of which contained copyrighted elements.

In 1996, Wal–Mart briskly sold the so-called knockoffs, generating more than $1.15 million in gross profits.

In June 1996, a buyer for JCPenney called a representative at Samara to complain that she had seen Samara garments on sale at Wal–Mart for a lower price than JCPenney was allowed to charge under its contract with Samara. The Samara representative told the buyer that Samara did not supply its clothing to Wal–Mart. Their suspicions aroused, however, Samara officials launched an investigation, which disclosed that Wal–Mart and several other major retailers—Kmart, Caldor, Hills, and Goody's— were selling the knockoffs of Samara's outfits produced by Judy–Philippine.

After sending cease-and-desist letters, Samara brought this action in the United States District Court for the Southern District of New York against Wal–Mart, Judy–Philippine, Kmart, Caldor, Hills, and Goody's for copyright infringement under federal law, consumer fraud and unfair competition under New York law, and—most relevant for our purposes— infringement of unregistered trade dress under § 43(a). All of the defendants except Wal–Mart settled before trial.

After a weeklong trial, the jury found in favor of Samara on all of its claims. Wal–Mart then renewed a motion for judgment as a matter of law, claiming, inter alia, that there was insufficient evidence to support a conclusion that Samara's clothing designs could be legally protected as distinctive trade dress for purposes of § 43(a). The District Court denied the motion and awarded Samara damages, interest, costs, and fees totaling almost $1.6 million, together with injunctive relief. The Second Circuit affirmed and we granted certiorari.

The Lanham Act provides for the registration of trademarks, which it defines in § 45 to include "any word, name, symbol, or device, or any combination thereof [used or intended to be used] to identify and distinguish [a producer's] goods ... from those manufactured or sold by others and to indicate the source of the goods...." 15 U.S.C. § 1127. Registration of a mark under § 2 of the Lanham Act, 15 U.S.C. § 1052, enables the owner to sue an infringer under § 32, 15 U.S.C. § 1114; it also entitles the owner to a presumption that its mark is valid, see § 7(b), 15 U.S.C. § 1057(b), and ordinarily renders the registered mark incontestable after five years of continuous use, see § 15, 15 U.S.C. § 1065. In addition to protecting registered marks, the Lanham Act, in § 43(a), gives a producer a cause of action for the use by any person of "any word, term, name, symbol, or device, or any combination thereof ... which ... is likely to cause confusion ... as to the origin, sponsorship, or approval of his or her goods...." 15 U.S.C. § 1125(a). It is the latter provision that is at issue in this case.

The breadth of the definition of marks registrable under § 2, and of the confusion-producing elements recited as actionable by § 43(a), has been held to embrace not just word marks, such as "Nike," and symbol marks, such as Nike's "swoosh" symbol, but also "trade dress"—a category that originally included only the packaging, or "dressing," of a product, but in recent years has been expanded by many Courts of Appeals to encompass the design of a product.

The text of § 43(a) provides little guidance as to the circumstances under which unregistered trade dress may be protected. It does require that a producer show that the allegedly infringing feature is not "functional," see § 43(a)(3), and is likely to cause confusion with the product for which protection is sought, see § 43(a)(1)(A), 15 U.S.C. § 1125(a)(1)(A). Nothing in § 43(a) explicitly requires a producer to show that its trade dress is distinctive, but courts have universally imposed that requirement, since without distinctiveness the trade dress would not "cause confusion . . . as to the origin, sponsorship, or approval of [the] goods," as the section requires. Distinctiveness is, moreover, an explicit prerequisite for registration of trade dress under § 2, and "the general principles qualifying a mark for registration under § 2 of the Lanham Act are for the most part applicable in determining whether an unregistered mark is entitled to protection under § 43(a)." *Two Pesos, Inc. v. Taco Cabana, Inc.*, 505 U.S. 763, 768 (1992) (citations omitted).

In evaluating the distinctiveness of a mark under § 2 (and therefore, by analogy, under § 43(a)), courts have held that a mark can be distinctive in one of two ways. First, a mark is inherently distinctive if "[its] intrinsic nature serves to identify a particular source." Ibid. In the context of word marks, courts have applied the now-classic test originally formulated by Judge Friendly, in which word marks that are "arbitrary" ("Camel" cigarettes), "fanciful" ("Kodak" film), or "suggestive" ("Tide" laundry detergent) are held to be inherently distinctive. Second, a mark has acquired distinctiveness, even if it is not inherently distinctive, if it has developed secondary meaning, which occurs when, "in the minds of the public, the primary significance of a [mark] is to identify the source of the product rather than the product itself."

[Author's note: The Court, in a footnote, discussed secondary meaning as follows: "The phrase 'secondary meaning' originally arose in the context of word marks, where it served to distinguish the source-identifying meaning from the ordinary, or 'primary,' meaning of the word. 'Secondary meaning' has since come to refer to the acquired, source-identifying meaning of a nonword mark as well. It is often a misnomer in that context, since nonword marks ordinarily have no 'primary' meaning. Clarity might well be served by using the term 'acquired meaning' in both the word-mark and the nonword-mark contexts—but in this opinion we follow what has become the conventional terminology."]

The judicial differentiation between marks that are inherently distinctive and those that have developed secondary meaning has solid foundation in the statute itself. Section 2 requires that registration be granted to any trademark "by which the goods of the applicant may be distinguished from the goods of others"—subject to various limited exceptions. It also provides, again with limited exceptions, that "nothing in this chapter shall prevent the registration of a mark used by the applicant which has become distinctive of the applicant's goods in commerce"—that is, which is not inherently distinctive but has become so only through secondary meaning. Nothing in § 2, however, demands the conclusion that every category of mark necessarily includes some marks "by which the goods of the applicant may be distinguished from the goods of others" without secondary meaning—that in every category some marks are inherently distinctive.

Indeed, with respect to at least one category of mark—colors—we have held that no mark can ever be inherently distinctive. [In *Qualitex Co. v. Jacobson Products Co.*, 514 U.S. 159 (1995)], petitioner manufactured and sold green-gold dry-cleaning press pads. After respondent began selling pads of a similar color, petitioner brought suit under § 43(a), then added a claim under § 32 after obtaining registration for the color of its pads. We held that a color could be protected as a trademark, but only upon a showing of secondary meaning. Reasoning by analogy to the *Abercrombie & Fitch* test developed for word marks, we noted that a product's color is unlike a "fanciful," "arbitrary," or "suggestive" mark, since it does not "almost automatically tell a customer that [it] refer[s] to a brand." However, we noted that, "over time, customers may come to treat a particular color on a product or its packaging . . . as signifying a brand." Because a color, like a "descriptive" word mark, could eventually "come to indicate a product's origin," we concluded that it could be protected upon a showing of secondary meaning.

It seems to us that design, like color, is not inherently distinctive. The attribution of inherent distinctiveness to certain categories of word marks and product packaging derives from the fact that the very purpose of attaching a particular word to a product, or encasing it in a distinctive packaging, is most often to identify the source of the product. Although the words and packaging can serve subsidiary functions—a suggestive word mark (such as "Tide" for laundry detergent), for instance, may invoke positive connotations in the consumer's mind, and a garish form of packaging (such as Tide's squat, brightly decorated plastic bottles for its liquid laundry detergent) may attract an otherwise indifferent consumer's attention on a crowded store shelf—their predominant function remains source identification. Consumers are therefore predisposed to regard those symbols as indication of the producer, which is why such symbols "almost automatically tell a customer that they refer to a brand," and "immediately . . . signal a brand or a product 'source'". And where it is not reasonable to assume consumer predisposition to take an affixed word or packaging as indication of source—where, for example, the affixed word is descriptive of the product ("Tasty" bread) or of a geographic origin ("Georgia" peaches)—inherent distinctiveness will not be found. That is why the statute generally excludes, from those word marks that can be registered as inherently distinctive, words that are "merely descriptive" of the goods or "primarily geographically descriptive of them." In the case of product design, as in the case of color, we think consumer predisposition to equate the feature with the source does not exist. Consumers are aware of the reality that, almost invariably, even the most unusual of product designs—such as a cocktail shaker shaped like a penguin—is intended not to identify the source, but to render the product itself more useful or more appealing.

The fact that product design almost invariably serves purposes other than source identification not only renders inherent distinctiveness problematic; it also renders application of an inherent-distinctiveness principle more harmful to other consumer interests. Consumers should not be deprived of the benefits of competition with regard to the utilitarian and esthetic purposes that product design ordinarily serves by a rule of law that facilitates plausible threats of suit against new entrants based upon alleged inherent distinctiveness. How easy it is to mount a plausible suit depends, of course, upon the clarity of the test for inherent distinctiveness, and where product design is concerned we have little confidence that a reasonably clear test can be devised.

It is true, of course, that the person seeking to exclude new entrants would have to establish the nonfunctionality of the design feature. Competition is deterred, however, not merely by successful suit but by the plausible threat of successful suit, and given the unlikelihood of inherently source-identifying design, the game of allowing suit based upon alleged inherent distinctiveness seems to us not worth the candle. That is especially so since the producer can ordinarily obtain protection for a design that is inherently source identifying (if any such exists), but that does not yet have secondary meaning, by securing a design patent or a copyright for the design—as, indeed, respondent did for certain elements of the designs in this case. The availability of these other protections greatly reduces any harm to the producer that might ensue from our conclusion that a product design cannot be protected under § 43(a) without a showing of secondary meaning.

Respondent contends that our decision in *Two Pesos* forecloses a conclusion that product-design trade dress can never be inherently distinctive. In that case, we held that the trade dress of a chain of Mexican restaurants, which the plaintiff described as "a festive eating atmosphere having interior dining and patio areas decorated with artifacts, bright colors, paintings and murals," could be protected under § 43(a) without a showing of secondary meaning. *Two Pesos* unquestionably establishes the legal principle that trade dress can be inherently distinctive, but it does not establish that product-design trade dress can be. Two Pesos is inapposite to our holding here because the trade dress at issue, the decor of a restaurant, seems to us not to constitute product design. It was either product packaging—which, as we have discussed, normally is taken by the consumer to indicate origin—or else some tertium quid that is akin to product packaging and has no bearing on the present case.

Respondent replies that this manner of distinguishing *Two Pesos* will force courts to draw difficult lines between product-design and product-packaging trade dress. There will indeed be some hard cases at the margin: a classic glass Coca–Cola bottle, for instance, may constitute packaging for those consumers who drink the Coke and then discard the bottle, but may constitute the product itself for those consumers who are bottle collectors, or part of the product itself for those consumers who buy Coke in the classic glass bottle, rather than a can, because they think it more stylish to drink from the former. We believe, however, that the frequency and the difficulty of having to distinguish between product design and product packaging will be much less than the frequency and the difficulty of having to decide when a product design is inherently distinctive. To the extent there are close cases, we believe that courts should err on the side of caution and classify ambiguous trade dress as product design, thereby requiring secondary meaning. The very closeness will suggest the existence of relatively small utility in adopting an inherent-distinctiveness principle, and relatively great consumer benefit in requiring a demonstration of secondary meaning.

We hold that, in an action for infringement of unregistered trade dress under § 43(a) of the Lanham Act, a product's design is distinctive, and therefore protectible, only upon a showing of secondary meaning. The judgment of the Second Circuit is reversed, and the case is remanded for further proceedings consistent with this opinion.

2. Famous Marks

THANE INTERNATIONAL, INC. v. TREK BICYCLE CORPORATION

United States Court of Appeals, Ninth Circuit, 2002.
305 F.3d 894.

BERZON, CIRCUIT JUDGE

Background

I. Trek

Trek, a Wisconsin corporation, has manufactured bicycles under the TREK mark since 1977. Trek also uses the TREK label on a variety of bicycle accessories including clothing, hats, packs, wrist watches, bags, video games, toys, computer games, helmets, and gloves. In all, Trek identifies over 1,000 products with the TREK mark. Trek products are sold through more than 1,600 independent dealers in 2,000 locations across the country. Surveys published in Bicycling Magazine in 1995, 1997, and 1999, each indicate that, according to the magazine's subscribers, Trek is the country's most popular and most respected bicycle brand.

In 1981, Trek was granted a United States trademark for the use of TREK on bicycles and bicycle frames. Since then, Trek has been awarded several other trademarks based on variations of the word "trek" including: "TREKKING" in 1996 for bicycles; "TREK 100" in 1996 for providing support services during charitable bicycle rides; "TREK BMX" in 1998 for bicycles and bicycle frames; and "ELEC TREK" in 1999 for bicycles, bicycle frames and parts. Additionally, Trek registered TREK on May 12, 1997, for "exercise equipment, namely stationary exercise cycles."

Trek spends between $3 million and $5 million per year on advertising. Publications including Rolling Stone Magazine, Men's Journal, Outside Magazine, Spin, Playboy, Women's Sport & Fitness, Bicycling Magazine, Mountain Bike, Backpacker, and Velonews run Trek's ads. Trek estimates that its website attracts 4.5 million visitors annually. Trek's other advertising comes through a variety of promotional efforts, including sponsoring athletes to use its equipment. The most prominent athlete Trek sponsors is cancer-survivor Lance Armstrong, who has used TREK bicycles to capture several Tour de France titles. The world press has chronicled Armstrong's victories, generating considerable publicity for Trek. Pictures of Armstrong with a TREK bicycle have appeared in The New York Times and on Wheaties boxes. When Armstrong presented a TREK bicycle to President Clinton, coverage of that event also made its way into papers across the country.

In 1993, Trek entered the stationary exercise machine market by introducing six models of exercise bikes bearing the TREK mark. Thane maintains that this venture was a failure. Three years later, Trek sold its TREK Fitness line to Vision Fitness, a small company founded by two former Trek employees. The transaction included a license allowing Vision Fitness to use the TREK mark for exercise equipment until September 1997. Trek claims that some dealers continued to advertise and sell stationary exercise cycles bearing the TREK logo through March 31, 1999.

In January 1998, Trek began considering another foray into the stationary exercise machine market by preparing a "new product evaluation" for a new stationary trainer. This stationary trainer would not have pedals, a seat, or handlebars. Instead, the device would allow the user to convert her mobile bicycle into a stationary one for indoor use. At the time of the summary judgment motions, Trek planned to begin selling these trainers in the summer of 2000.

II. Thane

Based in La Quinta, California, Thane operates in the "direct response marketing" field. It airs lengthy "infomercials" on television broadcast and cable stations, encouraging viewers to use the telephone, direct mail, or the Internet to purchase products directly from Thane.

In 1997, Thane developed the OrbiTrek, characterized as a "dual directional elliptical glider stationary exercise machine for indoor use." The OrbiTrek has rectangular platform pedals large enough to support a person's entire foot. The pedals move in an elliptical motion "designed to simulate the body's natural stride." Movable handlebars extend straight up from the OrbiTrek's base and provide upper body exercise. The OrbiTrek has no seat, because it is meant to be used while standing.

Thane began airing its 28–minute infomercial for the OrbiTrek in December 1997. The infomercial stated that the OrbiTrek sells for the "unbelievable price of only \$299.95," but if you "[c]all right now [ ] the exciting new OrbiTrek will be shipped to you immediately for the unheard of low price of only \$199.95."

Thane explains that the Trek part of the OrbiTrek mark had an inspiration entirely independent of Trek bicycles and other equipment. Thane's executive vice-president, Denise DuBarry, was married to an actor who appeared in the original pilot for the television Star Trek show. DuBarry has long watched the Star Trek television series and attended Star Trek conventions. By using a word associated with Star Trek, Thane believes it depicts the OrbiTrek as a "space-age, high-tech, and futuristic product." Indeed, Thane claims none of its employees had heard of TREK bicycles prior to the current dispute. Thane did not perform a trademark search for TREK before adopting OrbiTrek as the name for its exercise machine.

III. Proceedings

Thane filed an application with the United States Patent and Trademark Office to register "ORBITREK" for goods described as "stationary exercise machines." Trek thereupon filed a Notice of Opposition with the Trademark Trial and Appeal Board. On February 11, 1999, Thane filed a complaint and demand for jury trial in federal district court, seeking a declaration that it had not violated trademark laws under the Lanham Act, state common law, or state statutory law. Trek responded with a counter-claim and demand for jury trial. Its opposition to Thane's trademark application was suspended pending the outcome of this case.

The parties then filed cross-motions for summary judgment on all claims. The district court granted Thane's motion for summary judgment and denied Trek's, holding that "any reasonable juror would conclude that there is no likelihood of confusion between Trek Bicycle Corporation's 'Trek' mark and Thane's 'OrbiTrek' mark." Trek now appeals the district court's denial of its summary judgment motion and the district court's grant of Thane's summary judgment motion.

[Author's Note: The court reversed the grant of summary judgment for Thane, finding that a reasonable jury could find a likelihood of confusion under the Polaroid/Lapp/Sleekcraft factors for trademark infringement that we will discuss in the next section. The court remanded for a trial on trademark infringement. The court also considered the dilution claim which requires that the mark be famous. The court's analysis of what constitutes a famous mark follows. Note that we will discuss the dilution cause of action in greater detail in the next section.]

* * *

B. Famousness

Aside from establishing the identity or near identity of the marks, a party alleging dilution must satisfactorily prove that "(1) its mark is famous; (2) the defendant is making commercial use of the mark in commerce; (3) the defendant's use began after the plaintiff's mark became famous; and (4) the defendant's use presents a likelihood of dilution of the distinctive value of the mark." As we conclude that a reasonable factfinder could not find TREK famous in any relevant market segment, we need not proceed beyond the first prong of this inquiry.

(1) General Principles: The federal anti-dilution statute limits protection to the owners "of a famous mark." § 1125(c)(1). To help "determin[e] whether a mark is distinctive and famous," the statute, in keeping with trademark law's apparent penchant for flexible eight-factor tests, lists eight non-exclusive factors "a court may consider." § 1125(c)(1). The only case in this circuit [*Avery Dennison Corp. v. Sumpton*, 189 F.3d 868, 875 (9th Cir.1999)] to explicate the "famousness" requirement stressed that fame in the dilution context must be very narrow: "Dilution is a cause of action invented and reserved for a select class of marks—those marks with such powerful consumer associations that even non-competing uses can impinge their value." As a result, "to meet the famousness element of protection under the dilution statutes a mark must be truly prominent and renowned."

This limitation on dilution protection created by the narrow definition of famousness, like the identical or nearly identical requirement already discussed, is critical. Antidilution is "the most potent form of trademark protection" and has the potential of "over-protecting trademarks." Further, the concept of dilution is more abstract than the concept of trademark infringement, which is anchored by the likelihood of confusion standard. Absent strict policing of the famousness requirement, neither participants in the commercial market-place nor courts are likely to apply dilution statutes in a predictable fashion. It is one thing to determine whether consumers are likely to transfer associations evoked by a truly famous mark to an unrelated product; we can say with some certainty that nearly anyone in the civilized world buying a product titled "Coca–Cola" will associate that product with the soft drink, its packaging, and its advertisements. It is quite another to determine whether a less well known mark will evoke such associations. With respect to less well known marks, inquiries into consumers' mindsets become fuzzier, as likely associations become more dependent on individual backgrounds and experiences.

(2) Fame in a Niche Market: Despite its repeated admonition that only truly prominent and renowned marks deserve protection under § 1125(c)(1), *Avery Dennison* held that marks famous in only a limited geographic area or a specialized market segment can be "famous" for the purposes of the federal anti-dilution statute. We are bound by *Avery Dennison* to accept and apply the niche fame concept, despite its apparent tension with *Avery Dennison*'s overall message cautioning restraint in applying dilution protections.

Niche fame protection is, however, limited. The statute protects a mark only when a mark is famous within a niche market and the alleged diluter uses the mark within that niche.

Applying that concept here, we conclude, first, that a reasonable fact-finder could find that Trek and Thane operate in the same "narrow market segment." *Avery Dennison* indicated that a company providing integrated customer care to telephone and Internet customers operates in the same market segment as a company that provides engineering and installation services to the telecommunications industry. Similarly, a factfinder could conclude that stationary exercise bicycle manufacturers and stationary elliptical trainer manufacturers share the same market segment.

A reasonable factfinder could not, however, conclude that mobile bicycles and elliptical orbit machines operate in the same narrow market segment for purposes of the niche fame concept, although both products can be used for exercise. To maintain coherence, the niche fame concept must focus on highly specialized market segments with an identifiable customer base. Where those conditions obtain, participants are likely to make associations between marks that the general public will not make. As the market segments in which the senior and junior products operate become less specialized and less unitary, the notion that participants in those diverse markets will necessarily recognize and form mental associations with an established mark becomes increasingly questionable.

In this case, the smallest market segment that bicycles and elliptical orbit machines could be said to share is the sporting goods market. This is a widely diverse market that encompasses everything from football helmets to ice skates. There is no reason why participants in this broad market will have any particular knowledge about products in submarkets in which they do not participate.

Although a factfinder could conclude that stationary exercise bicycle manufacturers and stationary elliptical trainer manufacturers share the same market segment, it could not reasonably find that TREK is a famous mark in that niche market segment, as opposed to in the market segment frequented by bicycle enthusiasts. One of the eight statutory factors for adjudging famousness is "the duration and extent of use of the mark in connection with the goods and services with which the mark is used." § 1125(c)(1)(B). Trek stationary bicycles were sold for a fairly short time. If not extinct at the time OrbiTrek began selling its elliptical exercise machines, they were at least a threatened species.

Any future plans Trek may have had to reenter the stationary exercise machine market is not pertinent to the famousness inquiry. The federal statute applies only if the junior use "begins after the mark has become famous." § 1125(c)(1). Therefore, any fame Trek may acquire for its mark in the future in the stationary exercise machine market could not preclude OrbiTrek from using its mark in that market.

Where famousness is the question, the extent and duration of the use of a mark within a particular market segment will often be dispositive. No matter the degree of distinctiveness, § 1125(c)(1)(A), the geographic reach of the mark in the pertinent market segment, § 1125(c)(1)(D), the extent to which third parties use similar marks, § 1125(c)(1)(G), or the registration status of the mark, § 1125(c)(1)(H), a mark that is not widely associated with a particular product within a particular niche market is almost surely not famous in that market. The focus of the antidilution statute is on preventing junior users from appropriating or distorting the goodwill and positive associations that a famous mark has developed over the years. Where there has been no successful, long-term development of goodwill with respect to particular markets, asserting fame within that specialized market is simply inconsistent with the purpose of the antidilution protection.

[Author's Note: In a footnote, the court addressed the statutory factors to determine a famous mark as follows: The other three statutory fame factors are either not pertinent here or have already been taken into account implicitly in the above analysis. There is no record evidence concerning the "duration and extent of advertising and publicity" of the TREK mark within the stationary exercise equipment market. As to factors five and six—the "channels of trade" for Trek stationary exercise equipment and the degree of recognition of the TREK mark in Trek's trading channels and areas and in Thane's, § 1125(c)(1)(E) & (F)—the niche fame analysis subsumes those factors by focusing exclusively on the areas of overlap between the channels of trade and trading areas for the two products.]

Trek, it is true, primarily sells bicycles and bicycle accessories, and the evidence is more than sufficient to allow a trier of fact to find that TREK is a famous mark within the narrow market segment devoted to non-stationary bicycle production and sales. But there is no reason to expect that the typical purchaser of stationary exercise machines—particularly those who buy their exercise machines as a result of seeing television infomercials—buys bicycles or bicycle-related products, reads bicycle magazines or watches bicycle competitions on television, any more than anybody else does. That the mark "TREK" is famous with bicycle enthusiasts is therefore of little pertinence in gauging the fame of the mark in the market segment occupied by Thane, the junior user.

(3) Fame Outside a Niche Market: Finally, we consider whether TREK is famous outside any specialized market. While the antidilution statute can protect marks under the niche fame concept from dilution within their specialized markets, the main thrust of the statute is to provide select marks with broad anti-appropriation protection both within and beyond their specialized markets. Such protection is both more potent and more difficult to obtain than niche fame protection. It is more potent because, with important exceptions, § 1125(c)(4), the statute prohibits the use of its mark by any business, regardless of its industry or location. And it is more difficult to obtain because a finding of fame within only a specialized market is not sufficient for protection outside the niche fame context.

The statute does not indicate just how famous a mark must be in order to benefit from the anti-dilution statute's general protection. § 1125(c). As the Second Circuit has observed, "the word 'famous' is susceptible to widely different understandings," including some that would deem a mark famous even if only a small fraction of the population has heard of it. If § 1125(c) provided protection to marks that were famous under these broader understandings, the statute would have a crippling effect on the marketing of products, as more and more marks would be off limits for use in any market.

Because some limitation on what qualifies as famous is necessary and because the statutory language provides no guidance in shaping this limitation, Congress likely passed § 1125(c) "counting on courts to understand the legislature's intentions and to interpret the word or phrase in a sensible manner to carry out those intentions." To conduct this task we turn to a consideration of the statute's purposes, as expressed in its legislative history.

The legislative history does not contain an express statement regarding how famous a mark must be to merit protection, but it does provide lengthy explanations into the statute's purposes. These purposes provide significant insight into the famousness threshold Congress intended.

Congress passed the anti-dilution measure seeking to protect unauthorized users of famous marks from "attempt[ing] to trade upon the goodwill and established renown of such marks," regardless of whether such use causes a likelihood of confusion about the product's origin. The legislative history speaks of protecting those marks that have an "aura" and explains that the harm from dilution occurs "when the unauthorized use of a famous mark reduces the public's perception that the mark signifies something unique, singular, or particular." For example, such harm occurs in the hypothetical cases of "DUPONT shoes, BUICK aspirin, and KODAK pianos," according to the legislative history.

It is clear, then, that for the harm envisioned by Congress to occur, a mark must have achieved enough fame that someone operating a business in a completely different industry than the mark owner could reasonably believe that the mark possesses goodwill from which he could benefit. Congress' hypothetical piano manufacturer can free ride on the aura imbued in KODAK only because potential piano buyers have positive associations with that mark. These potential piano purchasers have warm feelings for KODAK not because the piano and photography industries have any particular overlap—they do not—but because KODAK has achieved fame throughout the population at large. Because the general public, and not just those with special knowledge about photography, perceive KODAK as unique, businesses in all industries may be tempted to trade on KODAK's name.

Thus, only marks that have achieved fame among the general consuming public, as opposed to a more particularized segment of the public, are susceptible to the kind of out-of-market free riding that Congress sought to prevent in passing the antidilution statute. Marks that have not achieved such fame are not susceptible to this free riding outside their own narrow market segment. If a piano manufacturer selects the mark of a photography business little known by the general public but well known to photographers, the piano firm will not benefit much from the goodwill associated with that mark, given the small number of professional photographers in the world. Most of the piano firm's potential customers will not have heard of the mark and will thus have no preconceived perception that the mark symbolizes something "unique, singular, or particular."

In short, for purposes of § 1125(c), a mark usually will achieve broad-based fame only if a large portion of the general consuming public recognizes that mark. Put another way, as a district court recently did, the mark must be a household name.

In many cases, the list of famousness factors contained in the statute can be quite useful in assisting a fact-finder to determine whether a mark is famous. § 1125(c)(1)(A) to (H). But the party seeking protection must initially make at least a minimal showing of the requisite level of fame. In this case, Trek has presented no evidence that its TREK mark has achieved fame among the general consuming public, as opposed to simply among bicycle enthusiasts.

The closest Trek has come to demonstrating this type of fame has been to produce evidence showing that the champion bicycle racer Lance Armstrong has often been pictured with a Trek bicycle in prominent displays, such as the front page of large circulation newspapers and on Wheaties boxes. This incidental appearance of a Trek bicycle does not by itself constitute evidence that the bicycle brand is famous. Many products receive broad incidental media coverage. Such promotion does not lead to the conclusion that their trademarks have become a part of the collective national consciousness. On the other hand, surveys showing that a large percentage of the general public recognizes the brand, press accounts about the popularity of the brand, or pop-culture references involving the brand would provide evidence of fame.

According to the continuum typically used to determine the distinctiveness or "strength" of a mark, TREK is a suggestive mark because "trek" means a long journey, and one can undertake a long journey on a bicycle. See *Entrepreneur,* [279 F.3d 1135, 1141 (9th Cir. 2002)]. As a suggestive mark, TREK has more distinctiveness than a merely descriptive mark and deserves some trademark protection. However, it does not belong to the highest category of distinctiveness, that reserved for arbitrary and fanciful marks, and thus does not deserve as much protection. Id. Because famousness is such a hard standard to achieve, the fact that TREK does not belong to this highest category of distinctiveness indicates—although it does not compel the conclusion—that TREK is not famous.

Similarly, the famousness factor suggesting that courts consider "the nature and extent of use of the same or similar marks by third parties," also strongly suggests that TREK is not famous. § 1125(c)(1)(G). Although the parties dispute how much third party use of the word "trek" exists, it is clear that others have incorporated this common English language word into their trademark. Notably, the "Star Trek" television and movie series have developed a cult following of considerable size. The glow of this celebrity makes it difficult for Trek to obtain fame using the same word.

Because TREK has produced no evidence from which a reasonable fact-finder could find that TREK is famous among members of the general consuming public, we conclude that, for reasons different from those given by the district court, Trek's dilution cause of action cannot succeed. Summary judgment was properly granted to OrbiTrek on that cause of action.

NOTES

1. The *Taco Cabana* decision provides a discussion of Section 43(a) of the Lanham Act and the concept of trade dress. What is trade dress? Is it the general impression of a restaurant? Or a compilation of parts that add up to whole? Think of other examples of trade dress. Would the design of a telephone, say in the shape of an animal or a cartoon character constitute trade dress? What about the layout of a newspaper or a web page? for a critical treatment of the Lanham Act's treatment of trade dress, see Glynn S. Lunney, Jr., *The Trade Dress Emperor's New Clothes: Why Trade Dress Does Not Belong On the Principal Register*, 51 Hastings L. J. 1131 (2000). For the argument that there is a tendency towards coherence in the case law on trade dress, especially in the development of a functionality doctrine, see Mark Alan Thurmon, *The Rise and Fall of Trademark Law's Functionality Doctrine*, 56 FLA. L. REV. 243 (2004).

2. What makes the trade dress in *Taco Cabana* inherently distinctive? Notice that the jury found that Taco Cabana's trade dress did not have secondary meaning. Therefore, the only way that Taco Cabana could obtain trade dress protection, short of overturning a jury verdict, is if its trade dress was inherently distinctive. Think of the logic of the decision. Trade dress can be protected as a trademark. A trademark has to be distinctive either because it is inherently distinctive or because it has acquired distinctiveness. Here, Taco Cabana's trade dress does not have acquired distinctiveness. Does it follow from this chain of propositions that Taco Cabana's trade dress is inherently distinctive? Notice that once the Court rules that trade dress can be inherently distinctive for trademark protection, then Taco Cabana wins. But one fact that is somewhat troubling about the case is what makes the trade dress inherently distinctive. In thinking about this issues, note that the district court judge in *Taco Cabana* instructed the jury as follows:

> Distinctiveness is a term used to indicate that a trade dress serves as a symbol of origin. If it is shown, by a preponderance of the evidence, that Taco Cabana's trade dress distinguishes its products and services from those of other restaurants and is not descriptive and not functional, then you should find that Taco Cabana's trade dress is inherently distinctive.

Note that the dress cannot be descriptive or functional and must serve to distinguish the produce and service from other restaurants. What is inherent in the Taco Cabana trade dress that is distinctive?

Consider the following definition of inherently distinctive trade dress. Trade dress is inherently distinctive if it "is of such a design that a buyer will immediately rely on it to differentiate the product from those of competing manufacturers." *Tone Bros., Inc. v. Sysco Corp.*, 28 F.3d 1192, 1206 (Fed.Cir. 1994). The Supreme Court states that a mark is inherently distinctive if its "intrinsic nature serves to identify a particular source." *Two Pesos, Inc. v. Taco Cabana, Inc.*, 505 U.S. 763, 768, 112 S.Ct. 2753, 120 L.Ed.2d 615 (1992). Which of these two definitions seems more helpful? For a discussion of these issues pre-Samara, see Graeme B. Dinwoodie, *Reconceptualizing the Inherent Distinctiveness of Product Design Trade Dress*, 75 N.C. L. REV. 471 (1997).

3. The Court's opinion in *Samara Brothers* provides a nice summary of the law of trade dress after *Taco Cabana*. The movement is towards requiring secondary meaning for protection of elements of trade dress such as color and product design. This shift represents a greater concern of the Court with what it calls "strike suits" in the *Samara Brothers* case. These suits are anticompetitive uses of trademark law brought by a trademark owner against a competitor to prevent the development of its business. The Court's decision in *Qualitex* is not reproduced here, but one thing to note is that Justice Breyer, who was not on the Court when Taco Cabana was heard, was on the Court when *Qualitex* was reviewed. In fact, Justice Breyer wrote the unanimous opinion in *Qualitex* that held that color can be protected as a trademark only upon a showing of secondary meaning. This is important because Justice Breyer is very conscious of the effects of intellectual property protection on markets, as is shown in his famous critique of copyright law. See Stephen Breyer, *The Uneasy Case for Copyright: A Study of Copyright in Books, Photocopies, and Computer Programs*, 84 HARV. L. REV. 281 (1970).

4. Once the Court requires secondary meaning for protection of elements of trade dress, it has to square its decision with the holding of *Taco Cabana*. In *Samara Brothers*, Justice Scalia suggests a distinction between product packaging and product design or configuration. Trade dress that is product packaging can be protected without a showing of secondary meaning while trade dress that is product design requires secondary meaning for protection. The example he offers is the Coke bottle which can be seen as either a container for the product (packaging) or part of the product itself (design). What Justice Scalia seems to be getting at is a type of product feature that is not functional. Notice that the current version of Section 43(a), as amended in 1996, requires the person seeking protection for trade to show that the dress is not functional. Perhaps a cleaner way to understand the distinction is as follows. A product's feature that is functional cannot be protected as a trademark. A product's feature that is ornamental can be protected as a trademark if the mark has secondary meaning. Finally, if the feature is ornamental packaging, then it can be protected even if it does not have secondary meaning. Of course, an even simpler way to distinguish *Taco Cabana* is to say that secondary meaning is not required if the trade dress is restaurant decor. The Court almost suggests this interpretation, but it is obviously too narrow. In light of these developments, there is a strong

argument that *Taco Cabana* was simply wrongly decided, but it is unlikely that this chestnut of trademark law will be overruled.

5. The Court in *Samara* uses the phrase "tertium quid" to categorize the type of trade dress at issue in Taco Cabana. By including this nebulous category, the Court seems to leave open the development of the law in the next trade dress case. What "third thing" could the trade dress have been other than packaging or configuration?

6. The *Trek* case provides a thorough discussion of some of the issues that arise in determining whether a mark is famous for federal anti-dilution purposes. The Lanham Act, under 1125(c)(1), a part of the Federal Anti–Dilution Statute, lists the following eight factors to be used in determining whether a mark is famous:

(A) the degree of inherent or acquired distinctiveness of the mark;

(B) the duration and extent of use of the mark in connection with the goods or services with which the mark is used;

(C) the duration and extent of advertising and publicity of the mark;

(D) the geographical extent of the trading area in which the mark is used;

(E) the channels of trade for the goods or services with which the mark is used;

(F) the degree of recognition of the mark in the trading areas and channels of trade used by the marks' owner and the person against whom the injunction is sought;

(G) the nature and extent of use of the same or similar marks by third parties; and

(H) whether the mark was registered under the Act of March 3, 1881, or the Act of February 20, 1905, or on the principal register.

Notice that federal registration is only one factor to be considered, but not a requirement for a mark to be famous. Is the market analysis applied by the court consistent with these factors? Is it clear from the case what constitutes a "niche market"?

7. Domain names are handled under a separate registration system and can give rise to a separate cause of action called cybersquatting, which we discuss in the next section. Domain names, however, can also be registered as a trademark. The USPTO in its guidelines for trademark examination procedures states the following about registering domain names as a trademark:

When a trademark, service mark, collective mark or certification mark is composed, in whole or in part, of a domain name, neither the beginning of the URL (http://www.) nor the TLD have any source indicating significance. Instead, those designations are merely devices that every Internet site provider must use as part of its address. Today, advertisements for all types of products and services routinely include a URL for the web site of the advertiser. Just as the average person with no special knowledge recognizes "800" or "1–800" followed by seven digits or letters as one of the prefixes used for every toll-free phone number, the average person familiar with the Internet recognizes the format for a domain name and understands that "http," "www," and a TLD are a part of every URL.

Applications for registration of marks consisting of domain names are subject to the same requirements as all other applications for federal trademark registration. This Examination Guide identifies and discusses some of the issues that commonly arise in the examination of domain name mark applications.

See Examination Guide 2–99 (September 29, 1999), available at http://www. uspto.gov/web/ offices/tac/ notices/guide299.htm. The Guide also states:

> If the proposed mark is used in a way that would be perceived as nothing more than an address at which the applicant can be contacted, registration must be refused. Examples of a domain name used only as an Internet address include a domain name used in close proximity to language referring to the domain name as an address, or a domain name displayed merely as part of the information on how to contact the applicant.
>
> Example: The mark is WWW.XYZ.COM for on-line ordering services in the field of clothing. Specimens of use consisting of an advertisement that states "visit us on the web at www.xyz.com" do not show service mark use of the proposed mark.
>
> Example: The mark is XYZ.COM for financial consulting services. Specimens of use consisting of a business card that refers to the service and lists a phone number, fax number, and the domain name sought to be registered do not show service mark use of the proposed mark.

This refusal is consistent with not allowing trademark registration for advertising uses alone. See *In re Eilberg*, 49 USPQ 2d 1955 (TTAB 1998) (refusing registration of mark when included solely on attorney's business card); *Microstrategy Inc. v. Motorola, Inc.*, 245 F.3d 335 (4th Cir. 2001) (not finding use when mark used on business cards and for advertising as opposed to brand product or service).

II. HOW TRADEMARKS ARE PROTECTED

The Lanham Act creates the following causes of action:

- a claim under 15 USC § 1114(a) (sometimes referred to as § 32(a)) for the unauthorized reproduction, counterfeit, copy or colorable imitation of a registered mark in the sale, offering for sale, distribution, or advertising of a good or service that is likely to cause confusion, to cause mistake, or to deceive;

- a claim under 15 USC § 1125(a) (sometimes referred to as § 43(a)) for the use of a trademark, either registered or unregistered, or of any false designation of origin, false or misleading description of fact, or false or misleading representation of fact that is likely to cause confusion, mistake or deception as to affiliation OR misrepresents the nature, characteristic, quality, or geographic origin of the product of service;

- a claim under 15 USC § 1125(c) (sometimes referred to as § 43(c)) for the use of a famous mark in a way that causes dilution of the mark;

- a claim under 15 USC § 1125(d) (sometimes referred to as § 43(d)) for the registration, trafficking, or use of a domain name that contains a federally protected trademark with a bad faith intent to profit from the mark.

An example will illustrate these causes of action. Suppose a company uses the registered mark Porsche as a label on and in advertising for cars that are not Porsches. This gives rise to claims under both § 1114 and § 1125(a). If, in addition, the company imitates the trade dress of Porsche in its cars, then a cause of action under § 1125(a), but not § 1114, arises since the trade dress is not registered. To the extent that the word Porsche and the trade dress are both famous and the use dilutes the mark by blurring or tarnishing it, there is a cause of action under § 1125(c). Finally, if the company registers the domain name www.porsche.com with a bad faith intent to profit from the mark, the company has violated § 1125(d). The following table summarizes the causes of action.

	Registered Mark	Unregistered Mark
Infringement 15 USC 1114	likelihood of confusion	N/A
Unfair Competition 15 USC 1125(a)	likelihood of confusion as to source or association	likelihood of confusing as to source or association
Dilution 15 USC 1125(c)	likelihood of dilution of famous mark	likelihood of dilution of famous mark
Anticybersquatting 15 USC 1125(d)	domain name that is identical or confusingly similar to trademark or dilutive of famous mark	domain name that is identical or confusingly similar to trademark or dilutive of famous mark

A. REGISTERED MARKS: INFRINGEMENT CLAIMS UNDER 15 USC §§ 1114 AND 1125(a)

BRENNAN'S, INC. v. BRENNAN'S RESTAURANT, LLC

United States Court of Appeals, Second Circuit, 2004.
360 F.3d 125.

CARDAMONE, CIRCUIT JUDGE.

This is an appeal from the denial of a preliminary injunction in a trademark infringement suit. The suit involves a dispute between two restaurant owners over the use of the name "Brennan's." The owner of a widely-renowned New Orleans restaurant named "Brennan's" moved for a preliminary injunction against the owners of a New York City restaurant called "Terrance Brennan's Seafood & Chop House." Plaintiff's motion was denied * * *.

This trademark infringement suit is focused on the protectibility as a mark of plaintiff's use of the family name Brennan. In trademark law, names are important identifiers of the source of goods or services marketed to the public consumer. Names, of course, are not constant like the northern star, but are changeable, as some—like show-business people, some newly married women, and recent immigrants—shed their birth names like old coats and happily don new ones they prefer. But others, like plaintiff and defendant in this case, think their names are treasures to be safeguarded jealously. From the surname Brennan, plaintiff's predecessor coined a trademark he used for his restaurant. Defendant, also named Brennan, attached to that surname his first name of Terrance and used these names as a mark for his restaurant. Thus, the stage for the trademark litigation before us was set.

Background

Plaintiff Brennan's, Inc. (Brennan's New Orleans, plaintiff, or appellant) owns and operates the restaurant "Brennan's," founded in 1946 in New Orleans, Louisiana. Plaintiff registered the name Brennan's pursuant to the Lanham Act as a trademark for its restaurant services. The validity of that mark is not disputed. Plaintiff operates one other restaurant, "Owen Brennan's Restaurant," in Memphis, Tennessee, but owns no restaurants in the New York City area.

Terrance Brennan, so named at birth, is a New York City chef who, prior to this litigation, opened two restaurants in New York City, "Picholine" and "Artisanal." He is a well-known "name" chef whose reputation attracts customers. At the center of this controversy is his newest enterprise, "Terrance Brennan's Seafood & Chop House" (Terrance Brennan's), located in Manhattan. Defendants originally called the new restaurant "Brennan's Seafood & Chop House," but after receiving a cease-and-desist letter from plaintiff's lawyers, they added the first name "Terrance" to their mark.

Brennan's New Orleans sought a preliminary injunction on the grounds that the name Terrance Brennan's Seafood & Chop House infringed its rights in the name Brennan's and was likely to cause consumer confusion. After expedited limited discovery and a two-day hearing, Judge McKenna denied the motion for a preliminary injunction. We affirm.

Discussion

The Lanham Act creates a cause of action against any person who, in connection with goods or services, uses in commerce any word, term, name, symbol, or device, or any combination thereof, or any false designation of origin * * * which—(A) is likely to cause confusion, or to cause mistake, or to deceive as to the ... connection ... of such person with another person, or as to the origin, sponsorship, or approval of his or her goods, [or] services. . . .

The key for a plaintiff in proving infringement of its trademark is to show the likelihood of consumer confusion. See Restatement (Third) of Unfair Competition § 21 cmt. a (1995) ("The test for infringement is whether the actor's use of a designation as a trademark ... creates a likelihood of confusion....").

A party seeking a preliminary injunction must establish (1) irreparable harm and (2) either (a) a likelihood of success on the merits or (b) a sufficiently serious question going to the merits and a balance of hardships tipping decidedly in the moving party's favor. In a trademark infringement case, proof of a likelihood of confusion establishes both a likelihood of success on the merits and irreparable harm.

Because we review a district court's denial of a preliminary injunction for an abuse of discretion, it is not surprising that appellant has a formidable hurdle to overcome.

Plaintiff also brought dilution and state law unfair competition claims in the district court, but the only issue before us on appeal is the trademark infringement claim. On that issue, the district court ruled that plaintiff had not demonstrated a likelihood of success on the merits. In particular, it noted the minimal evidence of actual confusion, the use of Terrance Brennan's first name in his mark, the sophistication of the relevant consumer market, and the substantial geographic distance—more than 1,000 miles—separating the two Brennan restaurants. Although we are doubtful about certain aspects of the district court's findings, we are at the same time persuaded that Judge McKenna's ultimate determination that plaintiff was not entitled to a preliminary injunction did not constitute an abuse of his discretion.

Plaintiff's claim of trademark infringement is brought under the federal trademark laws, 15 U.S.C. §§ 1114 (imitation of registered mark) and 1125(a) (false designation of origin). To prevail on a claim of trademark infringement, a plaintiff must show, first, that its mark merits protection, and, second, that the defendant's use of a similar mark is likely to cause consumer confusion. The parties do not dispute that plaintiff has a valid, registered mark in the name Brennan's that has become incontestable by operation of law. We turn therefore to consider the pivotal question: the likelihood of confusion.

To evaluate the likelihood of consumer confusion, we apply the multi-factor test set forth by Judge Friendly in *Polaroid Corp. v. Polarad Elecs. Corp.*, 287 F.2d 492, 495 (2d Cir. 1961). This test requires analysis of several non-exclusive factors, including: (1) the strength of the mark, (2) the degree of similarity between the two marks, (3) the competitive proximity of the products, (4) actual confusion, (5) the likelihood the plaintiff will bridge the gap, (6) the defendant's good faith in adopting its mark, (7) the quality of the defendant's products, and (8) the sophistication of the purchasers. No single factor is dispositive, nor is a court limited to consideration of only these factors. Further, "each factor must be evaluated in the context of how it bears on the ultimate question of likelihood of confusion as to the source of the product." *Lois Sportswear, U.S.A., Inc. v. Levi Strauss & Co.*, 799 F.2d 867, 872 (2d Cir. 1986).

In reviewing the district court's evaluation of the Polaroid factors, each individual factor is reviewed under a clearly erroneous standard, but the ultimate determination of the likelihood of confusion is a legal issue subject to de novo review.

The district court's findings with respect to each factor were as follows: (1) plaintiff has a strong mark; (2) the marks are similar, but Terrance Brennan's use of the first name "Terrance" in its mark reduces their similarity and reduces potential confusion; (3) the competing restaurants are not proximate competitors since they are more than 1,000 miles apart; (4) there is no indication that Brennan's New Orleans has any intention of bridging the gap by operating in or near New York City; (5) there is little or no evidence of actual confusion; (6) diners in the high-end restaurants tend to be sophisticated, and thus less likely to be confused; (7) there is no evidence of bad faith on the part of defendants; and (8) the high quality of Terrance Brennan's restaurant is not likely to diminish the reputation of Brennan's New Orleans. The district court concluded that the first factor favored plaintiff, the second partially favored plaintiff, and the remaining factors favored defendant. Accordingly, it refused to grant an injunction.

We find no clear error in most of the district court's findings, and we share its view that plaintiff has not at this point demonstrated a likelihood of confusion. We think, however, that three of the Polaroid factors warrant further discussion: the strength of plaintiff's mark, the degree of similarity of the two marks, and the proximity of the services.

A.   *Strength of the Mark*

The strength of a mark refers to its ability to identify the source of the goods being sold under its aegis. There are two components of a mark's strength: its inherent distinctiveness and the distinctiveness it has acquired in the marketplace. The former, inherent distinctiveness, examines a mark's theoretical potential to identify plaintiff's goods or services without regard to whether it has actually done so. The latter, acquired distinctiveness, refers to something entirely different. This measure looks solely to that recognition plaintiff's mark has earned in the marketplace as a designator of plaintiff's goods or services.

1.   *Inherent Distinctiveness of Family Names*

Courts assess inherent distinctiveness by classifying a mark in one of four categories arranged in increasing order of inherent distinctiveness: (a) generic, (b) descriptive, (c) suggestive, or (d) fanciful or arbitrary. A proper name such as Brennan's is descriptive because it does not by itself identify a product; however, if a name develops secondary meaning, it may come to identify a product as originating from a single source. The name of a person, therefore, like other descriptive marks, is protectible only if it has acquired secondary meaning.

Of course, a registered mark in continuous use for five consecutive years after registration, and still in use, becomes incontestable. Because of this statutory incontestability, Brennan's New Orleans, which would ordinarily be accorded only minimal protection as a descriptive mark, in the district court's view became a strong mark entitled to protection under the Lanham Act. This statutory incontestability was bolstered by the district court's finding that plaintiff's mark had acquired secondary meaning through its long history and numerous media reviews.

In the case at hand plaintiff and defendant have a common last name. And, it is one they share with many others. We take judicial notice that a current Manhattan telephone book lists 184 residences and 20 businesses with the name Brennan. Because the thrust of trademark law aims to avoid confusion as to the product's source it is unhelpful to draw rigid rules when dealing with a common last name. For our purposes in deciding this appeal, for example, it would be incorrect to insist that defendant is always entitled to use his own name in business, and it is equally incorrect to maintain that defendant is never entitled to the use of his own name to compete with the same and perhaps more famous business name of plaintiff.

While the law recognizes the unfairness of letting one person trade on the reputation or the name of another, at the same time it also recognizes that one's surname given at birth creates associations attached to that name which identify the individual. As a consequence, courts generally are hesitant to afford strong protection to proper names, since to do so preempts others with the same name from trading on their own reputation. "To prevent all use of [a man's personal name] is to take away his identity; without it he cannot make known who he is to those who may wish to deal with him; and that is so grievous an injury that courts will avoid imposing it, if they possibly can."

As a common last name, we think at this point and contrary to the district court that plaintiff's mark is inherently weak. A common last name implicates both the minimal level of protection traditionally granted to descriptive marks and the policy of not protecting last names to a degree that unnecessarily precludes other users from trading on their own names' reputation. Further, the more common a last name is, the lower the likelihood that a competitor will effectively appropriate the goodwill of the senior user since consumers will be unlikely to assume that the two brands with the same name refer to the same goods.

2. *Plaintiff Has Not Acquired Distinctiveness in New York*

Nevertheless, even a common name mark may warrant protection as a strong mark if it has achieved distinctiveness in the marketplace, the second component of a mark's strength. Yet, to achieve the status of a strong mark, plaintiff must demonstrate distinctiveness in the relevant market, for if the mark is not recognized by the relevant consumer group, a similar mark will not deceive those consumers and thereby increase search costs. In this case, the relevant market is the pool of actual and potential customers of Terrance Brennan's, for it is those patrons whose potential confusion is at issue.

To support its conclusion that plaintiff's mark was strong, the district court cited media notices regarding Brennan's New Orleans from various newspapers around the country, and observed that Brennan's New Orleans "has had almost two million customers and generated over $84 million in revenues, spending more than $4,600,000 on advertising and promotion." While media and advertising figures are relevant to the analysis, the district court made no findings with respect to advertising expenditures or media exposure in New York City.

We do not doubt that Brennan's New Orleans's history is notable. But virtually all the articles and reviews discuss Brennan's New Orleans in the context of the City of New Orleans or a trip to New Orleans. This evidence in no way demonstrates that potential diners in New York City who find the word Brennan's on a restaurant awning will have any reason to think the restaurant is connected with Brennan's New Orleans, or even will have heard of Brennan's New Orleans. This is especially true because Brennan's New Orleans has not expanded in or near New York, defendant Terrance Brennan has his own reputation in New York, and Brennan is a common name.

We recognize, of course, that some last names do achieve such a degree of secondary meaning that they can become strong identifiers of source (e.g., Bacardi for rum, Ford for automobiles, Smucker for jam). Considering however the importance of permitting a person's good faith use of his own name, courts have taken great care to ensure that injunctions are no broader than necessary to preserve the senior user's rights. To enjoin Terrance Brennan's use of his own name, Brennan's New Orleans must make a showing that its mark has achieved such potency in Terrance Brennan's market that his use of his own name will cause consumer confusion as to source.

The current record suggests to us at most that plaintiff has a strong mark among New Orleans diners and visitors to New Orleans. * * * Absent from the district court's analysis was any demonstration of acquired distinctiveness in the relevant market, namely the actual and potential New York City diners of Terrance Brennan's. Because the district court's legal analysis on this matter was insufficient, its findings do not at present support the conclusion that plaintiff has a strong mark. The district court may want to revisit this issue at trial in light of further proof it may have before it.

B. Similarity of the Marks

When evaluating the similarity of marks, courts consider the overall impression created by a mark. Each mark must be compared against the other as a whole; juxtaposing fragments of each mark does not aid in deciding whether the compared marks are confusingly similar. The fact that the two marks appear similar is not dispositive. Rather, the question is whether such similarity is more likely than not to cause consumer confusion.

We agree with the district court that the addition of the first name "Terrance" to defendant's mark is meaningful. Judge McKenna found that Terrance Brennan, through his restaurants Picholine and Artisanal, has become a well-known chef in Manhattan, and that the use of his first name suggests a restaurant connected with the Terrance Brennan of Picholine and Artisanal instead of a restaurant connected with Brennan's in New Orleans. This finding is not clearly erroneous.

Because the ultimate issue is the likelihood of confusion, analysis focuses on the particular industry where the marks compete. This is relevant because likelihood of confusion is related to consumer expectations. In the restaurant industry, it is not uncommon to name a restaurant after its chef, particularly with high-end restaurants where that chef has developed a reputation in the public's mind. Instances would be: Nobu/Matsuhisa (New York/Los Angeles), Charlie Trotter's (Chicago), Daniel/Café Boulud (New York), Jean Georges (New York), Hamersley's Bistro (Boston), Morimoto (Philadelphia), and Emeril's (multiple locations). These examples suggest the awareness diners have when connecting the name of a restaurant to a particular chef. They also suggest the importance of permitting a chef to use his own name, since forcing a junior user to change his mark imposes costs that may be substantial in the high-class restaurant business.

Plaintiff is concerned that the name Terrance Brennan's Seafood & Chop House will, in practice, simply be truncated to Brennan's in daily use. The district court found that on several occasions, people answering the telephone at Terrance Brennan's identified the restaurant as Brennan's Seafood and Chop House or simply Brennan's. But the court credited Terrance Brennan's testimony that he has since instructed his staff that the first name Terrance is always to be used. Whether and to what extent the practice of truncation may play a role in increasing consumer confusion need not concern us here because plaintiff has not demonstrated that any truncation in this case is of a confusing nature.

C. *Proximity of the Products*

The competitive proximity factor has two elements, market proximity and geographic proximity. Market proximity asks whether the two products are in related areas of commerce and geographic proximity looks to the geographic separation of the products. Both elements seek to determine whether the two products have an overlapping client base that creates a potential for confusion. In the instant case the services have close market proximity since both are upscale restaurants. The district court found that the two restaurants would, without question, compete for customers were they in the same city. The court also recognized the significance of the fact that the restaurants are geographically distant, with more than 1,000 miles separating them.

It is well established that a geographically remote mark may nevertheless gain protection in a distant market, at least where there is extensive advertising or evidence of strong reputation in the distant market. Although registration presumptively creates nationwide protection, the Lanham Act only permits an injunction against a party where that party's use of a similar mark is likely to cause confusion.

We agree with the district court that geographic remoteness is critical in this case. In the restaurant industry, especially where individual restaurants rather than chains are competing, physical separation seems particularly significant to the inquiry into consumer confusion. Even in this age of rapid communication and travel, plaintiff faces a high hurdle to demonstrate that a single restaurant in New Orleans and a single restaurant in New York City compete for the same customers. That is particularly the case here where the dining services require a customer's physical presence and cannot rely, for instance, on Internet or mail-order sales.

To succeed on an infringement claim, plaintiff must show that it is probable, not just possible, that consumers will be confused. The district court concluded that, even crediting plaintiff's contention that over seven percent of its business comes from New York State, the substantial distance between the restaurants coupled with the fact that plaintiff has never had an establishment in New York City meant it was unlikely that an appreciable number of ordinarily prudent purchasers were likely to be confused.

Geography is relevant to our analysis of a mark's strength, particularly with marks requiring secondary meaning. Likewise, strength analysis can inform proximity analysis, for the more arbitrary or fanciful a mark, the more likely that geographically distant customers with knowledge of the senior mark might presume that two similar marks are related. With a common last name, we consider it less likely that consumers in a distant market would be surprised to find two unrelated entities using the same common last name.

Certain businesses such as hotels, and to a lesser degree restaurants, attract the traveling public. Courts have recognized that even businesses that are separated by large distances may attract overlapping clientele due to the ease of travel. We do not disagree with this possibility, but only note that, in the absence of actual confusion or bad faith, substantial geographic separation remains a significant indicator that the likelihood of confusion is slight. Geography alone is not decisive, but the plaintiff still has the burden to demonstrate that an appreciable number of relevant consumers are likely to be confused. We find no such demonstration on this record.

As to the remaining *Polaroid* factors, we agree with the district court for substantially the reasons set forth in its memorandum and order. Having failed at this early stage to establish a likelihood of success on the merits, plaintiff is not entitled to a preliminary injunction.

FREEDOM CARD, INC. v. JPMORGAN CHASE & CO.

United States Court of Appeals, Third Circuit, 2005.
432 F.3d 463.

McKEE, CIRCUIT JUDGE.

In December 2000, UTN began offering its FREEDOM CARD in conjunction with CompuCredit Corporation. The FREEDOM CARD was offered to extend credit and financial services to the "sub-prime" credit market that is disproportionately comprised of African–American consumers. UTN focused its promotional efforts on "people who [had] bad credit or [had] filed bankruptcy recently and [were] looking to start all over." UTN entered into a contract with Queen Latifah, a prominent African American entertainer, as part of its efforts to promote the FREEDOM CARD. The majority of FREEDOM CARD customers had credit lines of $300. On average, they were charged annual fees and interest amounting to 140% over and above their principal balance. CompuCredit stopped marketing and issuing new accounts for the FREEDOM CARD card after December 2001. The district court found, FREEDOM CARD peaked at 28,193 accounts.

For a number of years, Chase and Shell Oil Company had issued a co-branded credit card called "CHASE Shell MasterCard." The card offered cash rewards on purchases of Shell gasoline. In March 2002, Shell notified Chase that it was terminating their relationship. Chase owned the Shell accounts and in order to retain those accounts it began developing a new credit card product that would serve existing accounts as well as generate new ones.

Chase's research eventually lead to a rewards program that allowed Chase's customers to use its card at any gasoline company's filling station and receive rebates on gasoline as well as other purchases. Chase claims that it named the card "CHASE FREEDOM card," because of the freedom it afforded cardholders to purchase gasoline wherever the cardholder chose. On January 11, 2003, Chase sent a letter to its Shell account holders notifying them that their Shell cards would be automatically converted to CHASE FREEDOM cards.

The CHASE FREEDOM card was officially announced in a January 27, 2003, advertisement in the Wall Street Journal, more than a year after the FREEDOM CARD card stopped being issued. "The CHASE FREEDOM card [was] a reissue of the CHASE Shell MasterCard. The CHASE FREEDOM portfolio consisted of approximately 1.5 million converted Shell accounts and fewer than 10,000 accounts acquired after the January 27, 2003 launch.

Chase maintains that the converted account holders were generally between the ages of 46 and 55, had a FICO score of 800 or higher, owned their own homes, and were married with average annual incomes between $40,000 and $50,000. Of the acquired account holders, 80% owned their own home and 60% had a FICO score of 780 or higher. Chase claims that the majority of CHASE FREEDOM cardholders had credit lines of $5,000—$10,000, with no annual fee and an annual percentage rate of between 12.4% and 14.4%.

The Wall Street Journal advertisement for CHASE FREEDOM card was the only advertisement that ever appeared. Upon seeing the Wall Street Journal advertisement the day it first appeared, Wesley Buford, UTN's Chief Executive Officer, contacted Chase and complained that Chase was infringing UTN's FREEDOM CARD mark. After Buford objected, Chase immediately halted its advertising and marketing efforts for "CHASE FREEDOM," and refrained from acquiring any new customers.

Thereafter, representatives of Chase and UTN met to discuss the problem. Chase claims that discussions broke down after UTN threatened to "have people protesting around [Chase's] branches" and to have demonstrations calling attention to "the evils of Chase and this Freedom Mastercard [sic]" and thereby "cause [Chase] a great deal of harm." UTN claims that these meetings were "positive and friendly" rather than confrontational and, based upon prior positive communication between the parties and Chase's prompt cessation of CHASE FREEDOM card, Buford still believed that the matter could be resolved amicably. As a consequence of that belief, UTN claims that it maintained its relationship with Queen Latifah and even executed another commercial production agreement with her on February 19, 2003.

On February 4, 2003, Chase filed the instant action in district court seeking a declaration that its use of the CHASE FREEDOM mark did not infringe any of UTN's rights in the FREEDOM CARD mark. UTN counterclaimed asserting third-party claims for trademark infringement in violation of 15 U.S.C. § 1114, and unfair competition in violation of 15 U.S.C. § 1125(a)(1)(A).

The district court granted Chase's motion for summary judgment upon determining that there was no likelihood of confusion between "CHASE FREEDOM" and FREEDOM CARD. This appeal followed. * * *

IV. General principles.

There are two types of "likelihood of confusion" claims—"direct confusion" claims and "reverse confusion" claims. As we noted at the outset, we are primarily concerned with a claim of reverse confusion because that is how UTN argues this appeal. Although direct confusion and reverse confusion have developed as two separate doctrines, they are not as analytically distinct as may, at first blush, appear. "Isolated instances of direct confusion may occur in a reverse confusion case, and vice-versa." Accordingly, although we are resolving UTN's claim of reverse confusion, we can not ignore the doctrine of direct confusion.

A. Direct Confusion

The essence of a direct confusion claim is that a junior user of a mark attempts to free-ride on the reputation and goodwill of the senior user by adopting a similar or identical mark. In deciding whether similar marks create a likelihood of confusion, we have adopted a non-exhaustive test using 10 factors that have come to be known as the "Lapp factors," for determining the likelihood of confusion between two marks where direct confusion is alleged. Pursuant to that analysis, we examine:

(1) the degree of similarity between the owner's mark and the alleged infringing mark;

(2) the strength of the owner's mark;

(3) the price of the goods and other factors indicative of the care and attention expected of consumers when making a purchase;

(4) the length of time the defendant has used the mark without evidence of actual confusion arising;

(5) the intent of the defendant in adopting the mark;

(6) the evidence of actual confusion;

(7) whether the goods, though not competing, are marketed through the same channels of trade and advertised through the same media;

(8) the extent to which the targets of the parties' sales efforts are the same;

(9) the relationship of the goods in the minds of consumers because of the similarity of function;

(10) other factors suggesting that the consuming public might expect the prior owner to manufacture a product in the defendant's market, or that he is likely to expand into that market.

Interpace Corp. v. Lapp, Inc., 721 F.2d 460, 463 (3d Cir. 1983) (citation omitted). The Lapp factors were originally used to determine likelihood of confusion for non-competing goods. Where goods that were the subject of a trademark infringement action directly competed with each other, we originally held that a "court need rarely look beyond the mark itself" to determine likelihood of confusion. However, we have since held that the Lapp factors should be used for both competing and non-competing goods. In either event, "the Lapp test is a qualitative inquiry. Not all factors will be relevant in all cases; further, the different factors may properly be accorded different weights depending on the particular factual setting. A district court should utilize the factors that seem appropriate to a given situation

B. *Reverse Confusion*

"Reverse confusion occurs when a larger, more powerful company uses the trademark of a smaller, less powerful senior owner and thereby causes likely confusion as to the source of the senior user's goods or services." Thus, the "junior" user is junior in time but senior in market dominance or size. In reverse confusion, the junior user saturates the market with a similar trademark and overwhelms the senior user. The public comes to assume the senior user's products are really the junior user's or that the former has become somehow connected to the latter. The result is that the senior user loses the value of the trademark—its product identity, corporate identity, control over its goodwill and reputation, and ability to move into new markets.

Without the recognition of reverse confusion, smaller senior users would have little protection against larger, more powerful companies who want to use identical or confusingly similar trademarks. The logical consequence of failing to recognize reverse confusion would be the immunization from unfair competition liability of a company with a well established trade name and with the economic power to advertise extensively for a product name taken from a competitor. If the law is to limit recovery to passing off, anyone with adequate size and resources can adopt any trademark and develop a new meaning for the trademark as identification of the second user's products. Thus, "the doctrine of reverse confusion is designed to prevent ... a larger, more powerful company usurping the business identity of a smaller senior user."

As noted above, UTN presents its Lanham Act Section 43(a) unfair competition claim as a reverse confusion claim. [I]n a typical case alleging reverse confusion, as in a case of direct confusion, a court should apply the Lapp factors in assessing likelihood of confusion. However, economic reality and common sense require that some of the Lapp factors be analyzed differently when reverse discrimination is at issue. Thus, the strength of the parties' marks (Lapp factor (2)), the intent in adopting the marks (factor (5)), and the evidence of actual confusion (factor (6)), are analyzed differently from the method employed in a typical direct confusion case.

We [have] summarized the test for reverse confusion as follows:

[I]n the typical case in which there is a claim of reverse confusion, a court should examine the following factors [in determining] whether or not there is a likelihood of confusion:

(1) the degree of similarity between the owner's mark and the alleged infringing mark;

(2) the strength of the two marks, weighing both a commercially strong junior user's mark and a conceptually strong senior user's mark in the senior user's favor;

(3) the price of the goods and other factors indicative of the care and attention expected of consumers when making a purchase;

(4) the length of time the defendant has used the mark without evidence of actual confusion arising;

(5) the intent of the defendant in adopting the mark;

(6) the evidence of actual confusion;

(7) whether the goods, competing or not competing, are marketed through the same channels of trade and advertised through the same media;

(8) the extent to which the targets of the parties' sales efforts are the same;

(9) the relationship of the goods in the minds of consumers, whether because of the near-identity of the products, the similarity of function, or other factors;

(10) other facts suggesting that the consuming public might expect the larger, more powerful company to manufacture both products, or expect the larger company to manufacture a product in the plaintiff's market, or expect that the larger company is likely to expand into the plaintiff's market.

Here again, "no one factor is dispositive." The weight given each factor can vary with the circumstances of a particular case.

V.   Discussion

UTN's underlying contention before us is that the district court did not properly apply the Lapp factors in the context of its reverse confusion claim * * *. [W]e have serious doubts that UTN's claim is really a claim of reverse confusion to begin with. The essence of reverse confusion is that the more powerful junior user saturates the market with a similar trademark and overwhelms the smaller senior user.

Here, Chase did not overwhelm UTN's FREEDOM CARD at all. It is undisputed that CompuCredit FREEDOM CARD was not promoted or marketed after December 2001. Thus, FREEDOM CARD was out of the market for more than a year before Chase launched the CHASE FREE-DOM card on January 27, 2003. We are therefore hard-pressed to understand how CHASE FREEDOM card could have overwhelmed UTN's FREEDOM CARD when FREEDOM CARD was not even participating in the market when CHASE FREEDOM was launched. Moreover, any claim that Chase heavily promoted and advertised CHASE FREEDOM card and thereby overwhelmed UTN's FREEDOM CARD via marketing and promotion would be fanciful at best. On the contrary, Chase published a single advertisement for CHASE FREEDOM in a single publication on a single day. Chase thereafter stopped its marketing and advertising efforts once it was contacted by Buford of UTN. UTN attempts to extend Chase's marketing efforts by pointing to the aforementioned news article in Newsweek magazine that reported about the CHASE FREEDOM card. However, even if Chase is somehow deemed responsible for "planting" and/or exploiting that article, it would still only amount to an additional one-paragraph news item. Even when combined with the single advertisement in the Wall Street Journal, that would hardly support a claim that Chase created confusion in the market by overwhelming FREEDOM CARD, the senior mark.

Nevertheless, "if we were to create a rigid division between direct and reverse confusion evidence, we would run the risk of denying recovery to meritorious plaintiffs." Accordingly, despite real doubts about whether UTN's claim can properly be characterized as a claim of reverse confusion, we must nevertheless determine whether the district court properly applied the Lapp factors to it.

UTN contends that the district court failed to properly analyze the similarity of the marks; the strength of the marks; and any facts indicating that the parties will expand into each other's markets. UTN also contends that the district court erred in analyzing some of the remaining Lapp factors including: consumer care when making a purchase; actual confusion; and intent. [Author's note: Here we include only the court's discussion of the actual confusion issue. The court affirmed the district court on the other factors considered.]

D. Actual confusion.

The district court concluded that "UTN [did] not come forward with any competent evidence of actual confusion. Thus, this factor also weighs significantly against a finding of likelihood of confusion." UTN argues that this was error because the district court (1) ignored the length of time that it had used the mark and (2) ignored anecdotal evidence of actual confusion.

UTN faults the district court's concern over the absence of evidence of actual confusion, reminding us that it was driven from the marketplace. However, that is yet another frivolous rejoinder since UTN stopped marketing the FREEDOM CARD approximately one year before Chase introduced its CHASE FREEDOM card. Chase's short-lived launch of its card, and its willingness to stop marketing CHASE FREEDOM immediately after being contacted by UTN, is uncontradicted. Moreover, even if we credit UTN's claim that CompuCredit refused to continue its relationship with UTN because of Chase's CHASE FREEDOM card, UTN could still not prevail on this record because UTN and Chase were in different markets. The district court found that "the undisputed evidence in this case indicates that [CHASE FREEDOM] and [FREEDOM CARD] are targeted at different groups of consumers * * *. Mr. Buford, UTN's CEO, made the distinction saying, 'Chase is targeting the high-income level and FreedomCard is targeting the middle-to-low income level.' " Absent more than appears here, this seriously undermines UTN's claim of likelihood of confusion.

Nevertheless, UTN attempts to argue the significance of anecdotal evidence of actual confusion that it introduced. UTN claims that the district court ignored evidence that UTN's accountant, Richard Moon, believed that CHASE FREEDOM was a joint venture between UTN and Chase. However, the district court did not credit that evidence because it was based on Buford's deposition testimony rather than anything Moon testified to. UTN had every opportunity to explore that issue during Moon's own deposition but refrained from doing so. UTN now invites us to ignore Moon's silence and focus on Buford's uncorroborated and self serving proclamations. That is an invitation we must decline.

UTN correctly reminds us that anecdotal evidence can be both relevant and probative, and argues the district court improperly dismissed the anecdotal evidence of Moon's confusion. * * ** That argument ignores the fact that, unlike the cases UTN relies upon, the anecdotal evidence here was de minimis just as the district court concluded. Accordingly, we do not think the district court erred in analyzing the evidence of actual confusion on this record.

[Author's note: The court addressed UTN's claim that the district court erred in not addressing all the Lapp factors. The court found that the district court had overlooked factors 7, 9 and 10 because they did not apply to directly competing goods and that UTN failed to show how this failure prejudiced the outcome. The district court's ruling for Chase was affirmed.]

NOTES

1. The two cases illustrate how courts approach the likelihood of confusion standard as it arises under both § 1114(a) and § 1125(a). In general, the standard is the same under the two statutes. The principal difference is that § 1114(a) applies only to registered marks, while § 1125(a) applies to both registered and unregistered marks. In the next section, we will consider a fact pattern involving an unregistered mark which gives rise to a § 1125(a) claim, but not a § 1114(a) claim. While the likelihood of confusion standard, as set out in the multi-factor *Polaroid* or *Lapp* factors (or west of the Mississippi, the *Sleekcraft* factors. See *AMF, Inc. v. Sleekcraft Boats*, 599 F.2d 341 (9th Cir. 1979)), is shared by both the 1114(a) and 1125(a) claims, the two largely differ in the presumptions of validity that are provided by federal registration. If the mark is not federally registered, the plaintiff has the burden to establish validity of the mark.

2. Make sure you understand the different types of confusion at issue in these cases. In *Chase*, the court distinguishes between direct and reverse confusion. Direct confusion occurs when a consumer thinks that a product produced by the junior user of the mark actually comes from the senior user when the senior user is the owner of the trademark. Reverse confusion is the opposite: the consumer thinks the product produced by the senior user comes from the junior user when the junior user is the owner of the trademark. Suppose a coffee shop starts selling a sandwich called the Big Mac. If consumers think this sandwich comes from McDonald's, the senior user who owns the mark, this is a case of direct confusion. But suppose the coffee shop sells a new dessert called The Ice Cream Headache. McDonald's starts selling its own dessert and calls it The Ice Cream Headache. If consumers start thinking that McDonald's dessert actually has as its source the coffee shop, we have a case of reverse confusion. Notice the problem. In both cases, the confused consumer goes to the infringer to buy the branded product, but the nature of the confusion is different. In both cases, however, there is potential confusion as to affiliation between the coffee shop and McDonald's, an affiliation that neither may want. Trademarks serve to distinguish products

and services, but also allow different companies to establish their own identity and goodwill in the marketplace.

For a discussion of the standards for confusion in trademark law, see Ann Bartow, *Likelihood of Confusion*, 41 SAN DIEGO L. REV. 721 (2004) (arguing that the standard for confusion is ridiculously low and is not applied in a gender neutral way); Jacob Jacoby, *The Psychological Foundations of Trademark Law: Secondary Meaning, Genericism, Fame, Confusion, and Dilution*, 91 TRADEMARK REP. 1013 (2001) (proposing a unifying psychological theory of trademark law). For a discussion of the expansive role of trademark law to include merchandising rights, see Stacey L. Dogan & Mark A, Lemley, *The Merchandising Right: Fragile Theory or Fait Accompli?*, 54 EMORY L. J. 461 (2005). See, also, Glynn S. Lunney, *Trademark Monopolies*, 48 EMORY L. J. 367 (1999) (presenting a broader context for trademark law in the law against monopolies).

3. Note that products and services do not have to be directly competing for there to be a finding of likelihood of confusion. For this reason, causes of action under 1114(a) and 1125(a) may include litigation between companies in two different marketplaces. This is also the case for dilution actions under 1125(c). But keep in mind the differences among the causes of action. When a company sues a non-competitor under 1114(a) or 1125(a), the claim is that the similarity of the marks is likely to confuse consumers as to source and as to an affiliation between the two companies. When a company sues a non-competitor under 1125(c), the claim is that the use of the market dilutes the value of the mark, either by blurring the association between the mark and a product or service or by tarnishing the mark by associating it with products or services that have a bad connotation.

4. There is a geographic scope to trademark rights that can be seen in the *Polaroid/Lapp/Sleekcraft* factors. In general, federal trademark registration gives the owner rights in the mark throughout the nation, even in regions it has not used the mark yet. These rights are subject to prior user rights of people who have used the mark prior to federal registration as a brand on their product or service. Nationwide protection is an important implication of federal trademark registration. Unregistered marks are protected largely in the area where they have been used. For a critical discussion of trademark law and protection of geographic markets, see Stephen L. Carter, *Comment: The Trouble with Trademark*, 99 YALE L. J. 759 (1990).

5. For a discussion of different types of actionable confusion, see *Gibson Guitar Corp. v. Paul Reed Smith Guitars, LP*, 423 F.3d 539 (6th Cir. 2005), a case involving infringement of a registered mark consisting of the two dimensional shape of a guitar. the court provides an engaging discussion of point of sale confusion (confusion that occurs at the point at which the buying decision is made), post sale confusion (confusion that occurs among the public after the sale is made), and initial interest confusion (confusion that occurs when the consumer is deciding where to make a purchase). Initial interest confusion is discussed in more detail below in the context of the *Falwell* case, under the heading of trademark infringement on the Internet. In *Gibson Guitar*, the court rejected the trademark owner's theory of "smoky bar confusion," the confusion that arises when a fan sees a musician playing the

infringing guitar in a bar and thinking the guitar was made by Gibson, the trademark owner. To the extent that this type of confusion would spur sales of Gibson guitars, the court concluded that it helped rather than harmed the trademark owner.

B. REGISTERED OR UNREGISTERED MARKS

1. Infringement Claims Under 15 USC § 1125(A)

TUMBLEBUS, INC. v. CRANMER

United States Court of Appeals, Sixth Circuit, 2005.
399 F.3d 754.

MOORE, CIRCUIT JUDGE.

In 1987, Brenda Scharlow ("Scharlow") launched Tumblebus Inc., a company which provides gymnastics and physical education instruction to children. Tumblebus Inc., which bills itself as a "mobile gym on wheels," furnishes such instruction on-site at day-care centers, birthday parties, and the like through the use of school buses retrofitted with gymnastics and other athletic equipment. Tumblebus Inc. currently operates three to four buses on a regular basis, marketing its services in the greater Louisville, Kentucky area.

Tumblebus Inc.'s business has also expanded to include the sale of retrofitted school buses to other persons wishing to enter the mobile-gymnastics-instruction market. Tumblebus Inc. has sold over two hundred retrofitted school buses to persons across the United States. Buses sold by Tumblebus Inc. seem to be similar in appearance to those used by Tumblebus Inc. in its own gymnastics-instruction business. Tumblebus Inc. permits purchasers to use the "Tumblebus" name when marketing their services, and many purchasers operate under names that include the word "Tumblebus." For approximately six years, Tumblebus Inc.'s training session for new bus purchasers has included a presentation by Donna Dugan ("Dugan"), owner of the Hot Fonts printing company, who offers for sale pre-designed letterhead, flyers, and other marketing materials containing the Tumblebus name and iconography.

According to Scharlow, Tumblebus Inc.'s expansion into selling retrofitted buses to other operators began somewhat informally, and the decision was made early on not to structure the business as a franchise because franchising would require too much on-site monitoring of individual franchisees' operations. Tumblebus Inc.'s record-keeping also appears rather informal, and according to Scharlow, Tumblebus Inc. does not have a complete list of all persons who have purchased retrofitted buses. Tumblebus Inc., however, has maintained contact with some purchasers, distributing new lesson plans and business development ideas.

In November 2001, Tara Pate ("Pate") purchased a retrofitted bus from Tumblebus Inc. When Pate first discussed her potential purchase with Scharlow, she indicated that she planned to operate in Lexington,

Kentucky. Scharlow, however, informed Pate that two other persons were already operating in Lexington, but suggested that Pate could instead service Elizabethtown, Brandenburg, Mt. Washington, Bardstown, and Radcliff, Kentucky. According to Scharlow and her husband, Pate orally agreed to operate in this area but not to expand into Louisville, where Tumblebus Inc. was based. The Scharlows admit, however, that they forgot to put this agreement in writing. Testimony at the hearing also indicates that during a meeting between Pate, Pate's mother, and Scharlow, Scharlow refused to include a territory provision in Pate's purchase contract. When asked what would prevent Pate from operating in the Louisville area, Scharlow apparently responded that there would be nothing that she could do to stop Pate from soliciting customers in the Louisville area, but that she was confident in her customers' loyalty to Tumblebus Inc.

In January 2002, Scharlow learned that Pate had distributed flyers advertising her business to day-care centers in the Louisville area. Scharlow contacted Pate, reminding Pate that she was not supposed to be operating in that area. Pate explained that she was having difficulty in obtaining customers in Elizabethtown and the surrounding areas, to which Scharlow responded that Pate could expand her operations into north Bullitt County, Kentucky, which included a day-care center that Tumblebus Inc. previously had serviced. Ultimately, however, Pate decided to leave the mobile-gymnastics-instruction market and listed her bus for sale in a Louisville newspaper.

Cranmer noticed Pate's advertisement in the Louisville newspaper and contacted Tumblebus Inc. in order to determine, for comparison purposes, what a newly retrofitted bus from Tumblebus Inc. would cost. Scharlow testified that when Cranmer called, she noticed that Cranmer's telephone number had a Louisville area code, so she asked Cranmer from where she was calling. When Cranmer explained that she was calling from Louisville, Scharlow apparently responded that she would not sell Cranmer a bus in Louisville because other Tumblebus operators were already in that area. Cranmer then stated that her sister was interested in purchasing a bus for operation in Bloomington, Indiana, and the discussion continued.

In April 2002, Cranmer purchased Pate's Tumblebus and began operating in the Louisville area under the name "Tumblebus." Upon learning that Cranmer was operating in Louisville, Scharlow contacted Cranmer. Cranmer and Scharlow discussed the possibility of Cranmer changing or adding something to the name of Cranmer's business, and Scharlow suggested such names as "Meredith's Tumblebus," "Fun Bus," and "Gym on Wheels." Cranmer eventually listed her business in the fall 2002 Louisville telephone book (with the same Louisville telephone number previously used by Pate) under the name "Tumblebus of Louisville." Tumblebus Inc. also appeared in the fall 2002 Louisville telephone book, but was listed after "Tumblebus of Louisville," appeared in smaller typeface, and included a New Albany, Indiana telephone number. Scharlow then began insisting that Cranmer remove the word "Tumblebus" from her business's name.

Scharlow claims that Tumblebus Inc. has suffered adverse consequences because of Cranmer's operation in the Louisville area. During the preliminary hearing, Scharlow recounted incidents in which customers apparently confused the two businesses, such as customers sending their payments to the wrong business and persons who had contracted with Cranmer telephoning Tumblebus Inc. when Cranmer failed to show up for scheduled appointments. According to Scharlow, Tumblebus Inc.'s income has declined as a result.

In July 2003, Tumblebus Inc. filed suit against Cranmer in the U.S. District Court for the Western District of Kentucky, accusing Cranmer of trademark infringement, trade dress infringement, and false advertising in violation of § 43 of the Lanham Act, 15 U.S.C. § 1125(a), as well as trademark infringement, trade dress infringement, and unfair competition under Kentucky common law. The district court issued its preliminary injunction order, and Cranmer timely appealed to this court.

Section 43(a) of the Lanham Act, 15 U.S.C. § 1125(a), provides a federal cause of action for infringement of marks and trade dress that have not obtained federal registration. When evaluating a Lanham Act claim for infringement of an unregistered mark, courts must determine whether the mark is protectable, and if so, whether there is a likelihood of confusion as a result of the would-be infringer's use of the mark.

1.   Existence Of A Protectable Mark

First, we must consider whether the district court erred in concluding that TUMBLEBUS is a protectable mark whose infringement can give rise to liability under § 43(a) of the Lanham Act. The protectability of the TUMBLEBUS mark depends on the level of the mark's distinctiveness. In the case at bar, the district court appears to have concluded that the TUMBLEBUS mark is protectable as a suggestive mark, a finding which we review for clear error.

Cranmer contends that Tumblebus Inc. is unlikely to succeed on the merits of its mark infringement claim because TUMBLEBUS is a generic term not entitled to Lanham Act protection. In Cranmer's view, the two constituent parts of TUMBLEBUS—"tumble" and "bus"—are generic terms that, when combined, are the most concise, easily understood way of referring to the services provided by Cranmer and Tumblebus Inc.

In support of her argument that TUMBLEBUS is a generic term, Cranmer cites Scharlow's testimony that TUMBLEBUS was a "natural" choice because Tumblebus Inc.'s business was "tumbling on a bus," and that TUMBLEBUS was "the most descriptive name [Scharlow] could think of." This statement by Scharlow, however, does not prove that TUMBLEBUS is in fact generic. First, Scharlow subsequently clarified during her testimony that the term "preschool gym on wheels" would be more descriptive of Tumblebus Inc.'s business than TUMBLEBUS. Moreover, many of the Tumblebus advertising materials, including those used by Tumblebus Inc., bear phrases such as "gym on wheels," which indicates that the term TUMBLEBUS alone has not been sufficient to convey the nature of Tumblebus Inc.'s services. Thus, we conclude that the district court did not clearly err in finding that TUMBLEBUS is not a generic term incapable of obtaining protected status.

Moreover, upon consideration of the record before us, the district court's apparent categorization of TUMBLEBUS as a suggestive, rather than merely descriptive, mark is not clear error. The line between merely descriptive and suggestive marks is admittedly hazy and can be difficult to discern. Nevertheless, the TUMBLEBUS mark shares a closer kinship with those marks previously designated as suggestive than those labeled merely descriptive because of the degree of inferential reasoning necessary for a consumer to discern that the TUMBLEBUS mark relates to the provision of on-site gymnastics and fitness instruction to children. Although the word "tumble" does describe a subset of the activities which occur inside Tumblebus Inc.'s "bus," the connection between "tumble" and "bus" is not so obvious that a consumer seeing TUMBLEBUS in isolation would know that the term refers to mobile-gymnastics instruction, and not, for instance, a mobile laundry service using tumble-dryers. Again, the fact that Tumblebus Inc. has found it necessary to include explanatory phrases such as "gym on wheels" in its advertising materials indicates that the term TUMBLEBUS does not merely describe the services provided by Tumblebus Inc. As a result, we conclude that the district court did not clearly err in classifying TUMBLEBUS as an inherently distinctive, suggestive mark.

2. Likelihood Of Confusion

To recover on a claim of mark infringement, a mark's owner must establish not only that the mark is protectable, but also that use of the mark by the opposing party is likely to cause confusion. When evaluating the likelihood of confusion, a district court must balance the following factors:

1. strength of the plaintiff's mark;
2. relatedness of the goods;
3. similarity of the marks;
4. evidence of actual confusion;
5. marketing channels used;
6. likely degree of purchaser care;
7. defendant's intent in selecting the mark; [and]
8. likelihood of expansion of the product lines.

We conclude that the TUMBLEBUS mark's relative strength as a suggestive mark and the record evidence of actual confusion weigh in favor of finding a likelihood of confusion, and that, based on the record before us, none of the other Frisch factors militate against such a finding. Thus, Tumblebus Inc. has made a sufficient showing of likely confusion to sustain entry of a preliminary injunction with respect to the TUMBLEBUS mark.

3.   Asserted Defenses

a.   *Abandonment Of Rights In A Mark Through Naked Licensing*

Cranmer argues that Tumblebus Inc. is unlikely to succeed on the merits of its mark infringement claim because Tumblebus Inc. has abandoned any rights it might have to the TUMBLEBUS mark through "naked licensing," * * * which occurs "[w]hen a trademark owner fails to exercise reasonable control over the use of a mark by a licensee," such that "the presence of the mark on the licensee's goods or services misrepresents their connection with the trademark owner since the mark no longer identifies goods or services that are under the control of the owner of the mark" and the mark can no longer provide "a meaningful assurance of quality." Restatement (Third) of Unfair Competition § 33 cmt. b (1995).

According to Cranmer, Tumblebus Inc.'s pattern of allowing its purchasers to use the term "Tumblebus" in their businesses has resulted in the TUMBLEBUS mark losing its significance in the greater Louisville area. The record before us, however, contains insufficient evidence for us to conclude that Cranmer's defense of abandonment is so strong as to make it unlikely that Tumblebus Inc. will succeed on the merits of its trademark infringement claim. First, based on the testimony presented at the evidentiary hearing, it is unclear whether the relationship between Tumblebus Inc. and the purchasers of its buses with respect to the TUMBLEBUS mark is most aptly categorized as a license, a consent-to-use agreement, or neither. See 2 MCCARTHY ON TRADEMARKS AND UNFAIR COMPETITION § 18:79 (4th ed. 2004) ("In a license, the licensee is engaging in acts which would infringe the licensor's mark but for the permission granted in the license. In that event, quality control is essential * * *. A consent agreement does not require quality control because by the very essence of the agreement, the parties recognize that concurrent usage does not lead customers to link the goods or services of the parties. Whereas a license brings the parties together into a common public image and a joint enterprise, a consent agreement keeps the parties apart at a defined distance.").

Moreover, Cranmer's abandonment defense lacks force because it relies on abandonment of the TUMBLEBUS mark in other parts of the United States to effectuate a forfeiture of Tumblebus Inc.'s rights to the mark in the greater Louisville area. In support of her abandonment defense, Cranmer asserts that, in creating the Lanham Act, Congress recognized the need for nationalization of trademark law in light of the increasing nationalization of trade and commerce. Arguably, some of our prior decisions have suggested that a junior mark-user's operation in a different geographic region from the senior mark-user might not, by itself, foreclose the senior mark-user's claim for infringement against the junior user. These cases would be turned on their heads, however, if we were to conclude that, because trademark rights may extend beyond the particular geographic area in which a business operates, a trademark holder may also lose any rights it has in a mark anywhere in the United States by abandoning the mark in one part of the country or by failing to establish a mark with national significance. Indeed, contrary to Cranmer's suggestion otherwise, there is considerable support for the concept that rights in a mark may be abandoned in certain geographic areas but not others (i.e., "partial geographic abandonment").

In the end, we must return to the statutory mandate of § 1127, which provides that abandonment occurs when a term "lose[s] its significance as a mark." So long as the TUMBLEBUS mark retains its significance in the greater Louisville area, we fail to see why Tumblebus Inc. should be foreclosed from asserting its rights in the TUMBLEBUS mark in that market. Given the lack of evidence in the record suggesting that the TUMBLEBUS mark has in fact lost its significance in the greater Louisville area, we conclude that the district court did not err in determining that Tumblebus Inc. is likely to succeed on its mark infringement claim notwithstanding Cranmer's asserted defense of abandonment.

b. "First–Sale" Defense

Cranmer also argues that Tumblebus Inc. is unlikely to succeed on the merits of its mark infringement claim because the exhaustion (or "first-sale") defense insulates Cranmer from liability. The first-sale doctrine provides that "a purchaser who does no more than stock, display, and resell a producer's product under the producer's trademark violates no right conferred upon the producer by the Lanham Act." This is true because, when a retailer merely resells a genuine, unaltered good under the trademark of the producer, the use of the producer's trademark by the reseller will not deceive or confuse the public as to the nature, qualities, and origin of the good. See Restatement (Third) of Unfair Competition § 24 cmt. b.

The first-sale doctrine does not apply in the case at bar, however, because Cranmer is not using the TUMBLEBUS mark to resell a genuine good produced by Tumblebus Inc., but rather is using the mark to promote her own mobile-gymnastics service. Unlike goods, which can be sold and resold without change to their nature, quality, and genuineness, services such as gymnastics and fitness instruction inherently vary depending on who is providing such services. Even assuming Cranmer and Tumblebus Inc. use identical retrofitted school buses when providing their gymnastics and fitness-instruction services, other factors, such as the quality of instructors and lesson plans, necessarily distinguish the services provided by the two companies, such that the public could be confused as to what qualities the TUMBLEBUS mark embodies. Thus, Cranmer's assertion of the first-sale defense does not render it unlikely that Tumblebus Inc. will prevail on the merits of its mark infringement claim.

c.   Trade–Dress Infringement

In addition to enjoining Cranmer's use of the TUMBLEBUS mark, the district court's preliminary injunction order also provides that Cranmer is prohibited from "using the vehicle color markings and color scheme of plaintiff (i.e., the 'TUMBLEBUS trade dress') on any vehicle used for Ms. Cranmer's mobile gymnastics business" and that Cranmer must "remove indicia of the TUMBLEBUS trade dress from her bus" when it is operated in the greater Louisville area. Cranmer asserts that this portion of the district court's preliminary injunction cannot stand because the district court failed to make the requisite findings on the record necessary to sustain such an order. We agree.

To recover for trade-dress infringement under § 43(a) of the Lanham Act, a party must first identify what particular elements or attributes comprise the protectable trade dress. Then, the party must show by a preponderance of the evidence that its trade dress is distinctive in the marketplace, that its trade dress is primarily nonfunctional, and that the defendant's trade dress is confusingly similar to the party's protected trade dress. In the case at bar, the district court failed to make any findings on the record as to what particular aspects of Tumblebus Inc.'s vehicular design qualify as distinctive trade dress that is primarily nonfunctional and confusingly similar to Cranmer's vehicular design, thus hampering our ability to review whether Tumblebus Inc. is likely to succeed on the merits of its trade-dress infringement claim and what particular trade-dress usage should be enjoined. Thus, we vacate the district court's preliminary injunction order to the extent that it relates to the issue of trade dress and remand to the district court for further factfinding on the record as to whether Tumblebus Inc. is likely to succeed on the merits of its trade-dress-infringement claim.

For the reasons set forth above, we AFFIRM the district court's preliminary injunction order as it relates to Cranmer's use of the TUMBLEBUS mark, we VACATE the district court's preliminary injunction order as it relates to Cranmer's use of the TUMBLEBUS trade dress, and we REMAND for further proceedings consistent with this opinion.

NOTES

1.   As pointed out in the previous section, the likelihood of confusion standard is the same for 1114(a) and 1125(a) claims. This overlap is also true for unregistered marks. Notice, however, that the unregistered mark gets none of the benefits of the presumption of validity that attaches to registered marks. The trademark owner has to establish validity in order to make a claim for trademark infringement of an unregistered mark. Note the distinction of geographic protection that arises in the discussion of abandonment. A registered mark offers protection nationwide with protections for prior users in the region of use before the owner's registration.

2.   The *Tumblebus* case includes a discussion of several defenses. These defenses also apply to 1114(a) claims. The first defense is one of abandon-

ment, particularly abandonment through naked licensing. Abandonment, in general, is a defense that can arise from nonuse of the trademark. Naked licensing, however, is a type of abandonment that arises from overuse, particularly the licensing of a trademark without the accompanying goodwill that the mark is supposed to protect. One problem with the defense, as asserted here, is that the defendant fails to show the nature of the agreement. The larger problem is one of geographic scope of abandonment. Abandonment anywhere does not mean abandonment everywhere. A trademark owner may decide to quit a particular market in which she has been using a mark without prejudicing rights in other markets, as long as use continues in that market.

3. The first-sale defense is also raised in the case. This is a very important defense, which also arises in patent and copyright law. The trademark owner upon selling the trademarked product or service relinquishes rights to control subsequent sales of the product or service in an unaltered form. The problem with the defense here is that the defendant's use of the mark is not a resale of the branded product, but the use of the mark in association with another product or service.

4. The court also discusses trade dress infringement. We will explore this claim in more depth below. The court vacates the lower court's preliminary injunction because it failed to establish what aspects of Tumblebus' product were protected as trade dress. It would be a good exercise to revisit the facts of this after reading the *Yankee Candle* case below to determine what aspects of the product would qualify for trade dress protection.

2. Infringement Claims Under 15 USC § 1125(c)

STARBUCKS CORP. v. WOLFE'S BOROUGH COFFEE, INC.

United States Court of Appeals for the Second Circuit, 2009.
588 F.3d 97.

MINER, CIRCUIT JUDGE:

Starbucks, a company primarily engaged in the sale of coffee products, was founded in Seattle, Washington in 1971. Since its founding, Starbucks has grown to over 8,700 retail locations in the United States, Canada, and 34 foreign countries and territories. In addition to operating its retail stores, Starbucks supplies its coffees to hundreds of restaurants, supermarkets, airlines, sport and entertainment venues, motion picture theaters, hotels, and cruise ship lines. Starbucks also maintains an internet site that generates over 350,000 "hits" per week from visitors.

In conducting all of its commercial activities, Starbucks prominently displays its registered "Starbucks" marks (the "Starbucks Marks") on its products and areas of business. The Starbucks Marks include, inter alia, the tradename "Starbucks" and its logo, which is circular and generally contains a graphic of a mermaid-like siren encompassed by the phrase "Starbucks Coffee." Starbucks "has been the subject of U.S. trademark registrations continuously since 1985" and has approximately 60 U.S.

trademark registrations. Starbucks also has foreign trademark registrations in 130 countries.

From fiscal years 2000 to 2003, Starbucks spent over $136 million on advertising, promotion, and marketing activities. These promotional activities included television and radio commercials, print advertising, and in-store displays, and "prominently feature[d] (or, in the case of radio, mention[ed]) the Starbucks Marks, which Starbucks considers to be critical to the maintenance of its positive public image and identity." Starbucks also enhanced its commercial presence by permitting the use of its products and retail stores in Hollywood films and popular television programs. These films and programs contained scenes in which the Starbucks Marks were also "prominently displayed."

As may be expected from its spending "substantial time, effort and money advertising and promoting the Starbucks Marks throughout the United States and elsewhere," Starbucks devotes "substantial effort to policing its registered Starbucks Marks." Starbucks "has a regular practice of using watch services and other methods to identify potential infringers of the Starbucks Marks," and it "routinely sends cease and desist letters and, if necessary, commences litigation in support of these efforts."

Black Bear, also a company engaged in the sale of coffee products, has its principal place of business in Tuftonboro, New Hampshire. In contrast to Starbucks, Black Bear is a relatively small company owned by Jim Clark and his wife. It is a family-run business that "manufactures and sells . . . roasted coffee beans and related goods via mail order, internet order, and at a limited number of New England supermarkets." Black Bear also sold coffee products from a retail outlet called "The Den," in Portsmouth, New Hampshire. To help operate its business, Black Bear hires some part-time employees, such as "one girl who comes in two days a week and helps with packaging," but Black Bear is otherwise operated by Mr. and Mrs. Jim Clark, with the occasional help of their two daughters.

In April 1997, Black Bear began selling a "dark roasted blend" of coffee called "Charbucks Blend" and later "Mister Charbucks" (together, the "Charbucks Marks"). Charbucks Blend was sold in a packaging that showed a picture of a black bear above the large font "BLACK BEAR MICRO ROASTERY." The package informed consumers that the coffee was roasted and "Air Quenched" in New Hampshire and, in fairly large font, that "You wanted it dark . . . You've got it dark!" Mister Charbucks was sold in a packaging that showed a picture of a man walking above the large font "Mister Charbucks." The package also informed consumers that the coffee was roasted in New Hampshire by "The Black Bear Micro Roastery" and that the coffee was "Roasted to the Extreme . . . For those who like the extreme."

Not long after making its first sale of Charbucks Blend, in August 1997, Starbucks demanded that Black Bear cease use of the Charbucks

Marks. Having felt wrongly threatened by Starbucks, and believing that "[w]e hadn't done anything wrong," Black Bear ultimately decided to continue selling its "Charbucks Blend" and "Mister Charbucks." Mr. Clark later testified, "[m]y main objection was that basically this was a large corporation coming at me and saying, telling us what to do, and, oh, by the way you're going to pay for it, too. . . . [S]ome of the requests that they were making were really off the wall."

After failed negotiations with Black Bear, on July 2, 2001, Starbucks filed a complaint in the District Court, alleging trademark dilution in violation of 15 U.S.C. §§ 1125(c), 1127; trademark infringement in violation of 15 U.S.C. § 1114(1); unfair competition in violation of 15 U.S.C. § 1125(a); trademark dilution in violation of New York Gen. Bus. Law § 360–l; deceptive acts and business practices and false advertising in violation of New York Gen. Bus. Law §§ 349, 350; and unfair competition in violation of New York common law.

A two-day bench trial was held on March 15, 2005, and March 17, 2005. Among the evidence proffered during trial, Starbucks introduced the testimony of Warren J. Mitofsky ("Dr. Mitofsky"), a scientist in the field of consumer research and polling. His testimony explained the results of his survey, which concluded in part that "[t]he number one association of the name 'Charbucks' in the minds of consumers is with the brand 'Starbucks' . . . [and that] [t]he name 'Charbucks' creates many negative associations in the mind of the consumer when it comes to describing coffee." Dr. Mitofsky testified that the surveyed sample of persons were "designed to be representative of the United States" and that he believed a telephone survey of 600 adults in the United States would "do a good job of random sampling." Dr. Mitofsky summarized the scope of his survey: "Well, if you want to know the reaction to the name Charbucks, then the telephone is perfectly adequate. If you want to measure the reaction or the familiarity with other visual cues, then it's not the right method."

On December 22, 2005, the District Court issued an opinion and order ruling in favor of Black Bear and dismissing Starbucks' complaint. Among its findings, the court determined that there was neither actual dilution to establish a violation of the federal trademark laws nor any likelihood of dilution to establish a violation of New York's trademark laws. The court also found that Starbucks failed to prove its trademark infringement and unfair competition claims because there was no likelihood that consumers would confuse the Charbucks Marks for the Starbucks Marks.

Starbucks appealed the District Court's judgment, and, while the appeal was pending, Congress amended the trademark laws by passing the Trademark Dilution Revision Act of 2005 (the "TDRA"). * * *The TDRA was in response to the Supreme Court's decision in *Moseley v. V Secret Catalogue, Inc.*, 537 U.S. 418, 433, 123 S.Ct. 1115, 155 L.Ed.2d 1 (2003), in which the Supreme Court held that the Federal Trademark Dilution Act required a showing of "actual dilution" in order to establish a dilution claim. * * *The TDRA amended the Federal Trademark Dilution Act to provide, inter alia, that the owner of a famous, distinctive mark is entitled to an injunction against the use of a mark that is "likely" to cause dilution of the famous mark. 15 U.S.C. § 1125(c)(1). In light of the change in law, we vacated the judgment of the District Court and remanded for further proceedings. * * * In so doing, we noted that "[a]lthough the district court also considered whether Starbucks had shown a likelihood of dilution under New York Gen. Bus. Law § 360–l, it is not clear that that statute is coextensive with the amended statute." Id.

On remand, the District Court accepted additional briefing from both parties. Both parties agreed that no further evidentiary proceedings were required. On June 5, 2008, the District Court again entered judgment in favor of Black Bear, finding-for substantially the same reasons detailed in the court's December 2005 decision but with additional analysis with respect to the federal dilution claim-that Starbucks failed to demonstrate an entitlement to relief on its federal and state claims. Starbucks timely appealed the District Court's June 5, 2008 judgment.

On appeal, Starbucks primarily argues (1) that the District Court erred in finding that the Charbucks Marks are not likely to dilute the Starbucks Marks under federal and state law; and (2) that the District Court erred in its factual findings and balancing of the relevant factors for determination of "likelihood of confusion" with respect to Starbucks' infringement and unfair competition claims.

B. Federal Trademark Dilution

Under federal law, an owner of a "famous, distinctive mark" is entitled to an "injunction against the user of a mark that is 'likely to cause dilution' of the famous mark." * * *Although the requirement that the mark be "famous" and "distinctive" significantly limits the pool of marks that may receive dilution protection, see *Savin Corp. v. Savin Group*, 391 F.3d 439, 449 (2d Cir.2004), that the Starbucks Marks are "famous" within the meaning of 15 U.S.C. § 1125(c) is not disputed by the parties in this case. Rather, the focus of this appeal is on dilution itself. As specified by statute, federal dilution is actionable in two situations: (1) dilution by "blurring" and (2) dilution by "tarnishment." 15 U.S.C. § 1125(c).

1. Dilution by Blurring

Dilution by blurring is an "association arising from the similarity between a mark or trade name and a famous mark that impairs the distinctiveness of the famous mark," 15 U.S.C. § 1125(c)(2)(B), and may be found "regardless of the presence or absence of actual or likely confusion, of competition, or of actual economic injury," 15 U.S.C. § 1125(c)(1).* * *

Federal law specifies six non-exhaustive factors for the courts to consider in determining whether there is dilution by blurring:

(i) The degree of similarity between the mark or trade name and the famous mark.

(ii) The degree of inherent or acquired distinctiveness of the famous mark.

(iii) The extent to which the owner of the famous mark is engaging in substantially exclusive use of the mark.

(iv) The degree of recognition of the famous mark.

(v) Whether the user of the mark or trade name intended to create an association with the famous mark.

(vi) Any actual association between the mark or trade name and the famous mark.

15 U.S.C. § 1125(c)(2)(B)(i)–(vi).* * *The District Court found that the second, third, and fourth factors favored Starbucks, and those findings are not challenged in this appeal.

With respect to the first factor-the degree of similarity between the marks-the District Court did not clearly err in finding that the Charbucks Marks were minimally similar to the Starbucks Marks. Although "Ch"arbucks is similar to "St"arbucks in sound and spelling, it is evident from the record that the Charbucks Marks-as they are presented to consumers-are minimally similar to the Starbucks Marks. The Charbucks line of products are presented as either "Mister Charbucks" or "Charbucks Blend" in packaging that displays the "Black Bear" name in no subtle manner, and the packaging also makes clear that Black Bear is a "Micro Roastery" located in New Hampshire.* * * Moreover, Black Bear's package design for Charbucks coffee is "different in imagery, color, and format from Starbucks' logo and signage." For example, either a graphic of a bear or a male person is associated with Charbucks, and those marks are not comparable to the Starbucks graphic of a siren in pose, shape, art-style, gender, or overall impression. Indeed, the Starbucks siren appears nowhere on the Charbucks package. To the extent the Charbucks Marks are presented to the public through Black Bear's website, the dissimilarity between the marks is still evident as the Charbucks brand of coffee is accompanied by Black Bear's domain name, www. blackbear coffee. com, and other products, such as shirts and cups, displaying Black Bear's name.

Furthermore, we note that it is unlikely that "Charbucks" will appear to consumers outside the context of its normal use, since "Charbucks" is not directly identifiable with the actual product, i.e., coffee beans. Cf. *Nabisco v. PF Brands, Inc.*, 191 F.3d 208, 213, 218 (2d Cir.1999) (observing that Pepperidge Farm's famous "goldfish" mark may be identified outside of the packaging because the goldfish cracker itself is the famous mark). The term "Charbucks" appears only on the packaging and on Black Bear's website-both mediums in which the Charbucks Marks' similarity with Starbucks is demonstratively minimal-and Starbucks has not identified any other method by which the Charbucks Marks likely would be presented to the public outside the context of its normal use. Cf. id. at

218 ("[M]any consumers of [the defendant's] crackers will not see the box; they will find goldfish-shaped cheddar cheese crackers served in a dish at a bar or restaurant or friend's house, looking very much like the familiar Pepperidge Farm Goldfish product."). To be sure, consumers may simply refer to "Mister Charbucks" or "Charbucks Blend" in conversation; however, it was not clearly erroneous for the District Court to find that the "Mister" prefix or "Blend" suffix lessened the similarity between the Charbucks Marks and the Starbucks Marks in the court's overall assessment of similarity.

Inasmuch as Starbucks argues that the District Court clearly erred in concluding that Charbucks is not a stand-alone identifier of Black Bear's products, we find Starbucks' argument to be unpersuasive. Starbucks asserts that the District Court should have ignored the term "Mister" or "Blend" before or after "Charbucks" in assessing the "degree of similarity" factor because those terms are generic and "too weak to serve a brand-identifying function." This argument to ignore relevant evidence is unfounded in the law. See 15 U.S.C. § 1125(c)(2)(B); accord H.R. Report No. 109–23, at 7 (2005), reprinted in 2006 U.S.C.C.A.N. 1091, 1096 (emphasizing that "a court is permitted to consider all relevant factors in determining the presence of dilution by blurring"). And in any event, even if the core term "Charbucks" were used to identify a product as a stand-alone term, such finding would not be dispositive of the District Court's overall assessment of the degree of similarity. * * *In this case, the District Court's reasons for a finding of minimal similarity between the Charbucks Marks and the Starbucks Marks were well supported by the record, as explained above.

Upon its finding that the marks were not substantially similar, however, the District Court concluded that "[t]his dissimilarity alone is sufficient to defeat [Starbucks'] blurring claim, and in any event, this factor at a minimum weighs strongly against [Starbucks] in the dilution analysis." We conclude that the District Court erred to the extent it required "substantial" similarity between the marks, and, in this connection, we note that the court may also have placed undue significance on the similarity factor in determining the likelihood of dilution in its alternative analysis.

Prior to the TDRA, this Court has held that "[a] plaintiff cannot prevail on a state or federal dilution claim unless the marks at issue are 'very' or 'substantially similar.' " * * *Notably, under the pre-TDRA law, the federal statute provided a remedy for dilution of famous marks but did not define "dilution," much less inform the courts of the importance of "similarity" in the dilution analysis.

> The owner of a famous mark shall be entitled, subject to the principles of equity and upon such terms as the court deems reasonable, to an injunction against another person's commercial use in commerce of a mark or trade name, if such use begins after the mark has become famous and causes dilution of the distinctive quality of the mark. . . .

15 U.S.C. § 1125(c) (2000). Our adoption of a "substantially similar" requirement for federal dilution claims, * * * can likely be attributed to the lack of guidance under the former federal statute and the existence of a "substantially similar" requirement under state dilution statutes, which were better defined.* * *

The post-TDRA federal dilution statute, however, provides us with a compelling reason to discard the "substantially similar" requirement for federal trademark dilution actions. The current federal statute defines dilution by blurring as an "association arising from the similarity between a mark ... and a famous mark that impairs the distinctiveness of the famous mark," and the statute lists six non-exhaustive factors for determining the existence of an actionable claim for blurring. 15 U.S.C. § 1125(c)(2)(B). Although "similarity" is an integral element in the definition of "blurring," we find it significant that the federal dilution statute does not use the words "very" or "substantial" in connection with the similarity factor to be considered in examining a federal dilution claim. See 15 U.S.C. § 1125(c); *Bonime v. Avaya, Inc.*, 547 F.3d 497, 502 (2d Cir.2008) ("In determining the proper interpretation of a statute, this court will look first to the plain language of a statute and interpret it by its ordinary, common meaning." (internal quotation marks omitted)).

Indeed, one of the six statutory factors informing the inquiry as to whether the allegedly diluting mark "impairs the distinctiveness of the famous mark" is "[t]he degree of similarity between the mark or trade name and the famous mark." 15 U.S.C. § 1125(c)(2)(B)(i) (emphasis added). Consideration of a "degree" of similarity as a factor in determining the likelihood of dilution does not lend itself to a requirement that the similarity between the subject marks must be "substantial" for a dilution claim to succeed. See *Bonime*, 547 F.3d at 502. Moreover, were we to adhere to a substantial similarity requirement for all dilution by blurring claims, the significance of the remaining five factors would be materially diminished because they would have no relevance unless the degree of similarity between the marks are initially determined to be "substantial." Such requirement of substantial similarity is at odds with the federal dilution statute, which lists "degree of similarity" as one of several factors in determining blurring. * * *

Turning to the remaining two disputed factors-(1) whether the user of the mark intended to create an association with the famous mark, and (2) whether there is evidence of any actual association between the mark and the famous mark-we conclude that the District Court also erred in considering these factors.

The District Court determined that Black Bear possessed the requisite intent to associate Charbucks with Starbucks but that this factor did not weigh in favor of Starbucks because Black Bear did not act in "bad faith." The determination of an "intent to associate," however, does not require the additional consideration of whether bad faith corresponded with that intent. The plain language of section 1125(c) requires only the consideration of "[w]hether the user of the mark or trade name intended to create an association with the famous mark." See 15 U.S.C. § 1125(c)(2)(B)(v). Thus, where, as here, the allegedly diluting mark was created with an intent to associate with the famous mark, this factor favors a finding of a likelihood of dilution.

The District Court also determined that there was not an "actual association" favoring Starbucks in the dilution analysis. Starbucks, however, submitted the results of a telephone survey where 3.1% of 600 consumers responded that Starbucks was the possible source of Charbucks. The survey also showed that 30.5% of consumers responded "Starbucks" to the question: "[w]hat is the first thing that comes to mind when you hear the name 'Charbucks.'" In rejecting Starbucks' claim of actual association, the District Court referred to evidence supporting the absence of "actual confusion" to conclude that "the evidence is insufficient to make the ... factor weigh in [Starbucks'] favor to any significant degree." (internal quotation marks and original alteration omitted). This was error, as the absence of actual or even of a likelihood of confusion does not undermine evidence of trademark dilution.* * *

Accordingly, in light of the foregoing, we remand to the District Court for consideration of Starbucks' claim of trademark dilution by blurring under 15 U.S.C. § 1125(c)(2)(B).

2. Dilution by Tarnishment

Dilution by tarnishment is an "association arising from the similarity between a mark or trade name and a famous mark that harms the reputation of the famous mark." 15 U.S.C. § 1125(c)(2)(C). "A trademark may be tarnished when it is linked to products of shoddy quality, or is portrayed in an unwholesome or unsavory context, with the result that the public will associate the lack of quality or lack of prestige in the defendant's goods with the plaintiff's unrelated goods." *Hormel Foods Corp. v. Jim Henson Productions, Inc.*, 73 F.3d 497, 507 (2d Cir.1996) (internal quotation marks omitted). A trademark may also be diluted by tarnishment if the mark loses its ability to serve as a "wholesome identifier" of plaintiff's product. Id.; accord *Chemical Corp. v. Anheuser-Busch, Inc.*, 306 F.2d 433 (5th Cir.1962) (finding that use of exterminator's slogan "where there's life, ... there's Bugs" tarnished the use of beer company's slogan "where there's life, ... there's Bud."); *Steinway & Sons v. Robert Demars & Friends*, 210 U.S.P.Q. 954 (C.D.Cal.1981) (finding that use of "STEIN–WAY CO." to sell clip-on beverage handles tarnished high-end musical instrument company's use of its name of "STEINWAY & SONS"); *Eastman Kodak Co. v. Rakow*, 739 F.Supp. 116 (W.D.N.Y.1989) (finding that comedian's stage name "Kodak" tarnished the mark of the Eastman Kodak Company because the comedian's act "includes humor that relates to bodily functions and sex ... and ... uses crude, off-color language repeatedly" (internal quotation marks omitted)); *Dallas Cowboys Cheerleaders, Inc. v. Pussycat Cinema, Ltd.*, 467 F.Supp. 366 (S.D.N.Y.) (finding that pornographic depiction of a Dallas Cowboys

Cheerleader-style cheerleader in an adult film tarnished the professional mark of the Dallas Cowboys Cheerleaders), aff'd, 604 F.2d 200 (2d Cir.1979).

To the extent Starbucks relies on the survey, a mere association between "Charbucks" and "Starbucks," coupled with a negative impression of the name "Charbucks," is insufficient to establish a likelihood of dilution by tarnishment. That a consumer may associate a negative-sounding junior mark with a famous mark says little of whether the consumer views the junior mark as harming the reputation of the famous mark. The more relevant question, for purposes of tarnishment, would have been how a hypothetical coffee named either "Mister Charbucks" or "Charbucks Blend" would affect the positive impressions about the coffee sold by Starbucks. We will not assume that a purportedly negative-sounding junior mark will likely harm the reputation of the famous mark by mere association when the survey conducted by the party claiming dilution could have easily enlightened us on the matter. Indeed, it may even have been that "Charbucks" would strengthen the positive impressions of Starbucks because it brings to the attention of consumers that the "Char" is absent in "Star"bucks, and, therefore, of the two "bucks," Starbucks is the "un-charred" and more appealing product. Juxtaposition may bring to light more appealing aspects of a name that otherwise would not have been brought to the attention of ordinary observers.

Starbucks also argues that "Charbucks" is a pejorative term for Starbucks' coffee, and, therefore, the Charbucks "name has negative associations that consumers are likely to associate with Starbucks' coffee." Although the term "Charbucks" was once used pejoratively during the so-called "coffee-wars" in Boston, Massachusetts, Black Bear is not propagating that negative meaning but, rather, is redefining "Charbucks" to promote a positive image for its brand of coffee. Black Bear sells "Charbucks" as its own product, and, consistent with its intent on profiting from selling Charbucks, the Charbucks line of coffee is of "[v]ery high quality. It's our life. We put everything into it." In short, Black Bear is promoting "Charbucks" and not referring to it in a way as to harm the reputation of Starbucks' coffees. Cf. *Deere & Co.*, 41 F.3d at 45 (stating that the likelihood of dilution by tarnishment means "the possibility that consumers will come to attribute unfavorable characteristics to a mark and ultimately associate the mark with inferior goods and services").

Moreover, that the Charbucks line of coffee is marketed as a product of "[v]ery high quality"-as Starbucks also purports its coffee to be-is inconsistent with the concept of "tarnishment." See *Hormel Foods Corp.*, 73 F.3d at 507 (citing cases finding tarnishment where challenged marks were either "seamy" or substantially of lesser quality than the famous mark). Certainly, the similarity between Charbucks and Starbucks in that they are both "[v]ery high quality" coffees may be relevant in determining dilution, see 15 U.S.C. 1125(c)(2)(B), (c)(2)(C), but such similarity in this case undercuts the claim that Charbucks harms the reputation of Starbucks. See *Deere & Co. v. MTD Prods., Inc.*, 41 F.3d 39, 43 (2d Cir.1994) (

" 'Tarnishment' generally arises when the plaintiff's trademark is linked to products of shoddy quality, or is portrayed in an unwholesome or unsavory context likely to evoke unflattering thoughts about the owner's product."). Accordingly, we conclude that the District Court did not err in rejecting Starbucks' claim of dilution by tarnishment.

3.   The Parody Exception

Even if its use of "Charbucks" constituted dilution by either blurring or tarnishment, Black Bear appears to argue in the alternative that Charbucks is a parody and thus falls under an exception to 15 U.S.C. § 1125(c). Section 1125(c)(3), which was added in 2006 pursuant to the TDRA, specifies that the following uses of a mark "shall not be actionable as dilution by blurring or dilution by tarnishment":

> (A) Any fair use, including a nominative or descriptive fair use, or facilitation of such fair use, of a famous mark by another person other than as a designation of source for the person's own goods or services, including use in connection with-
>
> (i) advertising or promotion that permits consumers to compare goods or services; or
>
> (ii) identifying and parodying, criticizing, or commenting upon the famous mark owner or the goods or services of the famous mark owner.
>
> (B) All forms of news reporting and news commentary.
>
> (C) Any noncommercial use of a mark.

15 U.S.C. § 1125(c)(3) (emphasis added).

As evident from the statutory language, Black Bear's use of the Charbucks Marks cannot qualify under the parody exception because the Charbucks Marks are used "as a designation of source for [Black Bear's] own goods[, i.e., the Charbucks line of coffee]." See 15 U.S.C. § 1125(c)(3)(A). Although Black Bear cites to several cases in support of its argument that the parody exception may still apply even if the parody were used to "identify the source of the defendants' goods," those cases were decided before the TDRA and are thus inapposite to the extent they are inconsistent with the amended section 1125(c)(3). See *Louis Vuitton Malletier S.A. v. Haute Diggity Dog, LLC*, 507 F.3d 252, 266 (4th Cir.2007).

Inasmuch as Black Bear's argument may be construed as advocating for consideration of parody in determining the likelihood of dilution by blurring-such as is recognized by the Fourth Circuit, see id. at 267-we need not adopt or reject *Louis Vuitton*'s parody holding. We conclude that Black Bear's use of the Charbucks Marks is not a parody of the kind which would favor Black Bear in the dilution analysis even if we were to adopt the Fourth Circuit's rule.

In the Fourth Circuit's *Louis Vuitton* case, Louis Vuitton Malletier S.A.-the famous maker of luxury luggage, handbags, and accessories-asserted, inter alia, a trademark dilution claim against Haute Diggity Dog,

LLC, a manufacturer of pet toys that named its products to "parody elegant high-end brands of products such as perfume, cars, shoes, sparkling wine, and handbags." Id. at 256, 258. Among its parodies, Haute Diggity Dog, LLC's "Chewy Vuiton" product was alleged by Louis Vuitton Malletier S.A. as infringing and dilutive of the "Louis Vuitton" mark. Id. at 256.

Addressing the dilution claim, the Fourth Circuit initially noted that the fair use exception for parodies as specified in 15 U.S.C. § 1125(c)(3)(A) "does not extend . . . to parodies used as a trademark. . . . [P]arodying a famous mark is protected by the fair use defense only if the parody is not 'a designation of source for the person's own goods or services.'" *Louis Vuitton*, 507 F.3d at 266. The Fourth Circuit then held, however, that the defendant's use of a parody "may [still] be considered in determining whether the plaintiff-owner of a famous mark has proved its claim that the defendant's use of a parody mark is likely to impair the distinctiveness of the famous mark [, i.e., whether the plaintiff has proved a likelihood of dilution by blurring under 15 U.S.C. § 1125(c)(2)(B)]." Id. at 267. In justifying its consideration of a parody element in conducting the blurring analysis under section 1125(c)(2)(B), the Fourth Circuit explained:

> [F]actor (v) (whether the defendant intended to create an association with the famous mark) and factor (vi) (whether there exists an actual association between the defendant's mark and the famous mark) directly invite inquiries into the defendant's intent in using the parody, the defendant's actual use of the parody, and the effect that its use has on the famous mark. While a parody intentionally creates an association with the famous mark in order to be a parody, it also intentionally communicates, if it is successful, that it is not the famous mark, but rather a satire of the famous mark. That the defendant is using its mark as a parody is therefore relevant in the consideration of these statutory factors.

Similarly, factors (i), (ii), and (iv)-the degree of similarity between the two marks, the degree of distinctiveness of the famous mark, and its recognizability-are directly implicated by consideration of the fact that the defendant's mark is a successful parody. Indeed, by making the famous mark an object of the parody, a successful parody might actually enhance the famous mark's distinctiveness by making it an icon. The brunt of the joke becomes yet more famous.

Id. (internal citations omitted). The Fourth Circuit then concluded that "Chewy Vuiton" did not dilute "Louis Vuitton" primarily because Chewy Vuiton "convey[ed] the . . . message that it was not in fact a source of [Louis Vuitton] products. . . . [A]s a parody, it separated itself from the [Louis Vuitton] marks in order to make fun of them." Id. at 267–68 ("[B]ecause [Louis Vuitton's] mark is particularly strong and distinctive, it becomes more likely that a [successful] parody will not impair the distinctiveness of the mark.").

Here, unlike in Louis Vuitton, Black Bear's use of the Charbucks Marks is, at most, a subtle satire of the Starbucks Marks. Although we recognize some humor in "Char"bucks as a reference to the dark roast of the Starbucks coffees, Black Bear's claim of humor fails to demonstrate such a clear parody as to qualify under the Fourth Circuit's rule. As the owner of Black Bear affirmed during his testimony, "[t]he inspiration for the term Charbucks comes directly from Starbucks' tendency to roast its products more darkly than that of other major roasters." The owner of Black Bear further testified that the Charbucks line of products "is the darkest roasted coffee that we do" and is of "[v]ery high quality." Thus, the Charbucks parody is promoted not as a satire or irreverent commentary of Starbucks but, rather, as a beacon to identify Charbucks as a coffee that competes at the same level and quality as Starbucks in producing dark-roasted coffees. See *Harley Davidson, Inc. v. Grottanelli*, 164 F.3d 806, 813 (2d Cir.1999) ("[P]arodic use is sharply limited" in circumstances where "an alleged parody of a competitor's mark [is used] to sell a competing product."); cf. *Louis Vuitton*, 507 F.3d at 260–61 (permitting parodic use where the parody marketed its products to a significantly different class of consumers than the famous mark); id. ("The [Louis Vuitton] handbag is provided for the most elegant and well-to-do celebrity, to proudly display to the public and the press, whereas the imitation 'Chewy Vuiton' 'handbag' is designed to mock the celebrity and be used by a dog.").

Therefore, because the Charbucks Marks do not effect an "increase [in] public identification [of the Starbucks Marks with Starbucks]," the purported Charbucks parody plays no part in undermining a finding of dilution under the Fourth Circuit's rule. See generally *Hormel Foods Corp.*, 73 F.3d at 506; Louis Vuitton, 507 F.3d at 260 ("[A] parody relies upon a difference from the original mark, presumably a humorous difference, in order to produce its desired effect." (internal quotation marks omitted)). Accordingly, we conclude that Black Bear's incantation of parody does nothing to shield it from Starbucks' dilution claim in this case.

C.   State Trademark Dilution

New York law provides that a "[l]ikelihood of injury to business reputation or of dilution of the distinctive quality of a mark or trade name shall be a ground for injunctive relief ... notwithstanding the absence of competition between the parties or the absence of confusion as to the source of goods or services." N.Y. Gen. Bus. Law § 360–l. Similar to federal trademark dilution law under 15 U.S.C. § 1125(c), section 360–l has been interpreted to provide for protection against both dilution by blurring and tarnishment. See *Hormel Foods Corp.*, 73 F.3d at 506–07. Unlike federal trademark dilution law, however, New York's trademark dilution law does not require a mark to be "famous" for protection against dilution to apply. Compare 15 U.S.C. § 1125(c), with N.Y. Gen. Bus. Law § 360–l. Nor are the factors that are considered for determining dilution by blurring under New York law coextensive with the factors for determining dilution by blurring under federal law. Compare *New York Stock Exchange, Inc. v. New York, New York Hotel LLC*, 293 F.3d 550, 558 (2d Cir.2002) ("To determine the likelihood of blurring, we have looked to six factors, including: (i) the similarity of the marks; (ii) the similarity of the products covered; (iii) the sophistication of the consumers; (iv) the existence of predatory intent; (v) the renown of the senior mark; and (vi) the renown of the junior mark."), with 15 U.S.C. § 1125(c)(2)(B)(i)–(vi). Most important to the distinction here, New York law does not permit a dilution claim unless the marks are "substantially" similar.* * *

Because we conclude that the District Court did not clearly err in finding that the Charbucks Marks are not substantially similar to the Starbucks Marks, the court did not err in denying Starbucks relief under New York dilution law. Moreover, for the reasons stated supra, Part II(B)(2) (Dilution by Tarnishment), we agree with the District Court that Starbucks failed to establish dilution by tarnishment under New York law. Accordingly, we hold that the District Court did not err in finding that there was no likelihood of dilution under New York law in this case.* * *

NOTES

1. The Supreme Court's decision in *Moseley v. V Secret Catalogue, Inc*, 537 U.S. 418, 123 S.Ct. 1115, 155 L.Ed.2d 1 (2003), was a closely watched and controversial one. The trademark bar was concerned that the Court would do exactly what it ended up doing: interpret the statute literally to require proof of actual dilution to make a claim. State dilution statutes required only proof of likelihood of dilution shown through a multi-factor test much like the Polaroid/Lapp/Sleekcraft factors used for proof of likelihood of confusion.

2. As was expected, Congress passed legislation in September, 2006, amending Section 43(c) to change the standard from actual dilution to likelihood of dilution. The amendment also clarified the distinction between dilution by blurring and dilution by tarnishment and clarified the standard for injunctive relief. The President signed the bill into law on October 6, 2006. The *Starbucks* decision illustrates how courts apply the new federal statute. Notice the discussion of state antidilution claims at the end of the opinion. Omitted is the court's analysis that Starbucks failed to establish likelihood of confusion under federal trademark and unfair competition law. What does the anti-dilution claim add to traditional trademark law?

3. For analyses of the dilution standard, see Clarissa Long, *Dilution*, 106 COLUM. L. REV. 1029 (2006) (demonstrating that dilution enforcement has been declining over time); Thomas R. Lee, *Demystifying Dilution*, 84 B.U. L. REV. 859 (2004) (providing standards for enforcing dilution claims in light the history of the cause of action); Brian A. Jacobs, *Note: Trademark Dilution on the Constitutional Edge*, 104 COLUM. L. REV. 161 (2004) (addressing First Amendment issues and proposing an economic test for determining dilution).

3. Special Issues

a. *Trade Dress*

YANKEE CANDLE COMPANY, INC. v. BRIDGEWATER CANDLE COMPANY, LLC

United States Court of Appeals, First Circuit, 2001.
259 F.3d 25.

TORRUELLA, CIRCUIT JUDGE.

Yankee Candle Company ("Yankee"), a leading manufacturer of scented candles, sued competitor Bridgewater Candle Company ("Bridgewater") on counts of copyright infringement and trade dress infringement under federal law, as well as on state claims of common law trade dress infringement, tortious interference, and deceptive trade practices. The district court granted summary judgment to Bridgewater on all claims except those of tortious interference and of [deceptive trade practices].

Yankee's [claim] for trade dress infringement, is brought pursuant to § 43(a) of the Lanham Act, which provides protection against the use of "any word, term, name, symbol, or device" that "is likely to cause confusion, or to cause mistake, or to deceive" as to the source of a product. 15 U.S.C. § 1125(a). The Lanham Act extends protection not only to words and symbols, but also to "trade dress," defined as "the design and appearance of a product together with the elements making up the overall image that serves to identify the product presented to the consumer." The primary purpose of trade dress protection is to protect that which identifies a product's source. Courts recognize trade dress claims based both on product packaging and on "product design/configuration." See, e.g., *Wal-Mart Stores v. Samara Bros., Inc.*, 529 U.S. 205, 213–14 (2000).

In order for trade dress to be protected under § 43(a), a plaintiff must prove that the dress is: (i) used in commerce; (ii) non-functional; and (iii) distinctive. Distinctiveness may be either "inherent," that is, the "intrinsic nature [of the trade dress] serves to identify a particular source," Wal-Mart, 529 U.S. at 210 (citing *Two Pesos, Inc. v. Taco Cabana, Inc.*, 505 U.S. 763, 768 (1992)), or "acquired," i.e., the trade dress has acquired a "secondary meaning" whereby the public views its "primary significance . . . as identify[ing] the source of the product rather than the product itself." Id. at 211. Finally, to prove infringement of protected trade dress, the plaintiff must show that another's use of a similar trade dress is likely to cause confusion among consumers as to the product's source.

The district court identified three ways in which Yankee claimed that Bridgewater had infringed its trade dress: (i) by copying Yankee's method of shelving and displaying candles in its stores, called the "Vertical Display System"; (ii) by copying the overall "look and feel" of Yankee's Housewarmer line of candles; and (iii) by copying the design of Yankee's merchandise catalog, specifically its one fragrance per page layout. The court first held that the Vertical Display System was "manifestly functional," both in its arrangement of candles by color and in its use of wooden shelving, and concluded that "Yankee cannot invoke the Lanham Act to appropriate such a conventional method of presenting its wares."

The court then turned to the "look and feel" of the Housewarmer line of candles and the layout of the Yankee catalog. It concluded, with little explanation, that both claims alleged trade dress infringement of a product design/configuration, rather than infringement of product packaging. In accordance with the Supreme Court's decision in Wal–Mart, the district court thus held that neither aspect of Yankee's trade dress could be inherently distinctive as a matter of law. The district court therefore turned to a determination of whether a genuine issue of material fact existed with respect to secondary meaning.

As to the Housewarmer line of candles, the district court determined that the evidence introduced by Yankee had fallen far short of the "vigorous" evidentiary standard required to show secondary meaning in a product design/configuration case. First, Yankee had failed to introduce any survey evidence, which this Court has described as the "preferred" manner of demonstrating secondary meaning. Second, Yankee had not introduced any circumstantial evidence indicating that the public had made a conscious connection between the trade dress at issue and Yankee as the source of that trade dress.

As for the catalog, the district court simply concluded that "there is no question that Bridgewater's catalog is indeed Bridgewater's and not Yankee's," and that "[n]o fair minded person, looking at Bridgewater's document, could possibly view it as an attempt to 'pass off' the Bridgewater catalogue as the Yankee one."

Lastly, although it had not found any of Yankee's trade dress sufficiently distinctive to qualify for protection, the district court held in the alternative that "no reasonable juror could conclude that there is a likelihood of confusion, where clearly marked company names are featured on the face of the products and catalogues."

Yankee argues that the distinct combination of elements comprising its candle sizes and shapes, quantities sold, labels, Vertical Design System, and catalog stem from "arbitrary" choices and are thus "inherently distinctive" and entitled to trademark protection. Certain types of trade dress, however, can never be inherently distinctive. Wal–Mart, 529 U.S. at 212–14 (product design/configuration cannot be inherently distinctive); Qualitex Co. v. Jacobson Prods. Co., 514 U.S. 159, 162 (1995) (color cannot be inherently distinctive). We find that Yankee's combination claim falls under the category of product design/configuration, and thus Yankee must prove that the dress has attained secondary meaning in order for it to be protected under the Lanham Act. Wal–Mart, 529 U.S. at 215.

Yankee argues that because its products are candles, all the trappings associated with the sale of the candle—i.e., the candle-holders, the Vertical Display System, the labels, and the catalog—constitute product packaging, or at the very least a "tertium quid ... akin to product packaging," categories of trade dress that may be inherently distinctive. See *Wal–Mart*, 529 U.S. at 215 (citing *Two Pesos*, 505 U.S. at 773, 112 S.Ct. 2753).

Although, as we explain below, Yankee's Housewarmer labels are product packaging and thus may be inherently distinctive, when combined with actual candle features, candle containers, the catalog, and the in-store display system, the claim is no longer clearly a product-packaging one. Nor can the claim be categorized as product design/configuration, as that term has generally been defined to be limited to features inherent to the actual physical product: here, the candles. See *Wal–Mart*, 529 U.S. at 212 (describing cocktail shaker shaped as penguin as a product design). We also do not see this claim as akin to the restaurant decor upheld as potentially inherently distinctive in *Two Pesos*, which the Supreme Court later described as a "tertium quid that is akin to product packaging." *Wal–Mart*, 529 U.S. at 215. Yankee has not made a claim as to the overall appearance of an entire store, but has instead isolated certain characteristics of its candle display in stores. This strikes us as far closer to the design/configuration category. The fact that Yankee points to particular aspects of the candles themselves, namely their shapes and sizes, only confirms our categorization.

Yankee also claims that unique features of its Housewarmer labels constitute an inherently distinctive trade dress. The district court found that the labels were also product configuration/design, and thus could not be inherently distinctive as a matter of law. We disagree. Detachable labels are a classic case of product packaging, and therefore may be inherently distinctive. Although the district court did not determine whether the Housewarmer labels were inherently distinctive, we are convinced that the label elements highlighted by Yankee do not meet the inherent distinctiveness test. We therefore uphold the district court's grant of summary judgment on this basis.

Trademarks are divided into five categories: generic, descriptive, suggestive, arbitrary, and fanciful. If a mark falls into one of the latter three categories, it is deemed to be inherently distinctive. [I]nherent distinctiveness [has been] determined by reference to: (i) whether the design was a common or basic one; (ii) whether it was "unique or unusual" in the field; (iii) whether it was a refinement of a common form of ornamentation; and (iv) "whether it was capable of creating a commercial impression distinct from the accompanying words."

Furthermore, in evaluating the inherent distinctiveness of Yankee's packaging, we must consider the fact that although Yankee's Housewarmer labels have obvious similarities, they also differ significantly from one another, in that they necessarily display different pictures corresponding to their particular candle fragrance. In other words, Yankee seeks to protect features common to a set of labels, as opposed to a specific label common to a host of Yankee goods. A trade dress plaintiff seeking to protect a series or line of products faces a particularly difficult challenge, as it must show that the appearance of the several products is "sufficiently distinct and unique to merit protection." Moreover, trade dress claims across a line of products present special concerns in their ability to artificially limit competition, as such claims are generally broader in scope than claims relating to an individual item.

Yankee has focused on the "arbitrary" choices it made in designing its label, and has for this reason introduced into evidence numerous possibilities of alternative label designs. While we appreciate that there are many different potential ways of creating a candle label, we think Yankee's approach ignores the focus of the inherent distinctiveness inquiry. As we detailed in the copyright section of this opinion, Yankee's label is essentially a combination of functional and common features. Although such a combination may be entitled to protection where secondary meaning is shown, it is less likely to qualify as inherently distinctive. While the particular combination of common features may indeed be "arbitrary," we do not think that any reasonable juror could conclude that these elements are so "unique and unusual" that they are source-indicative in the absence of secondary meaning.

Having concluded that neither trade dress claim made by Yankee qualifies for protection based on its inherent distinctiveness, we next address whether Yankee has introduced sufficient evidence to survive summary judgment on the question of secondary meaning. As evidence of secondary meaning, Yankee points to: (i) its advertising campaign featuring pictures of its products with the claimed trade dress; (ii) its continuous and virtually exclusive use of its trade dress since 1995; (iii) its high sales figures for Housewarmer candles; (iv) evidence from Bridgewater's files indicating that retailers identify a resemblance between Bridgewater's styles and Yankee's; (v) testimony by a Bridgewater's sales agent as to the distinctiveness of the Yankee trade dress; (vi) testimony by Bridgewater and Yankee employees as to the distinctiveness of Yankee's claimed trade dress; (vii) evidence of actual consumer confusion between Bridgewater and Yankee products; and (viii) evidence of intentional copying by Bridgewater.

Yankee has introduced no survey evidence here. Yankee also cites no evidence that individual consumers associate the particular features at issue with Yankee.

Secondary meaning may also be proven through circumstantial evidence, specifically the length and manner of the use of the trade dress, the nature and extent of advertising and promotion of the trade dress, and the efforts made to promote a conscious connection by the public between the trade dress and the product's source. Other factors may include the product's "established place in the market" and proof of intentional copying. Yankee has introduced substantial evidence that the Housewarmer line of candles and corresponding display have been in circulation since 1995, that Yankee spends significant resources advertising its Housewarmer line, and that sales of Housewarmer candles have been extremely successful. However, in concluding that Yankee had not made a sufficient evidentiary showing of secondary meaning, the district court focused on the lack of evidence as to advertising of the specific trade dress claimed, as well as the lack of evidence demonstrating a conscious connection by the public between the claimed trade dress and the product's source.

We believe the district court emphasized the relevant issues in conducting its analysis of secondary meaning. Proof of secondary meaning requires at least some evidence that consumers associate the trade dress with the source. Although evidence of the pervasiveness of the trade dress may support the conclusion that a mark has acquired secondary meaning, it cannot stand alone. To find otherwise would provide trade dress protection for any successful product, or for the packaging of any successful product * * *. In the absence of any evidence that the claimed trade dress actually does identify a product's source, the trade dress should not be entitled to protection.

That being said, Yankee argues that, because its advertising contained pictures of its products incorporating the claimed trade dress, it was the type of "look-for" advertising that can, on its own, support a finding of secondary meaning. In other words, it is advertising that specifically directs a consumer's attention to a particular aspect of the product. To be probative of secondary meaning, the advertising must direct the consumer to those features claimed as trade dress. Merely "featuring" the relevant aspect of the product in advertising is no more probative of secondary meaning than are strong sales; again, to provide protection based on extensive advertising would extend trade dress protection to the label (or to the combination claim) without any showing that the consumer associated the dress with the product's source. The district court found that Yankee's advertising did not emphasize any particular element of its trade dress, and thus could not be probative of secondary meaning. We agree.

We also do not find Yankee's evidence of intentional copying probative of secondary meaning. First, to the extent Yankee seeks to use such evidence as secondary meaning of its combination trade dress, intent plays a particularly minor role in product design/configuration cases. Given the highly functional nature of certain elements of Yankee's claimed combination trade dress, the concern that protection could prevent healthy competition in the scented candle field weighs heavily in this case.

The testimony that Bridgewater designers were, at times, told to make the labels look more like Yankee's is more troubling. However, the relevant intent is not just the intent to copy, but to "pass off" one's goods as those of another. Id. Given that Bridgewater prominently displayed its trade name on its candles, we do not think that the evidence of copying was sufficiently probative of secondary meaning.

In sum, Yankee has not introduced any of the direct evidence—surveys or consumer testimony—traditionally used to establish secondary meaning. Although it has introduced some of the circumstantial evidence often used to support such a finding, the lack of any evidence that actual consumers associated the claimed trade dress with Yankee, as well as the lack of evidence as to confusion on the part of actual consumers, renders this circumstantial evidence insufficient for a reasonable juror to find that the trade dress had acquired a secondary meaning. Yankee has not made the vigorous evidentiary showing required by this Court. The grant of summary judgment on Yankee's Lanham Act claim is affirmed.

NOTES

1. The *Yankee Candle* case presents a useful discussion of the packaging/design distinction made in *Samara*. Does the distinction make more sense now? Is the determination of whether trade dress is packaging or design less complicated than whether trade dress is inherently distinctive or trade dress has secondary meaning? The court, for example, states that the labels are product packaging, and therefore can be inherently distinctive, but when combined with other elements of the products, the trade dress is product design, requiring secondary meaning. Would not it be easier either to allow inherent distinctiveness or to require secondary meaning for all trade dress claims? Is the packaging/design distinction adding anything to the analysis?

2. Read the discussion of how to show secondary meaning. The evidentiary discussion would apply to all situations where secondary meaning is an issue, not just trade dress claims. The discussion should give you a sense of why trademark owners are wary of having to show secondary meaning. It is a very fact intensive inquiry that requires evidence of association in the consumer's mind between the mark and the source of the product or service. Inherent distinctiveness, on the other hand, requires consideration of the mark alone. But as the Court stated in *Samara*, allowing protection only through inherent distinctiveness of the mark may make it too easy to use trademark law in an anticompetitive way through strike suits. The packaging/design distinction really does not address the underlying tension in trade dress protection between granting protection to truly creative trade dress and using trademark infringement suits anticompetitively. The case can be made that simply requiring secondary meaning, with perhaps a slightly lower evidentiary threshold than the one described in *Yankee Candle*, might be the best compromise. For a critical discussion of secondary meaning and the enforcement of trademarks, see Robert Bone, *Enforcement Costs and Trademark Puzzles*, 90 VA. L. REV. 2099, 2155–2181 (2004) (recommending an expansion of the functionality bar to prevent the creation of product monopolies through trademark).

b. Internet

LAMPARELLO v. FALWELL
United States Court of Appeals, Fourth Circuit, 2005.
420 F.3d 309.

DIANA GRIBBON MOTZ, CIRCUIT JUDGE.

Christopher Lamparello appeals the district court's order enjoining him from maintaining a gripe website critical of Reverend Jerry Falwell. For the reasons stated below, we reverse.

Reverend Falwell is "a nationally known minister who has been active as a commentator on politics and public affairs." He holds the common law trademarks "Jerry Falwell" and "Falwell," and the registered trademark "Listen America with Jerry Falwell." Jerry Falwell Ministries can be found online at "www.falwell.com," a website which receives 9,000 hits (or visits) per day.

Lamparello registered the domain name "www.fallwell.com" on February 11, 1999, after hearing Reverend Falwell give an interview "in which he expressed opinions about gay people and homosexuality that [Lamparello] considered ... offensive." Lamparello created a website at that domain name to respond to what he believed were "untruths about gay people." Lamparello's website included headlines such as "Bible verses that Dr. Falwell chooses to ignore" and "Jerry Falwell has been bearing false witness (Exodus 20:16) against his gay and lesbian neighbors for a long time." The site also contained in-depth criticism of Reverend Falwell's views. For example, the website stated:

> Dr. Falwell says that he is on the side of truth. He says that he will preach that homosexuality is a sin until the day he dies. But we believe that if the reverend were to take another thoughtful look at the scriptures, he would discover that they have been twisted around to support an anti-gay political agenda ... at the expense of the gospel.

Although the interior pages of Lamparello's website did not contain a disclaimer, the homepage prominently stated, "This website is NOT affiliated with Jerry Falwell or his ministry"; advised, "If you would like to visit Rev. Falwell's website, you may click here"; and provided a hyperlink to Reverend Falwell's website.

At one point, Lamparello's website included a link to the Amazon.com webpage for a book that offered interpretations of the Bible that Lamparello favored, but the parties agree that Lamparello has never sold goods or services on his website. The parties also agree that "Lamparello's domain name and web site at www.fallwell.com," which received only 200 hits per day, "had no measurable impact on the quantity of visits to [Reverend Falwell's] web site at www.falwell.com."

Nonetheless, Reverend Falwell sent Lamparello letters in October 2001 and June 2003 demanding that he cease and desist from using www.fallwell.com or any variation of Reverend Falwell's name as a domain name. Ultimately, Lamparello filed this action against Reverend Falwell and his ministries (collectively referred to hereinafter as "Reverend Falwell"), seeking a declaratory judgment of noninfringement. Reverend Falwell counter-claimed, alleging trademark infringement under 15 U.S.C. § 1114 (2000), false designation of origin under 15 U.S.C. § 1125(a), and cybersquatting under 15 U.S.C. § 1125(d).

The district court granted summary judgment to Reverend Falwell, enjoined Lamparello from using Reverend Falwell's mark at www.fallwell.com, and required Lamparello to transfer the domain name to Reverend

Falwell. However, the court denied Reverend Falwell's request for statutory damages or attorney fees, reasoning that the "primary motive" of Lamparello's website was "to put forth opinions on issues that were contrary to those of [Reverend Falwell]" and "not to take away monies or to profit."

Trademark law serves the important functions of protecting product identification, providing consumer information, and encouraging the production of quality goods and services. But protections " 'against unfair competition' " cannot be transformed into " 'rights to control language.' " "Such a transformation" would raise serious First Amendment concerns because it would limit the ability to discuss the products or criticize the conduct of companies that may be of widespread public concern and importance. Much useful social and commercial discourse would be all but impossible if speakers were under threat of an infringement lawsuit every time they made reference to a person, company or product by using its trademark.

Lamparello and his amici argue at length that application of the Lanham Act must be restricted to "commercial speech" to assure that trademark law does not become a tool for unconstitutional censorship.

In its two most significant recent amendments to the Lanham Act, the Federal Trademark Dilution Act of 1995 ("FTDA") and the Anticybersquatting Consumer Protection Act of 1999 ("ACPA"), Congress left little doubt that it did not intend for trademark laws to impinge the First Amendment rights of critics and commentators. The dilution statute applies to only a "commercial use in commerce of a mark," 15 U.S.C. § 1125(c)(1), and explicitly states that the "[n]oncommercial use of a mark" is not actionable. Id. § 1125(c)(4). Congress explained that this language was added to "adequately address [ ] legitimate First Amendment concerns," H.R.Rep. No. 104–374, at 4 (1995), reprinted in 1995 U.S.C.C.A.N. 1029, 1031, and "incorporate[d] the concept of 'commercial' speech from the 'commercial speech' doctrine." Id. at 8, reprinted in 1995 U.S.C.C.A.N. at 1035. Similarly, Congress directed that in determining whether an individual has engaged in cybersquatting, the courts may consider whether the person's use of the mark is a "bona fide noncommercial or fair use." 15 U.S.C. § 1125(d)(1)(B)(i)(IV). The legislature believed this provision necessary to "protect[ ] the rights of Internet users and the interests of all Americans in free speech and protected uses of trademarked names for such things as parody, comment, criticism, comparative advertising, news reporting, etc." S.Rep. No. 106–140 (1999), 1999 WL 594571, at *8.

In contrast, the trademark infringement and false designation of origin provisions of the Lanham Act (Sections 32 and 43(a), respectively) do not employ the term "noncommercial." They do state, however, that they pertain only to the use of a mark "in connection with the sale, offering for sale, distribution, or advertising of any goods or services," 15 U.S.C. § 1114(1)(a), or "in connection with any goods or services," id.

§ 1125(a)(1). But courts have been reluctant to define those terms narrowly. Rather, as the Second Circuit has explained, "[t]he term 'services' has been interpreted broadly" and so "[t]he Lanham Act has ... been applied to defendants furnishing a wide variety of non-commercial public and civic benefits." *United We Stand Am., Inc. v. United We Stand, Am. N.Y., Inc.*, 128 F.3d 86, 89–90 (2d Cir. 1997). [W]e [have] noted that a website need not actually sell goods or services for the use of a mark in that site's domain name to constitute a use " 'in connection with' goods or services."

Thus, even if we accepted Lamparello's contention that Sections 32 and 43(a) of the Lanham Act apply only to commercial speech, we would still face the difficult question of what constitutes such speech under those provisions. In the case at hand, we need not resolve that question or determine whether Sections 32 and 43(a) apply exclusively to commercial speech because Reverend Falwell's claims of trademark infringement and false designation fail for a more obvious reason. The hallmark of such claims is a likelihood of confusion—and there is no likelihood of confusion here.

Lamparello can only be liable for infringement and false designation if his use of Reverend Falwell's mark would be likely to cause confusion as to the source of the website found at www.fallwell.com. This likelihood-of-confusion test "generally strikes a comfortable balance" between the First Amendment and the rights of markholders.

We have identified seven factors helpful in determining whether a likelihood of confusion exists as to the source of a work: "(a) the strength or distinctiveness of the mark; (b) the similarity of the two marks; (c) the similarity of the goods/services the marks identify; (d) the similarity of the facilities the two parties use in their businesses; (e) the similarity of the advertising used by the two parties; (f) the defendant's intent; (g) actual confusion."

Reverend Falwell's mark is distinctive, and the domain name of Lamparello's website, www.fallwell.com, closely resembles it. But, although Lamparello and Reverend Falwell employ similar marks online, Lamparello's website looks nothing like Reverend Falwell's; indeed, Lamparello has made no attempt to imitate Reverend Falwell's website. Moreover, Reverend Falwell does not even argue that Lamparello's website constitutes advertising or a facility for business, let alone a facility or advertising similar to that of Reverend Falwell. Furthermore, Lamparello clearly created his website intending only to provide a forum to criticize ideas, not to steal customers.

Most importantly, Reverend Falwell and Lamparello do not offer similar goods or services. Rather they offer opposing ideas and commentary. Reverend Falwell's mark identifies his spiritual and political views; the website at www.fallwell.com criticizes those very views. After even a quick glance at the content of the website at www.fallwell.com, no one seeking Reverend Falwell's guidance would be misled by the domain name—www.fallwell.com—into believing Reverend Falwell authorized the content of that website. No one would believe that Reverend Falwell sponsored a site criticizing himself, his positions, and his interpretations of the Bible.

Finally, the fact that people contacted Reverend Falwell's ministry to report that they found the content at www.fallwell.com antithetical to Reverend Falwell's views does not illustrate, as Reverend Falwell claims, that the website engendered actual confusion. To the contrary, the anecdotal evidence Reverend Falwell submitted shows that those searching for Reverend Falwell's site and arriving instead at Lamparello's site quickly realized that Reverend Falwell was not the source of the content therein.

For all of these reasons, it is clear that the undisputed record evidences no likelihood of confusion. In fact, Reverend Falwell even conceded at oral argument that those viewing the content of Lamparello's website probably were unlikely to confuse Reverend Falwell with the source of that material.

Nevertheless, Reverend Falwell argues that he is entitled to prevail under the "initial interest confusion" doctrine. This relatively new and sporadically applied doctrine holds that "the Lanham Act forbids a competitor from luring potential customers away from a producer by initially passing off its goods as those of the producer's, even if confusion as to the source of the goods is dispelled by the time any sales are consummated." According to Reverend Falwell, this doctrine requires us to compare his mark with Lamparello's website domain name, www.fallwell.com, without considering the content of Lamparello's website. Reverend Falwell argues that some people who misspell his name may go to www.fallwell.com assuming it is his site, thus giving Lamparello an unearned audience— albeit one that quickly disappears when it realizes it has not reached Reverend Falwell's site. This argument fails for two reasons.

First, we have never adopted the initial interest confusion theory; rather, we have followed a very different mode of analysis, requiring courts to determine whether a likelihood of confusion exists by "examin[ing] the allegedly infringing use in the context in which it is seen by the ordinary consumer."

[Our case law] simply outlines the parameters of the parody defense; it does not adopt the initial interest confusion theory or otherwise diminish the necessity of examining context when determining whether a likelihood of confusion exists. Indeed, in *PETA* [*v. Doughney*, 263 F.3d 359 (4th Cir. 2001)] itself, rather than embracing a new approach, we reiterated that "[t]o determine whether a likelihood of confusion exists, a court should not consider how closely a fragment of a given use duplicates the trademark, but must instead consider whether the use in its entirety creates a likelihood of confusion." Id. at 366 (internal quotation marks and citation omitted) (emphasis added). When dealing with domain names, this means a court must evaluate an allegedly infringing domain name in conjunction with the content of the website identified by the domain name.

Moreover, even if we did endorse the initial interest confusion theory, that theory would not assist Reverend Falwell here because it provides no basis for liability in circumstances such as these. The few appellate courts that have followed the Ninth Circuit and imposed liability under this theory for using marks on the Internet have done so only in cases involving a factor utterly absent here—one business's use of another's mark for its own financial gain.

Profiting financially from initial interest confusion is thus a key element for imposition of liability under this theory. When an alleged infringer does not compete with the markholder for sales, "some initial confusion will not likely facilitate free riding on the goodwill of another mark, or otherwise harm the user claiming infringement. Where confusion has little or no meaningful effect in the marketplace, it is of little or no consequence in our analysis." For this reason, even the Ninth Circuit has stated that a firm is not liable for using another's mark in its domain name if it "could not financially capitalize on [a] misdirected consumer [looking for the markholder's site] even if it so desired." *Interstellar Starship Servs., Ltd. v. Epix, Inc.,* 304 F.3d 936, 946 (9th Cir. 2002).

[Author's Note: In a footnote, the court provides this useful string cite of cases involving initial interest confusion outside the Internet: "Offline uses of marks found to cause actionable initial interest confusion also have involved financial gain. See *Elvis Presley Enters., Inc. v. Capece,* 141 F.3d 188, 204 (5th Cir. 1998); *Mobil Oil Corp. v. Pegasus Petroleum Corp.,* 818 F.2d 254, 260 (2d Cir. 1987). And even those courts recognizing the initial interest confusion theory of liability but finding no actionable initial confusion involved one business's use of another's mark for profit. See, e.g., *Savin Corp. v. The Savin Group,* 391 F.3d 439, 462 n. 13 (2d Cir. 2004); *AM Gen. Corp. v. DaimlerChrysler Corp.,* 311 F.3d 796, 827–28 (7th Cir. 2002); *Checkpoint Sys., Inc. v. Check Point Software Techs., Inc.,* 269 F.3d 270, 298 (3d Cir. 2001); *Hasbro, Inc. v. Clue Computing, Inc.,* 232 F.3d 1, 2 (1st Cir. 2000); *Syndicate Sales, Inc. v. Hampshire Paper Corp.,* 192 F.3d 633, 638 (7th Cir. 1999); *Rust Env't & Infrastructure, Inc. v. Teunissen,* 131 F.3d 1210, 1217 (7th Cir. 1997)."]

This critical element—use of another firm's mark to capture the markholder's customers and profits—simply does not exist when the alleged infringer establishes a gripe site that criticizes the markholder. See Hannibal Travis, *The Battle For Mindshare: The Emerging Consensus that the First Amendment Protects Corporate Criticism and Parody on the Internet,* 10 VA. J.L. & TECH. 3, 85 (Winter 2005) ("The premise of the 'initial interest' confusion cases is that by using the plaintiff's trademark to divert its customers, the defendant is engaging in the old 'bait and switch.' But because ... Internet users who find [gripe sites] are not sold anything, the mark may be the 'bait,' but there is simply no 'switch.'") (citations omitted). Applying the initial interest confusion theory to gripe sites like Lamparello's would enable the markholder to insulate himself from criticism—or at least to minimize access to it.

In sum, even if we were to accept the initial interest confusion theory, that theory would not apply in the case at hand. Rather, to determine whether a likelihood of confusion exists as to the source of a gripe site like that at issue in this case, a court must look not only to the allegedly infringing domain name, but also to the underlying content of the website. When we do so here, it is clear, as explained above, that no likelihood of confusion exists. Therefore, the district court erred in granting Reverend Falwell summary judgment on his infringement, false designation, and unfair competition claims.

NOTES

1. The *Lamparello* case offers a nice example of trademark infringement on the Internet and the First Amendment issues that can be implicated. Notice that as far as the underlying legal standard for infringement, the fact that the allegedly infringing activity occurs on the Internet does not change the likelihood of confusion standards. However, it may be worth thinking whether the context of the Internet makes the application of the *Polaroid/Lapp/Sleekcraft* factors easier or harder to establish trademark infringement. Furthermore, the First Amendment limitations on trademark may be stronger on the Internet, since all that is ultimately being distributed through web sites is content, than in the brick and mortar world. Then again, if your view is that the Internet is one giant shopping mall with very little noncommodified space, then perhaps trademark infringement is easier to show.

2. One way that trademark infringement is different on the Internet is the claim of initial interest confusion. The idea behind initial interest confusion is that adopting a mark similar to an identified trademark allows customers to come into the door. Suppose I make my retail establishment look exactly like a McDonald's except when customers enter, they find a clothing store rather than a fast food franchise. McDonald's would have a claim against me for initial interest confusion, among other things, for the use of their trade dress and marks to draw customers in. Falwell raised initial interest confusion here because it may have been difficult to establish other types of confusion. But note the commercial/non-commercial distinction made here and the discussion of cases where initial interest confusion was found. Does the court make a correct distinction? What about Falwell's, or other markholders', interest in protecting the goodwill and reputation of his name against someone who uses it to divert users in a non-commercial way to a cause he opposes? Should not trademark protect Falwell's interests in that situation?

For critical commentary on initial interest confusion, see Jennifer Rothman, *Initial Interest Confusion: Standing at the Crossroads of Trademark Law*, 27 CARDOZO L. REV. 105 (2005); Michael Grynberg, *The Road Not Taken: Initial Interest Confusion, Consumer Search Costs, and The Challenge of the Internet*, 28 SEATTLE U. L. REV. 97 (2004); Lisa M. Sharrock, *Realigning the Initial Interest Confusion Doctrine With The Lanham Act*, 25 WHITTIER L. REV.

53 (2003); Note, *Confusion in Cyberspace: Defending and Recalibrating the Initial Interest Confusion Doctrine*, 117 HARV. L. REV. 2387 (2004). For a case discussing the emerging problem of search engines and trademark infringement, see *800–JR Cigar, Inc. v. GoTo.com, Inc.*, 437 F.Supp.2d 273 (D.N.J. 2006) (holding that use of trademarks as a search term in a search engine can constitute trademark use). For innovative discussions of Internet search engines and trademark law, see Mark Bartholomew, *Making a Mark in the Internet Economy: A Trademark Analysis of Search Engine Advertising*, 58 OKLA. L. REV. 179 (2005); Eric Goldman, *Deregulating Relevancy in Internet Trademark Law*, 54 EMORY L. J. 507 (2005).

C. CYBERSQUATTING CLAIMS UNDER 15 USC § 1125(d)

LAMPARELLO v. FALWELL

United States Court of Appeals, Fourth Circuit, 2005.
420 F.3d 309.

[Author's Note: The excerpt below discusses the cybersquatting issues raised by the Lamparello case, cited above. Please refer back to that case for the facts of this dispute.]

We evaluate Reverend Falwell's cybersquatting claim separately because the elements of a cybersquatting violation differ from those of traditional Lanham Act violations. To prevail on a cybersquatting claim, Reverend Falwell must show that Lamparello: (1) "had a bad faith intent to profit from using the [www.fallwell.com] domain name," and (2) the domain name www.fallwell.com "is identical or confusingly similar to, or dilutive of, the distinctive and famous [Falwell] mark." PETA, 263 F.3d at 367 (citing 15 U.S.C. § 1125(d)(1)(A)).

"The paradigmatic harm that the ACPA was enacted to eradicate" is "the practice of cybersquatters registering several hundred domain names in an effort to sell them to the legitimate owners of the mark." *Lucas Nursery & Landscaping, Inc. v. Grosse*, 359 F.3d 806, 810 (6th Cir.2004). The Act was also intended to stop the registration of multiple marks with the hope of selling them to the highest bidder, "distinctive marks to defraud consumers" or "to engage in counterfeiting activities," and "well-known marks to prey on consumer confusion by misusing the domain name to divert customers from the mark owner's site to the cybersquatter's own site, many of which are pornography sites that derive advertising revenue based on the number of visits, or 'hits,' the site receives." S.Rep. No. 106–140, 1999 WL 594571, at *5–6. The Act was not intended to prevent "noncommercial uses of a mark, such as for comment, criticism, parody, news reporting, etc.," and thus they "are beyond the scope" of the ACPA. Id. at *9.

To distinguish abusive domain name registrations from legitimate ones, the ACPA directs courts to consider nine nonexhaustive factors:

(I) the trademark or other intellectual property rights of the person, if any, in the domain name;

(II) the extent to which the domain name consists of the legal name of the person or a name that is otherwise commonly used to identify that person;

(III) the person's prior use, if any, of the domain name in connection with the bona fide offering of any goods or services;

(IV) the person's bona fide noncommercial or fair use of the mark in a site accessible under the domain name;

(V) the person's intent to divert consumers from the mark owner's online location to a site accessible under the domain name that could harm the goodwill represented by the mark, either for commercial gain or with the intent to tarnish or disparage the mark, by creating a likelihood of confusion as to the source, sponsorship, affiliation, or endorsement of the site;

(VI) the person's offer to transfer, sell, or otherwise assign the domain name to the mark owner or any third party for financial gain without having used, or having an intent to use, the domain name in the bona fide offering of any goods or services, or the person's prior conduct indicating a pattern of such conduct;

(VII) the person's provision of material and misleading false contact information when applying for the registration of the domain name, the person's intentional failure to maintain accurate contact information, or the person's prior conduct indicating a pattern of such conduct;

(VIII) the person's registration or acquisition of multiple domain names which the person knows are identical or confusingly similar to marks of others that are distinctive at the time of the registration of such domain names, or dilutive of famous marks of others that are famous at the time of registration of such domain names, without regard to the goods or services of the parties; and

(IX) the extent to which the mark incorporated in the person's domain name registration is or is not distinctive and famous within the meaning of subsection (c)(1) of this section.

15 U.S.C. § 1125(d)(1)(B)(i); see also H.R.Rep. No. 106–412 (1999), 1999 WL 970519, at *10.

These factors attempt "to balance the property interests of trademark owners with the legitimate interests of Internet users and others who seek to make lawful uses of others' marks, including for purposes such as comparative advertising, comment, criticism, parody, news reporting, fair use, etc." H.R. Rep. No. 106–412, 1999 WL 970519, at *10 (emphasis added). "The first four [factors] suggest circumstances that may tend to indicate an absence of bad-faith intent to profit from the goodwill of a mark, and the others suggest circumstances that may tend to indicate that such bad-faith intent exists." Id. However, "[t]here is no simple formula for evaluating and weighing these factors. For example, courts do not simply count up which party has more factors in its favor after the evidence is in." *Harrods Ltd. v. Sixty Internet Domain Names*, 302 F.3d 214, 234 (4th Cir.2002). In fact, because use of these listed factors is permissive, "[w]e need not ... march through" them all in every case. *Virtual Works, Inc. v. Volkswagen of Am., Inc.*, 238 F.3d 264, 269 (4th Cir.2001). "The factors are given to courts as a guide, not as a substitute for careful thinking about whether the conduct at issue is motivated by a bad faith intent to profit."

After close examination of the undisputed facts involved in this case, we can only conclude that Reverend Falwell cannot demonstrate that Lamparello "had a bad faith intent to profit from using the [www.fallwell. com] domain name." Lamparello clearly employed www.fallwell.com simply to criticize Reverend Falwell's views. Factor IV of the ACPA, 15 U.S.C. § 1125(d)(1)(B)(i)(IV), counsels against finding a bad faith intent to profit in such circumstances because "use of a domain name for purposes of ... comment, [and] criticism," H.R.Rep. No. 106–412, 1999 WL 970519, at *11, constitutes a "bona fide noncommercial or fair use" under the statute, 15 U.S.C. § 1125(d)(1)(B)(i)(IV). That Lamparello provided a link to an Amazon.com webpage selling a book he favored does not diminish the communicative function of his website. The use of a domain name to engage in criticism or commentary "even where done for profit" does not alone evidence a bad faith intent to profit, H.R.Rep. No. 106–412, 1999 WL 970519, at *11, and Lamparello did not even stand to gain financially from sales of the book at Amazon.com. Thus factor IV weighs heavily in favor of finding Lamparello lacked a bad faith intent to profit from the use of the domain name.

[Author's note: In a footnote, the court discusses noncommercial sites: "We note that factor IV does not protect a faux noncommercial site, that is, a noncommercial site created by the registrant for the sole purpose of avoiding liability under the FTDA, which exempts noncommercial uses of marks, see 15 U.S.C. § 1125(c)(4)(B), or under the ACPA. As explained by the Senate Report discussing the ACPA, an individual cannot avoid liability for registering and attempting to sell a hundred domain names incorporating famous marks by posting noncommercial content at those domain names. See S.Rep. No. 106–140, 1999 WL 594571, at *14 (citing *Panavision Int'l v. Toeppen*, 141 F.3d 1316 (9th Cir.1998)). But Lamparello's sole purpose for registering www.fallwell.com was to criticize Reverend Falwell, and this noncommercial use was not a ruse to avoid liability. Therefore, factor IV indicates that Lamparello did not have a bad faith intent to profit."]

Equally important, Lamparello has not engaged in the type of conduct described in the statutory factors as typifying the bad faith intent to profit essential to a successful cybersquatting claim. First, we have already held, supra Part II.B, that Lamparello's domain name does not create a likelihood of confusion as to source or affiliation. Accordingly, Lamparello has not engaged in the type of conduct—"creating a likelihood of confusion as to the source, sponsorship, affiliation, or endorsement of the site," 15 U.S.C. § 1125(d)(1)(B)(i)(V)—described as an indicator of a bad faith intent to profit in factor V of the statute.

Factors VI and VIII also counsel against finding a bad faith intent to profit here. Lamparello has made no attempt—or even indicated a willingness—"to transfer, sell, or otherwise assign the domain name to [Reverend Falwell] or any third party for financial gain." 15 U.S.C. § 1125(d)(1)(B)(i)(VI). Similarly, Lamparello has not registered "multiple domain names," 15 U.S.C. § 1125(d)(1)(B)(i)(VIII); rather, the record indicates he has registered only one. Thus, Lamparello's conduct is not of the suspect variety described in factors VI and VIII of the Act.

Notably, the case at hand differs markedly from those in which the courts have found a bad faith intent to profit from domain names used for websites engaged in political commentary or parody. For example, in *Coca–Cola Co. v. Purdy*, 382 F.3d 774 (8th Cir.2004), the Eighth Circuit found an anti-abortion activist who had registered domain names incorporating famous marks such as "Washington Post" liable for cybersquatting because he had registered almost seventy domain names, had offered to stop using the Washington Post mark if the newspaper published an opinion piece by him on its editorial page, and posted content that created a likelihood of confusion as to whether the famous markholders sponsored the anti-abortion sites and "ha[d] taken positions on hotly contested issues." Id. at 786. In contrast, Lamparello did not register multiple domain names, he did not offer to transfer them for valuable consideration, and he did not create a likelihood of confusion.

Instead, Lamparello, like the plaintiffs in two cases recently decided by the Fifth and Sixth Circuits, created a gripe site. Both courts expressly refused to find that gripe sites located at domain names nearly identical to the marks at issue violated the ACPA. In *TMI, Inc. v. Maxwell*, 368 F.3d 433, 434–35 (5th Cir.2004), Joseph Maxwell, a customer of homebuilder TMI, registered the domain name "www.trendmakerhome.com," which differed by only one letter from TMI's mark, TrendMaker Homes, and its domain name, "www.trend makerhomes.com." Maxwell used the site to complain about his experience with TMI and to list the name of a contractor whose work pleased him. After his registration expired, Maxwell registered "www.trendmakerhome.info." TMI then sued, alleging cybersquatting. The Fifth Circuit reversed the district court's finding that Maxwell violated the ACPA, reasoning that his site was noncommercial and designed only "to inform potential customers about a negative experience with the company." Id. at 438–39.

Similarly, in *Lucas Nursery & Landscaping, Inc.* [*v. Grosse*, 359 F.3d 806 (6th Cir. 2004)], a customer of Lucas Nursery registered the domain name "www.lucasnursery.com" and posted her dissatisfaction with the company's landscaping services. Because the registrant, Grosse, like Lamparello, registered a single domain name, the Sixth Circuit concluded that her conduct did not constitute that which Congress intended to pro-scribe—i.e., the registration of multiple domain names. *Lucas Nursery & Landscaping,* 359 F.3d at 810. Noting that Grosse's gripe site did not create any confusion as to sponsorship and that she had never attempted to sell the domain name to the markholder, the court found that Grosse's conduct was not actionable under the ACPA. The court explained: "One of the ACPA's main objectives is the protection of consumers from slick internet peddlers who trade on the names and reputations of established brands. The practice of informing fellow consumers of one's experience with a particular service provider is surely not inconsistent with this ideal." Id. at 811.

Like Maxwell and Grosse before him, Lamparello has not evidenced a bad faith intent to profit under the ACPA. To the contrary, he has used www.fallwell.com to engage in the type of "comment[ ][and] criticism" that Congress specifically stated militates against a finding of bad faith intent to profit. See S. Rep. No. 106–140, 1999 WL 594571, at *14. And he has neither registered multiple domain names nor attempted to transfer www.fallwell.com for valuable consideration. We agree with the Fifth and Sixth Circuits that, given these circumstances, the use of a mark in a domain name for a gripe site criticizing the markholder does not consti-tute cybersquatting.

NOTES

1. The anticybersquatting provisions of the Lanham Act were imple-mented in 1999 to protect trademark owners against individuals who register marks as domain names in order to make money by making the owners buy the domain names back. A presumption behind the provisions is that owner-ship of a trademark entitles the owner to the domain name that uses the mark. But if the registrant does use the domain name and does not trade off the goodwill of the trademark owner, there is no cause of action for cybers-quatting. The problem arises when someone registers many trademarks and their variants as domain names without any use of the domain names. Do you think Lamparello was a cybersquatter? Would he be one if he had never used the domain name? If he had used it to market and sell a book critical of Falwell?

2. In addition to the Lanham Act, trademark owners have rights under the Uniform Dispute Resolution Process (UDRP) that all registrants submit to when they register a domain name. This process says that the domain name registrant agrees to resolve disputes over rights in the domain name through a dispute resolution process that is administered by the World Intellectual Property Organization in Geneva. The following is a table that summarizes the main difference between UDRP and 1125(d) of the Lanham Act. Note that undergoing mediation under the UDRP does not foreclose bringing an 1125(d) claim. For a discussion of UDRP procedures and cybers-quatting more generally, see Jacqueline Lipton, *Beyond Cybersquatting: Tak-ing Domain Name Disputes Past Trademark Policy,* 40 WAKE FOREST L. REV. 1361 (2005).

D. INTERNET SEARCH ENGINES

RESCUECOM CORP. v. GOOGLE INC.

United States Court of Appeals for the Second Circuit, 2009
562 F.3d 123

LEVAL, CIRCUIT JUDGE:

* * *Rescuecom is a national computer service franchising company that offers on-site computer services and sales. Rescuecom conducts a substantial amount of business over the Internet and receives between 17,000 to 30,000 visitors to its website each month. It also advertises over the Internet, using many web-based services, including those offered by Google. Since 1998, "Rescuecom" has been a registered federal trademark, and there is no dispute as to its validity.

Google operates a popular Internet search engine, which users access by visiting www.google.com. Using Google's website, a person searching for the website of a particular entity in trade (or simply for information about it) can enter that entity's name or trademark into Google's search engine and launch a search. Google's proprietary system responds to such a search request in two ways. First, Google provides a list of links to websites, ordered in what Google deems to be of descending relevance to the user's search terms based on its proprietary algorithms. Google's search engine assists the public not only in obtaining information about a provider, but also in purchasing products and services. If a prospective purchaser, looking for goods or services of a particular provider, enters the provider's trademark as a search term on Google's website and clicks to activate a search, within seconds, the Google search engine will provide on the searcher's computer screen a link to the webpage maintained by that provider (as well as a host of other links to sites that Google's program determines to be relevant to the search term entered). By clicking on the link of the provider, the searcher will be directed to the provider's website, where the searcher can obtain information supplied by the provider about its products and services and can perhaps also make purchases from the provider by placing orders.

The second way Google responds to a search request is by showing context-based advertising. When a searcher uses Google's search engine by submitting a search term, Google may place advertisements on the user's screen. Google will do so if an advertiser, having determined that its ad is likely to be of interest to a searcher who enters the particular term, has purchased from Google the placement of its ad on the screen of the searcher who entered that search term. What Google places on the searcher's screen is more than simply an advertisement. It is also a link to the advertiser's website, so that in response to such an ad, if the searcher clicks on the link, he will open the advertiser's website, which offers not only additional information about the advertiser, but also perhaps the option to purchase the goods and services of the advertiser over the

Internet. Google uses at least two programs to offer such context-based links: AdWords and Keyword Suggestion Tool.

AdWords is Google's program through which advertisers purchase terms (or keywords). When entered as a search term, the keyword triggers the appearance of the advertiser's ad and link. An advertiser's purchase of a particular term causes the advertiser's ad and link to be displayed on the user's screen whenever a searcher launches a Google search based on the purchased search term. Advertisers pay Google based on the number of times Internet users "click" on the advertisement, so as to link to the advertiser's website. For example, using Google's AdWords, Company Y, a company engaged in the business of furnace repair, can cause Google to display its advertisement and link whenever a user of Google launches a search based on the search term, "furnace repair." Company Y can also cause its ad and link to appear whenever a user searches for the term "Company X," a competitor of Company Y in the furnace repair business. Thus, whenever a searcher interested in purchasing furnace repair services from Company X launches a search of the term X (Company X's trademark), an ad and link would appear on the searcher's screen, inviting the searcher to the furnace repair services of X's competitor, Company Y. And if the searcher clicked on Company Y's link, Company Y's website would open on the searcher's screen, and the searcher might be able to order or purchase Company Y's furnace repair services.

In addition to AdWords, Google also employs Keyword Suggestion Tool, a program that recommends keywords to advertisers to be purchased. The program is designed to improve the effectiveness of advertising by helping advertisers identify keywords related to their area of commerce, resulting in the placement of their ads before users who are likely to be responsive to it. Thus, continuing the example given above, if Company Y employed Google's Keyword Suggestion Tool, the Tool might suggest to Company Y that it purchase not only the term "furnace repair" but also the term "X," its competitor's brand name and trademark, so that Y's ad would appear on the screen of a searcher who searched Company X's trademark, seeking Company X's website.

Once an advertiser buys a particular keyword, Google links the keyword to that advertiser's advertisement. The advertisements consist of a combination of content and a link to the advertiser's webpage. Google displays these advertisements on the search result page either in the right margin or in a horizontal band immediately above the column of relevance-based search results. These advertisements are generally associated with a label, which says "sponsored link." Rescuecom alleges, however, that a user might easily be misled to believe that the advertisements which appear on the screen are in fact part of the relevance-based search result and that the appearance of a competitor's ad and link in response to a searcher's search for Rescuecom is likely to cause trademark confusion as to affiliation, origin, sponsorship, or approval of service. This can occur, according to the Complaint, because Google fails to label the ads in a manner which would clearly identify them as purchased ads rather than search results. The Complaint alleges that when the sponsored links appear in a horizontal bar at the top of the search results, they may appear to the searcher to be the first, and therefore the most relevant, entries responding to the search, as opposed to paid advertisements.

Google's objective in its AdWords and Keyword Suggestion Tool programs is to sell keywords to advertisers. Rescuecom alleges that Google makes 97% of its revenue from selling advertisements through its Ad-Words program. Google therefore has an economic incentive to increase the number of advertisements and links that appear for every term entered into its search engine.

Many of Rescuecom's competitors advertise on the Internet. Through its Keyword Suggestion Tool, Google has recommended the Rescuecom trademark to Rescuecom's competitors as a search term to be purchased. Rescuecom's competitors, some responding to Google's recommendation, have purchased Rescuecom's trademark as a keyword in Google's Ad-Words program, so that whenever a user launches a search for the term "Rescuecom," seeking to be connected to Rescuecom's website, the competitors' advertisement and link will appear on the searcher's screen. This practice allegedly allows Rescuecom's competitors to deceive and divert users searching for Rescuecom's website. According to Rescuecom's allegations, when a Google user launches a search for the term "Rescuecom" because the searcher wishes to purchase Rescuecom's services, links to websites of its competitors will appear on the searcher's screen in a manner likely to cause the searcher to believe mistakenly that a competitor's advertisement (and website link) is sponsored by, endorsed by, approved by, or affiliated with Rescuecom.

The District Court granted Google's 12(b)(6) motion and dismissed Rescuecom's claims.* * * The district court explained its decision saying that even if Google employed Rescuecom's mark in a manner likely to cause confusion or deceive searchers into believing that competitors are affiliated with Rescuecom and its mark, so that they believe the services of Rescuecom's competitors are those of Rescuecom, Google's actions are not a "use in commerce" under the Lanham Act because the competitor's advertisements triggered by Google's programs did not exhibit Rescuecom's trademark.* * *

DISCUSSION

* * *Sections 32 and 43 of the Act, which we also refer to by their codified designations, 15 U.S.C. §§ 1114 & 1125, inter alia, impose liability for unpermitted "use in commerce" of another's mark which is "likely to cause confusion, or to cause mistake, or to deceive," § 1114, "as to the affiliation ... or as to the origin, sponsorship or approval of his or her goods [or] services ... by another person." § 1125(a)(1)(A). The *1–800 [Contacts Inc. v. WhenUCom, Inc., 414 F.3d 400 (2d Cir. 2005)]* opinion looked to the definition of the term "use in commerce" provided in § 45 of the Act, 15 U.S.C. § 1127. That definition provides in part that "a mark shall be deemed to be in use in commerce ... (2) on services when it is

used or displayed in the sale or advertising of services and the services are rendered in commerce." 15 U.S.C. § 1127. Our court found that the plaintiff failed to show that the defendant made a "use in commerce" of the plaintiff's mark, within that definition.

At the outset, we note two significant aspects of our holding in *1–800*, which distinguish it from the present case. A key element of our court's decision in *1–800* was that under the plaintiff's allegations, the defendant did not use, reproduce, or display the plaintiff's mark at all. The search term that was alleged to trigger the pop-up ad was the plaintiff's website address. 1–800 noted, notwithstanding the similarities between the website address and the mark, that the website address was not used or claimed by the plaintiff as a trademark. Thus, the transactions alleged to be infringing were not transactions involving use of the plaintiff's trademark.

* * *The present case contrasts starkly with* * *important aspects of the *1–800* decision. First, in contrast to *1–800*, where we emphasized that the defendant made no use whatsoever of the plaintiff's trademark, here what Google is recommending and selling to its advertisers is Rescuecom's trademark. Second, in contrast with the facts of 1–800 where the defendant did not "use or display," much less sell, trademarks as search terms to its advertisers, here Google displays, offers, and sells Rescuecom's mark to Google's advertising customers when selling its advertising services. In addition, Google encourages the purchase of Rescuecom's mark through its Keyword Suggestion Tool. Google's utilization of Rescuecom's mark fits literally within the terms specified by 15 U.S.C. § 1127. According to the Complaint, Google uses and sells Rescuecom's mark "in the sale ... of [Google's advertising] services ... rendered in commerce." § 1127.

Google, supported by amici, argues that *1–800* suggests that the inclusion of a trademark in an internal computer directory cannot constitute trademark use. Several district court decisions in this Circuit appear to have reached this conclusion. See e.g., S & L Vitamins, Inc. v. Australian Gold, Inc., 521 F.Supp.2d 188, 199–202 (E.D.N.Y.2007) (holding that use of a trademark in metadata did not constitute trademark use within the meaning of the Lanham Act because the use "is strictly internal and not communicated to the public"); Merck & Co., Inc. v. Mediplan Health Consulting, Inc., 425 F.Supp.2d 402, 415 (S.D.N.Y.2006) (holding that internal use of a keyword to trigger advertisements did not qualify as trademark use). This over-reads the *1–800* decision. First, regardless of whether Google's use of Rescuecom's mark in its internal search algorithm could constitute an actionable trademark use, Google's recommendation and sale of Rescuecom's mark to its advertising customers are not internal uses. Furthermore, *1–800* did not imply that use of a trademark in a software program's internal directory precludes a finding of trademark use. Rather, influenced by the fact that the defendant was not using the plaintiff's trademark at all, much less using it as the basis of a commercial transaction, the court asserted that the particular use before it did not constitute a use in commerce.* * * We did not imply in *1–800* that an alleged infringer's use of a trademark in an internal software program insulates the alleged infringer from a charge of infringement, no matter how likely the use is to cause confusion in the marketplace. If we were to adopt Google and its amici's argument, the operators of search engines would be free to use trademarks in ways designed to deceive and cause consumer confusion. This is surely neither within the intention nor the letter of the Lanham Act.

Google and its amici contend further that its use of the Rescuecom trademark is no different from that of a retail vendor who uses "product placement" to allow one vender to benefit from a competitors' name recognition. An example of product placement occurs when a store-brand generic product is placed next to a trademarked product to induce a customer who specifically sought out the trademarked product to consider the typically less expensive, generic brand as an alternative.* * * Google's argument misses the point. From the fact that proper, non-deceptive product placement does not result in liability under the Lanham Act, it does not follow that the label "product placement" is a magic shield against liability, so that even a deceptive plan of product placement designed to confuse consumers would similarly escape liability. It is not by reason of absence of a use of a mark in commerce that benign product placement escapes liability; it escapes liability because it is a benign practice which does not cause a likelihood of consumer confusion. In contrast, if a retail seller were to be paid by an off-brand purveyor to arrange product display and delivery in such a way that customers seeking to purchase a famous brand would receive the off-brand, believing they had gotten the brand they were seeking, we see no reason to believe the practice would escape liability merely because it could claim the mantle of "product placement." The practices attributed to Google by the Complaint, which at this stage we must accept as true, are significantly different from benign product placement that does not violate the Act.

Unlike the practices discussed in *1–800*, the practices here attributed to Google by Rescuecom's complaint are that Google has made use in commerce of Rescuecom's mark. Needless to say, a defendant must do more than use another's mark in commerce to violate the Lanham Act. The gist of a Lanham Act violation is an unauthorized use, which "is likely to cause confusion, or to cause mistake, or to deceive as to the affiliation, . . . or as to the origin, sponsorship, or approval of . . . goods [or] services." See 15 U.S.C. § 1125(a); Estee Lauder Inc. v. The Gap, Inc., 108 F.3d 1503, 1508–09 (2d Cir.1997). We have no idea whether Rescuecom can prove that Google's use of Rescuecom's trademark in its AdWords program causes likelihood of confusion or mistake. Rescuecom has alleged that it does, in that would-be purchasers (or explorers) of its services who search for its website on Google are misleadingly directed to the ads and websites of its competitors in a manner which leads them to believe mistakenly that these ads or websites are sponsored by, or affiliated with Rescuecom. This is particularly so, Rescuecom alleges, when the advertiser's link appears in a horizontal band at the top of the list of search results in a manner which makes it appear to be the most relevant search result and not an advertisement. What Rescuecom alleges is that by the manner of Google's display of sponsored links of competing brands in response to a search for Rescuecom's brand name (which fails adequately to identify the sponsored link as an advertisement, rather than a relevant search result), Google creates a likelihood of consumer confusion as to trademarks. If the searcher sees a different brand name as the top entry in response to the search for "Rescuecom," the searcher is likely to believe mistakenly that the different name which appears is affiliated with the brand name sought in the search and will not suspect, because the fact is not adequately signaled by Google's presentation, that this is not the most relevant response to the search. Whether Google's actual practice is in fact benign or confusing is not for us to judge at this time. We consider at the 12(b)(6) stage only what is alleged in the Complaint.

We conclude that the district court was mistaken in believing that our precedent in 1–800 requires dismissal. [VACATED AND REMANDED]

NOTES

1.   One purpose of trademark law is to facilitate consumer search and avoid consumer confusion. The theory is that consumers associate a trademark with a certain product or service. Trademark infringement serves to upset that association and thereby confuse consumers in the marketplace. Is this notion of search consistent with the court's analysis in *Rescuecom*? Is consumer search different from search in the bricks and mortar world? One difference of course is that the consumer has greater opportunities to ignore search results on the Internet and therefore can engage in more self-protection. If this observation is true, should that make a difference? Alternatively, one could take the view that search is the same in both the Internet and the non-Internet environment. Under this view, the court reached the wrong decision in *1–800*, the case the *Rescuecom* court distinguishes.

2.   Note that the court separates out the "use in commerce" element of trademark infringement from "likelihood of confusion." Is there an advantage to creating this separate prong? Why not fold the use analysis into the likelihood of confusion analaysis? What would the result be in *Rescuecom* under a likelihood of confusion analysis?

3.   The *Rescuecom* opinion contains a lengthy appendix, not included here, which discusses an inconsistency in the statute's use of the phrase "use in commerce." Both Sections 1114 and 1125, which impose liability for trademark infringement, require that the defendant "use in commerce" without permission of the trademark owner the protected trademark. However, section 1127 of the Lanham Act defines "use in commerce" in part as follows:

> The term "use in commerce" means the bona fide use of a mark in the ordinary course of trade, and not made merely to reserve a right in a mark. For purposes of this chapter, a mark shall be deemed to be in use in commerce—

(1) on goods when—

(A) it is placed in any manner on the goods or their containers or the displays associated therewith or on the tags or labels affixed thereto, or if the nature of the goods makes such placement impracticable, then on documents associated with the goods or their sale, and

(B) the goods are sold or transported in commerce....

15 U.S.C. § 1127. In the appendix, the court identifies a confusion from this definition. If the defendant is infringing, then use of the mark cannot be bona fide. Therefore, there cannot be a use in commerce and the element of infringement is not satisfied. The court resolves this confusion by pointing out that when the Lanham Act was first enacted, "use in commerce" included only the second part of the definition, but not the "bona fide" language. The "bona fide" language was added as Congress introduced the "intent to use" application and was applicable only to the showing of use in commerce for the purposes of registration. The problem is how to reconcile the term "use in commerce" for infringement purposes with the amended definition when the amendment was intended to apply only to registration, but not to infringement. In its appendix, the court suggests that the "bona fide" language should be ignored for the purposes of infringement analysis. The court, however, also makes clear that the appendix is dicta and urges Congress to clarify the definition.

4. Recall that in the beginning of the chapter, a trademark was defined as involving a three part relationship among the source, the mark, and the product or service. Is the court's analysis of trademark use consistent with this view of trademarks? In the context of search engines, such as Google, how is this three part relationship taken apart? Does a search engine potentially separate a mark from a reference to source? If so, is that the potential problem rising to a claim for trademark infringement?

	UDRP	1125(d)
Process	Mediation	Adjudication (in rem jurisdiction)
Elements of claim	Bad faith registration and use	Bad faith intent to profit and registration, use, or trafficking of distinctive trademark
Burdens	1. Trademark owner shows elements 2. Domain name registrant shows legitimate interests	1. Trademark owner establishing elements 2. Domain name registrant believed and had reasonable grounds to believe that use of the domain name was fair use or otherwise legal
Remedies	Transfer of domain name	Transfer of domain name with possibility of damages in cases of willfulness

III. THE SCOPE OF TRADEMARK RIGHTS

A. DEFENSES

1. Fair Use

KP PERMANENT MAKE–UP, INC. v. LASTING IMPRESSION I, INC.

Supreme Court of the United States, 2004.
543 U.S. 111, 125 S.Ct. 542, 160 L.Ed.2d 440.

JUSTICE SOUTER delivered the opinion of the Court.

The question here is whether a party raising the statutory affirmative defense of fair use to a claim of trademark infringement, 15 U.S.C. § 1115(b)(4), has a burden to negate any likelihood that the practice complained of will confuse consumers about the origin of the goods or services affected. We hold it does not.

Each party to this case sells permanent makeup, a mixture of pigment and liquid for injection under the skin to camouflage injuries and modify nature's dispensations, and each has used some version of the term "micro color" (as one word or two, singular or plural) in marketing and selling its product. Petitioner KP Permanent Make–Up, Inc., claims to have used the single-word version since 1990 or 1991 on advertising flyers and since 1991 on pigment bottles. Respondents Lasting Impression I, Inc., and its licensee, MCN International, Inc. (Lasting, for simplicity), deny that KP began using the term that early, but we accept KP's allegation as true for present purposes; the District and Appeals Courts took it to be so, and the disputed facts do not matter to our resolution of the issue. In 1992, Lasting applied to the United States Patent and Trademark Office (PTO) under 15 U.S.C. § 1051 for registration of a trademark consisting of the words "Micro Colors" in white letters separated by a green bar within a black square. The PTO registered the mark to Lasting in 1993, and in 1999 the registration became incontestable. § 1065.

It was also in 1999 that KP produced a 10–page advertising brochure using "microcolor" in a large, stylized typeface, provoking Lasting to demand that KP stop using the term. Instead, KP sued Lasting in the Central District of California, seeking, on more than one ground, a declaratory judgment that its language infringed no such exclusive right as Lasting claimed. Lasting counterclaimed, alleging, among other things, that KP had infringed Lasting's "Micro Colors" trademark.

KP sought summary judgment on the infringement counterclaim, based on the statutory affirmative defense of fair use, 15 U.S.C. § 1115(b)(4). After finding that Lasting had conceded that KP used the term only to describe its goods and not as a mark, the District Court held that KP was acting fairly and in good faith because undisputed facts showed that KP had employed the term "microcolor" continuously from a time before Lasting adopted the two-word, plural variant as a mark. Without inquiring whether the practice was likely to cause confusion, the court concluded that KP had made out its affirmative defense under § 1115(b)(4) and entered summary judgment for KP on Lasting's infringement claim.

The Court of Appeals for the Ninth Circuit thought it was error for the District Court to have addressed the fair use defense without delving into the matter of possible confusion on the part of consumers about the origin of KP's goods. The reviewing court took the view that no use could be recognized as fair where any consumer confusion was probable, and although the court did not pointedly address the burden of proof, it appears to have placed it on KP to show absence of consumer confusion. Since it found there were disputed material facts relevant under the Circuit's eight-factor test for assessing the likelihood of confusion, it reversed the summary judgment and remanded the case.

We granted KP's petition for certiorari to address a disagreement among the Courts of Appeals on the significance of likely confusion for a fair use defense to a trademark infringement claim, and the obligation of a party defending on that ground to show that its use is unlikely to cause consumer confusion. We now vacate the judgment of the Court of Appeals.

The Trademark Act of 1946, known for its principal proponent as the Lanham Act, 60 Stat. 427, as amended, 15 U.S.C. § 1051 et seq., provides the user of a trade or service mark with the opportunity to register it with the PTO, §§ 1051, 1053. If the registrant then satisfies further conditions including continuous use for five consecutive years, "the right . . . to use such registered mark in commerce" to designate the origin of the goods specified in the registration "shall be incontestable" outside certain listed exceptions. § 1065.

The holder of a registered mark (incontestable or not) has a civil action against anyone employing an imitation of it in commerce when "such use is likely to cause confusion, or to cause mistake, or to deceive." § 1114(1). Although an incontestable registration is "conclusive evidence . . . of the registrant's exclusive right to use the . . . mark in commerce," § 1115(b), the plaintiff's success is still subject to "proof of infringement as defined in section 1114," § ibid.(b). And that, as just noted, requires a showing that the defendant's actual practice is likely to produce confusion in the minds of consumers about the origin of the goods or services in question. This plaintiff's burden has to be kept in mind when reading the relevant portion of the further provision for an affirmative defense of fair use, available to a party whose "use of the name, term, or device charged to be an infringement is a use, otherwise than as a mark, . . . of a term or device which is descriptive of and used fairly and in good faith only to describe the goods or services of such party, or their geographic origin. . . ." § 1115(b)(4).

Two points are evident. Section 1115(b) places a burden of proving likelihood of confusion (that is, infringement) on the party charging infringement even when relying on an incontestable registration. And Congress said nothing about likelihood of confusion in setting out the elements of the fair use defense in § 1115(b)(4).

Starting from these textual fixed points, it takes a long stretch to claim that a defense of fair use entails any burden to negate confusion. It is just not plausible that Congress would have used the descriptive phrase "likely to cause confusion, or to cause mistake, or to deceive" in § 1114 to describe the requirement that a markholder show likelihood of consumer confusion, but would have relied on the phrase "used fairly" in § 1115(b)(4) in a fit of terse drafting meant to place a defendant under a burden to negate confusion.

Nor do we find much force in Lasting's suggestion that "used fairly" in § 1115(b)(4) is an oblique incorporation of a likelihood-of-confusion test developed in the common law of unfair competition. Lasting is certainly correct that some unfair competition cases would stress that use of a term by another in conducting its trade went too far in sowing confusion, and would either enjoin the use or order the defendant to include a disclaimer. But the common law of unfair competition also tolerated some degree of confusion from a descriptive use of words contained in another person's trademark. While these cases are consistent with taking account of the likelihood of consumer confusion as one consideration in deciding whether a use is fair, see Part II–B, infra, they do not stand for the proposition that an assessment of confusion alone may be dispositive. Certainly one cannot get out of them any defense burden to negate it entirely.

Finally, a look at the typical course of litigation in an infringement action points up the incoherence of placing a burden to show nonconfusion on a defendant. If a plaintiff succeeds in making out a prima facie case of trademark infringement, including the element of likelihood of consumer confusion, the defendant may offer rebutting evidence to undercut the force of the plaintiff's evidence on this (or any) element, or raise an affirmative defense to bar relief even if the prima facie case is sound, or do both. But it would make no sense to give the defendant a defense of showing affirmatively that the plaintiff cannot succeed in proving some element (like confusion); all the defendant needs to do is to leave the factfinder unpersuaded that the plaintiff has carried its own burden on that point. A defendant has no need of a court's true belief when agnosticism will do. Put another way, it is only when a plaintiff has shown likely confusion by a preponderance of the evidence that a defendant could have any need of an affirmative defense, but under Lasting's theory the defense would be foreclosed in such a case. Nor would it make sense to provide an affirmative defense of no confusion plus good faith, when merely rebutting the plaintiff's case on confusion would entitle the defendant to judgment, good faith or not.

Lasting tries to extenuate the anomaly of this conception of the affirmative defense by arguing that the oddity reflects the "vestigial" character of the fair use defense as a historical matter. Lasting argues that, because it was only in 1988 that Congress added the express provision that an incontestable markholder's right to exclude is "subject to proof of infringement," Trademark Law Revision Act of 1988, § 128(b)(1), 102 Stat. 3944, there was no requirement prior to 1988 that a markholder prove likelihood of confusion. Before 1988, the argument goes, it was sensible to get at the issue of likely confusion by requiring a defendant to prove its absence when defending on the ground of fair use. When the 1988 Act saddled the markholder with the obligation to prove confusion likely, § 1115(b), the revision simply failed to relieve the fair use defendant of the suddenly strange burden to prove absence of the very confusion that a plaintiff had a new burden to show in the first place.

But the explanation does not work. It is not merely that it would be highly suspect in leaving the claimed element of § 1115(b)(4) redundant and pointless. The main problem of the argument is its false premise: Lasting's assumption that holders of incontestable marks had no need to prove likelihood of confusion prior to 1988 is wrong.

Since the burden of proving likelihood of confusion rests with the plaintiff, and the fair use defendant has no free-standing need to show confusion unlikely, it follows (contrary to the Court of Appeals's view) that some possibility of consumer confusion must be compatible with fair use, and so it is. The common law's tolerance of a certain degree of confusion on the part of consumers followed from the very fact that in cases like this one an originally descriptive term was selected to be used as a mark, not to mention the undesirability of allowing anyone to obtain a complete monopoly on use of a descriptive term simply by grabbing it first. The Lanham Act adopts a similar leniency, there being no indication that the statute was meant to deprive commercial speakers of the ordinary utility of descriptive words. This right to describe is the reason that descriptive terms qualify for registration as trademarks only after taking on secondary meaning as "distinctive of the applicant's goods," 15 U.S.C. § 1052(f), with the registrant getting an exclusive right not in the original, descriptive sense, but only in the secondary one associated with the markholder's goods.

While we thus recognize that mere risk of confusion will not rule out fair use, we think it would be improvident to go further in this case, for deciding anything more would take us beyond the Ninth Circuit's consideration of the subject. It suffices to realize that our holding that fair use can occur along with some degree of confusion does not foreclose the relevance of the extent of any likely consumer confusion in assessing whether a defendant's use is objectively fair. Two Courts of Appeals have found it relevant to consider such scope, and commentators and amici here have urged us to say that the degree of likely consumer confusion bears not only on the fairness of using a term, but even on the further question whether an originally descriptive term has become so identified as a mark that a defendant's use of it cannot realistically be called descriptive.

Since we do not rule out the pertinence of the degree of consumer confusion under the fair use defense, we likewise do not pass upon the position of the United States, as amicus, that the "used fairly" requirement in § 1115(b)(4) demands only that the descriptive term describe the goods accurately. Accuracy of course has to be a consideration in assessing fair use, but the proceedings in this case so far raise no occasion to evaluate some other concerns that courts might pick as relevant, quite apart from attention to confusion. The Restatement raises possibilities like commercial justification and the strength of the plaintiff's mark. Restatement § 28. As to them, it is enough to say here that the door is not closed.

In sum, a plaintiff claiming infringement of an incontestable mark must show likelihood of consumer confusion as part of the prima facie case, 15 U.S.C. § 1115(b), while the defendant has no independent burden to negate the likelihood of any confusion in raising the affirmative defense that a term is used descriptively, not as a mark, fairly, and in good faith, § 1115(b)(4).

Because we read the Court of Appeals as requiring KP to shoulder a burden on the issue of confusion, we vacate the judgment and remand the case for further proceedings consistent with this opinion.

CENTURY 21 REAL ESTATE CORP. v. LENDINGTREE, INC.

United States Court of Appeals, Third Circuit, 2005.
425 F.3d 211.

RENDELL, CIRCUIT JUDGE.

This case presents an opportunity for us to consider the contours of the traditional test for trademark infringement where the defendant asserts the defense of "nominative fair use." More specifically, we must determine what role likelihood of confusion plays in a trademark infringement case where the defendant claims that its use was nominative and fair.

Appellees, Century 21, Coldwell Banker and ERA ("CCE") complain that Appellant Lending Tree ("LT"), in the process of marketing its mortgage services, improperly referenced CCE's trademarked services. LT contends that its use was nominative and fair, and permitted as a matter of law.

"Nominative" fair use is said to occur "when the alleged infringer uses the mark to describe the [trademark holder's] product, even if the alleged infringer's ultimate goal is to describe his own product. Nominative fair use also occurs if the only practical way to refer to something is to use the trademarked term." *KP Permanent Make–Up, Inc. v. Lasting Impression I, Inc.*, 328 F.3d 1061, 1072 (9th Cir.2003) (rev'd. on other grounds) (quotations omitted). By contrast, "classic" fair use occurs where the defendant uses the plaintiff's mark to describe the defendant's own product. *New Kids on the Block v. News America Pub., Inc.*, 971 F.2d 302, 308 (9th Cir.1992).

The use of the term "Volkswagen" by a car mechanic in an ad describing the types of cars he repairs has been held to constitute a nominative fair use. Clearly, the mechanic is referring to another's product, but does so in order to describe what he does. On the other hand, the use of the term "micro-colors," a registered trademark of one make-up company, referring to the pigments of the product of a different and competing make-up company that it used in its own product, was classified as a classic fair use. See *KP Permanent Make–Up, Inc.*, 328 F.3d at 1072. There, the reference to the mark of another was made in describing its own product and its attributes.

Traditionally, we have looked to whether a trademark is likely to cause confusion in order to determine whether a violation of the Lanham Act has occurred and, thus, whether the use should be enjoined and prohibited. However, it is unclear what role "likelihood of confusion" plays in the analysis when "fair use" is asserted as a defense. Recently, the United States Supreme Court provided guidance to the courts regarding the test for classic fair use in *KP Permanent Make–Up, Inc. v. Lasting Impression I, Inc.*, 543 U.S. 111 (2004). The issue before us is the extent to which its reasoning applies to the nominative fair use analysis as well.

It must be recognized at the outset that "fair use" presents a fact pattern different from that of a normal infringement suit. The typical situation in a trademark case involves the defendant's having passed off another's mark as its own or having used a similar name, confusing the public as to precisely whose goods are being sold. Likelihood of confusion is the sole issue. But the fair use defense, by reason of the circumstances giving rise to its applicability, alters the premise somewhat. The defendant is not purporting to be selling goods or services that the plaintiff has trademarked, but, rather, is using plaintiff's mark in order to refer to defendant's own goods or to the goods of the trademark owner in a way that might confuse the public as to the relationship between the two. Accordingly, the legal framework still involves a showing that A's reference to B's mark will likely confuse the public, but the analysis does not end there, for the use may nonetheless be permissible if it is "fair."

In *KP Permanent Make–Up, Inc. v. Lasting Impression I, Inc.*, 543 U.S. 111, 125 S.Ct. 542, 545–46, 160 L.Ed.2d 440 (2004), the Supreme Court rejected the notion that, in the context of classic fair use, the party asserting the fair use defense to a claim of trademark infringement had any burden to negate the likelihood that the practice complained of will confuse consumers about the origin of the services or goods affected. Instead, plaintiff has the exclusive burden to demonstrate likelihood of confusion, and then defendant's burden is only to show the affirmative defense of fair use. The Supreme Court stated, "[s]ince the burden of proving likelihood of confusion rests with the plaintiff, and the fair use defendant has no free-standing need to show confusion unlikely ... it follows that some possibility of consumer confusion must be compatible with fair use...." Id. at 550, 125 S.Ct. 542. Thus, consumer confusion and fair use are not mutually exclusive. The latter will in essence rebut or excuse the former so that the use is permissible.

Before the Supreme Court spoke on the issue of classic fair use, the Court of Appeals for the Ninth Circuit had charted a path through a different fair use analysis—nominative fair use. In *New Kids on the Block*, 971 F.2d at 308, the Court of Appeals for the Ninth Circuit adopted its own test governing the nominative fair use analysis where the marks are used, as they are here and in the case of the mechanic's ad described above that referenced Volkswagen, to refer to the plaintiff trademark owner's product in order to help better describe the defendant's product or service.

The Court distinguished "nominative" fair use from "classic" fair use, noting that if defendant's use of the trademark referred to something other than the plaintiff's product, traditional fair use inquiry would continue to govern. The court then articulated its own test for nominative fair use:

> [W]here the defendant uses a trademark to describe the plaintiff's product, rather than its own, we hold that a commercial user is entitled to a nominative fair use defense provided he meets the following three requirements: First, the product or service in question must be one not readily identifiable without use of the trademark; second, only so much of the mark or marks may be used as is reasonably necessary to identify the product or service; and third, the user must do nothing that would, in conjunction with the mark, suggest sponsorship or endorsement by the trademark holder. Id.

In announcing this new test, *New Kids On The Block* rejected traditional trademark infringement analysis. It held that this test replaces the "likelihood of confusion" test for trademark cases where nominative fair use is asserted.

While we agree with the Ninth Circuit Court of Appeals that a distinct analysis is needed for nominative fair use cases, we do not accept the legal basis or advisability of supplanting the likelihood of confusion test entirely. First, we do not see nominative fair use as so different from classic fair use as to warrant such different treatment. The Ninth Circuit Court of Appeals believed that the two types of fair use could be distinguished on the basis that nominative fair use makes it clear to consumers that the plaintiff, not the defendant, is the source of the trademarked product or service, while classic fair use does not. Thus, the Ninth Circuit Court of Appeals believed that a different analysis was appropriate for nominative fair use and that it could abandon the need for proof of confusion in these circumstances. *New Kids On The Block*, 971 F.2d at 307–08. Yet, it is clear to us that even a defendant's nominative use has the potential of confusing consumers with respect to its products or services. Since the defendant ultimately uses the plaintiff's mark in a nominative case in order to describe its own product or services, even an accurate nominative use could potentially confuse consumers about the plaintiff's endorsement or sponsorship of the defendant's products or services. Thus, we disagree with the fundamental distinction the Ninth Circuit Court of Appeals drew between classic and nominative fair use.

Today we adopt a two-step approach in nominative fair use cases. The plaintiff must first prove that confusion is likely due to the defendant's use of plaintiff's mark. * * * Once plaintiff has met its burden of proving that confusion is likely, the burden then shifts to defendant to show that its nominative use of plaintiff's mark is nonetheless fair. To demonstrate fairness, the defendant must satisfy a three-pronged nominative fair use test, derived to a great extent from the one articulated by the Court of Appeals for the Ninth Circuit. Under our fairness test, a defendant must show: (1) that the use of plaintiff's mark is necessary to describe both the plaintiff's product or service and the defendant's product or service; (2) that the defendant uses only so much of the plaintiff's mark as is necessary to describe plaintiff's product; and (3) that the defendant's conduct or language reflect the true and accurate relationship between plaintiff and defendant's products or services.

As an initial matter, we recognize that our concurring colleague rejects the bifurcated approach that we now adopt. He argues instead that the factors we consider under the fairness test should be incorporated into the likelihood of confusion analysis. In his view, our bifurcated approach places a heavy burden on the defendant to negate confusion and is judicially unmanageable. However, our approach does nothing of the kind.

We conclude that the broad based likelihood of confusion test our concurring colleague proposes is misplaced for several reasons. First, it is largely out of sync with the existing jurisprudence on fair use. The concurrence's test allows no real possibility of the co-existence of fair use with some likelihood of confusion, yet this is precisely what the Supreme Court's holding in *KP Permanent Make–Up* specifically contemplates. See *KP Permanent Make–Up*, 125 S.Ct. at 550 ("[S]ome possibility of consumer confusion must be compatible with fair use. . . ."). In addition, our concurring colleague rejects the notion that nominative fair use could be used as an affirmative defense, viewing it instead as a confusion substitute. Yet, the Supreme Court clearly views fair use (albeit classic fair use) as an affirmative defense. Id. at 548–49 (referring to the affirmative defense of fair use). The concurrence fails to explain why *KP Permanent Make–Up* should neither control nor inform our analysis here, choosing instead to ignore the Court's dictates in that case as they apply to nominative fair use. After that decision, it seems to us that neither classic or nominative fair use should rise and fall based on a finding of likelihood of confusion. Classic fair use and nominative fair use are different in certain respects, but it is unclear to us why we should ask radically different questions when analyzing a defendant's ability to refer to a plaintiff's mark in the two contexts. As we have already stated, in both nominative and classic fair use cases the defendant uses the plaintiff's mark descriptively in a way that potentially confuses consumers about the relationship between the plaintiff and the defendant's product or services. In the classic fair use context, the defendant uses the mark to describe its own product, and in the nominative context, the defendant references plaintiff's product in order to describe its own. The key first inquiry in both situations should be whether there is a likelihood of confusion. The only other court to consider the application of nominative fair use doctrine since *KP Permanent Make–Up* has embraced this logic.

Second, while the concurrence worries that a nominative use defendant will be overly burdened under our bifurcated approach, we believe that his approach is actually more burdensome to such a defendant. If the factors for determining fairness were incorporated into the likelihood of confusion test, a plaintiff's showing of confusion might well overwhelm a defendant's showing of fair use. This would essentially force a defendant asserting nominative fair use to negate all likelihood of confusion to succeed, a proposition that the Supreme Court rejected in *KP Permanent Make–Up*. Under our approach, the defendant has no duty to negate confusion as such, but rather must merely show that its use of the plaintiff's mark is fair, a burden which, by contrast, is not cumbersome. Thus, it is our view that the bifurcated approach is ultimately less burdensome to a nominative use defendant than the analysis the concurrence proposes.

Finally, we believe that the bifurcated approach that we adopt today is more workable than a unified confusion/fairness test. We leave the now familiar test for likelihood of confusion largely intact and in the form in which district courts are accustomed to applying it. Our test for nominative fair use considers distinct factors that are readily susceptible to judicial inquiry. By contrast, the concurrence would incorporate several new considerations into the already lengthy ten-part test for confusion and ask district courts to balance a plaintiff's showing of confusion against a defendant's showing of fair use. Because confusion and fairness are separate and distinct concepts that can co-exist, blending them together into one test is, to our mind, a much less manageable approach.

[Author's note: The court remanded the case to the district court for application of the new standard.]

FISHER, CIRCUIT JUDGE, [concurring and dissenting].

As the majority correctly concludes, proper nominative use is permissible use, leaving the critical question of how to frame the nominative use analysis. I concur with the majority's "firm conviction that the burden of proving likelihood of confusion should remain with the plaintiff in a trademark infringement case." I also concur in its conclusion that this Court's *Lapp* factors, where relevant, must be used in the analysis. I therefore join in the majority's judgment remanding the case for further proceedings.

I depart from majority, however, in its adoption of a bifurcated analysis that looks first to a truncated *Lapp*-factor test, followed by an affirmative defense of "nominative fair use." Despite professing a "firm conviction" that the burden of proving likely confusion remains on plaintiffs, the majority formulates an affirmative defense that shifts to defendant the burden of negating confusion. In so doing, the majority flouts binding caselaw holding that proper nominative use is use that is not likely to confuse, and that a plaintiff alone bears the burden of establishing likely confusion. Moreover, to the extent the majority places any burden on plaintiffs at all, it is so watered-down that plaintiffs might prove likely confusion on one *Lapp* factor alone. The majority's bifurcated test is also judicially unmanageable because it requires courts to address identical factors on both sides of the equation.

Accordingly, I dissent. I first review nominative use cases and conclude that precedent, binding and otherwise, shows that the question of nominative use is a question of likely confusion and not an affirmative defense. Second, I address the majority's bifurcated analysis, and conclude that it runs afoul of the Lanham Act and binding precedent because it places on defendant the burden of negating likely confusion. I also conclude that the test is judicially unmanageable because it requires courts to examine identical likelihood of confusion factors on both sides of the analysis. Finally, I propose that in nominative use cases, courts apply a modified likelihood of confusion inquiry based on Lapp factors two through ten, with the burden resting where it must, on plaintiffs. Because proper nominative use is use that is not likely to confuse, it is the majority's "nominative fair use" test that is unfair, because it places the burden where it should never be, on the defendant.

2. First Amendment

For an example of the First Amendment defense in trademark law, see the analysis in *Lamparello v. Falwell*, above. Also consider the following excerpt from *Bosley Medical Institute, Inc. v. Kremer*, 403 F.3d 672 (9th Cir. 2005), in which the defendant created a web site to criticize the services of the plaintiff, who sued for trademark infringement:

> The dangers that the Lanham Act was designed to address are simply not at issue in this case. The Lanham Act, expressly enacted to be applied in commercial contexts, does not prohibit all unauthorized uses of a trademark. Kremer's use of the Bosley Medical mark simply cannot mislead consumers into buying a competing product—no customer will mistakenly purchase a hair replacement service from Kremer under the belief that the service is being offered by Bosley. Neither is Kremer capitalizing on the good will Bosley has created in its mark. Any harm to Bosley arises not from a competitor's sale of a similar product under Bosley's mark, but from Kremer's criticism of their services. Bosley cannot use the Lanham Act either as a shield from Kremer's criticism, or as a sword to shut Kremer up. * * *

403 F. 3d at 679–80 (appellate court affirming on finding of no trademark infringement because use of mark was noncommercial, but remanding on issue of anticybersquatting since trademark owner was not given the opportunity for discovery on the bad faith intent to profit issue).

NOTES

1. The defenses discussed in this section illustrate that trademarks are a type of language, used to signify to consumers the source of a product or service. But a single symbol may have both a trademark significance and another significance. The defenses of fair use and the First Amendment serve to cabin trademark rights so as not to interfere with the other purposes of language.

2. Trademark fair use should be distinguished from copyright fair use. In copyright, fair use was originally a justification for infringement that developed along equitable lines. In situations where the copyright infringer was using the copyrighted expression to further some other end, such as criticism or research, as opposed to interfering with the copyright owner's rights in her expression, the infringing use was deemed fair. The 1976 Copyright Act codified fair use into a multifactor test, the most important of which has become the effect on the potential market for the copyrighted work. If the infringing use interferes with this potential market, then the use is most likely not fair. Trademark law, by contrast, is more straightforward. If the infringer uses the mark to refer to the trademark owner's product or service or to refer to his own product or service, then the trademark infringing use is fair. While copyright fair use mandates the application of a multifactor test, trademark fair use asks whether the mark is being used in a trademark sense or in a descriptive sense. For example, if the mark Exxon is used as shorthand to refer to the company or its product, as opposed to branding some other goods, then the use of the mark is fair.

3. The *KP Permanent Make–Up* case addresses the question of how trademark fair use relates to likelihood of confusion. Copyright fair use has roots in the law of justification, and therefore there is a strong argument that the alleged infringer had the burden to establish fair use as an affirmative defense. For a discussion of how complicated the burden of proof issue can become, see Thomas A. Mitchell, *Undermining the Initial Allocation of Rights: Copyright Versus Contract and the Burden of Proof*, 27 HASTINGS COMM. & ENT. L. J. 525 (2005). But some lower courts held that trademark fair use required the defendant to show that the use of the mark was not likely to be confusing. The Supreme Court resolved this issue by holding that the defendant did not have to show lack of confusion. The implication is that an infringer is allowed to make fair use of a trademark even if there is some likelihood of confusion. The argument can be made that the Court's holding in *KP Permanent Make–Up* undermines the goal of trademarks to police confusing use of marks in the marketplace. But there may be different degrees of confusion. For example, I may see the mark Exxon being used by a company. That may, at first, be confusing. Is the mark Exxon being used to sell Exxon–Mobil's product? Or is it being used by a competitor to trick me into buying his product? Fair use requires consumers to ask another question: is the mark being used as a

trademark or as a descriptive word? The Court's decision in *KP Permanent Make-Up* recognizes that what is confusing in the marketplace is a matter of degree. Whenever consumers see a mark, they should be able to distinguish uses of a mark as a brand and uses that are meant to be descriptive. Even though on the surface the Court's holding seems to countenance some confusion in the marketplace, a more accurate interpretation is that the fair use of a trademark cannot be confusing because consumers understand the difference.

4. The *Century 21* case illustrates some of the difficulties lower courts have had in applying the holding of *KP Permanent Make-Up*. The difficulties, in part, stem from the lack of guidance in the Lanham Act. They also arise from the development of the nominative fair use defense. As stated in the cases, nominative fair use is the use of a mark to refer to the trademark owner's product or service but not as a brand. If a story on the evening news refers to Exxon, that use is nominative fair use. Of course, in this example, consumers are unlikely to be confused about an affiliation between the company and the news program. But consider the example of the Volkswagen. If a service station says they fix Volkswagens, is there an implication that they are authorized by Volkswagen to fix their cars? If a lawsuit arises under these facts, who should have the burden to show how the word Volkswagen is being used? Under the *KP Permanent Make-Up* approach, the trademark owner would first establish likelihood of confusion and then the defendant would show fair use without having to show that there was no possibility of confusion from this use. As we stated above, the implication is that there might be some confusion as to the affiliation between the service station and Volkswagen, but consumers can sort that out presumably. Some courts are concerned that the defendant might nonetheless be free riding on the value of the trademarked brand. Suppose the service station stated they fix Jaguars. Non-Jaguar owners may go to the station, thinking if the station is good enough to fix Jaguars, it can fix my car. In response, to this type of confusion, some circuits, like the Ninth, required the defendant raising nominative fair use as a defense to show that the use of the mark does not create any impression of endorsement or affiliation. This approach was adopted before *KP Permanent Make-Up* and therefore the question is to what extent did the Supreme Court's holding apply to nominative fair use as well as the type of fair use associated with KP's use of "micro colors." The *Century 21* case illustrates one recent attempt to deal with that issue. The excluded portion of the opinion included a discussion of how the *Polaroid/Lapp/Sleekcraft* factors would have to be adopted in order to accommodate the nominative fair use defense. Specifically, the court held that similarity of the mark and strength of the mark were not relevant when nominative fair use is raised because in all cases involving nominative fair use, they would weigh against the defendant.

An important factor in the availability of the fair use defense is the good faith of the alleged infringer. See *Institute for Scientific Info. Inc. v. Gordon and Breach, Science Publishers, Inc.*, 931 F.2d 1002 (3rd Cir. 1991) (denying fair use defense when defendant was shown not to have acted in good faith).

5. One way to limit the effects of trademark law on speech is, of course, through the First Amendment. Trademarks are a form of commercial speech,

and so the application of trademark law to limit speech would be subject to intermediate scrutiny under the First Amendment. In other words, infringers could not absolutely hide behind the First Amendment nor is trademark infringing speech completely unprotected by the First Amendment. The *Bosley* case illustrates how courts strike this balance. Kremer is not asserting the First Amendment as a defense per se. Instead, the policies behind the First Amendment are used to interpret and apply the Lanham Act to the facts of the case. Notice especially how this approach works for anticybersquatting. The fact that Kremer was registering the trademark as a domain name in order to exercise his speech rights is to be taken into consideration in determining whether he acted in bad faith. First Amendment values are used to interpret and apply the statute to ensure that it does not overreach. See Lisa P. Ramsey, *Descriptive Trademarks and the First Amendment*, 70 TENN. L. REV. 1095 (2003); Mark A. Lemley & Eugene Volokh, *Freedom of Speech and Injunctions in Intellectual Property Cases*, 48 DUKE L. J. 147 (1998).

6.   The federal antidilution statute contains the following defenses:

- Fair use of a famous mark by another person in comparative commercial advertising or promotion to identify the competing goods or services of the owner of the famous mark.

- Fair use of a famous mark by another person, other than as a designation of source (e.g., identifying, parodying, criticizing, commenting).

- All forms of news reporting and news commentary.

See 15 USC § 1125(c)(3). Notice that the first and second defenses are analogous to the defense of fair use under 1115(b)(4).

7.   The first sale doctrine is another important defense to trademark infringement. In general, a purchaser of a branded product has the right to resell the product as long as there is no material alteration to the product or trademark. See, e.g., *Davidoff & Cie, S.A. v. PLD International Corp.*, 263 F.3d 1297 (11th Cir. 2001). The first sale defense arises most frequently in the context of international trade involving gray market goods. We will discuss this issue in Chapter Eight in the context of *American Circuit Breaker Corp. v. Oregon Breakers, Inc.*, 406 F.3d 577 (9th Cir. 2005).

B.   REMEDIES

The following table summarizes the remedies available under the Lanham Act. The two cases that follow provide some illustrations of these remedies.

	Injunctive Relief	Damages
1114(a) AND 1125(a)	• Equitable relief available under §1116 • Destruction of infringing article available under §1118	Available under §1117 • profits, that can be enhanced or diminished by judge • damages that can be trebled • attorney's fees in exceptional cases • statutory damages for counterfeit marks
1125(c)	• Injunctive relief is primary remedy under §1125(c)(2) • If willful dilution, then destruction of infringing article available under §1118	If willful dilution, then profits, damages and attorney's as under §1117
1125(d)	Forfeiture or cancellation of domain name under §1125(d)(1)(C)	• Actual damages and profits or statutory damages under §1117(d) • No damages for an in rem action under §1125(d)(2)

GRACIE v. GRACIE

United States Court of Appeals, Ninth Circuit, 2000.
217 F.3d 1060.

O'SCANNLAIN, CIRCUIT JUDGE:

We must resolve a variety of issues in this complex trademark litigation arising out of the U.S. activities of two members of the large and prominent Gracie family of Brazil, known for popularizing, competing in, and teaching a form of the martial art jiu-jitsu.

Carley Gracie ("Carley") and Rorion Gracie ("Rorion") are first cousins. More than 38 members of this Brazilian family have been involved in jiu-jitsu competition or teaching. Both Carley and Rorion operate California-based jiu-jitsu instruction businesses.

Carley came to the United States from Brazil in the early 1970s. Carley began teaching jiu-jitsu in the eastern United States as early as 1974 and in California sometime after he arrived in the state in 1979. Carley has used the name "Gracie" in identifying his jiu-jitsu instruction business.

In the late 1970s, Rorion came to the United States and began teaching the "Gracie method" of jiu-jitsu in Southern California. He used the term "Gracie Jiu–Jitsu" to identify his business, which now consists of a nationwide chain of training facilities. Rorion publicized his jiu-jitsu instruction business through national advertising which used the term "Gracie Jiu–Jitsu" and the Triangle Design logo, which consists of two grappling jiu-jitsu figures outlined by an open triangle. In 1988, Rorion applied for and obtained a California registration for the Triangle Design logo. In 1989, Rorion applied for and obtained federal registrations for the "Gracie Jiu–Jitsu" service mark and the Triangle Design logo. Rorion has actively enforced his rights in "Gracie Jiu–Jitsu" and the Triangle Design logo through litigation.

In December 1994, Carley sued Rorion, challenging the validity of the term "Gracie Jiu–Jitsu" and the Triangle Design logo as service marks. Carley's first amended complaint alleged the following federal and state causes of action: (1) cancellation of registration, (2) damages for false or fraudulent registration, (3) untrue or misleading advertising, (4) defamation, (5) interference with prospective business relationships, (6) infringement of common law service marks under California law, (7) unfair competition, (8) attempt to monopolize in violation of the Sherman Act, and (9) false advertising in violation of 15 U.S.C. § 1125(a). Rorion counterclaimed, alleging that Carley infringed registered marks for "Gracie Jiu–Jitsu" and the Triangle Design logo * * *.

On November 18, 1997, the district court granted Carley's motion to dismiss all defendants other than Rorion himself. On November 19, 1997, the jury returned a verdict in which it found that (1) Rorion did not have a valid federal service mark for "Gracie Jiu–Jitsu," (2) Rorion did have a valid federal service mark for the registered Triangle Design logo, (3) Carley infringed the registered Triangle Design logo, (4) Carley's infringement was "willful," and (5) Carley profited from the infringement in the amount of $108,000 * * *.

We must first decide whether the district court erred in refusing to order cancellation of Rorion's federal registration for "Gracie Jiu–Jitsu" pursuant to its power over registrations under 15 U.S.C. § 1119. Consistent with the jury verdict finding that Rorion did not have a valid federal service mark for "Gracie Jiu–Jitsu," the district court issued an amended judgment containing the following language: "It is also ORDERED, ADJUDGED, and DECREED that defendants do not have a valid service mark for the name GRACIE JIU–JITSU." Carley argues that the district court erred in refusing to order cancellation of Rorion's federal registration for "Gracie Jiu–Jitsu" following the jury's finding of invalidity.

Although there is a paucity of case law on point (perhaps because the situation at hand is rather unusual), the issue before us is not difficult to resolve. Once the district court gave the jury the power to determine the validity of Rorion Gracie's federal service mark, refusing to cancel the registration for "Gracie Jiu–Jitsu" after the jury declared it to be incapable of serving as a mark was inconsistent with the court's duty to give effect to a jury verdict, and as such erroneous. While a general verdict in favor of Carley on Rorion's "Gracie Jiu–Jitsu" infringement claim could have been reconciled with the district court's refusal to cancel Rorion's federal registration, because a jury could have found Carley not liable for infringement without passing on the validity of Rorion's mark, a special verdict presents an entirely different case.

In cases not involving jury trials, district courts have been reversed for refusing to order the cancellation of registrations for claimed marks found to be incapable of serving as valid marks. * * * These cases support our conclusion that the district court erred in refusing to cancel a mark found to be invalid. While it was within the district court's power to reject the jury's verdict of invalidity as against the weight of the evidence, the district court did not do so, explicitly denying Rorion's motion for judgment as a matter of law after the jury verdict of invalidity. In light of the jury verdict, which the district court allowed to stand, the district court should have ordered cancellation of Rorion's federal registration for "Gracie Jiu–Jitsu." * * *

Carley contends that there was no basis for the court's award of $108,000 to Rorion for Carley's infringement of the Triangle Design logo. According to Carley, this award was erroneous because Lanham Act damages cannot be recovered in the absence of evidence of actual consumer confusion. Because there was no evidence that any of Rorion's customers were confused by Carley's use of a triangular logo similar to the registered Triangle Design logo, Carley argues, no damages should have been awarded.

In response, Rorion argues that Carley's objection is both untimely and misplaced. First, Rorion points out that Carley failed to object at trial to the applicable sections of (1) the jury instructions, which did not require the jury to find proof of actual confusion in order to grant a recovery of profits for infringement, and (2) the verdict form, which asked the jury to "state the total profits made by Carley Gracie" if it found Carley liable for infringement. Second, Rorion argues that evidence of actual confusion was not required because "[w]illful infringement, not actual confusion, is the touchstone for an award of damages or accounting of profits." In this case, because the jury verdict found that Carley's infringement of Rorion's Triangle Design logo was "willful," an accounting of profits was a proper remedy.

We conclude that Rorion has the better of the argument. The Lanham Act provision upon which Rorion's trademark infringement claim rested, 15 U.S.C. § 1114, does not require actual consumer confusion for recovery of profits. Rather, by its terms § 1114 requires only a likelihood of confusion combined with willful infringement: "[T]he registrant shall not be entitled to recover profits or damages unless the acts have been committed with knowledge that such imitation is intended to cause confusion, or to cause mistake, or to deceive." While actual confusion may be relevant as evidence of the likelihood of confusion (which is required for an award of profits under § 1114), under our precedents a showing of actual confusion is not necessary to obtain a recovery of profits. * * *

Carley argues that the district court abused its discretion in deciding to award attorneys' fees to Rorion on the counterclaim for infringement of the Triangle Design logo. Carley also challenges the amount of the $620,000 award. We address these contentions in turn.

The Lanham Act permits an award of attorneys' fees to the prevailing party in "exceptional cases." 15 U.S.C. § 1117(a). "While the term 'exceptional' is not defined in the statute, generally a trademark case is exceptional for purposes of an award of attorneys' fees when the infringement is malicious, fraudulent, deliberate or willful." Lindy Pen, [982 F.2d 1400, 1409 (9th Cir. 1993)]. Carley contends that the case at bar is not an "exceptional case" within § 1117 so as to permit an award of attorneys' fees.

Carley's argument is difficult to advance successfully. Here the jury explicitly found that Carley engaged in "willful" infringement of Rorion's Triangle Design logo. The district court's decision to make a fee award to Rorion thus flows quite naturally from the jury's finding of willful infringement and the legal standard for "exceptional cases" under § 1117.

In trying to escape the effect of the jury's finding of willful infringement, Carley argues that the jury was not properly instructed regarding willfulness. * * * This argument lacks merit. The jury in this case was instructed that "you may find that [plaintiffs] intentionally infringed the [ ] service marks, if you find that they acted 'willfully,' or deliberately and in bad faith, in order to trade upon Rorion Gracie's good will." Thus the jury was properly instructed as to the bad faith component of willfulness * * *. In sum, because a properly instructed jury found that Carley willfully infringed Rorion's Triangle Design logo, the district court did not abuse its discretion in deciding to make a fee award.

The district court granted the entire fee award requested by Rorion, awarding him over $620,000 in attorneys' fees. We note that this award is a substantial one, almost six times the size of the damages awarded to Rorion in this case. Carley challenges the size of the award by arguing that the court could only award attorneys' fees under the Lanham Act for fees "incurred in prosecuting a Lanham Act claim on which that party prevails." Carley claims that the district court abused its discretion in awarding to Rorion the entire amount of attorneys' fees requested by Rorion (in excess of $620,000), which included fees for legal work related to both non-Lanham Act claims and Lanham Act claims on which Rorion did not prevail.

The Lanham Act simply provides that "[t]he court in exceptional cases may award reasonable attorney fees to the prevailing party," 15 U.S.C. § 1117(a); it does not address the proper procedure for determining reasonable attorney fees in a case involving non-Lanham Act claims and unsuccessful Lanham Act claims, in addition to successful claims under the Act. We have not yet addressed the question of whether the correct determination of attorneys' fees in cases like the one at bar requires allocation or apportionment between Lanham Act and non-Lanham Act claims.

We note that among the handful of district courts that have addressed calculation of a Lanham Act fee award in a case involving Lanham Act and non-Lanham Act claims, the following rule appears to be emerging: In an award of "reasonable attorney fees" pursuant to the Lanham Act, a party cannot recover legal fees incurred in litigating non-Lanham Act claims unless "the Lanham Act claims and non-Lanham Act claims are so intertwined that it is impossible to differentiate between work done on claims." John W. Crittenden & Eugene M. Pak, *Monetary Relief Under Lanham Act Section 35*, in Litigating Copyright, Trademark & Unfair Competition Cases for the Experienced Practitioner 1998, at 419 (PLI Pat., Copyrights, Trademarks and Literary Property Course Handbook Series No. 537, 1998) (surveying district court cases, including Neva) (emphasis added); see also Robin C. Larner, *Award of attorneys' fees under § 35(A) of Lanham Act*, 82 A.L.R. FED. 143, 198 (1987) (comparing two district court decisions, one allowing recovery of legal fees incurred on state law claims related to Lanham Act claims and one denying recovery of such legal fees). Thus, despite the general rule of apportionment, in a specific case apportionment might not be required if "it is impossible to differentiate between work done on claims." We hold, however, that the impossibility of making an exact apportionment does not relieve the district court of its duty to make some attempt to adjust the fee award in an effort to reflect an apportionment. In other words, apportionment or an attempt at apportionment is required unless the court finds the claims are so inextricably intertwined that even an estimated adjustment would be meaningless.

Based on the record before us, we must remand for the district court to attempt an apportionment or to make findings that apportionment would be impossible. In declining to apportion fees, the district court here stated that "it would be impossible to estimate the exact percentage of the defendants' fees that are attributable to Lanham Act claims." While calculating an "exact percentage" may be impossible, this does not relieve the district court of its duty to make some attempt to adjust the fee award to reflect, even if imprecisely, work performed on non-Lanham Act claims.

In addition to its failure to apportion fees between Lanham Act and non-Lanham Act claims, the district court also erred by not developing an adequate record to establish the reasonableness of the total fee award. A remand is therefore appropriate to permit the district court to conduct a more detailed and thorough inquiry into what would constitute a reasonable amount of attorneys' fees in this case.

In the case at bar, the district court expressed its exasperation with the "dilatory conduct" of plaintiff's counsel before making the following brief, somewhat conclusory statement regarding the reasonableness of the requested fee award: "Given the number of motions filed in this case, the number of delays and continuances, the eventual length of the trial, and the number of witnesses, the defendants' requested attorneys' fee award of $620,238.43 is reasonable." The district court made no findings as to the rates and hours it determined to be reasonable. [T]he district court here uncritically accepted a party's representations as to the time and money reasonably spent on the case. [T]he district court did not determine a presumptive lodestar figure. The underdeveloped record with respect to the fee award in this case prevents us from reviewing its adequacy. [Author's Note: A lodestar is used to calculate statutorily authorized attorney's fees and is equal to the number of hours reasonably expended multiplied by the prevailing hourly rate in the community for similar work, adjusted for the nature of the suit and the quality of representation.]

Accordingly, we remand the fee award of $620,000 for reconsideration in light of the principles set forth above. On remand, the district court should (1) make an apportionment between Lanham Act and non-Lanham Act claims, as well as claims on which Rorion prevailed and claims on which he did not, in setting a reasonable fee; and (2) determine a presumptive lodestar figure, subject to possible adjustment * * *.

Finally, Carley challenges the district court's decision not to award him attorneys' fees on his successful defense of the counterclaim for infringement of the service mark registration for "Gracie Jiu–Jitsu."

As Carley correctly notes (in challenging the fee award to Rorion), the Lanham Act permits, but does not mandate, an award of attorneys' fees to a prevailing party in "exceptional circumstances." 15 U.S.C. § 1117(a). Exceptional circumstances can be found when the non-prevailing party's case "is groundless, unreasonable, vexatious, or pursued in bad faith." *Interstellar Starship Servs., Ltd. v. Epix Inc.*, 184 F.3d 1107, 1112 (9th Cir. 1999) (internal quotation marks omitted). The above standard for exceptional circumstances applies to prevailing defendants as well as prevailing plaintiffs under the Lanham Act. See *Stephen W. Boney, Inc. v. Boney Servs., Inc.*, 127 F.3d 821, 827 (9th Cir. 1997). Here, Carley seeks attorneys' fees as a successful defendant, for prevailing in Rorion's counterclaim for infringement.

A party alleging that the district court erred by failing to award attorneys' fees under § 1117 faces an uphill battle. "The text of section 1117 places a heavy burden of an attorney arguing that the district court abused its discretion in refusing to award attorneys' fees," as we explained in *Polo Fashions, Inc. v. Dick Bruhn, Inc.*, 793 F.2d 1132, 1134 (9th Cir. 1986). "First, the remedy is available only in 'exceptional cases.' Second, the statute provides that the court 'may' award fees; it does not require them. Finally, the Senate Report expressly commends this decision to the discretion of the [trial] court." Id.

Carley's conclusory statements regarding Rorion's supposed bad faith are insufficient to carry Carley's burden under *Polo Fashions*. Carley uses strong language to call into question Rorion's motives in filing the "Gracie

Jiu–Jitsu" counterclaim, but Carley fails to cite any specific record evidence to support his aggressive speculation regarding Rorion's state of mind. As noted by the district court, "[p]laintiffs make no showing of any improper purpose in Defendants' filing the counterclaim for trademark infringement. They present no proof that Defendants acted in bad faith or filed the counterclaim unreasonably." In light of the Lanham Act's requirement of "exceptional circumstances," as interpreted—rather narrowly—by our past decisions, the district court did not abuse its discretion in denying the motion for attorneys' fees * * *.

[The appellate court held that the district court should have cancelled the registration of the service mark and award any relief consistent with the cancellation. The court upheld the accounting of profits, but remanded for recalculation and apportionment of the attorney's fees.]

NOTES

1. The principal case presents the analysis of remedies fairly comprehensively and should give you a sense of the issues that arise in determining how to remedy trademark infringement. There are several points worth highlighting:

- Injunctive relief is a standard remedy subject to the usual equitable defenses, but is discretionary. However, likelihood of success on the merits (which in the context of trademark, means likelihood of confusion) is usually enough to establish that there is irreparable injury that only an injunction can remedy. See *Dial–A–Mattress Operating Corp. v. Mattress Madness, Inc.*, 841 F.Supp. 1339 (E.D.N.Y. 1994).

- An injunction will not be granted to prevent trademark use in a geographic area that the trademark owner has not entered. In such situations, the possibility of confusion is not considered grave enough to merit injunctive relief. See *Dawn Donut Company, Inc. v. Hart's Food Stores, Inc.*, 267 F.2d 358 (2d Cir. 1959); *National Association for Healthcare Communications, Inc. v. Central Arkansas Area Agency on Aging, Inc.*, 257 F.3d 732 (8th Cir. 2001).

- Profits and damages are both recoverable, but there cannot be double recovery. To the extent, that the defendant's profits are money that the plaintiff would have made absent infringement, the plaintiff cannot recover that amount twice, once as disgorged profits and once as damages. See *Sands, Taylor & Wood Co. v. Quaker Oats Co.*, 978 F.2d 947 (7th Cir. 1992).

- The award of profits and damages are subject to the principles of equity. Since profits are viewed as a form of unjust enrichment, some courts do not award profits unless the defendant has acted in bad faith. See *Quick Technologies, Inc. v. The Sage Group, PLC*, 313 F.3d 338 (5th Cir. 2002) (reviewing the conflict and rejecting the requirement of bad faith).

- To establish profits, the trademark owner must establish the amount of the defendant's sales. The defendant has the burden to establish its costs in selling the infringing items. The difference between the sales as established by the plaintiff and the costs as established by the defendant are the profits that can be disgorged to the trademark owner. See *George Basch Co. v. Blue Coral, Inc.*, 968 F.2d 1532 (2d Cir. 1992).

- The court has the discretion to enhance or diminish the profits award if they are deemed inadequate or excessive. The court also has the discretion to increase the damage award up to three times the amount awarded by the jury. The statute states that the enhancement of either profits or damages is for the purposes of compensation, and not punishment. See *Sands, Taylor*, supra.

- Attorney's fees and costs and awarded to the prevailing party in "exceptional cases" under § 1117(a). Courts vary in the standard for exceptional cases, with some courts requiring willful or malicious conduct (see *Gracie v. Gracie*, above), some requiring the plaintiff failing to show any damage (see *CJC Holdings, Inc. v. Wright & Lato, Inc.*, 979 F.2d 60 (5th Cir. 1992)), and others appealing to equitable principles to determine when a case is exceptional (see *Securacomm Consulting, Inc. v. Securacom, Inc.*, 224 F.3d 273 (3rd Cir. 2000).

CHAPTER SIX

STATE LAWS GOVERNING INTELLECTUAL PROPERTY

■ ■ ■

OVERVIEW

While this text primarily focuses on federal intellectual property laws having nationwide scope and impact, state laws also impose some important restrictions on the use of intellectual works. The most important body of state intellectual property law—trade secret law—is addressed in Chapter 2. This chapter describes several additional types of state protections for intellectual property.

In some instances, state laws such as state trademark laws govern the same types of intellectual property as corresponding federal laws, providing protections to those types of property within the states involved that differ from federal protections in either the steps needed to gain protection or in the rights afforded to interest holders. These sorts of protections that directly parallel federal protections are covered in the chapters dealing with their related federal protections and are not discussed further here.

The protections considered here involve types of intellectual works and property rights not addressed by federal laws. The chapter begins with a discussion of the circumstances in which, in light of federalism concerns, states cannot enact intellectual property laws and related legal standards that differ from federal laws. This discussion considers two types of preemption of state laws by federal intellectual property laws: statutory preemption in which the scope of preemptive effect on state laws is defined by the statutory terms of a federal enactment and Constitutional preemption in which a federal enactment says nothing specifically about preemption of state standards but some such standards must be treated as preempted and unenforceable in order for the intended purpose of the federal enactment to be achieved.

Following this discussion of preemption issues, the chapter goes on to examine several distinctive types of intellectual property that are protected under state laws. The discussions in this portion of the chapter emphasize how state intellectual property laws extend to types of works that are not covered by federal intellectual property laws or establish rights not provided by such federal laws. The discussions also consider the reasons why states have sought to afford additional protections to intellectual property beyond the considerable protections already granted under federal intellectual property laws.

I. INTRODUCTION TO INTELLECTUAL PROPERTY FEDERALISM

A. STATUTORY PREEMPTION

In enacting statutes based on the powers granted to the federal government under the Constitution, Congress generally can choose to specify explicitly in the statutes when the statutes will preempt (that is, preclude) attempts by states to enact and enforce laws governing the same subject matters or rights. The scope of this power to define the preemptive effects of federal enactments is itself limited by the Tenth Amendment to the Constitution and other constitutional provisions restricting Congressional actions.

In the case of the federal Copyright Act, Congress adopted a very specific statutory test defining when state enactments are preempted by the provisions of the Act. The preemption standards specified in the Act are as follows:

Copyright Act of 1976 (as amended)

§ 301.   Preemption with respect to other laws

(a) On and after January 1, 1978, all legal or equitable rights that are equivalent to any of the exclusive rights within the general scope of copyright as specified by [federal copyright laws] in works of authorship that are fixed in a tangible medium of expression and come within the subject matter of copyright as specified by [federal copyright laws], whether created before or after that date and whether published or unpublished, are governed exclusively by this title. Thereafter, no person is entitled to any such right or equivalent right in any such work under the common law or statutes of any State.

(b) Nothing in this title annuls or limits any rights or remedies under the common law or statutes of any State with respect to—

(1) subject matter that does not come within the subject matter of copyright as specified by [federal copyright laws], including works of authorship not fixed in any tangible medium of expression; or

(2) any cause of action arising from undertakings commenced before January 1, 1978;

(3) activities violating legal or equitable rights that are not equivalent to any of the exclusive rights within the general scope of copyright as specified by [federal copyright laws]; or

(4) State and local landmarks, historic preservation, zoning, or building codes, relating to architectural works protected under [federal copyright laws].

(c) With respect to sound recordings fixed before February 15, 1972, any rights or remedies under the common law or statutes of any State shall not be annulled or limited by this title until February 15, 2067. The preemptive provisions of subsection (a) shall apply to any such rights and remedies pertaining to any cause of action arising from undertakings commenced on and after February 15, 2067. [N]o sound recording fixed before February 15, 1972, shall be subject to copyright under this title before, on, or after February 15, 2067.

(d) Nothing in this title annuls or limits any rights or remedies under any other Federal statute.

(e) The scope of Federal preemption under this section is not affected by the adherence of the United States to the Berne Convention or the satisfaction of obligations of the United States thereunder.

(f)(1) On or after [June 1, 1991], all legal or equitable rights that are equivalent to any of the rights [of attribution and integrity conferred by the Copyright Act as amended by the Visual Artists Rights Act of 1990 are governed exclusively by the provisions of the Copyright Act dealing with rights of attribution and integrity.] Thereafter, no person is entitled to any such right or equivalent right in any work of visual art under the common law or statutes of any State.

(2) Nothing in paragraph (1) annuls or limits any rights or remedies under the common law or statutes of any State with respect to—

(A) any cause of action from undertakings commenced before [June 1, 1991];

(B) activities violating legal or equitable rights that are not equivalent to any of the rights conferred by [the Copyright Act as amended by the Visual Artists Rights Act of 1990] with respect to works of visual art; or

(C) activities violating legal or equitable rights which extend beyond the life of the author.

17 U.S.C. § 301. The special provisions of this section addressing federal preemption of state laws governing artists' rights are analyzed in subsequent portions of this chapter discussing state moral rights statutes.

The House Report on the Copyright Act of 1976 summarized the intended effect of these statutory preemption tests as follows.

House Report No. 94–1476

HOUSE REPORT NO. 94–1476 UNITED STATES HOUSE OF REPRESENTATIVES

Committee on the Judiciary.
Sept. 3, 1976.

SECTION 301.   FEDERAL PREEMPTION OF RIGHTS EQUIVALENT TO COPYRIGHT

Single Federal system

Section 301, one of the bedrock provisions of the bill, would accomplish a fundamental and significant change in the present law. Instead of a dual system of "common law copyright" for unpublished works and statutory copyright for published works, which has been the system in effect in the United States since the first copyright statute in 1790, the bill adopts a single system of Federal statutory copyright from creation. Under section 301 a work would obtain statutory protection as soon as it is "created" or, as that term is defined in section 101, when it is "fixed in a copy or phonorecord for the first time." Common law copyright protection for works coming within the scope of the statute would be abrogated, and the concept of publication would lose its all-embracing importance as a dividing line between common law and statutory protection and between both of these forms of legal protection and the public domain.

By substituting a single Federal system for the present anachronistic, uncertain, impractical, and highly complicated dual system, the bill would greatly improve the operation of the copyright law and would be much more effective in carrying out the basic constitutional aims of uniformity and the promotion of writing and scholarship. The main arguments in favor of a single Federal system can be summarized as follows:

1.   One of the fundamental purposes behind the copyright clause of the Constitution, as shown in Madison's comments in The Federalist, was to promote national uniformity and to avoid the practical difficulties of determining and enforcing an author's rights under the differing laws and in the separate courts of the various States. Today, when the methods for dissemination of an author's work are incomparably broader and faster than they were in 1789, national uniformity in copyright protection is even more essential than it was then to carry out the constitutional intent.

* * *

4.   Adoption of a uniform national copyright system would greatly improve international dealings in copyrighted material. No other country has anything like our present dual system. In an era when copyrighted works can be disseminated instantaneously to every country on the globe, the need for effective international copyright relations, and the concomitant need for national uniformity, assume ever greater importance.

Under section 301, the statute would apply to all works created after its effective date, whether or not they are ever published or disseminated. With respect to works created before the effective date of the statute and still under common law protection, section 303 of the statute would provide protection from that date on, and would guarantee a minimum period of statutory copyright.

Preemption of State law

The intention of section 301 is to preempt and abolish any rights under the common law or statutes of a State that are equivalent to copyright and that extend to works coming within the scope of the Federal copyright law. The declaration of this principle in section 301 is intended to be stated in the clearest and most unequivocal language possible, so as to foreclose any conceivable misinterpretation of its unqualified intention that Congress shall act preemptively, and to avoid the development of any vague borderline areas between State and Federal protection.

Under section 301(a) all "legal or equitable rights that are equivalent to any of the exclusive rights [granted by the Copyright Act] are governed exclusively by the Federal copyright statute if the works involved are 'works of authorship' that are fixed in a tangible medium of expression and come within the [range of works covered by the Copyright Act]." All corresponding State laws, whether common law or statutory, are preempted and abrogated. Regardless of when the work was created and whether it is published or unpublished, disseminated or undisseminated, in the public domain or copyrighted under the Federal statute, the States cannot offer it protection equivalent to copyright. Section 1338 of title 28, United States Code, also makes clear that any action involving rights under the Federal copyright law would come within the exclusive jurisdiction of the Federal courts. The preemptive effect of section 301 is limited to State laws; as stated expressly in subsection (d) of section 301, there is no intention to deal with the question of whether Congress can or should offer the equivalent of copyright protection under some constitutional provision other than the patent-copyright clause of article 1, section 8.

As long as a work fits within one of the general subject matter categories of [works potentially qualifying for federal copyright protection], the bill prevents the States from protecting it even if it fails to achieve Federal statutory copyright because it is too minimal or lacking in originality to qualify, or because it has fallen into the public domain. On the other hand, section 301(b) explicitly preserves common law copyright protection for one important class of works: works that have not been "fixed in any tangible medium of expression." Examples would include choreography that has never been filmed or notated, an extemporaneous speech, 'original works of authorship' communicated solely through conversations or live broadcasts, and a dramatic sketch or musical composition improvised or developed from memory and without being recorded or written down. [U]nfixed works are not included in the specified "subject matter of copyright." They are therefore not affected by the preemption of section 301, and would continue to be subject to protection under State statute or common law until fixed in tangible form.

The preemption of rights under State law is complete with respect to any work coming within the scope of the bill, even though the scope of exclusive rights given the work under the bill is narrower than the scope of common law rights in the work might have been.

* * *

In a general way subsection (b) of section 301 represents the obverse of subsection (a). It sets out, in broad terms and without necessarily being exhaustive, some of the principal areas of protection that preemption would not prevent the States from protecting.

* * *

COMPUTER ASSOCIATES INTERNATIONAL, INC. v. ALTAI, INC.

United States Court of Appeals, Second Circuit, 1992.
982 F.2d 693.

WALKER, CIRCUIT JUDGE:

In recent years, the growth of computer science has spawned a number of challenging legal questions, particularly in the field of copyright law. As scientific knowledge advances, courts endeavor to keep pace, and sometimes—as in the area of computer technology—they are required to venture into less than familiar waters. This is not a new development, though. "From its beginning, the law of copyright has developed in response to significant changes in technology."

* * *

II. Facts

[Computer Associates (CA)] is a Delaware corporation, with its principal place of business in Garden City, New York. Altai is a Texas corporation, doing business primarily in Arlington, Texas. Both companies are in the computer software industry—designing, developing and marketing various types of computer programs.

The subject of this litigation originates with one of CA's marketed programs entitled CA–SCHEDULER. CA–SCHEDULER is a job scheduling program designed for IBM mainframe computers. Its primary functions are straightforward: to create a schedule specifying when the computer should run various tasks, and then to control the computer as it executes the schedule. CA–SCHEDULER contains a sub-program entitled ADAPTER, also developed by CA. ADAPTER is not an independently marketed product of CA; it is a wholly integrated component of CA–SCHEDULER and has no capacity for independent use.

* * *

Discussion

* * *

Altai has conceded liability for the copying of ADAPTER into [an Altair software product named] OSCAR 3.4 and raises no challenge to the award of $364,444 in damages on that score. Thus, we address only CA's appeal from the district court's rulings that: (1) Altai was not liable for copyright infringement in developing OSCAR 3.5; and (2) in developing both OSCAR 3.4 and 3.5, Altai was not liable for misappropriating CA's trade secrets.

* * *

CA maintains that the district court erroneously concluded that its state law trade secret claims had been preempted by the federal Copyright Act.

* * *

II. Trade Secret Preemption

In its complaint, CA alleged that Altai misappropriated the trade secrets contained in the ADAPTER program. Prior to trial, while the proceedings were still before Judge Mishler, Altai moved to dismiss and for summary judgment on CA's trade secret misappropriation claim. Altai argued that section 301 of the Copyright Act preempted CA's state law cause of action. Judge Mishler denied Altai's motion, reasoning that " '[t]he elements of the tort of appropriation of trade secrets through the breach of contract or confidence by an employee are not the same as the elements of a claim of copyright infringement.' "

The parties addressed the preemption issue again, both in pre-and post-trial briefs. Judge Pratt then reconsidered and reversed Judge Mishler's earlier ruling. The district court concluded that CA's trade secret claims were preempted because "CA—which is the master of its own case—has pleaded and proven facts which establish that one act constituted both copyright infringement *and* misappropriation of trade secrets [namely, the] copying of ADAPTER into OSCAR 3.4 * * *."

In our original opinion, *Computer Assocs. Int'l, Inc. v. Altai, Inc.,* Nos. 91–7893, 91–7935, slip op. 4715, 4762–69, 1992 WL 139364 (2d Cir. June 22, 1992), we affirmed Judge Pratt's decision. CA petitioned for rehearing on this issue. In its petition for rehearing, CA brought to our attention portions of the record below that were not included in the appendix on appeal. CA argued that these documents, along with Judge Mishler's disposition of Altai's motion to dismiss and for summary judgment, established that CA advanced non-preempted trade secret misappropriation claims before both Judge Mishler and Judge Pratt. CA further contended that Judge Pratt failed to consider its theory that Altai was liable for wrongful acquisition of CA's trade secrets through [the acts of an employee of CA who brought the trade secrets to Altai.] Upon reconsideration, we have granted the petition for rehearing, withdrawn our initial opinion, and conclude in this amended opinion that the district court's preemption ruling on CA's trade secret claims should be vacated. We accordingly vacate the judgment of the district court on this point and remand CA's trade secret claims for a determination on the merits.

A. General Law of Copyright Preemption Regarding Trade Secrets and Computer Programs

Congress carefully designed the statutory framework of federal copyright preemption. In order to insure that the enforcement of these rights remains solely within the federal domain, section 301(a) of the Copyright Act expressly preempts

> all legal or equitable rights that are equivalent to any of the exclusive rights within the general scope of copyright as specified by section 106 in works of authorship that are fixed in a tangible medium of expression and come within the subject matter of copyright as specified by sections 102 and 103 * * *.

17 U.S.C. § 301(a). This sweeping displacement of state law is, however, limited by section 301(b), which provides, in relevant part, that

> [n]othing in this title annuls or limits any rights or remedies under the common law or statutes of any State with respect to * * * activities violating legal or equitable rights that are not equivalent to any of the exclusive rights within the general scope of copyright as specified by section 106 * * *.

17 U.S.C. § 301(b)(3). Section 106, in turn, affords a copyright owner the exclusive right to: (1) reproduce the copyrighted work; (2) prepare derivative works; (3) distribute copies of the work by sale or otherwise; and, with respect to certain artistic works, (4) perform the work publicly; and (5) display the work publicly. See 17 U.S.C. § 106(1)–(5).

Section 301 thus preempts only those state law rights that "may be abridged by an act which, in and of itself, would infringe one of the exclusive rights" provided by federal copyright law. But if an "extra element" is "required instead of or in addition to the acts of reproduction, performance, distribution or display, in order to constitute a state-created cause of action, then the right does not lie 'within the general scope of copyright,' and there is no preemption."

A state law claim is not preempted if the "extra element" changes the "nature of the action so that it is *qualitatively* different from a copyright infringement claim." To determine whether a claim meets this standard, we must determine "what plaintiff seeks to protect, the theories in which the matter is thought to be protected and the rights sought to be enforced." An action will not be saved from preemption by elements such as awareness or intent, which alter "the action's scope but not its nature * * *."

Following this "extra element" test, we have held that unfair competition and misappropriation claims grounded solely in the copying of a plaintiff's protected expression are preempted by section 301. We also have held to be preempted a tortious interference with contract claim grounded in the impairment of a plaintiff's right under the Copyright Act to publish derivative works.

However, many state law rights that can arise in connection with instances of copyright infringement satisfy the extra element test, and thus are not preempted by section 301. These include unfair competition claims based upon breaches of confidential relationships, breaches of fiduciary duties and trade secrets.

Trade secret protection, the branch of unfair competition law at issue in this case, remains a "uniquely valuable" weapon in the defensive arsenal of computer programmers. Precisely because trade secret doctrine protects the discovery of ideas, processes, and systems which are explicitly precluded from coverage under copyright law, courts and commentators alike consider it a necessary and integral part of the intellectual property protection extended to computer programs.

The legislative history of section 301 states that "[t]he evolving common law rights of * * * trade secrets * * * would remain unaffected as long as the causes of action contain elements, such as * * * a breach of trust or confidentiality, that are different in kind from copyright infringement." Congress did not consider the term "misappropriation" to be "necessarily synonymous with copyright infringement," or to serve as the talisman of preemption.

Trade secret claims often are grounded upon a defendant's breach of a duty of trust or confidence to the plaintiff through improper disclosure of confidential material. The defendant's breach of duty is the gravamen of such trade secret claims, and supplies the "extra element" that qualitatively distinguishes such trade secret causes of action from claims for copyright infringement that are based solely upon copying.

B. Preemption in this Case

The district court stated that:

> Were CA's [trade secret] allegations premised on a theory of illegal *acquisition* of a trade secret, a charge that might have been alleged against Arney, who is not a defendant in this case, the preemption analysis might be different, for there seems to be no corresponding right guaranteed to copyright owners by § 106 of the copyright act.

However, the court concluded that CA's trade secret claims were not grounded in a theory that Altai violated a duty of confidentiality to CA. Rather, Judge Pratt stated that CA proceeded against Altai solely "on a theory that the misappropriation took place by Altai's *use* of ADAPTER— the same theory as the copyright infringement count." The district court reasoned that "the right to be free from trade secret misappropriation through 'use', and the right to exclusive reproduction and distribution of a copyrighted work are not distinguishable." Because he concluded that there was no qualitative difference between the elements of CA's state law trade secret claims and a claim for federal copyright infringement, Judge Pratt ruled that CA's trade secret claims were preempted by section 301.

We agree with CA that the district court failed to address fully the factual and theoretical bases of CA's trade secret claims. The district court relied upon the fact that [Claude F. Arney, III ("Arney"), a computer programmer who worked for CA]—not Altai—allegedly breached a duty to CA of confidentiality by stealing secrets from CA and incorporating those secrets into OSCAR 3.4. However, under a wrongful acquisition theory based on Restatement (First) of Torts § 757 (1939), [James P. Williams ("Williams"), then an employee of Altai and later its President] and Altai may be liable for violating CA's right of confidentiality. Section 757 states in relevant part:

> One who discloses or uses another's trade secret, without a privilege to do so, is liable to another if * * *. (c) he learned the secret from a third person with notice of the fact that it was a secret and that the third person discovered it by improper means or that the third person's disclosure of it was otherwise a breach of his duty to the other * * *.

Actual notice is not required for such a third party acquisition claim; constructive notice is sufficient. A defendant is on constructive notice when, "from the information which he has, a reasonable man would infer [a breach of confidence], or if, under the circumstances, a reasonable man would be put on inquiry and an inquiry pursued with reasonable intelligence and diligence would disclose the [breach]."

We agree with the district court that New Jersey's governing governmental interest choice of law analysis directs the application of Texas law to CA's trade secret misappropriation claim. Texas law recognizes trade secret misappropriation claims grounded in the reasoning of Restatement section 757(c), and the facts alleged by CA may well support such a claim.

It is undisputed that, when Arney stole the ADAPTER code and incorporated it into his design of OSCAR 3.4, he breached his confidentiality agreement with CA. The district court noted that while such action might constitute a valid claim against Arney, CA is the named defendant in this lawsuit. Additionally, the district court found, as a matter of fact, that "[n]o one at Altai, other than Arney, knew that Arney had the ADAPTER code * * *." However, the district court did not consider fully Altai's potential liability for improper trade secret acquisition. It did not consider the question of Altai's trade secret liability in connection with OSCAR 3.4 under a constructive notice theory, or Altai's potential liability under an actual notice theory in connection with OSCAR 3.5.

The district court found that, prior to CA's bringing suit, Altai was not on actual notice of Arney's theft of trade secrets, and incorporation of those secrets into OSCAR 3.4. However, by virtue of Williams' close relationship with Arney, Williams' general familiarity with CA's programs (having once been employed by CA himself), and the fact that Arney used the ADAPTER program in an office at Altai adjacent to Williams during a period in which he had frequent contact with Williams regarding the OSCAR/VSE project, Williams (and through him Altai) may well have been on constructive notice of Arney's breach of his duty of confidentiality toward CA. The district court did not address whether Altai was on constructive notice, thereby placing it under a duty of inquiry; rather the court's finding that only Arney affirmatively knew of the theft of CA's trade secrets and incorporation of those secrets into OSCAR 3.4 simply disposed of the issue of actual notice in connection with the creation of OSCAR 3.4. CA's claim of liability based on constructive notice, never considered in the district court's opinion, must be determined on remand.

With respect to actual notice, it is undisputed that CA's first complaint, filed in August 1988, informed Altai of Arney's trade secret violations in connection with the creation of OSCAR 3.4. The first complaint alleged that Arney assisted in the development of ADAPTER, thereby obtaining knowledge of CA's related trade secrets. It also alleged that Altai misappropriated CA's trade secrets by incorporating them into [an Altai program.]

In response to CA's complaint, Altai rewrote OSCAR 3.4, creating OSCAR 3.5. While we agree with the district court that OSCAR 3.5 did not contain any expression protected by copyright, it may nevertheless still have embodied many of CA's trade secrets that Arney brought with him to Altai. Since Altai's rewrite was conducted with full knowledge of Arney's prior misappropriation, in breach of his duty of confidentiality, it follows that OSCAR 3.5 was created with actual knowledge of trade secret violations. Thus, with regard to OSCAR 3.5, CA has a viable trade secret claim against Altai that must be considered by the district court on remand. This claim is grounded in Altai's alleged use of CA's trade secrets in the creation of OSCAR 3.5, while on actual notice of Arney's theft of trade secrets and incorporation of those secrets into OSCAR 3.4. The district court correctly stated that a state law claim based *solely* upon Altai's "use", by copying, of ADAPTER's non-literal elements could not satisfy the governing "extra element" test, and would be preempted by section 301. However, where the use of copyrighted expression is simultaneously the violation of a duty of confidentiality established by state law, that extra element renders the state right qualitatively distinct from the federal right, thereby foreclosing preemption under section 301.

We are also convinced that CA adequately pled a wrongful acquisition claim before Judge Mishler and Judge Pratt. In ruling that CA failed to properly plead a non-preempted claim, Judge Pratt relied heavily upon two allegations in CA's amended complaint. They read as follows:

¶ 57. By reason of the facts stated in paragraph 39 and by copying from CA–SCHEDULER into [several Altai programs] the various elements stated in paragraphs 39–51, 54 and 55, defendant Altai has infringed [CA's] copyright in CA–SCHEDULER.

* * *

¶ 73. Defendant's incorporation into its * * * programs of the various elements contained in the ADAPTER component of [CA's] CA–SCHEDULER program as set out in paragraphs 39–51, 54 and 55 constitutes the willful misappropriation of the proprietary property and trade secrets of plaintiff [CA].

From these pleadings, Judge Pratt concluded that the very same act, i.e., Altai's copying of various elements of CA's program, was the basis for both CA's copyright infringement and trade secret claims. We agree with Judge Pratt that CA's allegations are somewhat inartfully stated. However, when taken together, the terms "incorporation" and "misappropriation" in paragraph 73 above suggest to us an act of a qualitatively different nature than the infringement pled in paragraph 57. *House Report,* at 5748 (" '[m]isappropriation' is not necessarily synonymous with copyright infringement").

In support of our reading, we note that paragraphs 65–75 of CA's amended complaint alleged facts that reasonably comprise the elements of a wrongful acquisition of trade secrets claim. CA averred that, while he was employed at CA, Arney learned CA's trade secrets regarding the ADAPTER program. CA further alleged that, after Arney went to work for Altai, Altai misappropriated those trade secrets by incorporating CA's ADAPTER program into its own product. Finally, CA claimed that the trade secret misappropriation was carried out "in a willful, wanton and reckless manner in disregard of [CA's] rights." In other words, Altai could have reasonably inferred from CA's allegations that CA's claim, in part, rested on Williams' "wanton and reckless" behavior in the face of constructive notice.

In addition, while responding to Altai's preemption argument in its motion to dismiss and for summary judgment, CA specifically argued in its brief to Judge Mishler that "it can easily be inferred that Mr. Arney was hired by Altai to misappropriate [CA's] confidential source code for Altai's benefit." At oral argument, CA further contended that:

The circumstances of Mr. Arney's hiring suggested that Mr. Williams wanted more than Mr. Arney's ability and in fact got exactly what he wanted. And that is Computer Associates' confidential Adapter technology.

* * *

[Arney testified that he] surreptitiously took that code home from Computer Associates after giving notice he was going to go to work for Altai, and after being hired by Mr. Williams to come to Altai and reconstruct Zeke, to work on the MVS operating system.

In the aftermath of Judge Mishler's ruling in its favor on Altai's motion to dismiss and for summary judgment, CA reasonably believed that it had sufficiently alleged a non-preempted claim. And, in light of CA's arguments and Judge Mishler's ruling, Altai clearly was on notice that the amended complaint placed non-preempted trade secret claims in play.

Accordingly, we vacate the judgment of the district court and remand for reconsideration of those aspects of CA's trade secret claims related to Altai's alleged constructive notice of Arney's theft of CA's trade secrets and incorporation of those secrets into OSCAR 3.4. We note, however, that CA may be unable to recover damages for its trade secrets which are embodied in OSCAR 3.4 since Altai has conceded copyright liability and damages for its incorporation of ADAPTER into OSCAR 3.4. CA may not obtain a double recovery where the damages for copyright infringement and trade secret misappropriation are coextensive.

However, additional trade secret damages may well flow from CA's creation of OSCAR 3.5. Judge Pratt correctly acknowledged that "[i]f CA's claim of misappropriation of trade secrets did not fail on preemption grounds, it would be necessary to examine in some detail the conflicting claims and evidence relating to the process by which Altai rewrote OSCAR and ultimately produced version 3.5." Since we hold that CA's trade secret claims are not preempted, and that, in writing OSCAR 3.5, Altai had actual notice of Arney's earlier trade secret violations, we vacate and remand for such further inquiry anticipated by the district court. If the district court finds that CA was injured by Altai's unlawful use of CA's trade secrets in creating OSCAR 3.5, CA is entitled to an award of damages for trade secret misappropriation, as well as consideration by the district court of CA's request for injunctive relief on its trade secret claim.

NOTES

1. What was the "additional element" that distinguished Computer Associates' trade secret misappropriation claims from its copyright infringement claims? How might the company have stated its claims to make clearer the distinction between its trade secret claims and its claims covered by federal copyright laws?

2. Do the purposes underlying copyright and trade secret laws affect the scope of preemption of the latter under the Copyright Act? How should the respective purposes of these bodies of law be evaluated? Does the court in *Computer Associates* care about the goals of these laws or just the elements that must be proven to establish claims? How are these elements and purposes related?

NATIONAL BASKETBALL ASSOCIATION
v. MOTOROLA, INC.

United States Court of Appeals, Second Circuit, 1997.
105 F.3d 841.

WINTER, CIRCUIT JUDGE:

Motorola, Inc. and Sports Team Analysis and Tracking Systems ("STATS") appeal from a permanent injunction entered by Judge Preska. The injunction concerns a handheld pager sold by Motorola and marketed under the name "SportsTrax," which displays updated information of professional basketball games in progress. The injunction prohibits appellants, absent authorization from the National Basketball Association and NBA Properties, Inc. (collectively the "NBA"), from transmitting scores or other data about NBA games in progress via the pagers, STATS's site on America On–Line's computer dial-up service, or "any equivalent means."

The crux of the dispute concerns the extent to which a state law "hot-news" misappropriation claim based on *International News Service v. Associated Press*, 248 U.S. 215, 39 S.Ct. 68, 63 L.Ed. 211 (1918) ("*INS*"), survives preemption by the federal Copyright Act and whether the NBA's claim fits within the surviving *INS*-type claims. We hold that a narrow "hot-news" exception does survive preemption. However, we also hold that appellants' transmission of "real-time" NBA game scores and information tabulated from television and radio broadcasts of games in progress does not constitute a misappropriation of "hot news" that is the property of the NBA.

The NBA cross-appeals from the dismissal of its Lanham Act claim. We hold that any misstatements by Motorola in advertising its pager were not material and affirm.

I. Background

The facts are largely undisputed. Motorola manufactures and markets the SportsTrax paging device while STATS supplies the game information that is transmitted to the pagers. The product became available to the public in January 1996, at a retail price of about $200. SportsTrax's pager has an inch-and-a-half by inch-and-a-half screen and operates in four basic modes: "current," "statistics," "final scores" and "demonstration." It is the "current" mode that gives rise to the present dispute.[26] In that mode, SportsTrax displays the following information on NBA games in progress: (i) the teams playing; (ii) score changes; (iii) the team in possession of the

---

26. The other three SportsTrax modes involve information that is far less contemporaneous than that provided in the "current" mode. In the "statistics" mode, the SportsTrax pager displays a variety of player and team statistics, such as field goal shooting percentages and top scorers. However, these are calculated only at half-time and when the game is over. In the "final scores" mode, the unit displays final scores from the previous day's games. In the "demonstration" mode, the unit merely simulates information shown during a hypothetical NBA game. The core issue in the instant matter is the dissemination of continuously-updated real-time NBA game information in the "current" mode. Because we conclude that the dissemination of such real-time information is lawful, the other modes need no further description or discussion.

ball; (iv) whether the team is in the free-throw bonus; (v) the quarter of the game; and (vi) time remaining in the quarter. The information is updated every two to three minutes, with more frequent updates near the end of the first half and the end of the game. There is a lag of approximately two or three minutes between events in the game itself and when the information appears on the pager screen.

SportsTrax's operation relies on a "data feed" supplied by STATS reporters who watch the games on television or listen to them on the radio. The reporters key into a personal computer changes in the score and other information such as successful and missed shots, fouls, and clock updates. The information is relayed by modem to STATS's host computer, which compiles, analyzes, and formats the data for retransmission. The information is then sent to a common carrier, which then sends it via satellite to various local FM radio networks that in turn emit the signal received by the individual SportsTrax pagers.

Although the NBA's complaint concerned only the SportsTrax device, the NBA offered evidence at trial concerning STATS's America On–Line ("AOL") site. Starting in January, 1996, users who accessed STATS's AOL site, typically via a modem attached to a home computer, were provided with slightly more comprehensive and detailed real-time game information than is displayed on a SportsTrax pager. On the AOL site, game scores are updated every 15 seconds to a minute, and the player and team statistics are updated each minute. The district court's original decision and judgment did not address the AOL site, because "NBA's complaint and the evidence proffered at trial were devoted largely to SportsTrax." Upon motion by the NBA, however, the district court amended its decision and judgment and enjoined use of the real-time game information on STATS's AOL site. Because the record on appeal, the briefs of the parties, and oral argument primarily addressed the SportsTrax device, we similarly focus on that product. However, we regard the legal issues as identical with respect to both products, and our holding applies equally to SportsTrax and STATS's AOL site.

The NBA's complaint asserted six claims for relief: (i) state law unfair competition by misappropriation; (ii) false advertising under Section 43(a) of the Lanham Act, 15 U.S.C. § 1125(a); (iii) false representation of origin under Section 43(a) of the Lanham Act; (iv) state and common law unfair competition by false advertising and false designation of origin; (v) federal copyright infringement; and (vi) unlawful interception of communications under the Communications Act of 1934, 47 U.S.C. § 605. Motorola counterclaimed, alleging that the NBA unlawfully interfered with Motorola's contractual relations with four individual NBA teams that had agreed to sponsor and advertise SportsTrax.

The district court dismissed all of the NBA's claims except the first—misappropriation under New York law. The court also dismissed Motorola's counterclaim. Finding Motorola and STATS liable for misappropriation, Judge Preska entered the permanent injunction, reserved the calculation of damages for subsequent proceedings, and stayed execution of the injunction pending appeal. Motorola and STATS appeal from the injunction, while NBA cross-appeals from the district court's dismissal of its Lanham Act false-advertising claim. The issues before us, therefore, are the state law misappropriation and Lanham Act claims.

II. The State Law Misappropriation Claim

A. Summary of Ruling

Because our disposition of the state law misappropriation claim rests in large part on preemption by the Copyright Act, our discussion necessarily goes beyond the elements of a misappropriation claim under New York law, and a summary of our ruling here will perhaps render that discussion—or at least the need for it—more understandable.

The issues before us are ones that have arisen in various forms over the course of this century as technology has steadily increased the speed and quantity of information transmission. Today, individuals at home, at work, or elsewhere, can use a computer, pager, or other device to obtain highly selective kinds of information virtually at will. *International News Service v. Associated Press*, 248 U.S. 215, 39 S.Ct. 68, 63 L.Ed. 211 (1918) ("*INS*") [(reproduced in Chapter 9 of this text)] was one of the first cases to address the issues raised by these technological advances, although the technology involved in that case was primitive by contemporary standards. *INS* involved two wire services, the Associated Press ("AP") and International News Service ("INS"), that transmitted newsstories by wire to member newspapers. INS would lift factual stories from AP bulletins and send them by wire to INS papers. INS would also take factual stories from east coast AP papers and wire them to INS papers on the west coast that had yet to publish because of time differentials. The Supreme Court held that INS's conduct was a common-law misappropriation of AP's property.

With the advance of technology, radio stations began "live" broadcasts of events such as baseball games and operas, and various entrepreneurs began to use the transmissions of others in one way or another for their own profit. In response, New York courts created a body of misappropriation law, loosely based on *INS,* that sought to apply ethical standards to the use by one party of another's transmissions of events.

Federal copyright law played little active role in this area until 1976. Before then, it appears to have been the general understanding—there being no caselaw of consequence—that live events such as baseball games were not copyrightable. Moreover, doubt existed even as to whether a recorded broadcast or videotape of such an event was copyrightable. In 1976, however, Congress passed legislation expressly affording copyright protection to simultaneously-recorded broadcasts of live performances such as sports events. Such protection was not extended to the underlying events.

The 1976 amendments also contained provisions preempting state law claims that enforced rights "equivalent" to exclusive copyright protections when the work to which the state claim was being applied fell within the area of copyright protection. Based on legislative history of the 1976 amendments, it is generally agreed that a "hot-news" *INS*-like claim survives preemption. However, much of New York misappropriation law after *INS* goes well beyond "hot-news" claims and is preempted.

We hold that the surviving "hot-news" *INS*-like claim is limited to cases where: (i) a plaintiff generates or gathers information at a cost; (ii) the information is time-sensitive; (iii) a defendant's use of the information constitutes free riding on the plaintiff's efforts; (iv) the defendant is in direct competition with a product or service offered by the plaintiffs; and (v) the ability of other parties to free-ride on the efforts of the plaintiff or others would so reduce the incentive to produce the product or service that its existence or quality would be substantially threatened. We conclude that SportsTrax does not meet that test.

* * *

C. The State–Law Misappropriation Claim

The district court's injunction was based on its conclusion that, under New York law, defendants had unlawfully misappropriated the NBA's property rights in its games. The district court reached this conclusion by holding: (i) that the NBA's misappropriation claim relating to the underlying games was not preempted by Section 301 of the Copyright Act; and (ii) that, under New York common law, defendants had engaged in unlawful misappropriation. We disagree.

1. Preemption Under the Copyright Act

a) Summary

When Congress amended the Copyright Act in 1976, it provided for the preemption of state law claims that are interrelated with copyright claims in certain ways. Under 17 U.S.C. § 301, a state law claim is preempted when: (i) the state law claim seeks to vindicate "legal or equitable rights that are equivalent" to one of the bundle of exclusive rights already protected by copyright law under 17 U.S.C. § 106—styled the "general scope requirement"; and (ii) the particular work to which the state law claim is being applied falls within the type of works protected by the Copyright Act under Sections 102 and 103—styled the "subject matter requirement."

The district court concluded that the NBA's misappropriation claim was not preempted because, with respect to the underlying games, as opposed to the broadcasts, the subject matter requirement was not met. The court dubbed as "partial preemption" its separate analysis of misappropriation claims relating to the underlying games and misappropriation claims relating to broadcasts of those games. The district court then relied on a series of older New York misappropriation cases involving radio broadcasts that considerably broadened *INS*. We hold that where the challenged copying or misappropriation relates in part to the copyrighted broadcasts of the games, the subject matter requirement is met as to both the broadcasts and the games. We therefore reject the partial preemption doctrine and its anomalous consequence that "it is possible for a plaintiff to assert claims both for infringement of its copyright in a broadcast and misappropriation of its rights in the underlying event." We do find that a properly-narrowed *INS* "hot-news" misappropriation claim survives preemption because it fails the general scope requirement, but that the broader theory of the radio broadcast cases relied upon by the district court were preempted when Congress extended copyright protection to simultaneously-recorded broadcasts.

b) "Partial Preemption" and the Subject Matter Requirement

The subject matter requirement is met when the work of authorship being copied or misappropriated "fall[s] within the ambit of copyright protection." We believe that the subject matter requirement is met in the instant matter and that the concept of "partial preemption" is not consistent with Section 301 of the Copyright Act. Although game broadcasts are copyrightable while the underlying games are not, the Copyright Act should not be read to distinguish between the two when analyzing the preemption of a misappropriation claim based on copying or taking from the copyrightable work. We believe that:

> [O]nce a performance is reduced to tangible form, there is no distinction between the performance and the recording of the performance for the purposes of preemption under § 301(a). Thus, if a baseball game were not broadcast or were telecast without being recorded, the Players' performances similarly would not be fixed in tangible form and their rights of publicity would not be subject to preemption. By virtue of being videotaped, however, the Players' performances are fixed in tangible form, and any rights of publicity in their performances that are equivalent to the rights contained in the copyright of the telecast are preempted.

[*Baltimore Orioles, Inc. v. Major League Baseball Players Assn.*, 805 F.2d 663, 675 (7th Cir. 1986), *cert. denied*, 480 U.S. 941 (1987)] (citation omitted).

Copyrightable material often contains uncopyrightable elements within it, but Section 301 preemption bars state law misappropriation claims with respect to uncopyrightable as well as copyrightable elements. In *Harper & Row,* for example, we held that state law claims based on the copying of excerpts from President Ford's memoirs were preempted even with respect to information that was purely factual and not copyrightable. We stated:

> [T]he [Copyright] Act clearly embraces "works of authorship," including "literary works," as within its subject matter. The fact that portions of the Ford memoirs may consist of uncopyrightable material * * * does not take the work as a whole outside the subject matter protected by the Act. Were this not so, states would be free to expand the perimeters of copyright protection to their own liking, on the

theory that preemption would be no bar to state protection of material not meeting federal statutory standards.

[*Harper & Row, Publishers, Inc. v. Nation Enter.*, 723 F.2d 195, 200 (2d Cir. 1983), *rev'd on other grounds*, 471 U.S. 539, 105 S.Ct. 2218, 85 L.Ed.2d 588 (1985)] (citation omitted). The legislative history supports this understanding of Section 301(a)'s subject matter requirement. The House Report stated:

> As long as a work fits within one of the general subject matter categories of sections 102 and 103, the bill prevents the States from protecting it even if it fails to achieve Federal statutory copyright because it is too minimal or lacking in originality to qualify, or because it has fallen into the public domain.

H.R. No. 94–1476 at 131, *reprinted in* 1976 U.S.C.C.A.N. at 5747. *See also Baltimore Orioles*, 805 F.2d at 676 (citing excerpts of House Report 94–1476).

Adoption of a partial preemption doctrine—preemption of claims based on misappropriation of broadcasts but no preemption of claims based on misappropriation of underlying facts—would expand significantly the reach of state law claims and render the preemption intended by Congress unworkable. It is often difficult or impossible to separate the fixed copyrightable work from the underlying uncopyrightable events or facts. Moreover, Congress, in extending copyright protection only to the broadcasts and not to the underlying events, intended that the latter be in the public domain. Partial preemption turns that intent on its head by allowing state law to vest exclusive rights in material that Congress intended to be in the public domain and to make unlawful conduct that Congress intended to allow. This concern was recently expressed in *ProCD, Inc. v. Zeidenberg*, 86 F.3d 1447 (7th Cir.1996), a case in which the defendants reproduced non-copyrightable facts (telephone listings) from plaintiffs' copyrighted software. In discussing preemption under Section 301(a), Judge Easterbrook held that the subject matter requirement was met and noted:

> ProCD's software and data are "fixed in a tangible medium of expression", and the district judge held that they are "within the subject matter of copyright". The latter conclusion is plainly right for the copyrighted application program, and the judge thought that the data likewise are "within the subject matter of copyright" even if, after *Feist*, they are not sufficiently original to be copyrighted. [*ProCD, Inc. v. Zeidenberg*,] 908 F.Supp. [640] at 656–57 [(W.D. Wis. 1996)]. *Baltimore Orioles, Inc. v. Major League Baseball Players Ass'n*, 805 F.2d 663, 676 (7th Cir.1986), supports that conclusion, with which commentators agree * * *. One function of § 301(a) is to prevent states from giving special protection to works of authorship that Congress has decided should be in the public domain, which it can accomplish only if "subject matter of copyright" includes all

works of a *type* covered by sections 102 and 103, even if federal law does not afford protection to them.

ProCD, 86 F.3d at 1453 (citation omitted). We agree with Judge Easterbrook and reject the separate analysis of the underlying games and broadcasts of those games for purposes of preemption.

c) The General Scope Requirement

Under the general scope requirement, Section 301 "preempts only those state law rights that 'may be abridged by an act which, in and of itself, would infringe one of the exclusive rights' provided by federal copyright law." *Computer Assoc. Int'l, Inc. v. Altai, Inc.,* 982 F.2d 693, 716 (2d Cir. 1992) (quoting *Harper & Row,* 723 F.2d at 200). However, certain forms of commercial misappropriation otherwise within the general scope requirement will survive preemption if an "extra-element" test is met. As stated in *Altai:*

> But if an "extra element" is "required instead of or in addition to the acts of reproduction, performance, distribution or display, in order to constitute a state-created cause of action, then the right does not lie 'within the general scope of copyright,' and there is no preemption."

Id. (quoting 1 *Nimmer on Copyright* § 1.01[B] at 1–15).

ProCD was in part an application of the extra-element test. Having held the misappropriation claims to be preempted, Judge Easterbrook went on to hold that the plaintiffs could bring a state law contract claim. The court held that the defendants were bound by the software's shrink-wrap licenses as a matter of contract law and that the private contract rights were not preempted because they were not equivalent to the exclusive rights granted by copyright law. In other words, the contract right claims were not preempted because the general scope requirement was not met.

We turn, therefore, to the question of the extent to which a "hot-news" misappropriation claim based on *INS* involves extra elements and is not the equivalent of exclusive rights under a copyright. Courts are generally agreed that some form of such a claim survives preemption. This conclusion is based in part on the legislative history of the 1976 amendments. The House Report stated:

> "Misappropriation" is not necessarily synonymous with copyright infringement, and thus a cause of action labeled as "misappropriation" is not preempted if it is in fact based neither on a right within the general scope of copyright as specified by section 106 nor on a right equivalent thereto. For example, state law should have the flexibility to afford a remedy (under traditional principles of equity) against a consistent pattern of unauthorized appropriation by a competitor of the facts (i.e., not the literary expression) constituting "hot" news, whether in the traditional mold of *International News Service v. Associated Press,* 248 U.S. 215 [39 S.Ct. 68, 63 L.Ed. 211]

(1918), or in the newer form of data updates from scientific, business, or financial data bases.

H.R. No. 94–1476 at 132, *reprinted in* 1976 U.S.C.C.A.N. at 5748 (footnote omitted); see also *FII,* 808 F.2d at 209 (" 'misappropriation' of 'hot' news, under *International News Service,* [is] a branch of the unfair competition doctrine not preempted by the Copyright Act according to the House Report" (citation omitted)). The crucial question, therefore, is the *breadth* of the "hot-news" claim that survives preemption.

In *INS,* the plaintiff AP and defendant INS were "wire services" that sold news items to client newspapers. AP brought suit to prevent INS from selling facts and information lifted from AP sources to INS-affiliated newspapers. One method by which INS was able to use AP's news was to lift facts from AP news bulletins. Another method was to sell facts taken from just-published east coast AP newspapers to west coast INS newspapers whose editions had yet to appear. The Supreme Court held (prior to *Erie R. Co. v. Tompkins,* 304 U.S. 64, 58 S.Ct. 817, 82 L.Ed. 1188 (1938)), that INS's use of AP's information was unlawful under federal common law. It characterized INS's conduct as

> amount[ing] to an unauthorized interference with the normal operation of complainant's legitimate business precisely at the point where the profit is to be reaped, in order to divert a material portion of the profit from those who have earned it to those who have not; with special advantage to defendant in the competition because of the fact that it is not burdened with any part of the expense of gathering the news.

INS, 248 U.S. at 240, 39 S.Ct. at 72–73.

The theory of the New York misappropriation cases relied upon by the district court is considerably broader than that of *INS.* For example, the district court quoted at length from *Metropolitan Opera Ass'n v. Wagner–Nichols Recorder Corp.,* 199 Misc. 786, 101 N.Y.S.2d 483 (N.Y.Sup.Ct.1950), *aff'd,* 279 A.D. 632, 107 N.Y.S.2d 795 (1st Dep't 1951). *Metropolitan Opera* described New York misappropriation law as standing for the "broader principle that property rights of commercial value are to be and will be protected from any form of commercial immorality"; that misappropriation law developed "to deal with business malpractices offensive to the ethics of [ ] society"; and that the doctrine is "broad and flexible." 939 F.Supp. at 1098–1110 (quoting *Metropolitan Opera,* 101 N.Y.S.2d at 492, 488–89).

However, we believe that *Metropolitan Opera*'s broad misappropriation doctrine based on amorphous concepts such as "commercial immorality" or society's "ethics" is preempted. Such concepts are virtually synonymous for wrongful copying and are in no meaningful fashion distinguishable from infringement of a copyright. The broad misappropriation doctrine relied upon by the district court is, therefore, the equivalent of exclusive rights in copyright law.

Indeed, we said as much in [*Financial Information, Inc. v. Moody's Investors Service, Inc.*, 808 F.2d 204 (2d Cir.1986), *cert. denied,* 484 U.S. 820, 108 S.Ct. 79, 98 L.Ed.2d 42 (1987) (*"FII"*)]. That decision involved the copying of financial information by a rival financial reporting service and specifically repudiated the broad misappropriation doctrine of *Metropolitan Opera.* We explained:

> We are not persuaded by FII's argument that misappropriation is not "equivalent" to the exclusive rights provided by the Copyright Act * * *. Nor do we believe that a possible exception to the general rule of preemption in the misappropriation area—for claims involving "any form of commercial immorality," * * * quoting *Metropolitan Opera Ass'n v. Wagner–Nichols Recorder Corp.*, 199 Misc. 786, 101 N.Y.S.2d 483, * * *—should be applied here. We believe that no such exception exists and reject its use here. Whether or not reproduction of another's work is "immoral" depends on whether such use of the work is wrongful. If, for example, the work is in the public domain, then its use would not be wrongful. Likewise, if, as here, the work is unprotected by federal law because of lack of originality, then its use is neither unfair nor unjustified.

FII, 808 F.2d at 208. In fact, *FII* only begrudgingly concedes that even narrow "hot news" *INS*-type claims survive preemption. *Id.* at 209.

Moreover, *Computer Associates Intern., Inc. v. Altai Inc.* indicated that the "extra element" test should not be applied so as to allow state claims to survive preemption easily. "An action will not be saved from preemption by elements such as awareness or intent, which alter 'the action's scope but not its nature' * * *. Following this 'extra element' test, we have held that unfair competition and misappropriation claims grounded solely in the copying of a plaintiff's protected expression are preempted by section 301."

In light of cases such as *FII* and *Altai* that emphasize the narrowness of state misappropriation claims that survive preemption, most of the broadcast cases relied upon by the NBA are simply not good law. Those cases were decided at a time when simultaneously-recorded broadcasts were not protected under the Copyright Act and when the state law claims they fashioned were not subject to federal preemption. For example, *Metropolitan Opera,* 101 N.Y.S.2d 483, involved the unauthorized copying, marketing, and sale of opera radio broadcasts. As another example, in *Mutual Broadcasting System v. Muzak Corp.*, 177 Misc. 489, 30 N.Y.S.2d 419 (Sup.Ct.1941), the defendant simultaneously retransmitted the plaintiff's baseball radio broadcasts onto telephone lines. As discussed above, the 1976 amendments to the Copyright Act were specifically designed to afford copyright protection to simultaneously-recorded broadcasts, and *Metropolitan Opera* and *Muzak* could today be brought as copyright infringement cases. Moreover, we believe that they would *have* to be brought as copyright cases because the amendments affording broadcasts copyright protection also preempted the state law misappropriation claims under which they were decided.

Our conclusion, therefore, is that only a narrow "hot-news" misappropriation claim survives preemption for actions concerning material within the realm of copyright.[27]

In our view, the elements central to an *INS* claim are: (i) the plaintiff generates or collects information at some cost or expense; (ii) the value of the information is highly time-sensitive; (iii) the defendant's use of the information constitutes free-riding on the plaintiff's costly efforts to generate or collect it; (iv) the defendant's use of the information is in direct competition with a product or service offered by the plaintiff; [and] (v) the ability of other parties to free-ride on the efforts of the plaintiff would so reduce the incentive to produce the product or service that its existence or quality would be substantially threatened.

INS is not about ethics; it is about the protection of property rights in time-sensitive information so that the information will be made available to the public by profit seeking entrepreneurs. If services like AP were not assured of property rights in the news they pay to collect, they would cease to collect it. The ability of their competitors to appropriate their product at only nominal cost and thereby to disseminate a competing product at a lower price would destroy the incentive to collect news in the first place. The newspaper-reading public would suffer because no one would have an incentive to collect "hot news."

We therefore find the extra elements—those in addition to the elements of copyright infringement—that allow a "hotnews" claim to survive preemption are: (i) the time-sensitive value of factual information, (ii) the free-riding by a defendant, and (iii) the threat to the very existence of the product or service provided by the plaintiff.

2. *The Legality of SportsTrax*

We conclude that Motorola and STATS have not engaged in unlawful misappropriation under the "hot-news" test set out above. To be sure, some of the elements of a "hot-news" *INS* claim are met. The information transmitted to SportsTrax is not precisely contemporaneous, but it is nevertheless time-sensitive. Also, the NBA does provide, or will shortly do so, information like that available through SportsTrax. It now offers a service called "Gamestats" that provides official play-by-play game sheets and half-time and final box scores within each arena. It also provides such information to the media in each arena. In the future, the NBA plans to enhance Gamestats so that it will be networked between the various arenas and will support a pager product analogous to SportsTrax. SportsTrax will of course directly compete with an enhanced Gamestats.

---

27. State law claims involving breach of fiduciary duties or trade-secret claims are not involved in this matter and are not addressed by this discussion. These claims are generally not preempted because they pass the "extra elements" test. *See Altai,* 982 F.2d at 717.

However, there are critical elements missing in the NBA's attempt to assert a "hot-news" *INS*-type claim. As framed by the NBA, their claim compresses and confuses three different informational products. The first product is generating the information by playing the games; the second product is transmitting live, full descriptions of those games; and the third product is collecting and retransmitting strictly factual information about the games. The first and second products are the NBA's primary business: producing basketball games for live attendance and licensing copyrighted broadcasts of those games. The collection and retransmission of strictly factual material about the games is a different product: e.g., box-scores in newspapers, summaries of statistics on television sports news, and real-time facts to be transmitted to pagers. In our view, the NBA has failed to show any competitive effect whatsoever from SportsTrax on the first and second products and a lack of any free-riding by SportsTrax on the third.

With regard to the NBA's primary products—producing basketball games with live attendance and licensing copyrighted broadcasts of those games—there is no evidence that anyone regards SportsTrax or the AOL site as a substitute for attending NBA games or watching them on television. In fact, Motorola markets SportsTrax as being designed "for those times when you cannot be at the arena, watch the game on TV, or listen to the radio * * *"

The NBA argues that the pager market is also relevant to a "hot-news" *INS*-type claim and that SportsTrax's future competition with Gamestats satisfies any missing element. We agree that there is a separate market for the real-time transmission of factual information to pagers or similar devices, such as STATS's AOL site. However, we disagree that SportsTrax is in any sense free-riding off Gamestats.

An indispensable element of an *INS* "hot-news" claim is free riding by a defendant on a plaintiff's product, enabling the defendant to produce a directly competitive product for less money because it has lower costs. SportsTrax is not such a product. The use of pagers to transmit real-time information about NBA games requires: (i) the collecting of facts about the games; (ii) the transmission of these facts on a network; (iii) the assembling of them by the particular service; and (iv) the transmission of them to pagers or an on-line computer site. Appellants are in no way free-riding on Gamestats. Motorola and STATS expend their own resources to collect purely factual information generated in NBA games to transmit to SportsTrax pagers. They have their own network and assemble and transmit data themselves.

To be sure, if appellants in the future were to collect facts from an enhanced Gamestats pager to retransmit them to SportsTrax pagers, that would constitute free-riding and might well cause Gamestats to be unprofitable because it had to bear costs to collect facts that SportsTrax did not. If the appropriation of facts from one pager to another pager service were allowed, transmission of current information on NBA games to pagers or similar devices would be substantially deterred because any potential transmitter would know that the first entrant would quickly encounter a lower cost competitor free-riding on the originator's transmissions.

However, that is not the case in the instant matter. SportsTrax and Gamestats are each bearing their own costs of collecting factual information on NBA games, and, if one produces a product that is cheaper or otherwise superior to the other, that producer will prevail in the marketplace. This is obviously not the situation against which *INS* was intended to prevent: the potential lack of any such product or service because of the anticipation of free-riding.

For the foregoing reasons, the NBA has not shown any damage to any of its products based on free-riding by Motorola and STATS, and the NBA's misappropriation claim based on New York law is preempted.[28]

NOTES

1. Would the "partial preemption" theory rejected by the court in the preceding case have produced a different result in this case? In what circumstances would this theory produce different outcomes than the more broadly encompassing preemption theory accepted by the court? What are the difficulties raised by a preemption standard that distinguishes a live performance from a copyrighted depiction of that performance for purposes of determining the scope of federal preemption of state intellectual property protections?

2. How were the practices in transmitting sports information to SportsTrax devices different from the news transmission practices successfully challenged in *International News Service v. Associated Press,* 248 U.S. 215, 39 S.Ct. 68, 63 L.Ed. 211 (1918) ("*INS*")? More information about the latter case can be obtained from the Court's opinion and those of several dissenting justices reproduced in Chapter 9 of this text. Were the defendants in both cases relying on the news value of information developed by the plaintiffs? If so, how did the impacts of the practices of the defendant in the preceding case differ from those of the defendant in *INS*? Is it true, as the court concludes, that SportsTrax devices would be likely to have little or no competitive impact on the commercial value of the NBA's primary products? Was the provision of a service like that associated with the SportsTrax devices likely to preclude the NBA from offering a similar service in a commercially advantageous manner? Was the loss of this opportunity a meaningful commercial impact of the SportsTrax devices? If so, why did the NBA not suffer a misappropriation of intellectual property similar to that which supported a successful claim in *INS*?

B. CONSTITUTIONAL PREEMPTION

Where Congress has not specified the scope of preemption of state laws in the provisions of a federal statute, the range of preemption of state laws resulting from the enactment of the federal statute must be deter-

---

28. In view of our disposition of this matter, we need not address appellants' First Amendment and laches defenses.

mined from basic constitutional principles. The supremacy clause of the federal Constitution requires that the enforcement of state laws and rights be preempted where such enforcement would interfere with the achievement of the goals of a federal statute. Hence, under a constitutional analysis, the goals underlying federal enactments often determine the scope of state law preemption resulting from the federal enactments.

In evaluating the impacts of federal intellectual laws in preempting state laws, courts have sometimes struggled to determine Congress' goals in placing limits on the rights of intellectual property holders. In particular, courts have had difficulty in ascertaining if limits on intellectual property rights were intended by Congress to make certain uses of intellectual works freely available to the public, at least under some circumstances. Where such a purpose of protecting public freedom to use works is found, it provides a basis for preempting any state laws or rights that would restrict the use of the works in a manner inconsistent with the free use protected by federal law.

Federal patent and trademark laws lack the sorts of statutory preemption standards found in federal copyright laws. Hence, a number of constitutional preemption controversies have revolved around the impact of federal patent and trademark laws on state laws. The following case describes the diverse types of state laws that have been claimed to be preempted by federal patent laws and the criteria used by courts in resolving these constitutional preemption claims.

BONITO BOATS, INC. v. THUNDER CRAFT BOATS, INC.

Supreme Court of the United States, 1989.
489 U.S. 141, 109 S.Ct. 971, 103 L.Ed.2d 118.

JUSTICE O'CONNOR delivered the opinion of the Court.

We must decide today what limits the operation of the federal patent system places on the States' ability to offer substantial protection to utilitarian and design ideas which the patent laws leave otherwise unprotected. In *Interpart Corp. v. Italia,* 777 F.2d 678 (1985), the Court of Appeals for the Federal Circuit concluded that a California law prohibiting the use of the "direct molding process" to duplicate unpatented articles posed no threat to the policies behind the federal patent laws. In this case, the Florida Supreme Court came to a contrary conclusion. It struck down a Florida statute which prohibits the use of the direct molding process to duplicate unpatented boat hulls, finding that the protection offered by the Florida law conflicted with the balance struck by Congress in the federal patent statute between the encouragement of invention and free competition in unpatented ideas. We granted certiorari to resolve the conflict and we now affirm the judgment of the Florida Supreme Court.

I

In September 1976, petitioner Bonito Boats, Inc. (Bonito), a Florida corporation, developed a hull design for a fiberglass recreational boat which it marketed under the trade name Bonito Boat Model 5VBR. Designing the boat hull required substantial effort on the part of Bonito. A set of engineering drawings was prepared, from which a hardwood model was created. The hardwood model was then sprayed with fiberglass to create a mold, which then served to produce the finished fiberglass boats for sale. The 5VBR was placed on the market sometime in September 1976. There is no indication in the record that a patent application was ever filed for protection of the utilitarian or design aspects of the hull, or for the process by which the hull was manufactured. The 5VBR was favorably received by the boating public, and "a broad interstate market" developed for its sale.

In May 1983, after the Bonito 5VBR had been available to the public for over six years, the Florida Legislature enacted Fla.Stat. § 559.94 (1987). The statute makes "[i]t * * * unlawful for any person to use the direct molding process to duplicate for the purpose of sale any manufactured vessel hull or component part of a vessel made by another without the written permission of that other person." The statute also makes it unlawful for a person to "knowingly sell a vessel hull or component part of a vessel duplicated in violation of subsection (2)." Damages, injunctive relief, and attorney's fees are made available to "[a]ny person who suffers injury or damage as the result of a violation" of the statute. The statute was made applicable to vessel hulls or component parts duplicated through the use of direct molding after July 1, 1983.

On December 21, 1984, Bonito filed this action in the Circuit Court of Orange County, Florida. The complaint alleged that respondent here, Thunder Craft Boats, Inc. (Thunder Craft), a Tennessee corporation, had violated the Florida statute by using the direct molding process to duplicate the Bonito 5VBR fiberglass hull, and had knowingly sold such duplicates in violation of the Florida statute. Bonito sought "a temporary and permanent injunction prohibiting [Thunder Craft] from continuing to unlawfully duplicate and sell Bonito Boat hulls or components," as well as an accounting of profits, treble damages, punitive damages, and attorney's fees. Respondent filed a motion to dismiss the complaint, arguing that under this Court's decisions in *Sears, Roebuck & Co. v. Stiffel Co.*, 376 U.S. 225, 84 S.Ct. 784, 11 L.Ed.2d 661 (1964), and *Compco Corp. v. Day–Brite Lighting, Inc.*, 376 U.S. 234, 84 S.Ct. 779, 11 L.Ed.2d 669 (1964), the Florida statute conflicted with federal patent law and was therefore invalid under the Supremacy Clause of the Federal Constitution. The trial court granted respondent's motion and a divided Court of Appeals affirmed the dismissal of petitioner's complaint.

On appeal, a sharply divided Florida Supreme Court agreed with the lower courts' conclusion that the Florida law impermissibly interfered with the scheme established by the federal patent laws. The majority read our decisions in *Sears* and *Compco* for the proposition that "when an article is introduced into the public domain, only a patent can eliminate the inherent risk of competition and then but for a limited time." Relying on the Federal Circuit's decision in the *Interpart* case, the three dissenting judges argued that the Florida antidirect molding provision "does not prohibit the copying of an unpatented item. It prohibits one method of copying; the item remains in the public domain."

II

Article I, § 8, cl. 8, of the Constitution gives Congress the power "[t]o promote the Progress of Science and useful Arts, by securing for limited Times to Authors and Inventors the exclusive Right to their respective Writings and Discoveries." The Patent Clause itself reflects a balance between the need to encourage innovation and the avoidance of monopolies which stifle competition without any concomitant advance in the "Progress of Science and useful Arts." As we have noted in the past, the Clause contains both a grant of power and certain limitations upon the exercise of that power. Congress may not create patent monopolies of unlimited duration, nor may it "authorize the issuance of patents whose effects are to remove existent knowledge from the public domain, or to restrict free access to materials already available."

From their inception, the federal patent laws have embodied a careful balance between the need to promote innovation and the recognition that imitation and refinement through imitation are both necessary to invention itself and the very lifeblood of a competitive economy. Soon after the adoption of the Constitution, the First Congress enacted the Patent Act of 1790, which allowed the grant of a limited monopoly of 14 years to any applicant that "hath * * * invented or discovered any useful art, manufacture, * * * or device, or any improvement therein not before known or used." In addition to novelty, the 1790 Act required that the invention be "sufficiently useful and important" to merit the 14-year right of exclusion. Section 2 of the Act required that the patentee deposit with the Secretary of State, a specification and if possible a model of the new invention, "which specification shall be so particular, and said models so exact, as not only to distinguish the invention or discovery from other things before known and used, but also to enable a workman or other person skilled in the art or manufacture * * * to make, construct, or use the same, to the end that the public may have the full benefit thereof, after the expiration of the patent term."

The first Patent Act established an agency known by self-designation as the "Commissioners for the promotion of Useful Arts," composed of the Secretary of State, the Secretary of the Department of War, and the Attorney General, any two of whom could grant a patent. Thomas Jefferson was the first Secretary of State, and the driving force behind early federal patent policy. For Jefferson, a central tenet of the patent system in a free market economy was that "a machine of which we were possessed, might be applied by every man to any use of which it is susceptible." He viewed a grant of patent rights in an idea already disclosed to the public as akin to an *ex post facto* law, "obstruct[ing] others in the use of what they possessed before." Jefferson also played a large role in the drafting of our Nation's second Patent Act, which became law in 1793. The Patent Act of

1793 carried over the requirement that the subject of a patent application be "not known or used before the application." A defense to an infringement action was created where "the thing, thus secured by patent, was not originally discovered by the patentee, but had been in use, or had been described in some public work anterior to the supposed discovery of the patentee." Thus, from the outset, federal patent law has been about the difficult business "of drawing a line between the things which are worth to the public the embarrassment of an exclusive patent, and those which are not."

Today's patent statute is remarkably similar to the law as known to Jefferson in 1793. Protection is offered to "[w]hoever invents or discovers any new and useful process, machine, manufacture, or composition of matter, or any new and useful improvement thereof." Since 1842, Congress has also made protection available for "any new, original and ornamental design for an article of manufacture." To qualify for protection, a design must present an aesthetically pleasing appearance that is not dictated by function alone, and must satisfy the other criteria of patentability. The novelty requirement of patentability is presently expressed in 35 U.S.C. §§ 102(a) and (b), which provide:

"A person shall be entitled to a patent unless—

(a) the invention was known or used by others in this country, or patented or described in a printed publication in this or a foreign country, before the invention thereof by the applicant for patent, or

(b) the invention was patented or described in a printed publication in this or a foreign country or in public use or on sale in this country more than one year prior to the date of application for patent in the United States * * *."

Sections 102(a) and (b) operate in tandem to exclude from consideration for patent protection knowledge that is already available to the public. They express a congressional determination that the creation of a monopoly in such information would not only serve no socially useful purpose, but would in fact injure the public by removing existing knowledge from public use. From the Patent Act of 1790 to the present day, the public sale of an unpatented article has acted as a complete bar to federal protection of the idea embodied in the article thus placed in public commerce.

In the case of *Pennock v. Dialogue*, 2 Pet. 1, 7 L.Ed. 327 (1829), Justice Story applied these principles under the patent law of 1800. The patentee had developed a new technique for the manufacture of rubber hose for the conveyance of air and fluids. The invention was reduced to practice in 1811, but letters patent were not sought and granted until 1818. In the interval, the patentee had licensed a third party to market the hose, and over 13,000 feet of the new product had been sold in the city of Philadelphia alone. The Court concluded that the patent was invalid due to the prior public sale, indicating that, "if [an inventor] suffers the thing he invented to go into public use, or to be publicly sold for use" "[h]is voluntary act or acquiescence in the public sale and use is an abandonment of his right." The Court noted that under the common law of England, letters patent were unavailable for the protection of articles in public commerce at the time of the application and that this same doctrine was immediately embodied in the first patent laws passed in this country.

As the holding of *Pennock* makes clear, the federal patent scheme creates a limited opportunity to obtain a property right in an idea. Once an inventor has decided to lift the veil of secrecy from his work, he must choose the protection of a federal patent or the dedication of his idea to the public at large. As Judge Learned Hand once put it: "[I]t is a condition upon the inventor's right to a patent that he shall not exploit his discovery competitively after it is ready for patenting; he must content himself with either secrecy or legal monopoly." *Metallizing Engineering Co. v. Kenyon Bearing & Auto Parts Co.,* 153 F.2d 516, 520 (CA2), cert. denied, 328 U.S. 840, 66 S.Ct. 1016, 90 L.Ed. 1615 (1946).

In addition to the requirements of novelty and utility, the federal patent law has long required that an innovation not be anticipated by the prior art in the field. Even if a particular combination of elements is "novel" in the literal sense of the term, it will not qualify for federal patent protection if its contours are so traced by the existing technology in the field that the "improvement is the work of the skillful mechanic, not that of the inventor." In 1952, Congress codified this judicially developed requirement in 35 U.S.C. § 103, which refuses protection to new developments where "the differences between the subject matter sought to be patented and the prior art are such that the subject matter as a whole would have been obvious at the time the invention was made to a person of ordinary skill in the art to which said subject matter pertains." The nonobviousness requirement extends the field of unpatentable material beyond that which is known to the public under § 102, to include that which could readily be deduced from publicly available material by a person of ordinary skill in the pertinent field of endeavor. Taken together, the novelty and nonobviousness requirements express a congressional determination that the purposes behind the Patent Clause are best served by free competition and exploitation of either that which is already available to the public or that which may be readily discerned from publicly available material. See *Aronson v. Quick Point Pencil Co.,* 440 U.S. 257, 262, 99 S.Ct. 1096, 1099, 59 L.Ed.2d 296 (1979) ("[T]he stringent requirements for patent protection seek to ensure that ideas in the public domain remain there for the use of the public").

The applicant whose invention satisfies the requirements of novelty, nonobviousness, and utility, and who is willing to reveal to the public the substance of his discovery and "the best mode * * * of carrying out his invention," 35 U.S.C. § 112, is granted "the right to exclude others from making, using, or selling the invention throughout the United States," for a period of 17 years. 35 U.S.C. § 154. The federal patent system thus embodies a carefully crafted bargain for encouraging the creation and disclosure of new, useful, and nonobvious advances in technology and design in return for the exclusive right to practice the invention for a period of years. "[The inventor] may keep his invention secret and reap its fruits indefinitely. In consideration of its disclosure and the consequent benefit to the community, the patent is granted. An exclusive enjoyment is guaranteed him for seventeen years, but upon expiration of that period, the knowledge of the invention inures to the people, who are thus enabled without restriction to practice it and profit by its use." *United States v. Dubilier Condenser Corp.,* 289 U.S. 178, 186–187, 53 S.Ct. 554, 557, 77 L.Ed. 1114 (1933).

The attractiveness of such a bargain, and its effectiveness in inducing creative effort and disclosure of the results of that effort, depend almost entirely on a backdrop of free competition in the exploitation of unpatented designs and innovations. The novelty and nonobviousness requirements of patentability embody a congressional understanding, implicit in the Patent Clause itself, that free exploitation of ideas will be the rule, to which the protection of a federal patent is the exception. Moreover, the ultimate goal of the patent system is to bring new designs and technologies into the public domain through disclosure. State law protection for techniques and designs whose disclosure has already been induced by market rewards may conflict with the very purpose of the patent laws by decreasing the range of ideas available as the building blocks of further innovation. The offer of federal protection from competitive exploitation of intellectual property would be rendered meaningless in a world where substantially similar state law protections were readily available. To a limited extent, the federal patent laws must determine not only what is protected, but also what is free for all to use. Cf. *Arkansas Electric Cooperative Corp. v. Arkansas Public Service Comm'n,* 461 U.S. 375, 384, 103 S.Ct. 1905, 1912, 76 L.Ed.2d 1 (1983) ("[A] federal decision to forgo regulation in a given area may imply an authoritative federal determination that the area is best left *un* regulated, and in that event would have as much pre-emptive force as a decision *to* regulate") (emphasis in original).

Thus our past decisions have made clear that state regulation of intellectual property must yield to the extent that it clashes with the balance struck by Congress in our patent laws. The tension between the desire to freely exploit the full potential of our inventive resources and the need to create an incentive to deploy those resources is constant. Where it is clear how the patent laws strike that balance in a particular circumstance, that is not a judgment the States may second-guess. We have long held that after the expiration of a federal patent, the subject matter of the patent passes to the free use of the public as a matter of federal law. Where the public has paid the congressionally mandated price for disclosure, the States may not render the exchange fruitless by offering patent-like protection to the subject matter of the expired patent. "It is self-evident that on the expiration of a patent the monopoly created by it ceases to exist, and the right to make the thing formerly covered by the patent becomes public property."

In our decisions in *Sears, Roebuck & Co. v. Stiffel Co.,* 376 U.S. 225, 84 S.Ct. 784, 11 L.Ed.2d 661 (1964), and *Compco Corp. v. Day–Brite Lighting, Inc.,* 376 U.S. 234, 84 S.Ct. 779, 11 L.Ed.2d 669 (1964), we found that publicly known design and utilitarian ideas which were unprotected by patent occupied much the same position as the subject matter of an expired patent. The *Sears* case involved a pole lamp originally designed by the plaintiff Stiffel, who had secured both design and mechanical patents on the lamp. Sears purchased unauthorized copies of the lamps, and was able to sell them at a retail price practically equivalent to the wholesale price of the original manufacturer. Stiffel brought an action against Sears in Federal District Court, alleging infringement of the two federal patents and unfair competition under Illinois law. The District Court found that Stiffel's patents were invalid due to anticipation in the prior art, but nonetheless enjoined Sears from further sales of the duplicate lamps based on a finding of consumer confusion under the Illinois law of unfair competition. The Court of Appeals affirmed, coming to the conclusion that the Illinois law of unfair competition prohibited product simulation even in the absence of evidence that the defendant took some further action to induce confusion as to source.

This Court reversed, finding that the unlimited protection against copying which the Illinois law accorded an unpatentable item whose design had been fully disclosed through public sales conflicted with the federal policy embodied in the patent laws. The Court stated:

> "In the present case the 'pole lamp' sold by Stiffel has been held not to be entitled to the protection of either a mechanical or a design patent. An unpatentable article, like an article on which the patent has expired, is in the public domain and may be made and sold by whoever chooses to do so. What Sears did was to copy Stiffel's design and sell lamps almost identical to those sold by Stiffel. This it had every right to do under the federal patent laws."

376 U.S., at 231, 84 S.Ct., at 789.

A similar conclusion was reached in *Compco,* where the District Court had extended the protection of Illinois' unfair competition law to the functional aspects of an unpatented fluorescent lighting system. The injunction against copying of an unpatented article, freely available to the public, impermissibly "interfere[d] with the federal policy, found in Art. I, § 8, cl. 8, of the Constitution and in the implementing federal statutes, of allowing free access to copy whatever the federal patent and copyright laws leave in the public domain."

The pre-emptive sweep of our decisions in *Sears* and *Compco* has been the subject of heated scholarly and judicial debate. Read at their highest level of generality, the two decisions could be taken to stand for the proposition that the States are completely disabled from offering any form of protection to articles or processes which fall within the broad scope of patentable subject matter. Since the potentially patentable includes "anything under the sun that is made by man," *Diamond v. Chakrabarty,* 447

U.S. 303, 309, 100 S.Ct. 2204, 2207, 65 L.Ed.2d 144 (1980) (citation omitted), the broadest reading of *Sears* would prohibit the States from regulating the deceptive simulation of trade dress or the tortious appropriation of private information.

That the extrapolation of such a broad pre-emptive principle from *Sears* is inappropriate is clear from the balance struck in *Sears* itself. The *Sears* Court made it plain that the States "may protect businesses in the use of their trademarks, labels, or distinctive dress in the packaging of goods so as to prevent others, by imitating such markings, from misleading purchasers as to the source of the goods." Trade dress is, of course, potentially the subject matter of design patents. Yet our decision in *Sears* clearly indicates that the States may place limited regulations on the circumstances in which such designs are used in order to prevent consumer confusion as to source. Thus, while *Sears* speaks in absolutist terms, its conclusion that the States may place some conditions on the use of trade dress indicates an implicit recognition that all state regulation of potentially patentable but unpatented subject matter is not *ipso facto* preempted by the federal patent laws.

What was implicit in our decision in *Sears,* we have made explicit in our subsequent decisions concerning the scope of federal pre-emption of state regulation of the subject matter of patent. Thus, in *Kewanee Oil Co. v. Bicron Corp.,* 416 U.S. 470, 94 S.Ct. 1879, 40 L.Ed.2d 315 (1974), we held that state protection of trade secrets did not operate to frustrate the achievement of the congressional objectives served by the patent laws. Despite the fact that state law protection was available for ideas which clearly fell within the subject matter of patent, the Court concluded that the nature and degree of state protection did not conflict with the federal policies of encouragement of patentable invention and the prompt disclosure of such innovations.

Several factors were critical to this conclusion. First, because the public awareness of a trade secret is by definition limited, the Court noted that "the policy that matter once in the public domain must remain in the public domain is not incompatible with the existence of trade secret protection." Second, the *Kewanee* Court emphasized that "[t]rade secret law provides far weaker protection in many respects than the patent law." This point was central to the Court's conclusion that trade secret protection did not conflict with either the encouragement or disclosure policies of the federal patent law. The public at large remained free to discover and exploit the trade secret through reverse engineering of products in the public domain or by independent creation. Thus, the possibility that trade secret protection would divert inventors from the creative effort necessary to satisfy the rigorous demands of patent protection was remote indeed. Finally, certain aspects of trade secret law operated to protect noneconomic interests outside the sphere of congressional concern in the patent laws. As the Court noted, "[A] most fundamental human right, that of privacy, is threatened when industrial espionage is condoned or is made profitable." There was no indication that Congress had considered this interest in the balance struck by the patent laws, or that state protection for it would interfere with the policies behind the patent system.

We have since reaffirmed the pragmatic approach which *Kewanee* takes to the pre-emption of state laws dealing with the protection of intellectual property. See *Aronson,* 440 U.S., at 262, 99 S.Ct., at 1099 ("State law is not displaced merely because the contract relates to intellectual property which may or may not be patentable; the states are free to regulate the use of such intellectual property in any manner not inconsistent with federal law"). At the same time, we have consistently reiterated the teaching of *Sears* and *Compco* that ideas once placed before the public without the protection of a valid patent are subject to appropriation without significant restraint.

At the heart of *Sears* and *Compco* is the conclusion that the efficient operation of the federal patent system depends upon substantially free trade in publicly known, unpatented design and utilitarian conceptions. In *Sears,* the state law offered "the equivalent of a patent monopoly" in the functional aspects of a product which had been placed in public commerce absent the protection of a valid patent. While, as noted above, our decisions since *Sears* have taken a decidedly less rigid view of the scope of federal pre-emption under the patent laws, we believe that the *Sears* Court correctly concluded that the States may not offer patent-like protection to intellectual creations which would otherwise remain unprotected as a matter of federal law. Both the novelty and the nonobviousness requirements of federal patent law are grounded in the notion that concepts within the public grasp, or those so obvious that they readily could be, are the tools of creation available to all. They provide the baseline of free competition upon which the patent system's incentive to creative effort depends. A state law that substantially interferes with the enjoyment of an unpatented utilitarian or design conception which has been freely disclosed by its author to the public at large impermissibly contravenes the ultimate goal of public disclosure and use which is the centerpiece of federal patent policy. Moreover, through the creation of patent-like rights, the States could essentially redirect inventive efforts away from the careful criteria of patentability developed by Congress over the last 200 years. We understand this to be the reasoning at the core of our decisions in *Sears* and *Compco,* and we reaffirm that reasoning today.

III

We believe that the Florida statute at issue in this case so substantially impedes the public use of the otherwise unprotected design and utilitarian ideas embodied in unpatented boat hulls as to run afoul of the teaching of our decisions in *Sears* and *Compco.* It is readily apparent that the Florida statute does not operate to prohibit "unfair competition" in the usual sense that the term is understood. The law of unfair competition has its roots in the common-law tort of deceit: its general concern is with protecting *consumers* from confusion as to source. While that concern may result in the creation of "quasi-property rights" in communicative symbols, the focus is on the protection of consumers, not the protection of producers as an incentive to product innovation. Judge Hand captured the distinction well in *Crescent Tool Co. v. Kilborn & Bishop Co.,* 247 F. 299, 301 (CA2 1917), where he wrote:

> "[T]he plaintiff has the right not to lose his customers through false representations that those are his wares which in fact are not, but he may not monopolize any design or pattern, however trifling. The defendant, on the other hand, may copy plaintiff's goods slavishly down to the minutest detail: but he may not represent himself as the plaintiff in their sale."

With some notable exceptions, including the interpretation of the Illinois law of unfair competition at issue in *Sears* and *Compco,* the common-law tort of unfair competition has been limited to protection against copying of nonfunctional aspects of consumer products which have acquired secondary meaning such that they operate as a designation of source. The "protection" granted a particular design under the law of unfair competition is thus limited to one context where consumer confusion is likely to result; the design "idea" itself may be freely exploited in all other contexts.

In contrast to the operation of unfair competition law, the Florida statute is aimed directly at preventing the exploitation of the design and utilitarian conceptions embodied in the product itself. The sparse legislative history surrounding its enactment indicates that it was intended to create an inducement for the improvement of boat hull designs. See Tr. of Meeting of Transportation Committee, Florida House of Representatives, May 3, 1983, reprinted at App. 22 ("[T]here is no inducement for [a] quality boat manufacturer to improve these designs and secondly, if he does, it is immediately copied. This would prevent that and allow him recourse in circuit court"). To accomplish this goal, the Florida statute endows the original boat hull manufacturer with rights against the world, similar in scope and operation to the rights accorded a federal patentee. Like the patentee, the beneficiary of the Florida statute may prevent a competitor from "making" the product in what is evidently the most efficient manner available and from "selling" the product when it is produced in that fashion. Compare 35 U.S.C. § 154. The Florida scheme offers this protection for an unlimited number of years to all boat hulls and their component parts, without regard to their ornamental or technological merit. Protection is available for subject matter for which patent protection has been denied or has expired, as well as for designs which have been freely revealed to the consuming public by their creators.

In this case, the Bonito 5VBR fiberglass hull has been freely exposed to the public for a period in excess of six years. For purposes of federal law, it stands in the same stead as an item for which a patent has expired or been denied: it is unpatented and unpatentable. See 35 U.S.C. § 102(b). Whether because of a determination of unpatentability or other commercial concerns, petitioner chose to expose its hull design to the public in the marketplace, eschewing the bargain held out by the federal patent system of disclosure in exchange for exclusive use. Yet, the Florida statute allows petitioner to reassert a substantial property right in the idea, thereby constricting the spectrum of useful public knowledge. Moreover, it does so without the careful protections of high standards of innovation and limited monopoly contained in the federal scheme. We think it clear that such protection conflicts with the federal policy "that all ideas in general circulation be dedicated to the common good unless they are protected by a valid patent."

That the Florida statute does not remove all means of reproduction and sale does not eliminate the conflict with the federal scheme. In essence, the Florida law prohibits the entire public from engaging in a form of reverse engineering of a product in the public domain. This is clearly one of the rights vested in the federal patent holder, but has never been a part of state protection under the law of unfair competition or trade secrets. See *Kewanee,* 416 U.S., at 476, 94 S.Ct., at 1883 ("A trade secret law, however, does not offer protection against discovery by * * * so-called reverse engineering, that is by starting with the known product and working backward to divine the process which aided in its development or manufacture"); see also *Chicago Lock Co. v. Fanberg,* 676 F.2d 400, 405 (CA9 1982) ("A lock purchaser's own reverse-engineering of his own lock, and subsequent publication of the serial number-key code correlation, is an example of the independent invention and reverse engineering expressly allowed by trade secret doctrine"). The duplication of boat hulls and their component parts may be an essential part of innovation in the field of hydrodynamic design. Variations as to size and combination of various elements may lead to significant advances in the field. Reverse engineering of chemical and mechanical articles in the public domain often leads to significant advances in technology. If Florida may prohibit this particular method of study and recomposition of an unpatented article, we fail to see the principle that would prohibit a State from banning the use of chromatography in the reconstitution of unpatented chemical compounds, or the use of robotics in the duplication of machinery in the public domain.

Moreover, as we noted in *Kewanee,* the competitive reality of reverse engineering may act as a spur to the inventor, creating an incentive to develop inventions that meet the rigorous requirements of patentability. The Florida statute substantially reduces this competitive incentive, thus eroding the general rule of free competition upon which the attractiveness of the federal patent bargain depends. The protections of state trade secret law are most effective at the developmental stage, before a product has been marketed and the threat of reverse engineering becomes real. During this period, patentability will often be an uncertain prospect, and to a certain extent, the protection offered by trade secret law may "dovetail" with the incentives created by the federal patent monopoly. In contrast, under the Florida scheme, the would-be inventor is aware from the outset of his efforts that rights against the public are available regardless of his ability to satisfy the rigorous standards of patentability. Indeed, it appears that even the most mundane and obvious changes in the design of a boat hull will trigger the protections of the statute. See Fla.Stat. § 559.94(2) (1987) (protecting "any manufactured vessel hull or component part"). Given the substantial protection offered by the Florida scheme, we cannot dismiss as hypothetical the possibility that it will become a significant competitor to the federal patent laws, offering investors similar protection without the *quid pro quo* of substantial creative effort required by the federal statute. The prospect of all 50 States establishing similar protections for preferred industries without the rigorous requirements of patentability prescribed by Congress could pose a substantial threat to the patent system's ability to accomplish its mission of promoting progress in the useful arts.

Finally, allowing the States to create patent-like rights in various products in public circulation would lead to administrative problems of no small dimension. The federal patent scheme provides a basis for the public to ascertain the status of the intellectual property embodied in any article in general circulation. Through the application process, detailed information concerning the claims of the patent holder is compiled in a central location. The availability of damages in an infringement action is made contingent upon affixing a notice of patent to the protected article. The notice requirement is designed "for the information of the public" and provides a ready means of discerning the status of the intellectual property embodied in an article of manufacture or design. The public may rely upon the lack of notice in exploiting shapes and designs accessible to all. See *Devices for Medicine, Inc. v. Boehl*, 822 F.2d 1062, 1066 (CA Fed.1987) ("Having sold the product unmarked, [the patentee] could hardly maintain entitlement to damages for its use by a purchaser uninformed that such use would violate [the] patent").

The Florida scheme blurs this clear federal demarcation between public and private property. One of the fundamental purposes behind the Patent and Copyright Clauses of the Constitution was to promote national uniformity in the realm of intellectual property. See The Federalist No. 43, p. 309 (B. Wright ed. 1961). Since the Patent Act of 1800, Congress has lodged exclusive jurisdiction of actions "arising under" the patent laws in the federal courts, thus allowing for the development of a uniform body of law in resolving the constant tension between private right and public access. Recently, Congress conferred exclusive jurisdiction of all patent appeals on the Court of Appeals for the Federal Circuit, in order to "provide nationwide uniformity in patent law." H.R.Rep. No. 97–312, p. 20 (1981). This purpose is frustrated by the Florida scheme, which renders the status of the design and utilitarian "ideas" embodied in the boat hulls it protects uncertain. Given the inherently ephemeral nature of property in ideas, and the great power such property has to cause harm to the competitive policies which underlay the federal patent laws, the demarcation of broad zones of public and private right is "the type of regulation that demands a uniform national rule." Absent such a federal rule, each State could afford patent-like protection to particularly favored home industries, effectively insulating them from competition from outside the State.

Petitioner and its supporting *amici* place great weight on the contrary decision of the Court of Appeals for the Federal Circuit in *Interpart Corp. v. Italia*. In upholding the application of the California "antidirect molding" statute to the duplication of unpatented automobile mirrors, the Federal Circuit stated: "The statute prevents unscrupulous competitors from obtaining a product and using it as the 'plug' for making a mold. The statute does not prohibit copying the design of the product in any other way; the latter if in the public domain, is free for anyone to make, use or sell." The court went on to indicate that "the patent laws 'say nothing about the right to copy or the right to use, they speak only in terms of the right to exclude.' "

We find this reasoning defective in several respects. The Federal Circuit apparently viewed the direct molding statute at issue in *Interpart* as a mere regulation of the use of chattels. Yet, the very purpose of antidirect molding statutes is to "reward" the "inventor" by offering substantial protection against public exploitation of his or her idea embodied in the product. Such statutes would be an exercise in futility if they did not have precisely the effect of substantially limiting the ability of the public to exploit an otherwise unprotected idea. As *amicus* points out, the direct molding process itself has been in use since the early 1950's. Indeed, U.S. Patent No. 3,419,646, issued to Robert L. Smith in 1968, explicitly discloses and claims a method for the direct molding of boat hulls. The specifications of the Smith Patent indicate that "[i]t is a major object of the present invention to provide a method for making large molded boat hull molds at very low cost, once a prototype hull has been provided." In fact, it appears that Bonito employed a similar process in the creation of its own production mold. It is difficult to conceive of a more effective method of creating substantial property rights in an intellectual creation than to eliminate the most efficient method for its exploitation. *Sears* and *Compco* protect more than the right of the public to contemplate the abstract beauty of an otherwise unprotected intellectual creation—they assure its efficient reduction to practice and sale in the marketplace.

Appending the conclusionary label "unscrupulous" to such competitive behavior merely endorses a policy judgment which the patent laws do not leave the States free to make. Where an item in general circulation is unprotected by patent, "[r]eproduction of a functional attribute is legitimate competitive activity."

Finally, we are somewhat troubled by the *Interpart* court's reference to the *Mine Safety* case for the proposition that the patent laws say "nothing about the right to copy or the right to use." As noted above, the federal standards for patentability, at a minimum, express the congressional determination that patent-like protection is unwarranted as to certain classes of intellectual property. The States are simply not free in this regard to offer equivalent protections to ideas which Congress has determined should belong to all. For almost 100 years it has been well established that in the case of an expired patent, the federal patent laws *do* create a federal right to "copy and to use." *Sears* and *Compco* extended that rule to potentially patentable ideas which are fully exposed to the public. The *Interpart* court's assertion to the contrary is puzzling and flies in the face of the same court's decisions applying the teaching of *Sears* and *Compco* in other contexts. See *Power Controls Corp. v. Hybrinetics, Inc.,* 806 F.2d 234, 240 (CA Fed. 1986) ("It is well established * * * that an action for unfair competition cannot be based upon a functional design"); *Gemveto Jewelry Co. v. Jeff Cooper Inc.,* 800 F.2d 256, 259 (CA Fed.1986) (vacating injunction against copying of jewelry designs issued under state law of unfair competition "in view of the *Sears* and *Compco* decisions which hold that copying of the article itself that is unprotected by the federal patent and copyright laws cannot be protected by state law").

Our decisions since *Sears* and *Compco* have made it clear that the Patent and Copyright Clauses do not, by their own force or by negative implication, deprive the States of the power to adopt rules for the promotion of intellectual creation within their own jurisdictions. Thus, where "Congress determines that neither federal protection nor freedom from restraint is required by the national interest," the States remain free to promote originality and creativity in their own domains.

Nor does the fact that a particular item lies within the subject matter of the federal patent laws necessarily preclude the States from offering limited protection which does not impermissibly interfere with the federal patent scheme. As *Sears* itself makes clear, States may place limited regulations on the use of unpatented designs in order to prevent consumer confusion as to source. In *Kewanee,* we found that state protection of trade secrets, as applied to both patentable and unpatentable subject matter, did not conflict with the federal patent laws. In both situations, state protection was not aimed exclusively at the promotion of invention itself, and the state restrictions on the use of unpatented ideas were limited to those necessary to promote goals outside the contemplation of the federal patent scheme. Both the law of unfair competition and state trade secret law have coexisted harmoniously with federal patent protection for almost 200 years, and Congress has given no indication that their operation is inconsistent with the operation of the federal patent laws.

Indeed, there are affirmative indications from Congress that both the law of unfair competition and trade secret protection are consistent with the balance struck by the patent laws. Section 43(a) of the Lanham Act, 60 Stat. 441, 15 U.S.C. § 1125(a), creates a federal remedy for making "a false designation of origin, or any false description or representation, including words or other symbols tending falsely to describe or represent the same * * *." Congress has thus given federal recognition to many of the concerns that underlie the state tort of unfair competition, and the application of *Sears* and *Compco* to nonfunctional aspects of a product which have been shown to identify source must take account of competing federal policies in this regard. Similarly, as Justice Marshall noted in his concurring opinion in *Kewanee:* "State trade secret laws and the federal patent laws have co-existed for many, many, years. During this time, Congress has repeatedly demonstrated its full awareness of the existence of the trade secret system, without any indication of disapproval. Indeed, Congress has in a number of instances given explicit federal protection to trade secret information provided to federal agencies." The case for federal pre-emption is particularly weak where Congress has indicated its awareness of the operation of state law in a field of federal interest, and has nonetheless decided to "stand by both concepts and to tolerate whatever tension there [is] between them." The same cannot be said of the Florida statute at issue here, which offers protection beyond that available under the law of unfair competition or trade secret, without any showing of consumer confusion, or breach of trust or secrecy.

The Florida statute is aimed directly at the promotion of intellectual creation by substantially restricting the public's ability to exploit ideas that the patent system mandates shall be free for all to use. Like the interpretation of Illinois unfair competition law in *Sears* and *Compco,* the Florida statute represents a break with the tradition of peaceful co-existence between state market regulation and federal patent policy. The Florida law substantially restricts the public's ability to exploit an unpatented design in general circulation, raising the specter of state-created monopolies in a host of useful shapes and processes for which patent protection has been denied or is otherwise unobtainable. It thus enters a field of regulation which the patent laws have reserved to Congress. The patent statute's careful balance between public right and private monopoly to promote certain creative activity is a "scheme of federal regulation * * * so pervasive as to make reasonable the inference that Congress left no room for the States to supplement it."

Congress has considered extending various forms of limited protection to industrial design either through the copyright laws or by relaxing the restrictions on the availability of design patents. Congress explicitly refused to take this step in the copyright laws and despite sustained criticism for a number of years, it has declined to alter the patent protections presently available for industrial design. It is for Congress to determine if the present system of design and utility patents is ineffectual in promoting the useful arts in the context of industrial design. By offering patent-like protection for ideas deemed unprotected under the present federal scheme, the Florida statute conflicts with the "strong federal policy favoring free competition in ideas which do not merit patent protection." We therefore agree with the majority of the Florida Supreme Court that the Florida statute is preempted by the Supremacy Clause, and the judgment of that court is hereby affirmed.

It is so ordered.

NOTES

1. Congress responded to the holding in *Bonito Boats* with the enactment of federal legislation protecting boat hull designs. In 1998, Congress enacted a sui generis form of intellectual property protection to protect boat hulls from unauthorized copying. *See* Vessel Hull Design Protection Act, Pub. L. No. 105–304, tit. V, 112 Stat. 2905 (1998) (codified at 17 U.S.C. §§ 1301–1332 (Supp. V 1999)). The United States Copyright Office, which administers the system of hull design registrations provided for under the Act, has summarized the provisions of the Vessel Hull Design Protection Act as follows:

> [The Vessel Hull Design Protection Act (VHDPA)] added chapter 13 to title 17 of the United States Code, thereby establishing protection of original vessel hull designs. The statute defines a "vessel" as a craft that is designed and capable of independently steering a course on or through water through its own means of propulsion, and that is designed and capable of carrying and transporting one or more passengers. 17 U.S.C. § 1301(b)(3). A "hull" is the frame or body of a vessel, including its deck, but exclusive of the masts, sails, yards, and rigging. *Id.* § 1301(b)(4). In addition to the hull, design protection under chapter 13 extends to the plugs and molds used to manufacture the hull. A "plug" is "a device or model used to make a mold for the purpose of exact duplication, regardless of whether the device or model has an intrinsic utilitarian function that is not only to portray the appearance of the product or convey information." *Id.* § 1301(b)(5).

> A "mold" means "a matrix or form in which a substance for material is used, regardless of whether the matrix or form has an intrinsic utilitarian function that is not only to portray the appearance of the product or to convey information." *Id.* § 1301(b)(6).

> Design protection for vessel hulls is for a period of ten years and is available only for original designs that are embodied in an actual vessel hull: no protection is available for designs that exist only in models, drawings, or representations. Staple or commonplace designs, "such as a standard geometric figure, a familiar symbol, an emblem, or a motif, or another shape, pattern, or configuration that has become standard, common, prevalent or ordinary" are not protected. *Id.* § 1302. The statute also sets forth several circumstances under which an otherwise original design does not receive protection. A design that is embodied in a vessel hull "that was made public by the designer or owner in the United States or a foreign country more than two years before the date of application for registration" of the design is not eligible. *Id.* § 1302 (5). Section 1332 states that there is no retroactive protection: no protection is "available for any design that has been made public under '§ 1310(b) before" October 28, 1998. *Id.* § 1332. And vessel hulls may not be protected under chapter 13 of title 17 if they have design patent protection under title 35 of the United States Code. See id. § 1329. As a result, vessel hulls protected under chapter 13 lose that protection if they acquire U.S. design patent protection.

Unlike copyright law, where protection arises at the moment of creation, an original vessel hull design is not protected under chapter 13 until it is made public or the registration of the design with the Copyright Office is published, whichever date is earlier. Once a design is made public, an application for registration must be made no later than two years from the date on which the design was made public. Making a design public is defined as publicly exhibiting it, distributing it or offering it for sale (or selling it) to the public with the design owner's consent. *Id.* § 1310(b). Only the owner of a design may make an application for registration. *Id.* § 1310(c).

United States Copyright Office, The Vessel Hull Design Protection Act: Overview and Analysis 2–4 (November, 2003), http://www.copyright.gov/reports/vhdpa-report.pdf (last visited on 9/10/2006).

2.   Because of the provisions of the federal Vessel Hull Design Protection Act (VHDPA) summarized in note 1, publicly disclosed boat hull designs qualifying for protection under this federal legislation are not now freely available for copying in the manner sought to be protected by the Court in *Bonito Boats*. In passing the VHDPA, Congress stated a different rule on free access to hull designs that superseded its earlier rule derived from the Patent Act (as interpreted in *Bonito Boats*).

However, with respect to other types of useful intellectual works not covered by this or other special federal legislation, the Court's approach in *Bonito* Boats in analyzing the implications of federal patent laws regarding state laws purporting to extend protections to useful types of intellectual works continues to be important. In general, the Court has indicated that patent laws govern not only the range of intellectual works that are potentially protected by federal patent rights, but, by negative implication, the types of works that can not be protected and that must be left freely available to the public by state law schemes. What features will make a work or category of works freely available to the public due to the negative implications of the patent statute, according to the Court's analysis in *Bonito Boats*? Is this controlled by the nature of the works or their handling or both?

3.   The Court's analyses in *Bonito Boats* describe public interests in free access to at least three types of useful intellectual works: 1) patentable inventions for which patents have issued and expired, 2) patentable inventions for which patents were either not sought or not sought properly resulting in an unenforceable patent, and 3) unpatentable works falling outside the patentable subject matter standards of the Patent Act. Are the justifications for protecting public access to these types of works the same for all three types? Why do the provisions of the Patent Act indicate that, in passing this federal statute, Congress intended to express a public policy in favor of free access to some or all of these types of works?

4.   What types of intellectual works can be protected by state laws after *Bonito Boats* and why? Does the Court hold that all types of useful inventions that can not qualify for patent protections under the federal Patent Act can not be protected under state laws such as the legislation in that case? If not, what was the specific feature of the useful designs at issue in *Bonito Boats* that caused their protection under state law to be preempted?

5. The Court mentions in *Bonito Boats* that its analysis and those in earlier Supreme Court cases would allow states to continue to enforce trade secret laws, even as to types of useful designs which could qualify for patent protection. How does this square with the view expressed in *Bonito Boats* that federal patent laws should determine the scope of rights afforded to intellectual works having practical utility? State trade secret laws can be used to protect types of intellectual works that are not useful devices, materials, or processes (for example, secret customer lists) and that therefore do not involve patentable subject matter. These laws can also be used to protect designs for useful devices or processes that would not qualify for patents because of their lack of novelty or their mere obvious variation from publicly known designs (for example, a secret design for a manufacturing technique that is a close counterpart to a publicly known design and an obvious, nonpatentable variation from that design). How do the protections that trade secret laws afford to items such as these avoid federal preemption?

II. MORAL RIGHTS

A. OVERVIEW OF STATE PROVISIONS

WAIVER OF MORAL RIGHTS IN VISUAL ARTWORKS

United States Copyright Office.
March 1, 1996.

State Law Models for Protecting Moral Rights

1. The European moral rights model

Originating in Europe, the concept and observance of moral rights, or "droit moral", addresses the personal, rather than the economic, relationship between an author and his or her work. The rights uphold the integrity of an author's personality and the integrity of his or her work by preventing separation of the creator's personality from his or her work of authorship; the indelible impression of the artist's intellectual creation remains part of the work, even though it is more intangible than the economic rights in that work. France was the first to embody moral rights within the copyright law; other western European and Latin American countries followed France's lead. Moral rights were later added to the Berne Convention in 1928.[29] Berne generally affords greater personal protection for more works of authorship than given by the United States under [the federal Visual Artists Rights Act of 1990 (VARA)].[30]

---

29. [The Berne Convention concerning the Creation of an International Union for the Protection of Literary and Artistic Works (Sept. 9, 1886, revised in 1908, 1928, 1948, 1967, 1971), 25 U.S.T. 1341 (hereinafter "Berne Convention")] at Art. 6bis. provides that:

Independently of the author's economic rights, and even after the transfer of the said rights, the author shall have the right to claim authorship of the work and to object to any distortion, mutilation or other modification of, or other derogatory action in relation to, the said work, which would be prejudicial to his honor or reputation.

30. The Berne Convention's moral rights protection encompasses: the right to claim authorship of a work, and the right to protect the integrity of the work, i.e., the right to object to any distortion, mutilation, or other modification of a work, or other action which would be prejudicial to the author's honor or reputation. *See* Berne Convention (Paris Act 1971), *supra* note [29]; *see*

Before adhering to Berne, the United States had relied, for international copyright protection, on its bilateral treaties and on the Universal Copyright Convention (UCC), a multilateral copyright treaty to which the United States adhered as a founding member on September 16, 1955. Neither the bilaterals nor the UCC required moral rights protection.

On March 1, 1989, the United States adhered to the 1971 Paris text of the Berne Convention. In its review of whether the United States should adhere to Berne, Congress considered whether or not additional provisions for moral rights had to be added to United States Copyright law in order to meet the obligations of Berne's Article 6bis. By requiring certain minimum rights, the Berne Convention promotes harmonization among the laws of member nations. The Convention allows countries to implement the provisions in their national laws. This framework allowed the Congress to determine that existing law satisfied the minimum standard for protection of moral rights required by Berne. Because Congress also provided that Berne is not self-executing in the United States, moral rights cannot be claimed here directly on the basis of the Berne text.

The Berne Convention Implementation Act (BCIA) reflected Congress' opinion that at the time the United States joined Berne, our domestic law was adequate to satisfy the minimum obligations of membership. Moral rights protection, Congress maintained, could be found in the Lanham Act[31] and common law or First Amendment principles such as libel, privacy, defamation, misrepresentation or unfair competition. This view had been articulated by the Ad Hoc Working Group of private sector and government attorneys formed specifically for the purpose of comparing United States law with Berne requirements. The Working Group published its findings in a final report. The report maintained that, although there are no explicit moral rights provisions in the 1976 Copyright Act, relevant federal statutory provisions including 17 U.S.C. §§ 106(2) (exclusive right to make derivative works), 101 (definition of "derivative work") and 115(a)(2) (mechanical license) afford protection of a type envisioned by Berne. In addition, the Working Group cited protection under section 43(a) of the Lanham Act and decisions made under that law, as well as state common law principles and state statutes protecting rights equivalent to the Berne Convention's Article 6bis. The Group concluded that:

> Although the United States does not have a statute that grants, *in haec verba*, the moral rights set forth in Article 6bis, there are substantial grounds for concluding that the totality of U.S. law provides protection for the rights of paternity and integrity sufficient to comply with 6bis, as it is applied by various Berne countries.

Regarding transferability and waiver of moral rights, the Group noted that in some countries authors' moral rights are alienable, although courts

---

also Sam Ricketson, The Berne Convention for the Protection of Literary and Artistic Works: 1886–1986 at 467–472 (1987).

31. *See* Lanham Act, § 43(a), 15 U.S.C. § 1125(a)(1946).

may interpret application of the rights in different ways, depending on the facts of each case. The Group also noted that a 1986 British White Paper on copyright revision stated that proposed legislation in the United Kingdom would provide that "an author will be able to waive his moral rights, and such waiver will override any inheritance or bequest." Hence, Article 6bis principles were not always followed to the letter by other Berne member countries. For example, Berne is silent on waiver, but its spirit would seem to be more honored without provision for waiver. In sum, by enacting VARA Congress responded to a perceived public interest in protecting works of art against mutilation and destruction, and in providing for proper attribution of authorship.

2. *Moral rights in state statutes*

Before the United States enacted VARA, several states passed legislation that specifically protected artists' rights. In addition, New Mexico enacted legislation in 1995 to protect art in public buildings. Three basic state law models exist: the preservation model, the moral rights model, and the public works model. The preservation model is used to protect artistic works from destruction, as well as to protect rights of attribution and integrity. The moral rights model provides the rights of attribution and integrity.[32] The public works category, which is more related to state police power than to copyright administration, seeks to protect works from vandalism. These laws safeguard state treasures, antiques. and other works of historic or other value as part of a normal exercise of keeping the peace. A summary of state statutes follows.

a. *Preservation Statutes*

(i) California. In 1979, California became the first state to enact moral rights legislation.[33] The California Art Preservation Act seeks to preserve works of fine art and to protect the personality of the artist. The preamble to the Act states that "the act serves the dual purpose of protecting the artist's reputation and of protecting the public interest in preserving the integrity of cultural and artistic creations." The Act prohibits the intentional "physical defacement, mutilation, alteration, or destruction of a work of fine art." Where the alleged mutilation is associated with an effort to conserve a work of fine art, evidence of gross negligence is required to support an action.

The artist also has a right of attribution, and "for just and valid reason," the right "to disclaim authorship of his or her work of fine art." The rights of attribution and integrity may be waived by written contract. Owners of buildings who wish to remove a work of fine art that can be removed without mutilation are subject to liability under the act unless they attempt to notify the artist of their intention and provide the artist

---

32. Destruction is not, strictly speaking, a violation of a moral right in states using that model, since where the work is destroyed, the moral right can be considered extinguished because nothing is left to which the right can attach.

33. Cal. Civ. Code § 987 (West Supp. 1995).

with an opportunity to remove the work. Where the work cannot be removed without mutilation or destruction, moral rights are deemed to be waived unless the artist has reserved them in writing.

(ii) Connecticut. The 1988 Connecticut law, another preservation statute, covers works of fine art including calligraphy, craft works, and photographs with a minimum market value of $2500 or more.[34] Works made for hire are excluded from the definition of works of fine art. Under this act, the artist may waive his or her rights in writing. As amended in 1988, the Connecticut act provides a life-of-the-author plus fifty year duration for moral rights. The provisions on removing art from buildings are similar to those in the California Act, except that in Connecticut, the artist's reservation of rights must be recorded in the states real property, records.

(iii) Massachusetts. The 1984 Massachusetts statute prohibits "the intentional commission of any physical defacement, mutilation, alteration, or destruction of a work of fine art."[35] The artist retains a right of attribution and the right to disclaim authorship "for just and valid reason." If a work of fine art cannot be removed from a building without substantial alteration, the prohibitions of the Act are suspended unless a written obligation signed by the owner of the building has been recorded. If the work is capable of being removed without mutilation, the prohibitions of the act apply unless the owner notifies the artist and provides the artist with an opportunity to remove it.

(iv) Pennsylvania. The 1986 Pennsylvania Fine Arts Preservation Act prohibits destruction of works of fine art and establishes moral rights for those works.[36] Similar to the California law, the Pennsylvania Act applies to works of recognized quality. In addition to providing special rules for removing works of art from buildings, the Pennsylvania law excuses from liability, for alteration or destruction, those owners who remove works of art in "emergency situations." Conservation activities that are not grossly negligent are also not actionable.

b. Artists' Moral Rights Statutes

(i) Louisiana. Louisiana's Artists' Authorship Rights Act of 1986 protects visual or graphic works of recognized quality in any medium reproduced in not more than 300 copies.[37] Motion pictures, however, are excluded, as are works prepared under contract for advertising and trade, unless the contract provides otherwise. The Act grants rights of attribution and integrity, but does not cover the destruction of works with the exception of art on buildings. Rights in such works are subject to a special reservation, similar to reservations found in several other states' statutes. Alterations that occur as a result of conservation efforts are not actionable

---

34. Conn. Gen. Stat. Ann. § 42–116s—42–116t (West 1995).

35. Mass. Gen. Laws Ann. ch. 231, § 855 (West Supp. 1995).

36. Pa. Stat. Ann. tit. §§ 2101–2110 (Prudon Supp. 1995).

37. La. Rev. Stat. Ann. §§ 51:2151–2156 (Purdon West 1995).

unless the alteration is the result of gross negligence. Louisiana's rights attach upon public display of the work.

(ii) <u>Maine</u>. In 1985, Maine enacted moral rights for artists of visual or graphic works without restriction as to the quality of the work.[38] Similar to the Louisiana act, the Maine act attaches the rights to public display within the state, and excuses conservation activities except for gross negligence. The artist can claim authorship or disclaim it "for just and valid reasons," which include modification likely to cause damage to the author's reputation. No special requirements are established for removing works of art from buildings.

(iii) <u>New Jersey</u>. The New Jersey Artists Right Act of 1986 provides protection similar to that of Maine.[39] It excludes motion pictures and makes no special provisions for removing art from buildings.

(iv) <u>New York</u>. In 1984, New York passed its New York Artists' Authorship Rights Act.[40] The Act prohibits the display of an "altered, defaced, mutilated, or modified form" of a work of fine art which damages the artist's reputation. The artist additionally has a right of attribution, and the right to disclaim authorship for good cause. Conservation does not constitute alteration. defacement, mutilation, or modification unless the conservation is done negligently.

(v) <u>Rhode Island</u>. In 1987, Rhode Island passed attribution and integrity rights legislation for works of fine art that are knowingly displayed, published or reproduced in a place accessible to the public.[41] If definition of works of fine art, identical to that of Maine, New York, and New Jersey, is not limited to works of recognized quality. "Alteration, defacement, mutilation or modification of a work of fine art resulting from the passage of time or the inherent nature of the materials," in the absence of gross negligence, is not a violation of the Act.

c. *Art in Public Buildings*

New Mexico's Art in Public Buildings Act is an example of extensive rights in a very limited area.[42] The Act protects against alteration and destruction and provides attribution rights for works displayed in public buildings, thereby limiting its scope to works that are publicly displayed by the state. The Act includes special provisions for works of art that are incorporated in buildings. If the artist is deceased, the state's attorney general is authorized to assert moral rights on behalf of the author.

Preemption Issues Raised by Vara

Congress intended section 301 of the Copyright Act's "Preemption with respect to other laws," to "preempt and abolish any rights under the

---

38. Me. Rev. Stat. Ann. tit. 27, § 303 (West 1995).

39. N.J. Stat. Ann. §§ 2A:24A–I—2A:24A–S (West 1995).

40. N.Y. Arts & Cult. Af. Law §§ 14.01 *et seq.* (McKinney 1995).

41. R.I. Gen. Laws §§ 5–62–2 to 5–62–6 (Michie 1994).

42. N.M. Stat. Ann. §§ 13–4B–2 to 13–4B–3 (Lexis, states library, NMCODE file 1995).

common law or statutes of a State that are equivalent to copyright and that extend to works coming within the scope of the Federal copyright law." Section 301 was amended by the Visual Artists Rights Act of 1990 by adding subsection (f).[43] Following other copyright preemption provisions, this section preempts post-VARA state law causes of action that are equivalent to rights under VARA in subject matter covered by the federal statute. One writer labeled VARA's preemption provision as "one battleground of the near future."

The Supreme Court has used the supremacy clause of the Constitution in case law analyses as authority for validating the preemption doctrine. The definition of "equivalent right" can be unclear when comparing state and federal statutes. When comparing moral rights codes, even larger problems may arise because no body of case law interpreting VARA currently exists. The House Report on VARA states that:

> Consistent with current law on preemption for economic rights, the new Federal law will not preempt State causes of action relating to works that are not covered by the law. Similarly, State artists' rights laws that grant rights not equivalent to those accorded under the proposed law are not preempted, even when they relate to works covered by [VARA].

Courts decide on a case-by-case basis whether or not rights protected by state or other laws are preempted by equivalent federal rights. The method often used to analyze preemption issues relating to copyright is to break down the state right into elements, and then to compare those elements with rights granting by the Copyright Act. If extra elements are found in the state right that are not found in the federal law, the state right is not preempted.

Previously, preemption of states' rights by federal copyright law concerned only equivalent legal or equitable rights within the subject matter of copyright, and these rights were economic. Preemption under VARA will focus both on whether moral rights and subject matter are equivalent. Thus, to prevail on a VARA preemption argument, one will need to prove "prejudice to honor or reputation," in addition to equivalent

---

43. 17 U.S.C. § 301(f) reads as follows:

(f)(1) On or after the effective date set forth in section 610(a) of the Visual Artists Rights Act of 1990, all legal or equitable rights that are equivalent to any of the rights conferred by section 106A with respect to works of visual art to which the rights conferred by section 106A apply are governed exclusively by section 106A and 113(d) and the provisions of this title relating to such sections. Thereafter, no person is entitled to any such right or equivalent right in any work of visual art under the common law or statutes of any State.

(2) Nothing in paragraph (1) annuls or limits any rights or remedies under the common law or statutes of any State with respect to—

(A) any cause of action from undertakings commenced before the effective date set forth in section 610(a) of the Visual Artists Rights Act of 1990:

(B) activities violating legal or equitable rights that are not equivalent to any of the rights conferred by section 106A with respect to works of visual art: or

(C) activities violating legal or equitable rights which extend beyond the life of the author.

subject matter. The extent to which state statutes will be preempted awaits case law development.

It is expected that a number of state laws will continue to have effect either because they protect additional elements or VARA was not in effect at the time the cause of action arose.

* * *

NOTES

1. The federal Visual Artists Rights Act (VARA) provides parties who create works of visual art with certain moral rights. One court summarized the protections afforded by VARA as follows:

> Its principal provisions afford protection only to authors of works of visual art—a narrow class of art defined to include paintings, drawings, prints, sculptures, or photographs produced for exhibition purposes, existing in a single copy or limited edition of 200 copies or fewer. 17 U.S.C. § 101 (Supp. III 1991). With numerous exceptions, VARA grants three rights: the right of attribution, the right of integrity and, in the case of works of visual art of "recognized stature," the right to prevent destruction. 17 U.S.C. § 106A (Supp. III 1991). For works created on or after June 1, 1991—the effective date of the Act—the rights provided for endure for the life of the author or, in the case of a joint work, the life of the last surviving author. The rights cannot be transferred, but may be waived by a writing signed by the author. Copyright registration is not required to bring an action for infringement of the rights granted under VARA, or to secure statutory damages and attorney's fees. 17 U.S.C. §§ 411, 412 (1988 & Supp. III 1991). All remedies available under copyright law, other than criminal remedies, are available in an action for infringement of moral rights. 17 U.S.C. § 506 (1988 & Supp. III 1991).

Carter v. Helmsley–Spear, Inc., 71 F.3d 77, 83 (2d Cir. 1995), *cert. denied*, 517 U.S. 1208, 116 S.Ct. 1824, 134 L.Ed.2d 930 (1996).

2. At least one lower court has concluded that New York's Artists' Authorship Rights Act creates moral rights of "attribution" and "integrity" that are the equivalent of rights arising under the federal Visual Artists Rights Act (VARA) and that the portions of the New York Act establishing these sorts of moral rights are hence preempted by this federal legislation. *See Board of Managers of Soho International Arts Condominium v. City of New York*, 2003 WL 21403333 at *11 to *15 (S.D.N.Y. 2003). However, the Visual Artists Rights Act establishes moral rights protections that are distinguishable in several respects from the rights arising under state moral rights legislation like the California statutes described in the next subsection of this text. These distinctions will be important in determining the types of state rights that survive preemption under VARA. In the view of one commentator:

> Since the 1990 [Visual Artists Rights] Act explicitly does not preempt state laws creating rights that are not the "equivalent" of rights under the 1990 Act, the interpretation of this language is highly significant. The language of the preemption provision, as well as its legislative history,

make it clear that state statutes affecting works which fall outside the definition of a "work of visual art" are not preempted by the 1990 Act. The legislative history also states that Congress did not intend to preempt state laws providing moral rights in areas specifically exempted from protection by the 1990 Act, such as misattribution of authorship of a reproduction of a work of visual art. Similarly, the legislative history states that Congress did not intend to preempt state laws granting substantive rights unrelated to the rights granted by the 1990 Act, even if those rights affect works covered within the federal definition of "works of visual art."

* * *

On the other hand, when Congress provided that state laws granting rights "equivalent" to the rights created by the 1990 Act are preempted, Congress apparently intended to preempt all state statutes granting rights of attribution, disavowal, and integrity to artists with respect to works of visual art covered by the 1990 Act, even if the state law protections are not identical to the federal protections.

Joseph Zuber, *The Visual Artists Rights Act of 1990—What it Does, and What it Preempts*, 23 PAC. L.J. 445, 473–92 (1992).

VARA does not preempt state laws creating moral rights in works other than the "works of visual art" covered by the Act. For purposes of determining the coverage and preemptive impacts of VARA, the following definitions apply:

A "work of visual art" is—

(1) a painting, drawing, print, or sculpture, existing in a single copy, in a limited edition of 200 copies or fewer that are signed and consecutively numbered by the author, or, in the case of a sculpture, in multiple cast, carved, or fabricated sculptures of 200 or fewer that are consecutively numbered by the author and bear the signature or other identifying mark of the author; or

(2) a still photographic image produced for exhibition purposes only, existing in a single copy that is signed by the author, or in a limited edition of 200 copies or fewer that are signed and consecutively numbered by the author.

A work of visual art does not include—

(A)(i) any poster, map, globe, chart, technical drawing, diagram, model, applied art, motion picture or other audiovisual work, book, magazine, newspaper, periodical, data base, electronic information service, electronic publication, or similar publication;

(ii) any merchandising item or advertising, promotional, descriptive, covering, or packaging material or container;

(iii) any portion or part of any item described in clause (i) or (ii);

(B) any work made for hire; or

(C) any work not subject to copyright protection under this title.

17 U.S.C. § 101. State laws creating moral rights regarding types of works falling outside this definition are not affected by the passage of VERA.

For works within this definition, state laws are still not preempted by VERA if they create rights that are not equivalent to those established by VERA. The types of rights that will be deemed equivalent to the rights established by VERA are still uncertain. Controversies over the equivalency of rights created by federal and state laws governing works of visual art seem likely to continue for some time, leaving the enforceability of state moral rights laws regarding such works in doubt. See Zuber, *supra,* at 502–04.

B. CALIFORNIA ART PRESERVATION ACT

The following provisions from the California Art Preservation Act provide good examples of the statutory standards that some states have used to protect the moral and economic interests of artists. State laws focusing on artists' rights provide distinctive protections for artists regarding moral rights in their works and further economic interests in the resale of their works, but these special protections are often severely limited. State measures like the California statute below typically have three features that limit the scope of their impact. First, they tend to create highly specialized types of rights in artists that are different from the rights provided to artists under federal copyright laws, thereby avoiding preemption of the state measures under the statutory preemption standards of the federal Copyright Act. Second, the state statutes typically apply only to narrowly defined types of works and artists. Third, the conduct that will violate the statutes is frequently defined in very narrow ways. In many states, conduct adversely affecting artists' works must be undertaken in bad faith or with gross negligence in order to violate artist protection statutes and give rights of action to the affected artists.

The two statutory sections reproduced below address very different aspects of artists' rights. The first section provides a *droit de suite* or resale royalty right, entitling an artist to a percentage of the price received when her works are resold by their owners. This type of right gives an artist an interest in the resale prices realized for early works that are initially sold for low prices, thereby ensuring that, as higher resale prices are produced over time when an artist becomes increasingly popular, some of the resulting benefit accrues to the artist. See John L. Solow, *An Economic Analysis of the Droit de Suite*, http://www.biz.uiowa.edu/econ/ papers/uia/ARTLAW3.PDF. The second section addresses moral rights, protecting artists against certain types of physical alteration or destruction of fine art works.

CALIFORNIA CIVIL CODE

§ 986. Work of fine art; sale; payment of percentage to artist or deposit for Arts Council; failure to pay; action for damages; exemptions

(a) Whenever a work of fine art is sold and the seller resides in California or the sale takes place in California, the seller or the seller's agent shall pay to the artist of such work of fine art or to such artist's agent 5 percent of the amount of such sale. The right of the artist to receive an amount equal to 5 percent of the amount of such sale may be waived only by a contract in writing providing for an amount in excess of 5 percent of the amount of such sale. An artist may assign the right to collect the royalty payment provided by this section to another individual or entity. However, the assignment shall not have the effect of creating a waiver prohibited by this subdivision.

(1) When a work of fine art is sold at an auction or by a gallery, dealer, broker, museum, or other person acting as the agent for the seller the agent shall withhold 5 percent of the amount of the sale, locate the artist and pay the artist.

(2) If the seller or agent is unable to locate and pay the artist within 90 days, an amount equal to 5 percent of the amount of the sale shall be transferred to the Arts Council.

(3) If a seller or the seller's agent fails to pay an artist the amount equal to 5 percent of the sale of a work of fine art by the artist or fails to transfer such amount to the Arts Council, the artist may bring an action for damages within three years after the date of sale or one year after the discovery of the sale, whichever is longer. The prevailing party in any action brought under this paragraph shall be entitled to reasonable attorney fees, in an amount as determined by the court.

(4) Moneys received by the council pursuant to this section shall be deposited in an account in the Special Deposit Fund in the State Treasury.

(5) The Arts Council shall attempt to locate any artist for whom money is received pursuant to this section. If the council is unable to locate the artist and the artist does not file a written claim for the money received by the council within seven years of the date of sale of the work of fine art, the right of the artist terminates and such money shall be transferred to the council for use in acquiring fine art pursuant to the Art in Public Buildings program set forth in Chapter 2.1 (commencing with Section 15813) of Part 10b of Division 3 of Title 2, of the Government Code.

(6) Any amounts of money held by any seller or agent for the payment of artists pursuant to this section shall be exempt from enforcement of a money judgment by the creditors of the seller or agent.

(7) Upon the death of an artist, the rights and duties created under this section shall inure to his or her heirs, legatees, or personal representative, until the 20th anniversary of the death of the artist. The provisions of this paragraph shall be applicable only with respect to an artist who dies after January 1, 1983.

(b) Subdivision (a) shall not apply to any of the following:

(1) To the initial sale of a work of fine art where legal title to such work at the time of such initial sale is vested in the artist thereof.

(2) To the resale of a work of fine art for a gross sales price of less than one thousand dollars ($1,000).

(3) Except as provided in paragraph (7) of subdivision (a), to a resale after the death of such artist.

(4) To the resale of the work of fine art for a gross sales price less than the purchase price paid by the seller.

(5) To a transfer of a work of fine art which is exchanged for one or more works of fine art or for a combination of cash, other property, and one or more works of fine art where the fair market value of the property exchanged is less than one thousand dollars ($1,000).

(6) To the resale of a work of fine art by an art dealer to a purchaser within 10 years of the initial sale of the work of fine art by the artist to an art dealer, provided all intervening resales are between art dealers.

(7) To a sale of a work of stained glass artistry where the work has been permanently attached to real property and is sold as part of the sale of the real property to which it is attached.

(c) For purposes of this section, the following terms have the following meanings:

(1) "Artist" means the person who creates a work of fine art and who, at the time of resale, is a citizen of the United States, or a resident of the state who has resided in the state for a minimum of two years.

(2) "Fine art" means an original painting, sculpture, or drawing, or an original work of art in glass.

(3) "Art dealer" means a person who is actively and principally engaged in or conducting the business of selling works of fine art for which business such person validly holds a sales tax permit.

* * *

§ 987. Preservation of works of art

(a) [Legislative findings and declarations] The Legislature hereby finds and declares that the physical alteration or destruction of fine art, which is an expression of the artist's personality, is detrimental to the artist's reputation, and artists therefore have an interest in protecting their works of fine art against any alteration or destruction; and that there is also a public interest in preserving the integrity of cultural and artistic creations.

(b) [Definitions] As used in this section:

(1) "Artist" means the individual or individuals who create a work of fine art.

(2) "Fine art" means an original painting, sculpture, or drawing, or an original work of art in glass, of recognized quality, but shall not include work prepared under contract for commercial use by its purchaser.

(3) "Person" means an individual, partnership, corporation, limited liability company, association or other group, however organized.

(4) "Frame" means to prepare, or cause to be prepared, a work of fine art for display in a manner customarily considered to be appropriate for a work of fine art in the particular medium.

(5) "Restore" means to return, or cause to be returned, a deteriorated or damaged work of fine art as nearly as is feasible to its original state or condition, in accordance with prevailing standards.

(6) "Conserve" means to preserve, or cause to be preserved, a work of fine art by retarding or preventing deterioration or damage through appropriate treatment in accordance with prevailing standards in order to maintain the structural integrity to the fullest extent possible in an unchanging state.

(7) "Commercial use" means fine art created under a work-for-hire arrangement for use in advertising, magazines, newspapers, or other print and electronic media.

(c) [Mutilation, alteration, or destruction of work]

(1) No person, except an artist who owns and possesses a work of fine art which the artist has created, shall intentionally commit, or authorize the intentional commission of, any physical defacement, mutilation, alteration, or destruction of a work of fine art.

(2) In addition to the prohibitions contained in paragraph (1), no person who frames, conserves, or restores a work of fine art shall commit, or authorize the commission of, any physical defacement, mutilation, alteration, or destruction of a work of fine art by any act constituting gross negligence. For purposes of this section, the term "gross negligence" shall mean the exercise of so slight a degree of care as to justify the belief that there was an indifference to the particular work of fine art.

(d) [Authorship] The artist shall retain at all times the right to claim authorship, or, for a just and valid reason, to disclaim authorship of his or her work of fine art.

(e) [Remedies] To effectuate the rights created by this section, the artist may commence an action to recover or obtain any of the following:

(1) Injunctive relief.

(2) Actual damages.

(3) Punitive damages. In the event that punitive damages are awarded, the court shall, in its discretion, select an organization or organizations engaged in charitable or educational activities involving the fine arts in California to receive any punitive damages.

(4) Reasonable attorneys' and expert witness fees.

(5) Any other relief which the court deems proper.

(f) [Determination of recognized quality] In determining whether a work of fine art is of recognized quality, the trier of fact shall rely on the opinions of artists, art dealers, collectors of fine art, curators of art museums, and other persons involved with the creation or marketing of fine art.

(g) [Rights and duties] The rights and duties created under this section:

(1) Shall, with respect to the artist, or if any artist is deceased, his or her heir, beneficiary, devisee, or personal representative, exist until the 50th anniversary of the death of the artist.

(2) Shall exist in addition to any other rights and duties which may now or in the future be applicable.

(3) Except as provided in paragraph (1) of subdivision (h), may not be waived except by an instrument in writing expressly so providing which is signed by the artist.

(h) [Removal from building; waiver]

(1) If a work of fine art cannot be removed from a building without substantial physical defacement, mutilation, alteration, or destruction of the work, the rights and duties created under this section, unless expressly reserved by an instrument in writing signed by the owner of the building, containing a legal description of the property and properly recorded, shall be deemed waived. The instrument, if properly recorded, shall be binding on subsequent owners of the building.

(2) If the owner of a building wishes to remove a work of fine art which is a part of the building but which can be removed from the building without substantial harm to the fine art, and in the course of or after removal, the owner intends to cause or allow the fine art to suffer physical defacement, mutilation, alteration, or destruction, the rights and duties created under this section shall apply unless the owner has diligently attempted without success to notify the artist, or, if the artist is deceased, his or her heir, beneficiary, devisee, or personal representative, in writing of his or her intended action affecting the work of fine art, or unless he or she did provide notice and that person failed within 90 days either to remove the work or to pay for its removal. If the work is

removed at the expense of the artist, his or her heir, beneficiary, devisee, or personal representative, title to the fine art shall pass to that person.

(3) If a work of fine art can be removed from a building scheduled for demolition without substantial physical defacement, mutilation, alteration, or destruction of the work, and the owner of the building has notified the owner of the work of fine art of the scheduled demolition or the owner of the building is the owner of the work of fine art, and the owner of the work of fine art elects not to remove the work of fine art, the rights and duties created under this section shall apply, unless the owner of the building has diligently attempted without success to notify the artist, or, if the artist is deceased, his or her heir, beneficiary, devisee, or personal representative, in writing of the intended action affecting the work of fine art, or unless he or she did provide notice and that person failed within 90 days either to remove the work or to pay for its removal. If the work is removed at the expense of the artist, his or her heir, beneficiary, devisee, or personal representative, title to the fine art shall pass to that person.

(4) Nothing in this subdivision shall affect the rights of authorship created in subdivision (d) of this section.

(i) [Limitation of actions] No action may be maintained to enforce any liability under this section unless brought within three years of the act complained of or one year after discovery of the act, whichever is longer.

(j) [Operative date] This section shall become operative on January 1, 1980, and shall apply to claims based on proscribed acts occurring on or after that date to works of fine art whenever created.

(k) [Severability of provisions] If any provision of this section or the application thereof to any person or circumstance is held invalid for any reason, the invalidity shall not affect any other provisions or applications of this section which can be effected without the invalid provision or application, and to this end the provisions of this section are severable.

NOTES

1. While galleries and other parties selling fine art works in California may be aware of the provisions of the first statutory section reproduced above and comply with its provisions calling for payments to artists, what sorts of administrative (and perhaps jurisdictional) difficulties are raised by the provisions of this statute requiring payments to artists regarding out of state sales by sellers residing in California? Will sellers be likely to be aware of this requirement and comply with it in connection with sales conducted outside of the state? If not, will out of state galleries or other parties participating in sales be aware of this payment obligation concerning a work being sold by a party who is a California resident?

2. Does it make sense to provide for a 5 percent payment to an artist for every sale? Should the amount of the required payment be based on the full amount of a sale (as is the case in the California statute reproduced here) or based on the profit being made by the seller? If the obligation to make a 5 percent payment makes particular transfers unprofitable or economically unattractive to sellers, have the economic interests of artists been well served? For example, suppose that an artist sells a painting to an initial owner for $1,000. Ten years later, the painting sells for $10,000, then a year later sells for $15,000 and a year after that sells for $16,000. The first sale is exempt from the 5 percent payment obligation under the statute (presumably because the artist has obtained the full purchase price as the seller). The second, third, and fourth sales would appear to trigger obligations to pay the artist $500, $750, and $800 respectively. However, this last payment is over half of the profit from the sale that would otherwise be made by the party conducting the last sale, calculating this profit as $16,000 minus $15,000 or $1,000. Will this type of profit splitting discourage certain types of fine art sales? Will it cut down on the number of such sales? Will it encourage fine art owners to hold on to works longer to allow them to appreciate more between sales and cut down on the number of payments that will need to be made to artists?

3. While the preceding California provisions creating moral rights in artists contain extensive definitional provisions, the statute fails to describe the types of acts that will entail the "mutilation, alteration, or destruction" of a work. How should these terms be defined? While the destruction of a work probably requires changes that terminate the existence of the work entirely, a mutilation or alteration clearly can occur through less substantial changes. Does a party alter a work if it is displayed in highly unflattering florescent lighting that distorts the colors of the work? Would a party alter or mutilate a work if he sprayed the work with an over coating that had some color content and that caused the colors in the work to be altered in the same way that displaying the work under florescent lighting caused? What if the effort to spray the work was part of a good faith effort to conserve the work? Would it matter that the color shift resulting from the spraying was unexpected and that the expected result was a sealing of the work to protect it from subsequent decay? What if the party engaging in the spraying of the over coating was a private owner of the work having no special background in art conservation?

4. Suppose that a party displays a work of fine art in a highly polluted city with knowledge that, over time, the pollution will attack the work and substantially alter its appearance. Is the mere act of displaying the work under these circumstances an instance of alteration or mutilation?

III. RIGHTS OF PUBLICITY

Rights of publicity provide individuals with control over the use of their names and likenesses for commercial purposes. These rights are defined by statute in many states—most notably California—but courts have also recognized many common law rights in this field in recent years. In general, common law and statutory rights of publicity protect the commercial value of a person's identity. Claims for violations of rights of publicity arise when a party appropriates the commercial value of a person's identity, for example by using the person's name, likeness, or other indicia of identity for commercial purposes without the person's consent. *See* Restatement (Third) of Unfair Competition § 46 (1995).

There is some dispute among courts over whether rights of publicity protect all parties or just famous public figures, such as well-known actors, athletes and musicians. *See generally* Roger E. Schechter & John R. Thomas, Intellectual Property: The Law of Copyrights, Patents and Trademarks 268 (2003). However, most courts and the Restatement (Third) of Unfair Competition accept the view that rights of publicity extend to all parties, with the fame of the protected individual only affecting the scope of damages when improper commercial use is made of the personal identity of an individual. *See* Restatement (Third) of Unfair Competition § 46 (1995) (comment d).

A number of rationales support the recognition of rights of publicity. Protections afforded to rights of publicity aid in protecting an individual's interest in personal dignity and autonomy. Enforcement of rights of publicity can help well known individuals in protecting the commercial value of their fame and in preventing the unjust enrichment of others who might otherwise appropriate that value for themselves. Control over the extent of commercial exploitation of a person's identity can be maintained through enforcement of rights of publicity, thereby preventing overuse that might dilute the value of the identity. Rights of publicity can also protect against use of a person's identity in a manner that would raise false suggestions of endorsement or sponsorship of a product or activity. Finally, financial rewards associated with enforcement of rights of publicity can encourage parties to undertake the types of efforts needed to build up and maintain famous identities. *See generally* Restatement (Third) of Unfair Competition § 46 (1995) (comment c).

However, there are also several policy concerns that suggest rights of publicity should be strictly limited if recognized at all. The commercial value of a person's identity often is the result of entertainment or sports activities that entail substantial compensation of themselves, making further incentives created through the recognition of rights of publicity superfluous. Sometimes, commercial value associated with a person's identity arises by chance and minimal actions rather than through diligent efforts, undercutting any need for rights of publicity as a means to achieve just compensation when the individual's identity is used to the commercial advantage of another. Protections against false statements or implications of endorsements can be achieved through other means than enforcement of rights of publicity. Most importantly, recognition of broadly applicable rights of publicity can restrict or raise uncertainty about the legitimacy of valuable types of subsequent intellectual works involving the use of features of a party's identity.

Controversies over the proper scope of rights of publicity have been numerous in recent years. As summarized by two leading observers:

> For years, courts have struggled to make sense of two dimensions of [the right of publicity]—what it means to use a name or likeness "commercially," and what aspects of a person's "likeness" are protected against appropriation. In the absence of any clear theoretical foundation for the right of publicity, the meanings of these terms have steadily swelled, to the point at which virtually any reference to an individual that brings financial benefit to someone else qualifies as a violation of the right of publicity. At the same time, the courts have developed no meaningful counterweight to this ever-expanding right. Instead, they have created a few ad hoc exceptions in cases where the sweeping logic of the right of publicity seems to lead to results they consider unfair.
>
> Two types of publicity claims have raised particular problems for the courts. The first involves "merchandising" claims, in which individuals claim violation of their publicity right not by the use of a name in advertising, but by the sale of products that bear their names or likenesses. Courts have generally resolved these claims by making a distinction between "news" or "speech," on the one hand, and "merchandise," on the other. But as art and information become increasingly commodified, this distinction—if it ever made sense—has become ever harder to sustain. The second type of problematic claim involves cases in which a use draws attention away from the celebrity or arguably sullies the celebrity's reputation in some way that harms the overall value of her identity. Properly limited, such a cause of action might have some theoretical appeal, but courts have applied it in ways that exceed any plausible theoretical justification, particularly when First Amendment considerations enter the fray.

Stacey L. Dogan & Mark A. Lemley, *What the Right of Publicity Can Learn from Trademark Law*, 58 STAN. L. REV. 1161, 1162 (2006).

The following cases explore these types of problematic claims and several others. Four principle aspects of rights of publicity are addressed in these cases: 1) the range of conduct of famous parties in performances or otherwise that can lead to protectable rights, 2) the features of an artist, such as a distinctive vocal quality, that can form the basis for protections independent of any particular performance, 3) the scope of rights of famous parties to control uses of their names or likenesses, and 4) the countervailing public interests—such as the promotion of free news reporting—that may specially limit rights of publicity and reduce the control of famous parties over uses of their names and likenesses.

In considering how the courts in the following cases have addressed these features of rights of publicity, focus on whether the courts have implemented standards emphasizing property rights (placing primary control over the subsequent use of a name or likeness in the hands of the relevant celebrity) or regulatory concerns (recognizing a public interest in certain types of uses of names and likenesses and restricting the control of a celebrity accordingly).

CARSON v. HERE'S JOHNNY PORTABLE TOILETS, INC.

United States Court of Appeals for the Sixth Circuit, 1983.
698 F.2d 831.

Bailey Brown, Senior Circuit Judge.

This case involves claims of unfair competition and invasion of the right of privacy and the right of publicity arising from appellee's adoption of a phrase generally associated with a popular entertainer.

Appellant, John W. Carson (Carson), is the host and star of "The Tonight Show," a well known television program broadcast five nights a week by the National Broadcasting Company. Carson also appears as an entertainer in night clubs and theaters around the country. From the time he began hosting "The Tonight Show" in 1962, he has been introduced on the show each night with the phrase "Here's Johnny." This method of introduction was first used for Carson in 1957 when he hosted a daily television program for the American Broadcasting Company. The phrase "Here's Johnny" is generally associated with Carson by a substantial segment of the television viewing public. In 1967, Carson first authorized use of this phrase by an outside business venture, permitting it to be used by a chain of restaurants called "Here's Johnny Restaurants."

Appellant Johnny Carson Apparel, Inc. (Apparel), formed in 1970, manufactures and markets men's clothing to retail stores. Carson, the president of Apparel and owner of 20% of its stock, has licensed Apparel to use his name and picture, which appear on virtually all of Apparel's products and promotional material. Apparel has also used, with Carson's consent, the phrase "Here's Johnny" on labels for clothing and in advertising campaigns. In 1977, Apparel granted a license to Marcy Laboratories to use "Here's Johnny" as the name of a line of men's toiletries. The phrase "Here's Johnny" has never been registered by appellants as a trademark or service mark.

Appellee, Here's Johnny Portable Toilets, Inc., is a Michigan corporation engaged in the business of renting and selling "Here's Johnny" portable toilets. Appellee's founder was aware at the time he formed the corporation that "Here's Johnny" was the introductory slogan for Carson on "The Tonight Show." He indicated that he coupled the phrase with a second one, "The World's Foremost Commodian," to make "a good play on a phrase."

Shortly after appellee went into business in 1976, appellants brought this action alleging unfair competition, trademark infringement under federal and state law, and invasion of privacy and publicity rights. They sought damages and an injunction prohibiting appellee's further use of the phrase "Here's Johnny" as a corporate name or in connection with the sale or rental of its portable toilets.

After a bench trial, the district court issued a memorandum opinion and order, which served as its findings of fact and conclusions of law. The court ordered the dismissal of the appellants' complaint. On the unfair competition claim, the court concluded that the appellants had failed to satisfy the "likelihood of confusion" test. On the right of privacy and right of publicity theories, the court held that these rights extend only to a "name or likeness," and "Here's Johnny" did not qualify.

* * *

II.

The appellants * * * claim that the appellee's use of the phrase "Here's Johnny" violates the common law right of privacy and right of publicity.[51] The confusion in this area of the law requires a brief analysis of the relationship between these two rights.

In an influential article, Dean Prosser delineated four distinct types of the right of privacy: (1) intrusion upon one's seclusion or solitude, (2) public disclosure of embarrassing private facts, (3) publicity which places one in a false light, and (4) appropriation of one's name or likeness for the defendant's advantage. Prosser, *Privacy*, 48 Calif. L.Rev. 383, 389 (1960). This fourth type has become known as the "right of publicity." Henceforth we will refer to Prosser's last, or fourth, category, as the "right of publicity."

Dean Prosser's analysis has been a source of some confusion in the law. His first three types of the right of privacy generally protect the right "to be let alone," while the right of publicity protects the celebrity's pecuniary interest in the commercial exploitation of his identity. Thus, the right of privacy and the right of publicity protect fundamentally different interests and must be analyzed separately.

We do not believe that Carson's claim that his right of privacy has been invaded is supported by the law or the facts. Apparently, the gist of this claim is that Carson is embarrassed by and considers it odious to be associated with the appellee's product. Clearly, the association does not appeal to Carson's sense of humor. But the facts here presented do not, it appears to us, amount to an invasion of any of the interests protected by the right of privacy. In any event, our disposition of the claim of an invasion of the right of publicity makes it unnecessary for us to accept or reject the claim of an invasion of the right of privacy.

The right of publicity has developed to protect the commercial interest of celebrities in their identities. The theory of the right is that a

---

51. Michigan law, which governs these claims, has not yet clearly addressed the right of publicity. But the general recognition of the right, see W. Prosser, HANDBOOK OF THE LAW OF TORTS § 117, at 805 (4th ed. 1971), suggests to us that the Michigan courts would adopt the right. Michigan has recognized a right of privacy. Beaumont v. Brown, 401 Mich. 80, 257 N.W.2d 522 (1977).

celebrity's identity can be valuable in the promotion of products, and the celebrity has an interest that may be protected from the unauthorized commercial exploitation of that identity. In *Memphis Development Foundation v. Factors Etc., Inc.*, 616 F.2d 956 (6th Cir.), *cert. denied*, 449 U.S. 953, 101 S.Ct. 358, 66 L.Ed.2d 217 (1980), we stated: "The famous have an exclusive legal right during life to control and profit from the commercial use of their name and personality." *Id.* at 957.

The district court dismissed appellants' claim based on the right of publicity because appellee does not use Carson's name or likeness. It held that it "would not be prudent to allow recovery for a right of publicity claim which does not more specifically identify Johnny Carson." We believe that, on the contrary, the district court's conception of the right of publicity is too narrow. The right of publicity, as we have stated, is that a celebrity has a protected pecuniary interest in the commercial exploitation of his identity. If the celebrity's identity is commercially exploited, there has been an invasion of his right whether or not his "name or likeness" is used. Carson's identity may be exploited even if his name, John W. Carson, or his picture is not used.

In *Motschenbacher v. R.J. Reynolds Tobacco Co.*, 498 F.2d 821 (9th Cir.1974), the court held that the unauthorized use of a picture of a distinctive race car of a well known professional race car driver, whose name or likeness were not used, violated his right of publicity. In this connection, the court said:

> We turn now to the question of "identifiability." Clearly, if the district court correctly determined as a matter of law that plaintiff is not identifiable in the commercial, then in no sense has plaintiff's identity been misappropriated nor his interest violated.

> Having viewed a film of the commercial, we agree with the district court that the "likeness" of plaintiff is itself unrecognizable; however, the court's further conclusion of law to the effect that the driver is not identifiable as plaintiff is erroneous in that it wholly fails to attribute proper significance to the distinctive decorations appearing on the car. As pointed out earlier, these markings were not only peculiar to the plaintiff's cars but they caused some persons to think the car in question was plaintiff's and to infer that the person driving the car was the plaintiff.

Id. at 826 827 (footnote omitted).

In *Ali v. Playgirl, Inc.*, 447 F.Supp. 723 (S.D.N.Y. 1978), Muhammad Ali, former heavyweight champion, sued Playgirl magazine under the New York "right of privacy" statute and also alleged a violation of his common law right of publicity. The magazine published a drawing of a nude, black male sitting on a stool in a corner of a boxing ring with hands taped and arms outstretched on the ropes. The district court concluded that Ali's right of publicity was invaded because the drawing sufficiently identified him in spite of the fact that the drawing was captioned "Mystery Man." The district court found that the identification of Ali was made certain because of an accompanying verse that identified the figure as "The Greatest." The district court took judicial notice of the fact that "Ali has regularly claimed that appellation for himself."

In *Hirsch v. S.C. Johnson & Son, Inc.*, 90 Wis.2d 379, 280 N.W.2d 129 (1979), the court held that use by defendant of the name "Crazylegs" on a shaving gel for women violated plaintiff's right of publicity. Plaintiff, Elroy Hirsch, a famous football player, had been known by this nickname. The court said:

> The fact that the name, "Crazylegs," used by Johnson, was a nickname rather than Hirsch's actual name does not preclude a cause of action. All that is required is that the name clearly identify the wronged person. In the instant case, it is not disputed at this juncture of the case that the nickname identified the plaintiff Hirsch. It is argued that there were others who were known by the same name. This, however, does not vitiate the existence of a cause of action. It may, however, if sufficient proof were adduced, affect the quantum of damages should the jury impose liability or it might preclude liability altogether. Prosser points out "that a stage or other fictitious name can be so identified with the plaintiff that he is entitled to protection against its use." 49 Cal.L.Rev., supra at 404. He writes that it would be absurd to say that Samuel L. Clemens would have a cause of action if that name had been used in advertising, but he would not have one for the use of "Mark Twain." If a fictitious name is used in a context which tends to indicate that the name is that of the plaintiff, the factual case for identity is strengthened. Prosser, supra at 403.

280 N.W.2d at 137.

In this case, Earl Braxton, president and owner of Here's Johnny Portable Toilets, Inc., admitted that he knew that the phrase "Here's Johnny" had been used for years to introduce Carson. Moreover, in the opening statement in the district court, appellee's counsel stated:

> Now, we've stipulated in this case that the public tends to associate the words "Johnny Carson", the words "Here's Johnny" with plaintiff, John Carson and, Mr. Braxton, in his deposition, admitted that he knew that and probably absent that identification, he would not have chosen it.

That the "Here's Johnny" name was selected by Braxton because of its identification with Carson was the clear inference from Braxton's testimony irrespective of such admission in the opening statement.

We therefore conclude that, applying the correct legal standards, appellants are entitled to judgment. The proof showed without question that appellee had appropriated Carson's identity in connection with its corporate name and its product.

Although this opinion holds only that Carson's right of publicity was invaded because appellee intentionally appropriated his identity for commercial exploitation, the dissent, relying on its interpretation of the authorities and relying on policy and constitutional arguments, would hold that there was no invasion here. We do not believe that the dissent can withstand fair analysis.

The dissent contends that the authorities hold that the right of publicity is invaded only if there has been an appropriation of the celebrity's "name, likeness, achievements, identifying characteristics or actual performances." After so conceding that the right is at least this broad, the dissent then attempts to show that the authorities upon which the majority opinion relies are explainable as involving an appropriation of one or more of these attributes. The dissent explains *Motschenbacher, supra,* where the advertisement used a photograph, slightly altered, of the plaintiff's racing car, as an "identifying characteristic" case. But the dissent fails to explain why the photograph any more identified Motschenbacher than the phrase "Here's Johnny" identifies appellant Carson. The dissent explains *Hirsch, supra,* by pointing out that there the use of the appellation "Crazylegs" by the defendant was in a "context" that suggested a reference to Hirsch and that therefore Hirsch was identified by such use. Here, the dissent states, there is no evidence of the use of "Here's Johnny" in such a suggestive "context." Putting aside the fact that appellee also used the phrase "The World's Foremost Commodian," we fail to see why "context" evidence is necessary where appellee's president admitted that it adopted the name "Here's Johnny" because it identified appellant Carson. We do not understand appellee to even contend that it did not successfully accomplish its intended purpose of appropriating his identity. The dissent explains *Ali, supra,* by pointing out that in that case the magazine used a drawing that "strongly suggests" it to be a representation of the famous fighter, but it is also true that the court put emphasis on the fact that the subject of the drawing was referred to as "The Greatest," which "further implied" that the individual was Ali.

It should be obvious from the majority opinion and the dissent that a celebrity's identity may be appropriated in various ways. It is our view that, under the existing authorities, a celebrity's legal right of publicity is invaded whenever his identity is intentionally appropriated for commercial purposes. We simply disagree that the authorities limit the right of publicity as contended by the dissent. It is not fatal to appellant's claim that appellee did not use his "name." Indeed, there would have been no violation of his right of publicity even if appellee had used his name, such as "J. William Carson Portable Toilet" or the "John William Carson Portable Toilet" or the "J.W. Carson Portable Toilet." The reason is that, though literally using appellant's "name," the appellee would not have appropriated Carson's identity as a celebrity. Here there was an appropriation of Carson's identity without using his "name."

With respect to the dissent's general policy arguments, it seems to us that the policies there set out would more likely be vindicated by the majority view than by the dissent's view. Certainly appellant Carson's achievement has made him a celebrity which means that his identity has a pecuniary value which the right of publicity should vindicate. Vindication of the right will tend to encourage achievement in Carson's chosen field. Vindication of the right will also tend to prevent unjust enrichment by persons such as appellee who seek commercially to exploit the identity of celebrities without their consent.

The dissent also suggests that recognition of the right of publicity here would somehow run afoul of federal monopoly policies and first amendment proscriptions. If, as the dissent seems to concede, such policies and proscriptions are not violated by the vindication of the right of publicity where the celebrity's "name, likeness, achievements, identifying characteristics or actual performances" have been appropriated for commercial purposes, we cannot see why the policies and proscriptions would be violated where, as here, the celebrity's identity has admittedly been appropriated for commercial exploitation by the use of the phrase "Here's Johnny Portable Toilets."

The judgment of the district court is vacated and the case remanded for further proceedings consistent with this opinion.

CORNELIA G. KENNEDY, CIRCUIT JUDGE, dissenting.

I respectfully dissent from that part of the majority's opinion which holds that appellee's use of the phrase "Here's Johnny" violates appellant Johnny Carson's common law right of publicity. While I agree that an individual's identity may be impermissibly exploited, I do not believe that the common law right of publicity may be extended beyond an individual's name, likeness, achievements, identifying characteristics or actual performances, to include phrases or other things which are merely associated with the individual, as is the phrase "Here's Johnny." The majority's extension of the right of publicity to include phrases or other things which are merely associated with the individual permits a popular entertainer or public figure, by associating himself or herself with a common phrase, to remove those words from the public domain.

The phrase "Here's Johnny" is merely associated with Johnny Carson, the host and star of "The Tonight Show" broadcast by the National Broadcasting Company. Since 1962, the opening format of "The Tonight Show," after the theme music is played, is to introduce Johnny Carson with the phrase "Here's Johnny." The words are spoken by an announcer, generally Ed McMahon, in a drawn out and distinctive manner. Immediately after the phrase "Here's Johnny" is spoken, Johnny Carson appears to begin the program. This method of introduction was first used by Johnny Carson in 1957 when he hosted a daily television show for the American Broadcasting Company. This case is not transformed into a "name" case simply because the diminutive form of John W. Carson's given name and the first name of his full stage name, Johnny Carson, appears in it. The first name is so common, in light of the millions of persons named John, Johnny or Jonathan that no doubt inhabit this world, that, alone, it is meaningless or ambiguous at best in identifying Johnny Carson, the celebrity. In addition, the phrase containing Johnny Carson's first stage name was certainly selected for its value as a double entendre. Appellee manufactures portable toilets. The value of the phrase to appellee's product is in the risque meaning of "john" as a toilet or bathroom. For this reason, too, this is not a "name" case.

Appellee has stipulated that the phrase "Here's Johnny" is associated with Johnny Carson and that absent this association, he would not have chosen to use it for his product and corporation, Here's Johnny Portable Toilets, Inc. I do not consider it relevant that appellee intentionally chose to incorporate into the name of his corporation and product a phrase that is merely associated with Johnny Carson. What is not protected by law is not taken from public use. Research reveals no case in which the right of publicity has been extended to phrases or other things which are merely associated with an individual and are not part of his name, likeness, achievements, identifying characteristics or actual performances. Both the policies behind the right of publicity and countervailing interests and considerations indicate that such an extension should not be made.

I. Policies Behind Right of Publicity

The three primary policy considerations behind the right of publicity are succinctly stated in Hoffman, *Limitations on the Right of Publicity*, 28 Bull. Copr. Soc'y, 111, 116–22 (1980). First, "the right of publicity vindicates the economic interests of celebrities, enabling those whose achievements have imbued their identities with pecuniary value to profit from their fame." Second, the right of publicity fosters "the production of intellectual and creative works by providing the financial incentive for individuals to expend the time and resources necessary to produce them." Third, "[t]he right of publicity serves both individual and societal interests by preventing what our legal tradition regards as wrongful conduct: unjust enrichment and deceptive trade practices."

None of the above mentioned policy arguments supports the extension of the right of publicity to phrases or other things which are merely associated with an individual. First, the majority is awarding Johnny Carson a windfall, rather than vindicating his economic interests, by protecting the phrase "Here's Johnny" which is merely associated with him. In *Zacchini*, the Supreme Court stated that a mechanism to vindicate an individual's economic rights is indicated where the appropriated thing is "the product of * * * [the individual's] own talents and energy, the end result of much time, effort and expense." There is nothing in the record to suggest that "Here's Johnny" has any nexus to Johnny Carson other than being the introduction to his personal appearances. The phrase is not part of an identity that he created. In its content "Here's Johnny" is a very simple and common introduction. The content of the phrase neither originated with Johnny Carson nor is it confined to the world of entertainment. The phrase is not said by Johnny Carson, but said of him. Its association with him is derived, in large part, by the context in which it is said generally by Ed McMahon in a drawn out and distinctive voice[52] after

---

52. Ed McMahon arguably has a competing publicity interest in this same phrase because it is said by him in a distinctive and drawn out manner as his introduction to entertainers who appear on "The Tonight Show," including Johnny Carson.

the theme music to "The Tonight Show" is played, and immediately prior to Johnny Carson's own entrance. Appellee's use of the content "Here's Johnny," in light of its value as a double entendre, written on its product and corporate name, and therefore outside of the context in which it is associated with Johnny Carson, does little to rob Johnny Carson of something which is unique to him or a product of his own efforts.

The second policy goal of fostering the production of creative and intellectual works is not met by the majority's rule because in awarding publicity rights in a phrase neither created by him nor performed by him, economic reward and protection is divorced from personal incentive to produce on the part of the protected and benefited individual. Johnny Carson is simply reaping the rewards of the time, effort and work product of others.

Third, the majority's extension of the right of publicity to include the phrase "Here's Johnny" which is merely associated with Johnny Carson is not needed to provide alternatives to existing legal avenues for redressing wrongful conduct. The existence of a cause of action under section 43(a) of the Lanham Act, 15 U.S.C.A. § 1125(a) (1976) and Michigan common law does much to undercut the need for policing against unfair competition through an additional legal remedy such as the right of publicity. The majority has concluded, and I concur, that the District Court was warranted in finding that there was not a reasonable likelihood that members of the public would be confused by appellee's use of the "Here's Johnny" trademark on a product as dissimilar to those licensed by Johnny Carson as portable toilets. In this case, this eliminates the argument of wrongdoing. Moreover, the majority's extension of the right of publicity to phrases and other things merely associated with an individual is not conditioned upon wrongdoing and would apply with equal force in the case of an unknowing user. With respect to unjust enrichment, because a celebrity such as Johnny Carson is himself enriched by phrases and other things associated with him in which he has made no personal investment of time, money or effort, another user of such a phrase or thing may be enriched somewhat by such use, but this enrichment is not at Johnny Carson's expense. The policies behind the right of publicity are not furthered by the majority's holding in this case.

II. Countervailing Interests and Considerations

The right of publicity, whether tied to name, likeness, achievements, identifying characteristics or actual performances, etc. conflicts with the economic and expressive interests of others. Society's interests in free enterprise and free expression must be balanced against the interests of an individual seeking protection in the right of publicity where the right is being expanded beyond established limits. In addition, the right to publicity may be subject to federal preemption where it conflicts with the provisions of the Copyright Act of 1976.

A. Federal Policy: Monopolies

Protection under the right of publicity creates a common law monopoly that removes items, words and acts from the public domain. That federal policy favors free enterprise was recently reaffirmed by the Supreme Court in *National Society of Professional Engineers v. United States*, 435 U.S. 679, 98 S.Ct. 1355, 55 L.Ed.2d 637 (1978), in which the Supreme Court indicated that outside of the "rule of reason," only those anticompetitive restraints expressly authorized by Congress would be permitted to stand. Concern for the impact of adopting an overbroad approach to the right of publicity was also indicated in this Court's decision in *Memphis Development Foundation v. Factors Etc., Inc.*, 616 F.2d 956 (6th Cir.), *cert. denied*, 449 U.S. 953, 101 S.Ct. 358, 66 L.Ed.2d 217 (1980). In *Memphis Development*, this Court held that the right of publicity does not survive a celebrity's death under Tennessee law. In so holding, this Court recognized that commercial and competitive interests are potentially compromised by an expansive approach to the right of publicity. This Court was concerned that an extension of the right of publicity to the exclusive control of the celebrity's heirs might compromise the efficiency, productivity and fairness of our economic system without enlarging the stock or quality of the goods, services, artistic creativity, information, invention or entertainment available and detract from the equal distribution of economic opportunity available in a free market system. *Memphis Development* recognized that the grant of a right of publicity is tantamount to the grant of a monopoly, in that case, for the life of the celebrity. The majority's grant to Johnny Carson of a publicity right in the phrase "Here's Johnny" takes this phrase away from the public domain, giving him a common law monopoly for it, without extracting from Johnny Carson a personal contribution for the public's benefit.

Protection under the right of publicity confers a monopoly on the protected individual that is potentially broader, offers fewer protections and potentially competes with federal statutory monopolies. As an essential part of three federal monopoly rights, copyright, trademark and patents, notice to the public is required in the form of filing with the appropriate governmental office and use of an appropriate mark. This apprises members of the public of the nature and extent of what is being removed from the public domain and subject to claims of infringement. The right of publicity provides limited notice to the public of the extent of the monopoly right to be asserted, if one is to be asserted at all. As the right of privacy is expanded beyond protections of name, likeness and actual performances, which provide relatively objective notice to the public of the extent of an individual's rights, to more subjective attributes such as achievements and identifying characteristics, the public's ability to be on notice of a common law monopoly right, if one is even asserted by a given famous individual, is severely diminished. Protecting phrases and other things merely associated with an individual provides virtually no notice to the public at all of what is claimed to be protected. By ensuring the invocation of the adjudicative process whenever the commercial use of a phrase or other associated thing is considered to have been wrongfully appropriated, the public is left to act at their peril. The result is a chilling effect on commercial innovation and opportunity.

* * *

B. Federal Policy: Free Expression and Use of Intellectual Property

The first amendment protects the freedom of speech, including commercial speech. Strong federal policy permits the free use of intellectual property, words and ideas that are in general circulation and not protected by a valid copyright, patent or trademark. The federal copyright statute only protects original works that fix the author's particular expression of an idea or concept in a tangible form. State statutory or common law protection against activities violating rights that are not equivalent to those granted under copyright law or protection of subject matter which is not copyrightable, including works that are not fixed in any tangible form of expression, are not preempted. Apart from the technical arguments regarding preemption, if federal law and policy does not protect phrases such as "Here's Johnny," which is certainly not an original combination of words, state law should not protect them either under a right of publicity for want of a sufficient interest justifying protection. In addition, because copyright does not restrain the use of a mere idea or concept but only protects particular tangible expressions of an idea or concept, it has been held not to run afoul of first amendment challenges. The protected tangible expressions are asserted to not run afoul of first amendment challenges because the notice requirements and limited duration of copyright protection balances the interest of individuals seeking protection under the copyright clause and the first amendment. Because the phrase "Here's Johnny" is more akin to an idea or concept of introducing an individual than an original protectable fixed expression of that idea and because the right of publicity in this instance is not complemented by saving notice or duration requirements, phrases such as "Here's Johnny" should not be entitled to protection under the right of publicity as a matter of policy and concern for the first amendment.

Apart from the possibility of outright federal preemption, public policy requires that the public's interest in free enterprise and free expression take precedence over any interest Johnny Carson may have in a phrase associated with his person.

III. Case Law

The common law right of publicity has been held to protect various aspects of an individual's identity from commercial exploitation: name, likeness, achievements, identifying characteristics, actual performances, and fictitious characters created by a performer. Research reveals no case which has extended the right to publicity to phrases and other things which are merely associated with an individual.

The three cases cited by the majority in reaching their conclusion that the right of privacy should be extended to encompass phrases and other things merely associated with an individual and one other case merit further comment. *Hirsch v. S.C. Johnson & Son, Inc.*, 90 Wis.2d 379, 280 N.W.2d 129 (1979), *Ali v. Playgirl, Inc.*, 447 F.Supp. 723 (S.D.N.Y.1978), and *Motschenbacher v. R.J. Reynolds Tobacco Co.*, 498 F.2d 821 (9th Cir.1974), are factually and legally distinguishable from the case on appeal. *Hirsch* simply stands for the principle accepted by the commentators, if not by the courts, that the right of publicity extends not only to an individual's name but to a nickname or stage name as well. *Hirsch* required that the name clearly identify the wronged person. *Hirsch* goes on to state that if a fictitious name is used, context may be sufficient to link the fictitious name with the complaining individual, and therefore give rise to protection under a right of publicity. In the *Hirsch* case, context supplied the missing link which is not present here. Hirsch, a/k/a "Crazylegs," was a famous football player and all around athlete. He is described as the superstar of the era. He made a number of commercials and advertisements during his career and a movie was produced on his life. His unique running style, which was described by the Hirsch court as looking something like a whirling egg beater, earned him his nickname. The defendant in *Hirsch*, S.C. Johnson & Son, marketed a moisturizing shaving gel for women under the name of "Crazylegs." The context linking this product to Hirsch was Johnson's first promotion of its product at a running event for women, the use of a cheer in a television commercial similar to the "Crazylegs" cheer initiated at a college where Hirsch became athletic director, and the fact that the product was for women's legs. Based on this evidence of "context," the Wisconsin appellate court found a question of fact for the jury as to whether "Crazylegs" identified Hirsch. In this case, not only is the majority not dealing with a nickname or a stage name, but there is not a scintilla of evidence to support the context requirement of *Hirsch*. Appellee has only used the content of the "Here's Johnny" phrase on its product and its corporate name as transfigured by the double meaning of "John."

In *Ali*, Muhammad Ali sought protection under the right of publicity for the unauthorized use of his picture in Playgirl Magazine. *Ali* is a "likeness" case reinforced by the context in which the likeness occurs and further bolstered by a phrase, "the Greatest," commonly stated by Ali regarding himself. The essence of the case, and the unauthorized act from which Ali claims protection, is a drawing of a nude black man seated in the corner of a boxing ring with both hands taped and outstretched resting on the ropes on either side. The *Ali* court found that even a cursory inspection of the picture suggests that the facial characteristics of the man are those of Ali. The court stated: "The cheekbones, broad nose and wideset brown eyes, together with the distinctive smile and close cropped black hair are recognizable as the features of * * * [Ali]." Augmenting this likeness and reinforcing its identification with Ali was the context in which the likeness appeared in a boxing ring. The court found that identification of the individual depicted as Ali was further implied by the accompanying phrase "the Greatest." Based on these facts, the court had no difficulty concluding that the drawing was Ali's portrait or picture. To the extent the majority uses the phrase "the Greatest" to support is position that the right of publicity encompasses phrases or other things which are merely associated with an individual, they misstate the law of *Ali*. Once again, *Ali* is clearly a "likeness" case. To the extent the likeness was not a photographic one free from all ambiguity, identification with Muhammad Ali was reinforced by context and a phrase "the Greatest" stated by Ali about himself. The result in that case is so dependent on the identifying features in the drawing and the boxing context in which the man is portrayed that the phrase "the Greatest" may not be severed from this whole and the legal propositions developed by the *Ali* court in response to the whole applied to the phrase alone. To be analogous, a likeness of Johnny Carson would be required in addition to the words "Here's Johnny" suggesting the context of "The Tonight Show" or the *Ali* court would have to have enjoined all others from using the phrase "the Greatest." In short, Ali does not support the majority's holding.

Motschenbacher, the third case cited by the majority, is an "identifying characteristics" case. Motschenbacher, a professional driver of racing cars who is internationally known, sought protection in the right of publicity for the unauthorized use of a photograph of his racing car, slightly altered, in a televised cigarette commercial. Although he was in fact driving the car at the time it was photographed, his facial features are not visible in the commercial. The Ninth Circuit found as a matter of California law, that the right of publicity extended to protect the unauthorized use of photographs of Motschenbacher's racing car as one of his identifying characteristics. Identifying characteristics, such as Motschenbacher's racing car, are not synonymous with phrases or other things which are merely associated with an individual. In *Motschenbacher*, the Ninth Circuit determined that the car driver had "consistently 'individualized' his cars to set them apart from those of other drivers and to make them more readily identifiable as his own." Since 1966, each car had a distinctive narrow white pinstripe appearing on no other car. This decoration has always been in the same place on the car bodies, which have uniformly been red. In addition, his racing number "11" has always been against an oval background in contrast to the circular white background used by other drivers. In the commercial, the photo of Motschenbacher's car was altered so that the number "11" was changed to "71," a spoiler with the name "Winston" was added, and other advertisements removed. The remainder of the individualized decorations remained the same. Despite these alterations, the Ninth Circuit determined that car possessed identifying characteristics peculiar to Motschenbacher. This case is factually and legally distinguishable from the case on appeal. Motschenbacher's racing car was not merely associated with him but was the vehicle, literally and figuratively, by which he achieved his fame. The identifying characteristics, in the form of several decorations peculiar to his car, were the product of his personal time, energy, effort and expense and as such are inextricably interwoven with him as his individual work product, rather than being merely associated with him. Furthermore, the number and combination of the peculiar decorations on his cars results in a set of identifying characteristics, which although inanimate, are unique enough to resist duplication other than by intentional copying. This uniqueness provides notice to the public of what is claimed as part of his publicity right, as does an individual's name, likeness or actual performance, and narrowly limits the scope of his monopoly. In contrast to Motschenbacher, Johnny Carson's fame as a comedian and talk show host is severable from the phrase with which he is associated, "Here's Johnny." This phrase is not Johnny Carson's "thumbprint"; it is not his work product; it is not original; it is a common, simple combination of a direct object, a contracted verb and a common first name; divorced from context, it is two dimensional and ambiguous. It can hardly be said to be a symbol or synthesis, i.e., a tangible "expression" of the "idea," of Johnny Carson the comedian and talk show host, as Motschenbacher's racing car was the tangible expression of the man.

Finally, *Lombardo v. Doyle, Dane & Bernbach, Inc.*, 58 A.D.2d 620, 396 N.Y.S.2d 661 (App.Div.1977), which although not cited by the majority is discussed by a number of the commentators with the cases cited by the majority, does not go so far as to extend the right of publicity to phrases or things which are merely associated with an individual. In *Lombardo*, an advertising agency and foreign automobile manufacturer entered into negotiations with the band leader, Guy Lombardo, for the purpose of producing a television commercial designed to depict Lombardo and his orchestra in New Year's Eve party hats, playing "Auld Lang Syne" while models of cars rotated in the foreground. After negotiations between the parties fell through, the agency and manufacturer proceeded with the commercial. An actor was employed to lead a band playing "Auld Lang Syne" in the same musical beat as developed by Lombardo, using the same gestures as Lombardo employed in conducting his band. Lombardo then instituted suit claiming that the agency and manufacturer had used a "likeness and representation" of himself without his consent, violating his statutory right to privacy under New York law and his common law right to be free from the misappropriation of his cultivated public persona as "Mr. New Year's Eve." The *Lombardo* court found no statutory violation but did find a cause of action to be stated under Lombardo's common law theory. *Lombardo* appears to be in part a "likeness" case based on impersonation reinforced by context, and in part an "identifying characteristics" case like *Motschenbacher*. The "likeness" aspect comes from the actor portraying a bandleader, Lombardo's profession and vehicle for his fame, while using the same gestures employed by Lombardo and a musical beat linked to him. As in *Ali*, likeness is reinforced by context the trappings of New Year's Eve, balloons, party hats and the band playing "Auld Lang Syne." Like Motschenbacher,

Lombardo's gestures while conducting are part of his "thumbprint" and his musical beat and rendition of "Auld Lang Syne" on New Year's Eve are probably inseverable from his fame. *Lombardo*, however, is a less compelling case for finding a right of privacy than *Motschenbacher* and his similarities to the case on appeal. Unlike the several individualized decorations on Motschenbacher's car, only the conducting gestures and musical beat are unique to Lombardo. The very elements that he urged tied him to his persona as "Mr. New Year's Eve" are not peculiar to him but are shared with numerous bandleaders on New Year's Eve balloons, party hats and "Auld Lang Syne." The commonness of these crucial alleged "identifying characteristics" undercuts the value of their combination by Lombardo. In *Motschenbacher*, the combination of several individualized decorations peculiar to Motschenbacher resulted in relatively clear notice to the public of what the extent of Motschenbacher's monopoly right was and resulted in this monopoly right being very narrow; it protected only the unauthorized use of photographs or depictions of a particular set of identical cars. In contrast, in *Lombardo*, the net result of the court's opinion would seem to be that Lombardo has a monopoly right enforceable against anyone who wishes to duplicate a bandleader playing "Auld Lang Syne" amid the trappings of a New Year's Eve party. The *Lombardo* court did not explore the anticompetitive or free expression ramifications of its decision. As with the holiday New Year's Eve, the song "Auld Lang Syne" and party trappings such as balloons and party hats in *Lombardo*, the phrase "Here's Johnny" is very common and hardly peculiar to a particular individual. Unlike the combination of common and unique (gestures and musical beat) elements in *Lombardo*, the phrase "Here's Johnny" as used here does not exist in combination with other elements, with the exception of the pun, the "Great Commodium," an indirect reference to Johnny Carson, to narrow the monopoly right proposed or apprise the public of what is claimed. Unlike the situation in *Motschenbacher* and *Lombardo*, the phrase contains nothing personal to Carson in the sense of being caused by him or a product of his time, effort and energies. Therefore, while questioning the merits of extending the right or privacy as far as the court did in *Lombardo*, primarily for the court's lack of policy analysis concerning anticompetitive consequences and first amendment problems, I believe that *Lombardo* is distinguishable.

Accordingly, neither policy nor case law supports the extension of the right of publicity to encompass phrases and other things merely associated with an individual as in this case. I would affirm the judgment of the District Court on this basis * * *.

NOTES

1. Is the point of dispute between the majority and the dissenting judge in the preceding case 1) the degree of association between Johnny Carson and the disputed phrase "Here's Johnny," 2) the type of proof that should be needed to establish such an association, 3) the extension of rights of publicity

and associated private controls to the use of particular phrases, 4) the potential impact of the majority's approach in curtailing subsequent free speech, or 5) some combination of these?

2. Was the disputed use of the phrase "Here's Johnny" a cleaver parody? Should this have affected the outcome of the case?

3. Why was the contested phrase in the case associated with Johnny Carson rather than with Ed McMahan who uttered "Here's Johnny" in a distinctive manner at the beginning of every Tonight Show program that Carson hosted? Why should the target of a descriptive phrase have a right to control its use rather than the party who made the phrase famous?

4. Suppose the phrase at issue in the preceding case did not describe a famous person. For example, the "Laugh In" comedy show opened with an introduction in which an announcer indicated that the show was "Live from beautiful downtown Burbank." Assuming that this phrase gained some notoriety, could the announcer that uttered it control the subsequent use of the phrase? Would it matter whether the announcer was famous and associated in the public's mind with the phrase? If the phrase was famous—largely due to the efforts of the announcer in delivering it in an entertaining manner—but the announcer was not famous, would it be fair to withhold rights of publicity regarding subsequent use of the phrase? Isn't the type of appropriation that would result from subsequent commercial use of such a phrase similar to that which was found sufficient to support a claim in the *Carson* case?

MIDLER v. FORD MOTOR COMPANY

United States Court of Appeals for the Ninth Circuit, 1988.
849 F.2d 460.

NOONAN, CIRCUIT JUDGE:

This case centers on the protectability of the voice of a celebrated chanteuse from commercial exploitation without her consent. Ford Motor Company and its advertising agency, Young & Rubicam, Inc., in 1985 advertised the Ford Lincoln Mercury with a series of nineteen 30 or 60 second television commercials in what the agency called "The Yuppie Campaign." The aim was to make an emotional connection with Yuppies, bringing back memories of when they were in college. Different popular songs of the seventies were sung on each commercial. The agency tried to get "the original people," that is, the singers who had popularized the songs, to sing them. Failing in that endeavor in ten cases the agency had the songs sung by "sound alikes." Bette Midler, the plaintiff and appellant here, was done by a sound alike.

Midler is a nationally known actress and singer. She won a Grammy as early as 1973 as the Best New Artist of that year. Records made by her since then have gone Platinum and Gold. She was nominated in 1979 for an Academy award for Best Female Actress in *The Rose,* in which she portrayed a pop singer. *Newsweek* in its June 30, 1986 issue described her as an "outrageously original singer/comedian." *Time* hailed her in its

March 2, 1987 issue as "a legend" and "the most dynamic and poignant singer-actress of her time."

When Young & Rubicam was preparing the Yuppie Campaign it presented the commercial to its client by playing an edited version of Midler singing "Do You Want To Dance," taken from the 1973 Midler album, "The Divine Miss M." After the client accepted the idea and form of the commercial, the agency contacted Midler's manager, Jerry Edelstein. The conversation went as follows: "Hello, I am Craig Hazen from Young and Rubicam. I am calling you to find out if Bette Midler would be interested in doing * * *? Edelstein: "Is it a commercial?" "Yes." "We are not interested."

Undeterred, Young & Rubicam sought out Ula Hedwig whom it knew to have been one of "the Harlettes" a backup singer for Midler for ten years. Hedwig was told by Young & Rubicam that "they wanted someone who could sound like Bette Midler's recording of [Do You Want To Dance]." She was asked to make a "demo" tape of the song if she was interested. She made an a capella demo and got the job.

At the direction of Young & Rubicam, Hedwig then made a record for the commercial. The Midler record of "Do You Want To Dance" was first played to her. She was told to "sound as much as possible like the Bette Midler record," leaving out only a few "aahs" unsuitable for the commercial. Hedwig imitated Midler to the best of her ability.

After the commercial was aired Midler was told by "a number of people" that it "sounded exactly" like her record of "Do You Want To Dance." Hedwig was told by "many personal friends" that they thought it was Midler singing the commercial. Ken Fritz, a personal manager in the entertainment business not associated with Midler, declares by affidavit that he heard the commercial on more than one occasion and thought Midler was doing the singing.

Neither the name nor the picture of Midler was used in the commercial; Young & Rubicam had a license from the copyright holder to use the song. At issue in this case is only the protection of Midler's voice. The district court described the defendants' conduct as that "of the average thief." They decided, "If we can't buy it, we'll take it." The court nonetheless believed there was no legal principle preventing imitation of Midler's voice and so gave summary judgment for the defendants. Midler appeals.

The First Amendment protects much of what the media do in the reproduction of likenesses or sounds. A primary value is freedom of speech and press. The purpose of the media's use of a person's identity is central. If the purpose is "informative or cultural" the use is immune; "if it serves no such function but merely exploits the individual portrayed, immunity will not be granted." Moreover, federal copyright law preempts much of the area. "Mere imitation of a recorded performance would not constitute a copyright infringement even where one performer deliberately sets out to simulate another's performance as exactly as possible." It is in the context of these First Amendment and federal copyright distinctions that we address the present appeal.

Nancy Sinatra once sued Goodyear Tire and Rubber Company on the basis of an advertising campaign by Young & Rubicam featuring "These Boots Are Made For Walkin'," a song closely identified with her; the female singers of the commercial were alleged to have imitated her voice and style and to have dressed and looked like her. The basis of Nancy Sinatra's complaint was unfair competition; she claimed that the song and the arrangement had acquired "a secondary meaning" which, under California law, was protectible. This court noted that the defendants "had paid a very substantial sum to the copyright proprietor to obtain the license for the use of the song and all of its arrangements." To give Sinatra damages for their use of the song would clash with federal copyright law. Summary judgment for the defendants was affirmed. If Midler were claiming a secondary meaning to "Do You Want To Dance" or seeking to prevent the defendants from using that song, she would fail like Sinatra. But that is not this case. Midler does not seek damages for Ford's use of "Do You Want To Dance," and thus her claim is not preempted by federal copyright law. Copyright protects "original works of authorship fixed in any tangible medium of expression." A voice is not copyrightable. The sounds are not "fixed." What is put forward as protectible here is more personal than any work of authorship.

Bert Lahr once sued Adell Chemical Co. for selling Lestoil by means of a commercial in which an imitation of Lahr's voice accompanied a cartoon of a duck. Lahr alleged that his style of vocal delivery was distinctive in pitch, accent, inflection, and sounds. The First Circuit held that Lahr had stated a cause of action for unfair competition, that it could be found "that defendant's conduct saturated plaintiff's audience, curtailing his market." That case is more like this one. But we do not find unfair competition here. One-minute commercials of the sort the defendants put on would not have saturated Midler's audience and curtailed her market. Midler did not do television commercials. The defendants were not in competition with her.

California Civil Code section 3344 is also of no aid to Midler. The statute affords damages to a person injured by another who uses the person's "name, voice, signature, photograph or likeness, in any manner." The defendants did not use Midler's name or anything else whose use is prohibited by the statute. The voice they used was Hedwig's, not hers. The term "likeness" refers to a visual image not a vocal imitation. The statute, however, does not preclude Midler from pursuing any cause of action she may have at common law; the statute itself implies that such common law causes of action do exist because it says its remedies are merely "cumulative."

The companion statute protecting the use of a deceased person's name, voice, signature, photograph or likeness states that the rights it recognizes are "property rights." By analogy the common law rights are also property rights. Appropriation of such common law rights is a tort in California. *Motschenbacher v. R.J. Reynolds Tobacco Co.,* 498 F.2d 821 (9th Cir.1974). In that case what the defendants used in their television commercial for Winston cigarettes was a photograph of a famous professional racing driver's racing car. The number of the car was changed and a wing-like device known as a "spoiler" was attached to the car; the car's features of white pinpointing, an oval medallion, and solid red coloring were retained. The driver, Lothar Motschenbacher, was in the car but his features were not visible. Some persons, viewing the commercial, correctly inferred that the car was his and that he was in the car and was therefore endorsing the product. The defendants were held to have invaded a "proprietary interest" of Motschenbacher in his own identity.

Midler's case is different from Motschenbacher's. He and his car were physically used by the tobacco company's ad; he made part of his living out of giving commercial endorsements. But, as Judge Koelsch expressed it in *Motschenbacher,* California will recognize an injury from "an appropriation of the attributes of one's identity." It was irrelevant that Motschenbacher could not be identified in the ad. The ad suggested that it was he. The ad did so by emphasizing signs or symbols associated with him. In the same way the defendants here used an imitation to convey the impression that Midler was singing for them.

Why did the defendants ask Midler to sing if her voice was not of value to them? Why did they studiously acquire the services of a sound-alike and instruct her to imitate Midler if Midler's voice was not of value to them? What they sought was an attribute of Midler's identity. Its value was what the market would have paid for Midler to have sung the commercial in person.

A voice is more distinctive and more personal than the automobile accouterments protected in *Motschenbacher.* A voice is as distinctive and personal as a face. The human voice is one of the most palpable ways identity is manifested. We are all aware that a friend is at once known by a few words on the phone. At a philosophical level it has been observed that with the sound of a voice, "the other stands before me." A fortiori, these observations hold true of singing, especially singing by a singer of renown. The singer manifests herself in the song. To impersonate her voice is to pirate her identity.

We need not and do not go so far as to hold that every imitation of a voice to advertise merchandise is actionable. We hold only that when a distinctive voice of a professional singer is widely known and is deliberately imitated in order to sell a product, the sellers have appropriated what is not theirs and have committed a tort in California. Midler has made a showing, sufficient to defeat summary judgment, that the defendants here for their own profit in selling their product did appropriate part of her identity.

NOTES

1. In its analysis, the court points out that Nancy Sinatra failed in an earlier case to prevent another party from using a song closely associated with her in a commercial without her authorization, primarily because the use of the song in question was authorized by the copyright holder. Based on the court's analysis in *Midler*, should Sinatra still have been able to stop the airing of the commercial she objected to? What aspects of the commercial challenged by Sinatra would she be able to claim violated her rights of publicity?

2. To what extent did the producers of the commercial challenged in *Midler* essentially admit to a goal of appropriating the commercial value of Midler's voice by seeking her as a performer and then having another singer mimic Midler's voice? What if the appropriation of Midler's vocal style had been inadvertent? For example, suppose the singer hired to perform in the disputed commercial had mimicked Midler's style without any intent to do so and without any direction of the producers to adopt this style. Would this sort of "innocent" appropriation of Midler's style—without knowledge that it is happening—be a proper basis for a rights of publicity claim?

WHITE v. SAMSUNG ELECTRONICS AMERICA, INC.

United States Court of Appeals for the Ninth Circuit, 1992.
971 F.2d 1395.

GOODWIN, SENIOR CIRCUIT JUDGE:

This case involves a promotional "fame and fortune" dispute. In running a particular advertisement without Vanna White's permission, defendants Samsung Electronics America, Inc. (Samsung) and David Deutsch Associates, Inc. (Deutsch) attempted to capitalize on White's fame to enhance their fortune. White sued, alleging infringement of various intellectual property rights, but the district court granted summary judgment in favor of the defendants. We affirm in part, reverse in part, and remand.

Plaintiff Vanna White is the hostess of "Wheel of Fortune," one of the most popular game shows in television history. An estimated forty million people watch the program daily. Capitalizing on the fame which her participation in the show has bestowed on her, White markets her identity to various advertisers.

The dispute in this case arose out of a series of advertisements prepared for Samsung by Deutsch. The series ran in at least half a dozen publications with widespread, and in some cases national, circulation. Each of the advertisements in the series followed the same theme. Each depicted a current item from popular culture and a Samsung electronic product. Each was set in the twenty-first century and conveyed the message that the Samsung product would still be in use by that time. By hypothesizing outrageous future outcomes for the cultural items, the ads created humorous effects. For example, one lampooned current popular notions of an unhealthy diet by depicting a raw steak with the caption: "Revealed to be health food. 2010 A.D." Another depicted irreverent "news"-show host Morton Downey Jr. in front of an American flag with the caption: "Presidential candidate. 2008 A.D."

The advertisement which prompted the current dispute was for Samsung video-cassette recorders (VCRs). The ad depicted a robot, dressed in a wig, gown, and jewelry which Deutsch consciously selected to resemble White's hair and dress. The robot was posed next to a game board which is instantly recognizable as the Wheel of Fortune game show set, in a stance for which White is famous. The caption of the ad read: "Longest-running game show. 2012 A.D." Defendants referred to the ad as the "Vanna White" ad. Unlike the other celebrities used in the campaign, White neither consented to the ads nor was she paid.

Following the circulation of the robot ad, White sued Samsung and Deutsch in federal district court under: (1) California Civil Code § 3344; (2) the California common law right of publicity; and (3) § 43(a) of the Lanham Act, 15 U.S.C. § 1125(a). The district court granted summary judgment against White on each of her claims. White now appeals.

I.   Section 3344

White first argues that the district court erred in rejecting her claim under section 3344. Section 3344(a) provides, in pertinent part, that "[a]ny person who knowingly uses another's name, voice, signature, photograph, or likeness, in any manner, * * * for purposes of advertising or selling, * * * without such person's prior consent * * * shall be liable for any damages sustained by the person or persons injured as a result thereof."

White argues that the Samsung advertisement used her "likeness" in contravention of section 3344. In *Midler v. Ford Motor Co.,* 849 F.2d 460 (9th Cir.1988), this court rejected Bette Midler's section 3344 claim concerning a Ford television commercial in which a Midler "sound-alike" sang a song which Midler had made famous. In rejecting Midler's claim, this court noted that "[t]he defendants did not use Midler's name or anything else whose use is prohibited by the statute. The voice they used was [another person's], not hers. The term 'likeness' refers to a visual image not a vocal imitation."

In this case, Samsung and Deutsch used a robot with mechanical features, and not, for example, a manikin molded to White's precise features. Without deciding for all purposes when a caricature or impressionistic resemblance might become a "likeness," we agree with the district court that the robot at issue here was not White's "likeness" within the meaning of section 3344. Accordingly, we affirm the court's dismissal of White's section 3344 claim.

II.   Right of Publicity

White next argues that the district court erred in granting summary judgment to defendants on White's common law right of publicity claim.

In *Eastwood v. Superior Court,* 149 Cal.App.3d 409, 198 Cal.Rptr. 342 (1983), the California court of appeal stated that the common law right of publicity cause of action "may be pleaded by alleging (1) the defendant's use of the plaintiff's identity; (2) the appropriation of plaintiff's name or likeness to defendant's advantage, commercially or otherwise; (3) lack of consent; and (4) resulting injury." *Id.* at 417, 198 Cal.Rptr. 342 (citing Prosser, Law of Torts (4th ed. 1971) § 117, pp. 804–807). The district court dismissed White's claim for failure to satisfy *Eastwood's* second prong, reasoning that defendants had not appropriated White's "name or likeness" with their robot ad. We agree that the robot ad did not make use of White's name or likeness. However, the common law right of publicity is not so confined.

The *Eastwood* court did not hold that the right of publicity cause of action could be pleaded only by alleging an appropriation of name or likeness. *Eastwood* involved an unauthorized use of photographs of Clint Eastwood and of his name. Accordingly, the *Eastwood* court had no occasion to consider the extent beyond the use of name or likeness to which the right of publicity reaches. That court held only that the right of publicity cause of action "may be" pleaded by alleging, *inter alia,* appropriation of name or likeness, not that the action may be pleaded *only* in those terms.

The "name or likeness" formulation referred to in *Eastwood* originated not as an element of the right of publicity cause of action, but as a description of the types of cases in which the cause of action had been recognized. The source of this formulation is Prosser, *Privacy,* 48 Cal. L.Rev. 383, 401–07 (1960), one of the earliest and most enduring articulations of the common law right of publicity cause of action. In looking at the case law to that point, Prosser recognized that right of publicity cases involved one of two basic factual scenarios: name appropriation, and picture or other likeness appropriation. *Id.* at 401–02, nn. 156–57.

Even though Prosser focused on appropriations of name or likeness in discussing the right of publicity, he noted that "[i]t is not impossible that there might be appropriation of the plaintiff's identity, as by impersonation, without the use of either his name or his likeness, and that this would be an invasion of his right of privacy." At the time Prosser wrote, he noted however, that "[n]o such case appears to have arisen."

Since Prosser's early formulation, the case law has borne out his insight that the right of publicity is not limited to the appropriation of name or likeness. In *Motschenbacher v. R.J. Reynolds Tobacco Co.,* 498 F.2d 821 (9th Cir.1974), the defendant had used a photograph of the plaintiff's race car in a television commercial. Although the plaintiff appeared driving the car in the photograph, his features were not visible. Even though the defendant had not appropriated the plaintiff's name or likeness, this court held that plaintiff's California right of publicity claim should reach the jury.

In *Midler,* this court held that, even though the defendants had not used Midler's name or likeness, Midler had stated a claim for violation of her California common law right of publicity because "the defendants * * * for their own profit in selling their product did appropriate part of her identity" by using a Midler sound-alike.

In *Carson v. Here's Johnny Portable Toilets, Inc.,* 698 F.2d 831 (6th Cir.1983), the defendant had marketed portable toilets under the brand name "Here's Johnny"—Johnny Carson's signature "Tonight Show" introduction—without Carson's permission. The district court had dismissed Carson's Michigan common law right of publicity claim because the defendants had not used Carson's "name or likeness." In reversing the district court, the sixth circuit found "the district court's conception of the right of publicity * * * too narrow" and held that the right was implicated because the defendant had appropriated Carson's identity by using, *inter alia,* the phrase "Here's Johnny."

These cases teach not only that the common law right of publicity reaches means of appropriation other than name or likeness, but that the specific means of appropriation are relevant only for determining whether the defendant has in fact appropriated the plaintiff's identity. The right of publicity does not require that appropriations of identity be accomplished through particular means to be actionable. It is noteworthy that the *Midler* and *Carson* defendants not only avoided using the plaintiff's name or likeness, but they also avoided appropriating the celebrity's voice, signature, and photograph. The photograph in *Motschenbacher* did include the plaintiff, but because the plaintiff was not visible the driver could have been an actor or dummy and the analysis in the case would have been the same.

Although the defendants in these cases avoided the most obvious means of appropriating the plaintiffs' identities, each of their actions directly implicated the commercial interests which the right of publicity is designed to protect. As the *Carson* court explained:

> [t]he right of publicity has developed to protect the commercial interest of celebrities in their identities. The theory of the right is that a celebrity's identity can be valuable in the promotion of products, and the celebrity has an interest that may be protected from the unauthorized commercial exploitation of that identity * * *. If the celebrity's identity is commercially exploited, there has been an invasion of his right whether or not his "name or likeness" is used.

Carson, 698 F.2d at 835. It is not important *how* the defendant has appropriated the plaintiff's identity, but *whether* the defendant has done so. *Motschenbacher, Midler,* and *Carson* teach the impossibility of treating the right of publicity as guarding only against a laundry list of specific means of appropriating identity. A rule which says that the right of publicity can be infringed only through the use of nine different methods of appropriating identity merely challenges the clever advertising strategist to come up with the tenth.

Indeed, if we treated the means of appropriation as dispositive in our analysis of the right of publicity, we would not only weaken the right but effectively eviscerate it. The right would fail to protect those plaintiffs most in need of its protection. Advertisers use celebrities to promote their products. The more popular the celebrity, the greater the number of people who recognize her, and the greater the visibility for the product. The identities of the most popular celebrities are not only the most attractive for advertisers, but also the easiest to evoke without resorting to obvious means such as name, likeness, or voice.

Consider a hypothetical advertisement which depicts a mechanical robot with male features, an African–American complexion, and a bald head. The robot is wearing black hightop Air Jordan basketball sneakers, and a red basketball uniform with black trim, baggy shorts, and the number 23 (though not revealing "Bulls" or "Jordan" lettering). The ad depicts the robot dunking a basketball one-handed, stiff-armed, legs extended like open scissors, and tongue hanging out. Now envision that this ad is run on television during professional basketball games. Considered individually, the robot's physical attributes, its dress, and its stance tell us little. Taken together, they lead to the only conclusion that any sports viewer who has registered a discernible pulse in the past five years would reach: the ad is about Michael Jordan.

Viewed separately, the individual aspects of the advertisement in the present case say little. Viewed together, they leave little doubt about the celebrity the ad is meant to depict. The female-shaped robot is wearing a long gown, blond wig, and large jewelry. Vanna White dresses exactly like this at times, but so do many other women. The robot is in the process of turning a block letter on a game-board. Vanna White dresses like this while turning letters on a game-board but perhaps similarly attired Scrabble-playing women do this as well. The robot is standing on what looks to be the Wheel of Fortune game show set. Vanna White dresses like this, turns letters, and does this on the Wheel of Fortune game show. She is the only one. Indeed, defendants themselves referred to their ad as the "Vanna White" ad. We are not surprised.

Television and other media create marketable celebrity identity value. Considerable energy and ingenuity are expended by those who have achieved celebrity value to exploit it for profit. The law protects the celebrity's sole right to exploit this value whether the celebrity has achieved her fame out of rare ability, dumb luck, or a combination thereof. We decline Samsung and Deutch's invitation to permit the evisceration of the common law right of publicity through means as facile as those in this case. Because White has alleged facts showing that Samsung and Deutsch had appropriated her identity, the district court erred by rejecting, on summary judgment, White's common law right of publicity claim.

* * *

ALARCON, CIRCUIT JUDGE, concurring in part, dissenting in part:

* * *

II.

RIGHT TO PUBLICITY

I must dissent from the majority's holding on Vanna White's right to publicity claim. The district court found that, since the commercial advertisement did not show a "likeness" of Vanna White, Samsung did not improperly use the plaintiff's identity. The majority asserts that the use of a likeness is not required under California common law. According to the majority, recovery is authorized if there is an appropriation of one's "identity." I cannot find any holding of a California court that supports this conclusion. Furthermore, the record does not support the majority's finding that Vanna White's "identity" was appropriated.

The district court relied on *Eastwood v. Superior Court*, 149 Cal. App.3d 409, 198 Cal.Rptr. 342, (1983), in holding that there was no cause of action for infringement on the right to publicity because there had been no use of a likeness. In *Eastwood*, the California Court of Appeal described the elements of the tort of "commercial appropriation of the right of publicity" as "(1) the defendant's use of the plaintiff's identity; (2) the appropriation of plaintiff's name or likeness to defendant's advantage, * * *; (3) lack of consent; and (4) resulting injury."

All of the California cases that my research has disclosed hold that a cause of action for appropriation of the right to publicity requires proof of the appropriation of a name or likeness. See, *e.g.*, *Lugosi v. Universal Pictures*, 25 Cal.3d 813, 603 P.2d 425, 160 Cal.Rptr. 323 (1979) ("The so called right of publicity means in essence that the reaction of the public to name and likeness * * * endows the name and likeness of the person involved with commercially exploitable opportunities."); *Guglielmi v. Spelling Goldberg Prods.*, 25 Cal.3d 860, 603 P.2d 454, 457, 160 Cal.Rptr. 352, 355 (1979) (use of name of Rudolph Valentino in fictional biography allowed); *Eastwood v. Superior Court*, *supra* (use of photo and name of actor on cover of tabloid newspaper); *In re Weingand*, 231 Cal.App.2d 289, 41 Cal.Rptr. 778 (1964) (aspiring actor denied court approval to change name to "Peter Lorie" when famous actor Peter Lorre objected); *Fairfield v. American Photocopy Equip. Co.*, 138 Cal.App.2d 82, 291 P.2d 194 (1955), *later app.* 158 Cal.App.2d 53, 322 P.2d 93 (1958) (use of attorney's name in advertisement); *Gill v. Curtis Publishing Co.*, 38 C.2d 273, 239 P.2d 630 (1952) (use of photograph of a couple in a magazine).

Notwithstanding the fact that California case law clearly limits the test of the right to publicity to name and likeness, the majority concludes that "the common law right of publicity is not so confined." Majority opinion at p. 1397. The majority relies on two factors to support its innovative extension of the California law. The first is that the *Eastwood* court's statement of the elements was permissive rather than exclusive. The second is that Dean Prosser, in describing the common law right to publicity, stated that it might be possible that the right extended beyond name or likeness. These are slender reeds to support a federal court's attempt to create new law for the state of California.

In reaching its surprising conclusion, the majority has ignored the fact that the California Court of Appeal in *Eastwood* specifically addressed the differences between the common law right to publicity and the statutory cause of action codified in California Civil Code section 3344. The court explained that "[t]he differences between the common law and the statutory actions are: (1) Section 3344, subdivision (a) requires knowing use whereas under case law, mistake and inadvertence are not a defense against commercial appropriation and (2) section 3344, subdivision (g) expressly provides that its remedies are cumulative and in addition to any provided by law." *Eastwood*, 149 Cal.App.3d at n. 6, 198 Cal.Rptr. 342 (emphasis in original). The court did not include appropriations of identity by means other than name or likeness among its list of differences between the statute and the common law.

The majority also relies on Dean Prosser's statement that "[i]t is not impossible that there might be an appropriation of the plaintiff's identity, as by impersonation, without the use of either his name or his likeness, and that this would be an invasion of his right of privacy." Prosser, *Privacy*, 48 Cal.L.Rev. 383, 401 n. 155 (1960). As Dean Prosser noted, however, "[n]o such case appears to have arisen." *Id.*

The majority states that the case law has borne out Dean Prosser's insight that the right to publicity is not limited to name or likeness. As noted above, however, the courts of California have never found an infringement on the right to publicity without the use of the plaintiff's name or likeness.

The interest of the California Legislature as expressed in California Civil Code section 3344 appears to preclude the result reached by the majority. The original section 3344 protected only name or likeness. In 1984, ten years after our decision in *Motschenbacher v. R.J. Reynolds Tobacco Company*, 498 F.2d 821 (9th Cir.1974) and 24 years after Prosser speculated about the future development of the law of the right of publicity, the California legislature amended the statute. California law now makes the use of someone's voice or signature, as well as name or likeness, actionable. Thus, California, after our decision in *Motschenbacher* specifically contemplated protection for interests other than name or likeness, but did not include a cause of action for appropriation of another person's identity. The ancient maxim, *inclusio unius est exclusio alterius*, would appear to bar the majority's innovative extension of the right of publicity. The clear implication from the fact that the California Legislature chose to add only voice and signature to the previously protected interests is that it wished to limit the cause of action to enumerated attributes.

The majority has focused on federal decisions in its novel extension of California Common Law. Those decisions do not provide support for the majority's decision.

In each of the federal cases relied upon by the majority, the advertisement affirmatively represented that the person depicted therein was the plaintiff. In this case, it is clear that a metal robot and not the plaintiff, Vanna White, is depicted in the commercial advertisement. The record does not show an appropriation of Vanna White's identity.

* * *

The case before this court is distinguishable from the factual showing made in *Motschenbacher*, *Midler*, and *Carson*. It is patently clear to anyone viewing the commercial advertisement that Vanna White was not being depicted. No reasonable juror could confuse a metal robot with Vanna White.

The majority contends that "the individual aspects of the advertisement * * * [v]iewed together leave little doubt about the celebrity the ad is meant to depict." It derives this conclusion from the fact that Vanna White is "the only one" who "dresses like this, turns letters, and does this on the Wheel of Fortune game show." In reaching this conclusion, the majority confuses Vanna White, the person, with the role she has assumed as the current hostess on the "Wheel of Fortune" television game show. A recognition of the distinction between a performer and the part he or she plays is essential for a proper analysis of the facts of this case. As is discussed below, those things which Vanna White claims identify her are not unique to her. They are, instead, attributes of the role she plays. The representation of those attributes, therefore, does not constitute a representation of Vanna White.

Vanna White is a one role celebrity. She is famous solely for appearing as the hostess on the "Wheel of Fortune" television show. There is nothing unique about Vanna White or the attributes which she claims identify her. Although she appears to be an attractive woman, her face and figure are no more distinctive than that of other equally comely women. She performs her role as hostess on "Wheel of Fortune" in a simple and straight forward manner. Her work does not require her to display whatever artistic talent she may possess.

The majority appears to argue that because Samsung created a robot with the physical proportions of an attractive woman, posed it gracefully, dressed it in a blond wig, an evening gown, and jewelry, and placed it on a set that resembles the Wheel of Fortune layout, it thereby appropriated Vanna White's identity. But an attractive appearance, a graceful pose, blond hair, an evening gown, and jewelry are attributes shared by many women, especially in Southern California. These common attributes are particularly evident among game show hostesses, models, actresses, singers, and other women in the entertainment field. They are not unique attributes of Vanna White's identity. Accordingly, I cannot join in the majority's conclusion that, even if viewed together, these attributes identify Vanna White and, therefore, raise a triable issue as to the appropriation of her identity.

The only characteristic in the commercial advertisement that is not common to many female performers or celebrities is the imitation of the "Wheel of Fortune" set. This set is the only thing which might possibly lead a viewer to think of Vanna White. The Wheel of Fortune set, however, is not an attribute of Vanna White's identity. It is an identifying characteristic of a television game show, a prop with which Vanna White interacts in her role as the current hostess. To say that Vanna White may bring an action when another blond female performer or robot appears on such a set as a hostess will, I am sure, be a surprise to the owners of the show.

The record shows that Samsung recognized the market value of Vanna White's identity. No doubt the advertisement would have been more effective if Vanna White had appeared in it. But the fact that Samsung recognized Vanna White's value as a celebrity does not necessarily mean that it appropriated her identity. The record shows that Samsung dressed a robot in a costume usually worn by television game show hostesses, including Vanna White. A blond wig, and glamorous clothing are not characteristics unique to the current hostess of Wheel of Fortune. This evidence does not support the majority's determination that the advertisement was meant to depict Vanna White. The advertisement was intended to depict a robot, playing the role Vanna White currently plays on the Wheel of Fortune. I quite agree that anyone seeing the commercial advertisement would be reminded of Vanna White. Any performance by another female celebrity as a game show hostess, however, will also remind the viewer of Vanna White because Vanna White's celebrity is so closely associated with the role. But the fact that an actor or actress became famous for playing a particular role has, until now, never been sufficient to give the performer a proprietary interest in it. I cannot agree with the majority that the California courts, which have consistently taken a narrow view of the right to publicity, would extend law to these unique facts.

Notes

1.   Is it true, as Judge Alarcon asserts in his dissent, that "[i]t is patently clear to anyone viewing the commercial advertisement that Vanna White was not being depicted?" Was some aspect of her personal being depicted? If the viewer of the robot in question called up an image of White in the viewer's mind, does this mean that the robot image achieved the same result as a picture of White? Could the parody sought to be achieved through the robot be accomplished without calling up an image of White and her well known means of performance? Why should a depiction of a portion of White's features or performance be treated differently than a more complete depiction so long as the public associates the partial depiction with White?

2. Should *White* be viewed as a case testing the limits of the right of publicity in controlling subsequent creativity and the commercial value of works derived from the features of a famous person? Assuming that the robotic recasting of White and her efforts involved substantial creativity, both in concept and visual execution, why should White be able to limit the commercial use of this newly created work? Is it enough that some of the commercial value of the robot and its actions link back to White? Should there be no room for commercial use of this type of cleaver recasting of the characteristics of a famous person? Would it matter if the features of the robot and its actions were mostly original, with only a small fraction being derived from and publicly associated with White?

3. Should the result in this type of case be the same if White was being made fun of or criticized as part of a commentary or competitive process? For example, suppose that a review of the game show White performs on included a depiction of her as a robot as a means to emphasize that she performs in a mechanical manner. Or suppose that a producer of a game show used a robot like that in the preceding case to illustrate that White's game show operated by rote and that viewers should shift their attention to a new show being offered by the producer? Would these sorts of commercial uses of White's persona be objectionable? Would it matter that similar points could be made without using a robot featuring White's characteristics?

ZACCHINI v. SCRIPPS–HOWARD BROADCASTING COMPANY

Supreme Court of the United States, 1977.
433 U.S. 562, 97 S.Ct. 2849, 53 L.Ed.2d 965.

M<small>R</small>. J<small>USTICE</small> W<small>HITE</small> delivered the opinion of the Court.

Petitioner, Hugo Zacchini, is an entertainer. He performs a "human cannonball" act in which he is shot from a cannon into a net some 200 feet away. Each performance occupies some 15 seconds. In August and September 1972, petitioner was engaged to perform his act on a regular basis at the Geauga County Fair in Burton, Ohio. He performed in a fenced area, surrounded by grandstands, at the fair grounds. Members of the public attending the fair were not charged a separate admission fee to observe his act.

On August 30, a freelance reporter for Scripps–Howard Broadcasting Co., the operator of a television broadcasting station and respondent in this case, attended the fair. He carried a small movie camera. Petitioner noticed the reporter and asked him not to film the performance. The reporter did not do so on that day; but on the instructions of the producer of respondent's daily newscast, he returned the following day and video-taped the entire act. This film clip, approximately 15 seconds in length, was shown on the 11 o'clock news program that night, together with favorable commentary.[53]

---

53. The script of the commentary accompanying the film clip read as follows:

Petitioner then brought this action for damages, alleging that he is "engaged in the entertainment business," that the act he performs is one "invented by his father and ... performed only by his family for the last fifty years," that respondent "showed and commercialized the film of his act without his consent," and that such conduct was an "unlawful appropriation of plaintiff's professional property." Respondent answered and moved for summary judgment, which was granted by the trial court.

The Court of Appeals of Ohio reversed. The majority held that petitioner's complaint stated a cause of action for conversion and for infringement of a common-law copyright, and one judge concurred in the judgment on the ground that the complaint stated a cause of action for appropriation of petitioner's "right of publicity" in the film of his act. All three judges agreed that the First Amendment did not privilege the press to show the entire performance on a news program without compensating petitioner for any financial injury he could prove at trial.

Like the concurring judge in the Court of Appeals, the Supreme Court of Ohio rested petitioner's cause of action under state law on his "right to the publicity value of his performance." The opinion syllabus, to which we are to look for the rule of law used to decide the case, declared first that one may not use for his own benefit the name or likeness of another, whether or not the use or benefit is a commercial one, and second that respondent would be liable for the appropriation over petitioner's objection and in the absence of license or privilege, of petitioner's right to the publicity value of his performance. The court nevertheless gave judgment for respondent because, in the words of the syllabus:

> "A TV station has a privilege to report in its newscasts matters of legitimate public interest which would otherwise be protected by an individual's right of publicity, unless the actual intent of the TV station was to appropriate the benefit of the publicity for some non-privileged private use, or unless the actual intent was to injure the individual."

We granted certiorari to consider an issue unresolved by this Court: whether the First and Fourteenth Amendments immunized respondent from damages for its alleged infringement of petitioner's state law "right of publicity." Insofar as the Ohio Supreme Court held that the First and Fourteenth Amendments of the United States Constitution required judgment for respondent, we reverse the judgment of that court.

I

* * *

'This ... now ... is the story of a true spectator sport ... the sport of human cannonballing ... in fact, the great Zacchini is about the only human cannonball around, these days ... just happens that, where he is, is the Great Geauga County Fair, in Burton ... and believe me, although it's not a long act, it's a thriller ... and you really need to see it in person ... to appreciate it....' [Emphasis from original removed.]

There is no doubt that petitioner's complaint was grounded in state law and that the right of publicity which petitioner was held to possess was a right arising under Ohio law. It is also clear that respondent's claim of constitutional privilege was sustained. The source of this privilege was not identified in the syllabus. It is clear enough from the opinion of the Ohio Supreme Court, which we are permitted to consult for understanding of the syllabus, that in adjudicating the crucial question of whether respondent had a privilege to film and televise petitioner's performance, the court placed principal reliance on *Time, Inc. v. Hill*, 385 U.S. 374, 87 S.Ct. 534, 17 L.Ed.2d 456 (1967), a case involving First Amendment limitations on state tort actions. It construed the principle of that case, along with that of *New York Times Co. v. Sullivan*, 376 U.S. 254, 84 S.Ct. 710, 11 L.Ed.2d 686 (1964), to be that "the press has a privilege to report matters of legitimate public interest even though such reports might intrude on matters otherwise private," and concluded, therefore, that the press is also "privileged when an individual seeks to publicly exploit his talents while keeping the benefits private." The privilege thus exists in cases "where appropriation of a right of publicity is claimed." The court's opinion also referred to Draft 21 of the relevant portion of Restatement (Second) of Torts (1975), which was understood to make room for reasonable press appropriations by limiting the reach of the right of privacy rather than by creating a privileged invasion. The court preferred the notion of privilege over the Restatement's formulation, however, reasoning that "since the gravamen of the issue in this case is not whether the degree of intrusion is reasonable, but whether First Amendment principles require that the right of privacy give way to the public right to be informed of matters of public interest and concern, the concept of privilege seems the more useful and appropriate one."

* * *

II

The Ohio Supreme Court held that respondent is constitutionally privileged to include in its newscasts matters of public interest that would otherwise be protected by the right of publicity, absent an intent to injure or to appropriate for some nonprivileged purpose. If under this standard respondent had merely reported that petitioner was performing at the fair and described or commented on his act, with or without showing his picture on television, we would have a very different case. But petitioner is not contending that his appearance at the fair and his performance could not be reported by the press as newsworthy items. His complaint is that respondent filmed his entire act and displayed that film on television for the public to see and enjoy. This, he claimed, was an appropriation of his professional property. The Ohio Supreme Court agreed that petitioner had "a right of publicity" that gave him "personal control over commercial display and exploitation of his personality and the exercise of his talents."[54] This right of "exclusive control over the publicity given to his performances" was said to be such a "valuable part of the benefit which may be attained by his talents and efforts" that it was entitled to legal protection. It was also observed, or at least expressly assumed, that petitioner had not abandoned his rights by performing under the circumstances present at the Geauga County Fair Grounds.

The Ohio Supreme Court nevertheless held that the challenged invasion was privileged, saying that the press "must be accorded broad latitude in its choice of how much it presents of each story or incident, and of the emphasis to be given to such presentation. No fixed standard which would bar the press from reporting or depicting either an entire occurrence or an entire discrete part of a public performance can be formulated which would not unduly restrict the 'breathing room' in reporting which freedom of the press requires." Under this view, respondent was thus constitutionally free to film and display petitioner's entire act.[55]

The Ohio Supreme Court relied heavily on *Time, Inc. v. Hill*, 385 U.S. 374, 87 S.Ct. 534, 17 L.Ed.2d 456 (1967), but that case does not mandate a media privilege to televise a performer's entire act without his consent. Involved in *Time, Inc. v. Hill* was a claim under the New York "Right of Privacy" statute that Life Magazine, in the course of reviewing a new play, had connected the play with a long-past incident involving petitioner and his family and had falsely described their experience and conduct at that time. The complaint sought damages for humiliation and suffering flowing from these nondefamatory falsehoods that allegedly invaded Hill's privacy. The Court held, however, that the opening of a new play linked to an actual incident was a matter of public interest and that Hill could not recover without showing that the Life report was knowingly false or was published with reckless disregard for the truth, the same rigorous standard that had been applied in *New York Times Co. v. Sullivan*, 376 U.S. 254, 84 S.Ct. 710, 11 L.Ed.2d 686 (1964).

Time, Inc. v. Hill, which was hotly contested and decided by a divided Court, involved an entirely different tort from the "right of publicity"

---

54. The court relied on Housh v. Peth, 165 Ohio St. 35, 133 N.E.2d 340, 341 (1956), the syllabus of which held:

"An actionable invasion of the right of privacy is the unwarranted appropriation or exploitation of one's personality, the publicizing of one's private affairs with which the public has no legitimate concern, or the wrongful intrusion into one's private activities in such a manner as to outrage or cause mental suffering, shame or humiliation to a person of ordinary sensibilities."

The court also indicated that the applicable principles of Ohio law were those set out in Restatement (Second) § 652C of Torts (Tent. Draft No. 13, 1967), and the comments thereto, portions of which were stated in the footnotes of the opinion. * * *

55. The court's explication was as follows:

"The proper standard must necessarily be whether the matters reported were of public interest, and if so, the press will be liable for appropriation of a performer's right of publicity only if its actual intent was not to report the performance, but, rather, to appropriate the performance for some other private use, or if the actual intent was to injure the performer. It might also be the case that the press would be liable if it recklessly disregarded contract rights existing between the plaintiff and a third person to present the performance to the public, but that question is not presented here."

recognized by the Ohio Supreme Court. As the opinion reveals in *Time, Inc. v. Hill*, the Court was steeped in the literature of privacy law and was aware of the developing distinctions and nuances in this branch of the law. The Court, for example, cited W. Prosser, Law of Torts 831–832 (3d ed. 1964), and the same author's well-known article, *Privacy*, 48 Calif. L. Rev. 383 (1960), both of which divided privacy into four distinct branches.[56] The Court was aware that it was adjudicating a "false light" privacy case involving a matter of public interest, not a case involving "intrusion," "appropriation" of a name or likeness for the purposes of trade, or "private details" about a non-newsworthy person or event. It is also abundantly clear that *Time, Inc. v. Hill* did not involve a performer, a person with a name having commercial value, or any claim to a "right of publicity." This discrete kind of "appropriation" case was plainly identified in the literature cited by the Court and had been adjudicated in the reported cases.

The differences between these two torts are important. First, the State's interests in providing a cause of action in each instance are different. "The interest protected" in permitting recovery for placing the plaintiff in a false light "is clearly that of reputation, with the same overtones of mental distress as in defamation." By contrast, the State's interest in permitting a "right of publicity" is in protecting the proprietary interest of the individual in his act in part to encourage such entertainment. As we later note, the State's interest is closely analogous to the goals of patent and copyright law, focusing on the right of the individual to reap the reward of his endeavors and having little to do with protecting feelings or reputation. Second, the two torts differ in the degree to which they intrude on dissemination of information to the public. In "false light" cases the only way to protect the interests involved is to attempt to minimize publication of the damaging matter, while in "right of publicity" cases the only question is who gets to do the publishing. An entertainer such as petitioner usually has no objection to the widespread publication of his act as long as the gets the commercial benefit of such publication. Indeed, in the present case petitioner did not seek to enjoin the broadcast of his act; he simply sought compensation for the broadcast in the form of damages.

Nor does it appear that our later cases, such as *Rosenbloom v. Metromedia, Inc.*, 403 U.S. 29, 91 S.Ct. 1811, 29 L.Ed.2d 296 (1971); *Gertz v. Robert Welch, Inc.*, 418 U.S. 323, 94 S.Ct. 2997, 41 L.Ed.2d 789 (1974); and *Time, Inc. v. Firestone*, 424 U.S. 448, 96 S.Ct. 958, 47 L.Ed.2d 154 (1976), require or furnish substantial support for the Ohio court's privi-

---

56. "The law of privacy comprises four distinct kinds of invasion of four different interests of the plaintiff, which are tied together by the common name, but otherwise have almost nothing in common except that each represents an interference with the right of the plaintiff * * * 'to be let alone.'" Prosser, Privacy, 48 Calif. L. Rev., at 389. Thus, according to Prosser, some courts had recognized a cause of action for "intrusion" upon the plaintiff's seclusion or solitude; public disclosure of "private facts" about the plaintiff's personal life; publicity that places the plaintiff in a "false light": in the public eye; and "appropriation" of the plaintiff's name or likeness for commercial purposes. One may be liable for "appropriation" if he "pirate(s) the plaintiff's identity for some advantage of his own."

lege ruling. These cases, like *New York Times*, emphasize the protection extended to the press by the First Amendment in defamation cases, particularly when suit is brought by a public official or a public figure. None of them involve an alleged appropriation by the press of a right of publicity existing under state law.

Moreover, *Time, Inc. v. Hill*, *New York Times*, *Metromedia*, *Gertz*, and *Firestone* all involved the reporting of events; in none of them was there an attempt to broadcast or publish an entire act for which the performer ordinarily gets paid. It is evident, and there is no claim here to the contrary, that petitioner's state-law right of publicity would not serve to prevent respondent from reporting the newsworthy facts about petitioner's act.[57] Wherever the line in particular situations is to be drawn between media reports that are protected and those that are not, we are quite sure that the First and Fourteenth Amendments do not immunize the media when they broadcast a performer's entire act without his consent. The Constitution no more prevents a State from requiring respondent to compensate petitioner for broadcasting his act on television than it would privilege respondent to film and broadcast a copyrighted dramatic work without liability to the copyright owner, or to film and broadcast a prize fight or a baseball game where the promoters or the participants had other plans for publicizing the event. There are ample reasons for reaching this conclusion.

The broadcast of a film of petitioner's entire act poses a substantial threat to the economic value of that performance. As the Ohio court recognized, this act is the product of petitioner's own talents and energy, the end result of much time, effort, and expense. Much of its economic value lies in the "right of exclusive control over the publicity given to his performance"; if the public can see the act free on television, it will be less willing to pay to see it at the fair.[58] The effect of a public broadcast of the performance is similar to preventing petitioner from charging an admission fee. "The rationale for (protecting the right of publicity) is the straightforward one of preventing unjust enrichment by the theft of good

---

57. W. Prosser, Law of Torts 806–807 (4th ed. 1971), generalizes on the cases:

"The New York courts were faced very early with the obvious fact that newspapers and magazines, to say nothing of radio, television and motion pictures, are by no means philanthropic institutions, but are operated for profit. As against the contention that everything published by these agencies must necessarily be 'for purposes of trade,' they were compelled to hold that there must be some closer and more direct connection, beyond the mere fact that the newspaper itself is sold; and that the presence of advertising matter in adjacent columns, or even the duplication of a news item for the purpose of advertising the publication itself, does not make any difference. Any other conclusion would in all probability have been an unconstitutional interference with the freedom of the press. Accordingly, it has been held that the mere incidental mention of the plaintiff's name in a book or a motion picture is not an invasion of his privacy; nor is the publication of a photograph or a newsreel in which he incidentally appears." (Footnotes omitted.)

Cf. Restatement (Second) of Torts s 652C, Comment d (Tent. Draft No. 22, 1976).

58. It is possible, of course, that respondent's news broadcast increased the value of petitioner's performance by stimulating the public's interest in seeing the act live. In these circumstances, petitioner would not be able to prove damages and thus would not recover. But petitioner has alleged that the broadcast injured him to the extent of $25,000 and we think the State should be allowed to authorize compensation of this injury if proved.

will. No social purpose is served by having the defendant get free some aspect of the plaintiff that would have market value and for which he would normally pay." Moreover, the broadcast of petitioner's entire performance, unlike the unauthorized use of another's name for purposes of trade or the incidental use of a name or picture by the press, goes to the heart of petitioner's ability to earn a living as an entertainer. Thus, in this case, Ohio has recognized what may be the strongest case for a "right of publicity" involving, not the appropriation of an entertainer's reputation to enhance the attractiveness of a commercial product, but the appropriation of the very activity by which the entertainer acquired his reputation in the first place.

Of course, Ohio's decision to protect petitioner's right of publicity here rests on more than a desire to compensate the performer for the time and effort invested in his act; the protection provides an economic incentive for him to make the investment required to produce a performance of interest to the public. This same consideration underlies the patent and copyright laws long enforced by this Court. As the Court stated in *Mazer v. Stein*, 347 U.S. 201, 219, 74 S.Ct. 460, 471, 98 L.Ed. 630 (1954):

> "The economic philosophy behind the clause empowering Congress to grant patents and copyrights is the conviction that encouragement of individual effort by personal gain is the best way to advance public welfare through the talents of authors and inventors in 'Science and useful Arts.' Sacrificial days devoted to such creative activities deserve rewards commensurate with the services rendered."

These laws perhaps regard the "reward to the owner (as) a secondary consideration," but they were "intended definitely to grant valuable, enforceable rights" in order to afford greater encouragement to the production of works of benefit to the public. The Constitution does not prevent Ohio from making a similar choice here in deciding to protect the entertainer's incentive in order to encourage the production of this type of work. *Cf. Goldstein v. California*, 412 U.S. 546, 93 S.Ct. 2303, 37 L.Ed.2d 163 (1973); *Kewanee Oil Co. v. Bicron Corp.*, 416 U.S. 470, 94 S.Ct. 1879, 40 L.Ed.2d 315 (1974).[59]

---

59. Goldstein involved a California statute outlawing 'record piracy'—the unauthorized duplication of recordings of performances by major musical artists. Petitioners there launched a multifaceted constitutional attack on the statute, but they did not argue that the statute violated the First Amendment. In rejecting this broad-based constitutional attack, the Court concluded:

> "The California statutory scheme evidences a legislative policy to prohibit 'tape piracy' and 'record piracy,' conduct that may adversely affect the continued production of new recordings, a large industry in California. Accordingly, the State has, by statute, given to recordings the attributes of property. No restraint has been placed on the use of an idea or concept; rather, petitioners and other individuals remain free to record the same compositions in precisely the same manner and with the same personal as appeared on the original recording.

> Until and unless Congress takes further action with respect to recordings * * *, the California statute may be enforced against acts of piracy such as those which occurred in the present case."

412 U.S., at 571, 93 S.Ct., at 2317. (Emphasis added.)

We note that Federal District Courts have rejected First Amendment challenges to the federal copyright law on the ground that 'no restraint (has been) placed on the use of an idea or concept.'

There is no doubt that entertainment, as well as news, enjoys First Amendment protection. It is also true that entertainment itself can be important news. But it is important to note that neither the public nor respondent will be deprived of the benefit of petitioner's performance as long as his commercial stake in his act is appropriately recognized. Petitioner does not seek to enjoin the broadcast of his performance; he simply wants to be paid for it. Nor do we think that a state-law damages remedy against respondent would represent a species of liability without fault contrary to the letter or spirit of *Gertz v. Robert Welch, Inc.*, 418 U.S. 323, 94 S.Ct. 2997, 41 L.Ed.2d 789 (1974). Respondent knew that petitioner objected to televising his act, but nevertheless displayed the entire film.

We conclude that although the State of Ohio may as a matter of its own law privilege the press in the circumstances of this case, the First and Fourteenth Amendments do not require it to do so.

Reversed.

MR. JUSTICE POWELL, with whom MR. JUSTICE BRENNAN and MR. JUSTICE MARSHALL join, dissenting.

Disclaiming any attempt to do more than decide the narrow case before us, the Court reverses the decision of the Supreme Court of Ohio based on repeated incantation of a single formula: "a performer's entire act." The holding today is summed up in one sentence:

> "Wherever the line in particular situations is to be drawn between media reports that are protected and those that are not, we are quite sure that the First and Fourteenth Amendments do not immunize the media when they broadcast a performer's entire act without his consent."

I doubt that this formula provides a standard clear enough even for resolution of this case.[60] In any event, I am not persuaded that the Court's

---

United States v. Bodin, 375 F.Supp. 1265, 1267 (W.D.Okl.1974). *See also Walt Disney Productions v. Air Pirates*, 345 F.Supp. 108, 115–116 (N.D.Cal.1972) (citing Nimmer, *Does Copyright Abridge The First Amendment Guarantees of Free Speech and Press?*, 17 UCLA Rev. 1180 (1970), who argues that copyright law does not abridge the First Amendment because it does not restrain the communication of ideas or concepts); *Robert Stigwood Group Ltd. v. O'Reilly*, 346 F.Supp. 376 (Conn.1972) (also relying on Nimmer, *supra*). Of course, this case does not involve a claim that respondent would be prevented by petitioner's "right of publicity" from staging or filming its own "human cannonball" act.

In *Kewanee* this Court upheld the constitutionality of Ohio's trade-secret law, although again no First Amendment claim was presented. Citing *Goldstein*, the Court stated:

> "Just as the States may exercise regulatory power over writings so may the States regulate with respect to discoveries. States may hold diverse viewpoints in protecting intellectual property relating to invention as they do in protecting the intellectual property relating to the subject matter of copyright. The only limitation on the States is that in regulating the area of patents and copyrights they do not conflict with the operation of the laws in this area passed by Congress...."

416 U.S., at 479, 94 S.Ct., at 1885.

Although recognizing that the trade-secret law resulted in preventing the public from gaining certain information, the Court emphasized that the law had "a decidedly beneficial effect on society," and that without it, "organized scientific and technological research could become fragmented, and society, as a whole, would suffer."

60. Although the record is not explicit, it is unlikely that the "act" commenced abruptly with the explosion that launched petitioner on his way, ending with the landing in the net a few opinion is appropriately sensitive to the First Amendment values at stake, and I therefore dissent.

Although the Court would draw no distinction, I do not view respondent's action as comparable to unauthorized commercial broadcasts of sporting events, theatrical performances, and the like where the broadcaster keeps the profits. There is no suggestion here that respondent made any such use of the film. Instead, it simply reported on what petitioner concedes to be a newsworthy event, in a way hardly surprising for a television station by means of film coverage. The report was part of an ordinary daily news program, consuming a total of 15 seconds. It is a routine example of the press' fulfilling the informing function so vital to our system.

The Court's holding that the station's ordinary news report may give rise to substantial liability[61] has disturbing implications, for the decision could lead to a degree of media self-censorship. Hereafter, whenever a television news editor is unsure whether certain film footage received from a camera crew might be held to portray an "entire act,"[62] he may decline coverage even of clearly newsworthy events or confine the broadcast to watered-down verbal reporting, perhaps with an occasional still picture. The public is then the loser. This is hardly the kind of news reportage that the First Amendment is meant to foster.

In my view the First Amendment commands a different analytical starting point from the one selected by the Court. Rather than begin with a quantitative analysis of the performer's behavior [to determine whether] this is or is not his entire act, we should direct initial attention to the actions of the news media: what use did the station make of the film footage? When a film is used, as here, for a routine portion of a regular news program, I would hold that the First Amendment protects the station from a "right of publicity" or "appropriation" suit, absent a strong showing by the plaintiff that the news broadcast was a subterfuge or cover for private or commercial exploitation.

---

seconds later. One may assume that the actual firing was preceded by some fanfare, possibly stretching over several minutes, to heighten the audience's anticipation: introduction of the performer, description of the uniqueness and danger, last-minute checking of the apparatus, and entry into the cannon, all accompanied by suitably ominous commentary from the master of ceremonies. If this is found to be the case on remand, then respondent could not be said to have appropriated the 'entire act' in its 15–second newsclip and the Court's opinion then would afford no guidance for resolution of the case. Moreover, in future cases involving different performances, similar difficulties in determining just what constitutes the "entire act" are inevitable.

61. At some points the Court seems to acknowledge that the reason for recognizing a cause of action asserting a "right of publicity" is to prevent unjust enrichment. But the remainder of the opinion inconsistently accepts a measure of damages based not on the defendant's enhanced profits but on harm to the plaintiff regardless of any gain to the defendant. Indeed, in this case there is no suggestion that respondent television station gained financially by showing petitioner's flight (although it no doubt received its normal advertising revenue for the news program— revenue it would have received no matter which news items appeared). Nevertheless, in the unlikely event that petitioner can prove that his income was somehow reduced as a result of the broadcast, respondent will apparently have to compensate him for the difference.

62. Such doubts are especially likely to arise when the editor receives film footage of an event at a local fair, a circus, a sports competition of limited duration (e. g., the winning effort in a ski-jump competition), or a dramatic production made up of short skits, to offer only a few examples.

I emphasize that this is a "reappropriation" suit, rather than one of the other varieties of "right of privacy" tort suits identified by Dean Prosser in his classic article. Prosser, *Privacy*, 48 Calif.L.Rev. 383 (1960). In those other causes of action the competing interests are considerably different. The plaintiff generally seeks to avoid any sort of public exposure, and the existence of constitutional privilege is therefore less likely to turn on whether the publication occurred in a news broadcast or in some other fashion. In a suit like the one before us, however, the plaintiff does not complain about the fact of exposure to the public, but rather about its timing or manner. He welcomes some publicity, but seeks to retain control over means and manner as a way to maximize for himself the monetary benefits that flow from such publication. But having made the matter public—having chosen, in essence, to make it newsworthy—he cannot, consistent with the First Amendment, complain of routine news reportage.

Since the film clip here was undeniably treated as news and since there is no claim that the use was subterfuge, respondent's actions were constitutionally privileged. I would affirm.

NOTES

1.   Was the problem with the news reporting in *Zacchini* that, by depicting the entirety of the plaintiff's act, the reporting rendered the act significantly less valuable in performances before subsequent audiences? What sorts of showings on television would preempt public interest in seeing further instance of the same conduct live? Wouldn't some types of news reports actually enhance public interest in a live performance, thereby aiding rather than injuring the performer? Why wasn't the news reporting in *Zacchini* viewed as helpful rather than harmful?

2.   Does the analysis of the Court in the preceding case suggest that it felt that the television station went too far in broadcasting the full performance of the plaintiff when it could have presented an adequate news report showing just a part of the performance? What part of being shot out of a cannon, if portrayed in a news broadcast, would adequately convey the nature of this event? To what extent are the commercially valuable components of the plaintiff's performance different than the portions of the performance which would need to be shown to portray its most important features in a new broadcast? If most of the dramatic features of Zacchini's performance needed to be portrayed to adequately describe the performance in a news broadcast, wouldn't effective news broadcasting about the performance necessarily have a substantial impact on the subsequent novelty and commercial value of like performances?

3.   Various courts have sought to better define the relationship between First Amendment protections and rights of publicity since the Supreme Court's decision in *Zacchini*. These courts have developed several tests for reconciling First Amendment interests with claims of commercial misuse of elements of an identity as protected through rights of publicity.

Some courts have used a balancing test. Under this type of test, the impacts of speech restrictions resulting from enforcement of rights of publicity are compared to the public benefits resulting from those rights to determine which are more significant. See *Cardtoons, L.C. v. Major League Baseball Players Ass'n*, 95 F.3d 959, 972 (10th Cir. 1996) (in determining if enforcement of rights of publicity will improperly interfere with activities protected by the First Amendment, a court should "directly balance the magnitude of the speech restriction against the asserted governmental interest in protecting the intellectual property right").

Other courts have emphasized the importance of a "transformative use" in assessing whether a party's use of aspects of a person's identity should qualify for First Amendment protections. Where a use of a party's identity entails the addition of creative changes which substantially alter or "transform" the features of the party's identity, courts applying a transformative use standard will tend to find that this creative contribution deserves protection under the First Amendment and justifies withholding liability for violations of the affected individual's rights of publicity. However, absent such a transformative use, the replication of elements of an individual's identity in a product or other work will generally support liability for violation of the individual's rights of publicity. See, *e.g.*, *Comedy III Productions, Inc. v. Gary Saderup, Inc.*, 25 Cal.4th 387, 106 Cal.Rptr.2d 126, 21 P.3d 797 (2001).

Additional courts have used a purpose test for determining if the use of elements of an individual's identity for commercial purposes should trigger liability for violation of the affected individual's rights of publicity. Under this approach, such liability would not be recognized where the primary purpose for the use was to make an expressive comment about the individual whose features were portrayed, but would be imposed is the use was undertaken for other purposes. See *Doe v. TCI Cablevision*, 110 S.W.3d 363 (Mo. 2003).

IV. MISAPPROPRIATION OF INTELLECTUAL WORKS

Misappropriation of property generally involves an unfair or improper use of something recognized in the law as the property of another. In the context of intellectual works, misappropriation claims based on common law standards frequently involve difficult questions about the sorts of intellectual works that should be deemed to be the property of their creators and the circumstances in which the use of those works by others should be deemed to be sufficiently improper to constitute misappropriation. The flexibility of misappropriation claims is a source of both strengths and weaknesses. While such claims can suffice to remedy a broad range of arguably unfair practices, misappropriation claims can also loom as uncertain threats regarding the use of various types of intellectual works and thereby deter conduct that is actually proper and in the public interest.

Courts have struggled to define the role of misappropriation claims regarding intellectual property for some years and to reconcile the scope of these claims with the rights that are available under intellectual property statutes. The views of the Supreme Court on what makes an intellectual work an item of property capable of being protected through misappropriation claims are explored in *International News Service v. Associated Press*, 248 U.S. 215, 39 S.Ct. 68, 63 L.Ed. 211 (1918), reproduced in Chapter 9 of this text. The following case provides a more modern application of misappropriation standards and a good summary of recent claims based on misappropriation of intellectual works.

BOARD OF TRADE OF THE CITY OF CHICAGO v. DOW JONES & COMPANY, INC.

Appellate Court of Illinois, First District, 1982.
108 Ill.App.3d 681, 64 Ill.Dec. 275, 439 N.E.2d 526.

STAMOS, PRESIDING JUSTICE:

Plaintiff Board of Trade of the City of Chicago (the Board) brought a declaratory judgment action in the circuit court of Cook County seeking a declaration that its proposed stock market index contract, which is based on the stock market index and averages devised and published by defendant Dow Jones & Company, Inc. (Dow Jones), would not violate any proprietary rights of Dow Jones. * * *

The Board of Trade of the City of Chicago is a not-for-profit, non-stock membership corporation created in 1859 pursuant to a special charter from the Illinois legislature. The corporation was organized for the purpose of maintaining an exchange for the trading of commodity futures contracts. The Board is the oldest and largest such exchange in the United States, and today the Board offers a wide variety of contracts in agricultural products, precious metals and financial instruments. The business of the Board, and all trading on its exchange, is conducted at the Board of Trade building on Jackson Boulevard in Chicago. The activities of the Board, and of all other commodity exchanges in the United States, are regulated by the Commodities Futures Trading Commission (CFTC), a federal agency. The CFTC must approve any futures contract which is traded on an exchange, and no exchange may trade in a contract until the CFTC has designated it as a contract market for that contract.

Dow Jones is a Delaware corporation with its principal office in New York City. It is primarily a news gathering and publishing organization. Dow Jones publishes the *Wall Street Journal, Barron's,* and the *Asian Wall Street Journal,* and operates several wire services which transmit financial news to subscribers by means of ticker tape, computer linkups and the like. The Dow Jones activity which is relevant to this case is its computation of the Dow Jones Averages, in particular the Dow Jones Industrial Average. Dow Jones has been producing and publishing a price average of industrial stocks since 1896. The average has encompassed the stock issues of thirty separate highly capitalized industrial companies since 1928. The identity of the firms whose stocks make up the average has changed from time to time over the years. The selection of stocks used to compute the average is arrived at through the use of considerable financial expertise and experience and is based on Dow Jones's determination of which stocks are likely to reflect the overall activity of the stock market in their individual fluctuations in price. The Dow Jones Industrial Average is computed by adding together the current prices of the thirty constituent stocks and dividing the total by a number called the "divisor." The purpose of the divisor is to retain continuity in the overall average. The divisor is adjusted to account for changes in per-stock value which are caused by technical factors such as stock splits or stock dividends. The use of the divisor keeps the average within a range of numbers which is recognizable as the "Dow Jones Average" to the public. The divisor, list of stocks and method of calculating the average are all made public by Dow Jones. Dow Jones itself computes the value of its index once a day. Licensees of Dow Jones compute the value of the index on a "real time" basis throughout the day and disseminate that information via television, tape and electronic readouts to a large number of subscribers, including banks, brokerage houses, securities exchanges and commodities exchanges. The Board is a subscriber to such a service and, pursuant to that subscription, it displays the "real time" Dow Jones Average on its trading floor in order to aid its traders in making investment decisions. It is undisputed, as are most of the facts in this case, that the Dow Jones Averages have achieved high public regard as a source of information about the current performance of the stock market.

The events leading up to this litigation began in February 1980 when the Board submitted a proposal to the CFTC which asked that it be designated as a contract market for several new futures contracts which were to be based on indices composed of groups of stocks listed on the New York Stock Exchange. The indices were formulated entirely by the Board after two years of research and labor. In December 1981, the CFTC entered into a jurisdictional agreement with the Securities and Exchange Commission. Part of that agreement allowed the CFTC to permit trading on stock market index contracts only if the contracts were based on widely known and well established stock market indices. This agreement effectively precluded CFTC approval of a contract based on any new indices, including the index which had been devised by the Board.

The Board approached Dow Jones with a proposal that would have paid between $1 million and $2 million yearly to Dow Jones in return for its sponsorship of a contract based on its index. Dow Jones turned down the proposal for the asserted reason that it determined that any connection on its part with the speculative field of futures trading would damage its image as an advocate of conservativism in investment policy. Other prominent stock market indices, notably Standard & Poor's 500 and the Value Line Index, were licensed by their publishers to commodity futures exchanges for the purpose of trading a contract based on those indices at about the time that the parties here were negotiating.

On February 26, 1982, the Board submitted a proposal to the CFTC asking that it be designated as a contract market for a stock market index futures contract that would be based on the Dow Jones Industrial Index and Average. The contract would be called the Chicago Board of Trade

Stock Market Index (CBT Index). The proposal specifies that the CBT Index is identical to the Dow Jones Industrial Index and Average. The contracts are to be settled four times a year, and the value of the CBT Index will be calculated only on the last day of each of those trading periods. The value of the contract is $50 times the value of the index (*i.e.,* the average) on the last day of trading, with "longs" (buyers) and "shorts" (sellers) settling the contracts through an exchange of certified promissory notes for the appropriate sum. Because the value of the CBT Index will be calculated only when the contracts are to be settled, the "spot" value of the contracts during the trading period will be ascertainable only through reference to the current Dow Jones Average. On May 13, 1982, the CFTC designated the Board as a contract market for the CBT Index contract.

While the Board's proposal was pending before the CFTC, the Board filed this action in the circuit court of Cook County, seeking a declaration that its proposed contract would violate no proprietary rights of Dow Jones in the index and averages. On June 4, 1982, the trial court issued a 27–page opinion, holding that the burden of proof in the declaratory judgment action should be on Dow Jones; that Dow Jones has a property right and a valuable interest in the Dow Jones Index and Averages and a wrongful use of that property is actionable at law and in equity; and that the Board's proposed use of the averages was not a misappropriation of Dow Jones's property and therefore the Board was free to offer its CBT Index contract for trading. The court made this ruling conditioned on the use of a disclaimer on the CBT Index contract disavowing any association with or sponsorship by Dow Jones.

* * *

[T]he dispositive body of law in this case is the common law doctrine of misappropriation. The parties base their theories concerning this body of law upon the law of Illinois, New York, and other jurisdictions. It should be noted at the outset that misappropriation is a species of unfair competition. Unfair competition is a tort and the law of the state with the most significant relationship to the parties and to the relevant occurrence governs the action. Dow Jones, a Delaware corporation headquartered in New York, has offices and a registered agent in Illinois. It transmits its averages into Illinois directly and through licensees, where the Board proposes to make use of them as the basis of the CBT Index contract. The Board does business solely in Illinois, and the contract will be traded exclusively in Illinois. Illinois has the most significant relationship of any state to the parties and to the Board's proposed activities and, therefore, Illinois law properly governs this action.

The doctrine of misappropriation is recognized in Illinois. However, any discussion of the doctrine must make repeated reference to the law of other jurisdictions, particularly New York, where the doctrine has been most fully delineated.

The doctrine was first enunciated by the United States Supreme Court in the case of *International News Service v. Associated Press* (1918), 248 U.S. 215, 39 S.Ct. 68, 63 L.Ed. 211[, reproduced in Chapter 9 of this text]. In that case, the defendant news service received reports pertaining to World War I, which were transmitted over a "wire" by the plaintiff. Defendant copied the news stories and transmitted them to its subscribing newspapers on the west coast for publication. The defendant argued that the plaintiff lost the right to control the uses made of its news stories by virtue of the plaintiff's wide public dissemination of the stories, and that it had the same right as any purchaser of a newspaper containing the stories to communicate the information in the stories to others. The Court stated that the rights of the defendant to use the information provided by the plaintiff should not be gauged by the rights of the plaintiff as against the general public, but should be evaluated by a consideration of the rights of the plaintiff and the defendant, competitors in the news business, as between themselves. The Court further stated that the transmission of the stories for commercial use by the defendant involved the implicit admission that:

> "it is taking material which has been acquired by the complainant as the result of organization and the expenditure of labor, skill, and money, and which is salable by complainant for money, and that defendant in appropriating it and selling it as his own is endeavoring to reap where it has not sown, * * *. Stripped of all disguises, the process amounts to an unauthorized interference with the normal operation of complainant's legitimate business precisely at the point where the profit is to be reaped, in order to divert a material portion of the profit from those who have earned it to those who have not; * * *. The transaction speaks for itself, and a court of equity ought not to hesitate long in characterizing it as unfair competition in business."

The Court went on to describe the new species of unfair competition that it had created:

> "[D]efendant's conduct differs from the ordinary course of unfair competition in trade principally in this that, instead of selling its own goods as those of complainant, it substitutes misappropriation in the place of misrepresentation, and sells complainant's goods as its own."

248 U.S. at 242, 39 S.Ct. at 73.

As the Board points out, the majority of the cases applying the misappropriation doctrine involve direct competition between the parties, an element which is missing in the instant case. However, it has been stated that:

> "[T]he modern view as to the law of unfair competition does not rest solely on the ground of direct competitive injury, but on the broader principle that property rights of commercial value are to be and will be protected from any form of unfair invasion or infringement."

Metropolitan Opera Association v. Wagner–Nichols Recorder Corp. (Sup. Ct. 1950), 199 Misc. 786, 101 N.Y.S.2d 483, 492, *aff'd* (1st Dept. 1951), 279 App. Div. 632, 107 N.Y.S.2d 795.

In the *Metropolitan Opera* case, the defendant was engaged in the practice of recording performances of the plaintiff opera company from the radio and manufacturing and selling phonograph records of those performances. The opera association licensed the exclusive right to make and sell recordings of its performances to Columbia Records, also a plaintiff in the case. Although the defendant was in direct competition solely with Columbia, the court found the defendant guilty of unfair competition as to both plaintiffs. As to the opera company, the court held that the defendant was unjustifiably interfering with its contract with a third party, as well as violating the opera company's right to control its name and reputation.

There can be no question but that the name and reputation of Dow Jones figures heavily in the Board's plans. The Board can gain CFTC approval for a stock market index contract only if the contract is based on a widely known and well established stock index. When the Board became aware that the index which it had devised could not be used as the basis for its contracts, it approached Dow Jones in order to secure Dow Jones's sponsorship of the contracts. When Dow Jones rejected this offer, the Board proposed the CBT Index. The CBT Index is based directly on the Dow Jones Index and must in all events perform identically to the Dow Jones Index. The "spot" value of the CBT Index can be ascertained only from the "real time" Dow Jones value displayed on the trading floor of the Board of Trade. Although the contract itself will not use the trade name "Dow Jones," except to disclaim any connection with that company, the value of the contract at any particular time during the trading period will be ascertained by traders by reference to the Dow Jones Average. It is clear that the trading public will be entirely aware that trading the CBT Index contract is the same as trading a Dow Jones Index contract, and whatever aura of reliability, respectability, or expertise would adhere to a Dow Jones contract, if one existed, will adhere to the CBT Index contract, with or without the use of the Dow Jones name.

Not every commercial use of the name and reputation of another is an actionable misappropriation. In *National Football League v. Governor of the State of Delaware* (D. Del. 1977), 435 F.Supp. 1372, the State of Delaware was conducting a lottery called "Scoreboard" which essentially required players to bet on the final scores of N.F.L. games. The court held that there was no actionable misappropriation in the use of the N.F.L. scores as the basis of the lottery. The court reasoned that although one has a right to reap the profits of one's business without interference, this right does not preclude others from profiting from the demand for "collateral" services created by the popularity of that business. The court also stated that the N.F.L.'s claim that the State was appropriating the N.F.L.'s "good will" or "reputation" was, in that case, simply another way of saying that the lottery was profiting from a demand to gamble on the outcome of N.F.L. games that the popularity of those games had created.

The crucial distinction between that case and the case before us is that the product which the Board seeks to sell is not as "collateral" to the business of Dow Jones as the lottery was to the business of the N.F.L. The N.F.L. is in the business of presenting professional football contests of a high caliber to fans of that sport who watch the games in person or through the media. The games, not the scores, are the product that the N.F.L. offers for sale. The collection and dissemination of the scores is performed by the news media, and the N.F.L. does not "produce" those scores in any meaningful sense.

Dow Jones is in the business of collecting and tabulating financial information on companies which are carefully selected based on Dow Jones's financial expertise and acumen. That information is filtered through a "divisor" of Dow Jones's invention, and by that process the raw figures which were originally collected are freed from distortions which reflect factors other than the objective economic performance of the stocks in the index. Finally, Dow Jones is in the business of disseminating the resultant average to investors. The use of the Dow Jones Index as the basis for the CBT Index contract is a far cry from the use of football scores as the basis for a lottery. Traders in the contract are not merely "betting" on the index "numbers." The Board asserts that institutional investors and others will use the CBT contract as a "hedge," that is, to manage the risk in their stock portfolios. The strong correlation of the Dow Jones Average to the general pattern of stock market activity is essential to the usefulness of the CBT Index contract as a hedging device, and it is that correlation which will give "hedgers" confidence in the contract. That correlation exists solely as a result of Dow Jones's expertise, and has garnered considerable good will and respect for Dow Jones in the minds of the public. If a less reliable index and average were used, the CBT Index contract would be no more than a gambling device and would not gain CFTC approval. Thus, the Board's use of the Dow Jones Averages is not a "collateral" service or product which utilizes the good will of Dow Jones in an attenuated fashion.[64] The use of the Dow Jones Averages is not aimed at appealing to that segment of the public which is interested in the activities of Dow Jones. The contract is intended to appeal to the customers of the Board who are interested in trading stock market index futures, and the contract is designed to give those traders the sense of confidence that knowing that the contract is identical to a "Dow Jones contract" will surely produce.

Recently, the United States District Court for the Southern District of New York, Judge Milton Pollack presiding, granted Standard & Poor's Corporation's request for a preliminary injunction to prevent Commodity Exchange, Inc. (Comex) from trading in its proposed "Comex 500" con-

---

64. Good will is recognized as a business asset, and it figures significantly in the valuation of a business. Harm done to the good will of a business has been recognized as a proper element of consequential damages in actions sounding in contract and in tort. When a business is sold, its good will can be transferred along with its other assets. It follows that, in some circumstances, the good will of a business can be appropriated to another's use, and a wrongful appropriation of that property right is actionable.

tracts. (*Standard & Poor's Corp., Inc. v. Commodity Exchange, Inc.* (Docket No. 82–2545) (S.D.N.Y. May 13, 1982)), 14 S.R.L.R. 976, *aff'd* (2d Cir. 1982), 683 F.2d 704.)) The Comex 500 contract was based on Standard & Poor's 500 (S & P 500) Stock Index. The holding in that case was the subject of extensive analysis by the trial court, and that case has been thoroughly briefed in this court. The facts of that case can be summarized as follows. Beginning in 1979, Comex entered into negotiations with Standard & Poor's (S & P) in order to obtain a license to trade stock market index contracts based upon the S & P 500. S & P ultimately granted a license to trade in such a contract to the Chicago Mercantile Exchange. In December 1980, Comex applied to the CFTC for designation as the contract market for the Comex 500 contract. In the application, Comex referred to the "Comex 500" and the "S & P 500" interchangeably. Comex never proposed to calculate or use its own index of 500 stocks, instead stating that its contract was to be quoted in terms of and settled on the basis of the current quotation for the S & P 500. Prior to the CFTC ruling on the contract, Comex published a brochure featuring S & P's name prominently and stating that the Comex 500 was to be settled based on the S & P 500. The court found that Comex planned to use the S & P name and reputation in a way that would cause confusion as to the sponsorship of the contract, and that Comex's proposed use of the S & P 500 was a misappropriation of S & P's property without authority from and over the objection of S & P.

The trial court, in the instant case, found that the *S & P* case was distinguishable for four reasons: (1) Unlike Dow Jones, S & P does not make the method by which its index is calculated completely public. Although the list of stocks in the index and the general formula for computing the average are public knowledge, the "real time" calculations of the index by S & P's licensees depend on the input of confidential information provided by S & P. The court found that this factor makes it impossible to calculate the S & P Index without the "direct participation" of S & P, while the Dow Jones Index may be calculated without any secret information from Dow Jones; (2) The name of the Comex 500 contract is perilously close to the S & P 500 trademark. In the instant case, the Board's contract was to make no use of the Dow Jones name, although the disclaimer required by the trial court will have the effect of placing Dow Jones's name on every contract; (3) Comex never disclaimed an association with S & P. Instead, it tried to create the impression that the contract was sponsored by S & P. The Board does and will continue to disclaim any association with Dow Jones; and (4) Comex used the S & P name to promote the contract, while the Board will make no promotional use of the Dow Jones name.

The distinctions drawn by the trial court as to the differing use by the two exchanges of the trademarks and trade names of the index producers are significant. The absence of the Dow Jones name from the Board's promotional materials and the use of an unambiguous disclaimer of sponsorship clearly make the Board's planned activity less egregious than

Comex's. The use of the disclaimer may obviate any possible confusion as to the sponsorship of the contract, although this court has noted that a disclaimer does not adequately protect the rights of the complaining party if the connection inherent in the product itself is sufficiently strong. However, the misappropriation complained of in this case is not a misappropriation of Dow Jones's name, but of the property right of Dow Jones in its averages and the good will and public respect attendant to them.

* * *

The Board's conduct is within the boundaries of the doctrine of misappropriation. That doctrine will extend to protect the complaining party from unfair competition or trade practices regardless of how novel or ingenious those practices are. The doctrine is "adaptable and capacious" and has been described as "encompassing any form of commercial immorality." The controlling question in a misappropriation case is whether the commercial practice at issue is fair or unfair.

The facts in the instant case amply demonstrate that the appropriation of the Dow Jones Index and Averages by the Board for use as a trading vehicle is unfair. We hold that the Board's proposed actions are a misappropriation of the Dow Jones Index and Averages.

NOTES

1. What are the boundaries of intellectual property misappropriation as described in *Dow Jones*? How can a party considering a use of information or intellectual works developed by another party know that the use is unfair and a basis for a misappropriation claim? Do the standards used by the court in *Dow Jones* afford persons with enough notice of the threshold of liability for misappropriation of intellectual works to give users of those works a chance to detect risks of liability and to plan their activities accordingly?

2. For what subject matters or situations will a misappropriation claim provide a creator of an intellectual work with rights that differ from those arising under other intellectual property laws? What does the tort of misappropriation as applied to intellectual works add to the overall picture of controls over intellectual works?

3. Is the merit of the misappropriation tort its flexibility and adaptability to different situations and types of works? Or is the lack of detailed specifications regarding the types of intellectual works that can be misappropriated and the forms of misuse of works that will constitute misappropriation likely to produce disparate results in factually similar cases? Is there a risk of over-deterrence of legitimate conduct as persons who are contemplating proper uses of works fear that misappropriation standards will be applied in unpredictable ways to impose liability on them?

4. Are the protections afforded through misappropriation claims concerning intellectual works coextensive with the range of free rider problems concerning the use of such works? At what point should free rider problems be seen as being extensive enough to justify the recognition of misappropria-

tion liability in order to reduce such problems? How does the scope of other intellectual property laws affect the significance of free rider problems regarding different types of works and the corresponding need for misappropriation claims regarding such works?

5. The court's opinion in *National Basketball Association v. Motorola, Inc.*, 105 F.3d 841 (2d Cir. 1997), reprinted earlier in this chapter in the section on federalism, provides another good example of a recent intellectual property misappropriation claim, as well as a discussion of the extent to which broad claims of this sort may be preempted by the Copyright Act or other federal intellectual property statutes.

V. TRESPASS TO CHATTELS

Claims for trespass typically turn on physical intrusions into legally controlled property, such as when a person enters into the real property of another without permission or some other special basis for entry. Trespass in the context of personal property involves exerting control over personal property without the owner's consent in a manner that deprives the owner of the control over the property normally associated with personal property ownership. Some recent cases have recognized a type of trespass to chattels involving misappropriations of intellectual property and other information (although, as discussed in the notes at the end of this chapter, some courts have narrowed the application of this legal theory by requiring substantial evidence of harm to a physical chattel before ordering relief). The following case illustrates this type of trespass to chattels claim, and describes some of the ways that this legal theory may supplement and extend grounds for relief under more traditional claims of intellectual property misappropriation.

EBAY, INC. v. BIDDER'S EDGE, INC.

United States District Court, N.D. California, 2000.
100 F.Supp.2d 1058.

ORDER GRANTING PRELIMINARY INJUNCTION

Plaintiff eBay, Inc.'s ("eBay") motion for preliminary injunction was heard by the court on April 14, 2000. The court has read the moving and responding papers and heard the argument of counsel. For the reasons set forth below, the court preliminarily enjoins defendant Bidder's Edge, Inc. ("BE") from accessing eBay's computer systems by use of any automated querying program without eBay's written authorization.

I. BACKGROUND

eBay is an Internet-based, person-to-person trading site. eBay offers sellers the ability to list items for sale and prospective buyers the ability to search those listings and bid on items. The seller can set the terms and conditions of the auction. The item is sold to the highest bidder. The transaction is consummated directly between the buyer and seller without eBay's involvement. A potential purchaser looking for a particular item can access the eBay site and perform a key word search for relevant auctions and bidding status. eBay has also created category listings that identify items in over 2500 categories, such as antiques, computers, and dolls. Users may browse these category listing pages to identify items of interest.

Users of the eBay site must register and agree to the eBay User Agreement. Users agree to the seven page User Agreement by clicking on an "I Accept" button located at the end of the User Agreement. The current version of the User Agreement prohibits the use of "any robot, spider, other automatic device, or manual process to monitor or copy our web pages or the content contained herein without our prior expressed written permission." It is not clear that the version of the User Agreement in effect at the time BE began searching the eBay site prohibited such activity, or that BE ever agreed to comply with the User Agreement.

eBay currently has over 7 million registered users. Over 400,000 new items are added to the site every day. Every minute, 600 bids are placed on almost 3 million items. Users currently perform, on average, 10 million searches per day on eBay's database. Bidding for and sales of items are continuously ongoing in millions of separate auctions.

A software robot is a computer program which operates across the Internet to perform searching, copying and retrieving functions on the web sites of others. A software robot is capable of executing thousands of instructions per minute, far in excess of what a human can accomplish. Robots consume the processing and storage resources of a system, making that portion of the system's capacity unavailable to the system owner or other users. Consumption of sufficient system resources will slow the processing of the overall system and can overload the system such that it will malfunction or "crash." A severe malfunction can cause a loss of data and an interruption in services.

The eBay site employs "robot exclusion headers." A robot exclusion header is a message, sent to computers programmed to detect and respond to such headers, that eBay does not permit unauthorized robotic activity. Programmers who wish to comply with the Robot Exclusion Standard design their robots to read a particular data file, "robots.txt," and to comply with the control directives it contains.

To enable computers to communicate with each other over the Internet, each is assigned a unique Internet Protocol address. When a computer requests information from another computer over the Internet, the requesting computer must offer its IP address to the responding computer in order to allow a response to be sent. These IP addresses allow the identification of the source of incoming requests. eBay identifies robotic activity on its site by monitoring the number of incoming requests from each particular IP address. Once eBay identifies an IP address believed to be involved in robotic activity, an investigation into the identity, origin and owner of the IP address may be made in order to determine if the activity is legitimate or authorized. If an investigation reveals unauthorized robotic activity, eBay may attempt to ignore ("block") any further requests from that IP address. Attempts to block requests from particular IP addresses are not always successful.

Organizations often install "proxy server" software on their computers. Proxy server software acts as a focal point for outgoing Internet requests. Proxy servers conserve system resources by directing all outgoing and incoming data traffic through a centralized portal. Typically, organizations limit the use of their proxy servers to local users. However, some organizations, either as a public service or because of a failure properly to protect their proxy server through the use of a "firewall," allow their proxy servers to be accessed by remote users. Outgoing requests from remote users can be routed through such unprotected proxy servers and appear to originate from the proxy server. Incoming responses are then received by the proxy server and routed to the remote user. Information requests sent through such proxy servers cannot easily be traced back to the originating IP address and can be used to circumvent attempts to block queries from the originating IP address. Blocking queries from innocent third party proxy servers is both inefficient, because it creates an endless game of hide-and-seek, and potentially counterproductive, as it runs a substantial risk of blocking requests from legitimate, desirable users who use that proxy server.

BE is a company with 22 employees that was founded in 1997. The BE web site debuted in November 1998. BE does not host auctions. BE is an auction aggregation site designed to offer on-line auction buyers the ability to search for items across numerous on-line auctions without having to search each host site individually. As of March 2000, the BE web site contained information on more that five million items being auctioned on more than one hundred auction sites. BE also provides its users with additional auction-related services and information. The information available on the BE site is contained in a database of information that BE compiles through access to various auction sites such as eBay. When a user enters a search for a particular item at BE, BE searches its database and generates a list of every item in the database responsive to the search, organized by auction closing date and time. Rather than going to each host auction site one at a time, a user who goes to BE may conduct a single search to obtain information about that item on every auction site tracked by BE. It is important to include information regarding eBay auctions on the BE site because eBay is by far the biggest consumer to consumer on-line auction site.

On June 16, 1997, over a year before the BE web site debuted, Peter Leeds wrote an email in response to an email from Kimbo Mundy, co-founder of BE. Mundy's email said, "I think the magazines may be overrating sites' ability to block. The early agent experiments, like Arthur Anderson's *BargainFinder* were careful to check the robots.txt file on every site and desist if asked." Mundy wrote back: "I believe well-behaved robots are still expected to check the robots.txt file.... Our other concern was also legal. It is one thing for customers to use a tool to check a site and quite another for a single commercial enterprise to do so on a repeated basis and then to distribute that information for profit."

In early 1998, eBay gave BE permission to include information regarding eBay-hosted auctions for Beanie Babies and Furbies in the BE database. In early 1999, BE added to the number of person-to-person auction sites it covered and started covering a broader range of items hosted by those sites, including eBay. On April 24, 1999, eBay verbally approved BE crawling the eBay web site for a period of 90 days. The parties contemplated that during this period they would reach a formal licensing agreement. They were unable to do so.

It appears that the primary dispute was over the method BE uses to search the eBay database. eBay wanted BE to conduct a search of the eBay system only when the BE system was queried by a BE user. This reduces the load on the eBay system and increases the accuracy of the BE data. BE wanted to recursively crawl the eBay system to compile its own auction database. This increases the speed of BE searches and allows BE to track the auctions generally and automatically update its users when activity occurs in particular auctions, categories of auctions, or when new items are added.

In late August or early September 1999, eBay requested by telephone that BE cease posting eBay auction listings on its site. BE agreed to do so. In October 1999, BE learned that other auction aggregations sites were including information regarding eBay auctions. On November 2, 1999, BE issued a press release indicating that it had resumed including eBay auction listings on its site. On November 9, 1999, eBay sent BE a letter reasserting that BE's activities were unauthorized, insisting that BE cease accessing the eBay site, alleging that BE's activities constituted a civil trespass and offering to license BE's activities. eBay and BE were again unable to agree on licensing terms. As a result, eBay attempted to block BE from accessing the eBay site; by the end of November, 1999, eBay had blocked a total of 169 IP addresses it believed BE was using to query eBay's system. BE elected to continue crawling eBay's site by using proxy servers to evade eBay's IP blocks.

Approximately 69% of the auction items contained in the BE database are from auctions hosted on eBay. BE estimates that it would lose one-third of its users if it ceased to cover the eBay auctions.

The parties agree that BE accessed the eBay site approximate 100,000 times a day. eBay alleges that BE activity constituted up to 1.53% of the number of requests received by eBay, and up to 1.10% of the total data transferred by eBay during certain periods in October and November of 1999. BE alleges that BE activity constituted no more than 1.11% of the requests received by eBay, and no more than 0.70% of the data transferred by eBay. eBay alleges that BE activity had fallen 27%, to 0.74% of requests and 0.61% of data, by February 20, 2000. eBay alleges damages due to BE's activity totaling between $45,323 and $61,804 for a ten month period including seven months in 1999 and the first three months in 2000. However, these calculations appear flawed in that they assume the maximal BE usage of eBay resources continued over all ten months. Moreover, the calculations attribute a pro rata share of eBay expenditures to BE activity, rather than attempting to calculate the incremental cost to eBay due to BE activity. eBay has not alleged any specific incremental damages due to BE activity.

It appears that major Internet search engines, such as Yahoo!, Google, Excite and AltaVista, respect the Robot Exclusion Standard.

eBay now moves for preliminary injunctive relief preventing BE from accessing the eBay computer system based on nine causes of action: trespass, false advertising, federal and state trademark dilution, computer fraud and abuse, unfair competition, misappropriation, interference with prospective economic advantage and unjust enrichment. However, eBay does not move, either independently or alternatively, for injunctive relief that is limited to restricting how BE can use data taken from the eBay site.

II. LEGAL STANDARD

To obtain preliminary injunctive relief, a movant must demonstrate "either a likelihood of success on the merits and the possibility of irreparable injury, or that serious questions going to the merits were raised and the balance of hardships tips sharply in its favor." The alternatives in the above standard represent "extremes of a single continuum," rather than two separate tests. "The critical element in determining the test to be applied is the relative hardship to the parties. If the balance of harm tips decidedly toward the plaintiff, then the plaintiff need not show as robust a likelihood of success on the merits as when the balance tips less decidedly." *Alaska v. Native Village of Venetie*, 856 F.2d 1384, 1389 (9th Cir. 1988). A "serious question" is one on which the movant has a "fair chance of success on the merits." *Sierra On–Line, Inc. v. Phoenix Software, Inc.*, 739 F.2d 1415, 1421 (9th Cir. 1984). Generally, the "balance of harm" evaluation should precede the "likelihood of success analysis" because until the balance of harm has been evaluated the court cannot know how strong and substantial the plaintiff's showing of the likelihood of success must be.

III. ANALYSIS

A. *Balance of Harm*

eBay asserts that it will suffer four types of irreparable harm if preliminary injunctive relief is not granted: (1) lost capacity of its computer systems resulting from to BE's use of automated agents; (2) damage to eBay's reputation and goodwill caused by BE's misleading postings; (3) dilution of the eBay mark; and (4) BE's unjust enrichment. The harm eBay alleges it will suffer can be divided into two categories. The first type of harm is harm that eBay alleges it will suffer as a result of BE's automated query programs burdening eBay's computer system ("system harm"). The second type of harm is harm that eBay alleges it will suffer as a result of BE's misrepresentations regarding the information that BE obtains through the use of these automated query programs ("reputational harm").

As noted above, eBay does not seek an injunction that is tailored to independently address the manner in which BE uses the information it obtains from eBay. Even without accessing eBay's computer systems by robot, BE could inflict reputational harm by misrepresenting the contents of eBay's auction database or by misusing eBay's trademark. Moreover, allowing frequent and complete recursive searching of eBay's database (which would presumably exacerbate the system harm), requiring appropriate disclaimers regarding the accuracy of BE's listings, or limiting BE's use of the eBay mark would all reduce or eliminate the possibility of reputational harm, without requiring the drastic remedy of enjoining BE from accessing eBay's database. Since eBay does not move independently or alternatively for injunctive relief tailored toward the alleged reputational harm, the court does not include the alleged reputational harm in the balance of harm analysis, nor does the court address the merits of the causes of action based on the alleged reputational harm in the likelihood of success analysis.

According to eBay, the load on its servers resulting from BE's web crawlers represents between 1.11% and 1.53% of the total load on eBay's listing servers. eBay alleges both economic loss from BE's current activities and potential harm resulting from the total crawling of BE and others. In alleging economic harm, eBay's argument is that eBay has expended considerable time, effort and money to create its computer system, and that BE should have to pay for the portion of eBay's system BE uses. eBay attributes a pro rata portion of the costs of maintaining its entire system to the BE activity. However, eBay does not indicate that these expenses are incrementally incurred because of BE's activities, nor that any particular service disruption can be attributed to BE's activities. eBay provides no support for the proposition that the pro rata costs of obtaining an item represent the appropriate measure of damages for unauthorized use. In contrast, California law appears settled that the appropriate measure of damages is the actual harm inflicted by the conduct:

Where the conduct complained of does not amount to a substantial interference with possession or the right thereto, but consists of intermeddling with or use of or damages to the personal property, the owner has a cause of action for trespass or case, and may recover only the actual damages suffered by reason of the impairment of the property or the loss of its use. Moreover, even if BE is inflicting incremental maintenance costs on eBay, potentially calculable monetary damages are not generally a proper foundation for a preliminary injunction. Nor does eBay appear to have made the required showing that this is the type of extraordinary case in which monetary damages may support equitable relief.

eBay's allegations of harm are based, in part, on the argument that BE's activities should be thought of as equivalent to sending in an army of 100,000 robots a day to check the prices in a competitor's store. This analogy, while graphic, appears inappropriate. Although an admittedly formalistic distinction, unauthorized robot intruders into a "brick and mortar" store would be committing a trespass to real property. There does not appear to be any doubt that the appropriate remedy for an ongoing trespass to business premises would be a preliminary injunction. More importantly, for the analogy to be accurate, the robots would have to make up less than two out of every one-hundred customers in the store, the robots would not interfere with the customers' shopping experience, nor would the robots even be seen by the customers. Under such circumstances, there is a legitimate claim that the robots would not pose any threat of irreparable harm. However, eBay's right to injunctive relief is also based upon a much stronger argument.

If BE's activity is allowed to continue unchecked, it would encourage other auction aggregators to engage in similar recursive searching of the eBay system such that eBay would suffer irreparable harm from reduced system performance, system unavailability, or data losses. BE does not appear to seriously contest that reduced system performance, system unavailability or data loss would inflict irreparable harm on eBay consisting of lost profits and lost customer goodwill. Harm resulting from lost profits and lost customer goodwill is irreparable because it is neither easily calculable, nor easily compensable and is therefore an appropriate basis for injunctive relief. Where, as here, the denial of preliminary injunctive relief would encourage an increase in the complained of activity, and such an increase would present a strong likelihood of irreparable harm, the plaintiff has at least established a possibility of irreparable harm.

* * *

BE correctly observes that there is a dearth of authority supporting a preliminary injunction based on an ongoing to trespass to chattels. In contrast, it is black letter law in California that an injunction is an appropriate remedy for a continuing trespass to real property. If eBay were a brick and mortar auction house with limited seating capacity, eBay would appear to be entitled to reserve those seats for potential bidders, to refuse entrance to individuals (or robots) with no intention of bidding on any of the items, and to seek preliminary injunctive relief against non-customer trespassers eBay was physically unable to exclude. The analytic difficulty is that a wrongdoer can commit an ongoing trespass of a computer system that is more akin to the traditional notion of a trespass to real property, than the traditional notion of a trespass to chattels, because even though it is ongoing, it will probably never amount to a conversion. The court concludes that under the circumstances present here, BE's ongoing violation of eBay's fundamental property right to exclude others from its computer system potentially causes sufficient irreparable harm to support a preliminary injunction.

* * *

B. *Likelihood of Success*

As noted above, eBay moves for a preliminary injunction on all nine of its causes of action. These nine causes of action correspond to eight legal theories: (1) trespass to chattels, (2) false advertising under the Lanham Act, (3) federal and state trademark dilution, (4) violation of the Computer Fraud and Abuse Act, (5) unfair competition, (6) misappropriation, (7) interference with prospective economic advantage and (8) unjust enrichment. The court finds that eBay has established a sufficient likelihood of prevailing on the trespass claim to support the requested injunctive relief. Since the court finds eBay is entitled to the relief requested based on its trespass claim, the court does not address the merits of the remaining claims or BE's arguments that many of these other state law causes of action are preempted by federal copyright law. The court first addresses the merits of the trespass claim, then BE's arguments regarding copyright preemption of the trespass claim, and finally the public interest.

1. *Trespass*

Trespass to chattels "lies where an intentional interference with the possession of personal property has proximately cause injury." *Thrifty–Tel v. Bezenek*, 46 Cal.App.4th 1559, 1566, 54 Cal.Rptr.2d 468 (1996). Trespass to chattels "although seldom employed as a tort theory in California" was recently applied to cover the unauthorized use of long distance telephone lines. *Id.* Specifically, the court noted "the electronic signals generated by the [defendants'] activities were sufficiently tangible to support a trespass cause of action." *Id.* at n. 6. Thus, it appears likely that the electronic signals sent by BE to retrieve information from eBay's computer system are also sufficiently tangible to support a trespass cause of action.

In order to prevail on a claim for trespass based on accessing a computer system, the plaintiff must establish: (1) defendant intentionally and without authorization interfered with plaintiff's possessory interest in the computer system; and (2) defendant's unauthorized use proximately resulted in damage to plaintiff. *See Thrifty–Tel*, 46 Cal.App.4th at 1566, 54 Cal.Rptr.2d 468; see also *Itano v. Colonial Yacht Anchorage*, 267 Cal. App.2d 84, 90, 72 Cal.Rptr. 823 (1968) ("When conduct complained of consists of intermeddling with personal property 'the owner has a cause of action for trespass or case, and may recover only the actual damages suffered by reason of the impairment of the property or the loss of its use.'") (quoting *Zaslow v. Kroenert*, 29 Cal.2d 541, 550, 176 P.2d 1 (1946)). Here, eBay has presented evidence sufficient to establish a strong likelihood of proving both prongs and ultimately prevailing on the merits of its trespass claim.

a. BE's Unauthorized Interference

eBay argues that BE's use was unauthorized and intentional. eBay is correct. BE does not dispute that it employed an automated computer program to connect with and search eBay's electronic database. BE admits that, because other auction aggregators were including eBay's auctions in their listing, it continued to "crawl" eBay's web site even after eBay demanded BE terminate such activity.

BE argues that it cannot trespass eBay's web site because the site is publicly accessible. BE's argument is unconvincing. eBay's servers are private property, conditional access to which eBay grants the public. eBay does not generally permit the type of automated access made by BE. In fact, eBay explicitly notifies automated visitors that their access is not permitted. "In general, California does recognize a trespass claim where the defendant exceeds the scope of the consent." *Baugh v. CBS, Inc.*, 828 F.Supp. 745, 756 (N.D.Cal.1993).

Even if BE's web crawlers were authorized to make individual queries of eBay's system, BE's web crawlers exceeded the scope of any such consent when they began acting like robots by making repeated queries. Moreover, eBay repeatedly and explicitly notified BE that its use of eBay's computer system was unauthorized. The entire reason BE directed its queries through proxy servers was to evade eBay's attempts to stop this unauthorized access. The court concludes that BE's activity is sufficiently outside of the scope of the use permitted by eBay that it is unauthorized for the purposes of establishing a trespass.

eBay argues that BE interfered with eBay's possessory interest in its computer system. Although eBay appears unlikely to be able to show a substantial interference at this time, such a showing is not required. Conduct that does not amount to a substantial interference with possession, but which consists of intermeddling with or use of another's personal property, is sufficient to establish a cause of action for trespass to chattel. Although the court admits some uncertainty as to the precise level of possessory interference required to constitute an intermeddling, there does not appear to be any dispute that eBay can show that BE's conduct amounts to use of eBay's computer systems. Accordingly, eBay has made a strong showing that it is likely to prevail on the merits of its assertion that BE's use of eBay's computer system was an unauthorized and intentional interference with eBay's possessory interest.

b. Damage to eBay's Computer System

A trespasser is liable when the trespass diminishes the condition, quality or value of personal property. *See CompuServe, Inc. v. Cyber Promotions*, 962 F.Supp. 1015 (S.D.Ohio 1997). The quality or value of personal property may be "diminished even though it is not physically damaged by defendant's conduct." *Id.* at 1022. The Restatement offers the following explanation for the harm requirement:

The interest of a possessor of a chattel in its inviolability, unlike the similar interest of a possessor of land, is not given legal protection by an action for nominal damages for harmless intermeddlings with the chattel. In order that an actor who interferes with another's chattel may be liable, his conduct must affect some other and more important interest of the possessor. Therefore, one who intentionally intermeddles with another's chattel is subject to liability only if his intermeddling is harmful to the possessor's materially valuable interest in the physical condition, quality, or value of the chattel, or if the possessor is deprived of the use of the chattel for a substantial time, or some other legally protected interest of the possessor is affected.... Sufficient legal protection of the possessor's interest in the mere inviolability of his chattel is afforded by his privilege to use reasonable force to protect his possession against even harmless interference.

Restatement (Second) of Torts § 218 cmt. e (1977).

eBay is likely to be able to demonstrate that BE's activities have diminished the quality or value of eBay's computer systems. BE's activities consume at least a portion of plaintiff's bandwidth and server capacity. Although there is some dispute as to the percentage of queries on eBay's site for which BE is responsible, BE admits that it sends some 80,000 to 100,000 requests to plaintiff's computer systems per day. Although eBay does not claim that this consumption has led to any physical damage to eBay's computer system, nor does eBay provide any evidence to support the claim that it may have lost revenues or customers based on this use, eBay's claim is that BE's use is appropriating eBay's personal property by using valuable bandwidth and capacity, and necessarily compromising eBay's ability to use that capacity for its own purposes.

* * *

2. Copyright Preemption

BE argues that the trespass claim, along with eBay's other state law causes of action, "is similar to eBay's originally filed but now dismissed copyright infringement claim, and each is based on eBay's assertion that Bidder's Edge copies eBay's auction listings, a right within federal copyright law." BE is factually incorrect to the extent it argues that the trespass claim arises out of what BE does with the information it gathers by accessing eBay's computer system, rather than the mere fact that BE accesses and uses that system without authorization.

A state law cause of action is preempted by the Copyright Act if, (1) the rights asserted under state law are "equivalent" to those protected by the Copyright Act, and (2) the work involved falls within the "subject matter" of the Copyright Act as set forth in 17 U.S.C. §§ 102 and 103. "In order not to be equivalent, the right under state law must have an extra element that changes the nature of the action so that it is qualitatively different from a copyright infringement claim." *Xerox Corp. v. Apple Computer, Inc.*, 734 F.Supp. 1542, 1550 (N.D.Cal.1990). Here, eBay asserts a right not to have BE use its computer systems without authorization. The right to exclude others from using physical personal property is not equivalent to any rights protected by copyright and therefore constitutes an extra element that makes trespass qualitatively different from a copyright infringement claim.

3. *Public Interest*

The traditional equitable criteria for determining whether an injunction should issue include whether the public interest favors granting the injunction. *American Motorcyclist Ass'n v. Watt,* 714 F.2d 962, 965 (9th Cir.1983). The parties submit a variety of declarations asserting that the Internet will cease to function if, according to eBay, personal and intellectual property rights are not respected, or, according to BE, if information published on the Internet cannot be universally accessed and used. Although the court suspects that the Internet will not only survive, but continue to grow and develop regardless of the outcome of this litigation, the court also recognizes that it is poorly suited to determine what balance between encouraging the exchange of information, and preserving economic incentives to create, will maximize the public good. Particularly on the limited record available at the preliminary injunction stage, the court is unable to determine whether the general public interest factors in favor of or against a preliminary injunction.

BE makes the more specific allegation that granting a preliminary injunction in favor of eBay will harm the public interest because eBay is alleged to have engaged in anticompetitive behavior in violation of federal antitrust law. The Ninth Circuit has noted that in evaluating whether to issue a preliminary injunction, the district court is under no obligation to consider the merits of any antitrust counterclaims once the plaintiff has demonstrated a likelihood of success on the merits. Although anticompetitive behavior may be appropriately considered in the context of a preliminary injunction based on trademark infringement, where misuse is an affirmative defense, it does not appear to be appropriately considered here, because there is no equivalent affirmative defense to trespass to chattels. Accordingly, the court concludes the public interest does not weigh against granting a preliminary injunction.

IV. ORDER

Bidder's Edge, its officers, agents, servants, employees, attorneys and those in active concert or participation with them who receive actual notice of this order by personal service or otherwise, are hereby enjoined pending the trial of this matter, from using any automated query program, robot, web crawler or other similar device, without written authorization, to access eBay's computer systems or networks, for the purpose of copying any part of eBay's auction database. As a condition of the preliminary injunction, eBay is ordered to post a bond in the amount of $2,000,000 to secure payment of any damages sustained by defendant if it is later found to have been wrongfully enjoined. This order shall take effect 10 days from the date on which it is filed.

Nothing in this order precludes BE from utilizing information obtained from eBay's site other than by automated query program, robot, web crawler or similar device. The court denies eBay's request for a preliminary injunction barring access to its site based upon BE's alleged trademark infringement, trademark dilution and other claims. This denial is without prejudice to an application for an injunction limiting or conditioning the use of any information obtained on the theory that BE's use violates some protected right of eBay.

NOTES

1. The trespass to chattel theory embraced in *eBay* as a means to limit information transfers has been recognized by courts in diverse factual contexts. *See generally* Dan L. Burk, *The Trouble With Trespass, 4* J. Small & Emerging Bus. L. 27 (2000). An early decision found such a trespass where children gained unauthorized access to a long-distance telephone system, initially by manually entering randomly guessed telephone authorization codes and later by using software to conduct high-speed automated searches for access codes. *Thrifty–Tel, Inc. v. Bezenek,* 46 Cal.App.4th 1559, 54 Cal. Rptr.2d 468, 471 (1996). In a later case that received considerable attention, CompuServe, then a leading supplier of computer information services via a proprietary computer network, successfully claimed that it suffered a trespass to chattels where a commercial service transmitted unsolicited e-mail messages in bulk—typically referred to as "spam"—to thousands of user addresses on the CompuServe network. *CompuServe Inc. v. Cyber Promotions, Inc.,* 962 F.Supp. 1015, 1021–24 (S.D. Ohio 1997). A trespass to chattels was recognized under New York law in the context of an Internet domain name registration system in *Register.com, Inc. v. Verio, Inc.,* 126 F.Supp.2d 238 (S.D.N.Y. 2000), *aff'd as modified,* 356 F.3d 393 (2d Cir. 2004). There, the defendant's web hosting and development site robotically searched a registrar's database of newly registered domain names in search of business leads- in and the court found that the threatened harm if others emulated the defendant's practices provided sufficient evidence to support the issuance of a preliminary injunction. *See* 126 F.Supp.2d at 250–51.

2. To support a claim of trespass to chattels of the sort accepted in *eBay,* a plaintiff must show some harm to a chattel or its usefulness. The degree of harm necessary has been the subject of considerable dispute. In *eBay,* it was the specter of potential harm if others joined in the defendant's practices that established sufficient harm to support the preliminary injunction in that case. What are the risks of allowing injunctive relief based on such speculation about future activities and their harmful consequences? Does such a standard offer too easy a means to restrict access to intellectual property and information?

3. How much must the harm associated with unauthorized use of a computer or other device relate to the physical equipment involved in order to make out a trespass to chattels claim? When will impairment of the value of

the intellectual property or other information acquired through such actions be enough to establish this type of trespass claim? When will other harm suffice?

The harm to chattels and an owner's business activities needed to support a trespass to chattels claim was the focus of the California Supreme Court's analysis in *Intel Corp. v. Hamidi*, 30 Cal.4th 1342, 1 Cal.Rptr.3d 32, 71 P.3d 296 (2003). There, the defendant, a former Intel employee, sent e-mails criticizing Intel's employment practices to numerous current employees on Intel's electronic mail system on six occasions over almost two years. The messages and the process of sending them caused neither physical damage nor functional disruption to the company's computers, nor did they at any time deprive Intel of the use of its computers. The contents of the messages, however, caused adverse discussion of Intel among employees and managers. Intel brought suit, claiming that by communicating with its employees over the company's e-mail system Hamidi committed the tort of trespass to chattels. The trial court granted Intel's motion for summary judgment and enjoined Hamidi from any further mailings. A divided Court of Appeal affirmed. The California Supreme Court reversed on the ground that, under California law, the tort of trespass to chattels is not committed where an electronic communication is sent that neither damages the computer system involved nor impairs its functioning. The court found that "[s]uch an electronic communication does not constitute an actionable trespass to personal property, i.e., the computer system, because it does not interfere with the possessor's use or possession of, or any other legally protected interest in, the personal property itself." *Id.* at 1347.

The court concluded that Intel's claims that it was injured by the content of Hamidi's communications or by the loss of employee productivity as employees read and discussed the communications did not allege sufficient types of harms to support a trespass to chattels claim. The court's analysis of the harm needed was as follows:

> [The] theory of "impairment by content" (Burk, *The Trouble with Trespass*, [4 J. Small & Emerging Bus.L. 27, 37 (2000)]) threatens to stretch trespass law to cover injuries far afield from the harms to possession the tort evolved to protect. Intel's theory would expand the tort of trespass to chattels to cover virtually any unconsented-to communication that, solely because of its content, is unwelcome to the recipient or intermediate transmitter. As the dissenting justice below explained, " 'Damage' of this nature—the distraction of reading or listening to an unsolicited communication—is not within the scope of the injury against which the trespass-to-chattel tort protects, and indeed trivializes it. After all, '[t]he property interest protected by the old action of trespass was that of possession; and this has continued to affect the character of the action.' (Prosser & Keeton on Torts [(5th ed.1984)] § 14, p. 87.) Reading an e-mail transmitted to equipment designed to receive it, in and of itself, does not affect the possessory interest in the equipment. [¶] Indeed, if a chattel's receipt of an electronic communication constitutes a trespass to that chattel, then not only are unsolicited telephone calls and faxes trespasses to chattel, but unwelcome radio waves and television signals also constitute a trespass to chattel every time the viewer inadvertently sees or hears the

unwanted program." We agree. While unwelcome communications, electronic or otherwise, can cause a variety of injuries to economic relations, reputation and emotions, those interests are protected by other branches of tort law; in order to address them, we need not create a fiction of injury to the communication system.

Nor may Intel appropriately assert a property interest in its employees' time. "The Restatement test clearly speaks in the first instance to the impairment of the chattel.... But employees are not chattels (at least not in the legal sense of the term)." (Burk, *The Trouble with Trespass*, *supra*, 4 J. Small & Emerging Bus.L. at p. 36.) Whatever interest Intel may have in preventing its employees from receiving disruptive communications, it is not an interest in personal property, and trespass to chattels is therefore not an action that will lie to protect it. Nor, finally, can the fact Intel staff spent time attempting to block Hamidi's messages be bootstrapped into an injury to Intel's possessory interest in its computers. To quote, again, from the dissenting opinion in the Court of Appeal: "[I]t is circular to premise the damage element of a tort solely upon the steps taken to prevent the damage. Injury can only be established by the completed tort's consequences, not by the cost of the steps taken to avoid the injury and prevent the tort; otherwise, we can create injury for every supposed tort."

Intel connected its e-mail system to the Internet and permitted its employees to make use of this connection both for business and, to a reasonable extent, for their own purposes. In doing so, the company necessarily contemplated the employees' receipt of unsolicited as well as solicited communications from other companies and individuals. That some communications would, because of their contents, be unwelcome to Intel management was virtually inevitable. Hamidi did nothing but use the e-mail system for its intended purpose—to communicate with employees. The system worked as designed, delivering the messages without any physical or functional harm or disruption. These occasional transmissions cannot reasonably be viewed as impairing the quality or value of Intel's computer system. We conclude, therefore, that Intel has not presented undisputed facts demonstrating an injury to its personal property, or to its legal interest in that property, that support, under California tort law, an action for trespass to chattels.

Id. at 1358–60. See also *Pearl Investments, LLC v. Standard I/O, Inc.,* 257 F.Supp.2d 326, 354 (D.Me. 2003) (finding no evidence that defendant's unauthorized access to a computer network impaired the network's condition, quality, or value); *DirecTV, Inc. v. Chin,* 2003 WL 22102144, at *2 (W.D.Tex. 2003) (trespass to chattels claim dismissed where claimant alleged no specific facts indicating harm to computer system); *Ticketmaster Corp. v. Tickets.com, Inc.,* 2000 WL 1887522 at *4 (C.D.Cal. 2000) (noting that a trespass to chattel claim might lie based on unauthorized use of a computer system coupled with some extraction of information from the system, but finding insufficient interference with the plaintiff's business activities to support a preliminary injunction).

VI. IDEA SUBMISSIONS

Claims for compensation regarding ideas submitted to companies typically involve contract or quantum meruit theories. The former depend on criteria for payments to an idea submitter that have been agreed to by the submitter and the idea recipient, either explicitly or implicitly. The latter depend on the degree of benefit obtained by the recipient of an idea and the unfairness of allowing the recipient to gain such benefit without compensating the idea submitter. Both types of claims are complicated by the uncertainty surrounding the nature and value of a submitted idea until it is received and evaluated by its recipient.

The following cases explore these bases for claims by idea submitters in situations where their ideas proved valuable to the idea recipients. In reading each case, consider the steps that both the submitter and the recipient of the idea in question could have taken to avoid uncertainty about the circumstances in which compensation would be given and the scope of that compensation.

REEVES v. ALYESKA PIPELINE SERVICE COMPANY

Supreme Court of Alaska, 1996.
926 P.2d 1130.

PER CURIAM.

I. INTRODUCTION

This case raises issues concerning the protection of ideas. It arises out of John Reeves' claims that in 1991 Alyeska Pipeline Service Company (Alyeska) appropriated his idea for a visitor center at a popular turnout overlooking the Trans–Alaska Pipeline. The superior court granted summary judgment to Alyeska. We reverse in part and remand for further proceedings.

II. FACTS AND PROCEEDINGS

In 1985 Alyeska created a visitor turnout at Mile 9 of the Steese Highway between Fox and Fairbanks. The turnout had informational signs and provided visitors a view of the Trans–Alaska Pipeline. Before Alyeska constructed the turnout, visitors gained access to the pipeline by a nearby road and trespassed on the Trans–Alaska Pipeline right-of-way.

John Reeves, owner of Gold Dredge No. 8, a tourist attraction outside Fairbanks and near the turnout, contacted Alyeska in January 1991 to discuss a tourism idea he had. He spoke with Keith Burke, Alyeska's Fairbanks Manager. After receiving Burke's assurance that the tourism idea was "between us," Reeves orally disclosed his idea to build a visitor center at the turnout. He proposed that Alyeska lease him the land and he build the center, sell Alyeska merchandise, and display a "pig"[65] and a cross-section of pipe.

Burke told him the idea "look[ed] good" and asked Reeves to submit a written proposal, which Reeves did two days later. The proposal explained Reeves' idea of operating a visitor center on land leased to him by Alyeska. The proposal included plans to provide small tours, display a "pig," pipe valve, and section of pipe, sell refreshments and pipeline memorabilia, and plant corn and cabbage.

After submitting the proposal, Reeves met with Burke once again. At this meeting Burke told Reeves the proposal looked good and was exactly what he wanted. In Reeves' words, Burke told him, "We're going to do this deal, and I'm going to have my Anchorage lawyers draw it." Reeves claimed he and Burke envisioned that the visitor center would be operating by the 1991 summer tourist season.

Reeves alleges that Alyeska agreed during this meeting (1) to grant access to the turnout for twenty years; (2) to allow Reeves to construct and operate an information center; and (3) to allow Reeves to sell merchandise and charge a $2.00 admission fee. Reeves stated that, in exchange, he agreed to pay Alyeska ten percent of gross receipts.

Over the next several months, Burke allegedly told Reeves that the deal was "looking good" and not to worry because it takes time for a large corporation to move. However, in spring 1991, Burke told Reeves that the visitor center was such a good idea that Alyeska was going to implement it without Reeves. By August 1991 Alyeska had installed a portable building at the turnout to serve as a visitor center; it built a permanent log cabin structure in 1992.

The members of the Alyeska Pipeline Club North (APCN) operated the visitor center and sold T-shirts, hats, and other items.[66] APCN does not charge admission. A section of pipeline and a "pig" are on display. APCN employees provide information and answer visitors' questions. Members of APCN had suggested in 1987 that Alyeska create a visitor center at the turnout. However, Alyeska had rejected the idea at that time. Before meeting with Reeves, Burke did not know that APCN's visitor center idea had been raised and rejected by Alyeska in 1987.

Approximately 100,000 people visited the visitor center each summer in 1992 and 1993. It grossed over $50,000 in sales each year. The net profit for 1993 was calculated to be $5,000–$15,000. APCN received all the profit.

Reeves filed suit in May 1993. By amended complaint, he alleged a variety of tort and contract claims. Judge Charles R. Pengilly granted Alyeska's motion for summary judgment on all claims; Reeves appeals.
* * *

---

65. A "pig" is a device which passes through the pipeline to clean interior pipe walls, survey interior pipe shape and detect corrosion.

66. Alyeska Pipeline Club North is a non-profit corporation run by Alyeska employees. It raises money to fund activities such as picnics and Christmas parties for Alyeska employees.

III. DISCUSSION

* * *

Reeves sued Alyeska on claims of breach of oral contract, promissory estoppel, breach of implied contract, quasi-contract (unjust enrichment and quantum meruit), breach of the covenant of good faith and fair dealing, breach of license and/or lease agreement, and various torts related to the contractual relationships alleged.

This case presents several questions of first impression concerning the protection of business ideas. Reeves claims that Alyeska contracted for both the disclosure and use of his idea. Alyeska maintains that Reeves' "idea" was not novel or original and that an Alyeska employee had proposed an identical idea in 1987. Therefore, Alyeska argues that most of Reeves' claims fail because his idea was not novel or original. Alyeska also argues that Reeves' claims are barred by the statute of frauds. Before reaching the merits of Reeves' claims we must first briefly discuss the law relating to the protection of ideas and the roles of novelty and originality.

A. *Protection of Ideas*

The law pertaining to the protection of ideas must reconcile the public's interest in access to new ideas with the perceived injustice of permitting some to exploit commercially the ideas of others. Federal law addresses the protection of new inventions and the expression of ideas. Federal patent law protects inventors of novel, nonobvious, and useful inventions by excluding others from "making, using, or selling the invention" for a period of seventeen years. Federal copyright law protects an individual's tangible *expression* of an idea, but not the intangible idea itself. Copyright law creates a monopoly for the author that allows him or her to benefit economically from the author's creative efforts. It does not create a monopoly on the idea from which the expression originates; the idea remains available for all to use. Reeves' claims do not fall under these federal protections because his idea is not a new invention, nor is it expressed in a copyrighted work. Nevertheless, federal law is not the only protection available to individuals and their ideas.

Creating a middle ground between no protection and the legal monopolies created by patent and copyright law, courts have protected ideas under a variety of contract and contract-like theories. These theories protect individuals who spend their time and energy developing ideas that may benefit others. It would be inequitable to prevent these individuals from obtaining legally enforceable compensation from those who voluntarily choose to benefit from the services of the "idea-person." The California Supreme Court expressed this concept in the following manner:

> Generally speaking, ideas are as free as the air and as speech and the senses, and as potent or weak, interesting or drab, as the experiences, philosophies, vocabularies, and other variables of the speaker and listener may combine to produce, to portray, or to comprehend. But there can be circumstances when neither air nor ideas may be

acquired without cost. The diver who goes deep in the sea, even as the pilot who ascends high in the troposphere, knows full well that for life itself he, or someone on his behalf, must arrange for air (or its respiration-essential element, oxygen) to be specifically provided at the time and place of need. The theatrical producer likewise may be dependent for his business life on the procurement of ideas from other persons as well as the dressing up and portrayal of his self-conceptions; he may not find his own sufficient for survival.

Desny v. Wilder, 46 Cal.2d 715, 299 P.2d 257, 265 (1956). The scope of idea protection, although primarily raised in the entertainment field, is not limited to that industry; it may also apply to business and scientific ideas.

We have not had occasion to address these theories in the context of the protection of ideas. In addressing each of Reeves' claims we must determine whether the special nature of ideas affects the application of traditional contract and contract-like claims. In making these determinations we are mindful of the competing policies of retaining the free exchange of ideas and compensating those who develop and market their ideas. On the one hand, protecting ideas by providing compensation to the author for their use or appropriation rewards the idea person and encourages the development of creative and intellectual ideas which will benefit humankind. On the other hand, protecting ideas also inevitably restricts their free use, potentially delaying or restricting the benefit any given idea might confer on society.

Reeves argues that requiring novelty and originality, as did the trial court, erroneously imports property theories into contract-based claims. He contends that so long as the parties bargained for the disclosure of the idea, the disclosure serves as consideration and the idea itself need not have the qualities of property. Alyeska argues that novelty and originality should be employed as limiting factors in idea cases because these cases are based on a theory of idea as intellectual property. Alyeska contends that in order to be protected, an idea must have "not been suggested to or known by the public at any prior time."

We find that the manner in which requirements such as novelty or originality are applied depends largely on which theory of recovery is pursued. Thus, we will address the parties' arguments concerning novelty as they apply to each of Reeves' theories of recovery.

B. Express Contract Claims

Reeves argues that he and Alyeska entered into three different oral contracts: (1) a confidentiality or disclosure agreement by which Alyeska promised not to use Reeves' idea without his participation, if Reeves disclosed the idea; (2) a lease agreement by which Alyeska promised to lease the turnout to Reeves in exchange for a percentage of the center's profits; and (3) a memorialization agreement by which Alyeska promised to commit the agreement to writing.

Alyeska argues that Reeves alleged a *single contract* which "consisted of an agreement to keep Reeves' idea confidential, an agreement to lease land and an agreement to reduce the terms of the prior agreement to writing." It contends that to allow Reeves to argue he had three independent contracts would be inconsistent with his position at summary judgment and should therefore be precluded on appeal.

We disagree with Alyeska's analysis. Reeves has consistently argued that there were three agreements. It is of minor importance that he sometimes refers to these agreements as "a single binding contract." If any of the alleged agreements possesses the necessary elements to form a contract, Reeves is entitled to seek damages for breach of that agreement. We must analyze the legal relationships created by the parties' words and actions rather than the semantic tags the parties attach to their arguments.

* * *

Reeves alleges that in exchange for the disclosure of his idea, Alyeska promised to keep the idea confidential and not to use the idea without entering into a contract with Reeves to implement the idea. Reeves' deposition testimony, when all inferences are taken in his favor, supports the existence of a disclosure agreement. Reeves testified that in his early conversations with Burke, he told Burke that he was in the tourism industry and had an idea that would help Alyeska. Reeves stated that Burke told him the idea "was between us." Reeves testified that he "didn't offer anything to Keith Burke until [Reeves] was told by [Burke] that we had a deal. This was between me and him, and this was going no place else." Reeves also testified that Burke had promised confidentiality and that Reeves believed that he and Burke had a "done deal."

Alyeska does not respond separately to Reeves' disclosure agreement claim. It instead argues that, notwithstanding Reeves' assertion there were three agreements, Reeves actually alleged only one contract, which included a purported twenty-year lease agreement. It argues that the statute of frauds applies because the alleged agreement concerns a lease for a period longer than one year and because performance would not be completed within one year.

We conclude that the statute of frauds does not apply to the alleged disclosure agreement. That alleged agreement was to be completed within one year. If Alyeska chose to implement the idea, it was to enter into a lease agreement with Reeves by the summer tourist season. Moreover, Reeves' disclosure to Alyeska constituted full performance of his side of the contract for disclosure. The statute of frauds consequently does not apply.

* * *

C. Implied-in-Fact Contract

The trial court's opinion did not address whether Reeves established a contract implied-in-fact. Reeves argues that he "submitted uncontroverted evidence sufficient to find as a matter of law that Alyeska's actions established a contract implied in fact." We conclude that Alyeska failed to carry its burden of showing that it is entitled to judgment as a matter of law on this claim.

Reeves has made out a prima facie case for an implied contract. We have held that an implied-in-fact contract, like an express contract, is based on the intentions of the parties. "It arises where the court finds from the surrounding facts and circumstances that the parties intended to make a contract but failed to articulate their promises and the court merely implies what it feels the parties really intended."

In *Aliotti v. R. Dakin & Co.,* 831 F.2d 898, 902 (9th Cir. 1987), the court listed the requirements for demonstrating an implied-in-fact contract under California law:

> [O]ne must show: that he or she prepared the work; that he or she disclosed the work to the offeree for sale; under all circumstances attending disclosure it can be concluded that the offeree voluntarily accepted the disclosure knowing the conditions on which it was tendered (i.e., the offeree must have the opportunity to reject the attempted disclosure if the conditions were unacceptable); and the reasonable value of the work.

There are three primary factual scenarios under which ideas may be submitted to another. The first involves an unsolicited submission that is involuntarily received. The idea is submitted without warning; it is transmitted before the recipient has taken any action which would indicate a promise to pay for the submission. Under this scenario, a contract will not be implied.

The second involves an unsolicited submission that is voluntarily received. In this situation, the idea person typically gives the recipient advance warning that an idea is to be disclosed; the recipient has an opportunity to stop the disclosure, but through inaction allows the idea to be disclosed. Under California law, if the recipient at the time of disclosure understands that the idea person expects to be paid for the disclosure of the idea, and does not attempt to stop the disclosure, inaction may be seen as consent to a contract.

This view has been criticized as unfairly placing a duty on the recipient to take active measures to stop the submission. The critics argue that inaction generally should not be considered an expression of consent to a contract.

We believe that a contract should not be implied under this scenario. An implied-in-fact contract is based on circumstances that demonstrate that the parties intended to form a contract but failed to articulate their promises. Only under exceptional circumstances would inaction demonstrate an intent to enter a contract.[67]

---

67. We recognize the possibility of a rare case in which inaction could express intent to form a contract. For example, a contract would be implied if the parties' history of dealings demonstrat-

The third scenario involves a solicited submission. Here, a request by the recipient for disclosure of the idea usually implies a promise to pay for the idea if the recipient uses it. Nimmer states,

> The element of solicitation of plaintiff's idea by defendant is therefore of great importance in establishing an implied contract. If defendant makes such a request, even if he attempts to frame the request in ambiguous or exculpatory language, most courts will nevertheless imply a promise to pay if the idea is used.

[3 David Nimmer, *Nimmer on Copyright* § 16.01, at 16–40 to 16–41 (1994).]

Reeves argues that Alyeska solicited his idea. He alleges that Burke asked him what the idea was, and later requested a written proposal. He contends that the request and Alyeska's later use of the idea created an implied contract for payment. These allegations are sufficient to survive summary judgment. A reasonable fact-finder could determine that Burke's actions implied a promise to pay for the disclosure of Reeves' idea. A fact-finder could also determine that Reeves volunteered the idea before Burke took any affirmative action that would indicate an agreement to pay for the disclosure. These possible conclusions present genuine issues of material fact.

Relying largely on cases from New York, Alyeska argues that novelty and originality should be required in an implied-in-fact claim. Reeves responds that we should follow California's example and not require novelty as an essential element of this sort of claim.

Idea-based claims arise most frequently in the entertainment centers of New York and California, but New York requires novelty, whereas California does not.

We prefer the California approach. An idea may be valuable to the recipient merely because of its timing or the manner in which it is presented. In *Chandler v. Roach,* 156 Cal.App.2d 435, 319 P.2d 776 (1957), the court stated that "the fact that the [recipient of the idea] may later determine, with a little thinking, that he could have had the same ideas and could thereby have saved considerable money for himself, is no defense against the claim of the [idea person]. This is so even though the material to be purchased is abstract and unprotected material." *Id.* 319 P.2d at 781.

Implied-in-fact contracts are closely related to express contracts. Each requires the parties to form an intent to enter into a contract. It is ordinarily not the court's role to evaluate the adequacy of the consideration agreed upon by the parties. The bargain should be left in the hands of the parties. If parties voluntarily choose to bargain for an individual's services in disclosing or developing a non-novel or unoriginal idea, they have the power to do so. The *Desny* court analogized the services of a

---

ed that they had entered into similar contracts in the past, or if it were proven in a particular field or industry that a recipient's silence constitutes agreement to pay for an idea upon use.

writer to the services of a doctor or lawyer and determined there was little difference; each may provide a product that is not novel or original. It held that it would not impose an additional requirement of novelty on the work. Although Reeves is not a writer, his ideas are entitled to no less protection than those of writers, doctors, or lawyers. Therefore, Reeves should be given the opportunity to prove the existence of an implied-in-fact contract for disclosure of his idea.

D. Promissory Estoppel

Reeves claims that the trial court erred in granting summary judgment to Alyeska on his promissory estoppel claim. He argues that there were genuine fact questions. Alyeska argues that Reeves presented no evidence of detrimental reliance.

Under Alaska law, a promissory estoppel claim has four requirements:

1) The action induced amounts to a substantial change of position;

2) it was either actually foreseen or reasonably foreseeable by the promisor;

3) an actual promise was made and itself induced the action or forbearance in reliance thereon; and

4) enforcement is necessary in the interest of justice.

[*Zeman v. Lufthansa German Airlines,* 699 P.2d 1274, 1284 (Alaska 1985).] Reference to a set formula does not determine whether particular promises and actions satisfy the requirements of promissory estoppel; all circumstances are to be considered.

Reeves contends that in reliance on promises made by Alyeska in context of separate disclosure, lease, and memorialization agreements, he took two actions that changed his position: he disclosed the idea, and he failed to hire an attorney to draft the contract. Although forbearance may sometimes be considered an action that changes one's position, Reeves' failure to hire an attorney did not amount to a substantial change of position. As noted above, even if Reeves had presented a written contract to Alyeska, no evidence permits an inference Alyeska would have executed it.

By disclosing his idea, however, Reeves substantially changed his position. Once he disclosed the idea, Reeves' ability to bargain for terms was significantly reduced. It was reasonably foreseeable that a promise of confidentiality and a promise to allow Reeves to participate in any use of the idea would induce disclosure. There was evidence permitting an inference Alyeska's alleged promises induced the disclosure. Consequently, genuine fact disputes exist regarding the first three requirements for promissory estoppel.

The fourth requirement, that enforcement is necessary in the interest of justice, presents fact questions that ordinarily should not be decided on summary judgment. The record demonstrates that this issue presents fact questions. It is therefore necessary to remand Reeves' promissory estoppel claim based on his disclosure of the idea in reliance on promises of confidentiality and participation.

Reeves also argues promissory estoppel applies because he was induced to disclose his idea in reliance on promises to lease or memorialize the contract. We reject that argument because neither alleged promise could have induced disclosure. An agreement to lease necessarily assumes that Alyeska was aware of the visitor center idea, meaning that disclosure must have preceded the promise. Similarly, there is no evidence the parties entered into a memorialization agreement before Reeves disclosed the idea.

E.   Quasi–Contract Claim

Reeves argues that Alyeska was unjustly enriched because it solicited and received Reeves' services, ideas, and opinions without compensating Reeves. He argues that the trial court erred in granting summary judgment to Alyeska on his quasi-contract cause of action.[68]

We have required the following three elements for a quasi-contract claim:

1) a benefit conferred upon the defendant by the plaintiff;

2) appreciation by the defendant of such benefit; and

3) acceptance and retention by the defendant of such benefit under such circumstances that it would be inequitable for him to retain it without paying the value thereof.

Alaska Sales and Serv., Inc. v. Millet, 735 P.2d 743, 746 (Alaska 1987). Quasi-contracts are "judicially-created obligations to do justice." "Consequently, the obligation to make restitution that arises in quasi-contract is not based upon any agreement between the parties, objective or subjective."

The trial court understood Reeves to be arguing that his idea was a property right that was stolen by Alyeska. Reeves, however, argues that "Alyeska took Reeves' concept, proposal *and services* without any payment to Reeves." (Emphasis added.) Reeves' quasi-contract claims must be divided into two categories. His claim that Alyeska appropriated his idea for a visitor center is necessarily a property-based claim that seeks recovery for the value of the idea itself; Reeves seeks a recovery based on "his" idea. His claims that Alyeska benefited from his proposal and services, however, do not necessarily rely on the visitor center idea being property; these claims are based on his services of disclosing and drafting the proposal. The property and non-property claims are treated differently.

---

68. The concepts of quasi-contract, unjust enrichment, contract implied in law, and quantum meruit are very similar and interrelated. Unjust enrichment is not itself a theory of recovery. "Rather, it is a prerequisite for the enforcement of the doctrine of restitution; that is, if there is no unjust enrichment, there is no basis for restitution." Restitution also is not a cause of action; it is a remedy for various causes of action. Quasi-contract is one of the causes of action Reeves has pursued.

An idea is usually not regarded as property because our concept of property implies something that can be owned and possessed to the exclusion of others. To protect an idea under a property theory requires that the idea possess property-like traits. Courts consider the elements of novelty or originality necessary for a claim of "ownership" in an idea or concept. These elements distinguish protectable ideas from ordinary ideas that are freely available for others to use. It is the element of originality or novelty that lends value to the idea itself.

If the idea is not distinguished in this manner, its use cannot satisfy the requirements of a quasi-contract claim. The idea, even if beneficial to the defendant, cannot be conferred if the plaintiff has no right of possession. With no right of possession, the idea cannot be said to have been conferred by the plaintiff.[69] Despite Reeves' protestations, the idea of establishing a visitor center near the pipeline is neither original nor novel.

Nevertheless, not all of Reeves' quasi-contract claims require that his idea be considered property and consequently novel or original. Reeves argues that Alyeska was unjustly enriched "by Reeves' efforts on its behalf, not merely on the 'concept that [Reeves'] idea was intellectual property.' " Therefore, we must analyze whether the parties' transactions give rise to a quasi-contract.

The facts alleged by Reeves demonstrate that Burke specifically asked Reeves to draw up a proposal and that Alyeska was going to "do this deal." There is also evidence Reeves was familiar with the Fairbanks summer tourist industry and had special expertise in that area. These facts present a genuine issue of fact as to whether Alyeska benefited from Reeves' experience or his written plan. Thus, there is a question of fact whether Reeves' idea had value to Alyeska in its timing or in how it was presented, rather than in its novelty or originality. Reeves' endorsement of the idea, in combination with his experience in the Fairbanks tourism industry, may have also been valuable to Alyeska. The fact that Alyeska rejected a similar idea in 1987 may indicate that some feature of Reeves' plan or presentation caused Alyeska to go forward with a visitor center. If Reeves' services unjustly enriched Alyeska, he should be compensated for the value of those services.

F. Reeves' Claim for Breach of the Implied Covenant of Good Faith and Fair Dealing

The trial court granted summary judgment to Alyeska on Reeves' claim for breach of the implied covenant of good faith and fair dealing. It stated that although the covenant of good faith and fair dealing is implied in every contract governed by Alaska law, it concluded that this claim must fail because it believed that no contract existed. See *Guin v. Ha*, 591 P.2d 1281, 1291 (Alaska 1979) (recognizing the covenant of good faith and fair dealing implied in all contracts); *O.K. Lumber Co. v. Providence*

---

69. The court correctly granted summary judgment on Reeves' conversion claim for the same reason. If an idea is not considered property, it cannot be converted.

Washington Ins. Co., 759 P.2d 523, 526 (Alaska 1988) (declining to recognize a tort duty of good faith and fair dealing independent of the contractual relationship). Reeves argues that because there is evidence of three distinct contracts, the claim of breach of the covenant of good faith and fair dealing raises a factual question for the jury. Because we hold that there is evidence of a contract for disclosure of the idea, we must remand Reeves' claim for good faith and fair dealing in regard to that agreement.

G. Reeves' Tort Claims

The trial court granted summary judgment to Alyeska on Reeves' tort claims of fraud and negligent misrepresentation because Reeves cited no evidence of detrimental reliance. Because Reeves presented evidence of detrimental reliance in regard to disclosing the idea, we remand the fraud and negligent misrepresentation claims which are based on a disclosure agreement. However, the trial court did not err in dismissing the tort claims that are dependent on [other agreements alleged by Reeves].

NOTES

1. Is there any reason why a court should not enforce a contract calling for payment in exchange for gaining access to an idea or design for a useful item or practice? How do such contracts differ, if at all, from other types of contracts? Why might certain grounds for invalidity or unenforceability be unusually prevalent with respect to contracts addressing the submission of ideas?

2. Why did most of the plaintiff's quasi-contract claims fail? How did these claims differ from his contract claims? Why were the claims based on the plaintiff's services not dismissed? How did these claims differ from the quasi-contract claims based on his ideas? Wasn't the value of his services equal to the value of his resulting ideas? Why does the plaintiff have a claim for appropriation of the value of his services but not one for the appropriation of the value of his ideas?

3. What incentives do the standards applied by the court in this case create regarding the development and disclosure of useful ideas? Does this case place a premium on clear contracting regarding such submissions? What are some of the difficulties surrounding the drafting of a clear contract regarding an idea disclosure before the idea is disclosed?

4. Suppose that a large company is engaging in a wide range of product development in a given field before a party submits an idea for a new product in that same field. What might be the risks to the company in agreeing to compensate the submitter for the value of his or her idea? Indeed, what are the risks associated with even receiving the idea and reviewing it? What kinds of contractual commitments can a large company with many product development sources safely agree to in dealing with an idea submitter?

DOWNEY v. GENERAL FOODS CORPORATION

Court of Appeals of New York, 1972.
31 N.Y.2d 56, 334 N.Y.S.2d 874, 286 N.E.2d 257.

FULD, CHIEF JUDGE.

The plaintiff, an airline pilot, brought this action against the defendant General Foods Corporation to recover damages for the alleged misappropriation of an idea. It is his claim that he suggested that the defendant's own gelatin product, "Jell–O," be named "Wiggley" or a variation of that word, including "Mr. Wiggle," and that the product be directed towards the children's market; that, although the defendant disclaimed interest in the suggestion, it later offered its product for sale under the name "Mr. Wiggle." The defendant urges—by way of affirmative defense—that the plaintiff's "alleged 'product concept and name' was independently created and developed" by it. The plaintiff moved for partial summary judgment "on the question of liability" on 5 of its 14 causes of action and the defendant cross-moved for summary judgment dismissing the complaint. The court at Special Term denied both motions, and the Appellate Division affirmed, granting leave to appeal to this court on a certified question.

The plaintiff relies chiefly on correspondence between himself and the defendant, or, more precisely, on letters over the signature of a Miss Dunham, vice-president in charge of one of its departments. On February 15, 1965, the plaintiff wrote to the defendant, stating that he had an "excellent idea to increase the sale of your product JELL–O * * * making it available for children". Several days later, the defendant sent the plaintiff an "Idea Submittal Form" (ISF) which included a form letter and a space for explaining the idea.[70] In that form, the plaintiff suggested, in essence, that the produce be packaged & distributed to children under the name "WIG–L–E" (meaning wiggly or wiggley) or "WIGGLE–E" or "WIGGLE–EEE" or "WIGLEY." He explained that, although his children did not "get especially excited about the name JELL–O, or wish to eat it", when referred to by that name, "the kids really took to it fast" when his wife "called it 'wiggle-y,'" noting that they then "associate(d) the name to the 'wiggleing' dessert." Although this is the only recorded proof of his idea, the plaintiff maintains that he sent Miss Dunham two handwritten letters in which he set forth other variations of "Wiggiley," including "Mr. Wiggley, Wiggle, Wiggle-e."

A letter, dated March 8, 1965, over the signature of Miss Dunham, acknowledged the submission of the ISF and informed the plaintiff that it had no interest in promoting his suggestion. However, in July, the

---

70. The form letter—signed and returned by the plaintiff—recited that "I submit this suggestion with the understanding, which is conclusively evidenced by my use and transmittal to you of this form, that this suggestion is not submitted to you in confidence, that no confidential relationship has been or will be established between us and that the use, if any, to be made of this suggestion by you and the compensation to be paid therefor, if any, if you use it, are matters resting solely in your discretion."

defendant introduced into the market a Jell–O product which it called "Mr. Wiggle." The plaintiff instituted the present action some months later. In addition to general denials, the answer contains several affirmative defenses, one of which, as indicated above, recites that the defendant independently created the product's concept and name before the plaintiff's submission to it.

In support of its position, the defendant pointed to depositions taken by the plaintiff from its employees and from employees of Young & Rubicam, the firm which did its advertising. From these it appears that the defendant first began work on a children's gelatin product in May, 1965—three months after the plaintiff had submitted his suggestion—in response to a threat by Pillsbury Company to enter the children's market with a product named "Jiggly." Those employees of the defendant in charge of the project enlisted the aid of Young & Rubicam which, solely on its own initiative, "came up with the name 'Mr. Wiggle.' " In point of fact, Miss Dunham swore in her deposition that she had had no knowledge whatever of the plaintiff's idea until late in 1966, shortly before commencement of his suit; that ideas submitted by the general public were kept in a file by an assistant of hers 'under lock and key'; and that no one from any other of the defendant's departments ever asked to research those files. The assistant, who had alone handled the correspondence with the plaintiff over Miss Dunham's signature—reproduced by means of a signature duplicating machine—deposed that she had no contact whatsoever with Young & Rubicam and had never discussed the name "Wiggle" or "Mr. Wiggle" with any one from that firm.

In addition to the depositions of its employees and the employees of its advertising agency, the defendant submitted documentary proof of its prior use of some form of the word "wiggle" in connection with its endeavor to sell Jell–O to children. Thus, it submitted (1) a copy of a report which Young & Rubicam furnished it in June of 1959 proposing "an advertising program directed at children as a means of securing additional sales volume"; (2) a copy of a single dimensional reproduction of a television commercial, prepared in 1959 and used thereafter by the defendant in national and local television broadcasts, which contained the phrase, "ALL THAT WIGGLES IS NOT JELL–O"; and (3) a copy of a newspaper advertisement that appeared in 1960, depicting an Indian "squaw" puppet and her "papoose" preparing Jell–O—the "top favorite in every American tepee"—and suggesting to mothers that they "(m)ake a wigglewam of Jell–O for your tribe tonight!"

The critical issue in this case turns on whether the idea suggested by the plaintiff was original or novel. An idea may be a property right. But, when one submits an idea to another, no promise to pay for its use may be implied, and no asserted agreement enforced, if the elements of novelty and originality are absent, since the property right in an idea is based upon these two elements. The Bram case is illustrative; in reversing Special Term and granting summary judgment dismissing the complaint, the Appellate Division made it clear that, despite the asserted existence of an agreement, the plaintiff could not recover for his idea if it was not original and had been used before: "The idea submitted by the plaintiff to the defendants, the concept of depicting an infant in a highchair eating and enjoying yogurt, was lacking in novelty and had been utilized by the defendants * * * prior to its submission. Lack of novelty in an idea is fatal to any cause of action for its unlawful use. In the circumstances a question of fact as to whether there existed an oral agreement between the parties would not preclude summary judgment."

In the case before us, the record indisputably establishes, first, that the idea submitted—use of a word ("wiggley" or "wiggle") descriptive of the most obvious characteristic of Jell–O, with the prefix "Mr." added— was lacking in novelty and originality and, second, that the defendant had envisaged the idea, indeed had utilized it, years before the plaintiff submitted it. As already noted, it had made use of the word "wiggles" in a 1959 television commercial and the word "wigglewam" in a 1960 newspaper advertisement. It was but natural, then, for the defendant to employ some variation of it to combat Pillsbury's entry into the children's market with its "Jiggly." Having relied on its own previous experience, the defendant was free to make use of 'Mr. Wiggle' without being obligated to compensate the plaintiff.

It is only necessary to add that, in light of the complete pretrial disclosure in this case of every one who had any possible connection with the creation of the name, the circumstance, adverted to by the courts below, that the facts surrounding the defendant's development of the name were within the knowledge of the defendant and its advertising agency does not preclude a grant of summary judgment. In the present case, it was shown beyond peradventure that there was no connection between Miss Dunham's department and the defendant's other employees or the employees of the advertising outfit who took part in the creation of "Mr. Wiggle." In exhaustive discovery proceedings—which included examinations of all parties concerned either with that name or the defendant's idea files—the plaintiff was furnished with every conceivable item of information in the defendant's possession bearing on the privacy and confidentiality of such files and on the absence of access to them by those outside of Miss Dunham's department. The hope, expressed by the plaintiff that he may be able to prove that the witnesses who gave testimony in examinations before trial lied, is clearly insufficient to create an issue of fact requiring a trial or defeat the defendant's motion for summary judgment.

The order appealed from should be reversed, without costs, the question certified answered in the negative and the defendant's motion for summary judgment dismissing the complaint granted.

NOTES

1. Why does the novelty of the idea at issue matter in this case? Is it because novelty is a threshold condition for value stemming from the idea? Or

is novelty important here because the absence of novelty suggests that the defendant may have gotten (or could easily have gotten) the same idea from a source other than the plaintiff? Does a lack of novelty matter because it indicates that the plaintiff may have misrepresented or overstated the value of his idea?

2. Is novelty a contextual or absolute characteristic as considered in this case? Suppose that the product ideas at issue were new to both the plaintiff and defendant at the time of the disclosure, but were later found to have been well known to third parties? Should this change the outcome of the case?

3. Should novelty alone be enough to establish a claim based on the submission of a concrete idea for a useful product or practice? Suppose that the submitted idea is new, but just an obvious alteration of an old design. Should the submission of this type of novel idea support a claim? If so, should the obviousness of the idea affect the amount of recovery available to the idea submitter?

TATE v. SCANLAN INTERNATIONAL, INC.

Court of Appeals of Minnesota, 1987.
403 N.W.2d 666.

FORSBERG, JUDGE.

This case arises from respondent Karen Tate's action against Scanlan International for damages as a result of Scanlan's use of Tate's unpatented idea for a surgical supply product. Tate's claims were for breach of express or implied contract, unjust enrichment, conversion and breach of confidence. A jury trial resulted in a verdict for Tate in the amount of $520,313.

Scanlan moved for judgment notwithstanding the verdict (jnov) or for a new trial and sought a reduction of prejudgment interest awarded respondent. The trial court denied the jnov and new trial motions and partially reduced the award of prejudgment interest. We affirm in part and reverse in part.

Facts

Respondent has been an operating room nurse at the University of Minnesota for the past 19 years. In 1978 she came up with an idea to solve a common problem experienced by operating room nurses working with Prolene suture which, although possessing great tensile strength, was extremely delicate and often broke when clamped in place during surgery. Nurses had developed a practice of cutting pieces of catheter tubing to fit over the ends of the clamps to allow for a firm grip while protecting the suture from damage. Yet, this method was time consuming, the pieces of tubing were uneven and were not radiopaque (capable of being seen under x-ray), and it was difficult to keep track of the number of pieces cut, making mandatory accounting of operating room supplies difficult. Respondent's idea was to have available pre-cut uniform shods or tips to put on the ends of the clamps. The tips would be accessible, easily accountable, radiopaque, sterile, and able to hold the suture.

In September of 1979, respondent contacted Timothy Scanlan, president of appellant Scanlan International, a designer and marketer of surgical supplies. Respondent set up a meeting with Scanlan to present her idea, with the understanding that he would keep her idea confidential and that if he used her idea, she would be compensated. At the meeting, respondent explained the problem of working with the Prolene suture. She brought a "Kittner" sponge holder to illustrate a possible method for achieving some of the characteristics of the product she envisioned. The Kittner holder is a foam block with holes which secures the sponges until use, but allows them to be extracted with only one hand holding a clamp. With Kittners, nurses can determine from the number of empty holes in the block how many sponges are still in a patient's body.

Scanlan later wrote respondent that he liked her idea and that the company was going to look into it, including a package of "Tip–Guards" as an example after which they might model the proposed product. Tip–Guards, manufactured by appellant, were unsterilized, uniform plastic tips sold in bulk, and used to protect the ends of surgical instruments.

After their initial meeting, and over the course of the next two years, respondent was kept apprised of developments of the product by Scanlan, who consulted with her on various aspects of the design of the prototype such as color, number per package, and serrated vs. non-serrated surface ridges. Respondent gave Scanlan a list of potential customers.

In April of 1980, respondent and Scanlan met again, at which time respondent inquired as to her compensation. Scanlan told respondent that she would make money when the company made money, but no definite terms were discussed.

In February of 1981, respondent and Scanlan met to examine prototypes prepared by appellant. Respondent approved of the design of the prototype, and Scanlan told her that his company planned to sell a box of the products called "Suture Boots" for about $6.00 and that she would receive about $.35 per box, which would have been slightly less than six percent of gross sales.

When Suture Boots hit the market in May of 1981, each package contained one foam block which held ten plastic tips. The block had an adhesive strip on the bottom, and its entire contents were sterile. On June 22, 1981, appellant sent respondent two contract proposals. The first contract proposed payment of a royalty of 5% of appellant's net profit on Suture Boots for five years. Net profit was $2.00 per box. The alternative proposal was the immediate and final payment of $3,000. These proposals were revoked by letter dated July 7, 1981, before respondent had an opportunity to respond to either of them.

Appellant revoked the offers after learning from its patent attorney that the foam holder from the Kittner sponges that respondent had brought to the first meeting with Scanlan, and which had been incorporated into Suture Boots, had been previously patented (the Chapel patent). Appellant consequently revoked its contract proposals to respondent, and by letter dated September 2, 1981, presented her with a new proposal. The new proposal offered respondent $1,000 for her time and help plus a commission on any sales by her to customers. Respondent did not respond to this offer, and instead instituted this action against Scanlan International.

Appellant subsequently entered into a licensing agreement with the patent holder, Surgicott, to permit the use of the block in Suture Boots. This agreement required appellant to pay Surgicott a royalty of slightly more than 2% of gross sales.

At trial, testimony from patent attorneys was conflicting on the issue of whether Suture Boots actually infringed on the Chapel patent. Testimony revealed that appellant had previously investigated the idea of using plastic tips over the ends of clamps to aid in grasping suture. In the 1970's, Timothy Scanlan and Dr. Jose Ernesto Molina had unsuccessfully experimented with permanently affixing plastic to clamp jaws. Dr. Molina and Dr. Walton Lillehei testified that prior to May of 1981, there was no product on the market designed to handle the suture without damage or slippage.

On the question of respondent's damages, in addition to testimony relating to previous offers by Scanlan to Tate and Scanlan's license agreement with Surgicott, Thomas McGoldrick, a medical marketing expert, testified that a reasonable royalty for a "niche" product such as Suture Boots would be 30% of sales. McGoldrick's determination was based on an analysis of actual profit and profit objective for Suture Boots, the need for and risk involved in marketing the product, and possible competition. McGoldrick acknowledged that 30% was high, but noted that the 60% net profit appellant made on the product was very high for the medical field. John Heinmiller, an accountant, testified that sales of Suture Boots would increase 4.5 percent per year for the next five years.

The case was submitted to the jury by special verdict. The jury found respondent's idea was novel and concrete; that her idea was not covered by a patent; that respondent communicated her idea to appellant with the understanding that the idea would be kept confidential were it not used; that appellant expressly or impliedly agreed to compensate respondent if it profitably marketed a product using her idea; and that appellant breached its agreement with respondent. The jury awarded Tate $245,033 for the use of her idea up to the time of trial, and $275,280 in future damages.

Appellant moved for judgment notwithstanding the verdict and for a new trial, and sought an order reducing the amount of prejudgment interest as claimed in respondent's notice of taxation of costs and disbursements. The trial court denied appellant's motions, but reduced prejudgment interest for the period of September 17, 1985 through April 13, 1986, based on a continuance granted to respondent in September.

Appellant appeals from the trial court's denial of its motions. Respondent appeals from the reduction of prejudgment interest.

Issues

I. Was the evidence sufficient to support the jury's findings:

A. that respondent's idea was novel;

B. that respondent's idea was concrete;

C. that 30% of the net profit on sales of Suture Boots was a reasonable royalty?

* * *

Analysis

* * *

I.

Generally, abstract ideas are not protectable property interests. In order for an abstract idea to be the subject of an express or implied contract or to be otherwise protected by the law, it must be novel and concrete. Appellant argues that respondent's idea was neither novel nor concrete, and that the evidence was insufficient to support these findings by the jury.

A. *Novelty.*

A novel idea is an original idea, something that is not already known or in use. The novelty essential to a protected property right cannot arise solely from the fact that something already known and in use is put to a new use. *Id.* In order for the aggregation of known elements to satisfy the novelty requirement, their conjunction must contribute something, that is, the whole must exceed the sum of its parts.

Appellant asserts that respondent's idea is an obvious combination of previously developed products (Tip Guards, and the Kittner Sponge foam block), and is therefore not novel and not subject to legal protection. This argument requires an analogy to patent cases, in which the question of novelty often hinges on whether the subject of the patent is obvious.

The test for determining obviousness, or anticipation precluding patentability of an idea is whether the prior art discloses all elements of the claimed combinations, or their [obvious equivalents]. The linchpin in this analysis is not whether the individual components of the patent were obvious at the time of the invention, but whether the aggregation produced a new or different result or achieved a synergistic effect. In answering this question, secondary considerations tending toward a showing of nonobviousness include commercial success of the product, copying, long felt but unsolved need, and failure of others.

Here, there was no dispute that respondent did not design any of the individual elements of Suture Boots. However, respondent's idea was for a *system* to assist operating room nurses in firmly handling delicate suture. The need for such a product was evidenced by the prior dissatisfaction with the method of cutting catheter tubing to shod clamps. Evidence showed that prior experimentation into a method for achieving such a system had been unsuccessful, and that Suture Boots was a commercially successful product, despite copies which had emerged on the market.

The question of novelty is a question of fact for the jury and it is not a question upon which there is likely to be uniformity of thought in every given factual context. Here, the jury found that respondent's idea was novel. This conclusion finds much support in the evidence and will not be disturbed.

B.   *Concreteness.*

Concreteness of an idea pertains to the requisite developmental stage of the idea when it is presented. An idea is a protectable property interest, if it is sufficiently developed to be ready for immediate use without additional embellishment. If an idea requires extensive investigation, research, and planning before it is ripe for implementation, it is not concrete.

Appellant argues that since the key to Suture Boots as a new product was the foam block, and respondent admitted she provided only an example, expecting appellant to develop a suitable holder, the idea was not sufficiently developed so as to be usable, and was therefore not concrete.

The evidence here showed that respondent developed an idea for a system of elements, using something like the Kittner foam block to hold plastic, radiopaque, sterile tips to fit on the ends of clamps and provide strength and sensitivity in a convenient, efficient way. Respondent orally presented her specific idea to Scanlan, demonstrating the elements of the product and its goal. Respondent expected Scanlan to develop the idea further—by producing the parts of the product as she had specified. With respondent's help, Scanlan researched the idea and produced just what respondent had ordered in Suture Boots.

Oral presentations and demonstrations of ideas and written proposals of ideas have been held to be sufficiently developed to be "usable," and thus satisfy the concreteness requirement. See *Bergman v. Electrolux Corp.*, 558 F.Supp. 1351 (D.Nev. 1983) (salesman's oral presentation of idea was sufficiently concrete to create a jury question); *Galanis v. Procter and Gamble Corp.*, 153 F.Supp. 34 (S.D.N.Y. 1957) (plaintiff's letter describing idea about a new detergent combining two other products and called "Blue" was sufficiently concrete to create a jury question); [*Belt v. Hamilton Nat'l Bank*, 108 F.Supp. 689 (D.D.C. 1952)] (oral presentation of radio program sufficiently concrete); *Liggett & Meyer Tobacco Co. v. Meyer*, 101 Ind.App. 420, 194 N.E. 206 (1935) (plaintiff's letter describing idea for a new advertisement sufficiently concrete); see also *Dewey v.*

American Stair Glide Corp., 557 S.W.2d 643 (Mo.Ct.App. 1977) (plaintiff's drawing and nonworkable mock-up were sufficiently concrete).

The undisputed testimony of Mr. McGoldrick was that "concrete" in the field of medical marketing meant that the concept was very well defined, with reasonable access to all parts necessary to develop it. He also testified that in this field a working model of an idea was rarely presented. A review of the evidence adduced at trial shows that there was more than adequate support for the jury's determination that respondent's idea was usable and was concrete.

C. Reasonable Royalty.

Appellant argues that the jury's award of 30% of the net profit as a reasonable royalty is unreasonable, excessive, and not supported by the evidence. In patent cases, a reasonable royalty is determined by applying the "willing buyer-willing seller" test. This test measures what two free and uncoerced bargainers would have agreed upon as of the date when infringement began, and takes into account anticipated, as well as actual, profits.

* * *

The evidence on this issue included previous offers by appellant to respondent, detailed negotiations between the parties, and the licensing agreement between appellant and Surgicott (2% of net profit for use of patented foam block). In addition, Mr. McGoldrick testified that in this case, a reasonable royalty would be 30%. McGoldrick's undisputed testimony revealed that he arrived at this figure through consideration of actual profits and profitability, popularity and the portion of the selling price customary in the industry. McGoldrick stated that 30% was somewhat high, but not in relation to the unusually high 60% net profit realized by Scanlan.

The jury's determination that 30% was a reasonable royalty was based on extensive testimony relating to matters generally considered in such a determination. Thus it had sufficient basis in the evidence, and was not so excessive or unreasonable as to "shock the conscience" of the court or mandate reversal.

NOTES

1. How does the definition of the features of the plaintiff's "idea" affect the determination of the idea's novelty in this case? If the plaintiff did not develop any of the elements of the product at issue, what was her idea? Why was she in a good position to develop this idea?

2. Why should concreteness of a design be a requirement for an idea submission claim? Does concreteness depend on the state of knowledge about a useful idea or the completeness with which the idea is described when disclosed or both? How should concreteness be evaluated? What is the impact on the concreteness evaluation where, as here, both the idea submitter and

the idea recipient specified features of the product that resulted from the submitted idea?

3.   The court in this case evaluated the royalty awarded to the plaintiff using damage standards applied in patent infringement cases. Does the awarding of damages comparable to patent infringement damages make sense in this case? Did the plaintiff in this case have exclusive rights or control over the product design at issue of the sort that a patent holder would have? If not, why should the plaintiff receive damages in this case that are comparable to the patent infringement damages that a patent holder with complete control over an invention could demand from an infringer?

CHAPTER SEVEN

DIGITAL RIGHTS MANAGEMENT: COPYRIGHT, PRESENT INTERESTS AND SUSTAINABLE FUTURES

■ ■ ■

OVERVIEW

Chapter seven focuses on digital rights management in the use and protection of digital content. In this context, protection means securing copyrighted content to limit unauthorized (a) access, (b) alteration, (c) copying, (d) transmission, (e) rebroadcast or (f) use of said materials in a radio, video or other playback device. Absent the ability to functionally secure content, it can be copied and distributed without restriction. This in turn diminishes or destroys the economic value of the content holder's rights.

What distinguishes the threat to digital content of copying from prior analog formats? Traditional limitations on individual access, ability to copy, transmit and distribute primal quality content have been minimized or eliminated in the digital context. The ability to locate and secure access to copyrighted materials has been enhanced by search engine technologies that index content through web crawling (searching the web to locate items programmed in the search instruction) and then providing links for access. These technologies have been treated as a causal factor for infringement with liability for inducement or contributory infringement imposed on the enabler. It is in this context that we find the questions of this chapter. How to protect existing private rights while at the same time balancing the collateral implications of protective mechanisms with rights of the end user and general public? How will the legislature and courts craft rules in the face of rapidly changing technological contexts and interfaces?

Section I introduces Rights Management issues inherent in digitalization through an examination of early digital content use. The Audio Home Recording Act (AHRA) of 1992 remains a threshold legislative response addressing both infringement and the mechanisms for infringement. The AHRA was intended to protect digital music content, broadcast and recorded. Its' application, as well its limitations, were the subject of litigation in *Recording Industry Association of America, Alliance of Artists and Recording Companies v. Diamond Multimedia Systems Inc.*, 180 F.3d 1072 (9th Cir. 1999). [hereinafter *Diamond Rio*]. The AHRA was buttressed six years later by the Digital Millennium Copyright Act (DMCA) in 1998 (infra, section III) together representing significant legislative attempts to protect the integrity of "intellectual property" against those that would unlawfully appropriate it to their own purposes.

Section II addresses file sharing and P2P protocol controversies. The widespread use of peer-to-peer technologies for file sharing altered the mechanisms and magnitude of content misappropriation. It confirmed the understanding that protection for digital content was best directed at the controlling links as a limiting factor. The Supreme Court in *Metro–Goldwyn–Mayer Studios Inc. v. Grokster, Ltd.*, 545 U.S. 913, 125 S.Ct. 2764, 162 L.Ed.2d 781 (2005) found that *Grokster* neither directly infringed by copying, nor maintained a central server, two key elements in finding Napster liable. Grokster was found liable, however, of inducement based on the technology and software it provided, as well by representations of both the ease of locating and downloading copyrighted files. Grokster did this with full knowledge of the infringing conduct of those who used their software. Lingering doubt as to how the rules would be applied led a number of other file sharing entities to settle, including Limewise and Kazaa. That uncertainty may be partially resolved by the application of the rules set forth in further *Grokster* proceedings involving *Streamcase, Metro–Goldwyn–Mayer Studios, Inc. v. Grokster Ltd.*, 454 F.Supp.2d 966 (U.S.D.C. C.D. Cal. 2006) and the case against BitTorrent. The acquisition of YouTube by Google in October 2006 constitutes another step yet to be taken into account in establishing a workable "brightline."

Section III involves application of The Digital Millennium Copyright Act of 1999, which attempts to provide protections for and prevent the circumvention of devices and encryption technologies used as barriers to copying. The DMCA was at first applied to movies and other entertainment content released on DVDs. DVDs were believed to be a secure format through the use of highly sophisticated encryption technology, itself protected under the act. The security of the format was inadvertently compromised by the publication of the key (DeCSS) used to unlock the DVD content. The incorporation of the DeCSS in commercial applications to permit copying, as well as the distribution of DeCSS over the internet was the subject of *Universal City Studios, Inc. v. Reimerdes*, 111 F. Supp. 2d 294 (S.D.N.Y. 2000). [Hereinafter *Reimerdes* or *321 Studios*] This was the first of several diverse actions attempting to apply the DMCA to protect encrypted content. See *Lexmark International, Inc. v. Static Control Components, Inc.*, 253 F.Supp.2d 943, 969 (E.D.Ky.2003) [Hereinafter *Lexmark*] and *The Chamberlain Group, Inc. v. Skylink Technologies, Inc.*, 381 F.3d 1178 (Fed. Cir. 2004) [Hereinafter *Skylink*], which considered the use of encryption to foreclose access to unprotected content.

Section IV informs that Digital Rights Management issues continue to evolve in the context of digital broadcast and social networking.

Throughout this chapter, bear in mind the perspectives of early concern with digital content and balance with public domain use: *See generally* Lessig, *Code and Other Laws of Cyberspace* (Basic Books (1999)) and Lessig, *The Future of Ideas: The Fate of the Commons in a Connected World* (Random House (2001)); Jessica Litman, *Digital Copyright* (Prometheus Books (2001)); Siva Vaidhyanathan, *Copyrights and Copywrongs: The Rise of Intellectual Property and How It Threatens Creativity* (New York University Press (2003); Symposium, *The Public Domain*, 66 Law & Contemp. Prob. 1 (Winter/Spring, 2003).

I. DIGITAL RIGHTS MANAGEMENT: CONCEPTUALIZING CONTROL FACTORS—THE AUDIO HOME RECORDING ACT OF 1992

The AHRA reflects one late 20th century response to basic paradigm changes affecting the creation, production, distribution and use of music and the arts. The very nature of concurrent changes in digital technologies and user interfaces are understood to defy long-term projections of the road ahead. Consider some obvious examples, which serve to illustrate historic uses and the digital paradox.

Through the end of the 19th and into the early portion of the 20th centuries, if one wanted opera, they went to the opera house, which controlled production and access to the performance. Radio and analog recording technologies altered the time, space and place of engagement, but did so within basic paradigms of control over the component elements of production and distribution.

Proximate in real time, but ancient history in the span of technological change, the use of video capture devices to record over the air content enabled individuals to engage in activities potentially affecting the historic control exercised by content providers. This was the subject of *Sonybetax*, where, justified as "fair use" time shifting, in fact enabled end users to share and distribute "copyrighted" content. The high cost of copy equipment, acceptance and learning curve in its use, and fair to poor quality of video reproduction operated as a limiting set of factors on the primary paradigm.

The parallel in the progression of audio performance exists with early formats of reel-to-reel tape decks, eight track tapes and then cassettes. From AC to DC, from miniaturization to portability, changes in form and technology, but still subject to many of the same quality and cost factors that limited widespread public enablement or alteration of the paradigm of production and distribution. The primary threats to the content industry were individuals and entities that produced "counterfeit" goods, characterized by the industry as "pirates." Their impact on the content value and market place was limited by the fact that the basic paradigm of control and distribution was not itself implicated.

It is the advent of digitalization that initiated the paradigm paradox, one that changed the market place, the means of capture, production, distribution and ability to exercise controls that protected content value. Why would this be called a paradox? Why would continued attempts to secure by law or "code" prior methods of content control be likened to Don Quixote jousting with windmills?

Think about what digitalization has changed relative to the means of capture, production, distribution, copying, quality, time shifting, sharing and the like. Think about music compression and storage formats, miniaturization of digital storage devices that facilitate sharing, ever expanding internet and digital and satellite bandwidth and then think about the quandary of digital rights management. Thank about recent content concerns relating to digital satellite transmission of radio and video, such as XM and Sirius radio and home recording. The 21st century has borne out that anyone can create, produce, publish, distribute or broadcast using basic, affordable and ubiquitous means enabled by digitalization, the personal computer and the internet.

The cases and materials in this chapter provide multiple contexts necessary to an understanding of the complex relationships, not only of legal regimes, rules and market structures, but of underlying dependencies of viable legal structures on normative social behavior and inherent constraints.

At the time of the Audio Home Recording Act (1992) this snapshot provides a reasonable view of the issues surrounding digital file copying. The situation changed as discrete factors that operates as limitations on unlawful copying was removed. It was the juxtaposition of new compression technologies (MP3), the internet as a distribution and file sharing component and PC based recording capabilities (CD R/W devices) that removed any of these elements as a functional limiting factor preventing widespread copying of copyrighted content. See generally, Blackowicz, *Legal Update: RIAA V. Napster: Defining Copyright for the Twenty–First Century?* 7 B.U. J. SCI. & TECH. L. 182 (Winter, 2001); Wendy J. Gordon, *Fair Use as Market Failure: A Structural and Economic Analysis of the Betamax Case and Its Predecessors*, 82 Colum. L. Rev. 1600 (1982).

RECORDING INDUSTRY ASSOCIATION OF AMERICA, ALLIANCE OF ARTISTS AND RECORDING COMPANIES v. DIAMOND MULTIMEDIA SYSTEMS, INC.

United States Court of Appeals, Ninth Circuit, 1999.
180 F.3d 1072.

O'SCANNLAIN, CIRCUIT JUDGE:

In this case involving the intersection of computer technology, the Internet, and music listening, we must decide whether the Rio portable music player is a digital audio recording device subject to the restrictions of the Audio Home Recording Act of 1992.

I

This appeal arises from the efforts of the Recording Industry Association of America and the Alliance of Artists and Recording Companies (collectively, "RIAA") to enjoin the manufacture and distribution by Diamond Multimedia Systems ("Diamond") of the Rio portable music player. The Rio is a small device (roughly the size of an audio cassette) with headphones that allows a user to download MP3 audio files from a computer and to listen to them elsewhere. The dispute over the Rio's design and function is difficult to comprehend without an understanding of the revolutionary new method of music distribution made possible by digital recording and the Internet; thus, we will explain in some detail the brave new world of Internet music distribution.

A

The introduction of digital audio recording to the consumer electronics market in the 1980's is at the root of this litigation. Before then, a person wishing to copy an original music recording—e.g., wishing to make a cassette tape of a record or compact disc—was limited to analog, rather than digital, recording technology. With analog recording, each successive generation of copies suffers from an increasingly pronounced degradation in sound quality. For example, when an analog cassette copy of a record or compact disc is itself copied by analog technology, the resulting "second-generation" copy of the original will most likely suffer from the hiss and lack of clarity characteristic of older recordings. With digital recording, by contrast, there is almost no degradation in sound quality, no matter how many generations of copies are made. Digital copying thus allows thousands of perfect or near perfect copies (and copies of copies) to be made from a single original recording. Music "pirates" use digital recording technology to make and to distribute near perfect copies of commercially prepared recordings for which they have not licensed the copyrights.

Until recently, the Internet was of little use for the distribution of music because the average music computer file was simply too big: The digital information on a single compact disc of music required hundreds of computer floppy discs to store, and downloading even a single song from the Internet took hours. However, various compression algorithms (which make an audio file "smaller" by limiting the audio bandwidth) now allow digital audio files to be transferred more quickly and stored more efficiently. MPEG-1 Audio Layer 3 (commonly known as "MP3") is the most popular digital audio compression algorithm in use on the Internet, and the compression it provides makes an audio file "smaller" by a factor of twelve to one without significantly reducing sound quality. MP3's popularity is due in large part to the fact that it is a standard, non-proprietary compression algorithm freely available for use by anyone, unlike various proprietary (and copyright-secure) competitor algorithms. Coupled with the use of cable modems, compression algorithms like MP3 may soon allow an hour of music to be downloaded from the Internet to a personal computer in just a few minutes.

These technological advances have occurred, at least in part, to the traditional music industry's disadvantage. By most accounts, the predominant use of MP3 is the trafficking in illicit audio recordings, presumably because MP3 files do not contain codes identifying whether the compressed audio material is copyright protected. Various pirate websites offer free downloads of copyrighted material, and a single pirate site on the Internet may contain thousands of pirated audio computer files.

RIAA represents the roughly half-dozen major record companies (and the artists on their labels) that control approximately ninety percent of the distribution of recorded music in the United States. RIAA asserts that Internet distribution of serial digital copies of pirated copyrighted material will discourage the purchase of legitimate recordings, and predicts that losses to digital Internet piracy will soon surpass the $300 million that is allegedly lost annually to other more traditional forms of piracy. RIAA fights a well-nigh constant battle against Internet piracy, monitoring the Internet daily, and routinely shutting down pirate websites by sending cease-and-desist letters and bringing lawsuits. There are conflicting views on RIAA's success—RIAA asserts that it can barely keep up with the pirate traffic, while others assert that few, if any, pirate sites remain in operation in the United States and illicit files are difficult to find and download from anywhere online.

In contrast to piracy, the Internet also supports a burgeoning traffic in legitimate audio computer files. Independent and wholly Internet record labels routinely sell and provide free samples of their artists' work online, while many unsigned artists distribute their own material from their own websites. Some free samples are provided for marketing purposes or for simple exposure, while others are teasers intended to entice listeners to purchase either mail order recordings or recordings available for direct download (along with album cover art, lyrics, and artist biographies). Diamond cites a 1998 "Music Industry and the Internet" report by Jupiter Communications which predicts that online sales for pre-recorded music will exceed $1.4 billion by 2002 in the United States alone.

Prior to the invention of devices like the Rio, MP3 users had little option other than to listen to their downloaded digital audio files through headphones or speakers at their computers, playing them from their hard drives. The Rio renders these files portable. More precisely, once an audio file has been downloaded onto a computer hard drive from the Internet or some other source (such as a compact disc player or digital audio tape machine), separate computer software provided with the Rio (called "Rio Manager") allows the user further to download the file to the Rio itself via a parallel port cable that plugs the Rio into the computer. The Rio device is incapable of effecting such a transfer, and is incapable of receiving audio files from anything other than a personal computer equipped with Rio Manager.

Generally, the Rio can store approximately one hour of music, or sixteen hours of spoken material (e.g., downloaded newscasts or books on tape). With the addition of flash memory cards, the Rio can store an additional half-hour or hour of music. The Rio's sole output is an analog audio signal sent to the user via headphones. The Rio cannot make duplicates of any digital audio file it stores, nor can it transfer or upload such a file to a computer, to another device, or to the Internet. However, a flash memory card to which a digital audio file has been downloaded can be removed from one Rio and played back in another.

B

RIAA brought suit to enjoin the manufacture and distribution of the Rio, alleging that the Rio does not meet the requirements for digital audio recording devices under the Audio Home Recording Act of 1992, 17 U.S.C. § 1001 *et seq.* (the "Act"), because it does not employ a Serial Copyright Management System ("SCMS") that sends, receives, and acts upon information about the generation and copyright status of the files that it plays. *See id.* § 1002(a)(2). RIAA also sought payment of the royalties owed by Diamond as the manufacturer and distributor of a digital audio recording device. *See id.* § 1003.

The district court denied RIAA's motion for a preliminary injunction, holding that RIAA's likelihood of success on the merits was mixed and the balance of hardships did not tip in RIAA's favor. *See generally Recording Indus. Ass'n of America, Inc. v. Diamond Multimedia Sys., Inc.,* 29 F.Supp.2d 624 (C.D.Cal.1998) ("*RIAA I*"). RIAA brought this appeal.

II

The initial question presented is whether the Rio falls within the ambit of the Act. The Act does not broadly prohibit digital serial copying of copyright protected audio recordings. Instead, the Act places restrictions only upon a specific type of recording device. Most relevant here, the Act provides that "[n]o person shall import, manufacture, or distribute any *digital audio recording device* ... that does not conform to the Serial Copy Management System ["SCMS"] [or] a system that has the same functional characteristics." 17 U.S.C. § 1002(a)(1), (2) (emphasis added). The Act further provides that "[n]o person shall import into and distribute, or manufacture and distribute, any *digital audio recording device* ... unless such person records the notice specified by this section and subsequently deposits the statements of account and applicable royalty payments." *Id.* § 1003(a) (emphasis added). Thus, to fall within the SCMS and royalty requirements in question, the Rio must be a "digital audio recording device," which the Act defines through a set of nested definitions.

The Act defines a "digital audio recording device" as:

any machine or device of a type commonly distributed to individuals for use by individuals, whether or not included with or as part of some other machine or device, the digital recording function of which is designed or marketed for the primary purpose of, and that is capable of, making a *digital audio copied recording* for private use. . . .

Id. § 1001(3) (emphasis added).

A "digital audio copied recording" is defined as:

a reproduction in a digital recording format of a *digital musical recording,* whether that reproduction is made directly from another digital musical recording or indirectly from a transmission.

Id. § 1001(1) (emphasis added).

A "digital musical recording" is defined as:

a material object—

(i) in which are fixed, in a digital recording format, *only sounds, and material, statements, or instructions incidental to those fixed sounds,* if any, and

(ii) from which the sounds and material can be perceived, reproduced, or otherwise communicated, either directly or with the aid of a machine or device.

Id. § 1001(5)(A) (emphasis added).

In sum, to be a digital audio recording device, the Rio must be able to reproduce, either "directly" or "from a transmission," a "digital music recording."

III

We first consider whether the Rio is able directly to reproduce a digital music recording—which is a specific type of material object in which only sounds are fixed (or material and instructions incidental to those sounds). *See id.*

a

The typical computer hard drive from which a Rio directly records is, of course, a material object. However, hard drives ordinarily contain much more than "only sounds, and material, statements, or instructions incidental to those fixed sounds." *Id.* Indeed, almost all hard drives contain numerous programs (e.g., for word processing, scheduling appointments, etc.) and databases that are not incidental to any sound files that may be stored on the hard drive. Thus, the Rio appears not to make copies from digital music recordings, and thus would not be a digital audio recording device under the Act's basic definition unless it makes copies from transmissions.

Moreover, the Act expressly provides that the term "digital musical recording" does not include:

a material object—

(i) in which the fixed sounds consist entirely of spoken word recordings, or

(ii) *in which one or more computer programs are fixed,* except that a digital recording may contain statements or instructions constituting the fixed sounds and incidental material, and statements or instructions to be used directly or indirectly in order to bring about the perception, reproduction, or communication of the fixed sounds and incidental material.

Id. § 1001(5)(B) (emphasis added). As noted previously, a hard drive is a material object in which one or more programs are fixed; thus, a hard drive is excluded from the definition of digital music recordings. This provides confirmation that the Rio does not record "directly" from "digital music recordings," and therefore could not be a digital audio recording device unless it makes copies "from transmissions."

b

The district court rejected the exclusion of computer hard drives from the definition of digital music recordings under the statute's plain language (after noting its "superficial appeal") because it concluded that such exclusion "is ultimately unsupported by the legislative history, and contrary to the spirit and purpose of the [Act]." *RIAA I,* 29 F.Supp.2d at 629. We need not resort to the legislative history because the statutory language is clear. *See City of Auburn v. United States,* 154 F.3d 1025, 1030 (9th Cir.1998) ("[W]here statutory command is straightforward, 'there is no reason to resort to legislative history.'" (quoting *United States v. Gonzales,* 520 U.S. 1, 6, 117 S.Ct. 1032, 137 L.Ed.2d 132 (1997))). Nevertheless, we will address the legislative history here, because it is consistent with the statute's plain meaning and because the parties have briefed it so extensively.

1

The Senate Report states that "if the material object contains computer programs or data bases that are not incidental to the fixed sounds, then the material object would not qualify" under the basic definition of a digital musical recording. S. Rep. 102–294 (1992), *reprinted at* 1992 WL 133198, at *118–19. The Senate Report further states that the definition "is intended to cover those objects commonly understood to embody sound recordings and their underlying works." * * * A footnote makes explicit that this definition only extends to the material objects in which songs are normally fixed: "[t]hat is recorded compact discs, digital audio tapes, audio cassettes, long-playing albums, digital compact cassettes, and mini-discs." *Id.* at n. 36. There are simply no grounds in either the plain language of the definition or in the legislative history for interpreting the term "digital musical recording" to include songs fixed on computer hard drives.

RIAA contends that the legislative history reveals that the Rio does not fall within the specific exemption from the digital musical recording definition of "a material object in which one or more computer programs are fixed." 17 U.S.C. § 1001(5)(B)(ii). The House Report describes the exemption as "revisions reflecting exemptions for talking books and *computer programs.*" H.R. Rep. 102–873(I) (1992), *reprinted at* 1992 WL 232935, at *35 (emphasis added); *see also id.* at *44 ("In addition to containing an *express exclusion of computer programs* in the definition of 'digital musical recording'....") (emphasis added). We first note that limiting the exemption to computer programs is contrary to the plain meaning of the exemption. As Diamond points out, a computer program is not a material object, but rather, a literary work, *see, e.g., Apple Computer, Inc. v. Franklin Computer Corp.,* 714 F.2d 1240, 1249 (3d Cir.1983) ("[A] computer program ... is a 'literary work.'"), that can be fixed in a variety of material objects, *see* 17 U.S.C. § 101 ("'Literary works' are works ... expressed in words, numbers, or other verbal or numerical symbols or indicia, *regardless of the nature of the material objects, such as books ... tapes, disks, or cards, in which they are embodied.*") (emphasis added). Thus, the plain language of the exemption at issue does not exclude the copying of programs from coverage by the Act, but instead, excludes copying from various types of material objects. Those objects include hard drives, which indirectly achieve the desired result of excluding copying of programs. But by its plain language, the exemption is not limited to the copying of programs, and instead extends to any copying from a computer hard drive.

Moreover, RIAA's assertion that computer hard drives do not fall within the exemption is irrelevant because, regardless of that portion of the legislative history which addresses the *exemption* from the definition of digital music recording, *see id.* § 1001(5)(B)(ii), the Rio does not reproduce files from something that falls within the plain language of the basic *definition* of a digital music recording, *see id.* § 1001(5)(A).

2

The district court concluded that the exemption of hard drives from the definition of digital music recording, and the exemption of computers generally from the Act's ambit, "would effectively eviscerate the [Act]" because "[a]ny recording device could evade [ ] regulation simply by passing the music through a computer and ensuring that the MP3 file resided momentarily on the hard drive." *RIAA I,* 29 F.Supp.2d at 630. While this may be true, the Act seems to have been expressly designed to create this loophole.

a

Under the plain meaning of the Act's definition of digital audio recording devices, computers (and their hard drives) are not digital audio recording devices because their "primary purpose" is not to make digital audio copied recordings. *See* 17 U.S.C. § 1001(3). Unlike digital audio tape machines, for example, whose primary purpose is to make digital audio copied recordings, the primary purpose of a computer is to run various programs and to record the data necessary to run those programs and perform various tasks. The legislative history is consistent with this interpretation of the Act's provisions, stating that "the typical personal computer would not fall within the definition of 'digital audio recording device,'" S. Rep. 102–294, at *122, because a personal computer's "recording function is designed and marketed primarily for the recording of data and computer programs," *id.* at *121. Another portion of the Senate Report states that "[i]f the 'primary purpose' of the recording function is to make objects other than digital audio copied recordings, then the machine or device is not a 'digital audio recording device,' *even if the machine or device is technically capable of making such recordings.*" *Id.* (emphasis added). The legislative history thus expressly recognizes that computers (and other devices) have recording functions capable of recording digital musical recordings, and thus implicate the home taping and piracy concerns to which the Act is responsive. Nonetheless, the legislative history is consistent with the Act's plain language—computers are *not* digital audio recording devices.

b

In turn, because computers are not digital audio recording devices, they are not required to comply with the SCMS requirement and thus need not send, receive, or act upon information regarding copyright and generation status. *See* 17 U.S.C. § 1002(a)(2). And, as the district court found, MP3 files generally do not even carry the codes providing information copyright and generation status. *See RIAA I,* 29 F.Supp.2d. at 632. Thus, the Act seems designed to allow files to be "laundered" by passage through a computer, because even a device with SCMS would be able to download MP3 files lacking SCMS codes from a computer hard drive, for the simple reason that there would be no codes to prevent the copying.

Again, the legislative history is consistent with the Act's plain meaning. As the Technical Reference Document that describes the SCMS system explains, "[d]igital audio signals ... that have no information concerning copyright and/or generation status *shall be recorded* by the [digital audio recording] device so that the digital copy is copyright asserted and original generation status." *Technical Reference Document for the Audio Home Recording Act of 1992,* II–A, ¶ 10, *reprinted in* H.R. Rep. 102–780(I), 32, 43 (1992) (emphasis added). Thus, the incorporation of SCMS into the Rio would allow the Rio to copy MP3 files lacking SCMS codes so long as it marked the copied files as "original generation status." And such a marking would allow another SCMS device to make unlimited further copies of such "original generation status" files, *see, e.g.,* H.R. Rep. 102–873(I), at *47 ("Under SCMS ... consumers will be able to make an unlimited number of copies from a digital musical recording."), despite the fact that the Rio does not permit such further copies to be made because it simply cannot download or transmit the files that it stores to any other device. Thus, the Rio without SCMS inherently allows *less* copying than SCMS permits.

C

In fact, the Rio's operation is entirely consistent with the Act's main purpose—the facilitation of personal use. As the Senate Report explains, "[t]he purpose of [the Act] is to ensure the right of consumers to make analog or digital audio recordings of copyrighted music for their *private, noncommercial use*." S. Rep. 102–294, at *86 (emphasis added). The Act does so through its home taping exemption, *see* 17 U.S.C. § 1008, which "protects all noncommercial copying by consumers of digital and analog musical recordings," H.R. Rep. 102–873(I), at *59. The Rio merely makes copies in order to render portable, or "space-shift," those files that already reside on a user's hard drive. *Cf. Sony Corp. of America v. Universal City Studios*, 464 U.S. 417, 455, 104 S.Ct. 774, 78 L.Ed.2d 574 (1984) (holding that "time-shifting" of copyrighted television shows with VCR's constitutes fair use under the Copyright Act, and thus is not an infringement). Such copying is paradigmatic noncommercial personal use entirely consistent with the purposes of the Act.

IV

Even though it cannot directly reproduce a digital music recording, the Rio would nevertheless be a digital audio recording device if it could reproduce a digital music recording "from a transmission." 17 U.S.C. § 1001(1).

A

The term "transmission" is not defined in Act, although the use of the term in the Act implies that a transmission is a communication to the public. *See id.* § 1002(e) (placing restrictions upon "[a]ny person who transmits or *otherwise communicates to the public* any sound recording in digital format") (emphasis added). In the context of copyright law (from which the term appears to have been taken), "[t]o 'transmit' a performance or display is to communicate it by any device or process whereby images or sounds are received beyond the place from which they are sent." 17 U.S.C. § 101. The legislative history confirms that the copyright definition of "transmission" is sufficient for our purposes here. The Act originally (and circularly) provided that "[a] 'transmission' is any audio or audiovisual transmission, now known or later developed, whether by a broadcast station, cable system, multipoint distribution service, subscription service, direct broadcast satellite, or other form of analog or digital communication." S. Rep. 102–294, at *10. The Senate Report provides a radio broadcast as an example of a transmission. *See id.*, at *119 (referring to "a transmission (e.g., a radio broadcast of a commercially released audio cassette)."). The parties do not really dispute the definition of transmission, but rather, whether *indirect* reproduction of a transmission of a digital music recording is covered by the Act.

B

RIAA asserts that indirect reproduction of a transmission is sufficient for the Rio to fall within the Act's ambit as a digital audio recording device. *See* 17 U.S.C. § 1001(1) (digital audio recording devices are those devices that are capable of making "a reproduction in a digital recording format of a digital musical recording, whether that reproduction is made directly from another digital musical recording or *indirectly* from a transmission") (emphasis added). Diamond asserts that the adverb "indirectly" modifies the recording of the underlying "digital music recording," rather than the recording "from the transmission." Diamond effectively asserts that the statute should be read as covering devices that are capable of making a reproduction of a digital musical recording, "whether that reproduction is made directly[,] from another digital musical recording[,] or indirectly[,] from a transmission."

While the Rio can only directly reproduce files from a computer hard drive via a cable linking the two devices (which is obviously not a transmission), the Rio can indirectly reproduce a transmission. For example, if a radio broadcast of a digital audio recording were recorded on a digital audio tape machine or compact disc recorder and then uploaded to a computer hard drive, the Rio could indirectly reproduce the transmission by downloading a copy from the hard drive. Thus, if indirect reproduction of a transmission falls within the statutory definition, the Rio would be a digital audio recording device.

1

RIAA's interpretation of the statutory language initially seems plausible, but closer analysis reveals that it is contrary to the statutory language and common sense. The focus of the statutory language seems to be on the two means of reproducing the underlying digital music recording—either directly from that recording, or indirectly, by reproducing the recording from a transmission. RIAA's interpretation of the Act's language (in which "indirectly" modifies copying "from a transmission," rather than the copying of the underlying digital music recording) would only cover the indirect recording of transmissions, and would omit restrictions on the direct recording of transmissions (e.g., recording songs from the radio) from the Act's ambit. This interpretation would significantly reduce the protection afforded by the Act to transmissions, and neither the statutory language nor structure provides any reason that the Act's protections should be so limited. Moreover, it makes little sense for the Act to restrict the indirect recording of transmissions, but to allow unrestricted direct recording of transmissions (e.g., to regulate second-hand recording of songs from the radio, but to allow unlimited direct recording of songs from the radio). Thus, the most logical reading of the Act extends protection to direct copying of digital music recordings, and to indirect copying of digital music recordings from transmissions of those recordings.

2

Because of the arguable ambiguity of this passage of the statute, recourse to the legislative history is necessary on this point. *Cf. Moyle v. Director, Office of Workers' Compensation Programs*, 147 F.3d 1116, 1120

(9th Cir.1998) ("[I]f the statute is ambiguous, [this court] consult[s] the legislative history, to the extent that it is of value, to aid in [its] interpretation."), *cert. denied,* 526 U.S. 1064, 119 S.Ct. 1454, 143 L.Ed.2d 541 (1999). The Senate Report states that "a digital audio recording made from a commercially released compact disc or audio cassette, or *from a radio broadcast* of a commercially released compact disc or audio cassette, would be a 'digital audio copied recording.' " S. Rep. 102–294, at *119 (emphasis added). This statement indicates that the recording of a transmission need not be indirect to fall within the scope of the Act's restrictions, and thus refutes RIAA's proposed interpretation of the relevant language. Moreover, the statement tracks the statutory definition by providing an example of direct copying of a digital music recording from that recording, and an example of indirect copying of a digital music recording from a transmission of that recording. Thus the legislative history confirms the most logical reading of the statute, which we adopt: "indirectly" modifies the verb "is made"—in other words, modifies the making of the reproduction of the underlying digital music recording. Thus, a device falls within the Act's provisions if it can indirectly copy a digital music recording by making a copy from a transmission of that recording. Because the Rio cannot make copies from transmissions, but instead, can only make copies from a computer hard drive, it is not a digital audio recording device.

V

For the foregoing reasons, the Rio is not a digital audio recording device subject to the restrictions of the Audio Home Recording Act of 1992. The district court properly denied the motion for a preliminary injunction against the Rio's manufacture and distribution. Having so determined, we need not consider whether the balance of hardships or the possibility of irreparable harm supports injunctive relief.

Affirmed.

NOTES

1. For an excellent review of Diamond Rio, see, *Berkeley Technology Law Journal Annual Review of Law and Technology: I Intellectual Property,* 15 Berkeley Tech. L.J. 67 (2000).

2. Content rights and their requisite protections encompass multiple forms of entertainment and media, visual and audible, encompassing music, motion pictures, television broadcasts, radio and any combination thereof. The court in *Diamond Rio* focused on music, MP3 compression, and portable playback devices that served as a medium of storage and retrieval of digital files. The case itself was early in the evolution of digital technologies and transitional in understanding the breadth of factors inherent in copyright protection.

3. Was the court's approach to both the legislation and facts of the case influenced by the analog treatment accorded the VCR in *Sony Betamax?* While

the court notes that digital copies are perfect and can be distributed using the internet, did it understand the consequences of not applying the AHRA to the device or activity? Do you think the court read the AHRA too narrowly, or misunderstood the functionality devices represented by *Diamond Rio*? Make a list of factors that support your response from the decision. Take into account the next paragraph which is introductory to both *Napster* and *Grokster* following.

4. The perspective of the court in *Sony Betamax* might be said to have been informed by limitations inherent in copy and recording technologies as they existed in analog devices such as VCR, reel-to-reel tape, and cassette tape recorders. These analog characteristics functionally operated as a limiting factor on copy activities. That is to say, the first copy is degraded and each successive copy from a copy further degrades. This not only defined the value of each copy but the harm to the content right holder as well. In contrast to *Diamond Rio, Sony Betamax* copies were not highly transportable, nor were they easily transformative.

Which of these factors did the RIAA argue and how would you think the court should have adapted the paradigms set by *Sony Betamax* to situations of perfect copies without inherent limitations? Did *Diamond Rio* represent copies? Did it represent recording? Is storing the functional equivalent of recording? How would the treatment of the court compare with the underlying premises of *Sony* regarding fair use and the balance between private rights and the public beneficial interest? What implications does the forthcoming transition to pure digital broadcast of both music and television present for DRM? How will these implications impact rights to copy and rights to time shift? *See generally, The Times they are a Changing: The Digital Performance Right in the Sound Recordings Act of 1995 and the Digital Millennium Copyright Act of 1998, 1 Vand. J. Ent. L. & Prac. 46 (Spring 1999).*

5. It is interesting that neither *Diamond Rio* nor any of the cases that immediately followed addressed any number of underlying technologies that could alter file sharing paradigms. Technologies exist which permit the recording to a computer hard drive of any sound source played through a computer's sound card or chip. This includes a CD or DVD audio, regardless of present encryption status. It also permits the recording of licensed online streaming of audio from sources such as Rhapsody. One recording program is distributed online by High Criteria, an English based entity—http://www.highcriteria.com. The program not only allows recording sound, but also permits selection of format such as wav, mp3 and any number of compressions. The program, called Total Recorder, operates essentially as any recorder in appearance. It also allows post editing of the digital file stream.

6. This view will change dramatically as recent litigation regarding XM Radio recording devices have cast a new perspective on the Audio Home Recording Act treating satellite subscription and management services distinct from over the air broadcasts. Both the nature of the broadcaster's rights and the services of facilitating "copying" of copyrighted materials raised issues addressed and rule upon in *Napster* and *Grokster*. See *Atlantic Recording Corporation, Inc. v. XM Satellite Radio, Inc.*, 2007 WL 136186 (S.D.N.Y.).

II. FILE SHARING: ENABLEMENT, INDUCEMENT AND CONTRIBUTORY INFRINGEMENT

Napster played a role in what was to become a revolution in file sharing. It became a significant link in the process of file sharing by facilitating users as to the location of sites that contained specific music content. Pre–Napster the difficulty of finding content operated as a "limiting factor" extending protection to content rights by preventing massive appropriation. What were Napster's innovations? They included use of peer to peer (P2P) file sharing structures, creation and maintenance of a central index server and software that enabled users to identify files available online and permit that file to be downloaded from the source on the remote computer. Napster's central server allowed files to be shared in both directions in what amounted to a global swap arrangement for MP3 audio files. Do you think it was fair to say Napster not only removed a limiting factor protecting content, but was also an enabler and inducer for individual misappropriation of copyrighted materials under the bright line set forth in *Sonybetamax*?

Would it have been reasonable to believe that by removing *Napster* from the equation P2P file share would diminish and content would be protected? Some of the factors shedding light on this question were addressed in two cases that followed: *In re Aimster Copyright Litigation*, 334 F.3d 643 (7th Cir. 2003) and *Metro–Goldwyn–Mayer Studios Inc. v. Grokster, Ltd.*, 545 U.S. 913, 125 S.Ct. 2764, 162 L.Ed.2d 781 (2005).

METRO–GOLDWYN–MAYER STUDIOS INC. v. GROKSTER, LTD.

Supreme Court of the United States, 2005.
545 U.S. 913, 125 S.Ct. 2764, 162 L.Ed.2d 781.

JUSTICE SOUTER delivered the opinion of the Court.

The question is under what circumstances the distributor of a product capable of both lawful and unlawful use is liable for acts of copyright infringement by third parties using the product. We hold that one who distributes a device with the object of promoting its use to infringe copyright, as shown by clear expression or other affirmative steps taken to foster infringement, is liable for the resulting acts of infringement by third parties.

I

A

Respondents, Grokster, Ltd., and StreamCast Networks, Inc., defendants in the trial court, distribute free software products that allow computer users to share electronic files through peer-to-peer networks, so called because users' computers communicate directly with each other, not through central servers. The advantage of peer-to-peer networks over information networks of other types shows up in their substantial and growing popularity. Because they need no central computer server to mediate the exchange of information or files among users, the high-bandwidth communications capacity for a server may be dispensed with, and the need for costly server storage space is eliminated. Since copies of a file (particularly a popular one) are available on many users' computers, file requests and retrievals may be faster than on other types of networks, and since file exchanges do not travel through a server, communications can take place between any computers that remain connected to the network without risk that a glitch in the server will disable the network in its entirety. Given these benefits in security, cost, and efficiency, peer-to-peer networks are employed to store and distribute electronic files by universities, government agencies, corporations, and libraries, among others.

Other users of peer-to-peer networks include individual recipients of Grokster's and StreamCast's software, and although the networks that they enjoy through using the software can be used to share any type of digital file, they have prominently employed those networks in sharing copyrighted music and video files without authorization. A group of copyright holders (MGM for short, but including motion picture studios, recording companies, songwriters, and music publishers) sued Grokster and StreamCast for their users' copyright infringements, alleging that they knowingly and intentionally distributed their software to enable users to reproduce and distribute the copyrighted works in violation of the Copyright Act, 17 U.S.C. § 101 *et seq.* (2000 ed. and Supp. II). MGM sought damages and an injunction.

Discovery during the litigation revealed the way the software worked, the business aims of each defendant company, and the predilections of the users. Grokster's eponymous software employs what is known as Fast-Track technology, a protocol developed by others and licensed to Grokster. StreamCast distributes a very similar product except that its software, called Morpheus, relies on what is known as Gnutella technology. A user who downloads and installs either software possesses the protocol to send requests for files directly to the computers of others using software compatible with FastTrack or Gnutella. On the FastTrack network opened by the Grokster software, the user's request goes to a computer given an indexing capacity by the software and designated a supernode, or to some other computer with comparable power and capacity to collect temporary indexes of the files available on the computers of users connected to it. The supernode (or indexing computer) searches its own index and may communicate the search request to other supernodes. If the file is found, the supernode discloses its location to the computer requesting it, and the requesting user can download the file directly from the computer located. The copied file is placed in a designated sharing folder on the requesting user's computer, where it is available for other users to download in turn, along with any other file in that folder.

In the Gnutella network made available by Morpheus, the process is mostly the same, except that in some versions of the Gnutella protocol there are no supernodes. In these versions, peer computers using the protocol communicate directly with each other. When a user enters a search request into the Morpheus software, it sends the request to computers connected with it, which in turn pass the request along to other connected peers. The search results are communicated to the requesting computer, and the user can download desired files directly from peers' computers. As this description indicates, Grokster and StreamCast use no servers to intercept the content of the search requests or to mediate the file transfers conducted by users of the software, there being no central point through which the substance of the communications passes in either direction.

Although Grokster and StreamCast do not therefore know when particular files are copied, a few searches using their software would show what is available on the networks the software reaches. MGM commissioned a statistician to conduct a systematic search, and his study showed that nearly 90% of the files available for download on the FastTrack system were copyrighted works. Grokster and StreamCast dispute this figure, raising methodological problems and arguing that free copying even of copyrighted works may be authorized by the rightholders. They also argue that potential noninfringing uses of their software are significant in kind, even if infrequent in practice. Some musical performers, for example, have gained new audiences by distributing their copyrighted works for free across peer-to-peer networks, and some distributors of unprotected content have used peer-to-peer networks to disseminate files, Shakespeare being an example. Indeed, StreamCast has given Morpheus users the opportunity to download the briefs in this very case, though their popularity has not been quantified.

As for quantification, the parties' anecdotal and statistical evidence entered thus far to show the content available on the FastTrack and Gnutella networks does not say much about which files are actually downloaded by users, and no one can say how often the software is used to obtain copies of unprotected material. But MGM's evidence gives reason to think that the vast majority of users' downloads are acts of infringement, and because well over 100 million copies of the software in question are known to have been downloaded, and billions of files are shared across the FastTrack and Gnutella networks each month, the probable scope of copyright infringement is staggering.

Grokster and StreamCast concede the infringement in most downloads, Brief for Respondents 10, n. 6, and it is uncontested that they are aware that users employ their software primarily to download copyrighted files, even if the decentralized FastTrack and Gnutella networks fail to reveal which files are being copied, and when. From time to time, moreover, the companies have learned about their users' infringement directly, as from users who have sent e-mail to each company with questions about playing copyrighted movies they had downloaded, to whom the companies have responded with guidance. App. 559–563, 808–816, 939–954. And MGM notified the companies of 8 million copyrighted files that could be obtained using their software.

Grokster and StreamCast are not, however, merely passive recipients of information about infringing use. The record is replete with evidence that from the moment Grokster and StreamCast began to distribute their free software, each one clearly voiced the objective that recipients use it to download copyrighted works, and each took active steps to encourage infringement.

After the notorious file-sharing service, Napster, was sued by copyright holders for facilitation of copyright infringement, *A & M Records, Inc. v. Napster, Inc.,* 114 F.Supp.2d 896 (N.D.Cal.2000), aff'd in part, rev'd in part, 239 F.3d 1004 (C.A.9 2001), StreamCast gave away a software program of a kind known as OpenNap, designed as compatible with the Napster program and open to Napster users for downloading files from other Napster and OpenNap users' computers. Evidence indicates that "[i]t was always [StreamCast's] intent to use [its OpenNap network] to be able to capture email addresses of [its] initial target market so that [it] could promote [its] StreamCast Morpheus interface to them," App. 861; indeed, the OpenNap program was engineered " 'to leverage Napster's 50 million user base,' " *id.,* at 746.

StreamCast monitored both the number of users downloading its OpenNap program and the number of music files they downloaded. *Id.,* at 859, 863, 866. It also used the resulting OpenNap network to distribute copies of the Morpheus software and to encourage users to adopt it. *Id.,* at 861, 867, 1039. Internal company documents indicate that StreamCast hoped to attract large numbers of former Napster users if that company was shut down by court order or otherwise, and that StreamCast planned to be the next Napster. *Id.,* at 861. A kit developed by StreamCast to be delivered to advertisers, for example, contained press articles about StreamCast's potential to capture former Napster users, *id.,* at 568–572, and it introduced itself to some potential advertisers as a company "which is similar to what Napster was," *id.,* at 884. It broadcast banner advertisements to users of other Napster-compatible software, urging them to adopt its OpenNap. *Id.,* at 586. An internal e-mail from a company executive stated: " 'We have put this network in place so that when Napster pulls the plug on their free service . . . or if the Court orders them shut down prior to that . . . we will be positioned to capture the flood of their 32 million users that will be actively looking for an alternative.' " *Id.,* at 588–589, 861.

Thus, StreamCast developed promotional materials to market its service as the best Napster alternative. One proposed advertisement read: "Napster Inc. has announced that it will soon begin charging you a fee. That's if the courts don't order it shut down first. What will you do to get around it?" *Id.,* at 897. Another proposed ad touted StreamCast's software as the "#1 alternative to Napster" and asked "[w]hen the lights went off at Napster ... where did the users go?" *Id.*, at 836 (ellipsis in original). StreamCast even planned to flaunt the illegal uses of its software; when it launched the OpenNap network, the chief technology officer of the company averred that "[t]he goal is to get in trouble with the law and get sued. It's the best way to get in the new[s]." *Id.*, at 916.

The evidence that Grokster sought to capture the market of former Napster users is sparser but revealing, for Grokster launched its own OpenNap system called Swaptor and inserted digital codes into its Web site so that computer users using Web search engines to look for "Napster" or "[f]ree filesharing" would be directed to the Grokster Web site, where they could download the Grokster software. *Id.*, at 992–993. And Grokster's name is an apparent derivative of Napster.

StreamCast's executives monitored the number of songs by certain commercial artists available on their networks, and an internal communication indicates they aimed to have a larger number of copyrighted songs available on their networks than other file-sharing networks. *Id.*, at 868. The point, of course, would be to attract users of a mind to infringe, just as it would be with their promotional materials developed showing copyrighted songs as examples of the kinds of files available through Morpheus. *Id.*, at 848. Morpheus in fact allowed users to search specifically for "Top 40" songs, *id.*, at 735, which were inevitably copyrighted. Similarly, Grokster sent users a newsletter promoting its ability to provide particular, popular copyrighted materials. Brief for Motion Picture Studio and Recording Company Petitioners 7–8.

In addition to this evidence of express promotion, marketing, and intent to promote further, the business models employed by Grokster and StreamCast confirm that their principal object was use of their software to download copyrighted works. Grokster and StreamCast receive no revenue from users, who obtain the software itself for nothing. Instead, both companies generate income by selling advertising space, and they stream the advertising to Grokster and Morpheus users while they are employing the programs. As the number of users of each program increases, advertising opportunities become worth more. Cf. App. 539, 804. While there is doubtless some demand for free Shakespeare, the evidence shows that substantive volume is a function of free access to copyrighted work. Users seeking Top 40 songs, for example, or the latest release by Modest Mouse, are certain to be far more numerous than those seeking a free Decameron, and Grokster and StreamCast translated that demand into dollars.

Finally, there is no evidence that either company made an effort to filter copyrighted material from users' downloads or otherwise impede the sharing of copyrighted files. Although Grokster appears to have sent e-mails warning users about infringing content when it received threatening notice from the copyright holders, it never blocked anyone from continuing to use its software to share copyrighted files. *Id.*, at 75–76. StreamCast not only rejected another company's offer of help to monitor infringement, *id.*, at 928–929, but blocked the Internet Protocol addresses of entities it believed were trying to engage in such monitoring on its networks, *id.*, at 917–922.

B

After discovery, the parties on each side of the case cross-moved for summary judgment. The District Court limited its consideration to the asserted liability of Grokster and StreamCast for distributing the current versions of their software, leaving aside whether either was liable "for damages arising from *past* versions of their software, or from other past activities." 259 F.Supp.2d 1029, 1033 (C.D.Cal.2003). The District Court held that those who used the Grokster and Morpheus software to download copyrighted media files directly infringed MGM's copyrights, a conclusion not contested on appeal, but the court nonetheless granted summary judgment in favor of Grokster and StreamCast as to any liability arising from distribution of the then current versions of their software. Distributing that software gave rise to no liability in the court's view, because its use did not provide the distributors with actual knowledge of specific acts of infringement. Case No. CV 01 08541 SVW (PJWx) (CD Cal., June 18, 2003), App. 1213.

The Court of Appeals affirmed. 380 F.3d 1154 (C.A.9 2004). In the court's analysis, a defendant was liable as a contributory infringer when it had knowledge of direct infringement and materially contributed to the infringement. But the court read *Sony Corp. of America v. Universal City Studios, Inc.*, 464 U.S. 417, 104 S.Ct. 774, 78 L.Ed.2d 574 (1984), as holding that distribution of a commercial product capable of substantial noninfringing uses could not give rise to contributory liability for infringement unless the distributor had actual knowledge of specific instances of infringement and failed to act on that knowledge. The fact that the software was capable of substantial noninfringing uses in the Ninth Circuit's view meant that Grokster and StreamCast were not liable, because they had no such actual knowledge, owing to the decentralized architecture of their software. The court also held that Grokster and StreamCast did not materially contribute to their users' infringement because it was the users themselves who searched for, retrieved, and stored the infringing files, with no involvement by the defendants beyond providing the software in the first place.

The Ninth Circuit also considered whether Grokster and StreamCast could be liable under a theory of vicarious infringement. The court held against liability because the defendants did not monitor or control the use of the software, had no agreed-upon right or current ability to supervise its use, and had no independent duty to police infringement. We granted certiorari. 543 U.S. 1032, 125 S.Ct. 686, 160 L.Ed.2d 518 (2004).

II

A

MGM and many of the *amici* fault the Court of Appeals' holding for upsetting a sound balance between the respective values of supporting creative pursuits through copyright protection and promoting innovation in new communication technologies by limiting the incidence of liability for copyright infringement. The more artistic protection is favored, the more technological innovation may be discouraged; the administration of copyright law is an exercise in managing the trade-off. See *Sony Corp. v. Universal City Studios, supra,* at 442, 104 S.Ct. 774; see generally Ginsburg, Copyright and Control Over New Technologies of Dissemination, 101 Colum. L.Rev. 1613 (2001); Lichtman & Landes, Indirect Liability for Copyright Infringement: An Economic Perspective, 16 Harv. J.L. & Tech. 395 (2003).

The tension between the two values is the subject of this case, with its claim that digital distribution of copyrighted material threatens copyright holders as never before, because every copy is identical to the original, copying is easy, and many people (especially the young) use file-sharing software to download copyrighted works. This very breadth of the software's use may well draw the public directly into the debate over copyright policy, Peters, Brace Memorial Lecture: Copyright Enters the Public Domain, 51 J. Copyright Soc. 701, 705–717 (2004) (address by Register of Copyrights), and the indications are that the ease of copying songs or movies using software like Grokster's and Napster's is fostering disdain for copyright protection, Wu, When Code Isn't Law, 89 Va. L.Rev. 679, 724–726 (2003). As the case has been presented to us, these fears are said to be offset by the different concern that imposing liability, not only on infringers but on distributors of software based on its potential for unlawful use, could limit further development of beneficial technologies. See, *e.g.,* Lemley & Reese, Reducing Digital Copyright Infringement Without Restricting Innovation, 56 Stan. L.Rev. 1345, 1386–1390 (2004); Brief for Innovation Scholars and Economists as *Amici Curiae* 15–20; Brief for Emerging Technology Companies as *Amici Curiae* 19–25; Brief for Intel Corporation as *Amicus Curiae* 20–22.

The argument for imposing indirect liability in this case is, however, a powerful one, given the number of infringing downloads that occur every day using StreamCast's and Grokster's software. When a widely shared service or product is used to commit infringement, it may be impossible to enforce rights in the protected work effectively against all direct infringers, the only practical alternative being to go against the distributor of the copying device for secondary liability on a theory of contributory or vicarious infringement. See *In re Aimster Copyright Litigation,* 334 F.3d 643, 645–646 (C.A.7 2003).

One infringes contributorily by intentionally inducing or encouraging direct infringement, see *Gershwin Pub. Corp. v. Columbia Artists Management, Inc.,* 443 F.2d 1159, 1162 (C.A.2 1971), and infringes vicariously by profiting from direct infringement while declining to exercise a right to stop or limit it, *Shapiro, Bernstein & Co. v. H.L. Green Co.,* 316 F.2d 304, 307 (C.A.2 1963). Although "[t]he Copyright Act does not expressly render anyone liable for infringement committed by another," *Sony Corp. v. Universal City Studios,* 464 U.S., at 434, 104 S.Ct. 774, these doctrines of secondary liability emerged from common law principles and are well established in the law, *id.,* at 486, 104 S.Ct. 774 (Blackmun, J., dissenting); *Kalem Co. v. Harper Brothers,* 222 U.S. 55, 62–63, 32 S.Ct. 20, 56 L.Ed. 92 (1911); *Gershwin Pub. Corp. v. Columbia Artists Management, supra,* at 1162; 3 M. Nimmer & D. Nimmer, Copyright, § 12.04[A] (2005).

B

Despite the currency of these principles of secondary liability, this Court has dealt with secondary copyright infringement in only one recent case, and because MGM has tailored its principal claim to our opinion there, a look at our earlier holding is in order. In *Sony Corp. v. Universal City Studios, supra,* this Court addressed a claim that secondary liability for infringement can arise from the very distribution of a commercial product. There, the product, novel at the time, was what we know today as the videocassette recorder or VCR. Copyright holders sued Sony as the manufacturer, claiming it was contributorily liable for infringement that occurred when VCR owners taped copyrighted programs because it supplied the means used to infringe, and it had constructive knowledge that infringement would occur. At the trial on the merits, the evidence showed that the principal use of the VCR was for " 'time-shifting,' " or taping a program for later viewing at a more convenient time, which the Court found to be a fair, not an infringing, use. *Id.,* at 423–424, 104 S.Ct. 774. There was no evidence that Sony had expressed an object of bringing about taping in violation of copyright or had taken active steps to increase its profits from unlawful taping. *Id.,* at 438, 104 S.Ct. 774. Although Sony's advertisements urged consumers to buy the VCR to " 'record favorite shows' " or " 'build a library' " of recorded programs, *id.,* at 459, 104 S.Ct. 774 (Blackmun, J., dissenting), neither of these uses was necessarily infringing, *id.,* at 424, 454–455, 104 S.Ct. 774.

On those facts, with no evidence of stated or indicated intent to promote infringing uses, the only conceivable basis for imposing liability was on a theory of contributory infringement arising from its sale of VCRs to consumers with knowledge that some would use them to infringe. *Id.,* at 439, 104 S.Ct. 774. But because the VCR was "capable of commercially significant noninfringing uses," we held the manufacturer could not be faulted solely on the basis of its distribution. *Id.,* at 442, 104 S.Ct. 774.

This analysis reflected patent law's traditional staple article of commerce doctrine, now codified, that distribution of a component of a patented device will not violate the patent if it is suitable for use in other ways. 35 U.S.C. § 271(c); *Aro Mfg. Co. v. Convertible Top Replacement Co.,* 377 U.S. 476, 485, 84 S.Ct. 1526, 12 L.Ed.2d 457 (1964) (noting codification of cases); *id.,* at 486, n. 6, 84 S.Ct. 1526 (same). The doctrine was devised to identify instances in which it may be presumed from distribution of an article in commerce that the distributor intended the article to be used to infringe another's patent, and so may justly be held liable for that infringement. "One who makes and sells articles which are only adapted to be used in a patented combination will be presumed to intend the natural consequences of his acts; he will be presumed to intend that they shall be used in the combination of the patent." *New York Scaffolding Co. v. Whitney,* 224 F. 452, 459 (C.A.8 1915); see also *James Heekin Co. v. Baker,* 138 F. 63, 66 (C.A.8 1905); *Canda v. Michigan Malleable Iron Co.,* 124 F. 486, 489 (C.A.6 1903); *Thomson–Houston Electric Co. v. Ohio Brass Co.,* 80 F. 712, 720–721 (C.A.6 1897); *Red Jacket Mfg. Co. v. Davis,* 82 F. 432, 439 (C.A.7 1897); *Holly v. Vergennes Machine Co.,* 4 F. 74, 82 (C.C.D.Vt.1880); *Renwick v. Pond,* 20 F.Cas. 536, 541 (No. 11,702) (C.C.S.D.N.Y.1872).

In sum, where an article is "good for nothing else" but infringement, *Canda v. Michigan Malleable Iron Co., supra,* at 489, there is no legitimate public interest in its unlicensed availability, and there is no injustice in presuming or imputing an intent to infringe, see *Henry v. A.B. Dick Co.,* 224 U.S. 1, 48, 32 S.Ct. 364, 56 L.Ed. 645 (1912), overruled on other grounds, *Motion Picture Patents Co. v. Universal Film Mfg. Co.,* 243 U.S. 502, 37 S.Ct. 416, 61 L.Ed. 871 (1917). Conversely, the doctrine absolves the equivocal conduct of selling an item with substantial lawful as well as unlawful uses, and limits liability to instances of more acute fault than the mere understanding that some of one's products will be misused. It leaves breathing room for innovation and a vigorous commerce. See *Sony Corp. v. Universal City Studios, supra,* at 442, 104 S.Ct. 774; *Dawson Chemical Co. v. Rohm & Haas Co.,* 448 U.S. 176, 221, 100 S.Ct. 2601, 65 L.Ed.2d 696 (1980); *Henry v. A.B. Dick Co., supra,* at 48, 32 S.Ct. 364.

The parties and many of the *amici* in this case think the key to resolving it is the *Sony* rule and, in particular, what it means for a product to be "capable of commercially significant noninfringing uses." *Sony Corp. v. Universal City Studios, supra,* at 442, 104 S.Ct. 774. MGM advances the argument that granting summary judgment to Grokster and StreamCast as to their current activities gave too much weight to the value of innovative technology, and too little to the copyrights infringed by users of their software, given that 90% of works available on one of the networks was shown to be copyrighted. Assuming the remaining 10% to be its noninfringing use, MGM says this should not qualify as "substantial," and the Court should quantify Sony to the extent of holding that a product used "principally" for infringement does not qualify. See Brief for Motion Picture Studio and Recording Company Petitioners 31. As mentioned before, Grokster and StreamCast reply by citing evidence that their software can be used to reproduce public domain works, and they point to copyright holders who actually encourage copying. Even if infringement is the principal practice with their software today, they argue, the noninfringing uses are significant and will grow.

We agree with MGM that the Court of Appeals misapplied *Sony,* which it read as limiting secondary liability quite beyond the circumstances to which the case applied. *Sony* barred secondary liability based on presuming or imputing intent to cause infringement solely from the design or distribution of a product capable of substantial lawful use, which the distributor knows is in fact used for infringement. The Ninth Circuit has read *Sony's* limitation to mean that whenever a product is capable of substantial lawful use, the producer can never be held contributorily liable for third parties' infringing use of it; it read the rule as being this broad, even when an actual purpose to cause infringing use is shown by evidence independent of design and distribution of the product, unless the distributors had "specific knowledge of infringement at a time at which they contributed to the infringement, and failed to act upon that information." 380 F.3d, at 1162 (internal quotation marks and alterations omitted). Because the Circuit found the StreamCast and Grokster software capable of substantial lawful use, it concluded on the basis of its reading of *Sony* that neither company could be held liable, since there was no showing that their software, being without any central server, afforded them knowledge of specific unlawful uses.

This view of *Sony,* however, was error, converting the case from one about liability resting on imputed intent to one about liability on any theory. Because *Sony* did not displace other theories of secondary liability, and because we find below that it was error to grant summary judgment to the companies on MGM's inducement claim, we do not revisit *Sony* further, as MGM requests, to add a more quantified description of the point of balance between protection and commerce when liability rests solely on distribution with knowledge that unlawful use will occur. It is enough to note that the Ninth Circuit's judgment rested on an erroneous understanding of *Sony* and to leave further consideration of the *Sony* rule for a day when that may be required.

C

Sony's rule limits imputing culpable intent as a matter of law from the characteristics or uses of a distributed product. But nothing in *Sony* requires courts to ignore evidence of intent if there is such evidence, and the case was never meant to foreclose rules of fault-based liability derived from the common law. *Sony Corp. v. Universal City Studios,* 464 U.S., at 439, 104 S.Ct. 774 ("If vicarious liability is to be imposed on Sony in this case, it must rest on the fact that it has sold equipment with constructive knowledge" of the potential for infringement). Thus, where evidence goes beyond a product's characteristics or the knowledge that it may be put to infringing uses, and shows statements or actions directed to promoting infringement, *Sony's* staple-article rule will not preclude liability.

The classic case of direct evidence of unlawful purpose occurs when one induces commission of infringement by another, or "entic[es] or persuad[es] another" to infringe, Black's Law Dictionary 790 (8th ed.2004), as by advertising. Thus at common law a copyright or patent defendant who "not only expected but invoked [infringing use] by advertisement" was liable for infringement "on principles recognized in every part of the law." *Kalem Co. v. Harper Brothers,* 222 U.S., at 62–63, 32 S.Ct. 20 (copyright infringement). See also *Henry v. A.B. Dick Co.,* 224 U.S., at 48–49, 32 S.Ct. 364 (contributory liability for patent infringement may be found where a good's "most conspicuous use is one which will cooperate in an infringement when sale to such user is invoked by advertisement" of the infringing use); *Thomson–Houston Electric Co. v. Kelsey Electric R. Specialty Co.,* 75 F. 1005, 1007–1008 (C.A.2 1896) (relying on advertisements and displays to find defendant's "willingness ... to aid other persons in any attempts which they may be disposed to make towards [patent] infringement"); *Rumford Chemical Works v. Hecker,* 20 F.Cas. 1342, 1346 (No. 12,133) (C.C.D.N.J.1876) (demonstrations of infringing activity along with "avowals of the [infringing] purpose and use for which it was made" supported liability for patent infringement).

The rule on inducement of infringement as developed in the early cases is no different today. Evidence of "active steps ... taken to encourage direct infringement," *Oak Industries, Inc. v. Zenith Electronics Corp.,* 697 F.Supp. 988, 992 (N.D.Ill.1988), such as advertising an infringing use or instructing how to engage in an infringing use, show an affirmative intent that the product be used to infringe, and a showing that infringement was encouraged overcomes the law's reluctance to find liability when a defendant merely sells a commercial product suitable for some lawful use, see, *e.g., Water Technologies Corp. v. Calco, Ltd.,* 850 F.2d 660, 668 (C.A.Fed.1988) (liability for inducement where one "actively and knowingly aid [s] and abet[s] another's direct infringement" (emphasis omitted)); *Fromberg, Inc. v. Thornhill,* 315 F.2d 407, 412–413 (C.A.5 1963) (demonstrations by sales staff of infringing uses supported liability for inducement); *Haworth Inc. v. Herman Miller Inc.,* 37 U.S.P.Q.2d 1080, 1090, 1994 WL 875931 (W.D.Mich.1994) (evidence that defendant "demonstrate[d] and recommend[ed] infringing configurations" of its product could support inducement liability); *Sims v. Mack Trucks, Inc.,* 459 F.Supp. 1198, 1215 (E.D.Pa.1978) (finding inducement where the use "depicted by the defendant in its promotional film and brochures infringes the ... patent"), overruled on other grounds, 608 F.2d 87 (C.A.3 1979). Cf. W. Keeton, D. Dobbs, R. Keeton, & D. Owen, Prosser and Keeton on Law of Torts 37 (5th ed. 1984) ("There is a definite tendency to impose greater responsibility upon a defendant whose conduct was intended to do harm, or was morally wrong").

For the same reasons that *Sony* took the staple-article doctrine of patent law as a model for its copyright safe-harbor rule, the inducement rule, too, is a sensible one for copyright. We adopt it here, holding that one who distributes a device with the object of promoting its use to infringe copyright, as shown by clear expression or other affirmative steps taken to foster infringement, is liable for the resulting acts of infringement by third parties. We are, of course, mindful of the need to keep from trenching on regular commerce or discouraging the development of technologies with lawful and unlawful potential. Accordingly, just as *Sony* did not find intentional inducement despite the knowledge of the VCR manufacturer that its device could be used to infringe, 464 U.S., at 439, n. 19, 104 S.Ct. 774, mere knowledge of infringing potential or of actual infringing uses would not be enough here to subject a distributor to liability. Nor would ordinary acts incident to product distribution, such as offering customers technical support or product updates, support liability in themselves. The inducement rule, instead, premises liability on purposeful, culpable expression and conduct, and thus does nothing to compromise legitimate commerce or discourage innovation having a lawful promise.

III

A

The only apparent question about treating MGM's evidence as sufficient to withstand summary judgment under the theory of inducement goes to the need on MGM's part to adduce evidence that StreamCast and Grokster communicated an inducing message to their software users. The classic instance of inducement is by advertisement or solicitation that broadcasts a message designed to stimulate others to commit violations. MGM claims that such a message is shown here. It is undisputed that StreamCast beamed onto the computer screens of users of Napster-compatible programs ads urging the adoption of its OpenNap program, which was designed, as its name implied, to invite the custom of patrons of Napster, then under attack in the courts for facilitating massive infringement. Those who accepted StreamCast's OpenNap program were offered software to perform the same services, which a factfinder could conclude would readily have been understood in the Napster market as the ability to download copyrighted music files. Grokster distributed an electronic newsletter containing links to articles promoting its software's ability to access popular copyrighted music. And anyone whose Napster or free file-sharing searches turned up a link to Grokster would have understood Grokster to be offering the same file-sharing ability as Napster, and to the same people who probably used Napster for infringing downloads; that would also have been the understanding of anyone offered Grokster's suggestively named Swaptor software, its version of OpenNap. And both companies communicated a clear message by responding affirmatively to requests for help in locating and playing copyrighted materials.

In StreamCast's case, of course, the evidence just described was supplemented by other unequivocal indications of unlawful purpose in the internal communications and advertising designs aimed at Napster users ("When the lights went off at Napster ... where did the users go?" App. 836 (ellipsis in original)). Whether the messages were communicated is not to the point on this record. The function of the message in the theory of inducement is to prove by a defendant's own statements that his unlawful purpose disqualifies him from claiming protection (and incidentally to point to actual violators likely to be found among those who hear or read the message). See *supra,* at 2779–2780. Proving that a message was sent out, then, is the preeminent but not exclusive way of showing that active steps were taken with the purpose of bringing about infringing acts, and of showing that infringing acts took place by using the device distributed. Here, the summary judgment record is replete with other evidence that Grokster and StreamCast, unlike the manufacturer and distributor in

Sony, acted with a purpose to cause copyright violations by use of software suitable for illegal use. See *supra,* at 2772–2774.

Three features of this evidence of intent are particularly notable. First, each company showed itself to be aiming to satisfy a known source of demand for copyright infringement, the market comprising former Napster users. StreamCast's internal documents made constant reference to Napster, it initially distributed its Morpheus software through an OpenNap program compatible with Napster, it advertised its OpenNap program to Napster users, and its Morpheus software functions as Napster did except that it could be used to distribute more kinds of files, including copyrighted movies and software programs. Grokster's name is apparently derived from Napster, it too initially offered an OpenNap program, its software's function is likewise comparable to Napster's, and it attempted to divert queries for Napster onto its own Web site. Grokster and StreamCast's efforts to supply services to former Napster users, deprived of a mechanism to copy and distribute what were overwhelmingly infringing files, indicate a principal, if not exclusive, intent on the part of each to bring about infringement.

Second, this evidence of unlawful objective is given added significance by MGM's showing that neither company attempted to develop filtering tools or other mechanisms to diminish the infringing activity using their software. While the Ninth Circuit treated the defendants' failure to develop such tools as irrelevant because they lacked an independent duty to monitor their users' activity, we think this evidence underscores Grokster's and StreamCast's intentional facilitation of their users' infringement.

Third, there is a further complement to the direct evidence of unlawful objective. It is useful to recall that StreamCast and Grokster make money by selling advertising space, by directing ads to the screens of computers employing their software. As the record shows, the more the software is used, the more ads are sent out and the greater the advertising revenue becomes. Since the extent of the software's use determines the gain to the distributors, the commercial sense of their enterprise turns on high-volume use, which the record shows is infringing. This evidence alone would not justify an inference of unlawful intent, but viewed in the context of the entire record its import is clear.

The unlawful objective is unmistakable.

B

In addition to intent to bring about infringement and distribution of a device suitable for infringing use, the inducement theory of course requires evidence of actual infringement by recipients of the device, the software in this case. As the account of the facts indicates, there is evidence of infringement on a gigantic scale, and there is no serious issue of the adequacy of MGM's showing on this point in order to survive the companies' summary judgment requests. Although an exact calculation of infringing use, as a basis for a claim of damages, is subject to dispute, there is no question that the summary judgment evidence is at least adequate to entitle MGM to go forward with claims for damages and equitable relief.

* * *

In sum, this case is significantly different from *Sony* and reliance on that case to rule in favor of StreamCast and Grokster was error. *Sony* dealt with a claim of liability based solely on distributing a product with alternative lawful and unlawful uses, with knowledge that some users would follow the unlawful course. The case struck a balance between the interests of protection and innovation by holding that the product's capability of substantial lawful employment should bar the imputation of fault and consequent secondary liability for the unlawful acts of others.

MGM's evidence in this case most obviously addresses a different basis of liability for distributing a product open to alternative uses. Here, evidence of the distributors' words and deeds going beyond distribution as such shows a purpose to cause and profit from third-party acts of copyright infringement. If liability for inducing infringement is ultimately found, it will not be on the basis of presuming or imputing fault, but from inferring a patently illegal objective from statements and actions showing what that objective was.

There is substantial evidence in MGM's favor on all elements of inducement, and summary judgment in favor of Grokster and StreamCast was error. On remand, reconsideration of MGM's motion for summary judgment will be in order.

The judgment of the Court of Appeals is vacated, and the case is remanded for further proceedings consistent with this opinion.

It is so ordered.

JUSTICE GINSBURG, with whom THE CHIEF JUSTICE and JUSTICE KENNEDY join, concurring

I concur in the Court's decision, which vacates in full the judgment of the Court of Appeals for the Ninth Circuit, *ante,* at 2783, and write separately to clarify why I conclude that the Court of Appeals misperceived, and hence misapplied, our holding in *Sony Corp. of America v. Universal City Studios, Inc.,* 464 U.S. 417, 104 S.Ct. 774, 78 L.Ed.2d 574 (1984). There is here at least a "genuine issue as to [a] material fact," Fed. Rule Civ. Proc. 56(c), on the liability of Grokster or StreamCast, not only for actively inducing copyright infringement, but also or alternatively, based on the distribution of their software products, for contributory copyright infringement. On neither score was summary judgment for Grokster and StreamCast warranted.

At bottom, however labeled, the question in this case is whether Grokster and StreamCast are liable for the direct infringing acts of others. Liability under our jurisprudence may be predicated on actively encouraging (or inducing) infringement through specific acts (as the Court's opinion develops) or on distributing a product distributees use to infringe copyrights, if the product is not capable of "substantial" or "commercially significant" noninfringing uses. *Sony*, 464 U.S., at 442, 104 S.Ct. 774; see also 3 M. Nimmer & D. Nimmer, Nimmer on Copyright § 12.04[A] [2] (2005). While the two categories overlap, they capture different culpable behavior. Long coexisting, both are now codified in patent law. Compare 35 U.S.C. § 271(b) (active inducement liability), with § 271(c) (contributory liability for distribution of a product not "suitable for substantial noninfringing use").

In *Sony*, 464 U.S. 417, 104 S.Ct. 774, the Court considered Sony's liability for selling the Betamax video cassette recorder. It did so enlightened by a full trial record. Drawing an analogy to the staple article of commerce doctrine from patent law, the *Sony* Court observed that the "sale of an article ... adapted to [a patent] infringing use" does not suffice "to make the seller a contributory infringer" if the article "is also adapted to other and lawful uses." *Id.*, at 441, 104 S.Ct. 774 (quoting *Henry v. A.B. Dick Co.*, 224 U.S. 1, 48, 32 S.Ct. 364, 56 L.Ed. 645 (1912), overruled on other grounds, *Motion Picture Patents Co. v. Universal Film Mfg. Co.*, 243 U.S. 502, 517, 37 S.Ct. 416, 61 L.Ed. 871 (1917)).

"The staple article of commerce doctrine" applied to copyright, the Court stated, "must strike a balance between a copyright holder's legitimate demand for effective—not merely symbolic—protection of the statutory monopoly, and the rights of others freely to engage in substantially unrelated areas of commerce." *Sony*, 464 U.S., at 442, 104 S.Ct. 774. "Accordingly," the Court held, "the sale of copying equipment, like the sale of other articles of commerce, does not constitute contributory infringement if the product is widely used for legitimate, unobjectionable purposes. Indeed, it need merely be capable of substantial noninfringing uses." *Ibid.* Thus, to resolve the *Sony* case, the Court explained, it had to determine "whether the Betamax is capable of commercially significant noninfringing uses." *Ibid.*

To answer that question, the Court considered whether "a significant number of [potential uses of the Betamax were] noninfringing." *Ibid.* The Court homed in on one potential use—private, noncommercial time-shifting of television programs in the home (*i.e.*, recording a broadcast TV program for later personal viewing). Time-shifting was noninfringing, the Court concluded, because in some cases trial testimony showed it was authorized by the copyright holder, *id.*, at 443–447, 104 S.Ct. 774, and in others it qualified as legitimate fair use, *id.*, at 447–455, 104 S.Ct. 774. Most purchasers used the Betamax principally to engage in time-shifting, *id.*, at 421, 423, 104 S.Ct. 774, a use that "plainly satisfie[d]" the Court's standard, *id.*, at 442, 104 S.Ct. 774. Thus, there was no need in *Sony* to "give precise content to the question of how much [actual or potential] use is commercially significant." *Ibid.* Further development was left for later days and cases.

The Ninth Circuit went astray, I will endeavor to explain, when that court granted summary judgment to Grokster and StreamCast on the charge of contributory liability based on distribution of their software products. Relying on its earlier opinion in *A & M Records, Inc. v. Napster, Inc.,* 239 F.3d 1004 (C.A.9 2001), the Court of Appeals held that "if substantial noninfringing use was shown, the copyright owner would be required to show that the defendant had reasonable knowledge of specific infringing files." 380 F.3d 1154, 1161 (C.A.9 2004). "A careful examination of the record," the court concluded, "indicates that there is no genuine issue of material fact as to noninfringing use." *Ibid.* The appeals court pointed to the band Wilco, which made one of its albums available for free downloading, to other recording artists who may have authorized free distribution of their music through the Internet, and to public domain literary works and films available through Grokster's and StreamCast's software. *Ibid.* Although it acknowledged MGM's assertion that "the vast majority of the software use is for copyright infringement," the court concluded that Grokster's and StreamCast's proffered evidence met *Sony's* requirement that "a product need only be *capable* of substantial noninfringing uses." 380 F.3d, at 1162.

This case differs markedly from *Sony.* Cf. Peters, Brace Memorial Lecture: Copyright Enters the Public Domain, 51 J. Copyright Soc. 701, 724 (2004) ("The *Grokster* panel's reading of *Sony* is the broadest that any court has given it. . . ."). Here, there has been no finding of any fair use and little beyond anecdotal evidence of noninfringing uses. In finding the Grokster and StreamCast software products capable of substantial noninfringing uses, the District Court and the Court of Appeals appear to have relied largely on declarations submitted by the defendants. These declarations include assertions (some of them hearsay) that a number of copyright owners authorize distribution of their works on the Internet and that some public domain material is available through peer-to-peer networks including those accessed through Grokster's and StreamCast's software. 380 F.3d, at 1161, 259 F.Supp.2d 1029, 1035–1036 (C.D.Cal. 2003); App. 125–171.

The District Court declared it "undisputed that there are substantial noninfringing uses for Defendants' software," thus obviating the need for further proceedings. 259 F.Supp.2d, at 1035. This conclusion appears to rest almost entirely on the collection of declarations submitted by Grokster and StreamCast. *Ibid.* Review of these declarations reveals mostly anecdotal evidence, sometimes obtained second-hand, of authorized copyrighted works or public domain works available online and shared through peer-to-peer networks, and general statements about the benefits of peer-to-peer technology. * * * These declarations do not support summary judgment in the face of evidence, proffered by MGM, of overwhelming use of Grokster's and StreamCast's software for infringement.

Even if the absolute number of noninfringing files copied using the Grokster and StreamCast software is large, it does not follow that the products are therefore put to substantial noninfringing uses and are thus immune from liability. The number of noninfringing copies may be reflective of, and dwarfed by, the huge total volume of files shared. Further, the District Court and the Court of Appeals did not sharply distinguish between uses of Grokster's and StreamCast's software products (which this case is about) and uses of peer-to-peer technology generally (which this case is not about).

In sum, when the record in this case was developed, there was evidence that Grokster's and StreamCast's products were, and had been for some time, overwhelmingly used to infringe, *ante,* at 2772; App. 434–439, 476–481, and that this infringement was the overwhelming source of revenue from the products, *ante,* at 2774; 259 F.Supp.2d, at 1043–1044. Fairly appraised, the evidence was insufficient to demonstrate, beyond genuine debate, a reasonable prospect that substantial or commercially significant noninfringing uses were likely to develop over time. On this record, the District Court should not have ruled dispositively on the contributory infringement charge by granting summary judgment to Grokster and StreamCast.

If, on remand, the case is not resolved on summary judgment in favor of MGM based on Grokster and StreamCast actively inducing infringement, the Court of Appeals, I would emphasize, should reconsider, on a fuller record, its interpretation of *Sony's* product distribution holding.

JUSTICE BREYER, with whom JUSTICE STEVENS and JUSTICE O'CONNOR join, concurring.

I agree with the Court that the distributor of a dual-use technology may be liable for the infringing activities of third parties where he or she actively seeks to advance the infringement. *Ante,* at 2770. I further agree that, in light of our holding today, we need not now "revisit" *Sony Corp. of America v. Universal City Studios, Inc.,* 464 U.S. 417, 104 S.Ct. 774, 78 L.Ed.2d 574 (1984). *Ante,* at 2778–2779. Other Members of the Court, however, take up the *Sony* question: whether Grokster's product is "capable of 'substantial' or 'commercially significant' noninfringing uses." *Ante,* at 2783 (Ginsburg, J., concurring) (quoting *Sony, supra,* at 442, 104 S.Ct. 774). And they answer that question by stating that the Court of Appeals was wrong when it granted summary judgment on the issue in Grokster's favor. *Ante,* at 2772. I write to explain why I disagree with them on this matter.

I

The Court's opinion in *Sony* and the record evidence (as described and analyzed in the many briefs before us) together convince me that the Court of Appeals' conclusion has adequate legal support.

A

I begin with *Sony's* standard. In *Sony,* the Court considered the potential copyright liability of a company that did not itself illegally copy protected material, but rather sold a machine—a Video Cassette Recorder

(VCR)—that could be used to do so. A buyer could use that machine for *non* infringing purposes, such as recording for later viewing (sometimes called " 'time-shifting,' " *Sony,* 464 U.S., at 421, 104 S.Ct. 774) uncopyrighted television programs or copyrighted programs with a copyright holder's permission. The buyer could use the machine for infringing purposes as well, such as building libraries of taped copyrighted programs. Or, the buyer might use the machine to record copyrighted programs under circumstances in which the legal status of the act of recording was uncertain (*i.e.,* where the copying may, or may not, have constituted a "fair use," *id.,* at 425–426, 104 S.Ct. 774). Sony knew many customers would use its VCRs to engage in unauthorized copying and " 'library-building.' " *Id.,* at 458–459, 104 S.Ct. 774 (Blackmun, J., dissenting). But that fact, said the Court, was insufficient to make Sony itself an infringer. And the Court ultimately held that Sony was not liable for its customers' acts of infringement.

In reaching this conclusion, the Court recognized the need for the law, in fixing *secondary* copyright liability, to "strike a balance between a copyright holder's legitimate demand for effective—not merely symbolic— protection of the statutory monopoly, and the rights of others freely to engage in substantially unrelated areas of commerce." *Id.,* at 442, 104 S.Ct. 774. It pointed to patent law's "staple article of commerce" doctrine, *ibid.,* under which a distributor of a product is not liable for patent infringement by its customers unless that product is "unsuited for any commercial noninfringing use." *Dawson Chemical Co. v. Rohm & Haas Co.,* 448 U.S. 176, 198, 100 S.Ct. 2601, 65 L.Ed.2d 696 (1980). The Court wrote that the sale of copying equipment, "like the sale of other articles of commerce, does not constitute contributory infringement if the product is widely used for legitimate, unobjectionable purposes. *Indeed, it need merely be capable of substantial noninfringing uses.*" *Sony,* 464 U.S., at 442, 104 S.Ct. 774 (emphasis added). The Court ultimately characterized the legal "question" in the particular case as "whether [Sony's VCR] is *capable of commercially significant noninfringing uses*" (while declining to give "precise content" to these terms). *Ibid.* (emphasis added).

It then applied this standard. The Court had before it a survey (commissioned by the District Court and then prepared by the respondents) showing that roughly 9% of all VCR recordings were of the type— namely, religious, educational, and sports programming—owned by producers and distributors testifying on Sony's behalf who did not object to time-shifting. See Brief for Respondent Universal Studios et al. O.T.1983, No. 81–1687, pp. 52–53; see also *Sony, supra,* at 424, 104 S.Ct. 774 (7.3% of all Sony VCR use is to record sports programs; representatives of the sports leagues do not object). A much higher percentage of VCR *users* had at one point taped an authorized program, in addition to taping unauthorized programs. And the plaintiffs—not a large class of content providers as in this case—owned only a small percentage of the total available *un*authorized programming. See *ante,* at 2786, and n. 3 (Ginsburg, J., concurring). But of all the taping actually done by Sony's customers, only around 9% was of the sort the Court referred to as authorized.

The Court found that the magnitude of authorized programming was "significant," and it also noted the "significant potential for future authorized copying." 464 U.S., at 444, 104 S.Ct. 774. The Court supported this conclusion by referencing the trial testimony of professional sports league officials and a religious broadcasting representative. *Id.*, at 444, and n. 24, 104 S.Ct. 774. It also discussed (1) a Los Angeles educational station affiliated with the Public Broadcasting Service that made many of its programs available for home taping, and (2) Mr. Rogers' Neighborhood, a widely watched children's program. *Id.*, at 445, 104 S.Ct. 774. On the basis of this testimony and other similar evidence, the Court determined that producers of this kind had authorized duplication of their copyrighted programs "in significant enough numbers to create a *substantial* market for a noninfringing use of the" VCR. *Id.*, at 447, n. 28, 104 S.Ct. 774 (emphasis added).

The Court, in using the key word "substantial," indicated that these circumstances alone constituted a sufficient basis for rejecting the imposition of secondary liability. See *id.*, at 456, 104 S.Ct. 774 ("Sony demonstrated a significant likelihood that *substantial* numbers of copyright holders" would not object to time-shifting (emphasis added)). Nonetheless, the Court buttressed its conclusion by finding separately that, in any event, *un* authorized timeshifting often constituted not infringement, but "fair use." *Id.*, at 447–456, 104 S.Ct. 774.

B

When measured against *Sony's* underlying evidence and analysis, the evidence now before us shows that Grokster passes *Sony's* test—that is, whether the company's product is capable of substantial or commercially significant noninfringing uses. *Id.*, at 442, 104 S.Ct. 774. For one thing, petitioners' (hereinafter MGM) own expert declared that 75% of current files available on Grokster are infringing and 15% are "likely infringing." ... cf. *ante*, at 2772 (opinion of the Court). That leaves some number of files near 10% that apparently are noninfringing, a figure very similar to the 9% or so of authorized time-shifting uses of the VCR that the Court faced in *Sony.*

As in *Sony*, witnesses here explained the nature of the noninfringing files on Grokster's network without detailed quantification. Those files include:

— Authorized copies of music by artists such as Wilco, Janis Ian, Pearl Jam, Dave Matthews, John Mayer, and others. ...

— Free electronic books and other works from various online publishers, including Project Gutenberg. ....

— Public domain and authorized software, such as WinZip 8.1. *Id.*, at 170, ...

— Licensed music videos and television and movie segments distributed via digital video packaging with the permission of the copyright holder. *Id.,* at 70 . . .

The nature of these and other lawfully swapped files is such that it is reasonable to infer quantities of current lawful use roughly approximate to those at issue in *Sony.* At least, MGM has offered no evidence sufficient to survive summary judgment that could plausibly demonstrate a significant quantitative difference. See *ante,* at 2772 (opinion of the Court); see also Brief for Motion Picture Studio and Recording Company Petitioners (referring to "at least 90% of the total use of the services"); but see *ante,* at 2786, n. 3 (Ginsburg, J., concurring). To be sure, in quantitative terms these uses account for only a small percentage of the total number of uses of Grokster's product. But the same was true in *Sony,* which characterized the relatively limited authorized copying market as "substantial." (The Court made clear as well in *Sony* that the amount of material then presently available for lawful copying—if not actually copied—was significant, see 464 U.S., at 444, 104 S.Ct. 774, and the same is certainly true in this case.)

Importantly, *Sony* also used the word "capable," asking whether the product is *"capable of"* substantial noninfringing uses. Its language and analysis suggest that a figure like 10%, if fixed for all time, might well prove insufficient, but that such a figure serves as an adequate foundation where there is a reasonable prospect of expanded legitimate uses over time. See *ibid.* (noting a "significant potential for future authorized copying"). And its language also indicates the appropriateness of looking to potential future uses of the product to determine its "capability."

Here the record reveals a significant future market for noninfringing uses of Grokster-type peer-to-peer software. Such software permits the exchange of *any* sort of digital file—whether that file does, or does not, contain copyrighted material. As more and more uncopyrighted information is stored in swappable form, it seems a likely inference that lawful peer-to-peer sharing will become increasingly prevalent. . . .

And that is just what is happening. Such legitimate noninfringing uses are coming to include the swapping of: *research information* (the initial purpose of many peer-to-peer networks); *public domain films* (e.g., those owned by the Prelinger Archive); *historical recordings and digital educational materials* (e.g., those stored on the Internet Archive); *digital photos* (OurPictures, for example, is starting a P2P photo-swapping service); *"shareware" and "freeware"* (e.g., Linux and certain Windows software); *secure licensed music and movie files* (Intent MediaWorks, for example, protects licensed content sent across P2P networks); *news broadcasts past and present* (the BBC Creative Archive lets users "rip, mix and share the BBC"); *user-created audio and video files* (including "podcasts" that may be distributed through P2P software); *and all manner of free "open content" works collected by Creative Commons* (one can search for Creative Commons material on StreamCast). See Brief for Distributed

Computing Industry Association as *Amicus Curiae* 15–26; Merges, A New Dynamism in the Public Domain, 71 U. Chi. L.Rev. 183 (2004). I can find nothing in the record that suggests that this course of events will *not* continue to flow naturally as a consequence of the character of the software taken together with the foreseeable development of the Internet and of information technology. Cf. *ante,* at 2770 (opinion of the Court) (discussing the significant benefits of peer-to-peer technology).

There may be other now-unforeseen noninfringing uses that develop for peer-to-peer software, just as the home-video rental industry (unmentioned in *Sony*) developed for the VCR. But the foreseeable development of such uses, when taken together with an estimated 10% noninfringing material, is sufficient to meet *Sony's* standard. And while *Sony* considered the record following a trial, there are no facts asserted by MGM in its summary judgment filings that lead me to believe the outcome after a trial here could be any different. The lower courts reached the same conclusion.

Of course, Grokster itself may not want to develop these other noninfringing uses. But *Sony's* standard seeks to protect not the Grok-sters of this world (which in any event may well be liable under today's holding), but the development of technology more generally. And Grokster's desires in this respect are beside the point.

II

The real question here, I believe, is not whether the record evidence satisfies *Sony*. As I have interpreted the standard set forth in that case, it does. And of the Courts of Appeals that have considered the matter, only one has proposed interpreting *Sony* more strictly than I would do—in a case where the product might have failed under *any* standard. *In re Aimster Copyright Litigation,* 334 F.3d 643, 653 (C.A.7 2003) (defendant "failed to show that its service is *ever* used for any purpose other than to infringe" copyrights (emphasis added)); see *Matthew Bender & Co., Inc. v. West Pub. Co.,* 158 F.3d 693, 706–707 (C.A.2 1998) (court did not *require* that noninfringing uses be "predominant," it merely found that they *were* predominant, and therefore provided no analysis of *Sony's* boundaries); but see *ante,* at 2784 n. 1 (Ginsburg, J., concurring); see also *A & M Records v. Napster, Inc.,* 239 F.3d 1004, 1020 (C.A.9 2001) (discussing *Sony*); *Cable/Home Communication Corp. v. Network Productions, Inc.,* 902 F.2d 829, 842–847 (C.A.11 1990) (same); *Vault Corp. v. Quaid Software, Ltd.,* 847 F.2d 255, 262 (C.A.5 1988) (same); cf. *Dynacore Holdings Corp. v. U.S. Philips Corp.,* 363 F.3d 1263, 1275 (C.A.Fed.2004) (same); see also *Doe v. GTE Corp.,* 347 F.3d 655, 661 (C.A.7 2003) ("A person may be liable as a contributory infringer if the product or service it sells has no (or only slight) legal use").

Instead, the real question is whether we should modify the *Sony* standard, as MGM requests, or interpret *Sony* more strictly, as I believe Justice Ginsburg's approach would do in practice. Compare *ante,* at 2784–2787 (concurring) (insufficient evidence in this case of both present lawful uses and of a reasonable prospect that substantial noninfringing uses would develop over time), with *Sony,* 464 U.S., at 442–447, 104 S.Ct. 774 (basing conclusion as to the likely existence of a substantial market for authorized copying upon general declarations, some survey data, and common sense).

As I have said, *Sony* itself sought to "strike a balance between a copyright holder's legitimate demand for effective—not merely symbolic— protection of the statutory monopoly, and the rights of others freely to engage in substantially unrelated areas of commerce." *Id.,* at 442, 104 S.Ct. 774. Thus, to determine whether modification, or a strict interpretation, of *Sony* is needed, I would ask whether MGM has shown that *Sony* incorrectly balanced copyright and new-technology interests. In particular: (1) Has *Sony* (as I interpret it) worked to protect new technology? (2) If so, would modification or strict interpretation significantly weaken that protection? (3) If so, would new or necessary copyright-related benefits outweigh any such weakening?

A

The first question is the easiest to answer. *Sony's* rule, as I interpret it, has provided entrepreneurs with needed assurance that they will be shielded from copyright liability as they bring valuable new technologies to market.

Sony's rule is clear. That clarity allows those who develop new products that are capable of substantial noninfringing uses to know, *ex ante,* that distribution of their product will not yield massive monetary liability. At the same time, it helps deter them from distributing products that have no other real function than—or that are specifically intended for—copyright infringement, deterrence that the Court's holding today reinforces (by adding a weapon to the copyright holder's legal arsenal).

Sony's rule is strongly technology protecting. The rule deliberately makes it difficult for courts to find secondary liability where new technology is at issue. It establishes that the law will not impose copyright liability upon the distributors of dual-use technologies (who do not themselves engage in unauthorized copying) unless the product in question will be used *almost exclusively* to infringe copyrights (or unless they actively induce infringements as we today describe). *Sony* thereby recognizes that the copyright laws are not intended to discourage or to control the emergence of new technologies, including (perhaps especially) those that help disseminate information and ideas more broadly or more efficiently. Thus *Sony's* rule shelters VCRs, typewriters, tape recorders, photocopiers, computers, cassette players, compact disc burners, digital video recorders, MP3 players, Internet search engines, and peer-to-peer software. But *Sony's* rule does not shelter descramblers, even if one could *theoretically* use a descrambler in a noninfringing way. 464 U.S., at 441–442, 104 S.Ct. 774; Compare *Cable/Home Communication Corp., supra,* at 837–850 (developer liable for advertising television signal descrambler), with *Vault Corp., supra,* at 262 (primary use infringing but a substantial noninfringing use).

Sony's rule is forward looking. It does not confine its scope to a static snapshot of a product's current uses (thereby threatening technologies that have undeveloped future markets). Rather, as the VCR example makes clear, a product's market can evolve dramatically over time. And *Sony*—by referring to a *capacity* for substantial noninfringing uses—recognizes that fact. *Sony's* word "capable" refers to a plausible, not simply a theoretical, likelihood that such uses will come to pass, and that fact anchors *Sony* in practical reality. Cf. *Aimster, supra,* at 651.

Sony's rule is mindful of the limitations facing judges where matters of technology are concerned. Judges have no specialized technical ability to answer questions about present or future technological feasibility or commercial viability where technology professionals, engineers, and venture capitalists themselves may radically disagree and where answers may differ depending upon whether one focuses upon the time of product development or the time of distribution. Consider, for example, the question whether devices can be added to Grokster's software that will filter out infringing files. MGM tells us this is easy enough to do, as do several *amici* that produce and sell the filtering technology. See, *e.g.,* Brief for Motion Picture Studio Petitioners 11; Brief for Audible Magic Corp. et al. as *Amicus Curiae* 3–10. Grokster says it is not at all easy to do, and not an efficient solution in any event, and several apparently disinterested computer science professors agree. See Brief for Respondents 31; Brief for Computer Science Professors as *Amicus Curiae* 6–10, 14–18. Which account should a judge credit? *Sony* says that the judge will not necessarily have to decide.

Given the nature of the *Sony* rule, it is not surprising that in the last 20 years, there have been relatively few contributory infringement suits—based on a product distribution theory—brought against technology providers (a small handful of federal appellate court cases and perhaps fewer than two dozen District Court cases in the last 20 years). I have found nothing in the briefs or the record that shows that *Sony* has failed to achieve its innovation-protecting objective.

B

The second, more difficult, question is whether a modified *Sony* rule (or a strict interpretation) would significantly weaken the law's ability to protect new technology. Justice Ginsburg's approach would require defendants to produce considerably more concrete evidence—more than was presented here—to earn *Sony's* shelter. That heavier evidentiary demand, and especially the more dramatic (case-by-case balancing) modifications that MGM and the Government seek, would, I believe, undercut the protection that *Sony* now offers.

To require defendants to provide, for example, detailed evidence—say business plans, profitability estimates, projected technological modifications, and so forth—would doubtless make life easier for copyright holder plaintiffs. But it would simultaneously increase the legal uncertainty that surrounds the creation or development of a new technology capable of being put to infringing uses. Inventors and entrepreneurs (in the garage, the dorm room, the corporate lab, or the boardroom) would have to fear (and in many cases endure) costly and extensive trials when they create, produce, or distribute the sort of information technology that can be used for copyright infringement. They would often be left guessing as to how a court, upon later review of the product and its uses, would decide when necessarily rough estimates amounted to sufficient evidence. They would have no way to predict how courts would weigh the respective values of infringing and noninfringing uses; determine the efficiency and advisability of technological changes; or assess a product's potential future markets. The price of a wrong guess—even if it involves a good-faith effort to assess technical and commercial viability—could be large statutory damages (not less than $750 and up to $30,000 *per infringed work*). 17 U.S.C. § 504(c)(1). The additional risk and uncertainty would mean a consequent additional chill of technological development.

C

The third question—whether a positive copyright impact would outweigh any technology-related loss—I find the most difficult of the three. I do not doubt that a more intrusive *Sony* test would generally provide greater revenue security for copyright holders. But it is harder to conclude that the gains on the copyright swings would exceed the losses on the technology roundabouts.

For one thing, the law disfavors equating the two different kinds of gain and loss; rather, it leans in favor of protecting technology. As *Sony* itself makes clear, the producer of a technology which *permits* unlawful copying does not himself *engage* in unlawful copying—a fact that makes the attachment of copyright liability to the creation, production, or distribution of the technology an exceptional thing. See 464 U.S., at 431, 104 S.Ct. 774 (courts "must be circumspect" in construing the copyright laws to preclude distribution of new technologies). Moreover, *Sony* has been the law for some time. And that fact imposes a serious burden upon copyright holders like MGM to show a need for change in the current rules of the game, including a more strict interpretation of the test. See, *e.g.*, Brief for Motion Picture Studio Petitioners 31 (*Sony* should not protect products when the "primary or principal" use is infringing).

In any event, the evidence now available does not, in my view, make out a sufficiently strong case for change. To say this is not to doubt the basic need to protect copyrighted material from infringement. The Constitution itself stresses the vital role that copyright plays in advancing the "useful Arts." Art. I, § 8, cl. 8. No one disputes that "reward to the author or artist serves to induce release to the public of the products of his creative genius." *United States v. Paramount Pictures, Inc.*, 334 U.S. 131, 158, 68 S.Ct. 915, 92 L.Ed. 1260 (1948). And deliberate unlawful copying is no less an unlawful taking of property than garden-variety theft. See, *e.g.*, 18 U.S.C. § 2319 (criminal copyright infringement); § 1961(1)(B) (copyright infringement can be a predicate act under the Racketeer

Influenced and Corrupt Organizations Act); § 1956(c)(7)(D) (money laundering includes the receipt of proceeds from copyright infringement). But these highly general principles cannot by themselves tell us how to balance the interests at issue in *Sony* or whether *Sony's* standard needs modification. And at certain key points, information is lacking.

Will an unmodified *Sony* lead to a significant diminution in the amount or quality of creative work produced? Since copyright's basic objective is creation and its revenue objectives but a means to that end, this is the underlying copyright question. See *Twentieth Century Music Corp. v. Aiken,* 422 U.S. 151, 156, 95 S.Ct. 2040, 45 L.Ed.2d 84 (1975) ("Creative work is to be encouraged and rewarded, but private motivation must ultimately serve the cause of promoting broad public availability of literature, music, and the other arts"). And its answer is far from clear.

Unauthorized copying likely diminishes industry revenue, though it is not clear by how much. Compare S. Liebowitz, Will MP3 Downloads Annihilate the Record Industry? The Evidence So Far, p. 2 (June 2003), http://www.utdallas.edu/liebowit/intprop/records.pdf (all Internet materials as visited June 24, 2005, and available in Clerk of Court's case file) (file sharing has caused a decline in music sales), and Press Release, Informa Media Group Report (citing Music on the Internet (5th ed.2004)) (estimating total lost sales to the music industry in the range of $2 billion annually), at http://www.informatm.com, with F. Oberholzer & K. Strumpf, The Effect of File Sharing on Record Sales: An Empirical Analysis, p. 24 (Mar.2004), www.unc.edu/cigar/papers/FileSharing_ March 2004.pdf (academic study concluding that "file sharing has no statistically significant effect on purchases of the average album"), and McGuire, Study: File–Sharing No Threat to Music Sales (Mar. 29, 2004), http://www.washingtonpost.com/ac2/wp-dyn/A34300–2004   Mar29?   language=printer (discussing mixed evidence).

The extent to which related production has actually and resultingly declined remains uncertain, though there is good reason to believe that the decline, if any, is not substantial. See, *e.g.,* M. Madden, Pew Internet & American Life Project, Artists, Musicians, and the Internet, p. 21, http://www.pewinternet.org/pdfs/PIP_Artists.Musicians_ Report.pdf (nearly 70% of musicians believe that file sharing is a minor threat or no threat at all to creative industries); Benkler, *Sharing Nicely: On Shareable Goods and the Emergence of Sharing as a Modality of Economic Production,* 114 Yale L. J. 273, 351–352 (2004) ("Much of the actual flow of revenue to artists—from performances and other sources—is stable even assuming a complete displacement of the CD market by peer-to-peer distribution.... [I]t would be silly to think that music, a cultural form without which no human society has existed, will cease to be in our world [because of illegal file swapping]").

More importantly, copyright holders at least potentially have other tools available to reduce piracy and to abate whatever threat it poses to creative production. As today's opinion makes clear, a copyright holder may proceed against a technology provider where a provable specific intent to infringe (of the kind the Court describes) is present. *Ante,* at 2782 (opinion of the Court). Services like Grokster may well be liable under an inducement theory.

In addition, a copyright holder has always had the legal authority to bring a traditional infringement suit against one who wrongfully copies. Indeed, since September 2003, the Recording Industry Association of America (RIAA) has filed "thousands of suits against people for sharing copyrighted material." Walker, New Movement Hits Universities: Get Legal Music, Washington Post, Mar. 17, 2005, p. E1. These suits have provided copyright holders with damages; have served as a teaching tool, making clear that much file sharing, if done without permission, is unlawful; and apparently have had a real and significant deterrent effect. See, *e.g.,* L. Rainie, M. Madden, D. Hess, & G. Mudd, Pew Internet Project and comScore Media Metrix Data Memo: The state of music downloading and file-sharing online, pp. 2, 4, 6, 10 (Apr.2004), www.pewinternet.org/ pdfs/PIP_Filesharing_April_04.pdf (number of people downloading files fell from a peak of roughly 35 million to roughly 23 million in the year following the first suits; 38% of current downloaders report downloading fewer files because of the suits); M. Madden & L. Rainie, Pew Internet Project Data Memo: Music and video downloading moves beyond P2P, p. 7 (March 2005), www.pewinternet.org/pdfs/PIP_Filesharing_March05.pdf (number of downloaders has "inched up" but "continues to rest well below the peak level"); Groennings, Note, Costs and Benefits of the Recording Industry's Litigation Against Individuals, 20 Berkeley Technology L. J. 571 (2005); but see Evangelista, Downloading Music and Movie Files is as Popular as Ever, San Francisco Chronicle, Mar. 28, 2005, p. E1 (referring to the continuing "tide of rampant copyright infringement," while noting that the RIAA says it believes the "campaign of lawsuits and public education has at least contained the problem").

Further, copyright holders may develop new technological devices that will help curb unlawful infringement. Some new technology, called "digital 'watermarking' " and "digital fingerprint[ing]," can encode within the file information about the author and the copyright scope and date, which "fingerprints" can help to expose infringers. RIAA Reveals Method to Madness, Wired News, Aug. 28, 2003, http://www.wired.com/news/ digiwood/0,1412,60222,00.html; Besek, Anti–Circumvention Laws and Copyright: A Report from the Kernochan Center for Law, Media and the Arts, 27 Colum. J. L. & Arts 385, 391, 451 (2004). Other technology can, through encryption, potentially restrict users' ability to make a digital copy. See J. Borland, Tripping the Rippers, C/net News.com (Sept. 28, 2001), http://news.com.com/Tripping + the + rippers/2009 = 1023_3 = 27361 9.html; but see Brief for Bridgemar Services Ltd. as *Amicus Curiae* 5–8 (arguing that peer-to-peer service providers can more easily block unlawful swapping).

At the same time, advances in technology have discouraged unlawful copying by making *lawful* copying (*e.g.,* downloading music with the copyright holder's permission) cheaper and easier to achieve. Several services now sell music for less than $1 per song. (Walmart.com, for example, charges $0.88 each). Consequently, many consumers initially attracted to the convenience and flexibility of services like Grokster are now migrating to lawful paid services (services with copying permission) where they can enjoy at little cost even greater convenience and flexibility without engaging in unlawful swapping. See Wu, When Code Isn't Law, 89 Va. L.Rev. 679, 731–735 (2003) (noting the prevalence of technological problems on unpaid swapping sites); K. Dean, P2P Tilts Toward Legitimacy, wired.com, Wired News (Nov. 24, 2004), http://www.wired.com/news/digiwood/0,1412,65836,00.html; M. Madden & L. Rainie, March 2005 Data Memo, *supra,* at 6–7 (percentage of current downloaders who have used paid services rose from 24% to 43% in a year; number using free services fell from 58% to 41%).

Thus, lawful music downloading services—those that charge the customer for downloading music and pay royalties to the copyright holder—have continued to grow and to produce substantial revenue. See Brief for Internet Law Faculty as *Amici Curiae* 5–20; Bruno, Digital Entertainment: Piracy Fight Shows Encouraging Signs (Mar. 5, 2005), available at LEXIS, News Library, Billboard File (in 2004, consumers worldwide purchased more than 10 times the number of digital tracks purchased in 2003; global digital music market of $330 million in 2004 expected to double in 2005); Press Release, Informa Media Report, *supra* (global digital revenues will likely exceed $3 billion in 2010); Ashton, [International Federation of the Phonographic Industry] Predicts Downloads Will Hit the Mainstream, Music Week, Jan. 29, 2005, p. 6 (legal music sites and portable MP3 players "are helping transform the digital music market" into "an everyday consumer experience"). And more advanced types of *non*-music-oriented P2P networks have also started to develop, drawing in part on the lessons of Grokster.

Finally, as *Sony* recognized, the legislative option remains available. Courts are less well suited than Congress to the task of "accommodat[ing] fully the varied permutations of competing interests that are inevitably implicated by such new technology." *Sony,* 464 U.S., at 431, 104 S.Ct. 774; see, *e.g.,* Audio Home Recording Act of 1992, 106 Stat. 4237 (adding 17 U.S.C., ch. 10); Protecting Innovation and Art While Preventing Piracy: Hearing Before the Senate Comm. on the Judiciary, 108th Cong., 2d Sess. (July 22, 2004).

I do not know whether these developments and similar alternatives will prove sufficient, but I am reasonably certain that, given their existence, a strong demonstrated need for modifying *Sony* (or for interpreting *Sony's* standard more strictly) has not yet been shown. That fact, along with the added risks that modification (or strict interpretation) would impose upon technological innovation, leads me to the conclusion that we should maintain *Sony,* reading its standard as I have read it. As so read, it requires affirmance of the Ninth Circuit's determination of the relevant aspects of the *Sony* question.

* * *

For these reasons, I disagree with Justice Ginsburg, but I agree with the Court and join its opinion.

NOTES

1. Identify the issues the court either directly or indirectly acknowledged and whether there was a response or non-response to the issue. Did the court property narrow the issues to the matter at hand? Did they appropriately "avoid" by minimization some of the larger policy questions?

2. What is the actual holding of the court? Are the concurring opinions of Justice Ginsburg and Justice Breyer consistent with this narrow holding?

3. Is this case about "retribution" and "flaunting" with clear and convincing evidence that Grokster knew, intended and encouraged the primary use of their P2P program would be for illegal file sharing touting their protection under the Sony Betamax bright line?

4. In the amicus briefs, one argument supporting application of the rule set forth in Sony Betamax to provide a safe harbor for Grokster was that there were clear non-infringing uses of P2P file sharing that would be compromised by holding the provider of the enabling technology liable. The Majority and concurring opinions characterize these assertions as "anecdotal" and, according to Justice Ginsburg, Justice Beyer's opinion put together a "motley" collection of such uses. For the most part, the majority gave little, if any weight to these present or future alleged legitimate uses. Why? And, was this characterization necessary to the holding of the decision?

5. There was almost no disagreement on all sides of this controversy that copying and sharing of copyrighted work was unlawful and that direct violators should be punished. Actions against direct violators in the past have resulted in convictions or settlements. This didn't satisfy the "content" rights holders—why? What role does deterrence play in the efficacy of rules prohibiting unlawful copying and sharing of protected content? What role does respect for the law play as an independent factor in the function of law? Do you agree with the assertions of counsel for the content rights holders that the number of unlawful file sharing actors and activities rendered copyright meaningless in the identification and prosecution of violators because of direct transaction costs and the potential alienation of the public? Were the actions against Reimerdes, Aimster and Grokster examples of growing frustration with rights protection under contemporary legal structures? Why bring actions against those that "enable" by serving as a conduit, or catalyst instead of the direct infringers?

6. Have any of the prior victories in court against an "enabler" produced a sustainable result to protect content rights holders? See specifically, *Universal City Studios, Inc. v. Shawn C. Reimerdes,* 111 F.Supp.2d 294 (S.D.N.Y. 2000) later in this chapter and ask yourself are DVD formats protected significantly more effectively since that decision? Or, was the cat

forever out of the bag? Napster no longer provides illegal file sharing services, nor does any one else appear to maintain a central server list to facilitate access. Grokster decentralized such that shutting down part or most of the components of P2P won't make it go away. The underlying premises of the Court may need to be questioned. Does shutting down Grokster mean that P2P and illegal file sharing will disappear? Does it mean that there won't be further changes and improvements in code and programs? Does it mean that as additional controls are imposed by law there will be a reduction in P2P file sharing activities?

The ultimate reality test lies in appreciating a USAToday article which states that the day after the decision of the court in *Grokster* that there were an average of 5.2 to 5.4 million downloads per hour of files using file sharing technologies.

> LOS ANGELES—Digital copies of songs and movies flowed freely across the Internet on Tuesday, a day after the Supreme Court ruled that online file-sharing services can be held liable when their users pirate music and video. Big Champagne, a firm that measures Internet traffic, says 5.2 million to 5.4 million people were using file-sharing networks at any given moment Tuesday." See Jefferson Graham, *File-sharing beat goes on*, USA TODAY (USATODAY.com—File-sharing beat goes on http://usatoday)

In several interviews on that Tuesday, it was reported that downloading was no different than before the Supreme Court decision and several individuals stated they would continue to download despite the decision. Does this indicate a paradigm shift based on normative behavioral changes, digital globalization and changing contexts of jurisdiction power and control?

7.   One may ask the question whether this form of legislative action is a question of risk assessment. Who is at greater risk under these circumstances, the individual software writer, a company like Grokster, or a well endowed Microsoft? Will this have a chilling affect on innovation by raising the specter of holding those that innovate liable where that which they enable allows others to avoid legal proscriptions?

8.   Do you think the action of the Court consistent with their stated policy of restraint and recognition that Congress had been granted the power under the Constitution regarding Intellectual Activities?

9.   There are two elements of Grokster that are worthy of further note:

The first is the fact that Justice Stevens, relegated to the role of concurrence in *Grokster*, authored the majority opinion in *Sony Betamax*.

The second is the "Inducing Infringement of Copyrights Act of 2004" which was presented to the Senate on June 22, 2004 by two Senators who also filed an amicus brief in Grokster. The text of the act is as follows:

108th CONGRESS 2d Session **S. 2560**

To amend chapter 5 of title 17, United States Code, relating to inducement of copyright infringement, and for other purposes.

IN THE SENATE OF THE UNITED STATES

June 22, 2004

Mr. HATCH (for himself, Mr. LEAHY, Mr. FRIST, Mr. DASCHLE, Mr. GRAHAM of South Carolina, and Mrs. BOXER) introduced the following bill; which was read twice and referred to the Committee on the Judiciary

———

A BILL

To amend chapter 5 of title 17, United States Code, relating to inducement of copyright infringement, and for other purposes.

Be it enacted by the Senate and House of Representatives of the United States of America in Congress assembled,

SECTION 1. SHORT TITLE.

This Act may be cited as the 'Inducing Infringement of Copyrights Act of 2004'.

SEC.2. INTENTIONAL INDUCEMENT OF COPYRIGHT INFRINGEMENT

Section 501 of title 17, United States Code, is amended by adding at the end the following:

'(g)(1) In this subsection, the term 'intentionally induces' means intentionally aids, abets, induces, or procures, and intent may be shown by acts from which a reasonable person would find intent to induce infringement based upon all relevant information about such acts then reasonably available to the actor, including whether the activity relies on infringement for its commercial viability.

'(2) Whoever intentionally induces any violation identified in subsection (a) shall be liable as an infringer.

'(3) Nothing in this subsection shall enlarge or diminish the doctrines of vicarious and contributory liability for copyright infringement or require any court to unjustly withhold or impose any secondary liability for copyright infringement.'.

A bill to amend chapter 5 of title 17, United States Code, relating to inducement of copyright infringement, and for other purposes" was sent to the Judiciary Committee. It was introduced by Senators Hatch and Leahy. Senator Hatch in the introduction of the bill said of programs for file sharing:

"Users of these programs routinely violate criminal laws relating to copyright infringement and pornography distribution. Criminal law defines "inducement" as "that which leads or tempts to the commission of crime." Some P2P software appears to be the definition of criminal inducement captured in computer code."

The bill was never passed. How closely did the decision of the court comport with the language of the proposed legislation? Should the fact that Congress considered and failed to enact inducement legislation have been taken into account by the court? Is this decision consistent with the position of the court in *Eldred* deferring to the primary delegation of powers to Congress over copyright in the Constitution? If not, why not?

10.   The Supreme Court decision remanded the case to the Circuit Court, which in turn remanded the case to the district court for trial, *Metro–Goldwyn–Mayer Studios, Inc. v. Grokster Ltd.*, 419 F.3d 1005 (9th Cir. 2005). While uncertainty has been a force in its own right, many answers left unresolved as to activities which would lead to inducement and contributory liability for infringement were at issue in *Metro–Goldwyn–Mayer Studios, Inc. v. Grokster, Ltd.*, 454 F.Supp.2d 966 (U.S. D.C. C.D. Cal., 2006).[Hereinafter *Steamcast*] In reviewing this case note (1) the extraordinary detail on the underlying technology of Napster through current file sharing models, (2) the clear evidence of an intent to infringe using changing file sharing practices, (3) the disdain for filters described in the opinion to permit tracking and and payment of lawful licensing fees, (4) the refusal to use filters to block the download of copyrighted material, and finally, (5) both active inducement and knowledge that the primary function of their services were to infringe copyrights by facilitating downloading. The case represents a maturing appreciation of technology, infringing business models and evolving DRM alternatives through filtering, fingerprinting and tracking to ensure appropriate licensing fees for content rights holders.

METRO–GOLDWYN–MAYER STUDIOS, INC. v. GROKSTER, LTD.

(U.S.D.C. C.D.Cal., Sept. 27, 2006).
454 F.Supp.2d 966.

WILSON, DISTRICT J.

* * *

V.   Secondary Liability

A.   *The Inducement Doctrine*

Plaintiffs have moved for summary judgment on StreamCast's liability for the infringement committed by its users on the basis of the inducement doctrine set forth by the Supreme Court in *Grokster*. As the Supreme Court held, "one who distributes a device with the object of promoting its use to infringe copyright, as shown by clear expression or other affirmative steps taken to foster infringement, is liable for the resulting acts of infringement by third parties." *Grokster*, 125 S.Ct. at 2770. The Supreme Court further explained,

> [M]ere knowledge of infringing potential or of actual infringing uses would not be enough here to subject a distributor [of the device] to liability. Nor would ordinary acts incident to product distribution, such as offering customers technical support or product updates, support liability in themselves. The inducement rule, instead, premises liability on purposeful, culpable expression and conduct, and thus does nothing to compromise legitimate commerce or discourage inno-

vation having a lawful promise. *Id.* at 2780. Importantly, liability may attach even if the defendant does not induce specific acts of infringement. *Id.* at 2782 n. 13.

An unlawful objective to promote infringement can be shown by a variety of means. "The classic instance of inducement is by advertisement or solicitation that broadcasts a message designed to stimulate others to commit violations." *Id.* at 2780. However, showing that the defendant sent out such a message is "not [the] exclusive way of" demonstrating inducement. *Id.* With respect to StreamCast, the Supreme Court highlighted three facts from which a reasonable factfinder could infer an intent to foster infringement. First, some internal StreamCast communications and advertising designs expressed an intent to target Napster users, a community well-known for copyright infringement. Although it was not known whether some of the advertising designs were actually communicated to the public, "whether the messages were communicated is not to the point on this record." *Id.* at 2781. "The function of the message in the theory of inducement is to prove by a defendant's own statements that his unlawful purpose disqualifies him from claiming protection." *Id.* Second, StreamCast did not attempt to develop filtering tools or other means of diminishing the use of its products for infringement. Although this fact alone would be insufficient to support liability, viewed in conjunction with other evidence it underscored StreamCast's unlawful objective. *Id.* at 2781 n. 12. Third, StreamCast's business model depended on high-volume use of its software, which was overwhelmingly infringing. *Id.* at 2781–82. Again, this evidence would not alone justify the imposition of liability, but it supported an inference of unlawful intent when viewed in context with other evidence in the record. *Id.*

StreamCast argues that a defendant could be found liable for secondary infringement only if it: (1) for the purpose of inducing infringement, (2) took actions beyond distributing infringement-enabling technology, and (3) which actually resulted in specific instances of infringement. * * * In StreamCast's view, even if it distributed peer-to-peer software with the intent for it to be used for infringement, liability does not attach unless it took further actions, such as offering instructions on infringing use, that actually caused specific acts of infringement. Much of StreamCast's brief is devoted to arguing that Plaintiffs failed in proving the second and third elements of its proposed test. However, StreamCast's legal theory is plainly contrary to the Supreme Court's holding in *Grokser.* As the Supreme Court explained,

> It is not only that encouraging a particular consumer to infringe a copyright can give rise to secondary liability for the infringement that results. Inducement liability goes beyond that, and the distribution of a product can itself give rise to liability where evidence shows that the distributor intended and encouraged the product to be used to infringe. In such a case, the culpable conduct is not merely the encouragement of infringement but also the distribution of the tool intended for infringing use.

125 S.Ct. at 2782 n. 13. Thus, Plaintiffs need not prove that StreamCast undertook specific actions, beyond product distribution, that caused specific acts of infringement. Instead, Plaintiffs need prove only that Stream-Cast distributed the product with the intent to encourage infringement. Since there is no dispute that StreamCast did distribute an infringement-enabling technology, the inquiry focuses on the defendant's intent, which can be shown by evidence of the defendant's expression or conduct. "If liability for inducing infringement is ultimately found, it will not be on the basis of presuming or imputing fault, but from inferring a patently illegal objective from statements and actions showing what that objective [is]." *Id.* at 2782.

In the record before the Court, evidence of StreamCast's unlawful intent is overwhelming.

B. *StreamCast's Software Was Used Overwhelmingly for Infringement*

Plaintiffs have presented studies showing that StreamCast products facilitated massive infringement of their copyrighted content. * * * Plaintiffs' expert witness Dr. Ingram Olkin is a professor of statistics at Stanford University. He devised a random sampling procedure in which words were randomly selected from the American Heritage Electronic Dictionary and then used to search for files using Morpheus software. If a search results in a list of file names, a random number generator was used to choose a file for downloading. The search procedure was implemented in a study supervised by Charles Hausman, an anti-piracy executive at the Motion Picture Association of America. The study showed that 87.33% of the files offered for distribution on the Morpheus network were infringing or highly likely to be infringing. The randomly selected files were downloaded, and then uploaded to determine the percentage of file download requests from Morpheus users that were aimed at the infringing files. Almost 97% of the files actually requested for downloading were infringing or highly likely to be infringing. While infringing use by third parties is not by itself evidence of StreamCast's intent, the staggering scale of infringement makes it more likely that StreamCast condoned illegal use, and provides the backdrop against which all of StreamCast's actions must be assessed.

The only evidence StreamCast offers to rebut Plaintiffs' studies is a declaration from StreamCast counsel Wendy Goodkin, who testfied that she was able to locate some public domain content, such as the Declaration of Independence, using the Morpheus software. However, Goodkin did not use a random sampling procedure. Her declaration says nothing about the percentage of files available on the network that are infringing. It follows that Plaintiffs' showing of massive infringement on StreamCast's network is undisputed.

C. *StreamCast's Targeting of Napster Users*

StreamCast staved off closure at the start of 2001 by launching its OpenNap/MusicCity network to attract Napster users to is servers. As the

Supreme Court has noted, StreamCast's courting of the Napster community, which was notorious for copyright infringement, indicated an intent to foster infringement. *Grokster,* 125 S.Ct. at 2779. StreamCast now insists that it targeted the Napster community because it wanted to find a way to distribute Morpheus Toolbar, and Napster users represented a technology-savvy audience that any software company would want as a customer base. However, uncontroverted evidence shows that StreamCast purposefully targeted Napster users, not merely to market to them, but to convert them into StreamCast users by offering them the same file-sharing service that Napster had itself offered. Michael Weiss, Stream-Cast's CEO, himself stated in an email from early 2001 that "it was always our intent to use [OpenNap] to be able to capture email addresses of our initial target market so that we could promote our StreamCast Morpheus interface to them." * * *

StreamCast selected the OpenNap precisely because it was a Napster-compatible file-sharing application. Moreover, in the early days of Open-Nap, StreamCast measured its progress by comparing itself to Napster and by monitoring the amount of files available for download in the MusicCity network, many if not most of which were copyrighted works. StreamCast also sent its agents into Internet chatrooms to encourage Napster users to migrate to MusicCity, and ran advertisements promoting itself as an alternative to Napster. StreamCast's internal documents demonstrated its intent to exploit Napster's legal problems by enticing users to MusicCity in the event that Napster was forced to shut down or filter out copyrighted files by court order. StreamCast even ran online banner advertisements that stated: "When the lights went off at Napster ... where did the users go?" StreamCast rejoins that the banner advertisement merely promoted the use of its products, and did not expressly tell users to infringe. But that is besides the point. Clearly, StreamCast sought to offer the same exact service Napster did to the same group of users, even after a federal court had entered a preliminary injunction against Napster for secondary infringement. StreamCast's current position that it merely wanted to market Morpheus Toolbar to a desirable demographic does not controvert the fact that StreamCast chose a means—the establishment and promotion of a Napster-compatible file-sharing service to a community known for infringement—that manifested an intent to encourage copyright infringement. Such intent was also expressed in an email from CEO Weiss; he started a survey finding that 70% of Napster users would defect if Napster asked them to pay for music, and that those users were precisely the ones that StreamCast targeted for acquisition. * * *

Notwithstanding the fact that it actively marketed OpenNap/MusicCity to Napster users, StreamCast argues that it "fell upon these users by accident," and that Napster users discovered and migrated to MusicCity on their own. It is possible that StreamCast's marketing efforts were wholly ineffective and its user base grew primarily by word of mouth. Even if the Court assumes that to be true, StreamCast's promotional efforts, internal communications, advertising designs, and actual advertisements constitute clear expressions of its unlawful intent.

D. StreamCast's Assistance to Infringing Users

It is undisputed that StreamCast provided users with technical assistance for playback of copyrighted content. The files that users reported having trouble playing back included such popular copyrighted content as Seinfeld, the Matrix, Tomb Raider, and Shrek. StreamCast argues that the evidence is immaterial because the technical assistance concerned the use of third party software such as Microsoft's Windows Media Player, not Morpheus. However, those users sought assistance from StreamCast because the music and movies they wanted to play back were downloaded from OpenNap/MusicCity or Morpheus. StreamCast's incentive to help is obvious: if users could not enjoy the files they downloaded through Morpheus, they would be less likely to use Morpheus in the future. It is not surprising that, in one instance, StreamCast even suggested to a user that he upload copyrighted content for sharing. * * * While knowledge of infringing use per se cannot give rise to secondary liability, by providing technical assistance to help users enjoy copyrighted content they illegally downloaded, StreamCast demonstrated an intent to encourage use of its technology for infringement.

E. StreamCast Ensured Its Technology Had Infringing Capabilities

Infringing use was undisputably on StreamCast's mind when it developed Morpheus; indeed, StreamCast took steps to ensure that the technology it deployed would be capable of infringing use. Before deciding to license FastTrack technology for Morpheus, StreamCast chairman Griffin evaluated FastTrack by searching for Garth Brooks songs on the Fast-Track network. While Morpheus was in beta testing, StreamCast employees identified the insufficient quantity of popular copyrighted content on the network as an important problem. Griffin continued to focus on the availability of Garth Brooks songs, while art director Margauz Schaffer reported difficulties finding music from Elton John. * * * Software engineer Panetti, for his part, tested the system by downloading tracks by Britney Spears. * * * As an example of the Morpheus interface's capabilities, StreamCast also created screenshots of a search for music by Sting. * * * StreamCast would not have evaluated Morpheus by its infringing capabilities if it did not intend widespread infringing use. * * *

When StreamCast negotiated licensing FastTrack from Consumer Empowerment to replace the OpenNap architecture, Smith told Consumer Empowerment that StreamCast maintained a database of two million songs and wanted to enable users to conduct a "product/artist" search. * * * It is not clear whether that proposal was implemented, but it is undisputed that the Morpheus interface also contains a search category for "Top 40" songs. "Top 40" is a term typically used to refer to the best-selling or most frequently broadcast pop music songs at a given time. * * * Such songs are almost invariably copyrighted. StreamCast explains that Morpheus software does not itself identify particular files as Top 40 content. Rather, the Top 40 feature enables a user to search for files that other users have designated as Top 40 content. Even though StreamCast's peer-to-peer architecture gives users responsibility for categorizing content, the fact remains that StreamCast implemented a feature that made it easier for users to share copyrighted content. The inference of intent to promote infringement is particularly forceful when considered alongside the fact that StreamCast tested the system by searching for infringing content.

In addition, StreamCast took active steps to protest illegal file trading from the enforcement efforts of copyright holders. In May 2001, StreamCast became aware of MediaEnforcer, a software program that enabled copyright owners to track infringement on the Internet. As documented in a series of emails, StreamCast immediately undertook action to block MediaEnforcer from the Morpheus network. * * * StreamCast also blocked from its network Plaintiffs' law firm Mitchell Silverberg and the anti-piracy firm NetPD, which StreamCast described in an email as "hackers for RIAA and Metallica." * * * StreamCast also deployed encryption technology so that Plaintiffs could not see what files were being transferred through Morpheus. * * * StreamCast's current protestations that it was merely protecting the privacy of its users—as stated in Weiss's affidavit—is belied by these internal documents and deposition testimony showing its concern about copyright enforcement efforts. As chairman Griffin has explained, "[w]ith the continued litigious nature of the media companies at the time, we were always looking for ways to find a more anonymous solution" for its users. * * *

F. StreamCast's Business Model Depended on Massive Infringing Use

In *Grokster,* the Supreme Court identified StreamCast's reliance on revenue from infringing use as evidence of unlawful intent. 125 S.Ct. at 2781–82. Until 2004, StreamCast did not sell its Morpheus software, but gave it to away to users without cost. Revenue was generated by displaying advertising on the software's user interface. "[T]he more the software is used, the more ads are sent out and the greater the advertising revenue becomes. Since the extent of the software's use determines the gain to the distributors, the commercial sense of their enterprise turns on high-volume use, which the record shows is infringing." *Id.* In 2001, nearly all of StreamCast's revenue came from advertising. In 2002, advertising still made up nearly two-thirds of StreamCast's total revenue. In 2003, advertising's share of total revenue sunk to 19%, but it increased back to 26% in 2004. As of early 2006, advertising made up about half of total revenue. * * *

The record shows that StreamCast knew its business model depended on massive infringing use, and acted to grow its business accordingly. Smith has testified that StreamCast's objective in advertising to Napster users was to "increase the number of users by increasing the amount of file-sharing, because the more files that were physically available, the more users would come." * * * Shortly after launching the OpenNap/Music City network, Weiss measured the company's progress by tracking the number of files that were available, which he told employees had increased from 316,000 to 15,006,322 MP3 files in less than two weeks. * * * A month later, art director Schaffer produced presentation slides boasting that OpenNap/MusicCity had more files available for sharing than Napster. * * * The large number of users who were drawn to StreamCast by the files available for download was an asset for StreamCast's advertising business. For example, StreamCast sales executive Trey Bowles touted StreamCast to a prospective advertiser by pointing out that "Morpheus has such a high media content with almost every user interested in music in many capacities." * * * Of course, it helped StreamCast's profitability that it did not incur any costs to obtain the content that was used to attract users. As a PowerPoint presentation stated, a strength of its model was "that it had "[n]o product costs to acquire music" and an "[a]bility to get all the music." "

* * *

StreamCast emphasizes that it intended—as documented by business plans and strategy papers—to pay for licensed content, and also to derive revenue from instant messaging and an internet telephone service. StreamCast also blames Plaintiffs for their difficult licensing terms, which StreamCast believes prevented it from launching a successful, legal business with licensed content. StreamCast has submitted declarations from its executives stating that StreamCast wanted to be a legitimate business, and that infringing users took up its products through no fault of its own. Whatever its subjective intentions were about eventually securing licenses and developing revenue streams that did not depend on infringement, the business that actually materialized was one that thrived only because of the massive infringement enabled by Morpheus and OpenNap/MusicCity. And as recounted above, undisputed objective evidence shows that Stream-Cast distributed its software with the goal of facilitating and profiting from infringing use.

G. StreamCast Has Taken No Meaningful Affirmative Steps to Prevent Infringement

The Supreme Court held that a defendant's failure to prevent infringing use may indicate an intent to facilitate infringement. *Grokster,* 125 S.Ct. at 2781. Although secondary liability may not be premised on this factor alone, it may be considered along with other circumstances in determining the defendant's motive. *Id.* at 2781 n. 12. By implication, although StreamCast is not required to prevent all the harm that is facilitated by the technology, it must at least make a good faith attempt to mitigate the massive infringement facilitated by its technology.

Plaintiffs point out, and StreamCast does not dispute, that Stream-Cast has never implemented a system to filter out copyrighted content from the Morpheus network. However, the parties vigorously dispute whether filtering is technologically feasible. Generally, two potential methods of filtering exist. The first is based on acoustic fingerprinting technology, which involves the creation of unique digital signatures for each music file and the identification of the files on the basis of that signature through comparison of a database of copyrighted content. The file-sharing client application would then be programmed to block files that match the signatures of known copyrighted content. Plaintiffs have submitted declarations from executives of acoustic fingerprinting technology companies to show that acoustic fingerprinting is a readily available solution for stopping rampant copyright infringement in file-sharing networks. StreamCast rejoins that acoustic finger-printing does not work. A StreamCast witness' affidavit states that he was able to find copyrighted content made available for sharing on the iMesh network, a StreamCast competitor, inspite of iMesh's implementation of acoustic fingerprinting-based filtering. StreamCast has requested further discovery pursuant to Rule 56(f) to evaluate the effectiveness of acoustic fingerprinting technology.

The second potential filtering method is based on metadata. Metadata is data that describes the properties of a digital file. A music file typically has such metadata as song title and artist name. Morpheus itself executes file searches on the basis of metadata, such as song names. Conversely, the search function could be programmed to filter out copyrighted files on the basis of metadata. FastTrack-based versions of Morpheus already contain a feature that, if activated by the user, filters out pornographic content on the basis of file name. Plaintiffs argue that the technology behind the pornography filter could easily be reconfigured to filter out copyrighted content. For example, the client software could be configured to filter out all files bearing the names "Jay–Z" or "the Beatles." StreamCast counters that metadata filtering would be burdensome and overbroad, as it would block all files that share common words in metadata, even if the file is not copyrighted. There is less concern with overinclusive filtering for pornography because there are only a few terms commonly associated with pornography; in contrast, a list that contains of all copyrighted music and movies owned by Plaintiffs would contain many generic terms, with correspondingly greater potential for overinclusive filtering. StreamCast also argues that, with regard to FastTrack-based versions of Morpheus, StreamCast did not have the ability to directly modify the FastTrack source code, which the licensor controlled, to implement copyright filtering. StreamCast also emphasizes that former chief technology officer Smith, who is now cooperating with Plaintiffs, has given inconsistent testimony on the feasibility and ease of filtering technology; his current testimony is far more optimistic about the feasibility of metadata filtering than when he was still employed by StreamCast.

Based on the foregoing, a jury could reasonably agree with StreamCast that copyright-filtering does not work perfectly, and implementing it would negatively impact usability. However, the ultimate question for this Court's inquiry is to examine StreamCast's intent. Even if filtering technology does not work perfectly and contains negative side effects on usability, the fact that a defendant fails to make some effort to mitigate abusive use of its technology may still support an inference of intent to encourage infringement.

However, the technological issue is beside the point, considering StreamCast's expressed attitude toward filtering. In the record, there is no hint that StreamCast was at all troubled by the fact that its products were used to commit copyright infringement on a massive scale. While Stream-Cast executives were quick to express concern and devise technological solutions to prevent Plaintiffs from enforcing their copyrights, they were positively resistant to the possibility of copyright filtering. That is not surprising, because StreamCast's business depended on attracting users by providing them with the ability to pirate copyrighted content. As Weiss stated, "[w]e did not care what was on those files [traded by the users], we only cared that we were able to compare ourselves favorably with the much larger and firmly entrenched Napster." * * *

According to Smith's undisputed testimony, he had discussed the possibility of metadata-based copyright filtering on OpenNap/MusicCity and FastTrack/Morpheus, but Kallman and Weiss both rejected the idea. * * *

In fact, StreamCast saw its resistance to filtering as a competitive advantage. In another conversation, Griffin and Weiss discussed the possibility that Napster might be judicially ordered to implement copyright filters. * * *

Not surprisingly, StreamCast was unreceptive when it was approached in 2002 by GraceNote, a company that had worked with Napster on a way to use acoustic fingerprinting technology to identify copyrighted music and pay copyright holders. Jody Pace, the StreamCast employee responsible for responding to GraceNote's offer emailed Trey Bowles for instructions: "I know this is something we DO NOT want to do, but I am not sure how I need to word that." * * * Indeed, Smith, who as chief technology officer would be involved in any major technical decision, testified in 2002 that he has never conducted major research into the viability of new acoustic fingerprinting technology. Nor had he ever been asked to investigate the availability of databases that might be used for filtering. * * *

This Court recognizes that StreamCast blocked certain users from its network when asked to do so by copyright holders. However, its effort was half-hearted at best. As described above, StreamCast used encryption technology to defeat Plainitffs' monitoring efforts. Morever, blocking users was not very effective because a user could simply create a new username to re-enter the network under a different identity. StreamCast had the capability of automatically blocking these users on a rolling basis, but expressly decided not to do so. * * *

H. StreamCast Cannot Reasonably Claim Ignorance of Infringement

StreamCast contends that it was unaware of the copyrights at issue until November 2001, when it was served in the instant action. Stream-

Cast further argues that any evidence of its intent prior to November 2001—such as internal documents surrounding the launch of Open-Nap/MusicCity in January 2001—cannot be used to prove its intent to induce infringement, simply because it could not logically intend to infringe copyrights of which it was not aware.

This argument is implausible. StreamCast cannot seriously argue that it did not know that the popular music and movies traded on its network were copyrighted, particularly in light of the publicity surrounding the Napster litigation and StreamCast's clear plans to exploit Napster's legal troubles. StreamCast relies on a series of patent cases—*see, e.g., L.A. Gear, Inc. v. E.S. Originals, Inc.*, 859 F.Supp. 1294, 1300 (C.D.Cal.1994)—for the proposition that a defendant cannot be found to have intended and encouraged patent infringement unless it was actually aware of the infringed patent. However, while whether a particular technical process is patented may not be immediately obvious, it is common knowledge that most popular music and movies are copyrighted.

I. Summary of Inducement Liability

In sum, evidence of StreamCast's objective of promoting infringement is overwhelming. Indeed, in *Groskter* the Supreme Court had hinted that summary judgment should be granted for Plaintiffs after reviewing much of the same evidence. 125 S.Ct. at 2782. After carefully and independently considering the evidence presented by the parties, the this Court finds that no reasonable factfinder can conclude that StreamCast provided OpenNap services and distributed Morpheus without the intent to induce infringement. The only remaining question is whether StreamCast can show that a continuance of this summary judgment motion is warranted.

* * *

VII. Conclusion

For the foregoing reasons, this Court GRANTS Plaintiffs' motion for summary judgment as to StreamCast's liability for inducing copyright infringement through MusicCity/OpenNap and Morpheus. * * *

IT IS SO ORDERED.

COLUMBIA PICTURES, INDUSTRIES, INC. v. FUNG

United States District Court for the Central District of California, 2009.
2009 WL 6355911.

STEPHEN V. WILSON

ORDER GRANTING PLAINTIFFS' MOTION FOR SUMMARY JUDGMENT ON LIABILITY

* * *

II. FACTUAL BACKGROUND

A. The Torrent Structure

Plaintiffs own or control a large quantity of copyrights within the entertainment and popular media fields. Defendant Fung maintains and operates a number of websites, including www.isohunt.com, www. torrentbox.com, www.podtropolis.com, and www.ed2k-it.com (collectively "Fung sites" or "Defendants' sites"), that allow users to download files to their computers.

Plaintiffs maintain that Fung and his websites facilitate their users' infringement of copyrighted files. Specifically, Plaintiffs assert that, through his operation and promotion of the websites, Fung allows users to download infringing copies of popular movies, television shows, sound recordings, software programs, video games, and other copyrighted content free of charge. Users of the Fung sites have downloaded works that are copyrighted by Plaintiffs; these downloads have taken place without authorization from Plaintiffs.

The Fung sites are an evolutionary modification of traditional "peer-to-peer" sharing sites such as Napster and Grokster. A peer-to-peer service provides a method for users of a network to exchange files quickly and easily between the individuals on the network—other "peers". See, e.g., Metro–Goldwyn–Mayer Studios, Inc. v. Grokster, Ltd, 545 U.S. 913, 919, 125 S. Ct. 2764, 162 L. Ed. 2d 781 (2005). The content of the files shared therefore resides on the computers of individual users rather than on central servers.

Through use of the Fung sites, which are commonly known as "BitTorrent" or "torrent" sites, users download content directly from the computers of other users and not directly from the servers of the Defendants, thus operating as a sharing service of the peer-to-peer variety. In a BitTorrent network, however, the download process is unique from that of previous systems such as Napster and Grokster. Rather than downloading a file from an individual user, users of a bit-torrent network will select the file that they wish to download, and, at that point, the downloading will begin from a number of host computers that possess the file simultaneously. BitTorrent technology relies on a variety of mechanisms in order to accomplish the ultimate downloading of an given file, including: (1) a software application that users download, which is commonly referred to as a "client application"; (2) websites, also known as "torrent sites," which allow users to select "dot-torrent files" that they wish to download; and (3) servers, also known as "trackers," that manage the download process. The client applications and trackers work together through the use of a "BitTorrent protocol" which standardizes the client-client and client-tracker communications. These components essentially work together to allow individuals to visit a torrent site, download files, and keep track of those downloads—as well as discover additional persons to download from—through the use of trackers. In such a system the downloading of the desired content is occurring from multiple source points at the same time and allowing larger downloads to move more expeditiously. During this simultaneous downloading process users form what is known as a "swarm," which allows for quick exchange of the downloading material.

Accordingly, in order to download files from others in a BitTorrent network, users must engage in a number of steps. First, users must install a BitTorrent client application. Standing alone, a BitTorrent client application does not possess the ability to search other computers for files. Instead, as part of the second step, users must visit a torrent site for the purpose of locating dot-torrent files containing the content that they wish to download. These torrent sites maintain indexes of available torrent files for download that users may search, or, in the alternative, users may upload torrent files to share with others through the torrent site. These torrent files are referred to as "dot-torrent" files in reference to their file extension name. The dot-torrent files do not contain the actual content item searched for; rather, the dot-torrent file contains the data used by the BitTorrent client to retrieve the content through a peer-to-peer transfer. In the third step, once the user clicks on the desired dot-torrent file, the BitTorrent client will locate and download the actual content item. This is accomplished through the use of trackers that are contained within the dot-torrent file. The dot-torrent file contains "hash" values that are used to identify the various pieces of the content file and the location of those pieces in the network. The BitTorrent client application then simultaneously downloads the pieces of the content file from as many users as are available at the time of the request, and then reassembles the content file on the requesting computer when the download is complete. Once a user downloads a given content file, he also becomes a source for future requests and downloads.

B. Sites Maintained by Defendant Fung

Defendant Fung operates a number of websites, including www. isohunt.com ("Isohunt"), www.torrentbox.com ("Torrentbox"), www. podtropolis.com ("Podtropolis"), and www.ed2k-it.com ("eDonkey"). The structure and manner in which users download files from these sites differs in certain respects. The BitTorrent websites—Isohunt, Torrentbox, and Podtropolis—all provide users the ability to search for and download BitTorrent files. As explained by Defendants' expert Steven Gribble, "the defendants' Web sites collect, receive, index, and make available descriptions of content, including so-called 'dot-torrent files,' and they also provide access to 'open-access' BitTorrent Trackers."

Users of BitTorrent websites click on a "download torrent" button or link on the website that will begin the downloading process described above. The elements of the downloading process work together to bring the desired content to the user's computer without any further actions by the user. As one of Plaintiffs' experts explains: "[t]he only purpose of a dot-torrent file is to enable users to identify, locate, and download a copy of the actual content item referenced by the dot-torrent file.... Once a user has clicked the 'download' torrent button or link, the ... desired content file should begin downloading to the user's computer without any further action or input from the user."

The BitTorrent websites, as set forth in further detail below, also contain a number of categories from which users can select files to download, including "Top Searches," "Top 20 Movies," "Top 20 TV Shows," "Box Office Movies." For example, the Isohunt home page contains a listing of "Top Searches," which provides a listing of the most commonly searched-for terms by users of the websites. This category contained code filtering out pornography-related terms from the "Top Searches" display. The items found within the "Top Searches" category are all associated with copyrighted content. Much the same holds true for the "Top 20 Most Downloaded Torrents" on Defendant Fung's Torrentbox site. Another of Defendants' sites, Podtropolis, simply contains lists of the "Top 20 Movies" and "Top 20 TV Shows," all of which correspond to copyrighted content. The ed2k-it website contains files in lists entitled "High Quality DVD Rips" and "TV Show Releases," all of which correspond to copyrighted content.

Plaintiffs note that the meta tags used on Fung's websites often included the term "warez" as a header for every page. Plaintiffs also point to certain other elements of the webpage that related to known copyrighted material. Defendants, on the home page of the Isohunt website, asked users to upload dot-torrent files of Box Office Movies and also maintained a list of the top twenty grossing movies in U.S. theaters at the time. These lists served the function of getting users to upload dot-torrent files of the latest blockbuster films and have them posted on the Isohunt website.

* * *. According to Plaintiffs' expert Richard Waterman, approximately 95% of downloads occurring through Defendants' sites are downloads of copyright-infringing content. * * * Waterman further states that 95.6% of all dot-torrent files downloaded from Torrentbox are for either copyrighted or highly likely copyrighted material. In a study of the Isohunt website, Waterman found that approximately 90% of files available and 94% of dot-torrent files downloaded from the site are copyrighted or highly likely copyrighted. * * * Despite Defendants' repeated assertions that the evidence is based on "junk science," Defendants fail to rebut Waterman's statement that he relied on the standard statistical sampling techniques used in his field. It is also noteworthy that numerous courts have relied on such statistical sampling. See Arista Records, 633 F. Supp. 2d at 144–45; *MGM Studios, Inc. v. Grokster, Ltd.*, 454 F. Supp. 2d 966, 985 (C.D. Cal. 2006); *A & M Records, Inc. v. Napster*, 114 F. Supp. 2d 896, 902–03 (N.D. Cal. 2000), aff'd, 239 F.3d 1004 (9th Cir. 2001).

In any event, for the purposes of this case, the precise percentage of infringement is irrelevant: the evidence clearly shows that Defendants' users infringed on a significant scale. It simply does not matter whether 75% (to pick a number) of available materials were copyrighted or 95% of available materials were copyrighted; and even if this distinction did matter, * * *

C. Fung's Participation in the Websites

In addition to the general structure of the pages maintained by Defendants, Defendant Fung has personally made a number of statements regarding the copyrighted nature of the works available on his sites. In one such post on the Isohunt website Defendant Fung responded to a user's post by stating "they accuse us for [sic] thieves, and they r [sic] right. Only we r [sic] 'stealing' from the lechers (them) and not the originators (artists)." In an interview Fung stated: "Morally, I'm a Christian. 'Thou shalt not steal.' But to me, even copyright infringement when it occurs may not necessarily be stealing." In another post Fung stated: "We completely oppose RIAA & Co. so do not be alarmed by our indexing activities...." In another interview Fung also stated that users were attracted to his website by the availability of a blockbuster film of the time, The Da Vinci Code. Fung's other statements included references to aiding individuals in the download of then-popular movie titles such as The Matrix Reloaded and The Lord of the Rings: Return of the King, pointing users to links where they could download copies of these movies through the torrent sites. Other statements made on the website encouraged or made available the downloading of illegal content by users who were browsing the discussion forums on Fung's websites.

Plaintiffs also provide details relating to the assistance that Fung would give website users in downloading copyrighted material within the forum discussions of the various websites. In one such instance, in response to a user query on how to make a DVD from a downloaded copy of the film Pirates of the Caribbean, Fung provided a link to a website that would allow the individual to burn a DVD of the downloaded copy. Fung provided users with assistance on a number of occasions regarding how they could go about playing or extracting the copyrighted films that they downloaded from the Defendants' websites. Fung also provided assistance to a user who was searching for episodes of the television series Star Trek: Enterprise; Fung provided links to search possible search queries that would turn up the work. Fung also provided technical advice regarding the use of "trackers" in response to emails containing dot-torrent files connected with copyrighted television programs, such as the NBC series The Office.

IV. ANALYSIS

A. Preliminary Issues Regarding Secondary Liability

1. Secondary Theories of Liability

Plaintiffs move for summary judgment against defendants on three separate grounds: inducement of copyright infringement, material contribution to copyright infringement, and vicarious copyright infringement. The Court will only address the first theory, because Defendants' inducement liability is overwhelmingly clear. * * *

The first two theories (material contribution and inducement) are known collectively as "contributory liability." Perfect 10 v. Visa Int'l Serv.

Ass'n, 494 F.3d 788, 795 (9th Cir. 2007) ("One contributorily infringes when he (1) has knowledge of another's infringement and (2) either (a) materially contributes to or (b) induces that infringement."), cert. denied, 128 S. Ct. 2871, 171 L. Ed. 2d 811 (2008). Despite the analytical similarities between the inducement and material contribution theories, it is now established in this Circuit that inducement and material contribution are distinct theories of contributory liability through which defendants can be found liable. Id.; see also Metro–Goldwyn–Mayer Studios, Inc. v. Grokster, Ltd., 518 F. Supp. 2d 1197, 1227 (C.D. Cal. 2007) ("Grokster V") ("material contribution and inducement are two doctrinal subsets of the contributory infringement theory of liability."). Generally, inducement requires that the defendant has undertaken purposeful acts aimed at assisting and encouraging others to infringe copyright, see Metro–Goldwyn–Mayer Studios, Inc. v. Grokster, 545 U.S. 913, 936–37, 125 S. Ct. 2764, 162 L. Ed. 2d 781 (2005) ("Grokster III"); in contrast, material contribution (in the context of "computer system operator[s]") applies if the defendant "has actual knowledge that specific infringing material is available using its system, and can take simple measures to prevent further damage to copyrighted works, yet continues to provide access to infringing works." Perfect 10, Inc. v. Amazon.com, Inc., 508 F.3d 1146, 1172 (9th Cir. 2007) (internal citations and quotations omitted) (emphasis in original). The third theory, vicarious liability, is similar to contributory liability but includes some contours that differ from these other theories of liability. A defendant "infringes vicariously by profiting from direct infringement while declining to exercise a right to stop or limit it." Grokster III, 545 U.S. at 930.

2. Actual Infringement by Defendants' Users

With respect to all three of Plaintiffs' theories of liability, Plaintiffs must first demonstrate that there has been direct infringement of their copyrights by third parties. Amazon, 508 F.3d at 1169 (citing A & M Records, Inc. v. Napster, Inc., 239 F.3d 1004, 1013 n.2 (9th Cir. 2001)) ("Secondary liability for copyright infringement does not exist in the absence of direct infringement by a third party."). Plaintiffs have provided direct evidence of copyright infringement by Defendants' users, and Defendants have not introduced any evidence creating a triable issue of fact on this issue.

To establish copyright infringement, Plaintiffs must show that they own the copyrights that have been infringed, and that third parties have made unauthorized copies, downloads, or transfers of this material. 17 U.S.C. § 106(1), (3). Implicit in 17 U.S.C. § 106 is a further requirement at issue in the present case: that the infringement of Plaintiffs' copyrights occur inside the United States. The Ninth Circuit has determined that "United States copyright laws do not reach acts of infringement that take place entirely abroad." Subafilms, Ltd. v. MGM–Pathe Comm'ns Co., 24 F.3d 1088, 1098 (9th Cir. 1994) (en banc), cert. denied sub nom. Subafilms, Ltd. v. United Artists Corp., 513 U.S. 1001, 115 S. Ct. 512, 130 L.

Ed. 2d 419 (1994). As a later panel of that court wrote, "in order for U.S. copyright law to apply, at least one alleged infringement must be completed entirely within the United States." Allarcom Pay Television, Ltd. v. Gen'l Instrument Corp., 69 F.3d 381, 387 (9th Cir. 1995).

In the context of secondary liability, an actor may be liable for "activity undertaken abroad that knowingly induces infringement within the United States." 3 Nimmer on Copyright, § 12.04(D)(2) (citing Armstrong v. Virgin Records, Ltd., 91 F. Supp. 2d 628, 634 (S.D.N.Y. 2000); Blue Ribbon Pet Prods., Inc. v. Rolf C. Hagen (USA) Corp., 66 F. Supp. 2d 454, 462–64 (E.D.N.Y. 1999)). Once Plaintiffs have established that an act of infringement has taken place within the United States, Defendants may be held liable for their conduct that constitutes inducement, material contribution, or vicarious infringement, even if Defendants' conduct took place abroad. Id.

Here, there is not a genuine factual dispute over whether the users of Fung's websites infringed Plaintiffs' copyrights. It is undisputed that Plaintiffs "own or control the copyrights, or exclusive rights under copyright" for the works at issue in this case. * * * It is also undisputed that Plaintiffs have not authorized the distribution of their copyrighted works by Defendants or Defendants' users. * * *

The only purported dispute with respect to third parties' direct infringement is whether Plaintiffs have provided any evidence that users of Fung's sites have violated 17 U.S.C. § 106(1) and § 106(3) by reproducing and distributing Plaintiffs' copyrighted works. * * *

Defendants argue that Plaintiffs must provide evidence that both the transferor and the transferee are located in the United States. However, United States copyright law does not require that both parties be located in the United States. Rather, the acts of uploading and downloading are each independent grounds of copyright infringement liability. Uploading a copyrighted content file to other users (regardless of where those users are located) violates the copyright holder's § 106(3) distribution right. Downloading a copyrighted content file from other users (regardless of where those users are located) violates the copyright holder's § 106(1) reproduction right. A & M Records, Inc. v. Napster, Inc., 239 F.3d 1004, 1014 (9th Cir. 2001). Accordingly, Plaintiffs need only show that United States users either uploaded or downloaded copyrighted works; Plaintiffs need not show that a particular file was both uploaded and downloaded entirely within the United States.

Plaintiffs' broad statistical evidence is corroborated by evidence of specific instances of downloads and transfers of copyrighted works through Defendants' websites. In his deposition, Defendant Fung admitted to using the Isohunt website to download copyrighted broadcast television shows such as The Simpsons and Lost. Similarly, Fung admitted to downloading the copyrighted film The Lord of the Rings: The Fellowship of the Ring. Declarant Chris Masciarelli stated that he used Defendants' website isohunt.com to download a copyrighted work entitled Family Guy Presents Stewie Griffin: The Untold Story.

Although Defendants argue that there is no clear evidence that any infringement took place in the United States, Plaintiffs have presented admissible evidence of domestic infringement involving a copyright owned by each of Plaintiffs. Plaintiffs provide evidence based on internet protocol ("IP") address data and usage-summary data produced by Defendants themselves. Plaintiffs have also have used IP-address data to locate Defendants' users and show that particular infringing downloads took place in the United States. Further, in an examination of roughly 400 downloads (the only available evidence containing users' IP addresses), approximately 50% of the actual downloads using Defendants websites were made from the United States.

Plaintiffs have also provided evidence that, contrary to Defendants' wholly unsupported assertions, dot-torrent files downloaded from Defendants' sites correspond to and automatically cause the downloading of Plaintiffs' copyrighted content. Finally, Plaintiffs have linked the United States-based downloads (as identified by Plaintiffs' experts) with copyrighted works owned by each of the individual Plaintiffs.

Accordingly, Plaintiffs' evidence conclusively establishes that individuals located in the United States have used Fung's sites to download copies of copyrighted works. Defendants fail to introduce any evidence that raises a triable issue regarding the fact that Plaintiffs' copyrights have been infringed by third parties.

B.   Inducement of Infringement

Plaintiffs first seek summary judgment under the "inducement" theory articulated in the Supreme Court case *Metro–Goldwyn–Mayer Studios, Inc. v. Grokster*, 545 U.S. 913, 125 S. Ct. 2764, 162 L. Ed. 2d 781 (2005) ("Grokster III"). In an opinion by Justice Souter, the Supreme Court held that "one who distributes a device with the object of promoting its use to infringe copyright, as shown by clear expression or other affirmative steps taken to foster infringement, is liable for the resulting acts of infringement by third parties." Grokster III, 545 U.S. at 936–37. The Supreme Court further explained,

[M]ere knowledge of infringing potential or of actual infringing uses would not be enough here to subject a distributor [of the device] to liability. Nor would ordinary acts incident to product distribution, such as offering customers technical support or product updates, support liability in themselves. The inducement rule, instead, premises liability on purposeful, culpable expression and conduct, and thus does nothing to compromise legitimate commerce or discourage innovation having a lawful promise.

Id. at 937 (emphasis added). Importantly, liability may attach even if the defendant does not induce specific acts of infringement. Id. at 940 n.13 (emphasis added).19 Instead, the court may "infer[ ] a patently illegal objective from statements and actions showing what [the defendant's] objective was." Id. at 941.

An unlawful objective to promote infringement can be shown by a variety of means. "The classic instance of inducement is by advertisement or solicitation that broadcasts a message designed to stimulate others to commit violations." Id. at 937; see also Visa Int'l., 494 F.3d at 800. For example, in Grokster III, the defendants "respond[ed] affirmatively to requests for help in locating and playing copyrighted materials." 545 U.S. at 938.

However, showing that the defendant sent out a specific message is "not [the] exclusive way of" demonstrating inducement. Grokster III, 545 U.S. at 938. The Supreme Court in Grokster III highlighted three facts from which a reasonable factfinder could infer intent to foster infringement in that case. First, the Court noted that the defendant's owns communications and advertising designs had expressed an intent to target Napster users, a community well-known for copyright infringement. Although it was not known whether some of the advertising designs were actually communicated to the public, "whether the messages were communicated is not to the point on this record." Id. at 938. "The function of the message in the theory of inducement is to prove by a defendant's own statements that his unlawful purpose disqualifies him from claiming protection." Id. Second, the Court found it probative that defendants did not attempt to develop filtering tools or other means of diminishing the use of its products for infringement. Taken alone, the failure to develop a filter would be insufficient to support liability; but viewed in conjunction with other evidence it underscored the defendants' unlawful objective. Id. at 939 n.12. Third, the Court considered the fact that the defendants' business model depended on high-volume use of its software, which was overwhelmingly infringing, as circumstantial evidence of intent to induce infringement. Id. at 939–40. Again, this evidence would not alone justify the imposition of liability, but it supported an inference of unlawful intent when viewed in context with other evidence in the record. Id. Based on these elements of the factual record, the Court held that the defendants' "unlawful objective is unmistakable." Id. at 940.

On remand from the Supreme Court, the District Court took into account other factors in finding the defendants' intent to induce infringement, including the "the staggering scale of infringement" occurring through use of defendants' products, technical assistance provided by the defendants to users for the playback of copyrighted content, and affirmative steps taken by defendants to ensure that their products would be capable of infringing use. Metro–Goldwyn–Mayer Studios, Inc. v. Grokster, Ltd., 454 F. Supp. 2d 966, 985–92 (C.D. Cal. 2006) ("Grokster IV").

Upon review of all the evidence in the present case, the Court determines that evidence of Defendants' intent to induce infringement is overwhelming and beyond reasonable dispute.

1. Defendants' message to users

Plaintiffs present a variety of undisputed evidence that Defendants disseminated a message "designed to stimulate others" to commit infringements. Grokster III, 545 U.S. at 916. The clearest instance of Defendants' solicitation of infringing activity is the "Box Office Movies" feature of Defendants' Isohunt site. As Defendant Fung admitted in his deposition, this feature essentially involved Defendants' periodic posting of a list of the top 20 highest-grossing films then playing in United States, which linked to detailed web-pages concerning each film. Each of these pages contained "upload torrent" links allowing users to upload dot-torrent files for the films. Though Defendants eventually discontinued this feature, they did not remove pages that had already been created. By implementing this feature, therefore, Defendants engaged in direct solicitation of infringing activity. Defendant Fung, in his subsequent declaration filed with Defendants' Opposition, denies that this feature was intended to induce copyright infringement and asserts that the web-pages "did not lead anywhere." However, "actions speak louder than words," Arista Records, 633 F. Supp. 2d at 153 n.20, and Fung cannot dispute the objective historical fact that the websites included a "Box Office Movies" feature at one time. This feature evidences Defendants' intent to encourage their users' infringement.

In addition to the "Box Office Movies" feature, Plaintiffs present other evidence that Defendants disseminated messages designed to stimulate inducement. In particular, Plaintiffs demonstrate that, Defendants' websites present available torrent files (the vast majority of which contain infringing content) in browseable categories and provide further information about the works contained in the files. Defendants also generate lists of the most popular files in categories like "Top 20 Movies." Defendants do not dispute the presence of such information on their web-site, but instead merely assert that the lists' content originates from users or from automated processes that simply reflect user activity. Defendants' assertions ignore the material fact that Defendants designed the websites and included a feature that collects users' most commonly searched-for titles. The fact that these lists almost exclusively contained copyrighted works and that Defendants never removed these lists is probative of Defendants' knowledge of ongoing infringement and failure to stop this infringement.

Plaintiffs also provide evidence of what the Supreme Court has termed the "classic instance of inducement"—a statement that "broadcasts a message designed to stimulate others to commit violations." Grokster III, 545 U.S. at 938. Defendant Fung made statements on the Isohunt website encouraging or assisting infringement. He posted on his website a message telling the website's users that they should "try Peer Guardian," a software application that can be used to frustrate copyright enforcement against file sharers. Accord Grokster III, 545 U.S. at 937–38. Fung also provided a link to a torrent file for the recent film Lord of the Rings: Return of the King on the Isohunt site and stated, "if you are curious, download this." Additionally, Fung created a promotional page inviting users to upload torrent files for Matrix Reloaded, another recent film.

It is also undisputed that certain key terms known to the pirating community, such as "warez," were meta tags embedded in the websites for reference by search engines. Additionally, the Fung websites have honorary ranking systems for those who posted a certain number of forum users messages; ranks include titles such as "I pir4te, therefore I am" and "All Day I Dream About W4rez." In other words, the websites bestowed honors by identifying users as copyright infringers. This is strong circumstantial evidence that Defendants promoted their users' infringing activities by consciously fostering a community that encouraged—indeed, celebrated—copyright infringement.

Perhaps most tellingly, Fung has personally engaged in a broad campaign of encouraging copyright infringement. In a statement on the Isohunt website, Fung stated: "they accuse us for [sic] thieves, and they r [sic] right. Only we r [sic] 'stealing' from the lechers (them) and not the originators (artists)." In an interview with another website Fung stated: "Morally, I'm a Christian. 'Thou shalt not steal.' But to me, even copyright infringement when it occurs may not necessarily be stealing." Fung's statements provide further evidence that he has encouraged third parties to engage in copyright infringement. These statements also provide probative evidence regarding Fung's intent in creating the Defendant websites to aid others' infringement.

2.   Defendants' assistance to users engaging in infringement

There is also evidence that Defendants directly assisted users in engaging in infringement. As in Grokster III, Defendants in the present case have "respond[ed] affirmatively to requests for help in locating and playing copyrighted materials." 545 U.S. at 938.

Defendant Fung personally posted messages in the Isohunt discussion forums in which he provided technical assistance to users seeking copyrighted works. Specifically, in response to an Isohunt user who posted a message stating he did not know how to watch a file containing Lord of the Rings: Return of the King which he had recently downloaded, Defendant Fung provided directions on how to extract and play the video file. The record is replete with such instances of technical assistance provided to users by Defendant Fung through the forum. (Fung provided technical assistant to users who downloaded the film Kill Bill); (Fung provided assistance to user searching for Star Trek: Enterprise episodes by giving search tips); (Fung explained how to attach a tracker URL to a dot-torrent file sent to him by an Isohunt user, and recommended the user use the tracker at torrentbox.com).)

In addition to Fung's personal statements, statements by the "moderators" of Fung's websites provide further evidence of the Defendant websites' active inducement of infringing activities. There are numerous individuals who are known as "moderators" or "admins." The term "moderators" refers to "individuals whose job it is to look after the running of the forums from day to day." Moderators can edit, delete, and reorganize postings in the forums. Some moderators, referred to as "admins," also have the ability to ban selected abusive users and remove user-posted dot-torrent files. There is no substantive dispute by Defendants regarding their relationship to these individuals. Defendants assign this status and give these individuals authority to moderate the forums and user discussions. These individuals were under the control of Defendants and assigned duties related to the administration of the web forums. Therefore, there is an agency relationship between these individual moderators (or "admins") and Defendants.

The Defendant websites are full of statements by moderators who assisted users seeking to download files or provided links to other websites containing the requested items. In a post on the Isohunt forums, moderator "Estranged" provided instructions regarding DVD ripping and conversion. In a post on Torrentbox, moderator "Skull and Bones" referred a user to 353 dot-torrent files including King Kong and Silent Hill, which were "very good quality" and stated that "[m]ost of your films are here at Torrentbox or search on isohunt.com." In a post on the website Podtropolis, moderator "NewAgePirate" responded to a user who posted a list with films such as The Godfather, A Clockwork Orange, and One Flew Over the Cuckoo's Nest, with a post that stated "Great list by the way man. Great to have you here." All of these statements demonstrate that there was an active role played by the administrators of the websites within the forum, encouraging and providing technical assistance for users seeking to engage in infringing activities.

All of these statements demonstrate the assistance Defendant Fung and the corporate Defendant provided to the websites' users in infringing Plaintiffs' copyrights. Such actions demonstrate that Defendants did not maintain a hands-off approach to the operation of the sites. Instead, various of Defendants' representatives gave technical assistance and aid in the organized forum discussions that furthered the third parties' infringement using the sites.

* * *

3. Defendants' implementation of technical features promoting copyright infringement

Defendants' implementation of certain technical features in their web-sites is also probative of Defendants' intent to induce copyright infringement. Most obviously, Defendants' websites allow users to locate dot-torrent files * * *

Defendant Fung also implemented a "spider" program, which locates and obtains copies of dot-torrent files from other web-sites, including well-known infringing sites such as "The Pirate Bay." Defendant Fung additionally directs the program to specific web pages containing terms like "seinfeld-videos," which one would infer contains infringing content from the television show Seinfeld. Defendants do not rebut this obvious inference. Defendants also organized files using a program that matches content filenames with specific terms. Some of the specific terms used by the program describe likely infringing content, such as "Screener" or "PPV".

Defendants no do not dispute these facts except to assert that the spider programs were automated, generic components that operated in a copyright-neutral manner. Essentially, Defendants argue that they merely assembled a website that combined already-existing technologies, and that they did not include any unique innovations that were specifically tailored to assist the distribution of copyrighted works. These assertions are inapposite. The unrebutted factual evidence shows that Fung designed programs which improved the functioning of his websites with respect to infringing uses. Combined with other evidence regarding Defendants' improper purposes, these technological features support a finding of inducement liability.

4. Defendants' business model depends on massive infringing use

Plaintiffs assert that Defendants' business model depended on massive infringing use. In the instant litigation, just as with the programs at issue in Grokster III, Defendants' business generates its revenue almost exclusively by selling advertising space on the sites. Similarly, the revenue depends on users visiting Defendants' sites and viewing the advertising. As discussed previously, Defendant Fung acknowledges that the availability of popular works is what attracts users to the sites. Defendant Fung also solicited advertisement on the basis of the availability of works on his website. For example, in an email to a potential advertiser, movie-goods.com, Fung wrote that Isohunt would "make a great partner, since TV and movies are at the top of the most frequently searched by our visitors."

In short, there is no factual dispute that the availability of copyright material was a major draw for users of Fung's websites, and there is no dispute that Defendants derive revenue from the websites and that this revenue increases along with the number of users. This is further evidence of Defendants' intent to assist infringing uses.

5. Additional Considerations

Throughout their legal memoranda and supporting evidentiary papers, Defendants argue that there is no evidence of infringing activity. This argument obviously fails in light of the evidence discussed supra, Part IV.A.2. However, to the extent that Defendants subjectively believe that their users have not engaged in copyright infringement, Defendants' "ostrich-like refusal to discover the extent to which its system was being used to infringe copyright is merely another piece of evidence" of Defendants' purposeful, culpable conduct in inducing third party infringement. See *In re Aimster Copyright Litig.*, 334 F.3d 643, 655 (7th Cir. 2003).

V. DEFENDANTS' DIGITAL MILLENNIUM COPYRIGHT ACT AFFIRMATIVE DEFENSES

The Digital Millennium Copyright Act provides affirmative defenses for providers of certain internet services. In many ways, the Digital

Millennium Copyright Act is simply a restatement of the legal standards establishing secondary copyright infringement—in many cases, if a defendant is liable for secondary infringement, the defendant is not entitled to Digital Millennium Copyright Act immunity; if a defendant is not liable for secondary infringement, the defendant is entitled to Digital Millennium Copyright Act immunity. The two sets of rules do not entirely overlap, but this framework is helpful for understanding the Act's statutory text and structure. Cf. *A&M Records, Inc. v. Napster, Inc.*, 239 F.3d 1004, 1025 (9th Cir. 2001) ("We do not agree that ... potential liability for contributory and vicarious infringement renders the Digital Millennium Copyright Act inapplicable per se.").

Here, the relevant section of the Digital Millennium Copyright Act, 17 U.S.C. § 512(d), reads:

Information location tools.—A service provider shall not be liable for monetary relief, or, except as provided in subsection (j), for injunctive or other equitable relief, for infringement of copyright by reason of the provider referring or linking users to an online location containing infringing material or infringing activity, by using information location tools, including a directory, index, reference, pointer, or hypertext link, if the service provider-

(1) (A) does not have actual knowledge that the material or activity is infringing;

(B) in the absence of such actual knowledge, is not aware of facts or circumstances from which infringing activity is apparent; or

(C) upon obtaining such knowledge or awareness, acts expeditiously to remove, or disable access to, the material;

(2) does not receive a financial benefit directly attributable to the infringing activity, in a case in which the service provider has the right and ability to control such activity; and

(3) upon notification of claimed infringement as described in subsection (c)(3), responds expeditiously to remove, or disable access to, the material that is claimed to be infringing or to be the subject of infringing activity, except that, for purposes of this paragraph, the information described in subsection (c)(3)(A)(iii) shall be identification of the reference or link, to material or activity claimed to be infringing, that is to be removed or access to which is to be disabled, and information reasonably sufficient to permit the service provider to locate that reference or link.

17 U.S.C. § 512(d).

In other words, a provider of "information location tools" (such as Defendants' websites) must satisfy the three conjunctive requirements of § 512(d) in order to obtain safe harbor. These three safe harbor requirements are that the defendant: [1] does not know (§ 512(d)(1)(A)) or have reason to know (§ 512(d)(1)(B)) of infringing activities, or does not remove infringing materials upon receipt of such knowledge (§ 512(d)(1)(C); and [2] does not profit from infringement where it has the power to control the infringement (§ 512(d)(2)); and [3] upon receiving notice (in the statutorily-prescribed manner) from the copyright holder, removes the infringing material (§ 512(d)(3)).

In the present case, Plaintiffs have established that Defendants have reason to know of their users' infringing activities. Defendants have not satisfied their summary judgment burden by identifying facts showing that Defendants were "not aware of facts or circumstances from which infringing activity [wa]s apparent." 17 U.S.C. § 512(d)(1)(B). Further, Defendants have not introduced any evidence that they "act[ed] expeditiously to remove, or disable access to, the [infringing] material" once they became aware that this infringing activity was apparent. (See generally Defs.' SGI PP eee-lll.) Thus, Defendants are not entitled to statutory safe harbor under 17 U.S.C. § 512(d).

In order to obtain safe harbor, a defendant cannot have knowledge of ongoing infringing activities. This "knowledge" standard is defined as "actual knowledge" or "willful ignorance." According to the widely-cited House and Senate Report on the law, "if the service provider becomes aware of a 'red flag' from which infringing activity is apparent, it will lose the limitation of liability if it takes no action." H.R. Rep. 105–551(II), at 53; see also Perfect 10, Inc. v. CCBill LLC, 488 F.3d 1102, 1114 (9th Cir. 2007). The Congressional Report notes that the service provider is only liable if it "turned a blind eye to 'red flags' of obvious infringement." H.R. Rep. 105–551(II), at 57. Other courts have applied this test as requiring "willful ignorance of readily apparent infringement." UMG Recordings, Inc. v. Veoh Networks Inc., F. Supp. 2d, 2009 U.S. Dist. LEXIS 86932, 2009 WL 3422839, at *7 (C.D. Cal. 2009) (citing Corbis Corp. v. Amazon.com, Inc., 351 F. Supp. 2d 1090, 1108 (W.D. Wash. 2004)).

Even under this stringent "willful ignorance" test, it is apparent that Defendants have "turned a blind eye to 'red flags' of obvious infringement." See H.R. Rep. 105–551(II), at 57. Most importantly, Defendant Fung himself has engaged in unauthorized downloads of copyrighted material; even if those downloads were done abroad and were not actionable under United States copyright law (and thus would not provide "actual knowledge" of illegal activity for purposes of 17 U.S.C. § 512(d)(1)(A)), Fung's actions show that Fung was aware that infringing material was available on the Defendant websites. Given the "worldwide" nature of the world-wide web, it would have been obvious that United States-based users could access these same infringing materials and thus engage in infringing acts. Defendants provide no evidence to rebut this obvious conclusion that United States-based users would have been able to download the same copyrighted works that Fung himself downloaded.

Furthermore, Plaintiffs introduce evidence produced by Defendants themselves that shows that approximately 25% of Defendants' websites' users were based in the United States. This evidence further shows that, at its height, over ten million unique users visited Defendants' websites each month, which strongly suggests that some 2.5 million United States citizens visited Defendants' websites each month. Further, this evidence shows that at one point, Defendants' websites were accessed over 50 million times from the United States in a single month. Upon accessing Defendants' websites, these American users would have found that 90% to 95% of the available materials contained copyrighted content. Defendants fail to introduce any evidence rebutting this overwhelming evidence, and thus fail to raise a triable issue of fact as to whether Defendants had actual knowledge of copyright infringement or were willfully ignorant of ongoing copyright infringement.

There is a variety of other evidence of Defendants' willful ignorance to ongoing infringement. Defendants designed their website to include lists such as "Top Searches," "Top 20 Movies," "Top 20 TV Shows," and "Box Office Movies," and Defendants designed these lists to automatically update to reflect user activities. These lists included numerous copyrighted works. See Grokster, 454 F. Supp. 2d at 992 ("it is common knowledge that most popular music and movies are copyrighted"). Thus, unless Defendants somehow refused to look at their own webpages, they invariably would have been known that (1) infringing material was likely to be available and (2) most of Defendants' users were searching for and downloading infringing material.

In addition, Plaintiffs submit overwhelming statistical evidence of the prevalence of copyrighted material available through Defendants' websites. This evidence shows that 90%–95% of the material was likely to be copyright infringing, a percentage that is nearly identical to the facts in Napster, in which "eighty-seven percent of the files available on Napster may be copyrighted." 239 F.3d at 1011. In that case, the district court rejected the defendant's plainly meritless arguments seeking safe harbor under § 512(d). A & M Records, Inc. v. Napster, Inc., 114 F. Supp. 2d 896, 919 & n.24 (N.D. Cal. 2000), aff'd in part and rev'd in part, 239 F.3d 1004 (9th Cir. 2001). Given that Defendants' own statistics show that millions of Defendants' users are located in the United States Defendants were certainly "aware of a 'red flag' from which infringing activity is apparent." H.R. Rep. 105–551(II), at 57. Defendants do not introduce any evidence to raise a triable issue of fact on this question.

In light of this overwhelming evidence, the only way Defendants could have avoided knowing about their users' infringement is if they engaged in an "ostrich-like refusal to discover the extent to which [their] system[s] w[ere] being used to infringe copyright." See In re Aimster Copyright Litig., 334 F.3d 643, 655 (7th Cir. 2003). In other words, to avoid actual knowledge of infringement, Defendants would have had to engage in willful blindness.

There is one last reason why Defendants are unable to benefit from the 17 U.S.C. § 512 safe harbors. As stated by Judge Posner in In re Aimster Copyright Litig., 334 F.3d 643, 655 (7th Cir. 2003):

The common element of its safe harbors is that the service provider must do what it can reasonably be asked to do to prevent the use of its service by 'repeat infringers.' 17 U.S.C. § 512(i)(1)(A). Far from doing anything to discourage repeat infringers of the plaintiffs' copyrights, Aimster invited them to do so, showed them how they could do so with ease using its system, and by teaching its users how to encrypt their unlawful distribution of copyrighted materials disabled itself from doing anything to prevent infringement.

In other words, inducement liability and the Digital Millennium Copyright Act safe harbors are inherently contradictory. Inducement liability is based on active bad faith conduct aimed at promoting infringement; the statutory safe harbors are based on passive good faith conduct aimed at operating a legitimate internet business. Here, as discussed supra, Defendants are liable for inducement. There is no safe harbor for such conduct. Accordingly, Defendants are not entitled to the affirmative defenses provided by the Digital Millennium Copyright Act.

VII. CONCLUSION

This case contains the same general pattern presented in *Metro–Goldwyn–Mayer Studios, Inc. v. Grokster, Ltd.*, 545 U.S. 913, 125 S. Ct. 2764, 162 L. Ed. 2d 781 (2005), *A & M Records, Inc. v. Napster, Inc.*, 239 F.3d 1004 (9th Cir. 2001), and, more recently, *Arista Records LLC v. Usenet.com, Inc.*, 633 F. Supp. 2d 124 (S.D.N.Y. 2009). The Defendants in the present case attempt to distinguish their situation on three main grounds: first, that the BitTorrent technology is different from the other technologies because users do not download content files through Defendants' websites; second that Defendants' conduct is protected by the First Amendment; and third, that Defendants' users are located across the globe, not just in the United States.

On the evidence presented to the Court, none of these arguments raises a triable question of fact for the jury to decide. Defendants' technology is nothing more than old wine in a new bottle. Instead of logging into a proprietary network in order to download files from each others' computers, Defendants' users access Defendants' generally-accessible website in order to download those files. And instead of downloading content files directly through Defendants' website, Defendants' users download dot-torrent files that automatically trigger the downloading of content files. These technological details are, at their core, indistinguishable from the previous technologies. In fact, Defendants' technologies appear to improve upon the previous technologies by permitting faster downloads of large files such as movies. Such an improvement quite obviously increases the potential for copyright infringement.

Regarding Defendants' second main argument, caselaw establishes that Defendants are misguided if they think that the First Amendment provides blanket protection to all internet-based activities, particularly where those activities involve copyright infringement. Finally, Defendants third main argument ignores the unrebutted fact that millions of United States citizens have accessed Defendants' websites, and a substantial proportion of the files made available to them through those websites contained copyrighted or highly-likely copyrighted works. Further, Plaintiffs have provided undisputed evidence of specific infringing acts done in the United States.

Thus, as in Grokster, summary judgment is appropriate on the question of inducement liability. For the foregoing reasons, the Court GRANTS Plaintiff' Motion for Summary Judgment on Liability as to inducement of infringement.

NOTES

1.　Does *Streamcast* represent a step forward in providing a "bright line" to supplement *Sony Betamax*? If so, how would you state the "bright line" and identify the controlling elements?

2.　Google continues to challenge existing and future paradigms of Digital Rights Management and Intellectual Property content protection. See *Perfect 10, Inc. v. Amazon.com, Inc.*, 508 F.3d 1146 (9th Cir. 2007) (communication of thumbnail images was direct infringement and basis for contributory infringement, but Google's framing of thumbnails was not display or distribution and would constitute fair use).

After what appears to have been a short courtship, Google's wooing of YouTube, resulted in a 1.65 billion dollar acquisition of the later by Google during the first week in October, 2006. YouTube is an online video and content source for just about anything someone with home to professional video equipment may wish to share with others. The widespread distribution of digital video cameras and editing applications allow the posting and publication of content of vacations, the last birthday part, or how to do just about anything, such as how to properly screw in a light bulb, or exotic adventures in the South Seas. In fact, it has been noted that there is more content being viewed on YouTube than some cable TV channels and the content available is doubling every couple of months. Coupled with Google's search engine capabilities, the door is open to finding video content for just about anything.

What makes this combination the foundation for paradigm change? Certainly taking the largest internet search entity and coupling it with the scale of content provided by YouTube is noteworthy. But the major potential lies in factors just below the obvious.

First, YouTube is one of the first online file sharing entity comprised primarily of recognized public domain content, not subject to copyright limitations. While it might be noted that some content posted by users will be copyrighted and constitute infringing activity, the question shifts to asking whether this meets the standards of both *Sony Betamax* and *Grokster* to protect YouTube and Google from vicarious liability for either inducement to infringe or contributory infringement. Does the fact that most of the content is "lawful" protect these entities from the posting and downloading of copyrighted content third parties? Google and YouTube seem to believe that notice by the copyright holder and removal of protected content by them will suffice to insulate them from liability. There will always be some content that slips through the cracks, but is this just a risk that any content owner must assume? Would holding Google and YouTube liable under these circumstances constitute a collateral cost for protection of content holder rights that is unreasonable? Many of these questions will be addressed along with other issues before the court in *Viacom Int'l Inc. v. You Tube Inc.*, 2007 WL 775695 (complaint) (S.D.N.Y.), complaint filed 3/13/07 [case number unavailable].

Second, Google's "presence" in digital content utilization continues to grow. Google's search engine capabilities, their attempts to digitalize entire libraries, their entrée into video and their acquisition of YouTube position them as a dominant force for locating and providing content. With that comes not only the profit of entrepreneurial ventures, but also political recognition and stature. The question then becomes whether Google becomes a factor in balancing the rights of content holders with those of the public in the use of distributive technologies, such as peer to peer file sharing.

III. DIGITAL RIGHTS MANAGEMENT: ENCRYPTION AND MECHANICAL CONTROLS

Title 17. Copyrights DMCA

Chapter 12. Copyright Protection and Management Systems

§ 1201. Circumvention of copyright protection systems

(a) **Violations regarding circumvention of technological measures.**—(1)(A) No person shall circumvent a technological measure that effectively controls access to a work protected under this title. The prohibition contained in the preceding sentence shall take effect at the end of the 2–year period beginning on the date of the enactment of this chapter.

(B) The prohibition contained in subparagraph (A) shall not apply to persons who are users of a copyrighted work which is in a particular class of works, if such persons are, or are likely to be in the succeeding 3–year period, adversely affected by virtue of such prohibition in their ability to make noninfringing uses of that particular class of works under this title, as determined under subparagraph (C).

(C) During the 2–year period described in subparagraph (A), and during each succeeding 3–year period, the Librarian of Congress, upon the recommendation of the Register of Copyrights, who shall consult with the Assistant Secretary for Communications and Information of the Department of Commerce and report and comment on his or her views in making such recommendation, shall make the determination in a rulemaking proceeding for purposes of subparagraph (B) of whether persons who are users of a copyrighted work are, or are likely to be in the succeeding 3–year period, adversely affected by the prohibition under subparagraph (A) in their ability to make noninfringing uses under this title of a particular class of copyrighted works. In conducting such rulemaking, the Librarian shall examine—

(i) the availability for use of copyrighted works;

(ii) the availability for use of works for nonprofit archival, preservation, and educational purposes;

(iii) the impact that the prohibition on the circumvention of technological measures applied to copyrighted works has on criticism, comment, news reporting, teaching, scholarship, or research;

(iv) the effect of circumvention of technological measures on the market for or value of copyrighted works; and

(v) such other factors as the Librarian considers appropriate.

* * *

(2) No person shall manufacture, import, offer to the public, provide, or otherwise traffic in any technology, product, service, device, component, or part thereof, that—

(A) is primarily designed or produced for the purpose of circumventing a technological measure that effectively controls access to a work protected under this title;

(B) has only limited commercially significant purpose or use other than to circumvent a technological measure that effectively controls access to a work protected under this title; or

(C) is marketed by that person or another acting in concert with that person with that person's knowledge for use in circumventing a technological measure that effectively controls access to a work protected under this title.

(3) As used in this subsection—

(A) to "circumvent a technological measure" means to descramble a scrambled work, to decrypt an encrypted work, or otherwise to avoid, bypass, remove, deactivate, or impair a technological measure, without the authority of the copyright owner; and

(B) a technological measure "effectively controls access to a work" if the measure, in the ordinary course of its operation, requires the application of information, or a process or a treatment, with the authority of the copyright owner, to gain access to the work.

* * *

(2) As used in this subsection—

(A) to "circumvent protection afforded by a technological measure" means avoiding, bypassing, removing, deactivating, or otherwise impairing a technological measure; and

(B) a technological measure "effectively protects a right of a copyright owner under this title" if the measure, in the ordinary course of its operation, prevents, restricts, or otherwise limits the exercise of a right of a copyright owner under this title.

(c) Other rights, etc., not affected.—**(1)** Nothing in this section shall affect rights, remedies, limitations, or defenses to copyright infringement, including fair use, under this title.

(2) Nothing in this section shall enlarge or diminish vicarious or contributory liability for copyright infringement in connection with any technology, product, service, device, component, or part thereof.

* * *

(4) Nothing in this section shall enlarge or diminish any rights of free speech or the press for activities using consumer electronics, telecommunications, or computing products.

(d) Exemption for nonprofit libraries, archives, and educational institutions.

* * *

(f) Reverse engineering.—**(1)** Notwithstanding the provisions of subsection (a)(1)(A), a person who has lawfully obtained the right to use a copy of a computer program may circumvent a technological measure that effectively controls access to a particular portion of that program for the sole purpose of identifying and analyzing those elements of the program that are necessary to achieve interoperability of an independently created computer program with other programs, and that have not previously been readily available to the person engaging in the circumvention, to the extent any such acts of identification and analysis do not constitute infringement under this title.

(2) Notwithstanding the provisions of subsections (a)(2) and (b), a person may develop and employ technological means to circumvent a technological measure, or to circumvent protection afforded by a technological measure, in order to enable the identification and analysis under paragraph (1), or for the purpose of enabling interoperability of an independently created computer program with other programs, if such means are necessary to achieve such interoperability, to the extent that doing so does not constitute infringement under this title.

* * *

(g) Encryption research.—

(1) Definitions.—For purposes of this subsection—

(A) the term "encryption research" means activities necessary to identify and analyze flaws and vulnerabilities of encryption technologies applied to copyrighted works, if these activities are conducted to advance the state of knowledge in the field of encryption technology or to assist in the development of encryption products; and

(B) the term "encryption technology" means the scrambling and descrambling of information using mathematical formulas or algorithms.

(2) Permissible acts of encryption research.—Notwithstanding the provisions of subsection (a)(1)(A), it is not a violation of that subsection for a person to circumvent a technological measure as applied to a copy, phonorecord, performance, or display of a published work in the course of an act of good faith encryption research if—

(A) the person lawfully obtained the encrypted copy, phonorecord, performance, or display of the published work;

(B) such act is necessary to conduct such encryption research;

(C) the person made a good faith effort to obtain authorization before the circumvention; and

(D) such act does not constitute infringement under this title or a violation of applicable law other than this section, including section 1030 of title 18 and those provisions of title 18 amended by the Computer Fraud and Abuse Act of 1986.

(3) Factors in determining exemption.—In determining whether a person qualifies for the exemption under paragraph (2), the factors to be considered shall include—

(A) whether the information derived from the encryption research was disseminated, and if so, whether it was disseminated in a manner reasonably calculated to advance the state of knowledge or development of encryption technology, versus whether it was disseminated in a manner that facilitates infringement under this title or a violation of applicable law other than this section [17 U.S.C.A. § 1 et seq.], including a violation of privacy or breach of security;

(B) whether the person is engaged in a legitimate course of study, is employed, or is appropriately trained or experienced, in the field of encryption technology; and

(C) whether the person provides the copyright owner of the work to which the technological measure is applied with notice of the findings and documentation of the research, and the time when such notice is provided.

* * *

(k) Certain analog devices and certain technological measures.—

(1) Certain analog devices.—

(A) Effective 18 months after the date of the enactment of this chapter, no person shall manufacture, import, offer to the public, provide or otherwise traffic in any—

(i) VHS format analog video cassette recorder unless such recorder conforms to the automatic gain control copy control technology;

(ii) 8mm format analog video cassette camcorder unless such camcorder conforms to the automatic gain control technology;

(iii) Beta format analog video cassette recorder, unless such recorder conforms to the automatic gain control copy control technology, except that this requirement shall not apply until there are 1,000 Beta format analog video cassette recorders sold in the United States in any one calendar year after the date of the enactment of this chapter;

(iv) 8mm format analog video cassette recorder that is not an analog video cassette camcorder, unless such recorder conforms to the automatic gain control copy control technology, except that this requirement shall not apply until there are 20,000 such recorders sold in the United States in any one calendar year after the date of the enactment of this chapter; or

(v) analog video cassette recorder that records using an NTSC format video input and that is not otherwise covered under clauses (i) through (iv), unless such device conforms to the automatic gain control copy control technology.

UNIVERSAL CITY STUDIOS, INC.
v. SHAWN C. REIMERDES

United States District Court, S.D. New York, 2000.
111 F.Supp.2d 294.

Opinion

KAPLAN, DISTRICT JUDGE.

Plaintiffs, eight major United States motion picture studios, distribute many of their copyrighted motion pictures for home use on digital versatile disks ("DVDs"), which contain copies of the motion pictures in digital form. They protect those motion pictures from copying by using an encryption system called CSS. CSS-protected motion pictures on DVDs may be viewed only on players and computer drives equipped with licensed technology that permits the devices to decrypt and play—but not to copy—the films.

Late last year, computer hackers devised a computer program called DeCSS that circumvents the CSS protection system and allows CSS-protected motion pictures to be copied and played on devices that lack the licensed decryption technology. Defendants quickly posted DeCSS on their Internet web site, thus making it readily available to much of the world. Plaintiffs promptly brought this action under the Digital Millennium Copyright Act (the "DMCA") to enjoin defendants from posting DeCSS and to prevent them from electronically "linking" their site to others that post DeCSS. Defendants responded with what they termed "electronic civil disobedience"—increasing their efforts to link their web site to a large number of others that continue to make DeCSS available.

Defendants contend that their actions do not violate the DMCA and, in any case, that the DMCA, as applied to computer programs, or code, violates the First Amendment. This is the Court's decision after trial, and the decision may be summarized in a nutshell.

Defendants argue first that the DMCA should not be construed to reach their conduct, principally because the DMCA, so applied, could prevent those who wish to gain access to technologically protected copyrighted works in order to make fair—that is, non-infringing—use of them from doing so. They argue that those who would make fair use of technologically protected copyrighted works need means, such as DeCSS, of circumventing access control measures not for piracy, but to make lawful use of those works.

Technological access control measures have the capacity to prevent fair uses of copyrighted works as well as foul. Hence, there is a potential tension between the use of such access control measures and fair use. Defendants are not the first to recognize that possibility. As the DMCA made its way through the legislative process, Congress was preoccupied with precisely this issue. Proponents of strong restrictions on circumvention of access control measures argued that they were essential if copyright holders were to make their works available in digital form because digital works otherwise could be pirated too easily. Opponents contended that strong anti-circumvention measures would extend the copyright monopoly inappropriately and prevent many fair uses of copyrighted material.

Congress struck a balance. The compromise it reached, depending upon future technological and commercial developments, may or may not prove ideal. But the solution it enacted is clear. The potential tension to which defendants point does not absolve them of liability under the statute. There is no serious question that defendants' posting of DeCSS violates the DMCA.

Defendants' constitutional argument ultimately rests on two propositions—that computer code, regardless of its function, is "speech" entitled to maximum constitutional protection and that computer code therefore essentially is exempt from regulation by government. But their argument is baseless.

Computer code is expressive. To that extent, it is a matter of First Amendment concern. But computer code is not purely expressive any more than the assassination of a political figure is purely a political statement. Code causes computers to perform desired functions. Its expressive element no more immunizes its functional aspects from regulation than the expressive motives of an assassin immunize the assassin's action.

In an era in which the transmission of computer viruses—which, like DeCSS, are simply computer code and thus to some degree expressive—can disable systems upon which the nation depends and in which other computer code also is capable of inflicting other harm, society must be able to regulate the use and dissemination of code in appropriate circumstances. The Constitution, after all, is a framework for building a just and democratic society. It is not a suicide pact.

I. The Genesis of the Controversy

As this case involves computers and technology with which many are unfamiliar, it is useful to begin by defining some of the vocabulary.

A. The Vocabulary of this Case

1. Computers and Operating Systems

A computer is "a digital information processing device.... consist[ing] of central processing components ... and mass data storage.... certain peripheral input/output devices ..., and an operating system." Personal computers ("PCs") are computers designed for use by one person at a time. "[M]ore powerful, more expensive computer systems known as 'servers' ... are designed to provide data, services, and functionality through a digital network to multiple users."

An operating system is "a software program that controls the allocation and use of computer resources (such as central processing unit time, main memory space, disk space, and input/output channels). The operating system also supports the functions of software programs, called 'applications,' that perform specific user-oriented tasks.... Because it supports applications while interacting more closely with the PC system's hardware, the operating system is said to serve as a 'platform.'"

Microsoft Windows ("Windows") is an operating system released by Microsoft Corp. It is the most widely used operating system for PCs in the United States, and its versions include Windows 95, Windows 98, Windows NT and Windows 2000.

Linux, which was and continues to be developed through the open source model of software development, also is an operating system. It can be run on a PC as an alternative to Windows, although the extent to which it is so used is limited. Linux is more widely used on servers.

2. Computer Code

"[C]omputers come down to one basic premise: They operate with a series of on and off switches, using two digits in the binary (base 2) number system—0 (for off) and 1 (for on)." All data and instructions input to or contained in computers therefore must be reduced the numerals 1 and 0.

"The smallest unit of memory in a computer," a bit, "is a switch with a value of 0(off) or 1(on)." A group of eight bits is called a byte and represents a character—a letter or an integer. A kilobyte ("K") is 1024 bytes, a megabyte ("MB") 1024 kilobytes, and a gigabyte ("GB") 1024 megabytes.

Some highly skilled human beings can reduce data and instructions to strings of 1's and 0's and thus program computers to perform complex tasks by inputting commands and data in that form. But it would be inconvenient, inefficient and, for most people, probably impossible to do so. In consequence, computer science has developed programming languages. These languages, like other written languages, employ symbols and syntax to convey meaning. The text of programs written in these languages is referred to as source code. And whether directly or through the medium of another program, the sets of instructions written in programming languages—the source code—ultimately are translated into machine "readable" strings of 1's and 0's, known in the computer world as object code, which typically are executable by the computer.

The distinction between source and object code is not as crystal clear as first appears. Depending upon the programming language, source code may contain many 1's and 0's and look a lot like object code or may contain many instructions derived from spoken human language. Programming languages the source code for which approaches object code are referred to as low level source code while those that are more similar to spoken language are referred to as high level source code.

All code is human readable. As source code is closer to human language than is object code, it tends to be comprehended more easily by humans than object code.

3. The Internet and the World Wide Web

The Internet is "a global electronic network, consisting of smaller, interconnected networks, which allows millions of computers to exchange information over telephone wires, dedicated data cables, and wireless links. The Internet links PCs by means of servers, which run specialized operating systems and applications designed for servicing a network environment.

Internet Relay Chat ("IRC") is a system that enables individuals connected to the Internet to participate in live typed discussions. Participation in an IRC discussion requires an IRC software program, which sends messages via the Internet to the IRC server, which in turn broadcasts the messages to all participants. The IRC system is capable of supporting many separate discussions at once.

The World Wide Web (the "Web") is "a massive collection of digital information resources stored on servers throughout the Internet. These resources are typically provided in the form of hypertext documents, commonly referred to as 'Web pages,' that may incorporate any combination of text, graphics, audio and video content, software programs, and other data. A user of a computer connected to the Internet can publish a page on the Web simply by copying it into a specially designated, publicly accessible directory on a Web server. Some Web resources are in the form of applications that provide functionality through a user's PC system but actually execute on a server."

A web site is "a collection of Web pages [published on the Web by an individual or organization].... Most Web pages are in the form of 'hypertext'; that is, they contain annotated references, or 'hyperlinks,' to other Web pages. Hyperlinks can be used as cross-references within a single document, between documents on the same site, or between documents on different sites."

A home page is "one page on each Web site ... [that typically serves as] the first access point to the site. The home page is usually a hypertext document that presents an overview of the site and hyperlinks to the other pages comprising the site."

A Web client is "software that, when running on a computer connected to the Internet, sends information to and receives information from Web servers throughout the Internet. Web clients and servers transfer data using a standard known as the Hypertext Transfer Protocol ('HTTP'). A 'Web browser' is a type of Web client that enables a user to select, retrieve, and perceive resources on the Web. In particular, Web browsers provide a way for a user to view hypertext documents and follow the hyperlinks that connect them, typically by moving the cursor over a link and depressing the mouse button."

4. *Portable Storage Media*

Digital files may be stored on several different kinds of storage media, some of which are readily transportable. Perhaps the most familiar of these are so called floppy disks or "floppies," which now are 3 1/2 inch magnetic disks upon which digital files may be recorded. For present purposes, however, we are concerned principally with two more recent developments, CD–ROMs and digital versatile disks, or DVDs.

A CD–ROM is a five-inch wide optical disk capable of storing approximately 650 MB of data. To read the data on a CD–ROM, a computer must have a CD–ROM drive.

DVDs are five-inch wide disks capable of storing more than 4.7 GB of data. In the application relevant here, they are used to hold full-length motion pictures in digital form. They are the latest technology for private home viewing of recorded motion pictures and result in drastically improved audio and visual clarity and quality of motion pictures shown on televisions or computer screens.

5. *The Technology Here at Issue*

CSS, or Content Scramble System, is an access control and copy prevention system for DVDs developed by the motion picture companies, including plaintiffs. It is an encryption-based system that requires the use of appropriately configured hardware such as a DVD player or a computer DVD drive to decrypt, unscramble and play back, but not copy, motion pictures on DVDs. The technology necessary to configure DVD players and drives to play CSS-protected DVDs has been licensed to hundreds of manufacturers in the United States and around the world.

DeCSS is a software utility, or computer program, that enables users to break the CSS copy protection system and hence to view DVDs on unlicensed players and make digital copies of DVD movies. The quality of motion pictures decrypted by DeCSS is virtually identical to that of encrypted movies on DVD.

DivX is a compression program available for download over the Internet. It compresses video files in order to minimize required storage space, often to facilitate transfer over The Internet or other networks.

B. Parties

Plaintiffs are eight major motion picture studios. Each is in the business of producing and distributing copyrighted material including motion pictures. Each distributes, either directly or through affiliates, copyrighted motion pictures on DVDs. Plaintiffs produce and distribute a large majority of the motion pictures on DVDs on the market today.

Defendant Eric Corley is viewed as a leader of the computer hacker community and goes by the name Emmanuel Goldstein, after the leader of the underground in George Orwell's classic, *1984*. He and his company, defendant 2600 Enterprises, Inc., together publish a magazine called *2600: The Hacker Quarterly,* which Corley founded in 1984, and which is something of a bible to the hacker community. The name "2600" was derived from the fact that hackers in the 1960's found that the transmission of a 2600 hertz tone over a long distance trunk connection gained access to "operator mode" and allowed the user to explore aspects of the telephone system that were not otherwise accessible. Mr. Corley chose the name because he regarded it as a "mystical thing," commemorating something that he evidently admired. Not surprisingly, *2600: The Hacker Quarterly* has included articles on such topics as how to steal an Internet domain name, access other people's e-mail, intercept cellular phone calls, and break into the computer systems at Costco stores and Federal Express. One issue contains a guide to the federal criminal justice system for readers charged with computer hacking. In addition, defendants operate a web site located at <http://www.2600.com> ("2600.com"), which is managed primarily by Mr. Corley and has been in existence since 1995.

Prior to January 2000, when this action was commenced, defendants posted the source and object code for DeCSS on the 2600.com web site, from which they could be downloaded easily. At that time, 2600.com contained also a list of links to other web sites purporting to post DeCSS.

C. The Development of DVD and CSS

The major motion picture studios typically distribute films in a sequence of so-called windows, each window referring to a separate channel of distribution and thus to a separate source of revenue. The first window generally is theatrical release, distribution, and exhibition. Subsequently, films are distributed to airlines and hotels, then to the home market, then to pay television, cable and, eventually, free television broadcast. The home market is important to plaintiffs, as it represents a significant source of revenue.

Motion pictures first were, and still are, distributed to the home market in the form of video cassette tapes. In the early 1990's, however, the major movie studios began to explore distribution to the home market in digital format, which offered substantially higher audio and visual quality and greater longevity than video cassette tapes. This technology, which in 1995 became what is known today as DVD, brought with it a new problem—increased risk of piracy by virtue of the fact that digital files, unlike the material on video cassettes, can be copied without degradation from generation to generation. In consequence, the movie studios became concerned as the product neared market with the threat of DVD piracy.

Discussions among the studios with the goal of organizing a unified response to the piracy threat began in earnest in late 1995 or early 1996. They eventually came to include representatives of the consumer electronics and computer industries, as well as interested members of the public, and focused on both legislative proposals and technological solutions. In 1996, Matsushita Electric Industrial Co. ("MEI") and Toshiba Corp., presented—and the studios adopted—CSS.

CSS involves encrypting, according to an encryption algorithm, the digital sound and graphics files on a DVD that together constitute a motion picture. A CSS-protected DVD can be decrypted by an appropriate decryption algorithm that employs a series of keys stored on the DVD and the DVD player. In consequence, only players and drives containing the appropriate keys are able to decrypt DVD files and thereby play movies stored on DVDs.

As the motion picture companies did not themselves develop CSS and, in any case, are not in the business of making DVD players and drives, the technology for making compliant devices, i.e., devices with CSS keys, had to be licensed to consumer electronics manufacturers. In order to ensure that the decryption technology did not become generally available and that compliant devices could not be used to copy as well as merely to play CSS-protected movies, the technology is licensed subject to strict security requirements. Moreover, manufacturers may not, consistent with their licenses, make equipment that would supply digital output that could be used in copying protected DVDs. Licenses to manufacture compliant devices are granted on a royalty-free basis subject only to an administrative fee. At the time of trial, licenses had been issued to numerous hardware and software manufacturers, including two companies that plan to release DVD players for computers running the Linux operating system.

With CSS in place, the studios introduced DVDs on the consumer market in early 1997. All or most of the motion pictures released on DVD were, and continue to be, encrypted with CSS technology. Over 4,000 motion pictures now have been released in DVD format in the United States, and movies are being issued on DVD at the rate of over 40 new titles per month in addition to re-releases of classic films. Currently, more than five million households in the United States own DVD players, and players are projected to be in ten percent of United States homes by the end of 2000.

DVDs have proven not only popular, but lucrative for the studios. Revenue from their sale and rental currently accounts for a substantial percentage of the movie studios' revenue from the home video market. Revenue from the home market, in turn, makes up a large percentage of the studios' total distribution revenue.

D.   The Appearance of DeCSS

In late September 1999, Jon Johansen, a Norwegian subject then fifteen years of age, and two individuals he "met" under pseudonyms over the Internet, reverse engineered a licensed DVD player and discovered the CSS encryption algorithm and keys. They used this information to create DeCSS, a program capable of decrypting or "ripping" encrypted DVDs, thereby allowing playback on non-compliant computers as well as the copying of decrypted files to computer hard drives. Mr. Johansen then posted the executable code on his personal Internet web site and informed members of an Internet mailing list that he had done so. Neither Mr. Johansen nor his collaborators obtained a license from the DVD CCA.

Although Mr. Johansen testified at trial that he created DeCSS in order to make a DVD player that would operate on a computer running the Linux operating system, DeCSS is a Windows executable file; that is, it can be executed only on computers running the Windows operating system. Mr. Johansen explained the fact that he created a Windows rather than a Linux program by asserting that Linux, at the time he created DeCSS, did not support the file system used on DVDs. Hence, it was necessary, he said, to decrypt the DVD on a Windows computer in order subsequently to play the decrypted files on a Linux machine. Assuming that to be true, however, the fact remains that Mr. Johansen created DeCSS in the full knowledge that it could be used on computers running Windows rather than Linux. Moreover, he was well aware that the files, once decrypted, could be copied like any other computer files.

In January 1999, Norwegian prosecutors filed charges against Mr. Johansen stemming from the development of DeCSS. The disposition of the Norwegian case does not appear of record.

E.   The Distribution of DeCSS

In the months following its initial appearance on Mr. Johansen's web site, DeCSS has become widely available on the Internet, where hundreds of sites now purport to offer the software for download. A few other applications said to decrypt CSS-encrypted DVDs also have appeared on the Internet.

In November 1999, defendants' web site began to offer DeCSS for download. It established also a list of links to several web sites that purportedly "mirrored" or offered DeCSS for download. The links on defendants' mirror list fall into one of three categories. By clicking the mouse on one of these links, the user may be brought to a page on the linked-to site on which there appears a further link to the DeCSS software. If the user then clicks on the DeCSS link, download of the software begins. This page may or may not contain content other than the DeCSS link. Alternatively, the user may be brought to a page on the linked-to site that does not itself purport to link to DeCSS, but that links, either directly or via a series of other pages on the site, to another page on the site on which there appears a link to the DeCSS software. Finally, the user may be brought directly to the DeCSS link on the linked-to site such that download of DeCSS begins immediately without further user intervention.

F. The Preliminary Injunction and Defendants' Response

The movie studios, through the Internet investigations division of the Motion Picture Association of America ("MPAA"), became aware of the availability of DeCSS on the Internet in October 1999. The industry responded by sending out a number of cease and desist letters to web site operators who posted the software, some of which removed it from their sites. In January 2000, the studios filed this lawsuit against defendant Eric Corley and two others.

After a hearing at which defendants presented no affidavits or evidentiary material, the Court granted plaintiffs' motion for a preliminary injunction barring defendants from posting DeCSS. At the conclusion of the hearing, plaintiffs sought also to enjoin defendants from linking to other sites that posted DeCSS, but the Court declined to entertain the application at that time in view of plaintiffs' failure to raise the issue in their motion papers.

Following the issuance of the preliminary injunction, defendants removed DeCSS from the 2600.com web site. In what they termed an act of "electronic civil disobedience," however, they continued to support links to other web sites purporting to offer DeCSS for download, a list which had grown to nearly five hundred by July 2000. Indeed, they carried a banner saying "Stop the MPAA" and, in a reference to this lawsuit, proclaimed:

"We have to face the possibility that we could be forced into submission. For that reason it's especially important that as many of you as possible, all throughout the world, take a stand and mirror these files."

Thus, defendants obviously hoped to frustrate plaintiffs' recourse to the judicial system by making effective relief difficult or impossible.

At least some of the links currently on defendants' mirror list lead the user to copies of DeCSS that, when downloaded and executed, successfully decrypt a motion picture on a CSS-encrypted DVD.

G. Effects on Plaintiffs

The effect on plaintiffs of defendants' posting of DeCSS depends upon the ease with which DeCSS decrypts plaintiffs' copyrighted motion pictures, the quality of the resulting product, and the convenience with which decrypted copies may be transferred or transmitted.

As noted, DeCSS was available for download from defendants' web site and remains available from web sites on defendants' mirror list. Downloading is simple and quick—plaintiffs' expert did it in seconds. The program in fact decrypts at least some DVDs. Although the process is computationally intensive, plaintiffs' expert decrypted a store-bought copy of *Sleepless in Seattle* in 20 to 45 minutes. The copy is stored on the hard drive of the computer. The quality of the decrypted film is virtually identical to that of encrypted films on DVD. The decrypted file can be copied like any other.

The decryption of a CSS-protected DVD is only the beginning of the tale, as the decrypted file is very large—approximately 4.3 to 6 GB or more depending on the length of the film—and thus extremely cumbersome to transfer or to store on portable storage media. One solution to this problem, however, is DivX, a compression utility available on the Internet that is promoted as a means of compressing decrypted motion picture files to manageable size.

DivX is capable of compressing decrypted files constituting a feature length motion picture to approximately 650 MB at a compression ratio that involves little loss of quality. While the compressed sound and graphic files then must be synchronized, a tedious process that took plaintiffs' expert between 10 and 20 hours, the task is entirely feasible. Indeed, having compared a store-bought DVD with portions of a copy compressed and synchronized with DivX (which often are referred to as "DivX'd" motion pictures), the Court finds that the loss of quality, at least in some cases, is imperceptible or so nearly imperceptible as to be of no importance to ordinary consumers.

The fact that DeCSS-decrypted DVDs can be compressed satisfactorily to 650 MB is very important. A writeable CD–ROM can hold 650 MB. Hence, it is entirely feasible to decrypt a DVD with DeCSS, compress and synchronize it with DivX, and then make as many copies as one wishes by burning the resulting files onto writeable CD–ROMs, which are sold blank for about one dollar apiece. Indeed, even if one wished to use a lower compression ratio to improve quality, a film easily could be compressed to about 1.3 GB and burned onto two CD–ROMs. But the creation of pirated copies of copyrighted movies on writeable CD–ROMs, although significant, is not the principal focus of plaintiffs' concern, which is transmission of pirated copies over the Internet or other networks.

Network transmission of decrypted motion pictures raises somewhat more difficult issues because even 650 MB is a very large file that, depending upon the circumstances, may take a good deal of time to transmit. But there is tremendous variation in transmission times. Many home computers today have modems with a rated capacity of 56 kilobits per second. DSL lines, which increasingly are available to home and business users, offer transfer rates of 7 megabits per second. Cable modems also offer increased bandwidth. Student rooms in many universities are equipped with network connections rated at 10 megabits per second. Large institutions such as universities and major companies often have networks with backbones rated at 100 megabits per second. While effective transmission times generally are much lower than rated maximum capacities in consequence of traffic volume and other considerations, there are many environments in which very high transmission rates may be achieved. Hence, transmission times ranging from three to twenty minutes to six hours or more for a feature length film are readily achievable, depending upon the users' precise circumstances.

At trial, defendants repeated, as if it were a mantra, the refrain that plaintiffs, as they stipulated, have no direct evidence of a specific occasion on which any person decrypted a copyrighted motion picture with DeCSS and transmitted it over the Internet. But that is unpersuasive. Plaintiffs' expert expended very little effort to find someone in an IRC chat room who exchanged a compressed, decrypted copy of *The Matrix,* one of plaintiffs' copyrighted motion pictures, for a copy of *Sleepless in Seattle.* While the simultaneous electronic exchange of the two movies took approximately six hours, the computers required little operator attention during the interim. An MPAA investigator downloaded between five and ten DVD-sourced movies over the Internet after December 1999. At least one web site contains a list of 650 motion pictures, said to have been decrypted and compressed with DivX, that purportedly are available for sale, trade or free download. And although the Court does not accept the list, which is hearsay, as proof of the truth of the matters asserted therein, it does note that advertisements for decrypted versions of copyrighted movies first appeared on the Internet in substantial numbers in late 1999, following the posting of DeCSS.

The net of all this is reasonably plain. DeCSS is a free, effective and fast means of decrypting plaintiffs' DVDs and copying them to computer hard drives. DivX, which is available over the Internet for nothing, with the investment of some time and effort, permits compression of the decrypted files to sizes that readily fit on a writeable CD–ROM. Copies of such CD–ROMs can be produced very cheaply and distributed as easily as other pirated intellectual property. While not everyone with Internet access now will find it convenient to send or receive DivX'd copies of pirated motion pictures over the Internet, the availability of high speed network connections in many businesses and institutions, and their growing availability in homes, make Internet and other network traffic in pirated copies a growing threat.

These circumstances have two major implications for plaintiffs. First, the availability of DeCSS on the Internet effectively has compromised plaintiffs' system of copyright protection for DVDs, requiring them either to tolerate increased piracy or to expend resources to develop and implement a replacement system unless the availability of DeCSS is terminated. It is analogous to the publication of a bank vault combination in a national newspaper. Even if no one uses the combination to open the vault, its mere publication has the effect of defeating the bank's security system, forcing the bank to reprogram the lock. Development and implementation of a new DVD copy protection system, however, is far more difficult and costly than reprogramming a combination lock and may carry with it the added problem of rendering the existing installed base of compliant DVD players obsolete.

Second, the application of DeCSS to copy and distribute motion pictures on DVD, both on CD–ROMs and via the Internet, threatens to reduce the studios' revenue from the sale and rental of DVDs. It threatens also to impede new, potentially lucrative initiatives for the distribution of motion pictures in digital form, such as video-on-demand via the Internet.

In consequence, plaintiffs already have been gravely injured. As the pressure for and competition to supply more and more users with faster and faster network connections grows, the injury will multiply.

II.   *The Digital Millennium Copyright Act*

A.   *Background and Structure of the Statute*

In December 1996, the World Intellectual Property Organization ("WIPO"), held a diplomatic conference in Geneva that led to the adoption of two treaties. Article 11 of the relevant treaty, the WIPO Copyright Treaty, provides in relevant part that contracting states "shall provide adequate legal protection and effective legal remedies against the circumvention of effective technological measures that are used by authors in connection with the exercise of their rights under this Treaty or the Berne Convention and that restrict acts, in respect of their works, which are not authorized by the authors concerned or permitted by law."

The adoption of the WIPO Copyright Treaty spurred continued Congressional attention to the adaptation of the law of copyright to the digital age. Lengthy hearings involving a broad range of interested parties both preceded and succeeded the Copyright Treaty. As noted above, a critical focus of Congressional consideration of the legislation was the conflict between those who opposed anti-circumvention measures as inappropriate extensions of copyright and impediments to fair use and those who supported them as essential to proper protection of copyrighted materials in the digital age. The DMCA was enacted in October 1998 as the culmination of this process.

The DMCA contains two principal anticircumvention provisions. The first, Section 1201(a)(1), governs "[t]he act of circumventing a technological protection measure put in place by a copyright owner to control access to a copyrighted work," an act described by Congress as "the electronic equivalent of breaking into a locked room in order to obtain a copy of a book." The second, Section 1201(a)(2), which is the focus of this case, "supplements the prohibition against the act of circumvention in paragraph (a)(1) with prohibitions on creating and making available certain technologies ... developed or advertised to defeat technological protections against unauthorized access to a work." As defendants are accused here only of posting and linking to other sites posting DeCSS, and not of using it themselves to bypass plaintiffs' access controls, it is principally the second of the anticircumvention provisions that is at issue in this case.

B. Posting of DeCSS

1. Violation of Anti–Trafficking Provision

Section 1201(a)(2) of the Copyright Act, part of the DMCA, provides that:

"No person shall ... offer to the public, provide or otherwise traffic in any technology ... that—

"(A) is primarily designed or produced for the purpose of circumventing a technological measure that effectively controls access to a work protected under [the Copyright Act];

"(B) has only limited commercially significant purpose or use other than to circumvent a technological measure that effectively controls access to a work protected under [the Copyright Act]; or

"(C) is marketed by that person or another acting in concert with that person with that person's knowledge for use in circumventing a technological measure that effectively controls access to a work protected under [the Copyright Act]."

In this case, defendants concededly offered and provided and, absent a court order, would continue to offer and provide DeCSS to the public by making it available for download on the 2600.com web site. DeCSS, a computer program, unquestionably is "technology" within the meaning of the statute. "[C]ircumvent a technological measure" is defined to mean descrambling a scrambled work, decrypting an encrypted work, or "otherwise to avoid, bypass, remove, deactivate, or impair a technological measure, without the authority of the copyright owner," so DeCSS clearly is a means of circumventing a technological access control measure. In consequence, if CSS otherwise falls within paragraphs (A), (B) or (C) of Section 1201(a)(2), and if none of the statutory exceptions applies to their actions, defendants have violated and, unless enjoined, will continue to violate the DMCA by posting DeCSS.

a. Section 1201(a)(2)(A)

(1) CSS Effectively Controls Access to Copyrighted Works

During pretrial proceedings and at trial, defendants attacked plaintiffs' Section 1201(a)(2)(A) claim, arguing that CSS, which is based on a 40–bit encryption key, is a weak cipher that does not "effectively control" access to plaintiffs' copyrighted works. They reasoned from this premise that CSS is not protected under this branch of the statute at all. Their post-trial memorandum appears to have abandoned this argument. In any case, however, the contention is indefensible as a matter of law.

First, the statute expressly provides that "a technological measure 'effectively controls access to a work' if the measure, in the ordinary course of its operation, requires the application of information or a process or a treatment, with the authority of the copyright owner, to gain access to a work." One cannot gain access to a CSS-protected work on a DVD without application of the three keys that are required by the software. One cannot lawfully gain access to the keys except by entering into a license with the DVD CCA under authority granted by the copyright owners or by purchasing a DVD player or drive containing the keys pursuant to such a license. In consequence, under the express terms of the statute, CSS "effectively controls access" to copyrighted DVD movies. It does so, within the meaning of the statute, whether or not it is a strong means of protection.

This view is confirmed by the legislative history, which deals with precisely this point. The House Judiciary Committee section-by-section analysis of the House bill, which in this respect was enacted into law, makes clear that a technological measure "effectively controls access" to a copyrighted work if its *function* is to control access:

> "The bill does define the *functions* of the technological measures that are covered—that is, what it means for a technological measure to 'effectively control access to a work' ... and to 'effectively protect a right of a copyright owner under this title'.... The practical, common-sense approach taken by H.R.2281 is that if, in the ordinary course of its operation, a technology actually works in the defined ways to control access to a work ... then the 'effectiveness' test is met, and the prohibitions of the statute are applicable. This test, which focuses on the function performed by the technology, provides a sufficient basis for clear interpretation."

Further, the House Commerce Committee made clear that measures based on encryption or scrambling "effectively control" access to copyrighted works, although it is well known that what may be encrypted or scrambled often may be decrypted or unscrambled. As CSS, in the ordinary course of its operation—that is, when DeCSS or some other decryption program is not employed—"actually works" to prevent access to the protected work, it "effectively controls access" within the contemplation of the statute.

Finally, the interpretation of the phrase "effectively controls access" offered by defendants at trial—viz, that the use of the word "effectively" means that the statute protects only successful or efficacious technological means of controlling access—would gut the statute if it were adopted. If a technological means of access control is circumvented, it is, in common parlance, ineffective. Yet defendants' construction, if adopted, would limit the application of the statute to access control measures that thwart circumvention, but withhold protection for those measures that can be circumvented. In other words, defendants would have the Court construe the statute to offer protection where none is needed but to withhold protection precisely where protection is essential. The Court declines to do so. Accordingly, the Court holds that CSS effectively controls access to plaintiffs' copyrighted works.

(2) DeCSS Was Designed Primarily to Circumvent CSS

As CSS effectively controls access to plaintiffs' copyrighted works, the only remaining question under Section 1201(a)(2)(A) is whether DeCSS was designed primarily to circumvent CSS. The answer is perfectly obvious. By the admission of both Jon Johansen, the programmer who principally wrote DeCSS, and defendant Corley, DeCSS was created solely for the purpose of decrypting CSS—that is all it does. Hence, absent satisfaction of a statutory exception, defendants clearly violated Section 1201(a)(2)(A) by posting DeCSS to their web site.

b.   Section 1201(a)(2)(B)

As the only purpose or use of DeCSS is to circumvent CSS, the foregoing is sufficient to establish a *prima facie* violation of Section 1201(a)(2)(B) as well.

c.   The Linux Argument

Perhaps the centerpiece of defendants' statutory position is the contention that DeCSS was not created for the purpose of pirating copyrighted motion pictures. Rather, they argue, it was written to further the development of a DVD player that would run under the Linux operating system, as there allegedly were no Linux compatible players on the market at the time. The argument plays itself out in various ways as different elements of the DMCA come into focus. But it perhaps is useful to address the point at its most general level in order to place the preceding discussion in its fullest context.

As noted, Section 1201(a) of the DMCA contains two distinct prohibitions. Section 1201(a)(1), the so-called basic provision, "aims against those who engage in unauthorized circumvention of technological measures.... [It] focuses directly on wrongful conduct, rather than on those who facilitate wrongful conduct...." Section 1201(a)(2), the anti-trafficking provision at issue in this case, on the other hand, separately bans offering or providing technology that may be used to circumvent technological means of controlling access to copyrighted works. If the means in question meets any of the three prongs of the standard set out in Section 1201(a)(2)(A), (B), or (C), it may not be offered or disseminated.

As the earlier discussion demonstrates, the question whether the development of a Linux DVD player motivated those who wrote DeCSS is immaterial to the question whether the defendants now before the Court violated the anti-trafficking provision of the DMCA. The inescapable facts are that (1) CSS is a technological means that effectively controls access to plaintiffs' copyrighted works, (2) the one and only function of DeCSS is to circumvent CSS, and (3) defendants offered and provided DeCSS by posting it on their web site. Whether defendants did so in order to infringe, or to permit or encourage others to infringe, copyrighted works in violation of other provisions of the Copyright Act simply does not matter for purposes of Section 1201(a)(2). The offering or provision of the program is the prohibited conduct—and it is prohibited irrespective of why the program was written, except to whatever extent motive may be germane to determining whether their conduct falls within one of the statutory exceptions.

2. *Statutory Exceptions*

Earlier in the litigation, defendants contended that their activities came within several exceptions contained in the DMCA and the Copyright Act and constitute fair use under the Copyright Act. Their post-trial memorandum appears to confine their argument to the reverse engineering exception. In any case, all of their assertions are entirely without merit.

a. *Reverse engineering*

Defendants claim to fall under Section 1201(f) of the statute, which provides in substance that one may circumvent, or develop and employ technological means to circumvent, access control measures in order to achieve interoperability with another computer program provided that doing so does not infringe another's copyright and, in addition, that one may make information acquired through such efforts "available to others, if the person [in question] ... provides such information solely for the purpose of enabling interoperability of an independently created computer program with other programs, and to the extent that doing so does not constitute infringement...." They contend that DeCSS is necessary to achieve interoperability between computers running the Linux operating system and DVDs and that this exception therefore is satisfied. This contention fails.

First, Section 1201(f)(3) permits information acquired through reverse engineering to be made available to others only by the person who acquired the information. But these defendants did not do any reverse engineering. They simply took DeCSS off someone else's web site and posted it on their own.

Defendants would be in no stronger position even if they had authored DeCSS. The right to make the information available extends only to dissemination "solely for the purpose" of achieving interoperability as defined in the statute. It does not apply to public dissemination of means of circumvention, as the legislative history confirms. These defendants, however, did not post DeCSS "solely" to achieve interoperability with Linux or anything else.

Finally, it is important to recognize that even the creators of DeCSS cannot credibly maintain that the "sole" purpose of DeCSS was to create a Linux DVD player. DeCSS concededly was developed on and runs under Windows—a far more widely used operating system. The developers of

DeCSS therefore knew that DeCSS could be used to decrypt and play DVD movies on Windows as well as Linux machines. They knew also that the decrypted files could be copied like any other unprotected computer file. Moreover, the Court does not credit Mr. Johansen's testimony that he created DeCSS solely for the purpose of building a Linux player. Mr. Johansen is a very talented young man and a member of a well-known hacker group who viewed "cracking" CSS as an end it itself and a means of demonstrating his talent and who fully expected that the use of DeCSS would not be confined to Linux machines. Hence, the Court finds that Mr. Johansen and the others who actually did develop DeCSS did not do so solely for the purpose of making a Linux DVD player if, indeed, developing a Linux-based DVD player was among their purposes.

Accordingly, the reverse engineering exception to the DMCA has no application here.

b. Encryption research

Section 1201(g)(4) provides in relevant part that:

"Notwithstanding the provisions of subsection (a)(2), it is not a violation of that subsection for a person to—

"(A) develop and employ technological means to circumvent a technological measure for the sole purpose of that person performing the acts of good faith encryption research described in paragraph (2); and

"(B) provide the technological means to another person with whom he or she is working collaboratively for the purpose of conducting the acts of good faith encryption research described in paragraph (2) or for the purpose of having that other person verify his or her acts of good faith encryption research described in paragraph (2)."

Paragraph (2) in relevant part permits circumvention of technological measures in the course of good faith encryption research if:

"(A) the person lawfully obtained the encrypted copy, phonorecord, performance, or display of the published work;

"(B) such act is necessary to conduct such encryption research;

"(C) the person made a good faith effort to obtain authorization before the circumvention; and

"(D) such act does not constitute infringement under this title . . . ."

In determining whether one is engaged in good faith encryption research, the Court is instructed to consider factors including whether the results of the putative encryption research are disseminated in a manner designed to advance the state of knowledge of encryption technology versus facilitation of copyright infringement, whether the person in question is engaged in legitimate study of or work in encryption, and whether the results of the research are communicated in a timely fashion to the copyright owner.

Neither of the defendants remaining in this case was or is involved in good faith encryption research. They posted DeCSS for all the world to see. There is no evidence that they made any effort to provide the results of the DeCSS effort to the copyright owners. Surely there is no suggestion that either of them made a good faith effort to obtain authorization from the copyright owners. Accordingly, defendants are not protected by Section 1201(g).

c. *Security testing*

Defendants contended earlier that their actions should be considered exempt security testing under Section 1201(j) of the statute. This exception, however, is limited to "assessing a computer, computer system, or computer network, solely for the purpose of good faith testing, investigating, or correcting [of a] security flaw or vulnerability, with the authorization of the owner or operator of such computer system or computer network."

The record does not indicate that DeCSS has anything to do with testing computers, computer systems, or computer networks. Certainly defendants sought, and plaintiffs' granted, no authorization for defendants' activities. This exception therefore has no bearing in this case.

d. *Fair use*

Finally, defendants rely on the doctrine of fair use. Stated in its most general terms, the doctrine, now codified in Section 107 of the Copyright Act, limits the exclusive rights of a copyright holder by permitting others to make limited use of portions of the copyrighted work, for appropriate purposes, free of liability for copyright infringement. For example, it is permissible for one other than the copyright owner to reprint or quote a suitable part of a copyrighted book or article in certain circumstances. The doctrine traditionally has facilitated literary and artistic criticism, teaching and scholarship, and other socially useful forms of expression. It has been viewed by courts as a safety valve that accommodates the exclusive rights conferred by copyright with the freedom of expression guaranteed by the First Amendment.

The use of technological means of controlling access to a copyrighted work may affect the ability to make fair uses of the work. Focusing specifically on the facts of this case, the application of CSS to encrypt a copyrighted motion picture requires the use of a compliant DVD player to view or listen to the movie. Perhaps more significantly, it prevents exact copying of either the video or the audio portion of all or any part of the film. This latter point means that certain uses that might qualify as "fair" for purposes of copyright infringement—for example, the preparation by a film studies professor of a single CD–ROM or tape containing two scenes from different movies in order to illustrate a point in a lecture on cinematography, as opposed to showing relevant parts of two different DVDs—would be difficult or impossible absent circumvention of the CSS encryption. Defendants therefore argue that the DMCA cannot properly be construed to make it difficult or impossible to make any fair use of plaintiffs' copyrighted works and that the statute therefore does not reach their activities, which are simply a means to enable users of DeCSS to make such fair uses.

Defendants have focused on a significant point. Access control measures such as CSS do involve some risk of preventing lawful as well as unlawful uses of copyrighted material. Congress, however, clearly faced up to and dealt with this question in enacting the DMCA.

The Court begins its statutory analysis, as it must, with the language of the statute. Section 107 of the Copyright Act provides in critical part that certain uses of copyrighted works that otherwise would be wrongful are "not ... infringement[s] of copyright." Defendants, however, are not here sued for copyright infringement. They are sued for offering and providing technology designed to circumvent technological measures that control access to copyrighted works and otherwise violating Section 1201(a)(2) of the Act. If Congress had meant the fair use defense to apply to such actions, it would have said so. Indeed, as the legislative history demonstrates, the decision not to make fair use a defense to a claim under Section 1201(a) was quite deliberate.

Congress was well aware during the consideration of the DMCA of the traditional role of the fair use defense in accommodating the exclusive rights of copyright owners with the legitimate interests of noninfringing users of portions of copyrighted works. It recognized the contention, voiced by a range of constituencies concerned with the legislation, that technological controls on access to copyrighted works might erode fair use by preventing access even for uses that would be deemed "fair" if only access might be gained. And it struck a balance among the competing interests.

The first element of the balance was the careful limitation of Section 1201(a)(1)'s prohibition of the act of circumvention to the act itself so as not to "apply to subsequent actions of a person once he or she has obtained authorized access to a copy of a [copyrighted] work...." By doing so, it left "the traditional defenses to copyright infringement, including fair use, ... fully applicable" provided "the access is authorized."

Second, Congress delayed the effective date of Section 1201(a)(1)'s prohibition of the act of circumvention for two years pending further investigation about how best to reconcile Section 1201(a)(1) with fair use concerns. Following that investigation, which is being carried out in the form of a rule-making by the Register of Copyright, the prohibition will not apply to users of particular classes of copyrighted works who demonstrate that their ability to make noninfringing uses of those classes of works would be affected adversely by Section 1201(a)(1).

Third, it created a series of exceptions to aspects of Section 1201(a) for certain uses that Congress thought "fair," including reverse engineering, security testing, good faith encryption research, and certain uses by nonprofit libraries, archives and educational institutions.

Defendants claim also that the possibility that DeCSS might be used for the purpose of gaining access to copyrighted works in order to make fair use of those works saves them under *Sony Corp. v. Universal City Studios, Inc.* But they are mistaken. *Sony* does not apply to the activities with which defendants here are charged. Even if it did, it would not govern here. *Sony* involved a construction of the Copyright Act that has been overruled by the later enactment of the DMCA to the extent of any inconsistency between *Sony* and the new statute.

Sony was a suit for contributory infringement brought against manufacturers of video cassette recorders on the theory that the manufacturers were contributing to infringing home taping of copyrighted television broadcasts. The Supreme Court held that the manufacturers were not liable in view of the substantial numbers of copyright holders who either had authorized or did not object to such taping by viewers. But *Sony* has no application here.

When *Sony* was decided, the only question was whether the manufacturers could be held liable for infringement by those who purchased equipment from them in circumstances in which there were many noninfringing uses for their equipment. But that is not the question now before this Court. The question here is whether the possibility of noninfringing fair use by someone who gains access to a protected copyrighted work through a circumvention technology distributed by the defendants saves the defendants from liability under Section 1201. But nothing in Section 1201 so suggests. By prohibiting the provision of circumvention technology, the DMCA fundamentally altered the landscape. A given device or piece of technology might have "a substantial noninfringing use, and hence be immune from attack under *Sony*'s construction of the Copyright Act—but nonetheless still be subject to suppression under Section 1201." Indeed, explicitly noted that Section 1201 does not incorporate *Sony.*

The policy concerns raised by defendants were considered by Congress. Having considered them, Congress crafted a statute that, so far as the applicability of the fair use defense to Section 1201(a) claims is concerned, is crystal clear. In such circumstances, courts may not undo what Congress so plainly has done by "construing" the words of a statute to accomplish a result that Congress rejected. The fact that Congress elected to leave technologically unsophisticated persons who wish to make fair use of encrypted copyrighted works without the technical means of doing so is a matter for Congress unless Congress' decision contravenes the Constitution, a matter to which the Court turns below. Defendants' statutory fair use argument therefore is entirely without merit.

C. Linking to Sites Offering DeCSS

Plaintiffs seek also to enjoin defendants from "linking" their 2600.-com web site to other sites that make DeCSS available to users. Their request obviously stems in no small part from what defendants themselves have termed their act of "electronic civil disobedience"—their attempt to defeat the purpose of the preliminary injunction by (a) offering the practical equivalent of making DeCSS available on their own web site by electronically linking users to other sites still offering DeCSS, and (b) encouraging other sites that had not been enjoined to offer the program. The dispositive question is whether linking to another web site containing DeCSS constitutes "offer[ing DeCSS] to the public" or "provid[ing] or otherwise traffic[king]" in it within the meaning of the DMCA. Answering this question requires careful consideration of the nature and types of linking.

Most web pages are written in computer languages, chiefly HTML, which allow the programmer to prescribe the appearance of the web page on the computer screen and, in addition, to instruct the computer to perform an operation if the cursor is placed over a particular point on the screen and the mouse then clicked. Programming a particular point on a screen to transfer the user to another web page when the point, referred to as a hyperlink, is clicked is called linking. Web pages can be designed to link to other web pages on the same site or to web pages maintained by different sites.

As noted earlier, the links that defendants established on their web site are of several types. Some transfer the user to a web page on an outside site that contains a good deal of information of various types, does not itself contain a link to DeCSS, but that links, either directly or via a series of other pages, to another page on the same site that posts the software. It then is up to the user to follow the link or series of links on the linked-to web site in order to arrive at the page with the DeCSS link and commence the download of the software. Others take the user to a page on an outside web site on which there appears a direct link to the DeCSS software and which may or may not contain text or links other than the DeCSS link. The user has only to click on the DeCSS link to commence the download. Still others may directly transfer the user to a file on the linked-to web site such that the download of DeCSS to the user's computer automatically commences without further user intervention.

The statute makes it unlawful to offer, provide or otherwise traffic in described technology. To "traffic" in something is to engage in dealings in it, conduct that necessarily involves awareness of the nature of the subject of the trafficking. To "provide" something, in the sense used in the statute, is to make it available or furnish it. To "offer" is to present or hold it out for consideration. The phrase "or otherwise traffic in" modifies and gives meaning to the words "offer" and "provide." In consequence, the anti-trafficking provision of the DMCA is implicated where one presents, holds out or makes a circumvention technology or device available, knowing its nature, for the purpose of allowing others to acquire it.

To the extent that defendants have linked to sites that automatically commence the process of downloading DeCSS upon a user being transferred by defendants' hyperlinks, there can be no serious question. Defendants are engaged in the functional equivalent of transferring the DeCSS code to the user themselves.

Substantially the same is true of defendants' hyperlinks to web pages that display nothing more than the DeCSS code or present the user only with the choice of commencing a download of DeCSS and no other content. The only distinction is that the entity extending to the user the option of downloading the program is the transferee site rather than defendants, a distinction without a difference.

Potentially more troublesome might be links to pages that offer a good deal of content other than DeCSS but that offer a hyperlink for downloading, or transferring to a page for downloading, DeCSS. If one assumed, for the purposes of argument, that the *Los Angeles Times* web site somewhere contained the DeCSS code, it would be wrong to say that anyone who linked to the *Los Angeles Times* web site, regardless of purpose or the manner in which the link was described, thereby offered, provided or otherwise trafficked in DeCSS merely because DeCSS happened to be available on a site to which one linked. But that is not this case. Defendants urged others to post DeCSS in an effort to disseminate DeCSS and to inform defendants that they were doing so. Defendants then linked their site to those "mirror" sites, after first checking to ensure that the mirror sites in fact were posting DeCSS or something that looked like it, and proclaimed on their own site that DeCSS could be had by clicking on the hyperlinks on defendants' site. By doing so, they offered, provided or otherwise trafficked in DeCSS, and they continue to do so to this day.

III. *The First Amendment*

Defendants argue that the DMCA, at least as applied to prevent the public dissemination of DeCSS, violates the First Amendment to the Constitution. They claim that it does so in two ways. First, they argue that computer code is protected speech and that the DMCA's prohibition of dissemination of DeCSS therefore violates defendants' First Amendment rights. Second, they contend that the DMCA is unconstitutionally overbroad, chiefly because its prohibition of the dissemination of decryption technology prevents third parties from making fair use of plaintiffs' encrypted works, and vague. They argue also that a prohibition on their linking to sites that make DeCSS available is unconstitutional for much the same reasons.

A. *Computer Code and the First Amendment*

The premise of defendants' first position is that computer code, the form in which DeCSS exists, is speech protected by the First Amendment. Examination of that premise is the logical starting point for analysis. And it is important in examining that premise first to define terms.

Defendants' assertion that computer code is "protected" by the First Amendment is quite understandable. Courts often have spoken of certain categories of expression as "not within the area of constitutionally protected speech," so defendants naturally wish to avoid exclusion by an unfavorable categorization of computer code. But such judicial statements in fact are not literally true. All modes of expression are covered by the First Amendment in the sense that the constitutionality of their "regulation must be determined by reference to First Amendment doctrine and analysis." Regulation of different categories of expression, however, is subject to varying levels of judicial scrutiny. Thus, to say that a particular form of expression is "protected" by the First Amendment means that the constitutionality of any regulation of it must be measured by reference to the First Amendment. In some circumstances, however, the phrase connotes also that the standard for measurement is the most exacting level available.

It cannot seriously be argued that any form of computer code may be regulated without reference to First Amendment doctrine. The path from idea to human language to source code to object code is a continuum. As one moves from one to the other, the levels of precision and, arguably, abstraction increase, as does the level of training necessary to discern the idea from the expression. Not everyone can understand each of these forms. Only English speakers will understand English formulations. Principally those familiar with the particular programming language will understand the source code expression. And only a relatively small number of skilled programmers and computer scientists will understand the machine readable object code. But each form expresses the same idea, albeit in different ways.

There perhaps was a time when the First Amendment was viewed only as a limitation on the ability of government to censor speech in advance. But we have moved far beyond that. All modes by which ideas may be expressed or, perhaps, emotions evoked—including speech, books, movies, art, and music—are within the area of First Amendment concern. As computer code—whether source or object—is a means of expressing ideas, the First Amendment must be considered before its dissemination may be prohibited or regulated. In that sense, computer code is covered or, as sometimes is said, "protected" by the First Amendment. But that conclusion still leaves for determination the level of scrutiny to be applied in determining the constitutionality of regulation of computer code.

B. The Constitutionality of the DMCA's Anti–Trafficking Provision

1. Defendants' Alleged Right to Disseminate DeCSS

Defendants first attack Section 1201(a)(2), the anti-trafficking provision, as applied to them on the theory that DeCSS is constitutionally protected expression and that the statute improperly prevents them from communicating it. Their attack presupposes that a characterization of code as constitutionally protected subjects any regulation of code to the highest level of First Amendment scrutiny. As we have seen, however, this does not necessarily follow.

Just as computer code cannot be excluded from the area of First Amendment concern because it is abstract and, in many cases, arcane, the long history of First Amendment jurisprudence makes equally clear that the fact that words, symbols and even actions convey ideas and evoke emotions does not inevitably place them beyond the power of government. The Supreme Court has evolved an analytical framework by which the permissibility of particular restrictions on the expression of ideas must determined.

Broadly speaking, restrictions on expression fall into two categories. Some are restrictions on the voicing of particular ideas, which typically are referred to as content based restrictions. Others have nothing to do with the content of the expression—i.e., they are content neutral—but they have the incidental effect of limiting expression.

In general, "government has no power to restrict expression because of its message, its ideas, its subject matter, or its content...." "[S]ubject only to narrow and well-understood exceptions, [the First Amendment] does not countenance governmental control over the content of messages expressed by private individuals." In consequence, content based restrictions on speech are permissible only if they serve compelling state interests by the least restrictive means available.

Content neutral restrictions, in contrast, are measured against a less exacting standard. Because restrictions of this type are not motivated by a desire to limit the message, they will be upheld if they serve a substantial governmental interest and restrict First Amendment freedoms no more than necessary.

Restrictions on the nonspeech elements of expressive conduct fall into the conduct-neutral category. The Supreme Court long has distinguished for First Amendment purposes between pure speech, which ordinarily receives the highest level of protection, and expressive conduct. Even if conduct contains an expressive element, its nonspeech aspect need not be ignored. "[W]hen 'speech' and 'nonspeech' elements are combined in the same course of conduct, a sufficiently important governmental interest in regulating the nonspeech element can justify incidental limitations on First Amendment freedoms." The critical point is that nonspeech elements may create hazards for society above and beyond the speech elements. They are subject to regulation in appropriate circumstances because the government has an interest in dealing with the potential hazards of the nonspeech elements despite the fact that they are joined with expressive elements.

Thus, the starting point for analysis is whether the DMCA, as applied to restrict dissemination of DeCSS and other computer code used to circumvent access control measures, is a content based restriction on speech or a content neutral regulation. Put another way, the question is the level of review that governs the DMCA's anti-trafficking provision as applied to DeCSS—the strict scrutiny standard applicable to content based regulations or the intermediate level applicable to content neutral regulations, including regulations of the nonspeech elements of expressive conduct.

Given the fact that DeCSS code is expressive, defendants would have the Court leap immediately to the conclusion that Section 1201(a)(2)'s prohibition on providing DeCSS necessarily is content based regulation of speech because it suppresses dissemination of a particular kind of expression. But this would be a unidimensional approach to a more textured reality and entirely too facile.

The "principal inquiry in determining content neutrality ... is whether the government has adopted a regulation of speech because of [agreement or] disagreement with the message it conveys." The computer code at issue in this case, however, does more than express the programmers' concepts. It does more, in other words, than convey a message. DeCSS, like any other computer program, is a series of instructions that causes a computer to perform a particular sequence of tasks which, in the aggregate, decrypt CSS-protected files. Thus, it has a distinctly functional, non-speech aspect in addition to reflecting the thoughts of the programmers. It enables anyone who receives it and who has a modicum of computer skills to circumvent plaintiffs' access control system.

The reason that Congress enacted the anti-trafficking provision of the DMCA had nothing to do with suppressing particular ideas of computer programmers and everything to do with functionality—with preventing people from circumventing technological access control measures—just as laws prohibiting the possession of burglar tools have nothing to do with preventing people from expressing themselves by accumulating what to them may be attractive assortments of implements and everything to do with preventing burglaries. Rather, it is focused squarely upon the effect of the distribution of the functional capability that the code provides. Any impact on the dissemination of programmers' ideas is purely incidental to the overriding concerns of promoting the distribution of copyrighted works in digital form while at the same time protecting those works from piracy and other violations of the exclusive rights of copyright holders.

These considerations suggest that the DMCA as applied here is content neutral, a view that draws support also from *City of Renton v. Playtime Theatres, Inc.* The Supreme Court there upheld against a First Amendment challenge a zoning ordinance that prohibited adult movie theaters within 1,000 feet of a residential, church or park zone or within one mile of a school. Recognizing that the ordinance did "not appear to fit neatly into either the 'content based or the 'content-neutral' category," it found dispositive the fact that the ordinance was justified without reference to the content of the regulated speech in that the concern of the municipality had been with the secondary effects of the presence of adult theaters, not with the particular content of the speech that takes place in them. As Congress' concerns in enacting the anti-trafficking provision of the DMCA were to suppress copyright piracy and infringement and to promote the availability of copyrighted works in digital form, and not to regulate the expression of ideas that might be inherent in particular anti-circumvention devices or technology, this provision of the statute properly is viewed as content neutral.

Congress is not powerless to adopt content neutral regulations that incidentally affect expression, including the dissemination of the functional capabilities of computer code. A sufficiently important governmental interest in seeing to it that computers are not instructed to perform particular functions may justify incidental restrictions on the dissemination of the expressive elements of a program. Such a regulation will be upheld if:

> "it furthers an important or substantial governmental interest; if the governmental interest is unrelated to the suppression of free expression; and if the incidental restriction on alleged First Amendment freedoms is no greater than is essential to the furtherance of that interest."

Moreover, "[t]o satisfy this standard, a regulation need not be the least speech-restrictive means of advancing the Government's interests." "Rather, the requirement of narrow tailoring is satisfied 'so long as the ... regulation promotes a substantial government interest that would be achieved less effectively absent the regulation.' "

The anti-trafficking provision of the DMCA furthers an important governmental interest—the protection of copyrighted works stored on digital media from the vastly expanded risk of piracy in this electronic age. The substantiality of that interest is evident both from the fact that the Constitution specifically empowers Congress to provide for copyright protection and from the significance to our economy of trade in copyrighted materials. Indeed, the Supreme Court has made clear that copyright protection itself is "the engine of free expression." That substantial interest, moreover, is unrelated to the suppression of particular views expressed in means of gaining access to protected copyrighted works. Nor is the incidental restraint on protected expression—the prohibition of trafficking in means that would circumvent controls limiting access to unprotected materials or to copyrighted materials for noninfringing purposes—broader than is necessary to accomplish Congress' goals of preventing infringement and promoting the availability of content in digital form.

This analysis finds substantial support in the principal case relied upon by defendants, *Junger v. Daley.* The plaintiff in that case challenged on First Amendment grounds an Export Administration regulation that barred the export of computer encryption software, arguing that the software was expressive and that the regulation therefore was unconstitutional. The Sixth Circuit acknowledged the expressive nature of computer code, holding that it therefore was within the scope of the First Amendment. But it recognized also that computer code is functional as well and said that "[t]he functional capabilities of source code, particularly those of encryption source code, should be considered when analyzing the governmental interest in regulating the exchange of this form of speech." Indeed, it went on to indicate that the pertinent standard of review was that established in *United States v. O'Brien,* the seminal speech-versus-conduct decision. Thus, rather than holding the challenged regulation unconstitutional on the theory that the expressive aspect of source code immunized it from regulation, the court remanded the case to the district court to determine whether the *O'Brien* standard was met in view of the functional aspect of code.

Notwithstanding its adoption by the Sixth Circuit, the focus on functionality in order to determine the level of scrutiny is not an inevitable consequence of the speech-conduct distinction. Conduct has immediate effects on the environment. Computer code, on the other hand, no matter how functional, causes a computer to perform the intended operations only if someone uses the code to do so. Hence, one commentator, in a thoughtful article, has maintained that functionality is really "a proxy for effects or harm" and that its adoption as a determinant of the level of scrutiny slides over questions of causation that intervene between the dissemination of a computer program and any harm caused by its use.

The characterization of functionality as a proxy for the consequences of use is accurate. But the assumption that the chain of causation is too attenuated to justify the use of functionality to determine the level of scrutiny, at least in this context, is not.

Society increasingly depends upon technological means of controlling access to digital files and systems, whether they are military computers, bank records, academic records, copyrighted works or something else entirely. There are far too many who, given any opportunity, will bypass those security measures, some for the sheer joy of doing it, some for innocuous reasons, and others for more malevolent purposes. Given the virtually instantaneous and worldwide dissemination widely available via the Internet, the only rational assumption is that once a computer program capable of bypassing such an access control system is disseminated, it will be used. And that is not all.

There was a time when copyright infringement could be dealt with quite adequately by focusing on the infringing act. If someone wished to make and sell high quality but unauthorized copies of a copyrighted book, for example, the infringer needed a printing press. The copyright holder, once aware of the appearance of infringing copies, usually was able to trace the copies up the chain of distribution, find and prosecute the infringer, and shut off the infringement at the source.

In principle, the digital world is very different. Once a decryption program like DeCSS is written, it quickly can be sent all over the world. Every recipient is capable not only of decrypting and perfectly copying plaintiffs' copyrighted DVDs, but also of retransmitting perfect copies of DeCSS and thus enabling every recipient to do the same. They likewise are capable of transmitting perfect copies of the decrypted DVD. The process potentially is exponential rather than linear. Indeed, the difference is illustrated by comparison of two epidemiological models describing the spread of different kinds of disease. In a common source epidemic, as where members of a population contract a non-contagious disease from a poisoned well, the disease spreads only by exposure to the common source. If one eliminates the source, or closes the contaminated well, the epidemic is stopped. In a propagated outbreak epidemic, on the other hand, the disease spreads from person to person. Hence, finding the initial source of infection accomplishes little, as the disease continues to spread even if the initial source is eliminated. For obvious reasons, then, a propagated outbreak epidemic, all other things being equal, can be far more difficult to control.

This disease metaphor is helpful here. The book infringement hypothetical is analogous to a common source outbreak epidemic. Shut down the printing press (the poisoned well) and one ends the infringement (the disease outbreak). The spread of means of circumventing access to copyrighted works in digital form, however, is analogous to a propagated outbreak epidemic. Finding the original source of infection (e.g., the author of DeCSS or the first person to misuse it) accomplishes nothing, as the disease (infringement made possible by DeCSS and the resulting availability of decrypted DVDs) may continue to spread from one person who gains access to the circumvention program or decrypted DVD to another. And each is "infected," i.e., each is as capable of making perfect copies of the digital file containing the copyrighted work as the author of the program or the first person to use it for improper purposes. The disease metaphor breaks down principally at the final point. Individuals infected with a real disease become sick, usually are driven by obvious self-interest to seek medical attention, and are cured of the disease if medical science is capable of doing so. Individuals infected with the "disease" of capability of circumventing measures controlling access to copyrighted works in digital form, however, do not suffer from having that ability. They cannot be relied upon to identify themselves to those seeking to control the "disease." And their self-interest will motivate some to misuse the capability, a misuse that; in practical terms, often will be untraceable.

These considerations drastically alter consideration of the causal link between dissemination of computer programs such as this and their illicit use. Causation in the law ultimately involves practical policy judgments. Here, dissemination itself carries very substantial risk of imminent harm because the mechanism is so unusual by which dissemination of means of circumventing access controls to copyrighted works threatens to produce virtually unstoppable infringement of copyright. In consequence, the causal link between the dissemination of circumvention computer programs and their improper use is more than sufficiently close to warrant selection of a level of constitutional scrutiny based on the programs' functionality.

Accordingly, this Court holds that the anti-trafficking provision of the DMCA as applied to the posting of computer code that circumvents measures that control access to copyrighted works in digital form is a valid exercise of Congress' authority. It is a content neutral regulation in furtherance of important governmental interests that does not unduly restrict expressive activities. In any case, its particular functional characteristics are such that the Court would apply the same level of scrutiny even if it were viewed as content based. Yet it is important to emphasize that this is a very narrow holding. The restriction the Court here upholds, notwithstanding that computer code is within the area of First Amendment concern, is limited (1) to programs that circumvent access controls to copyrighted works in digital form in circumstances in which (2) there is no other practical means of preventing infringement through use of the programs, and (3) the regulation is motivated by a desire to prevent performance of the function for which the programs exist rather than any message they might convey. One readily might imagine other circumstances in which a governmental attempt to regulate the dissemination of computer code would not similarly be justified.

2. Prior Restraint

Defendants argue also that injunctive relief against dissemination of DeCSS is barred by the prior restraint doctrine. The Court disagrees.

Few phrases are as firmly rooted in our constitutional jurisprudence as the maxim that "[a]ny system of prior restraints of expression comes to [a] Court bearing a heavy presumption against its constitutional validity." Yet there is a significant gap between the rhetoric and the reality. Courts often have upheld restrictions on expression that many would describe as prior restraints, sometimes by characterizing the expression as unprotected and on other occasions finding the restraint justified despite its presumed invalidity. Moreover, the prior restraint doctrine, which has expanded far beyond the Blackstonian model that doubtless informed the understanding of the Framers of the First Amendment, has been criticized as filled with "doctrinal ambiguities and inconsistencies result[ing] from the absence of any detailed judicial analysis of [its] true rationale" and, in one case, even as "fundamentally unintelligible." Nevertheless, the doctrine has a well established core: administrative preclearance requirements for and at least preliminary injunctions against speech as conventionally understood are presumptively unconstitutional. Yet that proposition does not dispose of this case.

The classic prior restraint cases were dramatically different from this one. *Near v. Minnesota* involved a state procedure for abating scandalous and defamatory newspapers as public nuisances. *New York Times Co. v. United States* dealt with an attempt to enjoin a newspaper from publishing an internal government history of the Vietnam War. *Nebraska Press Association v. Stuart* concerned a court order barring the reporting of certain details about a forthcoming murder case. In each case, therefore, the government sought to suppress speech at the very heart of First

Amendment concern—expression about public issues of the sort that is indispensable to self government. And while the prior restraint doctrine has been applied well beyond the sphere of political expression, we deal here with something new altogether—computer code, a fundamentally utilitarian construct, albeit one that embodies an expressive element. Hence, it would be a mistake simply to permit its expressive element to drive a characterization of the code as speech no different from the Pentagon Papers, the publication of a newspaper, or the exhibition of a motion picture and then to apply prior restraint rhetoric without a more nuanced consideration of the competing concerns.

In this case, the considerations supporting an injunction are very substantial indeed. Copyright and, more broadly, intellectual property piracy are endemic, as Congress repeatedly has found. The interest served by prohibiting means that facilitate such piracy—the protection of the monopoly granted to copyright owners by the Copyright Act—is of constitutional dimension. There is little room for doubting that broad dissemination of DeCSS threatens ultimately to injure or destroy plaintiffs' ability to distribute their copyrighted products on DVDs and, for that matter, undermine their ability to sell their products to the home video market in other forms. The potential damages probably are incalculable, and these defendants surely would be in no position to compensate plaintiffs for them if plaintiffs were remitted only to *post hoc* damage suits.

On the other side of the coin, the First Amendment interests served by the dissemination of DeCSS on the merits are minimal. The presence of some expressive content in the code should not obscure the fact of its predominant functional character—it is first and foremost a means of causing a machine with which it is used to perform particular tasks. Hence, those of the traditional rationales for the prior restraint doctrine that relate to inhibiting the transmission and receipt of ideas are of attenuated relevance here. Indeed, even academic commentators who take the extreme position that most injunctions in intellectual property cases are unconstitutional prior restraints concede that there is no First Amendment obstacle to injunctions barring distribution of copyrighted computer object code or restraining the construction of a new building based on copyrighted architectural drawings because the functional aspects of these types of information are "sufficiently nonexpressive."

To be sure, there is much to be said in most circumstances for the usual procedural rationale for the prior restraint doctrine: prior restraints carry with them the risk of erroneously suppressing expression that could not constitutionally be punished after publication. In this context, however, that concern is not persuasive, both because the enjoined expressive element is minimal and because a full trial on the merits has been held. Accordingly, the Court holds that the prior restraint doctrine does not require denial of an injunction in this case.

3. Overbreadth

Defendants' second focus is the contention that Section 1201(a)(2) is unconstitutional because it prevents others from making fair use of copyrighted works by depriving them of the means of circumventing plaintiffs' access control system. In substance, they contend that the anti-trafficking provision leaves those who lack sufficient technical expertise to circumvent CSS themselves without the means of acquiring circumvention technology that they need to make fair use of the content of plaintiffs' copyrighted DVDs.

As a general proposition, "a person to whom a statute constitutionally may be applied may not challenge that statute on the ground that it conceivably may be applied unconstitutionally to others in situations not before the Court." When statutes regulate speech, however, "the transcendent value to all society of constitutionally protected expression is deemed to justify 'attacks on overly broad statutes with no requirement that the person making the attack demonstrate that his own conduct could not be regulated by a statute drawn with the requisite narrow specificity.'" This is so because the absent third parties may not exercise their rights for fear of triggering "sanctions provided by a statute susceptible of application to protected expression." But the overbreadth doctrine "is 'strong medicine'. . . . employed . . . with hesitation, and then 'only as a last resort.'" because it conflicts with "the personal nature of constitutional rights and the prudential limitations on constitutional adjudication," including the importance of focusing carefully on the facts in deciding constitutional questions. Moreover, the limited function of the overbreadth doctrine " 'attenuates as the otherwise unprotected behavior that it forbids the State to sanction moves from 'pure speech' toward conduct and that conduct—even if expressive—falls within the scope of otherwise valid criminal laws. . . .'" As defendants concede, "where conduct and not merely speech is involved, . . . the overbreadth of a statute must not only be real, but substantial as well, judged in relation to the statute's plainly legitimate sweep."

Factors arguing against use of the overbreadth doctrine are present here. To begin with, we do not here have a complete view of whether the interests of the absent third parties upon whom defendants rely really are substantial and, in consequence, whether the DMCA as applied here would materially affect their ability to make fair use of plaintiffs' copyrighted works.

The copyrighted works at issue, of course, are motion pictures. People use copies of them in DVD and other formats for various purposes, and we confine our consideration to the lawful purposes, which by definition are noninfringing or fair uses. The principal noninfringing use is to play the DVD for the purpose of watching the movie—viewing the images and hearing the sounds that are synchronized with them. Fair uses are much more varied. A movie reviewer might wish to quote a portion of the verbal script in an article or broadcast review. A television station might want to broadcast part of a particular scene to illustrate a review, a news story about a performer, or a story about particular trends in motion pictures. A musicologist perhaps would wish to play a portion of a musical sound track. A film scholar might desire to create and exhibit to students small segments of several different films to make some comparative point about the cinematography or some other characteristic. Numerous other examples doubtless could be imagined. But each necessarily involves one or more of three types of use: (1) quotation of the words of the script, (2) listening to the recorded sound track, including both verbal and non-verbal elements, and (3) viewing of the graphic images.

All three of these types of use now are affected by the anti-trafficking provision of the DMCA, but probably only to a trivial degree. To begin with, all or substantially all motion pictures available on DVD are available also on videotape. In consequence, anyone wishing to make lawful use of a particular movie may buy or rent a videotape, play it, and even copy all or part of it with readily available equipment. But even if movies were available only on DVD, as someday may be the case, the impact on lawful use would be limited. Compliant DVD players permit one to view or listen to a DVD movie without circumventing CSS in any prohibited sense. The technology permitting manufacture of compliant DVD players is available to anyone on a royalty-free basis and at modest cost, so CSS raises no technological barrier to their manufacture. Hence, those wishing to make lawful use of copyrighted movies by viewing or listening to them are not hindered in doing so in any material way by the anti-trafficking provision of the DMCA. Nor does the DMCA materially affect quotation of language from CSS-protected movies. Anyone with access to a compliant DVD player may play the movie and write down or otherwise record the sound for the purpose of quoting it in another medium.

The DMCA does have a notable potential impact on uses that copy portions of a DVD movie because compliant DVD players are designed so as to prevent copying. In consequence, even though the fair use doctrine permits limited copying of copyrighted works in appropriate circumstances, the CSS encryption of DVD movies, coupled with the characteristics of licensed DVD players, limits such uses absent circumvention of CSS. Moreover, the anti-trafficking provision of the DMCA may prevent technologically unsophisticated persons who wish to copy portions of DVD movies for fair use from obtaining the means of doing so. It is the interests of these individuals upon which defendants rely most heavily in contending that the DMCA violates the First Amendment because it deprives such persons of an asserted constitutional right to make fair use of copyrighted materials.

As the foregoing suggests, the interests of persons wishing to circumvent CSS in order to make lawful use of the copyrighted movies it protects are remarkably varied. Some presumably are technologically sophisticated and therefore capable of circumventing CSS without access to defendants' or other purveyors' decryption programs; many presumably are not. Many of the possible fair uses may be made without circumventing CSS while others, i.e., those requiring copying, may not. Hence, the question whether Section 1201(a)(2) as applied here substantially affects rights, much less constitutionally protected rights, of members of the "fair use community" cannot be decided *in bloc,* without consideration of the circumstances of each member or similarly situated groups of members. Thus, the prudential concern with ensuring that constitutional questions be decided only when the facts before the Court so require counsels against permitting defendants to mount an overbreadth challenge here.

Second, there is no reason to suppose here that prospective fair users will be deterred from asserting their alleged rights by fear of sanctions imposed by the DMCA or the Copyright Act.

Third, we do not deal here with "pure speech." Rather, the issue concerns dissemination of technology that is principally functional in nature. The same consideration that warrants restraint in applying the overbreadth doctrine to statutes regulating expressive conduct applies here. For reasons previously expressed, government's interest in regulating the functional capabilities of computer code is no less weighty than its interest in regulating the nonspeech aspects of expressive conduct.

Finally, there has been no persuasive evidence that the interests of persons who wish access to the CSS algorithm in order to study its encryption methodology or to evaluate theories regarding decryption raise serious problems. The statute contains an exception for good faith encryption research.

Accordingly, defendants will not be heard to mount an overbreadth challenge to the DMCA in this context.

4. *Vagueness*

Defendants argue also that the DMCA is unconstitutionally vague because the terms it employs are not understandable to persons of ordinary intelligence and because they are subject to discriminatory enforcement.

As the Supreme Court has made clear, one who "engages in some conduct that is clearly proscribed [by the challenged statute] cannot complain of the vagueness of the law as applied to the conduct of others." There can be no serious doubt that posting a computer program the sole purpose of which is to defeat an encryption system controlling access to plaintiff's copyrighted movies constituted an "offer to the public" of "technology [or a] product" that was "primarily designed for the purpose of circumventing" plaintiffs' access control system. Defendants thus engaged in conduct clearly proscribed by the DMCA and will not be heard to complain of any vagueness as applied to others.

C. *Linking*

As indicated above, the DMCA reaches links deliberately created by a web site operator for the purpose of disseminating technology that enables the user to circumvent access controls on copyrighted works. The question is whether it may do so consistent with the First Amendment.

Links bear a relationship to the information superhighway comparable to the relationship that roadway signs bear to roads but they are more functional. Like roadway signs, they point out the direction. Unlike roadway signs, they take one almost instantaneously to the desired destination with the mere click of an electronic mouse. Thus, like computer code in general, they have both expressive and functional elements. Also like computer code, they are within the area of First Amendment concern. Hence, the constitutionality of the DMCA as applied to defendants' linking is determined by the same *O'Brien* standard that governs trafficking in the circumvention technology generally.

There is little question that the application of the DMCA to the linking at issue in this case would serve, at least to some extent, the same substantial governmental interest as its application to defendants' posting of the DeCSS code. Defendants' posting and their linking amount to very much the same thing. Similarly, the regulation of the linking at issue here is "unrelated to the suppression of free expression" for the same reason as the regulation of the posting. The third prong of the *O'Brien* test as subsequently interpreted—whether the "regulation promotes a substantial government interest that would be achieved less effectively absent the regulation"—is a somewhat closer call.

Defendants and, by logical extension, others may be enjoined from posting DeCSS. Plaintiffs may seek legal redress against anyone who persists in posting notwithstanding this decision. Hence, barring defendants from linking to sites against which plaintiffs readily may take legal action would advance the statutory purpose of preventing dissemination of circumvention technology, but it would do so less effectively than would actions by plaintiffs directly against the sites that post. For precisely this reason, however, the real significance of an anti-linking injunction would not be with U.S. web sites subject to the DMCA, but with foreign sites that arguably are not subject to it and not subject to suit here. An anti-linking injunction to that extent would have a significant impact and thus materially advance a substantial governmental purpose. In consequence, the Court concludes that an injunction against linking to other sites posting DeCSS satisfies the *O'Brien* standard. There remains, however, one further important point.

Links are "what unify the [World Wide] Web into a single body of knowledge, and what makes the Web unique." They "are the mainstay of the Internet and indispensable to its convenient access to the vast world of information." They often are used in ways that do a great deal to promote the free exchange of ideas and information that is a central value of our nation. Anything that would impose strict liability on a web site operator for the entire contents of any web site to which the operator linked therefore would raise grave constitutional concerns, as web site operators would be inhibited from linking for fear of exposure to liability. And it is equally clear that exposing those who use links to liability under the DMCA might chill their use, as some web site operators confronted with claims that they have posted circumvention technology falling within the statute may be more inclined to remove the allegedly offending link rather than test the issue in court. Moreover, web sites often contain a great variety of things, and a ban on linking to a site that contains DeCSS amidst other content threatens to restrict communication of this information to an excessive degree.

The possible chilling effect of a rule permitting liability for or injunctions against Internet hyperlinks is a genuine concern. But it is not unique to the issue of linking. The constitutional law of defamation provides a highly relevant analogy. The threat of defamation suits creates the same risk of self-censorship, the same chilling effect, for the traditional press as a prohibition of linking to sites containing circumvention technology poses for web site operators. Just as the potential chilling effect of defamation suits has not utterly immunized the press from all actions for defamation, however, the potential chilling effect of DMCA liability cannot utterly immunize web site operators from all actions for disseminating circumvention technology. And the solution to the problem is the same: the adoption of a standard of culpability sufficiently high to immunize the activity, whether it is publishing a newspaper or linking, except in cases in which the conduct in question has little or no redeeming constitutional value.

In the defamation area, this has been accomplished by a two-tiered constitutional standard. There may be no liability under the First Amendment for defamation of a public official or a public figure unless the plaintiff proves, by clear and convincing evidence, that the defendant published the offending statement with knowledge of its falsity or with serious doubt as to its truth. Liability in private figure cases, on the other hand, may not be imposed absent proof at least of negligence under *Gertz v. Robert Welch, Inc.* A similar approach would minimize any chilling effect here.

The other concern—that a liability based on a link to another site simply because the other site happened to contain DeCSS or some other circumvention technology in the midst of other perfectly appropriate content could be overkill—also is readily dealt with. The offense under the DMCA is offering, providing or otherwise trafficking in circumvention technology. An essential ingredient, as explained above, is a desire to bring about the dissemination. Hence, a strong requirement of that forbidden purpose is an essential prerequisite to any liability for linking.

Accordingly, there may be no injunction against, nor liability for, linking to a site containing circumvention technology, the offering of which is unlawful under the DMCA, absent clear and convincing evidence that those responsible for the link (a) know at the relevant time that the offending material is on the linked-to site, (b) know that it is circumvention technology that may not lawfully be offered, and (c) create or maintain the link for the purpose of disseminating that technology. Such a standard will limit the fear of liability on the part of web site operators just as the *New York Times* standard gives the press great comfort in publishing all sorts of material that would have been actionable at common law, even in the face of flat denials by the subjects of their stories. And it will not subject web site operators to liability for linking to a site containing proscribed technology where the link exists for purposes other than dissemination of that technology.

In this case, plaintiffs have established by clear and convincing evidence that these defendants linked to sites posting DeCSS, knowing that it was a circumvention device. Indeed, they initially touted it as a way to get free movies, and they later maintained the links to promote the dissemination of the program in an effort to defeat effective judicial relief. They now know that dissemination of DeCSS violates the DMCA. An anti-linking injunction on these facts does no violence to the First Amendment. Nor should it chill the activities of web site operators dealing with different materials, as they may be held liable only on a compelling showing of deliberate evasion of the statute.

IV.   Relief

A.   Injury to Plaintiffs

The DMCA provides that "[a]ny person injured by a violation of section 1201 or 1202 may bring a civil action in an appropriate United States court for such violation." For the reasons set forth above, plaintiffs obviously have suffered and, absent effective relief, will continue to suffer injury by virtue of the ready availability of means of circumventing the CSS access control system on their DVDs. Defendants nevertheless argue that they have not met the injury requirement of the statute. Their contentions are a farrago of distortions.

They begin with the assertion that plaintiffs have failed to prove that decrypted motion pictures actually are available. To be sure, plaintiffs might have done a better job of proving what appears to be reasonably obvious. They certainly could have followed up on more of the 650 movie titles listed on the web site described above to establish that the titles in fact were available. But the evidence they did adduce is not nearly as meager as defendants would have it. Dr. Shamos did pursue and obtain a pirated copy of a copyrighted, DivX'd motion picture from someone he met in an Internet chat room. An MPAA investigator downloaded between five and ten such copies. And the sudden appearance of listings of available motion pictures on the Internet promptly after DeCSS became available is far from lacking in evidentiary significance. In any case, in order to obtain the relief sought here, plaintiffs need show only a threat of injury by reason of a violation of the statute. The Court finds that plaintiffs overwhelmingly have established a clear threat of injury by reason of defendants' violation of the statute.

Defendants next maintain that plaintiffs exaggerate the extent of the threatened injury. They claim that the studios in fact believe that DeCSS is not a threat. But the only basis for that contention is a couple of quotations from statements that the MPAA or one or another studio made (or considered making but did not in fact issue) to the effect that it was not concerned about DeCSS or that it was inconvenient to use. These statements, however, were attempts to "spin" public opinion. They do not now reflect the actual state of affairs or the studios' actual views, if they ever did.

Third, defendants contend that there is no evidence that any decrypted movies that may be available, if any there are, were decrypted with DeCSS. They maintain that "[m]any utilities and devices ... can decrypt DVDs equally well and often faster and with greater ease than by using DeCSS." This is a substantial exaggeration. There appear to be a few other so-called rippers, but the Court finds that DeCSS is usable on a broader range of DVDs than any of the others. Further, there is no credible evidence that any other utility is faster or easier to use than DeCSS. Indeed, the Court concludes that DeCSS is the superior product, as evidenced by the fact that the web site promoting DivX as a tool for obtaining usable copies of copyrighted movies recommends the use of DeCSS, rather than anything else, for the decryption step and that the apparent availability of pirated motion pictures shot up so dramatically upon the introduction of DeCSS.

B. Permanent Injunction and Declaratory Relief

Plaintiffs seek a permanent injunction barring defendants from posting DeCSS on their web site and from linking their site to others that make DeCSS available.

The starting point, as always, is the statute. The DMCA provides in relevant part that the court in an action brought pursuant to its terms "may grant temporary and permanent injunctions on such terms as it deems reasonable to prevent or restrain a violation...." Where statutes in substance so provide, injunctive relief is appropriate if there is a reasonable likelihood of future violations absent such relief and, in cases brought by private plaintiffs, if the plaintiff lacks an adequate remedy at law.

In this case, it is quite likely that defendants, unless enjoined, will continue to violate the Act. Defendants are in the business of disseminating information to assist hackers in "cracking" various types of technological security systems. And while defendants argue that they promptly stopped posting DeCSS when enjoined preliminarily from doing so, thus allegedly demonstrating their willingness to comply with the law, their reaction to the preliminary injunction in fact cuts the other way. Upon being enjoined from posting DeCSS themselves, defendants encouraged others to "mirror" the information—that is, to post DeCSS—and linked their own web site to mirror sites in order to assist users of defendants' web site in obtaining DeCSS despite the injunction barring defendants from providing it directly. While there is no claim that this activity violated the letter of the preliminary injunction, and it therefore presumably was not contumacious, and while its status under the DMCA was somewhat uncertain, it was a studied effort to defeat the purpose of the preliminary injunction. In consequence, the Court finds that there is a substantial likelihood of future violations absent injunctive relief.

There also is little doubt that plaintiffs have no adequate remedy at law. The only potential legal remedy would be an action for damages under Section 1203(c), which provides for recovery of actual damages or, upon the election of the plaintiff, statutory damages of up to $2,500 per offer of DeCSS. Proof of actual damages in a case of this nature would be difficult if not virtually impossible, as it would involve proof of the extent to which motion picture attendance, sales of broadcast and other motion picture rights, and sales and rentals of DVDs and video tapes of movies were and will be impacted by the availability of DVD decryption technology. Difficulties in determining what constitutes an "offer" of DeCSS in a world in which the code is available to much of the world via Internet postings, among other problems, render statutory damages an inadequate means of redressing plaintiffs' claimed injuries. Indeed, difficulties such as this have led to the presumption that copyright and trademark infringement cause irreparable injury, i.e., injury for which damages are not an adequate remedy. The Court therefore holds that the traditional requirements for issuance of a permanent injunction have been satisfied. Yet there remains another point for consideration.

Defendants argue that an injunction in this case would be futile because DeCSS already is all over the Internet. They say an injunction would be comparable to locking the barn door after the horse is gone. And the Court has been troubled by that possibility. But the countervailing arguments overcome that concern.

To begin with, any such conclusion effectively would create all the wrong incentives by allowing defendants to continue violating the DMCA simply because others, many doubtless at defendants' urging, are doing so as well. Were that the law, defendants confronted with the possibility of injunctive relief would be well advised to ensure that others engage in the same unlawful conduct in order to set up the argument that an injunction against the defendants would be futile because everyone else is doing the same thing.

Second, and closely related, is the fact that this Court is sorely "troubled by the notion that any Internet user ... can destroy valuable intellectual property rights by posting them over the Internet." While equity surely should not act where the controversy has become moot, it ought to look very skeptically at claims that the defendant or others already have done all the harm that might be done before the injunction issues.

The key to reconciling these views is that the focus of injunctive relief is on the defendants before the Court. If a plaintiff seeks to enjoin a defendant from burning a pasture, it is no answer that there is a wild fire burning in its direction. If the defendant itself threatens the plaintiff with irreparable harm, then equity will enjoin the defendant from carrying out the threat even if other threats abound and even if part of the pasture already is burned.

These defendants would harm plaintiffs every day on which they post DeCSS on their heavily trafficked web site and link to other sites that post it because someone who does not have DeCSS thereby might obtain it. They thus threaten plaintiffs with immediate and irreparable injury. They will not be allowed to continue to do so simply because others may do so as well. In short, this Court, like others than have faced the issued, is "not persuaded that modern technology has withered the strong right arm of equity." Indeed, the likelihood is that this decision will serve notice on others that "the strong right arm of equity" may be brought to bear against them absent a change in their conduct and thus contribute to a climate of appropriate respect for intellectual property rights in an age in which the excitement of ready access to untold quantities of information has blurred in some minds the fact that taking what is not yours and not freely offered to you is stealing. Appropriate injunctive and declaratory relief will issue simultaneously with this opinion.

V. Miscellaneous Contentions

There remain for consideration two other matters, plaintiffs' application for costs and attorney's fees and defendants' pretrial complaints concerning discovery.

The DMCA permits awards of costs and attorney's fees to the prevailing party in the discretion of the Court. Insofar as attorney's fees are concerned, this is an exception to the so-called "American rule" pursuant to which each side in a litigation customarily bears its own attorney's fees. As this was a test case raising important issues, it would be inappropriate to award attorney's fees pursuant to the DMCA. There is no comparable reason, however, for failing to award costs, particularly as taxable costs are related to the excessive discovery demands that the Court already has commented upon.

A final word is in order in view of defendants' repeated pretrial claims that their discovery efforts were being thwarted. During the course of the trial, they applied for leave to take one deposition, which was granted. At no point did they make any showing that they were hampered in presenting their case or meeting the plaintiffs' case by virtue of any failure to obtain discovery. They applied for no continuance. They have not sought a new trial. And though they estimated that their case would take several weeks to present, the entire trial was completed in six days. Indeed, in the Court's view, the trial fully vindicated its pretrial assessment that there were, in actuality, very few genuinely disputed questions of material fact, and most of those involved expert testimony that was readily available to both sides. Examination of the trial record will reveal that virtually the entire case could have been stipulated, although the legal conclusions to be drawn from the stipulated facts of course would have remained a matter of controversy.

VI. Conclusion

In the final analysis, the dispute between these parties is simply put if not necessarily simply resolved.

Plaintiffs have invested huge sums over the years in producing motion pictures in reliance upon a legal framework that, through the law of copyright, has ensured that they will have the exclusive right to copy and distribute those motion pictures for economic gain. They contend that the advent of new technology should not alter this long established structure.

Defendants, on the other hand, are adherents of a movement that believes that information should be available without charge to anyone clever enough to break into the computer systems or data storage media in which it is located. Less radically, they have raised a legitimate concern about the possible impact on traditional fair use of access control measures in the digital era.

Each side is entitled to its views. In our society, however, clashes of competing interests like this are resolved by Congress. For now, at least, Congress has resolved this clash in the DMCA and in plaintiffs' favor. Given the peculiar characteristics of computer programs for circumventing encryption and other access control measures, the DMCA as applied to posting and linking here does not contravene the First Amendment. Accordingly, plaintiffs are entitled to appropriate injunctive and declaratory relief.

SO ORDERED.

NOTES

1.   One of the products and enterprises in *Reimerdes* was 321 Studios, producers of DVD Xcopy. DVD Xcopy an early software application that automated the DVD copying process. The program enabled end users to decrypt a DVD inserted in their computer and burn a copy to DVD. The *Reimerdes* injunction ordered them to cease and desist from further sales of this application and remove DeCSS from future applications they developed. The company made a tentative attempt to market products without DeCSS, but shortly thereafter appear to have gone "offshore" through a sale of the application to another entity. The program was marketed through that entity until circa 2005, It is not clear whether the demise of the program was due to the decision in *Reimerdes*, or because of the continued development, distribution and revision of shareware or freeware accomplishing the same result with increasing sophistication. DVDshrink was revised through 2005 when code writers became "bored" with further revisions. These programs are still available on the internet and include not only DVDshrink, but DVDdcryptor and a number of commercial products that have come forth.

2.   In light of the above observations, what affect did either the DMCA or decision in *Reimerdes* have? Did it put a stop to decrypting DVD movies? What segment of the market was affected? Offshore "pirates?" How does this inform regarding the efficacy of law and changing paradigms of normative behavior? Is this a failure of market structures, the copyright system, or changing patterns of respect for law? See also, *Universal City Studios, Inc. v. Corley,* 273 F.3d 429 (2d Cir. 2001) for extended discussion of free speech, research and fair use.

3. Fair use, free speech and any number of other perceived rights and values can be implicated by both the use of encryption and legal protections accorded content right holders under the DMCA. Movie and TV rating systems provide warnings regarding content that allows the public to make choices of what to view or show. The portion of the content that triggers the rating may be minimal and not even related to or necessary to the main story. Does fair use include the right to remove morally offending content from a movie? Would the removal of explicit violent or sexually related scenes have been permissible under the copyright statute? Does the DMCA create new rights through its protective measures concerning CSS and other DRM technologies? These and other questions concerning fair use are discussed at length in *Clean Flicks of Colo., LLC v. Soderbergh*, 433 F. Supp. 2d 1236 (D. Colo. 2006).

4. In *The Chamberlain Group, Inc. v. Skylink Technologies, Inc.*, 381 F.3d 1178 (Fed. Cir. 2004), the court concerned itself with application of the DMCA to a device that bypasses controls designed to prevent access to software itself unprotected under the Copyright Act. The quest for competitive advantage through the use of technologies that limit generic or third party capacity to compete, particularly in the supply or alternative accessory area raises classic trade issues. See also *Lexmark Int'l, Inc. v. Static Control Components, Inc.*, 387 F.3d 522 (6th Cir. 2004) where the court distinguished between a device that bypasses controls designed to prevent access to software " * * * uses that copyright law explicitly authorizes * * distinct from content which is not authorized. See generally, Pamela Samuelson, *Intellectual Property and the Digital Economy: Why the Anti–Circumvention Regulations Need to Be Revised*, 14 BERKELEY TECH. L. J. 519 (1999).

IV. EMERGING ISSUES: PROTECTION OF CONTENT RIGHTS AND RIGHTS OF USE, LIMITS OF PROTECTION, TECHNOLOGY ENTRAPMENT

A. EXPANDING DRM CONTROLS TO OVER THE AIR BROADCAST BY SIGNAL DEVICE

The proposed institution of extension of DRM controls to over the air broadcast came with the Audio Broadcast Flag Licensing Act of 2006 109th CONGRESS 2d Session H. R. 4861 proposal that was unceremoniously never enacted. The terms of the proposed act follows included provisions "To authorize the Federal Communications Commission to impose licensing conditions on digital audio radio to protect against the unauthorized distribution of transmitted content." The primary control device was a transmitted signal that would protect the digital transmission from being copied with a compliant device in each receiver. The terms of the proposed act included, among other provisions, the following:

> To authorize the Federal Communications Commission to impose licensing conditions on digital audio radio to protect against the unauthorized distribution of transmitted content.

'(a) Grant of Authority–The Commission has authority—

'(1) to require and enforce, subject to subsections (b) and (c), in conjunction with the in-band, on-channel technical standard for digital audio broadcast transmissions under consideration in MM Docket No. 99–235, or any successor regulations, that—

'(A) all technologies necessary to make transmission and reception devices compliant with such technical standard are licensed on reasonable and nondiscriminatory terms;

'(B) such licenses shall include prohibitions against unauthorized copying and redistribution of transmitted content through the use of a broadcast flag or similar technology, in a manner generally consistent with the purposes of other applicable law; and

'(C) licensees of the Commission providing digital audio broadcast service shall give effect to and comply with such prohibitions; and

'(2) to require and enforce, subject to subsections (b) and (c), as part of its regulation of satellite digital audio radio services (SDARS) pursuant to part 25 of the Commission rules, or any successor regulations, that—

'(A) all technologies necessary to make transmission and reception devices capable of receiving satellite digital audio radio transmissions are licensed on reasonable and nondiscriminatory terms;

'(B) such licenses shall include prohibitions against unauthorized copying and redistribution of transmitted content through the use of a broadcast flag or similar technology, in a manner generally consistent with the purposes of other applicable law; and

'(C) licensees of the Commission providing satellite digital audio radio services shall give effect to and comply with such prohibitions.

NOTES

1. Just when the dust started to settle, new broadcasting technologies raised new issues for the protection of content rights. The reception of this attempt to legislate protective measures through the use of the "broadcast flag" noted above was the catalyst for public interest pressures in Congress. These three articles are representative of the compromises that followed. See generally, *Comment and Recent Development: Progress on the WIPO Broadcasting and Webcasting Treaty*, 24 Cardozo Arts & Ent. L.J. 349 (2006); Note: *American Library Ass'n v. FCC: Charting The Future of Content Protection For Digital television*, 21 Berkeley Tech. L.J. 613 (2006); Comment, *A Postmortem of the Digital Television Broadcast Flag*, 42 Hous. L. Rev. 1129

(2005). What do you think should be the appropriate measure of balance between protection of the copyright holder's interests and the rights of the public use consistent with *Sony Betamax* and *Grokster*?

2. The Amici briefs in *Grokster* were replete with non-invasive suggestions for DRM controls. Digital signatures and keys were among existing technologies, as well several others in various stages of development. Many of these were detailed in the later itineration of *Groksert, Streamcast*. Here are a few additional examples of non-invasive protections that are in current use:

(a) Adobe Systems has effectively used the upgrade path to validate users. Online upgrades had disclosed multiple users and copies of purchased software. Adobe has refused the upgrade and voided the license key of suspect users. Users are able to reinstate their license with a new key on proof of purchase.

(b) Microsoft uses a variation on this theme which many consider to be somewhat more invasive. They use a program script to validate the license before permitting upgrades of the program or security patches.

(c) iMatch, a German based program, requires multiple keys to enter and then download upgrades. The keys change over time.

(d) Qimage Pro and Bibble Labs both issue new keys to purchasers as a path to "new" editions.

(e) Rhapsody uses online authentication for use and then monitors that use for streaming audio.

(f) The use of licensing agreements that give content right holders the ability to file state court actions for misuse or appropriation.

These examples are simply suggestive alternatives to the preemptive exclusionary implications of technology based measures represented by the DMCA, Inducing Infringement of Copyrights Act of 2004 and the proposed Audio Broadcast Flag licensing Act of 2006.

B. TECHNOLOGY, SOCIAL NETWORKING, CREATIVITY IN CYBERSPACE AND THE FUTURE

1. The Author's Guild (and now The Visual Artists) v. Google

The Google book project is one of numerous ventures under the Google umbrella that present a quandary of potential promise and enrichment of the public domain. The book scanning project presents conventional issues at the core of protecting copyright holders copyrighted materials. The Google project will copy all of both copyrighted and non-copyrighted materials. They will maintain these copies on their servers over which they exercise control. They will, as to some subject matter yet to be determined, either facilitate copies or point to lawful places of purchase of a copy. They will permit the public, through searches, to see small portions of the materials for the purpose of identification and possible pursuit of a complete copy for loan or purchase. Is there any question whether this does or does not serve the public interest? It does serve the purposes of copyright. It does create private right issues as currently constituted. It does create issues of "detriment" to the public. Certainly, there are any number of variants on the threshold of rights and interests above that are just a starting point for questions and analysis.

The question is whether this should be for the courts or congress to decide and what interests should be considered in the balance. These are issues with prominent social and intellectual consequence that raise concern about the propriety of the adjudicatory process to reconcile public and private interests. The absence of congressional activity for over thirty years since the 1976 Copyright Act, other than protecting private rights, is quite evident. Since the passage of the Copyright Act, there have been "revolutionary" changes affecting paradigms of innovation, technology and use that were non-existent or of limited public use at the time of that enactment. The first minimal personal computers, Apple and Tandy TRS 80 were in their first introduction. Microsoft and the contemporary PC was a half decade away. The internet, in 1976, was the play of national defense and of child geeks. The changing landscape of the present is clear. These are distributed technologies that have enabled global populations to create, find, use, communicate and share as no time in the history of humanity. The Google Book Scanning Project is the tip of the iceberg. Search engines and artificial intelligence in search capabilities are an essential of daily life. Social networking and the sharing of creativity in ventures YouTube "like" and Twitter have changed the use and exchange of multiple forms and formats of information. These activities present similar issues of public benefit and conflict with private rights management and protection. Some of this has been obvious with judicial treatment of the power of the search engine in locating, copying thumbnails and linking to sites where infringing materials may be found amongst the legitimate content on the internet. *Perfect 10 v. Google* noted in both this chapter and chapter Three. But, the real question lies in whether this should have been the subject of congressional attention to ensure the public beneficial use of search engine technologies, in the context of balancing private rights with public purpose. Present cases raise these fundamental issues of private rights and public purpose and the respective responsibilities of the court and the congress.

Chapter three, section XII sets forth the basic materials of the Google Book Scanning project. The question here is of the digitalization and distribution of these materials representing a distinct public interest element for DRM relative to the management of public rights. The attempt to treat this as an adjudication of private rights misses that underlying public interest. See generally, brief in opposition filed by Attorney General United States. (THE AUTHORS GUILD, INC. et al., Plaintiffs v. GOOGLE INC., Defendant., 2010 WL 979111 (Trial Filing) (S.D.N.Y. Feb. 4, 2010) Statement of Interest of the United States of America Regarding Proposed Amended Settlement Agreement (NO. 105CV08136)). As of April 18, 2010 there were approximately 96 filings, memorandum or submissions in the case itself or in support or oppositions to the settlement agreement from within the United State and other countries.

2. Twitter and the Library of Congress

The headline news all indicates that the Library of Congress is in the business of using technology to archive and distribute fundamental content and expression to the American public and the world. In the first instance the Library of Congress used a two million dollar grant to have the rare and historic books in their collection digitalized for archival and posterity purposes. (See generally, http://www1.voanews.com/english/news/a–13–2009–01–23–voa29–68795057.html?CFTOKEN=54521330 & jsessionid=de30b53d1c8c913edb7e7f1bb11c5d61701f & CFID=132918064) In the Twitter instance, they are looking to create history by digitalizing the social correspondence and uttering's of the public on the social web site "Twitter." The library of congress has made arrangements to "acquire" (which may simply mean copy) the entire collected works of the blogging service which represents millions of "tweets" on a daily basis. This is quite a departure from past archives which focused on "juried" works, such as articles, newspapers, books and magazines. Tweets will be the record for history of "ordinary people."

The article indicates that there are over 167 terabytes of digital materials that are already stored on the Twitter servers which is the equivalent of 21 million books. An amazing amount of "expression." There is concern for privacy rights, although that is dismissed since these writings were ostensibly published. Likewise, the social interactions of people will reflect that these casual commentaries will be "history" in the making and have a persistence that may inhibit and skew that use and communication of "Twistites,"or "Twittees."

None of the commentaries address the copyright issues directly, nor what may give Twitter and the Library of Congress the "right" to archive or disseminate this information. One might suppose that Twitter has terms of service with those that use it agree to, but does it really? Does this present issues that are or are not analogous to the Google Scanning Projects but for the intervention of "copyright" law. http://www.nytimes.com/2010/04/15/technology/15twitter.html?scp=6 & sq=twitter & st=cse

3. Viacom v. Google

YouTube is one of the first online file sharing entities comprised primarily of recognized public domain content, not subject to copyright limitations. Some content posted by users will be copyrighted and constitute infringing activity. Does this infringement meet the criteria set forth in Grokster and other file sharing cases necessary to render YouTube and Google vicariously liable for either inducement to infringe or contributory infringement? Does the fact that most of the content is "lawful" protect Google/Youtube from inferences that they condoned or encouraged the posting of copyrighted content by third parties? Google and YouTube seem to believe that (a) notice by the copyright holder and (b) removal of protected content by them will suffice to insulate them from liability. This is the subject of extended analysis by the court of both the DMCA provisions and the legislative reports evidencing the issues and purpose of congress in the DMCA.

There will always be some copyrighted content that slips through the cracks. Should the burden of monitoring be on the content right holder or the ISP? Is this not a risk and duty of diligence that every property owner should assume? Is the legislative analysis that holding Google and You-Tube liable under these circumstances constitute a collateral cost for protection of content holder rights that is unreasonable and damaging to development of the internet? Many of these questions raised in the pleadings were addressed along with other issues by the court.

Almost all the issues noted above and raised in questions below were set forth in clear and unequivocal terms by the court. Below the surface, however, are issues that are implicit or included by implication which would digress from the lineal clarity of the decision. A little further probing, however, might be helpful.

NOTES AND QUESTIONS

1. The ISP does not have a duty to monitor. Why didn't the court require Youtube to develop filtering technologies to identify infringing materials? The obligation of filtering was suggested in some of the secondary liability cases, such as *Perfect 10 v. Google* and others involving both peer to peer file sharing and search engines? In this instance, what language of the DMCA was noted and applied by the court to negate the affirmative obligation of Youtube to search for infringing materials?

2. There are two statutory responsible parties necessary for liability. The first applies to the copyright holder, which requires a duly authorized person with appropriate knowledge of the actual infringed copyrighted materials to give notice. The second person is the designee or responsible party of the ISP to whom notice must be served. What if the person who gives notice is not officially designated to do so? Why does that person have to be the dully designated party to give notice? What if the notice is incorrect or incomplete? What if it is given to the wrong person?

3. What if Google/Youtube generates revenue through advertising on Youtube? Does this taint the nature of the activity as it often does in secondary liability regimes outside the DMCA?

4. What evidence in the case indicates whether the inclusion of copyrighted material was the purpose of posting or incidental to these activities? Does this raise fair use or fair/transformative use issues? Could this ever be a relevant factor and, if so, how or why?

5. Is the operation of YouTube, as a mechanism for the publication of individual creative expression, consistent with the purposes of the Constitution and a factor in the decision of the case? Was this noted by the court and if not could it ever be a factor in buttressing the decision? See generally,

Robert I. Reis, The Sony Legacy: Secondary Liability Perspectives, 3 Akron Intellectual Property Journal 224 (2009).

VIACOM INTERNATIONAL INC. v. YOUTUBE, LLC, AND GOOGLE, INC.

United States District Court, S.D. New York, 2010.
___ F.Supp.2d ___, 2010 WL 2532404 (S.D.N.Y.) (Cite as:
2010 WL 2532404 (S.D.N.Y.)) (June 23, 2010).

OPINION AND ORDER

LOUIS L. STANTON, DISTRICT JUDGE.

Defendants move for summary judgment that they are entitled to the Digital Millennium Copyright Act's ("DMCA"), 17 U.S.C. § 512(c), "safe harbor" protection against all of plaintiffs' direct and secondary infringement claims, including claims for "inducement" contributory liability, because they had insufficient notice, under the DMCA, of the particular infringements in suit.

Plaintiffs cross-move for partial summary judgment that defendants are not protected by the statutory "safe harbor" provision, but "are liable for the intentional infringement of thousands of Viacom's copyrighted works, . . . for the vicarious infringement of those works, and for the direct infringement of those works . . . because: (1) Defendants had 'actual knowledge' and were 'aware of facts and circumstances from which infringing activity [was] apparent,' but failed to 'act[ ] expeditiously' to stop it; (2) Defendants 'receive[d] a financial benefit directly attributable to the infringing activity' and 'had the right and ability to control such activity;' and (3) Defendants' infringement does not result solely from providing 'storage at the direction of a user' or any other Internet function specified in section 512." * * *

Resolution of the key legal issue presented on the parties' cross-motions requires examination of the DMCA's "safe harbor" provisions, 17 U.S.C. § 512(c), (m) and (n) which state:

(c) Information residing on systems or networks at direction of users.

(1) In general. A service provider shall not be liable for monetary relief, or, except as provided in subsection (j), for injunctive or other equitable relief, for infringement of copyright by reason of the storage at the direction of a user of material that resides on a system or network controlled or operated by or for the service provider, if the service provider-

(A)(i) does not have actual knowledge that the material or an activity using the material on the system or network is infringing;

(ii) in the absence of such actual knowledge, is not aware of facts or circumstances from which infringing activity is apparent; or

(iii) upon obtaining such knowledge or awareness, acts expeditiously to remove, or disable access to, the material;

(B) does not receive a financial benefit directly attributable to the infringing activity, in a case in which the service provider has the right and ability to control such activity; and

(C) upon notification of claimed infringement as described in paragraph (3), responds expeditiously to remove, or disable access to, the material that is claimed to be infringing or to be the subject of infringing activity.

(2) Designated agent. The limitations on liability established in this subsection apply to a service provider only if the service provider has designated an agent to receive notifications of claimed infringement described in paragraph (3), by making available through its service, including on its website in a location accessible to the public, * * *

(3) Elements of notification.

(A) To be effective under this subsection, a notification of claimed infringement must be a written communication provided to the designated agent of a service provider that includes substantially the following

(i) A physical or electronic signature of a person authorized to act on behalf of the owner of an exclusive right that is allegedly infringed.

(ii) Identification of the copyrighted work claimed to have been infringed, or, if multiple copyrighted works at a single online site are covered by a single notification, a representative list of such works at that site.

(iii) Identification of the material that is claimed to be infringing or to be the subject of infringing activity and that is to be removed or access to which is to be disabled, and information reasonably sufficient to permit the service provider to locate the material.

(iv) Information reasonably sufficient to permit the service provider to contact the complaining party, such as an address, telephone number, and, if available, an electronic mail address at which the complaining party may be contacted.

(v) A statement that the complaining party has a good faith belief that use of the material in the manner complained of is not authorized by the copyright owner, its agent, or the law.

(vi) A statement that the information in the notification is accurate, and under penalty of perjury, that the complaining party is authorized to act on behalf of the owner of an exclusive right that is allegedly infringed.

(B)(i) Subject to clause (ii), a notification from a copyright owner or from a person authorized to act on behalf of the copyright owner that fails to comply substantially with the provisions of subparagraph (A) shall not be considered under paragraph (1)(A) in determining whether a service provider has actual knowledge or is aware of facts or circumstances from which infringing activity is apparent.

(ii) In a case in which the notification that is provided to the service provider's designated agent fails to comply substantially with all the provisions of subparagraph (A) but substantially complies with clauses (ii), (iii), and (iv) of subparagraph (A), clause (i) of this subparagraph applies only if the service provider promptly attempts to contact the person making the notification or takes other reasonable steps to assist in the receipt of notification that substantially complies with all the provisions of subparagraph (A).

* * *

Defendant YouTube, owned by defendant Google, operates a website at http://www.youtube.com onto which users may upload video files free of charge. Uploaded files are copied and formatted by YouTube's computer systems, and then made available for viewing on YouTube. Presently, over 24 hours of new video-viewing time is uploaded to the YouTube website every minute. As a "provider of online services or network access, or the operator of facilities therefor" as defined in 17 U.S.C. § 512(k)(1)(B), YouTube is a service provider for purposes of § 512(c).

From plaintiffs' submissions on the motions, a jury could find that the defendants not only were generally aware of, but welcomed, copyright-infringing material being placed on their website. Such material was attractive to users, whose increased usage enhanced defendants' income from advertisements displayed on certain pages of the website, with no discrimination between infringing and non-infringing content.

Plaintiffs claim that "tens of thousands of videos on YouTube, resulting in hundreds of millions of views, were taken unlawfully from Viacom's copyrighted works without authorization" . . . and that "Defendants had 'actual knowledge' and were 'aware of facts or circumstances from which infringing activity [was] apparent,' but failed to do anything about it." . . . (alteration in original).

However, defendants designated an agent, and when they received specific notice that a particular item infringed a copyright, they swiftly removed it. It is uncontroverted that all the clips in suit are off the YouTube website, most having been removed in response to DMCA takedown notices.

Thus, the critical question is whether the statutory phrases "actual knowledge that the material or an activity using the material on the system or network is infringing," and "facts or circumstances from which infringing activity is apparent" in § 512(c)(1)(A)(i) and (ii) mean a general awareness that there are infringements (here, claimed to be widespread and common), or rather mean actual or constructive knowledge of specific and identifiable infringements of individual items.

1.

Legislative History

The Senate Committee on the Judiciary Report, S.Rep. No. 105–190 (1998), gives the background at page 8:

Due to the ease with which digital works can be copied and distributed worldwide virtually instantaneously, copyright owners will hesitate to make their works readily available on the Internet without reasonable assurance that they will be protected against massive piracy. Legislation implementing the treaties provides this protection and creates the legal platform for launching the global digital on-line marketplace for copyrighted works. It will facilitate making available quickly and conveniently via the Internet the movies, music, software, and literary works that are the fruit of American creative genius. It will also encourage the continued growth of the existing off-line global marketplace for copyrighted works in digital format by setting strong international copyright standards.

At the same time, without clarification of their liability, service providers may hesitate to make the necessary investment in the expansion of the speed and capacity of the Internet. In the ordinary course of their operations service providers must engage in all kinds of acts that expose them to potential copyright infringement liability. For example, service providers must make innumerable electronic copies by simply transmitting information over the Internet. Certain electronic copies are made in order to host World Wide Web sites. Many service providers engage in directing users to sites in response to inquiries by users or they volunteer sites that users may find attractive. Some of these sites might contain infringing material. In short, by limiting the liability of service providers, the DMCA ensures that the efficiency of the Internet will continue to improve and that the variety and quality of services on the Internet will continue to expand.

It elaborates:

There have been several cases relevant to service provider liability for copyright infringement. Most have approached the issue from the standpoint of contributory and vicarious liability. Rather than embarking upon a wholesale clarification of these doctrines, the Committee decided to leave current law in its evolving state and, instead, to create a series of "safe harbors," for certain common activities of service providers. A service provider which qualifies for a safe harbor, receives the benefit of limited liability. * * *

When discussing section 512(d) of the DMCA which deals with information location tools, the Committee Reports contain an instructive explanation of the need for specificity (Senate Report at 48–49, House Report at 57–58):

Like the information storage safe harbor in section 512(c), a service provider would qualify for this safe harbor if, among other requirements, it "does not have actual knowledge that the material or activity is infringing" or, in the absence of such actual knowledge, it is "not aware of facts or circumstances from which infringing activity is apparent." Under this standard, a service provider would have no obligation to seek out copyright infringement, but it would not qualify for the safe harbor if it had turned a blind eye to "red flags" of obvious infringement.

For instance, the copyright owner could show that the provider was aware of facts from which infringing activity was apparent if the copyright owner could prove that the location was clearly, at the time the directory provider viewed it, a "pirate" site of the type described below, where sound recordings, software, movies or books were available for unauthorized downloading, public performance or public display. Absent such "red flags" or actual knowledge, a directory provider would not be similarly aware merely because it saw one or more well known photographs of a celebrity at a site devoted to that person. The provider could not be expected, during the course of its brief cataloguing visit, to determine whether the photograph was still protected by copyright or was in the public domain; if the photograph was still protected by copyright, whether the use was licensed; and if the use was not licensed, whether it was permitted under the fair use doctrine.

The important intended objective of this standard is to exclude sophisticated "pirate" directories-which refer Internet users to other selected Internet sites where pirate software, books, movies, and music can be downloaded or transmitted-from the safe harbor. Such pirate directories refer Internet users to sites that are obviously infringing because they typically use words such as "pirate," "bootleg," or slang terms in their uniform resource locator (URL) and header information to make their illegal purpose obvious to the pirate directories and other Internet users. Because the infringing nature of such sites would be apparent from even a brief and casual viewing, safe harbor status for a provider that views such a site and then establishes a link to it would not be appropriate. Pirate directories do not follow the routine business practices of legitimate service providers preparing directories, and thus evidence that they have viewed the infringing site may be all that is available for copyright owners to rebut their claim to a safe harbor.

In this way, the "red flag" test in section 512(d) strikes the right balance. The common-sense result of this "red flag" test is that online editors and catalogers would not be required to make discriminating judgments about potential copyright infringement. If, however, an Internet site is obviously pirate, then seeing it may be all that is needed for the service provider to encounter a "red flag." A provider proceeding in the face of such a red flag must do so without the benefit of a safe harbor.

Information location tools are essential to the operation of the Internet; without them, users would not be able to find the information they need. Directories are particularly helpful in conducting effective searches by filtering out irrelevant and offensive material. The Yahoo! Directory, for example, currently categorizes over 800,000 online locations and serves as a "card catalogue" to the World Wide Web, which over 35,000,000 different users visit each month. Directories such as Yahoo!'s usually are created by people visiting sites to categorize them. It is precisely the human judgment and editorial discretion exercised by these cataloguers which makes directories valuable.

This provision is intended to promote the development of information location tools generally, and Internet directories such as Yahoo!'s in particular, by establishing a safe-harbor from copyright infringement liability for information location tool providers if they comply with the notice and takedown procedures and other requirements of subsection (d). The knowledge or awareness standard should not be applied in a manner which would create a disincentive to the development of directories which involve human intervention. Absent actual knowledge, awareness of infringement as provided in subsection (d) should typically be imputed to a directory provider only with respect to pirate sites or in similarly obvious and conspicuous circumstances, and not simply because the provider viewed an infringing site during the course of assembling the directory.

The tenor of the foregoing provisions is that the phrases "actual knowledge that the material or an activity" is infringing, and "facts or circumstances" indicating infringing activity, describe knowledge of specific and identifiable infringements of particular individual items. Mere knowledge of prevalence of such activity in general is not enough. That is consistent with an area of the law devoted to protection of distinctive individual works, not of libraries. To let knowledge of a generalized practice of infringement in the industry, or of a proclivity of users to post infringing materials, impose responsibility on service providers to discover which of their users' postings infringe a copyright would contravene the structure and operation of the DMCA. As stated in *Perfect 10, Inc. v. CCBill LLC,* 488 F.3d 1102, 1113 (9th Cir.2007):

The DMCA notification procedures place the burden of policing copyright infringement-identifying the potentially infringing material and adequately documenting infringement-squarely on the owners of the copyright. We decline to shift a substantial burden from the copyright owner to the provider....

That makes sense, as the infringing works in suit may be a small fraction of millions of works posted by others on the service's platform, whose provider cannot by inspection determine whether the use has been licensed by the owner, or whether its posting is a "fair use" of the material, or even whether its copyright owner or licensee objects to its posting. The DMCA is explicit:

it shall not be construed to condition "safe harbor" protection on "a service provider monitoring its service or affirmatively seeking facts indicating infringing activity...." *Id.* § 512(m)(1); see Senate Report at 44, House Report at 53.

Indeed, the present case shows that the DMCA notification regime works efficiently: when Viacom over a period of months accumulated some 100,000 videos and then sent one mass take-down notice on February 2, 2007, by the next business day YouTube had removed virtually all of them.

2.

Case Law

In *CCBill LLC, supra,* the defendants provided web hosting and other services to various websites. The plaintiff argued that defendants had received notice of apparent infringement from circumstances that raised "red flags": websites were named "illegal.net" and "stolencelebritypics.com," and others involved "password-hacking." . . . . As to each ground, the Ninth Circuit disagreed, stating "We do not place the burden of determining whether photographs are actually illegal on a service provider"; and "There is simply no way for a service provider to conclude that the passwords enabled infringement without trying the passwords, and verifying that they enabled illegal access to copyrighted material. We impose no such investigative duties on service providers." *Id.*

The District Court in *UMG Recordings, Inc. v. Veoh Networks, Inc.,* 665 F.Supp.2d 1099, 1108 (C.D.Cal.2009), concluded that "*CCBill* teaches that if investigation of 'facts and circumstances' is required to identify material as infringing, then those facts and circumstances are not 'red flags.' " That observation captures the reason why awareness of pervasive copyright-infringing, however flagrant and blatant, does not impose liability on the service provider. It furnishes at most a statistical estimate of the chance any particular posting is infringing-and that is not a "red flag" marking any particular work.

In *Corbis Corp. v. Amazon.com, Inc.,* 351 F.Supp.2d 1090, 1108 (W.D.Wash.2004) the court stated that "The issue is not whether Amazon had a general awareness that a particular type of item may be easily infringed. The issue is whether Amazon actually knew that specific zShops vendors were selling items that infringed Corbis copyrights." It required a "showing that those sites contained the type of blatant infringing activity that would have sent up a red flag for Amazon." . . . . Other evidence of "red flags" was unavailing, for it "provides no evidence from which to infer that Amazon was aware of, but chose to ignore, red flags of blatant copyright infringement on specific zShops sites."

* * *

Although by a different technique, the DMCA applies the same principle, and its establishment of a safe harbor is clear and practical: if a service provider knows (from notice from the owner, or a "red flag") of specific instances of infringement, the provider must promptly remove the infringing material. If not, the burden is on the owner to identify the: infringement. General knowledge that infringement is "ubiquitous" does not impose a duty on the service provider to monitor or search its service for infringements.

3.

The *Grokster* Case

* * *

Grokster addressed the more general law of contributory liability for copyright infringement, and its application to the particular subset of service providers protected by the DMCA is strained. In a setting of distribution of software products that allowed computer-to-computer exchanges of infringing material, with the expressed intent of succeeding to the business of the notoriously infringing Napster (*see* 545 U.S. at 923–26) the *Grokster* Court held (*id.* at 919, 936–37):

... that one who distributes a device with the object of promoting its use to infringe copyright, as shown by clear expression or other affirmative steps taken to foster infringement, is liable for the resulting acts of infringement by third parties.

On these cross-motions for summary judgment I make no findings of fact as between the parties, but I note that plaintiff Viacom's General Counsel said in a 2006 e-mail that "... the difference between YouTube's behavior and Grokster's is staggering." Ex. 173 to Schapiro Opp. Affid., Dkt. No. 306, Att. 4. Defendants asserted in their brief supporting their motion (Dkt. No. 188, p. 60) and Viacom's response does not controvert (Dkt. No. 296, p. 29, ¶ 1.80) that:

It is not remotely the case that YouTube exists "solely to provide the site and facilities for copyright infringement." ... Even the plaintiffs do not (and could not) suggest as much. Indeed, they have repeatedly acknowledged the contrary.

The *Grokster* model does not comport with that of a service provider who furnishes a platform on which its users post and access all sorts of materials as they wish, while the provider is unaware of its content, but identifies an agent to receive complaints of infringement, and removes identified material when he learns it infringes. To such a provider, the DMCA gives a safe harbor, even if otherwise he would be held as a contributory infringer under the general law. In this case, it is uncontroverted that when YouTube was given the notices, it removed the material. It is thus protected "from liability for all monetary relief for direct, vicarious and contributory infringement" subject to the specific provisions of the DMCA. Senate Report at 40, House Report at 50.

4.

Other Points

(a)

Plaintiffs claim that the replication, transmittal and display of videos on YouTube fall outside the protection § 512(c)(1) of the DMCA gives to "infringement of copyright by reason of the storage at the direction of a user of material" on a service provider's system or network. That confines the word "storage" too narrowly to meet the statute's purpose.

In § 512(k)(1)(B) a "service provider" is defined as "a provider of online services or network access, or the operator of facilities therefor," and includes "an entity offering the transmission, routing, or providing of connections for digital online communications." Surely the provision of such services, access, and operation of facilities are within the safe harbor when they flow from the material's placement on the provider's system or network: it is inconceivable that they are left exposed to be claimed as unprotected infringements. As the Senate Report states (p. 8):

In the ordinary course of their operations service providers must engage in all kinds of acts that expose them to potential copyright infringement liability.... In short, by limiting the liability of service providers, the DMCA ensures that the efficiency of the Internet will continue to improve and that the variety and quality of services on the Internet will continue to expand.

As stated in *Io Group, Inc. v. Veoh Networks, Inc.,* 586 F.Supp.2d 1132, 1148 (N.D.Cal.2008), such "means of facilitating user access to material on its website" do not cost the service provider its safe harbor. *See also UMG Recordings, Inc. v. Veoh Networks, Inc.,* 620 F.Supp.2d 1081, 1089 (C.D.Cal.2008):

Although Veoh correctly observes that the language of § 512(c) is "broad," it does not venture to define its outermost limits. It is unnecessary for this Court to do so either, because the critical statutory language really is pretty clear. Common sense and widespread usage establish that "by reason of" means "as a result of" or "something that can be attributed to...." So understood, when copyrighted content is displayed or distributed on Veoh it is "as a result of" or "attributable to" the fact that users uploaded the content to Veoh's servers to be accessed by other means. If providing access could trigger liability without the possibility of DMCA immunity, service providers would be greatly deterred from performing their basic, vital and salutary function-namely, providing access to information and material for the public.

To the extent defendants' activities go beyond what can fairly be characterized as meeting the above-described collateral scope of "storage" and allied functions, and present the elements of infringements under existing principles of copyright law, they are not facially protected by § 512(c). Such activities simply fall beyond the bounds of the safe harbor and liability for conducting them must be judged according to the general law of copyright infringement. That follows from the language of § 512(c)(1) that "A service provider shall not be liable ... for infringement of copyright by reason of the storage...." However, such instances have no bearing on the coverage of the safe harbor in all other respects.

(b)

The safe harbor requires that the service provider "not receive a financial benefit directly attributable to the infringing activity, in a case in which the service provider has the right and ability to control such activity ..." § 512(c)(1)(B). The "right and ability to control" the activity requires knowledge of it, which must be item-specific. (See Parts 1 and 2 above.) There may be arguments whether revenues from advertising, applied equally to space regardless of whether its contents are or are not infringing, are "directly attributable to" infringements, but in any event the provider must know of the particular case before he can control it. As shown by the discussion in Parts 1 and 2 above, the provider need not monitor or seek out facts indicating such activity. If "red flags" identify infringing material with sufficient particularity, it must be taken down.

(c)

Three minor arguments do not singly or cumulatively affect YouTube's safe harbor coverage.

(1) YouTube has implemented a policy of terminating a user after warnings from YouTube (stimulated by its receipt of DMCA notices) that the user has uploaded infringing matter (a "three strikes" repeat-infringer policy). That YouTube counts as only one strike against a user both (1) a single DMCA takedown notice identifying multiple videos uploaded by the user, and (2) multiple take-down notices identifying videos uploaded by the user received by YouTube within a two-hour period, does not mean that the policy was not "reasonably implemented" as required by § 512(i)(1)(A). In *Corbis Corp. v. Amazon.com, Inc.,* 351 F.Supp.2d 1090, 1105 (W.D.Wash.2004), in evaluating whether Amazon complied with § 512(i), the Court stated that even DMCA-compliant notices "did not, in themselves, provide evidence of blatant copyright infringement." In *UMG Recordings, Inc. v. Veoh Networks, Inc.,* 665 F.Supp.2d 1099, 1116, 1118 (C.D.Cal.2009), the Court upheld Veoh's policy of terminating users after a second warning, even if the first warning resulted from a take-down notice listing multiple infringements. It stated:

As the *Corbis* court noted, "[t]he key term, 'repeat infringer,' is not defined.... The fact that Congress chose not to adopt such specific provisions when defining a user policy indicates its intent to leave the policy requirements, and the subsequent obligations of the service providers, loosely defined." *Corbis,* 351 F.Supp.2d at 1100–01. This Court finds that Veoh's policy satisfies Congress's intent that "those who repeatedly or flagrantly abuse their access to the Internet through disrespect for the intellectual property rights of others should know that there is a realistic threat of losing that access." H.R. Rep. 105–551(II), at 61.

. . .

(2) In its "Claim Your Content" system, YouTube used Audible Magic, a fingerprinting tool which removed an offending video automatically if it matched some portion of a reference video submitted by a copyright owner who had designated this service. It also removed a video if the rights-holder operated a manual function after viewing the infringing video. YouTube assigned strikes only when the rights-holder manually requested the video to be removed. Requiring the rights-holder to take that position does not violate § 512(i)(1)(A). *See UMG Recordings,* 665 F.Supp.2d at 1116–18 (automated Audible Magic filter "does not meet the standard of reliability and verifiability required by the Ninth Circuit in order to justify

terminating a user's account''); *see also Perfect 10, Inc. v. CCBill LLC,* 488 F.3d 1102, 1112 (9th Cir.2007) (''We therefore do not require a service provider to start potentially invasive proceedings if the complainant is unwilling to state under penalty of perjury that he is an authorized representative of the copyright owner, and that he has a good-faith belief that the material is unlicensed.'').

* * *

(3) Plaintiffs complain that YouTube removes only the specific clips identified in DMCA notices, and not other clips which infringe the same works. They point to the provision in § 512(c)(3)(A)(ii) that a notification must include ''Identification of the copyrighted work claimed to have been infringed, or, if multiple copyrighted works at a single online site are covered by a single notification, a representative list of such works at that site.'' This ''representative list'' reference would eviscerate the required specificity of notice (see discussion in Parts 1 and 2 above) if it were construed to mean a merely generic description (''all works by Gershwin'') without also giving the works' locations at the site, and would put the provider to the factual search forbidden by § 512(m). Although the statute states that the ''works'' may be described representatively, 512(c)(3)(A)(ii), the subsection which immediately follows requires that the identification of the infringing material that is to be removed must be accompanied by ''information reasonably sufficient to permit the service provider to locate the material.'' 512(c)(3)(A)(iii). See House Report at 55; Senate Report at 46: ''An example of such sufficient information would be a copy or description of the allegedly infringing material and the so-called ''uniform resource locator'' . . . which allegedly contains the infringing material.'' *See also UMG Recordings,* 665 F.Supp.2d at 1109–10 (DMCA notices which demanded removal of unspecified clips of video recordings by certain artists did not provide '' 'information reasonably sufficient to permit the service provider to locate [such] material.' ''). . . .

4.

Conclusion

Defendants are granted summary judgment that they qualify for the protection of U.S.C. § 512(c), as expounded above, against all of plaintiff's claims for direct and secondary copyright infringement. Plaintiff's motion for judgment are denied. * * *

So ordered.

CHAPTER EIGHT

GLOBAL CONTEXT OF INTELLECTUAL PROPERTY

■ ■ ■

OVERVIEW

The source of intellectual property rights is national law, consisting of statutes enacted by provincial and national legislatures and case law developed by courts. This means that nation states have varied in the scope of protection granted by intellectual property law. Several facts, however, challenge national sovereignty in defining the boundaries of intellectual property.

First, much inventive and creative activity is transnational. Research scientists sometimes work across borders. Book and music publishing are not limited to the borders of a particular state. Broadcasting technologies, starting from the development of radio and continuing, dramatically, with the spread of the Internet, permeate the porous boundaries of the nation state. The issue of how to reconcile sometimes conflicting national law inevitably follows from creative, inventive, and publishing activities that cannot be contained within national borders.

Second, intellectual property is often embodied in the international trade of goods and services. Copyright, patent, and trademark statutes acknowledge international trade by giving the intellectual property owner the right to exclude unauthorized imports of copyrighted, patented, or trademarked material into the nation state. Even if someone copies an original work of authorship or makes a patented invention outside a country's borders, the copyright or patent owner can still prevent the unauthorized work from crossing the borders. Even though the intellectual property owner may be limited in preventing infringement outside the borders, she can still protect her rights at the border through the exclusive right to import. This right highlights two important issues. The first issue is that of extraterritoriality, or the use of national law to reach conduct outside the nation's borders. We will provide a thorough discussion of this issue below and analyze when extraterritorial application of law is allowed. The second issue is that of free trade. The contemporary norm, going back to the development of the General Agreement on Tariffs and Trade (GATT), the precursor to the World Trade Organization (WTO), is one of free movement of goods across borders, a norm consistent with that of market competition. The intellectual property owner's ability to stop infringing goods at the border seems in conflict with this norm. The topic of gray market goods, the very last topic in this chapter, allows exploration of this conflict between the norm of market competition and intellectual property rights.

Third, global diplomacy places limits on the national character of intellectual property law. Countries engage in political interactions that reflect economic, political, and military interests. These interactions are embodied in treaties, which memorialize an agreement on how two or more countries commit to behave. Intellectual property has been an important part of global diplomacy as companies seek to open markets and combat piracy of intellectual property in international markets. Intellectual property is also central to the transfer of know-how and technology to the developing world as part of the spread of economic development and prosperity, which should converge with the spread of democracy and rule of law. Since the nineteenth century, intellectual property has been the subject of many treaties, including the Berne Convention, the Paris Convention, and the Patent Cooperation Treaty. The global debate over intellectual property has arguably culminated in the establishment of two international bodies, the World Intellectual Property Organization (a part of the United Nations) and the World Trade Organization. The World Intellectual Property Organization governs such important treaties as the Berne Convention, the Universal Copyright Convention, the Patent Cooperation Treaty, and the Madrid Protocol. The World Trade Organization, much younger than the World Intellectual Property Organization, governs the Trade Related Intellectual Property Systems Agreement (more commonly known as TRIPS).

International Intellectual Property is a vast subject, deserving of a course of its own. The chapter first addresses cross border issues that arise in United States courts. The focus is on questions of choice of law, choice of forum, and extraterritoriality when the parties to an infringement action in the United States come from different nations. The discussion of cross border issues is divided by field into copyright, patent, and trademark, respectively. The chapter ends with a case [about moral rights and a case] about gray market goods. The problem of gray market goods highlights a gap in the current intellectual property treaty regime. Consequently, the last case provides a bridge between cross border issues and the development of international treaty regimes.

I. CROSS–BORDER ISSUES

A. COPYRIGHT

1. Choice of Law

ITAR–TASS RUSSIAN NEWS AGENCY
v. RUSSIAN KURIER, INC.

United States Court of Appeals for the Second Circuit, 1998.
153 F.3d 82.

JON O. NEWMAN, CIRCUIT JUDGE:

This appeal primarily presents issues concerning the choice of law in international copyright cases and the substantive meaning of Russian copyright law as to the respective rights of newspaper reporters and newspaper publishers. The conflicts issue is which country's law applies to issues of copyright ownership and to issues of infringement. The primary substantive issue under Russian copyright law is whether a newspaper publishing company has an interest sufficient to give it standing to sue for copying the text of individual articles appearing in its newspapers, or whether complaint about such copying may be made only by the reporters who authored the articles. Defendants-appellants Russian Kurier, Inc. ("Kurier") and Oleg Pogrebnoy (collectively "the Kurier defendants") appeal from the March 25, 1997, judgment of the District Court for the Southern District of New York (John G. Koeltl, Judge) enjoining them from copying articles that have appeared or will appear in publications of the plaintiffs-appellees, mainly Russian newspapers and a Russian news agency, and awarding the appellees substantial damages for copyright infringement.

On the conflicts issue, we conclude that, with respect to the Russian plaintiffs, Russian law determines the ownership and essential nature of the copyrights alleged to have been infringed and that United States law determines whether those copyrights have been infringed in the United States and, if so, what remedies are available. We also conclude that Russian law, which explicitly excludes newspapers from a work-for-hire doctrine, vests exclusive ownership interests in newspaper articles in the journalists who wrote the articles, not in the newspaper employers who compile their writings. We further conclude that to the extent that Russian law accords newspaper publishers an interest distinct from the copyright of the newspaper reporters, the publishers' interest, like the usual ownership interest in a compilation, extends to the publishers' original selection and arrangement of the articles, and does not entitle the publishers to damages for copying the texts of articles contained in a newspaper compilation. We therefore reverse the judgment to the extent that it granted the newspapers relief for copying the texts of the articles. However, because one non-newspaper plaintiff-appellee is entitled to some injunctive relief and damages and other plaintiffs-appellees may be entitled to some, perhaps considerable, relief, we also remand for further consideration of this lawsuit.

The lawsuit concerns Kurier, a Russian language weekly newspaper with a circulation in the New York area of about 20,000. It is published in New York City by defendant Kurier. Defendant Pogrebnoy is president and sole shareholder of Kurier and editor-in-chief of Kurier. The plaintiffs include corporations that publish, daily or weekly, major Russian language newspapers in Russia and Russian language magazines in Russia or Israel; Itar–Tass Russian News Agency ("Itar–Tass"), formerly known as the Telegraph Agency of the Soviet Union (TASS), a wire service and news gathering company centered in Moscow, functioning similarly to the Associated Press; and the Union of Journalists of Russia ("UJR"), the professional writers union of accredited print and broadcast journalists of the Russian Federation.

The Kurier defendants do not dispute that Kurier has copied about 500 articles that first appeared in the plaintiffs' publications or were distributed by Itar–Tass. The copied material, though extensive, was a small percentage of the total number of articles published in Kurier. The Kurier defendants also do not dispute how the copying occurred: articles from the plaintiffs' publications, sometimes containing headlines, pictures, bylines, and graphics, in addition to text, were cut out, pasted on layout sheets, and sent to Kurier's printer for photographic reproduction and printing in the pages of Kurier.

Most significantly, the Kurier defendants also do not dispute that, with one exception, they had not obtained permission from any of the plaintiffs to copy the articles that appeared in Kurier. Pogrebnoy claimed at trial to have received permission from the publisher of one newspaper, but his claim was rejected by the District Court at trial. Pogrebnoy also claimed that he had obtained permission from the authors of six of the copied articles. The District Court made no finding as to whether this testimony was credible, since authors' permission was not pertinent to the District Court's view of the legal issues. * * *

Preliminarily, the Court ruled that the request for a preliminary injunction concerned articles published after March 13, 1995, the date that Russia acceded to the Berne Convention. The Court then ruled that the copied works were "Berne Convention work[s]," 17 U.S.C. § 101, and that the plaintiffs' rights were to be determined according to Russian copyright law.

The Court noted that under Russian copyright law authors of newspaper articles retain the copyright in their articles unless there has been a contractual assignment to their employer or some specific provision of law provides that the author's rights vest in the employer. Since the defendants alleged no claim of a contractual assignment, the Court next considered the provision of the 1993 Russian Federation Law on Copyright and Neighboring Rights ("Russian Copyright Law") (World Intellectual

Property Organization (WIPO) translation) concerning what the United States Copyrights Act calls "works made for hire," 17 U.S.C. § 201(b). That provision gives employers the exclusive right to "exploit" the "service-related work" produced by employees in the scope of their employment, absent some contractual arrangement. However, the Court noted, Article 14(4) specifies that subsection 2 does not apply to various categories of works, including newspapers. Accepting the view of plaintiffs' expert, Professor Vratislav Pechota, Judge Koeltl therefore ruled that the Russian version of the work-for-hire doctrine in Article 14(2), though exempting newspapers, applies to press agencies, like Itar–Tass.

Turning to the rights of the newspapers, Judge Koeltl relied on Article 11, captioned "Copyright of Compiler of Collections and Other Works." This Article contains two subsections. Article 11(1) specifies the rights of compilers generally:

> The author of a collection or any other composite work (compiler) shall enjoy copyright in the selection or arrangement of subject matter that he has made insofar as that selection or arrangement is the result of a creative effort of compilation.

> The compiler shall enjoy copyright subject to respect for the rights of the authors of each work included in the composite work.

> Each of the authors of the works included in the composite work shall have the right to exploit his own work independently of the composite work unless the author's contract provides otherwise....

Russian Copyright Law, Art. 11(1). Article 11(2), the interpretation of which is critical to this appeal, specifies the rights of compilers of those works that are excluded from the work-for-hire provision of Article 14(2):

> The exclusive right to exploit encyclopedias, encyclopedic dictionaries, collections of scientific works—published in either one or several installments—newspapers, reviews and other periodical publications shall belong to the editor thereof. The editor shall have the right to mention his name or to demand such mention whenever the said publications are exploited.

The authors of the works included in the said publications shall retain the exclusive rights to exploit their works independently of the publication of the whole work.

In another translation of the Russian Copyright Law, which was in evidence at the trial, the last phrase of Article 11(2) was rendered "independently from the publication as a whole." Because the parties' experts focused on the phrase "as a whole" in the Davis translation of Article 11(2), we will rely on the Davis translation for the rendering of this key phrase of Article 11(2), but all other references to the Russian Copyright Law will be to the WIPO translation.

The District Court acknowledged, as the plaintiffs' expert had stated, that considerable scholarly debate existed in Russia as to the nature of a publisher's right "in a work as a whole." Judge Koeltl accepted Professor

Pechota's view that the newspaper could prevent infringing activity "sufficient to interfere with the publisher's interest in the integrity of the work." Without endeavoring to determine what extent of copying would "interfere with" the "integrity of the work," Judge Koeltl concluded that a preliminary injunction was warranted because what Kurier had copied was "the creative effort of the newspapers in the compilation of articles including numerous articles for the same issues, together with headlines and photographs." The Court's preliminary injunction opinion left it unclear whether at trial the plaintiffs could obtain damages only for copying the newspapers' creative efforts as a compiler, such as the selection and arrangement of articles, the creation of headlines, and the layout of text and graphics, or also for copying the text of individual articles.

At trial, this unresolved issue was the focus of conflicting expert testimony. The plaintiffs' expert witness at trial was Michael Newcity, coordinator for the Center for Slavic, Eurasian and East European Studies at Duke University and an adjunct member of the faculty at the Duke University Law School. He opined that Article 11(2) gave the newspapers rights to redress copying not only of the publication "as a whole," but also of individual articles. He acknowledged that the reporters retained copyrights in the articles that they authored, but stated that Article 11(2) created a regime of parallel exclusive rights in both the newspaper publisher and the reporter. He rejected the contention that exclusive rights could not exist in two parties, pointing out that co-authors share exclusive rights to their joint work.

Newcity offered two considerations in support of his position. First, he cited the predecessor of Article 11(2), Article 485 of the Russian Civil Code of 1964. That provision was similar to Article 11(2), with one change that became the subject of major disagreement among the expert witnesses. Article 485 had given compilers, including newspaper publishers, the right to exploit their works "as a whole." The 1993 revision deleted "as a whole" from the first paragraph of the predecessor of Article 11(2), where it had modified the scope of the compiler's right, and moved the phrase to the second paragraph of revised Article 11(2), where it modifies the reserved right of the authors of articles within a compilation to exploit their works "independently of the publication as a whole."

Though Newcity opined that even under Article 485, reprinting of "one or two or three, at most," articles from a newspaper would have constituted infringement of the copyright "as a whole," he rested his reading of Article 11(2) significantly on the fact that the 1993 revision dropped the phrase "as a whole" from the paragraph that specified the publisher's right. This deletion, he contended, eliminated whatever ambiguity might have existed in the first paragraph of Article 485.

Second, Newcity referred to an opinion of the Judicial Chamber for Informational Disputes of the President of the Russian Federation ("Informational Disputes Chamber"), issued on June 8, 1995. That opinion had been sought by the editor-in-chief of one of the plaintiffs in this litigation, Moskovskie Novosti (Moscow News), who specifically called the tribunal's attention to the pending litigation between Russian media organizations and the publisher of Kurier. The Informational Disputes Chamber stated, in response to one of the questions put to it, "In the event of a violation of its rights, including the improper printing of one or two articles, the publisher [of a newspaper] has the right to petition a court for defense of its rights."

Defendants' experts presented a very different view of the rights of newspapers. Professor Peter B. Maggs of the University of Illinois, Urbana–Champaign, College of Law, testifying by deposition, pointed out that Article 11(2) gives authors the exclusive rights to their articles and accords newspaper publishers only the "exclusive rights to the publication as a whole, because that's the only thing not reserved to the authors." He opined that a newspaper's right to use of the compiled work "as a whole" would be infringed by the copying of an entire issue of a newspaper and probably by copying a substantial part of one issue, but not by the copying of a few articles, since the copyright in the articles belongs to the reporters. He also disagreed with Newcity's contention that exclusive rights to individual articles belonged simultaneously to both the newspaper and the reporter. Exclusive rights, he maintained, cannot be held by two people, except in the case of co-authors, who have jointly held rights against the world.

The defendants' first expert witness at trial was Michael Solton, who has worked in Moscow and Washington as an associate of the Steptoe & Johnson law firm. Under Article 11, he testified, authors retain exclusive rights to their articles in compilations, the compiler acquires a copyright in the selection and creative arrangement of materials in the compilation, and a newspaper publisher typically acquires the limited rights of the compiler by assignment from the compiler. The publisher, he said, does not acquire any rights to the individual articles. Solton declined to attach any significance to the decision issued by the Informational Disputes Chamber because, he explained, the bylaws of that body accord it authority only over limited matters concerning the mass media and explicitly preclude it from adjudicating matters that Russian law refers to courts of the Russian Federation, such as copyright law.

The defendants' second expert trial witness was Svetlana Rozina, a partner of the Lex International law firm, who has consulted for the Russian government. She wrote the first draft of what became the 1993 revision of the Russian Copyright Law. She also testified that authors of works in compilations retain the exclusive right to their works, and that publishers of compilations do not have any rights to individual articles. Turning to the change in the placement of the phrase "as a whole" from Article 11(1) to Article 11(2), she explained that no substantive change was intended; the shift was made "[f]or the purpose of Russian grammar." She also agreed with Solton that the Informational Disputes Chamber renders advice on matters concerning freedom of mass information and lacks the competence to adjudicate issues of copyright law.

The District Court resolved the dispute among the experts by accepting Newcity's interpretation of Russian copyright law.... Judge Koeltl recognized that newspapers acquire no rights to individual articles by virtue of Article 14 since the Russian version of the work-for-hire doctrine is inapplicable to newspapers. Nevertheless, Judge Koeltl accepted Newcity's view of Article 11, relying on both the movement of the phrase "as a whole" from the first paragraph of Article 11(2) to the second paragraph of Article 11(2), and the opinion of the Informational Disputes Chamber. He also reasoned that publishers have "the real economic incentive to prevent wholesale unauthorized copying," and that, in the absence of assignments of rights to individual articles, widespread copying would occur if publishers could not prevent Kurier's infringements.

I. Choice of Law

The threshold issue concerns the choice of law for resolution of this dispute. That issue was not initially considered by the parties, all of whom turned directly to Russian law for resolution of the case. Believing that the conflicts issue merited consideration, we requested supplemental briefs from the parties and appointed Professor William F. Patry as Amicus Curiae. Prof. Patry has submitted an extremely helpful brief on the choice of law issue.

Choice of law issues in international copyright cases have been largely ignored in the reported decisions and dealt with rather cursorily by most commentators. Examples pertinent to the pending appeal are those decisions involving a work created by the employee of a foreign corporation. Several courts have applied the United States work-for-hire doctrine, see 17 U.S.C. § 201(b), without explicit consideration of the conflicts issue.

The Nimmer treatise briefly (and perhaps optimistically) suggests that conflicts issues "have rarely proved troublesome in the law of copyright." Nimmer on Copyright § 17.05 (1998) ("Nimmer") (footnote omitted). Relying on the "national treatment" principle of the Berne Convention and the Universal Copyright Convention ("U.C.C."), Nimmer asserts, correctly in our view, that "an author who is a national of one of the member states of either Berne or the U.C.C., or one who first publishes his work in any such member state, is entitled to the same copyright protection in each other member state as such other state accords to its own nationals." Nimmer then somewhat overstates the national treatment principle: "The applicable law is the copyright law of the state in which the infringement occurred, not that of the state of which the author is a national, or in which the work is first published." The difficulty with this broad statement is that it subsumes under the phrase "applicable law" the law concerning two distinct issues—ownership and substantive rights, i.e., scope of protection. Another commentator has also broadly stated the principle of national treatment, but described its application in a way that does not necessarily cover issues of ownership. "The principle of national treatment also means that both the question of whether the right exists and the question of the scope of the right are to be answered in accordance with the law of the country where the protection is claimed." S.M. Stewart, International Copyright and Neighboring Rights § 3.17 (2d ed. 1989). We agree with the view of the Amicus that the Convention's principle of national treatment simply assures that if the law of the country of infringement applies to the scope of substantive copyright protection, that law will be applied uniformly to foreign and domestic authors. See *Murray v. British Broadcasting Corp.*, 906 F.Supp. 858 (S.D.N.Y. 1995), aff'd, 81 F.3d 287 (1996).

Source of conflicts rules. Our analysis of the conflicts issue begins with consideration of the source of law for selecting a conflicts rule. Though Nimmer turns directly to the Berne Convention and the U.C.C., we think that step moves too quickly past the Berne Convention Implementation Act of 1988, Pub. L. 100–568, 102 Stat. 2853, 17 U.S.C. § 101 note. Section 4(a)(3) of the Act amends Title 17 to provide: "No right or interest in a work eligible for protection under this title may be claimed by virtue of . . . the provisions of the Berne Convention. . . . Any rights in a work eligible for protection under this title that derive from this title . . . shall not be expanded or reduced by virtue of . . . the provisions of the Berne Convention." 17 U.S.C. § 104(c).

We start our analysis with the Copyrights Act itself, which contains no provision relevant to the pending case concerning conflicts issues. We therefore fill the interstices of the Act by developing federal common law on the conflicts issue.

This provision could be interpreted to be an example of the general conflicts approach we take in this opinion to copyright ownership issues, or an exception to some different approach. See Jane C. Ginsburg, *Ownership of Electronic Rights and the Private International Law of Copyright*, 22 COLUM.-VLA J.L. & ARTS 165, 171 (1998). We agree with Prof. Ginsburg and with the amicus, Prof. Patry, that section 104A(b) should not be understood to state an exception to any otherwise applicable conflicts rule. See Ginsburg, id.

The choice of law applicable to the pending case is not necessarily the same for all issues. See Restatement (Second) of Conflict of Laws § 222 ("The courts have long recognized that they are not bound to decide all issues under the local law of a single state."). We consider first the law applicable to the issue of copyright ownership.

Conflicts rule for issues of ownership. Copyright is a form of property, and the usual rule is that the interests of the parties in property are determined by the law of the state with "the most significant relationship" to the property and the parties. See id. The Restatement recognizes the applicability of this principle to intangibles such as "a literary idea." Id. Since the works at issue were created by Russian nationals and first published in Russia, Russian law is the appropriate source of law to determine issues of ownership of rights. That is the well-reasoned conclusion of the Amicus Curiae, Prof. Patry, and the parties in their supplemental briefs are in agreement on this point. In terms of the United States Copyrights Act and its reference to the Berne Convention, Russia is the "country of origin" of these works, see 17 U.S.C. § 101 (definition of "country of origin" of Berne Convention work); Berne Convention, Art. 5(4), although "country of origin" might not always be the appropriate country for purposes of choice of law concerning ownership.

To whatever extent we look to the Berne Convention itself as guidance in the development of federal common law on the conflicts issue, we find nothing to alter our conclusion. The Convention does not purport to settle issues of ownership, with one exception not relevant to this case. See Jane C. Ginsburg, *Ownership of Electronic Rights and the Private International Law of Copyright*, 22 COLUM.-VLA J.L. & ARTS 165, 167–68 (1998) (The Berne Convention "provides that the law of the country where protection is claimed defines what rights are protected, the scope of the protection, and the available remedies; the treaty does not supply a choice of law rule for determining ownership.").

Selection of Russian law to determine copyright ownership is, however, subject to one procedural qualification. Under United States law, an owner (including one determined according to foreign law) may sue for infringement in a United States court only if it meets the standing test of 17 U.S.C. § 501(b), which accords standing only to the legal or beneficial owner of an "exclusive right."

Conflicts rule for infringement issues. On infringement issues, the governing conflicts principle is usually lex loci delicti, the doctrine generally applicable to torts. We have implicitly adopted that approach to infringement claims, applying United States copyright law to a work that was unprotected in its country of origin. In the pending case, the place of the tort is plainly the United States. To whatever extent lex loci delicti is to be considered only one part of a broader "interest" approach, United States law would still apply to infringement issues, since not only is this country the place of the tort, but also the defendant is a United States corporation.

The division of issues, for conflicts purposes, between ownership and infringement issues will not always be as easily made as the above discussion implies. If the issue is the relatively straightforward one of which of two contending parties owns a copyright, the issue is unquestionably an ownership issue, and the law of the country with the closest relationship to the work will apply to settle the ownership dispute. But in some cases, including the pending one, the issue is not simply who owns the copyright but also what is the nature of the ownership interest. Yet as a court considers the nature of an ownership interest, there is some risk that it will too readily shift the inquiry over to the issue of whether an alleged copy has infringed the asserted copyright. Whether a copy infringes depends in part on the scope of the interest of the copyright owner. Nevertheless, though the issues are related, the nature of a copyright interest is an issue distinct from the issue of whether the copyright has been infringed. The pending case is one that requires consideration not simply of who owns an interest, but, as to the newspapers, the nature of the interest that is owned.

II.   Determination of Ownership Rights Under Russian Law

Since United States law permits suit only by owners of "an exclusive right under a copyright," 17 U.S.C. § 501(b), we must first determine whether any of the plaintiffs own an exclusive right. That issue of ownership, as we have indicated, is to be determined by Russian law.

Determination of a foreign country's law is an issue of law. See Fed.R.Civ.P. 44.1. Even though the District Court heard live testimony from experts from both sides, that Court's opportunity to assess the witnesses' demeanor provides no basis for a reviewing court to defer to the trier's ruling on the content of foreign law. In cases of this sort, it is not the credibility of the experts that is at issue, it is the persuasive force of the opinions they expressed.

Under Article 14 of the Russian Copyright Law, Itar–Tass is the owner of the copyright interests in the articles written by its employees. However, Article 14(4) excludes newspapers from the Russian version of the work-for-hire doctrine. The newspaper plaintiffs, therefore, must locate their ownership rights, if any, in some other source of law. They rely on Article 11. The District Court upheld their position, apparently recognizing in the newspaper publishers "exclusive" rights to the articles, even though, by virtue of Article 11(2), the reporters also retained "exclusive" rights to these articles.

Having considered all of the views presented by the expert witnesses, we conclude that the defendants' experts are far more persuasive as to the meaning of Article 11. In the first place, once Article 14 of the Russian Copyright Law explicitly denies newspapers the benefit of a work-for-hire doctrine, which, if available, would accord them rights to individual articles written by their employees, it is highly unlikely that Article 11 would confer on newspapers the very right that Article 14 has denied them. Moreover, Article 11 has an entirely reasonable scope if confined, as its caption suggests, to defining the "Copyright of Compilers of Collections and Other Works." That article accords compilers copyright "in the selection and arrangement of subject matter that he has made insofar as that selection or arrangement is the result of a creative effort of compilation." Russian Copyright Law, Art. 11(1). Article 11(2) accords a publisher of compilations the right to exploit such works, including the right to insist on having their names mentioned, while expressly reserving to "authors of the works included" in compilations the "exclusive rights to exploit their works independently of the publication of the whole work." As the defendants' experts testified, Article 11 lets authors of newspaper articles sue for infringement of their rights in the text of their articles, and lets newspaper publishers sue for wholesale copying of all of the newspaper or for copying any portions of the newspaper that embody their selection, arrangement, and presentation of articles (including head-lines)—copying that infringes their ownership interest in the compilation. * * *

Our disagreement with the District Court's interpretation of Article 11 does not mean, however, that the defendants may continue copying with impunity. In the first place, Itar–Tass, as a press agency, is within the scope of Article 14, and, unlike the excluded newspapers, enjoys the benefit of the Russian version of the work-for-hire doctrine. Itar–Tass is therefore entitled to injunctive relief to prevent unauthorized copying of its articles and to damages for such copying, and the judgment is affirmed as to this plaintiff.

Furthermore, the newspaper plaintiffs, though not entitled to relief for the copying of the text of the articles they published, may well be entitled to injunctive relief and damages if they can show that Kurier infringed the publishers' ownership interests in the newspaper compila-tions. Because the District Court upheld the newspapers' right to relief for copying the text of the articles, it had no occasion to consider what relief the newspapers might be entitled to by reason of Kurier's copying of the newspapers' creative efforts in the selection, arrangement, or display of the articles. Since Kurier's photocopying reproduced not only the text of articles but also headlines and graphic materials as they originally ap-peared in the plaintiffs' publication, it is likely that on remand the newspaper plaintiffs will be able to obtain some form of injunctive relief and some damages. On these infringement issues, as we have indicated, United States law will apply. * * *

[T]here remains for consideration what relief, if any, might be award-ed to UJR, acting on behalf of any of its members whose articles have been copied. In its opinion granting the newspapers a preliminary injunc-tion, the District Court noted that the plaintiffs had not "established the union's organizational standing to sue to enforce the rights of its mem-bers," an issue the Court expected would be considered later in the lawsuit. In its ruling on the merits, the District Court ruled that the UJR had standing to sue on behalf of its members. However, the Court noted that UJR sought only injunctive relief and then ruled that since UJR declined to furnish a list of its members, the Court was unable to frame an injunction that would be narrowly tailored and sufficient to give the defendants notice of its scope.

THE BRIDGEMAN ART LIBRARY, LTD. v. COREL CORPORATION

United States District Court, S.D. New York, 1999.
36 F. Supp. 2d 191.

KAPLAN, DISTRICT JUDGE.

On November 13, 1998, this Court granted defendant's motion for summary judgment dismissing plaintiff's copyright infringement claim on the alternative grounds that the allegedly infringed works—color transparencies of paintings which themselves are in the public domain—were not original and therefore not permissible subjects of valid copyright and, in any case, were not infringed. It applied United Kingdom law in determining whether plaintiff's transparencies were copyrightable. The Court noted, however, that it would have reached the same result under United States law.

Following the entry of final judgment, the Court was bombarded with additional submissions. On November 23, 1998, plaintiff moved for reargument and reconsideration, arguing that the Court erred on the issue of originality. It asserted that the Court had ignored the Register of Copyright's issuance of a certificate of registration for one of plaintiff's transparencies, which it takes as establishing copyrightability, and that the Court had misconstrued British copyright law in that it failed to follow Graves' Case, L.R. 4 Q.B. 715 (1869), which was decided in the Court of Queens Bench in 1869. At about the same time, the Court received an unsolicited letter from Professor William Patry, author of a copyright law treatise, which argued that the Court erred in applying the law of the United Kingdom to the issue of copyrightability. Plaintiff then moved for an order permitting the filing of an amicus brief by one of its associates, The Wallace Collection, to address the United Kingdom law issue. The Court granted leave for the submission of the amicus brief and invited the parties to respond to Professor Patry's letter. The matter now is ripe for decision.

Choice of Law

Professor Patry argues principally that there can be no choice of law issue with respect to copyrightability because the Copyright Clause of the Constitution permits Congress to enact legislation protecting only original works of authorship. In consequence, he contends, only original works, with originality determined in accordance with the meaning of the Copyright Clause, are susceptible of protection in United States courts.

Of course, the ability of Congress to extend the protection of copyright is limited by the Copyright Clause. Nevertheless, the constitutional issue is not as straightforward as Professor Patry suggests. Bridgeman claims that the infringed works are protected by United Kingdom copyrights and that the United States, by acceding to the Convention for the Protection of Literary and Artistic Works, popularly known as the Berne Convention, and the Universal Copyright Convention and by enacting the Berne Convention Implementation Act of 1988 (the "BCIA"), agreed to give effect to its United Kingdom copyrights.

The fact that plaintiff's rights allegedly derive from its claimed British copyrights arguably is material. Granting Professor Patry's point that Congress, in light of the originality requirement of the Copyright Clause, in ordinary circumstances may not extend copyright protection to works that are not original, the questions remain whether (1) the United States constitutionally may obligate itself by treaty to permit enforcement of a foreign copyright where that copyright originates under the law of a signatory nation which does not limit copyright protection to works that are original in the sense required by the United States Constitution and, if so, (2) the United States in fact has done so. Thus, Professor Patry's contention that the United States may not apply foreign law less restrictive than its own with respect to originality may be too narrow because it rests exclusively on the Copyright Clause. The legal effect and constitutionality of treaties also is implicated.

Article II, Section 2, of the Constitution provides that the President "shall have Power, by and with the Advice and Consent of the Senate, to make Treaties, provided two thirds of the Senators present concur." Treaties, by virtue of the Supremacy Clause, join the Constitution and federal statutes as "supreme law of the land." . . . And while it now is clear that the treaty power is "subject to the constitutional limitations that apply to all exercises of federal power, principally the prohibitions of the Bill of Rights," the treaty power retains considerable scope.

The Copyright Clause and the Copyright Act both recognize that the United States has an important interest in protecting the intellectual property of its citizens and of those whose creative efforts enrich our lives. In this increasingly interconnected world, securing appropriate protection abroad also is important. Hence, it cannot seriously be denied that international copyright protection is "properly the subject of negotiation with" foreign countries.

Decades ago, the Supreme Court held in *Missouri v. Holland* [252 U.S. 416 (1920)] that Congress could enact legislation necessary and proper to the implementation of a treaty which, absent the treaty, would have been beyond its powers. Although the case arose in a different context, it suggests that the Conventions, if their purported effect actually is to permit enforcement in the United States of foreign copyrights which do not meet U.S. standards of originality—in other words, if they require enforcement here of any copyright valid under the law of the signatory nation in which copyright attached, even if that copyright does not meet U.S. standards of validity—would not be obviously invalid.

In view of these considerations, the proposition advanced by Professor Patry—that the Copyright Clause forecloses any choice of law issue with respect to the validity of a foreign Berne Convention work, is not free from doubt. It is necessary to decide that question, however, only if the Conventions require application of foreign law in determining the existence of copyright and, if so, whether there is any true conflict of law in this case on that point.

In most circumstances, choice of law issues do not arise under the Berne and Universal Copyright Conventions. Each adopts a rule of national treatment. Article 5 of the Berne Convention, for example, provides that "[a]uthors shall enjoy, in respect of works for which they are protected under this Convention, in countries of the Union other than the country of origin, the rights which their respective laws do now or may hereafter grant to their nationals, as well as the rights specially granted by this convention" and that "the extent of protection, as well as the means of redress afforded to the author to protect his rights, shall be governed exclusively by the laws of the country where protection is claimed." Hence, the Conventions make clear that the holder of, for example, a British copyright who sues for infringement in a United States court is entitled to the same remedies as holders of United States copyrights and, as this Court previously held, to the determination of infringement under the same rule of law.

While the nature of the protection accorded to foreign copyrights in signatory countries thus is spelled out in the Conventions, the position of the subject matter of copyright thereunder is less certain. Do the Conventions purport to require signatory nations to extend national treatment with respect to such enforcement-related subjects as remedies for infringement only where the copyright for which protection is sought would be valid under the law of the nation in which enforcement is sought? Or do they purport to require also that a signatory nation in which enforcement is sought enforce a foreign copyright even if that copyright would not be valid under its own law? But there is an even more fundamental issue, viz. whether United States courts may give effect to any provisions of the Conventions which might require or suggest that the existence of copyright be determined under the law of another nation.

Although the Supreme Court has not yet decided the point, it seems quite clear at this point that the Berne Convention is not self-executing. Section 3(a) of the BCIA confirms this view, stating that:

"The provisions of the Berne Convention—

"(1) shall be given effect under title 17, as amended by this Act, and any other relevant provision of Federal or State law, including the common law, and

"(2) shall not be enforceable in any action brought pursuant to the provisions of the Berne Convention itself."

Section 4(c), now codified at 17 U.S.C. § 104(c), states in relevant part that "[n]o right or interest in a work eligible for protection under this title may be claimed by virtue of, or in reliance upon, the provisions of the Berne Convention or the adherence of the United States thereto." Thus, while the Copyright Act, as amended by the BCIA, extends certain protection to the holders of copyright in Berne Convention works as there defined, the Copyright Act is the exclusive source of that protection.

The statutory basis of the protection of published Berne Convention works such as the photographs here at issue is Section 104(b), which states in relevant part that:

"The works specified by sections 102 and 103, when published, are subject to protection under this title if—* * *(4) the work is a Berne Convention work ... 17 U.S.C. § 104(b).

Section 102(a) limits copyright protection in relevant part to "original works of authorship. . . ." Accordingly, there is no need to decide whether the Berne Convention adopts any rule regarding the law governing copyrightability or whether the treaty power constitutionally might be used to extend copyright protection to foreign works which are not "original" within the meaning of the Copyright Clause. Congress has made it quite clear that the United States' adherence to the Berne Convention has no such effect in the courts of this country. And while there is no comparable legislation with respect to the Universal Copyright Convention, the question whether that treaty is self-executing is of no real significance here because the substantive provisions of the UCC are "of very limited practical import . . . ."

Originality and Copyrightability

United States Law

The Court's prior opinion indicated that plaintiff's exact photographic copies of public domain works of art would not be copyrightable under United States law because they are not original. In view of the Court's conclusion here that U.S. law governs on this issue, it is appropriate to give a somewhat fuller statement of the Court's reasoning.

As the Nimmers have written, there "appear to be at least two situations in which a photograph should be denied copyright for lack of originality," one of which is directly relevant here: "where a photograph of a photograph or other printed matter is made that amounts to nothing more than slavish copying." The authors thus conclude that a slavish photographic copy of a painting would lack originality, although they suggest the possibility that protection in such a case might be claimed as a "reproduction of a work of art." But they immediately go on to point out that this suggestion is at odds with the Second Circuit's in banc decision in *L. Batlin & Son, Inc. v. Snyder*, 536 F.2d 486 (2d Cir. 1976).

Batlin involved the defendants' claim to copyright in a plastic reproduction, with minor variations, of a mechanical cast-iron coin bank that had been sold in the United States for many years and that had passed into the public domain. The Court of Appeals affirmed a district court order compelling the defendants to cancel a recordation of copyright in the plastic reproduction on the ground that the reproduction was not "original" within the meaning of the 1909 Copyright Act, holding that the requirement of originality applies to reproductions of works of art. Only "a distinguishable variation"—something beyond technical skill—will render the reproduction original. . . . The requisite "distinguishable variation," moreover, is not supplied by a change of medium, as "production of a work of art in a different medium cannot by itself constitute the originality required for copyright protection."

There is little doubt that many photographs, probably the overwhelming majority, reflect at least the modest amount of originality required for copyright protection. "Elements of originality . . . may include posing the subjects, lighting, angle, selection of film and camera, evoking the desired expression, and almost any other variant involved." But "slavish copying," although doubtless requiring technical skill and effort, does not qualify.... It therefore is not entirely surprising that an attorney for the Museum of Modern Art, an entity with interests comparable to plaintiff's and its clients, not long ago presented a paper acknowledging that a photograph of a two-dimensional public domain work of art "might not have enough originality to be eligible for its own copyright." Beverly Wolff, Copyright, in ALI–ABA Course of Study; Legal Problems of Museum Administration, C989 ALI–ABA 27, at *48 (available on Westlaw). See also Lynne A. Greenburg, *The Art of Appropriation: Puppies, Piracy, and Post–Modernism*, 11 CARDOZO ARTS & ENT. L.J. 1, 20–21 (1992) (photographic copies of original art photographs taken by the famous photographer, Edward Weston, which were made to "deconstruct the myth of the masterpiece" not copyrightable).

In this case, plaintiff by its own admission has labored to create "slavish copies" of public domain works of art. While it may be assumed that this required both skill and effort, there was no spark of originality— indeed, the point of the exercise was to reproduce the underlying works with absolute fidelity. Copyright is not available in these circumstances.

United Kingdom Law

While the Court's conclusion as to the law governing copyrightability renders the point moot, the Court is persuaded that plaintiff's copyright claim would fail even if the governing law were that of the United Kingdom.

Plaintiff's attack on the Court's previous conclusion that its color transparencies are not original and therefore not copyrightable under British law depends primarily on its claim that the Court failed to apply Graves' Case, a nisi prius decision and the supposedly controlling authority that plaintiff did not even cite in its opposition to defendant's motion for summary judgment.

Graves' Case in relevant part involved an application to cancel entries on the no longer extant Register of Proprietors of Copyright in Paintings, Drawings and Photographs for three photographs of engravings. In rejecting the contention that the photographs were not copyrightable because they were copies of the engravings, Justice Blackburn wrote:

> The distinction between an original painting and its copy is well understood, but it is difficult to say what can be meant by an original photograph. All photographs are copies of some object, such as a painting or statute. And it seems to me that a photograph taken from a picture is an original photograph, in so far that to copy it is an infringement of the statute." L.R. 4 Q.B. at 722.

Plaintiff and the amicus therefore argue that plaintiff's photographs of public domain paintings are copyrightable under British law. But they overlook the antiquity of *Graves' Case* and the subsequent development of the law of originality in the United Kingdom.

Laddie, a modern British copyright treatise the author of which now is a distinguished British judge, discusses the issue at Bar in a helpful manner:

"It is obvious that although a man may get a copyright by taking a photograph of some well-known object like Westminster Abbey, he does not get a monopoly in representing Westminister Abbey as such, any more than an artist would who painted or drew that building. What, then, is the scope of photographic copyright? As always with artistic works, this depends on what makes his photograph original. Under the 1988 Act the author is the person who made the original contribution and it will be evident that this person need not be he who pressed the trigger, who might be a mere assistant. Originality presupposes the exercise of substantial independent skill, labour, judgment and so forth. For this reason it is submitted that a person who makes a photograph merely by placing a drawing or painting on the glass of a photocopying machine and pressing the button gets no copyright at all; but he might get a copyright if he employed skill and labour in assembling the thing to be photocopied, as where he made a montage. It will be evident that in photography there is room for originality in three respects. First, there may be originality which does not depend on creation of the scene or object to be photographed or anything remarkable about its capture, and which resides in such specialties as angle of shot, light and shade, exposure, effects achieved by means of filters, developing techniques etc.: in such manner does one photograph of Westminster Abbey differ from another, at least potentially. Secondly, there may be creation of the scene or subject to be photographed. We have already mentioned photo-montage, but a more common instance would be arrangement or posing of a group ... Thirdly, a person may create a worthwhile photograph by being at the right place at the right time. Here his merit consists of capturing and recording a scene unlikely to recur, e.g. a battle between an elephant and a tiger ..."

Moreover, the authors go on to question the continued authority of *Graves' Case* under just this analysis:

It is submitted that *Graves' Case* (1869) LR 4 QB 715 (photograph of an engraving), a case under the Fine Arts Copyright Act 1862, does not decide the contrary, since there may have been special skill or labour in setting up the equipment to get a good photograph, especially with the rather primitive materials available in those days. Although the judgments do not discuss this aspect it may have been self-evident to any contemporary so as not to require any discussion. If this is wrong it is submitted that *Graves' Case* is no longer good law and in that case is to be explained as a decision made before the subject of originality had been fully developed by the courts. [Author's note: Citation omitted.]

This analysis is quite pertinent in this case. Most photographs are "original" in one if not more of the three respects set out in the treatise and therefore are copyrightable. Plaintiff's problem here is that it seeks protection for the exception that proves the rule: photographs of existing two-dimensional articles (in this case works of art), each of which reproduces the article in the photographic medium as precisely as technology permits. Its transparencies stand in the same relation to the original works of art as a photocopy stands to a page of typescript, a doodle, or a Michelangelo drawing.

Plaintiff nevertheless argues that the photocopier analogy is inapt because taking a photograph requires greater skill than making a photocopy and because these transparencies involved a change in medium. But the argument is as unpersuasive under British as under U.S. law.

The allegedly greater skill required to make an exact photographic, as opposed to Xerographic or comparable, copy is immaterial.... [T]he authors implicitly recognize that a change of medium alone is not sufficient to render the product original and copyrightable. Rather, a copy in a new medium is copyrightable only where, as often but not always is the case, the copier makes some identifiable original contribution

Here, as the Court noted in its earlier opinion, "[i]t is uncontested that Bridgeman's images are substantially exact reproductions of public domain works, albeit in a different medium." There has been no suggestion that they vary significantly from the underlying works. In consequence, the change of medium is immaterial.

Lady Bridgeman, plaintiff's principal, testified that the goal of the transparencies is to be as true to the original work as possible. The color bars (referred to in the prior opinion) are employed to make sure that "the transparency is a genuine reflection of the colors" of the original works of art. Plaintiff has argued "that in creating the transparencies ..., Bridgeman strives to make the transparency look as identical to the underlying work of art as possible ...."

Finally, the amicus argues that this result is contraindicated because public art collections in the United Kingdom charge fees for reproductions of photographic images of works in their collections, thus evidencing their view that the images are protected by copyright. But the issue here is not the position of an economically interested constituency on an issue that has not been litigated, at least in this century, but the content of the originality requirement of the British Copyright Act. Moreover, it is far from clear what the understanding of British art collections, if any, actually is. Certainly, for example, there are original works of art in British public art collections in which copyright subsists and is owned by the collections, in which case reproduction rights no doubt are a fit subject for exploitation.

For all of the foregoing reasons, the Court is persuaded that its original [decision] that Bridgeman's transparencies are not copyrightable under British law was correct.

NOTES

1. The Second Circuit provides a sensible resolution to the choice of law issue. Questions of copyright ownership are determined by the law of the country in which the work was created. Questions of copyright infringement are determined by the law of the country in which infringement allegedly occurred. Notice that this creates some interesting problems when a country, like Russia, does not recognize the work for hire doctrine, but does allow copyrights in compilation. What if the work is created in many places at once, such as through outsourcing? What about creations on the Internet? Should the country in which the server resides or the country in which the author resides determine ownership? These questions are raised by the court's decision. Why not simply apply the law of the country-forum? For one reason why this seemingly simple rule is problematic, see the discussion of extraterritoriality below. One argument in favor of the Second Circuit's conclusion is that it provides notice to the defendant of what law will govern his conduct. If a work is created in Country A, then that country's copyright law will determine ownership. If the defendant then infringes the work created in Country A in Country B, then the copyright law of Country B will determine infringement. The problem is that this rule may either weaken the law of Country B or broaden the law of Country A. If the goal is to harmonize copyright law so that it is applied consistently and fairly at the international level, does the Itar–Tass decision lead to harmonization? Would any choice of law rule lead to harmonization? One response to this question is that choice of law rules are about the efficient adjudication of disputes rather than harmonizing copyright law of different nations.

2. It is worth comparing copyright's treatment of these issues with patent law and trademark law's treatment of the same set of issues.

Suppose the plaintiff has patented an invention in Country A and the defendant has practiced the invention without permission in Country B. Plaintiff sues defendant in Country A. Since the infringing activity occurred in Country B, plaintiff's suit in Country A would most likely be dismissed unless there is extraterritorial application of patent law from Country A to activity in Country B. On this point, see the discussion below. Now suppose plaintiff sues defendant in Country B. If plaintiff did not have a patent on the invention in Country B, then the suit will be dismissed because plaintiff has no patent rights in Country B. Notice, the Itar–Tass approach is irrelevant here because patent rights are territorial. In order to bring the patent suit in Country B, the plaintiff would have had to have a patent in Country B, and Country B's patent law would govern the ownership and infringement issues. Country B cannot enforce a patent granted by Country A. The reason why the problem in Itar–Tass does not arise in the context of patent law is because patents are a grant from the sovereign, obtained through an administrative process. Copyrights, however, are automatic, the rights arising when a work is fixed in a tangible medium of expression.

3. Now suppose plaintiff has a trademark in Country A and defendant infringes the trademark in Country B. If plaintiff sues in Country A, the issue is one of extraterritorial application of Country A's trademark law to conduct

in Country B. We will see in our discussions of *Steele v. Bulova* and *Vanity Fair v. Eaton*, below, that this suit might proceed since extraterritorial application of trademark law can be quite broad, certainly broader than either patent or copyright. What if plaintiff sues in Country B? The question is whether plaintiff has trademark rights in Country B and that will be a matter of Country B's trademark law. Why not apply the rule of *Itar–Tass* and say that the court in Country B will look to Country A's trademark law to establish ownership and to Country B's trademark law to establish infringement? Trademark rights arise from use in commerce, and if there has been no use of the mark in Country B, then the fact that there are trademark rights in Country A is irrelevant to the lawsuit in Country B. In contrast, a work need not be used in order to establish copyright.

4. In *Bridgeman*, the Southern District of New York holds that United States law applied to determine the issue of originality. The court reaches this conclusion through application of the principle of national treatment as provided in the Berne Convention. The Second Circuit, however, based its decision on general conflict of laws principles in order to interpret the United States Copyright Act. Is *Itar–Tass* consistent with the obligation of national treatment? The principle of national treatment states that foreign nationals be treated the same as U.S. nationals in U.S. court. But national treatment does not mandate that U.S. law always be applied. Instead, what national treatment requires is that *if* U.S. law applies, then it be applied equally to U.S. and non-U.S. nationals. The *Bridgeman* court finesses the choice of law question by finding that the work does not receive copyright protection under either U.S. or U.K. copyright law.

5. Arguably, the *Bridgeman* court evaded addressing the choice of law issue explicitly. But under *Itar–Tass*, the court would have to look to U.K. law to establish ownership and then to U.S. law to establish infringement. The problem is that the issue of originality is implicated in both the ownership and the infringement inquiry. The plaintiff would have to show originality to establish ownership and to show that defendant appropriated original elements from the work to establish infringement. The *Itar–Tass* approach to conflict of law would require the court to analyze both U.S. and U.K. law to determine originality because of its key role in both elements of a claim for copyright infringement.

2. Choice of Forum

CREATIVE TECHNOLOGY, LTD. v. AZTECH SYSTEM PTE., LTD.

United States Court of Appeals for the Ninth Circuit, 1995.
61 F.3d 696.

FLOYD R. GIBSON, SENIOR CIRCUIT JUDGE.

Creative Technology appeals the district court's forum non conveniens dismissal of its copyright infringement action.... [W]e affirm.

Appellant Creative Technology, Ltd. (Creative) and Appellee Aztech Systems Pte. Ltd. (Aztech) are competing Singapore corporations in the business of developing, manufacturing, and distributing sound cards. Both Aztech's and Creative's principal place of business is Singapore. All the sound cards are designed, developed, and manufactured in Singapore. Creative markets its sound cards in the United States under the brand name "Sound Blaster" through Creative Labs, Inc., a California corporation and wholly owned subsidiary. Aztech, in turn, markets its sound cards in the United States under the brand name "Sound Galaxy" through Appellee Aztech Labs, Inc. (Aztech Labs), another California corporation and wholly owned subsidiary.

The present action arises from a protracted copyright dispute between Creative and Aztech. The first round of copyright litigation erupted in November of 1992 when Creative, which holds twelve registered United States copyrights in its Sound Blaster series, publicly accused Aztech of infringing on its copyrighted material through the manufacture and distribution of Aztech's Sound Galaxy series. Aztech filed the equivalent of a declaratory relief action in Singapore under the Singapore Copyright Act, ultimately resulting in a settlement agreement on December 7, 1992.

Following the repudiation of this agreement, Creative filed suit in the United States District Court for the Northern District of California, claiming that Aztech's reproduction, adaptation, and United States distribution of "Sound Blaster clones" violated Creative's exclusive rights under 17 U.S.C. §§ 106 and 501 (1988) of the United States Copyright Act. Aztech responded by filing an action against Creative in the High Court of Singapore, alleging breach of the settlement agreement and seeking declaratory relief once again under the Singapore Copyright Act. Creative, in turn, filed mandatory counterclaims in Singapore alleging copyright infringement based on the manufacture of "Sound Blaster clones" in Singapore and their distribution abroad. Aztech Labs has consented to Singapore jurisdiction and is now a party to the ongoing Singapore action.

Aztech filed a motion to dismiss the United States action under the forum non conveniens doctrine. The district court granted Aztech's motion, concluding that Singapore offered an adequate alternative forum and that the balance of public and private interest factors favored dismissing the action in favor of adjudication in Singapore. Creative appeals....

The party moving for forum non conveniens dismissal must demonstrate two things: (1) the existence of an adequate alternative forum; and (2) that the balance of relevant private and public interest factors favor dismissal. Creative raises three primary issues on appeal: (1) whether the district court erred in concluding that the forum non conveniens doctrine applies to the United States Copyright Act; (2) whether the district court abused its discretion in concluding that the High Court of Singapore will provide an adequate alternative forum; and (3) whether the district court abused its discretion in determining that the balance of relevant public and private interest factors favors dismissal.

A.   Applicability of the Forum Non Conveniens Doctrine

The forum non conveniens doctrine is inapplicable to certain federal statutes such as the Jones Act or the Federal Employers' Liability Act (FELA) which contain special provisions mandating venue in the United States district courts. Because of this, a choice of law determination must be made before the district court dismisses an action under the forum non conveniens doctrine. Creative argues that its claim is governed exclusively by the United States Copyright Act, 17 U.S.C. § 101 et seq. (1988). As a result, Creative contends that the forum non conveniens doctrine is inapplicable to its claim because 28 U.S.C. § 1338(a) invests the federal district courts with "exclusive" jurisdiction over claims arising under the United States Copyright Act.

Regardless of which nation's law applies, Creative's argument is without merit. The inapplicability of the forum non conveniens doctrine to the Jones Act and FELA is based on "[a] privilege of venue, granted by the legislative body which created this right of action. . . ." 28 U.S.C. § 1338(a) is not the same type of mandatory venue provision found in either the Jones Act or FELA. That statute merely states that United States district courts shall have exclusive jurisdiction of United States copyright claims over state courts.

Our conclusion is reinforced by this Court's previous decision in *Lockman Found. v. Evangelical Alliance Mission*, 930 F.2d 764 (9th Cir. 1991). In that decision, the plaintiff brought an action for certain non-copyright claims and for copyright infringement under both United States and Japanese law. Id. at 766. Following the forum non conveniens dismissal of its complaint by the district court, the plaintiff appealed both the dismissal of its noncopyright claims and the district court's refusal to allow it to amend its complaint to drop the copyright claims. Id. This Court affirmed both the district court's forum non conveniens dismissal and its decision to deny the plaintiff's motion to amend its complaint, concluding that the copyright and non-copyright claims were too closely intertwined to be severed. Id. at 772. Based on an analysis of the complaint as a whole, including the copyright claims, we concluded that "[i]n this case, there is no arguably applicable law that would end the forum non conveniens inquiry, so no potentially dispositive choice of law determination need have been made." Id. at 771. We believe this state-ment of the law to be equally applicable to the instant case.

The dissent inaccurately faults our decision for failing to take the principle of national treatment into account. Both the Universal Copyright Convention (U.C.C.) and the Berne Convention for the Protection of Literary and Artistic Works (Berne) mandate a policy of national treat-ment in which copyright holders are afforded the same protection in foreign nations that those nations provide their own authors. See U.C.C. Art. II; Berne, Art. V. The dissent accurately points out that the principle of national treatment implicates a rule of territoriality in which " '[t]he applicable law is the copyright law of the state in which the infringement occurred, not that of the state of which the author is a national or in which the work was first published.' " *Subafilms, Ltd. v. MGM–Pathe Comm.*, 24 F.3d 1088, 1097 (9th Cir.1994) (en banc) (quoting 3 David Nimmer and Melville B. Nimmer, Nimmer on Copyright § 17.05 at 17–39 (1994)).

The law of this forum, however, includes the forum non conveniens doctrine. The dissent argues that "the principle of national treatment requires that United States copyright law be applied in order to remedy infringing conduct that occurred in the United States." We do not agree with this sweeping conclusion. National treatment and territoriality are choice of law principles, and do not preclude the application of the forum non conveniens doctrine merely because a foreign author alleges copyright violations occurring within our borders. National treatment merely requires this Court to grant Creative the same copyright protection enjoyed by American authors. The dissent seems to imply that national treatment confers a special immunity from forum non conveniens analysis on foreign copyright plaintiffs. But United States nationals alleging violations of United States copyright law are subject to forum non conveniens analysis. We believe that the concepts of national treatment and territoriality require that foreign copyright holders be subject to the same standards, no more, no less.

B. Adequate Alternative Forum

The first step in forum non conveniens analysis is the determination of whether an adequate alternative forum exists. *Piper [Aircraft Co. v. Reyno]*, 454 U.S. [235, 254 (1981)]. The key determination is whether "the remedy provided by the alternative forum is so clearly inadequate or unsatisfactory that it is no remedy at all." Id. This requirement is generally satisfied if the defendant is amenable to service of process in the alternative forum. Id. at n. 22. In this case, all parties are either subject to or have submitted to the jurisdiction of the High Court of Singapore. More may be required, however, in "rare circumstances" where the remedy offered by the alternative forum is "clearly unsatisfactory." The Supreme Court has described such an inadequate forum as one which "does not permit litigation of the subject matter of the dispute." Id.

Creative argues that because the reach of the Singapore Copyright Act is limited to infringing acts occurring within Singapore, the High Court of Singapore is unable to grant Creative any relief for the alleged acts of copyright infringement arising from Creative's distribution of "Sound Blaster clones" within the United States. Creative further argues that 28 U.S.C. § 1338(a)'s grant of "exclusive" jurisdiction to the United States district courts over claims brought under the United States Copyright Act prevents the High Court of Singapore from applying United States copyright law to supplement the remedies afforded under the Singapore Copyright Act.

We reject Creative's argument on both fronts. We conclude that the Singapore Copyright Act offers Creative an adequate alternative remedy independent of United States copyright law. Even if it did not, we further conclude that the High Court of Singapore would be free to apply United States copyright law to Creative's counterclaim should the need arise.

1. Adequacy of Remedies under the Singapore Copyright Act

The forum non conveniens doctrine does not guarantee the plaintiff its choice of law, or even that United States law will be applied in the alternative forum.... Creative's claim that the territorial limits of the Singapore Copyright Act renders the High Court of Singapore incapable of protecting Creative's United States copyrights interests is belied by the scope of Creative's own Singapore counterclaim. That counterclaim seeks both monetary and permanent injunctive relief for all alleged acts of infringement arising from both the development of the "Sound Blaster clones" in Singapore and their distribution abroad. We conclude that the High Court of Singapore is capable of granting Creative the relief it seeks despite the territorial limitations of the Singapore Copyright Act.

First, lack of extraterritorial reach should not prevent the High Court of Singapore from subsuming the amount of damages incurred by Aztech Labs' alleged illegal distribution of pirated sound cards within the United States in the amount of damages awarded under the Singapore Copyright Act for Aztech's alleged infringing acts occurring in Singapore.... We see no barrier preventing the High Court of Singapore from following a similar course of remedy if it so desires.

Second, the territorial limits of the Singapore Copyright Act cannot prevent the High Court of Singapore from granting Creative's request to permanently enjoin Aztech's infringing conduct in Singapore. Indeed, we are unable to conceive of a more effective means of protecting Creative's United States copyright interests than by shutting off the pipeline of infringing goods at the source. Thus, regardless of whether the High Court of Singapore has jurisdiction to adjudicate acts of copyright infringement occurring outside Singapore, we believe that Court is capable of offering Creative an adequate monetary or injunctive remedy under the Singapore Copyright Act. While the scope of relief available in the High Court of Singapore may not be what Creative envisioned when it filed its claim in the United States district court, the forum non conveniens doctrine does not require it to be so.

2. Availability of United States Copyright Law

In addition, we are aware of nothing preventing the High Court of Singapore from applying United States Copyright law to Creative's counterclaim in the event that it determines the scope of remedies offered under the Singapore Copyright Act to be inadequate. The mere inability to adjudicate acts of infringement occurring in the United States under the Singapore Copyright Act should not impede that court from applying United States copyright law to those claims should the need arise. This Court has recognized the potential of American courts to entertain actions under the copyright laws of other nations. If our courts can entertain actions under the copyright laws of foreign nations, we see no reason why the High Court of Singapore is incapable of doing the same if need be.

Finally, there is simply no support for Creative's argument that 28 U.S.C. § 1338(a) bars the High Court of Singapore from applying United States copyright law. That statute clearly grants United States district courts jurisdiction over copyright claims "exclusive of the courts of the states," not exclusive of the courts of foreign nations. Creative urges this Court to interpret this provision as a grant of jurisdiction exclusive of foreign courts as well as courts of the fifty states. There is no support for this interpretation, however. Even if this Court were to adopt Creative's strained interpretation of 28 U.S.C. § 1338(a), that statute could not prevent the High Court of Singapore from applying United States copyright law if it wished to do so. As a foreign nation, Singapore is not bound by acts of Congress as the fifty states are under the Supremacy Clause of the United States Constitution. Creative can point to no barrier precluding the High Court of Singapore from applying United States copyright law to Creative's counterclaim should the need arise.

C. The Balance of Private and Public Interest Factors

While there is normally a strong presumption in favor of honoring the plaintiff's choice of forum, a foreign plaintiff's choice is afforded less deference. *Piper* 454 U.S. at 255–56, 102 S.Ct. at 265–66. The district court concluded that, on the whole, both the private and public interest factors pointed to Singapore as the appropriate forum. We agree.

1. *Private Interest Factors*

The private interest factors include: (1) relative ease of access to sources of proof; (2) the availability of compulsory process for attendance of unwilling witnesses, and cost of obtaining attendance of willing witnesses; (3) possibility of viewing subject premises; (4) all other factors that render trial of the case expeditious and inexpensive.

The district court concluded that the balance of the private interest factors favored dismissal. It weighed the first factor in favor of dismissal because all of the records and the majority of witnesses involved in the manufacture of the alleged "Sound Blaster clones" are located in Singapore. The district court also weighed the last factor in favor of dismissal because the parallel action in the High Court of Singapore was further advanced than the United States action. It weighed the second factor against dismissal because the majority of expert witnesses reside in California. The district court viewed the third factor as a neutral because there were no premises to view. We find no abuse of discretion in the district court's consideration of the private interest factors. Both primary parties, the key infringing conduct, and the bulk of the witnesses are located in Singapore, and the case can best be litigated there.

2. *Public Interest Factors*

The public interest factors include: (1) administrative difficulties flowing from court congestion; (2) imposition of jury duty on the people of a community that has no relation to the litigation; (3) local interest in having localized controversies decided at home; (4) the interest in having a diversity case tried in a forum familiar with the law that governs the action: (5) the avoidance of unnecessary problems in conflicts of law.

The district court determined that the public interest factors also favored dismissal. It weighed the second factor in favor of dismissal because both principal parties are residents of Singapore and the alleged wrongful acts of copyright design infringement occurred there. The district court viewed the first and fourth factors neutrally, reasoning that both the United States and Singapore judiciaries are overburdened and that, regardless of which court eventually adjudicated this case, an application of foreign law at some point was inevitable.

Creative argues that the district court should have weighed the second and third factors against dismissal due to the United States' strong interest in protecting United States' copyright interests, especially where the complaint alleges infringements occurring within the United States. Creative also argues that the fourth factor should have been weighed against dismissal because its claim was based solely on United States copyright law.

Once again, we find no abuse of discretion. This is essentially a dispute between two Singapore corporations as to which of them was the original developer of the disputed sound card technology. This is not a case involving the piracy of American made products or substantively involving American companies. As such, the United States' interest in resolving this controversy and the relation of the jury community to this controversy are extremely attenuated and do not sway the balance against dismissal. The presence of Aztech Labs, a wholly-owned subsidiary of a Singapore corporation, influences our analysis very little.

The dissent charges that our decision unfairly discounts what it views as the United States' strong public interest in resolving this copyright claim. It argues that "an American copyright is a valued benefit granted by the United States government for the primary purpose of benefitting the general public good; therefore, a copyright infringement claim must not be treated as a mere private cause of action like a tort or breach of contract." We disagree. "Federal copyright laws do not serve this purpose of protecting consumers. They are designed to protect the property rights of copyright owners." *Anderson v. Nidorf*, 26 F.3d 100, 102 (9th Cir. 1994) (per curiam) (citing *Wheaton v. Peters*, 33 U.S. 591, 603, 8 L.Ed. 1055 (1834)). As such, the key interests in this dispute lie with the Singapore corporations, not the American public.

We also agree with the district court's determination retaining this action would not have avoided the problem of having to apply foreign law. The scope of Creative's complaint necessarily implicates the legality of infringing acts occurring in Singapore. As such, an application of foreign law is likely inevitable, regardless of which forum adjudicates this controversy. Consequently, we conclude that the district court did not abuse its discretion in determining that the public interest factors favor dismissal.

FERGUSON, CIRCUIT JUDGE, dissenting:

Because the district court failed to properly exercise its discretion by dismissing for forum non conveniens a claim brought pursuant to United States copyright law, I dissent. A district court may dismiss an action on grounds of forum non conveniens upon a showing that 1) an adequate alternative forum exists, and 2) the balance of relevant public and private interest factors weighs in favor of dismissal. *Piper Aircraft Co. v. Reyno*, 454 U.S. 235, 257, 102 S.Ct. 252, 266, 70 L.Ed.2d 419 (1981). In this case, the district court erred by ignoring the unique nature and complexity of American copyright law in its analysis of both parts of the forum non conveniens test.

I must admit that I am astounded when I read that it is not convenient to try an American copyright case in an American court for copyright infringement that takes place solely in America. I am also astounded by a decision that the convenient place to hold the trial is in Singapore, particularly when the majority have not the slightest idea that a court in that nation would even recognize an American copyright.

I.

In determining that it is not convenient to try this case in its court, the district court and the majority have failed to take into account one of the abiding principles of American copyright law, particularly as it has developed pursuant to the Berne Convention: the principle of "national treatment." According to this principle, authors should enjoy in other countries the same protection for their works as those countries accord their own authors. See UCC Art. II; Berne Conv. Art. V. See generally 3 Nimmer on Copyright § 17.01 [B], at 17–8; H.Rep. (BCIA) at 14. Foreign authors who are granted American copyrights must be treated the same as American authors. Moreover, "it is commonly acknowledged that the national treatment principle implicates a rule of territoriality." *Subafilms, Ltd. v. MGM–Pathe Communications Co.*, 94 C.D.O.S. 3381, 3385 (9th Cir. 1994). See also 3 Nimmer, supra, § 17.05, at 17–39 ("The applicable law is the copyright law of the state in which the infringement occurred, not that of the state of which the author is a national ..."). For purposes of a forum non conveniens analysis, the principle of national treatment sets copyright cases apart from other kinds of cases. The national treatment principle requires that, where a copyright has been infringed in a particular country, the author has the right to pursue a remedy in that country.

The majority have failed to consider the adequacy of Singapore as an alternative forum in light of the principle of national treatment. They do not address the impact of the Berne Convention, which requires United States courts to treat foreign owners of American copyrights the same as American owners. Instead, the majority use the doctrine of forum non conveniens to hold that when foreign persons own American copyrights, it is not convenient for an American court to adjudicate their claims. Contrary to the majority's assertion, I simply advocate that we follow the Berne Convention by allowing foreign copyright owners the same opportunity that we give to American copyright owners to litigate their case in the United States when the alleged infringement takes place in the United States.

In this case, Creative alleges independent violations of the United States Copyright Act by acts of distribution which occurred in the United States. Our decision in this case should be obvious when put in the context of this court's analysis in cases such as *Timberlane Lumber Co. v. Bank of America*, 749 F.2d 1378 (9th Cir. 1984) and *Subafilms*. In *Timberlane*, 749 F.2d at 1386, this court affirmed a dismissal on grounds of forum non conveniens, because the "witnesses, the parties, and dastardly deeds were all Honduran; these suits would clearly require us to apply Honduran law ..." Similarly, in *Subafilms*, 94 C.D.O.S. at 3385, this court attempted to prevent "international discord" by holding that a claim of infringement based only on the authorization in the United States of infringing acts which occurred entirely outside the United States was not cognizable under the United States Copyright Act. In *Timberlane* and *Subafilms*, the territorial nature of copyright law precluded application of the United States Copyright Act to conduct that did not occur at all in the United States. By contrast, in this case, the principle of national treatment requires that United States copyright law be applied in order to remedy infringing conduct that occurred in the United States. Those works of Creative that are protected by United States copyrights and that were infringed by conduct which occurred in the United States must receive the benefit and the protection of the national treatment principle. Creative is entitled to protection under the United States Copyright Act.

Thus, the first part of the forum non conveniens test requires us to retain this action because the principle of national treatment precludes Singapore from being an adequate alternative forum. See *Piper Aircraft*, 454 U.S. at 257, 102 S.Ct. at 266. The national treatment principle requires that infringement occurring in the United States be adjudicated in the United States.

However, the majority conclude that the "High Court of Singapore is capable of granting Creative the relief it seeks." They conclude that the High Court can provide both a permanent injunction and sufficient damages to remedy the independent violations of importation and distribution under the United States Copyright Act. The majority have reached these conclusions without resort to any High Court case or other Singapore authority. Nor do the majority have any basis on which to conclude that the Singapore High Court will even "desire" to follow this course of remedy. Indeed, the only thing we really know about Singapore copyright law is that it is not even bound by the principles of the Berne Convention, because Singapore was not a signatory to that treaty. The record before us contains not a single Singapore statute or opinion authorizing the type of legal approach that the majority assumes the High Court will follow. In fact, the record does not tell us anything about Singapore law, its procedures, composition, or rules.

Thus, Singapore law is inadequate and inapplicable for the purposes of protecting Creative's United States copyrights. In this case, the "subject matter" of the dispute consists of twelve United States copyrights which are entitled to protection by American courts against infringement occurring in the United States. This is precisely the type of case in which "dismissal [is] not ... appropriate where the alternative forum does not permit litigation of the subject matter of the dispute." *Piper Aircraft*, 454 U.S. at 254, n. 22, 102 S.Ct. at 265, n. 22.

II.

In addition to determining whether an adequate alternative forum exists, a district court must judge the applicability of forum non conveniens by weighing the relevant public and private interest factors. *Piper Aircraft*, 454 U.S. at 257, 102 S.Ct. at 266.

It is clear enough from the complaint, which is based entirely upon American copyright law, that the district court abused its discretion by dismissing this action. The district court utterly ignored the public interest in having the federal courts of this country apply American copyright law to resolve this controversy.... Here, the applicable law is the United States Copyright Act and the situs of the alleged infringement is the United States. The district court erred in finding that any copyright law other than the United States Copyright Act would need to be applied in this case. Thus there is a strong public interest in avoiding conflict of law problems by having American courts resolve this controversy.... [T]here is a strong public interest in having American courts resolve this localized controversy. The district court abused its discretion by failing to consider these factors....

By dismissing this action on grounds of forum non conveniens, the district court also failed to understand the importance of the copyrightability of computer software in American jurisprudence. American copyright law has yet to resolve fully the extent of protection that is due computer software, firmware, and other computer products. See, e.g., 2 International Copyright Law and Practice, USA, § 2, at 37 (Paul E. Geller & Melville B. Nimmer eds., 1993) ("Computer software stands at the vortex of a hotly contested storm in United States copyright law at present"). We must not leave the resolution of this issue to a Singapore court. The enormous importance of both computers and computer-related copyrights to American society precludes such a simplistic and shortsighted solution.

A copyright may not be as important as the Congressional Medal of Honor, but the district court and the majority have completely disregarded the fact that an American copyright is a valued benefit granted by the United States government for the primary purpose of benefiting the general public good; therefore, a copyright infringement claim must not be treated as a mere private cause of action like a tort or breach of contract. The majority confuse the importance of copyright law to the public good with the importance of copyright law to the American consumer. Nowhere have I stated that the district court should have accounted for the importance of this case to American consumers. Rather, I maintain that the district court failed to consider the enormous impact on the general public good resulting from its decision to leave to a Singapore court unsettled issues relating to the intellectual freedom to create American copyrights to computer software in a rapidly expanding market.

The district court and the majority cite *Lockman Foundation v. Evangelical Alliance Mission*, 930 F.2d 764 (9th Cir.1991), for authority to dismiss this case. They fail to understand the difference between this case and *Lockman*. In *Lockman*, the plaintiff owned an American copyright of its English translation of the Bible. The alleged infringement was the translation in Asia of the Bible into several Asian languages for distribution almost exclusively in Asia. In addition, the plaintiff alleged a violation of Japanese copyright law plus several non-copyright counts. The district court dismissed all the counts on the ground that it was not convenient to try them in America. The plaintiff did not appeal the dismissal of the American copyright claim. This Court held that, because the American copyright claim was so intertwined with the non-copyright claims, a grant of leave to amend in order to eliminate the copyright claim would have been futile. That is not this case. It is readily apparent that the American public interest is non-existent for Asian language Bibles distributed in Asia. There was no finding that even one Asian Bible was distributed in the United States. No infringement took place in the United States. In *Lockman*, there simply was not, as the Supreme Court found in *Aiken*, the stimulation of artistic creativity for the general public good in America.

Finally, contrary to the majority's view, given the enormous importance to American society of copyright protection of computer products that are imported and distributed in this country, the interest of the United States in resolving this matter and the relation of the jury community to this task strongly favor retaining this case in the United States courts. There is no evidence presented in this case to demonstrate that Singapore courts are qualified to balance the creativity protected by American copyright law. A United States copyright is a privilege bestowed by our government upon the author in order to reward creativity. American copyright law involves a significant public interest.

Because there is no basis in claiming that it is not convenient to try this case in a United States District Court and because the public and private interest factors weigh in favor of retaining this action, I dissent. The district court erred in dismissing this action on grounds of forum non conveniens.

NOTES

1. The first lesson from the *Creative Technology* case is that the forum non conveniens doctrine does apply to copyright claims. Other courts have held that forum non conveniens also applies to patent and trademark claims. See *Kerotest Mfg. Co. v. C–O–Two Fire Equip. Co.*, 342 U.S. 180, 72 S.Ct. 219, 96 L.Ed. 200 (1952) (forum non conveniens in patent cases); *Gates Learjet Corp. v. Jensen*, 743 F.2d 1325 (9th Cir. 1984).

2. The majority finds no reason to conclude that the district court abused its discretion in concluding that Singapore provided a more convenient forum than the United States. The majority emphasized that there is nothing to indicate that Singapore law and Singapore courts could not handle this dispute involve U.S. copyrights. From a practical matter, the evidence involving infringement was in Singapore and therefore was more accessible to the court. Furthermore, the majority finds no compelling public interest weighing in favor of the U.S. forum. Does the majority adequately consider the fact that U.S. copyrights are at issue? What is the point of securing copyrights in the U.S. if the U.S. cannot be used as forum? Does the fact that the litigants are both Singaporean companies somehow trump the fact that the copyrights are U.S.?

3. You might consider what the result would have been if a U.S. patent or a registered U.S. trademark were at issue. Most likely, if a patent were at issue under an identical set of facts, the court would not dismiss the case since U.S. law is unique in many ways (definition of prior art, the standard of non-obviousness, the first to invent rule). As for trademark law, the key inquiry is likelihood of confusion and, specifically in this context, confusion by U.S. consumers. The case can be made that in the case of patent and trademarks, the U.S. would be the more convenient forum. So what makes copyright law different? Is it that copyright law, unlike patent law, does not have unique administrative rules? Or is it that copyright law, unlike trademark law, is not designed to protect consumers in a geographically defined marketplace, but rather the rights of authors, who might reside anywhere?

4. Judge Ferguson, in dissent, raises some of the points made in Note 3. He certainly thinks that the existence of a U.S. copyright creates a compelling public interest in litigating the case in the United States. He also points to the national treatment principle to argue that the majority's ruling does not treat U.S. and non-U.S. nationals equally. Is he right? National treatment says that if U.S. law applies, then U.S. and non-U.S. nationals have to be treated equally. Does that mean that non-U.S. nationals automatically have to have their U.S. copyright claims heard in U.S. court? Arguably, under Judge Ferguson's interpretation, the national treatment principle would trump forum non conveniens, unless one of the other factors was more compelling. On the other hand, the application of forum non conveniens would most likely have led to the same result if Creative Technology were a U.S. company and all the other facts remained the same.

3. Extraterritoriality Issues

EXPEDITERS INTERNATIONAL OF WASHINGTON, INC. v. DIRECT LINE CARGO MANAGEMENT SERVICES, INC.

United States District Court, District New Jersey, 1998.
995 F.Supp. 468.

PISANO, UNITED STATES MAGISTRATE JUDGE.

Factual Summary

This matter involves the alleged wrongful use of a computer software program. Plaintiff Expediters International ("EI") claims that a Taiwan company, Direct Line Cargo Management Services, Inc. ("CMS–Taiwan"), became affiliated with it and assigned to it the rights of an allegedly copyrighted software program. Prior to EI's affiliation with CMS–Taiwan, CMS–Taiwan was associated with the New Jersey defendant, Direct Line Cargo Management Services, Inc., ("DLCMS–USA"), and a group of affiliated Asian companies. During its association with the defendant, CMS–Taiwan issued a license to the defendant and its affiliates which permitted the companies to make limited use of the software. When CMS–Taiwan became associated with the plaintiff, however, this license expired. This lawsuit arises from the defendant's, and its affiliates,' alleged wrongful use of the software subsequent to the expiration of the license . . . . .

a. Extraterritoriality.

The defendant urges the Court to grant its [summary judgment] motion because the Asian companies allegedly copied the Software overseas, beyond the jurisdiction of the United States Copyright Act. DLCMS–USA argues that the mere authorization of these infringing acts abroad is not sufficient to establish primary liability so as to bring the plaintiff's action within the jurisdiction of this Court. It also argues that, even if the Court were to attach primary liability to the mere act of authorizing infringement, there is no evidence that the defendant, in fact, authorized the Asian affiliates to copy the Software.

Section 501 of the Copyright Act states that "[a]nyone who violates any of the exclusive rights of the copyright owner as provided by sections 106 through 118 . . . is an infringer of the copyright . . ." 17 U.S.C. § 501(a). According to Section 106 of this act:

> [T]he owner of a copyright . . . has the exclusive rights to do and to authorize any of the following:
>
> (1) to reproduce the copyrighted work in copies or phonorecords;
>
> (2) to prepare derivative works based upon the copyrighted work;
>
> (3) to distribute copies . . . of the copyrighted work to the public by sale or other transfer of ownership, or by rental, lease or lending . . .
> 17 U.S.C. § 106 (1996).

There is a division among courts as to whether a claim for infringement can be brought under the Copyright Act when the alleged infringing conduct consists solely of the authorization within the United States of acts that occur entirely abroad. For example, the Ninth Circuit has held that such authorization, by itself, cannot not support a United States infringement claim. See *Subafilms, Ltd. v. MGM–Pathe Communications Co.*, 24 F.3d 1088 (9th Cir. 1994). In contrast, a district court in the Sixth Circuit has held that, by authorizing the release of copyrighted music recordings overseas, a United States entity commits primary infringement that is actionable under Section 106. See *Curb v. MCA Records, Inc.*, 898 F.Supp. 586 (M.D.Tenn. 1995).

In *Subafilms*, the plaintiffs alleged that Warner Brothers violated its copyright in the Beatle's movie, "Yellow Submarine," by authorizing distributors to release video versions of the movie abroad. 24 F.3d 1088. The Court tied the authorization right in Section 106 solely to a claim of contributory infringement; it reasoned that a defendant in the United States could not be liable based on its authorization of infringing acts, where the overseas entity who actually copied the materials was not subject to United States Copyright Law. See id. at 1094. The Court noted that "to hold otherwise would produce the untenable anomaly, inconsistent with the general principles of third party liability, that a party could be held liable as an infringer for violating the 'authorization' right when the party that it authorized could not be considered an infringer under the Copyright Act." Id.

While the defendant urges the Court to apply Subafilms' interpretation of Section 106, the Court departs from the Ninth Circuit's interpretation and adopts the holding set forth in *Curb v. MCA Records, Inc.*, 898 F. Supp. 586. In Curb, the defendant counterclaimed that a music company violated its licensing agreement by authorizing infringing acts abroad. See id. The Court denied the plaintiff's summary judgment motion, finding that there was a genuine issue of material fact as to whether the plaintiff engaged in primary infringement by merely authorizing the release of copyrighted sound recordings overseas. See id. The court held that authorizing infringing acts may constitute primary infringement in light of both the language and legislative history of the Statute. See id. at 595–96. Furthermore, it reasoned that imposing direct liability for authorizing infringement more closely serves the underlying policies of the Copyright Act in this modern era. See id. at 595. Specifically, the Court noted:

> [P]iracy has changed since the Barbary days. Today, the raider need not grab the bounty with his own hands; he need only transmit his go-ahead by wire or telefax to start the presses in a distant land. Subafilms ignores this economic reality, and the economic incentives underpinning the Copyright clause designed to encourage creation of new works, and transforms infringement of the authorization right into a requirement of domestic presence by a primary infringer. Under this view, a phone call to Nebraska results in liability; the

same phone call to France results in riches. In a global marketplace, it is literally a distinction without a difference. Id.

This Court agrees with *Curb*'s literal interpretation of Section 106, which clearly lends "the owner of a copyright ... the exclusive rights to do and to authorize" the reproduction and distribution of copyrighted materials. 17 U.S.C. § 106 (emphasis supplied). Furthermore, the Court appreciates the policy observations set forth in *Curb*, which appear more closely adapted to our modern age of telefaxes, Internet communication, and electronic mail systems. The purpose behind the Copyright Act is to protect a copyright owner's right to be free from infringement in the United States. To allow an entity to curtail this right by merely directing its foreign agent to do its "dirty work" would be to hinder the deterrent effect of the statute and to thwart its underlying purpose. Because it is more closely aligned with the language, legislative history, and purpose of the statute, the Court adopts the *Curb* interpretation of Section 106 and finds that the mere authorization of infringing acts abroad constitutes direct infringement and is actionable under United States Copyright Law.

Having made this determination, the Court considers whether a reasonable jury could conclude that DLCMS–USA, in fact, authorized the Asian companies' actions. In light of DLCMS–USA's arguable motive and ability to control its affiliates, the Court cannot foreclose this possibility. A jury might reasonably infer that the defendant had a motive for authorizing the infringing acts, since the affiliates' use of the Software enabled the defendant to receive manifests and billing information to facilitate its consolidation ventures. McKenzie himself indicated that the Software was extremely valuable to the companies' business. In its Answer to the Complaint, DLCMS–USA asserts as an affirmative defense that it signed the License Agreement limiting its use of the Software because it was under duress. Furthermore, during oral argument, defense counsel admitted that DLCMS–USA continued to use the Software after November 15, 1993 at the insistence of its customers. Finally, the fact that the defendant negotiated to use the Software during a transition period suggests that the defendant continued to need the Software, even after the license had expired.

In addition to motive, a jury might reasonably infer that the defendant had the ability to authorize the alleged infringing acts, owing to its close interaction with the affiliates. To prove this point, EI calls attention to the joint business dealings, the mutual agency agreements, and the shared profits, leadership, and ownership among the Asian companies and the defendant. Furthermore, it points to the defendant's own characterization of itself and its Asian affiliates as a "family of companies."

In light of the defendant's possible motive and power to authorize its affiliates to use the Software, the Court cannot, as a matter of law, find that the defendant did not direct its affiliates' actions. For this reason, the Court rejects the defendant's extraterritoriality argument.

NOTES

1. The *Expediters* case illustrates a tension in the courts on the extraterritorial application of copyright law. Note the Ninth Circuit is the highest appellate court that has addressed this question. But district courts in other circuits have not followed the Ninth Circuit. Most likely, this tension will be the basis for a Supreme Court decision in the future, as soon as another appellate court affirms one of the contrary district courts.

2. The source of the tension is easy to recognize, but not that easy to resolve. The issue is how to interpret the word "authorize" in Section 106 of the Copyright Act. As we have discussed above in the chapter on Copyright Law, "authorize" is understood to mean "secondary liability." Legislative history supports this narrow reading, and the Ninth Circuit adopts it. The implication is the following: if a defendant in the U.S. tells someone in another country to engage in acts of copying, adapting, or distributing overseas, then the defendant cannot be held liable in the U.S. for "authorization." To put it simply, since authorization means secondary liability, the defendant cannot be held secondarily liable for encouraging acts that were not infringement under U.S. law. The alternative interpretation is understand authorization broadly: authorize not only means secondary liability, but also means granting someone permission to undertake one of the exclusive rights under Section 106. The narrow interpretation is consistent since a defendant cannot be held liable in the U.S. for authorizing copyright infringement unless there has been an act of direct infringement. The broader interpretation would impose liability on a defendant for authorizing acts even if these acts would not be direct infringement. Since this broad interpretation has not been applied when all acts have occurred wholly in the U.S., the broad interpretation serves as way to create liability for U.S. defendants that have facilitated acts of infringement that occurred outside the U.S.

3. Think about the choices open to a U.S. copyright holder against a non-U.S. infringer. The U.S. copyright holder would have to find some act of infringement by the infringer within the U.S. in order to bring suit. Alternatively, the U.S. copyright holder would have to seek enforcement in the country where the infringement occurred. Here, review our discussion of choice of law and choice of forum from above. Under the approach in *Expediters*, the U.S. copyright holder could, as yet another alternative, find a defendant in the U.S. who authorized the acts of infringement overseas and seek a remedy against them. This third option is not available under the Ninth Circuit approach. The Expediters approach, needless to say, is more favorable to copyright holders. But the Ninth Circuit approach recognizes that intellectual property is territorial and respects the sovereignty of nations to devise their own intellectual property laws. However, the Ninth Circuit approach seems to create a way to evade claims for copyright infringement. One limitation to this last argument is that the U.S. copyright holder can prevent unauthorized imports. Even if the infringing acts occur overseas, any imports into the U.S. of the unauthorized work would be actionable.

4. Compare the principle of extraterritoriality with remedies for copyright infringement. The principle of extraterritoriality does not limit the

ability of the copyright holder to recover damages for harms that may have occurred overseas that stem from acts of infringement within the U.S. Suppose that a defendant makes unauthorized copies of a work in the U.S. and then sells the work overseas. The sales overseas may be a basis for enhancing statutory damages. Alternatively, the sales overseas may constitute either profits that have to be disgorged by the infringer or damages to the copyright holder from loss in foreign sales. Therefore, even though the non-U.S. distribution is technically outside the reach of U.S. copyright law, the economic harm resulting from domestic infringement, even if they occur overseas, can still be the basis for recovery. Also note, however, that a U.S. court cannot enjoin infringing activities that occur outside the United States. We will consider some trademark cases that address this issue below.

B. PATENT

1. Prosecution

APPLICATION OF HILMER

United States Court of Customs and Patent Appeals, 1966.
359 F.2d 859.

RICH, JUDGE.

The sole issue is whether a majority of the Patent Office Board of Appeals erred in overturning a consistent administrative practice and interpretation of the law of nearly forty years standing by giving a United States patent effect as prior art as of a foreign filing date to which the patentee of the reference was entitled under 35 U.S.C. § 119.

Because it held that a U.S. patent, cited as a prior art reference under 35 U.S.C. § 102(e) and § 103, is effective as of its foreign 'convention' filing date, relying on 35 U.S.C. § 119, the board affirmed the rejection of claims 10, 16, and 17 of application serial No. 750,887, filed July 25, 1958, for certain sulfonyl ureas.

This opinion develops the issue, considers the precedents, and explains why, on the basis of legislative history, we hold that section 119 does not modify the express provision of section 102(e) that a reference patent is effective as of the date the application for it was 'filed in the United States.'

The two 'references' relied on are:

Habicht 2,962,530 Nov. 29, 1960 (filed in the United States January 23, 1958, found to be entitled to priority as of the date of filing in Switzerland on January 24, 1957)

Wagner et al. 2,975,212 March 14, 1961 (filed in the United States May 1, 1957)

The rejection here is the aftermath of an interference between appellants and Habicht, a priority dispute in which Habicht was the winning party on a single count. He won because appellants conceded priority of the invention of the count to him. The earliest date asserted by appellants for their invention is their German filing date, July 31, 1957, which, we note, is a few months later than Habicht's priority date of January 24, 1957.

After termination of the interference and the return of this application to the examiner for further ex parte prosecution, the examiner rejected the appealed claims on Habicht, as a primary reference, in view of Wagner et al., as a secondary reference, holding the claimed compounds to be 'unpatentable over the primary reference in view of the secondary reference which renders them obvious to one of ordinary skill in the art.'

... The board's conclusion is that the foreign priority date of a U.S. patent is its effective date as a reference.... Our conclusion is arrived at simply by considering sections 102(e) and the first paragraph of section 119 of the statute together. We find the reasoning at fault, however, and the interpretation untenable. To discuss it we must have section 119 before us, insofar as applicable:

> § 119. Benefit of earlier filing date in foreign country; right of priority
>
> An application for patent for an invention filed in this country by any person who has, or whose legal representatives or assigns have, previously regularly filed an application for a patent for the same invention in a foreign country which affords similar privileges in the case of applications filed in the United States or to citizens of the United States, shall have the same effect as the same application would have if filed in this country on the date on which the application for patent for the same invention was first filed in such foreign country, if the application in this country is filed within twelve months from the earliest date on which such foreign application was filed; but no patent shall be granted on any application for patent for an invention which had been patented or described in a printed publication in any country more than one year before the date of the actual filing of the application in this country, or which had been in public use or on sale in this country more than one year prior to such filing.

The board's construction is based on the idea that the language of the statute is plain, that it means what it says, and that what it says is that the application filed abroad is to have the same effect as though it were filed here—for all purposes. We can reverse the statement to say that the actual U.S. application is to have the same effect as though it were filed in the U.S. on the day when the foreign application was filed, the whole thing being a question of effective date. We take it either way because it makes no difference here.

Before getting into history, we note first that there is in the very words of the statute a refutation of this literalism. It says 'shall have the same effect' and it then says 'but' for several situations it shall not have the same effect, namely, it does not enjoy the foreign date with respect to any of the patent-defeating provisions based on publication or patenting anywhere in the world or public use or being on sale in this country more than one year before the date of actual filing in this country.

As to the other statute involved, we point out that the words of section 102(e), which the board 'simply' reads together with section 119, also seem plain. Perhaps they mean precisely what they say in specifying, as an express patent-defeating provision, an application by another describing the invention but only as of the date it is 'filed in the United States.'

The great logical flaw we see in the board's reasoning is in its premise (or is it an a priori conclusion?) that 'these two provisions must be read together.' Doing so, it says 119 in effect destroys the plain meaning of 102(e) but the board will not indulge the reverse construction in which the plain words of 102(e) limit the apparent meaning of 119. We see no reason for reading these two provisions together and the board has stated none. We believe, with the dissenting board member, that 119 and 102(e) deal with unrelated concepts and further that the historical origins of the two sections show neither was intended to affect the other, wherefore they should not be read together in violation of the most basic rule of statutory construction, the 'master rule,' of carrying out the legislative intent. Additionally, we have a long and consistent administrative practice in applying an interpretation contrary to the new view of the board, confirmed by legislation ratification in 1952. We will consider these matters separately.

Section 119

We shall now take up the history and purpose of section 119. The board opinion devotes the equivalent of four pages in the printed record to a scholarly and detailed review of the history of section 119 with all of which we agree, except for the interwoven conclusions as to its meaning as it bears on the effective date of a U.S. patent used as a reference. * * *

This priority right was a protection to one who was trying to obtain patents in foreign countries, the protection being against patent-defeating provisions of national laws based on events intervening between the time of filing at home and filing abroad. Under the heading 'Recapitulation of Advantages Secured by the Convention,' the Commission said, so far as relevant here (pp. 14–15):

> The advantages to our citizens in the matter of patents directly afforded by the convention may be thus recapitulated.

> First. The enjoyment in foreign countries of equal rights with subjects or citizens of those countries.

> Second. The 'delay of priority' of seven months within which to file applications abroad after filing in this country.

> Third. The privilege of introducing articles embodying the invention manufactured in this country into foreign countries to a certain

extent without thereby causing the forfeiture of the patents taken out there.

Note the emphasis repeatedly placed in the Commission Report on advantages to United States citizens. It was felt we should do what was necessary to comply with the reciprocity provisions to enjoy the benefits of the convention for our own citizens. It was also believed that by reason of Opinions of Attorneys General, Vol. 19, 273, 'the International Convention, in so far as the agreements therein contained are not in accordance with the present laws of the United States, is without force and effect; that it is not self-executing, but requires legislation to render it effective * * * and * * * it is our opinion that such legislation should be adopted * * *.' (Report p. 19.)

> Specific to the question here, the Commission Report says (p. 24):

> We are, therefore, of the opinion that an amendment to the law should be made, providing that the foreign application shall have, in case an application is filed in this country by the applicant abroad within the specified period, the same effect as if filed here on the day it was filed abroad.

The board thinks this 'shows the intention of the Commissioners' to create 'a status of (an application) having been filed in the U.S. for all purposes * * *.' * * *

> This so-called right of priority was provided for in the second paragraph of R.S. 4887 which is the basis for the first paragraph of section 119 of this title. * * * (he here states the 4 conditions for obtaining the right) * * * The new statute made no changes in these conditions of the corresponding part of the old statute except to revise the language slightly * * *.

> We need not guess what Congress has since believed to be the meaning of the disputed words in section 119, for it has spoken clearly. World wars interfere with normal commerce in industrial property. The one-year period of priority being too short for people in 'enemy' countries, we had after World War I a Nolan Act (41 Stat. 1313, Mar. 3, 1921) and after World War II a Boykin Act. Foreign countries had reciprocal acts. One purpose was to extend the period of priority. House Report No. 1498, January 28, 1946, by Mr. Boykin, accompanied H.R. 5223 which became Public Law 690 of the 79th Cong., 2d Sess., Aug. 8, 1946, 60 Stat. 940. Section 1 of the bill, the report says, was to extend 'the so-called period of priority,' which then existed under R.S. 4887. On p. 3 the report says:

> > In this connection, it may be observed that the portion of the statute which provides that the filing of a foreign application—shall have the same force and effect as the same application would have if filed in this country on the date on which the application for patent for the same invention, discovery, or design was first filed in such foreign country—is intended to mean 'shall have the same force and effect,' etc., insofar as applicant's right to a patent is concerned. This statuto-

ry provision has no bearing upon the right of another party to a patent except in the case of an interference where the two parties are claiming the same patentable invention. U.S.Code Congressional Service 1946, p. 1493.

We emphasize none of those words because we wish to emphasize them all. We cannot readily imagine a clearer, more definitive statement as to the legislature's own view of the words 'same effect,' which now appear in section 119. This statement flatly contradicts the board's vies. The board does not mention it.

For the foregoing reasons, we are clearly of the opinion that section 119 is not to be read as anything more than it was originally intended to be by its drafters, the Commission appointed under the 1898 Act of Congress, namely, a revision of our statutes to provide for a right of priority in conformity with the International Convention, for the benefit of United States citizens, by creating the necessary reciprocity with foreign members of the then Paris Union.

Section 102(e)

We have quoted this section above and pointed out that it is a patent-defeating section, by contrast with section 119 which gives affirmative 'priority' rights to applicants notwithstanding it is drafted in terms of 'An application.' The priority right is to save the applicant (or his application if one prefers to say it that way) from patent-defeating provisions such as 102(e); and of course it has the same effect in guarding the validity of the patent when issued.

Section 102(e), on the other hand, is one of the provisions which defeats applicants and invalidates patents and is closely related in fact and in history to the requirement of section 102(a) which prohibits a patent if

> (a) the invention was known or used by others in this country, or patented or described in a printed publication in this or a foreign country, before the invention thereof by the applicant for patent, * * *.

In fact, section 102(e) springs straight from 102(a)'s predecessor, R.S. 4886, by decision of the United States Supreme Court in 1926. It was pure case law until 1952 when, having become firmly established, that law was codified by incorporating it in the statute. * * *

We have seen that section 119 originated in 1903 and that its purpose was to grant protective priority rights so that the United States might be a participating member in the International Convention by giving reciprocal priority rights to foreign applicants with respect to the obtaining of patents. We have also seen that section 102(e) was the codification of a court-developed patent-defeating rule based on a statutory requirement that an applicant's invention must not have been previously known by others in this country. We see no such relation between these two rules of law as requires them to be read together and it is our view that section

119 should not be so read with 102(e) as to modify the express limitation of the latter to applications 'filed in the United States.' * * *

Section 102(e) was a codification of the *Milburn* doctrine. The *Milburn* case accorded a U.S. patent effect as a reference as of its U.S. filing date and stated that the policy of the statute on domestic inventions 'cannot be applied to foreign affairs.' No foreign date was involved in the case. The codifying statute specifies that the date as of which the patent has effect is the date of filing 'in the United States.'

R.S. 4887, predecessor of section 119, was in effect from 1903 to 1952 when it was incorporated unchanged in the present statutes. An examination of the legislative history of that statute fails to reveal a scintilla of evidence that it was ever intended to give 'status' to an application or to serve as a patent-defeating provision except insofar as the application, or patent issuing thereon, becomes involved in a priority contest. The *Milburn* rule, under which U.S. patents are used as prior art references for all matter disclosed in them as of their U.S. filing dates has been consistently and continuously applied since its inception in 1926, if not earlier under lower court decisions, by the United States Patent Office. That view was that R.S. 4887, and later section 119, does not make a U.S. patent effective as a reference as of a foreign priority date to which it may be entitled. This view was further actively promulgated by the patent Office in the first edition of its Manual of Patent Examining Procedure, Section 715.01, November, 1949, and so continued until May 27, 1964, after the expression by the board of its new view as exemplified in this case.

But over and above this as a basis of decision we feel there is a paramount principle which controls. The administrative agency known as the Patent Office pursued a uniform policy and interpretation contrary to the new view of the board for the 26 years from 1926 to 1952, at least. That interpretation was well publicized and well known and must be assumed to have been known to Congress in 1952 when it revised and codified the patent statutes into present Title 35, United States Code. In that codification section 119 reenacted R.S. 4887 with no change in substance, as above shown.

This legislative ratification of the interpretation of the statutes by the Patent Office determines the meaning and effect of section 119 for the future. Under that interpretation, section 119 does not affect the express provision of 102(e) as to filing 'in the United States' and the decision of the board that the Swiss filing date of Habicht is the effective date of his U.S. patent as a reference must be reversed.

NOTES

1. One reason patent law is more territorial than either copyright or trademark law is the administrative basis for the creation of patent rights. An inventor does not have a patent until the national agency governing patents says she does. The inventor, in turn, must follow administrative procedure to

ensure that the formalities and substance of patent law are met. Therefore, patent law is necessarily more localized than either copyright or trademark.

2.   The *Hilmer* case is a controversial decision on the effect of a foreign application on the determination of novelty and non-obviousness under U.S. law. The implications of *Hilmer* are easy to spell out. Suppose an inventor files a non-U.S. application and then files a U.S. application within a year. Under the Paris Convention, as enacted in section 119 of the Patent Act of 1952, the inventor can take advantage of the filing date of the non-U.S. application for most instances. What these instances are depend upon the patent statute. For example, the non-U.S. filing date can be used to establish constructive reduction to practice for the purposes of section 102(g) (priority of inventorship). The non-U.S. filing date can also be used to defeat prior art that arose before the date of invention under section 102(a). However, the non-U.S. filing date cannot be used for section 102(b) purposes because the provision refers specifically to "the date of the application for patent in the United States." The facts of *Hilmer* pertain to the applicability of the non-U.S. filing date to prior art under section 102(e) which includes an application filed in the U.S. before the date of invention but granted after the date of invention. According to *Hilmer*, the non-U.S. filing date can be used as a shield to avoid prior art, but cannot be used as a sword to defeat someone else's invention. The conclusion follows from considering the practice of the Patent Office in applying 102(e) prior art based on the U.S. filing date and the legislative history in its separate enactments of sections 119 and 102(e).

3.   There are two implications from *Hilmer*. First, in order to take advantage of the safe harbor under section 102(b), an applicant must file in the U.S. and cannot rely on a non-U.S. filing date. Keep in mind that outside the U.S., there is no safe harbor since most countries have adopted an absolute priority rule for novelty and non-obviousness. Second, non-U.S. filing dates can be used defensively, but not offensively. A non-U.S. filing date can serve to defeat prior art, but cannot serve to create the secret prior art that arises under section 102(e). This last situation creates an anomaly under U.S. patent practice. After losing the interference to Habicht, Hilmer filed an application for an obvious variation on the claims the he lost during the interference. Hilmer used his non-U.S. filing date on the original application as his date of invention for his second application. Hilmer's non-U.S. filing date preceded Habicht's U.S. filing date and therefore Habicth's application could not be used a prior art under section 102(e). The anomaly is that Hilmer could use his non-U.S. filing date, but Habicht could not.

4.   One source of the anomaly in the *Hilmer* case was the inability, at the time of the case, to use foreign inventorship for the purposes of establishing priority. Recent amendments to the U.S. patent act now allow evidence of foreign inventorship to establish priority in an interference. Evidence of foreign inventorship may have been useful in challenging Hilmer's application as a derivation from Habicht's invention.

5.   The result in *Hilmer* has also been addressed by amendments to section 102(e) that allow use of the non-U.S. filing date for (1) a PCT applications that designate the United States and are published in English

and (2) a U.S. patent when the international application designated the United States and was published in English.

2. Extraterritoriality

VODA v. CORDIS CORP.

United States Court of Appeals for the Federal Circuit, 2007.
476 F.3d 887.

GAJARSA, CIRCUIT JUDGE.

I. BACKGROUND

The plaintiff-appellee Voda is a resident of Oklahoma City, Oklahoma. The defendant-appellant Cordis is a U.S.-based entity incorporated in Florida. None of the several foreign Cordis affiliates is a party to the present action, and we note that they appear to be separate legal entities. These foreign affiliates have not been joined to this action. To prevent confusion, we refer to the defendant-appellant as "Cordis U.S."

The patents at issue relate generally to guiding catheters for use in interventional cardiology. * * * Voda sued Cordis U.S. in the United States District Court for the Western District of Oklahoma alleging infringement of his three U.S. patents. * * *

Voda then moved to amend his complaint to add claims of infringement of the European, British, Canadian, French, and German foreign patents. Voda's amended complaint alleges that "Cordis [U.S.] has commenced and continues acts of making, selling, offering for sale and selling at least the XB guiding catheter, which is covered by [the several foreign patents] without Dr. Voda's authority. Such acts constitute infringement, under corresponding foreign law of [these several foreign patents]." Cordis U.S. has admitted that "the XB catheters have been sold domestically and internationally since 1994. The XB catheters were manufactured in Miami Lakes, Florida from 1993 to 2001 and have been manufactured in Juarez, Mexico since 2001." Voda's amended complaint asks for damages, fees, and "such other and further relief as this Court deems just and proper." We resolve the jurisdictional issue based upon those allegations, accepting them to be true.

Cordis U.S. opposed Voda's attempt to amend its complaint to add foreign patent infringement claims on the basis that the district court lacked subject matter jurisdiction over such claims. * * * In a three-page order, the district court analyzed two circuit court cases discussing supplemental jurisdiction over patent claims, *Mars, Inc. v. Kabushiki–Kaisha Nippon Conlux*, 24 F.3d 1368 (Fed.Cir.1994) (finding no jurisdiction), and *Ortman v. Stanray*, 371 F.2d 154 (7th Cir.1967) (affirming district court's denial of a motion to dismiss foreign patent infringement claims). The district court determined that "[t]he allegations in the [proposed] amended complaint demonstrate that this case is more akin to *Ortman* than to *Mars*" and thus, that "it would have supplemental jurisdiction over the foreign patent[ ] claim[s]." *Voda v. Cordis*, No. CIV–03–1512–L, slip op. at

2, 2004 WL 3392022 (August 2, 2004). Therefore, the district court granted Voda's motion to file his amended complaint. Id.

III. DISCUSSION

2. Discretion

Section 1367 "reaffirms that the exercise of supplemental jurisdiction is within the discretion of the district court." *Mars*, 24 F.3d at 1374. * * * Section 1367(c) provides:

> The district courts may decline to exercise supplemental jurisdiction over a claim under subsection (a) if-
>
> (1) the claim raises a novel or complex issue of State law,
>
> (2) the claim substantially predominates over the claim or claims over which the district court has original jurisdiction,
>
> (3) the district court has dismissed all claims over which it has original jurisdiction, or
>
> (4) in exceptional circumstances, there are other compelling reasons for declining jurisdiction.

28 U.S.C. § 1367(c). The Supreme Court has noted that the "statute thereby reflects the understanding that, when deciding whether to exercise supplemental jurisdiction, 'a federal court should consider and weigh in each case, and at every stage of the litigation, the values of judicial economy, convenience, fairness, and comity.' " * * *

Voda asserts that such considerations "have nothing to do with, the certified question concerning existence of subject-matter jurisdiction." We disagree. * * * § 1367(c) constitutes an express statutory exception to the authorization of jurisdiction granted by § 1367(a). In this case, Cordis U.S. asserted that the district court should exercise its discretion to decline supplemental jurisdiction of Voda's foreign patent claims at the end of its opposition to Voda's motion to amend the complaint. The district court's order contained no § 1367(c) analysis. We find that considerations of comity, judicial economy, convenience, fairness, and other exceptional circumstances constitute compelling reasons to decline jurisdiction under § 1367(c) in this case and therefore, hold that the district court abused its discretion by assuming jurisdiction.

a. Treaties as the "supreme law of the land"

Article VI of the Constitution proclaims that "all treaties made, or which shall be made, under the authority of the United States, shall be the supreme law of the land." U.S. Const. art. VI, cl.2. The Supreme Court has accordingly stated that "a treaty ratified by the United States is not only the law of this land, see U.S. Const., Art. II, § 2, but also an agreement among sovereign powers." *El Al Isr. Airlines, Ltd. v. Tsui Yuan Tseng*, 525 U.S. 155, 167, 119 S.Ct. 662, 142 L.Ed.2d 576 (1999) (citation omitted).

The United States entered into Articles 13 through 30 of the Paris Convention for the Protection of Industrial Property ("Paris Convention") on September 5, 1970 and Articles 1 through 12 of the Paris Convention on August 25, 1973. Paris Convention, art. 13–30, 21 U.S.T. 1583; id., art. 1–12, 24 U.S.T. 2140. Article 4 bis of the Paris Convention states that U.S. patents "shall be independent of patents obtained for the same invention in other countries" and that the "foregoing provision is to be understood in an unrestricted sense, ... both as regards the grounds for nullity and forfeiture." In addition, Article 2(3) of the Paris Convention states that the "provisions of the laws of each of the countries of the Union relating to judicial and administrative procedure and to jurisdiction, ... which may be required by the laws on industrial property are expressly reserved." The Paris Convention thus clearly expresses the independence of each country's sovereign patent systems and their systems for adjudicating those patents. Nothing in the Paris Convention contemplates nor allows one jurisdiction to adjudicate the patents of another, and as such, our courts should not determine the validity and infringement of foreign patents. Accordingly, while the Paris Convention contains no express jurisdictional-stripping statute, we relied on it in Stein to hold that "[o]nly a British court, applying British law, can determine validity and infringement of British patents." 748 F.2d at 658.

Subsequently, the United States adopted the Patent Cooperation Treaty ("PCT") on January 24, 1978. Patent Cooperation Treaty, 28 U.S.T. 7645. As with the Paris Convention, the text of the PCT maintains the independence of each country's patents. Article 27(5) states: "Nothing in this Treaty and the Regulations is intended to be construed as prescribing anything that would limit the freedom of each Contracting State to prescribe such substantive conditions of patentability as it desires."

On January 1, 1995, the United States joined the World Trade Organization by entering the Marrakesh Agreement Establishing the World Trade Organization, which through Article II § 2 binds all of its members to the Agreement on Trade–Related Aspects of Intellectual Property Rights ("TRIPS"). 1867 U.N.T.S. 154, 33 I.L.M. 1144 (Apr. 15, 1994). The Agreement on TRIPS contains several provisions regarding the enforcement of patents. Article 41 § 1 of the Agreement on TRIPS specifies that each country "shall ensure that enforcement procedures as specified in this Part are available under their law so as to permit effective action against any act of infringement of intellectual property rights." In addition, § 4 states that "[p]arties to a proceeding shall have an opportunity for review by a judicial authority of final administrative decisions and, subject to jurisdictional provisions in a Member's law concerning the importance of a case," and § 5 states "[i]t is understood that this Part does not ... affect the capacity of Members to enforce their law in general." See also id., art. 41–49. Like the Paris Convention, nothing in the PCT or the Agreement on TRIPS contemplates or allows one jurisdiction to adjudicate patents of another. Canada, France, Germany, and the United Kingdom, which are the foreign sovereigns concerned in this case, are parties to each of these treaties. See World Intellectual Property Organization, "States Party to the PCT and the Paris Convention and

Members of the World Trade Organization" (2006), available at http://www. wipo. int/ pct/ en/ texts/ pdf/ pct_ paris_ wto. pdf. * * *

Based on the international treaties that the United States has joined and ratified as the "supreme law of the land," a district court's exercise of supplemental jurisdiction could undermine the obligations of the United States under such treaties, which therefore constitute an exceptional circumstance to decline jurisdiction under § 1367(c)(4). Accordingly, we must scrutinize such an exercise with caution

b. Comity and relations between sovereigns

"Comity refers to the spirit of cooperation in which a domestic tribunal approaches the resolution of cases touching the laws and interests of other sovereign states." *Sociét é Nationale Industrielle Aérospatiale v. U.S. Dist. Court for the S.D. of Iowa*, 482 U.S. 522, 543 n. 27, 107 S.Ct. 2542, 96 L.Ed.2d 461 (1987).

> Comity, in the legal sense, is neither a matter of absolute obligation, on the one hand, nor of mere courtesy and good will, upon the other. But it is the recognition which one nation allows within its territory to the legislative, executive or judicial acts of another nation, having due regard both to international duty and convenience, and to the rights of its own citizens or of other persons who are under the protection of its laws.

Id. * * *

In this case, these considerations of comity do not support the district court's exercise of supplemental jurisdiction over Voda's foreign patent infringement claims. First, Voda has not identified any international duty, and we have found none, that would require our judicial system to adjudicate foreign patent infringement claims. As discussed [above], while the United States has entered into the Paris Convention, the PCT, and the Agreement on TRIPS, nothing in those treaties contemplates or allows one jurisdiction to adjudicate the patents of another. Second, as discussed infra, Voda has not shown that it would be more convenient for our courts to assume the supplemental jurisdiction at issue. Third, with respect to the rights of our citizens, Voda has not shown that foreign courts will inadequately protect his foreign patent rights. Indeed, we see no reason why American courts should supplant British, Canadian, French, or German courts in interpreting and enforcing British, Canadian, European, French, or German patents. * * *

Fourth, assuming jurisdiction over Voda's foreign patent infringement claims could prejudice the rights of the foreign governments. None of the parties or amicus curiae have demonstrated that the British, Canadian, French, or German governments are willing to have our courts exercise jurisdiction over infringement claims based on their patents. Cf. 28 U.S.C. § 1338(a) (granting federal courts exclusive jurisdiction of claims relating to U.S. patents). * * *

The territorial limits of the rights granted by patents are similar to those conferred by land grants. A patent right is limited by the metes and bounds of the jurisdictional territory that granted the right to exclude. * * * Therefore, a patent right to exclude only arises from the legal right granted and recognized by the sovereign within whose territory the right is located. It would be incongruent to allow the sovereign power of one to be infringed or limited by another sovereign's extension of its jurisdiction. Therefore, while our Patent Act declares that "patents shall have the attributes of personal property," 35 U.S.C. § 261, and not real property, the local action doctrine constitutes an informative doctrine counseling us that exercising supplemental jurisdiction over Voda's foreign patent claims could prejudice the rights of the foreign governments.

Therefore, the four considerations enunciated by the Supreme Court in *Société* demonstrate that extending our jurisdiction through § 1367(a) in this case could undermine "the spirit of cooperation" underlying the comity doctrine. Because the purpose underlying comity is not furthered and potentially hindered in this case, adjudication of Voda's foreign patent infringement claims should be left to the sovereigns that create the property rights in the first instance. * * *

We would risk such interference by exercising supplemental jurisdiction over Voda's foreign patent infringement claims. Patents and the laws that govern them are often described as complex. Indeed, one of the reasons cited for why Congress established our court was because it "felt that most judges didn't understand the patent system and how it worked." Judge Pauline Newman, Origins of the Federal Circuit: The Role of Industry, 11 Fed. Cir. B.J. 541, 542 (2002). As such, Cordis U.S. and one of the amicus curiae assert, and Voda does not dispute, that the foreign sovereigns at issue in this case have established specific judges, resources, and procedures to "help assure the integrity and consistency of the application of their patent laws." Therefore, exercising jurisdiction over such subject matter could disrupt their foreign procedures.

By analogy, Congress unified our patent jurisprudence by creating the Federal Circuit and granting exclusive jurisdiction of appeals on patent claims. 28 U.S.C. § 1295. Foreign courts exercising jurisdiction over claims based on U.S. patents would destroy Congress's intent to foster uniformity and to preclude forum shopping. * * *

Accordingly, comity and the principle of avoiding unreasonable interference with the authority of other sovereigns dictate in this case that the district court decline the exercise supplemental jurisdiction under § 1367(c). * * *

e. Fairness

Lastly, the act of state doctrine may make the exercise of supplemental jurisdiction over foreign patent infringement claims fundamentally unfair. As "a 'principle of decision binding on federal and state courts alike,'" the act of state doctrine "requires that, in the process of deciding, the acts of foreign sovereigns taken within their own jurisdictions shall be deemed valid." *W.S. Kirkpatrick & Co., Inc. v. Envtl. Tectonics Corp., Int'l,* 493 U.S. 400, 406, 409, 110 S.Ct. 701, 107 L.Ed.2d 816 (1990) (citation omitted). In this case, none of the parties or amicus curiae have persuaded us that the grant of a patent by a sovereign is not an act of state. But see *Mannington Mills, Inc. v. Congoleum Corp.,* 595 F.2d 1287, 1293–94 (3d Cir.1979) (stating that Third Circuit was "unable to accept the proposition that the mere issuance of patents by a foreign power constitutes [ ] an act of state" under abstention analysis). Therefore, assuming arguendo that the act of state doctrine applies, the doctrine would prevent our courts from inquiring into the validity of a foreign patent grant and require our courts to adjudicate patent claims regardless of validity or enforceability. Given the number of U.S. patent cases that we resolve on validity or enforceability as opposed to infringement grounds, exercising such jurisdiction could be fundamentally unfair to the alleged infringer where, as one amicus curiae points out, "the patent is in fact invalid and the defendant would be excused from liability on that basis in a foreign forum." Voda has not shown in this case that the validity of the foreign patents would not be at issue. Indeed, Cordis U.S. asserts otherwise.

NEWMAN, CIRCUIT JUDGE, dissenting

I respectfully dissent, for the question here presented is not related to federalism and the federal/state relationship, or to pendent jurisdiction of state law issues; nor are disputes about foreign patents so unique as to call up the other theories collected by the panel majority to support this ousting of United States parties from access to United States courts. The certified question is concerned solely with the authority of a United States court, having personal jurisdiction of the parties, to exercise its discretion to accept the amended complaint concerning the foreign patents corresponding to the United States patent in suit. * * *

A foreign country is not a "state" in the constitutional context, and the judicial application of foreign law plays no role in the jurisdictional balance represented by federalism. The rules governing federal jurisdiction of supplemental state claims are irrelevant to whether a United States court has the authority and can exercise its discretion to decide questions that require the application of foreign law. * * *

Courts Routinely Apply Foreign Law

* * * United States courts have determined and applied foreign commercial law, foreign property law, foreign inheritance law, foreign citizenship law, foreign copyright law, foreign trademark law, foreign liability and negligence law, and other foreign law as appropriate to resolution of the dispute between the parties before the court. The principle is that a court should apply the same law that would be applied in the nation where the event occurred, or the law having the most significant relationship to the event in dispute. * * *

Judicial authority to decide questions of foreign law is not a matter of the federal/state relationship codified at 28 U.S.C. § 1367. Nonetheless, the elaboration in *United Mine Workers of America v. Gibbs,* 383 U.S. 715,

86 S.Ct. 1130, 16 L.Ed.2d 218 (1966) concerning federal supplemental jurisdiction of state law causes that have "a common nucleus of operative fact" is a useful analogy to the Voda/Cordis situation, for the "considerations of judicial economy, convenience and fairness to litigants" that are served by supplemental jurisdiction, 383 U.S. at 726, 86 S.Ct. 1130, are relevant to considerations of the exercise of judicial discretion. If these criteria are applied they reinforce, rather than negate, the district court's exercise of discretion to accept Voda's amended complaint. * * *

Enforcement Is Not An Issue

There is no issue raised by either party concerning enforcement by a foreign court of the district court's potential decision concerning any of the Voda foreign patents. This case does not raise issues of comity, treaty, and diplomacy, when judgments are sought to be enforced in another country. The complexities of enforcement of foreign judgments, at which my colleagues hint, indeed serve to protect litigants from abusive procedures, and under the various protocols and treaties that relate to foreign judgments, a foreign court can refuse to accept a decision of another nation's tribunal. * * *

The enforcement aspect was not raised by either party. The district court may have recognized that both Dr. Voda and Cordis Corporation, the manufacturer for all five countries, are within the district court's personal jurisdiction. In Forbo–Giubiasco, supra, the court explained that its findings with respect to the foreign patents were directed to the obligations of the parties to each other, and not to whether or how a foreign tribunal would view the decision.

The issues and relationships herein reinforce the district court's exercise of discretion to accept the amended complaint, and further impugns this court's withdrawal of the district court's discretion as to foreign patents. There is no sound reason why speculative concerns of enforcement in foreign countries warrant depriving the district court of its discretion to resolve this dispute between these United States parties. While we do not know the extent to which the district court might find liability and impose constraints in this case, the answer to this dispute is not to bar the court from hearing it.

The Role of Patent Treaties

The panel majority proposes that it would violate the Paris Convention for the Protection of Industrial Property, the Patent Cooperation Treaty, and the TRIPS Agreement of the World Trade Organization, if the United States were to consider the validity and infringement of Dr. Voda's foreign patents. None of these treaties prohibits resolution by a national court of private disputes that include foreign patent rights. The question is not as presented by the panel majority, whether any treaty imposes "an international duty" on a nation's courts to render decision concerning foreign patents. The question is whether any treaty prohibits a national court from resolving a dispute between entities under the personal jurisdiction of the court. No treaty bars such dispute resolution.

Comity, Harmonization, and the Future

Comity is a complex concept of international law, and its generalization to evict United States courts from their dispute-resolution obligation is not supported on any theory of comity. * * * Comity has no relevance to the need to apply foreign law and the obligation and authority to meet that need. * * *

Proponents of patent "harmonization" point to the similarity of the policies that underlie patent law of all industrialized nations, and stress that for most technologies the same scope of practical protection is available to industrial development in all nations. It would be anomalous indeed for the United States now to rule that the courts cannot understand patent principles as applied in other nations.

Preclusion and prejudgment are inappropriate and unnecessary. From my colleagues' extreme limitation and bar on the district court's exercise of discretion to receive and resolve foreign patent issues, I respectfully dissent.

JOHNS HOPKINS UNIVERSITY v. CELLPRO, INC.

United States Court of Appeals for the Federal Circuit, 1998.
152 F.3d 1342.

LOURIE, CIRCUIT JUDGE.

The '680 and '204 patents (the "Civin patents") issued from continuations of the same parent application and pertain generally to relatively pure suspensions of immature blood cells and monoclonal antibodies used to produce such suspensions. These immature cells, known as "stem" cells, develop into many different forms of mature blood cells, including lymphoid cells (T-cells and B-cells) and myeloid cells (red cells, platelets and granulocytes.

Because stem cells are killed by radiation therapy, these cells must be replaced in leukemia patients who have undergone this treatment. While bone marrow transplants can provide a patient with new stem cells, this procedure carries risks. Notably, the presence of mature cells in transplanted bone marrow can give rise to Graft Versus Host Disease (GVHD), a potentially fatal condition. Accordingly, one of the stated objectives of the invention of the Civin patents "is to provide a method for preparing a cell population useful for stem cell transplantation that is enriched in immature marrow cells and substantially free of mature myeloid and lymphoid cells."

In the early 1980s, scientists began making monoclonal antibodies that would recognize and bind to the antigens contained on the surface of blood cells. Once an antibody binds to an antigen on a cell surface, that cell is flagged and can be separated from other cells using known techniques such as the "FACS" method. Monoclonal antibodies, which are uniform in their binding properties, are produced by cloned cells known as hybridomas. Hybridomas grow and reproduce rapidly and can be frozen for later use to produce additional monoclonal antibodies.

Dr. Curt Civin, the inventor named in the '680 and '204 patents, discovered an antigen, which he named My–10, that appears on the surface of immature stem cells but not on the surface of mature cells. The patents' specifications disclose a monoclonal antibody, which Civin named anti-My–10, which recognizes the My–10 antigen and is useful in separating stem cells from mature cells. The patents further disclose how a hybridoma, which manufactures the anti-My–10 antibody, can be produced and note that a sample of the hybridoma has been deposited with the American Type Culture Collection (ATCC), ATCC Accession No. HB–8483, in Rockville, Maryland.

The '680 and '204 patents claim, respectively, a purified cell suspension of stem cells and monoclonal antibodies useful in producing such a suspension. The parties do not draw distinctions between the various claims in the patents, and instead premise their arguments as to each patent solely on independent claim 1 of each patent. These claims are set forth below with the disputed limitations from each claim emphasized:

> '680 Claim 1: "A suspension of human cells comprising pluripotent lympho-hemapoietic stem cells substantially free of mature lymphoid and myeloid cells."

> '204 Claim 1: "A monoclonal antibody which specifically binds to an antigen on nonmalignant, immature human marrow cells, wherein said antigen is stage specific and not lineage dependent, and said antigen is also specifically bound by the antibody produced by the hybridoma deposited under ATCC Accession No. HB–8483. . . ."

Hopkins, assignee of the Civin patents, and its licensees, Baxter Healthcare and Becton Dickinson, sued CellPro on March 8, 1994, alleging infringement of certain claims of the '204 patent. CellPro, inter alia, counterclaimed for a declaratory judgment of invalidity and noninfringement of certain claims of the '680 patent, prompting Hopkins to sue CellPro for infringement of that patent as well.

The case was tried to a jury beginning on July 24, 1995. The district court reserved construing the claims until after the presentation of evidence. At that time, the court considered but did not provide the jury with instruction concerning the meaning of the disputed limitations, concluding that the language contained therein could be understood according to its ordinary meaning. The jury returned a verdict entirely favorable to CellPro, concluding that all of the asserted claims of both patents were invalid for obviousness and lack of enablement, and that none of the asserted claims was infringed.

Hopkins brought a renewed motion for judgment as a matter of law and in the alternative moved for a new trial, asserting, inter alia, that the court had erred in its construction of the disputed claim limitations. The court agreed that its failure to construe the disputed limitations appeared to be in error, and revisited these and other questions in considering the motion. * * *

As part of the district court's permanent injunction order, the court ordered CellPro to repatriate to the United States "all clones or subclones of the 12.8 hybridoma cell line previously exported by it, as well as any further clones or subclones produced therefrom," and any antibodies produced therefrom. This order encompassed six vials of 12.8 hybridoma from CellPro's United States cell bank which CellPro sent to its Canadian business partner, Biomira, Inc., and cloned vials and antibodies produced therefrom in Canada. These six vials, like the other vials in the cell bank, were created prior to the issuance of the '204 patent, the only patent that is relevant to the 12.8 hybridoma, but were sent to Canada during the term of that patent. The six vials were never thawed or used in any manner prior to their export. One of the six vials was cloned in Canada to produce a working Canadian cell bank of 32 vials of 12.8 hybridoma. Under CellPro's contract with Biomira, Biomira thawed and used the hybridoma from the Canadian cell bank to make 12.8 antibodies for the performance of the Berenson cell separation technique in Canada. Title to the hybridoma, however, remained with CellPro.

In its memorandum opinion supporting its repatriation order, the court did not find compelling CellPro's argument that none of its activities concerning the six vials exported to Canada were infringing uses under 35 U.S.C. § 271 and that they were thus free of the court's equitable power to order repatriation. * * *

E. The Repatriation Order

CellPro's final argument is that the court exceeded the scope of its power when it ordered the repatriation and destruction of the six vials that it exported to its business partner, Biomira, in Canada, as well as cloned vials and antibodies produced therefrom. CellPro contends that it has not committed an infringing act with respect to the exported vials. CellPro summarizes its activities as follows: it produced approximately 100 vials of 12.8 hybridoma to create a United States master cell bank prior to the issuance of the '204 patent, it exported six of those vials to Canada after issuance, and it used those vials in Canada to supply markets outside of the United States. CellPro asserts that none of these acts—pre-issuance manufacture, export, or use outside of the United States—constitutes infringement under 35 U.S.C. § 271, and accordingly that such acts are beyond the scope of the court's equitable powers.

Hopkins responds that the district court's order was properly predicated on the determination that CellPro used (i.e., by cloning or testing) other vials from its United States cell bank in the United States after the issuance of the patent and thereby infringed with respect to the United States cell bank "as a whole." Hopkins asserts that the injunctive power of the district courts is not limited to the prohibition of those activities that constitute patent infringement, but also extends to prohibitions necessary in order to fashion a meaningful remedy for past infringement.

Hopkins argues that repatriation in this case is such a meaningful remedy and will prevent CellPro from unfairly capitalizing upon its infringement.

Section 283 of the Patent Code empowers the courts to "grant injunctions in accordance with the principles of equity to prevent the violation of any right secured by patent, on such terms as the court deems reasonable." 35 U.S.C. § 283 (1994). A "necessary predicate" for the issuance of a permanent injunction is therefore a determination of infringement. When deciding whether a district court abused the discretion provided by Section 283, we are mindful of the fact that the district courts are in the best position to fashion an injunction.

We agree with CellPro that the district court abused its discretion in ordering the repatriation and destruction of the exported vials. The repatriation aspect of the order does not enjoin activities that either have infringed the '204 patent or are likely to do so and thus does not prevent infringement—the proper purpose of an injunction under Section 283. It is clear that the six vials standing alone have not infringed the '204 patent. Mere possession of a product which becomes covered by a subsequently issued patent does not constitute an infringement of that patent until the product is used, sold, or offered for sale in the United States during the term of the patent. Likewise, neither export from the United States nor use in a foreign country of a product covered by a United States patent constitutes infringement. See 35 U.S.C. § 271(a) (1994) ("[W]hoever without authority makes, uses, offers to sell, or sells any patented invention, within the United States or imports into the United States any patented invention during the term of the patent therefor, infringes the patent."); see also *Paper Converting Mach. Co. v. Magna–Graphics Corp.*, 745 F.2d 11, 16, 223 USPQ 591, 594 (Fed.Cir. 1984) ("[B]y the terms of the patent grant, no activity other than the unauthorized making, using, or selling of the claimed invention can constitute direct infringement of a patent, no matter how great the adverse impact of that activity on the economic value of a patent.") (emphasis in original).

That CellPro used other vials from the cell bank in an infringing manner in the United States does not taint the six exported vials with infringement. The exported vials were not "guilty by association." One may consider the pre-issuance manufacture of two machines, one of which is used after the patent is issued and the other of which is exported. An injunction requiring return of the exported machine, which was never made, used, or sold during the term of the patent in the United States, is beyond the scope of Section 283 and hence an abuse of discretion. The same principle applies here to the vials exported to Canada. Accordingly, the court's conclusion that use of some of the vials of the cell bank constituted a use of the cell bank "as a whole" as a means of justifying its repatriation order was an abuse of discretion.

Moreover, there is also no evidentiary basis for concluding that the district court's order was necessary to prevent CellPro from committing further infringing activities. An injunction under Section 283 can reach extraterritorial activities such as those at issue here, even if these activities do not themselves constitute infringement. It is necessary however that the injunction prevent infringement of a United States patent . . . . .

The record in this case does not . . . suggest that the exported vials will be used in a manner which will infringe the patent. CellPro has stipulated, and Hopkins does not refute, that Biomira intended to produce antibodies for CellPro in Canada "for use in products to be sold outside of the United States." . . . Because the record is devoid of evidence upon which the district court could have concluded that its order would prevent further infringement, there was no basis for the court to order the exported hybridomas and its byproducts to be shipped to the United States.

We also do not find persuasive Hopkins' argument that the scope of the district court's order can be justified because it is necessary to fashion a meaningful remedy for CellPro's past infringement. Section 283 does not provide remedies for past infringement; it only provides for injunctive relief to prevent future infringement. The section under which a litigant must seek compensation for past infringement is Section 284. See 35 U.S.C. § 284, ¶ 1 (1994) ("Upon finding for the claimant the court shall award the claimant damages adequate to compensate for the infringement."). We do not understand Hopkins to seriously dispute that it has not received adequate compensation for CellPro's infringement. However, to the extent that Hopkins complains that CellPro's infringement has damaged its ability to service foreign markets, Hopkins must rely on foreign patent protection. See *Deepsouth*, 406 U.S. at 531, 92 S.Ct. 1700, 32 L.Ed.2d 273, 173 USPQ at 774 ("Our patent system makes no claim to extraterritorial effect. . . . To the degree that the inventor needs protection in markets other than those of this country, the wording of 35 U.S.C. §§ 154 and 271 reveals a congressional intent to have him seek it abroad through patents secured in countries where his goods are being used.") (citations and quotation omitted). Such a complaint cannot be remedied by the imposition of an injunction under Section 283.

Hopkins further argues, mimicking the district court's "as a whole" rationale, that it would be fair under the circumstances to order repatriation and destruction because CellPro has committed other clear acts of infringement with respect to other vials in the United States cell bank. We do not agree. As we have already stated, we disagree that this rationale provides a sufficient premise for the court's order given the facts of this case. Moreover, premising the order on this rationale amounts to punishment of CellPro for its infringement. This is not the proper purpose of injunctive relief under Section 283.

Those portions of the district court's permanent injunction order that ordered repatriation and destruction of vials exported by CellPro to Biomira and byproducts produced thereby are not consistent with the stated purpose of Section 283—to prevent infringement. Thus, the court abused its discretion, and those portions of the order are vacated.

NOTES

1. The Federal Circuit's decision in *Voda* provides a nice summary of international treaty obligations and the jurisdiction of federal district courts over non-United States patents. The excerpt also provides a good introduction to the conflicting policy issues surrounding international patent law. The majority adopts a strict territorial approach, with deference to the judgment of non-U.S. sovereigns. Judge Newman takes a pragmatic approach that emphasizes the need for dispute resolution and harmonization. Think of the positives and negatives of each approach. The majority's analysis rests on the competence of domestic courts to resolve disputes involving foreign patents and foreign law. The approach leads to diversity and pluralist approaches to patent law. Judge Newman's approach, on the other hand, leads to harmonization potentially. What happens under Judge Newman's approach if different courts come to different results with respect to patent infringement? Which approach is more likely to lead to problems like forum shopping?

2. As discussed in the materials on extraterritoriality of copyright, patent law is the most territorial of the three intellectual property laws. An inventor can enforce patent rights in a country only if he has been granted a patent in the country and the infringing activities have occurred in that country. Congress has expressly given patent law extraterritorial effect in enacting Section 271(f) of the Patent Act. The fact pattern governed by section 271(f) is relatively straightforward. Inventor has a patent on an invention. Defendant exports components of the invention and has them assembled overseas. Since the infringing activity occurred overseas, absent section 271(f) these acts would not violate the Patent Act. Section 271(f), however, imposes liability on the party for exporting the disassembled parts to make the patented invention. For a discussion of extraterritoriality and software components, see *Microsoft Corp. v. AT & T Corp.*, 550 U.S. 437, 127 S.Ct. 1746, 167 L.Ed.2d 737 (2007) (holding that a copy of software constitutes a component, but software in the abstract does not).

3. Section 271(g) also imposes liability for extraterritorial acts of a defendant. This provision covers the following fact pattern. Inventor has a patent on a process in the United States. The process is used to create a product that is unpatented. Defendant uses the patented process overseas and imports the unpatented product into the United States. The importation is actionable. The statute provides two exceptions: (i) the product is materially changed by subsequent processes, OR (ii) the product becomes a trivial and nonessential component of another product. See *Kinik Co. v. International Trade Comm'n*, 362 F.3d 1359 (Fed. Cir. 2004); *Zoltek Corp. v. United States*, 51 Fed.Cl. 829 (2002); *Eli Lilly & Co. v. Am. Cyanamid Co.*, 82 F.3d 1568 (Fed. Cir. 1996).

4. The *CellPro* case illustrates the extraterritorial reach of remedies. In general, a U.S. court cannot enjoin acts that occur outside the borders of the U.S. unless the injunction serves the purpose of preventing infringement within the United States. Recall Judge Newman's discussion of enforcement in her *Voda* dissent. Do you think the court could order Microsoft to destroy

the software code that it may be keeping outside the United States? How about any physical components that are part of the patented invention?

C. TRADEMARK

1. Extraterritoriality

STEELE v. BULOVA WATCH CO.

Supreme Court of the United States, 1952.
344 U.S. 280, 73 S.Ct. 252, 97 L.Ed. 319.

JUSTICE CLARK delivered the opinion of the Court.

The issue is whether a United States District Court has jurisdiction to award relief to an American corporation against acts of trade-mark infringement and unfair competition consummated in a foreign country by a citizen and resident of the United States.

Bulova Watch Company, Inc., a New York corporation, sued Steele, petitioner here, in the United States District Court for the Western District of Texas. The gist of its complaint charged that 'Bulova,' a trade-mark properly registered under the laws of the United States, had long designated the watches produced and nationally advertised and sold by the Bulova Watch Company; and that petitioner, a United States citizen residing in San Antonio, Texas, conducted a watch business in Mexico City where, without Bulova's authorization and with the purpose of deceiving the buying public, he stamped the name 'Bulova' on watches there assembled and sold. Basing its prayer on these asserted violations of the trade-mark laws of the United States, Bulova requested injunctive and monetary relief. Personally served with process in San Antonio, petitioner answered by challenging the court's jurisdiction over the subject matter of the suit and by interposing several defenses, including his due registration in Mexico of the mark 'Bulova' and the pendency of Mexican legal proceedings thereon, to the merits of Bulova's claim. The trial judge, having initially reserved disposition of the jurisdictional issue until a hearing on the merits, interrupted the presentation of evidence and dismissed the complaint 'with prejudice,' on the ground that the court lacked jurisdiction over the cause. This decision rested on the court's findings that petitioner had committed no illegal acts within the United States. With one judge dissenting, the Court of Appeals reversed; it held that the pleadings and evidence disclosed a cause of action within the reach of the Lanham Trade–Mark Act of 1946, 15 U.S.C. 1051 et seq., 15 U.S.C.A. § 1051 et seq. The dissenting judge thought that 'since the conduct complained of substantially related solely to acts done and trade carried on under full authority of Mexican law, and were confined to and affected only that Nation's internal commerce, (the District Court) was without jurisdiction to enjoin such conduct.'

Petitioner concedes, as he must, that Congress in prescribing standards of conduct for American citizens may project the impact of its laws beyond the territorial boundaries of the United States. Resolution of the jurisdictional issue in this case therefore depends on construction of exercised congressional power, not the limitations upon that power itself.

The Lanham Act, on which Bulova posited its claims to relief, confers broad jurisdictional powers upon the courts of the United States. The statute's expressed intent is 'to regulate commerce within the control of Congress by making actionable the deceptive and misleading use of marks in such commerce; to protect registered marks used in such comme(r)ce from interference by State, or territorial legislation; to protect persons engaged in such commerce against unfair competition; to prevent fraud and deception in such commerce by the use of reproductions, copies, counterfeits, or colorable imitations of registered marks; and to provide rights and remedies stipulated by treaties and conventions respecting trade-marks, trade names, and unfair competition entered into between the United States and foreign nations.' § 45, 15 U.S.C. § 1127, 15 U.S.C.A. § 1127. To that end, § 32(1) holds liable in a civil action by a trade-mark registrant '(a)ny person who shall, in commerce,' infringe a registered trade-mark in a manner there detailed. 'Commerce' is defined as 'all commerce which may lawfully be regulated by Congress.' § 45, 15 U.S.C. § 1127, 15 U.S.C.A. § 1127. The district courts of the United States are granted jurisdiction over all actions 'arising under' the Act, § 39, 15 U.S.C. § 1121, 15 U.S.C.A. § 1121, and can award relief which may include injunctions, 'according to the principles of equity,' to prevent the violation of any registrant's rights. § 34, 15 U.S.C. § 1116, 15 U.S.C.A. § 1116.

The record reveals the following significant facts which for purposes of a dismissal must be taken as true: Bulova Watch Company, one of the largest watch manufacturers in the world, advertised and distributed 'Bulova' watches in the United States and foreign countries. Since 1929, its aural and visual advertising, in Spanish and English, has penetrated Mexico. Petitioner, long a resident of San Antonio, first entered the watch business there in 1922, and in 1926 learned of the trade-mark 'Bulova.' He subsequently transferred his business to Mexico City and, discovering that 'Bulova' had not been registered in Mexico, in 1933 procured the Mexican registration of that mark. Assembling Swiss watch movements and dials and cases imported from that country and the United States, petitioner in Mexico City stamped his watches with 'Bulova' and sold them as such. As a result of the distribution of spurious 'Bulovas,' Bulova Watch Company's Texas sales representative received numerous complaints from retail jewelers in the Mexican border area whose customers brought in for repair defective 'Bulovas' which upon inspection often turned out not to be products of that company. Moreover, subsequent to our grant of certiorari in this case the prolonged litigation in the courts of Mexico has come to an end. On October 6, 1952, the Supreme Court of Mexico rendered a judgment upholding an administrative ruling which had nullified petitioner's Mexican registration of 'Bulova.'

On the facts in the record we agree with the Court of Appeals that petitioner's activities, when viewed as a whole, fall within the jurisdictional scope of the Lanham Act. This Court has often stated that the legislation of Congress will not extend beyond the boundaries of the United States unless a contrary legislative intent appears. The question thus is 'whether Congress intended to make the law applicable' to the facts of this case. For 'the United States is not debarred by any rule of international law from governing the conduct of is own citizens upon the high seas or even in foreign countries when the rights of other nations or their nationals are not infringed. With respect to such an exercise of authority there is no question of international law, but solely of the purport of the municipal law which establishes the duty of the citizen in relation to his own government.' *Skiriotes v. State of Florida*, 1941, 313 U.S. 69, 73, 61 S.Ct. 924, 927, 85 L.Ed. 1193. As Mr. Justice Minton, then sitting on the Court of Appeals, applied the principle in a case involving unfair methods of competition: 'Congress has the power to prevent unfair trade practices in foreign commerce by citizens of the United States, although some of the acts are done outside the territorial limits of the United States.' *Branch v. Federal Trade Commission*, 7 Cir., 1944, 141 F.2d 31, 35. Nor has this Court in tracing the commerce scope of statutes differentiated between enforcement of legislative policy by the Government itself or by private litigants proceeding under a statutory right. *Thomsen v. Cayser*, 1917, 243 U.S. 66. 37 S.Ct. 353, 61 L.Ed. 597; *Mandeville Island Farms v. American Crystal Sugar Co.*, 1948, 334 U.S. 219, 68 S.Ct. 996, 92 L.Ed. 1328; cf. *Vermilya–Brown Co. v. Connell*, 1948, 335 U.S. 377, 69 S.Ct. 140, 93 L.Ed. 76; *Foley Bros., Inc. v. Filardo*, supra. The public policy subserved is the same in each case. In the light of the broad jurisdictional grant in the Lanham Act, we deem its scope to encompass petitioner's activities here. His operations and their effects were not confined within the territorial limits of a foreign nation. He bought component parts of his wares in the United States, and spurious 'Bulovas' filtered through the Mexican border into this country; his competing goods could well reflect adversely on Bulova Watch Company's trade reputation in markets cultivated by advertising here as well as abroad. Under similar factual circumstances, courts of the United States have awarded relief to registered trade-mark owners, even prior to the advent of the broadened commerce provisions of the Lanham Act. Even when most jealously read, that Act's sweeping reach into 'all commerce which may lawfully be regulated by Congress' does not constrict prior law or deprive courts of jurisdiction previously exercised. We do not deem material that petitioner affixed the mark 'Bulova' in Mexico City rather than here, or that his purchases in the United States when viewed in isolation do not violate any of our laws. They were essential steps in the course of business consummated abroad; acts in themselves legal lose that character when they become part of an unlawful scheme. In sum, we do not think that petitioner by so simple a device can evade the thrust of the laws of the United States in a privileged sanctuary beyond our borders.

American Banana Co. v. United Fruit Co., 1909, 213 U.S. 347, 29 S.Ct. 511, 53 L.Ed. 826, compels nothing to the contrary. This Court there upheld a Court of Appeals' affirmance of the trial court's dismissal of a private damage action predicated on alleged violations of the Sherman Act, 15 U.S.C.A. §§ 1–7, 15. The complaint, in substance, charged United Fruit Company with monopolization of the banana import trade between Central America and the United States, and with the instigation of Costa Rican governmental authorities to seize plaintiff's plantation and produce in Panama. The Court of Appeals reasoned that plaintiff had shown no damage from the asserted monopoly and could not found liability on the seizure, a sovereign act of another nation. This Court agreed that a violation of American laws could not be grounded on a foreign nation's sovereign acts. Viewed in its context, the holding in that case was not meant to confer blanket immunity on trade practices which radiate unlawful consequences here, merely because they were initiated or consummated outside the territorial limits of the United States. Unlawful effects in this country, absent in the posture of the Banana case before us, are often decisive.... And, unlike the *Banana* case, whatever rights Mexico once conferred on petitioner its courts now have decided to take away.

Nor do we doubt the District Court's jurisdiction to award appropriate injunctive relief if warranted by the facts after trial. 15 U.S.C. §§ 1116, 1121, 15 U.S.C.A. §§ 1116, 1121. Mexico's courts have nullified the Mexican registration of 'Bulova'; there is thus no conflict which might afford petitioner a pretext that such relief would impugn foreign law. The question, therefore, whether a valid foreign registration would affect either the power to enjoin or the propriety of its exercise is not before us. Where, as here, there can be no interference with the sovereignty of another nation, the District Court in exercising its equity powers may command persons properly before it to cease or perform acts outside its territorial jurisdiction.

MR. JUSTICE REED, with whom MR. JUSTICE DOUGLAS joins, dissenting.

The purpose of the Lanham Act is to prevent deceptive and misleading use of trade-marks. § 45, 15 U.S.C. § 1127, 15 U.S.C.A. § 1127. To further that purpose the Act makes liable in an action by the registered holder of the trade-mark 'any person who shall, in commerce,' infringe such trade-mark. § 32(1), 15 U.S.C. § 1114(1), 15 U.S.C.A. § 1114(1). 'Commerce' is defined as being 'all commerce which may lawfully be regulated by Congress.' § 45, 15 U.S.C. § 1127, 15 U.S.C.A. § 1127.

The Court's opinion bases jurisdiction on the Lanham Act. In the instant case the only alleged acts of infringement occurred in Mexico. The acts complained of were the stamping of the name 'Bulova' on watches and the subsequent sale of the watches. There were purchases of assembly material in this country by petitioners. Purchasers from petitioners in Mexico brought the assembled watches into the United States. Assuming that Congress has the power to control acts of our citizens throughout the world, the question presented is one of statutory construction: Whether Congress intended the Act to apply to the conduct here exposed.

There are, of course, cases in which a statement of specific contrary intent will not be deemed so necessary. Where the case involves the construction of a criminal statute 'enacted because of the right of the government to defend itself against obstruction, or fraud * * * committed by its own citizens,' it is not necessary for Congress to make specific provisions that the law 'shall include the high seas and foreign countries'. *United States v. Bowman*, 260 U.S. 94, 98, 43 S.Ct. 39, 41, 67 L.Ed. 149. This is also true when it is a question of the sovereign power of the United States to require the response of a nonresident citizen. *Blackmer v. United States*, 284 U.S. 421, 52 S.Ct. 252, 76 L.Ed. 375. A similar situation is met where a statute is applied to acts committed by citizens in areas subject to the laws of no sovereign. See *Skiriotes v. State of Florida*, 313 U.S. 69, 61 S.Ct. 924, 85 L.Ed. 1193; *Old Dominion S. S. Co. v. Gilmore*, 207 U.S. 398, 28 S.Ct. 133, 52 L.Ed. 264.

In the instant case none of these exceptional considerations come into play. Petitioner's buying of unfinished watches in the United States is not an illegal commercial act. Nor can it be said that petitioners were engaging in illegal acts in commerce when the finished watches bearing the Mexican trade-mark were purchased from them and brought into the United States by such purchasers, all without collusion between petitioner and the purchaser. The stamping of the Bulova trade-mark, done in Mexico, is not an act 'within the control of Congress.' It should not be utilized as a basis for action against petitioner. The Lanham Act, like the Sherman Act, should be construed to apply only to acts done within the sovereignty of the United States. While we do not condone the piratic use of trade-marks, neither do we believe that Congress intended to make such use actionable irrespective of the place it occurred. Such extensions of power bring our legislation into conflict with the laws and practices of other nations, fully capable of punishing infractions of their own laws, and should require specific words to reach acts done within the territorial limits of other sovereignties.

VANITY FAIR MILLS, INC. v. THE T. EATON CO.

United States Court of Appeals for the Second Circuit, 1956.
234 F.2d 633.

WATERMAN, CIRCUIT JUDGE.

This case presents interesting and novel questions concerning the extraterritorial application of the Lanham Act, 15 U.S.C.A. § 1051 et seq., and the International Convention for the Protection of Industrial Property (Paris Union)....

Plaintiff, Vanity Fair Mills, Inc., is a Pennsylvania corporation, having its principal place of business at Reading, Pennsylvania. It has been engaged in the manufacture and sale of women's underwear under the trade-mark 'Vanity Fair' since about the year 1914 in the United States, and has been continuously offering its branded merchandise for sale in Canada since at least 1917. Plaintiff has publicized its trade-mark 'Vanity Fair' on feminine underwear in the United States since 1914, and since 1917 has regularly expended large sums of money in advertising and promoting its trademark both in the United States and Canada. As a result of the high quality of plaintiff's merchandise, and its extensive sales promotion and advertising, the name 'Vanity Fair' has become associated throughout the United States and Canada with plaintiff's products.

Beginning in 1914 plaintiff has protected its trade-mark rights by registrations with the United States Patent Office of the trade-mark 'Vanity Fair' as applying to various types of underwear. It has been continuously manufacturing and selling feminine underwear under these trade-mark registrations since about the year 1914.

Defendant, The T. Eaton Company, Limited, is a Canadian corporation engaged in the retail merchandising business throughout Canada, with its principal office in Toronto, Ontario. It has a regular and established place of business within the Southern District of New York. On November 3, 1915, defendant filed with the proper Canadian official an application for the registration in Canada of the trade-mark 'Vanity Fair,' claiming use in connection with the sale of 'Women's, Misses' and Children's Coats, Suits, Cloaks, Waists, Dresses, Skirts, Corsets, Knitted Goods, Gloves, Hosiery, Boots & Shoes, Outer Garments, and other Wearing Apparel.' On November 10, 1915, the proper Canadian official granted defendant's application for the registration of that mark. Plaintiff asserts that this registration applies only to feminine outerwear, and that in any event it is merely a 'paper registration' because of non-use. In 1919 plaintiff sought to register the trade-mark 'Vanity Fair' in Canada for 'ready made underwear,' but its application was rejected as a matter of course because of the prior registration of defendant. In 1933 defendant, in reply to a request of the Canadian Registrar of Trade–Marks, listed 'women's underwear, corsets, girdles and other foundation garments' as the goods in connection with which it had actually been using the mark 'Vanity Fair,' and its registration was modified accordingly. Plaintiff alleges that defendant, by this informal procedure, amended its trade-mark registration in Canada to include, for the first time, feminine underwear.

During the years 1945–1953 the defendant ceased to use its own 'Vanity–Fair' trade-mark, purchased branded merchandise from the plaintiff, and sold this merchandise under advertisements indicating that it was of United States origin and of plaintiff's manufacture. These purchases by defendant from plaintiff were made through defendant's New York office. In 1953 defendant resumed the use of its own trade-mark 'Vanity Fair' and, simultaneously, under the same trade-mark, sold plaintiff's branded merchandise and cheaper merchandise of Canadian manufacture. Defendant at this time objected to plaintiff's sales of its branded merchandise to one of defendant's principal competitors in Canada, the Robert Simpson

Company. The Simpson Company discontinued purchases of plaintiff's branded merchandise after being threatened with infringement suits by defendant.

Plaintiff alleges that these acts constitute a conspiracy on the part of the corporate defendant and its officers and agents to appropriate for their own benefit plaintiff's registered and common-law trade-mark. It asserts that defendant, by purchasing plaintiff's branded merchandise for a period of years and advertising and selling such merchandise as plaintiff's goods, attempted to associate plaintiff's trade-mark with itself, and, that purpose having been accomplished, defendant then began using the trade-mark 'Vanity Fair' in connection with its own inferior feminine underwear, discontinued purchases from plaintiff, and threatened its competitors in Canada with infringement suits if they continued to sell plaintiff's branded merchandise in Canada.

Finally, plaintiff asserts that defendant has advertised feminine underwear in the United States under the trade-mark 'Vanity Fair,' and that it has sold such underwear by mail to customers residing in the United States.

The complaint seeks injunctive relief against the use by defendant of the trade-mark 'Vanity Fair' in connection with women's underwear both in Canada and the United States, a declaration of the superior rights of the plaintiff in such trade-mark, and an accounting for damages and profits.

[Plaintiff] asserts that its claims arise under the laws of the United States and should be governed by those laws. The result sought—extraterritorial application of American law—is contrary to usual conflict-of-laws principles. First, the legal status of foreign nationals in the United States is determined solely by our domestic law—foreign law confers no privilege in this country that our courts are bound to recognize. And when trade-mark rights within the United States are being litigated in an American court, the decisions of foreign courts concerning the respective trade-mark rights of the parties are irrelevant and inadmissible. Similarly, the rights and liabilities of United States citizens who compete with foreign nationals in their home countries are ordinarily to be determined by the appropriate foreign law. This fundamental principle, although not without exceptions, is the usual rule, and is based upon practical considerations such as the difficulty of obtaining extraterritorial enforcement of domestic law, as well as on considerations of international comity and respect for national integrity. Second, the creation and extent of tort liability is governed, according to the usual rule, by the law of the place where the alleged tort was committed (lex loci delicti). The place of the wrong (locus delicti) is where the last event necessary to make an actor liable takes place. If the conduct complained of is fraudulent misrepresentation, the place of the wrong is not where the fraudulent statement was made, but where the plaintiff, as a result thereof, suffered a loss. Thus in cases of trade-mark infringement and unfair competition, the wrong takes place not where the deceptive labels are affixed to the goods or where the goods are wrapped in the misleading packages, but where the passing off occurs, i.e., where the deceived customer buys the defendant's product in the belief that he is buying the plaintiff's. In this case, with the exception of defendant's few mail order sales into the United States, the passing-off occurred in Canada, and hence under the usual rule would be governed by Canadian law.

Conflict-of-laws principles, however, are not determinative of the question whether the International Convention and/or the Lanham Act provide relief in American courts and under American law against acts of trade-mark infringement and unfair competition committed in foreign countries by foreign nationals. If the International Convention or the Lanham Act provide such relief, and if the provisions are within constitutional powers, American courts would be required to enforce these provisions. It is therefore necessary to determine whether the International Convention or the Lanham Act provide such relief. Only if it is determined that they do not provide such extensive relief, and hence that the only jurisdictional basis for the suit is diversity of citizenship, do we reach the question whether the district court abused its discretion in dismissing the complaint because of forum non conveniens.

I. The International Convention

Plaintiff asserts that the International Convention for the Protection of Industrial Property (Paris Union) ... to which both the United States and Canada are parties, is self-executing; that by virtue of Article VI of the Constitution it is a part of the law of this country which is to be enforced by its courts; and that the Convention has created rights available to plaintiff which protect it against trade-mark infringement and unfair competition in foreign countries. Plaintiff would appear to be correct in arguing that no special legislation in the United States was necessary to make the International Convention effective here, but it erroneously maintains that the Convention created private rights under American law for acts of unfair competition occurring in foreign countries.

The International Convention is essentially a compact between the various member countries to accord in their own countries to citizens of the other contracting parties trade-mark and other rights comparable to those accorded their own citizens by their domestic law. The underlying principle is that foreign nationals should be given the same treatment in each of the member countries as that country makes available to its own citizens. In addition, the Convention sought to create uniformity in certain respects by obligating each member nation 'to assure to nationals of countries of the Union an effective protection against unfair competition.'

The Convention is not premised upon the idea that the trade-mark and related laws of each member nation shall be given extraterritorial application, but on exactly the converse principle that each nation's law shall have only territorial application. Thus a foreign national of a member nation using his trade-mark in commerce in the United States is accorded extensive protection here against infringement and other types of unfair competition by virtue of United States membership in the Convention. But that protection has its source in, and is subject to the limitations of, American law, not the law of the foreign national's own country. Likewise, the International Convention provides protection to a United States trade-mark owner such as plaintiff against unfair competition and trade-mark infringement in Canada—but only to the extent that Canadian law recognizes the treaty obligation as creating private rights or has made the Convention operative by implementing legislation. Under Canadian law, unlike United States law, the International Convention was not effective to create any private rights in Canada without legislative implementation. However, the obligations undertaken by the Dominion of Canada under this treaty have been implemented by legislation, most recently by the Canadian Trade marks Act of 1953, 1–2 Elizabeth II, Chapter 49. If plaintiff has any rights under the International Convention (other than through 44 of the Lanham Act, discussed below), they are derived from this Canadian law, and not from the fact that the International Convention may be a self-executing treaty which is a part of the law of this country.

II. The Lanham Act

Plaintiff's primary reliance is on the Lanham Act, 15 U.S.C.A. 1051–1127, 60 Stat. 427, a complex statute conferring broad jurisdictional powers on the federal courts. Plaintiff advances two alternative arguments, the first one based on the decision of the Supreme Court in *Steele v. Bulova Watch Co.*, 1952, 344 U.S. 280, 73 S.Ct. 252, 97 L.Ed. 319, giving the provisions of the Lanham Act an extraterritorial application against acts committed in Mexico by an American citizen, and the second based specifically on § 44 of the Act, 15 U.S.C.A. § 1126, which was intended to carry out our obligations under the International Conventions.

A. General Extraterritorial Application of the Lanham Act—the Bulova Case.

Section 32(1)(a) of the Lanham Act, 15 U.S.C.A. § 1114(1)(a), one of the more important substantive provisions of the Act, protects the owner of a registered mark from use 'in commerce' by another that is 'likely to cause confusion or mistake or to deceive purchasers as to the source of origin' of the other's good or services. 'Commerce' is defined by the Act as 'all commerce which may lawfully be regulated by Congress.' § 45, 15 U.S.C.A. § 1127. Plaintiff, relying on *Steele v. Bulova Watch Co.*, 1952, 344 U.S. 280, 73 S.Ct. 252, 97 L.Ed. 319, argues that § 32(1)(a) should be given an extraterritorial application, and that this case falls within the literal wording of the section since the defendant's use of the mark 'Vanity Fair' in Canada had a substantial effect on 'commerce which may be lawfully be regulated by Congress.'

While Congress has no power to regulate commerce in the Dominion of Canada, it does have power to regulate commerce 'with foreign Nations, and among the several States.' Const. art. 1, § 8, cl. 3. This power is now generally interpreted to extend to all commerce, even intrastate and entirely foreign commerce, which has a substantial effect on commerce between the states or between the United States and foreign countries. Particularly is this true when a conspiracy is alleged with acts in further-ance of that conspiracy taking place in both the United States and foreign countries. Thus it may well be that Congress could constitutionally provide infringement remedies so long as the defendant's use of the mark has a substantial effect on the foreign or interstate commerce of the United States. But we do not reach this constitutional question because we do not think that Congress intended that the infringement remedies provided in 32(1)(a) and elsewhere should be applied to acts committed by a foreign national in his home country under a presumably valid trade-mark registration in that country.

The Lanham Act itself gives almost no indication of the extent to which Congress intended to exercise its power in this area. While § 45, 15 U.S.C.A. § 1127, states a broad definition of the "commerce" subject to the Act, both the statement of Congressional intent in the same section and the provisions of § 44, 15 U.S.C.A. § 1126, indicate Congressional regard for the basic principle of the International Conventions, i.e., equal application to citizens and foreign nationals alike of the territorial law of the place where the acts occurred. And the Supreme Court, in *Steele v. Bulova Watch Co.*, 1952, 344 U.S. 280, 73 S.Ct. 252, 97 L.Ed. 319, the only other extraterritorial case since the Lanham Act, did not intimate that the Act should be given the extreme interpretation urged upon us here.

In the *Bulova* case, supra, the Fifth Circuit, 194 F.2d 567, assuming that the defendant had a valid registration under Mexican law, found that the district court had jurisdiction to prevent the defendant's use of the mark in Mexico, on the ground that there was a sufficient effect on United States commerce. Subsequently, the defendant's registration was canceled in Mexican proceedings, and on review of the Fifth Circuit's decision, the Supreme Court noted that the question of the effect of a valid registration in the foreign country was not before it. The Court affirmed the Fifth Circuit, holding that the federal district court had jurisdiction to prevent unfair use of the plaintiff's mark in Mexico. In doing so the Court stressed three factors: (1) the defendant's conduct had a substantial effect on United States commerce; (2) the defendant was a United States citizen and the United States has a broad power to regulate the conduct of its citizens in foreign countries; and (3) there was no conflict with trade-mark rights established under the foreign law, since the defendant's Mexican registration had been canceled by proceedings in Mexico. Only the first factor is present in this case.

We do not think that the *Bulova* case lends support to plaintiff; to the contrary, we think that the rationale of the Court was so thoroughly based on the power of the United States to govern 'the conduct of its own citizens upon the high seas or even in foreign countries when the rights of other nations or their nationals are not infringed', that the absence of one of the above factors might well be determinative and that the absence of both is certainly fatal. Plaintiff makes some argument that many American citizens are employed in defendant's New York office, but it is abundantly clear that these employees do not direct the affairs of the company or in any way control its actions. The officers and directors of defendant who manage its affairs are Canadian citizens. Moreover, the action has only been brought against Canadian citizens. We conclude that the remedies provided by the Lanham Act, other than in § 44, should not be given an extraterritorial application against foreign citizens acting under presumably valid trade-marks in a foreign country.

B. Section 44 of the Lanham Act.

Plaintiff's alternative contention is that § 44 of the Lanham Act, which is entitled 'International Conventions,' affords to United States citizens all possible remedies against unfair competition by foreigners who are nationals of convention countries, including the relief requested in this case. Subsection (b) of § 44 specifies that nationals of foreign countries signatory to certain named conventions (including the Paris Union signed by Canada) are 'entitled to the benefits * * * (of the Act) to the extent * * * essential to give effect to (the conventions).' Subsection (g) then provides that the trade names of persons described in subsection (b), i.e., nationals of foreign countries which have signed the conventions, 'shall be protected without the obligation of filing or registration whether or not they form parts of marks', and subsection (h) provides that the same persons 'shall be entitled to effective protection against unfair competition * * * ' Finally, subsection (i) provides that 'citizens or residents of the United States shall have the same benefits as are granted by this section to persons described in subsection (b) * * * ' Thus § 44 first implements the international agreements by providing certain foreign nationals with the benefits contained in those agreements, then, in subsection (i), places American citizens on an equal footing by providing them with the same benefits. Since American citizens are given only the same benefits granted to eligible foreign nationals, the benefits conferred on foreign nationals must be examined to see whether they have any extraterritorial application.

The benefits provided by § 44 (without attempting to be exhaustive) may be summarized as follows: a foreign national may register his foreign mark upon the production of a certificate of registration issued by his country of origin, even though he has not used his mark in United States commerce, § 44(c), 15 U.S.C.A. § 1126(c); in determining priority of filing, if the foreign national has filed for registration in the United States within six months after filing abroad, he may make use of his foreign filing date but if his foreign registration antedates the six month period, he may use only his United States Filing date, § 44(d), 15 U.S.C.A. § 1126(d); a foreign national may register his foreign mark on the Principal Register if they are eligible, and, if not, on the Supplemental Register, § 44(e), 15 U.S.C.A. § 1126(e); a foreign national may prevent the importation into the United States of goods bearing infringing marks or names, § 42, 15 U.S.C.A. § 1124; once a foreign mark has been registered under the Lanham Act, its status in the United States is independent of the continued validity of its registration abroad, and its duration, validity, and transfer in the United States are governed by 'the provisions of this chapter', § 44(f), 15 U.S.C.A. § 1126(f). It will be noted that all of these benefits are internal to the United States in the sense that they confer on foreign nationals certain rights in the United States. None of them could have extraterritorial application, for all of them relate solely to the registration and protection of marks within the United States.

We now come to the two remaining benefits specified in § 44, and the ones upon which plaintiff relies: the provision in subsection (g) protecting trade-names names without the obligation of filing or registration, and the provision in subsection (h) entitling eligible foreign nationals 'to effective protection against unfair competition' and making available 'the remedies provided in this chapter for infringement of marks * * * so far as they may be appropriate in repressing acts of unfair competition.' Here again, we think that these benefits are limited in application to within the United States. It is true that they are not expressly so limited, but it seems inconceivable that Congress meant by this language to extend to all eligible foreign nationals a remedy in the United States against unfair competition occurring in their own countries. Moreover, if § 44 were so interpreted, it would apply to commerce which is beyond the Congressional power to regulate, and a serious constitutional question would be created. In the absence of any Congressional intent to provide remedies of such extensive application, we interpret § 44 in a manner which avoids constitutional questions and which carries out the underlying principle of the International Conventions sought to be implemented by § 44—the principle that each nation shall apply its national law equally to foreigners and citizens alike.

Since United States citizens are given by subsection (i) of § 44 only the same benefits which the Act extends to eligible foreign nationals, and since the benefits conferred on those foreign nationals have no extraterritorial application, the benefits accorded to citizens by this section can likewise have no extraterritorial application.

[The court also addressed the issue of forum non conveniens and ruled that the doctrine favored the Canadian defendant because of the prevailing issue of rights in the mark under Canadian law.]

NOTES

1. Of the three intellectual property regimes, trademark arguably has the greatest extraterritorial reach. The breadth of extraterritoriality rests on trademark's roots in Congress' power to regulate commerce between nations and among the states. The *Bulova* case illustrates how broad the law can be applied. Putting aside the important gloss on *Bulova* in the *Vanity Fair case*, did the Court go too far in permitting liability for unauthorized use of a

trademark on sales in Mexico? Where is the effect on United States commerce when the goods were manufactured and sold in Mexico? Keep the case in mind when you discuss the gray market materials below. Does the case reflect the universalist notion of trademark, as opposed to the more accepted territorial notion?

2.   One interpretation of *Bulova* is that while the trademark owner had a cause of action against the user of the mark in Mexico, the remedies might be limited. Damages might be minimal here if the trademark owner was not using the mark in Mexico. Furthermore, the Supreme Court does see some limits on injunctive relief if the court were to interfere with the sovereignty of a foreign nation. In this case, the Court did not see any interference since the mark had been cancelled in Mexico. Therefore, the court could enjoin sales of the branded product in Mexico without interfering with rights established under Mexican law.

3.   The *Vanity Fair* case provides a helpful three part approach to determining the extra-territorial reach of the Lanham Act. Note that the first element rests on the effect on U.S. commerce. What was the effect on U.S. commerce of the sales of the branded watches in Mexico? Was it the limitations on the trademark owner to expand his market into Mexico? Was it a loss to the value of the brand? Notice that the second element focuses on the nationality of the infringer. Why is this relevant? Is there some issue beyond the interference with sovereignty under the third element?

2.   Trademark Rights

STERLING DRUG, INCORPORATED v. BAYER AG

United States Court of Appeals for the Second Circuit, 1994.
14 F.3d 733.

JON O. NEWMAN, CHIEF JUDGE:

This appeal primarily concerns the permissible scope of an injunction issued to protect American trademark rights against infringement by a foreign corporation. The context of the dispute is the name and mark "Bayer" in which both an American corporation, Sterling Drug Inc. ("Sterling"), and a German corporation, Bayer AG, hold rights. The appeal is brought by Bayer AG, Bayer U.S.A. Inc., and Miles, Inc. from the July 22, 1992, judgment of the District Court for the Southern District of New York (Robert J. Ward, Judge), upholding Sterling's claims of breach of contract and trademark infringement and broadly enjoining Bayer AG from using the word "Bayer" in any advertisement or materials that are reasonably likely to be disseminated in the United States. We conclude that Sterling is entitled to prevail but that the injunction is overly broad and must be modified . . . . .

At the turn of the century, the rights to the "Bayer" name and mark in the United States were owned by Bayer AG. It lost those rights during World War I when Bayer AG's United States subsidiary, The Bayer Company, Inc., was seized by the United States Alien Property Custodian. In 1918, Sterling acquired rights to the "Bayer" name and mark by purchasing The Bayer Company from the Alien Property Custodian. That acquisition precipitated decades of controversy between Sterling and Bayer AG, marked by a series of lawsuits and agreements.

Sterling is a Delaware corporation with its principal place of business in New York. Sterling manufactures and sells prescription drugs and over-the-counter ("OTC") medicines, as well as home and personal care products. Ever since purchasing The Bayer Company, Sterling (which was itself acquired by the Eastman Kodak Company in 1988 and, since this lawsuit began, has changed its name to Sterling Winthrop, Inc.) has sold aspirin and related products in the United States under the "Bayer" trademark. Sterling's total sales in 1989 were $1.6 billion, of which $125 million was attributable to aspirin and related products using the "Bayer" trademark. Over the last five years, Sterling has spent approximately $50 million a year in promoting and advertising its "Bayer" trademark and products.

Bayer AG, founded in Germany some 125 years ago by Friedrich Bayer, is a large multinational corporation headquartered in Leverkusen, Germany, with worldwide sales in 1990 of $25.7 billion. The United States is Bayer AG's largest single market. In the United States, Bayer AG owns Miles, Inc., a pharmaceutical company, and Mobay Corporation, a chemical company. Bayer AG also owns Bayer USA Inc., a Delaware corporation, which is the subject of much of the pending controversy. Since the initiation of this lawsuit, Bayer USA and Mobay have been merged into Miles, and Bayer AG no longer uses "Bayer" as part of the name of any subsidiary in the United States.

In 1955, Bayer AG brought suit against Sterling in an ultimately unsuccessful effort to regain the right to use the "Bayer" mark in the United States. It sued under the antitrust laws, arguing that Sterling had improperly asserted trademark rights to the "Bayer" mark as a means of suppressing competition. The Third Circuit held against Bayer AG, ruling broadly that Sterling "acquired absolute rights to the exclusive use of the trademarks in question by its purchase of [The Bayer Company, Inc.]" The Court dismissed the suit, ruling that because Sterling had acted within its legal rights in using the mark, that use could not violate the antitrust laws.

Following this decision, Sterling and Bayer AG signed a contract in 1964 governing Bayer AG's use of the Bayer mark in the United States. The 1964 Agreement prohibited Bayer AG from using the Bayer name "in connection with Aspirin or other analgesics . . . [or] in the course of trade in any other goods." The Agreement recognized an exception that allowed Bayer AG to use its full name (then "Farbenfabriken Bayer A.G.") in packaging inserts for consumer goods including pharmaceutical products. The Agreement also permitted Bayer AG to use its full name for nonpharmaceutical and non-consumer goods, as long as it did not advertise them on radio or television.

In 1970, Bayer AG and Sterling signed another agreement, this time dealing with the use of the "Bayer" name and mark in all countries other than the United States and Cuba. Under this agreement, in return for a payment of $2.8 million, Sterling recognized Bayer AG's exclusive rights in the "Bayer" name and mark everywhere except the United States, Canada, and some Caribbean nations. In Canada, the parties agreed to concurrent use of the "Bayer" name, while in some Caribbean countries, Sterling was granted exclusive rights to the "Bayer" name and mark.

In 1971, the parties modified the 1964 Agreement in response to Bayer AG's plan to drop "Farbenfabriken" from its corporate name. Sterling consented to the use of Bayer AG's new name in the United States, but under more limited circumstances than had been permitted under the 1964 Agreement.

The late 1970's and early 1980's saw a major expansion of Bayer AG's U.S. operations. Bayer AG bought out its partner in the Mobay Corporation, acquired Cutter Laboratories and Miles Laboratories, and created a U.S. holding company called "Rhinechem." Bayer AG's higher U.S. profile led to further negotiations between Bayer AG and Sterling regarding the German firm's rights to use the "Bayer" name in the U.S. These negotiations culminated in a 1986 modification to the 1964 Agreement. The 1986 Agreement permitted Bayer AG to change the name of its U.S. holding company to "Bayer USA Inc." so long as this company remained "a non-operating holding company, i.e., [a company] not trading in goods." Sterling expressly agreed to concurrent use of the Bayer tradename and to registration of the "Bayer" trademark by Bayer AG for use "in the course of trade in non-consumer and non-pharmaceutical goods." The 1986 Agreement provided that "[t]hese uses shall include advertising to the relevant trade in the normal course of trade." Bayer for its part agreed not to use the mark "in communicating with the pharmaceutical industry or consumers in general through product, institutional or company-identifying advertising or promotion...." Bayer AG paid Sterling $25 million for Sterling's concessions under the 1986 Agreement.

Following execution of the 1986 Agreement, defendants began to make extensive use of the "Bayer" name and mark. Though Bayer AG characterizes these actions as being fully consistent with Sterling's contractual and legal rights, Sterling sees them as "more than a few innocent steps over the line."

Bayer AG began by obtaining federal registrations for the "Bayer" mark for industrial and agricultural chemicals and related products. It advertised these products in trade journals. In accordance with the 1986 Agreement, it renamed Rhinechem "Bayer USA Inc." Bayer AG expanded this subsidiary's managerial functions, employing 60 persons at Bayer USA Inc. where Rhinechem had employed none. During 1987 and 1988, Bayer USA conducted a corporate "image" campaign, placing a total of 67 advertisements in the Wall Street Journal, Forbes, Fortune, Business Week, and the "Business World" section of the Sunday New York Times.

The advertisements introduced Bayer USA as the "highest-ranked new company on the Fortune 500," and described Bayer USA as a "group of progressive, dynamic, forward-looking companies like Miles Laboratories and Mobay Corporation." The advertisements observed that Bayer USA's "businesses range from chemical to health and life sciences to imaging and graphic information systems." Miles also distributed press releases that identified it as "the health-care company of Bayer USA Inc." Bayer AG sponsored at least three international medical symposia held in the United States. Bayer AG used its name freely in these symposia, including it in the literature printed for the events, and sometimes even incorporating it into the name of the symposium, as, for example, in "Bayer AG Centenary Symposium: Perspectives in Antiinfective Therapy".

Bayer USA also sponsored numerous theater, opera, concert, and dance performances in its local community of Pittsburgh. The programs for these events included advertisements describing Bayer USA as consisting of a group of companies "in the areas of chemicals, health and life sciences, and imaging and graphic information systems." Bayer USA, either directly or through Miles, donated to various charitable foundations, usually requesting the organizations to credit the philanthropy to both Miles and Bayer USA. After receiving a contribution of $500,000 from Bayer USA, the public radio station in Pittsburgh renamed its broadcast facility the "Bayer USA Broadcast Center for the Arts," and posted a large sign with this name in front. The station advised Bayer USA that this sign would "be visible each day to thousands of commuters and visitors. . . ." Bayer USA sponsored a "German Hour" program on a Pittsburgh public radio station, during which the "Bayer" name was spoken over the airwaves, but always with the German pronunciation— "buy-er".

Bayer AG also added the word "Bayer" to six billboards maintained by Mobay in the Detroit area, including one that periodically displayed the word "Bayer" as part of a changing electronic display for Mobay automobile body panels. Bayer USA also erected a sign at its Pittsburgh headquarters with the words "Bayer USA Inc." The sign was visible from nearby highways. Bayer USA erected another sign on a busy highway from Pittsburgh to the airport that identified Mobay with Bayer USA. Bayer USA also distributed corporate promotional merchandise such as T-shirts and golf towels imprinted with "Bayer USA Inc." or "Bayer/Mobay." Miles also ran employment notices in general interest newspapers throughout the country in which it described itself as "a Bayer USA Inc. Company." . . .

Having concluded that Bayer AG did violate Sterling's contract and trademark rights, we now turn to the question of relief. With a few narrow exceptions, the District Court broadly enjoined Bayer AG and its subsidiaries from using the "Bayer" mark in the United States, or even abroad if such foreign use might make its way to the American public. Bayer AG primarily complains that the injunction's extraterritorial provisions interfere impermissibly with its rights under foreign laws. Bayer AG owns rights to the "Bayer" name and mark in its home country of Germany, as well as in over one hundred other countries. Germany, as amicus curiae, contends that the extraterritorial prohibitions of the injunction fail to respect its sovereign rights. Bayer AG also attacks various other provisions of the injunction on the grounds that (1) they are impermissibly vague; (2) they violate its rights under earlier agreements with Sterling; and (3) they violate its free speech rights. We review the scope of the injunction for abuse of discretion. See *George Basch Co., Inc. v. Blue Coral, Inc.*, 968 F.2d 1532, 1542 (2d Cir.), cert. denied, 506 U.S. 991, 113 S.Ct. 510, 121 L.Ed.2d 445 (1992).

1.   *Extraterritorial provisions of the injunction*

The District Court broadly enjoined Bayer AG or its subsidiaries from using the "Bayer" name or mark in:

> "any product, institutional or company-identifying advertisement or promotional materials published or reasonably likely to be disseminated in the United States" (¶ 1(g)(i));

> "any employment notice ... published or reasonably likely to be distributed within the United States (¶ 1(g)(ii));

> any radio or television broadcast ... or other electronic means of mass communication received through one or more stations, channels or services, or by subscribers, within the United States (¶ 1(g)(iv)); or

> any news release ... or informational materials distributed, or reasonably likely to be distributed, within the United States, or at any press conference held, or reasonably likely to be reported on, within the United States ..." (¶ 1(g)(vi)).

The Court allowed a few narrow exceptions to these prohibitions. Under the injunction, Bayer AG may use the mark in advertisements or employment notices: (1) in foreign print publications that have a U.S. circulation of 5,000 or less; and (2) in trade publications when the advertisements or employment notices refer only to non-pharmaceutical, non-consumer products or pharmaceutical intermediates or ingredients. With perhaps a nod towards corporate disclosure requirements, the District Court also allowed Bayer AG to use the mark in not more than two press releases a year "exclusively concerning extraordinary events involving Bayer AG, such as changes in corporate control." (¶ 1(g)(vi)). The Court allowed an exception for press conferences held abroad and attended primarily by foreign journalists if (1) such press conferences were not conducted in English; (2) the subject of the conference did not include "any discovery, invention, activity, event, product or service within the United States"; or (3) the conferences related exclusively to Bayer AG's worldwide activities, without any special prominence given to either health care matters or Bayer AG's activities within the United States. (¶ 1(g)(vi)(B)). The Court allowed the same three exceptions for press releases as long as the releases indicated that the information was "Not for Distribution or Release in the United States." (¶ 1(g)(vi)(C)).

The Court also allowed Bayer AG to use the mark in press releases exclusively concerning non-pharmaceutical, non-consumer products or pharmaceutical intermediates and ingredients, as long as these releases are disseminated only to print trade publications. (¶ ¶ 1(g)(vi)(D), (E)). Notwithstanding these exceptions, Bayer AG contends that the "extraterritorial injunctive provisions impair the ability of one of Europe's largest corporations to conduct its everyday business in its home country and around the world."

It is well-established that United States courts have jurisdiction to enforce the Lanham Act extraterritorially in order to prevent harm to United States commerce. The Supreme Court divined such a Congressional intent to project the Act extraterritorially in *Steele v. Bulova Watch Co., Inc.*, 344 U.S. 280, 73 S.Ct. 252, 97 L.Ed. 319 (1952). In that leading case, the Court applied the Act to prevent a U.S. citizen from selling fake "Bulova" watches in Mexico on the ground that his use of the "Bulova" name diverted sales in Mexico and the United States from the American trademark holder. But courts have also recognized limits on the application of the Lanham Act beyond our borders. In *Vanity Fair Mills, Inc. v. T. Eaton Co.*, 234 F.2d 633 (2d Cir.), cert. denied, 352 U.S. 871, 77 S.Ct. 96, 1 L.Ed.2d 76 (1956), an American clothing manufacturer that sold women's underwear in the U.S. and Canada using its "Vanity Fair" trademark sought to enjoin a Canadian retailer from selling women's undergarments using the same mark in Canada. We dismissed the claims against the defendant because it was a Canadian corporation using a mark to which it held presumably valid trademark rights in Canada. We explained the Supreme Court's application of the Lanham Act extraterritorially in *Steele v. Bulova* as resting on three factors: (1) whether the defendant's conduct has a substantial effect on United States Commerce; (2) whether the defendant is a citizen of the United States; and (3) whether there exists a conflict between defendant's trademark rights established under foreign law, and plaintiff's trademark rights established under domestic law. Id. at 642.

In the instant case, the District Court granted an injunction with extensive extraterritorial effects without adequately considering its power to do so under the Lanham Act. The Court did not examine the *Vanity Fair* factors to see whether they supported an extraterritorial injunction, nor did it explicitly eschew the *Vanity Fair* analysis as inadequate for the instant facts. Because the District Court failed to make the necessary findings to support the extraterritorial reach of its injunction, we vacate the injunction's extraterritorial provisions and remand for further analysis as to the scope of such extraterritorial relief as may be warranted. In this connection, the District Court may receive such additional proofs as it may deem appropriate.

Citing *Vanity Fair*, Bayer AG would have us forgo a remand in favor of a simple redrawing of the injunction to eliminate its extraterritorial provisions. Indeed, if we applied the *Vanity Fair* test mechanically to the instant case, we would forbid the application of the Lanham Act abroad against a foreign corporation that holds superior rights to the mark under foreign law. But such an unrefined application of that case might mean that we fail to preserve the Lanham Act's goals of protecting American consumers against confusion, and protecting holders of American trademarks against misappropriation of their marks. A more careful application of *Vanity Fair* is necessary because the instant case is not on all fours with Vanity Fair. In Vanity Fair, the plaintiff sought a blanket prohibition against the Canadian retailer's use of "Vanity Fair" in connection with the sale of defendant's products in Canada. Sterling, on the other hand, seeks to enjoin only those uses of the "Bayer" mark abroad that are likely to make their way to American consumers. Sterling is not concerned with Bayer AG's use of the mark abroad so long as that use does not enter the channels of international communication that lead to the United States. While the stringent *Vanity Fair* test is appropriate when the plaintiff seeks an absolute bar against a corporation's use of its mark outside our borders, that test is unnecessarily demanding when the plaintiff seeks the more modest goal of limiting foreign uses that reach the United States. Though Congress did not intend the Lanham Act to be used as a sword to eviscerate completely a foreign corporation's foreign trademark, it did intend the Act to be used as a shield against foreign uses that have significant trademark-impairing effects upon American commerce.

Sterling contends that whatever issues might arise from the concurrent rights of the parties to the "Bayer" mark under both German and United States law have been eliminated by the decision of the *Supreme Court in Hartford Fire Insurance Co. v. California*, 509 U.S. 764, 113 S.Ct. 2891, 125 L.Ed.2d 612 (1993). The Court there ruled that considerations of "international comity" were not a bar to the extraterritorial application of the Sherman Act to alleged boycotting activities with a "substantial effect" in the United States. 113 S.Ct. at 2909–10. In the context of the case before it, the Court found no "conflict" warranting a declination of jurisdiction because there was no claim that conformity with the requirements of United States law required the defendants to do any act in violation of British law. 113 S.Ct. at 2910–11. Though the Court's approach to the comity issue might not be limited to the antitrust context, see Restatement (Third) Foreign Relations Law § 403 cmt. e (1987), we think it is not automatically transferable to the trademark context, especially where the contending parties both hold rights in the same mark under the respective laws of their countries. It is one thing for the British reinsurers in Hartford Fire to be barred under United States law from boycotting activity that they might be free to engage in without violating British law. But it is quite a different thing for the holder of rights in a mark under German law to be ordered by a United States court to refrain from uses of that mark protected by German law. In Hartford Fire, the Supreme Court appeared to recognize that a different context, such as a trademark dispute, might implicate other concerns:

> We have no need in this case to address other considerations that might inform a decision to refrain from the exercise of jurisdiction on grounds of international comity. 113 S.Ct. at 2911.

We need not go so far as to limit the District Court's jurisdiction in order to oblige it to frame more carefully the scope of its injunction in light of the concurrent rights of the parties. "In establishing the parameters of injunctive relief in the case of lawful concurrent users, a court must take account of the realities of the marketplace." Restatement of the Law of Unfair Competition, Tentative Draft No. 3 § 35 cmt. f (1991) (approved 1993). In today's global economy, where a foreign TV advertisement might be available by satellite to U.S. households, not every activity of a foreign corporation with any tendency to create some confusion among American consumers can be prohibited by the extraterritorial reach of a District Court's injunction.

Upon remand, the District Court may grant an extraterritorial injunction carefully crafted to prohibit only those foreign uses of the mark by Bayer AG that are likely to have significant trademark-impairing effects on United States commerce. If the Court finds that Bayer AG's use of the mark abroad carries such significant effects in the United States, the District Court may require Bayer AG to take appropriate precautions against using the mark in international media in ways that might create confusion among United States consumers as to the source of "Bayer" pharmaceutical products in the United States. It might be appropriate, to take examples offered by appellee, to prevent Bayer AG from placing a full-page "Bayer" advertisement in the U.S. edition of a foreign magazine or newspaper, or inviting representatives of the U.S. press to an offshore briefing in which Bayer AG distributed materials describing "Bayer's" analgesics products for publication in the U.S. On the other hand, it might be inappropriate, to take examples offered by the amicus curiae, to leave the injunction so broad as to ban the announcement of new medical research in Lancet, or an employment notice in Handelsblatt, or a press conference in England to publicize a new over-the-counter remedy developed in the United States, or sponsorship of a German soccer team if that team might appear, wearing "Bayer" jerseys, on a television broadcast carried by an American sports cable channel. * * *

Where, as in the instant case, both parties have legitimate interests, consideration of those interests must receive especially sensitive accommodation in the international context. While Bayer AG suggests that we must accept these conflicts as the unavoidable result of an international community of nations in which each nation exercises the power to grant trademark rights, we prefer to allow the District Court to fashion an appropriately limited injunction with only those extraterritorial provisions reasonably necessary to protect against significant trademark-impairing effects on American commerce.

Sterling contends that if the extraterritorial provisions of the injunction cannot be sustained as a remedy for Bayer AG's Lanham Act violations, they should be sustained as a remedy for Bayer AG's contract violations. We disagree. The 1970 Agreement clearly recognized Bayer AG's "exclusive rights" to the "Bayer" mark outside the United States, Canada, and certain Caribbean nations. Indeed, it may be the case that the broad extraterritorial provisions of the injunction improperly rescind certain rights that Bayer AG purchased in the 1970 Agreement. The 1964 Agreement and the 1986 modification to that Agreement restrict Bayer AG's use of the mark only inside the United States.

Since Sterling has not claimed that New York's unfair competition and anti-dilution laws have any broader extraterritorial reach in this case than the Lanham Act, we have no occasion to consider what relief might appropriately be predicated in a proper case on those sources of law.

NOTES

The *Bayer* case presents two points. First, the facts illustrate the role of contract in determining trademark rights, especially in the transfer of trademark rights transnationally. Second, the opinion provides a helpful discussion of the ongoing applicability of *Bulova* and *Vanity Fair*, and their influence in shaping injunctive relief. How can the injunction be drafted to avoid some of the problems the court Notes and still protect the rights of the trademark owner?

3. Internet

PLAYBOY ENTERPRISES, INC. v. CHUCKLEBERRY PUBLISHING, INC.

United States District Court for the Southern District of New York, 1996.
939 F.Supp. 1032.

SCHEINDLIN, DISTRICT JUDGE:

In 1967, Tattilo began publishing a male sophisticate magazine in Italy under the name PLAYMEN. Although the magazine carried an English title, it was written entirely in Italian. In July 1979, Tattilo announced plans to publish an English language version of PLAYMEN in the United States. Shortly thereafter, PEI brought suit against Tattilo to enjoin Tattilo's use of the name PLAYMEN in connection with a male sophisticate magazine and related products. PEI has published the well-known male entertainment magazine "PLAYBOY" since 1953, which is sold throughout the world in a multitude of foreign languages. Plaintiff's suit for injunctive relief alleged trademark infringement, false designation of origin, unfair competition based on infringement of Plaintiff's common law trademark rights, and violations of the New York Anti–Dilution Statute.

A permanent injunction was awarded on April 1, 1981, and a judgment subsequently entered on June 26, 1981, permanently enjoining Tattilo from:

> a. using the word "PLAYMEN" or any word confusingly similar therewith as or in the title, as or in the subtitle, or anywhere else on the cover of a male sophisticate magazine, published, distributed or sold in the United States;

b. publishing, printing, distributing or selling in the United States and importing into or exporting from the United States an English language male sophisticate magazine which uses the word "PLAY-MEN" or any word confusingly similar therewith as or in the title, as or in the subtitle, or anywhere else on the cover of such magazine; and

c. using "PLAYBOY", "PLAYMEN" or any other word confusingly similar with either such word in or as part of any trademark, service mark, brand name, trade name or other business or commercial designation, in connection with the sale, offering for sale or distributing in the United States, importing into or exporting from the United States, English language publications and related products.

PEI was similarly successful in enjoining the use of the PLAYMEN name in the courts of England, France and West Germany. However, the Italian courts ruled that "lexically" PLAYBOY was a weak mark and not entitled to protection in that country. The publication of PLAYMEN in Italy continues to the present day.

On approximately January 22, 1996, PEI discovered that Tattilo had created an Internet site featuring the PLAYMEN name. This Internet site makes available images of the cover of the Italian magazine, as well as its "Women of the Month" feature and several other sexually explicit photographic images. Users of the Internet site also receive "special discounts" on other Tattilo products, such as CD ROMs and Photo CDs. Tattilo created this site by uploading these images onto a World Wide Web server located in Italy. These images can be accessed at the Internet address "http://www.playmen.it."

Two distinct services are available on the PLAYMEN Internet site. "PLAYMEN Lite" is available without a paid subscription, allowing users of the Internet to view moderately explicit images via computer. It appears that the main (if not sole) purpose of the PLAYMEN Lite service is to allow prospective users to experience a less explicit version of the PLAY-MEN product before committing to purchasing a subscription. In addition, the PLAYMEN Internet site offers the more sexually explicit service called "PLAYMEN Pro." PLAYMEN Pro is available only to users who have paid the subscription price.

In order to access the Lite version of the PLAYMEN Internet service, the prospective user must first contact Tattilo. The user will then receive a temporary user name and password via e-mail. To subscribe to PLAY-MEN Pro, the prospective user must fill out a form and send it via fax to Tattilo. Within 24 hours, the user receives by e-mail a unique password and login name that enable the user to browse the PLAYMEN Pro service.

The PLAYMEN Internet site is widely available to patrons living in the United States. More to the point, anyone in the United States with access to the Internet has the capacity to browse the PLAYMEN Internet site, review, and obtain print and electronic copies of sexually explicit pages of PLAYMEN magazine. All that is required to establish the account is the brief contact with Tattilo outlined above. . . .

The primary issue before the Court is whether the Defendant distributed or sold the PLAYMEN magazine in the United States when it established an Internet site containing pictorial images under the PLAYMEN name.

A. Whether the Injunction Could Have Been Violated

As an initial matter, the question arises whether a fifteen-year-old injunction prohibiting certain traditional publishing activities should be applied to the recent development of cyberspace and the Internet. If the dissemination of information over the Internet, in any form, cannot constitute a violation of the Injunction, then the inquiry is over.

Defendant argues that because this case involves the new technology of the Internet and World Wide Web—which purportedly did not exist when the Injunction was issued—the complained of activities cannot be "clearly and unambiguously" barred.

The 1981 Injunction was issued with respect to the publication and distribution in the United States of print magazines bearing on their cover the name P[LAYMEN]. Plainly, it does not bar the conduct at issue, placing pictorial images on the World Wide Web in Italy, which conduct was not contemplated by any of the parties involved in framing the 1981 Injunction, let alone addressed in that judgment.

This argument is premised on the belief that the Internet did not exist in 1981. While it is difficult, if not impossible, to establish a definite "birth date" for this new medium, it appears that the Internet did in fact exist in some form when the Injunction was entered fifteen years ago. See, e.g., The Birth of the Internet, Newsweek, August 8, 1994, at 56. The beginnings of the Internet date back to 1969, when the Department of Defense's Advanced Research Project Agency funded a project called ARPANET for the purpose of developing a computer network which would enable researchers around the country to share ideas. Id. On that date in 1969, four universities were linked by a computer network for the first time. The number of network sites, called "nodes," gradually increased to nearly two dozen in 1971 and 62 three years later. Id. By 1981, more than 200 network sites had been established. Today, users of publicly available news groups discuss "everything from particle physics to Barney the dinosaur." Id.

Nevertheless, I agree with the Defendant that the availability of pictorial images on the Internet could not have been contemplated at the time of the Injunction. While the Internet may have existed in some form in 1981, it was undeniably vastly different from today's extensive montage of data available in multimedia format. In 1981, the Internet was a means to exchange text-based information, primarily by posting messages on public electronic "bulletin boards" and by sending electronic mail. Today, of course, the Internet can be seen as its own thriving city, where citizens meet to exchange thoughts and ideas, where merchants buy and sell their wares, and where visitors take virtual tours of entire cities and buildings such as the White House and the Louvre. Certainly, only the most active imagination could have contemplated the public dissemination of pictorial images over the Internet when the Injunction was entered in 1981.

The key date, then, is the start of the Internet as it exists today. The Internet, defined narrowly, dates from the time that advanced computer technology made it possible to view, manipulate and exchange pictorial images electronically on a home computer. This was no earlier than the late 1980s, when the microprocessor speed and memory capacity of home computers first allowed large quantities of data to be stored and transferred quickly. Regardless of the exact date, this use could not have been contemplated at the time the Injunction was entered.

Defendant argues that because the Internet (as it now exists) could not have been contemplated by the parties in 1981, the distribution of pictorial images over that medium cannot be barred. Specifically, Defendant argues that "as Internet use was not contemplated by any of the participants who had a hand in shaping [the Injunction], . . . there is ground to doubt the wrongfulness of the defendant's conduct."

I disagree. That this use of the images could not have been contemplated by the parties does not prevent the Injunction from applying to the modern technology of the Internet and the World Wide Web. The purpose behind the Injunction was to restrict the ability of Defendant to distribute its product in the United States, where it has been found to infringe upon the trademark of Playboy. Allowing the Defendant to contravene the clear intent of the Injunction by permitting it to distribute its pictorial images over the Internet would emasculate the Injunction. The Injunction's failure to refer to the Internet by name does not limit its applicability to this new medium. Injunctions entered before the recent explosion of computer technology must continue to have meaning. . . .

In sum, the Injunction controls the activities complained of here, despite the fact that the Internet in its current form did not exist (and, moreover, could not have been contemplated by the parties) when the Injunction was entered. Prohibition of the sale or distribution of the PLAYMEN magazine within the United States thus extends to the Internet.

B. Whether the Injunction Was Violated

Subsection 1(c) of the Injunction permanently enjoined Tattilo from: using "PLAYBOY", "PLAYMEN" or any other word confusingly similar with either such word in or as part of any trademark, service mark, brand name, trade name or other business or commercial designation, in connection with the sale, offering for sale or distributing in the United States, importing into or exporting from the United States, English language publications and related products.

Three conditions must be met to support a finding of a violation of this provision. First, the word PLAYMEN must have been used as part of any trademark, service mark, brand name, trade name or other business or commercial designation. Second, such use must have been in connection with an English language publication or related product. Third, such use must have been made in connection with a sale or distribution within the United States.

There is ample evidence that the word PLAYMEN has been used as a trade name or business or commercial designation of the Internet site. As mentioned above, the site's URL, which typically remains displayed on the computer screen once the site is accessed, is "playmen.it." Moreover, the word PLAYMEN prominently appears (along with the PLAYMEN logo) in oversized font on the site's "home page," the electronic equivalent of a magazine cover and table of contents. The PLAYMEN name and logo appear in this same form at the top of each "page" accessed on the site. The site's address, and the prominence of the PLAYMEN name, demonstrate an association between the PLAYMEN name and the Internet site.

Similarly, the PLAYMEN name has been used in connection with an English language publication or related product. First, although there is an intriguing question as to whether an Internet site consisting of uploaded pictorial images constitutes a "publication," there is no doubt that the "related product" clause is satisfied by this use. Second, this product appears in the English language. Although a portion of the text is written in Italian, enough sections appear in English to allow an English-speaking user to navigate the site with ease. Paramount among these is the PLAYMEN page purportedly answering frequently asked questions about the Internet site, such as the price of a subscription ("$30 U.S., or 50000 [sic] Italian lire for 6 months, payable by all major credit cards"), benefits of a subscription ("You get a unique password, that can be used only by one person at a time, to browse on Playmen Pro, where you can find about 500 xxx rated pictures always updated, mpeg movies, photo cd images, and many other things"), and a description of the PLAYMEN magazine itself ("The 'Playmen' magazine is written in Italian, and is sold in Italy and all the major countries in Europe"). Therefore, the English language publication/related product requirement has been met.

The final condition—for a distribution or sale to have taken place within the United States—is analytically more difficult. The question of whether uploading pictorial images onto a computer which may be accessed by other users constitutes a "distribution" has been addressed by at least two courts. In *Playboy Enterprises, Inc. v. Frena*, 839 F. Supp. 1552 (M.D.Fla. 1993), Defendant Frena operated a subscription electronic bulletin board service accessible by computer modem. Once logged onto the service, subscribers could browse through different directories and view unauthorized copies of PEI's copyrighted photographs, as well as download and store these images on their home computers. Id. at 1554. The court held that the unauthorized uploading of copyrighted images with the knowledge that the images would be downloaded by other bulletin board subscribers constituted a distribution. Id. at 1556. Similarly, in *Religious Technology Center v. Netcom On–Line Communication Servs., Inc.*, 907 F. Supp. 1361 (N.D.Cal. 1995), copyright holders brought an infringement action against the operator of an Internet access provider, seeking to hold the defendant liable for copyright infringement committed by a bulletin board subscriber. In that case, the court refused to extend the Frena doctrine to an Internet access provider, because Netcom did not create or control the content of the information available to its subscribers.

Although the Internet consists of many different computers networked together, some of which may contain infringing files, it does not make sense to hold the operator of each computer liable as an infringer merely because his or her computer is linked to a computer with an infringing file. It would be especially inappropriate to hold liable a service that acts more like a conduit, in other words, one that does not itself keep an archive of files for more than a short duration. Finding such a service liable would involve an unreasonably broad construction of public distribution and display rights. * * *

Here, Defendant does more than simply provide access to the Internet. It also provides its own services, PLAYMEN Lite and PLAYMEN Pro, and supplies the content for these services. Moreover, as in Frena, these pictorial images can be downloaded to and stored upon the computers of subscribers to the service. In fact, Defendant actively invites such use: the Internet site allows the user to decide between viewing and downloading the images. Thus this use of Defendant's Internet site constitutes a distribution.

In order to violate the Injunction, however, Defendant must distribute the pictorial images within the United States. Defendant argues that it is merely posting pictorial images on a computer server in Italy, rather than distributing those images to anyone within the United States. A computer operator wishing to view these images must, in effect, transport himself to Italy to view Tattilo's pictorial displays. The use of the Internet is akin to boarding a plane, landing in Italy, and purchasing a copy of PLAYMEN magazine, an activity permitted under Italian law. Thus Defendant argues that its publication of pictorial images over the Internet cannot be barred by the Injunction despite the fact that computer operators can view these pictorial images in the United States.

Once more, I disagree. Defendant has actively solicited United States customers to its Internet site, and in doing so has distributed its product within the United States. When a potential subscriber faxes the required form to Tattilo, he receives back via e-mail a password and user name. By this process, Tattilo distributes its product within the United States.

Defendant's analogy of "flying to Italy" to purchase a copy of the PLAYMEN magazine is inapposite. Tattilo may of course maintain its Italian Internet site. The Internet is a world-wide phenomenon, accessible from every corner of the globe. Tattilo cannot be prohibited from operating its Internet site merely because the site is accessible from within one country in which its product is banned. To hold otherwise "would be tantamount to a declaration that this Court, and every other court throughout the world, may assert jurisdiction over all information providers on the global World Wide Web." Such a holding would have a devastating impact on those who use this global service. The Internet deserves special protection as a place where public discourse may be conducted without regard to nationality, religion, sex, age, or to monitors of community standards of decency.

However, this special protection does not extend to ignoring court orders and injunctions. If it did, injunctions would cease to have meaning and intellectual property would no longer be adequately protected. In the absence of enforcement, intellectual property laws could be easily circumvented through the creation of Internet sites that permit the very distribution that has been enjoined. Our long-standing system of intellectual property protections has encouraged creative minds to be productive. Diluting those protections may discourage that creativity.

While this Court has neither the jurisdiction nor the desire to prohibit the creation of Internet sites around the globe, it may prohibit access to those sites in this country. Therefore, while Tattilo may continue to operate its Internet site, it must refrain from accepting subscriptions from customers living in the United States. In accord with this holding, an Italian customer who subsequently moves to the United States may maintain his or her subscription to the Internet site.

I therefore conclude that Tattilo has violated subsection 1(c) of the Injunction by using its PLAYMEN Internet site to distribute its products in the United States. The clear intent of the Injunction was to prohibit Tattilo from selling its PLAYMEN magazine and related products to United States customers. Tattilo has knowingly attempted to circumvent the Injunction by selling its products over the Internet. Cyberspace is not a "safe haven" from which Tattilo may flout the Court's Injunction.

BARCELONA.COM, INCORPORATED v. EXCELENTISIMO AYUNTAMIENTO DE BARCELONA

United States Court of Appeals for the Fourth Circuit, 2003.
330 F.3d 617.

NIEMEYER, CIRCUIT JUDGE:

Barcelona.com, Inc. ("Bcom, Inc."), a Delaware corporation, commenced this action under the Anticybersquatting Consumer Protection Act against Excelentisimo Ayuntamiento de Barcelona (the City Council of Barcelona, Spain) for a declaratory judgment that Bcom, Inc.'s registration and use of the domain name <barcelona.com> is not unlawful under the Lanham Act. The district court concluded that Bcom, Inc.'s use of <barcelona.com> was confusingly similar to Spanish trademarks owned by the City Council that include the word "Barcelona." Also finding bad faith on the basis that Bcom, Inc. had attempted to sell the <barcelona.com> domain name to the City Council for a profit, the court ordered the transfer of the domain name to the City Council.

Because the district court applied Spanish law rather than United States law and based its transfer order, in part, on a counterclaim that the City Council never filed, we reverse the judgment of the district court denying Bcom, Inc. relief under the Anticybersquatting Consumer Protection Act, vacate its memorandum opinion and its order to transfer the domain name <barcelona.com> to the City Council, and remand for further proceedings consistent with this opinion.

In 1996, Mr. Joan Nogueras Cobo ("Nogueras"), a Spanish citizen, registered the domain name <barcelona.com> in the name of his wife, also a Spanish citizen, with the domain registrar, Network Solutions, Inc., in Herndon, Virginia. In the application for registration of the domain name, Nogueras listed himself as the administrative contact. When Nogueras met Mr. Shahab Hanif, a British citizen, in June 1999, they developed a business plan to turn <barcelona.com> into a tourist portal for the Barcelona, Spain, region. A few months later they formed Bcom, Inc. under Delaware law to own <barcelona.com> and to run the website, and Nogueras, his wife, and Hanif became Bcom, Inc.'s officers. Bcom, Inc. was formed as an American company in part because Nogueras believed that doing so would facilitate obtaining financing for the development of the website. Although Bcom, Inc. maintains a New York mailing address, it has no employees in the United States, does not own or lease office space in the United States, and does not have a telephone listing in the United States. Its computer server is in Spain.

Shortly after Nogueras registered the domain name <barcelona.com> in 1996, he placed some Barcelona-related information on the site. The site offered commercial services such as domain registry and web hosting, but did not offer much due to the lack of financing. Before developing the business plan with Hanif, Nogueras used a web-form on the City Council's official website to e-mail the mayor of Barcelona, Spain, proposing to "negotiate" with the City Council for its acquisition of the domain name <barcelona.com>, but Nogueras received no response. And even after the development of a business plan and after speaking with potential investors, Nogueras was unable to secure financing to develop the website.

In March 2000, about a year after Nogueras had e-mailed the Mayor, the City Council contacted Nogueras to learn more about Bcom, Inc. and its plans for the domain name <barcelona.com>. Nogueras and his marketing director met with City Council representatives, and after the meeting, sent them the business plan that was developed for Bcom, Inc.

On May 3, 2000, a lawyer for the City Council sent a letter to Nogueras demanding that Nogueras transfer the domain name <barcelona.com> to the City Council. The City Council owned about 150 trademarks issued in Spain, the majority of which included the word Barcelona, such as "Teatre Barcelona," "Barcelona Informacio I Grafic," and "Barcelona Informacio 010 El Tlefon Que Ho Contesta Tot." Its earlier effort in 1995 to register the domain name <barcelona.es>, however, was unsuccessful. The City Council's representative explained, "It was denied to Barcelona and to all place names in Spain." This representative also explained that the City Council did not try also to register <barcelona.com> in 1995 even though that domain name was available because "[a]t that time ... the world Internet that we know now was just beginning and it was not seen as a priority by the City Council." The City Council now took the position with Bcom, Inc. that its domain name <barcelona.com> was confusingly similar to numerous trademarks that the City Council owned.

A couple of days after the City Council sent its letter, Nogueras had the domain name <barcelona.com> transferred from his wife's name to Bcom, Inc., which he had neglected to do in 1999 when Bcom, Inc. was formed.

Upon Bcom, Inc.'s refusal to transfer <barcelona.com> to the City Council, the City Council invoked the Uniform Domain Name Dispute Resolution Policy ("UDRP") promulgated by the Internet Corporation for Assigned Names and Numbers ("ICANN") to resolve the dispute. Every domain name issued by Network Solutions, Inc. is issued under a contract, the terms of which include a provision requiring resolution of disputes through the UDRP. In accordance with that policy, the City Council filed an administrative complaint with the World Intellectual Property Organization ("WIPO"), an ICANN-authorized dispute-resolution provider located in Switzerland. The complaint sought transfer of the domain name <barcelona.com> to the City Council and relied on Spanish law in asserting that Bcom, Inc. had no rights to the domain name while the City Council had numerous Spanish trademarks that contained the word "Barcelona." As part of its complaint, the City Council agreed "to be subject to the jurisdiction of the registrant[']s residence, the Courts of Virginia (United States), only with respect to any challenge that may be made by the Respondent to a decision by the Administrative Panel to transfer or cancel the domain names that are [the] subject of this complaint."

The administrative complaint was resolved by a single WIPO panelist who issued a ruling in favor of the City Council on August 4, 2000. The WIPO panelist concluded that <barcelona.com> was confusingly similar to the City Council's Spanish trademarks, that Bcom, Inc. had no legitimate interest in <barcelona.com>, and that Bcom, Inc.'s registration and use of <barcelona.com> was in bad faith. To support his conclusion that Bcom, Inc. acted in bad faith, the WIPO panelist observed that the only purpose of the business plan was "to commercially exploit information about the City of Barcelona ... particularly ... the information prepared and provided by [the City Council] as part of its public service." The WIPO panelist ordered that Bcom, Inc. transfer the domain name <barcelona.com> to the City Council.

In accordance with the UDRP's provision that required a party aggrieved by the dispute resolution process to file any court challenge within ten business days, Bcom, Inc. commenced this action on August 18, 2000 under the provision of the Anticybersquatting Consumer Protection Act (the "ACPA") that authorizes a domain name owner to seek recovery or restoration of its domain name when a trademark owner has overstepped its authority in causing the domain name to be suspended, disabled, or transferred. See 15 U.S.C. § 1114(2)(D)(v). Bcom, Inc.'s complaint sought a declaratory judgment that its use of the name <barcelona.com> "does not infringe upon any trademark of defendant or cause confusion as to the origin, sponsorship, or approval of the website <barcelona.com>; . . . [and] that [the City Council] is barred from instituting any action against [Bcom, Inc.] for trademark infringement." While the City Council answered the complaint and stated, as an affirmative defense, that the court lacked jurisdiction over the City Council for any cause of action other than Bcom, Inc.'s "challenge to the arbitrator's Order issued in the UDRP domain name arbitration proceeding," the City Council filed no counterclaim to assert any trademark rights.

Following a bench trial, the district court entered a memorandum opinion and an order dated February 22, 2002, denying Bcom, Inc.'s request for declaratory judgment and directing Bcom, Inc. to "transfer the domain name barcelona.com to the [City Council] forthwith." Although the district court concluded that the WIPO panel ruling "should be given no weight and this case must be decided based on the evidence presented before the Court," the court proceeded in essence to apply the WIPO panelist opinion as well as Spanish law. The court explained that even though the City Council did not own a trademark in the name "Barcelona" alone, it owned numerous Spanish trademarks that included the word Barcelona, which could, under Spanish law as understood by the district court, be enforced against an infringing use such as <barcelona.com>. Adopting the WIPO panelist's decision, the court stated that "the WIPO decision was correct in its determination that [Bcom, Inc.] took 'advantage of the normal confusion' of an Internet user by using the 'Barcelona route' because an Internet user would 'normally expect to reach some official body . . . for . . . the information.'" Referring to the facts that Bcom, Inc. engaged in little activity and attempted to sell the domain name to the City Council, the court concluded that "these factors clearly demonstrate a bad faith intent on the part of the Plaintiff and its sole shareholders to improperly profit from their registration of the domain name barcelona.com." At bottom, the court concluded that Bcom, Inc. failed to demonstrate, as required by 15 U.S.C. § 1114(2)(D)(v), that its use of <barcelona.com> was "not unlawful."

In addition to concluding that Bcom, Inc. failed to establish its claim, the court stated that it was also deciding the City Council's counterclaim for relief under 15 U.S.C. § 1125 and determined that "the Spanish trademark 'Barcelona' is valid for purposes of the ACPA." Applying the factors of 15 U.S.C. § 1125(2)(d)(1)(B)(i), the court found that Nogueras and his wife acted with "bad faith intent" in registering <barcelona.com> as a domain name. The court also found that <barcelona.com> "is confusingly similar to the defendant's mark."

Bcom, Inc. contends that in deciding its claim under § 1114(2)(D)(v), the district court erred in applying the law of Spain rather than the law of the United States. Because the ACPA explicitly requires application of the Lanham Act, not foreign law, we agree.

Section 1114(2)(D)(v), the reverse domain name hijacking provision, states:

> A domain name registrant whose domain name has been suspended, disabled, or transferred under a policy described under clause (ii)(II) may, upon notice to the mark owner, file a civil action to establish that the registration or use of the domain name by such registrant is not unlawful under this chapter. The court may grant injunctive relief to the domain name registrant, including the reactivation of the domain name or transfer of the domain name to the domain name registrant. 15 U.S.C. § 1114(2)(D)(v).

Thus, to establish a right to relief against an "overreaching trademark owner" under this reverse hijacking provision, a plaintiff must establish (1) that it is a domain name registrant; (2) that its domain name was suspended, disabled, or transferred under a policy implemented by a registrar as described in 15 U.S.C. § 1114(2)(D)(ii)(II); (3) that the owner of the mark that prompted the domain name to be suspended, disabled, or transferred has notice of the action by service or otherwise; and (4) that the plaintiff's registration or use of the domain name is not unlawful under the Lanham Act, as amended.

The parties do not dispute that the first two elements are satisfied. Bcom, Inc. is a domain name registrant, and its domain name was suspended, disabled, or transferred under Network Solutions' policy, i.e., the UDRP incorporated into the domain name registration agreement for <barcelona.com>. Although the domain name had not actually been transferred from Bcom, Inc. as of the time that Bcom, Inc. commenced this action, the WIPO panelist had already ordered the transfer, and as a result of this order the transfer was certain to occur absent the filing of this action to stop it. By filing this suit, Bcom, Inc. obtained an automatic stay of the transfer order by virtue of paragraph 4(k) of the UDRP, which provides that the registrar will stay implementation of the administrative panel's decision if the registrant commences "a lawsuit against the complainant in a jurisdiction to which the complainant has submitted" under the applicable UDRP rule of procedure. Moreover, this suit for declaratory judgment and injunctive relief under § 1114(2)(D)(v) appears to be precisely the mechanism designed by Congress to empower a party whose domain name is subject to a transfer order like the one in the present case to prevent the order from being implemented.

It is the last element that raises the principal issue on appeal. Bcom, Inc. argues that the district court erred in deciding whether Bcom, Inc.

satisfied this element by applying Spanish law and then by concluding that Bcom, Inc.'s use of the domain name violated Spanish law.

It appears from the district court's memorandum opinion that it indeed did resolve the last element by applying Spanish law. Although the district court recognized that the City Council did not have a registered trademark in the name "Barcelona" alone, either in Spain or in the United States, it observed that "[u]nder Spanish law, when trademarks consisting of two or more words contain one word that stands out in a predominant manner, that dominant word must be given decisive relevance." The court noted that "the term 'Barcelona' has been included in many trademarks consisting of two or more words owned by the City Council of Barcelona. In most of these marks, the word 'Barcelona' is clearly the dominant word which characterizes the mark." These observations regarding the substance and effect of Spanish law led the court to conclude that the City Council of Barcelona "owns a legally valid Spanish trademark for the dominant word 'Barcelona.'" The district court then proceeded to determine whether Bcom's "use of the Barcelona trademark is 'not unlawful.'" In this portion of its analysis, the district court determined that there was a "confusing similarity between the barcelona.com domain name and the marks held by the Council," and that "the circumstances surrounding the incorporation of [Bcom, Inc.] and the actions taken by Nogueras in attempting to sell the domain name evidence[d] a bad faith intent to profit from the registration of a domain name containing the Council's mark". Applying Spanish trademark law in this manner, the court resolved that Bcom, Inc.'s registration and use of <barcelona.com> were unlawful.

It requires little discussion to demonstrate that this use of Spanish law by the district court was erroneous under the plain terms of the statute. The text of the ACPA explicitly requires application of the Lanham Act, not foreign law, to resolve an action brought under 15 U.S.C. § 1114(2)(D)(v). Specifically, it authorizes an aggrieved domain name registrant to "file a civil action to establish that the registration or use of the domain name by such registrant is not unlawful under this chapter." 15 U.S.C. § 1114(2)(D)(v). It is thus readily apparent that the cause of action created by Congress in this portion of the ACPA requires the court adjudicating such an action to determine whether the registration or use of the domain name violates the Lanham Act. Because the statutory language has a plain and unambiguous meaning that is consistent with the statutory context and application of this language in accordance with its plain meaning provides a component of a coherent statutory scheme, our statutory analysis need proceed no further.

By requiring application of United States trademark law to this action brought in a United States court by a United States corporation involving a domain name administered by a United States registrar, 15 U.S.C. § 1114(2)(D)(v) is consistent with the fundamental doctrine of territoriality upon which our trademark law is presently based. Both the United States and Spain have long adhered to the Paris Convention for the Protection of Industrial Property. See Convention for the Protection of Industrial Property of 1883 (the "Paris Convention"), opened for signature Mar. 20, 1883, 25 Stat. 1372, as amended at Stockholm, opened for signature July 14, 1967, 21 U.S.T. 1583. Section 44 of the Lanham Act, 15 U.S.C. § 1126, incorporates the Paris Convention into United States law, but only "to provide foreign nationals with rights under United States law which are coextensive with the substantive provisions of the treaty involved." *Scotch Whisky Ass'n v. Majestic Distilling Co.*, 958 F.2d 594, 597 (4th Cir. 1992). The relevant substantive provision in this case is Article 6(3) of the Paris Convention, which implements the doctrine of territoriality by providing that "[a] mark duly registered in a country of the [Paris] Union shall be regarded as independent of marks registered in the other countries of the Union, including the country of origin." Paris Convention, supra, art. 6(3). As one distinguished commentary explains, "the Paris Convention creates nothing that even remotely resembles a 'world mark' or an 'international registration.' Rather, it recognizes the principle of the territoriality of trademarks [in the sense that] a mark exists only under the laws of each sovereign nation." 4 J. Thomas McCarthy, McCarthy on Trademarks and Unfair Competition § 29:25 (4th ed.2002).

It follows from incorporation of the doctrine of territoriality into United States law through Section 44 of the Lanham Act that United States courts do not entertain actions seeking to enforce trademark rights that exist only under foreign law. See *Person's Co., Ltd. v. Christman*, 900 F.2d 1565, 1568–69 (Fed.Cir. 1990) ("The concept of territoriality is basic to trademark law; trademark rights exist in each country solely according to that country's statutory scheme"). Yet the district court's application of foreign law in this declaratory judgment action did precisely this and thereby neglected to apply United States law as required by the statute.

When we apply the Lanham Act, not Spanish law, in determining whether Bcom, Inc.'s registration and use of <barcelona.com> is unlawful, the ineluctable conclusion follows that Bcom, Inc.'s registration and use of the name "Barcelona" is not unlawful. Under the Lanham Act, and apparently even under Spanish law, the City Council could not obtain a trademark interest in a purely descriptive geographical designation that refers only to the City of Barcelona. See 15 U.S.C. § 1052(e)(2); see also Spanish Trademark Law of 1988, Art. 11(1)(c) (forbidding registration of marks consisting exclusively of "geographical origin"). Under United States trademark law, a geographic designation can obtain trademark protection if that designation acquires secondary meaning. On the record in this case, however, there was no evidence that the public—in the United States or elsewhere—associates "Barcelona" with anything other than the City itself. Indeed, the Chief Director of the City Council submitted an affidavit stating that "[t]he City does not own and is not using any trademarks in the United States, to identify any goods or services." Therefore, under United States trademark law, "Barcelona" should have been treated as a purely descriptive geographical term entitled to no trademark protection. See 15 U.S.C. § 1052(e)(2). It follows then that there was nothing unlawful about Nogueras' registration of <barcelona.com>, nor is there anything unlawful under United States trademark law about Bcom, Inc.'s continued use of that domain name.

For these reasons, we conclude that Bcom, Inc. established entitlement to relief under 15 U.S.C. § 1114(2)(D)(v) with respect to the domain name <barcelona.com>, and accordingly we reverse the district court's ruling in this regard.

NOTES

1. Needless to say, the Internet poses important problems for the reach of trademark law. Conceptually, one issue is the choice of law to govern disputes involving the Internet. Is the Internet sovereign territory, and if so, whose sovereignty applies? Alternatively, is the Internet a new type of domain, such as the high seas or outer space, requiring new governance rules? Finally, is the Internet no different from existing domains, allowing application of existing norms and practices of international law to define governance? In some ways, as we have seen in the case law of trademarks on the Internet, each of these are true. ICANN and the UDRP serve as a type of sovereignty, originating in the United States, that governs the Internet. Alternatively, informal norms seem to be developing, albeit slowly, to govern the use of words, phrases and images on the Internet. Finally, many of the governance rules seem to be tracking traditional trademark law as developed in the United States. Consider these three descriptions in reviewing the cases in this section.

2. The *Playmen* case illustrates the role of injunctive relief on the Internet. Review the injunction at issue in this case. How would you assess its effectiveness in protecting the trademark owner's rights? Is the injunction protective of the rights of the infringer? Pay special attention to the court's discussion of how new technologies affect the interpretation of an injunction. Is the court correct the uploading and downloading materials on the Internet is no different from importing or exporting goods and services across borders? Does that conclusion inevitably lead to the result that the Internet is no different from more traditional methods of distributing branded products? Does the conclusion somewhat artificially import geographic boundaries onto the seamless domain of the Internet?

3. The *Barcelona* case offers a nice review of trademark concepts that we have encountered previously as well as introduction to the use of the UDRP and the ACPA to resolve international disputes. Review the procedural history of the case to recall the relationship between the UDRP and the ACPA. Also review the discussion of geographic marks. Is there any case for secondary meaning here in order to establish trademark rights?

II. INTERNATIONAL TRADE AND INTELLECTUAL PROPERTY

A. MORAL RIGHTS

GILLIAM v. AMERICAN BROADCASTING COMPANIES, INC.

United States Court of Appeals for the Second Circuit, 1976.
538 F.2d 14.

LUMBARD, CIRCUIT JUDGE:

Plaintiffs, a group of British writers and performers known as "Monty Python," appeal from a denial by Judge Lasker in the Southern District of a preliminary injunction to restrain the American Broadcasting Company (ABC) from broadcasting edited versions of three separate programs originally written and performed by Monty Python for broadcast by the British Broadcasting Corporation (BBC). We agree with Judge Lasker that the appellants have demonstrated that the excising done for ABC impairs the integrity of the original work. We further find that the countervailing injuries that Judge Lasker found might have accrued to ABC as a result of an injunction at a prior date no longer exist. We therefore direct the issuance of a preliminary injunction by the district court.

Since its formation in 1969, the Monty Python group has gained popularity primarily through its thirty-minute television programs created for BBC as part of a comedy series entitled "Monty Python's Flying Circus." In accordance with an agreement between Monty Python and BBC, the group writes and delivers to BBC scripts for use in the television series. This scriptwriters' agreement recites in great detail the procedure to be followed when any alterations are to be made in the script prior to recording of the program. The essence of this section of the agreement is that, while BBC retains final authority to make changes, appellants or their representatives exercise optimum control over the scripts consistent with BBC's authority and only minor changes may be made without prior consultation with the writers. Nothing in the scriptwriters' agreement entitles BBC to alter a program once it has been recorded. The agreement further provides that, subject to the terms therein, the group retains all rights in the script.

Under the agreement, BBC may license the transmission of recordings of the television programs in any overseas territory. The series has been broadcast in this country primarily on non-commercial public broadcasting television stations, although several of the programs have been broadcast on commercial stations in Texas and Nevada. In each instance, the thirty-minute programs have been broadcast as originally recorded and broadcast in England in their entirety and without commercial interruption.

In October 1973, Time–Life Films acquired the right to distribute in the United States certain BBC television programs, including the Monty

Python series. Time–Life was permitted to edit the programs only "for insertion of commercials, applicable censorship or governmental ... rules and regulations, and National Association of Broadcasters and time segment requirements." No similar clause was included in the scriptwriters' agreement between appellants and BBC. Prior to this time, ABC had sought to acquire the right to broadcast excerpts from various Monty Python programs in the spring of 1975, but the group rejected the proposal for such a disjoined format. Thereafter, in July 1975, ABC agreed with Time–Life to broadcast two ninety-minute specials each comprising three thirty-minute Monty Python programs that had not previously been shown in this country.

Correspondence between representatives of BBC and Monty Python reveals that these parties assumed that ABC would broadcast each of the Monty Python programs "in its entirety." On September 5, 1975, however, the group's British representative inquired of BBC how ABC planned to show the programs in their entirety if approximately 24 minutes of each 90 minute program were to be devoted to commercials. BBC replied on September 12, "we can only reassure you that ABC have decided to run the programmes 'back to back,' and that there is a firm undertaking not to segment them."

ABC broadcast the first of the specials on October 3, 1975. Appellants did not see a tape of the program until late November and were allegedly "appalled" at the discontinuity and "mutilation" that had resulted from the editing done by Time–Life for ABC. Twenty-four minutes of the original 90 minutes of recording had been omitted. Some of the editing had been done in order to make time for commercials; other material had been edited, according to ABC, because the original programs contained offensive or obscene matter.

In early December, Monty Python learned that ABC planned to broadcast the second special on December 26, 1975. The parties began negotiations concerning editing of that program and a delay of the broadcast until Monty Python could view it. These negotiations were futile, however, and on December 15 the group filed this action to enjoin the broadcast and for damages. Following an evidentiary hearing, Judge Lasker found that "the plaintiffs have established an impairment of the integrity of their work" which "caused the film or program ... to lose its iconoclastic verve." According to Judge Lasker, "the damage that has been caused to the plaintiffs is irreparable by its nature." Nevertheless, the judge denied the motion for the preliminary injunction on the grounds that it was unclear who owned the copyright in the programs produced by BBC from the scripts written by Monty Python; that there was a question of whether Time–Life and BBC were indispensable parties to the litigation; that ABC would suffer significant financial loss if it were enjoined a week before the scheduled broadcast; and that Monty Python had displayed a "somewhat disturbing casualness" in their pursuance of the matter.

Judge Lasker granted Monty Python's request for more limited relief by requiring ABC to broadcast a disclaimer during the December 26 special to the effect that the group dissociated itself from the program because of the editing. A panel of this court, however, granted a stay of that order until this appeal could be heard and permitted ABC to broadcast, at the beginning of the special, only the legend that the program had been edited by ABC. We heard argument on April 13 and, at that time, enjoined ABC from any further broadcast of edited Monty Python programs pending the decision of the court. . . .

[After analyzing the contract and copyright issues, the court turned to the moral rights question.]

It also seems likely that appellants will succeed on the theory that, regardless of the right ABC had to broadcast an edited program, the cuts made constituted an actionable mutilation of Monty Python's work. This cause of action, which seeks redress for deformation of an artist's work, finds its roots in the continental concept of droit moral, or moral right, which may generally be summarized as including the right of the artist to have his work attributed to him in the form in which he created it. See 1 M. Nimmer, supra, at § 110.1.

American copyright law, as presently written, does not recognize moral rights or provide a cause of action for their violation, since the law seeks to vindicate the economic, rather than the personal, rights of authors. Nevertheless, the economic incentive for artistic and intellectual creation that serves as the foundation for American copyright law, *Goldstein v. California*, 412 U.S. 546, 93 S.Ct. 2303, 37 L.Ed.2d 163 (1973); *Mazer v. Stein*, 347 U.S. 201, 74 S.Ct. 460, 98 L.Ed. 630 (1954), cannot be reconciled with the inability of artists to obtain relief for mutilation or misrepresentation of their work to the public on which the artists are financially dependent. Thus courts have long granted relief for misrepresentation of an artist's work by relying on theories outside the statutory law of copyright, such as contract law, *Granz v. Harris*, 198 F.2d 585 (2d Cir. 1952) (substantial cutting of original work constitutes misrepresentation), or the tort of unfair competition, *Prouty v. National Broadcasting Co.*, 26 F. Supp. 265 (D.Mass. 1939). See Strauss, The Moral Right of the Author 128–138, in Studies on Copyright (1963). Although such decisions are clothed in terms of proprietary right in one's creation, they also properly vindicate the author's personal right to prevent the presentation of his work to the public in a distorted form. See *Gardella v. Log Cabin Products Co.*, 89 F.2d 891, 895–96 (2d Cir. 1937); Roeder, *The Doctrine of Moral Right*, 53 HARV.L.REV. 554, 568 (1940).

Here, the appellants claim that the editing done for ABC mutilated the original work and that consequently the broadcast of those programs as the creation of Monty Python violated the Lanham Act § 43(a), 15 U.S.C. § 1125(a). This statute, the federal counterpart to state unfair competition laws, has been invoked to prevent misrepresentations that may injure plaintiff's business or personal reputation, even where no registered trademark is concerned. See *Mortellito v. Nina of California*, 335 F. Supp. 1288, 1294 (S.D.N.Y. 1972). It is sufficient to violate the Act that a representation of a product, although technically true, creates a false impression of the product's origin. See *Rich v. RCA Corp.*, 390 F. Supp. 530 (S.D.N.Y. 1975) (recent picture of plaintiff on cover of album containing songs recorded in distant past held to be a false representation that the songs were new); *Geisel v. Poynter Products, Inc.*, 283 F. Supp. 261, 267 (S.D.N.Y. 1968).

These cases cannot be distinguished from the situation in which a television network broadcasts a program properly designated as having been written and performed by a group, but which has been edited, without the writer's consent, into a form that departs substantially from the original work. "To deform his work is to present him to the public as the creator of a work not his own, and thus makes him subject to criticism for work he has not done." Roeder, supra, at 569. In such a case, it is the writer or performer, rather than the network, who suffers the consequences of the mutilation, for the public will have only the final product by which to evaluate the work. Thus, an allegation that a defendant has presented to the public a "garbled," *Granz v. Harris*, supra (Frank, J., concurring), distorted version of plaintiff's work seeks to redress the very rights sought to be protected by the Lanham Act, 15 U.S.C. § 1125(a), and should be recognized as stating a cause of action under that statute. See *Autry v. Republic Productions, Inc.*, 213 F.2d 667 (9th Cir. 1954); *Jaeger v. American Int'l Pictures, Inc.*, 330 F. Supp. 274 (S.D.N.Y. 1971), which suggest the violation of such a right if mutilation could be proven.

During the hearing on the preliminary injunction, Judge Lasker viewed the edited version of the Monty Python program broadcast on December 26 and the original, unedited version. After hearing argument of this appeal, this panel also viewed and compared the two versions. We find that the truncated version at times omitted the climax of the skits to which appellants' rare brand of humor was leading and at other times deleted essential elements in the schematic development of a story line. We therefore agree with Judge Lasker's conclusion that the edited version broadcast by ABC impaired the integrity of appellants' work and represented to the public as the product of appellants what was actually a mere caricature of their talents. We believe that a valid cause of action for such distortion exists and that therefore a preliminary injunction may issue to prevent repetition of the broadcast prior to final determination of the issues. . . .

Complete relief for the alleged infringement and mutilation complained of may be accorded between Monty Python and ABC, which alone broadcast the programs in dispute. If ABC is ultimately found liable to appellants, a permanent injunction against future broadcasts and a damage award would satisfy all of appellants' claims. ABC's assertion that failure to join BBC and Time–Life may leave it subject to inconsistent verdicts in a later action against its licensors may be resolved through the process of impleader, which ABC has thus far avoided despite a suggestion from the district court to use that procedure. Finally, neither of the parties considered by ABC to be indispensable has claimed any interest in the subject matter of this litigation. See Fed.R.Civ.P. 19(a)(2).

For these reasons we direct that the district court issue the preliminary injunction sought by the appellants.

GURFEIN, CIRCUIT JUDGE (concurring):

I concur in my brother Lumbard's scholarly opinion, but I wish to comment on the application of Section 43(a) of the Lanham Act, 15 U.S.C. § 1125(a).

I believe that this is the first case in which a federal appellate court has held that there may be a violation of Section 43(a) of the Lanham Act with respect to a common-law copyright. The Lanham Act is a trademark statute, not a copyright statute. Nevertheless, we must recognize that the language of Section 43(a) is broad. It speaks of the affixation or use of false designations of origin or false descriptions or representations, but proscribes such use "in connection with any goods or services." It is easy enough to incorporate trade names as well as trademarks into Section 43(a) and the statute specifically applies to common law trademarks, as well as registered trademarks. Lanham Act § 45, 15 U.S.C. § 1127.

In the present case, we are holding that the deletion of portions of the recorded tape constitutes a breach of contract, as well as an infringement of a common-law copyright of the original work. There is literally no need to discuss whether plaintiffs also have a claim for relief under the Lanham Act or for unfair competition under New York law. I agree with Judge Lumbard, however, that it may be an exercise of judicial economy to express our view on the Lanham Act claim, and I do not dissent therefrom. I simply wish to leave it open for the District Court to fashion the remedy.

The Copyright Act provides no recognition of the so-called droit moral, or moral right of authors. Nor are such rights recognized in the field of copyright law in the United States. See 1 Nimmer on Copyright, § 110.2 (1975 ed.). If a distortion or truncation in connection with a use constitutes an infringement of copyright, there is no need for an additional cause of action beyond copyright infringement. Id. at § 110.3. An obligation to mention the name of the author carries the implied duty, however, as a matter of contract, not to make such changes in the work as would render the credit line a false attribution of authorship, *Granz v. Harris*, 198 F.2d 585 (2d Cir. 1952).

So far as the Lanham Act is concerned, it is not a substitute for droit moral which authors in Europe enjoy. If the licensee may, by contract, distort the recorded work, the Lanham Act does not come into play. If the licensee has no such right by contract, there will be a violation in breach of contract. The Lanham Act can hardly apply literally when the credit line correctly states the work to be that of the plaintiffs which, indeed it is, so far as it goes. The vice complained of is that the truncated version is not what the plaintiffs wrote. But the Lanham Act does not deal with artistic integrity. It only goes to misdescription of origin and the like. See *Societe Comptoir De L'Industrie Cotonniere Etablissements Boussac v. Alexander's Dept. Stores, Inc.*, 299 F.2d 33, 36 (2d Cir. 1962).

The misdescription of origin can be dealt with, as Judge Lasker did below, by devising an appropriate legend to indicate that the plaintiffs had not approved the editing of the ABC version. With such a legend, there is no conceivable violation of the Lanham Act. If plaintiffs complain that their artistic integrity is still compromised by the distorted version, their claim does not lie under the Lanham Act, which does not protect the copyrighted work itself but protects only against the misdescription or mislabelling.

So long as it is made clear that the ABC version is not approved by the Monty Python group, there is no misdescription of origin. So far as the content of the broadcast itself is concerned, that is not within the proscription of the Lanham Act when there is no misdescription of the authorship.

I add this brief explanation because I do not believe that the Lanham Act claim necessarily requires the drastic remedy of permanent injunction. That form of ultimate relief must be found in some other fountainhead of equity jurisprudence.

Notes

1. There were two important copyright treaties in effect before the adoption of the TRIPS Agreement: the Berne Convention, which dates back to the Nineteenth Century and the Universal Copyright Conventions (UCC), which dates back to the 1950's. The Berne Convention was entered into by European countries in order to ensure mutual recognition and enforcement of copyrights. The United States did not become a signatory under 1989. The UCC was enacted to meet the needs of developing countries and countries in the former Soviet Bloc which did not desire the strong copyright protections that were part of Western copyright law. Both were administered by the World Intellectual Property Organization (WIPO). Both have been eclipsed by the TRIPS Agreement, which was ratified in 1994 and went into effect in 1998.

2. The TRIPS Agreement did not incorporate Article 6bis of the Berne Convention, which deals with moral rights. As discussed in the chapter on copyright, moral rights are protections to authors of expressive works designed to enforce the rights of integrity, of paternity, of divulgation, and of withdrawal. The right of integrity allows the author to prevent adaptations or alterations of the work. The right of paternity allows the author to control the attribution of the work. The right of divulgation allows the author to control how and when the work is published. The right of withdrawal allows the author to remove the work from the public. Signatories of the Berne Convention are required moral right protection to authors under copyright law. The reluctance of the United States in joining Berne stemmed in part from the

reluctance to recognize moral rights within the utilitarian tradition of United States copyright law. As the United States recognized the utility of joining Berne in order to obtain international protection for its own copyright industries, the U.S. adopted some moral rights protection through the implementation of the Visual Artists Rights Act, codified in Section 106A of the Copyright Act.

3. The debate over protection of moral rights is the subtext to the *Gilliam* decision. The United States has relied on the *Gilliam* decision to show that its intellectual property law does offer protection for moral rights through other provisions, such as Section 43(a) of the Lanham Act and contract law. Review Judge Gurfein's concurrence and his warning against a reading of Section 43(a) into copyright law. Does the majority go too far? Is this really moral rights as described in Article 6bis?

4. Arguably, the holding of *Gilliam*, with its reading of Section 43(a), protects the author's right of integrity. The author's rights of divulgation and of withdrawal are protected through the distribution right. How about the right of attribution? In *Dastar v. Twentieth Century Fox*, 539 U.S. 23, 123 S.Ct. 2041, 156 L.Ed.2d 18 (2003), the Supreme Court addressed the issue of reverse passing off. Dastar had repackaged a videotape that had fallen into the public domain and sold it without attribution to Twentieth Century Fox or the creator of the videotape. Since the work was no longer copyrighted, the plaintiffs had no claim for copyright infringement and instead brought a claim under Section 43(a), alleging that Dastar by distributing the movie without attribution had created likelihood of confusion as to origin. The Court denied the claim unanimously (with Justice Breyer recusing himself). The Court ruled that "origin" under the Lanham Act meant source of the manufactured product and was different from "origin" under the Copyright Act, which meant source of the information content. Effectively, the Court rejected a right of attribution claim under section 43(a).

5. Are *Dastar* and *Gilliam* consistent? One argument is that *Dastar* repudiates the broad reach of section 43(a) as interpreted in *Gilliam*. But the Supreme Court did not discuss the *Gilliam* case in *Dastar*. A narrow way to reconcile the cases is to conclude that section 43(a) allows for right of integrity claims, but not right of attribution claims.

B. GRAY MARKETS

AMERICAN CIRCUIT BREAKER CORPORATION v. OREGON BREAKERS INC.

United States Court of Appeals for the Ninth Circuit, 2005.
406 F.3d 577.

McKEOWN, CIRCUIT JUDGE:

Few subjects have generated more ink and consternation in the trademark arena in recent years than the topic of parallel imports/gray market goods. In general terms, a gray market good, often referred to as a parallel import, is "[a] foreign-manufactured good, bearing a valid United States trademark, that is imported without the consent of the United

States trademark holder." *K Mart Corp. v. Cartier, Inc.*, 486 U.S. 281, 285, 108 S.Ct. 1811, 100 L.Ed.2d 313 (1988). Indeed, the debate is not a new one, as Congress jumped on the bandwagon in the early 1900s to provide United States trademark holders a remedy under the Tariff Act against importation of genuine goods bearing a United States trademark. Tariff Act of 1922 § 526, 42 Stat. 975 (later reenacted in identical form as Tariff Act of 1930 § 526, 19 U.S.C. § 1526). That legislation, amended over the years, did not quell the confusion and uncertainty, especially regarding the relationship between infringement claims under the Lanham Act and claims under the Tariff Act.

It is no surprise then that the parties to this dispute have diametrically opposed views as to how the case should be analyzed. At issue is the sale in the United States of circuit breakers imported from Canada under the trademark STAB–LOK. In an ironic twist, the circuit breakers are gray. Whether viewed as a gray market case or not, American Circuit Breaker Corporation ("ACBC") must establish a "likelihood of confusion" to prevail.

The essential facts are undisputed. ACBC holds the STAB–LOK trademark in the United States. Schneider Canada holds the STAB–LOK trademark in Canada. Federal Pioneer Limited ("Pioneer"), a subsidiary of Schneider Canada, manufactures circuit breakers for itself and ACBC. The circuit breakers sold by the companies are identical except for the casing color. Pioneer manufactures black circuit breakers for ACBC and gray ones for itself. The parties have stipulated that, except for the casing color, there are no material differences between the products, and that the gray circuit breakers are "genuine" versions of the black ones. This dispute arose because Oregon Breakers bought gray circuit breakers from a Canadian third-party supplier and, without permission from ACBC, sold them in the United States.

The question we address is whether the district court erred in dismissing ACBC's claims against Oregon Breakers for trademark infringement and unfair competition. We affirm the court's dismissal of the claims.

I.   Factual Background

Although the current relationships among the various companies are fairly straightforward, we briefly discuss the history of the STAB–LOK trademark because an understanding of where and when the parties derived their trademark rights provides useful background to our analysis.

In 1950, Federal Pacific Electric Company ("FPE") adopted the trademark STAB–LOK for circuit breakers. FPE eventually sold its U.S. circuit breaker business, including the U.S. STAB–LOK trademark, to Challenger Electric. In 1988, Challenger Electric sold the circuit breaker portion of its business to ACBC's predecessor, which in turn assigned all of its rights in the business and trademark to Provident Industries, Inc.

Provident Industries, Inc. changed its corporate name to American Circuit Breaker Corporation in late 1988.

Since 1950, ACBC and its predecessors have continuously used the trademark STAB–LOK on advertising, marketing, and sales of circuit breakers in the United States. ACBC is the record owner of the U.S. mark STAB–LOK, which was issued in 1988. Under the Lanham Act, the mark is incontestable and ACBC has the exclusive right to use the mark.

In 1952, Federal Electric Products Company, a U.S. company that was later merged into FPE, registered the trademark STAB–LOK in Canada. Until 1988, Pioneer, the manufacturer of the gray circuit breakers, was a Canadian subsidiary of FPE. The Canadian registration of STAB–LOK was assigned to Pioneer in 1986.

In 1988, FPE sold Pioneer to a Canadian company that had no relationship to Challenger Electric or any other predecessor of ACBC. In 1999, Pioneer assigned the Canadian trademark STAB–LOK to its parent company, Schneider Canada.

Prior to 1993, ACBC manufactured black STAB–LOK circuit breakers for the U.S. market at its plant in Albemarle, North Carolina, and Pioneer manufactured in Canada gray STAB–LOK circuit breakers for the Canadian market. Following an intellectual property dispute in the early 1990s, ACBC entered into an agreement with Pioneer and Schneider Canada.

Part of the dispute centered around Pioneer's claim that it had acquired rights to market under the STAB–LOK mark in the United States, as well as Canada. Although the details of the settlement agreement are confidential, the parties reveal the key elements in their briefs. Under the agreement, Pioneer manufactures black STAB–LOK circuit breakers for ACBC for sale in the United States and ACBC has agreed to purchase guaranteed minimums from Pioneer. Pioneer continues to manufacture gray STAB–LOK circuit breakers for sale in Canada by Pioneer. The agreement forbids Pioneer from selling its STAB–LOK circuit breakers in the United States for the term of the agreement. The effect of the agreement is that, although ACBC originally acquired its U.S. rights in the STAB–LOK mark from Challenger Electric, a U.S. company, ACBC's exclusivity of those trademark rights came about through the deal it struck with Pioneer, a Canadian company.

Accordingly, since 1993, both black and gray circuit breakers have been manufactured by Pioneer in Canada and both bear the STAB–LOK trademark, as well as an indication that "Federal Pioneer Limited" is the manufacturer and that the breakers are manufactured in Canada. The parties agree that there are no material differences between ACBC's black STAB–LOK circuit breakers and the gray STAB–LOK circuit breakers. Finally, the agreement provides that ACBC will assign its rights in the trademark STAB–LOK to Pioneer at the conclusion of the agreement.

From 1997 to 2000, Oregon Breakers sold gray Pioneer-manufactured STAB–LOK circuit breakers in the United States. Oregon Breakers purchased the circuit breakers from Merchant Pier, a Canadian distributor of circuit breakers and imported them into the United States for resale.

In sum, this case involves a U.S. trademark owner which contracts with a foreign, but historically affiliated manufacturer that owns the identical trademark in the foreign jurisdiction. The foreign trademark owner legitimately manufactures goods for both markets, which goods are identical except for color. A third party then imports identical goods manufactured under the foreign trademark into the United States, in competition with the U.S. trademark owner's products. . . .

III. Discussion

A. *Katzel* AND THE EMERGENCE OF TERRITORIALITY

It is now generally agreed and understood that trademark protection encompasses the notion of territoriality. The Supreme Court ushered in this concept more than eighty years ago in *A. Bourjois & Co. v. Katzel*, 260 U.S. 689, 43 S.Ct. 244, 67 L.Ed. 464 (1923). Understanding *Katzel* in the context of the transition from the notion of universality of trademarks to the emergence of territoriality sheds light on the dispute here.

As McCarthy, one of the leading commentators in the trademark arena Notes: "Early U.S. cases refused to protect U.S. trademark owners from parallel imports of genuine goods obtained from the foreign manufacturer." J. Thomas McCarthy, McCarthy on Trademarks and Unfair Competition, § 29:51 (4th ed. West 2005) (citing *Apollinaris Co. v. Scherer*, 27 F. 18 (C.C.N.Y. 1886)); *Fred Gretsch Mfg. Co. v. Schoening*, 238 F. 780 (2d Cir. 1916). These early cases were decided under the then-dominant principle of universality of trademarks. The universality principle stands for the proposition that a trademark serves the sole purpose of identifying the source of a product. Under this principle, a trademark is valid if it correctly identifies the origin or source of the product, regardless of where the consumer purchases the product. A gray market product does not violate trademark rights under the universality principle as long as it bears a genuine trademark that identifies the source of the product. Jerome Gilson, 1 Trademark Protection and Practice, § 4.05[5] (2004). *Katzel* came to the Supreme Court on a writ of certiorari from the Second Circuit. The plaintiff in *Katzel* purchased a French cosmetic firm's U.S. business, along with its goodwill and U.S. trademark "Java," which was used on face powder. *Katzel*, 260 U.S. at 690, 43 S.Ct. 244. The plaintiff continued to purchase the face powder from the French firm and used "substantially the same form of box and label as its predecessors" but "uses care in selecting colors suitable for the American market. . . ." Id. at 691, 43 S.Ct. 244. The Court pointed out that "the labels have come to be understood by the public here as meaning goods coming from the plaintiff." Id. The defendant was a third party who purchased the same face powder in France and resold it in the United States "in the French boxes which closely resemble those used by the plaintiff. . . ." Id.

Following precedent based on the principle of universality, the Second Circuit concluded that there was no trademark infringement. *A. Bourjois & Co. v. Katzel*, 275 F. 539, 540 (2d Cir. 1921) ("The question is whether the defendant has not the right to sell this article under the trade-marks which truly indicate its origin. We think she has."). In quick response to the ruling and with the intent of overruling the decision, Congress enacted § 526 of the Tariff Act of 1922, while *Katzel* was on appeal. See *K Mart*, 486 U.S. at 287–88, 108 S.Ct. 1811; see also *McCarthy*, supra, § 29:51. Section 526, which has since been reenacted as § 526 of the 1930 Tariff Act, 19 U.S.C. § 1526, prohibits importation of foreign-manufactured goods bearing a registered trademark owned by a U.S. citizen or corporation. Unlike a trademark infringement action under § 32 of the Lanham Act, the remedy under § 526 is prohibition of importation of the goods.

The Supreme Court subsequently reversed the Second Circuit and held that the plaintiff's trademark rights were infringed, though the Court did not reference the new legislation . . . . . The *Katzel* decision marked a dramatic change in trademark law by adopting the principle of "territoriality" of trademarks and moving away from the rule of "universality." See McCarthy, supra, § 29:51; Gilson, supra, § 4.05 [5]. Under the territoriality principle, a "trademark has a separate legal existence in each country and receives the protection afforded by the laws of that country." Gilson, supra, § 405[5].

Between the Supreme Court's decision in *Katzel* and the early 1980s "the legal journals [were] the main battleground" over the issue of whether a U.S. trademark holder could prevent the importation of "genuine" gray market goods. *Mamiya Co. v. Masel Supply Co.*, 548 F.Supp. 1063, 1065 (E.D.N.Y. 1982). Changing world economic conditions during the 1980s ushered in a dramatic increase in the number of cases dealing with the issue. See McCarthy, supra, § 29:46.

Some courts limited *Katzel* to its particular facts. See, e.g., *Weil Ceramics and Glass, Inc. v. Jalyn Corp.*, 878 F.2d 659, 669 (3d Cir. 1989) ("We do not read *Katzel* to extend beyond [its] circumstance."); *Olympus Corp. v. United States*, 792 F.2d 315, 321–22 (2d Cir. 1986) (holding that § 42 of the Lanham Act did not apply to genuine goods in cases that did not present the same equities as *Katzel*). . . . More recently, the principle of territoriality "has been criticized as obsolete in a world market where information products like computer programs cannot be located at a particular spot on the globe." McCarthy, supra, § 29:1. Nevertheless, *Katzel* remains good law and found expression in the more recent *K Mart* case.

B. *K Mart* AND GRAY MARKET GOODS

In 1988, the Supreme Court in *K Mart* provided a useful tutorial on gray market goods. *K Mart* involved a challenge to Customs Service regulations implementing § 526 of the Tariff Act. The Court began its opinion by explaining that "A gray-market good is a foreign-manufactured good, bearing a valid United States trademark, that is imported without the consent of the United States trademark holder." *K Mart*, 486 U.S. at 285, 108 S.Ct. 1811 (emphasis added). The Court then went on to describe the three general gray market scenarios.

The "prototypical" context, based on *Katzel*, see id. at 287, 108 S.Ct. 1811, arises where "a domestic firm ... purchases from an independent foreign firm the rights to register and use the latter's trademark as a United States trademark and to sell its foreign-manufactured products here." Id. at 286, 108 S.Ct. 1811. If the foreign manufacturer or a third party imports the products into the United States, they would be gray market goods competing with the trademark holder's goods. Id.

The second gray market scenario is where a domestic firm registers the U.S. trademark "for goods that are manufactured abroad by an affiliated manufacturer." Id. The Court detailed three variations that fit under this example: a) a foreign firm incorporates a subsidiary in the United States which then registers the U.S. trademark (which is identical to the foreign parent firm's trademark) in its own name; b) "an American-based firm establishes abroad a manufacturing subsidiary corporation"; or c) an American-based firm establishes abroad "its own unincorporated manufacturing division ... to produce its United States trademarked goods, and then imports them for domestic distribution." Id. at 286–87, 108 S.Ct. 1811. All of these variations involve "common control" of the United States and foreign trademark holders. See *Gilson*, supra, § 4.05[6].

The third gray market scenario is where the "domestic holder of a United States trademark authorizes an independent foreign manufacturer to use it." *K Mart*, 486 U.S. at 287, 108 S.Ct. 1811 (emphasis in original). "Usually the holder sells to the foreign manufacturer an exclusive right to use the trademark in a particular foreign location, but conditions the right on the foreign manufacturer's promise not to import its trademarked goods into the United States." Id. This situation usually arises when the U.S. firm owns both the domestic and foreign trademarks and licenses its use to a foreign manufacturer in a foreign country. See Gilson, supra, § 4.05[6].

The circumstances here most closely approximate *Katzel*, which is also *K Mart's* case 1. There are both similarities and differences between *Katzel* and the present case. In each case, separate companies owned the trademark in the United States and the trademark in the foreign jurisdiction. In both cases the plaintiff and the third party defendant acquired the product from the foreign manufacturer. And, in both cases the plaintiff's product has a valid U.S. trademark and the defendant's product has a valid trademark from the foreign trademark owner. Although ACBC did not purchase the U.S. trademark from a foreign company, its predecessor purchased those rights from a U.S. company that was a common predecessor to ACBC and Pioneer. And, unlike the labels in *Katzel*, the record here does not indicate that the black circuit breaker casing "ha[s] come to be understood by the public here as meaning goods coming from the plaintiff." *Katzel*, 260 U.S. at 691, 43 S.Ct. 244.

At least one prominent commentator has argued that the first K Mart context did not fit the definition of gray market at all because "the U.S. trademark owner did not own the mark abroad." Gilson, supra, § 4.05[6]. Indeed, determining whether such goods should be labeled as gray market is a bit tricky given the fact that the Supreme Court explained that gray market goods must have "a valid United States trademark," but also described the first *K Mart* context as the prototypical gray market situation. Caught up in the confusion, the parties spend a great deal of energy wrangling over whether this is a gray market case. ACBC claims it is not bringing a gray market claim because the marks are owned by independent corporations. Oregon Breakers argues that, as a result of the 1993 agreement, the companies are not truly unrelated and that the relationship fits within several of the *K Mart* criteria.

In the end, whether this is technically classified as a gray market case or not does not drive the solution. Ultimately, what is at issue is whether there is a likelihood of confusion as to source under the well established precedent of §§ 32 and 43(a) of the Lanham Act. Neither *Katzel* nor *K Mart* preclude a finding of trademark infringement as a matter of law in this context. As McCarthy Notes, "the ultimate issue in a trademark infringement suit against the importer of gray market imports is the factual question of likelihood of confusion of U.S. customers." McCarthy, supra, § 29.46; see *Brookfield Communications, Inc. v. West Coast Entm't Corp.*, 174 F.3d 1036, 1053 (9th Cir.1999) ("The core element of trademark infringement is the likelihood of confusion, i.e., whether the similarity of the marks is likely to confuse customers about the source of the products.") (citations omitted); *New West Corp. v. NYM Co.*, 595 F.2d 1194, 1201 (9th Cir.1979) ("Whether we call the violation infringement, unfair competition or false designation of origin, the test is identical is there a 'likelihood of confusion?' "); see also *Societe Des Produits Nestle v. Casa Helvetia, Inc.*, 982 F.2d 633, 640 (1st Cir.1992) ("Whether the fulcrum of plaintiffs' complaint is perceived as section 32(1)(a), section 42, or section 43(a), liability necessarily turns on the existence vel non of material differences between the products of a sort likely to create consumer confusion.").

C. ABSENCE OF THE LIKELIHOOD OF CONFUSION

The likelihood of confusion test centers on weighing the so-called Sleekcraft factors that range from the strength of the mark to the degree of care customers are likely to exercise. See *AMF Inc. v. Sleekcraft Boats*, 599 F.2d 341, 348–49 (9th Cir. 1979). These factors do not guide our analysis here, however, because the parties have, in effect, short circuited the case through their stipulation.

Determining whether the record sustains an infringement claim is not straightforward in this instance. This case is made more complicated by the parties' efforts to resolve it via stipulation and subsequent dismissal of claims. Rather than a clean set of district court findings or a comprehensive opinion, we are left to piece together the meaning of the final judgment, which incorporates but modifies the court's earlier Opinion and Order and encompasses the parties' factual stipulations. Reading the record in conjunction with the final judgment leads us to conclude that there is no material issue of fact with respect to infringement, that ACBC failed to establish infringement and, consequently, the dismissal of claims was appropriate.

The bulk of the record evidence relates to the nature of the circuit breakers sold by Oregon Breakers, namely whether they are genuine STAB–LOK circuit breakers and the quality control conditions of their manufacture. After much back and forth, the parties stipulated that there are no material differences between the black and the gray breakers, and that the gray breakers are "genuine" products in relation to the black breakers.

Because of this stipulation and the related court order, this case is governed by the rule we set out in *NEC Elecs. v. CAL Circuit Abco*, 810 F.2d 1506, 1510 (9th Cir. 1987) (citations omitted): "Trademark law generally does not reach the sale of genuine goods bearing a true mark even though such sale is without the mark owner's consent." Here, the parties have agreed that the goods were genuine vis-a-vis the ACBC goods bearing the same mark. The NEC rule makes good sense and comports with the consumer protection rationale of trademark law: "[T]rademark law is designed to prevent sellers from confusing or deceiving consumers about the origin or make of a product, which confusion ordinarily does not exist when a genuine article bearing a true mark is sold." Id.

The upshot of the stipulation between ACBC and Oregon Breakers is that consumers purchasing circuit breakers from Oregon Breakers are getting exactly the same circuit breaker, both in specification and quality, as they would purchase from ACBC. In other words, the goods are genuine. Rather than being confused, customers who purchase the gray STAB–LOK circuit breakers from Oregon Breakers get exactly what they expect. See *Iberia Foods Corp. v. Romeo*, 150 F.3d 298, 303 (3d Cir. 1998) ("[W]hen the differences between the products prove so minimal that consumers who purchase the alleged infringer's goods 'get precisely what they believed that they were purchasing,' consumers' perceptions of the trademarked goods are not likely to be affected by the alleged infringer's sales.") (internal citation omitted). In short, because there is no material fact as to infringement, ACBC's claims of trademark infringement and unfair competition must fail ..... We do not need to go as far as our sister circuit's circumscription of *Katzel* because the answer here is found in the parties' stipulated record as to genuine products.

NOTES

1. The TRIPS Agreement does not directly address the treatment of gray market goods. The argument can be made that permitting gray market goods limits the rights of the intellectual property holder to exclude imports of goods or services protected by trademark, copyright, or patent. On the other

hand, since the TRIPS Agreement is part of the World Trade Organization, whose mission following from its roots in GATT is to promote free trade, permitting gray market goods is consistent with competitive norms. This tension is reflected in Article 40(1): "Members agree that some licensing practices or conditions pertaining to intellectual property rights which restrain competition may have adverse effects on trade and may impede the transfer and dissemination of technology." Article 40 permits member states to enact legislation, such as antitrust laws or unfair competition laws, that place limits on intellectual property rights that interfere with competition. Allowing gray market goods is arguably consistent with Article 40. As of this date, there is no interpretation from the WTO of the scope of Article 40. The practices of member states may provide some guidance.

2.   The *American Circuit Breaker* case provides an excellent discussion of the law of trademark and gray market goods. Notice that the court ends up falling back on the likelihood of confusion principle to determine whether the gray market goods should be allowed. How does this compare with the Court's approach in *Bulova* and *Vanity Fair* in determining the extraterritorial application of the Lanham Act? Remember in those cases the court addressed the use of the Lanham Act to police trademark infringement outside the U.S. borders. Likelihood of confusion arguably would have worked against the trademark owner in those cases, especially *Bulova*. But likelihood of confusion seemed to play little role in the court's analysis. If *Bulova* suggests that the trademark owner has some universal rights in the mark, how can that suggestion be reconciled with the rejection of universality as discussed by the court in *American Circuit Breaker*?

3.   Gray market goods can implicate copyright and patents. For example, in *Quality King Distributors, Inc. v. L'anza Research International, Inc.*, 523 U.S. 135, 118 S.Ct. 1125, 140 L.Ed.2d 254 (1998), a manufacturer of hair care products in the United States challenged the importation of hair care products in boxes that were copyrighted. The imports had originated in the United States from the plaintiff who had sold them in a foreign market. The defendant had purchased the products with the intention of shipping and reselling the products in the United States. The Supreme Court held that the first sale doctrine protected the gray market products. The Court's ruling in *Quality King* permitted gray markets when the products could be traced to a sale from the U.S. copyright owner. A question left open by the Court was whether the first sale doctrine would apply to goods that are manufactured outside the United States. In *Omega S.A. v. Costco Wholesale Corp.*, 541 F.3d 982 (9th Cir. 2008), the United States Court of Appeals for the Ninth Circuit held that the *Quality King* decision applied only to the a round trip, that is copyrighted words make into the United States that were eventually exported and then reimported into the United States. In April, 2010, the Supreme Court granted a certiorari petition by Costco in order to clarify its *Quality King* decision.

4.   The Federal Circuit addressed patents and gray markets in *Jazz Photo Corp. v. International Trade Comm'n*, 264 F.3d 1094 (Fed. Cir. 2001). The case involved a challenge by Fujitsu, the patent holder in a particular type of disposable cameras, against Jazz Photo, who bought the used cameras and retrofitted for sale in the aftermarket. The court ruled the retrofitting

was protected from patent infringement as permitted repair and the resale of the cameras in the United States were permitted by the first sale doctrine. As in *Quality King*, the gray marketer was not found liable and was able to compete with the intellectual property owner.

5. Arguably, the most controversial gray market is the market for pharmaceuticals. The unauthorized production and sale of pharmaceuticals by a generic manufacturer is patent infringement. But consider the common practice of patients buying cheap versions of patented pharmaceuticals in Canada or Mexico and importing them for personal use into the United States. The importation is patent infringement. But is this a gray market that should be allowed? Notice that the first sale does not protect the practice for two reasons. First, the sale occurs outside the U.S. between the user and an unauthorized manufacturer of the product. Second, the sale, even if unauthorized, is often conditioned on a restriction on resale. The United States Senate has been contemplating legislation to immunize such activity from liability.

At the international level, generic manufacturers of drugs sometimes import unauthorized manufactures of drugs into a country where the drug is under patent and there is need for the product. Glaxo Smith Kline challenged such practices in South Africa by unauthorized manufactures of AIDS drugs. In 2003, a panel of the South African Competition Commission held that such restrictions on the gray market were inconsistent with South African competition law.

CHAPTER NINE

NEW HORIZONS: THE FUTURE OF INTELLECTUAL PROPERTY

■ ■ ■

OVERVIEW

Intellectual property laws govern the development and use of new types of creative works that often challenge our established views of applicable legal doctrines and policies. Many of the important issues that will shape the future characteristics of intellectual property laws will probably be dictated by the features of new types of intellectual works and means for using those works that we can not imagine today. As new categories of innovative products and expressive works—such as the new products, services, and creative works that have grown in importance with the rise of the Internet—are developed and brought to the public, fundamentally important intellectual property issues are likely to follow regarding who should control these products, services, and works and under what circumstances. The very unpredictability of the characteristics of future intellectual works makes the likelihood of new intellectual property controversies very high, but also frustrates our ability to accurately project the nature of these controversies.

Nonetheless, looking at the near future rather than at more dimly seen distant periods, a number of forces are already important in shaping changes in intellectual property laws and seem likely to continue to be significant for some time. This chapter introduces some of these presently important forces influencing changes in intellectual property laws. These forces are explored here through chapter subsections organized around several recent themes in the development of intellectual property laws. Each of the themes is largely independent of the others, so that various subsections of this chapter can be studied or omitted as time permits. The readings presented here introduce these themes both to suggest the frameworks within which future intellectual property reforms are likely to be developed and to better equip students entering into the legal profession (whether as intellectual property specialists or otherwise) to participate effectively in shaping future intellectual property laws in light of the developmental forces discussed here.

The themes addressed in this chapter concern basic criteria used to recognize property rights in intellectual works, the range of rights afforded to intellectual property owners, the proper interactions between intellectual property laws and other legal standards, and the impacts that intellectual property laws have on social values and public benefits from intellectual works. Collectively, these considerations define many of the substantive features, innovative influences, competitive impacts, and societal consequences of intellectual property laws. Questions about how these considerations should be resolved in the future represent many of the most important challenges facing our legal system as we seek to develop intellectual property laws for modern patterns of innovation, intellectual endeavors, and social practices.

I. EVOLVING JUSTIFICATIONS FOR PROPERTY CONTROLS OVER INTELLECTUAL WORKS

The nature of intellectual works in which parties should be recognized as having property rights continues to be poorly defined in intellectual property laws. As the features of intellectual works have grown more diverse and the circumstances in which they are created, distributed, and used have grown more complex, courts reviewing intellectual property laws have confronted increasingly difficult questions about what makes an intellectual work "property," as well as further questions about the consequences if property rights are or are not recognized in such a work. These questions are usually encountered in connection with works that do not fall within the scope of statutorily defined patent, copyright, trademark, or trade secret protections. Courts encountering property claims in these contexts have sometimes adopted very broadly inclusive views of protected property interests in intellectual works.

For example, in *Metropolitan Opera Ass'n v. Wagner–Nichols Recorder Corp.*, 199 Misc. 786, 101 N.Y.S.2d 483 (N.Y.Sup. 1950), a New York court applied a highly inclusive measure of property rights to recognize property interests in uncopyrighted radio broadcasts and related contract rights. In this case, the producers of the New York Metropolitan Opera sought to prevent a record company from making and selling phonograph records containing unauthorized recordings of opera performances taken from radio broadcasts of the performances. Prior to the initiation of this litigation, the Metropolitan Opera Association had transferred the exclusive right to broadcast its performances to the American Broadcasting Corporation and the exclusive right to record its performances to Columbia Records Incorporated.

The court in this case considered whether the making and distribution of the contested recordings constituted unfair competition under state law standards. It recognized that "[t]he modern view as to the law of unfair competition does not rest solely on the ground of direct competitive injury, but on the broader principle that property rights of commercial value are to be and will be protected from any form of unfair invasion or infringement and from any form of commercial immorality, and a court of equity will penetrate and restrain every guise resorted to by the wrong-doer." *Id.* at 492.

Whether or not the recordings in question infringed the property rights of the Metropolitan Opera Association was the key issue in this case. In finding that several types of protected property rights were at stake, the court reasoned as follows:

The defendants raise the further objection that the complaints fail to state a cause of action in that they set forth no property rights of the plaintiffs. Clearly, some property rights in the plaintiffs and interference with and misappropriation of them by defendants are necessary to a cause of action. However, "property rights," as has often been pointed out, are rights which are recognized and protected by the courts by excluding others therefrom. The designation is therefore more in the nature of a legal conclusion than a description.

The rights which the plaintiffs allege in their complaint are:

(1) The right of Metropolitan Opera to exclusive use, directly or indirectly, of the name and reputation which it has developed over a sixty-year period.

(2) The exclusive right of Metropolitan Opera to the productions which it creates by the use of its skill, artists, money and the organization it has developed.

(3) As a corollary of the latter the exclusive right to license the use of its performances and productions commercially in radio broadcasts, recordings and in other forms upon such terms as are agreed upon as to payments and the maintenance of artistic and technical standards in accord with the reputation of the Metropolitan Opera.

(4) The rights of plaintiffs Columbia Records and American Broadcasting being their exclusive recording and broadcasting rights derived from their agreements with Metropolitan Opera for which they have paid and in which they have invested substantial sums of money, time and skill.

The question presented is thus whether these rights are rights which the courts have recognized and protected and should recognize and protect as "property rights."

The Court of Appeals in *Fisher v. Star Company*, 231 N.Y. 414, 132 N.E. 133, 19 A.L.R. 937, quoted with approval the broad definition of property rights laid down by the Supreme Court of the United States in the *International News Service* case, [248 U.S. 215 (1918)]" * * *. The rule that a court of equity concerns itself only in the protection of property rights treats any civil right of a pecuniary nature as a property right * * *. And the right to acquire property by honest labor or the conduct of a lawful business is as much entitled to protection as the right to guard property already acquired * * *. It is this right that furnishes the basis of the jurisdiction in the ordinary case of unfair competition.

Id. at 493. In short, the court concluded that "property rights" are implicated where any civil right of pecuniary value is threatened and that such rights are present if they are acquired in exchange for "honest labor" or in the "conduct of a lawful business." According to the analysis adopted by this court, the law of unfair competition provides protections against interference with the full range of property rights mentioned above and is therefore a flexible enforcement tool of sweeping importance as the scope of property rights in intellectual works expands. If these broad views of property rights and unfair competition laws are applied, property interests can arise in intellectual works resulting from diverse types of labors and business activities. Through either unfair competition claims or claims for misappropriation of property interests, a person investing labor in the creation of an intellectual work or a business pursuing activities leading to the creation of such a work can develop extensive property rights and control regarding the resulting work.

The following case explores the justifications for recognizing property rights in a very simple yet important type of intellectual product—descriptive information about newsworthy activities. The justifications for property controls discussed in this case focus on the work leading to the news information at issue—that is, the intellectual endeavors of reporters and newspaper staff members in pursuing news gathering and promptly and effectively reporting the results.

The opinions in this case capture the views of several insightful jurists—including Justices Holmes and Brandeis—about the proper criteria for recognizing and enforcing property interests in products of intellectual endeavors. While the primary focus here is on news reporting, the insights and principles addressed in the several opinions below can be applied to questions regarding the proper scope of property rights in any form of intellectual work. In reaching different conclusions about whether the news reports at issue in this case constituted a form of property, the several justices apply substantially different tests for what constitutes intellectual property. In addition, the justices also struggle to define how the relationships between competing news reporting and distribution services should be regulated in the public interest and how such regulation should interact with property interests regarding news content. These sorts of boundary questions about the proper scope of property interests in various forms of intellectual works and the legitimate regulatory limits on the exercise of intellectual property rights continue to challenge courts. Such challenges are likely to grow more numerous as new forms of intellectual works and means of producing and distributing them emerge and intellectual property protections are sought to be extended into new settings and activities.

INTERNATIONAL NEWS SERVICE
v. ASSOCIATED PRESS

Supreme Court of the United States, 1918.
248 U.S. 215, 39 S.Ct. 68, 63 L.Ed. 211.

Mr. Justice Pitney delivered the opinion of the Court.

The parties are competitors in the gathering and distribution of news and its publication for profit in newspapers throughout the United States. The Associated Press, which was complainant in the District Court, is a co-operative organization, incorporated under the Membership Corporations Law of the state of New York, its members being individuals who are either proprietors or representatives of about 950 daily newspapers published in all parts of the United States. That a corporation may be organized under that act for the purpose of gathering news for the use and benefit of its members and for publication in newspapers owned or represented by them, is recognized by an amendment enacted in 1901 (Laws N. Y. 1901, c. 436). Complainant gathers in all parts of the world, by means of various instrumentalities of its own, by exchange with its members, and by other appropriate means, news and intelligence of current and recent events of interest to newspaper readers and distributes it daily to its members for publication in their newspapers. The cost of the service, amounting approximately to $3,500,000 per annum, is assessed upon the members and becomes a part of their costs of operation, to be recouped, presumably with profit, through the publication of their several newspapers. Under complainant's by-laws each member agrees upon assuming membership that news received through complainant's service is received exclusively for publication in a particular newspaper, language, and place specified in the certificate of membership, that no other use of it shall be permitted, and that no member shall furnish or permit any one in his employ or connected with his newspaper to furnish any of complainant's news in advance of publication to any person not a member. And each member is required to gather the local news of his district and supply it to the Associated Press and to no one else.

Defendant is a corporation organized under the laws of the state of New Jersey, whose business is the gathering and selling of news to its customers and clients, consisting of newspapers published throughout the United States, under contracts by which they pay certain amounts at stated times for defendant's service. It has widespread news-gathering agencies; the cost of its operations amounts, it is said, to more than $2,000,000 per annum; and it serves about 400 newspapers located in the various cities of the United States and abroad, a few of which are represented, also, in the membership of the Associated Press.

The parties are in the keenest competition between themselves in the distribution of news throughout the United States; and so, as a rule, are the newspapers that they serve, in their several districts.

Complainant in its bill, defendant in its answer, have set forth in almost identical terms the rather obvious circumstances and conditions under which their business is conducted. The value of the service, and of the news furnished, depends upon the promptness of transmission, as well as upon the accuracy and impartiality of the news; it being essential that the news be transmitted to members or subscribers as early or earlier than similar information can be furnished to competing newspapers by other news services, and that the news furnished by each agency shall not be furnished to newspapers which do not contribute to the expense of gathering it. And further, to quote from the answer:

> Prompt knowledge and publication of worldwide news is essential to the conduct of a modern newspaper, and by reason of the enormous expense incident to the gathering and distribution of such news, the only practical way in which a proprietor of a newspaper can obtain the same is, either through co-operation with a considerable number of other newspaper proprietors in the work of collecting and distributing such news, and the equitable division with them of the expenses thereof, or by the purchase of such news from some existing agency engaged in that business.

The bill was filed to restrain the pirating of complainant's news by defendant in three ways: First, by bribing employees of newspapers published by complainant's members to furnish Associated Press news to defendant before publication, for transmission by telegraph and telephone to defendant's clients for publication by them; second, by inducing Associated Press members to violate its by-laws and permit defendant to obtain news before publication; and, third, by copying news from bulletin boards and from early editions of complainant's newspapers and selling this, either bodily or after rewriting it, to defendant's customers.

The District Court, upon consideration of the bill and answer, with voluminous affidavits on both sides, granted a preliminary injunction under the first and second heads, but refused at that stage to restrain the systematic practice admittedly pursued by defendant, of taking news bodily from the bulletin boards and early editions of complainant's newspapers and selling it as its own. The court expressed itself as satisfied that this practice amounted to unfair trade, but as the legal question was one of first impression it considered that the allowance of an injunction should await the outcome of an appeal. Both parties having appealed, the Circuit Court of Appeals sustained the injunction order so far as it went, and upon complainant's appeal modified it and remanded the cause, with directions to issue an injunction also against any bodily taking of the words or substance of complainant's news until its commercial value as news had passed away. The present writ of certiorari was then allowed.

The only matter that has been argued before us is whether defendant may lawfully be restrained from appropriating news taken from bulletins issued by complainant or any of its members, or from newspapers published by them, for the purpose of selling it to defendant's clients. Complainant asserts that defendant's admitted course of conduct in this regard both violates complainant's property right in the news and constitutes unfair competition in business. And notwithstanding the case has proceeded only to the stage of a preliminary injunction, we have deemed it proper to consider the underlying questions, since they go to the very merits of the action and are presented upon facts that are not in dispute. As presented in argument, these questions are: (1) Whether there is any property in news; (2) Whether, if there be property in news collected for the purpose of being published, it survives the instant of its publication in the first newspaper to which it is communicated by the news-gatherer; and (3) whether defendant's admitted course of conduct in appropriating for commercial use matter taken from bulletins or early editions of Associated Press publications constitutes unfair competition in trade.

* * *

In considering the general question of property in news matter, it is necessary to recognize its dual character, distinguishing between the substance of the information and the particular form or collocation of words in which the writer has communicated it.

No doubt news articles often possess a literary quality, and are the subject of literary property at the common law; nor do we question that such an article, as a literary production, is the subject of copyright by the terms of the act as it now stands. In an early case at the circuit Mr. Justice Thompson held in effect that a newspaper was not within the protection of the copyright acts of 1790 and 1802. But the present act is broader; it provides that the works for which copyright may be secured shall include "all the writings of an author," and specifically mentions "periodicals, including newspapers." Evidently this admits to copyright a contribution to a newspaper, notwithstanding it also may convey news; and such is the practice of the copyright office, as the newspapers of the day bear witness.

But the news element—the information respecting current events contained in the literary production—is not the creation of the writer, but is a report of matters that ordinarily are publici juris; it is the history of the day. It is not to be supposed that the framers of the Constitution, when they empowered Congress "to promote the progress of science and useful arts, by securing for limited times to authors and inventors the exclusive right to their respective writings and discoveries," intended to confer upon one who might happen to be the first to report a historic event the exclusive right for any period to spread the knowledge of it.

* * *

Defendant insists that when, with the sanction and approval of complainant, and as the result of the use of its news for the very purpose for which it is distributed, a portion of complainant's members communicate it to the general public by posting it upon bulletin boards so that all may read, or by issuing it to newspapers and distributing it indiscriminately, complainant no longer has the right to control the use to be made of it; that when it thus reaches the light of day it becomes the common possession of all to whom it is accessible; and that any purchaser of a newspaper has the right to communicate the intelligence which it contains to anybody and for any purpose, even for the purpose of selling it for profit to newspapers published for profit in competition with complainant's members.

The fault in the reasoning lies in applying as a test the right of the complainant as against the public, instead of considering the rights of complainant and defendant, competitors in business, as between themselves. The right of the purchaser of a single newspaper to spread knowledge of its contents gratuitously, for any legitimate purpose not unreasonably interfering with complainant's right to make merchandise of it, may be admitted; but to transmit that news for commercial use, in competition with complainant—which is what defendant has done and seeks to justify—is a very different matter. In doing this defendant, by its very act, admits that it is taking material that has been acquired by complainant as the result of organization and the expenditure of labor, skill, and money, and which is salable by complainant for money, and that defendant in appropriating it and selling it as its own is endeavoring to reap where it has not sown, and by disposing of it to newspapers that are competitors of complainant's members is appropriating to itself the harvest of those who have sown. Stripped of all disguises, the process amounts to an unauthorized interference with the normal operation of complainant's legitimate business precisely at the point where the profit is to be reaped, in order to divert a material portion of the profit from those who have earned it to those who have not; with special advantage to defendant in the competition because of the fact that it is not burdened with any part of the expense of gathering the news. The transaction speaks for itself and a court of equity ought not to hesitate long in characterizing it as unfair competition in business.

The underlying principle is much the same as that which lies at the base of the equitable theory of consideration in the law of trusts—that he who has fairly paid the price should have the beneficial use of the property. It is no answer to say that complainant spends its money for that which is too fugitive or evanescent to be the subject of property. That might, and for the purposes of the discussion we are assuming that it would furnish an answer in a common-law controversy. But in a court of equity, where the question is one of unfair competition, if that which complainant has acquired fairly at substantial cost may be sold fairly at substantial profit, a competitor who is misappropriating it for the purpose of disposing of it to his own profit and to the disadvantage of complainant cannot be heard to say that it is too fugitive or evanescent to be regarded as property. It has all the attributes of property necessary for determining that a misappropriation of it by a competitor is unfair competition because contrary to good conscience.

The contention that the news is abandoned to the public for all purposes when published in the first newspaper is untenable. Abandonment is a question of intent, and the entire organization of the Associated Press negatives such a purpose. The cost of the service would be prohibited if the reward were to be so limited. No single newspaper, no small group of newspapers, could sustain the expenditure. Indeed, it is one of the most obvious results of defendant's theory that, by permitting indiscriminate publication by anybody and everybody for purposes of profit in competition with the news-gatherer, it would render publication profitless, or so little profitable as in effect to cut off the service by rendering the cost prohibitive in comparison with the return. The practical needs and requirements of the business are reflected in complainant's by-laws which have been referred to. Their effect is that publication by each member must be deemed not by any means an abandonment of the news to the world for any and all purposes, but a publication for limited purposes; for the benefit of the readers of the bulletin or the newspaper as such; not for the purpose of making merchandise of it as news, with the result of depriving complainant's other members of their reasonable opportunity to obtain just returns for their expenditures.

It is to be observed that the view we adopt does not result in giving to complainant the right to monopolize either the gathering or the distribution of the news, or, without complying with the copyright act, to prevent the reproduction of its news articles, but only postpones participation by complainant's competitor in the processes of distribution and reproduction of news that it has not gathered, and only to the extent necessary to prevent that competitor from reaping the fruits of complainant's efforts and expenditure, to the partial exclusion of complainant. and in violation of the principle that underlies the maxim 'sic utere tuo,' etc.

It is said that the elements of unfair competition are lacking because there is no attempt by defendant to palm off its goods as those of the complainant, characteristic of the most familiar, if not the most typical, cases of unfair competition. But we cannot concede that the right to equitable relief is confined to that class of cases. In the present case the fraud upon complainant's rights is more direct and obvious. Regarding news matter as the mere material from which these two competing parties are endeavoring to make money, and treating it, therefore, as quasi property for the purposes of their business because they are both selling it as such, defendant's conduct differs from the ordinary case of unfair competition in trade principally in this that, instead of selling its own goods as those of complainant, it substitutes misappropriation in the place of misrepresentation, and sells complainant's goods as its own.

* * *

There is some criticism of the injunction that was directed by the District Court upon the going down of the mandate from the Circuit Court of Appeals. In brief, it restrains any taking or gainfully using of the complainant's news, either bodily or in substance from bulletins issued by the complainant or any of its members, or from editions of their newspapers, *"until its commercial value as news to the complainant and all of its members has passed away."* The part complained of is the clause we have italicized; but if this be indefinite, it is no more so than the criticism. Perhaps it would be better that the terms of the injunction be made specific, and so framed as to confine the restraint to an extent consistent with the reasonable protection of complainant's newspapers, each in its own area and for a specified time after its publication, against the competitive use of pirated news by defendant's customers. But the case presents practical difficulties; and we have not the materials, either in the way of a definite suggestion of amendment, or in the way of proofs, upon which to frame a specific injunction; hence, while not expressing approval of the form adopted by the District Court, we decline to modify it at this preliminary stage of the case, and will leave that court to deal with the matter upon appropriate application made to it for the purpose.

The decree of the Circuit court of Appeals will be

Affirmed.

MR. JUSTICE HOLMES, dissenting.

When an uncopyrighted combination of words is published there is no general right to forbid other people repeating them—in other words there is no property in the combination or in the thoughts or facts that the words express. Property, a creation of law, does not arise from value, although exchangeable—a matter of fact. Many exchangeable values may be destroyed intentionally without compensation. Property depends upon exclusion by law from interference, and a person is not excluded from using any combination of words merely because some one has used it before, even if it took labor and genius to make it. If a given person is to be prohibited from making the use of words that his neighbors are free to make some other ground must be found. One such ground is vaguely expressed in the phrase unfair trade. This means that the words are repeated by a competitor in business in such a way as to convey a misrepresentation that materially injures the person who first used them, by appropriating credit of some kind which the first user has earned. The ordinary case is a representation by device, appearance, or other indirection that the defendant's goods come from the plaintiff. But the only reason why it is actionable to make such a representation is that it tends to give the defendant an advantage in his competition with the plaintiff and that it is thought undesirable that an advantage should be gained in that way. Apart from that the defendant may use such unpatented devices and uncopyrighted combinations of words as he likes. The ordinary case, I say, is palming off the defendant's product as the plaintiff's but the same evil may follow from the opposite falsehood—from saying whether in words or by implication that the plaintiff's product is the defendant's, and that, it seems to me, is what has happened here.

Fresh news is got only by enterprise and expense. To produce such news as it is produced by the defendant represents by implication that it has been acquired by the defendant's enterprise and at its expense. When it comes from one of the great news collecting agencies like the Associated Press, the source generally is indicated, plainly importing that credit; and that such a representation is implied may be inferred with some confidence from the unwillingness of the defendant to give the credit and tell the truth. If the plaintiff produces the news at the same time that the defendant does, the defendant's presentation impliedly denies to the plaintiff the credit of collecting the facts and assumes that credit to the defendant. If the plaintiff is later in Western cities it naturally will be supposed to have obtained its information from the defendant. The falsehood is a little more subtle, the injury, a little more indirect, than in ordinary cases of unfair trade, but I think that the principle that condemns the one condemns the other. It is a question of how strong an infusion of fraud is necessary to turn a flavor into a poison. The dose seems to me strong enough here to need a remedy from the law. But as, in my view, the only ground of complaint that can be recognized without legislation is the implied misstatement, it can be corrected by stating the truth; and a suitable acknowledgment of the source is all that the plaintiff can require. I think that within the limits recognized by the decision of the Court the defendant should be enjoined from publishing news obtained from the Associated Press for _____ hours after publication by the plaintiff unless it gives express credit to the Associated Press; the number of hours and the form of acknowledgment to be settled by the District Court.

MR. JUSTICE BRANDEIS, dissenting.

There are published in the United States about 2,500 daily papers. More than 800 of them are supplied with domestic and foreign news of general interest by the Associated Press—a corporation without capital stock which does not sell news or earn or seek to earn profits, but serves merely as an instrumentality by means of which these papers supply themselves at joint expense with such news. Papers not members of the Associated Press depend for their news of general interest largely upon agencies organized for profit. Among these agencies is the International News Service which supplies news to about 400 subscribing papers. It has, like the Associated Press, bureaus and correspondents in this and foreign countries; and its annual expenditures in gathering and distributing news is about $2,000,000. Ever since its organization in 1909, it has included among the sources from which it gathers news, copies (purchased in the open market of early editions of some papers published by members of the Associated Press and the bulletins publicly posted by them. These items, which constitute but a small part of the news transmitted to its subscribers, are generally verified by the International News Service before transmission; but frequently items are transmitted without verification; and occasionally even without being re-written. In no case is the fact disclosed that such item was suggested by or taken from a paper or bulletin published by an Associated Press member.

No question of statutory copyright is involved. The sole question for our consideration is this: Was the International News Service properly enjoined from using, or causing to be used gainfully, news of which it acquired knowledge by lawful means (namely, by reading publicly posted bulletins or papers purchased by it in the open market) merely because the news had been originally gathered by the Associated Press and continued to be of value to some of its members, or because it did not reveal the source from which it was acquired?

* * *

News is a report of recent occurrences. The business of the news agency is to gather systematically knowledge of such occurrences of interest and to distribute reports thereof. The Associated Press contended that knowledge so acquired is property, because it costs money and labor to produce and because it has value for which those who have it not are ready to pay; that it remains property and is entitled to protection as long as it has commercial value as news; and that to protect it effectively, the defendant must be enjoined from making, or causing to be made, any gainful use of it while it retains such value. An essential element of individual property is the legal right to exclude others from enjoying it. If the property is private, the right of exclusion may be absolute; if the property is affected with a public interest, the right of exclusion is qualified. But the fact that a product of the mind has cost its producer money and labor, and has a value for which others are willing to pay, is not sufficient to ensure to it this legal attribute of property. The general rule of law is, that the noblest of human productions—knowledge, truths ascertained, conceptions, and ideas—became, after voluntary communication to others, free as the air to common use. Upon these incorporeal productions the attribute of property is continued after such communication only in certain classes of cases where public policy has seemed to demand it. These exceptions are confined to productions which, in some degree, involve creation, invention, or discovery. But by no means all such are endowed with this attribute of property. The creations which are recognized as property by the common law are literary, dramatic, musical, and other artistic creations; and these have also protection under the copyright statutes. The inventions and discoveries upon which this attribute of property is conferred only by statute, are the few comprised within the patent law. There are also many other cases in which courts interfere to prevent curtailment of plaintiff's enjoyment of incorporal productions; and in which the right to relief is often called a property right, but is such only in a special sense. In those cases, the plaintiff has no absolute right to the protection of his production; he has merely the qualified right to be protected as against the defendant's acts, because of the special relation in which the latter stands or the wrongful method or means employed in acquiring the knowledge or the manner in which it is used. Protection of this character is afforded where the suit is based upon breach of contract or of trust or upon unfair competition.

The knowledge for which protection is sought in the case at bar is not of a kind upon which the law has heretofore conferred the attributes of property; nor is the manner of its acquisition or use nor the purpose to which it is applied, such as has heretofore been recognized as entitling a plaintiff to relief.

First. Plaintiff's principal reliance was upon the "ticker" cases [involving information on stock or commodities prices transmitted over specialized communication systems and governed by confidentiality obligations arising under contractual terms or fiduciary obligations]; but they do not support its contention. The leading cases on this subject rest the grant of relief, not upon the existence of a general property right in news, but upon the breach of a contract or trust concerning the use of news communicated; and that element is lacking here.

* * *

Second. Plaintiff also relied upon the cases which hold that the common law right of the producer to prohibit copying is not lost by the private circulation of a literary composition, the delivery of a lecture, the exhibition of a painting, or the performance of a dramatic or musical composition. These cases rest upon the ground that the common law recognizes such productions as property which, despite restricted communication, continues until there is a dedication to the public under the copyright statutes or otherwise. But they are inapplicable for two reasons: (1) At common law, as under the copyright acts, intellectual productions are entitled to such protection only if there is underneath something evincing the mind of a creator or originator, however modest the requirement. The mere record of isolated happenings, whether in words or by photographs not involving artistic skill, are denied such protection. (2) At common law, as under the copyright acts, the element in intellectual productions which secures such protection, is not the knowledge, truths, ideas, or emotions which the composition expresses, but the form or sequence in which they are expressed; that is, "some new collocation of visible or audible points—of lines, colors, sounds, or words." An author's theories, suggestions, and speculations, or the systems, plans, methods, and arrangements of an originator, derive no such protection from the statutory copyright of the book in which they are set forth; and they are likewise denied such protection at common law.

That news is not property in the strict sense is illustrated by the case of *Sports and General Press Agency, Ltd. v. 'Our Dogs' Publishing Co., Ltd.*, [1916] 2 K. B. 880, where the plaintiff, the assignee of the right to photograph the exhibits at a dog show, was refused an injunction against defendant who had also taken pictures of the show and was publishing them. The court said that, except in so far as the possession of the land occupied by the show enabled the proprietors to exclude people or permit them on condition that they agree not to take photographs (which condition was not imposed in that case), the proprietors had no exclusive right to photograph the show and could therefore grant no such right. And it was further stated that, at any rate, no matter what conditions might be imposed upon those entering the grounds, if the defendant had been on top of a house or in some position where he could photograph the show without interfering with the physical property of the plaintiff, the plaintiff would have no right to stop him. If, when the plaintiff creates the event recorded, he is not entitled to the exclusive first publication of the news (in that case a photograph) of the event, no reason can be shown why he should be accorded such protection as to events which he simply records and transmits to other parts of the world, though with great expenditure of time and money.

Third. If news be treated as possessing the characteristics not of a trade secret, but of literary property, then the earliest issue of a paper of general circulation or the earliest public posting of a bulletin which embodies such news would, under the established rules governing literary property, operate as a publication, and all property in the news would then cease. Resisting this conclusion, plaintiff relied upon the cases which hold that uncopyrighted intellectual and artistic property survives private circulation or a restricted publication; and it contended that in each issue of each paper, a restriction is to be implied, that the news shall not be used gainfully in competition with the Associated Press or any of its members. There is no basis for such an implication. But it is, also, well settled that where the publication is in fact a general one—even express words of restriction upon use are inoperative. In other words, a general publication is effective to dedicate literary property to the public, regardless of the actual intent of its owner. In the cases dealing with lectures, dramatic and musical performances, and art exhibitions, upon which plaintiff relied, there was no general publication in print comparable to the issue of daily newspapers or the unrestricted public posting of bulletins. The principles governing those cases differ more or less in application, if not in theory, from the principles governing the issue of printed copies; and in so far as they do differ, they have no application to the case at bar.

Fourth. Plaintiff further contended that defendant's practice constitutes unfair competition, because there is "appropriation without cost to itself of values created by" the plaintiff; and it is upon this ground that the decision of this court appears to be based. To appropriate and use for profit, knowledge and ideas produced by other men, without making compensation or even acknowledgment, may be inconsistent with a finer sense of propriety; but, with the exceptions indicated above, the law has heretofore sanctioned the practice. Thus it was held that one may ordinarily make and sell anything in any form, may copy with exactness that which another has produced, or may otherwise use his ideas without his consent and without the payment of compensation, and yet not inflict a legal injury; and that ordinarily one is at perfect liberty to find out, if he can by lawful means, trade secrets of another, however valuable, and then use the knowledge so acquired gainfully, although it cost the original owner much in effort and in money to collect or produce.

Such taking and gainful use of a product of another which, for reasons of public policy, the law has refused to endow with the attributes of property, does not become unlawful because the product happens to have been taken from a rival and is used in competition with him. The unfairness in competition which hitherto has been recognized by the law as a basis for relief lay in the manner or means of conducting the business; and the manner or means held legally unfair, involves either fraud or force or the doing of acts otherwise prohibited by law. In the 'passing off' cases (the typical and most common case of unfair competition), the wrong consists in fraudulently representing by word or act that defendant's goods are those of plaintiff. In the other cases, the diversion of trade was effected through physical or moral coercion, or by inducing breaches of contract or of trust or by enticing away employees. In some others, called cases of simulated competition, relief was granted because defendant's purpose was unlawful; namely, not competition but deliberate and wanton destruction of plaintiff's business.

* * *

Fifth. The great development of agencies now furnishing country-wide distribution of news, the vastness of our territory, and improvements in the means of transmitting intelligence, have made it possible for a news agency or newspapers to obtain, without paying compensation, the fruit of another's efforts and to use news so obtained gainfully in competition with the original collector. The injustice of such action is obvious. But to give relief against it would involve more than the application of existing rules of law to new facts. It would require the making of a new rule in analogy to existing ones. The unwritten law possesses capacity for growth; and has often satisfied new demands for justice by invoking analogies or by expanding a rule or principle. This process has been in the main wisely applied and should not be discontinued. Where the problem is relatively simple, as it is apt to be when private interests only are involved, it generally proves adequate. But with the increasing complexity of society, the public interest tends to become omnipresent; and the problems presented by new demands for justice cease to be simple. Then the creation or recognition by courts of a new private right may work serious injury to the general public, unless the boundaries of the right are definitely established and wisely guarded. In order to reconcile the new private right with the public interest, it may be necessary to prescribe limitations and rules for its enjoyment; and also to provide administrative machinery for enforcing the rules. It is largely for this reason that, in the effort to meet the many new demands for justice incident to a rapidly changing civilization, resort to legislation has latterly been had with increasing frequency.

The rule for which the plaintiff contends would effect an important extension of property rights and a corresponding curtailment of the free use of knowledge and of ideas; and the facts of this case admonish us of the danger involved in recognizing such a property right in news, without imposing upon news-gatherers corresponding obligations. A large majority of the newspapers and perhaps half the newspaper readers of the United States are dependent for their news of general interest upon agencies other than the Associated Press. The channel through which about 400 of these papers received, as the plaintiff alleges, "a large amount of news relating to the European war of the greatest importance and of intense interest to the newspaper reading public" was suddenly closed [due to restrictions imposed by foreign governments]. The closing to the International News Service of these channels for foreign news (if they were closed) was due not to unwillingness on its part to pay the cost of collecting the news, but to the prohibitions imposed by foreign governments upon its securing news from their respective countries and from using cable or telegraph lines running therefrom. For aught that appears, this prohibition may have been wholly undeserved; and at all events the 400 papers and their readers may be assumed to have been innocent. For aught that appears, the International News Service may have sought then to secure temporarily by arrangement with the Associated Press [reports from the latter's foreign news service, a request the Associated Press could ignore unless it was obligated to serve the public interest by sharing foreign news on a commercially reasonable basis].

* * *

Courts are ill-equipped to make the investigations which should precede a determination of the limitations which should be set upon any property right in news or of the circumstances under which news gathered by a private agency should be deemed affected with a public interest. Courts would be powerless to prescribe the detailed regulations essential to full enjoyment of the rights conferred or to introduce the machinery required for enforcement of such regulations. Considerations such as these should lead us to decline to establish a new rule of law in the effort to redress a newly disclosed wrong, although the propriety of some remedy appears to be clear.

NOTES

1. Under the analysis accepted by the majority in *International News*, how are property rights gained in an intellectual work? Is labor a critical basis for recognizing property rights in intellectual works because such rights are useful in ensuring that compensation is paid for the labor invested in creating the works? Or is the recognition of property rights an aspect of ensuring personal control over the fruits of intellectual labors and thereby promoting beneficial psychological and behavioral characteristics of individuals? Or is reserving control over intellectual works through property rights an aspect of respecting the "personhood" of creators of intellectual works and ensuring the status of these creators as independent actors exercising choices over conduct and its consequences within our legal system?

If labor in the creation of an intellectual work is important in justifying property rights concerning such a work, which aspects of news reporting should be deemed to be covered by property rights in news reports? Also, if the investment of labor in the production of works is the basis for recognizing property rights, what is the basis for recognizing property rights in an organization such as the Associated Press? Should an organization of this sort be deemed to have intellectual property rights upon the creation of a work or only if the organization is assigned such rights by the creator of the work? If rights should be seen as being held by an organization or corporation upon the creation of a work, under what circumstances should this be the case? What type of arrangement should be in place before rights resulting from the creation of an intellectual work should vest immediately in an organization or corporation rather then in the individual who has created the work?

2.   What sorts of public policy interests should override normal intellectual property rules to preclude the recognition of any rights in a given type of intellectual work? For example, Justices Holmes and Brandeis suggest that the public's interest in the free dissemination of news justifies a rule in which news reporters and organizations would have no property interests in the factual contents of news reports regardless of the degree of labor or creative effort invested in producing the reports. What features of news dissemination might justify this result? Is this result justified by the importance of news reporting alone? If news reporting is important to the public, should this justify less or more intellectual property incentives to encourage additional efforts to provide news reports?

Or does the justification for a limited range of property interests in news reports turn on the communication methods used to distribute news and the need, at least in the era of the *International News* case, for competing news distributors to have access to the full range of news reports to ensure that some newspaper readers were not shut out from important news reports? Are there comparable issues regarding the distribution of intellectual works today which should limit the range of property rights recognized in intellectual works?

3.   As discussed in Justice Brandeis' dissent, prior to the Supreme Court's ruling in *International News*, a number of courts had provided protection to news services when subscribers had used news reports in violation of the subscriber's contractual obligations to use reports only in specified manners and to keep these reports confidential except when being put to an authorized use. If no property rights are recognized in intellectual works such as news reports, when will privately negotiated contract terms between creators and users be an effective means for creators to maintain control over the works and to receive compensation from users? Does the range of situations in which contractual arrangements are potentially effective indicate that the further protections of intellectual property laws are not needed in these situations? Should intellectual property protections be reserved for situations where the formation or enforcement of contracts regarding the use of intellectual works is likely to be ineffective?

4.   Assuming that intellectual property rights are recognized in works such as news reports, the means to enforce these rights may still be problematic. For example, the injunction at issue in *International News* called for the International News Service to avoid "any bodily taking of the words or substance of complainant's news until its commercial value as news had

passed away." What would indicate that the "commercial value of news had passed away?" Also, if the International News Service produced or carried news reports on an event that was previously addressed in one of the Associated Press' news reports, how would a court determine if the International News Service had "bodily tak[en] the words or substance" of the report carried over the Associated Press news service?

What are the advantages, if any, of Justice Holmes' suggestion that other news services like International News Service should be precluded from using Associated Press reports for a specified number of hours? How would the proper number of hours be chosen? Would the proper number of hours vary with developing technologies for news gathering and distribution? Would a particular number of hours (say "2 hours") in which the Associated Press reports were deemed to be unavailable to other news services still be problematic?

5. Justices Holmes and Brandeis suggest that, even if property rights in news reports are not recognized, the interactions and competition between news services should be regulated to ensure that news delivery to the public is accomplished in a complete and beneficial manner. How would a system of regulation of news gathering through unfair competition laws (or through equivalent trade regulation standards imposed under antitrust laws) differ from a system where property rights in news reports were recognized? Could a regulatory system ensuring fair or publicly beneficial delivery of news reports by news agencies be implemented even if property rights were recognized in news reports? What would be the major differences between regulatory systems imposed with and without the recognition of property rights in news reports?

6. Justice Holmes indicates that, even in the absence of property rights in news reports, concern over the proper attribution of the source of news reports might still provide a basis for the regulation of news organizations under unfair competition laws. He suggests that the public's interest in proper attribution could be adequately served in the context of a case like *International News* by forcing a service that wished to use reports from the Associated Press to indicate that this organization was the source of the reports. Would this type of relief adequately protect the Associated Press? What sorts of harms might still prevail under a system which ensured that the source of news reports was properly described?

7. Justice Holmes emphasizes in his dissenting opinion that in his view the labor underlying the production of an intellectual work is not enough to justify property rights in such a work. Assuming that this is true, what alternative basis is there for recognizing property rights in intellectual works? Are these justifications the same across different types of intellectual works? For example, can we state a general theory that will justify the recognition of intellectual property rights in both useful designs of the sorts covered by patent laws and expressive works covered by copyright laws?

8. Justice Brandeis points out in a portion of his opinion that limitations imposed by certain foreign governments on the gathering and transmission of news by other news services made broad access to reports from the Associated Press particularly important. To what extent should barriers to the comple-

tion or delivery of comparable intellectual works by others limit the scope of rights recognized in the creator of an intellectual work? In situations where other competing or substitute works are unlikely be available, should holders of property rights in intellectual works be forced to make their works available? For example, should the limited availability of reports comparable to those being carried by the Associated Press have been the basis for an injunction forcing the Associated Press to license rights to other news organizations allowing those organizations to use reports from Associated Press on commercially reasonable terms? When should such a limitation on enforcement choices be imposed on an intellectual property rights holder in the public interest? Should these sorts of limitations on the full scope of controls normally afforded to intellectual property holders only be implemented to limit controls over intellectual property where the intellectual works involved are highly important to the public and where the production of competing or substitute works is peculiarly constrained by resource or legal limitations?

9.   Justice Brandeis asserted that enforcing the intellectual property rule advocated by the Associated Press in *International News* would involve "making of a new rule in analogy to existing ones." To what extent was the property rule at issue in *International News* a new or old rule? Will new types of intellectual works regularly test the limits of present intellectual property laws such that the sort of "new" rule at issue in *International News* must be confronted regularly? What are the advantages of deciding such cases by analogy to property rules applied in earlier cases involving personal or real property? What are the disadvantages of using such analogies? Are the risks and advantages the same if courts use earlier intellectual property standards by analogy—that is, if they use standards developed for one type of intellectual work to resolve cases involving new types of intellectual works? Which is a better presumption: that new types of intellectual works are not governed by any form of intellectual property rights until such rights are established by legislation or that new types of intellectual works are governed by rights derived from general principles of intellectual property law until the legislature assesses the balance of protection and free use of such works which best serves the public and steps in with associated legislation to clarify the scope of rights available regarding the new type of work?

10.   Claims of misappropriation of intellectual property under the theory embraced in *International News* have survived, at least in narrow forms, despite assertions that such claims are preempted by federal copyright laws. For a more complete discussion of the possible preemption of state "hot news" misappropriation claims by federal copyright laws, see the court's analyses in *National Basketball Association v. Motorola Inc.*, 105 F.3d 841 (2d Cir. 1997), reprinted in Chapter Six.

II. SCOPE OF PROTECTED SUBJECT MATTER

As advances in diverse fields have made possible significantly new types of useful inventions and expressive works, courts have repeatedly considered whether these new types of inventions and works fall within intellectual property laws and creation incentives. The resulting judicial analyses have progressively expanded the boundaries of intellectual property controls, leading to new controversies over the broad impacts of these expanded controls.

The expanded scope of intellectual property controls has produced two types of public policy controversies examined in this section.

In some settings, inventions or works covered by intellectual property rights are so central to further research or to beneficial practices and products that intellectual property rights and restrictions may harm the public by constraining access to these key inventions or works. Public policy debates in these areas focus on whether intellectual property controls should be relaxed or avoided altogether to ensure beneficial public access to these important inventions or works and additional advances or creative works derived from them.

In other contexts, the lure of broadly applied intellectual property rights may promote the development of goods or practices that have immoral or illegal features, suggesting that government actions should discourage rather than encourage the creation and commercialization of such goods or practices. In these settings, the questions that are the primary focus of public policy debates concern how uses of potentially harmful new technologies should be regulated and how the incentives of patent laws should be reconciled with regulatory restrictions on new technologies.

This section addresses three important types of public policy problems stemming from recent trends towards the recognition of intellectual property controls over broad subject matters. The first subsection addresses the features that discoveries derived from nature must have in order to be properly subject to patent incentives and rewards. The resolution of this issue has great significance in determining the limits that patents on biotechnology features such as genes may place on subsequent research activities and patient treatment methods. The second subsection examines patents that may restrict free access to methods of complying with substantive legal requirements in fields such as tax law or to technologies (such as pollution control equipment) that are essential or highly effective in complying with particular legal standards. This second subsection considers the degree to which patent protections (and associated payments to patent holders) should allow particular parties to capture economic benefits derived from legal requirements that compel or strongly encourage parties to use products or practices that are restricted by intellectual property laws. The third subsection considers the possibility that patents may encourage the creation of products that are sometimes (or even frequently) immoral or illegal when used and examines the degree to which the patent system should withhold incentives from the creation of such products.

A. RESTRICTING THE USE OF ITEMS AND PROCESSES DERIVED FROM NATURE

ASSOCIATION FOR MOLECULAR PATHOLOGY v. UNITED STATES PATENT AND TRADEMARK OFFICE

09 Civ. 4515 (RWS).

COMPLAINT

INTRODUCTION

1. Every person's body contains human genes, passed down to each individual from his or her parents. These genes determine, in part, the structure and function of every human body. This case challenges the legality and constitutionality of granting patents over this most basic element of every person's individuality.

2. The gene patents that are challenged in this case are patents covering the BRCA1 and BRCA2 genes, which relate to an increased risk of breast and/or ovarian cancer. Ease of access to genomic discoveries is crucial if basic research is to be expeditiously translated into clinical laboratory tests that benefit patients in the emerging era of personalized and predictive medicine. The patents make ease of access more restricted. Because of the patents, defendant Myriad has the right to prevent clinicians from independently looking at or interpreting a person's BRCA1 and BRCA2 genes to determine if the person is at a higher risk of breast and/or ovarian cancer. Because of the patents and because Myriad chooses not to license the patents broadly, women who fear they may be at an increased risk of breast and/or ovarian cancer are barred from having anyone look at their BRCA 1 and BRCA2 genes or interpret them except for the patent holder. Women are thereby prevented from obtaining information about their health risks from anyone other than the patent holder, whether as an initial matter or to obtain a second opinion. The patents also prevent doctors or laboratories from independently offering testing to their patients, externally validating the test, or working cooperatively to improve testing. Many women at risk cannot even be tested because they are uninsured and/or cannot afford the test offered by Myriad.

3. The patents cover the human genes themselves. In this respect, they cover the healthy gene and numerous variations of the gene, some of which Myriad identified, some of which it did not, and some of which have not yet been identified. Some of those variations correlate with an increased risk of breast and ovarian cancer. Some do not. The patents also cover any new methods of looking at the human genes that might be developed by others, the concept of comparing one BRCA 1 or BRCA2 gene to another BRCA1 or BRCA2 gene for the purpose of discerning differences, and the correlations found in nature between mutations in the human gene and an increased risk of breast or ovarian cancer.

4.   The patenting of human genes, the concept of looking at or comparing human genes, and correlations found in nature between certain genes and an increased risk of breast and/or ovarian cancer violates long established legal principles that prohibit the patenting of laws of nature, products of nature, and abstract ideas. These patents also violate the First Amendment and Article I, section 8, clause 8 of the United States Constitution

* * *

FACTS

31.   Defendant U.S. Patent Office has granted, and Myriad holds, either through ownership or exclusive license, numerous patents relating to the human genes known as BRCA1 and BRCA2.

32.   Plaintiffs challenge the legality and the constitutionality of four categories of claims in these patents:

> a.   Patent Claims Over Natural Human Genes: Claims 1, 2, 5, and 6 of patent 5,747,282 ('282) and claim 1 of patent 5,837,492 ('492).
>
> b.   Patent Claims Over Natural Human Genes With Natural Mutations: Claim 1 of patent 5,693,473 ('473), claim 7 of patent '282, and claims 6 and 7 of patent '492.
>
> c.   Patent Claims Over Any Method, Including Non–Patented Methods, Of Looking For Mutations in Natural Human Genes: Claim 1 of patent 5,709,999 ('999).
>
> d.   Patent Claims Over The Thought That Two Genes Are Different or Have Different Effects, Including But Not Limited To The Thought That The Differences Correlate With An Increased Risk Of Breast And/Or Ovarian Cancer: Claim 1 of patent 5,710,001 ('001), claim 1 of patent 5,753,441 ('441), claims I and 2 of patent 6,033,857 ('857) and claim 20 of patent '282.

33.   Every person's body is composed of cells. In the nucleus of each cell is the person's DNA. Genes are encoded by DNA. Genes instruct the body to create the proteins and gene products that that person's body uses to function. Human DNA and human genes consist of hundreds or thousands of nucleotides (i.e. bases) referred to as A, T, G, and C. A gene is represented in scientific research and the patents in this case, by the genomic sequence, the series of nucleotides (represented by the letters) corresponding to the bases.

34.   DNA is a chemical structure made by the body. However, the genetic sequence is informational both for clinicians and researchers and for the body itself.

35.   Not everyone's DNA or genes are identical. Genes vary in nature from one person to another and those variations are often called mutations or variants. Those variants can include such changes as a T appearing where an A normally appears or a G being deleted from the DNA sequence. Variants can be inherited and can also be acquired during a

lifetime. They can also include much larger variations such as sections of DNA that are missing or displaced. Some of these variants have effects on the body's ability to create proteins necessary for sound health.

36. To find out if a person has a T where an A normally appears, a genetic researcher or clinician looks at the sequence of an individual's gene. The researcher or clinician can sequence that gene—i.e. read the A, T, C, G letters of the gene. Once the sequence is known, the researcher or clinician can look at it to see if the letters show a healthy sequence, a sequence with mutations known to be associated with cancer, or a sequence with one or more variants of uncertain significance. Alternatively, the researcher or clinician can check just a small section of the sequence where a known mutation or variant is known to occur. The methods by which researchers or clinicians identify the sequence of either the whole gene or any part thereof are not patented in the claims at issue here and are well known in the field.

37. The genes covered by the patents in this case are called BRCA1 and BRCA2 because of their association with breast cancer. Every man and woman has BRCA1 and BRCA2 genes, but the genomic sequence of each person's BRCA genes can differ. Certain mutations in the genes are correlated with an increased risk of breast and/or ovarian cancer. Scientists also have found that mutations in these genes may be associated with other cancers, such as prostate and pancreatic cancers.

38. Breast cancer is one of the leading causes of death among women. Approximately 5–10% of the women who develop breast cancer are likely to have a mutation, inherited from one of their parents, in their BRCA1 or BRCA2 genes, that predisposes them to an increased risk of breast and/or ovarian cancer.

39. Women with one of these significant gene mutations in the BRCA1 or BRCA2 gene have an approximately 40–85% lifetime risk of developing breast cancer. Inherited mutations on the BRCA 1 and BRCA2 genes also increase the risk of ovarian cancer.

40. A BRCA1/BRCA2 genetic test result that is positive for one of these mutations can have a substantial impact on a woman's medical decisions and health. It can also have an impact on that woman's relatives. Many women will obtain earlier and more vigilant screening for breast and/or ovarian cancers, and some women may choose to have prophylactic surgery to remove their breasts and/or ovaries in order to reduce the risk of future cancers.

41. In the 1990's, a number of genetic researchers around the world began looking for a human gene that correlated with an increased risk of breast and/or ovarian cancer. Many of those researchers, including the researchers who ultimately formed defendant Myriad, were funded, at least in part, by the federal government.

42. Researchers, using techniques widely available in the profession, determined in 1990 that one gene that correlated with an increased risk of breast and/or ovarian cancer was located in the body on chromosome 17.

43. Another researcher team, eventually associated with defendant Myriad, also using techniques widely available in the profession, sequenced the precise BRCA1 gene. They subsequently formed Myriad. They sought, and ultimately obtained, several patents on this human BRCA 1 gene.

44. Scientists knew that BRCA1 was not the only gene that predisposed women to an increased risk of inherited breast and/or ovarian cancer. Researchers from all over the world began looking for other similar genes, again using techniques widely available in the profession.

45. Defendant Myriad, using techniques widely available in the profession, filed patents over the BRCA2 gene. Myriad ultimately obtained a series of patents over the human BRCA2 gene.

46. Defendant Myriad did not invent, create or in any way construct or engineer the human BRCA 1 and BRCA 2 genes. These genes are existing products of nature, naturally occurring within the human body. Myriad located them in nature and merely described their informational content as it exists and functions in nature.

47. Defendant Myriad did not invent, create or in any way construct the differences found when genes are compared or the correlations between certain mutations and an increased risk of breast and/or ovarian cancer. Nature did that. Myriad identified nature's laws.

48. As a result of the breadth of its patents, Myriad has the right to control all genetic testing related to breast and/or ovarian cancer linked to BRCA1 or BRCA2. Researchers and clinicians cannot develop or implement new tests for breast/ovarian cancer linked to BRCA1 or BRCA2 if development or implementation involves looking at BRCA 1 or BRCA2. Women cannot give their blood or DNA to a researcher or clinician and obtain a second opinion. The effect is to infringe on quality medical practice and to compromise quality assurance and improvement of testing.

49. Defendant Myriad has enforced its patent rights over BRCA1 and BRCA2 genes at least nine (9) times. For example, according to press reports, laboratories at Yale performed analyses of those genes, but they no longer do so as a direct result of a cease-and-desist letter received from defendant Myriad.

50. Defendant Myriad obtained its patents from defendant Patent Office pursuant to a formal written policy by the Patent Office which provides that naturally occurring genes can be patented if they are "isolated from their natural state and purified."

51. An "isolated and purified" human gene performs the exact same function as a non-isolated and purified human gene in a person's body. The information dictated by the gene is identical whether it is inside or outside of the body. According to the Patent Office policy, an "isolated and purified" gene includes one that is simply removed from the body and removed from other content of the cell. Removing a product of nature from its natural location does not make it any less a product of nature.

52. This policy permits the patenting of products of nature, laws of nature, natural phenomena, abstract ideas, and basic human knowledge and thought. It therefore violates the United States Constitution Article 1, section 8, clause 8 and the First Amendment, as well as 35 U.S.C. § 101 of the patent statute.

53. Defendant Myriad obtained its patents pursuant to the practice of the defendant United States Patent and Trademark Office that permits patenting of comparisons or correlations created by nature, but identified by a patent holder.

54. This practice permits the patenting of laws of nature and abstract ideas and basic human knowledge or thought. It therefore violates Article 1, section 8, clause 8 and the First Amendment of the United States Constitution, as well as 35 U.S.C. § 101.

PATENT CLAIMS OVER NATURAL HUMAN GENES

55. Several of the claims in Myriad's patents cover the human BRCA1 and BRCA2 genes in their natural, non-mutated form. These include claims 1, 2, 5, and 6 of patent '282 and claim I of patent '492.

56. Claim 1 of patent '282 covering BRCA 1 is for any strand of "isolated" DNA that creates a particular protein identified in the patent. This claim covers the DNA that includes the BRCA1 gene in its "wild-type" or non-mutated form. It also includes any DNA that creates any portion of the identified protein. It thus includes DNA sequences that are identical in structure and function to the DNA as it exists in every person's body. It also includes any DNA that creates a fragment of the protein.

57. Claim 2 of patent '282 is very similar, but somewhat narrower. It covers a specific DNA sequence listed in the patent as the DNA sequence for the BRCA 1 gene.

58. Claim 5 of patent '282 also covers BRCA1, but it covers any DNA that has "at least 15 nucleotides" of the DNA referenced in claim 1. A nucleotide is one base. Claim 5 thus explicitly covers small fragments of the BRCA 1 gene.

59. Claim 6 of patent '282 covers any isolated DNA that has "at least 15 nucleotides" of the DNA referenced in claim 2.

60. Claim 1 of patent '492 is for any strand of "isolated" DNA that creates a particular protein identified in the patent. This claim covers the DNA that includes the BRCA2 gene in its "wild-type" or non-mutated form. It also includes any DNA that creates the identified protein. It thus includes DNA sequences that are identical in structure and function to the DNA as it exists in every person's body.

PATENT CLAIMS OVER NATURAL HUMAN GENES WITH NATURAL MUTATIONS

61.   Several of the claims in Myriad's patents claim the human BRCA1 or BRCA2 gene that contains variants or mutations caused by nature. These include claim 1 of '473, claim 7 of '282, and claims 6 and 7 of '492.

62.   Myriad looked at human genes from many individuals. Some of those individuals had variants in BRCA 1 or BRCA2.Myriad recorded the DNA sequences of those individuals with those variants and obtained patents on the DNA with those naturally mutated sequences.

63.   Claim 1 of '473 claims "isolated DNA comprising an altered BRCA1 DNA having at least one" of the specified variants. Myriad asserts that some of the patented DNA containing specified variants correlate with an increased risk of breast and ovarian cancer. Myriad asserts that other patented DNA containing specified variants does not so correlate or that Myriad does not yet know their effect, if any.

64.   Claim 7 of '282 claims "an isolated DNA" that has specified variants. In the text of the patent, Myriad describes all of the variants as cancer predisposing mutations.

65.   Claim 6 of '492 claims any "isolated DNA" that creates any mutated form of the protein created by BRCA2 if the mutations correlate with a "susceptibility to cancer." In other words, the claim covers any yet-to-be discovered mutations—discovered by anyone—that correlate with an increased risk of any type of cancer.

66.   Claim 7 of '492 also claims isolated DNA if the DNA contains sequences that include any mutations that correlate with an increased risk of cancer.

67.   Claim 1 of '473, claim 7 of '282, and Claims 6 and 7 of '492 include DNA sequences that are identical in structure and function to the DNA inside the body of some people.

PATENT CLAIMS OVER ANY METHOD, INCLUDING NON–PATENT-ED METHODS, OF LOOKING FOR MUTATIONS IN NATURAL HU-MAN GENES

68.   Myriad's patents also claim any and all methods, including non-patented methods, of looking at natural human genes. This includes Claim 1 of patent '999.

69.   Claim 1 of patent '999 covers any method of analyzing a human being's BRCA 1 gene for the purpose of finding whether the human being has any of the specified germline [inherited] variants.

70.   The methods used to look at the gene are not patented and are well known in the field. All that is patented is the act of looking at the BRCA1 gene to see if the gene has the specified variants.

PATENT CLAIMS OVER THOUGHT OR ABSTRACT IDEAS

71.   Several of the claims in Myriad's patents include comparing two genes, correlations between mutations in the human BRCA1 and BRCA2 genes that are currently known to be associated with an increased risk of

breast and/or ovarian cancer, and correlations between cancer and mutations not now known, but identified in the future. These include claim 1 of '001, claim 1 of '441, claims 1 and 2 of patent '857, and claim 20 of '282.

72.   Specifically, claim 1 of '001 involves taking a tumor sample from a person and looking at the BRCA1 gene in that sample and comparing it to the BRCA1 gene from the same person taken from a part of the body in which there is no tumor and seeing if there are any differences. The methods by which this is done are not patented. What is patented is performing this comparison of the tumor and germline sequences to identify somatic mutations in the BRCA1 gene and thinking "there are differences and they must be somatic (environmentally caused)." What is patented is the abstract idea that nature has made the two forms of the BRCA1 genes different.

73.   Claim 1 of '441 similarly involves the comparison of two BRCA genes. This claim covers comparing the BRCA1 gene in a tissue sample taken from a person with the BRCA 1 gene in its "wild-type" or non-mutated state. The methods by which this is done are not patented. What is patented is performing this comparison of the BRCA1 gene from the tissue sample and the BRCA1 wild-type gene and thinking "there are differences." What is patented is the abstract idea that nature has made the two BRCA1 genes different.

74.   Patent '857 involves the comparison of two BRCA2 genes. Claim 1 involves comparing a BRCA2 gene taken from a person with a wild-type BRCA2 gene. The methods by which this is done are not patented. What is patented is performing this comparison for BRCA2 and thinking "there are differences" and that the differences reflect a mutation. What is patented is the abstract idea that nature has made the two BRCA2 genes different.

75.   Claim 2 of patent '857 involves the same comparison of two BRCA2 genes. The only difference is that the thought that is patented is "there are differences" and they "indicate a predisposition to [breast] cancer." What is patented is the abstract idea that nature has made the two genes different in a manner that increases that person's risk of breast cancer.

76.   Claim 20 of '282 involves "a method for screening potential cancer therapeutics." However, the method consists entirely of putting the potential therapeutic into contact with a cell that includes a BRCA1 mutation and looking to see if the cell grows more slowly with the therapeutic than without. That method simply describes a scientific method that has been in place for many years, specifically for a cell with a BRCA1 mutation. The only even arguably unique part of the method is the thought that the person has at the end of the process i.e. "this therapeutic worked" when used in the context of a BRCA1 mutation or "this therapeutic did not work" in that context.

77.   All of these claims (except claim 1 of '857 and claim 20 of '282) include comparisons not only of DNA, but of other derivatives of DNA such as RNA, and cDNA made from mRNA.

78. None of these claims is limited to identifying differences in genes that Myriad has itself identified as correlating with an increased risk of cancer. All identifying of differences, including those that are found in the future by anyone to correlate with an increased risk of cancer, are patented.

79. Myriad did not create any of the differences found in the genes. Nature did. Myriad did not cause any of the effects of those differences. Nature did. All of the effects of these differences occur in a person's body as well as outside the body.

80. None of these claims is limited to "isolated" DNA.

IMPACT OF THE PATENTS

81. Defendant Myriad utilizes its patents by offering a test to determine if an individual has any mutations in the human BRCA 1 or BRCA2 genes. The test consists of sequencing a person's gene, comparing it to either another gene in that person's body or one from another person, and reaching a conclusion about whether nature has caused a variant that increases that person's risk of breast and/or ovarian cancer.

82. There are thousands of doctors and scientists, including molecular pathologists, geneticists, and researchers, around the country, and the plaintiffs, who have the technical ability to look at human genes and who do so on a daily basis. The only thing that prevents those doctors and scientists from looking at the human BRCA1 and BRCA2 genes is Myriad's patents.

83. One of the conditions for receiving a patent is to disclose publicly all information about the patented thing. The purpose of that requirement is to enable others to "invent around" and build upon and improve the patented thing, thereby fostering scientific progress. Unlike most things that are granted patents, it is not possible to invent around the patented human BRCA1 and BRCA2 genes or correlations. These genes, their effects, and the correlations between the genes and disease were created by nature and exist in nature. They are pure information, and in order to build upon them, one needs to utilize the patented sequences, which is not permissible under the patents.

84. Because of its patents, Myriad maintains a monopoly over any genetic testing to determine the presence or absence of mutations on the human BRCA1 or BRCA2 genes. Thus, although others including plaintiffs have the technical ability to determine if a person has a mutation, and are willing to do so using non-patented methods, they can be prohibited from doing so because of the patents on the BRCA1 and BRCA2 genes and can't tell any patient the results because of Myriad's enforcement of its patents.

85. Because Myriad maintains a monopoly on clinical testing to determine the presence or absence of mutations on the human BRCA1 and BRCA2 genes, the only types of tests that are offered to patients and the only mutations examined are those dictated by Myriad.

86. Myriad maintains the largest database of BRCA 1 and BRCA2 data. It does not share the information in that database with the Breast Cancer Mutation Database set up by NIH to ensure the widest possible distribution of information about genes and breast cancer.

87. Myriad's monopoly has resulted in a disparity in the amount of information known about genetic mutations in BRCA1 and BRCA2 in ethnic groups other than Caucasians.

88. Gene patents can serve as a disincentive to innovation in molecular testing because they deny access to a vital baseline of genomic information that cannot be invented around. Moreover, threat of enforcement from a patent holder and ensuing litigation costs lead to a chilling effect as clinical laboratories are reluctant to develop new tests, even when new tests could directly benefit patients.

89. For at least some portions of the life of the patents, Myriad did not perform certain tests that were known to reveal additional mutations that increased the risk of breast and/or ovarian cancer. Myriad prohibited anyone else from offering those tests to patients even though it knew that they would provide women with essential information about their risk of developing life-threatening cancer. Eventually, Myriad began to offer this additional testing, but chose to package it separately from its standard test.

90. Because of its patents on the BRCA genes, Myriad has the power to bar patients from obtaining testing other than through its laboratory. There are women, such as plaintiff Girard and any other women who have obtained full sequencing from Myriad, who cannot obtain a second opinion on their BRCA testing and are compelled to make major medical decisions based on a test that they cannot confirm. Plaintiff Limary, who received the result of variant of uncertain significance from Myriad, wants to obtain further testing and for information about her variant to be freely disclosed and studied.

91. Laboratories, such as that operated by Dr. Ledbetter, are increasingly adopting new generations of genetic sequencing technology that will permit faster, more comprehensive and potentially less expensive testing. That testing will be impeded by patents on genes that they cannot test.

92. Myriad charges more than $3,000 for its exclusive Comprehensive BRACAnalysis test. Many researchers might be able to do the testing for a reduced cost.

93. There are women, including plaintiffs Ceriani and Fortune, who cannot afford the testing offered by Myriad and whose insurance Myriad will not accept. As a result, these women have not been tested.

94. Myriad offers another test, called BRACAnalysis Rearrangement Test or BART, that looks for large genetic rearrangements that are not caught by its standard Comprehensive BRACAnalysis test. Myriad will conduct BART testing for some women who meet its criteria at no additional cost.

However, other women must pay an additional price for BART testing—approximately $650.

95.   There are women, including plaintiffs Thomason and Raker, who have a significant personal or family history of cancer or who have been advised that they are appropriate candidates for BART testing by their doctors or genetic counselors, but whose BART testing was not included in the price of Myriad's standard Comprehensive BRACAnalaysis test. They have not been able to access the BART testing for large rearrangements. The BRCA gene patents gave Myriad the power to package this testing separately.

96.   Researchers who want to look at the human BRCA1 and BRCA2 genes for research purposes are prohibited from doing so by the patents without the permission of the patent-holder.

97.   Myriad has permitted some researchers to do pure research on the human BRCA1 and BRCA2 genes. Upon information and belief, Myriad has no official policy permitting the research and has not publicized its occasional permissiveness. At any time, Myriad can use its patents to prohibit researchers from doing research.

98.   Researchers are chilled from engaging in research on the human BRCA 1 and BRCA2 genes by the patents. Researchers are also chilled from engaging in research on other genes. It is increasingly clear that genes interact with other genes in ways that are not yet fully understood. Researchers are chilled from engaging in research on other genes that may interact with the BRCA1 and BRCA2 genes by the patents.

99.   Researchers, such as plaintiffs Dr. Chung and Dr. Ostrer, study women for genetic research. Dr. Chung and some other geneticists believe that if they obtain the results of a particular woman's BRCA1/BRCA2 test, they are morally obligated to provide that woman with the option to find out the results. Genetic test results used in clinical management should be performed by a CLIA certified clinical diagnostic laboratory, and Myriad is the only such laboratory performing testing for BRCA1/BRCA2 because Myriad will not permit other clinical laboratories to perform BRCA1/BRCA2 testing except to a very limited extent.

100.   The problems caused by patenting of DNA sequences are not limited to human genes inherited from one's parents. Every human body contains pathogens such as viruses and bacteria that also have DNA and genes. Modern medicine increasingly relies on analysis of the DNA of such entities to develop treatments for disease. If genes are patented, including human genes as well as their pathogens and commensals, there can be a serious and negative effect on diagnosis and treatment of disease.

101.   The effect of the patents has been to stifle clinical practice and research on the genetic pre-dispositions to breast and/or ovarian cancer. The public, and, in particular, women, have suffered unnecessarily as a result.

CAUSES OF ACTION

102. Because human genes are products of nature, laws of nature and/or natural phenomena, and abstract ideas or basic human knowledge or thought, the challenged claims are invalid under Article 1, section 8, clause 8 of the United States Constitution and 35 U.S.C. § 101.

103. All of the challenged claims represent patents on abstract ideas or basic human knowledge and/or thought and as such are unconstitutional under the First and Fourteenth Amendments to the United States Constitution.

PRAYER FOR RELIEF

For all of these reasons, plaintiffs respectfully ask the Court to:

1. Declare invalid and/or unenforceable

    a. Claim 1, 2, and 5, 6, 7 and 20 of patent 5,747,282

    b. Claims 1, 6, and 7 of patent 5,837,492

    c. Claim 1 of patent 5,693,473

    d. Claim 1 of patent 5,709,999

    e. Claim 1 of patent 5,710,001

    f. Claim 1 of patent 5,753,441

    g. Claims 1 and 2 of patent 6,033,857;

2. Enjoin defendants from taking any actions to enforce these claims of these patents;

3. Grant plaintiffs attorneys' fees and costs; and

4. For such other and further relief as the Court deems just and necessary.

Respectfully submitted,

Christopher A. Hansen
Aden Fine
American Civil Liberties Union

Lenora M. Lapidus
Sandra S. Park
Women's Rights Project
American Civil Liberties Union

Daniel B. Ravicher
Public Patent Foundation (PUBPAT)
Benjamin N. Cardozo School of Law

May 12, 2009

ASSOCIATION FOR MOLECULAR PATHOLOGY v. UNITED STATES PATENT AND TRADEMARK OFFICE

United States District Court, Southern District of New York, 2010.
702 F.Supp.2d 181, 2010 WL 1233416.

Plaintiffs Association for Molecular Pathology, et al. (collectively "Plaintiffs") have moved for summary judgment pursuant to Rule 56, Fed.R.Civ.P., to declare invalid fifteen claims (the "claims-in-suit") contained in seven patents (the "patents-in-suit") relating to the human BRCA1 and BRCA2 genes (Breast Cancer Susceptibility Genes 1 and 2) (collectively, "BRCA1/2") under each of (1) the Patent Act, 35 U.S.C. § 101 (1952), (2) Article I, Section 8, Clause 8 of the United States Constitution, and (3) the First and Fourteenth Amendments of the Constitution because the patent claims cover products of nature, laws of nature and/or natural phenomena, and abstract ideas or basic human knowledge or thought. The defendant United States Patent and Trademark Office ("USPTO") issued the patents-in-suit which are held by defendants Myriad Genetics and the University of Utah Research Foundation ("UURF") (collectively "Myriad" or the "Myriad Defendants"). Myriad has cross-moved under Rule 56, Fed.R.Civ.P., for summary judgment dismissing Plaintiffs' complaint, and the USPTO has cross-moved under Rule 12(c), Fed.R.Civ.P., for judgment on the pleadings. Based upon the findings and conclusions set forth below, the motion of Plaintiffs to declare the claims-in-suit invalid is granted, the cross-motion of Myriad is denied, and the motion of the USPTO is granted.

* * *

V.   CONCLUSIONS OF LAW

* * *

C.   The Composition Claims Are Invalid Under 35 U.S.C. § 101

[T]he issue presented by the instant motions with respect to the composition claims is whether or not claims directed to isolated DNA containing naturally-occurring sequences fall within the products of nature exception to § 101 [of the Patent Act defining patentable subject matter]. Based upon the reasons set forth below, it is concluded that the composition claims-in-suit are excepted.

* * *

2.   Patentable subject matter must be "markedly different" from a product of nature

Supreme Court precedent has established that products of nature do not constitute patentable subject matter absent a change that results in the creation of a fundamentally new product. In *American Fruit Growers* [*v. Brogdex Co.,* 283 U.S. 1 (1931)], the Supreme Court rejected patent claims covering fruit whose skin had been treated with mold-resistant borax. Acknowledging that the "complete article is not found in nature," and "treatment, labor and manipulation" went into producing the fruit, the Court nonetheless held that the fruit did not become an "article of manufacture" unless it "possesses a new or distinctive form, quality, or property" compared to the naturally-occurring article. The Court went on to observe:

> Manufacture implies a change, but every change is not manufacture, and yet every change in an article is the result of treatment, labor, and manipulation. But something more is necessary.... There must be transformation; a new and different article must emerge having a distinctive name, character, or use.

Id. at 12–13 (quoting *Anheuser–Busch Brewing Ass'n v. United States*, 207 U.S. 556, 562, 28 S.Ct. 204, 52 L.Ed. 336 (1908)) (internal citation and quotation marks omitted).

Similarly, in *Funk Brothers* [*v. Kalo Inoculant Co.*, 333 U.S. 127 (1948)], the Supreme Court considered whether a mixture of several naturally-occurring species of bacteria was patentable. 333 U.S. at 128–31. Each species of bacteria in the mixture could extract nitrogen from the air for plant usage. While the patent holder had created a mixture by selecting and testing for strains of bacteria that did not mutually inhibit one another, the Court concluded that the patent holder "did not create a state of inhibition or of non-inhibition in the bacteria. Their qualities are the work of nature. Those qualities are of course not patentable." *Id.* at 130.

Most recently, the Supreme Court addressed the application of § 101 to product claims in *Diamond v. Chakrabarty*, 447 U.S. 303, 100 S.Ct. 2204, 65 L.Ed.2d 144. In *Chakrabarty,* the Court considered whether a "live, human-made micro-organism is patentable subject matter under 35 U.S.C. § 101." *Id.* at 305. The microorganism in question was a bacterium that had been genetically engineered to break down multiple components of crude oil and possessed considerable utility in the treatment of oil spills. *Id.* In concluding that the man-made bacterial strain was patentable, the Court observed that the claim "is not to a hitherto unknown natural phenomenon, but to a nonnaturally occurring manufacture or composition of matter—a product of human ingenuity 'having a distinctive name, character [and] use.' " *Id.* at 309–10 (quoting *Hartranft v. Wiegmann*, 121 U.S. 609, 615, 7 S.Ct. 1240, 30 L.Ed. 1012 (1887)). The Court went on to contrast the Chakrabarty bacterium with the bacterial mixture at issue in *Funk Brothers*, stating that in Chakrabarty's case, "the patentee has produced a new bacterium with markedly different characteristics from any found in nature and one having the potential for significant utility. His discovery is not nature's handiwork, but his own...." *Id.* at 310. This requirement that an invention possess "markedly different characteristics" for purposes of § 101 reflects the oft-repeated requirement that an invention have "a new or distinctive form, quality, or property" from a product of nature. *Am. Fruit Growers*, 283 U.S. at 11; *In re Merz*, 25 C.C.P.A. 1314, 97 F.2d 599, 601 (C.C.P.A.1938) ("[M]ere purification of known materials does not result in a patentable product," unless "the product obtained in such a case had properties and characteristics which were different in kind from those of the known product rather than in degree.").

Courts have also specifically held that "purification" of a natural compound, without more, is insufficient to render a product of nature patentable. In *The American Wood–Paper Co. v. The Fibre Disintegrating Co.*, 90 U.S. (23 Wall.) 566, 23 L.Ed. 31 (1874), the Supreme Court held that refined cellulose, consisting of purified pulp derived from wood and vegetable, was un-patentable because it was "an extract obtained by the decomposition or disintegration of material substance." *Id.* at 593. As the Court observed:

> There are many things well known and valuable in medicine or in the arts which may be extracted from divers[e] substances. But the extract is the same, no matter from what it has been taken. A process to obtain it from a subject from which it has never been taken may be the creature of invention, but the thing itself when obtained cannot be called a new manufacture.

Id. at 593–94. Similarly, in *Cochrane v. Badische Anilin & Soda Fabrik*, 111 U.S. 293, 4 S.Ct. 455, 28 L.Ed. 433 (1884), the Court rejected a patent on an artificial version of a natural red dye called alizarine that was produced by manipulating another compound through acid, heat, water or distillation. *See generally, id.* Although the artificial version of the dye was of a brighter hue than the naturally occurring dye, the Court concluded that "[c]alling it artificial alizarine did not make it a new composition of matter, and patentable as such...." *Id.* at 311 (citing *Am. Wood–Paper*, 90 U.S. (23 Wall.) at 593).

* * *

3. The claimed isolated DNA is not "markedly different" from native DNA.

The question thus presented by Plaintiffs' challenge to the composition claims is whether the isolated DNA claimed by Myriad possesses "markedly different characteristics" from a product of nature. In support of its position, Myriad cites several differences between the isolated DNA claimed in the patents and the native DNA found within human cells. None, however, establish the subject matter patentability of isolated BRCA1/2 DNA.

The central premise of Myriad's argument that the claimed DNA is "markedly different" from DNA found in nature is the assertion that "[i]solated DNA molecules should be treated no differently than other chemical compounds for patent eligibility," and that the alleged "difference in the structural and functional properties of isolated DNA" render the claimed DNA patentable subject matter.

Myriad's focus on the chemical nature of DNA, however, fails to acknowledge the unique characteristics of DNA that differentiate it from other chemical compounds. As Myriad's expert Dr. Joseph Straus observed: "Genes are of double nature: On the one hand, they are chemical substances or molecules. On the other hand, they are physical carriers of information, i.e., where the actual biological function of this information is coding for proteins. Thus, inherently genes are multifunctional." This informational quality is unique among the chemical compounds found in our bodies, and it would be erroneous to view DNA as "no different[ ]" than other chemicals previously the subject of patents.

Myriad's argument that all chemical compounds, such as the adrenaline at issue in *Parke–Davis*, necessarily conveys some information ignores the biological realities of DNA in comparison to other chemical compounds in the body. The information encoded in DNA is not information about its own molecular structure incidental to its biological function, as is the case with adrenaline or other chemicals found in the body. Rather, the information encoded by DNA reflects its primary biological function: directing the synthesis of other molecules in the body—namely, proteins, "biological molecules of enormous importance" which "catalyze biochemical reactions" and constitute the "major structural materials of the animal body." DNA, and in particular the ordering of its nucleotides, therefore serves as the physical embodiment of laws of nature—those that define the construction of the human body. Any "information" that may be embodied by adrenaline and similar molecules serves no comparable function, and none of the declarations submitted by Myriad support such a conclusion. Consequently, the use of simple analogies comparing DNA with chemical compounds previously the subject of patents cannot replace consideration of the distinctive characteristics of DNA.

In light of DNA's unique qualities as a physical embodiment of information, none of the structural and functional differences cited by Myriad between native BRCA1/2 DNA and the isolated BRCA1/2 DNA claimed in the patents-in-suit render the claimed DNA "markedly different." This conclusion is driven by the overriding importance of DNA's nucleotide sequence to both its natural biological function as well as the utility associated with DNA in its isolated form. The preservation of this defining characteristic of DNA in its native and isolated forms mandates the conclusion that the challenged composition claims are directed to unpatentable products of nature.

Myriad argues that the § 101 inquiry into the subject matter patentability of isolated DNA should focus exclusively on the differences alleged to exist between native and isolated DNA, rather than considering the similarities that exist between the two forms of DNA. See, e.g., Myriad Reply at 8–9 ("[T]he observation that isolated DNA and native DNA share this single property [i.e. the same protein coding sequences] is irrelevant to the critical issue of whether there are *differences* in their properties. It is the *differences* that are legally relevant to the novelty inquiry under Section 101, not the properties held in common." (emphasis in original));

Myriad Br. at 8. Setting aside the fact that considerations such as novelty are irrelevant for § 101 purposes, Myriad offers no authorities supporting such an approach. To the contrary, the Supreme Court has held that "[i]n determining the eligibility of [a] claimed process for patent protection under § 101, [the] claims must be considered as a whole." Similarly, the Federal Circuit has expressly held that "[i]n the final analysis under § 101, the claimed invention, as a whole, must be evaluated for what it is."

Were Myriad's approach the law, it is difficult to discern how any invention could fail the test. For example, the bacterial mixture in *Funk Brothers* was unquestionably different from any preexisting bacterial mixture; yet the Supreme Court recognized that a patent directed to the mixture, considered as a whole, did no more than patent "the handiwork of nature." 333 U.S. at 131. There will almost inevitably be some identifiable differences between a claimed invention and a product of nature; the appropriate § 101 inquiry is whether, considering the claimed invention as a whole, it is sufficiently distinct in its fundamental characteristics from natural phenomena to possess the required "distinctive name, character, [and] use." *Chakrabarty*, 447 U.S. at 309–10.

None of Myriad's arguments establish the distinctive nature of the claimed DNA. Myriad's argument that association of chromosomal proteins with native DNA establishes the existence of "structural differences" between native and isolated DNA relies on an incorrect comparison between isolated DNA and chromatin, which are indeed different insofar as chromatin includes chromosomal proteins normally associated with DNA. The proper comparison is between the claimed isolated DNA and the corresponding native DNA, and the presence or absence of chromosomal proteins merely constitutes a difference in purity that cannot serve to establish subject matter patentability.

* * *

Myriad's argument that the functional differences between native and isolated DNA demonstrates that they are "markedly different" relies on the fact that isolated DNA may be used in applications for which native DNA is unsuitable, namely, in "molecular diagnostic tests (e.g., as probes, primers, templates for sequencing reactions), in biotechnological processes (e.g. production of pure BRCA1 and BRCA2 protein), and even in medical treatments (e.g. gene therapy)."

Isolated DNA's utility as a primer or a molecular probe (for example, for Southern blots) arises from its ability to "target and interact with other DNA molecules," that is, the ability of a given DNA molecule to bind exclusively to a specific DNA target sequence. Thus, for example, a 24 nucleotide segment of isolated BRCA1 DNA can be used as a primer because it will bind only to its corresponding location in the BRCA1 gene. However, the basis for this utility is the fact that the isolated DNA possesses the identical nucleotide sequence as the target DNA sequence, thus allowing target specific hybridization between the DNA primer and the portion of the target DNA molecule possessing the corresponding sequence. In contrast, another 24 nucleotide segment of DNA possessing the same nucleotide composition but a different nucleotide sequence would not have the same utility because it would be unable to hybridize to the proper location in the BRCA1 gene. Indeed, Myriad implicitly acknowledges this fact when it states that the usefulness of isolated DNA molecules "is based on their ability to target and interact with other DNA molecules, which is a function of their own individual structure and chemistry." Therefore, the cited utility of the isolated DNA as a primer or probe is primarily a function of the nucleotide sequence identity between native and isolated BRCA1/2 DNA.

Similarly, the utility of isolated DNA as a sequencing target relies on the preservation of native DNA's nucleotide sequence. Indeed, one need look no further than Myriad's BRACAnalysis testing, which relies on the sequencing of isolated DNA (i.e. the PCR amplified exons of BRCA1/2), to determine the sequence of the corresponding DNA coding sequences found in the cell. The entire premise behind Myriad's genetic testing is that the claimed isolated DNA retains, in all relevant respects, the identical nucleotide sequence found in native DNA. The use of isolated BRCA1/2 DNA in the production of BRCA1/2 proteins or in gene therapy also relies on the identity between the native DNA sequences and the sequences contained in the isolated DNA molecule. Were the isolated BRCA1/2 sequences different in any significant way, the entire point of their use—the production of BRCA1/2 proteins—would be undermined.

While the absence of proteins and other nucleotide sequences is currently required for DNA to be useful for the cited purposes, the purification of native DNA does not alter its essential characteristic—its nucleotide sequence—that is defined by nature and central to both its biological function within the cell and its utility as a research tool in the lab. The requirement that the DNA used be "isolated" is ultimately a technological limitation to the use of DNA in this fashion, and a time may come when the use of DNA for molecular and diagnostic purposes may not require such purification. The nucleotide sequence, however, is the defining characteristic of the isolated DNA that will always be required to provide the sequence-specific targeting and protein coding ability that allows isolated DNA to be used for the various applications cited by Myriad. For these reasons, the use of isolated DNA for the various purposes cited by Myriad does not establish the existence of differences "in kind" between native and isolated DNA that would establish the subject matter patentability of what is otherwise a product of nature.

Finally, the isolated BRCA1/2 DNA claimed in Myriad's patents bears comparison to the bacterial mixture in *Funk Brothers*. In explaining why the claimed mixture of bacteria did not constitute an invention, the Court observed that the first part of the claimed invention was the "[d]iscovery of the fact that certain strains of each species of these bacteria can be mixed without harmful effect to the properties of either" which was "a discovery of their qualities of non-inhibition. It is no more than the discovery of some of the handiwork of nature and hence is not patentable." 33 U.S. at 131. The Court went on to observe that the second part of the claimed invention was "[t]he aggregation of select strains of the several species into one product[,] an application of that newly-discovered natural principle. But however ingenious the discovery of that natural principle may have been, the application of it is hardly more than an advance in the packaging of the inoculants." *Id.*

According to Myriad, the invention claimed in its patents required the identification of the specific segments of chromosomes 17 and 13 that correlated with breast and ovarian cancer (BRCA1 and BRCA2) followed by the isolation of these sequences away from other genomic DNA and cellular components. Like the discovery of the mutual non-inhibition of the bacteria in *Funk Brothers*, discovery of this important correlation was a discovery of the handiwork of nature-the natural effect of certain mutations in a particular segment of the human genome. And like the aggregation of bacteria in *Funk Brothers*, the isolation of the BRCA1 and BRCA2 DNA, while requiring technical skill and considerable labor, was simply the application of techniques well-known to those skilled in the art. The identification of the BRCA1 and BRCA2 gene sequences is unquestionably a valuable scientific achievement for which Myriad deserves recognition, but that is not the same as concluding that it is something for which they are entitled to a patent. See *Funk Bros.*, 33 U.S. at 132 ("[O]nce nature's secret of the non-inhibitive quality of certain strains of the [nitrogen-fixing bacteria] was discovered, the state of the art made the production of a mixed inoculant a simple step. Even though it may have been the product of skill, it certainly was not the product of invention.").

Because the claimed isolated DNA is not markedly different from native DNA as it exists in nature, it constitutes unpatentable subject matter under 35 U.S.C. § 101.

D.   The Method Claims are Invalid Under 35 U.S.C. § 101

[The court concluded that the methods claimed in this case—processes involving (1) "analyzing" a BRCA1 sequence and noting whether or not the specified naturally-occurring mutations exist, (2) "comparing" two gene sequences to see if any differences exist, and (3) "comparing" the growth rates of cells in the presence or absence of a potential cancer therapeutic—were not patentable subject matter as they did not involve a distinct machine or physical transformation as required by the Federal Circuit court's standard for patentable subject matter as described in *In re Bilski*, 545 F.3d 943, 950 (Fed.Cir.2008) (en banc), *rev. in relevant part*, ___ U.S. ___, 130 S.Ct. 3218 (2010).]

E.   The Constitutional Claims Against the USPTO Are Dismissed

As determined above, the patents issued by the USPTO are directed to a law of nature and were therefore improperly granted. The doctrine of constitutional avoidance, which states that courts should not reach unnecessary constitutional questions, thereby becomes applicable. *See, e.g., Allstate Ins. Co. v. Serio*, 261 F.3d 143, 149–50 (2d Cir.2001) ("It is axiomatic that the federal courts should, where possible, avoid reaching constitutional questions.") (citing *Spector Motor Serv., Inc. v. McLaughlin*, 323 U.S. 101, 65 S.Ct. 152, 89 L.Ed. 101 (1944) ("If there is one doctrine more deeply rooted than any other in the process of constitutional adjudication, it is that we ought not to pass on questions of constitutionality ... unless such adjudication is unavoidable")); *see also Ashwander v. TVA*, 297 U.S. 288, 347, 56 S.Ct. 466, 80 L.Ed. 688 (1936) (Brandeis, J., concurring) ("[I]f a case can be decided on either of two grounds, one involving a constitutional question, the other a question of statutory construction or general law, the Court will decide only the latter."). This doctrine bears on the consideration of Plaintiffs' claims that the USPTO's policy permitting the grant of the Myriad patents violates Article I, Section 8, Clause 8 and the First Amendment of the Constitution.

The Plaintiffs have not addressed these authorities and have contended that "the doctrine of constitutional avoidance is inapplicable" because the invalidation of Myriad's claims pursuant to 35 U.S.C. § 101 "will not necessarily invalidate the USPTO's policy [in granting the patents]." However, a decision by the Federal Circuit or the Supreme Court affirming the holding set forth above would apply to both the issued patents as well as patent applications and would be binding on all patent holders and applicants, as well as the USPTO. See *Koninklijke Philips Electronics N.V. v. Cardiac Science*, 590 F.3d 1326, 1337 (Fed.Cir.2010) ("We remind the district court and the [USPTO] Board that they must follow judicial precedent...."). Thus, to the extent the USPTO examination policies are inconsistent with a final, binding ruling, the USPTO would conform its examination policies to avoid issuing patents directed to isolated DNA or the comparison or analysis of DNA sequences.

With the holding that the patents are invalid, the Plaintiffs have received the relief sought in the Complaint and the doctrine of constitutional avoidance precludes this Court from reaching the constitutional claims against the USPTO. Plaintiffs' claims for constitutional violations against the USPTO are therefore dismissed without prejudice.

VIII. CONCLUSION

For the reasons set forth above, Plaintiffs' motion for summary judgment is granted in part, Myriad's motion for summary judgment is denied, the USPTO's motion for judgment on the pleadings is granted, and the claims-in-suit are declared invalid pursuant to 35 U.S.C. § 101.

Submit judgment on notice.

It is so ordered.

NOTES

1. What types of research would be likely to be promoted by the availability of the patents in dispute in this case? What types of research would be impaired by the enforcement of the patents in dispute here? How

should these potential conflicts between the impacts of patents on basic research and efforts to make further advances be resolved?

2.   What types of patient treatment might be impaired by the enforcement of the patents in dispute in this case? Assuming that these types of treatment are highly important (because they help to prevent serious disease developments or because there are no treatment alternatives or both), does this suggest the need for stronger or weaker patent rights?

3.   Why are discoveries of naturally occurring materials with useful properties treated differently in our patent system than discoveries of non-naturally occurring materials (e.g., pharmaceutical drugs or laboratory-created chemicals) with similar useful properties?

4.   Should the ability of DNA molecules to record useful information mean that they are treated differently in the patent system than other useful materials as reasoned by the district court in this case? How can these information recording and transmitting molecules be distinguished from other means of transmitting information such as electronic communication equipment? Does the reasoning in this case concerning the patenting of information recording and transmitting materials threaten the patentability of advances in the computer and communications fields? If not, what is the distinction that retains the patentability of information recording and transmission advances in the latter fields?

5.   Is the characterization of DNA molecules as information recording and transmitting compositions simply a human-created construct that is applied to conveniently describe the ability of some molecules to hold and then transmit "information" through what is just "stage setting" for another round of chemical reactions? If this is the only sense in which DNA is an information recording device, how is this different than other chemical compounds that are useful because they facilitate or trigger further chemical reactions? Can't these last compounds be said to be holding "information" about what reactions should proceed next, in which case these should be excluded from the patent system under the court's analysis as information recording materials? Would this interpretation write most or all new chemical compounds out of the patent system?

6.   Under the court's reading of the doctrine of constitutional avoidance, when will a court ever reach the sorts of constitutional issues raised in this case? What were the differences between the plaintiffs' statutory arguments under the Patent Act (concerning the lack of patentable subject matter), under Article I, Section 8, Clause 8 of the Constitution (concerning Congress' lack of power to authorize patents such as those challenged in this case), and under the First Amendment (concerning the adverse impact of the challenged patents on free speech)?

B.   RESTRICTIONS ON MEANS FOR LAW COMPLIANCE: TAX METHOD PATENTS

A number of United States patents now apply to sequences of asset and income management steps that are aimed at achieving advantageous tax results for taxpayers.[1] The developers of these methods have claimed that their tax planning steps are significantly new and useful methods for achieving practical results and have accordingly obtained patents covering the methods. If valid, these patents will preclude other parties from using the patented methods without the patent holders' permission.

For intellectual property specialists, tax planning patents are simply the latest business method patents, reflecting the systemization of law practice and legal services and the ability of computer-enhanced financial management strategies to achieve highly valuable tax results under certain circumstances. For tax practitioners, tax planning patents strike at the heart of their professional services, raising the potential that they will be impeded in aiding clients to pursue lawful strategies for tax minimization if the best tax planning strategy for a given client is patented and cannot be used without the permission of the patent holder. In short, tax planning patents promise to reward and expand efforts to develop tax mitigation innovations while impeding the client-specific, individualized service activities of traditional tax practitioners.

The threats posed by tax planning patents are not hypothetical projections of future risks. The United States Patent and Trademark Office (USPTO) has issued a number of patents on tax planning methods,[2] and has even created a subject matter subclassification[3] in its records system in anticipation of the large volume of such patents to come. At least one such patent has been the subject of litigation[4] and the focus of

---

1. *See generally* Richard S. Gruner, *When Worlds Collide: Tax Planning Method Patents Meet Tax Practice, Making Attorneys the Latest Patent Infringers,* 2008 U. Ill. J.L. Tech. & Pol'y 33.

2. *See, e.g.,* U.S. Patent No. 6567790 (issued May 20, 2003).

3. In 2006, the USPTO added subclass 36T to Class 705 in its patent classification system to cover innovations involving tax strategies. Class 705 is a generic class which includes apparatus and corresponding methods for performing data processing operations related to the administration of management of a business or in the processing of financial data. *See* U.S. Patent & Trademark Office, Classification System—Classification Definitions, http://www. uspto.gov/web/ offices/ac/ido/ oeip/taf/def/ 705.htm (last visited on 7/17/2006).

As of July 13, 2006, there were 41 issued patents related to tax strategies classified in subcategory 36T of Class 705. In addition, 61 published patent applications, not yet examined, were classified in this subcategory. *See* James A. Toupin, General Counsel, USPTO, Statement Prepared in Connection with Hearing on "Issues Relating to the Patenting of Tax Advice," Subcommittee on Select Revenue Measures, House Committee on Ways and Means (July 13, 2006), http://waysand means.house.gov/hearings.asp?formmode=view & id=5103 (last visited on 7/17/2006).

4. *See Wealth Transfer Group v. Rowe,* No. 06CV00024 (D.Conn. filed Jan. 6, 2006). This litigation has gained considerable attention from tax practitioners. One tax specialist described this case as follows:

On January 6, 2006, the SOGRAT patent holder filed suit in the Connecticut United States Federal District Court for infringement of the SOGRAT patent [U.S. Patent No. 6567790]. The defendant in the lawsuit is Dr. John W. Rowe, the Executive Chairman of Aetna, Inc. The lawsuit is in the discovery stage and is anticipated to go to trial in 2007. Because I understand that the lawsuit is being prosecuted vigorously, the lawsuit cannot be considered a nuisance lawsuit. When this lawsuit was discussed at ACTEC's Estate and Gift Tax Committee on July 8, 2006, the vast majority of lawyers present (more than 100 experienced estate planning lawyers) indicated that they would not recommend to any client the use of a GRAT funded with nonqualified stock options without disclosing the existence of the SOGRAT patent and the pending lawsuit. In addition, these lawyers indicated that they would be reluctant to allow a client to use this technique without the permission of the patent holder.

further enforcement threats against attorneys who, according to the patent holder, have offered or were about to offer to aid clients in using the patented method without appropriate licenses.[5]

Patents regarding tax planning techniques are emerging as significant concerns within the tax planning community. Tax attorneys and other tax planning specialists have raised objections that patents will limit their ability to provide valuable services to their clients and will produce unexpected patent infringement liability for themselves and their clients. At the same time, parties seeking and obtaining these patents assert that they have developed advances in tax planning methods which are significant departures from earlier methods and deserving of the sorts of patent protections and rewards that have traditionally applied to useful advances.

According to Dennis I. Belcher, an experienced tax attorney writing on behalf of the American College of Trust and Estate Counsel, tax planning patents are problematic because:

1. Patents on tax planning methods can prevent taxpayers from exercising their rights to choose how to minimize their taxes within the limits of the law and avoiding the activity in question—the payment of taxes—is not an option;

2. Royalties charged for implementing a patented tax planning technique can unfairly increase a taxpayer's costs of tax law compliance; and

3. Because a patent on a tax planning technique can add credibility to the technique, patents on objectionable or aggressive tax planning techniques can hurt compliance with the federal tax laws.[6]

Additional concerns with tax planning patents stem from the types of benefits to taxpayers these patents promote. Assuming that patented techniques for tax liability reduction do help taxpayers to reduce the amounts of tax payments they are obligated to make, it is not clear that this type of benefit is within the range of utility that the patent system

Dennis I. Belcher, Statement Prepared in Connection with Hearing on "Issues Relating to the Patenting of Tax Advice," Subcommittee on Select Revenue Measures, House Committee on Ways and Means (July 13, 2006), http://waysandmeans.house.gov/hearings.asp?formmode=view & id=5103 (last visited on 7/20/2006).

5. This enforcement technique was described by one observer as involving the following steps and consequences:

One prominent practitioner recently told me that a holder of a tax strategy patent obtained the list of all the attendees at a meeting held to consider the area of tax law involved in the patent. The patent holder sent all of the attendees a letter saying that their business activities might be infringing his patent. Some of those who received the letter in fact paid royalties, as the least costly course of action; others went though the burden and expense of asking their lawyers to review the patent to ensure that they were not guilty of any infringement.

Ellen P. Aprill, Statement Prepared in Connection with Hearing on "Issues Relating to the Patenting of Tax Advice," Subcommittee on Select Revenue Measures, House Committee on Ways and Means (July 13, 2006), http://waysandmeans.house.gov/hearings.asp?formmode=view & id=5106 (last visited on 7/26/2006).

6. Statement of Dennis I. Belcher, Statement Prepared in Connection with Hearing on "Issues Relating to the Patenting of Tax Advice," Subcommittee on Select Revenue Measures, House Committee on Ways and Means (July 13, 2006), http://waysand means.house.gov/hearings.asp?formmode=view & id=5103 (last visited on 7/20/2006).

was intended to promote. At least two separate objections might be raised to this type of utility and the use of the patent system to promote it. First, the benefits achieved by carrying out many tax planning methods are mere "wealth transfers"—that is, monies which would otherwise end up in the hands of the government instead remain in the hands of taxpayers, with no net gains in efficiency, reductions in transaction costs, or other incremental benefits to society. Second, even if a net retention of greater amounts of money by a particular party without any overall expansion of societal wealth will qualify in some circumstances as a form of utility that is a proper target of a patentable invention, in the particular case of tax planning patents, the parties adversely affected by carrying out the patented methods include the government and, at least arguably, all citizens who share in the loss of the government services and benefits the lost tax revenues might otherwise have funded. Whether or not the patent system was intended to promote private activities that are against the interests of the government has not been confronted in prior patent controversies. The notion of one government agency (the USPTO) promoting tax payment reductions through the issuance of tax planning patents while another government agency (the IRS) seeks to increase tax payments through aggressive tax law enforcement represents a strange and, in all probability, unprecedented tug of war within the federal government in response to the strange new world of tax planning patents.

For its part, the USPTO has implicitly agreed that advances in tax planning methods can qualify for patents by issuing a substantial number of patents in this domain.[7] Responding to concerns that patented tax planning methods might implement abusive tax shelters or other misleading tax planning methods which are illegal of themselves or which promote illegal underreporting of tax liabilities, the USPTO has noted that the mere possibility that a patented method might be used illegally or might be against public policy is not, of itself, a basis for the USPTO to reject a patent on a particular tax planning method.[8] Rather, the USPTO contends that the responsibility to police the use of particular tax planning methods lies with the Internal Revenue Service and Congress and that the USPTO has neither the statutory charter nor the expertise to preclude patents for potentially abusive tax planning methods.

Notes

1.   One problem potentially raised by tax planning patents is that a given patent may allow a patent holder to control or "capture" means of compliance

---

7. *See* James A. Toupin, General Counsel, USPTO, Statement Prepared in Connection with Hearing on "Issues Relating to the Patenting of Tax Advice," Subcommittee on Select Revenue Measures, House Committee on Ways and Means (July 13, 2006), http://waysandmeans.house.gov/hearings.asp?formmode=view & id=5103 (last visited on 7/17/2006).

8. *See id.* The USPTO cites the Federal Circuit's decision in *Juicy Whip, Inc. v. Orange Bang, Inc.*, 185 F.3d 1364, 1366 (Fed. Cir. 1999) (discussed in the next subsection), as support for the view that potential illegal use of an innovation or public policy concerns regarding an innovation are not reasons to reject a patent on the innovation, even if these concerns may justify regulation or prohibition of the making or use of the innovation.

with particular tax law requirements. These concerns potentially apply to non-aggressive, clearly lawful tax planning methods that are restricted by patents. The concern here is that: "patent-holders could effectively claim ownership of certain routine planning tools, or even of a method which constitutes the most efficient (or, in the extreme, the only) manner of complying with the requirements of the Internal Revenue Code and administrative guidance thereunder." Joint Comm. on Taxation, Background and Issues Relating to the Patenting of Tax Advice 25 (2006), available at http://www.house.gov/jct/x–31–06.pdf.

If a patented method is the only means to comply with a particular legal requirement—or if the other alternatives are so inferior as to make their adoption economically unreasonable—there is a strong case for restricting absolute control by the patentee over the patented method. However, this concern is similar to those in areas other than tax law compliance where rights arising under patent laws intersect with requirements of statutory or regulatory regimes. *Id.* For example, imagine a governmental health and safety standard that can only be met by using a patented device or method. To reconcile patent rights and regulatory requirements in these sorts of circumstances, Professor Janice M. Mueller has suggested that "[w]hen government mandates a technology standard . . . any entity holding patent rights in the subject matter of the standard should be required to license all users at reasonable commercial terms," and failing that, "the government should consider the exercise of eminent domain over the patent." Janice M. Mueller, *Patent Misuse Through the Capture of Industry Standards*, 17 Berkeley Tech. L.J. 623, 684 (2002). Should this rule be limited to settings where government mandates a particular technology standard or should it extend to any patented invention that is materially useful in complying with a legal requirement? Should any patent rights be recognized regarding technologies or practices that aid in law compliance?

2. How do the wealth transfer benefits achieved through a successful tax reduction strategy differ from the benefits achieved by an improved billboard design that causes customers to buy more goods and thereby increases the revenues received by a retailer? If the latter can be patented as an improved business device, should the former be also be deemed to have sufficient utility to qualify for patenting?

3. What are the professional implications of threatening tax attorneys with patent infringement liability for aiding clients in implementing patented tax reduction strategies? Are tax attorneys likely to be able to accurately evaluate the risks of such infringement liability? Will such attorneys tend to overreact and shy away from advising clients about tax methods that are at least arguably covered by patent rights?

4. Does it make sense to hold clients (who can be found liable for patent infringement based on their unlicensed use of a patented tax reduction strategy even if they have no knowledge of the patent involved) more strictly accountable for the use of a patented tax planning method than the attorneys who advise them (who can only be held liable as inducers of patent infringement if the attorneys are aware of the relevant patent)?

5. When should a lawyer's actions in advising a client to implement a patented tax planning method without obtaining a license from the patent holder (or in failing to advise a client to use a patented tax planning method) be deemed to be professional malpractice? Is a tax attorney who is not authorized to implement a patented tax planning method obligated to recommend a client who would benefit from the method to another tax practitioner who is licensed by the patent holder and can aid with the implementation of the method?

C. PROMOTING MORALLY SUSPECT ACTIVITIES

Patent incentives promote the development of useful inventions of various types. Some of the devices and processes that patents promote have diverse moral and societal implications when used in different ways. For example, a gun with a better design encouraged by patent laws may be put to good or bad uses in different hands. Similarly, an improved cigarette design which produces a more pleasurable smoking experience may be seen as an improved entertainment device or a carcinogenic source of increased injury. The impacts of patent laws in encouraging the development of morally suspect inventions are considered in the next case, which involves a device that was designed, in part, to mislead consumers of drinks dispensed in restaurants about the source and character of the drinks. The invention at issue is illustrated in the following diagram showing the above-the-counter reservoir (device element 66) which was the apparent source of drinks as seen by customers and the below-the-counter equipment which was the actual source of drinks served to customers:

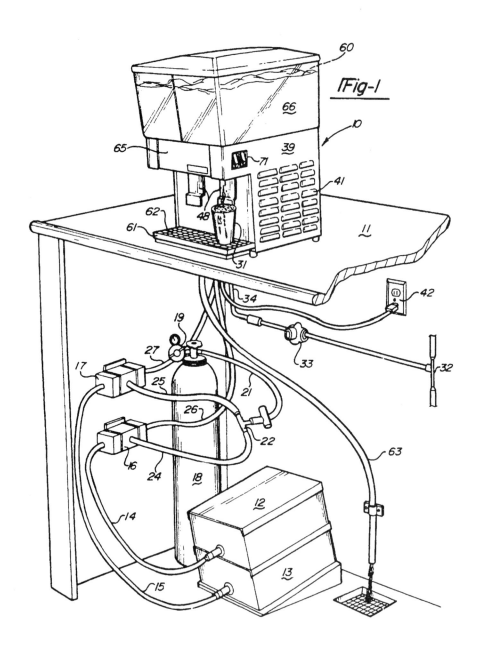

Fig-1

JUICY WHIP, INC. v. ORANGE BANG, INC.

United States Court of Appeals, Federal Circuit, 1999.
185 F.3d 1364.

The district court in this case held a patent invalid for lack of utility on the ground that the patented invention was designed to deceive customers by imitating another product and thereby increasing sales of a particular good. We reverse and remand.

I

Juicy Whip, Inc., is the assignee of United States Patent No. 5,575,-405, which is entitled "Post–Mix Beverage Dispenser With an Associated Simulated Display of Beverage." A "post-mix" beverage dispenser stores beverage syrup concentrate and water in separate locations until the beverage is ready to be dispensed. The syrup and water are mixed together immediately before the beverage is dispensed, which is usually after the consumer requests the beverage. In contrast, in a "pre-mix" beverage dispenser, the syrup concentrate and water are pre-mixed and the beverage is stored in a display reservoir bowl until it is ready to be dispensed. The display bowl is said to stimulate impulse buying by providing the consumer with a visual beverage display. A pre-mix display bowl, however, has a limited capacity and is subject to contamination by bacteria. It therefore must be refilled and cleaned frequently.

The invention claimed in the '405 patent is a post-mix beverage dispenser that is designed to look like a pre-mix beverage dispenser. The claims require the post-mix dispenser to have a transparent bowl that is filled with a fluid that simulates the appearance of the dispensed beverage and is resistant to bacterial growth. The claims also require that the dispenser create the visual impression that the bowl is the principal source of the dispensed beverage, although in fact the beverage is mixed immediately before it is dispensed, as in conventional post-mix dispensers.

Claim 1 is representative of the claims at issue. It reads as follows:

In a post-mix beverage dispenser of the type having an outlet for discharging beverage components in predetermined proportions to provide a serving of dispensed beverage, the improvement which comprises:

a transparent bowl having no fluid connection with the outlet and visibly containing a quantity of fluid;

said fluid being resistant to organic growth and simulating the appearance of the dispensed beverage;

said bowl being positioned relative to the outlet to create the visual impression that said bowl is the reservoir and principal source of the dispensed beverage from the outlet; and

said bowl and said quantity of fluid visible within said bowl cooperating to create the visual impression that multiple servings of the dispensed beverage are stored within said bowl.

Juicy Whip sued defendants Orange Bang, Inc., and Unique Beverage Dispensers, Inc., (collectively, "Orange Bang") in the United States District Court for the Central District of California, alleging that they were infringing the claims of the '405 patent. Orange Bang moved for summary judgment of invalidity, and the district court granted Orange Bang's motion on the ground that the invention lacked utility and thus was unpatentable under 35 U.S.C. § 101.

The court concluded that the invention lacked utility because its purpose was to increase sales by deception, i.e., through imitation of another product. The court explained that the purpose of the invention "is to create an illusion, whereby customers believe that the fluid contained in the bowl is the actual beverage that they are receiving, when of course it is not." Although the court acknowledged Juicy Whip's argument that the invention provides an accurate representation of the dispensed beverage for the consumer's benefit while eliminating the need for retailers to clean their display bowls, the court concluded that those claimed reasons for the patent's utility "are not independent of its deceptive purpose, and are thus insufficient to raise a disputed factual issue to present to a jury." The court further held that the invention lacked utility because it "improves the prior art only to the extent that it increases the salability of beverages dispensed from post-mix dispensers"; an invention lacks utility, the court stated, if it confers no benefit to the public other than the opportunity for making a product more salable. Finally, the court ruled that the invention lacked utility because it "is merely an imitation of the pre-mix dispenser," and thus does not constitute a new and useful machine.

II

Section 101 of the Patent Act of 1952, 35 U.S.C. § 101, provides that "[w]hoever invents or discovers any new and useful process, machine, manufacture, or composition of matter, or any new and useful improvement thereof," may obtain a patent on the invention or discovery. The threshold of utility is not high: An invention is "useful" under section 101 if it is capable of providing some identifiable benefit. See *Brenner v. Manson*, 383 U.S. 519, 534, 86 S.Ct. 1033, 16 L.Ed.2d 69 (1966); *Brooktree Corp. v. Advanced Micro Devices, Inc.*, 977 F.2d 1555, 1571 (Fed.Cir.1992) ("To violate § 101 the claimed device must be totally incapable of achieving a useful result"); *Fuller v. Berger*, 120 F. 274, 275 (7th Cir.1903) (test for utility is whether invention "is incapable of serving any beneficial end").

To be sure, since Justice Story's opinion in *Lowell v. Lewis*, 15 F. Cas. 1018 (C.C.D.Mass.1817), it has been stated that inventions that are "injurious to the well-being, good policy, or sound morals of society" are unpatentable. As examples of such inventions, Justice Story listed "a new invention to poison people, or to promote debauchery, or to facilitate private assassination." *Id.* at 1019. Courts have continued to recite Justice Story's formulation, but the principle that inventions are invalid if they are principally designed to serve immoral or illegal purposes has not been applied broadly in recent years. For example, years ago courts invalidated patents on gambling devices on the ground that they were immoral, see *e.g., Brewer v. Lichtenstein,* 278 F. 512 (7th Cir.1922); *Schultze v. Holtz,* 82 F. 448 (N.D.Cal.1897); *National Automatic Device Co. v. Lloyd,* 40 F. 89 (N.D.Ill.1889), but that is no longer the law, see *In re Murphy,* 200 USPQ 801 (PTO Bd.App.1977).

In holding the patent in this case invalid for lack of utility, the district court relied on two Second Circuit cases dating from the early years of this century, *Rickard v. Du Bon,* 103 F. 868 (2d Cir.1900), and *Scott & Williams v. Aristo Hosiery Co.,* 7 F.2d 1003 (2d Cir.1925). In the *Rickard* case, the court held invalid a patent on a process for treating tobacco plants to make their leaves appear spotted. At the time of the invention, according to the court, cigar smokers considered cigars with spotted wrappers to be of superior quality, and the invention was designed to make unspotted tobacco leaves appear to be of the spotted—and thus more desirable—type. The court noted that the invention did not promote the burning quality of the leaf or improve its quality in any way; "the only effect, if not the only object, of such treatment, is to spot the tobacco, and counterfeit the leaf spotted by natural causes." *Id.* at 869.

The *Aristo Hosiery* case concerned a patent claiming a seamless stocking with a structure on the back of the stocking that imitated a seamed stocking. The imitation was commercially useful because at the time of the invention many consumers regarded seams in stockings as an indication of higher quality. The court noted that the imitation seam did not "change or improve the structure or the utility of the article," and that the record in the case justified the conclusion that true seamed stockings were superior to the seamless stockings that were the subject of the patent. See *Aristo Hosiery,* 7 F.2d at 1004. "At best," the court stated, "the seamless stocking has imitation marks for the purposes of deception, and the idea prevails that with such imitation the article is more salable." *Id.* That was not enough, the court concluded, to render the invention patentable.

We decline to follow *Rickard* and *Aristo Hosiery,* as we do not regard them as representing the correct view of the doctrine of utility under the Patent Act of 1952. The fact that one product can be altered to make it look like another is in itself a specific benefit sufficient to satisfy the statutory requirement of utility.

It is not at all unusual for a product to be designed to appear to viewers to be something it is not. For example, cubic zirconium is designed to simulate a diamond, imitation gold leaf is designed to imitate real gold leaf, synthetic fabrics are designed to simulate expensive natural fabrics, and imitation leather is designed to look like real leather. In each case, the invention of the product or process that makes such imitation possible has "utility" within the meaning of the patent statute, and indeed there are numerous patents directed toward making one product imitate another. See, *e.g.,* U.S. Pat. No. 5,762,968 (method for producing imitation grill marks on food without using heat); U.S. Pat. No. 5,899,038 (laminated flooring imitating wood); U.S. Pat. No. 5,571,545 (imitation hamburger). Much of the value of such products resides in the fact that they appear to be something they are not. Thus, in this case the claimed post-mix dispenser meets the statutory requirement of utility by embodying the features of a post-mix dispenser while imitating the visual appearance of a pre-mix dispenser.

The fact that customers may believe they are receiving fluid directly from the display tank does not deprive the invention of utility. Orange Bang has not argued that it is unlawful to display a representation of the beverage in the manner that fluid is displayed in the reservoir of the invention, even though the fluid is not what the customer will actually receive. Moreover, even if the use of a reservoir containing fluid that is not dispensed is considered deceptive, that is not by itself sufficient to render the invention unpatentable. The requirement of "utility" in patent law is not a directive to the Patent and Trademark Office or the courts to serve as arbiters of deceptive trade practices. Other agencies, such as the Federal Trade Commission and the Food and Drug Administration, are assigned the task of protecting consumers from fraud and deception in the sale of food products. *Cf. In re Watson*, 517 F.2d 465, 474–76, 186 USPQ 11, 19 (CCPA 1975) (stating that it is not the province of the Patent Office to determine, under section 101, whether drugs are safe). As the Supreme Court put the point more generally, "Congress never intended that the patent laws should displace the police powers of the States, meaning by that term those powers by which the health, good order, peace and general welfare of the community are promoted." *Webber v. Virginia*, 103 U.S. (13 Otto) 344, 347–48, 26 L.Ed. 565 (1880).

Of course, Congress is free to declare particular types of inventions unpatentable for a variety of reasons, including deceptiveness. *Cf.* 42 U.S.C. § 2181(a) (exempting from patent protection inventions useful solely in connection with special nuclear material or atomic weapons). Until such time as Congress does so, however, we find no basis in section 101 to hold that inventions can be ruled unpatentable for lack of utility simply because they have the capacity to fool some members of the public. The district court therefore erred in holding that the invention of the '405 patent lacks utility because it deceives the public through imitation in a manner that is designed to increase product sales.

REVERSED and REMANDED.

NOTES

1. In its discussion of the *Rickard* and *Aristo Hosiery* cases, the court appears to reject the reasoning of these cases and to endorse the view that aims of the patent laws include encouraging developers to produce devices and processes that are better at misleading the public than prior devices and processes. Is the public served by this notion of patent law goals and patentable subject matter? Is there a difference between cubic zirconium

(which is aimed at simulating the appearance of a diamond) and a fraudulent sales methodology (which might tend to cause consumers to think that they are buying a diamond when they are not)? What types of misleading products are beneficial to consumers and within the legitimate scope of patentable subject matter?

2.   What are the limits to the scope of the court's rational in *Juicy Whip*? If an invention has nothing but illegal uses, does it lack sufficient utility for patenting? What about inventions that are illegal in some states but not others? A wide variety of patents have been issued for devices or practices that are illegal in certain states or contexts. Examples of these include patents covering a method of producing alcoholic liquids, which could have been used illegally during Prohibition, U.S. Patent No. 1,785,447 (filed June, 1926), a radar detector, which could be used to facilitate illegal speeding and is illegal to use of itself in some jurisdictions, U.S. Patent No. 7,023,374 (filed Oct. 6, 2002), a device for use in cock fights despite the fact that such fights are illegal in most jurisdictions, U.S. Patent No. 6,928,960 (filed Sept. 6, 2001), and a gambling device, the use of which would be illegal in most jurisdictions, U.S. Patent No. 6,540,609 (filed April 1, 2003).

III.   DIFFICULTIES IN MAINTAINING UNIFORM INTELLECTUAL PROPERTY LAWS ACROSS DIVERSE TECHNOLOGIES AND EXPRESSIVE CONTEXTS

Creativity in different fields involves disparate mechanisms that may be encouraged in different ways. In light of this, should intellectual property laws which are aimed at encouraging the production and dissemination of intellectual works vary from field to field? If so, does this require different laws for each field or is it sufficient to have one set of intellectual property laws for all fields which incorporate field-specific analyses and results when applied?

These sorts of policy issues are the focus of considerable debate among intellectual property scholars. For example, Dan L. Burk and Mark A. Lemley have detected what they feel is a clear trend of courts towards technology-specific views of patent laws:

> Fundamental shifts in technology and in the economic landscape are rapidly making the current system of intellectual property rights unworkable and ineffective. Designed more than 100 years ago to meet the simpler needs of an industrial era, it is an undifferentiated, one-size-fits-all system. Although treating all advances in knowledge in the same way may have worked when most patents were granted for new mechanical devices, today's brainpower industries pose challenges that are far more complex. Patent law has a general set of legal rules to govern the validity and infringement of patents in a wide variety of technologies. With very few exceptions, the statute does not distinguish between different technologies in setting and applying legal standards. Rather, those standards are designed to adapt flexibly

to new technologies, encompassing "anything under the sun made by man." In theory, then, we have a unified patent system that provides technology-neutral protection to all kinds of technologies.

Of late, however, we have noticed an increasing divergence between the rules themselves and the application of the rules to different industries. The best examples are biotechnology and computer software. In biotechnology cases, the Federal Circuit has bent over backwards to find biotechnological inventions nonobvious, even if the prior art demonstrates a clear plan for producing the invention. On the other hand, the court has imposed stringent enablement and written description requirements on biotechnology patents that do not show up in other disciplines. In computer software cases, the situation is reversed. The Federal Circuit has essentially excused software inventions from compliance with the enablement and best mode requirements, but has done so in a way that raises serious questions about how stringently it will read the nonobviousness requirements. As a practical matter, it appears that while patent law is technology-neutral in theory, it is technology-specific in application.

Dan L. Burk & Mark A. Lemley, *Is Patent Law Technology Specific?*, 17 BERKELEY TECH. L.J. 1155, 1155–56 (2002); see also Dan L. Burk & Mark A. Lemley, *Policy Levers in Patent* Law, 89 VA. L. REV. 1575 (2003).

In response to arguments like these, R. Polk Wagner has advocated a somewhat different vision of the technology specificity of patent laws. In his view Burk and Lemley's work:

> marks an important and insightful contribution to the growing literature on the institutional relationships of the patent law. And yet * * * I suggest an alternative view of Burk and Lemley's findings—specifically, that their exposition makes a rather compelling case against precisely the sort of judicial ventures into technologically-specific innovation policy that they recommend. Instead, their examples of the ongoing struggle to adapt the patent law to technological changes illuminate the undesirability of entangling the patent doctrine in broad, policy-driven technological exceptionalism. As befits an expansive regulatory regime concerned with innovation policy, the patent law is inextricably intertwined with the process and details of technological development. As courts and commentators alike have long recognized, both a challenge and strength of our patent system is the ongoing effort to adapt the legal infrastructure to an ever-changing environment. The patent law—by explicit design—is technologically flexible, with significant adjustment points built into the system. That distinctions in treatment will exist between various technologies is both expected and unremarkable; rather than leveraging these differences for policy effect, the goal should be to embrace the flexibility while retaining the essential strengths of the unified patent system.

[W]hile Burk and Lemley are undoubtedly correct in noting that there is technological-specificity in the patent law—that biotechnological inventions get "treated differently" than, say, software or mechanical inventions—this observation alone is certainly no cause for alarm. Submerged in the Burk and Lemley analysis is an important conceptual distinction between two types of technological-specificity: micro-specificity, which applies the variable legal rules to specific technological circumstances; and macro-specificity, which countenances distinct legal rules across different technologies, and relatively more similar application within related technologies. Determining which of these two forms best describes modern patent jurisprudence is critically important, for this explains whether the Federal Circuit has developed (or seeks to develop) an innovation regime especially for specific industries, or whether any observable distinctions are merely the expected consequence of the patent law's inherent flexibility.

R. Polk Wagner, *Of Patents and Path Dependency: A Comment on Burk and Lemley*, 18 BERKELEY TECH. L.J. 1341, 1342–43 (2003).

Ultimately, the resolution of concerns about the proper technology-specificity of intellectual property laws will depend on three considerations. First, how does innovation occur in various fields and how will intellectual property incentives affect this? Second, how is information about intellectual property advances disseminated to potential users in various fields and how will intellectual property laws aid or hinder these dissemination processes? Third, how will intellectual property laws and associated concepts of business value impact the production of capital, initiation of startup company operations, and ongoing competition among product providers and how should these impacts be adjusted to best serve consumer needs in various fields?

While a full treatment of these sorts of issues is beyond the scope of this text, the following reading identifies the substantially different ways that one intellectual property scheme—patent law—influences intellectual efforts and technology advancement practices in four different fields. These differences define the sorts of field-specific dynamics that variations in patent laws for particular fields may need to accommodate. The fields covered by this study—the pharmaceutical, biotechnology, Internet, and computer industries—involve some of the most important products and services affecting society today. These fields also involve technology development processes in which patent laws presently have many important impacts, both positive and negative. The significant differences in the ways that patent rewards and restrictions are perceived by participants in these diverse fields suggest the potential need for tailoring of patent laws and other intellectual property standards to ensure that useful incentives are established to promote technological advances in particular fields without imposing unnecessary costs on subsequent technology users.

TO PROMOTE INNOVATION: THE PROPER BALANCE OF COMPETITION AND PATENT LAW AND POLICY (EXCERPTS)

Federal Trade Commission October, 2003.

BUSINESS TESTIMONY: CURRENT INNOVATION LANDSCAPE IN SELECTED INDUSTRIES

Summary

Over six days of Hearings, business representatives from four high tech industries discussed the drivers of innovation in their industries. Representatives from the pharmaceutical, biotechnology, Internet, and computer hardware and software industries described their real world experience with how patents and competition affect incentives to innovate. * * * They highlighted both the benefits and costs of current patent and antitrust policies applied in their industries. This [reading] discusses the diverse views presented by the panelists, and also incorporates the results of business surveys and other industry specific scholarship.

The panelists identified various attributes that characterized innovation in the different industries. Panelists discussed whether innovation in their industries tends to be discrete or cumulative, building incrementally on prior discoveries. Panelists also addressed sources and amounts of capital required for entry, barriers to entry, the extent to which industries are vertically integrated, and difficulties in commercializing new products. They raised issues of fixed cost recovery, alternative appropriability mechanisms, and relationships between initial and follow on innovation * * *. According to both panelists and academics, factors such as these shape the role of competition and patents in spurring or discouraging innovation in their industries.

Pharmaceutical and biotechnology representatives testified that strong patent protection is essential to innovation in their industries. Business representatives characterized innovation in these industries as costly and unpredictable, requiring significant amounts of pioneering research to discover and test new drug products. By preventing rival firms from free riding on discoveries, patents allow pharmaceutical firms to recoup the substantial capital investments made to discover, test, and obtain regulatory approval of new drug products. Biotech representatives emphasized that patent protection is critical to attract the capital necessary to fund this high risk investment. Indeed, firms believed that the biotech industry would not exist but for patents. One concern involved patents on the research tools used to assist in the discovery of new drug products. Biotech representatives expressed concern that such patents could obstruct the commercialization of new products, thereby hindering follow on innovation. To date, however, evidence suggests that such problems have not emerged.

Pharmaceutical and biotech representatives testified that they use patent information disclosures required by the patent statutes to direct their research and development (R & D) into areas not claimed by the patents. Representatives from generic pharmaceutical firms discussed how patent disclosures guide their efforts to "design around" patents, so that they can develop non-infringing generic versions of brand name drug products.

By contrast, computer hardware and software industry representatives generally emphasized competition to develop more advanced technologies as a driver of innovation in these rapidly changing industries. These representatives, particularly those from the software industry, described an innovation process that is generally significantly less costly than in the pharmaceutical and biotech industries, and they spoke of a product life cycle that is generally much shorter. Some software representatives observed that copyrights or open source code policies facilitate the incremental and dynamic nature of software innovation. They discounted the value of patent disclosures, because they do not require the disclosure of a software product's underlying source code.

Computer hardware manufacturers noted that they often use trade secrets, rather than patents, to protect their inventions, because it is difficult to discover whether a rival firm has infringed a patented manufacturing invention. Computer hardware manufacturers generally would rather keep the invention secret than publicly disclose it and risk third party misappropriation of patent rights that they will be unable to discover. By contrast, computer hardware firms that specialize solely in hardware design and have no manufacturing responsibilities valued patent protection as a way to raise venture capital.

Representatives from both the computer hardware and software industries observed that firms in their industries are obtaining patents for defensive purposes at rapidly increasing rates. They explained that the increased likelihood of firms holding overlapping intellectual property rights creates a "patent thicket" that they must clear away to commercialize new technology. They discussed how patent thickets divert funds away from R & D, make it difficult to commercialize new products, and raise uncertainty and investment risks. Some computer hardware and software representatives highlighted their growing concern that companies operating in a patent thicket are increasingly vulnerable to threats to enjoin their production from non-practicing entities that hold patents necessary to make the manufacturer's product.

A global concern that representatives from each of the four industries described was that poor patent quality (e.g., a patent for which there is invalidating prior art, or a patent broader than was enabled) can blunt incentives to innovate. They described the costly nature of litigation to invalidate these patents, both in terms of dollars and resources diverted from R & D. They also discussed how a timely, less costly mechanism to review poor quality patents would enhance innovation in their industries.

These representatives also described how each industry has developed licensing practices to extract value from their patents or, in some cases, to obviate some of the problems raised by patent thickets. They raised concerns that uncertainty about the parameters of antitrust enforcement may be hindering the use of certain methods to extract patent value. For example, biotech representatives noted that antitrust concerns have contributed to uncertainty about the propriety of using reach through royalty provisions in research tool licenses.

Firms in the computer hardware and software industries indicated that antitrust concerns may be inhibiting joint discussions of licensing terms during the standard setting process. They noted that antitrust has traditionally been suspicious of joint discussions of licensing terms arising prior to the adoption of a standard. Some panelists suggested, however, that such conduct is necessary for the efficient establishment of new standards because some companies are using patents strategically.

NOTES

1. How might the following factors affect the proper scope of intellectual property laws aimed at optimally encouraging the creation of intellectual works in a particular field:

(a) The tendency of innovation or creative advances to occur through incremental changes rather than through significant "leaps" forward;

(b) The size of capital investments typically needed to support the creation and distribution of new intellectual works;

(c) The rate of change in intellectual works;

(d) The availability of alternatives to intellectual property rights as means to promote the creation of new intellectual works; and

(e) The disruptions that changes in intellectual property protections—that is, changes in either the subject matters protected by intellectual property rights or the strength of those rights—are likely to cause given existing expectations in the field about intellectual property rights?

IV. RECONCILING INTELLECTUAL PROPERTY AND COMPETITION LAWS

Intellectual property laws restricting the use of intellectual works can restrict competition at two levels. First, the rights of intellectual property interest holders may preclude other parties from using protected works as the basis for further intellectual works, thereby restricting competition among creative parties regarding the production of new works. Second, restrictions on how products incorporating new designs and works can be used can impact competition at the user level.

Concern over these types of competitive impacts have produced repeated efforts by legislatures, courts, and other policy makers to reconcile the rights granted by intellectual property laws with the requirements of antitrust statutes and other competition laws. The goal of these efforts has been to grant sufficient exclusivity to intellectual property owners to encourage the creation and distribution of valuable intellectual works while having as few additional impacts on competition as possible.

The following readings describe how intellectual property and competition laws have been reconciled in a number of contexts and the policy issues that govern the intersection of these two types of laws.

A. COMPETITION ISSUES RAISED BY INTELLECTUAL PROPERTY LAWS

COMPETITION AND INTELLECTUAL PROPERTY IN THE U.S.: LICENSING FREEDOM AND THE LIMITS OF ANTITRUST

R. Hewitt Pate Assistant Attorney General Antitrust
Division U.S. Department of Justice.
2005 EU Competition Workshop Florence, Italy June 3, 2005.

I. Introduction

Defining the relationship of intellectual property rights and competition law is an important economic issue in Europe and the United States. This paper attempts to outline some bedrock principles of intellectual property and antitrust policy in the United States, then discuss how they explain, and in some cases require, the current U.S. approach to a series of specific licensing practices. The basic U.S. approach, reflected in the 1995 DOJ/FTC Guidelines for the Licensing of Intellectual Property, calls for flexible application of economic analysis to licensing practices. And the recent trend has been one of increasing convergence in U.S. and European approaches to IP licensing questions, as seen in the new revisions to the Technology Transfer Block Exemption and accompanying guidelines.

The opening question for this workshop asks whether intellectual property is like other property. This question has been discussed to death many times over in recent years, without much improvement on the answer given ten years ago in the 1995 Guidelines. In short, for competition law purposes, intellectual property should be treated in essentially the same way as other forms of property, though this does not mean that it is in all respects the same as other forms of property. "Intellectual property is thus neither particularly free from scrutiny under the antitrust laws, nor particularly suspect under them."

This answer means rejection of the hostility toward intellectual property that held sway in the U.S. during the 1970's. During this era, the Antitrust Division had a section devoted to attacking IP licensing practices that we routinely applaud today. This was the era of the "Nine No Nos," during which we applied per se rules of illegality to many licensing practices. The contention that IP should be treated essentially like other forms of property at that time was meant as a call to curtail hostility toward IP rights, a call for the end of disfavored status for IP.

Today, in contrast, our policy is animated by the recognition that IP licensing is generally procompetitive. But the modern answer to the question of whether IP is like other forms of property also requires rejection of extreme claims of privilege on the part of IP owners. Today, the statement that IP is essentially like other forms of property is often heard in arguments against claims for complete exemption from antitrust scrutiny. The mere presence of an IP right that somehow figures in a course of otherwise anticompetitive conduct does not act as a talisman that wards off all antitrust enforcement. The classic statement on this point is contained in *United States v. Microsoft Corp.*, 253 F.3d 34 (D.C. Cir. 2001) ("Microsoft's primary copyright argument borders upon the frivolous. The company claims an absolute and unfettered right to use its intellectual property as it wishes * * *. That is no more correct than the proposition that use of one's personal property, such as a baseball bat, cannot give rise to tort liability.").

II. First Principles of U.S. Intellectual Property Law and Antitrust

Sound antitrust enforcement condemns anticompetitive conduct. It does not attempt to regulate the amount of competition in a general sense or address vague questions of fairness. It does not attempt to create an affirmative incentive for procompetitive conduct, by promising any specific reward or legal recognition for competitors who play by the rules. It focuses on specific anticompetitive actions, as judged by their effects on markets and consumer welfare. Although this narrow focus is a limitation, at the same time it is a great strength—it makes possible objectivity, predictability, and transparency.

Intellectual property laws, by contrast, provide a complex system of affirmative rewards for an important type of procompetitive behavior— innovation. They take consumer welfare into account, but in different ways than does antitrust. First, they reward innovators with exclusive rights that serve as an incentive to bring new and improved goods and services to market. The hope is that such innovations will lead to increased competition and increased consumer welfare in the long term. Second, they strike a balance between these rights and certain types of public access, such as fair use under copyright law or the disclosure requirement and the limited term of patents. They also include a fail-safe procedure under which a rival or a customer can sue to declare an intellectual property right noninfringed or unenforceable for a number of reasons. So the legislature, via the IP laws, has struck a balance between the rights of IP owners, the rights of consumers, and concerns for a competitive marketplace. This may or may not be the correct balance; nevertheless, it is the one the legislature has chosen.

It is important to understand precisely what reward is offered by the IP laws. Each type of IP right provides "exclusivity" for its owner. What does this exclusivity mean? It does not mean a right to commercialize any invention or creation. The owner of an improvement patent, for example, may find itself blocked from practicing its own patent if it cannot secure permission from the original patentee. Instead, what IP rights provide is the right to exclude others. The right to exclude is not simply one of the rights provided by intellectual property, it is the fundamental right, the foundation upon which the entire IP system is built.

III. Specific Practices and the Freedom to License

These bedrock principles of antitrust and intellectual property law inform the proper approach to specific licensing and IP-related practices. A decade's experience with the Guidelines, together with subsequent judicial precedent, provide reliable guidance on several issues in the U.S. On many, but not all, of these issues, it is also possible to rely on continued transatlantic convergence.

Unilateral Refusals to License Technology

The subject of unilateral refusals to license intellectual property is one in which the premise that IP is essentially like other forms of property has sometimes been stretched beyond sensible limits. Because, outside the area of IP, antitrust law holds out the possibility of rare exceptions to the principle that parties are free unilaterally to refuse to deal with others, the argument is that there must therefore be some circumstance in which the unilateral, unconditional refusal to license a patent must constitute an antitrust violation. With a single much-criticized exception, this is an argument that has never found support in any U.S. legal decision. At this point in the development of U.S. law, it is safe to say that this argument is without merit.

A unilateral, unconditional refusal to license a valid patent cannot, by itself, result in antitrust liability under U.S. law. It is instructive that the very notion of such liability was not even discussed in the 1995 Guidelines. Instead, the Guidelines unequivocally state that, even in the case of IP that conveys market or monopoly power, that power does not "impose on the intellectual property owner an obligation to license the use of that property to others." This is hardly surprising, as the right to choose whether the license has long been recognized by the U.S. Supreme Court as the core of the patent right. Although the Supreme Court decisions are not directly on point, lower courts have correctly held that the unilateral, unconditional refusal to license a valid patent does not give rise to liability as an improper refusal to deal under Section 2 of the Sherman Act. But of course, while an intellectual property owner has the right to decide not to license its technology, the owner does not have the right to impose conditions on licensees that would effectively extend an intellectual property right beyond the limits of the Patent Act.

The clarity of U.S. law on unilateral refusals was enhanced by last year's Supreme Court decision in *Verizon Communications Inc. v. Law Offices of Curtis V. Trinko, LLP.* In *Trinko,* the Supreme Court found that private plaintiffs did not state an antitrust claim when they alleged a failure by a communications provider, Verizon, to provide adequate assistance to its rivals. The Court showed great skepticism about expanding liability for the refusal to deal because such liability "may lessen the incentive for the monopolist, the rival, or both to invest in * * * economically beneficial facilities" and "also requires antitrust courts to act as central planners * * * a role for which they are ill-suited." The Court posed the question as being whether the narrow list of exceptions to the general rule against liability should be expanded. Although *Trinko* was not an intellectual property case—the rights in that case were governed by the Telecommunications Act—the Supreme Court would apply similar logic under the Patent Act. Given the many cases indicating that the right to exclude is a fundamental right embodied in the patent grant, it is safe to say that liability for the unilateral, unconditional refusal to license a valid patent is not going to be added to the narrow list of exceptions the Court mentioned.

When analyzing the effects of a unilateral refusal to deal, one cannot merely consider the effect on a rival that is refused a license; one must also consider the alternative world in which the IP owner would have had less of an incentive to innovate because he could not be assured of the right to refuse to license. Would that IP owner have chosen to innovate less? If so, would competition or consumer welfare have been better off with the present state of affairs, including the right to refuse? In the short term, it will always be more efficient to disregard the IP right and allow duplication. The IP system rests on the idea of long-term innovation incentives, so we must think about the long-term effects of a rule imposing liability in this context. That is entirely consistent with antitrust policy related to exclusionary conduct, which also focuses on dynamic competition and long-term effects. Where we cannot reliably predict the effects of enforcement decisions, false positives are likely, and the increased uncertainty itself will raise costs to businesses and enforcers.

It is useful to remember that the creation of intellectual property tends to add to consumer choices, rather than to reduce them. The development of intellectual property for new technological solutions usually does not cause older solutions to be withdrawn from a marketplace; instead, it increases competition, which tends to erode the prices of the old solutions over time, increasing choice and consumer welfare. Of course, a patent sometimes issues for an obvious or previously-known solution to a problem, but such a patent should be invalidated, and the proper remedy is to seek invalidation under the patent laws.

Does this mean that the policy on unilateral refusals conflicts with EU law as stated in *IMS Health*? At this time, that it is difficult to tell. The European Court of Justice decision, issued a year ago, began by stating that a refusal to license a copyright "cannot in itself" constitute an abuse of a dominant position. That seems to match the U.S. view on unilateral refusals to license. But the court added that liability might occur if: (1) the refusal prevents the emergence of a new product for which consumer demand exists; (2) the refusal is not justified by any objective considerations; and (3) the refusal excludes competition in a "secondary market." It is not clear how these three factors will be interpreted, or whether the same reasoning would apply to other contexts such as a refusal to license a patent. (Some have observed that the IP right asserted in IMS was relatively weak, and that the lack of a unified European system of IP rights may explain differing attitudes toward antitrust liability in this context.) * * *

"Excessive" Royalties in Standard Setting and Beyond

The Antitrust Division sometimes hears complaints about demands for large royalties. Most frequently, although not always, the complaints arise in the context of a technical standard. According to the complainants, one or more patent holders can "hold up" licensees by waiting until participants are locked into the standard, then charging an allegedly "excessive" royalty for patents that cover the standard. * * *

Bringing a complaint to the Antitrust Division about "excessive" royalties, without more, is a losing strategy. Antitrust enforcers are not in the business of price control. We protect a competitive process, not a particular result, and particularly not a specific price. In fact, if a monopoly is lawfully obtained, whether derived from IP rights or otherwise, we do not even object to setting a monopoly price. A high patent royalty rate, after all, might just reflect that the Patent Act is functioning correctly and the market is rewarding an inventor for a pioneering invention. When a complainant begins a presentation by telling the Antitrust Division that a royalty rate is "excessive," the staff responds that the complainant is putting the cart before the horse. A complaining party must first identify some anticompetitive conduct beyond a mere unilateral refusal to license and beyond the mere attempt to charge, where a lawful monopoly exists, a monopoly price.

Many situations of standard setting "hold up" can be mitigated by disclosure in the ex ante phase, before the standard is set. For example, if all participants are required to disclose their financial interest in any version of the standard—including any patents they own or are seeking on the technology—other participants can adjust their behavior accordingly. If a participant agrees to disclose but then fails to do so, it can be liable for breach of contract or fraud. Such liability would hinge on a pattern of breaches, frauds, or other unlawful conduct. If antitrust liability is also contemplated, it would require, in addition, proof of market effects.

Increasingly, standards development organizations are requiring "reasonable and non-discriminatory" (RAND) licensing, which is a partial solution. A difficulty of RAND, however, is that the parties tend to disagree later about what level of royalty rate is "reasonable." It would be useful to clarify the legal status of ex ante negotiations over price. Some standards development organizations have reported to the Department of Justice that they currently avoid any discussion of actual royalty rates, due in part to fear of antitrust liability. It would be a strange result if antitrust policy is being used to prevent price competition. There is a possibility of anticompetitive effects from ex ante license fee negotiations, but it seems only reasonable to balance that concern against the inefficiencies of ex post negotiations and licensing hold up. It is interesting to note that the EU licensing guidelines already address this point: in their Paragraph 225, the guidelines state that firms normally should be allowed to negotiate royalty rates before a standard setting effort, as well as after a standard is set.

Barriers to discussing licensing rates may not be entirely law-related. Some standard setting participants do not want the distraction of considering licensing terms. Engineers and other technical contributors may prefer to leave the lawyers at home and limit discussions to technical issues alone. So there may be powerful incentives to keep the status quo. If that is the case, this may be yet another area where the outcomes can be imperfect but antitrust does not provide a solution.

Compulsory Licensing

Compulsory licensing is another place where enforcers need to be fully aware of antitrust's limitations. Licensing can be an effective remedy in some contexts; for example, for merger cases, it can serve as a less drastic alternative to a divestiture. But in the first instance, there must be conduct that warrants a remedy—licensing is only a remedy, not a liability theory. And there are practical reasons to tread carefully when considering compulsory licensing: designing and enforcing such licenses is complex and can be an invitation to endless ancillary compliance litigation. As explained in the *Trinko* case, an enforcement agency should not impose a duty to deal that it cannot reasonably supervise, since this risks assuming the day-to-day controls characteristic of a regulatory agency. For these and other reasons, compulsory licensing of intellectual property as an antitrust remedy should be a rare beast.

"Excessive Patenting" and Patent Enforceability

There has been much talk in recent years, and perhaps worldwide, about whether there is a problem of "excessive patenting," meaning patents being granted too easily or in too great a number. Of course, it is the job of the U.S. Patent and Trademark Office in the Department of Commerce—not the Department of Justice—to make and regulate awards of patent rights. The PTO has mechanisms for reconsidering specific patents and hearing complaints about the patent system as a whole, and it employs untold hundreds of patent experts. The Federal Trade Commission, an independent agency, has issued a useful report on possible improvements to the patent system. The National Academies have also issued a report.

It is open to question whether antitrust analysis, which is specific and effects-based, can be applied to a question as broad as "excessive patenting." To know whether patenting is excessive, we would first have to make a conclusion about the "but-for" world. If fewer patents were granted, would innovation have decreased? Would firms have reduced their research and development in areas that currently are covered by patents, and would the result have been fewer benefits for consumers?

Antitrust enforcement is not well suited to answering such questions. These questions should be directed, instead, to the patent authorities or to legislators.

Of course, this point must not be overstated. Part of the patent system is court review of patent enforceability. In the appropriate case the Antitrust Division will examine enforceability and, if necessary, challenge the validity or scope of a patent as part of an antitrust claim. This is not necessary where a patent-related practice will be lawful (or at least, does not violate the antitrust laws) or unlawful regardless of the patent's enforceability. But if the conduct would have violated the antitrust laws in the absence of patent rights, it is difficult to address fundamental questions about the but-for world—here, meaning the world that would have existed without the allegedly anticompetitive patent-related practice—unless one knows whether the patent owner could have won an infringement claim. If the patent is valid, all entry before its expiration is a competitive "gift," but if it is invalid, any delay in entry due to threatened patent enforcement is a competitive harm. Just three months ago, an appellate court asserted this need to examine the but-for world in a case involving the antitrust analysis of a patent settlement. According to the court, it is impossible to measure a patent settlement's effect on competition unless one first makes a conclusion about the validity and enforceability of the patent. * * *

IP Rights and Market Power

Last on my list of specific issues is the concept of market power. Intellectual property cannot be presumed to establish market power. While intellectual property grants exclusive rights, these rights are not monopolies in the economic sense: they do not necessarily provide a large share of any commercial market and they do not necessarily lead to the ability to raise prices in a market. A single patent, for example, may have dozens of close substitutes. The mere presence of an intellectual property right does not permit an antitrust enforcer to skip the crucial steps of market definition and determining market effects.

In the view of the Department of Justice and the Federal Trade Commission, the idea that IP rights cannot be presumed to create market power is a settled question. Interestingly, however, there is still some debate in courts that decide private party antitrust claims. In the January 2005 case *Independent Ink*, the Federal Circuit—which handles all direct patent appeals in the United States—held that Supreme Court precedent compelled it to conclude that a patent does raise a presumption of market power in an IP tying case. But even the Federal Circuit disagreed with the presumption; in fact, the Federal Circuit's opinion invited the Supreme Court to reverse. [The Supreme Court accepted this invitation and held the presumption of market power to be improper following the Court's review of this case.]

Many other IP issues arise at the competition law interface. With respect to patent pools, the Antitrust Division has issued several "Business Review Letters" analyzing proposed licensing arrangements. Package licensing, bundling, and tying all receive some coverage in our Guidelines. Our general approach is to avoid rigid tests and instead rely on a review of the likely economic effects to the marketplace as a whole, both in the short term and over the long term, factoring in incentives for procompetitive innovation. Both IP law and competition law seek to maintain dynamic, robustly innovative markets far into the future, and to that end they properly are willing to tolerate—or rather, offer the inducement of—a degree of private reward and market power in the present day.

IV. Conclusion

We have made great strides in the United States in bringing sound economics to the antitrust analysis of intellectual property. Europe is doing the same with the newly revised Technology Transfer Block Exemption and its accompanying licensing guidelines, both of which embrace an effects-based analysis for licensing transactions. We have experienced significant international convergence in this area and we have every reason to expect more of the same. While some differences remain between the U.S., the EU, and our other important trading partners, the general trend toward convergence is continuing.

B. LIMITING ANTICOMPETITIVE CONSEQUENCES OF INTELLECTUAL PROPERTY LICENSING

ANTITRUST GUIDELINES FOR THE LICENSING OF INTELLECTUAL PROPERTY (EXCERPTS)

U.S. Department of Justice & Federal Trade Commission.
April 6, 1995.

1. Intellectual property protection and the antitrust laws

1.0   These Guidelines state the antitrust enforcement policy of the U.S. Department of Justice and the Federal Trade Commission (individually, "the Agency," and collectively, "the Agencies") with respect to the licensing of intellectual property protected by patent, copyright, and trade secret law, and of know-how. By stating their general policy, the Agencies hope to assist those who need to predict whether the Agencies will challenge a practice as anticompetitive. However, these Guidelines cannot remove judgment and discretion in antitrust law enforcement. Moreover, the standards set forth in these Guidelines must be applied in unforeseeable circumstances. Each case will be evaluated in light of its own facts, and these Guidelines will be applied reasonably and flexibly.

* * *

3. Antitrust concerns and modes of analysis

3.1   Nature of the concerns

While intellectual property licensing arrangements are typically welfare-enhancing and procompetitive, antitrust concerns may nonetheless arise. For example, a licensing arrangement could include restraints that adversely affect competition in goods markets by dividing the markets among firms that would have competed using different technologies. *See, e.g.*, Example 7. An arrangement that effectively merges the research and development activities of two of only a few entities that could plausibly engage in research and development in the relevant field might harm competition for development of new goods and services. An acquisition of intellectual property may lessen competition in a relevant antitrust market. The Agencies will focus on the actual effects of an arrangement, not on its formal terms.

The Agencies will not require the owner of intellectual property to create competition in its own technology. However, antitrust concerns may arise when a licensing arrangement harms competition among entities that would have been actual or likely potential competitors in a relevant market in the absence of the license (entities in a "horizontal relationship"). A restraint in a licensing arrangement may harm such competition, for example, if it facilitates market division or price-fixing. In addition, license restrictions with respect to one market may harm such competition in another market by anticompetitively foreclosing access to, or significantly raising the price of, an important input, or by facilitating coordination to increase price or reduce output. When it appears that such competition may be adversely affected, the Agencies will follow the analysis set forth below.

3.2   Markets affected by licensing arrangements

Licensing arrangements raise concerns under the antitrust laws if they are likely to affect adversely the prices, quantities, qualities, or varieties of goods and services either currently or potentially available. The competitive effects of licensing arrangements often can be adequately assessed within the relevant markets for the goods affected by the arrangements. In such instances, the Agencies will delineate and analyze only goods markets. In other cases, however, the analysis may require the delineation of markets for technology or markets for research and development (innovation markets).

3.2.1   Goods markets

A number of different goods markets may be relevant to evaluating the effects of a licensing arrangement. A restraint in a licensing arrangement may have competitive effects in markets for final or intermediate goods made using the intellectual property, or it may have effects upstream, in markets for goods that are used as inputs, along with the intellectual property, to the production of other goods. In general, for goods markets affected by a licensing arrangement, the Agencies will approach the delineation of relevant market and the measurement of market share in the intellectual property area as in section 1 of the U.S. Department of Justice and Federal Trade Commission Horizontal Merger Guidelines.

3.2.2   Technology markets

Technology markets consist of the intellectual property that is licensed (the "licensed technology") and its close substitutes—that is, the technologies or goods that are close enough substitutes significantly to constrain the exercise of market power with respect to the intellectual property that is licensed. When rights to intellectual property are marketed separately from the products in which they are used, the Agencies may rely on technology markets to analyze the competitive effects of a licensing arrangement.

EXAMPLE 2

Situation:

Firms Alpha and Beta independently develop different patented process technologies to manufacture the same off-patent drug for the treatment of a particular disease. Before the firms use their technologies internally or license them to third parties, they announce plans jointly to manufacture the drug, and to assign their manufacturing processes to the new manufacturing venture. Many firms are capable of using and have the incentive to use the licensed technologies to manufacture and distribute the drug; thus, the market for drug manufacturing and distribution is competitive. One of the Agencies is evaluating the likely competitive effects of the planned venture.

Discussion:

The Agency would analyze the competitive effects of the proposed joint venture by first defining the relevant markets in which competition may be affected and then evaluating the likely competitive effects of the joint venture in the identified markets. (*See* Example 4 for a discussion of the Agencies' approach to joint venture analysis.) In this example, the structural effect of the joint venture in the relevant goods market for the manufacture and distribution of the drug is unlikely to be significant, because many firms in addition to the joint venture compete in that market. The joint venture might, however, increase the prices of the drug produced using Alpha's or Beta's technology by reducing competition in the relevant market for technology to manufacture the drug.

The Agency would delineate a technology market in which to evaluate likely competitive effects of the proposed joint venture. The Agency would identify other technologies that can be used to make the drug with levels of effectiveness and cost per dose comparable to that of the technologies owned by Alpha and Beta. In addition, the Agency would consider the extent to which competition from other drugs that are substitutes for the drug produced using Alpha's or Beta's technology would limit the ability of a hypothetical monopolist that owned both Alpha's and Beta's technology to raise its price.

To identify a technology's close substitutes and thus to delineate the relevant technology market, the Agencies will, if the data permit, identify the smallest group of technologies and goods over which a hypothetical monopolist of those technologies and goods likely would exercise market power—for example, by imposing a small but significant and nontransitory price increase. The Agencies recognize that technology often is licensed in ways that are not readily quantifiable in monetary terms. In such circumstances, the Agencies will delineate the relevant market by identifying other technologies and goods which buyers would substitute at a cost comparable to that of using the licensed technology.

In assessing the competitive significance of current and likely potential participants in a technology market, the Agencies will take into account all relevant evidence. When market share data are available and accurately reflect the competitive significance of market participants, the Agencies will include market share data in this assessment. The Agencies also will seek evidence of buyers' and market participants' assessments of the competitive significance of technology market participants. Such evidence is particularly important when market share data are unavailable, or do not accurately represent the competitive significance of market participants. When market share data or other indicia of market power are not available, and it appears that competing technologies are comparably efficient, the Agencies will assign each technology the same market share. For new technologies, the Agencies generally will use the best available information to estimate market acceptance over a two-year period, beginning with commercial introduction.

3.2.3 Research and development: innovation markets

If a licensing arrangement may adversely affect competition to develop new or improved goods or processes, the Agencies will analyze such an impact either as a separate competitive effect in relevant goods or technology markets, or as a competitive effect in a separate innovation market. A licensing arrangement may have competitive effects on innovation that cannot be adequately addressed through the analysis of goods or technology markets. For example, the arrangement may affect the development of goods that do not yet exist. Alternatively, the arrangement may affect the development of new or improved goods or processes in geographic markets where there is no actual or likely potential competition in the relevant goods.

An innovation market consists of the research and development directed to particular new or improved goods or processes, and the close substitutes for that research and development. The close substitutes are research and development efforts, technologies, and goods that significantly constrain the exercise of market power with respect to the relevant research and development, for example by limiting the ability and incentive of a hypothetical monopolist to retard the pace of research and development. The Agencies will delineate an innovation market only when the capabilities to engage in the relevant research and development can be associated with specialized assets or characteristics of specific firms.

In assessing the competitive significance of current and likely potential participants in an innovation market, the Agencies will take into account all relevant evidence. When market share data are available and accurately reflect the competitive significance of market participants, the Agencies will include market share data in this assessment. The Agencies also will seek evidence of buyers' and market participants' assessments of the competitive significance of innovation market participants. Such evidence is particularly important when market share data are unavailable or do not accurately represent the competitive significance of market participants. The Agencies may base the market shares of participants in an innovation market on their shares of identifiable assets or characteristics upon which innovation depends, on shares of research and development expenditures, or on shares of a related product. When entities have comparable capabilities and incentives to pursue research and development that is a close substitute for the research and development activities of the parties to a licensing arrangement, the Agencies may assign equal market shares to such entities.

EXAMPLE 3

Situation:

Two companies that specialize in advanced metallurgy agree to cross-license future patents relating to the development of a new component for aircraft jet turbines. Innovation in the development of the component requires the capability to work with very high tensile strength materials for jet turbines. Aspects of the licensing arrangement raise the possibility that competition in research and development of this and related components will be lessened. One of the Agencies is considering whether to define an innovation market in which to evaluate the competitive effects of the arrangement.

Discussion:

If the firms that have the capability and incentive to work with very high tensile strength materials for jet turbines can be reasonably identified, the Agency will consider defining a relevant innovation market for development of the new component. If the number of firms with the required capability and incentive to engage in research and development of very high tensile strength materials for aircraft jet turbines is small, the Agency may employ the concept of an innovation market to analyze the likely competitive effects of the arrangement in that market, or as an aid in analyzing competitive effects in technology or goods markets. The Agency would perform its analysis as described in parts 3–5.

If the number of firms with the required capability and incentive is large (either because there are a large number of such firms in the jet turbine industry, or because there are many firms in other industries with the required capability and incentive), then the Agency will conclude that the innovation market is competitive. Under these circumstances, it is unlikely that any single firm or plausible aggregation of firms could acquire a large enough share of the assets necessary for innovation to have an adverse impact on competition.

If the Agency cannot reasonably identify the firms with the required capability and incentive, it will not attempt to define an innovation market.

EXAMPLE 4

Situation:

Three of the largest producers of a plastic used in disposable bottles plan to engage in joint research and development to produce a new type of plastic that is rapidly biodegradable. The joint venture will grant to its partners (but to no one else) licenses to all patent rights and use of know-how. One of the Agencies is evaluating the likely competitive effects of the proposed joint venture.

Discussion:

The Agency would analyze the proposed research and development joint venture using an analysis similar to that applied to other joint ventures. The Agency would begin by defining the relevant markets in which to analyze the joint venture's likely competitive effects. In this case, a relevant market is an innovation market—research and development for biodegradable (and other environmentally friendly) containers. The Agency would seek to identify any other entities that would be actual or likely potential competitors with the joint venture in that relevant market. This would include those firms that have the capability and incentive to undertake research and development closely substitutable for the research and development proposed to be undertaken by the joint venture, taking into account such firms' existing technologies and technologies under development, R & D facilities, and other relevant assets and business circumstances. Firms possessing such capabilities and incentives would be included in the research and development market even if they are not competitors in relevant markets for related goods, such as the plastics currently produced by the joint venturers, although competitors in existing goods markets may often also compete in related innovation markets.

Having defined a relevant innovation market, the Agency would assess whether the joint venture is likely to have anticompetitive effects in that market. A starting point in this analysis is the degree of concentration in the relevant market and the market shares of the parties to the joint venture. If, in addition to the parties to the joint venture (taken collectively), there are at least four other independently controlled entities that possess comparable capabilities and incentives to undertake research and development of biodegradable plastics, or other products that would be close substitutes for such new plastics, the joint venture ordinarily would be unlikely to adversely affect competition in the relevant innovation market. If there are fewer than four other independently controlled entities with similar capabilities and incentives, the Agency would consider whether the joint venture would give the parties to the joint venture an incentive and ability collectively to reduce investment in, or otherwise to retard the pace or scope of, research and development efforts. If the joint venture creates a significant risk of anticompetitive effects in the innovation market, the Agency would proceed to consider efficiency justifications for the venture, such as the potential for combining complementary R & D assets in such a way as to make successful innovation more likely, or to bring it about sooner, or to achieve cost reductions in research and development.

The Agency would also assess the likelihood that the joint venture would adversely affect competition in other relevant markets, including markets for products produced by the parties to the joint venture. The risk of such adverse competitive effects would be increased to the extent that, for example, the joint venture facilitates the exchange among the parties of competitively sensitive information relating to goods markets in which the parties currently compete or facilitates the coordination of competitive activities in such markets. The Agency would examine whether the joint venture imposes collateral restraints that might significantly restrict competition among the joint venturers in goods markets, and would examine whether such collateral restraints were reasonably necessary to achieve any efficiencies that are likely to be attained by the venture.

3.3   Horizontal and vertical relationships

As with other property transfers, antitrust analysis of intellectual property licensing arrangements examines whether the relationship among the parties to the arrangement is primarily horizontal or vertical in nature, or whether it has substantial aspects of both. A licensing arrangement has a vertical component when it affects activities that are in a complementary relationship, as is typically the case in a licensing arrangement. For example, the licensor's primary line of business may be in research and development, and the licensees, as manufacturers, may be buying the rights to use technology developed by the licensor. Alternatively, the licensor may be a component manufacturer owning intellectual property rights in a product that the licensee manufactures by combining the component with other inputs, or the licensor may manufacture the product, and the licensees may operate primarily in distribution and marketing.

In addition to this vertical component, the licensor and its licensees may also have a horizontal relationship. For analytical purposes, the Agencies ordinarily will treat a relationship between a licensor and its licensees, or between licensees, as horizontal when they would have been actual or likely potential competitors in a relevant market in the absence of the license.

The existence of a horizontal relationship between a licensor and its licensees does not, in itself, indicate that the arrangement is anticompetitive. Identification of such relationships is merely an aid in determining whether there may be anticompetitive effects arising from a licensing arrangement. Such a relationship need not give rise to an anticompetitive effect, nor does a purely vertical relationship assure that there are no anticompetitive effects.

The following examples illustrate different competitive relationships among a licensor and its licensees.

EXAMPLE 5

Situation:

AgCo, a manufacturer of farm equipment, develops a new, patented emission control technology for its tractor engines and licenses it to FarmCo, another farm equipment manufacturer. AgCo's emission control technology is far superior to the technology currently owned and used by FarmCo, so much so that FarmCo's technology does not significantly constrain the prices that AgCo could charge for its technology. AgCo's emission control patent has a broad scope. It is likely that any improved emissions control technology that FarmCo could develop in the foreseeable future would infringe AgCo's patent.

Discussion:

Because FarmCo's emission control technology does not significantly constrain AgCo's competitive conduct with respect to its emission control technology, AgCo's and FarmCo's emission control technologies are not close substitutes for each other. FarmCo is a consumer of AgCo's technology and is not an actual competitor of AgCo in the relevant market for superior emission control technology of the kind licensed by AgCo. Furthermore, FarmCo is not a likely potential competitor of AgCo in the relevant market because, even if FarmCo could develop an improved emission control technology, it is likely that it would infringe AgCo's patent. This means that the relationship between AgCo and FarmCo with regard to the supply and use of emissions control technology is vertical. Assuming that AgCo and FarmCo are actual or likely potential competitors in sales of farm equipment products, their relationship is horizontal in the relevant markets for farm equipment.

EXAMPLE 6

Situation:

FarmCo develops a new valve technology for its engines and enters into a cross-licensing arrangement with AgCo, whereby AgCo licenses its emission control technology to FarmCo and FarmCo licenses its valve technology to AgCo. AgCo already owns an alternative valve technology that can be used to achieve engine performance similar to that using FarmCo's valve technology and at a comparable cost to consumers. Before adopting FarmCo's technology, AgCo was using its own valve technology in its production of engines and was licensing (and continues to license) that technology for use by others. As in Example 5, FarmCo does not own or control an emission control technology that is a close substitute for the technology licensed from AgCo. Furthermore, as in Example 5, FarmCo is not likely to develop an improved emission control technology that would be a close substitute for AgCo's technology, because of AgCo's blocking patent.

Discussion:

FarmCo is a consumer and not a competitor of AgCo's emission control technology. As in Example 5, their relationship is vertical with regard to this technology. The relationship between AgCo and FarmCo in the relevant market that includes engine valve technology is vertical in part and horizontal in part. It is vertical in part because AgCo and FarmCo stand in a complementary relationship, in which AgCo is a consumer of a technology supplied by FarmCo. However, the relationship between AgCo and FarmCo in the relevant market that includes engine valve technology is also horizontal in part, because FarmCo and AgCo are actual competitors in the licensing of valve technology that can be used to achieve similar engine performance at a comparable cost. Whether the firms license their valve technologies to others is not important for the conclusion that the firms have a horizontal relationship in this relevant market. Even if AgCo's use of its valve technology were solely captive to its own production, the fact that the two valve technologies are substitutable at comparable cost means that the two firms have a horizontal relationship.

As in Example 5, the relationship between AgCo and FarmCo is horizontal in the relevant markets for farm equipment.

3.4   Framework for evaluating licensing restraints

In the vast majority of cases, restraints in intellectual property licensing arrangements are evaluated under the rule of reason. The Agencies' general approach in analyzing a licensing restraint under the rule of reason is to inquire whether the restraint is likely to have anticompetitive effects and, if so, whether the restraint is reasonably necessary to achieve procompetitive benefits that outweigh those anticompetitive effects.

In some cases, however, the courts conclude that a restraint's "nature and necessary effect are so plainly anticompetitive" that it should be treated as unlawful per se, without an elaborate inquiry into the restraint's likely competitive effect. Among the restraints that have been held per se unlawful are naked price-fixing, output restraints, and market division among horizontal competitors, as well as certain group boycotts and resale price maintenance.

To determine whether a particular restraint in a licensing arrangement is given per se or rule of reason treatment, the Agencies will assess whether the restraint in question can be expected to contribute to an efficiency-enhancing integration of economic activity. In general, licensing arrangements promote such integration because they facilitate the combination of the licensor's intellectual property with complementary factors of production owned by the licensee. A restraint in a licensing arrangement may further such integration by, for example, aligning the incentives of the licensor and the licensees to promote the development and marketing of the licensed technology, or by substantially reducing transactions costs. If there is no efficiency-enhancing integration of economic activity and if the type of restraint is one that has been accorded per se treatment, the Agencies will challenge the restraint under the per se rule. Otherwise, the Agencies will apply a rule of reason analysis.

Application of the rule of reason generally requires a comprehensive inquiry into market conditions. However, that inquiry may be truncated in certain circumstances. If the Agencies conclude that a restraint has no likely anticompetitive effects, they will treat it as reasonable, without an elaborate analysis of market power or the justifications for the restraint. Similarly, if a restraint facially appears to be of a kind that would always or almost always tend to reduce output or increase prices, and the restraint is not reasonably related to efficiencies, the Agencies will likely challenge the restraint without an elaborate analysis of particular industry circumstances.

EXAMPLE 7

Situation:

Gamma, which manufactures Product X using its patented process, offers a license for its process technology to every other manufacturer of Product X, each of which competes world-wide with Gamma in the manufacture and sale of X. The process technology does not represent an economic improvement over the available existing technologies. Indeed, although most manufacturers accept licenses from Gamma, none of the licensees actually uses the licensed technology. The licenses provide that each manufacturer has an exclusive right to sell Product X manufactured using the licensed technology in a designated geographic area and that no manufacturer may sell Product X, however manufactured, outside the designated territory.

Discussion:

The manufacturers of Product X are in a horizontal relationship in the goods market for Product X. Any manufacturers of Product X that control technologies that are substitutable at comparable cost for Gamma's process are also horizontal competitors of Gamma in the relevant technology market. The licensees of Gamma's process technology are technically in a vertical relationship, although that is not significant in this example because they do not actually use Gamma's technology.

The licensing arrangement restricts competition in the relevant goods market among manufacturers of Product X by requiring each manufacturer to limit its sales to an exclusive territory. Thus, competition among entities that would be actual competitors in the absence of the licensing arrangement is restricted. Based on the facts set forth above, the licensing arrangement does not involve a useful transfer of technology, and thus it is unlikely that the restraint on sales outside the designated territories contributes to an efficiency-enhancing integration of economic activity. Consequently, the evaluating Agency would be likely to challenge the arrangement under the per se rule as a horizontal territorial market allocation scheme and to view the intellectual property aspects of the arrangement as a sham intended to cloak its true nature.

If the licensing arrangement could be expected to contribute to an efficiency-enhancing integration of economic activity, as might be the case if the licensed technology were an advance over existing processes and used by the licensees, the Agency would analyze the arrangement under the rule of reason applying the analytical framework described in this section.

In this example, the competitive implications do not generally depend on whether the licensed technology is protected by patent, is a trade secret or other know-how, or is a computer program protected by copyright; nor do the competitive implications generally depend on whether the allocation of markets is territorial, as in this example, or functional, based on fields of use.

* * *

NOTES

1. Should intellectual property laws be interpreted as exceptions to generally prevailing policies favoring free competition as enforced through antitrust statutes and other business competition laws? How might the enforcement of intellectual property laws be limited (or at least focused on certain remedies) if such enforcement were required to have minimal impacts on competitive processes?

2. To what extent do economic and market forces create pressures on intellectual property holders to either produce and market works and products incorporating their intellectual property or to license others to do so? Given these forces, are refusals to license likely to have meaningful impacts on competition among potential users of intellectual property? Under what circumstances might a refusal to license others to use intellectual property have significant impacts on potential users of the intellectual property? How will these impacts on users affect competition between them?

3. What are the limitations of forced licensing as a means to reduce the impacts of intellectual property rights enforcement on competition among potential users of intellectual property?

V. INCREASING CRIMINALIZATION OF INTELLECTUAL PROPERTY LAW

The criminalization of intellectual property law is proceeding on at least three fronts. More and more substantive laws are extending criminal penalties to various forms of misappropriation and misuse of intellectual property. Prosecutors are bringing increasing numbers of cases under these laws in recognition of the importance of intellectual property protection to the American economy and the continued production of innovative works. Criminal penalties for intellectual property crimes are increasing in severity as Congress authorizes larger and larger penalties for intellectual property misuse and as the United States Sentencing Commission reacts to new criminal legislation with sentencing guidelines that call for substantial penalties for intellectual property crimes.[1]

The readings in this section describe some of the directions that the criminalization of intellectual property law is taking, particularly at the federal level. Further discussions of state criminal laws regarding trade secret theft are contained in Chapter 2.

A. CRIMINAL LAW ENFORCEMENT POLICIES REGARDING INTELLECTUAL PROPERTY PROTECTION

PROGRESS REPORT OF THE DEPARTMENT OF JUSTICE'S TASK FORCE ON INTELLECTUAL PROPERTY (EXCERPTS)

Department of Justice.
June, 2006.

http://www.usdoj.gov/criminal/cybercrime/2006
IPTF ProgressReport(6–19–06).pdf

Why Is Protecting Intellectual Property Important?

In our 21st century economy, intellectual property is one of the most valuable forms of property that exists. Whether it is the copyright of a blockbuster film, a patent on a breakthrough drug, a trade secret relating to an innovative product, or a trademark on one of the world's most valuable brands, intellectual property is a significant source of the growth of the American economy and a key driver of global economic activity. As America and more countries around the world move from an industrial to an information-based economy, the importance of protecting intellectual property will only continue to increase.

The negative effects of intellectual property theft make clear the need to protect intellectual property. First, to the extent that piracy diminishes

---

1. *See* United States Sentencing Commission, Sentencing Guidelines Manual § 2B5.3 (2005) (sentencing guidelines for criminal offenses related to intellectual property; reproduced in online casebook supplement).

incentives to create new forms of intellectual property, fewer new products will be created, and businesses and consumers will enjoy fewer options in the marketplace. Second, intellectual property theft hits the Nation's most innovative economic sectors the hardest, and it is those sectors that are increasingly responsible for ensuring America's continuing prosperity and competitiveness. Third, theft of intellectual property can threaten public health and safety by introducing dangerous counterfeit products into the marketplace. Finally, the sizeable profits that can be generated at relatively low risk through intellectual property theft can invite additional criminal activity.

The economic impact of intellectual property theft is enormous. According to the Office of the United States Trade Representative ("USTR"), intellectual property theft costs American corporations $250 billion every year. Among those affected are manufacturers, distributors, retailers, employees, artists, consumers, and governments.

These crimes also harm the economy through lost profits, taxes, and wages, and the loss of hundreds of thousands of jobs.

The costs of intellectual property theft are not solely economic. Intellectual property theft also affects the public's health and safety in costly ways. For instance, intellectual property thieves can make enormous profits from selling cheap counterfeit versions of products whose safety and reliability are essential—including pharmaceuticals, automotive parts, and electrical equipment.

In addition to serious consequences for the economy and public health and safety, intellectual property theft is a concern because it can fund other criminal activities. Modern technology has increased the innovativeness of companies and the amount of new intellectual property being created, but it has also made intellectual property theft easier and more anonymous. Computer technology and the Internet generate inexpensive and far-flung opportunities for piracy and distribution. Such ease and profitability attract organized criminal enterprises to these offenses, and some of those enterprises may even have ties to terrorist organizations.

* * *

What Principles Should Apply to Intellectual Property Enforcement?

The Department of Justice has developed a comprehensive, multidimensional strategy to fight intellectual property crime. This strategy addresses the many different, yet essential, aspects of intellectual property enforcement: criminal enforcement; international cooperation; civil and antitrust enforcement; and prevention. While the perspective and focus of each of these areas differ, they nonetheless are all united by underlying values that form the foundation of the Department of Justice's intellectual property efforts. The Task Force continues to adhere to these key principles that drive and shape the Department of Justice's intellectual property enforcement efforts, and provide a basis for recommending further actions. These principles are set forth below:

The laws protecting intellectual property rights must be enforced.

The Nation's economic security depends on the protection of valuable intellectual resources. The Department of Justice has a responsibility to enforce the criminal laws of the Nation that are designed to protect its economic security and the creativity and innovation of entrepreneurs.

The federal Government and intellectual property owners have a collective responsibility to take action against violations of federal intellectual property laws.

The federal Government has the primary responsibility for prosecuting violations of federal criminal laws involving intellectual property. The owners of intellectual property have the primary responsibility of protecting their creative works, marks, and trade secrets, and of pursuing civil enforcement actions.

The Department of Justice should take a leading role in the prosecution of the most serious violations of the laws protecting copyrights, marks, and trade secrets.

The Department of Justice has historically placed—and should continue to place—the highest priority on the prosecution of intellectual property crimes that are complex and large in scale, and that undermine our economic national security or threaten public health and welfare. The Department of Justice should continue to focus on these areas and enforce federal intellectual property laws as vigorously as resources will allow.

The federal Government should punish the misappropriation of innovative technologies rather than innovation itself.

The Department of Justice should enforce federal intellectual property laws in a manner that respects the rights of consumers, technological innovators, and content providers. The Department of Justice should prosecute those who misappropriate innovative technology or use technology to commit crimes, while ensuring that such enforcement efforts do not chill legitimate innovation.

Intellectual property enforcement must include the coordinated and cooperative efforts of foreign governments.

Violations of intellectual property laws are increasingly global in scope and involve offenders in many nations. Enforcement measures must therefore confront and deter foreign as well as domestic criminal enterprises. This requires the informal assistance of foreign governments and their law enforcement agencies, active enforcement of their own intellectual property laws, and formal international cooperation through treaties and international agreements.

B. FEDERAL CRIMINAL LAWS PROTECTING INTELLECTUAL PROPERTY

PROGRESS REPORT OF THE DEPARTMENT OF JUSTICE'S TASK FORCE ON INTELLECTUAL PROPERTY (EXCERPTS)

Department of Justice.
June, 2006.

http://www.usdoj.gov/criminal/cybercrime/2006
IPTFProgressReport(6–19–06).pdf

Trade Secrets

18 U.S.C. § 1831

Economic Espionage to Benefit a Foreign Government

Statutory maximum of 15 years in prison and a $500,000 fine or twice the gain/loss for an individual offender, $10 million fine or twice the gain/loss for a corporate offender. Criminal forfeiture is available. [The provisions of the Economic Espionage Act of 1996 addressing thefts of information to benefit foreign entities are discussed in depth in Chapter 2 of this text.]

18 U.S.C. § 1832

Commercial Theft of Trade Secrets

Statutory maximum penalty of 10 years in prison and a $250,000 fine or twice the gain/loss for an individual first-time offender (10 years for second offense); $5 million fine or twice the gain/loss for a corporate offender. Criminal forfeiture available. [The commercial theft provisions of the Economic Espionage Act of 1996 and their impacts on commercial activities are discussed in depth in Chapter 2 of this text.]

Copyright

17 U.S.C. § 506(a)(1)(A) [(formerly § 506(a)(1))] & 18 U.S.C. § 2319(b)

Copyright Infringement for Profit (Felony)

Statutory maximum penalty of 5 years in prison and a $250,000 fine or twice the gain/loss for an individual first-time offender (10 years for second offense); $500,000 fine or twice the gain/loss for a corporate offender. Civil and criminal forfeiture available.

17 U.S.C. § 506(a)(1)(B) [(formerly § 506(a)(2))] & 18 U.S.C. § 2319(c)

Large–Scale Copyright Infringement Without Profit Motive (Felony)

Statutory maximum penalty of 3 years in prison and $250,000 fine or twice the gain/loss for an individual first-time offender (6 years for second offense); $500,000 fine or twice gain/loss for corporate offender. Civil and criminal forfeiture available.

17 U.S.C. § 506(a)(1)(C) & 18 U.S.C. § 2319(d)

Distribution of Pre–Release Copyrighted Works or Material over Publicly–Accessible Computer Network

If infringement is effected for commercial purpose: Statutory maximum penalty of 5 years in prison and a $250,000 fine or twice the gross gain/loss for an individual first-time offender (10 years for second offense); $500,000 fine or twice the gain/loss for a corporate offender. Civil and criminal forfeiture available.

If infringement is not effected for commercial purpose: Statutory maximum penalty of 3 years in prison and $250,000 fine or twice the gain/loss for an individual first-time offender (6 years for second offense); $500,000 fine or twice the gain/loss for a corporate offender. Civil and criminal forfeiture available.

17 U.S.C. § 1204

Technology to Circumvent Anti–Piracy Protections Digital Millennium Copyright Act ("DMCA")

Statutory maximum penalty of 5 years in prison and a $500,000 fine or twice the gain/loss for an individual and corporate first-time offender. Statutory maximum penalty of 10 years in prison for a second offense and a $1 million dollars fine or twice the gain/loss. No forfeiture available.

18 U.S.C. § 2318

Counterfeit/Illicit Labels and Counterfeit Documentation and Packaging for Copyrighted Works

Statutory maximum penalty of 5 years in prison and a $250,000 fine or twice the gross gain/loss for an individual; $500,000 fine or twice the gain/loss for a corporate offender. Criminal and civil forfeiture available.

18 U.S.C. § 2319A

Bootleg Recordings of Live Musical Performances

Statutory maximum penalty of 5 years in prison and a $250,000 fine or twice the gain/loss for an individual first-time offender (10 years for second offense); $500,000 or twice the gain/loss for a corporate offender. Civil and criminal forfeiture available.

18 U.S.C. § 2319B

Camcording

Statutory maximum penalty of 3 years in prison and $250,000 fine or twice the gain/loss for an individual first-time offender (6 years for second offense); $500,000 fine or twice the gain/loss for a corporate offender. Criminal forfeiture available.

Trademarks, Service Marks, and Certification Marks

18 U.S.C. § 2320

Counterfeit Trademarks, Service Marks, and Certification Marks

Statutory maximum penalty of 10 years in prison and a $2 million fine or twice the gain/loss for an individual first-time offender; $5 million fine or twice the gain/loss for corporate offender. For second-time offenders statutory maximum penalty of 20 years in prison and a $5 million fine or twice the gain/loss for an individual; $15 million fine or twice the gain/loss for corporate offender. Civil and criminal forfeiture available.

C. EXAMPLES OF PROSECUTIONS RELATED TO INTELLECTUAL PROPERTY

PROGRESS REPORT OF THE DEPARTMENT OF JUSTICE'S TASK FORCE ON INTELLECTUAL PROPERTY (EXCERPTS)

Department of Justice.
June, 2006.

http://www.usdoj.gov/criminal/cybercrime/2006
IPTFProgressReport(6–19–06). pdf

Counterfeit Pharmaceuticals

Cholesterol Medication—The Department of Justice obtained convictions against eight people for selling counterfeit Lipitor tablets, a drug widely used to reduce cholesterol, and 13 people are awaiting trial in Kansas City, Missouri, for their alleged participation in a $42 million conspiracy to sell counterfeit, illegally imported, and misbranded Lipitor and other drugs. More than $2.2 million has been forfeited.

Antibiotics—In May 2005, the Department of Justice obtained the conviction of a former president of an Italian drug firm for violating the Federal Food, Drug, and Cosmetic Act by introducing an unapproved copy of the antibiotic Cefaclor. The defendant was sentenced to a year in confinement, fined $16,481,000, and required to forfeit $300,000. The corporate defendant pleaded guilty and paid criminal and civil penalties of more than $33 million.

Viagra and Cialis—In February 2006, the Department of Justice obtained a conviction in Houston against a United States citizen for importing from China counterfeit pharmaceuticals bearing the Viagra and Cialis trademarks. ICE Special Agents conducted an undercover operation in Beijing, China, involving the Internet site bestonlineviagra.com. The Internet site was owned and used by the defendant to distribute bulk quantities of counterfeit Viagra and Cialis manufactured in China. Chinese officials cooperated in the investigation, and 11 additional individuals in China were arrested by Chinese authorities for manufacturing and distributing counterfeit drugs. Chinese officials seized 600,000 counterfeit Viagra labels and packaging, 440,000 counterfeit Viagra and Cialis tablets, and 260 kilograms of raw materials used to manufacture counterfeit pharmaceuticals.

Viagra—In January 2005, the Department of Justice obtained the conviction of a Los Angeles man for manufacturing, importing, and distributing over 700,000 counterfeit Viagra tablets, valued at more than $5.5 million, over a four-year period.

Terrorism and Organized Crime

Terrorist Financing—In March 2006, a federal indictment was unsealed in Detroit charging 19 individuals with operating a racketeering enterprise that supported the terrorist organization Hizballah. The defendants are alleged to have financed their criminal enterprise by trafficking in counterfeit Viagra, by trafficking in counterfeit Zig–Zag papers and contraband cigarettes, and by producing counterfeit cigarette tax stamps.

Organized Crime—Yi Ging Organization—In April 2006, the Department of Justice obtained convictions against two Chinese nationals as part of a crackdown against a violent criminal group in New York known as the Yi Ging Organization. These defendants had been included, along with 39 others, in a September 2005 indictment charging racketeering offenses, including extortion, witness tampering, trafficking in counterfeit DVDs and CDs, money laundering, operating a large-scale illegal gambling business, and drug trafficking. The Yi Ging Organization allegedly generated millions of dollars in profits from their counterfeit DVD and CD business. Gang members traveled to China to obtain illegal copies of American and Chinese DVDs, which they then smuggled into the United States, copied, and sold along with pirated music CDs at stores the gang controlled in Manhattan and other parts of New York City.

Organized Crime—Operation Smoking Dragon—In Los Angeles, the Department of Justice obtained indictments against 30 defendants in August 2005 for allegedly, among other things, trafficking in counterfeit cigarettes and pharmaceuticals as part of Operation Smoking Dragon.

Software, Movie, and Music Piracy

International Enforcement Operations—The Department of Justice led the largest ever international enforcement efforts against organized online piracy in Operation FastLink and Operation Site Down. Each of these undercover operations by the FBI, involved coordinated law enforcement action among 12 countries and targeted elite, criminal organizations, known as "warez release groups," which are the first to provide pirated works on the Internet. Law enforcement agents conducted more than 200 searches and arrested numerous people worldwide, seized hundreds of thousands of pirated works conservatively valued at more than $100 million, and eliminated more than 20 major online distribution centers. To date, the Department of Justice has obtained convictions against 60 people in the United States on criminal copyright infringement charges.

Illegal Manufacturing of DVDs in China—In the first joint criminal intellectual property investigation by the United States and China, known as Operation Spring, the Department of Justice obtained a conviction against the ringleader in a conspiracy to import 2,000 counterfeit DVDs of motion pictures. The defendant was convicted in China, along with three other co-conspirators, for selling more than 133,000 pirated DVDs to customers in more than 20 countries. After returning to the United States, the defendant was convicted again in Mississippi, sentenced to 45 months in prison, and ordered to forfeit more than $800,000.

Optical Disc Piracy—Operation Remaster—On April 3, 2006, the Department of Justice obtained convictions against two California men who pleaded guilty to conspiracy to mass-produce pirated music and software CDs. The two men were among five arrested as part of an undercover investigation targeting large-scale suppliers of pirated music and software. Agents seized nearly half a million pirated CDs and 5,500 high-speed, high-quality stampers used to make bootleg products. The recording industry called Operation Remaster the largest music manufacturing piracy seizure in United States history.

Online Music Piracy—On May 19, 2006, the Department of Justice obtained sentences of up to 15 months for three members of pre-release music piracy groups. Two of the defendants belonged to the Internet piracy group Apocalypse Crew, also known as "APC," and the third to the group Chromance, also known as "CHR." Both groups sought to acquire digital copies of songs and albums before their commercial release in the United States, which they would then prepare for distribution to secure computer servers throughout the world. The stolen songs were then distributed globally and, within hours, filtered down to peer-to-peer and other public file-sharing networks.

Peer-to-Peer Piracy—Operation Gridlock—In January 2005, the Department of Justice obtained the first-ever criminal convictions for piracy through peer-to-peer networks when two operators of Direct Connect distribution centers pleaded guilty in Washington, D.C., to charges of conspiracy to commit criminal copyright infringement. Four defendants were convicted as a result of this FBI undercover investigation, code-named Operation Gridlock.

Counterfeit Software—In December 2005, the Department of Justice obtained convictions against a California man in Alexandria, Virginia, for selling copies of copyrighted software through his website, www.ibackups. net, and through the United States mail. The man sold, at prices substantially below the suggested retail price, more than $25 million in software products that were manufactured by Adobe Systems Inc., Macro-media, Inc., Microsoft Corporation, Sonic Solutions, and Symantec Corporation. He is believed to be the most prolific online commercial distributor of pirated software ever convicted in the United States.

First Federal Camcording Conviction—In June 2005, a jury convicted a former Hollywood, California, resident of eight federal criminal charges, including three counts of copyright infringement, related to his use of a video camcorder to covertly film the motion pictures "The Core," "8 Mile," and "Anger Management" at private screenings for the purpose of making money. The defendant fled from the custody of his attorney on the evening of his last scheduled trial in 2003 and remained a fugitive for 16 months until the United States Marshals Service apprehended him in Florida.

Movie Piracy—Operation Copycat—On April 6, 2006, the Department of Justice obtained charges against five individuals who were "first-providers" of stolen movies on the Internet. Operation Copycat, a San Jose-based FBI undercover investigation, was one of three investigations contributing to Operation Site Down. The Department of Justice has obtained charges against 36 individuals and convicted 28, including the first convictions under the newly enacted Family Entertainment and Copyright Act for camcording movies and distributing pre-release works on the Internet.

Trafficking in Pirated Movies—Operation Western Pirates—On November 23, 2005, two men were convicted by a Puerto Rico jury for copyright infringement and trafficking in pirated motion pictures. The convictions resulted from Operation Western Pirates, an FBI movie piracy investigation in which approximately 50,000 pirated motion pictures in DVD and VHS format were seized from more than 25 locations in western Puerto Rico, including 23 video rental stores and three laboratories where employees manufactured the pirated movies. Agents also seized more than $125,000 in currency and approximately 450 pieces of computer and other electronic equipment.

Satellite Signal Theft

DMCA Prosecution—In June 2005, the Department of Justice obtained the conviction of a New York man who violated the Digital Millennium Copyright Act ("DMCA") and mail fraud statutes by reprogramming Smart Cards to steal satellite programming from DISH Network. DISH Network electronically "scrambles" its satellite transmissions to prevent unauthorized viewing of its programming and, in order to receive services, its customers must purchase or lease satellite equipment that include Smart Cards inserted into the satellite receiver. The defendant sold approximately $308,000 of reprogrammed Smart Cards to others across the United States.

Luxury Goods

Trafficking in Counterfeit Hard Goods—In November 2005, the Department of Justice obtained indictments against four Massachusetts residents for laundering money and trafficking in more than 30,000 counterfeit luxury handbags and wallets, as well as the materials needed to make the counterfeits, worth more than $1.4 million. The defendants were alleged to have used 13 self-storage units in Massachusetts as the home base for one of New England's largest counterfeit goods operations, and they allegedly sold the counterfeit wallets and handbags at flea markets and to smaller gatherings at approximately 230 "purse parties" throughout the state.

Trade Secrets

Ohio Theft of Trade Secrets—The Department of Justice obtained convictions against an executive of an Ohio hydraulic pump manufacturer and a subsidiary of a South African competitor who stole the Ohio company's trade secrets. While still an employee of the Ohio company, the executive secretly assisted the South African subsidiary company by sharing financial and other confidential information in order to assist the competitor in establishing United States operations. The executive held clandestine meetings with representatives of the competitor in South Africa and elsewhere, and gave them surreptitious and unauthorized tours of the victim company's manufacturing facility.

Kentucky Theft of Trade Secrets—In April 2006, the Department of Justice obtained a 48–month prison sentence against a Kentucky man for conspiring to steal and sell trade secrets belonging to Corning, Inc. The defendant, while a Corning employee, stole drawings of Corning's Thin Filter Translator Liquid Crystal Display ("LCD") glass and sold the drawings to a corporation based in Taiwan that intended to compete with Corning in the production of LCD glass.

D. INTERNATIONAL CRIMINAL LAW ENFORCEMENT

TAKING ACTION: HOW COUNTRIES ARE FIGHTING INTELLECTUAL PROPERTY RIGHTS CRIME (EXCERPTS)

United States Department of State.
January, 2006.

http://usinfo.state.gov/products/pubs/intelprp/action.htm

Burkina Faso Targets Copyright Piracy

Burkina Faso, which has a vibrant and significant local music industry under assault by cut-rate imported pirated music products, is fighting back. In the fall of 2004, the Ministry of Culture, Arts, and Tourism and the Copyrights Office kicked off a three-day meeting to discuss anti-piracy strategies against the more than 10 million pirated cassettes that enter the country each year, 80 percent of them from neighboring countries. The meeting ended with the incineration of 17,000 pirated cassettes and CDs seized by the Copyrights Office and the Gendarmerie in Ouagadougou and Bobo–Dioulasso.

Before reporters covering the meeting, Mahamoudou Ouedraogo, minister of culture, arts, and tourism, called piracy "a cancer" for Burkina Faso and insisted that pirates should be prosecuted for their crimes. The director general of the government's Office for the Rights of Authors, in turn, outlined Burkina Faso's anti-piracy strategy. The strategy will include setting up an independent anti-piracy organization; issuing a common policy with the neighboring countries to secure the borders against pirated goods; setting up a subregional court in charge of copyrights; providing intellectual property rights (IPR) training to judges, gendarmes, police, and customs agents; and pressing criminal charges against pirates and sellers of pirated goods, of which there are an estimated 100,000 in Burkina Faso. The majority of these sellers are street hawkers.

Supporting IPR Through Improved Government–NGO Cooperation in Estonia

Estonia's Police Board and its Customs and Tax Board signed a cooperative agreement on December 27, 2004, that allows them to improve Estonia's IPR regime through the exchange of information on operations, investigations, and procedures. Both boards also are working more closely with the country's leading IPR nongovernmental organization (NGO), the Estonian Organization for Copyright Protection (EOCP), in gathering information and securing evidence on specific cases of IPR infringement.

EOCP and other Estonian NGOs also work independently to teach the younger generation about the importance of IPR. According to EOCP's managing director, Ilmar Harg, Internet piracy is a more worrisome problem than pirated CDs in Estonia, with an average of 50 web sites closed each month because of pirated content. In November of 2004, the NGO organized a media campaign in Estonia's leading newspapers explaining the criminal nature of IPR infringement on the Internet. The campaign materials reported that, beginning in 2005, the Estonian Police will step up its investigations and prosecutions of Internet piracy, and noted that the Estonian penal code calls for up to three years of imprisonment for those found guilty of Internet piracy.

The Estonian Computer Club, another local NGO that boasts about 4,500 members, is using a U.S. Embassy grant to organize several IPR-related seminars and Local Area Network (LAN) parties for young computer users. The seminars will be held in cooperation with EOCP and the Business Software Alliance.

In India, A Law Firm Combats Piracy With New Strategy

The Mumbai-based law firm of Krishna & Saurastri's new strategy for combating copyright infringement in India is to use the legal system to inconvenience the pirated material manufacturer through persistent search-and-seizure tactics and with recurrent civil and criminal litigation.

According to Sunil Krishna of Krishna & Saurastri, their strategy combats violations in the pharmaceutical, software, audio, and music industries. Owing to what Krishna describes as "the reluctance of local police to pursue" complaints about counterfeited goods, his firm now has turned to the "Anton Pillar" order along with other means to fight piracy. The "Anton Pillar" order allows for the appointment of court receivers to search and seize suspected counterfeit property for custodial purposes without any prior notification to the alleged perpetrator. The court also orders the police to provide protection to the receiver of the goods. Krishna claims that this method has proved extremely successful with pirated software.

After the seizure, Krishna says, he can obtain an injunction against the alleged perpetrator. This will prevent additional manufacturing and/or trading of the counterfeit products. Violating the court injunction is punishable by a minimum of six months to a maximum of three years' imprisonment. Krishna argues that this sentence serves as a deterrent against future counterfeiting operations.

The attorney cites two cases where both civil and criminal statutes were used in successfully eradicating a spurious pharmaceutical product. Krishna said this process is time-consuming, and involves filing hundreds of cases against the manufacturers of the fake goods. Convinced that it is a successful strategy "guaranteed" to make the manufacturer or trader of illegal goods close up shop permanently, Krishna says that the cost for this approach is less than 5 percent of the legitimate turnover of the company whose goods are being copied.

Krishna believes the government of India could make a few changes that would make his job easier. He favors the continual education of law enforcement officers about piracy. He recommends that Indian Customs be empowered to destroy counterfeit goods, something they cannot do now. He also suggests that pirated goods coming into or going out of India could be prosecuted under the Conservation of Foreign Exchange and Prevention of Smuggling Activities Act. The act allows for a one-year imprisonment without bail for the illegal import or export of any good.

Optical Disc Regulations Now Law in Indonesia

Former Indonesian President Megawati Soekarnoputri signed Indonesia's first-ever optical disc regulations on October 5, 2004. The long-awaited regulations require producers to register their production facilities, maintain and report production records, and open their factories to unannounced police and/or civil service investigators, among other measures. Then Minister of Industry and Trade Rini Soewandi signed the accompanying implementing ministerial regulations on October 19, her last day in office. In anticipation of a decision by incoming President Susilo Bambang Yudhoyono to split the Ministry of Industry and Trade into two separate ministries, Soewandi issued two separate implementing regulations, dividing issues and responsibilities between the two future ministries.

According to a local Indonesian Motion Picture Association consultant, who worked with Indonesian officials in drafting the new regulations, these will require existing and future companies with optical disc production facilities to:

    — Register each of their production facilities, the production capacity at each facility, and manager names at each facility with the Ministry of Industry.

— Hang company signs outside factories in a manner that makes them clearly visible to the public.

— Use and have in their possession only those production molds that are engraved with government-approved source identification codes (SID).

— Keep records of orders, the quantity of polycarbonate (the material used to make discs) purchased, numbers of disc copies produced, samples of each batch of discs produced, and copyright agreements.

— Register with an internationally accredited organization that issues SID codes, such as the International Federation of the Phonographic Industry (IFPI).

The regulations provide for the possibility of administrative sanctions, specifically the removal of a producer's registration. Since the optical disc regulations fall under Indonesia's copyright law, they call for criminal penalties of up to five years' imprisonment. These new regulations went into effect on April 18, 2005.

Paraguay: Use of Laws, Enforcement to Protect IPR

Paraguay moved forcefully in 2004 with legislation and enforcement actions that strengthen IPR protection. For instance, the government worked with the private sector and supported the introduction of two draft laws that increase penalties in criminal cases of IPR violations, one law for copyright piracy and the other for counterfeiting. The draft laws increase penalties to five years or more, avoiding provisions for crimes with lower penalties that provide the option of paying a fine in lieu of jail time.

Paraguay's Specialized Technical Unit, designed to act as an intelligence and inter-agency coordination unit for IPR enforcement, became part of the Ministry of Industry and Commerce, and gained a stronger focus on copyright piracy and falsification. This unit has participated in a significant number of enforcing actions, often in cooperation with private sector groups. Reviews of company registration data following increased cooperation (including data sharing) between the ministry and the Customs Service led to the closure of 56 importing companies and the cancellation of 73 import licenses.

A report prepared by the ministry in February 2005 states that between December 2003 through January 2004, for instance, action by the Paraguayan authorities resulted in: 11 million virgin CDs confiscated; 1,600 CD burners confiscated; five cigarette factories raided that were suspected of producing counterfeit cigarettes; three printers raided that were producing cartons and labels for counterfeit cigarettes; four warehouses raided where counterfeit cigarettes were stored; 15 operations resulting in the seizure of various counterfeit products, such as watches, toys, and cell phones; raids of 10 TV cable operator companies engaged in piracy of cable signals; two raids in Market 4 in Asunci, with 11 stores raided and the confiscation of thousands of pirated CDs and DVDs; and the investigation of five major organized crime groups that imported CDs for sound-recording piracy.

The ministry reached agreement in August 2004 with Fox Sports Latin America to cooperate in ending the theft of Fox's programming, among the most popular in Paraguay. The first such agreement signed by Fox in Latin America, it allows Fox and the ministry to use the powers of the country's communications regulator (CONATEL) to revoke the licenses of companies providing pirated cable signals, a more efficient method than relying solely on the courts. Since the agreement was reached, at least four cable TV providers have reached accords with Fox and stopped pirating the signals.

South Korea: Bringing Sound Recording Protection on the Internet Into the Public Eye

South Korean media headlines in January 2005 on the government's new action to protect sound recordings grabbed the attention of the Korean public. A drastic slide in revenues over the last three years for the music industry in South Korea, including both domestic and foreign rights holders, prompted the government to push through amendments to the country's Copyright Act that require prior permission from rights holders before anyone can download music from the Internet. In an effort to protect the "cultural future" of Korea—especially the "Korea wave" of popular music, TV dramas, and films that permeates Asia—the government has been very aggressively raising public consciousness about the new rules.

The Ministry of Culture and Tourism posted information on its web site to inform and educate the public regarding the practical consequences of the new amendments, which went into effect January 17. The web site unequivocally states that only performers and phonogram producers themselves can transmit their performance or phonograms over the Internet or other networks. If the general public, the users, want to transmit phonograms over the Internet, they must seek prior permission from the rights holders. The site lists acts now illegal in Korea, including uploading music files and other copyrighted works onto web sites, mini-homepages, Internet cafes, or blogs, and uploading music files with the purpose of file sharing to closed web sites, mini-homepages, Internet cafes, or blogs. The government's campaign seems to be bearing fruit: Recording companies report that they already have received inquiries from some of the smaller on-line music services asking for a meeting to discuss contract details.

In addition, three National Assembly members are sponsoring a bill to revise Korea's Copyright Act yet again. The bill would grant significant additional rights to producers and performers, including the right of communication to the public. The Ministry of Culture and Tourism's Game and Music Division, in turn, drafted a new Music Promotion Bill for consideration by the National Assembly that would introduce additional protections for sound recordings, as well as authorize the ministry to set up and run an inspection team to investigate and handle illegal phonogram cases.

Sri Lanka's Biggest Raid Discovers Illicit Disc–Printing Plant

Although the sale of counterfeit CDs and DVDs is common in Sri Lanka, authorities assumed discs on sale were being imported to Sri Lanka from other parts of Asia. Then, on the night of October 9, 2004, Sri Lankan police investigating other criminal activities raided a previously unknown CD manufacturing plant, Optical Media Pvt. Ltd. Owned and operated by Malaysian nationals, the plant had been in operation since early that year, ironically as a company approved by the Board of Investment, the government of Sri Lanka's foreign investment promotion agency. The police also raided the main bazaar in Colombo and confiscated a large number of optical media products. The news of the raids spread to other counterfeit CD sellers, and most of the shops have stopped displaying counterfeit copies of the Eagle brand produced by the plant.

The plant had counterfeited music, movie, and software products and produced CDs using polycarbonate resin, which will make it possible to calculate the number of CDs and DVDs that were pirated. Informants told the police that a truck had removed approximately 175,000 discs and some stampers the night before the raid. Officials assume that, because of the large number of discs involved and the presence of several hundred Chinese Microsoft discs, the plant must have manufactured illegal discs for export as well as local consumption.

The U.S. Embassy in Colombo reports that its public/private IPR Working Group is helping to coordinate private sector support, including that of Microsoft, for Sri Lankan authorities' continuing investigations.

Taiwan Strengthens Copyright Law

A new law passed by Taiwan's Legislative Yuan on August 24, 2004, closes loopholes in the version they passed in 2003. The new bill makes any technology or information used for circumventing "anti-piracy measures" a crime punishable by up to one year in prison and/or a fine of up to approximately U.S. $8000. It also allows Taiwan Customs to impound goods, pending determination of their authenticity. However, rights holders must still take measures to apply for attachment and/or initiate criminal or civil proceedings to protect their intellectual property rights within three days, or Customs is required to release the goods.

The 2003 law eliminated minimum sentences for counterfeiters, giving judges the discretion to allow violators to pay a fine instead of serving jail time. Most intellectual property pirates saw paying these minimal fines as a justifiable cost of doing business. The new law mandates that those involved in the sale or rent of copyright-infringing optical discs must be imprisoned between six months and five years, and also may be fined between U.S. $16,100 to U.S. $161,000.

NOTES

1.   Why should governmental resources in the form of efforts by investigators, prosecutors, criminal courts, and prison officials be used to protect private intellectual property rights? What can criminal investigations, prosecutions, and convictions achieve that private rights enforcement can not? What are the risks of over criminalizing intellectual property laws?

2.   In what settings involving intellectual property are criminal laws and enforcement actions most needed to supplement private rights enforcement?

3.   Given the limited resources available to prosecutors and their frequent inexperience with the high tech activities involved in many cases of intellectual property theft, are prosecutors likely to be able to develop criminal cases regarding intellectual property theft effectively and establish meaningful deterrents? What types of support for these prosecutions might be advantageous?

4.   How should private rights holders interact with investigators and prosecutors in the development of criminal cases involving intellectual property? Should holders of intellectual property rights be given the authority to invoke criminal processes—perhaps by giving them the ability to initiate proceedings leading to searches of premises of asserted trade secret thieves as is described in the reading on practices in the Indian legal system? If these sorts of actions are reserved solely to prosecutors, should private rights holders nonetheless be allowed to provide technical assistance to investigators and prosecutors or to reimburse the costs of special technical experts engaged by the government to develop and present a complex case of trade secret theft? What are the benefits and risks of such private support of prosecutorial efforts?

VI.   INTELLECTUAL PROPERTY IN DEVELOPING COUNTRIES

THE U.S. APPROACH: GENETIC RESOURCES, TRADITIONAL KNOWLEDGE, AND FOLKLORE

United States Department of State. January 2006.
by Jeanne Holden.

http://usinfo.state.gov/products/pubs/intelprp/approach.htm

A U.S. agency negotiates a collaborative agreement with a university research organization in Brazil to study plants in that country as potential sources of drugs to fight cancer.

Members of a Native–American tribe create a digital database in which they record all of their community's cultural knowledge, history, practices, and arts.

A U.S. corporation seeking to study microorganisms in Yellowstone National Park enters a Cooperative Research and Development Agreement with the U.S. government, stating that any benefits of commercialization will be shared.

Though these situations may seem unrelated, they have something in common: All are mechanisms aimed at protecting the value of genetic resources, traditional knowledge, and folklore, three elements that are often intertwined in daily life in indigenous communities. A traditional healing remedy, for example, may involve preparing a local plant according to a recipe passed down from generation to generation and consuming it as part of a cultural ceremony.

The United States respects and recognizes the importance of protecting genetic resources, traditional knowledge, and expressions of folklore by facilitating equitable benefit sharing, eliminating erroneously issued patents, eliminating misappropriation of traditional knowledge, and preserving expressions of folklore, says Linda Lourie, an attorney with the U.S. Patent and Trademark Office's (USPTO) International Relations Office.

As a country composed of people from all over the globe, as well as more than 560 Native–American tribes, the U.S. government has had to handle a myriad of concerns regarding these often-complex matters. "We've resolved these issues by national means," Lourie stressed. Some of these solutions utilize existing U.S. intellectual property laws, while others do not. Tribal businesses, for example, use established intellectual property laws, while Native–American expressions of folklore are protected by other types of laws, programs, and even museums.

In the international arena, the United States is at the forefront in developing benefit-sharing agreements with source countries regarding their genetic resources. "We have consistently led the world in negotiating these kinds of arrangements," she said, "and we certainly would encourage other countries to do so."

The United States is eager to share its experiences with other countries in international fora, said Lourie. "But," she cautioned, "each country has different issues that need to be resolved differently. One size does not fit all."

What Are the Issues?

In 1993, the Convention on Biological Diversity (CBD) came into force. It represents a commitment by nations to conserve biological diversity, to use biological resources sustainably, and to share the benefits arising from the use of genetic resources fairly and equitably. Article 8(j) of the convention draws a connection among traditional knowledge, folklore, and genetic resources by calling on nations to "respect, preserve, and maintain knowledge, innovations, and practices of indigenous and local communities" and to promote wider application with the approval of the holders of such knowledge and practices.

Since 1993, the international community has been working to better understand and implement Article 8(j) within the framework of the World Trade Organization (WTO) and the World Intellectual Property Organization (WIPO), among others. In these discussions, several developing countries have advocated creating new forms of legal protections for these resources at WIPO. In response, WIPO member states established an Intergovernmental Committee (IGC) as an international forum for discussing the relationship between intellectual property and genetic resources, traditional knowledge, and folklore.

But what is meant by these three terms? Ultimately there is no uniformity in definitions. The term "genetic resources" is defined in the Convention on Biological Diversity, Article 2, as "genetic material of actual or potential value." Genetic material refers to any material of plant, animal, microbial, or other origin containing functional units of heredity.

According to the International Bureau of WIPO, "traditional knowledge" refers to systems of knowledge, generally passed from generation to generation, pertaining to a particular people or territory, and including their creations, innovations, and cultural expressions. By definition, some form of traditional knowledge has existed for a long time. However, such knowledge is not static and can be constantly evolving in response to a changing environment. Traditional knowledge may focus on natural elements such as mineral deposits, location of salmon, healing properties of local plants, land management practices, or agricultural technologies.

The term "expressions of folklore" has also been defined by WIPO for purposes of its discussions. WIPO says this term refers to characteristic elements of "traditional artistic heritage" developed and maintained by a community or by individuals who reflect the traditional artistic expectations of such a community. Expressions of folklore may be oral, as in folktales; musical, as in songs; actions, as in folk dances, plays, or rituals; or tangible expressions, such as drawings, paintings, carvings, sculptures, pottery, woodwork, metal ware, jewelry, basket weaving, needlework, textiles, carpets, costumes, musical instruments, and architectural forms, among others.

The concerns of traditional knowledge holders within the United States and other countries include: loss of traditional knowledge; lack of respect for traditional knowledge; the misappropriation of traditional knowledge, including use without benefit sharing and offensive use; and the need to preserve and promote the use of traditional knowledge. Indigenous communities have many similar concerns regarding their traditional artistic expressions.

Holders of genetic resources worldwide also are largely focused on the issues of "protection," "preservation," and "equity," although even those terms have not been defined uniformly.

There have been calls for the creation of new international legal protections for these resources, but many questions remain unanswered. Who would be the beneficiaries of any protection measures created for genetic resources, traditional knowledge, or folklore? No country, international intergovernmental organization, or person has been able to identify the intended beneficiaries of these sought-after protection measures. Similarly, none has determined what the scope of such protection might be, what would constitute "fair use" or other exceptions of limitations, or even what enforcement mechanisms could be applied. How would an expatriate of an indigenous community from one country profit from, or have the right to use, genetic resources, traditional knowledge, or folklore from her past in her new home? How would combinations of traditions be protected? What about traditions or knowledge that span borders or continents or are universally practiced?

Some countries want to prevent others from using their traditions while others want to commercialize or profit from such use. How could any one system encompass all these interests? And, to make matters even more complex, there is no agreement as to what actual harm would be remedied by new means of protection.

In the United States, tribal enterprises can and do avail themselves of U.S. intellectual property laws, said Eric Wilson, an international program analyst with the U.S. Department of the Interior. The Mississippi Band of Choctaw, for example, holds annual seminars for tribal government and tribal industry managers on intellectual property. The tribe is engaged in manufacturing enterprises and wants to be able to avail itself of relevant intellectual property rights (IPR), he explained.

The current laws of intellectual property rights are not enough to cover all the concerns of indigenous peoples, and such laws alone cannot be expected to do so, Wilson stressed. "Indigenous values," as they are sometimes called, are quite broad and vary among the tribal communities, with some interests belonging to an entire tribe, a clan, or an individual.

In order to achieve protection of intellectual interests, Wilson suggested that some of the solutions will need to come from the indigenous communities themselves. He said that it would be appropriate for national governments to give legal recognition to customary indigenous law.

Traditional Knowledge

One approach taken to respond to traditional knowledge holders, said Linda Lourie, consists of ensuring that patents are not granted on known products or processes, including those that are considered traditional knowledge.

A patent is a grant by a national government to an inventor for the right to exclude others from making, using, or selling his or her invention. To qualify for patent protection in most countries, an invention must be new, it must be useful, and it must not be a trivial extension of what is already known. Some holders of traditional knowledge fear that others will seek patents based on their long-held knowledge and reap the benefits from it. But an applicant trying to patent traditional knowledge likely cannot meet the three necessary requirements, Lourie said. "Traditional knowledge is already known, so if it has been documented, it's no longer new."

According to the U.S. Patent Act (Title 35 U.S. Code, Section 102), if an invention a) was known or used by others in the United States, or patented or described in a printed publication in this or a foreign country before the invention thereof by the applicant for patent, or b) was patented or described in a printed publication in this or a foreign country or in public use or on sale in this country, more than one year prior to the date of the application for patent in the United States, then it is not entitled to a patent.

"However," Lourie explained, "if our patent examiners in Virginia do not know about traditional practices overseas, they cannot protect them."

Lack of information about a traditional remedy led to a problem in 1995 when a U.S. patent covering the use of the turmeric plant in healing wounds was mistakenly granted to Indian nationals from the University of Mississippi Medical Center. Turmeric has been used for a long time in India to heal wounds, and this had been documented in Indian publications. The Indian Council for Scientific and Industrial Research requested a reexamination of the patent, and the U.S. Patent and Trademark Office revoked the patent for lack of novelty. The ability of a third party to request reexamination and the eventual cancellation of the claims when a mistake has occurred demonstrate that the current patent system works well to correct itself.

The importance of publishing traditional knowledge and making that information available to patent examiners internationally cannot be over-emphasized, said Lourie. "If traditional knowledge is documented, that knowledge may not be the subject of a patent, even if it is not widely known in an industrialized country."

The United States is encouraging other countries to create digital databases to catalog their traditional knowledge and protect it from patent attempts. Digital databases would allow patent examiners all over the world to search and examine traditional knowledge. Several developing countries are working toward this end. India and China have been very involved in developing searchable digital libraries of their traditional knowledge, Lourie said. U.S. patent examiners regularly check the international databases that are already in use.

Lourie acknowledged that some traditional knowledge holders might want to keep certain aspects of their knowledge secret or limited to specific individuals or groups. If so, she said, they may want to take steps to guard their knowledge as a trade secret. In the United States, infringement of a trade secret is considered a type of unfair competition.

Within the United States, some Native–American tribes are cataloging their tribal values in a way that fulfills the need for documentation and the need to limit outsiders' access to information. According to Eric Wilson, the Tulalip Tribes in the U.S. state of Washington, for example, have developed a sophisticated digital computer inventory, named "Cultural Stories," that delineates who is to have access to what traditional information about their knowledge, history, culture, or practices. Some users have unlimited access, while others, such as U.S. patent examiners, may have limited access.

Some holders of traditional knowledge want to be sure that any new discoveries derived from their traditional knowledge include an equitable sharing of benefits. These communities may want to negotiate contractual benefit-sharing agreements regarding new products or processes created through research using their traditional knowledge. Lourie cautioned, however, that it could be a mistake to expect a windfall from such contracts; to date, very few financial benefits have accrued from commercialization of traditional knowledge.

Folklore

In the United States, expressions of folklore are protected in a variety of ways, ranging from standard U.S. intellectual property laws to laws and programs specifically designed to protect and preserve the cultural heritage of its indigenous peoples.

One mechanism is the Indian (Native American) Arts and Crafts Act, a federal law enacted in 1935 and amended in 1990. This truth-in-advertising law prohibits the marketing of products misrepresented as Native American-made. It covers all Indian and Indian-style traditional and contemporary arts and crafts, such as baskets, jewelry, masks, and rugs. An individual or business violating the act can face civil penalties or criminal penalties or both.

The Database of Official Insignia of Native–American Tribes was established at the USPTO in 2001 in response to Native–American concerns about the preservation of expressions of folklore. Official insignia are not trademarked designs; they are insignia that various federally and state-recognized Native–American tribes have identified as their official tribal emblem. Inclusion of official insignia in the database ensures that an examining attorney will be able to identify any official insignia that may preclude registration of a mark where the mark suggests a false connection with the tribe.

In addition, all trademark applications containing tribal names, recognizable likenesses of Native Americans, symbols perceived as being Native American in origin, and any other application that the USPTO believes suggests an association with Native Americans are examined by an attorney at the USPTO who has developed expertise and familiarity in this area.

The U.S. government has taken several other steps to protect and preserve its peoples' expressions of folklore. The American Folklife Center in the Library of Congress was created in 1976 by the U.S. Congress "to preserve and present American folk life" through programs of research, documentation, archival preservation, live performance, exhibition, public programs, and training. The center incorporates the Library's Archive of Folk Culture, established in 1928 as a repository for American folk music. The center holds more than 1,000,000 photographs, manuscripts, audio recordings, and moving images.

The U.S. government also maintains the Smithsonian Center for Folklife and Cultural Heritage to promote the understanding of grassroots cultures in the United States and abroad. Its collection includes many thousands of commercial discs, audiotapes, compact discs, still images, videotapes, and motion picture film. It produces annual folklife festivals, recordings, exhibitions, documentary films, and educational materials.

The newest U.S. effort to protect and preserve Native–American culture is the Smithsonian Institution's National Museum of the American Indian, which opened in Washington, D.C., on September 21, 2004. It is the first national museum in the United States dedicated to the preservation, study, and exhibition of the life, languages, history, and arts of Native Americans.

Genetic Resources

Throughout the world, many communities are focusing on issues of equity as well as protection and preservation of resources. Those communities have expressed their concern that industrialized-country companies could utilize source-country natural resources for agricultural and pharmaceutical products and assert intellectual property rights claims.

Many others believe that such concerns have been overstated. Where the U.S. government, including the National Cancer Institute (NCI), is involved in genetic resource research in other countries, it enters into benefit-sharing agreements with those countries to gain fair access to genetic resources and/or traditional knowledge, said Linda Lourie. "There are many success stories" involving collaborative agreements and contracts for cooperation negotiated on mutually beneficial terms.

"NCI was ahead of the Convention on Biological Diversity by about three or four years" in negotiating agreements with source countries regarding their resources, says scientist Dr. Gordon Cragg.

Cragg, chief of the Natural Products Branch of NCI's Developmental Therapeutics Program, explained that, in the 1980s, NCI started developing policies for collaborating with source countries on the use of their genetic resources in research aimed at finding more effective treatments for cancer. These agreements provided the source countries with short-term benefits that would accrue without having to wait and see whether promising discoveries were derived from their resources. The benefits included training source-country scientists in NCI laboratories or U.S. universities' laboratories and technology transfer, he said.

"The chances of a discovery becoming a commercial product is usually said to be one in 10,000," said Cragg, adding, "I think that is optimistic."

NCI, part of the U.S. National Institutes of Health, one arm of the U.S. Department of Health and Human Services, functions much like a non-profit pharmaceutical company. Established in 1937, NCI had evolved by the 1950s into a drug research and development center, collecting plants mostly in the United States, Mexico, Canada, and parts of Africa and Europe. In the 1980s, NCI began a collection program for plants and marine organisms in tropical regions.

This was the program in which NCI first developed policies for benefit-sharing with source countries. "We began letting out contracts to high-quality research organizations in the United States for collections overseas," explains Bjarne Gabrielsen, senior advisor for drug discovery and development in NCI's Technology Transfer Branch. "The Missouri Botanical Garden collected plants in Africa, the New York Botanical Garden collected in Latin America, the University of Illinois in Chicago collected in South Asia," he said. "The collections were done mainly in tropical and subtropical countries, mainly developing countries."

At this stage, Cragg's program started using Letters of Collection, agreements among NCI, a U.S. contractor organization, and a collecting organization in the source country. "The U.S. contractor goes into an area, obtains the necessary permits, and collects plants and marine organisms for us" with the source country organization, said Gabrielsen. "The NCI does the extraction and testing." In addition to short-term benefits, NCI requires that, if a promising potential drug is discovered and licensed to a pharmaceutical company, the company must negotiate an agreement so that benefits, such as part of the royalties, will be returned to the country.

Over time, in response to the Convention on Biological Diversity and to greater awareness on the part of source countries about the value of their resources, research organizations and pharmaceutical companies increasingly have adopted policies of equitable collaboration and compensation.

In this, too, NCI has been a leader. In the 1990s, NCI de-emphasized its collections in its plant-derived drug discovery program in favor of expanding closer collaboration with qualified source-country scientists and organizations under agreements called Memoranda of Understanding.

"Where source-country organizations have the skills, expertise, and knowledge and some reasonable infrastructure in their labs, we support them by helping them further their own drug discovery research programs," said Cragg. For example, he said, NCI's Developmental Therapeutics Program has provided a research organization at the Federal University of Ceara in Fortaleza, Brazil, with the training and cancer cell lines to establish their own cancer drug discovery program. This group is now screening materials from research programs all over Brazil.

"We have five such agreements in Brazil," said Cragg, as well as collaborations with organizations in Australia, Bangladesh, China, Costa Rica, Fiji, Iceland, South Korea, Mexico, New Zealand, Nicaragua, Pakistan, Panama, Papua New Guinea, South Africa, and Zimbabwe.

Through this type of collaboration, the developing-country organization may make a promising discovery in-country, said Cragg. Even if they send NCI a sample for more extensive testing, such testing is regarded as routine and NCI makes no intellectual property claim, he said. "The results are sent back to them and the source-country organization can take out the patent, if appropriate.

"To our minds," stressed Cragg, "it is an ideal process. * * * If a pharmaceutical company wants to use the discovery and the source-country organization has the patent, it must negotiate a licensing agreement and the source-country organization can dictate [the] terms.

"By establishing these close collaborations aimed at developing promising treatments for the U.S. and global cancer population, we achieve NCI's mission and also the goals of the Convention on Biological Diversity," said Cragg. "The source country is deriving significant benefit."

Linda Lourie pointed out that the U.S. government also requires a contract when companies want to collect genetic resources from federally owned lands or from the approximately 56 million acres of land the federal government holds in trust for U.S. tribes and individual Native Americans. For example, in order to study unique microorganisms in the hot springs of the U.S. government-owned Yellowstone National Park that can withstand great heat, researchers must enter into a Cooperative Research and Development Agreement (CRADA) with the U.S. government that includes benefit sharing, with milestone payments if the results are commercialized, she said.

"The U.S. view of protection of genetic resources," Lourie said, "is to encourage other countries to establish appropriate access and benefit-sharing regimes that provide benefit sharing on mutually agreed terms." Some countries develop policies limiting access by creating so many barriers as to almost prohibit collaboration, thus ruling themselves out of the potential benefits of collaboration, said Cragg.

Conclusion

The United States has developed a wide variety of mechanisms to respond to concerns regarding the protection of traditional knowledge, folklore, and genetic resources. In the U.S. view, intellectual property laws are and should continue to be available to indigenous individuals and peoples who meet the appropriate criteria for such legal protection.

The U.S. government supports the exchange of views on traditional knowledge, expressions of folklore, and genetic resources in international fora, particularly in WIPO, which has the necessary expertise and resources to tackle these complex and technical issues. WIPO activities have included fact-finding missions, case studies and surveys, sample contractual clauses, and examples of databases.

U.S. experts agree that intellectual property protections do not offer a solution for all of the issues involved in the protection, preservation, promotion, and use of traditional knowledge, expressions of folklore, and genetic resources worldwide. In the U.S. view, however, the key to resolving these issues satisfactorily is a solutions-oriented approach rooted in each country's national context.

NOTES

1.   To what extent are proposed extensions of legal rights of control over "traditional knowledge" aimed at different goals than present intellectual property laws? Is the protection of traditional knowledge aimed at producing more such knowledge or at some other goal?

2.   Should the aim of legal reforms concerning traditional knowledge be limited to ensuring that no rights granted to other parties interfere with the use and development of traditional knowledge by indigenous communities? Or should positive intellectual property rights be granted to indigenous communities allowing them to control and gain commercial returns from the use of traditional knowledge by others? If so, on what basis?

ROUNDTABLE: ENFORCEMENT, A PRIORITY FOR ALL COUNTRIES

United States Department of State.
January, 2006.

http://usinfo.state.gov/products/pubs/intelprp/enforce.htm

Many countries have adopted sophisticated laws to protect intellectual property in order to join international or regional accords and organizations. By doing this, a country has taken an important first step. However, the creation of laws alone will not enable a country to effectively enforce the rights of property holders. That requires the development of appropriate enforcement mechanisms.

Why does effective enforcement often lag behind the institution of law? What are the barriers to enforcement? Will the benefits of enforcement be shared by all countries or just a few?

The State Department's Bureau of International Information Programs (IIP) invited a panel of U.S. government experts to discuss these and other questions regarding the enforcement of intellectual property rights (IPR). Led by moderator Berta Gomez, then a senior writer-editor in IIP's Office of Economic Security, the roundtable discussion included: Michael Smith, an attorney adviser in the Office of Enforcement at the U.S. Patent and Trademark Office (USPTO); Jason Gull, a trial attorney with the U.S. Department of Justice's Computer Crimes and Intellectual Property Section; and Joseph Howard, a senior attorney adviser in the Intellectual Property Rights Branch of the U.S. Customs and Border Protection Service, part of the Department of Homeland Security.

According to these experts, effective enforcement of intellectual property rights should be a priority for all countries seeking economic growth and full participation in the world economy. The following is their discussion.

MODERATOR: First, where does enforcement fit into an overall intellectual property strategy?

SMITH: As the world economy develops and as economies are more reliant on high-technology sectors, the importance of protecting intellectual property rights is rising.

When the Patent and Trademark Office began conducting overseas training in 1997, the emphasis was on advising countries about drafting legislation that would conform to obligations under the World Trade Organization's Agreement on Trade–Related Aspects of Intellectual Property Rights (TRIPS). Over time, the focus has shifted from these laws to what countries actually are doing on a daily basis. We've found that many countries have laws on the books that are TRIPS-compliant, but that much remains to be done to actually enforce those rights at the borders and in the civil and criminal court systems.

As copyrights, trademarks, and patents become more important each year to the U.S. economy, our interest in protecting those rights abroad increases. And U.S. and other rights holders around the world are reluctant to invest in countries where, on a day-to-day basis, copyrights, patents, trademarks, and trade secrets are not adequately protected.

GULL: From our perspective at the Department of Justice, the harmonizing of intellectual property laws around the world through international agreements, going back even to the Berne Convention, is important to defining the rights of authors, inventors, and companies in products they develop. We would like to see countries come to a general agreement about what those rights should be.

But without effective enforcement, these laws are essentially empty promises. Effective enforcement of these rights is required so that authors and inventors can make rational decisions about whether they're going to publish, release, or invent something.

In the last few years, enforcement has become a much more significant issue. A combination of factors, including improvements in shipping, technology, telecommunications, and the Internet, has created markets that are increasingly global in scope.

Just as tangible things can move easily and cheaply across borders, IP problems can likewise be exported. For example, counterfeit products manufactured in East Asia have been a problem for a long time. But counterfeit production like this becomes an even greater problem as the products become less expensive and easier to ship to other parts of the world.

The Internet allows for instantaneous distribution of information around the world at essentially no cost. So, in addition to all the positive activity this technology allows, people are using the Internet to engage in massive infringement of intellectual property. This problem is growing as the digital sector of the economy is growing in the United States and in other countries.

MODERATOR: You said improvements in shipping make it easier for goods to cross borders. Is this one of the barriers to effective enforcement?

HOWARD: Perhaps the most critical obstacle to effective enforcement is the absence of a full understanding of the value of intellectual property rights to every nation that engages in international trade.

I've spoken in several countries overseas, and in each I was asked, "Why should we do this? Why are we protecting the wealthy nations or manufacturers who own these intellectual property rights?"

My response is that, first, if your country is governed by the rule of law and has signed certain international agreements, it is obligated to adhere to its agreements. Secondly, as your country develops its own sectors in which manufacturers, inventors, or artisans are creating intellectual property, it's important that you give them the full value of their rights.

Many times, people don't appreciate that protecting intellectual property is important to employment, which leads to growth and a better quality of life. If you don't respect intellectual property rights, no one wants to invest in your country. You won't attract the foreign capital that you need to improve the lifestyle of your nation's inhabitants.

Once people appreciate the value of the rule of law, then it's clearly not just benefiting the wealthy countries.

GULL: I, too, am asked by foreign audiences, "Why protect intellectual property when it's all American or rich countries' brands? Why should I do the bidding of these U.S. companies?" One answer is that, in much the same way that trademark owners must work to protect their brands, countries themselves must work to enforce IPR to protect the country's own reputation.

A trademark is simply a brand. It conveys information about the reputation of the manufacturer and the reputation of the product. If a particular trademark holder starts turning out poor-quality products, people will stop buying them. The reputation goes down.

To encourage investment, you need an effective legal regime that protects people's rights, including intellectual property rights. A country can help build its own brand image by ensuring effective IP enforcement. Conversely, countries that neglect IPR enforcement will tend to see their reputations, and the investment climate, suffer.

SMITH: Another key barrier to effective enforcement is a lack of political will. Without political will starting at the very top of the government, it's hard for enforcement authorities to look at these issues as important and to commit resources to solving them.

When the USPTO conducts technical assistance, we try to explain why enforcement is important to the local economy. For example, local music is not only an indigenous cultural heritage issue; it is a copyright issue of economic concern to local industries. We have found, particularly in Asia, that there's a link between the ability of the country to provide effective enforcement mechanisms and the growth of music made by local artists.

MODERATOR: But how does a government go about providing effective enforcement once it has decided to do so?

GULL: Although political will is certainly important, that is not to say that protecting intellectual property rights is just a matter of convincing the upper levels of government that this is an important issue, and that their decrees will trickle down to street-level enforcement.

The government also has to work on public awareness to make sure that the public agrees that intellectual property is worth protecting. Michael's point about indigenous music is an excellent one.

Of course, many pirated products are copies of goods produced by U.S. companies, such as Microsoft's software or American pop stars' CDs, which are then sold overseas. But if a country allows piracy to go unchecked, its own industries—music, or film, or software—will likely find their own products being pirated along American ones. Since the domestic creators of music, or movies, or software, tend to rely more heavily on their own domestic markets for their livelihoods, a high level of piracy at home may hurt these domestic producers most of all.

Piracy can make it even tougher for domestic industries to compete with large foreign companies. In countries where every kind of CD, DVD, or software is available for a couple of dollars per disc, a local film studio or software publisher will find it very difficult to compete, based on price, with the latest Silicon Valley software or Hollywood blockbuster.

Ironically, countries that want to avoid being overrun by American goods might consider strengthening their protection of intellectual property. That would serve local industry in the long run by allowing that industry to grow and encouraging investment.

If the public is on board with protecting intellectual property, then police officials will be willing to shut down street vendors selling pirated and counterfeit products. Prosecutors will be willing to pursue those cases because they won't face the wrath of an unhappy public. Judges will be more willing to mete out deterrent penalties, whether prison time or monetary damages.

HOWARD: It is particularly important for a country to have a mechanism whereby a foreign rights holder can bring a problem to the attention of authorities and have a realistic chance of receiving enforcement activity on his or her behalf. This overcomes the inertia that otherwise is present. It encourages the authorities to enforce rights.

MODERATOR: Can you describe the training or speaking that you do overseas?

HOWARD: I've gone to other countries, looked at legislation, and talked to people about what we do. I explain that it's reasonable, if you don't have the resources to have a database of all the intellectual property rights that might be infringed, to at least have a mechanism so that others can bring information to your attention. Many countries thought that that was useful.

The U.S. Customs Service also enforces exclusion orders (legally binding commands barring entry into the United States of goods that allegedly violate U.S. intellectual property rights) issuing from the U.S. International Trade Commission (USITC). Just as with intellectual property rights that are recorded with us, information about exclusion orders issued by the USITC is entered into the IPR module for dissemination to field officers. The public version of the IPR module1 can be easily accessed. The web address is http://www.cbp.gov. Click on the "Quick link" at that page for "Intellectual Property Rights," and at the next page click on "Intellectual Property Rights Search (IPRS)." The web site also contains a wealth of information about our intellectual property rights border enforcement program.

MODERATOR: And this is a case in which new technology actually helps enforcement?

HOWARD: Yes. But as my colleagues have pointed out, people have to want to do it. That's crucial.

MODERATOR: Do you have examples of countries in which you've seen progress and growing interest in protecting IPR?

HOWARD: I was in Egypt when they were talking about IP enforcement issues, and the people I spoke with said that they wanted a customs system like that in the United States. It seems people from all over the world look to our government for guidance on how to do certain things. They might not like what we say in some instances, but they're open to considering what we have to say.

SMITH: I think most countries would agree that the U.S. system for protecting intellectual property rights at the border is one of the most efficient systems in the world. But a lot of what is done in the United States is not practical for most countries. Certainly developing and least developed countries don't have nearly the resources that the U.S. government has. Also, most countries don't have as many border crossing points as the United States.

The customs services in these countries have to decide how best to utilize the resources that they have. In technical assistance programs overseas, the Patent Office uses that as a starting point to encourage compliance with a country's obligations under the TRIPS agreement. TRIPS provides minimum standards, such as establishing a system so that rights holders can go and record and seek enforcement of their rights.

Having said that, a country can be fully in compliance with the minimum obligations of the TRIPS agreement and still have a huge problem at its borders. For instance, the TRIPS agreement requires countries to provide for protection against imports of pirated copies of goods and goods bearing counterfeit trademarks. It does not require countries to provide protection at the border with regard to exportations of such goods or movements of such goods within the country that might be exported later.

So a primary concern of the U.S. government is the exportation of pirated and counterfeit goods that are produced in one country to other countries, for instance, within Europe or Asia. In that case, we would advocate for "TRIPS-plus" provisions. We do this in bilateral negotiations as part of the free trade agreements negotiation process. In training, we would emphasize why, although these are not TRIPS requirements, they are often needed in order to have an effective enforcement system.

MODERATOR: Are countries receptive to this?

SMITH: Definitely now more than 10 years ago. I think that, as countries have become more comfortable with their obligations under the TRIPS agreement and have had legislation in place for a while, they become more receptive.

Of particular importance to the U.S. government right now is regulating optical disc (i.e., CDs, VCDs, DVDs, etc.) piracy in countries where the production exceeds the amount of legitimate demand. Obviously, this overproduction of pirated material can't be supported by the local economy, so the product is being exported. In these instances, we would advocate export controls at the border and optical disc regulations.

MODERATOR: How big a problem is corruption as it relates to IPR?

GULL: Corruption is a significant problem in a number of countries around the world that are trying to enforce intellectual property rights.

Part of this is related to just how much money is at stake. When there's a lot of money involved in an illicit activity, there is bound to be some corruption.

Another aspect of intellectual property piracy and counterfeiting is organized crime. Criminal gangs, both within the United States and in many other parts of the world, are involved in the production and distribution of pirated and counterfeit goods at all different levels. Of course, corruption of public officials is by no means unique to intellectual property issues. But in those places where corruption is widespread, it's going to affect intellectual property enforcement.

SMITH: You asked, "What are the barriers to effective enforcement?" I think it depends on whether you are talking about civil, criminal, or border enforcement.

Criminal enforcement and border enforcement can be grouped together in that they are actions taken by the government. On the civil side, it's a private litigant going in and redressing harm in a civil courts system.

The problems on the civil side are similar in many countries around the world. The USPTO found that although lots of countries have legislation and a civil procedure code that provides for a rights holder to go into court and get interim relief or a temporary restraining order, those laws are not applied in practice.

We've also found that the damage awards that many courts give are so low that they are not actually a deterrent to those who engage in piracy or counterfeiting and do not adequately compensate rights holders for the harm they have suffered.

Finally, we've found that, in some countries, the infringing goods and the machinery used to produce those goods are not actually destroyed. They can enter back into the stream of commerce. That's obviously not in the best interest of the rights holders or the public.

On the government side, one barrier to border enforcement is that it's labor-intensive. You need customs officials at the border who are good consumers, familiar with the trademarks that have been recorded, and who have an interest in enforcing the rights of trademark holders. Without knowledgeable customs inspectors, you're going to have a problem with effective enforcement at the border.

On the criminal side, another problem is that countries initially might prosecute numerous cases of vendors selling pirated or counterfeit goods on the street. Although this might get the infringers off the street, it's not going to the source of the activity. In many countries, the infringement of intellectual property rights has its base in organized crime. Therefore, a more efficient use of a government's time and money would be to use their organized crime statutes to prosecute these cases at the source of the funding.

GULL: Yes, it's more effective to go after "big fish" than small ones because you cut off the supply. Generally, the biggest effect of going after street vendors is that piracy gets pushed a little off the street. That is, instead of a table full of pirated optical discs, you'll have one guy with a sign saying CDs and DVDs, and he'll burn you a copy or get you a counterfeit copy from a van or an apartment down the street.

Michael touched on the critical importance of having effective civil remedies. In the United States, the vast majority of enforcement is done by copyright holders or trademark owners who initiate actions. The United States has effective civil remedies: injunctions, seizures of counterfeit goods, and monetary damages. One has a realistic chance of actually obtaining those types of remedies here, and in many other countries with more established civil law mechanisms.

In some places, there isn't as mature a civil enforcement system. In those areas, for now at least, criminal and related border-enforcement mechanisms are the only realistic chance of making a dent in intellectual property infringement.

In some countries, a criminal prosecution or investigation cannot be initiated unless there is a complaint from a rights holder. This is a serious impediment because it's not practical for the rights holder to make a complaint in every instance. It means that, in some countries, police aren't empowered to seize offending goods that they recognize on the street or at a criminal enterprise. We encourage countries to eliminate this kind of requirement, whether it's in their actual law or merely a policy on the part of the police and prosecutors.

Also, some countries erect or maintain artificial barriers that make it more difficult to show ownership of a trademark or copyright. A court may require that there be testimony from the actual copyright owner, rather than simply allowing a certificate from a copyright office as "prima facie" (Ed. Note: Latin for "on its face," as it seems at first sight) evidence of copyright ownership. This sort of excessive formality can impede an effective enforcement regime. Often it's little things like this that persist even after the large steps of signing on to TRIPS, for example, have been accomplished.

MODERATOR: How important is participation on the part of the rights holder?

HOWARD: The U.S. Customs and Border Protection Program relies heavily on the rights holder who has recorded something with us to bring information about potential problems to us. Often the rights holder can pinpoint the date when infringing goods are going to arrive, the port or ship they're going to be on, or the mode of entry into the United States. That helps us to focus our efforts and not waste our limited resources.

Intellectual property rights holders also might help themselves by educating the consumer to understand that not all decisions should be based merely on price alone. A counterfeit product may be sold at a lower price, but may not have the same features as the actual product, or it may not be as safe or last as long. Equally or perhaps more important, you may not get the support that you would get from a legitimate manufacturer if the product is defective.

MODERATOR: Do health authorities have a role in telling consumers that counterfeit products may be unsafe or dangerous?

GULL: In the United States, a variety of federal laws and agencies protect against the kinds of counterfeit products that endanger health and safety. Selling a counterfeit drug on the Internet, like the fake Viagra advertised by "spammers" through e-mail, would likely be a violation of Food and Drug Administration laws regarding drug safety, as well as a federal trademark violation. It might violate laws in the individual 50 U.S. states as well.

When something is counterfeit, there's no way of tracing it to the true manufacturer. For example, counterfeit liquor is prevalent in a number of Eastern European countries. When genuine liquor violates health and safety standards, the origin of the product can be traced. The factory where it was made can be inspected and forced to improve. But with counterfeit goods, that's not possible because, by definition, the origin of the product is unknown.

SMITH: This ties in with public awareness. The government can play a role in educating the population that intellectual property protection is not only an economic issue, but also a health and safety issue. Counterfeit food products and counterfeit pharmaceuticals have resulted in deaths. Either they don't contain the components that they're supposed to or they contain components that are lethal to people, and people purchase them unwittingly.

Or consider airplane parts, where a pirated or counterfeit product is labeled as meeting laboratory standards of safety, but actually contains faulty components.

Health and safety issues can bring the discussion to a more personal level than the economic aspects of intellectual property protection. This is about people's lives.

NOTES

1. What are the limits of the arguments presented in this reading regarding the advantages to developing countries of bolstering intellectual property rights enforcement within their borders? At what point in the development of a country's economy—as it progresses towards the production of intellectual works—will strong enforcement of intellectual property rights be advantageous? Where residents of a country have a substantial capacity to produce new intellectual works, will the country gain an advantage from differential enforcement of intellectual property laws, providing strong enforcement regarding works created by domestic parties and weak enforcement regarding works originating from foreign sources?

2. To what extent can foreign governments create additional incentives for particular countries to strengthen their intellectual property rights enforcement? Should the United States or other countries impose economic sanctions on developing countries with weak intellectual property rights enforcement? If so, under what circumstances? What other sanctions or incentives might be used to encourage intellectual property rights enforcement in particular countries?

3. To what extent is a strategy of border interdiction—in which customs officials exclude goods from entry into the United States or other countries if the goods were produced or imported in violation of intellectual property laws—likely to be effective in creating incentives for the enforcement of intellectual property rights in the countries of origin of the goods? What are some of the weaknesses of an intellectual property rights enforcement strategy relying on enforcement at country boarders?

VII. INTELLECTUAL PROPERTY AND DISTRIBUTED MODES OF INNOVATION: THE OPEN SOURCE MOVEMENT

Open source innovation—primarily in the software field—constitutes a mode of innovation that is both mediated by and held largely immune from intellectual property protections. Open source development of software has proceeded through the efforts of a distributed community of innovators who have made their various improvements in software available to the general community. Well known open source software products include Linux (a widely used operating system), Apache (a popular Internet server program), and Perl (an Internet programming language).

While the software products produced through the open source movement are thought by many persons to be free of intellectual property restrictions, the truth of the situation is more complex. Open source software works are themselves subject to licensing terms (derived from copyright protections) which purport to allow parties to use and modify the works only if they agree to make resulting improvements available to subsequent generations of users. In this respect, intellectual property rights are paradoxically used to ensure a degree of user freedom. Access to restricted works is made available today as part of an intellectual property bargain to ensure free access to works tomorrow.

In addition to this unusual use of intellectual property rights to maintain a degree of free access to works, intellectual property rights are sometimes asserted in more traditional ways in attempts to limit the marketing of open source products. For example, a party holding intellectual property rights may assert that portions of protected works have been incorporated in an open source product without permission such that the continued replication, distribution, and use of that product will infringe the copyright or (less frequently) the patent of the rights holder. These sorts of claims, if successful or even colorable, will severely undercut user confidence in the continued availability and merit of open source products.

The following reading provides a good overview of the intellectual property issues surrounding the development, marketing, and use of open source products.

REPORT FOR CONGRESS: INTELLECTUAL PROPERTY, COMPUTER SOFTWARE AND THE OPEN SOURCE MOVEMENT

Congressional Research Service.
March 11, 2004.

by John R. Thomas Visiting Scholar in Entrepreneurship and Economic Growth Resources, Science, and Industry Division

http://www.ipmall.info/hosted_resources/crs/RL32268_040311.pdf#search=%22open%20source%22

Perhaps the most dramatic development in the contemporary computer industry is the "open source" software movement. The term "open source" refers to a computer program whose "source code" is made available to the public for modification or improvement as individual users desire. In contrast, the source code of "closed source" software is proprietary, not publicly distributed and subject to alteration only by the software manufacturer.

The rise of open source software has generated considerable discussion in recent years. Proponents of open source software contend that the open source system preserves the freedom of computer users and provides a superior development methodology as compared to the usual proprietary model. Other commentators have expressed concerns regarding the security of open source software and whether it will operate in a compatible fashion with other programs.

Intellectual property rights, including copyrights, patents and trade secrets, present another possible set of concerns with respect to open source software. Although a particular computer program may be designated as open source, it remains possible that an owner of intellectual property may enforce its rights against open source software developers and users. In addition, open source software is ordinarily accompanied by a license that requires users to maintain the program as open source. Some commentators have expressed concern that these licenses may overreach, converting proprietary programs into open source software even if only a portion of that program was derived from an open source original. Others have suggested that open source licenses may not be legally enforceable, which would allow users to obtain and assert intellectual property rights pertaining to software that was initially distributed as open source.

This report considers the impact of intellectual property rights upon open source software. This report commences with an introduction to the open source movement in the software industry. * * * After identifying issues of interface between open source software and the intellectual property laws, this report concludes with a discussion of possible legislative issues and approaches.

Introduction to the Open Source Movement

Fundamental Concepts

An understanding of the fundamentals of modern computer software technology will assist in an understanding of the open source movement. Software programmers typically write software programs using a high level computer language such as Basic, C++, or Java. By using the words, symbols and numbers that make up these high-level computer languages, the programmer tells the computer what to do. For instance, the command "ADD (X,Y)" instructs the computer to add the value of the variable X to the variable Y. A computer program written in this high level language is said to be in "source code" form.

Computers are incapable of reading the high-level instructions of source code, however. Rather, the computer responds to binary inputs—either a "0" or a "1"—that correspond to an open or closed electrical switch. The number "01001101" might tell a computer to add two numbers and save the result, for example. Thus, after writing the program in source code, the programmer ordinarily uses a compiler program to translate or "compile" the source code into the corresponding 1s and 0s that the computer can read. Source code that has been compiled into this series of 1s and 0s is called "object code."

Today, most computer programs are distributed in object code form. This distribution system is often referred to as the "proprietary software" model. When a consumer purchases a copy of, for example, WordPerfect software, that program comes on a CD–ROM into which the object code 1s and 0s have been encoded. One of the reasons that software developers distribute only the object code, and not the source code, is convenience. Software in object code format is ready for the computer to use.

This technique also protects the source code from disclosure. Because skilled programmers can easily read source code, a competitor could review this text in order to find out how a program works. As a result, if software were distributed in source code form, rival firms could readily take and reuse parts of the program in competing products. As this report discusses below, this appropriation of the original programmer's work may violate intellectual property laws. However, such violations may be difficult both to discover and stop. Distributing software in object code form is a more cost-efficient and effective means of preventing this infringement.

Some computer users have expressed dissatisfaction with the proprietary software model. End users of proprietary software must ordinarily rely upon the software publisher to fix mistakes in the code and develop additional features. As free software advocate Richard Stallman has explained, the proprietary software model "keeps users helpless and divided: the inner workings are secret." Stallman further opines that computer users "should be free to modify programs to fit their needs, and free to share software, because helping other people is the basis of society."

A loosely organized open source software community has resulted from this reaction to proprietary software development. In contrast to proprietary software, the source code of "open source" software is available to the public. Computer users are therefore able to examine the human-readable instructions that the programmer wrote to create the software. A number of well-known programs are "open source," including a widely used Internet server program, Apache; a popular Internet programming language, Perl; the program that routes more than 80 percent of all Internet email messages worldwide, Sendmail; the program that is the basis for the domain name system, Bind; and the fastest growing operating system in the world, Linux." Due to the open source status of these programs, members of the public may consult their source code as desired.

Open Source Software Licenses

It is important to note that the term "open source" implies more than merely distribution of source code along with the object code. In such circumstances, the publisher could continue to assert its intellectual property rights in the software, thereby limiting the ability of others to modify the program or redistribute it. Even though disclosed to the public, the source code would remain under the control of the publisher.

As a result, publishers of open source software ordinarily do more than simply provide copies of both the source code and the object code when they distribute computer programs to the public. In addition, they establish the terms of use of the software by means of a license. A license is a contract through which the publisher allows recipients to use and modify the software, subject to certain conditions specified in the license. For example, the license might require that anyone who redistributes the software also make the source code of that software publicly available. Contracts that provide users with a sufficient set of privileges to access and modify the software's source code are deemed to be "open source licenses."

The practice of preserving the rights of software users through a set of license provisions is sometimes called "copylefting." This term is a play on words on the term "copyright." Under this system, the copyright holder licenses the recipient of a copy of the software. The license permits the redistribution of further copies of the software—including software containing modifications—under the condition that those copies are subject to the same license. This legal framework ensures that derivatives of the licensed work remain open. If the licensee fails to distribute derivative works under the same license, then he may face legal consequences. In particular, the licensor could terminate the license, leaving the licensee without permission to copy, distribute, or modify the software.

Although no official definition specifies which software licenses qualify as open source licenses, an organization called the "Open Source Initiative," or OSI, has promulgated a widely followed set of standards. OSI describes itself as a "nonprofit corporation dedicated to managing and promoting the Open Source Definition through a certification program that it administers. To satisfy the Open Source Definition, the license must satisfy certain conditions, including:

1.   The publisher must provide both object and source code.

2.   The publisher must allow modification and redistribution of the code (with or without modifications by the licensee).

3.   The publisher must not limit distribution to certain fields of endeavor or products, or limit its use with other free software.

A number of different groups have promulgated a variety of open source licenses that OSI has certified as compliant with the Open Source Definition. Among these is the General Public License, or GPL. As compared to the Open Source Definition, the GPL imposes additional restrictions upon software publishers. As a result, a license may fulfill the conditions of the Open Source Definition but not qualify as a GPL. According to its sponsor, the Free Software Foundation, the GPL guarantees computer users the following "four freedoms":

The freedom to run the program, for any purpose.

The freedom to study how the program works, and adapt it to your needs.

The freedom to redistribute copies so you can help your neighbor.

The freedom to improve the program, and release your improvements to the public, so that the whole community benefits.

It is important to note that, in this context, the term "freedom" does not mean that the software has to be sold at no charge. Rather, it refers to permissible user activities, and in particular the principle that software should be openly available in all of its current and future forms to all those desiring to learn or benefit from it.

The chief distinction between the Open Source Definition and the GPL is that the Open Source Definition effectively allows users to appropriate privately any modifications that they make. For example, under the Open Source Definition, a user could refuse to disclose publicly the source code of any programs that include the user's modifications. The licensee could also claim intellectual property rights in any modifications they introduced into the software. Of course, in such cases, the licensee's software would not qualify as open source. In contrast, the GPL requires that the source code be kept open to the public, even if the recipient of the software made changes. Also, under the GPL, the licensee cannot restrict the ability of others to build upon any modifications that the licensee made.

For example, a computer programmer may use software under a license that minimally complies with the Open Source Definition. Suppose further that the programmer modifies the software, and then licenses the object code of the modified version with the additional restriction that no licensee could copy the modified version's object code. This practice is acceptable under the Open Source Definition. This practice would not comply with the Free Software Foundation's GPL, however.

* * *

Potential Conflicts Between Open Source Software and Intellectual Property

Conflicts potentially arise between open source standards and intellectual property rights. Some observers have expressed concerns that if open source software is incorporated into an otherwise proprietary program, then the terms of the open source license will apply to the entire program and defeat intellectual property rights that would otherwise exist. It is also possible that a party not bound by the terms of an open source license may raise claims of intellectual property infringement based upon the use of software that others believe to be open source. Finally, questions have arisen regarding the validity and enforceability of open source licenses. This report next reviews these issues.

The Alleged "Viral" Nature of Open Source Software

Certain open source licenses have sometimes been described as "viral" in character. Some individual open source licenses require that the terms of that license apply automatically to each copy of the software, as well as to any modified versions. Some observers have expressed concerns regarding situations where a programmer, perhaps unknowingly, incorporates some open source program code into a larger software package. In these circumstances, the open source portion of the software could "contaminate" the entire program. As a result, even though the publisher intended that the program be proprietary, it may be instead be distributed as the open source license stipulates. In this way, the open source software component would trump any intellectual property rights that the publisher hoped to claim.

Whether a particular open source software [product] is potentially "viral" or not depends upon the individual terms of the accompanying open source license. Some commentators have stated that the Free Software Foundation's GPL is one example of a potentially "viral" license. Under the GPL, anyone who uses or modifies the software must, upon further distributing that software or a modification of that software, make the source code fully available to the public, free of any proprietary interest. This limitation prevents the software written and distributed under the GPL from being subject to intellectual property rights. As a result, the GPL maintains the "open" nature of the open source code by allowing users to modify and redistribute the software, but requiring that such modifications be made available to anyone under the terms of the GPL.

Notably, under certain conditions the GPL allows users to incorporate open source-derived computer programs into proprietary software packages without subjecting the entire package to the GPL. According to the Free Software Foundation, in order to avoid the imposition of the GPL upon the entire program, software publishers "must make sure that the free and non-free programs communicate at arms length, that they are not combined in a way that would make them effectively a single program."

The Free Software Foundation offers as an example the combination of an editor program and a shell program. To expand upon this illustration, suppose that an editor program executes textual commands typed by the user. A shell, or user interface program, might provide a graphical, menu-driven interface so that the user doesn't have to memorize the text commands. The editor could be a proprietary program. The shell might have been developed for individuals who did not wish to learn the text commands, and distributed under the GPL. As the editor can work independently of the shell in this example, the proprietary nature of the editor would be maintained even though the shell was subject to the GPL.

The functional separation of proprietary and open source software provides one avenue for avoiding the broad application of an open source license to an entire software product. Some observers believe, however, that conformity with this exception imposes substantial compliance burdens. For example, attorneys James A. Harvey and Todd S. McClelland state:

> It is therefore a good practice to advise clients with respect to procedures designed to segregate software that can be licensed as

proprietary from that which must be distributed under an open source license. Developing and maintaining procedures to implement these administrative tasks can be very difficult in complex development environments.

Views differ on the supposed "viral" nature of some open source licenses. Representatives of proprietary software firms have expressed concerns that "open source is an intellectual-property destroyer," and have reportedly referred to open source software as a "cancer" and "un-American." Others believe that, in order for open source software to remain open to the public, all programs derived from an open source original should be treated as open source as well. And, as noted above, some open source licenses take an intermediate position. Although these licenses require that the original software that is distributed with the license remain open source, they allow modifications and upgrades to that code to be "taken private" and be treated as proprietary software.

Third Party Infringement Claims

Some open source licenses, such as the General Public License (GPL), effectively prevent individuals from asserting intellectual property rights in open source software. This restriction only applies to individuals who have consented to these licenses, however. Parties not subject to that license are therefore not necessarily prevented from enforcing their intellectual property rights against individuals who use the software. As a result, even though one individual has distributed software that it has designated as open source, another entity may possibly assert that the software infringes an intellectual property right. Such assertions lead to potential conflicts between the intellectual property rights owner and individuals who believe that the software is open to the public.

For example, suppose that a computer scientist, Alpha, invents a new method of sorting data useful for computer programs. Alpha then files a patent application at the USPTO claiming the method. Later, a programmer named Beta independently writes a software program that uses the same data sorting method that Alpha had claimed in his pending application. Unaware of Alpha's patent application, Beta distributes his own software to the public under the GPL. If the USPTO approves of Alpha's application, Alpha could assert claims of patent infringement against anyone using Beta's software. These users would be subject to legal liability, even though the software was believed to be open source, and even though no one had knowledge of the patent infringement.

This scenario is possible not only for open source software, but also for proprietary software. A software publishing firm may also discover that their products infringe a patent or other intellectual property. However, commercial enterprises may stand in a better position to consider the intellectual property ramifications of their published software than the more diffuse open source community. Such enterprises often perform audits or establish procedures to avoid the use of other's software in their own products. Members of the more loosely organized open source community may have less capability to engage in these sorts of efforts.

At least one member of the open source community has addressed possible patent issues with respect to open source software. Red Hat, Inc., a well-known distributor of the open source operating system program called Linux, has presented a "patent promise." Red Hat's promise states in part:

> Subject to any qualifications or limitations stated herein, to the extent any party exercises a Patent Right with respect to Open Source/Free Software which reads on any claim of any patent held by Red Hat, Red Hat agrees to refrain from enforcing the infringed patent against such party for such exercise * * *

This statement appears to immunize users of open source software from claims of patent infringement by Red Hat, subject to certain qualifications. Red Hat's promise expressly does not cover patents owned by anyone else, however. As a result, users of open source software theoretically face the possibility of infringement claims by anyone holding a pertinent patent.

The ongoing litigation between the SCO Group and IBM Corporation offers a notable example of third party infringement claims. SCO is the current owner of the source code, as well as certain intellectual property rights, associated with a computer program known as UNIX. UNIX, a widely used operating system program, coordinates use of the computer's resources (such as its disk drive or a printer) during the computer's operation. Publishers of certain versions of UNIX have declared their programs to be open source software.

On March 6, 2003, SCO filed a lawsuit against IBM, in part asserting that IBM had misappropriated SCO's trade secrets. More specifically, SCO contends that IBM accessed its proprietary information when it licensed the UNIX software code from SCO and its predecessors. SCO further asserts that IBM then introduced this proprietary UNIX code into its own operating system, AIX, and later into its Linux-based products. IBM has denied these charges and, in turn, has asserted that SCO products infringe IBM copyrights and patents. As of early 2004, two other open source software vendors, Novell and Red Hat, had also become party to that litigation or to related lawsuits.

In addition to commencing infringement litigation against IBM, SCO has reportedly sent 1,500 letters to other firms. These letters are said to explain that the recipient's use of Linux could expose them to liability, and also to extend an offer of a license. The requested fee is reportedly about $700 for each computer using the Linux code. This demand has in turn animated some observers, such as the Electronic Frontier Foundation, to organize protests against SCO. As well, a consortium of technology companies, including IBM and Intel, have contributed substantial amounts of money towards the "Linux Legal Defense Fund." Contributors intend that these sums be used to defray the legal expenses of open source software users who face charges of intellectual property infringement.

As of the publication date of this report, the lawsuit between SCO and IBM continues in the U.S. District Court for the District of Utah in Salt Lake City. The outcome of this litigation may significantly impact users of Linux and other open source software. It also illustrates the potential tension between intellectual property rights and the open source community. Regardless of the outcome of this particular case, the SCO–IBM dispute demonstrates the possibility of future intellectual property infringement claims against open source software, commenced by individuals who claim not to be subject to the license under which the software was distributed.

Validity of Open Source Licenses

No court has yet ruled on the enforceability of open source software licenses. Some observers have suggested that these agreements may be invalid, however. These commentators point to the doctrine of federal preemption, which invalidates state laws that are inconsistent with federal laws. Under this view, open source software licenses—which are enforced through the mechanisms of state contract laws—conflict with the federal copyright statute, and are therefore invalid.

The rule of federal preemption derives from the Supremacy Clause of the U.S. Constitution. That provision states that the "Constitution and the laws of the United States * * * shall be the supreme law of the land * * * anything in the constitutions or laws of any State to the contrary notwithstanding." In resolving cases under the Supremacy Clause, courts typically determine whether enforcement of a state law would either directly conflict with federal law or frustrate federal purposes. In addition, section 301 of the Copyright Act expressly exempts state laws "that are equivalent to any of the exclusive rights within the general scope of copyright" and that apply to "the types of works protected by the Copyright Act."

The ongoing litigation between SCO and IBM may offer a court the opportunity to decide whether the open source license known as the General Public License, or GPL, is preempted by the federal copyright law. In that litigation, IBM has in part argued that SCO cannot enforce whatever intellectual property rights SCO owns in Linux due to the terms of the GPL. According to IBM, SCO distributed Linux software under the GPL for many years. IBM observes that the GPL stipulates that software distributed under the GPL must be made available for copying by others. As a result, IBM has asserted that SCO cannot now demand payment for use of any intellectual property SCO might own in Linux.

In turn, SCO has in part asserted that the GPL is invalid. As part of its argument, SCO has reportedly pointed to section 117 of the Copyright Act. That statute provides that "it is not [a copyright] infringement for the owner of a copy of a computer program to make or authorize the making of another copy or adaptation of that computer program provided * * * that such new copy or adaptation is for archival purposes only * * *." Stated differently, the Copyright Act permits users to make a backup copy of their software without fear of infringement liability.

The GPL places limitations upon the ability of users to make copies of GPL-licensed software, however. In particular, the GPL requires that individuals receiving copies of the software also receive copies of the GPL, and that persons making copies of the software be able to access the program's source code. The GPL then states that "[a]ny attempt otherwise to copy, modify, sublicense or distribute the Program is void, and will automatically terminate your rights under this License." SCO has taken the position that because the GPL conflicts with the Copyright Act, the GPL is preempted and therefore unenforceable.

Notably, SCO and IBM have presented a number of other arguments to the court. The court may not need to address this issue to resolve their dispute. This aspect of the SCO–IBM litigation has nonetheless raised concerns in the open source software community. As explained by journalist William M. Bulkeley:

> If SCO's argument ultimately wins, free-software advocates worry it would create considerable uncertainty about the legal status of many industry products. Although most believe the industry could adapt, companies that use GPL-licensed software might be confronted by surprise copyright claims from software developers. In addition, creation of new programs might be slowed by the confusion.

Other observers believe that the possibility of a court striking down the GPL is small. For example, lawyer James Boyle, a member of the faculty of the Duke University Law School, has reportedly described the federal preemption argument as "simply ludicrous." Eben Moglen, a law professor at Columbia University, believes that the federal preemption argument is overly broad. In Moglen's view, this position would effectively invalidate all software licenses, even those for which people pay, and even for proprietary software. Moglen believes it unlikely that a court would wish to dispute this longstanding industry practice.

Possible Legislative Issues and Approaches

Given the wide recognition that intellectual property and the open source movement are of growing importance in the U.S. computer industry, the relationship between these fields is the subject of increasing attention. The policymakers of the 108th Congress have addressed the open source movement with respect to cybersecurity and other contexts. Should Congress choose to address this area directly, a variety of approaches are available. If the current interface between intellectual property rights and the open source movement is considered satisfactory, then no action need be taken. Indeed, growing awareness that intellectual property and open source software licenses can sometimes conflict may lead to more sophisticated treatment of intellectual property by members of the open source community, as well as continued refinement of the governing law in the courts.

Another approach is to provide governmental assistance to the open source movement in identifying intellectual properties that might bear upon a particular open source software product. For example, the U.S. Patent and Trademark Office could, upon request by a recognized open source software publisher or organization, conduct a search of pending patent applications and issued patents in order to determine whether these patents might bear upon a particular open source software program. This capability would allow members of the open source community to become more fully informed of intellectual property rights. It should be noted, however, that a number of patent research firms already exist that could conduct such a search for a fee, at least with respect to issued patents and published patent applications.

More far-reaching legal reforms are also possible. For example, one recognized source of legal uncertainty for the software industry concerns the enforceability of open source licenses. A legislative statement concerning the status of these licenses in terms of the federal preemption doctrine might allow software firms to make decisions concerning research, investment, and other commercial activities with more confidence.

The allegedly viral nature of open source software presents another source of concern. One possible legislative response is to allow a proprietary software publisher that discovers its product contains an open source component a fixed period of time to eliminate the open source component. If the publisher removes the open source component within the stipulated grace period, then the software would remain proprietary.

Any possible legal reform would be well-advised to recognize that the U.S. software industry is increasingly characterized both by rapid innovation and by a distinct community of knowledgeable users who wish to "opt out" of the intellectual property system. The possibility of intellectual property rights, and their attendant license fees and royalties, may provide a significant incentive for firms to innovate and to distribute software. On the other hand, some computer users believe that these incentives are unnecessary, and further hope to maintain a non-proprietary environment of software distribution and development. These two trends have sometimes led to conflicts between exclusive intellectual property rights and open source software. Striking a balance between promoting innovation, on one hand, and accommodating the demands of software developers and users, on the other, forms an important component of contemporary software policy.

NOTES

1. To what extent do the scope and long duration of copyright protections make copyrights a particularly good basis for open source licenses governing the development and distribution of computer software? Will other

types of intellectual property rights serve as similarly effective bases for open source licenses? Will copyrights serve as well as bases for open source licenses concerning the development of intellectual works outside the domain of computer software?

2.   To what extent can vendors of open source products such as Red Hat allay fears of consumers about intellectual property claims by agreeing in published statements not to enforce the vendors' intellectual property rights? Would vendors be more effective in responding to concerns of consumers over open source software if the vendors agreed to indemnify consumers from claims of intellectual property infringement resulting from purchases and use of the vendors' products? Under what circumstances might this sort of indemnification arrangement still be ineffective in eliminating consumers' risks from intellectual property claims related to open source software?

VIII.   THE CENTRAL BUSINESS ROLE OF INTELLECTUAL PROPERTY DEVELOPMENT AND DISTRIBUTION

Intellectual property interests play many key roles in modern business activities and lawyers capable of dealing with intellectual property interests effectively are increasingly important participants in business affairs. Intellectual property interests can be major considerations at all stages of company life, raising distinctive legal issues as businesses are founded, financed, expanded, transferred to others, or terminated. Intellectual property interests—both presently possessed and potentially acquired—can shape how businesses select their primary business activities, establish business operations, seek financing, handle confidential information and activities, transfer technologies to others, terminate their businesses, transfer business units through mergers and acquisitions, prepare for and conduct public offerings of stock, and respond to competitive threats. For further discussions of the legal issues surrounding intellectual property in these and other business contexts, see Richard S. Gruner, Shubha Ghosh, & Jay P. Kesan, Intellectual Property in Business Organizations (2006).

While the focus of the following reading is on the use of intellectual property in small-and medium-sized business organizations, many of the means for employing intellectual property in business activities that are addressed here are also important in larger business entities or in divisions or subsidiaries of those entities.

INTELLECTUAL PROPERTY FOR BUSINESS

World Intellectual Property Organization (WIPO) Small
and Medium–Sized Enterprises Division.

http://www.wipo.int/sme/en/ip_business/doc/ip_business.doc

(last visited on 9/8/2006)

Why is Intellectual Property Relevant to Your [Small-and Medium–Sized
Enterprise (SME)]?

Along with human creativity and inventiveness, intellectual property
is all around us. Every product or service that we use in our daily lives is
the result of a long chain of big or small innovations, such as changes in
designs, or improvements that make a product look or function the way it
does today. Take a simple product. For example, a pen. Ladislao Biro's
famous patent on ballpoint pens was in many ways a breakthrough. But,
like him, many others have improved the product and its designs and
legally protected their improvements through the acquisition of IP rights.
The trademark on your pen is also intellectual property, and it helps the
producer to market the product and develop a loyal clientele.

And this would be the case with almost any product or service in the
marketplace. Take a CD player. Patent protection is likely to have been
obtained for various technical parts of a CD player. Its design may be
protected by industrial design rights. The brand name is most probably
protected by a trademark and the music played in the CD player is (or has
been) protected by copyright.

So, How Does this Affect Your Business?

Regardless of what product your enterprise makes or what service it
provides, it is likely that it is regularly using and creating a great deal of
intellectual property. This being the case, you should systematically consider the steps required for protecting, managing and enforcing it, so as to
get the best possible commercial results from its ownership. If you are
using intellectual property that belongs to others, then you should consider buying it or acquiring the rights to use it by taking a license in order to
avoid a dispute and consequent expensive litigation.

Almost every SME has a trade name or one or more trademarks and
should consider protecting them. Most SMEs will have valuable confidential business information, from customers' lists to sales tactics that they
may wish to protect. A large number would have developed creative
original designs. Many would have produced, or assisted in the publication, dissemination or retailing of a copyrighted work. Some may have
invented or improved a product or service.

In all such cases, your SME should consider how best to use the IP
system to its own benefit. Remember that IP may assist your SME in
almost every aspect of your business development and competitive strategy: from product development to product design, from service delivery to

marketing, and from raising financial resources to exporting or expanding your business abroad through licensing or franchising.

* * *

How can Intellectual Property Enhance the Market Value of Your SME?

The value of intellectual property (IP) is often not adequately appreciated and its potential for providing opportunities for future profit is widely underestimated by SMEs. However, when IP is legally protected and there is demand for the IP-protected products and/or services in the marketplace, IP can become a valuable business asset.

- IP may generate an income for your SME through the licensing, sale, or commercialization of the IP-protected products or services that may significantly improve an enterprise's market share or raise its profit margins.
- IP rights can enhance the value or worth of your SME in the eyes of investors and financing institutions.
- In the event of a sale, merger or acquisition, IP assets may significantly raise the value of your enterprise, and at times may be the primary or only true assets of value.

The strategic utilization of IP assets can, therefore, substantially enhance the competitiveness of your SME. SMEs should make sure that they are ready to face the challenge and take measures to exploit their IP and protect it wherever possible. Like physical assets, IP assets must be acquired and maintained, accounted for, valued, monitored closely, and managed carefully in order to extract their full value. But before this can be done, SMEs must first acknowledge the value of IP and begin to see it as a valuable business asset.

Intellectual Property as a Business Asset

An enterprise's assets may be broadly divided into two categories: physical assets—including buildings, machinery, financial assets and infrastructure—and intangible assets—ranging from human capital and know-how to ideas, brands, designs and other intangible fruits of a company's creative and innovative capacity. Traditionally, physical assets have been responsible for the bulk of the value of a company, and were considered to be largely responsible for determining the competitiveness of an enterprise in the market place. In recent years, the situation has changed significantly. Increasingly, and largely as a result of the information technologies revolution and the growth of the service economy, companies are realizing that intangible assets are often becoming more valuable than their physical assets.

In short, large warehouses and factories are increasingly being replaced by powerful software and innovative ideas as the main source of income for a large and growing proportion of enterprises worldwide. And even in sectors where traditional production techniques remain dominant, continuous innovation and endless creativity are becoming the keys to greater competitiveness in fiercely competitive markets, be it domestic or international. Intangible assets are therefore taking center stage and SMEs should seek how to make best use of their intangible assets.

One crucial way of doing so is by legally protecting intangible assets and, where they meet the criteria for intellectual property protection, acquiring and maintaining IP rights. IP rights may be acquired in particular for the following categories of intangible assets:

- Innovative products and processes (through patents and utility models);

- Cultural, artistic and literary works including, in most countries, also for computer software and compilation of data (through copyright and related rights protection);

- Creative designs, including textile designs (through industrial design rights);

- Distinctive signs (mostly through protection of trademarks including collective and certification marks, but in some cases through geographical indications; see below);

- Microchips (through protection of layout-designs or topographies of integrated circuits);

- Denominations for goods of a given quality or reputation attributable to the geographical origin (through protection of geographical indication; and

- Trade secrets (through protection of undisclosed information of commercial value).

Intellectual Property Protection as an Investment

Making the right investments is crucial for enhancing the market value of your SME. Investing in equipment, property, product development, marketing and research can strongly enhance your company's financial situation by expanding its asset base and increasing future productivity. Acquiring intellectual property may have a similar effect. Markets will value your company on the basis of its assets, its current business operations and expectations of future profits. Expectations for future profit may be considerably affected by the acquisition of key patents. There are numerous examples of SMEs that have seen their market value increase overnight as a result of their acquisition of important patents in key technologies.

Similarly, a good trademark with a good reputation among consumers may also enhance your company's current value and may decisively contribute to making your company's products and services more attractive to consumers. Investment in developing a good IP portfolio is, therefore, much more than a defensive act against potential competitors. It is a way of increasing your company's market value and improving future profitability.

The Value of Intellectual Property Assets

A crucial point about legal protection of intellectual property is that it turns intangible assets into exclusive property rights, albeit for a limited period of time. It enables your SME to claim ownership over its intangible assets and exploit them to their maximum potential. In short, IP protection makes intangible assets "a bit more tangible" by turning them into valuable exclusive assets that can often be traded in the market place.

If the innovative ideas, creative designs and powerful brands of your SME are not legally protected by IP rights, then these may be freely and legally used by any other enterprise without limitation. However, when they are protected by IP rights, they acquire concrete value for your enterprise as they become property rights which cannot be commercialized or used without your authorization.

Increasingly, investors, stock market brokers and financial advisors are becoming aware of this reality and have begun to value IP assets highly. Enterprises worldwide are also more and more acknowledging the value of their IP assets, and, on occasions, have included them in their balance sheets. Many enterprises, including SMEs, have begun to undertake regular technology and IP audits. In a number of cases, enterprises have realized that their IP assets are in fact worth more than their physical assets. This is often the case for companies operating in knowledge-intensive and highly innovative sectors, or companies with a well-known brand name.

Auditing Your Intellectual Property

One way your SME may acquire a better position to capitalize on the potential benefits of its IP assets and extract their full value is by conducting an IP audit. Ideally, this should be done by professional IP auditors, but often a preliminary IP audit may be done within your company. This entails identifying, monitoring, valuing your SME's IP assets so as to make sure that you are making the most out of them. By doing so, your SME would be able to make informed decisions when it comes to:

- Acquiring IP assets—Knowledge of your company's intellectual property and of its value will assist you in deciding which type of IP rights to acquire and maintain, and how best to manage the IP assets of your SME.

- Mergers and acquisitions—Good knowledge of what IP assets your SME owns can lead to a significant increase in the value of your SME. This is because investors would value a company on the basis of their expectations of future profits, which may, to a considerable extent, be based on the exploitation of IP rights.

- Licensing—Your SME can increase its cash flow (revenue) by licensing out its IP rights to a third party. An IP audit will assist your SME in determining the value of your own IP in order to obtain maximum benefit from license agreements. The revenue resulting therefrom has the potential of increasing the market value of your SME.

- Collateral—A well-structured IP portfolio can also be used as collateral. In such cases lenders will use your IP assets to determine the credit worthiness of your SME.

- Enforcement—Knowing the value of your IP assets will assist your SME in taking decisions on whether it is worthwhile taking action against infringement and in what way this may be done on a case by case basis.

- Cost reduction—A well managed IP register would help you identify obsolete IP assets (thus enabling you to cut-down IP asset maintenance costs), avoid infringing other peoples IP rights, etc. This would undoubtedly lead to a reduction in costs.

By establishing a culture of identifying and cultivating IP assets and strategically using them, an enterprise can increase its revenue, have an edge over its competitors and position itself well in the market; these are strategies that may lead to an increased market value of your SME.

* * *

How do you Turn Inventions Into Profit-making Assets of Your SME?

Innovative and creative ideas are at the heart of most successful businesses. Ideas by themselves, however, have little value. They need to be developed, turned into innovative products or services and commercialized successfully so as to enable your SME to reap the benefits of your innovation and creativity. Intellectual Property (IP), patents in particular, can be crucial for turning innovative ideas and inventions into competitive products that significantly increase profit margins.

Your SME may also use patents to earn royalty revenue by licensing such patented inventions to other firms that have the capacity to commercialize them. This may not only save your SME money, but also provide you with a stream of income from your invention or the inventions of employees of your SME, without the need to invest in its commercialization.

* * *

Reasons for Patenting Your Inventions

- Exclusive rights—Patents provide the exclusive rights which usually allow your SME to use and exploit the invention for twenty years from the date of filing of the patent application.

- Strong market position—Through these exclusive rights, you are able to prevent others from commercially using your patented invention, thereby reducing competition and establishing yourself in the market as the pre-eminent player.

- <u>Higher returns on investments</u>—Having invested a considerable amount of money and time in developing innovative products, your SME could, under the umbrella of these exclusive rights, commercialize the invention enabling your SME to obtain higher returns on investments.

- <u>Opportunity to license or sell the invention</u>—If you chose not to exploit the patent yourself, you may sell it or license the rights to commercialize it to another enterprise which will be a source of income for your SME.

- <u>Increase in negotiating power</u>—If your SME is in the process of acquiring the rights to use the patents of another enterprise, through a licensing contract, your patent portfolio will enhance your bargaining power. That is to say, your patents may prove to be of considerable interest to the enterprise with whom you are negotiating and you could enter into a cross licensing arrangement where, simply put, the patent rights could be exchanged between your enterprise and the other.

- <u>Positive image for your enterprise</u>—Business partners, investors and shareholders may perceive patent portfolios as a demonstration of the high level of expertise, specialization and technological capacity within your company. This may prove useful for raising funds, finding business partners and raising your company's market value.

* * *

In many cases, where an enterprise has merely improved an existing product and the said improvement is not sufficiently inventive to be deemed patentable, utility models (or "petty patents" or "utility innovations") may represent a good alternative, if available in the country in question. On occasions, it may be advisable for your SME to keep its innovations as trade secrets which requires, in particular, that sufficient measures are taken to keep the information confidential.

It is highly advisable for SMEs engaging in inventive activities to consult patent databases to find out about existing technologies, identify licensing partners in case a technology already exists and avoid duplication of research activities. * * *

What Happens if you do not Patent Your Inventions?

- <u>Somebody else might patent them</u>—In most countries (with the exception of the United States), the first person or enterprise to apply for a patent for an invention will have the right to the patent. This may in fact mean that, if you do not patent your inventions or inventions of the employees of your SME, somebody else—who may have developed the same or an equivalent invention later—may do so and legitimately exclude your enterprise from the market, limit its activities to the continuation of prior use, where the patent legislation provides for such exception, or ask your SME to pay a licensing fee for using the invention.

- Competitors will take advantage of your invention—If the product is successful, many other competitor firms will be tempted to make the same product by using your invention but without having to pay for such use. Larger enterprises may take advantage of scale economies to produce the product more cheaply and compete at a more favorable market price. This may considerably reduce your company's market share for that product. Even small competing enterprises can produce the same product and often sell it at a lower price as they do not have to recoup research and development costs incurred by your SME.

- Possibilities to license, sell or transfer technology will be severely hindered—Without IP rights, transfers of technology would be difficult if not impossible. Transfer of technology presupposes ownership of a technology which can only be effectively obtained through appropriate IP protection. Moreover, wherever negotiations do take place for transferring a given technological development without IP protection over the technology in question, parties are suspicious of disclosing their inventions, fearing that the other side may "run away with the invention." IP protection, in particular patent protection, is crucial for acquiring technology through its licensing.

* * *

Why is Intellectual Property Crucial for Marketing the Products or Services of Your SME?

For most small and medium-sized enterprises (SMEs), marketing products or services is a major challenge. A marketing strategy should establish a clear link between your products or services and your SME, as the producer or provider of such products or services. That is to say, customers should be able to distinguish, at a glance, between your products or services and those of your competitors and associate them with certain desired qualities.

Intellectual property, when efficiently used, is an important tool in creating an image for your business in the minds of your current and potential customers and in positioning your business in the market. IP rights, combined with other marketing tools (such as advertisements and other sales promotion activities) are crucial for:

- Differentiating your products and services and making them easily recognizable

- Promoting your products or services and creating a loyal clientele

- Diversifying your market strategy to various target groups

- Marketing your products or services in foreign countries

Intellectual Property Rights and Marketing

Different IP rights may contribute to your marketing strategy in different ways:

Trade and Service Marks

A well-crafted mark is often a decisive tool for the success of your SME in the market place. It will enable consumers to distinguish products or services of your SME from those of your competitors and to associate your products or services with desired qualities. Furthermore, it may play an important part in the ability of your product or service to penetrate a new market, especially if care was taken while selecting or creating the mark so that it appeals to the target market. It is crucial that you search for conflicting marks prior to filing an application or using a new mark on your products or services. For this purpose, you may wish to use the services of a competent attorney or agent. This would save your SME from incurring unnecessary expenses if there is already an identical or conflicting mark in the target market.

Collective Marks

The use of a collective mark (by a cooperative or an association of enterprises) allows the member SMEs to benefit from a reputation acquired on the basis of the common origin or other common characteristics of the goods produced or services rendered by different enterprises. This is, particularly, the case where the origin or other common characteristics are the main contributing factor in determining the quality or good taste of a product or service. The use of a collective mark may foster an alliance or facilitate cooperation with other SMEs so as to take full advantage of common resources.

Industrial Designs

In today's highly competitive global economy, a visually attractive design alone may enable you to captivate a demanding and extremely diversified clientele. Through creative designs, your SME could reach out to and appeal to diverse groups of customers from different age groups, regions, cultures, etc. Having design rights on an attractive shape or style of a product may give you the much-needed edge over the competition.

Geographical Indications

Inherent in certain products from a particular region are characteristics that are due to the soil, climate or particular expertise of the people of that area which consumers of those products expect and have confidence in. Capitalizing on that reputation for your products that emanate from such area or benefit from such skills in your marketing strategy makes sound business sense in differentiating your products from those of others. It is important to note that in the case of such products, your SME must maintain the standards and quality expected of goods produced in that region or with such expertise. * * *

Patents

The market for your newly introduced product can effectively be protected by obtaining patent protection. Being a patent holder can also open other business avenues such as licensing or strategic alliances (see "How do you Turn Inventions Into Profit-making Assets of Your SME").

Utility Models

Effective utilization of utility models, where such protection is available, can help your SME stay abreast of its competitors. If strategically used, the protection of utility models can be an effective tool in positioning your SME in the marketplace especially if your SME is active in a business where technological advantage plays an important role in determining who holds a larger share of the market. By paying close attention to your competitors' products and their promise of benefits, you can always improve products of your SME in order to provide the same or even greater benefits and protect your innovation as utility models, especially if the criteria of patentability are not fully met.

Marketing Your Products and Services in the New Economy

Impact of Electronic Commerce on Intellectual Property and Your SME

While the Internet can open a lot of opportunities for SMEs, it may also pose a number of challenges for the effective protection and enforcement of intellectual property rights, in general, and for copyright and related rights, trademarks and patents, in particular. The protection of copyright and related rights in the digital environment, the protectability of e-commerce business methods by patents, the use of trademarks as "metatags" and keywords, the infringement of trademark rights through the use of a sign on the Internet, the scope of protection of well-known marks and unfair competition in electronic commerce are some of the controversial issues and challenges which your SME may have to face.
* * *

Domain Names

If you intend to do business via the Internet then you need an Internet address, technically known as a domain name. In spite of their different function, domain names often conflict with marks which are used to identify and distinguish your products or services from those of your competitors. Your SME should, therefore, avoid using a domain name that is already protected by another enterprise as a mark. When your SME is faced with the use of its mark as a domain name by a competitor, you may wish to seek advice on how a dispute can be settled efficiently and at a reasonable cost. While conflicts between marks and domain names can be resolved in courts, many SMEs may prefer to take advantage of faster and cheaper special procedures under alternative dispute settlement mechanisms. WIPO's Domain Name Dispute Resolution Services is a leading institution in this area.

* * *

Getting the Best out of Intellectual Property Protection

To make sure that your marketing program gets the best out of your IP rights, the following points are worth considering:

- Register or seek protection of your IP assets at the earliest in order to take full advantage of your IP rights while undertaking advertising and other promotional activities.

- Check carefully to make sure that your SME does not infringe the IP rights of others. In this respect, it is advisable to conduct trademarks and patent searches before commercializing products and services which may conflict with the IP rights protected by other persons or enterprises.

- Use, or make reference to, your IP rights in your advertisements and other promotional activities in order to make your customers and potential customers aware of the IP protection of your products and services.

- Monitor the market and be ready to contact an IP lawyer or an official enforcement authority wherever you detect infringement of your IP rights that may be damaging your SME's profits or reputation. IP rights in fact allow you to fight unauthorized copying, imitation and other kinds of infringement. National legislation or case law may also provide protection against unfair competition, such as false allegations aimed at discrediting your products or services, allegations aimed at misleading the public as to the characteristics of your products and services and acts which aim at creating confusion with your products and services.

Can Your SME use Intellectual Property Assets for Financing?

In recent years, there is growing awareness that intellectual property (IP) assets can be monetized. There are various ways to do so. IP can be sold, licensed, used as collateral or security for debt finance, or it can provide an additional or alternative basis for seeking equity from friends, family, private investors (the so-called "business angels" who invest in * * * small and medium-sized enterprises (SMEs) and often also provide experience and business skills), venture capitalists, specialized banks and some times even from regular banks.

In addition, in most countries, the Government provides encouragement and support to high-tech start-ups and other innovative SMEs through grants, guarantees, subsidies and/or soft loan schemes, which are provided via various public funding institutions and banks that directly or indirectly recognize the importance of intellectual property assets.

As an owner/manager of an SME, therefore, it is important for you to look after the intellectual property of your SME not only as a legal asset but also as a financial instrument.

Using Intellectual Property Assets to Finance Your Business

Intellectual property (IP) assets may help you to strengthen your case for obtaining business finance from investors/lenders. The investor/lender, be it a bank, a financial institution, a venture capitalist, or a business angel, in undertaking an appraisal of the request for equity assistance or loan, will assess whether the new or innovative product or service offered by the SME is protected by a patent, a utility model, a trademark, an industrial design, or copyright or related rights. Such protection is often a good indicator of the potential of your SME for doing well in the market-place.

IP ownership is thus important to convince investors/lenders of the market opportunities open to the enterprise for the commercialization of the product or service in question. On occasions, a single powerful patent may open doors to a number of financing opportunities.

Ownership of IP rights over the creative output or innovations related to the products or services that an enterprise intends to market, guarantees a certain degree of exclusivity and, thereby, a higher market share if the product/service proves successful among consumers.

Different investors/lenders may value your IP assets in different ways and may attach different degrees of importance to IP rights. A clear trend, however, is developing towards an increasing reliance on IP assets as a source of competitive advantage for firms. Thus investors/lenders are increasingly focusing on firms with a well-managed IP portfolio, even though they encounter, even in the developed countries, many new problems and issues while trying to perfect security interests in intellectual property.

As the owner/manager of an SME, you must therefore take steps to understand the commercial value of the IP assets of your SME, ensure their proper valuation by professionals if need be, and understand the requirement(s), if any, for their proper accounting in the accounts books and balance sheet. Above all, make sure to include the IP assets of your SME in your business plan when presenting it to potential investors/lenders.

The Securitization of Intellectual Property Assets—A New Trend

Lending partly or wholly against intellectual property (IP) assets is a recent phenomenon even in developed countries. Collateralizing commercial loans and bank financing by granting a security interest in IP is a growing practice, especially in the music business, Internet-based SMEs and in high technology sectors.

Securitization normally refers to the pooling of different financial assets and the issuance of new securities backed by those assets. In principle, these assets can be any claims that have reasonably predictable cash flows, or even future receivables that are exclusive. Thus securitization is possible for future royalty payments from licensing a patent, trademark or trade secret, or from musical compositions or recording rights of a musician. In fact, one of the most famous securitizations of recent years involved the royalty payments of a rock musician in the USA, namely, Mr. David Bowie.

At present, the markets for intellectual property asset-based securities are small, as the universe of buyers and sellers is limited. But if the recent proliferation of Intellectual Property Exchanges on the Internet is an indication, then it is only a matter of time before all concerned will develop greater interest and capacity to use IP assets for financing business start-ups and expansions. As more cash flows are generated by intellectual property, more opportunities will be created for securitization.

Importance of Proper Valuation of Intellectual Property for Obtaining Finance

While securitization appears to be gaining ground, conventional lending remains the main source of external finance for most SMEs. The practice of extending loans secured solely by IP assets is not very common; in fact, it is practiced more by venture capitalists than by banks. If you seek to use IP assets as collateral to obtain financing, your IP assets stand a greater chance of being accepted as collateral if you are able to prove their liquidity and that they can be valued separately from your business. Furthermore, you have to show that your IP assets are durable, at least for the period during which you have to repay the loan, and marketable in the event of foreclosure or bankruptcy.

In this respect, it is critical to identify all the IP assets of your SME and to obtain an objective valuation of the identified assets from a competent valuation firm. The value of IP management processes which identify, log, track and quantify your IP assets becomes increasingly important in the Internet economy. This is one more reason for you to increase in-house awareness of the extent and value of IP asset holdings, including trade secrets, which might be used to collateralize a loan.

It is true that until now the valuation of intellectual property is considered to be highly subjective by both lenders and borrowers. While well-founded valuation methodologies exist, they are either considered to be too subjective or are not generally understood by most people. However, the increasing use of royalty streams arising from licensing to determine the value of intellectual property is a welcome development in enhancing the acceptability of intellectual property assets as valuable assets providing security for debt financing and equity participation.

As an SME, it is therefore important to keep this aspect in mind while seeking financial assistance in particular, and while developing your business strategy and business plan in general.

* * *

How can Intellectual Property Enhance the Export Opportunities of Your SME?

Before embarking on an export operation, enterprises go through a series of crucial steps which range from identifying an appropriate export market and estimating demand, to finding channels of distribution, estimating costs and obtaining funds. Here we seek to outline the main reasons why you should also take intellectual property (IP) issues into account while planning your export strategy, and look into ways in which IP rights could enhance the competitiveness of your small or medium-sized enterprise (SME) in export markets.

As IP rights are "territorial", i.e., are only available to you in the country or region in which they had been applied for and granted, to enjoy exclusive IP rights in foreign markets, you would have to seek and obtain protection abroad (except when it is available automatically without the need to comply with formalities, e.g., through an international treaty mechanism such as the Berne Convention for the Protection of Literary and Artistic Works * * *). The main reasons for protecting IP in export markets are outlined below:

- IP rights, especially patents, may open up new export opportunities.

- IP rights, especially trademarks and industrial designs, may help you to develop an advantageous market position in export markets.

- IP rights enhance the opportunity of winning loyal clientele for your products and services in export markets.

Exporting Your Patented Products

Patent (or utility model) protection abroad allows you to enjoy an important competitive advantage in your export markets. Companies that have adequately protected their inventions abroad have a range of options for exporting their innovative products that may not be available otherwise. These options include:

- Producing the good domestically and exporting the protected good directly or through intermediaries, knowing that no other company will be able to legally produce, sell or exploit the same product in the selected market without your authorization (and that most patent laws no longer allow, in accordance with international obligations of the country, [a country] to issue non-voluntary licenses on the ground that the protected goods are not produced locally in the country of export destination).

- Licensing the invention to a foreign firm that will manufacture the product locally, in exchange for a lump-sum payment and/or royalty fees.

- Setting up joint ventures with other firms for manufacturing and/or commercialization of the product in the selected foreign markets.

Depending on your strategy, your enterprise will earn additional revenues either through direct sales of the product or through fees and/or royalties from a licensee.

Using Brands and Designs to Market Goods and Services Abroad

The reasons for protecting trademarks and industrial designs in the domestic market fully apply to foreign markets too. Trademark registration, in particular, enables you to maximize product differentiation, advertising and marketing, thus enhancing recognition of your product or service in international markets and establishing a direct link with the foreign consumers. Depending on the nature of your service, a franchising agreement with firms abroad could be a useful alternative way to earn revenue from your trademark abroad as well.

Companies that export unbranded products will face disadvantages such as:

- Lower revenues as consumers demand lower prices for unbranded goods.

- Lack of customer loyalty largely due to their inability to recognize the product and distinguish it from the products of competitors.

- Difficulties in marketing and advertising products or services abroad in the absence of a suitable symbol or easy identifier that links your products or services with your SME, as marketing an unbranded product is inherently much more difficult.

With regard to industrial designs, protection in export markets will help not only to strengthen your overall marketing strategy but may also be important for customizing products for specific target markets, creating new niche markets for your company's products, and strengthening your company's image and reputation by linking it to a specific design.

International Exhaustion and Parallel Importation

While developing your export strategy, you should verify, preferably by consulting a qualified professional, whether a buyer could legally resell in another market IP-protected goods bought from, or with the consent of, your SME without having to seek your consent. This issue will only arise if you have already protected or would be protecting your IP rights in the domestic as well as in export market(s). Similarly, if your SME has bought goods that are protected by a patent, trademark, industrial design and/or copyright, then you should ascertain whether you would need the formal agreement of the IP owner(s) to sell those goods abroad, that is, in another market(s) (i.e. whether the IP rights are considered to be "exhausted"). You may be surprised that the answers to these questions are rather complex and may not only be different from one country to another but may also depend on the kind of IP rights involved.

Before discussing these issues, we must define what is meant by "exhaustion" of IP rights. "Exhaustion" refers to one of the limits of intellectual property rights. Once a product protected by an IP right has been marketed either by your SME or by others with your consent, the IP rights of commercial exploitation over this given product can no longer be exercised by your SME, as they are "exhausted". Sometimes this limitation is also called the "first sale doctrine", as the rights of commercial exploitation for a given product end with the product's first sale. Unless otherwise specified by law, subsequent acts of resale, rental, lending or other forms of commercial use by third parties can no longer be controlled or opposed by your SME. There is a fairly broad consensus that this applies at least within the context of the domestic market.

There is less consensus as to what extent the sale of an IP protected product abroad can exhaust the IP rights over this product in the context of domestic law. The issue becomes relevant in cases of so-called "parallel importation". Parallel importation refers to the import of goods outside the distribution channels contractually negotiated by the manufacturer. Because the manufacturer/IP owner has no contractual connection with a parallel importer, the imported goods are sometimes referred to as "grey market goods", which in fact is somewhat misleading, as the goods as such are original, only the distribution channels are not controlled by the manufacturer/IP owner. Based upon the right of importation that an IP right confers upon the IP owner, the latter may try to oppose such importation in order to separate markets. If, however, marketing of the product abroad by the IP owner or with his consent leads to the exhaustion of the domestic IP right, * * * the right of importation [also] is exhausted and can thus no longer be invoked against such parallel importation.

The above principles have different implications depending on whether the country of importation, for reasons of law or policy, applies the concept of national, regional or international exhaustion. The concept of *national exhaustion* does not allow the IP owner to control the commercial exploitation of goods put on the domestic market by the IP owner or with his consent. However, the IP owner (or his authorized licensee) could still oppose the importation of original goods marketed abroad based on the right of importation. In the case of *regional exhaustion*, the first sale of the IP protected product by the IP owner or with his consent exhausts any IP rights over these given products not only domestically, but within the whole region, and parallel imports within the region can no longer be opposed based on the IP right. Where a country applies the concept of *international exhaustion*, the IP rights are exhausted once the product has been sold by the IP owner or with his consent in any part of the world.

* * *

NOTES

1. In what respects are elements of intellectual property and associated rights resources of businesses that can be developed and commercialized? How do these resources differ from other types of property such as personal and real property? What features of intellectual property will indicate that it should be used exclusively in one's own business? What features of intellectual property will indicate that it should be licensed to others to gain the full value of the property?

2.   How do intellectual property rights influence the ways in which intellectual property is developed, used, and disposed of by businesses? Is the scope of intellectual property protections likely to influence engineering directions of companies? How might the requirements of intellectual property laws—particularly patent and trade secret laws—affect the procedures used by companies in undertaking engineering and product development efforts? How can intellectual property rights ensure that companies take a long term view of the best way to develop intellectual works and related products?

3.   How should a company systematically detect and address threats to its operations from the intellectual property rights of others? What types of threats are most easily detectable? What types of threats are most serious to a given business? How is the timing of the discovery of intellectual property rights conflicting with company activities likely to affect the seriousness of the threats posed by those rights?

4.   What should the personal liability of company managers be for the mismanagement of a company's intellectual property and associated rights? Are the business risks associated with these interests materially different than other business risks confronted by business managers? If there are important differences, do these differences suggest needs for greater or lesser liability for individual managers to ensure that these managers adopt reasonable efforts to properly develop and manage the acquisition and use of intellectual property interests?

IX.   CONCLUSION: BALANCING RESTRICTIONS ON INTELLECTUAL WORKS TODAY WITH INTELLECTUAL FREEDOM TOMORROW

One of the most difficult problems in intellectual property law concerns striking the proper balance between protection and free availability of intellectual works to ensure the maximum public benefits from such works. Strong protections for new works may encourage the creation of more such works, but the enforcement of these protections may restrict effective use of the works once they are created. In addition, strong restrictions on the use of works may limit the use of the works as building blocks for additional works, thereby limiting the production of further generations of works.

Issues like these were at the heart of arguments over the legitimacy of copyright term extension legislation in *Eldred v. Ashcroft*, 537 U.S. 186, 123 S.Ct. 769, 154 L.Ed.2d 683 (2003). In that case, the Supreme Court held that Congress had broad discretion to choose the length of copyright protection that would properly encourage the creation and dissemination of copyrighted works. In the Court's view, this discretion extended to choices by Congress to increase the period of protection available for works already in existence and even to reassert protection for an additional period to some works which had fallen out of copyright protection.

Hence, the Court upheld the particular copyright term extension legislation at issue in that case. *Id.* at 221–22.

The Court's analysis in *Eldred* did not directly confront the policy issues governing the proper balance between the scope and duration of protection for intellectual works and free access to those works, indicating instead that this was a balance for Congress to strike. However, a number of observers recognized that the copyright term extensions at issue in this case directly implicated the balance between protection and access that would best serve the public. The following amicus brief describes a number of issues raised by tradeoffs between intellectual work protection and free access, issues that will continue to shape the future of copyright law and of intellectual property protections generally.

ELDRED v. ASHCROFT, BRIEF OF AMICI CURIAE AMERICAN ASSOCIATION OF LAW LIBRARIES, AMERICAN LIBRARY ASSOCIATION, ASSOCIATION OF RESEARCH LIBRARIES, DIGITAL FUTURE COALITION, MEDICAL LIBRARY ASSOCIATION AND SOCIETY OF AMERICAN ARCHIVIST IN SUPPORT OF PETITION FOR WRIT OF CERTIORARI

Peter Jaszi, Attorney for Amici Curiae.
December 13, 2001.

The U.S. Court of Appeals for the District of Columbia Circuit ("DC Circuit") erroneously held that Congress' grant of twenty additional years of copyright protection as set forth in the Copyright Term Extension Act (CTEA) is constitutional. The DC Circuit failed to recognize that Congress' act violates the constitutional language that empowers Congress to grant copyright protection for "limited times" as a means of "promoting" the arts and sciences. This balance struck by the Framers consisted of giving incentives for cultural production through limited rewards to creators, while providing for an ever-growing arena of ideas and materials available for the public. Central to this balance was the public domain, whose importance has been denigrated by the enactment of the CTEA.

The public domain is a vast expanse of knowledge, experience and ideas embodied in artistic creations, including written works, audio files, movies, and photographs, as well as historical documents and archives, held in common for all people to access, enjoy, research, and use as inspiration for future creations. The public domain results from the Framers' skepticism toward monopolies and remains an integral part of the balance between the protection of works and promotion of knowledge. Historically, copyright legislation and this Court's jurisprudence have recognized the importance of the public interest as embodied in this domain of information for the people.

The CTEA cannot promote the creation of works that already exist. But it will severely diminish the ability of modern creators to generate new art and new knowledge based on existing works—as did previous generations of authors and scholars. Artists, musicians, theatrical performers, scholars, educators, librarians, authors, publishers, archivists, and historians, among others, utilize the public domain. The CTEA harms these users by limiting their access to works through prohibitively expensive licensing fees and conditional permissions for use. The CTEA also prevents the timely preservation of works, deprives scholars of research materials, and reduces funds from educational institutions, thus hampering the preservation and dissemination of information, stories, and documentation of who we are as a people.

* * *

The architecture of U.S. Copyright law embodies the principle that works should be available to the public after a limited time, through the avenue of the public domain. The public domain is the priceless repository of works that are ineligible for copyright, were created before copyright law existed, have had their copyrights expire, or have been freely given to the public by their authors. The Framers of the Constitution believed that dissemination of information throughout society was a cornerstone of learning, and thus of the democratic participation of citizens in the cultural and political life of the nation. They were skeptical of all restraints on the free exchange of ideas, whether by public tyranny or private monopoly. Copyright operates as a monopoly for a limited time granted to the creator by the government for exclusive control over a work. This skepticism of the Framers shaped the constitutional "bargain" they struck between creators and the public: the grant of a limited monopoly in exchange for the subsequent deposit of works into the public domain.

The DC Circuit, in upholding the constitutionality of the Copyright Term Extension Act, abandoned this constitutional bargain by ruling, in effect, that Congress has the power to use repeated extensions of the length of copyright protection for existing works (as well as new ones), transforming a limited monopoly into a virtually limitless one. However, such ever-increasing periods of protection ignore the Constitution's clear directive to "Promote the progress of Science and useful Arts," and constitute a dangerous expansion of the monopoly created by copyright.

The dangers inherent in this expansion include rendering some older works inaccessible, some prohibitively expensive, and some available only upon restrictive conditions. Moreover, long terms of copyright mean that it is difficult or impossible even to determine who owns the rights that control the use of many cultural resources. This state of affairs differs dramatically from what the Framers envisioned.

* * *

Modern scholarship stresses the centrality of the public domain to the public purpose of copyright law. Professor Jessica Litman has stated:

> American ideas of freedom are bound up with a vision of information policy that counts information as social wealth owned by all. We

believe we are entitled to say what we think, to think what we want, and to learn whatever we're willing to explore. Part of the information ethos in the United States is that facts and ideas cannot be owned, suppressed, censored or regulated, they are meant to be found, studied, passed along and freely traded in the "marketplace of ideas."[119]

Further, Professor Yochai Benkler sees the public domain as a vehicle for "a robust democratic discourse, of diversity of antagonistic voices, and of individual expressive autonomy."[120]

* * *

The limited scope of the copyright holder's statutory monopoly, like the limited copyright term required by the Constitution, reflects a balance of competing claims upon the public interest: creative work is to be encouraged and rewarded, but private motivation must ultimately serve the cause of promoting broad public availability of literature, music, and the other arts.

* * *

The public domain benefits the public by providing inexpensive and ready access to many works of literary, scientific, historic, social and artistic importance, and by supporting innovation and the expansion of knowledge. Works within the public domain are the foundation for new creativity: creators rarely produce original works isolated from cultural tradition, but in every era authors have drawn extensively on public domain materials. While all works are not pastiche, even the most innovative incorporate previous ideas and expressions. For example, modern dance pioneer Martha Graham frequently expressed her indebtedness to public domain materials that encouraged her creative process and fostered acclaimed new works.

Similarly, the Walt Disney Company has used many stories and previous works from the public domain in creating its internationally recognized animated movies. The old tales of Snow White and the Seven Dwarves, Cinderella, and Sleeping Beauty, as well as modern works of authorship such as Pinocchio, the Jungle Book, and the Hunchback of Notre Dame, were public domain works utilized by Disney to produce some of American cinema's most memorable icons.[121]

---

119. Jessica Litman, Digital Copyright 1 (2001).

120. Yochai Benkler, Through the Looking Glass: Alice and the Constitutional Foundations of the Public Domain, (Nov. 2001) (unpublished Framing Paper, available at http://www.law.duke.edu/pd/papers.html) (last visited Nov. 29, 2001).

121. See Heidi Anne Heiner, Sur La Lune Annotated Fairy Tales (Oct. 14, 2000) at http://members. aol.com/rocketrder/frytales/snowhite/history.htm (last visited Nov. 18, 2001) (relating that Snow White was originally recorded by the Grimm brothers in 1818); see Tiffany Jensen, Cinderella The Evolution of a Story: An Examination of the Cultural Significance of Oral History, available at http://www.usu.edu/anthro/origins_of_writing/cindereua (last visited Nov. 18, 2001) (noting that Cinderella and Sleeping Beauty are both direct representatives of "Histoires ou Contes Du Temps Passe" [Tales of Times Past] by Charles Perrault, 1697); see Bob's World Literature Page at http://www.intac.com/rfrone/Lit/1106/1106-00.htm (last visited Nov 18, 2001)

Public domain status also gives the public new opportunities to appreciate older works. In 1993 Willa Gather's "My Antonio" entered the public domain and in 1994 seven new editions appeared (costing from $2 to $24) making the story available to many more people than had previously read it. Likewise, the children's book "The Velveteen Rabbit" became a widely popular classic once it passed into the public domain. Although the original version is still in print, newly illustrated versions that creatively interpret the story have been released, and seven different editions are now listed in Books in Print.

Generally, the CTEA extends the term (and therefore the economic reward) of copyright protection, creating disturbing consequences. Users must incur further costs for licensing fees (which effectively limit the amount of material available for public use), while many creators and scholars face costly impediments to identifying and locating rights holders for older, lesser-known works, which may entail multiple ownership tiers. Even the necessity of seeking permission to use such works may be prohibitive because of the high search and negotiation costs involved. The CTEA, under certain circumstances, may subject the public and institutions that disseminate information to additional expense and burdens with very uncertain benefits. As a consequence, institutions large and small may forgo use of those works. For example, the University of Texas, apparently conscious of potential liability, prohibits students, faculty or staff from using copyrighted works if permission cannot be obtained, even if a good faith effort is made to secure such permission, and even if a persuasive fair use argument may be made.

Specifically, the CTEA imposes a twenty-year moratorium on works entering the public domain. Were it not for the CTEA, the decades from 1998 to 2018 would have seen the entry into the public domain of a wide variety of works published in the United States between 1923 and 1943, in addition to many unpublished works by authors who died prior to 1968. The following examples illustrate the harms flowing from the general phenomenon of the erosion of the public domain by copyright extension.

1. Copyright Term Extension Harms Disseminators Of Information

Primary disseminators of information include educators, archivists and librarians. These individuals and their organizations serve the public without commercial gain, seeking only to benefit users through promoting accessible information, exposure to arts and sciences, and cultural enrichment, drawing in part on the public domain.

a. Educators and librarians:

Educators face many difficulties obtaining works by important authors at reasonable prices. The CTEA affects educational enterprises by

---

(explaining that Pinocchio was originally created in 1883 by Carlo Collodi, and released as a movie in 1940 by Disney). Jungle Book was written in 1894 by Rudyard Kipling (who died in 1936) but * * *, had CTEA's rules applied, would not have been available for use by Disney until 2007, 40 years after Disney released its version as a movie, at http://www. ricochet-jeunes.org/eng/biblio/author/kipling.html (last visited Nov. 18, 2001); and the Hunchback of Notre Dame appeared in 1831, at http://www.kirjasto.sci.fi/vhugo.htm (last visited Nov. 18, 2001).

adding to the cost of books that are commonly assigned for class use, such as The Great Gatsby and A Farewell to Arms.[122]

Copyright term extension also inhibits educators' efforts to provide students with texts in electronic form. Electronic teaching tools have become an important resource for educators, as evidenced by the success of The Dickens Web, a successful hypertextual research and educational site detailing the world of Charles Dickens. The creation of such pedagogical tools becomes difficult or impossible if the information needed remains under copyright protection. Thus, copyright concerns will continue to inhibit the development of similar resources for the study of twentieth-century culture.

2. Copyright Term Extension Harms Creative Users Of The Public Domain

Copyright term extension adversely affects not just institutional disseminators, but also a wide variety of creative users of public domain material. These include theatrical and musical performers, authors, publishers, and film scholars.

a. Theatrical and musical performers:

Without the public domain, every theater in the nation, be it a high school or the Kennedy Center, would first need to obtain permission from Shakespeare's heirs to perform any work by Shakespeare. In the future, under the current regime of repeated copyright term extension, this requirement of securing permission may be the case for the plays of Tennessee Williams and other twentieth-century playwrights for many decades to come. Term extension poses additional dilemmas for would-be performers of dramatic works. For example, a recently published play, "Painting Churches," includes the following direction to potential licensees: "Note: Permission to produce Painting Churches does not include permission to use this song ['Nothing Could Be Finer'], which ought to be procured from the copyright owner;" and on another page, "Note: This song is still under copyright protection. Permission to use it in productions of Painting Churches ought to be procured from the copyright owner." The potential producer must identify, locate, and receive permission from unnamed copyright owners, a costly and burdensome exercise.

Today, many regional theaters forgo performing classic American musicals because producers cannot afford the necessary licensing fees. Even if they can, the copyright holder may restrict the interpretation of the work to reflect contemporary times and issues. For example, theaters are barred by the Gershwin Family Trust from producing Porgy and Bess

---

122. See S.Rep. No. 104–315 at 34 (1996) (Statement of Sen. Hank Brown). In 1996 Bantam Books conducted a study and determined that almost 12 million literary classics are sold each year to high schools and colleges. One analysis concluded that if copyright were extended twenty years, consumers including schools and students would pay out an additional $345 million in royalties. *Id.* at 34. *See also* S. Rep. No. 104–315 at 37 (1996) (Statement of Sen. Herb Kohl). Moreover, firms like Scribners, publisher of Fitzgerald and Hemingway, long charged their educational customers high prices for reprints of modern classics. *Id.* at 37

(1934) with casts including white performers. Permission to perform Rodgers and Hammerstein works is also subject to strict conditions. Copyright extension reduces opportunities for new artists to expand on or reinterpret materials that would otherwise have been part of the public domain.

Merely singing songs in the most innocent of situations is touched by copyright extension. For example, restaurants where waiters serenade customers with "Happy Birthday" (in which the copyright now will not expire until at least 2030) might be forced to pay performance rights fees to copyright holders.

b.   Authors and publishers:

Term extension yields other examples of results completely disconnected from the incentive rationale for copyright protection. In one instance, a university press required the author of a book on city planning to pursue permissions for use of a previously unpublished photograph of Charles Mulford Robinson, who died in 1917. The photographer's name was unknown, and securing permission was impossible. In another instance, a television network required permission to use a similarly unpublished 1912 photograph of Jim Thorpe running on the deck of a ship en route to the Stockholm Olympics. The photograph, containing no indication of the photographer, established no clear evidence of ownership, and thus a clear path for securing permission could not be established. Even when creators can surmount the costs of permissions and invest the complicated and time-consuming effort, this requirement creates enormous burdens for scholarship, documentary filmmakers and authors.

In the domain of fiction, as well, excessive copyright can restrict, rather than promote, creative production. A notorious recent example of attempted private censorship utilizing copyright law is the case of Alice Randall's The Wind Done Gone. This work, offering a revisionist portrait of the antebellum South, is a creative and critical commentary on Margaret Mitchell's Gone With the Wind in the form of the first-person narrative of Scarlett O'Hara's black half-sister. Only because of copyright term extension could the Mitchell estate sue to suppress Randall's work. At the time of its first publication, Gone With the Wind was due to enter the public domain no later than 1992. However, because of successive term extensions, this work will not be freely available for public use until 2031 (presuming no further extensions by Congress).

3.   Copyright Term Extension Harms Scholarly Institutions And Scholars Who Utilize The Public Domain

a.   Archivists and historians:

Those who preserve and interpret history face similar problems. For example, important documents relating to World Wars I and II remain and will continue to remain inaccessible. Dwight D. Eisenhower died in 1969, so the copyright in his non-presidential papers will not expire until the end of 2039, restricting use of his letters ruminating on the conduct of

World War II until nearly a century after that war was fought. Meanwhile, Eisenhower's thoughts on his service in World War I cannot be fully utilized in historical scholarship without costs and/or restrictions until more than 121 years after the 1918 Armistice.

Copyright term extensions can severely limit the publication of scholarly works, as a recent article on the Civil War submitted to a historical journal demonstrates. The author used compelling excerpts from soldiers' diaries and letters to compare the perceptions and sentiments of western soldiers with those of their eastern counterparts. The journal would not accept the article unless the researcher obtained signed permissions from the families (and other copyright holders if applicable) of every soldier who was quoted, since the materials could conceivably still enjoy copyright protection. The last Civil War veteran died in 1959; thus, under the CTEA, the copyright on some previously unpublished letters could endure until 2030. Because archives include items of mixed and unknown provenance, the task of clearing such copyrights may involve genealogical and probate inquiries dwarfing the scope of the original research effort. The journal's reluctance to gamble on a potential copyright infringement action prevented the publication of this important article.

Similarly, archivists desiring to make digital copies of Civil War materials available to schools and universities to further public understanding are thwarted in their efforts by excessive copyright terms. As Roy Rosenzweig noted in a recent article in the Journal of American History, "[f]or historians, copyright protection has redlined * * * much twentieth-century history * * *." If copyright term extension survives constitutional challenge, opportunities for new artists to expand on the culture of the past will be fewer, and citizens will miss opportunities to be exposed to, and enriched by, primary historical documents and knowledge.

b. Film scholars and archivists:

A film scholar and author of the book Film, Form, & Culture, a textbook with an accompanying CD–ROM, chronicles the difficulty and cost of identifying and obtaining permission for use of films from the twentieth century. The Second Edition increased in cost when the author included clips from two "B" gangster films of the late 1940's and 50's, for which the copyright owner demanded $2,000 for 120 seconds of clips. This same author also could not use any clips of Disney-owned works, which are not licensed for CD–ROM use as a general policy. Although a modified version of Film, Form, and Culture was eventually published, the need to obtain permission may chill similar publications for decades to come, since under the CTEA many pre–1960 American films will be protected well into the twenty-first century.

Although the CTEA is sometimes characterized as promoting the preservation of America's film heritage, the reality is otherwise. Thousands of old movies sit on shelves deteriorating because the companies that hold the copyrights make no efforts to restore them or make them available, while their copyright status prevents others from preserving such works. By the time many of these works are finally available to enter the public domain, prints and negatives will have physically disintegrated. These endangered works include not only film "classics," but also industrial films, forgotten examples of silent cinema, footage from uncompleted projects (such as Orson Welles' Don Quixote), and kinescopes of programs from the "golden age" of television.

Conclusion

Unless the decision of the DC Circuit is reversed, the CTEA and subsequent extensions of copyright terms will continue to impede the growth of the public domain. Amici do not argue against licensing fees as an appropriate means of rewarding authors and creators, nor do we suggest that we are prevented from invoking the fair use doctrine in appropriate situations. However, the practical result of copyright term extension, by maintaining unnecessary barriers to the accessibility of information, diminishes the ability of the public to be educated, to be entertained, and to engage in debate. Through excessive copyright extension, copyright owners will continue to restrict access to and exert censorial control over millions of works, thereby chilling discourse and cultural development long after incentives for production have ceased to operate. The Framers of our Constitution envisioned a very different role for copyrights.

Every member of society, from the toddler who hears a fable for the first time to the archivist who meticulously inventories the wealth of information present on the World Wide Web, has the constitutional right to use and receive information. Amici urge this Court to recognize the breadth of the harms the public will suffer if the CTEA is not found unconstitutional and to reaffirm the Framer's intent for Congress to promote the public's interest through balanced copyright law.

NOTES

1.   Should there be a constitutionally protected right to "use and receive information?" Assuming that this is not a right but rather an interest to be promoted by copyright laws and other intellectual property laws, what types of protections will best promote the public's use and receipt of information? To what extent are the public's interests in the "use" and "receipt" of information different and likely to be furthered through different types of intellectual property standards?

2.   When are intellectual property protections—particularly trade secret protections—potentially justified for reasons other than the promotion of the public's use and receipt of information and intellectual works?

3.   What circumstances create a particularly strong case for emphasizing intellectual property protections over free use of intellectual works in defining intellectual property laws?

4.   What features should justify free public use of intellectual works normally protected by intellectual property laws? How do these factors com-

pare with the factors governing "fair use" of expressive works under copyright laws?

INDEX

References are to Pages

†